ISBN 978-0-266-96903-7
PIBN 10917151

JOURNAL OF THE PARLIAMENTS OF THE EMPIRE.

INDEX
TO
VOLUME III.

1922.

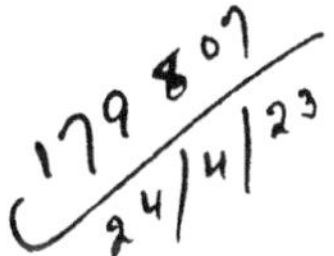

Issued under the Authority of the
EMPIRE PARLIAMENTARY ASSOCIATION
(United Kingdom Branch),
WESTMINSTER HALL, HOUSES OF PARLIAMENT,
LONDON, S.W.1.

ABBREVIATIONS.

A.	= Answer(s).
Adm.	= Admiral.
Af.	= Africa.
Agreet.	= Agreement.
Amendt.	= Amendment.
Art.	= Article.
Assocn.	= Association.
Aust.	= Australia. / = Australian.
Aust. Com.	= Australian Commonwealth.
B.C.	= British Columbia.
B. of T.	= Board of Trade.
Brit. Emp.	= British Empire.
Can.	= Canada. / = Canadian.
cf.	= *compare.*
C.L.	= Coalition Liberal.
Co.	= Company.
Col.	= Colonel.
Com.	= Commander.
Commdt.	= Commandant.
Con. Dem.	= Constitutional Democrat.
Conf.	= Conference.
Confs.	= Conferences.
Cons.	= Conservative.
Contrib.	= Contribution.
Conv.	= Convention.
Convs.	= Conventions.
C.P.	= Country Party.
C. U.	= Coalition Unionist.
Dept.	= Department.
E.	= East.
Employt.	= Employment.
Exam.	= Examination(s).
F. O.	= Foreign Office.
F. U.	= Farmers' Union.
Gen.	= General.
Gov.-Gen.	= Governor-General.
Govt.	= Government.
H. of A.	= House of Assembly.
H. of C.	= House of Commons.
H. of L.	= House of Lords.
H. of R.	= House of Representatives.
Ind.	= Independent.
Ind. Lib.	= Independent Liberal.
Ind. U.	= Independent Unionist.
infra	= *below.*
Internat.	= International.
Irish F. S.	= Irish Free State.
Lab.	= Labour.
Legis. Assemb.	= Legislative Assembly.
Legis. Conn.	= Legislative Council.
Lib.	= Liberal.
Lib.-Con.	= Liberal-Conservative.
L. of N.	= League of Nations.
Lt.-Col.	= Lieutenant-Colonel.
Maj.	= Major.
Maj.-Gen.	= Major-General.
N.	= North.
Nat.	= Nationalist.
Natl.	= National.
Nat. Prog.	= National Progressive.
Newfld.	= Newfoundland.
N.L. &. C.	= National Liberal and Conservative.
N.S.W.	= New South Wales.
N.Z.	= New Zealand.
Oppos.	= Opposition.
P.	= Party.
Parl.	= Parliamentary.
Parl. Lab. P.	= Parliamentary Labour Party.
Pref.	= Preference.
Pres.	= President.
Prog.	= Progressive.
Q.	= Question(s).
Q. & A.	= Question(s) and Answer(s).
Qsld.	= Queensland.
q.v.	= *quod vide.*
Rec. *or* Recs.	= Recommendation(s).
Ref.	= Reform.
Repres.	= Representative(s) *and* Representation.
Res.	= Resolution, *and* Resolutions.
Ry. *or* Rys.	= Railway *or* Railways.
S.	= South.
S. Af.	= South Africa. / = South African.
S.A.P.	= South African Party.
S. Aust.	= South Australia. / = South Australian.
Sec.	= Secretary.
Sen.	= Senator.
Soc.	= Socialist.
sqq.	= *sequitur* (*and following pages*).
supra	= *above.*
S.-W. Af.	= South-West Africa.
Tas.	= Tasmania.
T.U.	= Trade Union.
T.U.s	= Trade Unions.
U.	= Unionist.
U.K.	= United Kingdom.
Ulster U.	= Ulster Unionist.
Unemployt.	= Unemployment.
U.S.A.	= United States of America.
Vic.	= Victoria (Australia).
vide	= *see.*
W.	= West *or* Western.
W. Aust.	= Western Australia. / = West. Australian.

INDEX.

VACHER & SONS, LTD., Westminster House, S.W.1.—3730.

JOURNAL OF THE PARLIAMENTS OF THE EMPIRE

Vol. III.—No. 1. January, 1922.

Issued under the Authority of the
EMPIRE PARLIAMENTARY ASSOCIATION
(United Kingdom Branch),
WESTMINSTER HALL, HOUSES OF PARLIAMENT,
LONDON, S.W.1.

Price to Non-Members 10s. *Net.*

CONTENTS.

UNITED KINGDOM.

CANADA.

AUSTRALIA.

Commonwealth Parliament.

State Parliaments.

New South Wales.

Queensland.

NEW ZEALAND.

SOUTH AFRICA.

NEWFOUNDLAND.

INTRODUCTION.

The present issue constitutes the first number of the thirc year of the publication of the JOURNAL. It is not necessary to discuss the cordiality of the reception which the JOURNAI has received amongst Members of Parliament during the tw(years of its existence, but it may be useful to place on record at the commencement of the third year, that every Dominion Parliament decided during 1921 to make an annual financia contribution towards the cost of its production. It would b(perhaps difficult to obtain a more practical recognition thaı this of the value of the JOURNAL to Members of Parliament throughout the British Empire; and it may be now said tha an enterprise which was originally supported by only on(Parliament has now become the joint production of all th(Parliaments of the Empire.

Regarding the contents of the present JOURNAL, th(discussions in the Parliaments of New Zealand, the Australiaı Commonwealth and the United Kingdom contain a wealth o material that is of particular value to students of the constitu tional position and of the relationship of the Dominions to th(United Kingdom in the conduct of those affairs which are o common interest to all.

The discussions in the United Kingdom Parliament on th Irish Free State,* besides being of intimate concern to thos Members in the different countries of the Empire who hav worked for the settlement of an age-long controversy, calle forth a statement from the Prime Minister of the Unite Kingdom on the subject of Dominion status which will almos certainly remain on record as of first-rate importance. Th references to the same subject in the discussions occurring i the Dominions have revealed, as heretofore, differences o opinion as to methods, but a general tendency toward emphasising the elasticity of the bond which unites the Empir and the equality of political status of the nations which go t form the British Commonwealth.

The discussions dealing with Ireland (in the Unite Kingdom) and with the Conference of Prime Ministers of th Empire (in Australia and New Zealand) should be closel studied from the standpoint of the inter-relations of the natior within the Empire; while the discussions upon the Washingto Conference, League of Nations, Defence, Anglo-Japanes Treaty and the Pacific generally (in Australia, New Zealan and the United Kingdom) should be considered from the poir

* It has been thought well to give the full text of the Articles Agreement for the Treaty between Great Britain and the representativ

of view of the relationship of the Empire to the great world-problems of to-day.

Important as were the discussions on the Peace Treaty and other matters affecting Foreign Policy, which have been summarised in previous volumes of the JOURNAL, the Dominion Parliaments show clearly, in the Debates which are dealt with in the following pages, a broad conception of the world forces which are intimately affecting their own destinies and which require careful calculation before a policy, acceptable to the whole Empire, can be adequately evolved.

Apart from the special Session which was called to deal with the Irish problem in December, matters of interest to the whole Empire took place during the Session of the United Kingdom Parliament which ended on the 10th November. The statement on the Washington Conference by the Prime Minister showed that the representatives of the Dominions would form part of the British Empire Delegation, and this in itself has given rise to favourable comment oversea. The Resolution on the subject of the Conference was an indication of the feeling of the House of Commons upon the necessity for reducing the crushing burden of armaments. Of particular interest to oversea readers are the discussions in the United Kingdom upon Oversea Settlement and the Trade Facilities Bill. Though the latter was brought forward as one of the measures in connection with the unemployment problem, the principle of guaranteed loans embodied in the Act will naturally receive close attention from Members of the Dominion Parliaments. A great deal of discussion has taken place on the subject of unemployment generally, and these discussions, together with the terms of the Unemployed Workers' Dependants (Temporary Provision) Act, should receive attention from oversea readers. Other subjects in the United Kingdom Parliament which are of more than local interest affect International Labour, the Canadian Navy, the Canadian Cattle Embargo, the Air Mail to Australia and South African Import Restrictions.

In Canada, the main Parliamentary interest has naturally centred round the General Election which took place in December, and resulted in the formation of a Government by Mr. Mackenzie King. The subjects dealt with in the present JOURNAL mainly relate to some Acts of the Fifth Session which were held over from previous issues. The Copyright Act, the Patent Amendment Act, and the Bankruptcy Amendment Act all deal with subjects of general interest to other Parliaments; while the passage of the Criminal Code Amendment Bill through Parliament and its material alteration in the Senate is instructive to those who are interested in an alteration of the law regarding sexual offences.

In the Parliament of the Australian Commonwealth, attention has already been drawn to some of the subjects of wide Imperial importance which have been discussed. Many other matters, *e.g.*, those relating to Finance (including the elimination of double Income Tax), Tariff, the New Hebrides, New Guinea, Immigration, etc., have been considered. In the State Parliaments, the Motherhood Endowment Bill of New South Wales and the Bill dealing with the abolition of the Upper House in Queensland are of special significance.

In New Zealand, the measure relating to the future Government of Western Samoa and the discussion upon it, together with the reference to Chinese indentured labour in the discussion on the Treaties of Peace Extension Act, will interest those concerned not only with the government of native races but with the Mandate system generally. Other matters affecting the Licensing Law in the Dominion and Prohibition in Samoa and the Cook Islands should receive attention. Matters of more local interest relate to Banking and Commerce, though the Maintenance Orders (Facilities for Enforcement) Bill* should not be lost sight of in reference to the legislation in the United Kingdom upon the same subject.

Under South Africa, some subjects have been dealt with for which room could not be found in previous issues. The discussion during last Session on the subject of the Union Offices in London gave rise to some interesting observations upon the representation of South Africa in England. The discussion on an Empire News Service, and the terms of the Children's Protection Act Amendment Act will be of interest to other Parliaments.

In December last the Prime Minister of Newfoundland made an important statement in Parliament upon the general condition of the country and its activities. Matters which called for special comment related to finance, trade and unemployment.

THE EDITOR.

EMPIRE PARLIAMENTARY ASSOCIATION
(*United Kingdom Branch*),
WESTMINSTER HALL,
HOUSES OF PARLIAMENT,
LONDON, S.W.1.

25th January, 1922.

* *Vide* also under Queensland. Information has been received that the State Parliaments of South Australia and Tasmania have passed Acts dealing with this subject, and these will be summarised in the next issue of the JOURNAL.

UNITED KINGDOM.

A special Session—the fourth of the present Parliament—was opened by the King with full State ceremonial on 14*th December,* 1921, *for the purpose of enabling both Houses to express approval of the Articles of Agreement for a Treaty between Great Britain and Ireland signed by the representatives of the two countries at* 10, *Downing Street on* 6*th December. The debates in Parliament occupied three days and on* 19*th December, after an adjournment over the week-end, Parliament was prorogued until* 31*st January,* 1922.*

IRISH FREE STATE.

(Treaty between Great Britain and Ireland: Dominion Status, Foreign Affairs, Defence, Ireland and the Empire.)

The House of Commons met on 14th December, at the opening of the special Session, to discuss and approve the Treaty concluded with the representatives of Southern Ireland for the establishment of an Irish Free State. The following is the full text of the Articles of Agreement for the Treaty:—

The Irish Free State.

(1) Ireland shall have the same constitutional status in the community of nations known as the British Empire as the Dominion of Canada, the Commonwealth of Australia, the Dominion of New Zealand, and the Union of South Africa, with a Parliament having powers to make laws for the peace, order, and good government of Ireland, and an Executive responsible to that Parliament, and shall be styled and known as the Irish Free State.

The Canadian Model.

(2) Subject to the provisions hereinafter set out, the position of the Irish Free State in relation to the Imperial Parliament and Government and otherwise shall be that of the Dominion of Canada, and the law, practice, and constitutional usage governing the relationship of the Crown, or the representative of the Crown, and of the Imperial Parliament to the Dominion of Canada shall govern their relationship to the Irish Free State.

The Governor-General.

(3) The representative of the Crown in Ireland shall be appointed in like manner as the Governor-General of Canada, and in accordance with the practice observed in the making of such appointments.

---

* Subsequently altered to 7th February.

The Oath.

(4) The Oath to be taken by Members of the Parliament of the Irish Free State shall be in the following form :—

> I, ..., do solemnly swear true faith and allegiance to the Constitution of the Irish Free State as by law established, and that I will be faithful to H.M. King George V., his heirs and successors by law, in virtue of the common citizenship of Ireland with Great Britain, and her adherence to and membership of the group of nations forming the British Commonwealth of nations.

Debt Obligations.

(5) The Irish Free State shall assume liability for the service of the Public Debt of the United Kingdom as existing at the date hereof, and towards the payment of war pensions as existing at that date, in such proportion as may be fair and equitable having regard to any just claims on the part of Ireland by way of set-off or counter-claim, the amount of such sums being determined, in default of agreement, by the arbitration of one or more independent persons being citizens of the British Empire.

Naval Defence.

(6) Until an arrangement has been made between the British and Irish Governments whereby the Irish Free State undertakes her own coastal defence, the defence by sea of Great Britain and Ireland shall be undertaken by His Majesty's Imperial forces, but this shall not prevent the construction or maintenance by the Government of the Irish Free State of such vessels as are necessary for the protection of the revenue or the fisheries.

The foregoing provisions of this article shall be reviewed at a conference of representatives of the British and Irish Governments to be held at the expiration of five years from the date hereof with a view to the undertaking by Ireland of a share in her own coastal defence.

Harbour Facilities.

(7) The Government of the Irish Free State shall afford to His Majesty's Imperial Forces :—

> (A) In time of peace such harbour and other facilities as are indicated in the Annex hereto, or such other facilities as may fro time to time be agreed between the British Government and th Government of the Irish Free State ; and
>
> (B) In time of war or of strained relations with a Foreig Power such harbour and other facilities as the British Governmen may require for the purposes of such defence as aforesaid.

Military Defence.

(8) With a view to securing the observance of the principle o international limitation of armaments, if the Government of the Irisl Free State establishes and maintains a military defence force, th establishments thereof shall not exceed in size such proportion of th military establishments maintained in Great Britain as that which th population of Ireland bears to the population of Great Britain.

Freedom of Ports.

(9) The ports of Great Britain and the Irish Free State shall be freely open to the ships of the other country on payment of the customary port and other dues.

Police and Public Servants.

(10) The Government of the Irish Free State agrees to pay fair compensation on terms not less favourable than those accorded by the Act of 1920 to judges, officials, members of Police Forces, and other Public Servants, who are discharged by it or who retire in consequence of the change of government effected in pursuance hereof.

Provided that this agreement shall not apply to members of the Auxiliary Police Force or to persons recruited in Great Britain for the Royal Irish Constabulary during the two years next preceding the date hereof. The British Government will assume responsibility for such compensation or pensions as may be payable to any of these excepted persons.

Northern Ireland.

(11) Until the expiration of one month from the passing of the Act of Parliament for the ratification of this instrument, the powers of the Parliament and the Government of the Irish Free State shall not be exercisable as respects Northern Ireland, and the provisions of the Government of Ireland Act, 1920, shall, so far as they relate to Northern Ireland, remain of full force and effect, and no election shall be held for the return of Members to serve in the Parliament of the Irish Free State for constituencies in Northern Ireland, unless a resolution is passed by both Houses of the Parliament of Northern Ireland in favour of the holding of such elections before the end of the said month.

Ulster Boundaries.

(12) If, before the expiration of the said month, an Address is presented to His Majesty by both Houses of the Parliament of Northern Ireland to that effect, the powers of the Parliament and the Government of the Irish Free State shall no longer extend to Northern Ireland, and the provisions of the Government of Ireland Act, 1920 (including those relating to the Council of Ireland), shall, so far as they relate to Northern Ireland, continue to be of full force and effect, and this instrument shall have effect subject to the necessary modifications.

Provided that if such an Address is so presented a Commission consisting of three persons, one to be appointed by the Government of the Irish Free State, one to be appointed by the Government of Northern Ireland, and one who shall be Chairman, to be appointed by the British Government, shall determine in accordance with the wishes of the inhabitants, so far as may be compatible with economic and geographic conditions, the boundaries between Northern Ireland and the rest of Ireland, and for the purposes of the Government of Ireland Act, 1920, and of this instrument the boundary of Northern Ireland shall be such as may be determined by such Commission.

The Council of Ireland.

(13) For the purpose of the last foregoing article the powers of the Parliament of Southern Ireland under the Government of Ireland Act, 1920, to elect members of the Council of Ireland shall, after the Parliament of the Irish Free State is constituted, be exercised by that Parliament.

If Ulster accepts.

(14) After the expiration of the said month, if no such Address as is mentioned in article 12 hereof is presented, the Parliament and Government of Northern Ireland shall continue to exercise as respects Northern Ireland the powers conferred on them by the Government of Ireland Act, 1920, but the Parliament and Government of the Irish Free State shall in Northern Ireland have in relation to matters in respect of which the Parliament of Northern Ireland has not power to make laws under that Act (including matters which under the said Act are within the jurisdiction of the Council of Ireland) the same powers as in the rest of Ireland, subject to such other provisions as may be agreed in manner hereinafter appearing.

Safeguards for a Consenting Ulster.

(15) At any time after the date hereof the Government of Northern Ireland and the provisional Government of Southern Ireland, hereinafter constituted, may meet for the purpose of discussing the provisions subject to which the last foregoing article is to operate in the event of no such address as is therein mentioned being presented, and those provisions may include :—

(A) Safeguards with regard to patronage in Northern Ireland.

(B) Safeguards with regard to the collection of revenue in Northern Ireland.

(C) Safeguards with regard to import and export duties affecting the trade or industry of Northern Ireland.

(D) Safeguards for minorities in Northern Ireland.

(E) The settlement of the financial relations between Northern Ireland and the Irish Free State.

(F) The establishment and powers of a local militia in Northern Ireland and the relation of the Defence Forces of the Irish Free State and of Northern Ireland respectively.

And if at any such meeting provisions are agreed to, the same shall have effect as if they were included amongst the provisions subject to which the powers of the Parliament and the Government of the Irish Free State are to be exercisable in Northern Ireland under article 14 hereof.

Religious Freedom.

(16) Neither the Parliament of the Irish Free State nor the Parliament of Northern Ireland shall make any law so as either directly or indirectly to :—

Endow any religion or prohibit or restrict the free exercise thereof, or

Give any preference or impose any disability on account of religious belief or religious status, or

Affect prejudicially the right of any child to attend a school receiving public money without attending the religious instruction at the school, or

Make any discrimination as respects State aid between schools under the management of different religious denominations, or

Divert from any religious denomination or any educational institution any of its property except for public utility purposes and on payment of compensation.

Interim Provisional Government.

(17) By way of provisional arrangement for the administration of Southern Ireland during the interval which must elapse between the date hereof and the constitution of a Parliament and Government of the Irish Free State in accordance therewith, steps shall be taken forthwith for summoning a meeting of Members of Parliament elected for constituencies in Southern Ireland since the passing of the Government of Ireland Act, 1920, and for constituting a provisional Government, and the British Government shall take the steps necessary to transfer to such provisional Government the powers and machinery requisite for the discharge of its duties, provided that every member of such provisional Government shall have signified in writing his or her acceptance of this instrument. But this arrangement shall not continue in force beyond the expiration of twelve months from the date hereof.

Ratification.

(18) This instrument shall be submitted forthwith by His Majesty's Government for the approval of Parliament and by the Irish signatories to a meeting summoned for the purpose of the Members elected to sit in the House of Commons of Southern Ireland, and, if approved, shall be ratified by the necessary legislation.

(*Signed*)

On behalf of the British Delegation.

D. LLOYD GEORGE.
AUSTEN CHAMBERLAIN.
BIRKENHEAD.
WINSTON S. CHURCHILL.
L. WORTHINGTON-EVANS.
HAMAR GREENWOOD.
GORDON HEWART.

On behalf of the Irish Delegation.

ART Ó GRIOBHTHA.
MICHAÉL Ó COILEAIN.
RIOBÁRD BARTÚN.
E. S. Ó DUGAIN.
SEÓRSA GHABHÁIN ÚI DHUBHTHAIGH.

6th December, 1921.

ANNEX.

(1) The following are the specific facilities required :—

DOCKYARD PORT AT BEREHAVEN.

(A) Admiralty property and rights to be retained as at the date hereof. Harbour defences to remain in charge of British care and maintenance parties.

QUEENSTOWN.

(B) Harbour defences to remain in charge of British care and maintenance parties. Certain mooring buoys to be retained for use of His Majesty's ships.

BELFAST LOUGH.

(C) Harbour defences to remain in charge of British care and maintenance parties.

LOUGH SWILLY.

(D) Harbour defences to remain in charge of British care and maintenance parties.

AVIATION.

(E) Facilities in the neighbourhood of the above ports for coastal defence by air.

OIL FUEL STORAGE.

(F) Haulbowline and Rathmullen to be offered for sale to commercial companies under guarantee that purchasers shall maintain a certain minimum stock for Admiralty purposes.

(2) A Convention shall be made between the British Government and the Government of the Irish Free State to give effect to the following conditions :—

(A) That submarine cables shall not be landed or wireless stations for communication with places outside Ireland be established except by agreement with the British Government ; that the existing cable landing rights and wireless concessions shall not be withdrawn except by agreement with the British Government ; and that the British Government shall be entitled to land additional submarine cables or establish additional wireless stations for communication with places outside Ireland.

(B) That lighthouses, buoys, beacons, and any navigational marks or navigational aids shall be maintained by the Government of the Irish Free State as at the date hereof, and shall not be removed or added to except by agreement with the British Government.

(C) That war signal stations shall be closed down and left in charge of care and maintenance parties, the Government of the Irish Free State being offered the option of taking them over and working them for commercial purposes, subject to Admiralty inspection and guaranteeing the upkeep of existing telegraphic communication therewith.

(3) A Convention shall be made between the same Governments for the regulation of civil communication by air.

DEBATE IN HOUSE OF COMMONS.

Lieut.-Colonel Sir Samuel Hoare (Coalition Unionist, *Chelsea*) opened the debate by moving :—

"That an humble Address be presented to His Majesty as followeth :

"Most Gracious Sovereign, We, Your Majesty's most dutiful and loyal subjects, the Commons of the United Kingdom of Great Britain and Ireland, in Parliament assembled, beg leave to thank Your Majesty for the Most Gracious Speech which Your Majesty has addressed to both Houses of Parliament.

"Having taken into consideration the Articles of Agreement presented to us by Your Majesty's Command, we are ready to confirm and ratify these Articles in order that the same may be established for ever by the mutual consent of the peoples of Great Britain and Ireland, and we offer to Your Majesty our humble congratulations on the near accomplishment of that work of reconciliation to which Your Majesty has so largely contributed."

The turning point.

There were, the hon. and gallant Member said, some who believed in the sincerity of their hearts that they could settle Ireland by the sword. It had been left to the British Monarchy, in the person of the King, to point a better and surer way to settlement. His Majesty's Gracious Speech at Belfast was the turning point in the crisis. They were making a peace with Ireland, not because they had to make a peace, but because they wished to make a peace.

They wished to make the friendship between the two countries permanent and secure. They asked Ireland to take her place as a peer at the Round Table of the Empire's government. Not only did Great Britain make the invitation; it was an invitation from every one of the great self-governing Dominions of the British Empire. Ireland might bring to the service of the Empire a wealth of history and tradition and foreign influence such as was not possessed by any of the Dominions. More than that, she could bring to the service of the Irish Free State a unique wealth of political experience.

The Right Hon. G. Barnes (Labour, *Glasgow, Gorbals*), in seconding the motion, said they had to make up their minds as far as they could that Irishmen and Britishers would in future live on terms of amity, in the same way as they lived in amity with the peoples of Canada, Australia, and other overseas Dominions. They could not longer withhold from Irishmen the right to manage their own affairs—a right for which they had so long fought. That was the principle which had been progressively applied to the Dominions overseas until now, without conflict or ill-will, they had absolutely free hands so far as their own internal affairs were concerned.

Labour's eager approval.

The Right Hon. J. R. Clynes (Chairman of the Parliamentary Labour Party) regarded the Articles of Agreement as a triumph of national patriotism—a victory for an enduring national spirit over every obstacle and every form of force which that spirit had encountered for centuries. The truth was that nationhood once acquired would endure in spite of any acts of repression directed against it. The Articles travelled on the lines long advocated by Labour. He looked upon them as the instrument of a lasting and beneficent settlement between Ireland and Great Britain.

"The Agreement," said the right hon. gentleman, "is an act of justice and a manifestation to us of the futility of any attempt to govern peoples against their will. . . . It is essential to have unity between the South and the North of Ireland for the future prosperity of the whole of Ireland. I believe that, until the North and the South come together, they can never realise how much they have in common and how little fundamentally there is for conflict." The representatives of the North of Ireland had now a golden opportunity to secure not only all substantial safeguards for their interests, but to make a priceless contribution to the creation of a reconciled Ireland which would be a lasting friend and partner with Great Britain, and a welcome force for the future progress of mankind.

The Labour Party were eager to approve the Agreement, and were convinced that it had the support of the vast majority of the Irish people.

Prime Minister's speech.

The Prime Minister (the Right Hon. D. Lloyd George) remarked that no Agreement ever arrived at between two peoples had been received with so enthusiastic and so universal a welcome as the Agreement with the Irish representatives. The Articles had been received in every quarter in Great Britain with satisfaction and relief. They had been received throughout the whole of His Majesty's Dominions with acclaim. He saw that they were characterised in some quarters as a humiliation for Britain and for the Empire. "The Dominions of the Crown," said the Premier, "are not in the habit of rejoicing over acts of humiliation to the Empire for which they have sacrificed so much." At home, in the great Dominions of the Crown, among Britain's Allies, throughout the whole of the civilised world, the Agreement had been received not merely with satisfaction, but with delight and hope.

The main operation of the scheme was the raising of Ireland to the status of a Dominion of the British Empire—that of a Free State within the Empire, with a common citizenship, and by virtue of that membership in the Empire and that common citizenship owning allegiance to the King.

Mr. Ronald M'Neill (Coalition Unionist, *Canterbury*): "Owning allegiance!"

The Prime Minister: "And swearing allegiance to the King. . . . What does 'Dominion status' mean? It is difficult and dangerous to give a definition. When I made a statement at the request of the Imperial Conference to this House as to what had passed at our gathering, I pointed out the anxiety of all the Dominion Delegates not to have any rigid definitions. That is not the way of the British Constitution. We realise the danger of rigidity and the danger of limiting our constitution by too many finalities.

Dominion status freedom.

" Many of the Premiers delivered notable speeches in the course of that Conference emphasising the importance of not defining too precisely what the relations of the Dominions were with ourselves, what their powers were, and what was the limit of the power of the Crown.

" It is something that has never been defined by an Act of Parliament, even in this country, and yet it works perfectly. All we can say is that whatever measure of freedom Dominion status gives to Canada, Australia, New Zealand or South Africa, that will be extended to Ireland, and there will be the guarantee, contained in the mere fact that the status is the same, that wherever there is an attempt at encroaching upon the rights of Ireland, every Dominion will begin to feel that its own position is put in jeopardy.

" That is a guarantee which is of infinite value to Ireland. In practice it means complete control over their own internal affairs without any interference from any other part of the Empire. They are the rulers of their own hearth—finance, administration, legislation, so far as their domestic affairs are concerned—and the representatives of the Sovereign will act on the advice of the Dominion Ministers.

External affairs.

" The position of the Dominions in reference to external affairs has been completely revolutionised in the course of the last four years. . . . The Dominions since the War have been given equal rights with Great Britain in the control of the foreign policy of the Empire. That was won by the aid they gave us in the Great War. I wonder what Lord Palmerston would have said if a Dominion representative had come over here in 1856 and said, ' I am coming along to the Congress of Vienna.' I think he would have dismissed him with polite disdain and wondered where he came from. But the conditions were different. There was not a single platoon from the Dominions in the Crimean War.

" It would have been equally inconceivable that there should have been no representative of the Dominions at Versailles or at Washington. Why ? There had been a complete change of the conditions since 1856. What were they ? A million men . . . had gone from all the Dominions to help the Motherland in the hour of danger. Although they came to help the Empire in a policy which they had no share in passing, they felt that in future it was an unfair dilemma to impose on them. They said, ' You are putting us in this position : Either we have to support you in a policy which we might or might not approve, or we have to desert the old country in the time of trouble. That is a dilemma in which you ought never to put us.'

"That was right. That was just. That was advantageous to both Parties. We acceded to it gladly.

Foreign Policy: place of the Dominions.

"The machinery is the machinery of the British Government—the Foreign Office, the Ambassadors. The machinery must remain here. It is impossible that it could be otherwise, unless you had a Council of Empire, with representatives elected for the purpose. . . . The instrument of the foreign policy of the Empire is the British Foreign Office. That has been accepted by all the Dominions as inevitable. But they claim a voice in determining the lines of our future policy. At the last Imperial Conference they were there discussing our policy in Germany, our policy in Egypt, our policy in America, our policy all over the world; and we are now acting upon the mature general decisions arrived at with the common consent of the whole Empire.

"The sole control of Britain over foreign policy is now vested in the Empire as a whole. . . . The advantage to us is that joint control means joint responsibility, and when the burden of Empire has become so vast it is well that we should have the shoulders of these young giants under the burden to help us along. It restrains rash Ministers and it will stimulate timorous ones. It widens the prospect. When we took part in discussion at the Imperial Conference what struck us was this, that from the mere fact that representatives were there from the Pacific and the Indian Ocean, and from other ends of the world, with different interests, the discussion broadened into a world survey. That was an advantage.

"Our troubles were Upper Silesia, the Ruhr Valley, Angora and Egypt. They came there with other questions—with the problems of the Pacific, Honolulu, the Philippines, Nagasaki and Pekin. All these problems were brought into the common stock, and a wide survey was taken by all the representatives of the Empire, who would honour the policy decided upon and support that policy when it was challenged. They felt that there was not one of them who was not speaking for hundreds of thousands and millions of men, who were prepared to risk their fortunes and their lives for a great Empire."

Ireland and the Empire.

Proceeding the Premier showed how this development within the last four years had altered the argument about the union with Ireland. If Pitt had found that the question of treaties, alliances, peace and war were left, as they were now, to a great council of free peoples, each of them self-governing, and coming together with the Motherland to discuss their affairs and decide upon their policy, what he would have done then would have been to invite Ireland to come to that Council Chamber, to merge her interests and her ideals with the common ideals of the whole of those free peoples throughout the Empire.

" Ireland," the Premier continued, " will share the rights of the Empire and share the responsibilities of the Empire. She will take her part with other Free States in discussing the policy of the Empire. That, undoubtedly, commits her to responsibilities which I have no doubt her people will honour, whatever ensues as a result of the policy agreed upon in the Council Chamber of the Empire."

It was all very well to say " Dominion Home Rule " or " Dominion Self-Government," but the difficulties only began there—difficulties formidable and peculiar to Ireland. They did not settle great complicated problems the moment they uttered a good phrase about them. The Prime Minister went on to enumerate the things that made a settlement in Ireland difficult. " I hope we have found the solution," he said. " I never like to be too confident or too sanguine when I am talking of Ireland. Therefore I am not going to say that we have found the specific at last. It has been said so often—but we must try. At any rate, I can see nothing better."

Allegiance; Armed Forces, etc.

There had been complete acceptance of allegiance to the British Crown, of membership in the Empire, and of common citizenship. The first of the great difficulties was the security of Great Britain, if full and complete Dominion Government were conferred on Ireland. It was desirable in the interests of the Empire, in the interests of the world, in the interests of Ireland herself, that there should be a limitation imposed upon the raising of armaments and the training of armed men in Ireland. The limit was not beyond what was necessary for the purpose. If they took the most sanguine view the numbers would not exceed, for the whole of Ireland, 40,000 men.

The Right Hon. Sir F. Banbury (Coalition Unionist, *City of London*)**:** " How do you propose to enforce the limit ? "

The Prime Minister: " My right hon. friend inquires, if this Treaty is broken, what shall we do to enforce it ? I am quite willing to face it. It is not a question of one Article. It is a question of the whole of the Articles. If Ireland breaks faith, breaks her Treaty, if such a situation has arisen, the

British Empire has been quite capable of dealing with breaches of Treaties with much more formidable Powers than Ireland; but we want to feel perfectly clear that when she does so the responsibility is not ours, but entirely on other shoulders."

The Navy.

"With regard to the Navy," the Premier observed, "we felt that we could not allow the ordinary working of Dominion status to operate. Here we had the experience of the late War, which showed how vital Ireland was to the security of this country. The access to our ports is along the coasts of Ireland. For offence or defence Ireland is a post which is a key in many respects, and though I agree that Ireland is never likely to raise a great formidable navy which will challenge us upon the seas, I would remind the House that minelayers and submarines do not cost much, and that they were our trouble mostly in the War.

"As to naval accessibility to the ports of Ireland—the use of coastal positions for the defence of our commerce and the British Islands in time of war is vital. We could not leave that merely to good-will or the general interpretation of vague conditions of the Treaty. Good-will has been planted, but it must have time to grow, and must not be exposed too much to the winds of temptation. Therefore we felt that where the security of these islands was concerned we must leave nothing to chance."

Ireland and Defence.

The right hon. gentleman proceeded to say that Mr. Asquith had charged him with having stigmatised Dominion Home Rule as lunacy. He had never done so. What he said was that to allow Ireland the right to raise unlimited forces which would provoke civil war there and be a menace to Great Britain, to allow Ireland to raise a navy and any craft she chose when Ireland was so vital to the defence of Great Britain, was lunacy. He still said that. It was proposed that in five years the conditions should be reviewed, and the Government trusted it would then be possible to allocate a certain proportion of defence to Ireland herself.

He was reluctant to assent to any proposition which would involve Ireland having the right to impose tariffs upon British goods, although undoubtedly it was a Dominion right. Ultimately the British representatives assented to it for the reason that Ireland was more dependent upon Britain in the matter of trade than was Britain upon Ireland. It was very important that there should be a protection against any legislation which would exclude British ships from the coastal trade with Ireland, and that was inserted in the Agreement.

Ulster.

Coming to what he termed "the more vexed question of Ulster," the Premier said they had all given a definitely clear pledge that under no conditions would they agree to any proposals that would involve the coercion of Ulster. He had always been strongly of the view that they could not do it without provoking a conflict which would simply mean transferring the agony from the South to the North, thus unduly prolonging the Irish controversy instead of settling it. The British Government had never for a moment forgotten the pledge, but that did not preclude them from endeavouring to persuade Ulster to come into an All-Ireland Parliament. It could not be held that arguing a question and saying that a person ought to take a certain course was coercing him.

Ulster had her option either to join an All-Ireland Parliament or to remain exactly as she was. No change from her present position would be involved if she decided by an Address to the Crown to remain where she was. If she exercised her option with her full rights under the Act of 1920 she would remain without a single change except in respect of boundaries. The British Government were of opinion that it was desirable, if Ulster was to remain a separate unit, that there should be a readjustment of boundaries. There was no doubt, certainly since the Act of 1920, that the majority of the people of two counties* preferred being with their Southern neighbours to being in the Northern Parliament.

It was not proposed to have a readjustment of the boundaries of the six counties, but of the boundaries of the North of Ireland which would take into account where there were homogeneous populations of the same kind as that which was in Ulster, and where there were homogeneous populations of the same kind as they had in the South.

Prestige of the Empire enhanced.

After dealing with the machinery to be provided for giving effect to the Treaty, the Premier said the prestige of the Empire had been enormously enhanced by this Agreement. It had given the Empire a new strength. It had added to the conviction which the world already possessed that Britain somehow or other always got over her difficulties.

"The freedom of Ireland," the right hon. gentleman added, "increases the strength of the Empire by ending

* Tyrone and Fermanagh.

the conflict which has been carried on for centuries with varying success, but with unvarying discredit. Incidents of that struggle have done more to impair the honour of this country than any aspect of its world dominion throughout the ages. It was not possible to interchange views with the truest friends of Britain without feeling that there was something in reference to Ireland to pass over. This brings new credit to the Empire, and it brings new strength. It brings to our side a valiant comrade.

"It would be taking too hopeful a view of the future to imagine that the last peril of the British Empire has passed. There are still dangers lurking in the mists. Whence will they come? From what quarter? Who knows? But when they do come, I feel glad to know that Ireland will be there by our side, and the old motto that 'England's danger is Ireland's opportunity' will have a new meaning. As in the case of the Dominions in 1914, our peril will be her danger, our fears will be her anxieties, our victories will be her joy."

The Ulster view.

Captain C. Craig (Chairman of the Ulster Unionist Party) said that Ulster was no party to the Agreement and repudiated it so far as her own area was concerned. The Oath contained in the Agreement was a conglomeration of senseless words and not worth the paper it was written on. He believed that within a very few years Sinn Fein would throw off all the remaining trammels or bonds which would bind that party to Great Britain after the Act embodying the Agreement was passed, and would become a Republic. Whenever that happened, he did not believe England would raise a finger, or send a pinnace or a soldier, to recover Ireland's allegiance.

Ulster, at the present moment at any rate, had no intention whatever of coming into an All-Ireland Parliament. The Prime Minister had reiterated that Ulster was not to be coerced; but for the last two or three months Ulster had been subjected to a most unworthy form of coercion. The Press campaign against her, organised and fed by the Government, had been one of the most disgraceful features in connection with the Government. Nothing the Prime Minister could have done was more calculated to rouse the ire and suspicion of the Ulster people than the appointment of a Boundary Commission.

The Right Hon. Lord Hugh Cecil (Independent Unionist, *Oxford University*) said there would be no peace in Ireland until the mass of the Irish people had a higher conception of the moral duties of a citizen—until at any rate they had scruples about murder. Drive murder out of Irish life and they might be able to have political and civic freedom.

Mr. Asquith's endorsement.

When the debate was resumed on 15th December,

The Right Hon. H. H. Asquith (Leader of the Independent Liberal Party) said he had been preaching Dominion self-government for the last two years. He agreed whole-heartedly with those who said that Dominion status was a term which it was difficult—he would go further and say that he thought it would be dangerous—to regard as one that could be defined with mathematical or scientific precision. In an Empire so varied, it had been the real cause of their unique success in reconciling local autonomy with Imperial unity that Dominion status had never come out of a cast iron mould, but had been applied time after time in quarter after quarter with flexibility and elasticity.

It was because this Treaty between two peoples, as far as he could judge, gave the full substance of self-government without ignoring special local conditions that he heartily commended it to the acceptance of the House. Concluding with a solemn warning to the House, Mr. Asquith said it would be a great, almost a fatal, mistake when the Agreement had been ratified to suppose that they had come to an end of their difficulties. But if that great international pact was ratified they could start on their future relations with clean hands and a clear conscience.

An Amendment.

Colonel John Gretton (Unionist, ***Burton*****)** moved an amendment to the Address in these terms :—

> "This House regrets that the proposed settlement of the government of Ireland indicated in the Gracious Speech from the Throne involves the surrender of the rights of the Crown in Ireland, gives power to establish an independent Irish Army and Navy, violates pledges given to Ulster, and fails to safeguard the rights of the Loyalist population in Southern Ireland."

Mr. Rupert Gwynne (Coalition Unionist, ***Eastbourne*****)** seconded the amendment.

The Secretary of State for the Colonies (the Right Hon. Winston Churchill), having dealt with the origin of the negotiations, contended that every one of the conditions insisted on by the British Government had been embodied in the Treaty. If Irish unity could be achieved it could only be because the Government of the Irish Free State would have convinced Ulster of its loyal association with the British Empire and would have offered Ulster conditions of security and partnership in every way satisfactory to her. Of those conditions Ulster was the sole judge, and the initiative rested entirely with her.

"I do not believe," said the right hon. gentleman, "that Irish Republicans have consented to swear allegiance to the British Crown and Empire in the terms which are set forth . . . out of fear of a renewal of warfare, but in the hope that by so doing they will render possible that unity between North and South of their country for which more than anything else in the whole of this settlement they care, and on which they more than anything else have set their hearts, and for which they are prepared to make the greatest efforts and sacrifice." The Oath was far more precise and searching than the ordinary oath which was taken elsewhere.

Sir W. H. Davison (Coalition Unionist, *Kensington, S.*): "Why should they not take the Canadian Oath ?"

The Secretary of State for the Colonies: "The Oath they are asked to take is more carefully and precisely drawn than the existing Oath, and it was chosen because it was more acceptable to the people whose allegiance we are seeking." It was not, the right hon. gentleman said, as a humiliation that the Treaty was viewed by the world, or by the Empire. It was as a great, peculiar manifestation of British genius, over which the friends of England all over the world had rejoiced.

Mr. Bonar Law.

The Right Hon. A. Bonar Law (Coalition Unionist, *Glasgow, Central*) said that he was in favour of the Agreement. He had noticed that there seemed to be a bitter feeling growing up in Ulster on the ground that she had been betrayed, but he honestly thought it was not justified by anything in the Agreement. The only aspect of the Treaty which was open to serious objection was the appointment of a Boundary Commission, because if ever the Ulster people considered that anything was settled, and settled for ever, it was the boundaries.

The Secretary of State for War (the Right Hon. Sir Laming Worthington-Evans) denied a statement made in the course of the debate that there was power under the Agreement to establish an independent Irish Navy. What was agreed to was that at the end of five years there should be a conference to see whether Ireland should be asked to take over a part of her coastal defence in the same way that Canada, South Africa, and every Dominion of the Crown had done.

On 16th December—the third day of the debate—the discussion was continued by

The Right Hon. Arthur Henderson (Labour, *Widnes*), who said the outstanding fact of the Treaty was that it meant peace.

The Leader of the House (the Right Hon. Austen Chamberlain) remarked that Ulster remained under the Treaty, as he promised she should remain, mistress of her own fate. Until she had taken her decision the Parliament of the Irish Free State had no authority in Northern Ireland, and if her decision be, as evidently it was going to be, that at the present time she would not join in an Irish Free State, the Irish Free State Parliament in Dublin would never exercise any authority within the boundaries of Northern Ireland.

On a division the amendment was negatived by 401 votes against 58, and the Address was then agreed to.

DEBATE IN HOUSE OF LORDS.

The Articles of Agreement were debated in the House of Lords on 14th, 15th and 16th December.

Viscount Morley moved an Address in reply to the King's Speech in terms identical with that proposed in the Lower House.

The noble lord said he wondered whether any Englishman, any citizen of Great Britain, could look back upon the government of Ireland by Great Britain as an object of pride. Surely, so far from being that, the misrule of Ireland by Great Britain had been a catchword for an age or more. A great nation ought to have a good conscience. Could anybody defend the proposition that the government of Ireland all these years had been such as the political conscience could approve? He thought not. It was the naked government of another kingdom by irresponsible force—irresponsible, that was to say, as regarded those whom the system was to affect.

The Agreement and all the measures to carry it further in the way of good machinery, would depend upon the continuance, both in Great Britain and in Ireland, of the same spirit as marked that day.

Act of reconciliation.

The Earl of Dunraven, in seconding the motion, said they were met to approve a great act of reconciliation that would completely change the whole relations in the future between Great Britain and Ireland, would heal the feuds of centuries and bring about an era, he believed, of true friendship, understanding and fellowship between the two peoples. They could not expect a miracle, and it would be little short of a miracle for any people to take over that great responsibility without difficulty, and to put the whole machinery for complete self-government into operation without friction. Ireland, therefore, would want the help of all her friends, and he rejoiced to see that the Southern Unionists had received assurances from the chairman of the Irish Delegation* guaranteeing the safeguarding of their interests and asking for their help and support.

The Marquess of Crewe thought it might be fairly claimed on behalf of His Majesty's Government that the Agreement, taken as a whole, was not Separatist in any way in its effects. But it was bound to receive some opposition. The men who were the heirs of the Fenians of 1886 and the Invincibles of 1882 were not likely to be content with a measure of this kind. He could not believe, however, that they were numerous, nor could he believe that other opponents on the same side could be numerous—that was to say, those who were mere *doctrinaire* revolutionaries and clung to terms and forms more than they did to the essentials of such a proposal as that.

He apprehended the position of Ulster, and he did not think the British Government would be surprised if some hard things were said about them in Northern Ireland. But he did not comprehend in any sense the attitude of English Tories who were prepared to believe that a renewal of civil war, which was the only alternative, would be preferable to the carrying out of the Agreement.

The choice of title.

The Secretary of State for Foreign Affairs (the Marquess Curzon of Kedleston) remarked that there was nothing sinister about the selection of the title of Irish Free State. It was chosen not merely because it gratified the Irishmen, but because it rested upon a distinct historical precedent in recent history, viz., that of the Orange Free State. The draft of the constitution of the Irish Free State would be drawn up by the Provisional Government that was to be set up in Ireland. It was earnestly hoped that all parties in Ireland would participate in that act. Under the new Articles, Ireland was completely mistress of all forms of taxation, direct and indirect. She absolutely controlled her own Customs and Excise. The British Government trusted that this power would not be exercised in any way likely to impair the relations between the two islands.

" At the present moment," Lord Curzon proceeded, " the erection of tariffs between the States that were set up in Europe by the Treaty of Versailles has unquestionably impeded their recovery from the effects of the War. We do not in the least grudge to Ireland the power to protect new industries or to make safeguards of any sort that she may think necessary for her economic development; but we are very strongly of opinion that the freest possible trade between the two islands is best, and is, indeed, essential for both." Was this peace, if it were peace, honourable to Ireland? No one, he thought, would doubt that proposition. He could understand the contention that the British Government had given too much. They had to measure the price they paid for a commodity, however, not merely by the value of that commodity at the moment, but by its prospective value in the future. Here, he ventured to think, they were purchasing an article which would greatly appreciate in value as time went on.

Honourable to the Empire.

Was this a measure of peace that was honourable to Great Britain and the British Empire? He maintained that in the Agreement they had vindicated the three essential principles which had over and over again been laid down—(1) the position and supremacy of the Crown; (2) the security of the United Kingdom; and (3) the integrity of the Empire.

"For my own part," said the noble marquess, "I look for the vindication of this Agreement, not merely to its contents, but to its consequences. This will, as I hope, cover the whole of our national life, both at home and abroad. . . . There has not been a Foreign Minister in this country during the last 50 years who has not felt, and indeed often stated, that the strength of England was diminished and her moral influence jeopardised by the unsolved position of the Irish question. This was felt not merely in the Dominions, where the Irish had been so disturbing a factor, but most of all in the United States of America, where the understanding which we so warmly desire has not only been rendered difficult, but almost impossible, by the existence of the Irish question."

They would never have got this settlement, said Lord Curzon, had it not been that Ulster, by legislation passed in 1920, attained a separate being of her own, with her own rights entrenched therein behind an Act of Parliament. He did not know whether Ulster was going to accept this plan.

Lord Carson: "No."

The Secretary of State for Foreign Affairs: "That remains to be seen. I am quite sure that Nationalist Ireland would never have accepted it before."

Peaceful and prosperous.

"I contemplate," Lord Curzon added, "not merely a peaceful Ireland or a prosperous Ireland, taking advantage of her great resources; I contemplate an Ireland whic shall be a willing and a valuable member of the Common wealth of Nations that constitutes our Empire. During th last seven years, since the War began, I have realised, in manner which I should have deemed incredible before, th strength, the dignity and the independence enjoyed by thos constituent elements of our Empire. In domestic affairs the are practically independent. In Imperial affairs their Minister attend our Councils, they are kept informed of our policy they see all the most important papers.

"The day-by-day conduct of the foreign affairs of th Empire is, of course, in the hands of the Foreign Office; tha is determined by conditions of geography and convenience But from time to time those Ministers come here to review the whole field, and if any substantial change or departure i contemplated, either in their relations or in Imperial affairs it is only by the consent of the Imperial Conference, which ha insensibly developed into a sort of Imperial Cabinet, that th thing can be done.

"These are the conditions of peace. In war time thes Ministers take their seats at the council table; they becom Cabinet Ministers; they are responsible for the great decision that regulate the conduct of the war; they help to direct th war policy of the Empire, to determine the movement of troops the strategy of campaigns, and so forth. When war is con cluded, they attend the meetings of the Supreme Council wherever they are held; they sign the Peace Treaties; the are in a position of absolute equality with Great Britain; the are incorporated in the League of Nations—as Ireland, I hope will shortly be, for if this Agreement be accepted she has onl to ask it—and they enjoy an independent status there.

"These are the advantages, as I see them, which ar open to Ireland. Will her citizens be so blind as to refus them?"

Obsequies of the Unionist Party.

Lord Carson said the Unionist Party was dead and buri —strangled, without consultation with their followers, by tl leaders and trustees who were sent into the Government protect them. He suggested to the Marquess Curzon that was not in the least necessary, because he came down to tl House with his coat turned, that he should have tried to pictu himself in such a state of absolute nudity as his speech appear to indicate. The noble Marquess paid a generous and eloque tribute to Michael Collins—the head of the murder gang, Sir Hamar Greenwood described him only a few months a in the House of Commons.

The Secretary of State for Foreign Affairs: "I never mentioned him."

Lord Carson: "You mentioned the Delegates. Perhaps you did not know he was one of them. . . . He committed many murders with his own hands—the hand that you have now so willingly grasped." One thing the noble Marquess entirely forgot to tell them was how the Government came to the conclusion that the Articles of Agreement were so much for the benefit of the country. Unless as a matter of mere pretence there was not a noble lord who believed for a moment that the terms were passed upon the merits. Not at all. They were passed with a revolver pointed at the head of the British representatives.

An awful confession.

"When we are told," said Lord Carson, "that the reason why they had to pass these terms of Treaty, and the reason why they should not put down crime in Ireland, was because they had neither the men nor the money nor the backing, let me say that that is an awful confession to make to the British Empire. If you tell your Empire in India, in Egypt, and all over the world that you have not got the men, the money, the pluck, the inclination and the backing to restore law and order in a country within twenty miles of your own shores, you may as well begin to abandon the attempt to make British rule prevail throughout the Empire at all."

He defied anybody to show him anything in the Agreement but one provision—that was that Great Britain should scuttle out of Ireland. "You may talk of a Free State. You may put in window-dressing about the status of the Colonies and everything else; but from beginning to end of this document there is nothing you will find except that England, beaten to her knees by the gun of the assassin, says: 'We are willing to scuttle out of Ireland and to leave to the tender mercies of the assassins everybody who has supported us in the past.'"

They would find from the utterances of the Prime Minister that his enthusiasm for the preservation of the *status quo* had cooled as the number of murders multiplied in Ireland.

Ulster's "No."

A Treaty! On the very face of the document itself it was false. It said: "A Treaty between Great Britain and Ireland"—and before they signed it they never even asked Ulster. Like everybody else, they had betrayed Ulster.

"When Ulster refuses to accept these terms," Lord Carson remarked, "you proceed behind her back, having promised to submit new proposals to her which you never did until they were signed—you proceed to pass the Treaty, as you call it, which is now under discussion. Even then you must outrage her sentiments by putting her without her consent into what they call the Free State of Ireland. Why should you do that? Do you not know perfectly well that the way she takes that is this, and I am sure she is right—that you are throwing the whole weight of the British Government into the policy of compelling her to go under the Sinn Fein Parliament in Dublin? Why else did you put her in in that way, and how have you framed your Bill if she comes out? And I promise you she will come out. I promise you that she will come out within ten minutes of her hearing of the King's Assent being given to a Bill putting her in."

He advised his Ulster friends to stick to their old ideals of closer and closer connection with Great Britain.

A surrender.

The Marquess of Londonderry did not believe that Great Britain was so weary and so impoverished that a surrender of that description on the part of the Government could in the end receive a full measure of popular support. If it did it proclaimed one thing only—that sufficient force and crime could achieve any object its promoters desired.

The Archbishop of Canterbury said that when they were asked to say "yes" or "no" to a resolution accepting that proposal for a settlement, they gave a deliberate welcome to the endeavour. He hoped the vote would be cast on the side of hope, on the side of trustfulness, and on the side, as they believed, of ultimate peace.

The Earl of Midleton believed it was the feeling of the great mass of Southern Unionists that the future of Ireland depended on some arrangement being established which would bring together, in whatever form, the north and the south, and would bring the south into closer relations with Great Britain. So far as the Southern Unionists had any status or power in the new Government of Ireland it would be directed not to loosening, but to making firmer the ties with Great Britain.

Amendment moved.

The Duke of Northumberland moved the following amendment to the Address:—

"But we humbly represent to Your Majesty that this House regrets that the settlement of the Government of Ireland indicated in the gracious Speech from the Throne would involve the surrender of the rights of the

Crown in Ireland, give power to establish an independent Irish Army and Navy, would require further sacrifices from Ulster, and would not safeguard the rights of the loyalist population in Southern Ireland."

The noble Duke said that all the talk about national aspirations was nonsense. These aspirations were not those of the Irish people. "They are," he remarked, "the programme of a gang of conspirators who by a system of terror, by an alliance with our foreign enemies in time of war, and by the aid of a secret society have established one of the most awful tyrannies over the Irish people, and now pretend to be acting in their name. It is to this organisation, to this conspiracy, that we are going to hand over the wretched people of Ireland."

The Marquess of Salisbury said he had been a staunch fighter for the Union, but he knew that the cause of the Union was lost. They were defeated and they must accept the fact. There was no statesmanship in struggling against accomplished facts.

Government's alternatives.

The Lord Chancellor (Viscount Birkenhead), in winding up the debate, said adoption of the amendment meant that the House would have finally rejected the proposals to which the negotiators on both sides had set their individual hands. Did anybody suppose that if he at that moment could persuade the population of Ireland to continue the Union as that Union existed in the year 1905 he would be standing at the Woolsack to recommend these proposals, or to give his vote for them? But the Government could not remain idle and apathetic. Either they or some better Government must take some positive action.

The Government had to consider alternative courses. Either they had to invite no conference and to attempt more successfully to carry out their policy of coercion and repression, or they had to take the course, which in fact they had adopted. They reconsidered the whole military situation. He himself made a speech in that House in which he said plainly that in his judgment the kind of war in which they were at that moment engaged was not proceeding favourably to their cause, and a close examination was made. He did not at the present moment speak of the result in greater detail than this—that it was clear if they were to carry on the struggle it would be necessary for them to make an appeal for voluntary recruits to the young men of Great Britain and it would be equally necessary for them to make very large demands upon Parliament for credits.

Great things in a great way.

"This country," the Lord Chancellor observed, "raised in the War more millions in soldiers than there are men, women, and children of all ages in Ireland. Are we then to be told that we cannot accept this Agreement because we are making ourselves parties to national change and national humiliation. Is it not the truth that those who are great can afford to do great things in a great way? I shall be asked, 'Are you so confident that this is a great thing?' . . . I say it plainly that I do not tell your lordships too confidently. I am hopeful, but I will not dogmatise about the hope, for I see too many elements in the situation even now that make for uncertainty.

"The Irish people are a very strange, wayward, incalculable people. Nobody can ever say confidently whether they will do this or whether they will do the other thing in an unexpected contingency; but of this I am sure, that for the first time, with due and, as I think, adequate protection of the legitimate interests of Ulster, we have given a population which is overwhelmingly homogeneous an opportunity of taking its place side by side with the other communities which compose the British Empire." The Lord Chancellor went on to say that if the Government had resumed the war, and had broken the Irish people they would not have been any nearer an Irish settlement. At the conclusion of that war, with memories a thousand times more bitterly inflamed, they would have had to enter into negotiations with the Irish people.

He invited their Lordships to vote hoping that they would see in the future an Ireland which would at last after centuries be reconciled with this country.

On a division the amendment was negatived by 166 votes against 47, and the Address was, thereafter, agreed to.

CLOSE OF THE THIRD SESSION.

Parliament, which had stood adjourned since 19th August 1921, re-assembled on 18th October to conclude the business of the Third Session. The sittings lasted until 10th November when Parliament was formally prorogued after passing a series of measures dealing with the unemployment question.

WASHINGTON CONFERENCE.

(British and Dominion Delegates; Prime Minister's Statement; House of Commons Resolution.)

In reply to a question by the Right Hon. H. H. Asquith (Leader of the Independent Liberal Party), in the House of Commons on the 18th October, as to whether he could make any statement with regard to the Washington Conference,

The Prime Minister (the Right Hon. D. Lloyd George) said: "The Members of the British Empire Delegation will be as follows:—

Mr. Balfour.
Lord Lee of Fareham,

and I hope to go myself as soon as the Parliamentary and general situation renders this possible.*

"The British Ambassador to the United States, acting as a Delegate in the absence of myself or any other Delegate.

"As regards the Dominions and India, it was arranged at the recent Imperial Conference that His Majesty's Government should represent the whole Empire at Washington. In view, however, of the vital importance of the subjects to be considered at the Conference on Disarmament, it was felt to be very desirable that the Dominions should be represented by their Prime Ministers themselves, or, if this proved impossible, by persons nominated by them. None of the Prime Ministers of the Dominions has found it possible to attend in person, and the following have been nominated to represent their respective Dominions on the British Empire Delegation:—

Sir Robert Borden, for Canada;
Senator Pearce, for Australia;
Sir John Salmond, for New Zealand; as well as
Mr. Srinivása Sástri, for India.

"General Smuts has decided to leave the interests of the Union to the representatives of the British Government, who were made fully acquainted with his views at the recent Imperial Conference.

"Admiral-of-the-Fleet Earl Beatty will be the senior British Naval Expert at the outset of the Conference, and will be succeeded in due course by Admiral Chatfield.

"General the Earl of Cavan will be the principal Military Expert, and Vice-Air-Marshal Higgins will represent the Air Ministry.

---

* The course of the Irish negotiations and other matters subsequently prevented Mr. Lloyd George from fulfilling his intention to attend the Conference.

"Sir Maurice Hankey will be the British Secretary of the British Empire Delegation."

DEBATE IN HOUSE OF COMMONS.

A brief debate on the subject of the Washington Conference took place in the House of Commons on 4th November.

The Right Hon. J. R. Clynes (Chairman of the Parliamentary Labour Party) moved a resolution in these terms:—

> "That this House warmly approves of the meeting of the International Conference at Washington and trusts that a supreme effort will be made to arrive at such a measure of agreement as will secure a substantial and progressive reduction of the crushing burden of armaments."

The right hon. gentleman said the world was indebted to America for convening the Washington Conference. The League of Nations, which was the proposed instrument for an enduring peace following upon the War, was incomplete for its purpose. He regarded America as having taken a step which he hoped would carry further the main principles and objects to be attained by the League of Nations. The penalties of victory were so heavy and burdensome that it could not be claimed that any material benefit could be secured from war as war. Out of 35 nations who met in the previous year at Brussels at the International Financial Conference to discuss the financial situation, only four—Great Britain, the United States, India and Peru—raised enough money to cover their expenses.

Of the 31 other countries, only 11 raised more than three-quarters of their expenditure, nine raised between a half and three-quarters, and the remaining 11 raised less than half of what they spent.

Maintenance of Armaments.

Statements presented to the Brussels Conference showed that, on the average, some 20 per cent. of the national expenditure was being devoted to the maintenance of armaments now and to further preparations for war.

"When I first came into this House, some fifteen years ago," Mr. Clynes proceeded, "we were appalled at the figure of £1,000,000 for a battleship. We must now pay £8,000,000 or £10,000,000 for a battleship. This unproductive output, in our judgment, is a great contribution to economic unsettlement. It does find work, of course; but it also is the greatest contribution to national waste that can be made. . . . In the year before the War we spent upon our armaments £26,000,000 a year; now we spend over £100,000,000 a year.

In order to bring the world to an age of peace and security we can imagine nothing so effective as a reduction of armaments."

There were, he added, no moral, material and economic advantages in the expenditure on armaments. He ventured the opinion that narrow groupings of countries, however great and friendly, would not make for lasting peace. Future progress could be secured only by the whole of the great nations uniting together for the peace of the world. He pleaded for a universal alliance, for world friendship, and for the burying of the hate and jealously which had made war certain.

The Right Hon. Sir Donald Maclean (Chairman of the Independent Liberal Party in Parliament) observed that in the present year, three years after the conclusion of the Armistice, the United States, Great Britain, France, Italy, Japan, Belgium, Sweden, Holland and Denmark were jointly spending no less than £1,252,000,000 upon armaments. It was a melancholy reflection that in this country 4s. out of every pound of the Income Tax went to the cost of armaments. If they took the cost of past wars and of their present expenditure they were paying no less than 12s. of every pound of taxation for that purpose. " I hope," said Sir Donald, " that it is not too much to believe that heavy taxation, if other means fail, is the schoolmaster to bring us to peace."

Stark-naked Madness.

The Right Hon. G. N. Barnes (Labour, *Glasgow, Gorbals*) declared that war in the future from the human point of view would be hell let loose, and from a moral point of view sheer stark-naked madness. It could not be too often urged upon the working-men of this country, that, if they were going to play their part in securing their country's good, they must realise that, although war expenditure might bring a job to a few here and there, it must inevitably have the effect of reducing employment on the whole. The peoples of the world had their own little faults and follies, but he believed that they earnestly desired peace.

The Leader of the House (the Right Hon. Austen Chamberlain) said the invitation of President Harding was welcomed in Great Britain with a unanimity and thankfulness which it would be difficult to express in words. It was obviously true, as had been said by Mr. Clynes, that its acceptance was in no sense hostile or derogatory to the League of Nations. " Let us," said Mr. Chamberlain, "pursue every path that promises a possibility of our reaching the desired end. . . . It is in the realisation of the immensity of the cost which the world must pay for the struggle we have just fought, and the still greater horrors which must accompany any similar struggle in the future, that, perhaps, we shall find that determination to overcome difficulties which will enable the nations of the world to fulfil the purpose of the President when he summoned this Conference to lighten its armaments and to assure its peace.

"The policy of the British Government is to seek peace and to ensue it, and we join with the House at large in our prayer for the success of this Conference and in our earnest hope that it may bring relief to the overburdened nations of the world."

Bulwark to League of Nations Efforts.

The Right Hon. Lord Robert Cecil (Independent Unionist, *Hitchin*) said they could not have too many workers in the cause of peace. He welcomed the Washington Conference, not only as not antagonistic to and inconsistent with the League of Nations, but as a great assistance and great bulwark to the efforts which that institution was making in the same cause. The Assembly of the League had no question that the Washington Conference was an assistance to their work and in no way a hindrance to it.

Sir A. Shirley Benn (Coalition Unionist, *Plymouth, Drake*) said that as President of the Association of Chambers of Commerce he could state that there was a unanimous feeling among them that the best thing that could happen for Great Britain and the world at large was that the Washington Conference should be a success. Neither social progress nor happiness could exist in war time. Merchants and manufacturers of all countries realised, too, that no successful business could be conducted during war.

Colonel J. C. Wedgwood (Labour, *Newcastle-under-Lyme*) said it seemed to him that the present League of Nations was not so sure a foundation for future peace as cordial co-operation between England and America.

The resolution moved by Mr. Clynes was agreed to without a division.

CONFERENCE OF PRIME MINISTERS OF THE EMPIRE.

(Official Description.)

In the House of Commons on 27th October,

Mr. J. A. R. Marriott (Coalition Unionist, *Oxford*) asked the Secretary of State for the Colonies whether the meeting between representatives of the Imperial Government and the Prime Ministers and other representatives of the Overseas

Dominions and of India during the summer of 1921 was to be officially known as a cabinet or a conference; and whether he could state the reasons for the official appellation finally selected?

The Under-Secretary for the Colonies (Hon. Edward Wood), who replied, said: "It will be seen from the published summary of proceedings that the meeting held in the summer is officially known as 'Conference of Prime Ministers and Representatives of the United Kingdom, the Dominions and India.' It was so styled because, having regard to the character of the meetings, both the term 'Imperial Cabinet' and the term 'Imperial Conference' were thought unsuitable."

IMPERIAL PREFERENCE.

(British Industry Benefited.)

In the House of Commons on 2nd November,

Mr. Alfred T. Davies (Coalition Unionist, *Lincoln***)** asked the Secretary of State for the Colonies whether the Overseas Dominions were being systematically encouraged to give preference to British goods and British contracts; whether any tangible results had yet accrued to British industry; and, if so, the particulars?

The Secretary of the Overseas Trade Department (Sir Philip Lloyd-Greame), who replied, said: "The principle of Imperial Preference has already been confirmed by the Imperial War Conference at their meeting in London in 1917. The terms of a resolution passed unanimously are as follows:—

"The time has arrived when all possible encouragement should be given to the development of Imperial resources and especially to making the Empire independent of other countries in respect of food supplies, raw materials, and essential industries. With these objects in view this Conference expresses itself in favour of—

"The principle that each part of the Empire, having due regard to the interests of our Allies, shall give specially favourable treatment and facilities to the produce and manufactures of other parts of the Empire.

"With regard to the second part of the question, there is ample evidence that British industry has benefited by the preferences accorded by the Overseas Dominions."

OVERSEAS SETTLEMENT.

(Supplementary Estimate Voted.)

On 3rd November the House of Commons went into Committee of Supply and considered a supplementary estimate of

£330,000 for the Colonial Office in respect of grants in aid and other expenses connected with overseas settlement.

DEBATE IN HOUSE OF COMMONS.

The Hon. Gideon Murray (Coalition Unionist, *Glasgow, St. Rollox*) thought the Overseas Settlement Committee were much to be congratulated upon the manner in which they had carried out the operation of overseas settlement. He understood that some 60,000 people had been settled overseas since the Armistice, and that with the £330,000 now to be voted from 10,000 to 15,000 more were to go.

There were in addition, he understood, 60,000 applicants registered with the Overseas Settlement Committee who had expressed a desire to be given an opportunity to settle in the Dominions. Last February a State Conference sat in London at which certain proposals were put forward by Senator Millen on behalf of the Australian Government under which large State-aided schemes of fresh settlement in Australia should be entered into, and at least 20,000 men from Great Britain could be settled in that Dominion.

Only in the last few days there had appeared in *The Times* an article from the pen of Sir Joseph Carruthers, a well-known statesman in Australia, in which he advocated a much larger scheme than that proposed by Senator Millen. Since then Mr. Hughes, the Premier of Australia, who had as great a knowledge of the conditions in Great Britain as he had of the conditions in Australia, had put forward another suggestion under which some 100,000 men from this country were to be settled in Australia. It was by large schemes like those suggested by the three Australian statesmen he had named that it was possible to meet the present serious situation as regarded unemployment and the wishes of the many applicants who desired to settle in the Dominions overseas.

Labour and Emigration.

He agreed with a suggestion made by Mr. Clynes as to the necessity for Labour having a larger share in the supervision of emigration arrangements in Great Britain. He intended to ask the Government to consider the advisability of adding Labour representatives to the Overseas Settlement Committee. It was important that Labour should have every confidence in the arrangements for overseas settlement. He regarded overseas settlement as very important from the point of view of trade in Great Britain, and he urged the Government to take up the larger schemes of settlement to which he had referred.

Lieut.-Colonel J. Ward (Coalition Liberal, *Stoke-on-Trent*) hoped that the supplementary estimate was only a beginning. There were enormous territories in Australia that were uninhabited. It was impossible to suppose that those territories could be maintained for ever in their unoccupied and undeveloped condition so long as the pressure of the yellow races was as great as they knew it to be. If they could not people those parts of the British Dominions, it was a moral certainty they would be obliged to allow the people of Asiatic races to populate them.

If they did not consult the Labour organisations of this country from which they took the emigrants, and also the Labour organisations of the Dominions where they intended to settle them, they would have great difficulty. The suggestion had recently been made that the Federation of Trades Unions should call a conference of English-speaking people to discuss subjects from a purely British point of view. They had met the representatives of the Canadian trades unions and also an official deputation from the South African trades unions.

Views of Dominion Trade Unionists.

"It is a remarkable fact," said the hon. Member, "that the Canadian trades unions, the South African trades unions, and all the other parts of the British Dominions that have organised European labour in their midst, all insisted that the first item on the agenda of the conference, which is to be held in a year's time, should be the question of emigration. Mr. Crawford, not in any hostility, informed us that if we were to attempt at the present time to send miners to Johannesburg, or to South Africa generally, we should make a great mistake, because there is a surplus of mining labour already in existence there.

"On the other hand, he pointed out, in a lengthy discussion, that there are other forms of labour for which South Africa is almost entirely stopped, and the probabilities are that the South African Union Government would assist the British Government financially if they could only secure the kind of man and citizen that they want." The hon. Member advised the Colonial Office to extend their activities enormously along the lines suggested by the supplementary estimate.

Sir C. Kinloch-Cooke (Coalition Unionist, *Devonport*) said that migration was not an insular, but an Imperial problem, and if British settlers were to be attracted to the Dominions the overseas Governments must offer them greater advantages than they offered to foreigners coming in. On the other hand the Imperial Government must be prepared to grant further financial assistance for emigration. What was required was

State direction, State aid, and joint financial assistance. They had the State direction at last. They had the State aid. At present they had not the joint financial assistance, and until that came they would not have an Imperial system of migration.

Duty of the State.

The Right Hon. J. R. Clynes (Chairman of the Parliamentary Labour Party) observed that there was not any recorded Parliamentary Labour Party doctrine on that subject. The question should be viewed without the prejudices of either Party or class, and without regard for any view they might entertain concerning existing unemployment difficulties. He was glad the State was taking more notice than it did of this question, and was leaving it less to private agents. It no longer trusted the emigrant to the mercies of shipping agents, or to those who wanted to plant people upon the land in certain parts of the world for some particular private enterprise in which they were concerned. It was the business of the State, if it assisted people to leave the country, to assist them also until they were fairly well established in proper productive work and were able to maintain themselves under proper conditions.

"I take the view," said Mr. Clynes, "that with the existing unevenness of population in the various parts of the Empire it is the proper service of the State to step in and do what it can to make the distribution of population more helpful to the individual and better for the various parts of the Empire. It is an insular and parochial doctrine, never, I hope, to be entertained by any Party, that a Briton must not leave these shores, and that once established here he must stay here. That has never, to my mind, been part of any Labour or Socialist doctrine." Emigration was an industrial, an economic, and a labour question. Labour, therefore, had a right to be consulted by those who had the matter in their keeping.

"If we could have on these shores and on the other shores some share of effective labour supervision, I think," the right hon. gentleman added, "we would be able to look at this matter in a manner that would set up such conditions of mutual welfare as would remove the opposition and suspicions of those who are the opponents of immigration in other countries."

More should be done.

Major-General Sir Newton Moore (Coalition Unionist, *Islington, North*) impressed upon the Government the necessity of doing something more than was proposed in the estimate. Labour Governments in Australia—in fact every Government—were prepared to ensure proper supervision, so that people should not be dumped on a market where there were no facilities for employment.

Sir Frederick Young (Coalition Unionist, *Swindon*) said that those in the Dominions who were hostile to immigration had no real cause for the suspicion they showed. Nobody wished for any form of immigration which led to a reduction of the standard of living. Immigration to be effective, both as regarded the Dominion and the individual, must lie in the direction of importing those who would be willing, with proper assistance and guidance, to open up the immense areas of uncultivated soil still to be found. When such people were placed on the land they became, and through them the State became, great potential buyers of the things which Great Britain manufactured.

The Right Hon. Sir Donald Maclean (Chairman of the Independent Liberal Party in Parliament) remarked that there were certain conditions in which if women, especially young women, had proper opportunities of seeking a career in the British Dominions, it would be good for them and good for the Dominions.

Not a final contribution.

The Under-Secretary for the Colonies (Hon. Edward Wood) said that so far as it was possible to encourage and assist women, and so preserve the due proportion with men in the settlement scheme, it would be done. The present estimate was supplementary to a sum previously taken of something like £650,000 and did not represent the final contribution of the Government towards the partial solution of the great problem of State Empire emigration. The number assisted under the scheme was 60,000, distributed, roughly, as follows:—

Canada	25,000
Australia	20,000
New Zealand	10,000
South Africa	5,000

He hoped the Government would have it in their power to propose much larger sums to the House of Commons in respect of the scheme after they had had time to consider the proposals and decisions of the Imperial Conference last summer.

"The importance to my mind of the Imperial Conference," the Under-Secretary proceeded, "is that it emphasised two things that are worthy to be borne in mind. The first was that this problem of Empire settlement is not one that can possibly be treated by *ad hoc* measures, taken spasmodically, but is one that requires the continuous attention of the Government of this country and of the other parts of the Empire. . . . The second thing is that the problem will only be solved satisfactorily by not only co-operation between this country and the Dominions, but permanent co-operation between these. Of course, it did definitely move a stage further along the path of accepting definite State responsibility for endeavouring to do the best to assist the population of the Empire to find what, I think, Mr. Clynes called a more even distribution. All these were, I think, conclusions of great value.

Not a remedy for Unemployment.

" I must rather deprecate the tendency in some quarters to hitch this question of Empire settlement too closely to the problem of unemployment. It is certainly most true that it can never be a remedy for unemployment, and its warmest advocates would not suggest it. I think it is nearer the truth to say that the existence of unemployment reminds us of its perpetual importance. After all, it is worth remembering that the whole of this emigration, or practically the whole of it, is directed towards land settlement. It is also worth remembering that every man who settles on the land at once establishes in himself, and in the organised society that grows up around him, a growing and potential market for industry. Therefore it is both regrettable and unsound to lose sight of the second part of the matter when emphasising the first.

" The speech of Mr. Clynes satisfied, I think, the whole of the Committee that if you can get rid of misunderstanding and prejudice and one or two faults of administration there is really no objection in any quarter of the House to these proposals of Empire settlement and Empire migration. As he stated the case it really is unanswerable. Where you have on the one hand vast spaces with no population and on the other limited spaces with a great population, it is not only wisdom but common sense, as he said, that you should attempt to marry the two—in other words, that you should attempt to give elsewhere that scope for enterprise and initiative to those who lack it here."

Co-operation of the Dominions.

It had been said, the hon. gentleman continued, that the movement had suffered in the past from lack of efficien organisation and direction. He thought it was generally recognised that in many quarters the arrangements on the other side had not been nearly good enough. " It has worked out," Mr. Wood observed, " in conjunction with other things in this country, such as the bonus system and so on, almost in the nature of a traffic in human beings that was unworthy of the cause to which it was devoted. Hon. Members who are interested in that side of the question will be glad to know that the bonus system of payment for recruiting by results to third parties with the consent and co-operation of the Dominions is fast disappearing, if it has not already disappeared.

" I am very glad to be able to say that the Dominion Governments, in so far as improvement is required, are in co-operation with ourselves in effecting that improvement on their side, and we are endeavouring to make improvements in our selection and our arrangement where they require improvement on this side. It might also interest the Committee to know that . . . in Australia there has been formed a League under the title of the New Settlers' League, which is indeed unofficial, but which works in the closest conjunction with the Government, and is intended to permeate and have representation all over Australia as an organisation with which the new comers can get into touch, and which will be as it were a settler's friend all over the Australian continent."

Three essentials.

Three things were necessary if this policy was to bear its full fruit for the strength of the Empire, for the soundness and prosperity of the communities where it operated, and for the contentment of those who took advantage of it :—

(1) The closest co-operation between Governments.

(2) Good organisation and machinery, including careful selection.

(3) The cordial co-operation of organised Labour.

Labour was represented on the Overseas Settlement Committee, which also included representatives of the Dominions. He was sure he was speaking the sentiments of the Chairman of the Committee when he stated that he would welcome the opportunity of strengthening the representation of official Labour on that body.

The supplementary estimate was, after further debate, agreed to without a division.

Proposal of Australian Minister.

The subject of Empire Overseas Settlement* was raised in the House of Commons at Question time on 1st November.

The Hon. Gideon Murray asked the Prime Minister whether in view of the fact that the promotion of Empire overseas settlement by means of assisted passages, etc., was not likely to prove successful in the present and near future on account of the measure of unemployment which existed in the overseas Dominions, his attention had been drawn to the record of the proceedings of the Conference on State-aided Empire Settlement held in February, 1921.

Whether he would give earnest consideration to the desirability of adopting the proposals put forward by Senator the Hon. E. D. Millen† made on behalf of the Australian Government, recommending a scheme for establishing 20,000 British settlers on certain selected areas to be financed by a Commonwealth loan of £20,000,000 to be raised in five annual instalments, His Majesty's Government's assistance to take the form of a payment for five years of half the interest on each instalment of the loan, and the comprehensive settlement schemes to be promoted thereunder to include the work of the opening up of areas by railways and roads, the construction of other public works, and the clearing of land, etc. which would provide employment for many of the intending settlers, and, in addition, give employment to many workers in Great Britain in the manufacture of the necessary materials and steel rails, etc., required in connection with such schemes.

Whether, whereas 60,000 settlers had already been settled overseas since the War, there were another 60,000 applicants awaiting settlement in the Empire ?

Fresh proposals.

The Under-Secretary for the Colonies (Hon. Edward Wood), who replied, said : " The proposal put forward by Senator Millen goes beyond the scheme sanctioned by the Resolution of the Prime Ministers' Conference. Fresh proposals have, however, been under discussion recently Australia, similar to those put forward by Senator Mille and it is understood that further proposals of this kind a likely to be made. His Majesty's Government have und consideration the steps that can usefully be taken by them order to implement the Resolution passed by the Conferenc and, in deciding their general policy in this important proble of Empire settlement, careful regard will be paid to all su

* *Vide* also debate on Trade Facilities Bill, p. 52.

† Minister for Repatriation of the Australian Commonwealth.

proposals as those referred to above. The Government do not doubt that larger numbers of persons would be glad to avail themselves of increased opportunities for settlement overseas if, in concert with the Dominion Governments, the necessary arrangements can be made."

Sir Frederick Young: "Will the hon. gentleman bear in mind that, after all, this form of emigration is by far the most practical form, having regard to the conditions in our overseas possessions as well as here, and that every man established abroad under these conditions is a potential purchaser of British goods to a far greater extent than when he is in this country?"

The Under-Secretary for the Colonies: "I can assure my hon. friend that the Government are entirely alive to all those considerations, and, as I said in my answer, the fullest consideration will be given to these proposals when they are brought forward."

Colonel J. C. Wedgwood (Labour, *Newcastle-under-Lyme*)**:** "Are the Government also alive to the fact that people in this country would rather remain here with their friends and relations?"

The Under-Secretary for the Colonies: "All that I aimed at pointing out in my answer was that the Government were fully aware, as I think the House is aware, that if people in this country desire opportunities of going overseas those opportunities should be given them."

UNEMPLOYMENT.

(Proposals of the Government: Relief Works, Emigration, Assistance for Trade, etc.)

On 19th October the House of Commons went into Committee for the purpose of considering a Resolution on which the Government proposed to base the Trade Facilities Bill. By agreement the occasion was utilised for a general debate on the unemployment problem and the Government's proposals in respect thereof.

DEBATE IN HOUSE OF COMMONS.

The Prime Minister (the Right Hon. D. Lloyd George) said they were confronted with the worst period of unemployment that this country had seen probably for 100 years. They had seen nothing like it since the end of the Napoleonic wars, and the causes were the same. There were 1,750,000 workers, including women, boys and girls, unemployed at that moment. Every war had been followed by periods of depression and the depression had been in proportion to the magnitude of the war. This was the greatest depression that had been felt, certainly for 100 years, and they had just emerged from the greatest war ever witnessed. After the Napoleonic wars the Government left the problem of poverty to be dealt with locally; they did not take, at least for some time, large national action. The result was appalling, and the Government to-day unhesitatingly recommended the second course.

Defending the Government and Parliament against the criticism that nothing had been done to meet the situation, the Prime Minister said that in 1919 a considerable sum was voted by the House of Commons for the restoration of Central Europe. It had a considerable effect, not merely in averting a great deal of suffering. If it had not been done things would have been infinitely worse in Central Europe even than they were now, and probably they would have been driven into Bolshevism. The second step the Government took was the setting up of an export credits scheme with a sum of £26,000,000. In August, 1920, trade was so good that the unemployment was only 1·6 per cent., but, in spite of appearances to the contrary, the Government were advised that unemployment would increase.

Therefore they brought in a Bill that added 8,000,000 workers to the Insurance Fund. When that was done unemployment was not bad, but between then and now £48,000,000 had been distributed to unemployed families under the Unemployment Insurance Act.

Relief Works.

In August, 1920, the Cabinet appointed a special committee to consider unemployment and what further action was necessary in order that they might get ready to deal with it. The Committee instantly set on foot schemes for the provision of relief work for the unemployed.

> For arterial roads, £10,400,000 was allocated; £3,000,000 was voted for assisting local authorities in the provision of relief work.
>
> Other alternative work was provided in Government Departments. Local authorities were stimulated to provide emergency work by example and by subvention.
>
> £25,000,000 was spent on these various schemes, and at least 200,000 men had from time to time been provided with work under them.

An Hon. Member: " A drop in the bucket."

The Prime Minister: " Even in these days £48,000,000 is not a drop in the bucket."

Settlement in the Dominions.

" Steps were taken," the Prime Minister went on to say, "to enable ex-Service men to settle in the Dominions. A sum of £637,000 was voted for that purpose. Under the scheme, 60,000 have already settled in the various Dominions of the Empire. At the present moment the applications are coming in in much greater numbers. Australia has recently taken up an immigration policy. The result is that, as part of this present scheme, we propose to ask Parliament for another £300,000 to enable more ex-Service men to emigrate."

An Hon. Member: " To get rid of them."

The Prime Minister: " One thing the War taught us was not to get rid of them. Nor did our enemies get rid of them, either. There is no compulsory expatriation, and if men choose to settle under the flag under these favourable conditions I can conceive of nothing better, not merely for the Empire, but for this country. At the present moment we are more dependent upon our Dominions and upon the Empire for trade than at any previous period, and the more men you settle under the British flag the better it will be for the trade of this country and for unemployment in this land as well."

Continuing, the right hon. gentleman remarked that in every previous period of unemployment the trade that had suffered worst had been the building trade. But at the present time the building trade was engaged to the limit of its capacity upon public credit and public funds under an Act of Parliament passed by that House. When there were meetings of unemployed, full of despair, full of worry, and ready to be exasperated as people under those conditions always were, at any rate the truth ought to be told concerning what had been done.

Trade prospects: The Russian Agreement.

Turning to the subject of trade with Russia, the Prime Minister said that when the trading Agreement was going through the House of Commons was warned by the Government not to expect too much from it. They knew there was some trade to be done, but not to the extent of the anticipations of some friends of the trading Agreement. There had been no restrictions on the British side to any trading with Russia and the total trade from 1st January, 1921, to

31st August, 1921, was £3,150,000. That included re-exports of tea and other commodities that passed through Great Britain, largely produced in the British Dominions. It included the trade which was done direct and the trade done through some of the Baltic ports. Before the end of the year they might have trade with Russia to the amount of £5,000,000 or £6,000,000, and that was a contribution of value. But nothing was to be gained by creating the impression that there was an unlimited field for British or any other enterprise in Russia until that country was restored to a much better condition than she was in at the present time.

With regard to trade prospects generally, there were undoubted signs of a revival in some of the most important industries in this country, but there were others in which there was no such sign. "It is true," said the right hon. gentleman, "when trade begins to move, it moves along the whole front; but taking into account the economic and political condition of Europe, its impoverishment, its heavy burdens, its racial and political restlessness, the man would be sanguine who would predict a return to normal conditions at an early date, or who would predict that there will not be considerable unemployment for some time to come. Our best hope lies not in a short-lived and feverish boom, which would end in a worse reaction, but in a slow and steady improvement . . . and I think we shall get it."

Export Credits.

After speaking of the exhaustion of the supplementary means at the disposal of the working classes to provide against unemployment, the Prime Minister remarked that it was essential further steps should be taken. The best steps undoubtedly would be action that would provide employment for men in their own avocations. Great Britain was an exporting country and there was no doubt about the nee for their goods. The whole point was, "Could need be con verted into demand?" There was a still more importan question, "Could demand be converted into payment?' Unless they could give a satisfactory answer to those question they would have unemployment. It was no use stackin British goods in rotting pyramids in foreign depots. Thei export credits scheme, which was an attempt to stimulat legitimate trade, had shown that it needed amendment.

Parliament voted £26,000,000 for the purpose of facili tating the export of British goods to various countries. I order that they might trade with these "broken countries' it was proposed that the importer should find some security

At first he had some reserve for security in one way or another, but it had all gone. They were left with three kinds of security. One was Government Bonds in those countries. The League of Nations were trying to organise something which was known as the "Ter Meulen" scheme and which he had no doubt would be valuable if it came into operation. The next was that the banks guaranteed payment in sterling; but the banks were not in a hurry to do it.

The third class of security was the currency of the importing country. After quoting examples of the violent fluctuations of the exchanges, the Prime Minister said it was obvious that neither exporter nor importer could build up a trade on that acrobatic basis.

State guarantee.

Therefore, it came to be a question of the exporter's risk and whether the Government were prepared to share it —the exporter taking his risk upon a knowledge of the trader he was dealing with.

"We were guaranteeing 85 per cent. of the cost, with recourse against the exporter for half the uncovered risk," the Prime Minister explained. "That means our risk was 42½ per cent., but we were only guaranteeing 85 per cent. The trader says he cannot trade on those terms. He is quite willing to do so if the State guarantees 100 per cent. without altering his risk. The credit would be for one year as a maximum. That means that the State would guarantee 100 per cent., but the exporter would be liable on recourse to 57½ per cent., and the State risk would still be 42½ per cent.

An Hon. Member: "Gamble."

The Prime Minister: "If trade is to be started at all, I agree there is a risk in it, but the whole question for us is, 'On which side is the greater risk?' Is our risk greater in losing part of our money or in doing nothing to aid and restart trade? The conclusion we have come to is that our risk is much greater by standing still and doing nothing."

Dealing with other amendments of the scheme, the right hon. gentleman said that it had been necessary for the exporter to get sanction from the Department for each separate transaction. The proposal now was that there should be a maximum fixed for each firm and that it should be permitted to trade to the limit of that maximum. Another amendment was an extension of the area of the credit system. The first proposal was that the scheme should only apply to the countries whose credit was practically destroyed by the War. It was now proposed that the scheme should be extended to other countries as well; including the British Empire.

In some respects, perhaps, the most important amendment dealt with the question of the length of credit according to the quality of goods. What the world stood mostly in need of was equipment to start its trade—machinery and transport. "We have come to the conclusion that where there are large orders of that kind for heavy goods for countries which would take years to develop and complete, it is desirable that we should extend credit for five, or even six years. We believe that, under this amendment of the export credits scheme, it would be possible to give very considerable orders, especially in the engineering line, which is suffering most from unemployment at the present moment."

Trade facilities: £20,000,000 for Colonial development.

The right hon. gentleman next described the provision to be made for special trade facilities with foreign countries and the British Empire. They might expect two classes of orders to come to their markets. One was from countries which could, without British Government credit, finance their own demands; and the other was the class of order they might get from countries or enterprises which could not be financed without some Government guarantee. In the first class would be India, which had already raised a substantial sum of money on the British market and given substantial orders to this country. Then, in the British Colonies, they had gigantic areas awaiting development and repaying development.

If anyone would follow what was done by the late Mr. Chamberlain in Nigeria, he would realise at once how those great possessions of the Crown in Africa repaid expenditure for development. The Colonial Secretary was following that fine example in making a real endeavour to develop still further the resources of those great African possessions and of other parts of the Dominions of the Crown. He had already either actually raised in the market, or was making arrangements for raising, something like £20,000,000, upon the credit of those Colonies, without any British guarantee, for the purpose of development.

Turning to countries or enterprises in the second category, the Prime Minister said there was much to be done at home and abroad in loosening the wheels of the machinery of industry at the first point at which they were stuck. That was in the restoration and improvement of the means of production and of transport.

There were two reasons why orders were tarrying. One was that the cost of production was too high. The other was the difficulty of raising capital for some of these enterprises and the still greater difficulty of raising it at a price which would not unduly burden the enterprise. There, undoubtedly, the Government could assist.

Guaranteed loans.

"It is proposed," said the Premier, "that where the Government are satisfied that the proceeds of any loan to be raised by the Government of any part of the Dominions or the Colonies, any foreign Government, any public authority, or any corporation or other body of persons, are to be applied towards the carrying out of any capital undertaking, or in the purchase of articles to be manufactured within the United Kingdom required for the purposes of any such undertaking, the Government may, on such conditions as may be deemed proper, guarantee the payment of interest and principal of the loan. It is to be a condition of the guarantee that the application of the loan is calculated to promote employment in the United Kingdom."

That meant, the right hon. gentleman proceeded, enterprises—railway extensions, electrification and waterways, if there were schemes of that kind—which could produce immediate employment. The aggregate capital amount of the loans was not to exceed £25,000,000.

The Right Hon. H. H. Asquith (Leader of the Independent Liberal Party): "The total is £25,000,000. What does that represent ?"

The Prime Minister: "It represents the total of our liability under this proposal." Continuing, Mr. Lloyd George explained that it was proposed to set up a committee of men of high authority and great knowledge in financial, industrial and economic matters to administer the scheme. The committee would be instructed to consider each application in the light of the amount of fresh employment which the scheme would bring to this country, and of the benefits by way of increased and cheapened production and transport facilities which it would confer.

Relief Works: Grants for dependants of Unemployed.

Whatever the Government did, they could not bridge the great chasm of unemployment, and there would be a considerable amount of distress to be relieved. It was proposed to allocate a sum of £10,000,000 to assist the relief works which the Government had already undertaken, including a certain amount of provision for agricultural unemployment. A sum of money would be allocated for forestry and for land drainage, and there would be further proposals with regard to roads. With reference to the unemployment allowance, the Government were compelled by the exigencies of the public revenue and the fact that the Unemployment Insurance Fund was exhausted to reduce the benefit to 15s., which it was not pretended was an adequate sum.

The Government now proposed to introduce legislation establishing for a period of six months a fund to be called "The Unemployed Workers' Dependents' Fund." Out of it unemployed workers who were in receipt of unemployment benefit would receive grants towards the maintenance of their wives and dependent children. Those grants would, subject to a maximum limit of 9s., be at the weekly rate of 5s. for the wife and 1s. for each child. The necessary money would be obtained by means of a compulsory levy upon the contributors to the Unemployment Insurance Fund at the following rates :

In the case of men—Employer 2d., employed person 2d., State 3d.

In the case of women, girls, and boys under the age of 18—Employer 1d., employed person 1d., State 2d.

It was proposed that in the case of necessitous areas, where the Guardians found it impossible to cope with the difficulties, there should be a Government loan that would enable them to spread out the amount so as to carry them over the immediate difficulty with which they were confronted.

Public economy, cost of production, etc.

Trade recovery was what they had to look to for the ultimate solution of unemployment. That did not depend upon Governments.

Hon. Members : "Oh !" and "Taxation !"

The Prime Minister said there was no doubt that in every country heavy taxation, local and Imperial, must necessarily retard trade recovery. It was the business of every Government and of every Parliament to insist that the whole of the estimates of expenditure should be cut down ruthlessly. Nothing the Government could do in the way of economy could get rid of the fact that they had a debt of £8,000,000,000, and that everything cost twice as much as it did formerly. This was one of the two countries of the world where up to the present they had been able to make ends meet. There w the system whereby here and in America they had taxed the people to pay their way. There was the other system whe there were deficiencies and these were covered up by th printing of paper. That meant inflation. This country, believed, had probably touched bottom in regard to its trade. It had faced its obligations with courage, and courage would have its reward.

They must face the cost of production. It was for the employers and the workmen to come together. It was easy to excite prejudice by saying, "Oh, there is the old story; you are going to cut down wages." But if they did not do it they would have no wages at all.

Mr. G. Barker (**Labour,** *Abertillery*): "What about prices?"

The Prime Minister remarked that it was not a question of excessive profits. It was a question of no profits at all. There were orders to be taken in hand by the business men of this country to-day if they could be assured, not that they would make a profit, but that they would be able to meet expenses. Trade would not be restored to this country for years to come unless the problem of the cost of production was courageously faced. There was no doubt that political unrest, which was still fermenting, prevented trade from recovering. Peace and a good understanding between the nations of Europe was necessary.

"Let us get out of the atmosphere that if you talk about a German without a frown on your brow you are not a patriot," said the Premier. "In order to re-establish trade you must have peace, you must have good will, and you must have co-operation between the nations, yea, and between all classes."

Labour view: Parliament and the worker.

The Right Hon. J. R. Clynes (**Chairman of the Parliamentary Labour Party**) thought the speech of the Prime Minister had denoted the fact that Parliament must more and more in the future accept the task of governing the people of this country by providing the masses with two conditions—employment and contentment. The precedents set that day, and the obligations which were being accepted, could not remain precisely in the same position in which the Prime Minister's words had left them. They would have to be expanded and enlarged in a manner fully to cover the right of the workman to earn his living by labour, and no longer to be deprived by any conditions of an existing social system from earning his daily bread.

In principle he had no prejudices against emigration; but it was necessary to consider under what conditions it was to be arranged and encouraged. Recent reports from Australia, Canada, New Zealand and South Africa showed that those countries had their unemployed troubles and spoke of resolutions of protest against continued immigration. If workmen were to be asked to emigrate, Labour should take part in the supervision and conduct of any emigration arrangements. "We should be assured," said Mr. Clynes, "that when they land on strange . . . shores they are not to be faced with conditions of distress, that they are to be assisted adequately, and established in conditions of employment that will make their lot in the new world better than it was in the old."

He was not prepared to leave it to shipping agents or others who might be interested in the financial side of such a policy to say what facilities could be provided.

Trade and the Peace Treaty.

On the whole he welcomed the Prime Minister's announcement of certain proposals for assisting trade under the head of credits and loan arrangements. He hoped, however, that in any steps the Government might take they would act in the spirit of real co-operation and leave employers as free as they possibly could to manage their own affairs. The State must accept a much greater liability if the assistance of trade was to be worth while, and his view was that unless this part of the job was done very well indeed it was, perhaps, better to leave it alone altogether.

International trade was dislocated not merely because of the wastage of the War, but because of the terms of the Peace Treaty. Europe was in need of a Peace Treaty which would have enabled the defeated countries not only to pay for the damage wickedly done in Belgium and France, but to begin in their own countries internal works of reconstruction and economic development. Their prosperity would have made the prosperity of Great Britain more certain. Their injury, which the policy of Reparations was designed to secure, had come more nearly to securing the industrial and financial ruin of some of the victorious countries. No scheme of credit restoration, of trade development by artificial means, could succeed without international co-operation.

Immediate measures to stimulate export industries were necessary, and the Government alone could take them in an adequate form. The Government could be responsible in a very large measure for this country's export trade, paying manufacturers for their goods, and trusting to receive the money from European countries after business was done with them.

Russia: Diplomatic relations, etc.

Great Britain had entered into a trade arrangement with Russia, but had not entered into the full diplomatic relations of peace with that country. "There is good reason to believe . . . that the present Russian Government would be quite ready to enter into discussion with this Government as to the acceptance of debts contracted under the old Czarist *régime* in Russia, if this Government accept and recognise the Russian Government as one with which it is proper to have discussion and to trade."

As to the question of the cost of production, in a recent manifesto of the joint Labour bodies, Labour expressly stated that it was in the interests of the whole community that production should be increased and costs reduced. To reduce wages gave no guarantee at all of lessening the price of the article. Profits, interest, dividends, rents for land and premises, high salaries and maintenance charges, should all be subject to revision. Since the beginning of 1921 changes in rates of wages reported to the Ministry of Labour had resulted in a net reduction of over £3,800,000 in the weekly wages of nearly 6,700,000 workers. He did not say that under no circumstances should there be a reduction of wages, but the question must not be faced as though reduced wages was the short cut to a solution of the difficulty.

The question of reduced cost of production was of such vital importance in the solution of the unemployment problem that it was essential workmen should see that if they could make a contribution to reducing the cost of the article it was urgently necessary, primarily in their own interest, that they should do so. There was, he thought, a good deal of unworthy suspicion in the minds of employers as to workmen deliberately shirking the day's task. He did not know that anyone preached the idea of deliberate under-production, and so far as it was practised it must be by workmen ignorant of the real injury it did to them above all other classes. Scarcity was the shield of the profiteer, and the workman was just as bad a profiteer if he deliberately refrained from doing a fair day's work for a fair day's pay.

Condemnation of "doles."

Mr. Asquith said that everybody now believed that for a situation such as that with which they were now confronted the policy of doles—frankly giving money without exacting any return in the nature of work—was a demoralising, ineffectual, and in the long run a fatal procedure. With regard to the policy of developing the system of export credits, in the essence of things it was a gamble. He did not say that it was not a legitimate gamble, but it was a gamble in regard to which they ought, first of all, to realise what was the extent to which they might possibly, if things went wrong, be let in.

When they sought to increase their export trade with the Continent of Europe, the root difficulty was that they could not in business, while the state of exchange was as at present make any forward arrangements in regard to which they might not expose themselves to great loss and even ruin.

The root causes of unemployment were not domestic but international. Unemployment existed in quite as aggravated a form in almost all the other countries of the world That raised the necessity for a reconstruction of the whole problem of international indebtedness in both its aspects—first the indebtedness of the Allies to one another, and next the indebtedness of their late enemies to the Allies. One of the results of the War was that Great Britain had ceased to be the principal creditor nation of the world. The United States of America was at that moment a creditor of European countries—and he excluded Russia—for £2,240,000,000. There had been such a complete transformation of the relative position in regard to international indebtedness as to make this practically a new world.

German Reparations.

They knew the enormous obligations in regard to Reparations and Indemnities which had been imposed upon Germany by treaty. It was time these matters were reconsidered He wished to record the great satisfaction with which he read of the Loucheur-Rathnau Agreement for the delivery by Germany of machinery and material for French reconstruction to the value of something like £300,000,000 or £350,000,000 before October, 1935. That seemed to be a very good example of the way in which the process of what was called "Reparations" could be carried out in practice with a minimum of disturbance to the normal course of international trade Germany could only pay either by commodities or services

"We must," Mr. Asquith said, "get the international financial situation, particularly in this aspect of relative indebtedness, on to a sane foundation before we can ever grapple again, as we did before the War, with the great question of international competition." He thought too much attention was apt to be concentrated on the European situation. Taking the year before the War, the total export of British produce and manufactures amounted to £525,000,000 Of those, all European countries together, including Russia took only £150,000,000, and no less than £200,000,000, or thereabouts, went to British possessions. For many reasons it was all-important that they should develop that tendency He was not speaking of what might be called sentimenta reasons; he was on the lower plane of material advantage, and the diminution of unemployment.

Development of Imperial Trade.

"After all," the right hon. gentleman observed, "the things which Germany sends us, and is obliged to send us, are things which we really do not want, or which we can make ourselves. But the British Dominions send us things which we cannot make ourselves, things which are essential to us in the shape of food, material, or half-finished products. They are sending us things which we do need, and there is no reason whatever why, by a wise development of our inter-Imperial resources, assisted on sound lines by what would be really remunerative expenditure by the Imperial Government, you should not establish a healthy trade and a progressive trade between the Dominions and ourselves, which would overtop altogether the European trade with this country. I need not say . . . that I am not suggesting any artificial expedient. A natural and normal and well-conceived policy will do more than anything else to diminish the volume of unemployment in this country."

Three remedies.

The Right Hon. G. N. Barnes (Labour, *Glasgow, Gorbals*) said the unemployment problem was at the very basis of the social and industrial well-being of this country. The classes who had the running of the country would be judged in proportion as they could find or organise employment for the great mass of the people. He believed that the fundamental cause of most of their troubles was the private appropriation of land values. Industry, both employer and employed, was fined and taxed by landlords before it could proceed to increase the wealth of the community. But the cause of the abnormal unemployment was the War from 1914 to 1918 abroad, and the war from 1918 onwards at home. He placed the remedies for the existing state of affairs under three headings:—

(1) More hearty co-operation between employers and workmen.

(2) An easement of the burden of taxation upon industry.

(3) A greater degree of mutual aid amongst Governments in an international scheme.

Speaking with intimate knowledge of the engineering workshops in which he spent twenty-one years of his life, the right hon. gentleman said that, if the men and the employers were to put their hearts as well as their hands into their work, at least twice as much could be turned out without hurting anybody and with advantage even to the health of the average man concerned. Nothing was more irritating or demoralising than that a man should spend his time sitting waiting for the bell to ring. With regard to taxation the first matter to be considered was the cost of the immense armaments which still weighed upon industry.

Reparations an element of instability.

Sir A. Steel-Maitland (Coalition Unionist, ***Birmingham, Erdington*****)** said it was his conviction that the Reparation payments under the Peace Treaty were an element both in the instability of the world and also in the unemployment in this country. The trend of events, so far as could be foreseen, pointed to a *débâcle* in Germany in the near future if affairs were allowed to go on as at present. It was a matter for the most urgent consideration whether the question of the German Reparations should not be taken in hand from the point of view of reducing them to a compass that might prevent the *débâcle*, and possibly of postponing the next payment while taking security to prevent evasion of ultimate payments on the reduced scale.

After further debate the Resolution was agreed to in Committee.

Fluctuating exchanges.

On 20th October the Resolution was further debated in the House of Commons on the Report stage.

The Right Hon. Dr. Addison (ex-Minister of Health) remarked that the export credits scheme did not touch in any degree the difficulty of the fluctuating foreign exchanges. It only sought to patch up or add to a proposal which hitherto had been substantially inoperative.

The Minister of Health (the Right Hon. Sir Alfred Mond) said the export credits scheme was originally introduced not so much for the benefit of British trade, but as a help for some of the countries with damaged exchanges in Central Europe. It was obvious that a country with a damaged exchange was about the worst customer that they could hope to find; but they had extended the scheme to every country in the world and to the British Empire. They were now going out to the Far East, to South America, to people who had good exchanges. Before the War 75 per cent. of the British export trade was done overseas, and they must realise that there was an enormous field for that trade outside Europe.

Mr. A. Bigland (Coalition Unionist, *Birkenhead, E.*) remarked that the Prime Minister was right when he said that in future they must look more than ever before to the markets in their own Dominions. He was in a position in business to know how keenly every Empire in the world was trying to become self-supporting. They were increasingly frightened of the imports which they obtained from those countries where the exchange had broken down and were trying to protect themselves with even more tariffs.

Colonisation overseas.

The Prime Minister did not say a word about what the Imperial Conference had done with regard to overseas settlement. Trade unionists seemed to think it was derogatory to suggest that many of their able-bodied men should ever be spoken of as people who might go and settle in some other part of the Empire. "If we once get the idea," remarked the hon. Member, "that science has annihilated distance and that a man under the British flag in Canada and New Zealand is practically living in Greater Britain, though not in Britain itself, it will remove what I fear is a misconception in the minds of many people in this country, and those who realise the facts as we find them will see that one of the reliefs of unemployment must be the easier movement of the adventurous spirits amongst our people at home to found settlements overseas."

The Right Hon. Lord Robert Cecil (Independent Unionist, *Hitchin*) said he had always believed that what was absolutely essential to any permanent settlement of their difficulties was a frank acceptance of the principle of partnership between the employer and the employed. There had been utterances by important people on both sides which led one to hope that some settlement of that kind was not so impossible as certain critics would have them believe. The loss of foreign markets was the basis of a great part of the present unemployment, and he hoped the Government would make the principle of co-operation between nations more the guide of their policy than it had been in the past.

The economic difficulty.

The real difficulty to which the greater part of the attention of those who assembled at Paris ought to have been directed was the economic difficulty. Free commerce between the nations and free interchange of goods was the vital thing required for the restoration of the economic position and the radical diminution of unemployment. The Government proposals for stimulating production might be wise, but their success, after all, depended on whether the foreigner could buy. With regard to Russia, he believed there was not only the moral claim that they should go to the assistance of the famine-stricken people in that country, but that it was in the best interests of themselves that they should do so.

The Minister of Labour (the Right Hon. T. J. Macnamara) thought that through the winter they would probably have round about 1,500,000 people wholly unemployed.

The report of the Resolution was agreed to without a Division.

TRADE FACILITIES ACT.

(Help for Industrial enterprises; Guaranteed Loans; Preference to Dominions; Unemployment relief, etc.)

One of the special measures brought forward by the Government in connection with the unemployment problem was the Trade Facilities Bill, which was passed through both Houses, and received the Royal Assent on 10th November.

The Act provides that if the Treasury are satisfied that the proceeds of any loan proposed to be raised, whether within or without the United Kingdom, by any Government, public authority, corporation, or other body of persons are to be applied to the carrying out of any capital undertaking, or in the purchase of articles manufactured in the United Kingdom required for such undertaking, and that the application of the loan is calculated to promote employment in the United Kingdom, the Treasury may guarantee the payment of the interest and principal of the loan, or of either interest or principal.

The aggregate capital amount of the loans the principal or interest of which is guaranteed is not to exceed twenty-five million pounds, and no guarantee is to be given by the Treasury after the expiration of twelve months from the commencement of the Act.

The provisions of the Overseas Trade (Credits and Insurance) Act, 1920, as amended by the Act of 1921, are extended so as to authorise the granting of credits and the giving of guarantees in respect of export transactions between the United Kingdom and any other country whatsoever.

DEBATE IN HOUSE OF COMMONS.

The Bill was debated on the order for Second Reading ir the House of Commons on 25th October.

The Chancellor of the Exchequer (the Right Hon. Si Robert Horne) said the destruction of so much of the wealth o the world had the effect of paralysing trade and commerce

In this country they had built up on a very narrow base of agricultural life a huge superstructure of industrialism, and whenever there was depression of trade they felt it worse than anybody else. Moreover, Britain had built up her great position in the world by the fact that she had financed and carried out industrial enterprises in every region of the globe. Unfortunately there was no longer a flow of capital to such enterprises; indeed, the capital was not being asked for.

With regard to the difficulty of financing large enterprises, the Government proposed to guarantee loans to approved undertakings on condition that the money was to be spent on material and equipment within the United Kingdom. Such loans could be applied for by any Government or any undertaking in any part of the world. There were several small nations which if they could raise the money in the City of London for some of their railway enterprises would be enabled immediately to place orders in many British factories. There were great undertakings which many of the Dominions and Colonies could carry out that were only impeded by want of the necessary finance.

Preference to the Dominions.

"We, of course, shall favour proposals that come to us from our own Dominions," said the Chancellor of the Exchequer. "It is the first duty of this country to develop the great assets which it owns throughout the world, but entirely apart from that it is distinctly to our interest to do so. They are in truth our best customers, and they have proved that in time of difficulty they are our most loyal and most attached friends. Accordingly I think that in any scheme dealing with the matter we should be bound to give preference to the claims of our Dominions.

"Happily, many of these Dominions have already been raising money here for the purposes of undertakings within their own borders, and the energy of the Secretary for the Colonies has been applied with great vigour in recent times to that achievement. In point of fact a good deal of money has already been raised, and so far as the future is concerned, where any borrower, such as one of our Dominions, is able to raise money upon its own credit, no help will be given. But there are many Crown Colonies and Protectorates which require the aid which this Bill will afford, and accordingly we hope that such enterprises as I have described will go forward in the immediate future and thus help to alleviate unemployment in this country."

Colonel J. C. Wedgwood (**Labour**, *Newcastle-under-Lyme*): "Will the expenditure be ear-marked for this country?"

The Chancellor of the Exchequer: "It will be made a condition for guaranteeing loans that the expenditure on any goods that can be produced in this country shall be made here."

Colonel Wedgwood: "That will not apply to all the money?"

The Chancellor of the Exchequer: "No, and for this reason. A large amount of labour will be required to build the bridges, construct the railways and create the docks, and you cannot provide that the money for this purpose shall be spent in this country. It must necessarily be expended locally."

Cheaper borrowing.

"The Bill does not confine the guarantee of such loans to the cases of people overseas, whether apart from or belonging to our own Dominions. It deals also with the case of enterprises to be carried out within the borders of the United Kingdom. There are many such undertakings which are only waiting to be financed on suitable terms to go forward. There are light railways in several parts of the country. There are electrical undertakings; there are projects for the extension of docks and harbours. For all enterprises of that kind, which are particularly desirable under these circumstances, guarantees will be given for loans.

"The result of the Government guarantee in almost all instances will be to enable the borrower to obtain cheaper money than he would otherwise obtain for himself and that at the present time, in the condition of the world's finance, is a great factor in the problem for the people who are undertaking such enterprises as I have described." The right hon. gentleman explained that it was intended to set up a small expert committee to deal with applications, which must be made within twelve months from the passing of the Bill. The loans guaranteed were not to exceed £25,000,000 and in that connection he hoped the House would keep in mind the large obligations which the Government were undertaking at a time when the financial situation was one of great difficulty.

After discussing the provisions of the Bill with respect to the export credits scheme,* the right hon. gentleman referred to the problem of the exchanges, which, he said, would not be brought back to normal until they restored the production of wealth and the interchange of commodities.

A bad Peace; Insanity of Military expenditure.

The Right Hon. Sir Donald Maclean (Chairman of the Independent Liberal Party in Parliament) said the disastrous

* *Vide* general debate on unemployment problem, pp. 37 to 52.

War was followed by a bad Peace, and from the conditions of peace arose, undoubtedly, many of the main factors of the present unemployment. Since the days of the Armistice up to the end of the current financial year Britain would have spent on the Navy, the Army, and the Air Force little short of £1,000,000,000. Their example had been followed, or worsened, by the efforts of European countries, small and great, old and new The whole world must recognise that a revival of trade would never be fundamentally accomplished until that insanity of military expenditure was brought to an end.

It was said by the Chancellor of the Exchequer to be of the greatest importance in this effort to set business going again that they should remove all unnecessary obstacles in the way. One obstacle that could very readily be removed was the Safeguarding of Industries Act. The Government, while assisting their own manufacturers, were subsidising foreign traders and enabling them to get better goods at lower prices in the competitive world owing to the operation of that measure. He was not overstating the case when he said that until Germany got upon her trade legs again there was little or no hope of a real revival of trade in the Near East; there were goods of every kind of British manufacture in the Far East which had got there through German agents.

Russia not excluded.

That was the only way in which trade with Russia could begin to be re-established. Therefore he was glad that not only Germany, but Russia, was brought within the ambit of the measure.

The Secretary to the Overseas Trade Department (Sir Philip Lloyd-Greame) indicated dissent.

Lieut.-Com. the Hon. J. M. Kenworthy (Independent Liberal, *Hull, Central*): "What! Is Russia not in?"

Sir Donald Maclean: "Russia is a country, and the Bill says any country whatsoever."

The Chancellor of the Exchequer: "That is permissive on the part of the Board of Trade. . . . We are not excluding Russia."

Sir J. Fortescue Flannery (Coalition Unionist, *Maldon*) remarked that the presumption that the Treasury in guaranteeing new undertakings would be at an expense of £25,000,000 was an exaggeration. If the Committee and the Treasury made a wise selection of enterprises for guarantee they would perhaps run the risk of an amount equivalent to a premium at Lloyds of ·5 per cent. In that case the ultimate amount the Chancellor of the Exchequer would have to find out of the national purse would be something like £1,000,000 or £1,250,000. To his mind the great good in the Bill was the fact that there was an intention to give preferential treatment under it to the Crown Colonies.

For the self-governing Dominions, such as Australia and South Africa, there was, as shown by recent events in the City, no real difficulty in raising practically any amount they required. But the Crown Colonies were much less well known, and it was impossible for most of them without assistance from the Imperial Government by way of guarantee to raise the funds that were necessary. Every shilling that was wisely advanced to the Crown Colonies by the British investing public would come back a hundredfold in prosperity at home and in their future development.

Employers and Employed.

Sir W. H. Raeburn (Coalition Unionist, *Dumbarton*) did not think the cure for the high cost of production was always a reduction of wages. He would like to see wages kept at a good level so that men might be content; but if there was nothing out of which high wages could be paid it was futile to expect the Government to offer subsidies for the maintenance of what was called a standard rate of wages. A good deal had been done by amicable arrangement between employers and employed.

He found amongst sensible workmen a strong feeling in favour of such co-operation. Why should not trade union leaders drop the insane idea of the nationalisation of everything and try to work on practical lines? Men's minds had been so filled with suspicion that they never would believe that an employer could do anything from a good and high standpoint. It was that horrible spirit of antagonism that was to blame for a good deal of what was happening to-day.

The Right Hon. G. Lambert (Liberal, *Devon, South Molton*) said the fact must be recognised that high rates and taxes were potent causes of unemployment. He suggested that the Government should appoint a Commission or Committee to inquire into the root causes of unemployment. If they could get at the facts, the British public would face them.

Labour's support.

Mr. T. Myers (Labour, *Spen Valley*) said the Labour Party had decided to give general support to the Second Reading. The country had been going through a period of inflated prices and one of the causes of unemployment was that the reduction in prices had not been sufficiently great to render trade the assistance it required. One of the chief causes of the inflation of prices was notorious. In almost every industry they had been made acquainted with the procedure of writing-up capital and the issue of bonus shares.

Industries with increased capital had to make larger profits in order to pay larger dividends. As there was now a reduction in the demand for their goods the penalty for the inflation of prices was being shown. He asked whether the export credits scheme was to be applied for the purpose of propping up fictitious prices and seeking to maintain the inflation of capital. The conditions of industry in this country were an absolute menace to the State, and the £25,000,000 was nothing but a pill applied to a cancerous growth.

The Hon. Gideon Murray (Coalition Unionist, *Glasgow, St. Rollox*) remarked that after the Napoleonic wars Great Britain was in much the same condition economically as it was to-day. One important measure adopted was a State-aided scheme of emigration under which the Treasury expended different amounts in different years—£30,000 or £50,000—to relieve unemployment. At that time the solid foundation of the Empire was laid by that means. To-day they had the opportunity of building higher and stronger the foundations then laid.

Australia and Empire Settlement.

When the Conference on State-aided Empire Settlement was sitting, Senator Millen, the Australian representative, pointed out that the conditions in Australia had reached a point where unemployment was commencing and it was difficult to receive any more emigrants on the ordinary assisted basis. The Senator made the following helpful suggestion:—

> "As an indication of what Australia might be willing to do if she could secure the co-operation of His Majesty's Government, he put forward for consideration a scheme for establishing 20,000 British settlers on certain selected areas, to be financed by a Commonwealth loan of £20,000,000, to be raised in five annual instalments. On the analogy of the assistance given by the Commonwealth to the Australian States in connection with the Australian soldier settlement schemes, he suggested that the assistance of His Majesty's Government might take the form of a payment for five years of half the interest of each instalment of the loan."

Proceeding, the hon. Member suggested that the Bill might be so amended that it would be possible for His Majesty's Government to spend £3,000,000 out of the £25,000,000 in that way, and thus make a substantial contribution towards a solution of the unemployment problem.

The Bill was, thereafter, read a second time without a division. The Bill went through Committee on 27th October and was read a third time on 3rd November. It had a rapid passage through the House of Lords and became law on the date stated.

UNEMPLOYED WORKERS' DEPENDANTS (TEMPORARY PROVISION) ACT.

This Act—one of the emergency measures introduced by the Government in connection with their effort to meet the problem of unemployment—received the Royal Assent on 8th November. References to its provisions were made in the general debate on Unemployment which preceded the consideration of the Bills relating to this subject. (*Vide* pp. 37 to 52.)

The Act, which is to continue in force for six months, provides that during this special period grants will be payable to every person who is an unemployed worker within the meaning of the Act towards the maintenance of his wife and dependent children.

Where the husband of an unemployed worker is prevented by physical or mental infirmity from supporting himself and is maintained wholly or mainly by his wife the grant is payable to the wife towards the maintenance of her husband and her dependent children.

The following is the scale of the grant :—

	s.	d.	
In respect of a wife or husband	5	0	per week.
In respect of each dependent child	1	0	per week.

The weekly rate of the grant is not in any case to exceed 9s. No grant is payable in respect of a wife who is in receipt of benefit under the Unemployment Insurance Acts, 1920 and 1921, or is in regular wage-earning employment. A "dependent child" is a child under the age of 14 years who is maintained wholly or mainly at the cost of the person claiming the grant. The expression includes a step-child, an adopted child, and an illegitimate child.

Funds for the payment of these grants are to be provided by the following special weekly contributions :—

INSURED PERSONS AND EMPLOYERS.

From the insured person for each week :—

In the case of men	2d.
In the case of women, boys, and girls	1d.

From the employer for each week :—

In the case of an insured person being a man	2d.
In the case of an insured person being a woman, boy, or girl	1d.

OUT OF MONEYS PROVIDED BY PARLIAMENT.

For every contribution paid in respect of a man ..	3d.
For every contribution paid in respect of a woman, boy, or girl	2d.

If the amount of the contributions payable between 7th November, 1921, and 7th May, 1922 (the period covered by the Act), is insufficient to meet the charges on the fund the contributions are to be payable for such further period as is necessary for the purpose of meeting the deficiency.

DEBATE IN HOUSE OF COMMONS.

On 24th October the Bill was debated on the order for Second Reading in the House of Commons.

The Minister of Labour (the Right Hon. T. J. Macnamara) said the Unemployment Insurance Act had been of the greatest assistance during the long months of depression. Those who rather loosely used the word "dole" in connection with the benefit it furnished should remember that three-fourths of the help it brought was contributed by the workpeople and the employers themselves. A new period of sixteen weeks' benefit, which would be made twenty-two weeks as necessary, started at the close of the following week from that in which he was speaking. The benefit was 15s. for men and 12s. for women.

That was the second winter of hardship in succession, and trade union help was pretty well exhausted. The savings of the workers, and even their household resources, had been pressed into the service of providing daily maintenance. The Government, therefore, through the measure now before the House, had to try to do a little more along the line of the Insurance Act for married men and women with little children dependent upon them. The employer was already paying 1s. 1d. per week in respect of each workman for unemployment and health insurance. The workman himself, if he were lucky enough to be in work, was paying 1s. per week for the same purpose, to say nothing of his trade union contributions and special levies.

Tribute to Employers and Employed.

"The way these contributions have been paid by both employers and employed during this distressing period of depression," said the Minister of Labour, "confirms me in the view that, though we greatly regret the necessity, we can with confidence make this further appeal to the spirit of comradeship, of mutual solicitude, and of helpfulness which characterise our people." Proceeding, he explained that the special contributions now to be made would yield about £218,000 a week, or, unless employment became very much worse, £5,500,000 in the six months. The contributions would be divided roughly as follows :—

Employers	£1,500,000
Workmen	£1,500,000
State	£2,500,000

It was estimated that the amount of additional assistance represented by the grants would be given week by week through the winter in respect of about 700,000 wives and nearly double as many children. It was objected that the scheme did nothing for two classes outside the Insurance Act, namely, domestic servants and agricultural labourers. There was work open for domestic servants. In the last twelve months 270,000 vacancies for them were registered at the Employment Exchanges and only 158,000 were filled. Agricultural labourers were out of the Insurance Act because until quite recently they did not want to come in.

The right hon. gentleman added that originally it was not intended that the Bill should apply to Ireland; but in view of representations which had been made it would now be extended to that country.

Labour's objections.

The Right Hon. J. R. Clynes (Chairman of the Parliamentary Labour Party) moved the following amendment:—

> "That whilst anxious to take every step calculated to relieve distress during the present unemployment crisis, this House cannot assent to the Second Reading of a Bill which provides inadequate assistance to some working-class families and no assistance to others, which adds to the burden upon certain industries and imposes a further tax upon a section of the workers whilst exempting from direct contribution other and wealthier classes of the community, and which fails to recognise the full obligation of the State towards every citizen deprived of the means of livelihood."

The right hon. gentleman argued that the Bill did not provide the substantial measure of relief demanded by the situation. The sum suggested was far too low adequately to supplement anything which the workmen might be given from other sources. Contributions to this special fund and to the Unemployment Insurance Act were not the only payments workers were making towards relieving unemployment. Taking only nine of the largest trade unions of the country he found that in the twelve months ended 30th September, 1921, collectively they had paid to their members in unemployment benefit from their funds £4,267,119. It could not be said, therefore, that the men were not putting their hands deep in their pockets to relieve the distress of their own class.

On that account the Labour Party felt entitled to call upon the State to make not only a more generous, but a more general contribution for the purposes of that temporary relie fund. There were very deserving and proper cases which clearly were not covered by the terms of the Bill. He suggested to the Government that plans should be devised foı making some special collection of money for the fund from the classes that would be left untouched by the Bill as it stood. " Surely," he said, " those who ought to pay, if there is to be compulsory contribution to a fund for relief, are those who are best off, whose incomes are largest, and who are making no contribution whatever to the national reserve in the relief of unemployment."

Position of Trade Unions.

The Right Hon. G. H. Roberts (Labour, *Norwich*), who gave general support to the Bill, said it was wrong to delude the people into the belief that the Government had at their disposal some inexhaustible reservoir into which they could dip to furnish all of them with the needs of life. All classes of the community were bearing very heavy burdens, and if they imposed more on them in the shape of taxation they might defeat the purpose they had in view—the provision of employment. If the trade unions were in possession of accumulated funds, if they were able to continue paying out-of-work benefit as heretofore, the intervention of the State scheme would not be so necessary as it was.

" But we know," said Mr. Roberts, " what has happened in the trade union movement. Membership has fallen away, funds have become depleted; and—let us face the truth—workers have been rendered workless because of the policy of a section of their fellow workers."

Hon. Members : " Withdraw," and " Rot ! "

Mr. Roberts said his hon. friends knew it and admitted it privately. One of the inducements he had for supporting the Bill was the imperative necessity that existed for it, because of the unfortunate position in which trade unions were placed at the present time.

Viscountess Astor (Coalition Unionist, *Plymouth*) observed that in Bills of this kind the woman had not been brought up to the level at which they would like to see her.

Colonel Sir Godfrey Collins (Independent Liberal, *Greenock*) said it was a question whether it would not be wise to shoulder the burden of these proposals, which imposed a charge of £3,500,000 on industry, rather than allow that burden to fall on the shoulders of employers and employed, who, no doubt, would endeavour to transfer it to the general body of consumers. In a falling market that task could not easily be carried out, so that for six months the burden would rest on industry and to that extent would retard recovery.

After further debate the Labour Party's amendment was negatived by 226 votes against 70, and the Bill was read a second time.

Labour's disappointment.

During the Committee and Report stages in the House of Commons the Bill was amended in certain particulars.

On the motion for the Third Reading of the Bill, on 1st November,

Mr. T. Shaw (Labour, *Preston*) expressed the disappointment of the Labour Party at what they considered to be the very small contribution made by the Bill to a great necessity. Labour objected to what was a purely national calamity, aggravated by Government neglect, and, in some respects, incompetence, being dealt with in a piece-meal fashion at the expense largely of the people who were least easily able to bear the burden. The Bill left out of account many millions of workers not covered by the Insurance Scheme, and, as the result, unemployment would largely become a matter for the Poor Law authorities.

No one except the man who had lived with the workers knew the hatred they had of the thought of Poor Law relief. Once an honest workman had applied to the Parish for relief, generally speaking that man's sense of self-respect was dead. Labour objected also to the sum to be paid under the Bill, which meant in the vast majority of cases nothing less than under-feeding. They were told that when the War was over the workers would come into their own, and the workers now felt that they had been duped. Labour detested the principle of the Bill, but he and his friends, knowing the needs of the people, could not vote against it.

The Minister of Labour said that notwithstanding the severe criticism of the hon. Member, the Bill would provide real relief for women and children.

The Third Reading was agreed to and, after a rapid passage through the House of Lords, the Bill received the Royal Assent.

UNEMPLOYMENT RELIEF.

(Acts connected with Forestry; Powers of Local Authorities; Health Insurance.)

Other Acts passed during this period of the Session in connection with the Government's programme for the relief of unemployment included the following:—

Forestry Act: Enabling the Forestry Commission to expend within the ensuing six months a grant of £250,000 for the purpose of relieving unemployment in country districts.

Local Authorities (Financial Provisions) Act: Making a temporary extension of the charges on the Metropolitan Common Poor Fund in respect of the maintenance of paupers in workhouse or asylums, and of out-door relief; empowering precept issuing authorities to levy rates in the event of a metropolitan borough council refusing or neglecting to do so; enabling local authorities to seek a temporary bank overdraft to meet current expenses; and giving temporary power to local authorities to suspend sinking fund payments in the case of money borrowed for unremunerative works.

National Health Insurance (Prolongation of Insurance) Act: Making provision for maintaining in insurance contributors under the National Health Insurance Acts who would otherwise, through unemployment, fall out of benefit.

CANADIAN NAVY.

(Transfer of Warships and Stores.)

In the House of Commons on 1st November the question of the transfer of warships and stores to Canada was raised.

Dr. D. Murray (Independent, *Western Isles*) asked the Prime Minister whether two destroyers, two submarines, and one cruiser had been handed over to the Dominion of Canada; if so, by whom was this transfer authorised, and at whose request was it made; and whether any conditions were laid down as to the use of the ships and, if so, what?

The Civil Lord of the Admiralty (Commander B. M. Eyres-Monsell), who replied, said: "The answer to the first part of the question is in the affirmative. The transfer was authorised by the British Government, and was made as the result of an offer of surplus war vessels to Dominion Governments as gifts in cases where such vessels were needed to assist the Dominions in the development of their naval forces. No conditions were made beyond those implied in the terms of the offer, that is, that the vessels would be maintained as ships of war."

CANADIAN CATTLE EMBARGO.

(Report of Royal Commission.)

In the House of Commons on 20th October a number of questions were asked on the subject of the Report of the Royal Commission on the Importation of Store Cattle.

The Minister of Agriculture (the Right Hon. Sir A. Griffith-Boscawen) said that legislation would be necessary to give effect to the recommendations in the Report and such legislation could not be introduced that session.

In reply to Sir Beville Stanier* (Coalition Unionist, *Ludlow*),

The Minister of Agriculture said he had received information that the cost of consignment in the case of a cargo of Canadian cattle which recently arrived was £15 to £17 per head.

AIR MAIL TO AUSTRALIA.

(Postmaster-General and London to Australia Service.)

Questions relating to air mails between London and Australia were addressed to the Government in the House of Commons on 1st November.

Mr. A. Baldwin Raper (Coalition Unionist, *Islington, East*) asked the Postmaster-General whether, and at what rate, he would be willing to guarantee a ton of mail matter per week from London to Australia in the event of a firm, or combination of firms, of sufficient standing and repute being prepared to run a weekly aeroplane service in organised stages from London to Australia, the entire distance to be covered in, say, five days?

The Postmaster-General (the Right Hon. F. G. Kellaway): "If a weekly aeroplane service can be established from London to Australia, I shall be prepared to consider the question of employing it for the conveyance of mails. The quantity of mails available, and the price to be paid for their carriage, would depend on the amount of the extra fee which would have to be charged for the service, and on its speed and reliability, which it would, in present conditions, be difficult to determine beforehand."

Mr. Raper: "Will the right hon. gentleman be willing to consider the matter and give some sort of approximate idea of the amount of mails he could guarantee?"

The Postmaster-General: "I should like to see something like a definite undertaking that it is possible to carry out anything like the service which my hon. friend suggests. If he can give me that information, I shall be glad to consider it sympathetically."

---

* Sir Beville Stanier died on 16th December, 1921.

BOOT AND SHOE TRADE.*

(South African Import Restrictions.)

In the House of Commons on 20th October,

Mr. W. R. Smith (Labour, *Wellingborough*) asked the President of the Board of Trade if the importation of boots and shoes into South Africa from this country was being prohibited by the South African Government; whether this matter was discussed at the recent Imperial Conference; if so, what, if any, was the decision reached upon the matter; whether this action had intensified the problem of unemployment in this industry at home; and would he take steps to secure consideration being given to this matter with a view to the removal of the embargo?

The President of the Board of Trade (the Right Hon. Stanley Baldwin): "The prohibition to which the hon. Member refers is qualified by the grant of licences in respect of boots of classes not ordinarily made in the Union of South Africa. For boots which are ordinarily so made, of which schedules have been issued by the Union Government and published in the 'Board of Trade Journal,' licences are, it is true, only granted exceptionally, but I do not understand that the control thus established has greatly affected the volume of trade which could otherwise take place.

"I shall, however, be ready to consider any representations which the hon. Member may be in a position to send me, and to see what can be done. The matter was not discussed at the recent Imperial Conference."

INTERNATIONAL LABOUR CONFERENCE.

(Genoa Conventions on questions relating to Seamen.)

On 8th November a debate took place in the House of Commons on a motion submitted by the Government in respect of the Draft Conventions and Recommendations adopted by the International Labour Conference held at Genoa in June and July, 1920.

DEBATE IN HOUSE OF COMMONS.

The Minister of Labour (the Right Hon. T. J. Macnamara) moved a resolution expressing approval of the policy of His

* For Debate in South African House of Assembly *vide* JOURNAL, Vol. II. No. 4, p. 929.

Majesty's Government in relation to the Conventions and Recommendations. He said it was agreed by the Commission which framed the Labour section of the Peace Treaty at Paris that special questions concerning the minimum conditions to seamen should be dealt with at a special meeting of the International Labour Conference devoted exclusively to that subject. The Conference, held at Genoa, agreed to three draft Conventions and four Recommendations. No agreement was reached on the difficult question of the limitation of the hours of work of seamen. There was no Convention or Recommendation about it.

The Government proposed to accept the three Conventions that were adopted. The first draft Convention dealt with the establishment of a minimum age for the admission of children to employment at sea. With certain exceptions, the Convention took the minimum age of 14 years. It was covered by the Employment of Women, Young Persons, and Children Act, 1920, and was formally ratified by the British Government on 5th July, 1921.

Unemployment indemnities.

The second draft Convention provided for the payment of unemployment indemnities to seamen in cases of loss or foundering of their ship. The proposal was that indemnities should be paid for the days during which the seaman remained, in fact, unemployed, at the same rate as the wages payable under his contract, but that the total indemnity to any one seaman might be limited to two months' wages. The Government were prepared to accept the Convention, but they thought it better to postpone formal ratification until it had been carried into effect by an amendment of the Merchant Shipping Acts. The President of the Board of Trade would introduce a Merchant Shipping Bill when the pressure of Parliamentary business permitted.

The third Convention provided for the establishment of employment facilities either by representative associations of shipowners and seamen jointly, or, in the absence of such joint action, by the State itself. Shipowners and seamen were at present working together in this matter in Great Britain, and had established joint employment facilities in a number of ports, the expenses being conjointly borne by employers' and workmen's associations. But the system was not yet so fully developed as to provide complete compliance with this Convention. It would be agreed that if a system arranged by the industry itself could be so far extended as to cover the whole ground, that was infinitely the best procedure.

The Government proposal, therefore, was to accept this Convention, but postpone formal ratification, and, in the meantime, to watch the development of the existing voluntary system.

The Recommendations: hours of work in fishing industry.

The first of the Recommendations proposed the limitation of hours of work in the fishing industry. It was so drawn as to allow considerable latitude, but, even so, any sincere attempt to carry it into practice was open to many objections. The Recommendation was as follows:—

"In view of the declaration in the Treaties of Peace that all industrial communities should endeavour to adopt, so far as their special circumstances will permit, 'an eight-hours' day or a 48 hours' week as the standard to be aimed at where it has not already been obtained,' the International Labour Conference recommends that each member of the International Labour Organisation enact legislation limiting in this direction the hours of work of all workers employed in the fishing industry, with such special provisions as may be necessary to meet the conditions peculiar to the fishing industry in each country; and that in framing such legislation each Government consult with the organisations of employers and the organisations of workers concerned."

Amongst the difficulties involved in the proposal was the fact that the suggested reduction of hours would mean an increase of staff, for which, he was advised, room could not be found, in most of the British fishing craft. Further, the hours of work were necessarily governed by weather conditions, by the distances of the fishing grounds from the port, and by the fact that fish was a perishable commodity. In these circumstances the Government felt that they could not carry out the Recommendation in any real and satisfactory sense. Therefore, the fair and honest course to pursue was not to accept it.

Inland navigation.

The second Recommendation concerned the limitation of hours of work in inland navigation. This particular industry was one for which it was extremely difficult to prescribe conditions at the present time, because the circumstances were far from normal. The Government proposed, therefore, to postpone the consideration of the question as proposed in the Recommendation until the return of more settled conditions. The third Recommendation dealt with the establishment of national seamen's codes. It suggested that each member of a National Labour Organisation should undertake the embodiment in the seamen's code of its laws and regulations relating to seamen in their capacity as such. Effect would require to be given to the Recommendation by the passing of legislation consolidating the Merchant Shipping Acts. The Government proposed to accept the Recommendation, but intended to defer the necessary legislative action until the pressure of other urgent Parliamentary work decreased.

The fourth and last of the Recommendations concerned the establishment of schemes of unemployment insurance for seamen. Effect to that had already been given in the Unemployment Insurance Act, and, therefore, the Government proposed to inform the Secretary-General of the League of Nations that they were prepared to accept it. He submitted that the policy of the Government made a real endeavour to fall in with the decisions at Genoa.

After a brief debate the resolution was adopted without a division.

FAMINE RELIEF FOR RUSSIA.

(Action by British Government.)

In the House of Commons on 18th October questions were addressed to the Government on the subject of the famine in Russia.

The Right Hon. J. R. Clynes (Chairman of the Parliamentary Labour Party) asked whether the Minister for Overseas Trade was correctly expressing the views of His Majesty's Government in refusing to consider any grant or credit to the Soviet Government to mitigate the Russian famine unless the Soviet Government recognised the debts of former Russian Governments ?

The Secretary to the Overseas Trade Department (Sir Philip Lloyd-Greame): "The resolutions passed by the International Commission in Brussels drew a clear distinction between charitable relief and economic credits. As regards the first, they invited Governments to assist their respective Red Cross societies, a recommendation which has already been carried out by His Majesty's Government without any conditions. As regards the second, the reasoning and conclusions of the Commission are similar to those which were submitted to the House of Commons on the 16th August last, to the effect that the only way in which the necessary confidence can be restored is by establishing those conditions upon which alone credit can be given and maintained in all civilised commercial communities."

Colonel J. C. Wedgwood (Labour, *Newcastle-under-Lyme*)**:** "Is it not a fact that when we entered into the Trade Agreement with Russia we postponed the question of the recognition of pre-War debts till the time when peace was declared with Russia, and why have the Government changed their mind now that there is more urgent need than ever before to give credits to Russia ?"

The Secretary to the Overseas Trade Department: "No, the hon. and gallant gentleman is quite wrong in his statement of the policy of the Government, and the way in which it was expressed. It was made perfectly clear at the time the Trade Agreement was signed, and constantly in this House since, that credits would only be given to Russia if and when debts were acknowledged."

Hon. Members: "What debts ?"

The Secretary to the Overseas Trade Department: "All debts properly entered into, which is exactly the same condition on which credits were applied to other countries."

DENTISTS' ACT.

(Compulsory Registration.)

Before the adjournment of Parliament in August for the summer recess there was passed through both Houses a Bill providing for the registration of all dentists practising in Great Britain and Ireland. It received the Royal Assent on 28th July, 1921.

The Act provides that on and after 28th July, 1922 (one year, that is to say, from the date of the commencement of the Act), no person, unless registered in the Dentist's Register, will be allowed to practise, "or hold himself out, whether directly or by implication, as practising, or as being prepared to practise, dentistry." Contravention of the Statute will render the offender liable to a penalty of £100.

An exception to the above provision is made in the case of the practice of dentistry by a registered medical practitioner; the extraction of a tooth by a duly registered chemist where the case is urgent and no registered medical practitioner or registered dentist is available, and the operation is performed without the application of any general or local anæsthetic; or the performance in any public dental service of minor dental work by any person under the personal supervision of a registered dentist.

Provision is made for the establishment of a Dental Board of the United Kingdom, who will admit to the Dentists' Register persons satisfying the conditions laid down under the Act.

CANADA.

The following Summary deals with some matters held over from previous issues of the JOURNAL, *including the Budget statement and some further Acts of the Fifth Session of the Thirteenth Parliament (which opened on 14th February, and was prorogued on 4th June, 1921) and is in continuation of the Summaries published in Vol. II., Nos. 2, 3 and 4.*

General Election and New Government (Note).

Parliament having been dissolved, a General Election was held on 6th December, 1921, with the result that the Parties are represented in the House of Commons (235 members) as follows:

Liberal	117
National Progressive	65
Conservative	51
Labour	2
	235

Mr. Mackenzie King, the Leader of the Liberal Party, having been called upon to form a Ministry, the following were sworn into office on 29th December:—

Prime Minister and Minister of External Affairs	Hon. W. L. Mackenzie King, M.P.
Minister of Finance	Hon. W. S. Fielding, M.P.
Minister of Justice	Hon. Sir Lomer Gouin, M.P.
Minister of Railways	Hon. William Kennedy, M.P.
Minister of Militia, Defence and Naval Affairs	Hon. G. P. Graham, M.P.
Minister of Marine and Fisheries ..	Hon. Ernest Lapointe, M.P.
Minister of Trade and Commerce ..	Hon. James Robb, M.P.
Postmaster-General	Hon. Charles Murphy, M.P.
Minister of Labour	Hon. James Murdock, M.P.
Minister of Customs and Excise ..	Hon. Jacques Bureau, M.P.
Minister of Agriculture	Hon. W. R. Motherwell, M.P.
Minister of the Interior and Mines ..	Hon. Charles Stewart, M.P.
Minister of Public Works	Senator the Hon. Hewitt Bostock.*
Solicitor-General	Hon. D. D. Mackenzie, M.P.
Ministers without Portfolio ..	Hon. J. E. Sinclair, M.P. Senator the Hon. Raoul Dandurand. Hon. Thomas Low, M.P.

It will be noticed that Naval Affairs are united with the Ministry of Militia and Defence, and that the Department of Health, Immigration and Colonisation is abolished.

---

* After the swearing in of the Cabinet, the Prime Minister announced that on the meeting of Parliament Senator Bostock would be appointed Speaker of the Senate, and the Hon. Rodolphe Lemieux, M.P., Speaker of the House of Commons.

THE BUDGET.

(Annual Financial Statement.)

On 9th May, 1921, the Minister of Finance presented the annual financial statement to the House of Commons.

General position.

The Minister of Finance (Hon. Sir Henry Drayton) said that the past year had been a difficult one for business practically the world over, and Canada had suffered with other nations from the commercial and economic conditions obtaining. The year had been a year of deflation. During the first portion of the year the price of commodities, instead of declining after the cessation of hostilities, sharply rose. Extravagant and luxurious buying was common, and the cost of living in Canada was unreasonable. As a corrective measure, as well as for purposes of revenue, the taxes of last year, known as Luxury Taxes, were imposed. Extravagant buying was slowly but surely checked, and in November declines in commodity prices, both manufacturers' and wholesale, were well marked. Having served these main purposes, the Luxury Taxes were, with but trifling exceptions, abolished on 18th December, 1920. It was felt that working on the sure foundations of lower costs, the conditions of their trade and commerce ought steadily to revive.

Trade.

The previous year showed a total of imports and domestic exports of $2,304,008,267 as against $2,429,288,757 for the year ended 31st March last. This was a remarkable showing, more particularly in view of the fact that prices had materially declined during the last half of the year and that their heavy export of grain was made on the lower price level. The aggregate foreign trade *per capita* in 1920 was $293.30 for Canada, and $127.78 for the United States.

Canada had continued to be a large buyer. Their imports in the year had increased by $175,608,887, while their domestic exports had dropped from those of last year by $50,328,397. While it was perfectly true that Canada, relatively, was very much better off than many other nations, conditions were not as they would have them.

United States.—The unfortunate part of their international balances was that with the United States. Their exports to that market amounted to $542,304,456 of domestic and

$18,379,342 of foreign produce, while their imports amounted to $856,593,470, resulting in an unfavourable trade balance between the two countries of $295,909,672. This large unfavourable balance, coupled with the largely increased invisible payments which had to be made to American holders of Canadian securities, of necessity created a heavy demand for New York exchange, resulting in a premium on New York funds. If Canada was to continue to buy as much as she now did from the United States, she ought to sell a great deal more in that market. The position of their trade with the United States was likely, however, to be made still more unfavourable. The Emergency Tariff, commonly known as the Young Bill, which had already been favourably considered by both Houses of the American Congress, called for the imposition of taxes which would practically prohibit the importation of Canadian agricultural commodities which amounted in volume during the past year to $168,350,000.

United Kingdom.—Their business with the United Kingdom continued to be favourable, although it was unaccompanied by favourable balances as in the past. Last year their exports to the Mother Country amounted to $495,960,118, while their imports amounted to $126,359,249. This year their exports had fallen to $314,226,348, while their imports from the Mother Country had grown to $213,930,946. In view of the large holdings of Canadian securities in the United Kingdom, the net balance would be much reduced, if not indeed turned against them. He had much pleasure in calling attention to the remarkable recovery and extension of British trade in Canada. The increase in imports this year over last, although last year's were greater than those of any previous year except 1913, was over 69 per cent.

Revenue and Expenditure; Debt.

The revenue for the fiscal year (1920-21) would approximately reach $432,000,000 as compared against $349,746,334 for the year before. The estimated expenditure amounted to $533,368,077. The total expenditure had been met without new loans, being covered entirely by current revenue and cash reserves available at the close of last year. Consolidated fund charges connected with and growing out of the War approximated $225,000,000.

The net debt now amounted to $2,350,236,700. War obligations, current and capital, had been met and paid to the extent of $698,809,700.

The revenue for 1921-22 might be estimated at $372,600,000. The main Estimates tabled called for an expenditure of $582,062,698. The policy of the Government was to pay at least all current expenses, including capital charges, out of current income. The total to be raised was $435,360,971. It was obvious that additional revenues ought to be provided.

Tariff.

It was not proposed to put into effect now a general revision of the tariff schedules. While Canada must make her own tariff and while that tariff must be a tariff dictated in the interests of Canada and her people, it was not advisable that frequent changes should be made. It was idle to attempt to disguise the fact that any proper Canadian tariff must have consideration to the settled tariff conditions obtaining in the United States. Of their total trade of the past year 57 per cent. was with the United States. The temporary tariff legislation of the United States would place a barrier against their exports amounting to no less than $168,000,000. Such or similar action made permanent, of necessity, would require a careful and thorough revision of the Canadian tariff for the purpose of ensuring the proper continuance of Canadian business.

Changes in the schedules, however, became necessary for the purpose of implementing the trade pact with the West India Islands which had been ratified by both Houses and assented to. (*Vide infra* Customs Tariff Amendment Act.)

Dumping: Customs amendment.

Changes ought to be made in the Customs Act with a view to securing a more efficient carrying out of the principle of the dumping provisions. Much of the unemployment at present existing resulted from the importation into Canada of goods at prices below the cost of production. Goods ought to be valued for customs purposes, not at forced-sale prices, justified by temporary quotations in the foreign market, but having regard to the regular standard value in that market and to cost of production and a reasonable profit thereon. A further change should also be made having regard to the valuation of goods imported from foreign countries where currencies had greatly depreciated. It was, therefore, proposed to provide that any depreciation of a foreign currency greater than 50 per cent. should be disregarded and that the lowest valuation which could be made would be arrived at by a depreciation of 50 per cent. When the rate of exchange was adverse to Canada, the value for duty would be computed at the rate of exchange existing at the date of the shipment of the goods. (*Vide infra* Department of Customs and Excise Act.)

Marking of importations.

Representations had from time to time been made to the effect that the goods of one country were being palmed off on the Canadian public as the goods of another country. Especially had representatives of British business urged that many goods were being sold as British goods which had either not seen Great Britain or were merely collected in and forwarded from that country. A resolution would, therefore, be moved to provide that all goods imported into Canada capable of being marked, stamped, branded or labelled without injury should have indicated on them legibly in English or French the country of origin. (*Vide infra* Customs Tariff Amendment Act.)

Taxes.

Business Profits War Tax.—This tax would be dropped. With present business conditions it would in any event become largely inoperative—excess profits, generally speaking, would not be found. This tax was one which was only justifiable as an emergency measure in a time of inflation and national stress. It was a tax which worked harm to the general financial situation and business conditions in an ordinary period and more particularly in a period of business depression.

Excise Taxes.—The few remaining so-called Luxury Taxes would be abolished. In lieu thereof, having particular regard to the necessities of revenue, duties (increased) would be levied on playing cards and wine. It was proposed to grant a rebate of 99 per cent. of the duties paid on spirits actually used for medicinal purposes in *bona fide* hospitals. (*Vide infra* Inland Revenue Amendment Act and Special War Revenue Amendment Act.)

Sales Tax.—It was proposed to increase the rate of the sales tax. The principle of either a sales or turnover tax had been strongly advocated by many boards of trade and commercial bodies. Theoretically a general turnover tax on commodities and services had much to commend it. In practical administration the cost would be unduly great and the difficulties of collection many. Instead of extending the tax, it was proposed to confine its operation to the sales of manufacturers, wholesalers, jobbers and importers and to continue a list of special exemptions, which, broadly speaking, would cover foodstuffs, initial sales of farm produce by the farmer of his own production, as well as the first products of the fisheries, mines and forests. The 1 per cent. and 2 per cent. rates on domestic transactions would become 1½ per cent. and 3 per cent. respectively, and the present import rates would become 2½ per cent. and 4 per cent. (*Vide infra* Special War Revenue Act Amendment.)

DEPARTMENT OF CUSTOMS AND EXCISE ACT.

(Dumping of Foreign Goods.)

This Act, which was assented on 4th June, 1921, provides for the constitution of a Department of Customs and Excise, and amends the Customs Act to prevent the dumping of foreign goods.

Constitution of Department.

The Act provides that there shall be constituted a Department of Customs and Excise, presided over by a Minister of Customs and Excise, who is substituted for the Minister of Customs and Inland Revenue. The chief officer of the Department, called the Commissioner of Customs and Excise, shall be appointed by the Governor-in-Council. (*Sect.* 2.) The Minister's duties and powers shall apply to : (A) control and management of the collection of the duties of Customs and of matters incident thereto ; (B) collection of all duties of excise ; (C) collection of stamp duties, and the preparation and issue of stamps and stamped paper, except postage stamps ; (D) internal taxes, but not including income taxes ; (E) such other duties as may be assigned to the Minister by the Governor-in-Council. (*Sect.* 3 *and Schedule.*)

Invoice for Foreign Goods.

It is further provided that entry of goods in Canada is not perfect unless an invoice is produced, and unless in all cases of shipments from any country other than the United Kingdom, British Colonies and British Possessions, where the value for duty of the invoiced goods in terms of the standard dollar of Canada is $100 or over, such invoice bear thereon a certificate of a Canadian Trade Commissioner, British Consul or other duly accredited officer. (*Sect.* 6.)

Valuation for Duty.

The Customs Act is also amended by providing that the valuation for duty of goods imported into Canada shall in no case be lower than the wholesale price thereof, when sold for home consumption, and that the value for duty of new or unused goods shall in no case be less than the actual cost of production of similar goods at date of shipment direct to Canada, plus a reasonable profit thereon, the Minister of Customs and Excise being the sole judge of what shall constitute a reasonable profit in the circumstances. (*Sect.* 7.)

In computing the value for duty of the currency of an invoice, no reduction shall be allowed in excess of 50 per cent. of the value of the standard or proclaimed currency of the country from whence the goods are invoiced to Canada, irrespective of the rate of exchange existing between such country and Canada on the date of the shipment of the goods ; and in respect of goods shipped to Canada from a country when the rate of exchange is adverse to Canada, the value for duty of the currency of the invoice shall be computed at the rate of exchange existing between such country and Canada at the date of the shipment of the goods. (*Sect.* 8.)

CUSTOMS TARIFF AMENDMENT ACT.

(West Indies Trade Agreement.)

This Act, which was assented to on 4th June, 1921, amends the Customs Tariff, 1907, so as to give effect to the Customs clauses of the West Indies Trade Agreement Act (*vide* JOURNAL, Vol. II., No. 4, p. 813), and provide for the marking of imports into Canada.

The Act provides that all goods, other than tobaccos, spirituous or alcoholic liquors and articles specified in Schedule A. of the West Indies Trade Agreement Act, which are the produce or manufacture of British Honduras, Bermuda, the Bahamas, Jamaica, Turks and Caicos Islands, the Leeward Islands, the Windward Islands, Barbados, Trinidad and Tobago and British Guiana, when imported direct therefrom, shall not be liable for more than 50 per cent. of the duties imposed on similar goods as set forth in the general tariff.

It is further provided that all goods imported into Canada shall be marked, stamped, branded or labelled in legible English or French words, where this can be done without injury to the article, in a conspicuous place so as to indicate the country of origin. All goods which do not comply with these requirements shall be subject to an additional duty of 10 per cent. *ad valorem.*

INLAND REVENUE AMENDMENT ACT.

This Act, which increases the excise duties on spirits, and allows a drawback of 99 per cent. on spirits for university, scientific, research and hospital purposes, was assented to on 4th June, 1921.

SPECIAL WAR REVENUE AMENDMENT ACT.

This Act, which was assented to on 4th June, 1921, imposes increased excise taxes on playing cards and wines, and increases, with the exception of certain exempted articles, such as dairy produce, British and Canadian coin and foreign gold, newspapers and magazines, etc., the tax on sales in accordance with the Budget statement.

COPYRIGHT ACT.

The object of this Act is to amend and consolidate the law relating to copyright and to make the Canadian law concerning copyright conform to the provisions of the Berne Conference and similar laws existing in foreign countries. The Act was read a second time and referred to a Special Committee on 3rd May, and received the Royal Assent on 4th June.

Definitions.

For the purposes of the Act " copyright " means the sole right to produce or reproduce, to perform, or in the case of a lecture to deliver, the work or any substantial part thereof in public ; if the work is unpublished, to publish the work or any substantial part thereof, and includes the sole right :—

(A) To produce, reproduce, perform or publish any translation of the work ;

(B) In the case of a dramatic work, to convert it into a novel or other non-dramatic work ;

(C) In the case of a novel or other non-dramatic work, or of an artistic work, to convert it into a dramatic work, by way of performance in public or otherwise ;

(D) In the case of a literary, dramatic, or musical work, to make any record, perforated roll, cinematograph film, or other contrivance by means of which the work may be mechanically performed or delivered.

For the purposes of the Act (other than those relating to infringement of copyright) a work shall not be deemed to be published or performed or a lecture delivered in public if so published, performed or delivered without the consent of the author, his executors, administrators or assigns. A work shall be deemed to be first published within His Majesty's Dominions or within a foreign country to which the Act extends, notwithstanding that it has been published simultaneously in some other place ; and to be published simultaneously in two places, if the time between the publication does not exceed fourteen days or such longer period as may be fixed by Order in Council. Where in the case of an unpublished work, the making of the work is extended over a considerable period, the conditions of the Act conferring copyright shall be deemed to have been complied with if the author was, during any substantial part of that period, a British subject, or a subject of a foreign country to which the Act extends, or a resident within His Majesty's Dominions ; and the author shall be deemed to be a resident within His Majesty's Dominions if he is domiciled therein. (*Sect.* 3.)

Conditions and Term of Copyright.

Copyright shall subsist in Canada, during the life of an author and a period of fifty years after his death, in every original literary, dramatic, musical and artistic work (including records and other mechanical contrivances), if the author was at the date of the making of the work a British subject, a citizen or subject of a foreign country which has adhered to the Convention of Berne of 13th November, 1908, and the additional protocol thereto, or resident within His Majesty's Dominions; and if, in the case of a published work, the work was first published within His Majesty's Dominions or in such foreign country. The Minister may, under certain conditions, extend copyright to other countries. It is further provided that any time after the expiration of twenty-five years, or, in the case of a work in which copyright subsists at the passing of the Act, thirty years, from the death of the author of a published work, copyright in the work shall not be infringed by its reproduction for sale, subject to prescribed notice of reproduction being given and royalties of ten per cent. on the price at which the work is published being paid to the owner of the copyright. In cases of joint authorship copyright shall subsist during the life of the author who first dies and for a term of fifty years after his death, or during the life of the author who dies last, whichever period is the longer. In the case of photographs, records, etc., copyright shall subsist for fifty years from the making of the original negative or plate. Copyright in posthumous works shall subsist for fifty years after their first publication or performance. Without prejudice to any rights or privileges of the Crown, when any work has been prepared or published by or under the control of His Majesty or any Government Department, the copyright of the work shall, subject to any agreement with the author, belong to His Majesty, and shall continue for fifty years from the date of first publication. (*Sects.* 4–10.)

Ownership of Copyright.

The author of a work shall be the first owner of the copyright therein save when, in the case of an engraving, photograph or portrait, the original was ordered by some other person and was made for valuable consideration in pursuance of that order; or when the author was in the employment of some other person under a contract of service or apprenticeship and the work was made in the course of his employment, that person shall be the first owner of the copyright; but when the work is an article or other contribution to a newspaper, magazine or similar periodical there shall be reserved to the author a right to restrain the publication of the work, otherwise than as part of a newspaper, magazine or similar periodical. The owner of the copyright in any work may assign the right either wholly or partially, either generally or subject to territorial limitations; and either for the whole term of the copyright or part of it, and may grant any interest in the right by licence, provided that, when the author of the work is the first owner of the copyright therein, no assignment of the copyright, and no grant of any interest therein made by him otherwise than by will, shall be operative to vest in the assignee any rights with respect to the copyright in the work beyond the expiration of twenty-five years from the death of the author, and the reversionary interest in the copyright expectant on the termination of that period shall, on the death of the author, devolve on his legal representatives as part of his estate. (*Sect.* 11.)

Licences.

If at any time after the death of the author of a literary, dramatic or musical work which has been published or performed in public, a complaint is made to the Governor in Council that the owner of the copyright has refused to allow the republication or performance of the work, and that by reason of such refusal the work is withheld from the public, the owner of the copyright may be ordered to grant a licence to reproduce the work or perform the work in public. (*Sect.* 12.)

Any person, subject to certain conditions, may apply to the Minister for a licence to print and publish in Canada any book wherein copyright subsists if at any time after publication and within the duration of the copyright the owner of the copyright fails (A) to print the book or cause it to be printed in Canada, (B) to supply by means of copies so printed the reasonable demands of the Canadian market for such book. If the owner, on notice being given, does not proceed, the application may be granted; and the licence when issued shall entitle the licensee to the sole right to print and publish such book in Canada during a term not exceeding five years or for such editions as may be fixed by the licence, the licensee paying a royalty on the retail selling price of every copy. (*Sect.* 13.)

If the publication of a book is lawfully begun as a serial elsewhere than in His Majesty's Dominions, and the owner of the copyright has refused to grant a licence to any person in Canada, being a publisher of a periodical, to publish such book in serial form, a licence may at the discretion of the Minister be granted to such publisher to publish such book once in serial form, provided that a licence shall not be granted to more than one publisher in the same city.

Every licence issued under these sections shall be deemed to constitute a contract between the owner of the copyright and the licensee who shall be entitled to the same remedies as in the case of a contract. (*Sect.* 15.)

Infringement of Copyright.

Copyright in a work shall be deemed to be infringed by any person who, without the consent of the owner of the copyright, does anything the sole right to do which is by this Act conferred on the owner of the copyright. The following acts shall not, however, constitute an infringement :—(i.) Any fair dealing with a work for the purposes of private study, research, criticism, review or newspaper summary; (ii.) the use by the author, who is not the owner of the copyright, of any mould, sketch, model, etc., made by him for the purpose of the work, provided he does not repeat or imitate the main design of the work; (iii.) the making or publishing of paintings, engravings or photographs of a work of sculpture or artistic craftsmanship, if permanently situate in a public place or building, or of any architectural work of art; (iv.) the publication in a collection, under certain conditions, of short passages from published literary works intended for use in schools; (v.) the publication in a newspaper of a report of a lecture given in public, unless notice to the contrary is given. Copyright in a work shall be deemed to be infringed by any person who sells or lets for hire, distributes or exhibits in public for purposes of trade, or imports for sale or hire into Canada any work which to his knowledge infringes copyright or would infringe copyright if it had been made within Canada; or for his private profit permits any place of entertainment to be used for the performance in public of the work without the consent of the owner of the copyright. Reports in newspapers of political speeches are no infringement; and it shall not be deemed an infringement of copyright in any musical, literary or dramatic work for any person to make within Canada records, perforated rolls or other contrivances by means of which sounds may be reproduced provided that such contrivances have previously been made by or with the consent of the owner of the copyright and the proper royalties paid. (*Sects.* 16–18.)

Importation of Copies.

Copies made out of Canada of any work in which copyright subsists, which if made in Canada would infringe copyright and as to which the owner of the copyright gives notice in writing to the Department of Customs that such copies should not be so imported into Canada, shall not be imported, and shall be deemed to be included in Schedule C. to the Customs Tariff, 1907. The same applies where the right or licence to reproduce any book in Canada has been granted; and the Act also declares it unlawful to import into Canada copies of any book in which copyright subsists until fourteen days after publication thereof, the Minister being empowered to extend this period at his discretion if within the period an application for a licence has been made. It is lawful, however, for any person (A) to import for his own use not more than two copies of any work published in any country adhering to the Convention; (B) to import for use by any Department of His Majesty's Government for the Dominion or any of the Provinces of Canada, copies of any work, wherever published; (C) at any time before a work is printed or made in Canada to import any copies required for the use of any public library or institution of learning; (D) to import, subject to safeguards, any book lawfully printed in the United Kingdom or in a foreign country which has adhered to the Convention, and published for circulation among and sale to the public within either. (*Sects.* 26 *and* 27.)

Other Provisions.

The Act further provides for civil remedies for the infringement of copyright; summary remedies for the sale, exhibition, importation, etc., of infringing copies of works in which copyright subsists (*Sects.* 19–25); the administration of the Act by the Commissioner of Patents and the Registrar of Copyrights (*Sects.* 28–35); the registration of copyrights (*Sects.* 36–39); fees (*Sect.* 40); subsistence of substituted right (*Sect.* 41); and the Governor in Council is empowered to make such rules and regulations as appear to him necessary for the purposes of the Act. (*Sect.* 43.)

It is also provided that all the enactments relating to copyright passed by the Parliament of the United Kingdom are, so far as they are operative in Canada, repealed, provided that this repeal shall not prejudicially affect any legal rights existing at the time of the repeal. (*Sect.* 47.)

The Governor in Council may take such action as may be necessary to secure the adherance of Canada to the revised Convention of Berne of 13th November, 1908, and the additional protocol thereto. (*Sect.* 49.)

PATENT AMENDMENT ACT.

This Act, which was assented to on 4th June, 1921, makes certain amendments in the Patent Act.

Validity of, and Applications for, Patents.

The Act, after making alterations in the tariff of fees for patents, provides that no patent in force on 1st August, 1914, or subsequently granted shall be void through failure to construct or manufacture, or by the importation of, the invention covered by the patent between that date and 10th January, 1922. Fees which have become payable under the Patent Act since 1st August, 1914, may, at any time until the expiration of a period of one year from the coming into force of this Act, be paid with the same effect as if paid within the times prescribed by the Patent Act.

The above privileges in regard to payment of fees on patents already obtained and lapsed by reason of non-payment are granted under the Act only in favour of nationals and residents of Canada, but the Governor in Council may extend the same favour to citizens and subjects of all countries which have extended or which now extend or which, within six months of the passage of the Act, shall extend substantially reciprocal privileges to citizens and nationals of Canada. (*Sects.* 4 *and* 5.)

The rights provided by the Patent Act for the filing of applications for patents for invention, which rights had not expired on 1st August, 1914, or have arisen since that date shall be extended for a period of six months from the coming into force of this Act, this extension to apply to applications upon which patents have been granted as well as to those pending or filed within the said period. It is provided, however, that such extension shall in no way affect the right of any person, who, before the passage of this Act, was *bona fide* in possession of any rights in patents or applications for patents conflicting with rights granted or validated by reason of such extension, to exercise such rights himself personally or by agents, or licensees, as derived their rights from him before the passage of this Act; and such persons shall not be amenable to any action for infringement of any patent granted or validated by reason of such extension. (*Sect.* 6.)

It is further provided that a patent shall not be refused on an application filed between 1st August, 1914, and the expiration of a similar period of six months, nor shall a patent granted on such application be held invalid by reason of the invention having been patented in any other country or in any other of His Majesty's Dominions or Possessions or described in any printed publication or because it was in public use or on sale prior to the filing of the application, unless such patent, publication, etc., was issued prior to 1st August, 1913. No patent under these provisions shall, however, abridge the right of any person to continue any manufacture, use or sale commenced before the coming into force of this Act, nor shall the continued manufacture constitute an infringement. (*Sect.* 7.)

It is also provided that, in cases where a patent which has become void in consequence of the non-payment of fees or failure to manufacture, or because of the importation of the patented invention has been subsequently made valid, any person who has, during the period when such patent was void, commenced lawfully to manufacture, use or sell the invention covered by the patent, the patentee or proprietor of the patent shall not be entitled to any claim, and the Commissioner for Patents may impose such terms and conditions to which any revived patent shall be subject.

Rights under Treaty of Peace.

Nothing in the provisions of the above section shall be deemed in any way to affect any rights as to the revival of any lapsed rights or in respect of any patent of invention applied for or acquired under the provisions of this Act which may be claimed by any person under the stipulations of the Treaty of Peace between the Allied and Associated

Powers and Germany, or under any treaty entered into and ratified, or that may be entered into and ratified by His Majesty, acting on behalf of Canada, with any other Power with which the Allied and Associated Powers are, or have been at war, with regard to industrial property, or otherwise affecting patent rights. (*Sect.* 8.)

Validity of Patents under War Regulations.

The Act ratifies and confirms all orders which have been made under the orders and regulations respecting patents of invention made by the Governor in Council under the provisions of the War Measures Act, 1914, etc.; provided that nothing contained in this section shall affect the validity of any patent which is the subject of litigation before any court of record at the time of the passing of the Act. The above orders shall continue in force for one year from the date of the passing of the Act.

BANKRUPTCY AMENDMENT ACT.

This Act, which amends the Bankruptcy Act of 1919 in various particulars, was assented to on 4th June, 1921.

Interim Receiver.

The Act provides that if an authorised trustee is appointed interim receiver of the property of the debtor, he may, under the direction of the court, summarily dispose of any perishable goods and carry on the business of the debtor for all conservatory purposes. (*Sect.* 8.)

Composition of Debts and Scheme of Arrangement.

As soon as possible after an authorised trustee has been required to convene a meeting of creditors to consider a proposal of a composition, extension or scheme of arrangement, he shall fix a date for such meeting and send to every creditor: (A) notice of time and place of meeting; (B) condensed statement of debtor's assets and liabilities; (C) list of creditors; and (D) his proposals. If at the meeting of creditors a majority (holding two-thirds in amount of the proved debts) resolves to accept the proposal, it shall be deemed to be duly accepted by them, and, if approved by the court, binding on all the creditors. (*Sect.* 12.) A similar majority may by resolution appoint a committee of not more than five persons to represent the creditors; and such committee or majority thereof may, subject to the confirmation of the court upon the joint application of the trustee and the debtor and to any limitations imposed by the majority of the creditors, proceed by itself, its solicitors or agents, to investigate the affairs of the debtor in order to advise the creditors whether to accept or reject the proposal. Pending acceptance or rejection the court may authorise the committee, by itself or the debtor or jointly, to administer the estate or business of the debtor in the interests of the creditors, and in particular to: (i.) compromise any debts or claims of the debtor against others; (ii.) comprise the debts or claims of the creditors against the debtor; (iii.) mortgage or pledge the property of the debtor for the purpose of raising money for the payment of his debts. The action of the committee is binding upon all creditors, the costs and expenses to be fixed by court and payable out of the debtor's estate.

(*Sect.* 13.) On the application of the trustee the court may order that any action or other proceedings against a debtor shall stand stayed, pending consideration of the proposal of composition; and on the making of an authorised assignment or any order approving a proposal of composition every action for the recovery of a debt shall stand stayed subject to the rights of secured creditors to realise or otherwise deal with their securities. (*Sect.* 14.)

Appointment and Powers of Trustees.

If a majority of the creditors present at any meeting require it a trustee must give security by bond or otherwise to the registrar of the court in the amount required by the creditors for the due accounting, payment over and transfer of all property received by him in respect of the debtor's estate. (*Sect.* 15.) Creditors constituting a majority of those holding half or more of the proved debts of $25 or upward may substitute any other authorised trustee acting in the same bankruptcy district. (*Sect.* 16.) The trustee must insure all the insurable property of the debtor until sold or disposed of (*Sect.* 17); he may apply to the court for direction in relation to any matter affecting the administration of the estate of the bankrupt (*Sect.* 18); and, with the permission of the inspectors, elect to retain for the whole or part of its unexpired term, or to assign or disclaim any lease of or other temporary interest in any property forming part of the debtor's estate. (*Sect.* 19.) Any person claiming to own goods in the charge or possession of a debtor must give 15 days' notice to the trustee of his intention to remove them. (*Sect.* 21.) If the creditors refuse or neglect to repay to the trustee all money advances made by him or to secure the trustee to an extent adequate in his opinion or that of the court in respect of all liabilities incurred in carrying on the business of the debtor, the court may order that the property of the debtor be offered for sale by tender and apply the proceeds to the payment of the advances. If the tenders are insufficient the court may permit the trustee in his personal capacity to purchase the property, whereupon all rights and interests of the debtors and creditors in it or to it shall become determined and ended. (*Sect.* 24.)

Book Debts.

When a person engaged in any trade or business makes an assignment of his existing or future book debts, and is subsequently adjudicated bankrupt, or makes an authorised assignment, the assignment of book debts shall be void against the trustee in the bankruptcy or under the authorised assignment, as regards any book debts which have not been paid at the date of the presentation of the petition in bankruptcy or of the making of the authorised assignment unless there has been compliance with the provision of any statute in force in the province of the debtor; provided that this shall not render void any assignment of book debts, due at the date of assignment from specified debtors, or debts growing due under specified contracts, or any assignment of book debts included in a transfer of a business made *bona fide*, and for value, or in any authorised assignment. (*Sect.* 25.)

Contributories to Insolvent Corporations.

Misrepresentation or fraud in obtaining any subscription for shares or securities of a corporation shall not constitute a ground of defence in respect of any amount claimed to be payable by a contributory unless prior to the presentation of the bankruptcy petition against the corporation or the making of the authorised assignment by it the contributory has brought action to have his subscription cancelled on the same ground. (*Sect.* 27.) The court may, on the application of any contributory, adjust the rights of the contributories among themselves, and, for the purpose of facilitating such adjustment, may direct the trustee to intervene. (*Sect.* 28.) The court shall allow to the trustee, as against the contributories, such remuneration, expenses and costs as the court may deem just. (*Sect.* 29.)

Dividends.

The trustee may, at any time after the first meeting of creditors, give notice that if any person claiming to be a creditor does not prove his debt within thirty days, he will proceed to make a dividend or final dividend without regard to such person's claim, the court, however, being empowered to extend the time. (*Sect.* 31.) The trustee, having realised all the property of the bankrupt or authorised assignor or all thereof that can be realised without needlessly protracting the trusteeship and settled the claims of all creditors against the estate of the debtor, shall make a final dividend, and be at liberty to divide the property of the debtor among the creditors who have proved their debts without regard to other claimants. (*Sect.* 32.) No action for dividend unless improperly refused shall lie against the trustee. (*Sect.* 34.)

Remuneration and Discharge of Trustee.

The remuneration of the trustee in bankruptcy, excepting those rendered: (A) upon the adjustment of the rights of contributories as among themselves; and (B) in connection with the application of a bankrupt or authorised assignor for a discharge, shall be such as is voted to the trustee by a majority of creditors present at any general meeting. (*Sect.* 35.) The court may by order discharge an authorised trustee upon or, for sufficient cause, before full administration. A trustee shall be entitled to be discharged if another trustee has been substituted and his accounts are satisfactory, provided that three months have elapsed without any undisposed of claim having been made by the debtor or any creditor; or when his accounts have been approved and appeals settled, and a period of two and a half years has lapsed after payment of the final dividend. Nothing in this section shall discharge a trustee from fraud or breach of trust. (*Sect.* 36.)

Meeting of Creditors.

The chairman may accept telegraphic or cable communication as proof of the debt of a creditor who carries on business outside Canada, and as to the authority of anyone claiming to represent and vote on behalf of such creditor. (*Sect.* 37.)

Inspectors.

No inspector may acquire for himself or another any property of the estate for which he is an inspector unless with the prior approval of the court. (*Sect.* 38.)

Proof by Secured Creditors.

If a secured creditor does not realise or surrender his security he shall within thirty days of the receiving order or authorised assignment file with the trustee a statutory declaration stating full particulars of his security and its value. Every creditor must identify any property within the estate of the debtor on which he claims lien, and is only entitled to receive a dividend in respect of the balance due to him after deducting the assessed value of his security. (*Sect.* 40.)

Rights of Landlord.

The trustee shall be entitled to continue in occupation of the leased premises of the debtor for so long as he requires them for the purpose of the trust estate, and any payment to be made to the landlord in respect of accelerated rent shall be credited against the amount payable by the trustee for the period of his occupation. If he occupies for three months or more beyond the making of the receiving order the landlord shall be entitled to three months' notice of the trustee's intention to surrender possession or three months rent in lieu thereof. (*Sect.* 42.) The trustee may elect to retain the leased premises for the whole or any portion of the unexpired term, and may, upon payment to the landlord of all overdue rent, assign the lease to any person who will covenant to observe its terms, and agree to conduct upon the demised premises a business which is not reasonably of a more objectionable or hazardous nature than that conducted by the debtor, and shall be approved by the court. Security must, however, be given to the landlord by the assignee of the leased premises. (*Sect.* 43.) The trustee's entry into possession of the leased premises and their occupation by him while required for the purposes of the trust estate shall not be deemed to be evidence of his intention to elect to retain the premises, nor affect his right to disclaim possession, and if he elects to retain or assign the premises, his liability shall be limited to the payment of rent for the period during which he shall remain in possession for the purpose of the trust estate. (*Sect.* 44.) An underlease by the bankrupt or assignor, if disclaimed or assigned by the trustee, may be vested by the court in the underlessee of the debtor. (*Sect.* 45.)

Miscellaneous Provisions.

To the list of claims to be settled is added, last in order of priority, "all indebtedness of the bankrupt or assignor to any Workmen's Compensation Board or under any Workmen's Compensation Act established under the law of a province." (*Sect.* 41.)

The court may by warrant direct the seizure or search in behalf of the trustee of the property of the debtor whether in the possession of the debtor or of any other person, and for that purpose the breaking open of any building or place where the debtor or any part of his property is believed to be. (*Sect.* 49.)

For any purposes of the Act an incorporated company may act by any of its officers or employees authorised in that behalf, a firm may act by any of its members, and a lunatic may act by his committee or curator or by the curator or guardian of his property. (*Sect.* 50.)

Any person who without the permission of the trustee removes or attempts to remove the debtor's goods is liable to a fine not exceeding $5,000 or two years' imprisonment (*Sect.* 52); and when any offence under the Act has been committed by an incorporated company every officer, director or agent of the company who participates in the commission of the offence shall be liable to like penalties as the company, and as if he had committed the offence personally, and shall be so liable cumulatively with the company. (*Sect.* 53.)

CRIMINAL CODE AMENDMENT ACT.

(Sexual Offences; Age of Consent, &c.).

This Act, dealing with sexual offences, etc., was passed by the House of Commons on 26th May, 1921. It was subsequently amended by the Senate in several important details, and received assent on 4th June. Some of the original sections as passed by the House of Commons were of general interest, and it has therefore been thought desirable to place them on record together with a note of the Senate amendments.

Sexual offences.

The Bill as passed by the House of Commons provided for the repeal of Section 17 of the Criminal Code Amendment Act of 1920 (*vide* JOURNAL, Vol. I., No. 4, p. 677), which empowers the judge, in cases of seduction, to instruct the jury that if in their view the evidence does not show that the accused is wholly or chiefly to blame, they may find a verdict of acquittal.* (*Sect.* 1.)

The Criminal Code of 1906 is amended by raising the age up to which the consent of the child is no defence in cases of indecent assault, from fourteen to sixteen.* (*Sect.* 5.) Whipping is added to the punishments for rape. (*Sect.* 6.) Section 8 of the Criminal Code Amendment Act of 1920, which makes any person guilty of an indictable offence and liable to imprisonment for five years who carnally knows any girl of previous chaste character under the age of sixteen and above the age of fourteen, is amended by striking out the words "of previous chaste character."* (*Sect.* 7.)

Possession of bombs, firearms, etc.

The Criminal Code of 1906 is amended by making any person who without lawful excuse has in his possession any bomb, grenade or other device made or intended for a similar purpose, liable to seven years' imprisonment. (*Sect.* 2.) The Act also empowers the Governor in Council to forbid, for such period as he deems fit, the having in possession in such portion of Canada as may be named in the proclamation any firearm or other weapon without a permit. (*Sect.* 4.)

Other Provisions.

It is also an indictable offence to drive a motor while intoxicated (*Sect.* 4) and to play "three card monte" or similar game in a public place (*Sect.* 10); the minimum sentence for stealing a motor car is one year's imprisonment (*Sect.* 8); the penalty of whipping is added to the punishments for robbery and assault with intent to rob (*Sect.* 11); any person who wilfully and for any fraudulent or unlawful purpose burns any chattel having a greater value than $25 is made liable to fourteen years' imprisonment* (*Sect.* 12); the docking of animals,* except dogs, is forbidden. (*Sect.* 14.) Other clauses deal with the cruelly killing* and ill-treatment of animals, including failure to administer anæsthetics to animals when operated upon, the carriage of animals, etc. (*Sects.* 15 *and* 16); use of metal tokens as money (*Sect.* 17); etc.

---

* *Vide* Senate amendment below.

Senate Amendments.

The Senate amended the Bill by *inter alia* :—

Striking out Sections 1, 5 and 7.

Reducing the penalty in Section 12 from fourteen to five years' imprisonment, and raising the value prescribed for the article burned from $25 to $200.

Striking out Sections 14 (docking of tails) and 15 (cruelly killing animals).

These amendments were concurred in by the House of Commons on 2nd June.

OPIUM AND NARCOTIC DRUG AMENDMENT ACT.

This Act, which was assented to on 4th June, 1921, amends in certain details the Act summarised in the JOURNAL, Vol. II., No. 1, p. 80.

The Act amends Subsection 1 of Section 5, so as to prevent prescriptions for drugs being used more than once, by striking out the words "without the authority of the prescribing physician, veterinary surgeon or dentist," and by inserting after the word "occasion" the following words : "except where the preparation covered by the prescription might have lawfully been sold in the first instance without a written order or prescription" (*vide* above JOURNAL, p. 81, lines 6 and 8).

The Act further provides that any person who occupies, controls or is in possession of any building, room, vessel, vehicle, enclosure or place in which any drug is found, shall if charged with having such drug in possession without lawful authority, be deemed to have been so in possession unless he prove that the drug was there without his authority or knowledge, or that he was lawfully entitled to the possession thereof.

Any constable or other peace officer who has reasonable cause to suspect that any drug is kept for any purpose contrary to the Act in any dwelling-house, store, or other place, may search any such place by day or night.

CANADIAN BAR ASSOCIATION.

(Incorporation Act.)

This Act, which was assented to on 15th April, 1921, is the result of a petition on behalf of the Canadian Bar Association for incorporation.

The Act incorporates the Association and enumerates its objects, viz., to advance the science of jurisprudence ; promote the administration of justice and uniformity of legislation throughout Canada so far as is consistent with the preservation of the basic systems of law in the respective provinces; uphold the honour of the profession of the law and foster co-operation among the incorporated law societies, barristers' societies and general corporations of the Bars of the several provinces and cordial intercourse among the members of the Canadian Bar; encourage a high standard of legal education; and publish its own transactions, reports of cases and decisions concerning the law and its practice, etc.

Subject to the by-laws of the Association, power is given to constitute local branches and executives, provided that their powers are not in excess of those conferred on the Association by the Act.

The Act gives powers to the Association to make by-laws including those in regard to members and fees, the council and officers of the Association, meetings and administration.

Membership is divided into (A) active, (B) honorary and (C) other classes. Active members comprise the active members of the unincorporated Association, and all others who are from time to time admitted to active membership under the by-laws or rules of the Association; any member in good standing of the Bar of any province, and any judge or retired judge of a Court of Record in Canada appointed from such Bar shall be eligible to active membership.

GRAND TRUNK ARBITRATION ACT.

This Act, which was assented to on 3rd May, 1921, is pursuant to the Grand Trunk Railway Acquisition Act (*vide* JOURNAL, Vol. I., No. 1, p. 106) and the agreement of 8th March, 1920, entered into between the Government and the Grand Trunk Railway Company for the acquisition of the railway by the Government under the terms of the Act.

This Act empowers the Governor in Council to extend the time for the arbitrators' award fixed by the Agreement, but on conditions which will ensure to the satisfaction of the Government (A) that the directors of the Company and of others comprised in the System shall resign and nominees of the Government shall be appointed to the vacancies; (B) that the directors of the Company nominated by the Government shall hold office during pleasure and shall carry on the business of the Company without reference to the shareholders and without being subject to their vote or control; (C) that the meetings of the Board may be held in Canada or elsewhere; (D) that the directors shall exercise all the powers of the Committee of Management as provided for in the agreement; (E) that there shall be a committee of shareholders constituted by the present directors, which for the purpose of carrying on arbitration proceedings, shall be vested with the powers heretofore belonging to the directors; (F) that books and records, railways and properties may be open to inspection by the Committee; and (G) that on the substitution of the directors arbitration shall proceed as speedily as possible.

AUSTRALIA.

Commonwealth Parliament.

The following Summary is in continuation of the proceedings of the First Session of the Eighth Parliament, which commenced on 26th February, 1920, and concluded on 10th December.†*

CONFERENCE OF PRIME MINISTERS OF THE EMPIRE.

(Status of Dominions; Empire's Foreign Policy; Anglo-Japanese Treaty; Pacific Problem; Disarmament Conference; Constitutional Conference.)

On 30th September, 1921, the Prime Minister made a statement upon the work of the Conference of Prime Ministers of the Empire which had been held in London from 20th June to 5th August. This statement was followed by a debate, when questions relating to the Dominion and foreign affairs, etc., were discussed.

---

* On 21st December it was officially announced that the Federal Cabinet (*vide* JOURNAL, Vol. I., No. 2, p. 346) had been reconstituted as follows:—

Prime Minister and Minister for External Affairs	Rt. Hon. W. M. Hughes, K.C., M.P.
Minister for Home and Territories..	Sen. the Rt. Hon. G. F. Pearce.
Minister for Repatriation	Sen. the Hon. E. D. Millen.
Attorney-General	Hon. Littleton E. Groom, M.P.
Minister for Defence and the Navy ‡	Hon. W. Massy Greene, M.P.
Postmaster-General	Hon. A. Poynton, O.B.E., M.P.
Minister for Trade and Customs ..	Hon. A. S. Rodgers, M.P.
Treasurer	Hon. S. M. Bruce, M.P.
Minister for Works and Railways ..	Hon. R. W. Foster, M.P.
Assistant Minister for Defence ..	Hon. Sir Granville Ryrie, K.C.M.G., C.B., M.P.
Vice-President of the Executive Council	Sen. the Hon. J. Earle.
Assistant Minister for Repatriation	Hon. H. Lamond, M.P.

Mr. W. M. Marks (Nationalist, *Wentworth, N.S.W.*) has been appointed Under-Secretary assisting the Prime Minister.

The Hon. F. G. Tudor, Leader of the Opposition, died on 10th January, 1922, and later in the month, Mr. Matthew Charlton was selected to succeed him as Leader of the Opposition in the Federal Parliament.

† This information has been furnished by cable to the Press.

‡ It will be noted that, as in Canada, Naval and Military affairs are to come under the same Minister. (*Vide* p. 70.)

DEBATE IN HOUSE OF REPRESENTATIVES.

The Prime Minister (the Right Hon. W. M. Hughes), after calling attention to his statement in the House of 7th April, 1921,* said that the pledges given by him prior to his departure from Australia for the Conference had been carried out not only to the letter, but also in the spirit. The Commonwealth had not been committed to any expenditure. Everything done was subject to parliamentary approval, and Parliament would have the fullest opportunity of expressing its opinion.

Prior to the War, Imperial Conferences were ceremonious and social functions rather than serious attempts to co-ordinate the activities of a far-flung Empire. The experiences of war had clearly shown that as the safety of every part of the Empire depended upon united action, means for ensuring to each member an effective share in guiding its course must be devised.

Status of Dominions.

The War had changed many things. It had destroyed dynasties, uprooted ancient institutions, readjusted the boundaries of the nations, and created many difficult problems; but it had also given them a wider and more splendid concept of Empire. They had realised that the British Empire is a partnership of free nations, every one being free to act as it pleases, yet all united in council and in action. Australia had been a Dominion; the War had made her a nation within the Commonwealth of Nations.

The status granted in War had been confirmed in times of Peace. Mr. Lloyd George, in his opening speech to the Conference, said:—

> "In recognition of their services and achievements in the war the British Dominions have now been accepted fully into the comity of the nations of the whole world. They are signatories to the Treaty of Versailles and of all other Treaties of Peace; they are members of the Assembly of the League of Nations, and their representatives have already attended meetings of the League; in other words, they have achieved full national status, and they now stand beside the United Kingdom as equal partners in the dignities and responsibilities of the British Commonwealth. If there are any means by which that status can be rendered even more clear to their own communities and to the world at large we shall be glad to have them put forward at this Conference."

Continuing, Mr. Hughes asked the House and the country to note all that was involved in those words of the Prime

---

* *Vide* JOURNAL, Vol. II., No. 2, p. 354.

Minister of Britain, accepted by his colleagues and endorsed by the Conference, and to contrast this concept of a British Commonwealth comprised of free nations, each enjoying the status of nationhood, each claiming and being accorded an equal voice in shaping Empire policy, with that other concept, which, not many years ago, stood unchallenged—of Britain supreme in power and authority, deciding without question the destiny of all. But the years had passed; much water had run under the bridges, much blood had been shed; the Dominions had established their right to be treated as equals, and Britain, not waiting for formal demand, had been the first to acclaim and gladly welcome the Dominions as her equals, and to bid them sit with her at the Council table of Empire.

Foreign Policy.

As the great canvas of Foreign Policy was slowly unrolled by the Foreign Secretary and his colleagues, declared Mr. Hughes, and they saw the immensity of the stage on which it moved, they were able to appreciate to the full the greatness and majesty of the British Empire, and to realise still more vividly how great a privilege it was to be able to claim its citizenship.

Australia, remote as she was from the western world, was a western nation, and, though the farthest outpost of the western world, was profoundly affected by all that the Western nations think and do. The late War, unhappily, had made it only too clear that their remoteness, their isolation, could not save them from the cataclysm that burst over Europe.

And the modern world grew each day smaller, and the nations of the earth more interdependent. Not wars or the dangers of wars only concerned them, but the varying social and economic conditions of every country of the world. The corner-stone of their national, social and economic life, the "White Australia" policy, and those pillars of their national temple—the standard of living, the wages paid for labour, markets for their produce—were, or might be, affected, not only by what other nations did, but by what they said and thought.

Australia was great. She had already done great things in peace and in war. The splendid promise of her future beckoned them on; but whether they would achieve it or not depended upon themselves and, as he saw it, upon their remaining a partner of this great Commonwealth of Nations. In unity was their strength. And this was true, not only of Australia, but of every other part of the Empire.

The British Government recognised the right of Australia and the other Dominions to an equal voice in formulating the policy on foreign and Imperial affairs, and gave the Conference a very full and clear account of British foreign policy all over the world. This marked a great advance in Imperial relations, and was an auspicious augury for the future. The candour with which the Dominions had been met had established an atmosphere of complete confidence, which had had its effect on all the discussions which followed.

Anglo-Japanese Treaty.

The main reason for summoning the Conference in June of this year was to consider the Anglo-Japanese Treaty and the Pacific problems with which it was inseparably connected.

Briefly, said Mr. Hughes, the position in regard to the Treaty was as follows: In its original form the Treaty had been concluded by Lord Lansdowne in 1902. The present Treaty was signed by Sir Edward Grey in 1911. The 1911 Treaty contained a most important modification. Article 4 reads:—

> Should either High Contracting Party conclude a Treaty of General Arbitration with a third Power, it is agreed that nothing in the agreement shall entail upon such contracting party an obligation to go to war with the Power with whom such Treaty of Arbitration is in force.

At that time Lord Grey was endeavouring to negotiate a Treaty of Arbitration with America, but this was rejected by the United States Senate. In September, 1914, however, Lord Grey succeeded in concluding a Treaty, entitled "With regard to the establishment of a Peace Commission," under the terms of which all disputes between the contracting parties—Great Britain and the United States of America—were to be referred to a special Investigation Commission. Although not in terms an Arbitration Treaty, it was in effect equivalent thereto, and the then Government of Great Britain accordingly informed the Japanese Government that the "Peace Commission" was regarded by them as equivalent to an Arbitration Treaty, and that the conditions prescribed by Article 4 of the Treaty of 1911 applied. The Japanese Government accepted the interpretation without demur, and Article 4 has since been applied, thus precluding the possibility of the Anglo-Japanese Treaty leading to war between the United States of America and Great Britain.

It was well that the whole world should note this, for the facts flatly contradicted the opinions held in America and elsewhere that the Anglo-Japanese Treaty might possibly involve a conflict between America and Britain.

The position on the day the discussion opened was that the Treaty was held to expire within two weeks, viz., the 13th July, 1921, but three months' extension had been asked for by the British Government in order to give the Conference an opportunity of considering the question of renewal. The belief that the Treaty expired on 13th July arose from a joint notification made by Great Britain and Japan in June, 1920, to the League of Nations, intimating that as the Anglo-Japanese Treaty did not conform to the provisions of the Covenant, both parties desired that it should do so.

This notification was regarded by the British Law Officers as constituting a denunciation of the Treaty as provided in Clause 6, which stipulates that twelve months' notice of denunciation shall be given by either party before the Treaty can terminate. The question before the Conference when it turned to the discussion of the Treaty was whether it should be renewed in a form consistent with the Covenant of the League of Nations or be allowed to lapse. There were wide differences of opinion.

Explaining his attitude, Mr. Hughes quoted from his remarks at the Conference to the effect that, speaking broadly, Australia was in favour of the renewal of the Treaty. But there were certain difficulties which must be faced. One of these arose out of the attitude of America towards the Treaty. He was sure that he stated the opinion of Australia when he said that its people had a very warm corner in their hearts for America. They saw in America to-day what they themselves hoped in the future to become. They had a country very similar in extent and resources, and it might be laid down as a *sine qua non* that any future Treaty with Japan, to be satisfactory to Australia, must specifically exclude the possibility of war with the United States of America. In any Treaty they must guard against even the suspicion of hostility or unfriendliness to the United States.

Some of his colleagues, said Mr. Hughes, regarded America's objections as so strong that they felt it their duty to oppose the renewal of the Treaty on any terms. With these views he had not agreed. He was as warm a friend and as resolute a champion of the Union of English-speaking people as any man. He yielded to none in his desire to bring this about. But he did not mistake the voice of a noisy, anti-British faction in America for the sentiment of that great Republic. He had advocated an immediate declaration of their intention to renew the Treaty upon terms that would at once be compatible with the League of Nations Covenant, which would give America ample opportunity to be officially consulted, and which would exclude specifically, and in set terms, the possibilities of their being ranged in hostile array against America by virtue of that Treaty.

Disarmament Conference.

On the second day of the Conference he had thrown out two suggestions, one urging Mr. Lloyd George to invite the great nations of the world, in particular America, Japan and France, to a Conference in order to discuss Disarmament, and the other, that America and Japan should be invited to a Conference to discuss the terms of a tripartite treaty to take the place of the Anglo-Japanese Treaty, or, failing a tripartite treaty, to ascertain from America what form a treaty between Japan and Britain should take to be acceptable to her.

Negotiations on these lines were undertaken at once, but it became obvious as these proceeded that the suggested conference must consider not only the Anglo-Japanese Treaty, but many other Pacific questions, *e.g.*, the "open door" in China, and Immigration, for these questions were naturally related to the Anglo-Japanese Treaty, to naval rivalry in the Pacific, and so to Disarmament.

Before the negotiations with America and Japan, conducted through their respective Ambassadors, had resulted in any definite conclusion, President Harding's invitation to a Disarmament Conference was received. The Imperial Conference welcomed this invitation with enthusiasm. One most significant fact he would mention. Members of the Conference differed widely on many matters—on the Anglo-Japanese Treaty, the Constitution, Naval Defence—but upon Disarmament, and the preservation of the world's peace, there was complete and striking unanimity.

Although the Washington Conference had changed the situation, the Pacific problem and, of course, the question of the renewal of the Treaty still remained. This had not been definitely settled, though a majority favoured a renewal. It was evident that as the Treaty, according to the British law officers, expired on 13th July, and that even if the three months' extension were agreed to, a decision must be arrived at before the Imperial Conference disbanded and before the Washington Conference began. It was at this stage that the matter was referred to the Lord Chancellor for an opinion, views having been expressed at the Conference that the presentation of the Note by Britain and Japan to the League of Nations did not constitute an act of denunciation under Article 6. The Lord Chancellor, who considered the question with the Law Officers of the Crown, held that no notice of denunciation had been given. This then was the position. The Treaty was in force and would continue to operate until twelve months after the date on which either party gave notice of denunciation.

Pacific Problem.

The destiny of Australia lay in the Pacific. Before the War the strategic centre of the world was the North Sea. But the defeat of Germany, the re-grouping of the Central Powers, the collapse of Russia, and, of course, the opening of the Panama Canal, had entirely changed the position. It was on the vast stage of the Pacific that the great world drama of the future was to be played. The Pacific Ocean had become what the North Sea once was—the world's strategic centre.

For Australia the Pacific problem for all practical purposes was the problem of Japan. Here was a nation with nearly 70,000,000 of people crowded together in narrow islands; its population was increasing rapidly, and was already pressing on the margin of subsistence. She wanted room for her increasing millions of population, and markets for her manufactured goods. And she wanted both these very badly indeed. America and Australia say to her millions: "Ye cannot enter in." Japan is then faced with the great problem which has bred wars since time began. For when tribes and nations of the past outgrew the resources of their own territory they moved on and on, hacking their way to the fertile pastures of their neighbours. But where were the overflowing millions of Japan to find room? Not in Australia; not in America. Well, where then?

This then was one problem. There remained the other. The 70,000,000 Japanese could not possibly live except as a manufacturing nation. Their position was analogous to that of Great Britain. To a manufacturing nation, overseas markets were essential to its very existence. Japan saw across a narrow strip of water 400,000,000 Chinese gradually awakening to an appreciation of Western methods; and she saw in China the natural market for her goods. She felt that her geographical circumstances gave her a special right to the exploitation of the Chinese markets. But other countries wanted that market, too; and so came the demand for the "open door." What is Japan to do?

This was the problem of the Pacific—the modern riddle of the Sphinx, for which they must find an answer. Assuredly they would not solve the problem by turning their backs upon it, by ignoring it. These things were real and could not be dissolved by words, nor even by Conferences, unless these recognised facts and were prepared to consider Japan's point of view as well as that of other nations. Talk about Disarmament was idle unless the causes of naval armaments were removed. It had been for these reasons that he had strongly advocated a preliminary conference or meeting to discuss Pacific questions prior to the meeting of the Washington Conference. He regretted very much indeed that the American Government had not seen its way to accept the suggestion. The proposal to hold a Pacific Conference received the unanimous support of the Imperial Conference. Australia had much at stake. Peace in the Pacific meant more to her than to any other nation. Yet until the causes of war were removed, talk about peace could not be more than beating the air. Frankly, said Mr. Hughes, he saw no hope for Disarmament until the Pacific problems to which he had referred were settled, and this could only be done by a *modus vivendi* satisfactory to Japan, America and Australasia.

Naval Defence.

The Conference, having all the facts before it, and after most careful consideration of the whole field of foreign and Imperial politics, decided that the Empire must have a Navy at least equal to that of any other Power. Before the discussion on Naval and Military Defence could be concluded, President Harding issued his invitation to the Disarmament Conference, and further consideration of Imperial Defence was postponed until after the Washington Conference had concluded its labours.

Constitutional Conference.

It would be recalled that at the Imperial War Conference in 1917, at which Australia had not been represented, a resolution had been passed approving the summoning of a special Conference as soon as possible after the War to consider the constitutional relations between the component parts of the Empire. As he (Mr. Hughes) had stated before he left Australia, it was not proposed at the recent Conference to do more than deal with the agenda of this proposed Constitutional Conference, which was to be held in 1922.

There was some danger, however, that the constitutional question once raised by discussion of the agenda, and on procedure, might extend over the whole field, and result in substantive changes in the Constitution. As was well known to honourable Members, said Mr. Hughes, he had always opposed a Constitutional Conference, considering it both unnecessary and unwise; and he had taken the earliest opportunity of setting out his views before the Conference.

Suggestions made by some of the Dominion representatives at the Conference had filled him with apprehension as to what might happen if a Constitutional Conference were held. He had therefore strongly opposed it. He had said that no Conference was necessary; that to meddle with the Constitution was the surest way to dismember the Empire.

"I invite those of my colleagues," said Mr. Hughes, "to tell me what it is we cannot now do. I have said we cannot make treaties with foreign countries, so that if they want to make a treaty with a foreign country—I am sure they do not, and am only taking that as an illustration—I say they cannot do it as a nation within the Empire. That is the constitutional position; but, apart from that, where are the limitations upon our authority? What is it we cannot do? When I am told that we need more power, and there is something the Dominions have not got, I want to know what there is of substance that we yet lack. I know of nothing, but if there is anything, let us see what it is, examine it, and if necessary, grant it. But we ought not to be asked to a Constitutional Conference unless it can be shown that it will give us some advantage we do not enjoy, some real thing which we do not possess, and which cannot be given here and now. I do not believe there is any such thing. I am against a Constitutional Conference; it is not only unnecessary, it is dangerous. I am very strongly opposed to any attempt to reduce the Constitution to writing; I am against any flamboyant declaration of rights. The chief glory of our Constitution is its elasticity; under it nothing is impossible; under it we have already received everything we need as a self-governing nation. What we have become, what we are, we owe to this Constitution—this most wonderful, flexible, and efficient instrument of free government that the world has ever known. It is as boundless as freedom itself; it has no limitations. And where there are no limits, disputes about the ambit of power cannot enter in."

Mr. Hughes, continuing, said that this was undoubtedly one of the most important matters which had engaged the attention of the recent Conference or any other Conference. It only remained to add that the Conference unanimously decided that no Constitutional Conference was necessary or desirable, rejected every proposal to reduce the present Constitutional practice to writing, and adopted a resolution to the effect that continuous consultation could only be secured by a substantial improvement in the communications between the component parts of the Empire, and that the Prime Ministers of the United Kingdom and the Dominions, and the representatives of India, should aim at meeting annually, or at such longer intervals as may prove feasible.

Success of Conference.

Mr. Hughes, in conclusion, said that the Conference, marking as it did a new era in Empire Government, was most successful. They had not, it was true, completely solved that great problem insuring united action in foreign affairs, side by side with complete autonomy of the component parts, but they had gone far towards it. With improved and more effective communications, and with the lessening of distance by more rapid means of transit, they would go still further, and the influence of the Dominions in shaping and directing Foreign and Imperial affairs would grow. Meantime, it was good to know that a great change in Empire relationship had been initiated, not only without friction but with the enthusiastic co-operation of the Mother Country and every one of the self-governing Dominions.

While this spirit endured, they could face the future with confidence. In the course of time the great bulk of the white population of the British Empire would be outside Britain. The centre of the Empire might, indeed, come East; for who could set a limit to the growth of their own country?

By the Conference they had effected a great step forward in Imperial government, for they had demonstrated that the Empire could speak with one voice in peace as well as in war, and that the greatest experiment in free government in all human history had again proved by its wonderful adaptability that the principles upon which it rested were sound and fated to endure through the ages.

Addressing the House of Representatives at a later date (5th October), Mr. Hughes explained the results of the Imperial Conference in regard to Reparations; communication by land, air and sea, including wireless telegraphy and telephony; immigration; the position of British Indians within the Empire; Empire patents; nationality; and the Condominium in the New Hebrides.

Tribute to Mr. Lloyd George.

Referring to the work of Mr. Lloyd George, Mr. Hughes said that the Conference had been most fortunate in having that gentleman as its President. For the success which attended the Conference they owed him a great deal. He (Mr. Hughes) had never met a man who, by temperament and quality, was so admirably fitted for dealing with his fellow-men as Mr. Lloyd George.

Empire migration.

Dealing with this matter Mr. Hughes said that the position was that the British Government were willing to provide means up to £2,000,000 for settling British soldiers on the land. The condition was that the Dominions should grant £200 to each soldier to whom Great Britain had advanced this sum, in addition to passage money, which was covered by other arrangements now in force, and whatever was necessary to settle ex-soldiers on the land. The various Dominions expressed their assent subject to the qualifications set out in the Conference resolution, and, shortly, the position of Australia in regard to the matter was that, subject to financial considerations, she would be most happy to fall in with the proposal.

Anglo-Japanese Treaty.

Mr. Matthew Charlton (Labour, Acting Leader of the Opposition) said that when the Prime Minister (Mr. Hughes) was on the eve of his departure for the Imperial Conference they had been assured that it was absolutely necessary for Australia to be represented at that gathering in order that their views concerning the Anglo-Japanese Treaty and other matters vital to the welfare of Australia should be stated. It had been especially urged that nothing should be done in the new Treaty that would endanger their relations with the people of the United States of America. He ventured to say it must have struck honourable Members as more than passing strange that, though the main purpose of the Conference was to deal with the Anglo-Japanese Treaty, after the Conference had been dealing with business for several days it was suddenly found that the Treaty was still in existence and was not likely to expire.* This was a remarkable position, in view of the statement prior to the departure of the Prime Minister that, in consequence of Great Britain and Japan having informed the League of Nations that the Treaty then in existence did not come within the Covenant of the League, the British law authorities had held that there had been a denunciation of the Treaty in accordance with Article 6 of that document.†

He could not understand how it could have been held that there had been a denunciation. At all events, the Japanese Government did not hold that view. In consequence of a division of opinion in the Conference the matter had been submitted for the opinion of Lord Haldane,‡ who held that there had been no denunciation of the Treaty, thus supporting

* For explanation by Mr. Lloyd George *vide* JOURNAL, Vol. II., No. 4, p. 704, and Mr. W. M. Hughes, the present number of the JOURNAL, p. 93.

† The hon. Member quoted the words of Article 6, which provides for twelve months' notice of the intention of terminating the Agreement.

‡ Reference is apparently made to the Lord Chancellor (Lord Birkenhead) *vide* JOURNAL, Vol. II., No. 4, p. 704.

the Japanese contention. The Treaty had not expired, and would not expire until the necessary notice had been given. The subject of the greatest moment to the people of Australia had not been in question at all, and there had been no need to have a Conference to discuss it. So far as that aspect of the Imperial Conference was concerned nothing had been done.

Naval Defence.

The question of Naval Defence could not be dealt with. It had been deferred because the Anglo-Japanese Treaty was still in force. Those had been the two main questions to be considered, and so far as they were concerned they might as well have had no Conference.

The Treasurer (the Right Hon. Sir Joseph Cook)* : "It was deferred because some of the other Dominions would not foot the bill. It was stated in the Press cables."

Empire Constitution.

Mr. Charlton, continuing, agreed that good work had been done in connection with the constitutional question. They had been afraid, when it was listed on the agenda paper, that it might be leading to what might be called Imperialism. Most of the people of Australia did not want anything of that kind. It was pleasing to know that, after full consideration, it had been decided that there was no need to interfere with the present constitutional arrangements. The Prime Minister had shown that there had been considerable discussion on the subject, and it had been demonstrated that their unwritten Constitution served the purpose of the government of the Empire, and that to put anything down in writing which would be binding might lead, at some time, to the disintegration of the Empire. He thought Mr. Hughes was right in that respect.

The Right Hon. W. A. Watt (Nationalist, *Balaclava, Vic.*)**:** "Who proposed to do that? Was it proposed?"

Secrecy of Conference.

Mr. Charlton : "Unfortunately, we do not know anything at all as to that." The Conference was held in secret. The only information they had was that given by Mr. Hughes himself, and he had told them that he could not furnish an account of what was done or said by others, or state what voting took place, because the proceedings had been confidential. It was regrettable that in national affairs there was

* Sir Joseph Cook has been appointed High Commissioner for the Commonwealth of Australia in Great Britain, as from 11th November, 1922.

so much secrecy. There had been too much secret diplomacy. He had hoped that with the termination of the War they would have seen the end of such secret negotiations, but they were now no better off. If they had a mind to piece together the various reports of the representatives to their respective Parliaments they would ascertain what really occurred. The Prime Minister of New Zealand (Mr. Massey) had said that very little had been achieved at the Conference. He (Mr. Charlton) agreed with Mr. Massey that nothing of very great importance to the Empire had been finalised.

Immigration.

The Prime Minister (Mr. Hughes) had touched on immigration, and had said that nothing definite had been determined. He took it from that statement that anything which might emanate from the Conference in regard to an immigration scheme would be brought before the House for consideration, and that Parliament would then have a full opportunity to deal with the matter.

Disarmament and the League of Nations.

The League of Nations was only a skeleton. It required the breath of life to be put into it, and that could be done only by leading public men throughout the world making up their minds that it must be a living thing, and that it must achieve the purpose which President Wilson had in mind when he introduced it. Unless that was done the League would soon be a thing of the past, and war would be upon them, perhaps, before they realised it. Instead of making extra provision for defence, public men should be doing their best to reduce defence expenditure, and should turn their attention to measures whereby war could be prevented. He wished to make the position of Members on his side of the House quite clear. They were favourable to steps being taken to give effect to the Covenant of the League of Nations to bring about Disarmament, so that there might be world-peace. They stood for that principle. He ventured to say that every Member of the House stood for it also, and that the people of Australia had come to the conclusion, after the War, that every possible step should be taken to prevent a repetition of that awful tragedy. His contention was that everything possible was not being done for the purpose of galvanising the League into life. The members of the Opposition pinned their faith to the possibility of the League being placed in a position that would bring about Disarmament, and prevent future wars. He pinned his faith to the League of Nations, but that would not justify him in ignoring any other conference.

Dr. Earle Page (Leader of the Country Party) regretted that he could not congratulate the Prime Minister on what had transpired at the London Conference. There was an entire absence of frankness regarding the whole position. What they wanted to know was where the other Dominions stood. They should have been informed of the details of the arguments advanced by the Prime Ministers of Canada, South Africa and New Zealand. All the facts should be given concerning the views, intentions, aspirations and ideals of the Dominions. After the War it had been stated that open diplomacy was to be the international policy of the future. If that was the ideal in international affairs, surely there might be expected something like frankness and candour in dealing with the internal affairs of what was, after all, a great family circle. Concerning the matter of intra-Imperial relationship, he had to pay a tribute to the work of the Prime Minister, as it had been outlined.

The decisions at the Disarmament Conference would perhaps determine the size of the fleets; but the Imperial Conference discussions should have led to some definite conclusions as to the particular quotas to be allocated to each Dominion.

Trade with Germany.

As for the question of trading with Germany, one was given to understand that a resumption was not yet in operation. During the past year or two one had seen in Australia a great variety of goods which appeared to be identical with those made in Germany and imported to Australia before the War. They had been, and were being, sold in that country under some other label of origin. Why should this absurd situation be maintained? Why should the Government carry on the vendetta? The War was won and over.*

Advantages of Imperial Conference.

Mr. Watt thought that, reading the history of past Imperial Conferences, gatherings of the kind from which the Prime Minister had just returned, it would be admitted that they had always proved beneficial to the Empire and its constituent parts. At those earlier Conferences statesmen of the Empire had met to consider common problems, but in recent years the gatherings had assumed an intimacy of touch and spirit which

* *Vide* summary at p. 134 hereof.

former Conferences had lacked. It was quite clear to any one who had visited the Old Country or discoursed with representatives of other Dominions that they had totally different points of view on many fundamental questions throughout this Empire, and that the only way to harmonise these different objectives was to assemble around the Council table and talk about them with the utmost frankness. The Prime Minister, he thought, was right in saying that whatever else the Conference had achieved, however they might be disappointed with the decisions registered, or the lack of them, the advance made on this occasion was a marked one. He agreed that it represented a substantial advantage to Australia, and probably to Canada and the other Dominions, as well as to the Mother Country itself. But when they had acknowledged all that, he thought they ought to say candidly that that was practically all that had been done. It seemed to him, as he had read daily the cable communications from the other end of the world, when the Conference was taking place, and as he had listened to the speech of the Prime Minister, that the Conference was, from every other standard, practically resultless. They could not blame, if blame there be, any person who had taken part in that gathering. It had been clearly overshadowed by two great events of world-wide importance. The first event had been the attempt at Irish reconciliation. He could not imagine that the Prime Minister of Great Britain, or any of his colleagues, could have continued to pay sustained attention or given earnest consideration to even the problems of the Empire which the Dominion representatives had been considering, while that great event was moving on the stage. The other circumstance which had frustrated the hopes and rendered in some degree unnecessary the deliberations of the Conference had been the issue of an invitation by the new President of the United States of America to the Conference at Washington. This invitation went right into the centre of their gathering. Foreign policy was to be determined by relationships which were largely conditioned by the armament question. It was perfectly clear that whatever the Delegates did they could not continue to the point of finality the discussion of any of the questions they were considering.

League of Nations.

In reply to references by the Acting-Leader of the Opposition to the League of Nations, Mr. Watt said that the League could not flourish and function with power unless America was a member of it. If conditions changed in America, and she should decide to join the League, he thought that that would go further than anything else to secure peace in this world and justice to the small nations. Let them, however, hope that this implement, which had come from the most exalted brains of the world and had only the altruistic desire to improve and render safer the conditions of mankind regardless of colour or place, would grow into manhood, though it might be going through a very difficult period of babyhood.

WASHINGTON CONFERENCE.

(Australian Representation.)

In the House of Representatives, on 6th October, the Prime Minister made a statement regarding the representation of Australia at the Washington Disarmament Conference. A debate ensued on a motion by Mr. Hughes for the printing of the telegram from the Secretary of State for the Colonies, dated 3rd October, 1921, conveying the invitation of the Prime Minister of Great Britain to Australia to be represented on the British Empire Delegation at the Washington Conference.

DEBATE IN HOUSE OF REPRESENTATIVES.

The Prime Minister (the Right Hon. W. M. Hughes) said that when the Imperial Conference had reached the stage in its deliberations when it was quite obvious that the Government of the United States of America did not favour the suggestion of a preliminary Pacific Conference, and when, therefore, it appeared clear that all such questions would have to be postponed until the Washington Disarmament Conference was held, it was agreed that the British Government should represent the whole of the Empire at that Conference. That was the position when he returned to Australia, and it had remained the position until late on the previous Tuesday (4th October) when he received certain cablegrams* which had changed the position entirely. In an interview which he had given to the Press, he had stated that he was not favourable to a representation of Australia in a capacity which would exclude its representatives from the Conference.

* The other cablegrams submitted by Mr. Hughes refer to the constitution of the British Delegation, the tentative agenda, procedure, etc.

The first cablegram was from Mr. Lloyd George, and the relevant portion was in the following terms :—

> I am very anxious that the standpoint of Australia and New Zealand should be well represented on the British Empire Delegation at the Washington Conference. Your personal presence is, in my opinion, highly desirable, and I urge you to go if by any means possible. Failing this, a single Delegate may serve as representative of both Australia and New Zealand, as your standpoints are identical. I should greatly prefer you going yourself; but if you cannot, please consult Massey, and tell me what you propose. We will, of course, also welcome any officer whom you may wish to send to serve on the secretariat.

Continuing, Mr. Hughes said that honourable Members would quite appreciate that the British Government had acted in this, as they had acted, he thought he might fairly say, in all matters for many years past, with every regard for the welfare and interest of the Dominions. The cablegrams which he had read showed that upon mature consideration the British Government thought that the Empire Delegation would be greatly strengthened if it included direct representatives of the Dominions, or of some of them. It would be noticed that it was suggested that Australasia should have a representative. Mr. Lloyd George, in his cablegram, said that the interests of Australia and New Zealand in this matter were identical. For all practical purposes they might accept that view as a fair presentation of the position. In the face of the cablegrams there was clearly but one thing that Parliament could do, and that was to accept the invitation to send a Delegate. That the Government was resolved to do.

He thought that the representative of Australia should be one who was responsible to the people; he should go from that Parliament instructed—for that was the proper term—as to what the people of that country conceived to be that policy which would best conserve their interests, and at the conclusion of his mission he should come back and report to that Parliament of which he was a responsible Member, and then it would be for Parliament and the people of Australia to express approval or disapproval of what he had done. The Government considered that a Minister should go to Washington.

The world to-day was distracted and neurotic. Bleeding from a hundred wounds, it turned hither and thither seeking comfort and consolation. It was a fact that the burden of armaments to-day was from two to four times as great as it was before the War. The Prime Minister of Great Britain conceived, as he (Mr. Hughes) did, that it was idle to talk about peace or disarmament, or limitation of armaments, until the causes of armaments were removed; and these causes, so far as Australia was concerned, lay in the Pacific problems. The settlement of these problems would be no easy matter. Australia had more to lose than any other country. It had more at stake. A continent with a population of 5,500,000 was naturally more interested than any other country in a problem which had for its origin the position of Japan, with 70,000,000 people occupying a narrow strip of land which did not exceed in total area the islands handed over to Australia under the Mandate from the League of Nations. Australia had ideals which the world did not understand, and with which it might not sympathise. It was essential, therefore, that their views should be set out clearly at this Conference. The Government had considered the matter very carefully, and recommended to the House that the Commonwealth should send a representative, and that Senator Pearce (Minister for Defence) should be that representative. It had been suggested that he (Mr. Hughes) himself should go; but that had been found impossible; and other members of the Ministry, who would have made admirable representatives of Australia at Washington, were, for various reasons, disinclined, or unable, to go.

Mr. Matthew Charlton (Labour, Acting Leader of the Opposition) said the Washington Conference would be a very important one—really much more important than honourable Members and the country generally had been led to believe right up to the moment of the speech which had just been delivered by the Prime Minister. Prior to that day no one had possessed any specific knowledge concerning the work proposed to be undertaken at the Conference. Now, however, the actual details of the agenda paper had been made known. He found that among the subjects that would arise for consideration was the question of the limitation of armaments. No more vitally important question could come up for discussion at any international gathering. Upon the agenda paper, also, there was the matter of Naval Defence. This was vital to Australia and the Empire, seeing that it involved the future naval strengths of the fleets of the nations. He need scarcely stress the all-important nature of this subject, particularly to Australia, in relation to Pacific affairs. One other item had to do with the limitation of land armaments. In this regard the question was as to what sums of money should be expended by each of the various nations in connection with their land defences. Still another crucial feature of the agenda paper related to the mandated islands. He need not emphasise the fact of Australia being deeply involved in this subject. In view of the agenda paper—or of so much of it, at any rate, as he had just indicated—it became absolutely essential that Australia should be fully and amply represented at the Washington Conference. Honourable Members had now been informed that, at the Imperial Conference, this factor of Dominion representation at Washington had been considered, and that a decision had been reached that the direct representatives of Great Britain be regarded as sufficient and adequate to look after the interests of all parts of the Empire. In other words, the Imperial Conference, from the inception of President Harding's proposal, had decided that there was no need for the Dominions to be directly represented, but that the Delegates appointed by Great Britain would be capable of safeguarding Dominion interests.

The Prime Minister replied that the whole Conference was strongly of opinion that Australia and New Zealand ought to be represented at Washington, and had striven to secure representation. It was not until the United States of America objected to the separate representation of the Dominions that they had relinquished the effort.

Mr. Charlton asked why should not the British Government be asked to make representations to President Harding and to point out that Australia viewed the Washington Conference with vital concern; and that so far as the Pacific was concerned, the deliberations concerned their very life. President Harding ought to be asked if it were not possible for the Dominions, and the parties in the Dominions, to be represented, so as to make the deliberations of the Conference and its conclusions absolutely of a non-party character. Continuing, Mr. Charlton said that the Minister for Defence (Senator Pearce), who had been appointed to represent Australia at the Washington Conference, was the most unsuitable person that could have been selected, because, in the first place, he was not a Member of the House of Representatives, and therefore could not report to that branch of the Legislature on his return. On the other hand, the Minister for Defence did not give one the impression of being in favour of Disarmament, because he was endeavouring to commit Australia to unnecessary expenditure in the matter of Military Defence, notwithstanding that such a policy was contrary to the views of the majority of the people of the Commonwealth. In the circumstances the Government could not have made a more unwise selection. "We are in favour," said Mr. Charlton, "of everything possible being done to bring about the peace of the world, either through the League of Nations or through the medium of the Washington Conference or any other similar gathering. We cannot see the possibility of the Disarmament Conference being a success unless it comprises representatives of the different political Parties throughout the world." He therefore moved an amendment that Australia should be represented at the Conference by a representative of the Government and each of the other Parties, and that the decisions of the Conference should be subject to ratification by Parliament.*

Dr. Earle Page (Leader of Country Party) remarked that there should be some Australian representative in the Imperial Delegation. It was impossible to ask for separate representation in view of the attitude of America to the League of Nations. The suggestion that all Parties should be represented could be attributed only to a lack of appreciation of the relative importance of Australia at the forthcoming Conference. If one Delegation was sufficient for France, surely they could not expect a great entourage of Dominion representatives in the trail of the Delegates of Great Britain.

The Right Hon. W. A. Watt (Nationalist, *Balaclava, Vic.*) observed that he was sure the friends of Senator Pearce would absolve him from any desire to comment upon Senator Pearce's personal qualifications. They were high, but the man who was to go to Washington should have a higher responsibility than had the Minister for Defence. The choice should have fallen upon the head of the Government (Mr. Hughes). As to the domestic circumstances which might detain him, or discourage his attendance at the Conference, the right hon. gentleman and his colleagues were the best judges; but, speaking as a private Member of Parliament, he did not think that the Leader of the Government could divest himself of the responsibility resting upon him. Reading between the lines, it was clear that it was in the mind of the Prime Minister (Mr. Hughes) the idea of the Conference first originated. The view of Mr. Hughes had always been since the war ended that either through the League of Nations or through some special Conference the various nations of the world should get together and endeavour to understand one another's objectives, and agree either to the abolition of armaments or to a limitation or definite reduction of them.

Exclusion of Immigrants.

The Hon. J. M. Fowler (Nationalist, *Perth, W.A.*) said that Japan had exactly the same policy for the exclusion of immigrants as they had in Australia. The Japanese Government would not allow a single Chinese coolie or labourer to enter Japan. It was absurd, therefore, to suggest that their "White Australia" policy was menaced by Japan, because they were merely doing what Japan was doing herself. When they talked about a menace to a "White Australia" they should be prepared to indicate where it lay. Up to the present it

* The "other Parties" being the Labour Party (led by Mr. Charlton) and the Country Party (led by Dr. Earle Page).

could not be done. The danger, to his mind, was largely fictitious. Japan made certain claims for racial equality, and they were given to understand that these affected Australia, but they knew now, having possession of all the facts, that Japan had in mind the treatment of Japanese immigrants in the United States, and that the claim for racial equality had nothing to do with the "White Australia" policy. Japan had a perfect right to complain of the treatment of the Japanese in the United States of America. At first they were welcomed there as workers, but gradually they had acquired money and land, and had become competitors in many respects with the white people of the Pacific States. Then the trouble commenced. Japan objected to its emigrants not receiving the same treatment as those from other countries, and that was the basis of its claim for racial equality.

Mr. J. Mathews (**Labour,** *Melbourne Ports*, *Vic.*) said that it had been suggested that the Prime Minister should go to the Washington Disarmament Conference. He might just as well go as the Minister for Defence. He (Mr. Mathews) was of opinion that, however able any representative of Australia might be, his views would count for nothing at a Conference of men brought together, not to bring about Disarmament, but to maintain the commercial grasp which various nations had upon the world and assist its extension.

Mr. J. H. Prowse (**Country Party,** *Swan*, *W.A.*) thought that President Harding had properly regarded the British Empire as one entity. But he agreed with those who felt that the family attachment or expression should have representation at the Conference in the manner proposed. Although they were confident that the Government of the Mother Country would represent Australian interests satisfactorily to the full extent of their knowledge, there were matters concerning Australia with which they could not be expected to be fully acquainted.

On 7th October, Mr. Hughes' motion was agreed to by 36 votes to 16.

DEBATE IN THE SENATE.

Senator A. Gardiner (*N.S.W.*), on 11th October, during the Budget discussion, said he supposed that according to the "rules of the game," he should follow the lead taken by his colleagues in the House of Representatives and re-echo what they had said there, or, probably, owing to the advantage he had of closer personal knowledge of Senator Pearce, add a little more. He was not going to do that. This appointment was one of the most important that had ever been made in Australia; and, realising that, he felt that whoever went to the Conference must be viewed, not through Party spectacles, but in the light of his capacity worthily to represent that great country. Looking at Senator Pearce's record of service and achievements, Senator Gardiner knew of no man in the public life of the Commonwealth who could perform the responsible duties of a Delegate to such a Conference with more satisfaction. Of course, there was a feeling in the House of Representatives that a representative of the Commonwealth should have been selected from that Chamber. It was simply an attempt to reverse that axiom of Euclid which says that the whole is greater than the part. Honourable Members in the other Chamber had endeavoured to prove that the part was greater than the whole; but when one remembered that a Senator represented the whole of a State, whereas a Member of the House of Representatives represented only one-twenty-seventh, surely the latter was not of more importance or entitled to more consideration than the former. When it was a question of representation in other countries, they had only to consider the ability and capacity of the gentleman selected to carry out the important work.

He knew that many Australians by adoption could show as good a record as many Australians by birth; but he was glad that the Commonwealth was to be represented by an Australian-born Minister. He had endeavoured to look at the question in the right way, and to lift the criticism of a public man to a proper level, free from Party spirit and Party sentiment.

LEAGUE OF NATIONS.

(Report by Delegate on Second Assembly.)

Australia was represented at the Second Assembly of the League of Nations by Mr. S. M. Bruce (now Treasurer)* as the Senior Delegate and Mr. M. L. Shepherd (Acting High Commissioner in London for the Commonwealth) as the second Delegate. On 17th November, shortly after his return, Mr. Bruce submitted his report to Parliament, and at the same time addressed the House of Representatives on the work of the Assembly.

---

* Mr. S. M. Bruce was appointed Treasurer of the Commonwealth in the reconstructed Ministry of Mr. Hughes, *vide* p. 89.

Covenant.

Mr. S. M. Bruce (**Nationalist,** *Flinders, Vic.,*) in explaining the Covenant* of the League of Nations, pointed out that there were two sides to it. In the first place, the primary object of the Covenant was to substitute international justice for the hideous arbitrament of war; in the second place, to carry out great humanitarian objectives, which would improve the condition of mankind and add to the health, happiness and prosperity of the people of the world.

The first primary object—the doing away with war—was particularly covered by Articles 12, 13 and 15 of the Covenant. Under these Articles the nations signatory to the Peace Treaty and to the pact or covenant agree that they will submit their disputes either to arbitration or to the Council of the League of Nations for settlement. That was the great effort that was made to carry out the first of the primary objects of the League. The next object was the establishment of a Permanent Court of International Justice which came under Article 14. Another object was the "economic sanction," which meant that where any State in breach of its Covenant under the document proceeded to war, the other nations would cut off all commercial, financial and other intercourse. Then there was what was called an attempt to abolish secret diplomacy, viz., Article 18, which provided for the registration with the League Secretariat of all treaties or international engagements. Article 19, designed to carry out the intention of avoiding war, dealt with the reconsideration of treaties which had become inapplicable, and the consideration of international conditions which might endanger the peace of the world. The other great effort of the League was in the direction of Disarmament, which came under Article 8, providing for the reduction of armaments to the lowest point consistent with national safety, the prevention of the private manufacture of munitions and implements of war, etc.

The other side of the League's activities was humanitarian, and, roughly, the points mentioned in the Covenant were—fair and humane conditions for labour, as a result of which the International Labour Bureau had been established; the just treatment of native inhabitants in all the countries under the mandatory powers of a member of the League; traffic in women and children; traffic in opium and other dangerous drugs; the prevention and control of disease, and the encouragement of Red Cross organisations and similar enterprises.

---

* Mr. Bruce dealt very completely with this and other interesting phases, but space precludes more than is contained in this summary.

Relation of Assembly and Council.

There was no matter, he thought, on which people gene ally were less informed than the relative positions of these tw bodies, and the spheres in which their respective activiti were employed. The only definition contained in the Covena of the powers of the Assembly and the Council was a provisio that both might deal with any matter within the sphere action of the League, and affecting the peace of the worl The actual relations between these two bodies had been le to be defined in the future, and to grow as time passed an precedents were established. Whilst some of the natio might object to that, he thought that they who were of Britis descent, and knew how every one of their constitution institutions was founded upon just such a basis, would acce it as a hopeful augury for the future. The Assembly mig be described as, in a sense, equivalent to a Parliament, and th Council to the Executive. That description was by no mea exact, but it more or less described the relationship betwee the two bodies.

At the recent gathering the Assembly had taken a furth step forward by managing to establish clearly and unequivo ably its right to vote the annual Budget and approve th accounts of the League. As to the membership of these tw bodies, the Council was composed at the moment of the repr sentatives of eight countries. The four permanent membe were the British Empire, France, Japan and Italy, and th four non-permanent members were at that time Brazil, Belgiu China and Spain. Under the Covenant the permane members were to number five, but, unfortunately, the Unit States of America was not a member of the League, and d not take its position in the Council to-day. The first fo non-permanent members, who were still in office, had be appointed under the Covenant, and it was intended that th should be changed from time to time. Many suggestions h been made at the recent gathering as to an exact basis for t election of non-permanent members to the Council, but it w finally decided to re-elect the original four for another ye and leave it to the next Assembly to determine this matte

Tribute to Mr. Balfour.

Referring to Mr. Balfour, who was the leader of the Briti Delegation, Mr. Bruce said that he had worked in very clo contact with him at Geneva, and he was convinced that the was no other living Englishman better qualified to go America to do the great work that confronted him the Great Britain's representative at the Washington Conferen was the best who could have been obtained, and the interes of the whole of the Empire were safe in his hands.

Court of International Justice.

The distinction between the Court of International Justice and the Arbitration Courts that had been established under the Hague Convention was that the latter provided for the settlement of disputes purely and simply by arbitration. When a dispute between two nations was referred to the Hague for settlement, arbitrators were appointed by each side, and a chairman was placed between them; but the arbitrators were really advocates of the two sets of interests that were in conflict, and the decision, when it was arrived at, was merely the best compromise that could be made, taking into account the circumstances of the two parties at the moment.

Settlement by arbitration was not settlement in accordance with the rules of law; it was only the adoption of the best arrangement that could be come to for avoiding trouble. A Court of International Justice went much further; it was a Court of law in the same sense that every Court in Australia was a Court of law. Its procedure was governed by rules of justice and of international law. It would not consider how best to settle a dispute with the least friction, or what it could get the parties to agree to. Those who submitted to its jurisdiction must observe the rules of international law and of right conduct. Again, under the Hague Convention, the parties to a dispute determined under what law their dispute should be adjudicated; in the Court of International Justice it would be the rules of international law that would be applied. He hoped that hon. Members would see that the establishment of this Court was a great step forward. To his mind, had the League of Nations so far done nothing else, it would have fully justified its existence by having created this institution.

Economic sanction.

Mr. Maxwell (Nationalist, *Fawkner, Vic.*): "Is there any method provided for enforcing the judgments of the International Court?"

Mr. Bruce: "The methods of enforcing the judgments of the Court are exactly the same as those which the League of Nations can employ against any of its members who do anything in breach of the Covenant; there is the economic sanction, and the physical sanction—for which the world is not yet ready."

It had been said that the economic sanction was of no value; but with that statement he did not agree. At this moment it was of very great value; and it was a serious thing for any nation to contemplate in the future. The world to-day was in a state of chaos. Europe was in a particularly unfortunate position. The exchanges had fallen into such confusion that no man knew where he was. The great problem with which they were faced was how to regulate again the exchanges of the world, so that the various countries might trade with one another. When that had been done there would be such an interlocking of the nations that the mere threat or possibility that relations with other countries might be cut off would paralyse the most adventurous and unscrupulous nation. He believed that the economic sanction was of the greatest value, and the backbone of the Covenant of the League of Nations.

Disarmament.

Touching on the work of the League in connection with the question of Disarmament, Mr. Bruce remarked that during the past few days they had heard the most wonderful and almost unexpected news from the Washington Conference. There would appear to be some prospect of great results accruing from that gathering.

While it was no part of his to say anything about it, he suggested that what had happened there merely pointed more and more to the necessity of the League of Nations being ready to do the work that would undoubtedly lie in its hands if the Washington Conference should be successful. He believed the League of Nations itself looked to the Washington Conference to solve the one question which the League could not handle, namely, naval armaments, together with the position in the Pacific. If these matters could be got out of the way, be believed that the League felt that it could accomplish a great deal towards the diminution, at all events, of armaments. In his Address to the Assembly on this subject he had tried to express what he believed to be the views of Australia. The two points he had had in mind were that, above all things, Australia desired a reduction of armaments, but that, if it could not be secured, they were determined to go on, and that nothing would prevent them from guarding and preserving that country to themselves, and preventing any nation from wresting it from them.

Organisation of Secretariat and Labour Office.

Last year Senator E. D. Millen, representing Australia at the First Assembly,* had given a great deal of attention to the question of the organisation of the Secretariat and the Labour Office, and had done extremely good work in pointing

---

* *Vide* JOURNAL, Vol. II., No. 3, p. 618.

out the weak spots and insisting upon their removal. This year the whole matter had been gone into very fully. In the interval they had had the advantage of the report of a special committee, presided over by M. Noblemaire, a Frenchman, and the work done by it was quite invaluable. This Committee had suggested remedies, and he (Mr. Bruce) believed that what had been recommended had put the Secretariat itself and the International Labour Bureau on as business-like a footing as one could ask for in respect of any institution.

Achievements of the League.

Referring to the present position of the League and the prospect of its continuing a career of usefulness, Mr. Bruce observed that there were a great number of sceptics in the world; there were many people who said, through ignorance, that the League of Nations was no good, and would do nothing. There were other people who, throughout life, suffered from a dread of appearing to take an idealistic view of anything, instead of the practical view of a hard-headed, common-sense person, and those people had not the courage to say what they really thought. But any man who gave careful consideration to the whole question, and had regard to what the League had already done, could come to no other conclusion than that it had justified its existence up to date, and it was beyond the power of man to say what a factor for good it might prove in the future history of the world.

To substantiate his statement that the League had already done some good, he commended to the notice of the House some of its achievements. During the past year the League had settled the dispute regarding the Aaland Islands, and thus prevented war between Finland and Sweden. If the League had not been in existence there would have been no authority to which this question could have been referred.

To-day the League was administering two important territories, which involved most difficult diplomatic questions. He referred to the Saar Valley and the free city of Danzig. Without the League of Nations, what would the Supreme Council have done with the Saar Valley? The Supreme Council would have been in a terrible difficulty. The free city of Danzig was closely bound up with Poland's interest in securing an outlet to the sea. If the administration of that territory had been entrusted to any authority but the League, trouble would have arisen in a moment. If the League had done nothing else, the administration of these two territories was a valuable and continuing work, and heaven alone knew what other territories it might be necessary to ask the League to administer in the future.

At present the League was handling a dispute betw(Poland and Lithuania. He believed that the publication the League of the facts concerning this dispute had hac considerable influence on Poland and Lithuania, and efforts of the League, besides preventing war for the last t years, would probably bring about a settlement of the dispu

Another great achievement, and probably the great vindication to date of the League of Nations, was the hand over to it by the Allied Powers of the Upper Silesian questi Over this matter two of the greatest nations of the world l developed very strained relations, and if the League had been in existence how could this *impasse* have been overcom To whom could the dispute have been referred for settlem in a way that would have allowed both parties to retire w dignity and honour ? There was no authority, and there co be no authority, to decide between them.

To-day the League of Nations was handling the disp between Albania, Greece and the Serb-Croat-Slovene Sta The dispute, though small in itself, was fraught with dang inasmuch as it was one of those things which happening in Balkans before the War, as likely as not led to Europ(conflagration. Anybody who remembered what took pl in the Balkans before the War would realise what a men this small dispute would have been if there had been no Lea of Nations, before whose Assembly it could be threshed out, a given such publicity that the whole world might know w was happening.

Apart from these achievements, the whole of the prison of war in Russia had been repatriated through the League Nations. The transport and all other arrangements bringing 350,000 men out of Russia had been organised by League.

In conclusion, Mr. Bruce stated that he was absolut certain that the League had done a great deal of good up date. He was hopeful that it would do a great deal in future, but even if he believed neither of those things, he wo still say that they must not abolish the League of Nati(If they destroyed it there was nothing in the world to t its place, and the position then would be very much w(than it was, inasmuch as they should have attempted failed, and that failure would discourage others from this gr humanitarian effort, which, it seemed to him, there was a gr prospect of the present generation carrying to success.

(*Debate on the motion by Mr. Bruce for the printing of report will be summarised in the next issue of the* JOURNAL, *w the necessary numbers of the Parliamentary Reports will doubt be available.*)

THE BUDGET.

(Revenue and Expenditure; Elimination of Double Taxation; New Guinea Mandate; Immigration; Shipbuilding; Disarmament.)

On 29th September the Commonwealth Treasurer delivered his Budget Statement in the House of Representatives.

The Treasurer (the Right Hon. Sir Joseph Cook),* in the course of his statement, showed the position at the close of the financial year ended 30th June, 1921, and the estimates for the coming financial year to be as follows :—

PAST FINANCIAL YEAR, 1920-1921.

	£
Revenue	65,517,608
Expenditure out of Revenue	64,624,087
Leaving a surplus on the year's transactions of ..	893,521
Surplus brought forward from the previous year ..	5,724,806
Accumulated surplus at 30th June, 1921	£6,618,327

NEW FINANCIAL YEAR, 1921-1922.

	£
Estimated Revenue	61,787,350
Estimated Expenditure	64,604,458
Showing a deficiency of	2,817,108
Surplus available from previous year	6,618,327
Leaving an estimated surplus at 30th June, 1922, of	£3,801,219

Revenue Surplus.

It was estimated in last year's Budget, said the Treasurer, that the year would close with a surplus of £239,545, instead of which he had been able to bring forward to the present financial year the very substantial sum of £6,618,327. This meant not only that the surplus at the beginning of the past financial year, viz., £5,724,806, had been kept intact, but that it had been increased to the extent of £893,521.

The Revenue for the last financial year had exceeded the estimate by about £2,150,000. Of more importance, however, in the production of the surplus was the very large savings of 4¼ millions. While the present satisfactory surplus had been realised largely as the result of good seasons for the

* Now High Commissioner in London, *vide* p. 100, note

last year or two, with heavy imports at high prices as a contributing factor, the large savings in expenditure were the outcome of a determined resolution to save the public funds wherever possible. The surplus, following the previous practice, had been placed in Trust Fund for the purpose of meeting Old Age and Invalid Pensions and War Pensions during the present financial year.

Total Expenditure.

The total expenditure for the financial year 1920-21 was £92,874,314, of which £64,624,087 was from Revenue, £24,148,501 from War Loan, and £4,101,726 from Works Loan.

The estimated total expenditure for 1921-22 is £81,397,632, of which £64,604,458 is from Revenue, £11,196,000 from War Loan, and £5,597,174 from Works Loan. The decrease in the expenditure from War Loan as compared with the previous year is £12,952,501. The items of proposed expenditure out of War Loan are Soldier Land Settlement—£7,000,000; War Service Homes—£4,000,000; Forestry, etc.—£196,000.

Commonwealth Public Debt.

The gross Public Debt as at 30th June, 1921, was £401,720,025, including the War Debt of £359,606,719. This shows an increase during the year of £20,410,121. The net Public Debt was £332,009,032, being an actual reduction of £8,800,872 on the year. The Commonwealth's War indebtedness includes £234,800,000 owing to Australian bond holders, and £92,480,000 to the British Government. For purposes of the War and Repatriation £256,000,000 have been raised in Australia, and of this amount £11,598,590 have been redeemed.

Sinking Fund.

Payments to Loans Sinking Fund were made to the extent of £3,201,298 in 1920-21. The Loans Sinking Fund Act requires contributions to be made at not less than 10s. per cent. per annum on the War loan borrowings and on stock raised for works. The contributions made last year were at the rate of 1 per cent. on account of war loans and ½ per cent. on the stock raised for works (excepting a small portion upon which 5 per cent. contribution was made). It is proposed to continue contributions at approximately the same rates during 1921-22.

Under the terms of the recent arrangement for the funding of the indebtedness to Great Britain* an annual payment of 6 per cent. is made to cover both interest and sinking fund in respect of this debt.

* *Vide* p. 138.

Commonwealth Note Issue.

The profits from investments of the Australian Note Issue appear for the first time in the Treasury Accounts. They are payable to the Treasury by virtue of the Act passed last year, which placed the Note Issue under a special department of the Commonwealth Bank.* The estimated profits for the coming year are £1,400,000.

Elimination of Double Taxation.

It was proposed to adopt the scheme recommended by the sub-committee of the British Royal Commission on Taxation, which was specially appointed to consider the best means for eliminating double taxation of income within the Empire. The Commonwealth would, in respect of incomes taxed both in the United Kingdom and the Commonwealth, in all cases where the deduction at present allowed from the United Kingdom tax was not in itself sufficient to insure the payment only of the amount equivalent to the higher of the two taxes, grant such further relief as would effect that end. The ideal, namely, relief from triple income tax resulting from the taxation of the same income by the British, Commonwealth and State Governments, could not be attained until all the State Governments came into line in this matter, and so relieve not only the taxpayers of Australia, but also those of the Mother Country, of what he (Sir Joseph Cook) regarded as a very unfair and unjust exaction.†

New Guinea.

The Mandate for the government of the late German possessions in New Guinea having been received, steps were taken under the New Guinea Act, 1920,‡ to establish a civil administration to replace the military government of the territory. The change was made on 9th May last. On that day German law ceased to apply, and the government is now carried out under Ordinances made by the Governor-General of the Commonwealth. The Civil Administrator has been directed to give early attention to the formation of a policy for promoting the material and moral well-being of the natives, especially in regard to education, handicrafts, agriculture

---

* Commonwealth Bank Amendment (Note Issue) Act, *vide* JOURNAL, Vol. II., No. 2, p. 384. For particulars as to gold reserve, *vide* Vol. II., No. 1, p. 135.

† A Bill to give effect to this scheme was passed by the Commonwealth Parliament on 10th December and will be summarised in the next issue of the JOURNAL.

‡ For summary of New Guinea Act, *vide* JOURNAL, Vol. I., No. 4, p. 692, and Vol. II., No. 1, p. 113.

and health. Several Ordinances have been issued with a view to safeguarding the interests of the natives, which is a specific requirement of the Mandate. Under the power given in the Treaty of Versailles, the properties and businesses of German companies in the Territory have been expropriated and are now being managed by an Expropriation Board. The value of the properties (now estimated at from £3,000,000 to £5,000,000) will when ascertained by valuation or sale, be credited to Germany as part payment of the Reparations due to the Allies. The Estimates for the current financial year show revenue as £237,650, principally composed of: customs, £105,000; business tax, £10,000; native head tax, £25,000; earnings of inter-island ships, £40,000; wireless, £13,400. After considerable pruning, the expenditure estimates have been reduced to a sum not exceeding the estimated revenue.

Immigration.

Though the expenditure for last year was only £12,830, some thousands of settlers have come to Australia. The main expenditure on these settlers has been borne by the British Government, who generously grant free passages to all men who were engaged in the War and to their children, as well as to young women who were engaged in England in auxiliary work. This concession expires at the end of 1921, but its extension in full or in a modified form is now under discussion between the British and Dominion Governments. For the present financial year the Commonwealth was estimating to spend £250,000. If more could be usefully spent the Government would not hesitate to do so, and it was hoped that an appreciable addition to the rural population would result.

Capital Increases.

The total amount of nominal capital registered in Australia during 1920 was £185,207,917, and £102,037,406 during the first six months of 1921. It could not be stated how much of this nominal capital had been, or would be, issued, but it might be safely assumed that a considerable number of the companies registered had been formed for the purpose of carrying on industrial and producing operations in Australia.

Shipbuilding and Shipping.

One matter on which the Government had been subjected to a good deal of criticism was its shipbuilding and ship-owning policy. Although the entry of the Government into the list of shipowners was, in the first place, a War measure, it had proved very profitable. The net profit of the Commonwealth Government Line had been more than sufficient to pay the capital cost of the ships purchased. Moreover, the existence of the Commonwealth Line had forced competing shipowners to reduce their freight rates, with the result that shippers were in pocket to a very large amount.

Disarmament.

Stressing the economic side of the Disarmament question, the Treasurer said that in pre-War days Germany had always had an average of a million men in compulsory training. The economic equivalent of these men's work was not much less than £200,000,000 a year. In addition, she had been compulsorily relieved by the Allies of about £80,000,000 a year as the upkeep of her pre-War Defence establishments. If this latter sum were expressed in terms of to-day, it would represent a sum at least equal to that borne by the British Government, viz., £170,000,000 a year. Disarmament for Germany, therefore, meant financial and economic relief of an amount well over £300,000,000. This meant that, after payment of all Reparations, she would still be in a highly favoured position to conduct the economic war of competition in the future. Unless, therefore, something could be done to relieve the Empire of the tremendous handicap of armaments, they might as surely lose the economic struggle as they had won the military one.

Conclusion.

In concluding his speech, the Treasurer said : " The whole world is experiencing the greatest danger and difficulty in the passage from war to peace. The greatest need of the world to-day is peace, not only between the nations of the world, but also within our own borders and among ourselves. Another excellent year is in sight so far as our great staple industries are concerned."

DEBATE IN HOUSE OF REPRESENTATIVES.

On 19th October, in Committee of Supply,

Mr. Matthew Charlton (Labour, Acting Leader of the Opposition) said it was pleasing to note the very hopeful view the Treasurer took in regard to their primary products. The future welfare of the country depended largely upon the nature of the seasons they enjoyed. Fortunately, during the last few years, these had been very good, and there was every appearance of the incoming season being equally good.

Shipbuilding.

The Treasurer had pointed out that provision had been made on the Estimates for £3,000,000 to meet the cost of ships built in Great Britain. In connection with the Government shipbuilding policy, the time had arrived when they should build in the Commonwealth. He knew they would be told that ships could be built cheaper abroad than in Australia. That was probably true, but they must not lose sight of the fact that by building the ships in Australia they employed their own people, and in doing so assisted in maintaining a greater number of producers who, in turn, contributed to the revenue. The need for more population was upon everyone's lips; but what was the use of repeating such a cry when they were sending £3,000,000 out of the country to pay for ships that could be built in Australia? At the request of the Government, preparations had been made in Australia for the construction of ships of the dimensions that were being built abroad, and those controlling the shipbuilding industry had been informed at the time that the work would be permanent. But immediately after the War terminated the ship construction policy of the Government had been changed, and ships were now being built of material produced in enemy countries, whilst their own people were out of employment. It had always been contended that it was essential, in the interests of the Commonwealth, that they should have their own iron and steel works; but now that such works had been established on a sound basis, the Government were preventing industries in which iron and steel could be utilised from operating. Even if the cost of building in Australia were slightly higher, they should balance the position by expending the money in their own country, and finding employment for their own people.

Budget Deficit.

The estimated revenue for the year 1921-1922 was £61,787,350; and the expenditure, £64,604,158; showing a deficiency on the year's transactions of £2,817,108. The surplus available from the past year was £6,618,327, leaving an estimated surplus at 30th June, 1922, of £3,801,219. It would be seen that there was a deficiency of £2,817,108 on the year's transactions. They, on that side of the House, as a Party, desired to see the ledger squared, though not at the expense of employment in that country. They desired to expend as much as possible on services that were absolutely necessary to the welfare of the people, and the development of Australia.

War Debt.

The public debt had increased considerably, and, to be fair, one had to admit that the War was chiefly responsible. Those of them who had approved of entering the War must expect a bill of that kind, but to-day the newspapers that had urged Parliament and the people to leave no stone unturned, and to spend every shilling obtainable, to prosecute the War, were condemning Parliament because of the heavy expenditure. Whatever attitude Members took up, they ought to be fair and say that Parliament was responsible for committing the country to the War debt. That debt had to be carried, and, whatever else happened, it must be met. If it was necessary to impose additional taxation for the purpose of meeting it, the burden must be borne. They could not repudiate the debt.

It was satisfactory that the War expenditure from revenue was decreasing, and that it would be much less this year than it was during the last financial year; but, in bringing about a reduction in the War expenditure, they must be careful not to do an injustice to those who went overseas to fight.

Immigration.

On the question of immigration, might he suggest that they put their own house in order? Lord Northcliffe and others might feel constrained to plead for more population in Australia, but they should begin by finding employment for their own people, and making them contented. If they could place them on the land under a proper scheme, so soon as they reached those shores, without their coming into competition with the people already working there, the Labour Party would not object, but they could not lose sight of the fact that thousands of their own citizens were then unemployed, and there was no prospect of immediate improvement in the position. What was taking place in other parts of the world, as a result of the War, was being reflected in Australia, and they contended that, until they could find constant employment for their own people, no immigrants should be brought out. The first duty of Parliament was to make available land that would be most suitable for settlement. From one end of Australia to the other the best land was held by a few individuals. Advocates of immigration should begin by passing laws in the Federal and State Parliaments to compel the owners of large areas which were not being used to the best advantage to cut the land up and make it available for those who wished to come from overseas.

Income Tax Exemption.

He was sorry that the Treasurer in outlining the proposed amendments of the income tax legislation had not promised an increase of the exemption. If, when the cost of living was very much lower than it then was, and exemption of £150 was fair, the present exemption should be at least £300. It was never intended that the poorer persons in the community should be made to pay income tax; the tax was imposed so that those who were able to do so might contribute towards defraying the cost of the War. In the circumstances, there was no justification for leaving the general exemption at £150, and the exemption of single persons without dependants at £100.

Disarmament.

During the War it had been said from almost every platform that the War was a war to end war, and that the useless expenditure on armaments for the destruction of mankind would cease after they had won the War. The Labour Party stood behind every movement for bringing about disarmament. Its members supported the establishment of the League of Nations when prominent men threw cold water on it. They saw that it would make for the salvation of the peoples if they could be got to come together for the settlement of international disputes without recourse to the arbitrament of war. The Labour Party stood for the limitation of armaments, and, indeed, for the abolition of armaments at the earliest moment that it could be brought about.

Budget Deficit—Amendment.

In concluding, Mr. Charlton moved that the first item on the Estimates be reduced by £1 with a view to the reconsideration by the Government of the Estimates of Expenditure in order to reduce the expenditure proposed for Military, Navy and Air Services by £2,817,180, and so eliminate the expected deficit.

Dr. Earle Page (Leader of the Country Party) said he would oppose Mr. Charlton's amendment in its present form, because he did not think it was possible, in existing circumstances, to reduce the Defence Estimates by £2,817,000. He thought it would be possible to reduce the Estimates, as a whole, by that amount. The Country Party recognised the responsibility of making some very determined effort, whether the Government wished it or not, not only to square the ledger, so far as revenue and expenditure were concerned, but also to put the public finances in such a position that they could give a lead both to the States and to private enterprise in making some provision to meet the tremendous commitments of the next few years. They desired again to point out the folly of regarding such action as a Party matter, and the absurdity of making a vote on the matter of reduction of expenditure a question of want of confidence in the Government. He said that, not because he had any reason to wish that the Government should continue in office, but because their position was so serious that they must view this matter as they looked at some of the big national issues during the War—they must deal with it as a united, and not as a divided, nation.

Three years had elapsed since the close of the War. The days of inflated values and high prices were going out. The time had surely come, after the orgy of living for seven years at War rate of income and expenditure, to take stock of their position and face the issue of national solvency. The War had destroyed somewhere in the vicinity of £50,000,000,000 of actual wealth in the world, with the inevitable result of a general paralysis of industry and upsetting of exchange, and the Government of every country found itself burdened with huge financial commitments that hung like millstones round its neck. Australia, with a bare 5,500,000 people, owed £300,000,000 of War debt for which there was no tangible asset. It was manifest that there was only one sane policy for their Government, as for all Governments, to pursue; and that was one of national economy that would lift the weight off industry and stimulate production. National economy meant something more than not spending a few pounds here and discharging a man or two there. It meant more than just balancing expenditure with income. It meant the proper marshalling and mobilisation of all the resources, both human and material, of the nation to secure the greatest production, the maximum efficiency and the elimination of waste.

Australia's financial position and prospects of development were greatly complicated by their Federal system, and they would not secure effective economy or effective service except through the reorganisation of the whole system of government, from the top to the bottom, by means of the Federal Convention. What was needed was a revision of their constitutional machinery so as to define more clearly the Federal and State spheres of activity and of taxation, to simplify the system of government, to abolish all duplication of services, and to consolidate the public debts.

Dr. Page urged the Government to withdraw the Budget —to grasp the nettle firmly, and to do what every business house was doing, namely, try to square the ledger and prepare for the lean years.

Mr. A. Wienholt (Country Party, *Moreton*, **Q.)** said he was less concerned even with the amount of their public indebtedness than with the necessity for renewing their loans in the future, which was the outstanding financial menace to Australia. To his mind the system of taxation—Commonwealth and State—was absolutely unsound. The position was much as if two men, not on good speaking terms, were drawing cheques on the same banking account. In some cases they had three taxing authorities. For instance, the land tax was levied on the same taxpayer by a local governing authority, the State Government and the Commonwealth Government. Commonwealth and State finance were inseparable. If the States, through extravagance and wastefulness, became insolvent, the Commonwealth must go down, too; if the Commonwealth met with disaster through the same causes, it must drag the States with it. They were one people and one taxpayer, but there were many tax-gatherers.

He thought that there were many ways in which they could save, and many directions in which the Estimates could be reduced, including the Defence proposals. Last year the Imperial Government had paid off no less than £251,000,000 of debt. This year, they had budgeted a surplus of £175,000,000, whilst in Australia the Commonwealth Government had budgeted a deficit of something like £3,000,000.

Proposed Amendments.

Mr. Charlton's amendment, being put, was negatived by 37 votes to 20.

Dr. Earle Page thereupon moved:—

> That the item be reduced by 10s., and that it be taken as an instruction to the Government to reconsider the Estimates for the purpose of reducing the total expenditure from revenue by the sum of £2,817,108, the amount of the anticipated deficit, in order to square the ledger.

On 20th October,

The Prime Minister said that while the Government could not and would not accept Dr. Earle Page's amendment, or any general direction such as was contained therein, it fully recognised the need for economy and the general principle that it was desirable to live within their income. The Government would make an honest endeavour to do that. Further, the Government invited the Committee to indicate where economy could be effected; and, provided that that economy did not strike a vital blow at the policy of the Government, they would accept the decision of the Committee.

(On 27th October Dr. Earle Page's amendment was defeated by 33 votes to 32.)

On 11th November,

The Prime Minister said that four months of the financial year having expired, the heads of the various Departments were able more accurately to forecast the expenditure for the remaining portion. After further consideration of the Estimates, the Government would cause such reduction to be made as would effect a saving of £500,000 in the public expenditure from revenue. That reduction, and the taking into account of a sum of £835,000 which was lying to the credit of the Commonwealth Government in London, would improve the balance-sheet by a total of £1,335,000.

(The Estimates have been passed; but definite advice as to the extent to which they were finally reduced has not yet been received.)

DEFENCE ESTIMATES.

(Military Works; Disarmament; Washington Conference; Navy Estimates, etc.)

DEBATE IN HOUSE OF REPRESENTATIVES.

On 29th September,

Mr. W. G. Mahony (Labour, *Dalley, N.S.W.*), criticising a proposed Military vote for "Additions, New Works, Buildings, etc."—£1,134,251, said the House should have some explanation as to why the vote for military Defence purposes was to be increased this year by approximately £500,000. The Government had introduced Estimates for this increased vote notwithstanding that they had just passed through the turmoil of a great war, which they had been told was fought to save the world from military domination and the dictation of the military caste. Surely after having experienced the ravages of war it was time to call a halt in naval and military expenditure, more particularly in view of the fact that a great Conference was to be held at Washington for the purpose of considering the question of the general Disarmament of nations. The best example they could set would be to move in the direction of reducing their military

Estimates instead of asking for an increased vote. The Government spoke of economy and said that money could not be found to provide employment. Many citizens who had risked their lives in fighting against military domination were walking the streets in search of employment.

The Assistant Minister for Defence (Sir Granville Ryrie), in reply, said that it would be time enough to discuss the increase in the military expenditure when the main estimates were before the Committee. The vote in question was for new works. It was a portion of the Estimates of the Department,* and if it was necessary to expend more on new works this year he would give the reason.† Some Members seemed to think that because the recent War had terminated all military expenditure should cease. It was quite possible that wars might occur in the future, and were they to be totally unprepared? He believed in establishing an insurance fund for the Commonwealth—an insurance against foreign aggression. His firm belief was that the best way to prevent war was to be prepared for it, and he would go further, and say that if Great Britain had been prepared he did not believe that Germany would have set out in her mad endeavour to dominate the world. Germany had believed that Britain was absolutely unprepared, and it had been in that belief that she had sought to invade France. Germany had not counted upon their having such a brilliant soldier as the late Lord Kitchener, who had been able in such a short time to equip men and send them across the water in time to stem the tide of the German invasion of France. Preparedness for war was the best way to prevent it, and the Government's intention was to maintain the Defence Forces in Australia on a proper footing.

Disarmament: Defence Expenditure.

Mr. F. Brennan (Labour, ***Batman, Vic.*****)**: "Are not the Government going to support the policy of Disarmament?"

The Assistant Minister for Defence: "It remains to be seen whether the Washington Conference will be able to do anything with regard to Disarmament. I sincerely hope it

---

* The total Defence Department Vote is £3,250,000. The Minister for Defence, in a statement presented to Parliament, points out that the present estimated expenditure, having regard to the decreased purchasing power of money, is considerably less than the expenditure in 1913-14, which was £2,641,321.

† In explaining the increased vote, Sir Granville Ryrie instanced the increased cost of production of rifles, increased expenditure in connection with small arms, ammunition and munitions, and the establishment of an arsenal.

will be possible to stop this mad race among the nations for supremacy in armaments. But until we know, it would be suicidal for us to call a halt in connection with our preparations to maintain an efficient military force on a democratic basis. Nothing could be more democratic than the basis on which it is proposed to maintain our Military Force, namely, the basis of citizenship. Honourable Members opposite have always maintained that their Party inaugurated the present system of compulsory military service."*

Mr. S. R. Nicholls (Labour, *Macquarie, N.S.W.*): "For home defence."

The Assistant Minister for Defence: "It cannot be said that the proposals now under consideration are not for home defence."

Dr. Earle Page (Leader of the Country Party) said that the proposals for Works expenditure amounted to practically £3,000,000, of which over £2,000,000 was to provide for Defence. Last year there had been a surplus of £893,000; while this year the Treasurer had actually budgeted for a deficit. This was contrary to all established business principles.

Mr. Matthew Charlton (Acting Leader of the Opposition) believed that the expenditure of last year should not be exceeded pending, at least, the outcome of the Washington Conference and the deliberations of the League of Nations. Last year they had expended £693,255 on the items in question, and this year they estimated to expend £1,134,251. They were, therefore, practically doubling the Defence expenditure on additions, new works and buildings, apart from the Navy. He could not understand why they talked about Peace Conferences and meetings of the League of Nations for the purpose of bringing about Disarmament and, at the same time, proposed to spend money that they could ill afford, when they were heavily taxed to meet the indebtedness of the War. During the War they had said that it would be a war to end war, and that the great mass of the people would not again be called upon to pay heavy taxation for the purpose of armament. They had told the people that, instead of having to expend so much labour unproductively in the future, they would be able to use their money in productive channels. Instead of that, they were now asked to expend more money in providing munitions for the destruction of life.

Mr. A. Wienholt (Country Party, *Moreton, Q.*) said it was appalling to him to see such a large sum on the Defence Estimates, especially as they had only lately come through a tremendous war. He should have thought that they would have had harness, vehicles and equipment to burn. He was

* An outline of the Australian system of compulsory military training will be found in the JOURNAL, Vol. II., No. 1, p. 131.

not going to vote for a Budget that deliberately and in cold blood proposed that Australia should go further into debt this year, to the extent of something like £3,000,000 on the year's transactions.

Mr. J. E. Fenton (Labour, *Maribyrnong, Vic.*) said his reminder last year of the millions by which the British Government had reduced expenditure seemed to have had no effect on the Australian Government. If they were to continue this huge Defence expenditure in Australia, they would lose all the advantages, if any, which they had gained by the winning of the War. In support of that statement he would quote from the Budget Speech of the Treasurer:

> "Disarmament for Germany therefore means financial and economic relief to an amount of well over £300,000,000 per annum. This means that after payment of all reparations she will still be in a highly favoured position to conduct the economic war of competition in the future. Unless, therefore, something can be done to relieve us of the tremendous handicap of military armaments, we may as surely lose the economic struggle as we won the military one."*

In the general Estimates would be found a large increase in Defence expenditure proposed. In the Estimates for additions, new works and buildings, a considerable increased expenditure was also proposed, and in the Loan Estimates they would find that increased expenditure to the extent of something like £150,000 was proposed in connection with them. For all this proposed increase of expenditure the Assistant Minister for Defence had given one of the lamest excuses that Mr. Fenton had ever listened to from the mouth of a member of the Government. The Treasurer had told them that afternoon that if they continued to expend money in the way proposed on defence, they should be treading on the road to ruin. He hoped that the Treasurer would continue to preach that gospel; but he could not see how the Treasurer could reconcile it with the Estimates now submitted. They could not look for industrial advancement if they were to spend money on Defence in the way proposed by the Government, which was throwing money into a bottomless pit. In the face of what other nations were doing, the Australian Parliament, led by the present Ministry, was setting but a sorry example to the rest of the world. One of the greatest movements of modern times was the Disarmament Conference called by the President of the United States of America. If that Conference meant business Australia should be in it up to the hilt. There were many men wandering through the country looking in vain for the opportunity to earn a crust, and amongst them were men who had suffered and bled in the trenches of France and in

* For full statement in this connection by the Treasurer *vide* Budget summary under Disarmament, p. 121 hereof.

other war areas, and it was certainly the duty of that Parliament to do something which would lead to the industrial advancement of the country, rather than to indulge in the huge naval and military expenditure proposed by the Government.

Reduction of Estimates.

The Assistant Minister for Defence, speaking on 15th November, intimated that arrangements had been made to reduce the Defence Department Vote by £250,000.

Navy Estimates.

In a statement presented to the House of Representatives on 13th October,

The Minister for the Navy (Hon. W. H. Laird Smith) shows the Navy Estimates for the present financial year as £3,180,203. The expenditure in the previous year was £3,100,281. The provision for maintenance of fleet and establishments, reserves of stores and construction of fleet, and naval works, shows a reduction of £80,860. Reductions in personnel are again being effected this year by the return to the United Kingdom of Royal Navy officers and men lent to the Royal Australian Navy, whose period of loan has expired. The places of these ranks and ratings will not be filled. The cost per head of the population in respect of the Commonwealth Navy Estimates is 13s. as compared with 33s. per head in the case of Great Britain.

The recommendations of the Imperial Conference as to the Naval Defence of the Empire, and the decisions of the Commonwealth Government on these recommendations, as far as they affect Australia, were not available when the Estimates were drawn up. In consequence, the Estimates were prepared with a view to maintaining the present Naval Forces as far as possible in a state of efficiency. In order to keep within the amount available on the Estimates the Naval Board found it necessary to reduce the strength of the sea-going fleet to 2 light cruisers, 1 training cruiser, 2 sloops, 3 modern destroyers, 1 river class destroyer, 1 submarine parent ship, 3 " J " class submarines, and 1 yacht, or fourteen ships in all. H.M.A.S. *Australia* is now in commission for training purposes; and H.M.A.S. *Mallow* and 8 T.B.Ds. are in reserve, while *Encounter* and *Pioneer* are being utilised as depot ships. The numbers of officers and men required for the reduced fleet for which provision has been made are 501 officers, and 4,188 men.

(*Debate on the Navy and Air Service Estimates will be concluded in the next issue of the* JOURNAL, *when the necessary Parliamentary Reports will be available.*)

NEW HEBRIDES.

In the House of Representatives, on 4th November,

The Prime Minister (the Right Hon. W. M. Hughes), referring to an offer which had been made on behalf of the French proprietors of land in the New Hebrides to sell their interests for £500,000, said that honourable Members knew that the conditions under the Condominium were very unsatisfactory. The acceptance of the offer would place all the land in the New Hebrides under the control of British holders.

He was against acceptance, but the House might do as it pleased concerning it. The summary of the proposal with which he had been furnished was as follows :—

Since 1902 the Commonwealth Government has spent approximately £134,000 in New Hebrides—£22,000 for assistance to settlers in preparing land claims, £4,000 in refund of Customs Duties, and about £108,000 on a steamer service.

Australia naturally gets the bulk of the export trade as a result of this latter expenditure.

Our main interest, however, lies in the fact that the natives of New Hebrides are decreasing, and labour must be imported. The French own the bulk of the land, and, it is understood, are anxious to import Asiatic labour. The presence of any considerable number of Asiatics so near Australia, especially as we pursue a policy of exclusion in our own island territories, would be embarrassing and possibly dangerous.

The French own 600,000 hectares out of a total of 1,200,000 hectares of land. The natives own about 522,000 hectares.

A French Company, known as the Société Française des Nouvelles Hébrides, is the owner of the 600,000 hectares above mentioned, and in addition has been granted trading concessions in the group. The Company is willing to sell its property and trading concessions for 25,000,000 francs (about £500,000). All the bases and ports, except Port Olry, form part of the Company's land, and are susceptible of exclusive private ownership with unrestricted sea rights.

The possibility of the sale to British interests has been disclosec to the French Government, and it is stated that the transaction wil meet with no objection on their part.

The purchase of this property by British interests would revers the present position so far as dominant land ownership in the grou is concerned, and such would pass from French to British control.

It is understood that Japan is pressing the sellers for an offer failin Australian acceptance.

On the 13th October a cable was received making an offer to arrang payment by bonds maturing over five years—7,000,000 francs maturin the first year, 3,000,000 the second year, 5,000,000 each of the thre following years—bonds for full amount being deposited at time of purchas and maturing accordingly. It was added that if this offer did not sui an endeavour to meet Commonwealth wishes would be made; bu payment in francs was insisted on, or if in another currency in cash c security for which francs could be obtained now, in order to avoid possib loss of present advantageous exchange, which naturally greatly reduces the cost in sterling.

Mr. Hughes, continuing, said the reason why he was opposed to the acceptance of the offer was that he did not think the purchase of the land would place Australia in the position suggested in the summary. Even if it would, whether the land itself was worth the money was a matter on which he was not able to express an opinion. He did not know the land; he knew, however, that the Condominium, which it was proposed to continue, was most unsatisfactory.

Mr. W. M. Fleming (Nationalist, *Robertson, N.S.W.*): "But even if we did acquire in this way the whole of the French interest in the lands of the New Hebrides, that would not abrogate the control of the French over the New Hebrides."

The Prime Minister, in reply, said that the point raised by Mr. Fleming was a vital one. Labour laws had been the real cause of the trouble in the past, and even if they did acquire this land, the control would remain exactly as it was. It was an integral part of the Condominium. He had no doubt that the missionary societies would strongly favour the purchase of this land by the Commonwealth*; but the question was whether they would be able to get a good title to it. The file showed that of the 600,000 hectares of land in question, the title of the Company to 376,000 hectares was established. The rest of the land was only partially marked out, and the titles to it were not established.

(The Parliamentary Report covering the subsequent discussion will not reach London in time for inclusion in this number. It appears from recent Press cables, however, that the Government will reject the offer.)

TRADE WITH GERMANY AND AUSTRIA.

In the House of Representatives on 29th September, in reply to a question by the Hon. W. G. Higgs (Nationalist, *Capricornia, Q.*) as to the nature of the restrictions on trade with Germany and other late enemy countries,

The Minister for Trade and Customs (Hon. W. Massy Greene) gave the following answer:—

There are no restrictions on the exportation of goods from Australia to any ex-enemy countries, excepting on those goods specially gazetted as prohibited exports to any country. The prohibition on the importation

---

* The summary of an earlier discussion in the House of Representatives (12th June last), in which reference was made to unsatisfactory conditions under the Condominium, appeared in the last issue of the JOURNAL, p. 877.

of goods from all ex-enemy countries imposed by Proclamation dated 14th January, 1920, and published in *Commonwealth Gazette*, No. 3, dated 14th January, 1920, is still in force.

The Proclamation referred to prohibits the importation into the Commonwealth, except with the consent, in writing, of the Minister of State for Trade and Customs, of the following goods, namely :—

(A) goods manufactured or produced in, or brought directly or indirectly from, Germany, Austria-Hungary, Turkey, or Bulgaria. Goods shall be deemed to have been manufactured or produced in Germany, Austria-Hungary, Turkey, or Bulgaria if more than 5 per cent. of the invoice value thereof has been derived from the labour of persons resident in any of those countries and/or from material obtained from any of those countries, and the onus of proof of the country of manufacture or production within the meaning of this paragraph shall lie upon the importer ; and

(B) goods upon or in connection with which there is used a trade mark the registration of which, and all the rights conferred by the registration of which, are avoided or suspended by order of the Attorney-General made in exercise of the powers conferred upon him by the provisions of the Patents, Trade Marks, and Designs Act, 1914-1915, and the regulations thereunder.

(*Information has since been received that a Proclamation has been issued providing for the resumption of trade with ex-enemy countries as from* 1*st August next.*)

CUSTOMS TARIFF ACT.

(Free Trade and Protection, etc.)

The following summary of the debate in the Senate on the Bill to give legislative effect to the new Tariff is in continuation of the summary appearing in the last number of the JOURNAL commencing at page 879. This Bill was passed by the House of Representatives on 8th July last and was introduced into the Senate on 13th July. It was subsequently returned by the Senate to the House of Representatives with suggested modifications, which, however, did not materially affect the protective nature of the Tariff or its preferential provisions in respect of British manufactures. The Act was assented to on 16th December.

DEBATE IN THE SENATE.

Plea for Free Trade.

On 13th July,

Senator A. Gardiner (*N.S.W.*), on the motion for the First Reading, opposed the Bill. He said he stood as a Free Trader, with an absolute belief that Free Trade was the best policy for a country like Australia. He understood that Protection was a policy for the improvement of the community and the employment of the individuals in it. If the Protectionist argued that it would give more work, Senator Gardiner was prepared to concede that it would, with this addition, that it would give more work and more labour for less return than would a Free Trade policy. Thus, under a policy of Protection, to get the same amount of production and the same results there must be longer hours and more labour. Otherwise there would be less return. For fifty years the State of Victoria had had a policy of Protection, yet it was in no better a position than the Free Trade States. The attempt to bolster up industries in a country by a Protective Tariff was an absolute fallacy.

The new Tariff had been in operation since March of last year, and what was the result up to the present? They were then beginning to notice the unemployment on every hand. The War was over. He admitted that its disastrous effects had been felt everywhere. They had heard some saying that during the war period it had been shown that a Protective Tariff, such as the one under discussion, was absolutely essential. What was the position in Great Britain, which had had a Free Trade policy for a period of seventy years? It had not only carried the financial burdens of the War, but it was mainly owing to its industrial organisation that Free Trade England had been responsible for the successful termination of the great conflict.

He was assuming that under a Free Trade policy exchange of products to the amount of £20,000,000 could be effected with ten important countries, but by adopting a Protective Tariff and drawing a circle round their own country they were ceasing to trade with these people on the mistaken belief they would manufacture all they required. But as soon as they threw out of employment all the people engaged in producing the £200,000,000 worth of trade with the ten countries, the question arose as to what was to be done to replace that labour. Although the Tariff had been in operation only fifteen months, ships were lying idle everywhere. Why was that so? It was because they had a Tariff that had so enhanced the price of goods that the merchants in the Commonwealth were ceasing to purchase.

Senator H. E. Pratten (*N.S.W.*): "The importations during the last twelve months have been higher than ever."

Senator E. A. Drake-Brockman (*W.A.*): "The values are higher but the quantity is smaller."

Senator Gardiner, continuing, said that importations had been larger because they had had four or five years during which trade had been practically at a standstill, and in consequence the warehouses had become empty. When the War was over an effort was made to replenish stocks.

The Protective policy of the State of Victoria could be dated from 1870, and from that year until 1900 New South Wales was practically operating under a Free Trade policy. The result of the growth of those two States was that Victoria, which was leading in population by many thousands in 1870, after a race of thirty years, was greatly out-distanced by New South Wales, which not only made up her deficiency but also a lead of many thousands.

Senator the Hon. H. de Largie (*W.A.*) contended that the reason of the progress of New South Wales lay in her rich coal deposits.

Senator Gardiner, continuing, said that his argument was that Protection was costing the country £50,000,000 per annum, while Free Trade would cost them nothing. He claimed that wages were reduced by Protection. Wages were reduced when they ceased to purchase in proportion to their value. The policy hit Australia where it hurt most, which was the primary producing industries. The secondary industries should not be fostered at the expense of the primary industries.

Defence of Protection.

Senator the Hon. J. Earle (*Tas.*) said that Senator Gardiner's speech had come as a surprise. He had not known that there was such a pronounced Free Trader in Australia. He could not conceive that there was anything so paradoxical as a pronounced and consistent Labour representative in that Parliament subscribing to Free Trade views. It was inconceivable to him that a man who believed in a "White Australia," who would not allow Asiatics to enter the country, a man who believed in good conditions for the workers, reasonable hours of employment, good wages, good factory conditions, would allow the product of black labour to enter the country. It was impossible to build up a young nation in Australia unless they protected their industries against the cheap labour of the outside world. The question of Protection was one of far-reaching importance. Its success led to the creation of new industries, to the introduction of more people, more taxpayers, more consumers of the farmers' products, and more carriers of the gun to defend Australia if ever the necessity arose. Senator Gardiner's idea was to rely absolutely upon the development of their primary industries; but, as about three-fifths of their population were not employed in the primary industries, they must realise that without Protection their population would be considerably reduced, and their position as a growing nation would be very much worse than it was to-day. If there were no industries in Australia for the manufacture of any particular product, they were then at the mercy of the importer, and experience all over the world showed that if there were no local competition the price of an article, whether it were agricultural machinery or anything else, was a great deal higher than in those countries which had their own local industries.

The Vice-President of the Executive Council (Senator the Hon. E. J. Russell), in moving the Second Reading, said that since the signing of the Armistice capital to the extent of £100,000,000 had been invested in industries and in the extension of industries in Australia. They were under an obligation to those who had invested this money to assist production to see that they should not lose it The world had tried Free Trade. Even the Motherland, the home of Cobdenism and the Manchester School, had not only given up Free Trade, but had adopted Protective duties, with an additional 33 per cent. to balance rates of exchange. The abandonment of Free Trade by Great Britain was an admission that the principle was wrong. All countries should be self-sustaining, particularly in regard to the production of the raw materials of essential industries. No country in the world had finer iron deposits than were to be found in Australia. Why should they be left to lie idle whilst they had the men there to turn them into articles of use whilst Australia was at the same time importing every year hundreds of thousands of pounds' worth of machinery? Why should they place themselves at the mercy of the American Steel Trust? It had been said that they could not make engines for ships. To-day they were turning out engines for 12,000-ton boats of 23,000 tons displacement. This proved that given the opportunity the Australian artisan was the equal of any in the world. Agricultural implements manufactured in Australia were now used throughout the Commonwealth, and that industry would not have reached its present state of efficiency and security if it had not been for the protection it had received under a reasonable Tariff. In the Argentine, where there were no duties, the prices of agricultural implements were in excess of those ruling for similar machines in Australia, because the primary producers in that country had to depend solely upon importations. During the nineteen years that New South Wales had been working under a Protective policy, she had progressed and developed her territory to a greater extent than she had ever done before. He believed the Tariff was a scientific one, and although it might not be the last word in Tariffs, it would be the means of protecting existing industries and encouraging others to become established. They had been hewers of wood and drawers of water for other countries too long. They had lost millions of pounds sterling because they had been lacking in enterprise in establishing industries, but that time had passed. Although they had a small population, they had the raw material at their disposal, and should therefore have every opportunity of fully developing the country.

CUSTOMS TARIFF (INDUSTRIES PRESERVATION) ACT.

The Bill, the provisions of which were summarised in the last issue of the JOURNAL, pp. 893 *et seq.*, was finally passed by Parliament on 9th December. The percentage given in paragraphs (B) and (C) of the summary in connection with the definition of "reasonable price" and "reasonable selling price" has been reduced from 20 to 5 in each case.

WAR INDEBTEDNESS TO GREAT BRITAIN.

In the House of Representatives on 4th November, in reply to a question by the Hon. W. G. Higgs (Nationalist, *Capricornia, Q.*) on the subject of the funding arrangement in connection with the Commonwealth Government's War indebtedness to Great Britain,

The Minister for Trade and Customs (Hon. W. Massy Greene), for the Treasurer, stated that the total indebtedness of the Commonwealth under the funding arrangements with the British Government was £92,480,157, made up as follows:—

	£
4½ per cent. Bonds	11,500,000
3½ per cent. Book Debt	1,263,158
5 per cent. Book Debt	36,318,900
War Office Capitation	36,036,694
Admiralty Account	3,635,000
Ministry of Shipping	3,620,000
Ministry of Munitions	203,929
Railway Warrants	60,000
Bread Subsidy	60,000
Gross total	£92,697,681
Less moneys due by British Government	217,524
Net total	£92,480,157

The Commonwealth pays annually £5,548,810, being 6 per cent. on the total indebtedness. The amount is applied in the first half-year on £1,263,158 at 3½ per cent., £11,500,000 at 4½ per cent., and £79,716,998 at 5 per cent. per annum, and the balance is taken in reduction of principal. In subsequent half-years the amount is first applied in payment of interest at the before-mentioned rates on the balances of the principal sums outstanding, and the remainder is taken in reduction of principal. By this means, the indebtedness will be wiped out in 35¼ years, or in 1956.

State Parliaments.

New South Wales.

Resignation of Government (Note).

According to cable advices, the Government resigned on 13th December following on a defeat in the Legislative Assembly on a motion by the Opposition for adjournment requesting a dissolution. The resignation of the Speakership by the Hon. D. Levy (Nationalist), and the appointment of Mr. S. Hickey (Labour) to the Chair, had left the Government in a minority of one.

A coalition Government consisting of Nationalists and Progressives, with Sir George Fuller (Nationalist) as Premier, was sworn in on 20th December, but resigned the same day, being unable to command a majority in the House of Assembly. The Labour Government* thereupon resumed office, and carried on until 24th December, when Parliament was prorogued.

MOTHERHOOD ENDOWMENT BILL.

A Bill to provide for the endowment of motherhood under certain conditions was introduced in the Legislative Assembly on 20th September, 1921, by the Government, and passed the Third Reading on 22nd December. No advice has yet been received as to the introduction of the Bill in the Upper Chamber.

The main provisions of the Bill are :—

Endowment Allowance : Mothers.

Every mother of three or more living children under fourteen years of age shall be entitled to be paid, in respect of each such child other than the first two, six shillings per week, to be applied towards the maintenance of the child ; provided the income of the mother, or the combined income of the mother and her husband, does not exceed the living wage payable at the time to male employees, and that the total amount of endowment allowance is decreased by the extent to which such income exceeds the living wage.

(" Living wage " is that fixed by the New South Wales Board of Trade from time to time calculated on the cost of living, and is now £4 5s. per week.)

In the event of the death of the mother, or where the mother is not maintaining the child, payment may be made to some other person as approved by the Minister for the maintenance of the child.

---

* *Vide* JOURNAL, Vol. II., No. 4, p. 902.

Widows, etc.

Every widow who is the mother of one or more living children under fourteen years of age shall be entitled to six shillings per week, or, if the circumstances warrant it, at the discretion of the Minister, a sum not exceeding ten shillings per week, in respect of each such child, and also a further sum of ten shillings per week for her own use ; provided her income does not exceed the living wage payable at the time to female employees (£2 3s. per week), and that the amount of the allowances is decreased by the extent that such income exceeds the living wage.

(The term "widow" includes a mother whose husband is not supporting her, or who is incapacitated for work by physical or mental infirmity, or who is undergoing a term of imprisonment, provided such failure to support, etc., is continued for a period of not less than one month immediately prior to the application.)

Motherless Children.

Where the mother of a child is dead, or is not maintaining her child, and the child is without adequate means of support, payment may be made to an approved person of ten shillings per week in respect of every such child towards its maintenance. Any such payment may be terminated or varied by the Minister.

Illegitimate Children.

Payment may be made to the mother or to some approved person of a sum not exceeding ten shillings per week in respect of any illegitimate child under fourteen years of age which is satisfactorily proved to be without adequate means of support.

Children in Orphanages.

Six shillings per week may be paid to an orphanage or similar institution in respect of each child which is being maintained.

Exceptions.

No payment shall be made in respect of any child, if and so long as any payment is made for its maintenance under the State Children Relief Act, 1901, the Deserted Wives and Children Act, 1901, or the Infant Protection Act, 1904, or any Acts amending the same.

Calculation of Income.

Benefits or sick pay from a friendly society shall not be deemed to be part of the income. Five per centum of the capital value of any land or buildings owned or used, or used rent free, shall be included in the income, provided that a deduction may be made of any interest paid on a mortgage of the land or buildings. The value of any board or lodging given in part payment of wages, or otherwise, may be included as income.

Nationality and Residence Qualifications.

To be entitled to the endowment allowance the mother or widow must be British born or the wife or widow of a person who is or was British born, or is or was a naturalised British subject ; and must have been a *bona fide* resident of the State of New South Wales for a period of two years immediately prior to the date of each application for payment ; and also enrolled as a Parliamentary elector.

Revision of Payments, etc.

Provision is made for variation of the payments in accordance with the rise or fall in the cost of living; and for the cessation of payment in the case of conviction of offences against the Act, failure to satisfy the Minister as to character and repute, physical or mental incapacity, and improper use of the endowment payments.

No order shall be made by any Court of Justice for the attachment of any sum payable under the Act. Regulations and orders may fix a penalty not exceeding £20, or imprisonment not exceeding three months for breach thereof.

DEBATE IN LEGISLATIVE ASSEMBLY.

On 20th October, in moving the Second Reading,

The Minister for Labour and Public Health and Motherhood (Hon. J. J. G. McGirr) said that no one in New South Wales, more particularly among the social workers, could deny that on the basic wage as fixed by the Board of Trade (£4 5s. per week), which provided only for a man and wife and two children, although there were families of eight or ten children under 14 years of age, dire poverty and distressful conditions must exist.

Motherhood endowment was based on the fact that they wanted to populate Australia. They took it for granted that Australia needed population. Therefore it was essential that there should be some recompense to those to whom they looked to bring about an increase in the white Australian race. The mother who was rendering a social service—for it was a social service—should be recognised as so doing. The child whom she brought into the world must also be recognised. If it was a good thing to pay £17 or £18 per head towards bringing immigrants to Australia, it was a good thing to see that the mother who was helping to maintain their Australian race should be subsidised at least to the extent that she herself would not have to starve.

The estimated number of mothers affected by the Bill would be 44,000. There would be 15,000 widows, and 2,500 deserted wives, and also 40 orphanage institutions. The total net expenditure was estimated at £1,528,000 a year.

In concluding, Mr. McGirr said that the measure was only the first instalment of a comprehensive scheme of motherhood endowment. If returned after the next election he would bring forward a further instalment—a scheme for the endowment of all mothers in New South Wales, no matter what their incomes might be. Before very long they would find civilised countries throughout the world following the example of Australia.

The Hon. Sir George Fuller (Leader of the Opposition) said it would be a good thing if their finances could be put in such a position that they would not stand in the way of this and other matters proposed to be carried out in the interests of the community. But, unfortunately, they had to realise that the present financial position of the State was such that they must pause and consider before they entered on the expenditure of such a large sum of money as was involved in the measure.

Mr. T. J. Ley (Progressive, *St. George*) in opposing the Bill said that motherhood endowment had been in operation in New South Wales for many years, but there were defects in the scheme. He asked the Minister why he had not attempted to make good those defects instead of proceeding with this extraordinary measure. The State Children Relief Department had found itself handicapped. It could not in certain directions make the requisite allowance because of the want of sufficient money. That had been the trouble in the past. The State Children Relief Act provided for an allowance of ten shillings per week, and that Act should be suitably amended. It was unwise and ethically wrong to make an allowance to a person who was not in need of it. Before making an allowance to parents who were receiving the basic wage the Minister should increase the allowance in the case of those children who were not fortunate enough to have fathers who were earning the basic wage, instead of providing for a flat rate as in the measure under discussion. It would be far better to use the money on reproductive works, and in that way get over the difficulty, but where there was actual need for it relief should be given with proper safeguards.

Queensland.

CONSTITUTION AMENDMENT BILL.

A Bill for an Act to amend the Constitution of Queensland by abolishing the Legislative Council was passed by the Legislative Assembly on 25th October and by the Legislative Council on 26th October, and reserved for the King's Assent.

The principal provisions of the Bill as passed by both Houses are as follow :—

The Legislative Council of Queensland,* the office of Member of the Legislative Council, and all officers constituted in connection with the Legislative Council, are abolished.

---

* The present Legislative Council consists of 59 Members, appointed by the Governor. Members, other than the President and Chairman of Committees, receive no emoluments, but free passes on the State Railways are granted. The President receives an annual allowance of £1,000, and the Chairman of Committees, £700.

The Parliament of Queensland is declared to be constituted by His Majesty the King and the Legislative Assembly in Parliament assembled; and any reference in any Act, rule, regulation, etc., which would be deemed to include a reference to the Legislative Council shall be construed to refer only to His Majesty the King and the Legislative Assembly. All enactments or provisions in any Act or Order in Council relating to the Constitution of Queensland inconsistent with any of the provisions of this Act are repealed.

The Governor-in-Council may, by notification published in the *Gazette*, declare that the existing Members of the Legislative Council shall, during life or other period, retain and exercise the privilege of a free pass upon the railways of the State, the use of the Parliamentary library, etc.

DEBATE IN LEGISLATIVE ASSEMBLY.

On 25th October,

The Premier (Hon. E. G. Theodore), in moving the Second Reading in the Legislative Assembly, said that when the Legislative Council was originally established in Australia, it was stated that it would be a check upon the growing democracy of the people, and that, no doubt, was the justification for the establishment of Legislative Councils, based upon the nomination, by the Government of the day, of Members of those Councils, appointed for life. In some States the constitution of the Councils had been altered to make them elective; but the elective basis contained a restrictive qualification, resulting in the appointment, in most cases, of conservative Members. It was known what the Legislative Council had done in recent years to prevent popular measures becoming law. That obstruction did not now exist so far as Queensland was concerned, because their Council was now dominated by a majority of the supporters of the Government. It had been said that if they found their legislation was being blocked, they could have resorted to the Parliamentary Bills Referendum Act of 1908, and thus have got it carried into effect without abolishing the Council. But that procedure was cumbersome, and had practically never been resorted to.

The Labour Party had been pledged for many years to secure the abolition of the Council. On the other hand, Members opposite advocated the continuance of the bi-cameral system,* but proposed in place of the nominee Upper House,

* On the previous day, in the debate on the motion to introduce the Bill, Mr. W. J. Vowles (Leader of the Opposition) stated that the Country Party were in favour of the abolition of the Legislative Council as at present constituted, but desired to substitute therefor an elective council, and moved an amendment to that effect. A similar amendment was moved by Mr. J. S. Kerr, on behalf of the Nationalist Party, with the proviso that the election should be on the basis of adult franchise. Both amendments were defeated, the former by 40 votes to 21, and the latter by 41 votes to 15.

a House based on an elective franchise, and some considered that there should be a limited franchise with a property or educational qualification. He would point out that an Upper House, based on a broad franchise must be only an echo of what was known as the Lower House. The election of an Upper House upon a restricted franchise had often led to the thwarting of the will of the people, and would be merely carrying out the wishes of a limited number of people.

In 1917, a referendum was taken on the question of the Council's abolition, and resulted in a large majority in favour of its retention. The Government were not satisfied with the decision of the people, and it became an important issue again in the 1918 Election, and they had come back with a handsome endorsement from the electors to carry out that policy.

Constitutional aspect.

In years gone by the question had frequently arisen as to whether Parliament could constitutionally, by a mere Act of Parliament, abolish the Legislative Council. Prior to the passage of the Constitution Amendment Act of 1908, the Constitution Act itself could not be amended except by the consent of a two-thirds majority of the Legislative Council. The Amendment Act of 1908 removed that restriction, and allowed a simple majority in both Houses to amend the Constitution Act. The constitutionality of that Act itself was then called into question. That had, in his opinion, been entirely cleared up in consequence of the litigation arising from the earlier attempts of the Government to abolish the Legislative Council. A special case was stated in the High Court of Australia on behalf of some Members of the Legislative Council, and the High Court had decided that the Act of 1908 was valid.* The point also arose in the McCawley case. The decision† of the Privy Council in that case pointed out that no special formalities were required in order to secure an effective amendment of the Constitution. The judgment made it perfectly clear that it was quite within the power and the province of Parliament as at present constituted, by a simple Act of Parliament, to amend the Constitution, and, by implication, to abolish the Legislative Council.

The interests of the people would be as well safeguarded by a Parliament consisting of one Chamber as by a Parliament consisting of two Chambers; and would have an advantage inasmuch as legislation could be dealt with with dispatch,

---

* Taylor *v.* The Attorney-General of Queensland.—*Commonwealth Law Reports*, 1916-17, p. 463.

† McCawley *v.* The King.—*Commonwealth Law Reports*, 1921, p. 114.

and without the expense or the obstruction of the Legislative Council. If the Legislative Assembly, when it had supreme control, and constituted the Parliament of Queensland, did anything that was against the interests of Queensland, it could be called to book within three years. It would be answerable to the people.

This was an innovation in Queensland, but in Canada seven out of nine provinces had single Chambers. He thought he was right in saying that in South Africa the Provincial Parliaments consisted of only one Chamber. These Parliaments were not quite the same, because the Union Government exercised greater functions than the Federal Parliament did in Australia. In South Africa it was the opinion of many people that the Senate would disappear in about ten years from the date of the Union. The great Liberal Party in England, at a conference held just after the commencement of the War, had declared in favour of the complete abolition of the House of Lords without any proposal to substitute anything for it.

Proposed Revisory Committee.

The Bill provided for a standing revisory committee, which would perform all the useful functions of the Council. The Committee would be formed from the Assembly, and would never become obstructive, because if they did not report in the time stipulated the Bill would simply become law. The Committee would be useful only for making grammatical corrections or pointing out where it might be necessary more clearly to express the intention of the Government.

He did not believe that the Home Authorities would attempt to withhold assent to the Bill, for it was a matter dealing with the internal affairs of Queensland, and not affecting interest of the people in the other parts of the Empire in the slightest degree. If the Imperial Authorities considered that what that Parliament proposed to do with respect to the abolition of the Legislative Council was not a wise course, it was not for them to give a decision upon that; it was for them to allow the people of Queensland to correct the matter if they considered it wrong.

Mr. W. J. Vowles (Leader of the Opposition) said that the attitude of the Country Party in the matter, now that they had been deprived of the opportunity of having an elective Chamber, was to abolish the Council as at present constituted. Anybody who had any knowledge of the internal working of Parliament must have realised that the Upper House, as at present constituted, had no business in it, and the sooner it was got rid of the better. In the past when Members who had constituted that Chamber had had freedom of action and thought, when it had not been composed mainly of men who were bound by pledges which had curtailed their discretion, they had had good results. He agreed with the Premier that the combined Houses, with the assent of the Governor, had the power under the Constitution to amend it as they thought fit; but it was remarkable to him that while the Premier had complained that in the past there had been a body in the Upper House which set out to defeat his legislation, where he had had the opportunity of submitting those measures to the referendum of the people, he had never done so.

The Bill before him put him in a position that he could not support it. He had supported the principle of abolition, but the Bill contained something that was objectionable—that was, that they should reward those persons who had been put into the Upper House for their political perfidy by giving them privileges for the whole of their lives in the form of railway passes and the privileges of the House.

As to the suggestion that a memorial might be sent by the Opposition to the King objecting to the Bill as being unconstitutional, as Leader of the Country Party it was not his intention to send any memorial. If the Legislative Council had been a useful body, then he would not have taken exception to it. It was a misnomer to call it a Council at all, and he was prepared to do away with it.

Mr. C. Taylor (Leader of the Nationalist Party) said that the Premier in showing how Legislative Councils came to be introduced, and the restricted franchise which operated many years ago, did not go the whole way. The exigencies of the times caused the men who had lived in that period in Australia to think it necessary that there should be certain restrictions in parliamentary government. As time had gone by, those restrictions had been removed. No man could truthfully say that Australia was not now a democratic country, with a franchise such as it possessed at the present time. The Premier had told them that the Legislative Assembly was quite sufficient to carry out all the legislation necessary for the State, yet they had a provision in the Bill to appoint a standing Revisory Committee. Would the members of that Committee be appointed on Party lines, or selected from the whole Parliament? The Premier had said that the referendum had not been put to the people as it should have been, but out of seventy-two electorates either sixty-one or sixty-two had voted in favour of the Upper House being retained. The second Chamber had been a part of the Constitution of Australia and of Great Britain ever since Parliaments had existed. They were now asked to throw their second Chamber on one side and to put in its place a committee to revise Bills which were passed by that House. He claimed that a big national matter like that should be placed before the people of Queensland by referendum. The Premier need have no fear that the Royal Assent would be withheld if the passage of that legislation was backed up by the whole of the people of Queensland. He claimed that in so far as hasty legislation was concerned that the Legislative Council should be retained. He would sooner have a hostile nominee Upper Chamber than have no Upper Chamber at all. Even where, in the past, an Upper House had been hostile to the Government, the "popular" Chamber in the end had got its way.

Referendum proposed.

An amendment to the Second Reading, proposed by **Mr. H. E. Sizer** (Nationalist, *Nundah*), that the question be referred to the people by means of a referendum, was defeated by 35 votes to 34.

The Clause constituting the Revisory Committee was withdrawn by the Premier in the Committee stage, and the Bill passed through the Legislative Council without amendment.

MAINTENANCE ORDERS (FACILITIES ENFORCEMENT) ACT.

This Act, the object of which is to facilitate the enforcement in Queensland of maintenance orders made in England, Ireland and other parts of His Majesty's Dominions and Protectorates, and *vice versa*, was passed on 27th October. It is similar to and reciprocal with the Act passed by the British Parliament in 1920.

British Main Provisions.

Where a maintenance order, other than an affiliation order, has been made, whether before or after the passing of the Act, against any person resident in Queensland, by any court in England, Ireland or any reciprocating British Dominion or Protectorate, and a certified copy has been transmitted by the Secretary of State for the Colonies or the Governor of the reciprocating State, as the case may be, to the Governor of Queensland, the order shall be referred by the latter to a competent court in Queensland for registration. After registration, all proceedings may be taken on the order as if it had been an order originally obtained in the court in Queensland.

Where an order made outside Queensland is provisional only and requires confirmation by a court in Queensland the person against whom the Order is made may be summoned to appear before the court to show cause why the order should not be confirmed. It he does not appear, or fails to satisfy the court that the order ought not to be confirmed the court may confirm the order with or without modifications.

Provision is also made for the variation and rescission of orders, reference to the original court for further evidence, etc., and for the making of orders in Queensland against persons resident in reciprocating countries.

NEW ZEALAND.

The Third Session of the Twentieth Parliament of New Zealand began on 22nd September, 1921.

THE ADDRESS—GENERAL DISCUSSION.

(Governor-General's Speech: Conference of Prime Ministers, Dominion Trade, Samoa, Unemployment, Naval Service, New Customs Tariff, Mortgages Extension, Land and Income Tax, etc.)

The Speech of the Governor-General, Viscount Jellicoe, was delivered in the Legislative Council on 22nd September, 1921.

Conference of Prime Ministers.

Admiral the Viscount Jellicoe, in addressing both Houses, said details of matters that had been under discussion at the Conference of Prime Ministers in England would be laid before Parliament as soon as possible after Mr. Massey's arrival. The brief summary furnished by the Press had to a certain extent already enabled them to appreciate the gravity of the subjects dealt with by a Conference which by common consent had proved to be more important than any held in former years.

Fall in prices.

The result of the fall in the prices of wool and frozen meat had affected all classes of the community. The outlook at that time justified the hope that prices would gradually improve. The curtailment of expenditure had resulted in considerable unemployment and in a reduction in the volume of goods imported. Fortunately, the market price for dairy produce had been well maintained.

Western Samoa, etc.

The Speech also referred to the satisfactory result of negotiations with native landowners in regard to opening up a large area of land, hitherto idle, to a recent visit of the Minister of External Affairs to Western Samoa, and to the fact that, in substitution for the Orders in Council under which the Islands had hitherto been administered, legislation would be submitted to be exercised for the first time by the Parliament of the Dominion.

Naval Policy.

The arrival in New Zealand waters of H.M.S. *Chatham* during that year had marked the initiation of the policy of the Dominion's contribution to the maintenance of the Empire's Navy.

Financial matters.

In addressing the House of Representatives on the finances of the country, Lord Jellicoe referred to the 6 per cent. loan of £5,000,000 placed in London at £96 and which was almost immediately at a premium, affording gratifying proof of New Zealand's credit; to the new tariff which was to be submitted; and to certain amendments of the Land and Income Tax Act.

Forecast of legislation.

Finally, in foreshadowing the legislation of a general nature to be introduced, Lord Jellicoe said that for the existing Mortgages Extension Act would be substituted an Act providing for the gradual repayment of principal sums; a Bill to amend the law of libel; a Bill consolidating the land laws; a Forestry Act; a compilation of company law incorporating some of the provisions of the English Act of 1908 which did not appear in the New Zealand Act; and compilations, with amendments, of the Industrial Conciliation and Arbitration Act, and other Acts.

DEBATE IN LEGISLATIVE COUNCIL.

On 27th September,

The Hon. J. P. Campbell (*Auckland*) having moved the Address in reply, which was seconded by the Hon. W. H. McIntyre (*Millerton*),

Protest against postponement of Imperial Conference.

The Hon. Sir John Sinclair (*Dunedin*) said he wished to say a few words about the Prime Ministers' Conference, at which they had been so ably and so worthily represented by their Prime Minister—"whose name," said Sir John, "is now a household word in our Empire family." He wished to refer to a feature of the Conference that took a shape that he, at any rate, had not looked for—namely, its decision that the Constitutional Conference should not be held next year. From this it would appear, he said, that consideration of whether an Empire body should be set up to maintain continuous consultation between the different parts of their Commonwealth—"the question of the medium to regulate and control that touch"—was further off than ever. "Preparation for holding this long-promised Constitutional Conference," said Sir John, "which had been fixed after many delays to take place next year, at which this all-important question was to be discussed in terms of the resolution of the Imperial War Cabinet passed in 1917, was among the principal reasons for summoning the Prime Ministers' Conference that has just taken place." It would mean that that resolution, and all that had been built upon it, was to be abrogated.

Empire Representatives in England.

The need that day was for the setting up of an Empire consultative body broadly upon the lines of the War Cabinet; not an executive body, but a consultative body that would keep all parts in touch upon questions that concerned the welfare of their Commonwealth as a whole. It was an anomaly and a weakness of their constitution that no such body existed. Continuing, Sir John said: "A Dominion representative on the body that I have in mind, whether it should be a substantive body, or whether a graft upon the Foreign Office, would matter little. The Dominion representatives upon such a body would, alike with the representatives of the Mother Country, live in England; they would be on the spot; each would be in touch with the other, all would be in touch with the whole. There would be the finger upon the pulse of Empire. I submit that the time has arrived when the Dominions ought to be represented upon such a body in the Mother Country each by one of its own Ministers." In no other way could there be frequent consultations. Prolonged frequent absences by Prime Ministers were becoming more and more difficult. To pass over the resolution of the War Cabinet, with the promise it implied that a Constitutional Conference would be held, was to set back the hands of the clock. The reason for coming to that decision, as cabled, was: "Having regard to the constitutional development since 1917, no advantage would be gained by holding a Constitutional Conference." But whatever may have been the extent of that development, it had meant such heavier responsibility on the part of the Dominions as to make the need for such a body more urgent than ever.

View of Dominion Independence.

The reference to constitutional development was what they had heard a good deal about in general terms since the signing of the Peace Treaty, namely, to the change of status—status of independence—to the nationhood which the Dominions were said to have attained. That there had been some change they knew, but, happily, it fell far short of independence. By signing the Treaty of Versailles the Dominions shared with the Mother Country responsibility upon questions of foreign policy. And in addition the Dominions had been brought face to face, and quite rightly, with their heavier obligation to contribute to national defence. He had not seen that status of independence authoritatively defined, although he had looked for some deliverance on the question from the Prime Ministers' Conference. The plain fact was, it was not capable of definite statement and Prime Ministers were not even agreed as to its extent. The result was that there were wide differences as to what the position of a Dominion was. There might well be confusion on the part of outside countries, which might not be sure whether they should address certain questions to the Mother Country or to a Dominion.

League of Nations.

The League of Nations was to their people an outside body, although their nation was represented upon it; a system of super-world government whose tendency, in the case of a Commonwealth constituted as theirs, might be separatist; a body the measure of whose control, and the extent of the liability they had been brought under, the Dominions might not be able to realise for years to come.

Plea for Imperial Federation; Naval Contribution.

In conclusion, Sir John said that "while as a system a consultative body would lack something, it would fill a present need and be a step towards the goal we hope to reach some day—federation in the full sense, with a written Constitution."

The Hon. H. L. Michel (*Hokitika*) said there was no doubt that in the future they were going to be called upon to contribute a further substantial sum towards the upkeep of the British Navy—much greater than they had been paying up till the present. Any reasonable contribution would be willingly paid by all classes of the people in New Zealand.

Samoa and Native races.

Speaking of Samoa, Mr. Michel said an unfair attempt was being made to discredit New Zealand's management. He was certain that all the agitation arose from two causes, the first of which was the liquor question. Under the mandate they had to keep intoxicating liquors away from the native race. It was only a few traders who wanted liquor introduced; and they had, in his opinion, been the people who had been working up the discontent and unrest that existed. The other reason was the fall in the price of copra, cocoa, fruit, and other products of the islands; and the very men that had been making capital out of the liquor question were those who were now trying to make the native race believe that the fall in the price of those products had been the result of New Zealand's mismanagement.

Empire "written Constitution" criticised.

The Hon. W. H. Triggs (*Christchurch*), in referring to the speech of Sir John Sinclair, said that in one respect he thought they should both agree—that any form of central Parliament with a written Constitution and with power to levy taxation on the outlying portions of the Empire was quite opposed to the spirit of the Empire and would never be tolerated by the Dominions. One might sympathise with Sir John Sinclair's regret that the Imperial Conference, to have been held for the purpose of discussing the Constitution of the Empire, had been postponed, if not definitely abandoned. He would suggest that there were very strong practical reasons why that question should not have been pressed at the present time: first, the enormous weight of anxiety and responsibility which already rested upon the British Government. But he fancied there was probably another reason. Was it not plain that the Dominions themselves were not united on the question at present? And would there not have been a danger, if the Conference had met, of the result being either to show that they were a divided family, or it might have had to adjourn without coming to any definite decision? New Zealand, they knew, was thoroughly devoted to the Empire, and was quite content to regard herself as a grown-up daughter of the Mother State.

Conference practically an Executive.

After stating the views attributed to General Smuts and the Prime Minister of Canada, and remarking that it was largely owing to the efforts of Mr. Hughes that the Conference was definitely postponed, Mr. Triggs said that it seemed to him that the time was hardly opportune for pressing for a decision. He agreed with Sir John Sinclair that some form of clearing-house of opinion was necessary for the various portions of the Empire, because it would be disastrous if they appeared with divided views before an outside body such as the League of Nations; but the Conference of Prime Ministers was something to which they ought to cling until they had something else they could be quite certain was better to put in its place. That Conference, as carried out at present, was practically an executive body, such as a consultative council would not be.

When the Prime Ministers met, one might say that the decisions taken were practically final, because each Prime Minister knew that what he agreed to he would be able to carry in the Parliament he represented.

Washington Conference: "One voice for the Empire."

In referring to the Washington Conference, Mr. Triggs said he thought the Anglo-Japanese Alliance had played its part and had had its day, and that it was time it was replaced by an alliance on a broader basis, which should include an agreement not only with Japan but with the United States, and should also secure justice for China. He believed that that ideal was not far from being realised. Holding the views he did that the Empire should speak with one voice when dealing with the outside world, he was not altogether disappointed that President Harding had not seen fit on this occasion to invite representatives of the oversea Dominions to take part in that Conference. But he thought it of the utmost importance that some one should be present to keep the British representatives fully posted not only with their views on the question, but also with the local conditions which must be borne in mind before any sound decision even on broad lines could be arrived at.

British Empire League of Nations.

The Hon. G. J. Garland (*Auckland*) said the Peace Treaty gave them a new status among the nations, a new status in the Pacific, and they were that day enjoying a position which was envied by those who hated them, or, if they did not, he was led to believe so—he, referred to the Celestial. He (the Celestial) wanted to get to the Pacific. "But we are here," said the speaker. "We hear a great deal of talk about a League of Nations. Now, my idea of a league of nations is a league of nations of the British Empire. That is the only league of nations I have any faith in."

The Hon. J. P. Campbell (*Auckland*), in his reply, referred to the speeches of Sir John Sinclair and Mr. Triggs, saying that hon. Members were doubtless all in agreement that "the permanence of the tie between Great Britain and the Dominions is largely dependent upon its flexibility, and that any attempt to render that tie more stringent and inelastic by means of a written Constitution or other similar device would probably result in the weakening, and possibly the destruction, of such a tie."

On the point that the time had arrived when the Dominion ought to have permanent representatives in the Old Country he was somewhat doubtful. A great deal seemed to depend upon whether telegraphic and wireless communication between Great Britain and the Dominions could be so improved as to enable the Prime Minister to keep in continuous communication with the Imperial Government.

The Address was agreed to on 6th October.

DEBATE IN HOUSE OF REPRESENTATIVES.

On 27th September,

Mr. E. Dixon (Reform, *Patea*) moved the Address in reply, which was seconded by Mr. T. D. Burnett (Reform, *Temuka*).

"Want of Confidence" motion.

On 28th September,

Mr. T. M. Wilford (Leader of the Opposition) moved :—

> "That the Government, which does not represent a majority of the people of New Zealand, has forfeited the confidence of this House by its want of foresight and incompetent administration of the public finances, thereby being in a large degree directly responsible for the present financial crisis and consequent unemployment."

Government by minority.

Mr. Wilford said it seemed to him as if constitutional government was almost upside down when they had to sit Session after Session with the control exercised by a Party which represented a minority of the people. After quoting figures in connection with the General Election of 1919, Mr. Wilford said they had in the House a huge majority of Members sitting on the side of Reform representing 129,729 less votes than the votes cast against them. Turning to another question, he said, Ministers flitted from one portfolio to another. They had had at least four different Ministers of Railways during the past five years—perhaps more, and at least three during the last eighteen months.

Prime Minister's absence at Imperial Conferences.

Then there was the continued absence of the Prime Minister at Imperial Conferences—absences with which he entirely agreed, but with the result that the Departments supposed to be administered by the Prime Minister fell to the lot of other Ministers, who had no opportunity, with the time at their disposal, of being even conversant with the ramifications and details of those Departments. The natural result was disorganisation in every Department.

Protest against waste.

It had been well said by the Acting Prime Minister, Sir Francis Bell, that never had things been so bad as they were that day, since the days of Sir Harry Atkinson.* What was the chief reason for it? The most scandalous waste had taken place, and Ministers were regardless of that fact. Giving an instance, Mr. Wilford said that when he had been Minister of Marine and the *Philomel*, the ship provided for the purposes of a naval training-ship was tied up alongside the wharf there, it was settled—to his mind, at any rate—that she was useless for any purpose whatever. But what had happened since? The *Philomel* was that day at Auckland with her tail-shaft out, absolutely useless; but £18,000 had been spent on her recently for engineering work alone, apart from supervision and wages.

After making other charges against the Government of waste and extravagance, Mr. Wilford referred to the Royal Commissions that had been appointed, saying that if there was one farce more than another it was the way the Commissions had been run to death during the last two years.

Speaking of the attitude taken up by the Prime Minister and his Cabinet regarding the country's financial condition, he said that Mr. Massey had told them a few months ago that money would be easier after the 31st March. "And to-day," said Mr. Wilford, "local authorities are allowed to borrow money at 7½ per cent." Within a month of the Prime Minister's statement, they found Sir Francis Bell saying "the Treasury has run dry."

Land bought for Soldier-settlement.

The Government always stood for the big man; and when they paid the landowners for their land for soldier-settlement they squeezed every shilling out of the pockets of every patriotic man by getting him to purchase war bonds in order that they might hand the cash to the landowner instead of giving the landowner bonds. In the Discharged Soldiers' Settlement Act, 1916, there was power to take land compulsorily for soldier-settlement. If the Government had done so and had made the landowners take war bonds and accept the ordinary rate of interest which war bonds carried, those millions of money would have been available for industries and for the general requirements of the country. Everybody who took up war bonds knew that when in need of money he had to go into the market and sell a £100 bond less £17, or whatever was the discount.

* The late Sir Harry Atkinson was Prime Minister of New Zealand in the years 1876–7, 1883–4, 1887–91.

The Housing question.

In regard to housing, Mr. Wilford said the Government had no heart and no desire to help the people to get houses; they had tinkered with the question and the people that day were in such a position on account of the cost of dwellings that they did not know where to turn. In every city of the Dominion people were taking houses and letting single rooms at exorbitant prices, and that was all due to the fact that the Government had no policy.

After criticising the Government in regard to arrangements made to meet unemployment, Mr. Wilford made reference to taxation and asked hon. Members to insist that for the revision of the incidence of taxation in the country a body of experts should be called to overhaul the whole taxation system, and that it should not be left to politicians.

"Trusts."

Continuing, he remarked that the biggest octopus in the country that day was in oil. Three companies controlled it—the "Big Three"—and if the Government were not backing them they were winking at them. That oil concern was exploiting every man in the country by the prices charged for kerosene and petrol. Then they had got the American Tobacco Trust, and they had the Meat Trust, and there were others.

In conclusion, Mr. Wilford said that unless the Ministers got to work and understood their respective Departments and stopped the colossal waste that was occurring, the country was going to be faced with a worse position than it occupied that day.

Electoral Reform.

The Minister of Internal Affairs (Hon. W. Downie Stewart) said that the Leader of the Opposition had supported the first part of his amendment, setting forth that the Government did not represent a majority of the people of New Zealand, by an elaborate investigation of the last electoral returns. Everybody knew, said Mr. Downie Stewart, that at the last Election—and for some Elections past—except for the clear line of demarcation which existed between the official Labour Party and all other Parties, the question of who was to be returned for any particular constituency was largely a question of personal preference.

World conditions; unemployment.

It was not justifiable for the Leader of the Opposition to point merely to the financial stringency and to the unemployment, and to say that the Government was entirely to blame.

New Zealand was suffering from world conditions which would affect the country whatever steps the Government might take. In regard to Mr. Wilford's complaint that Mr. Massey was far too optimistic about New Zealand's prosperity, if he (Mr. Wilford) had read the speech carefully and given a fuller extract than he did, he would have found that the Prime Minister had forecast exactly what had been going on. In regard to unemployment, there was no country in the world where the problem of unemployment had been so successfully dealt with as in New Zealand. The Government were trying to meet the situation fairly and suspended till the last minute the retrenchment of employees. When he had heard members asking that millions of pounds be spent on housing, pensions, unemployed and a thousand and one other matters, he had thought he was in an unreal world, when one considered the tremendous strain the country was under financially. If they compared the flotation of their loans with those of other countries and Dominions, like South Africa, they would see that the credit of New Zealand stood high and that her position was perfectly sound.

Minority representation.

Mr. T. K. Sidey (Liberal, *Dunedin, South*) referring to the question of minority representation in the House, said that what was wrong was the electoral system which the Reform Government had promised to amend. Why had it not been reformed? The only reason was "because of political opportunism." While the Opposition was divided into separate factions it suited the Reform Party to continue the present system.

Unemployment Insurance.

Dealing with the question of unemployment, Mr. Sidey said that had the Government carried out their pledge to deal with unemployment insurance and put a scheme on the Statute Book, they would have been in a very different position that day to meet the unemployed difficulty.

After criticising the policy of the Government in regard to immigration and in regard to preference of employment to returned soldiers, Mr. Sidey concluded by saying that the Government were by their want of foresight in a large measure responsible for present conditions which otherwise would not have been so acute.

Electoral Reform.

Sir J. P. Luke (Reform, *Wellington, North*), speaking on the subject of electoral reform, and in reply to the remark of an hon. Member (Mr. P. Fraser, Labour, *Wellington, Central*) that there was Proportional Representation in Ireland, said: "Yes, for Ulster, as a compromise and an experiment." He added that the position as far as the Government of Great Britain was concerned was that, while there was a strong national sentiment there in favour of a new system of election, they had not come to a conclusion as to the methods to adopt.

Need for Immigration.

Speaking of immigration, Sir J. Luke said if the country was going to shoulder its burden of debt it became an absolute necessity that the population should be largely increased. The time would come when they must go in for a progressive policy of immigration, even if it had to be subsidised by the State, so that they might get an accretion of population.

Anglo-Japanese Alliance.

Mr. G. Mitchell (Independent, *Wellington, South*) said, in reference to the Anglo-Japanese Alliance: "I am of opinion that all our sympathies of race, of language, of tradition, and of colour are with the Americans rather than with the Japanese. I believe that there will yet be formed among the English-speaking peoples of the world an alliance that will be far stronger than any alliance with the Japanese. I believe it is in our interest to have an alliance with the American people, and I do hope that we have not in any way estranged them by the renewal of the Japanese alliance."

On the 5th October,

Mr. Wilford's amendment to the Address was negatived by 38 votes to 20, the Liberal and Labour members voting for the amendment.

Labour "Want of Confidence" motion.

On 6th October,

Mr. Henry Holland (Labour, *Buller*) moved as follows:—

> "That the following amendment by way of addition be made to the Address in Reply to His Excellency the Governor-General's Speech: 'We feel it, however, to be our duty to submit to Your Excellency that Your Excellency's Ministers do not possess the confidence of this House, for the reasons hereinafter given—namely, (1) their failure to bring down a financial policy necessary to the proper maintenance of the public services and the economic progress of the Dominion; (2) their failure to deal with the problem of unemployment on the basis of the right to work or adequate maintenance; (3) their failure to provide adequate housing for the people; (4) their wasteful policy of heavy coal importations instead of local production; and (5) their refusal to furnish information with respect to the cost of imported coal.'"

Unemployment.

Dealing with the question of unemployment, Mr. Holland said the Government told them they had an accumulated surplus of about £24,000,000. It was the duty of the Government to provide work for every man and woman willing to work. If they could not or would not do that, it was their duty to provide adequate maintenance. In speech after speech of Government supporters the predominant note had been the demand for wage reductions. There was no need for wage reductions, and whatever was wrong, was wrong with their system of taxation. He would go further than those who said taxation fell too heavily on people not able to bear it, and would say that it fell too lightly on the very wealthy people who were well able to bear it. The Labour Party would fight to the last ditch against any wage reductions so far as public servants were concerned. If they were to have reductions there was only one logical way to proceed, and that was to start right at the top of the tree with the £5,000-a-year men, and come down to the £500-a-year men, and not go below that.

The Prime Minister (the Right Hon. W. F. Massey): "There are no £5,000-a-year men."

Mr. Holland: "Yes there are. It does not matter to me what position the big-salaried men are in—whether they are on the Civil List or not—if it is necessary to retrench, then if these people are as loyal to this country as they are held to be they will not object to being retrenched heavily."

German "Reparation" coal.

Mr. Holland then proceeded to deal exhaustively with the coal question in New Zealand, saying that while they were importing coal heavily, the Government's publications stated that the coal resources of New Zealand were estimated to be 1,000,000,000 tons, while the "coal probable" was said to be 2,800,000,000 tons. In the year 1921—for the first six months—they had imported something like 490,000 tons. One might pause at that stage, said Mr. Holland, to ask the Government whether any German Reparation coal had come to New Zealand.

The Prime Minister: "Do you mean from Germany?"

Mr. Holland: "I mean the German Reparation coal which France is using to capture the European markets from the British mines."

The Prime Minister: "Then my answer is, No."

Mr. Holland, continuing, said he had a suspicion that some of the coal coming to New Zealand was German Reparation coal. If that was not so, most certainly the Welsh coal being dumped there then was a result of the capture of the European markets by German Reparation coal handled by France. Were they not entitled to ask what was the price of the imported coal? The Government had refused to tell the people what they were paying for it. There were hundreds of unemployed miners throughout New Zealand that day, and there were heaps of imported coal North and South. Meanwhile the shipping monopoly was being allowed to increase the sea freights for coal.

"Go slow" strike admitted.

After dealing with figures relating to the output of coal per man in New Zealand over forty-one years, in the course of which he remarked that in 1919 there was a "go slow" strike in New Zealand, and that "nobody denied it," Mr. Holland proceeded to criticise the conditions under which the miners were housed, and said men were unable to get decent living accommodation. The present method of coal production was wasteful and uneconomical, and that applied to distribution as well. In Wellington at that moment consumers were paying up to £4 per ton, and in some of the suburbs up to £6. The 1918 Government report said that it cost on an average 15s. 4d. to bring coal to the surface. Of that amount 7s. 1d. represented wages. Hon. Members who wanted to make their case against the coal-miner had to show what became of the difference between that sum and the £6 which the consumers paid. In conclusion, he wished to say that no case whatever could be made out against the coal-miner; the case was altogether against the Government, which had made it impossible for coal production to be carried on efficiently and under decent conditions, which failed utterly to provide proper housing accommodation for the miners, and which, having unnecessarily imported coal into the country in huge quantities, refused to give the people any information as to the price they had to pay for the Government's importing policy.

Attack on Immigration Policy.

Mr. F. N. Bartram (**Labour**, *Grey Lynn*) said the Speech as a whole was an attempt to cover up the shortcomings of the Government by ascribing the financial mess in which it found itself to world causes, when the greater part of it could well have been avoided by statesmanlike home administration. There need be no house shortage, no unemployment, and no one lacking the necessities of existence, if the Government were only big enough to shake itself free from the trammels of convention and get out of the groove which vested interests and class prejudice kept it trotting around in.

In conclusion, Mr. Bartram said that the policy of the Government with regard to immigration was, from the working-class standpoint, one of the chief reasons, at any rate, why he had absolutely no faith in them. He contended that it was an absolutely cruel thing to bring people out to that country under false pretences, as they had been brought out. The Labour Party had been charged by the Government with being opposed to immigration. They were not opposed to it. It was ridiculous to say that New Zealand should go on with an immigration scheme simply because Canada and some other countries had stopped it. They had no land policy there (in New Zealand) that was of any use to an immigrant. What was the good of bringing immigrants out to compete with an over-stocked labour market? It was only being done to reduce wages, and the whole of the Government's policy had been in that direction. The Master and Apprentice Act of 1920* was an attempt to flood that country with cheap boy labour. From a labour standpoint they (the Government) had no right to bring a solitary immigrant to those shores while they had insufficient housing accommodation and not enough work for the people who were there already.

Mr. Holland's motion was defeated by 40 votes against nine, the Reform and Liberal Members voting together against it.

The Address was agreed to on the same date.

CONFERENCE OF PRIME MINISTERS OF THE EMPIRE.

(Anglo-Japanese Treaty; Future Conferences; Constitutional Questions; Disarmament Conference; Empire Navy; League of Nations; an "Imperial Parliament"; Samoan Mandate, etc.)

DEBATE IN HOUSE OF REPRESENTATIVES.

On 13th October, 1921, the Prime Minister made his statement on the work of the Conference of Prime Ministers of the Empire.

The Prime Minister (the Right Hon. W. F. Massey) said that Members would understand that much of the work was confidential.

Proceeding, he remarked that there had been some doubt, in all parts of the Empire, prior to the Conference, as to

* *Vide* JOURNAL, Vol. II., No. 1, p. 189.

whether the different countries would be able to work together as sister nations. "Those doubts," said Mr. Massey, "have now been dispelled. The Representatives of the different countries of the Empire came together; they exchanged views, expressed their opinions one to another, arrived at an understanding, and I have no doubt, speaking for myself, that the foundation of a system has been laid which will assist in keeping the countries of the Empire together for many centuries to come."

Objection to written Constitution.

Continuing, Mr. Massey said it was generally admitted that the time had come when the Dominions should cease to be dependencies in the ordinary sense of the term, and become partners, although, perhaps for the time being, junior partners, in the Empire itself. That was the position to-day. There was no written Constitution for the British Empire; there were probably more objections to a written Constitution than in favour of it. Proceeding to give an account of the work of the Conference, Mr. Massey said that no information respecting the business of the Conference and State affairs of the Empire, especially foreign affairs, was kept back from the overseas representatives: "We were treated," he said, "in every way as the equals of the Ministers representing the United Kingdom." Members would recollect the trouble with regard to Silesia when, for a time, the international position looked just about as serious as it was possible to look. "That matter," said Mr. Massey, "was referred to the Imperial Conference, which arrived at a decision, and, for the first time in the history of the British Empire, the Empire was able to speak with one voice and with no uncertain sound." The effect of being able to do so had had a great deal to do with the settlement of the difficulties that had arisen. There were other problems: the difficulty with regard to Egypt, and trouble in Persia and in India; but the progress made with regard to each was in the right direction—progress in the direction of peace, and always peace with honour.

Anglo-Japanese Treaty.

Speaking of the Lord Chancellor's decision that the Anglo-Japanese Treaty had not come to an end, Mr. Massey said he believed that the peace of the world was much more likely to be secured by its continuance than if they had denounced the Treaty and a dissolution of the Alliance had taken place. Japan had been a faithful ally of Britain for twenty years, and had taken part in the Great War—not perhaps a very active part, but she had been willing to do anything that she was requested by Great Britain. He had a certain amount of inside knowledge, and he knew the Japanese were willing to do a great deal more. Japan was always able to make a good bargain for herself; still, she had stood by them and it would have been a very serious thing if she had deserted them and gone over to the enemy. He did not say there was ever any possibility of that; indeed, he did not think it possible in the case of Japan. The dissolution of the Treaty would undoubtedly be a weakening of the power and prestige of the British Empire.

Empire isolation.

Within the last few months many people had expressed the opinion that the time had come for the British Empire to stand alone, to decline to be associated with any other country, either by arrangement or by alliance. He did not agree with that view. There were other countries with which, for geographical reasons, Britain should continue to be associated, and more particularly at the present time, with France and with Belgium.

An alliance with America.

He would express the same opinion with regard to the American nation; he would have no objection, and, he thought, there would be no objection on the part of British statesmen or of the British people, to an alliance with the American people in order to promote the peace of the world. Such an alliance would probably be a great advantage to the American people and to the United Kingdom, Canada, Australia, New Zealand and South Africa. The world wanted a long rest from war; and if they were going to have peace for a lengthened period, that could only come about by a friendly arrangement between the three great naval Powers of the world, Britain, America and Japan.

Conferences in other parts of the Empire.

Mr. Lloyd George had expressed the hope that the Conference might be able to meet not less than once each year. Unless very important changes took place it would be impossible for the Prime Minister of New Zealand or Australia to leave his country for six months of every year. Other things being equal, he would say that the Conference should meet in London all the time. But there were good reasons why it should meet in other centres as well. It was not possible just now; but he believed that in years to come the Imperial Conference would meet periodically in the other centres of the Empire. He would give Canada the honour of furnishing the first of those meeting places. If he had his choice, it would be on the West Coast of Canada, Vancouver or Victoria. The representatives of Australia and New Zealand could reach one of those centres in about fifteen days from New Zealand, and three days longer from Australia. The United Kingdom representatives could reach even the West Coast of Canada in thirteen days quite easily; while the representative of South Africa would take a little longer. They could all get to one of those centres in Canada and take a month for the Conference, away from the somewhat disturbing influences of the London season.

An Hon. Member: "Oh!"

The Prime Minister, continuing, said they could get to Canada from Australia and New Zealand, do their business, and return within three months. At some future time the Conference would come to New Zealand itself. The statesmen at Home were devoted to the affairs of the Empire; but they needed to see the Empire for themselves.

Ireland and the Empire.

Speaking of Ireland, Mr. Massey said they had been informed that, as it was a matter for the Parliament of the United Kingdom, it was not intended to bring the Irish question before the Conference. He did not think any of them were particularly anxious to deal with it, but if it had been submitted, he believed that each and every Member would have done his best to settle the Irish difficulty, and at the same time make certain that the Empire would be kept intact, because that was really the most important point in connection with the trouble.

He thought it was realised that day by all thinking people in every country in the world that the British Empire was the most important factor for peace in the world at the present time, that it was the greatest Empire the world had ever seen.

Egypt and the Suez Canal.

The British Empire did not consist only of the United Kingdom and the Overseas Dominions and India. There were forty-three Crown Colonies, each presided over by a representative of the King, and they had huge populations. He was not quite certain what the Government of Egypt would be in the future; but whatever might happen, the British Empire could not give up control of Egypt. They spoke of the Suez Canal as theirs, but the country through which it passed was only held on lease, and some day or other the former owners would raise a claim to it. It would be absurd to think that that gateway of the Empire could pass into hands that might become enemy hands at any time.

They did not want to do any injustice to the former owners: they must abide by straight dealing with them and pay compensation, if necessary; but that gateway could not be given up. They who were entrusted with the affairs of the Empire must see that the confidence of the native races in the Empire and in its government would never be interfered with, would never be lessened. If those native races were left to shift for themselves they would be at the mercy, perhaps, of some of the stronger native races, and certainly at the mercy of some of the stronger countries. It would assuredly lead to chaos. It would be disaster not only for each country but for the whole Empire, disaster for the world.

Dominions' voice in Foreign Affairs.

Another very important phase of the Conference was that it was the first time that representatives of the Dominions had had a voice in the management of foreign affairs of the Empire. They were partners, and that was the important part.

"Cabinet" or "Conference."

When the Cabinet met—perhaps he should not use the word "Cabinet" in that connection but Mr. Lloyd George, when reporting to the House of Commons, used the word "Cabinet" five times, just as he (Mr. Massey) had used it at that moment; personally, while he had his mind made up, he did not trouble very much about the name. A Conference met, discussed certain proposals or very important subjects, arrived at a conclusion, and there stopped; it could not go any further.

Whatever decisions had been arrived at in the past had been left to the Government of the United Kingdom to give effect to through the only channel by consulting the King, and making a recommendation to him. There was no other way. "When you get to that stage," said Mr. Massey, "and the Ministers who are assembled together in Conference or in Cabinet—just as you choose to call it—have their minds made up that they are in a position to make a recommendation to the Sovereign and are qualified to do so, then, I say, they are to all intents and purposes a Cabinet. We are all partners and I, for one, believe that it is right and proper that we should be partners. But I was not thinking particularly of that; I was thinking that if we stopped short of sending a recommendation to the Sovereign our position would be weaker and much more easily broken than would be the case if we took up the position of a Cabinet. In the end the point was practically conceded." Upon Mr. Massey quoting the opinion expressed by Mr. Lloyd George to the effect that so long as the Dominions were represented at the Conference they carried the weight of a Cabinet,

Mr. R. McCallum (Liberal, *Wairau*): "Where does it bind this Parliament?"

The Prime Minister: "This Parliament is not bound. I am quite willing to deal with that point. It does not bind this Parliament in the slightest. . . . What has happened leaves us in the position we occupied before. . . . We manage our own affairs . . . our autonomy is not interfered with in the very slightest, and everything of importance has to go before the Parliaments of the different countries."

Mr. McCallum: "Then where is the partnership?"

The Prime Minister: "The partnership is with regard to the foreign affairs of the Empire, and particularly with regard to the defence of the Empire."

Mr. McCallum: "But you say we are not bound."

The Prime Minister: "Yes, I say so, except in honour and principle, and remembering always that we are subjects of the King. Do you remember what Burke . . . said . . . about the Empire? He said, 'If the Empire is to keep together it must be by bonds light as air but stronger than iron.'"

Mr. McCallum: "I am with you there."

The Prime Minister, continuing, said they ought to do everything they could to encourage patriotism, especially on the part of the rising generation in the different countries. It was not well to attempt too much by way of constitutional changes. They should probably fail, and perhaps do a great deal more harm than good. "I think," he said, "we have gone as far as at present it is safe to go."

Speaking of the King's constitutional position in relation to the Empire, Mr. Massey said that while the King consulted with his Ministers on every possible opportunity and discussed with them each proposal from the Empire point of view, or from the point of view of the United Kingdom, and adhered strictly to constitutional methods, the effect was that the government of the British Empire was that day the most democratic government in the world.

Dominion independence.

About the time they met there were some peculiar ideas as to what might possibly take place as a result of the Dominions and India having signed the Covenant of the League of Nations. He thought most of those ideas had since been got rid of; but there was no question about it; the opinion was held in many quarters that the different Dominions of the Empire had become independent. Those people seemed to have forgotten that they were subjects of the King and citizens of the Empire.

Standing out of a war.

Whatever changes had taken place, they were still subjects of the King. If the King went to war on the advice of his Ministers, every one of his subjects was at war. It was quite true that a section of the community might say, "We are not going to war. We are not going to risk our lives or lose our lives for the King or the Empire. We are going to stand out." "By so doing," said Mr. Massey, "such people would earn the contempt of every one of their fellow-citizens, and of the citizens of every civilised nation, and of the belligerents as well." Did anyone imagine, he continued, that, supposing the Empire were at war, and some or one of the Dominions stood out, the belligerent nation would take any notice of that? The enemy would sink their ships just as he would those of other countries of the Empire; and in the event of being successful he would see that they paid a part of the indemnity, and their territory, or a part of it, might be taken possession of. As to the idea that a Dominion could do what it liked—it could do nothing of the sort.

The King and Dominion Recommendations; "Prime Minister of the Empire."

Another idea had become prevalent, that the Government of any Dominion, although part of the Empire, might approach of its own volition the Sovereign with a recommendation. "Imagine," said Mr. Massey, "half-a-dozen representatives, of half-a-dozen Dominions, making recommendations to the King, perhaps on the same business. They could not possibly agree, they would probably be antagonistic to each other, and the result would be chaos, perhaps worse. The Sovereign can only be approached through the Government of the United Kingdom along with the representatives of the different Dominions and India. In each case, the British Prime Minister speaks for the Dominions. In effect to-day, the Right Hon. David Lloyd George is not only Prime Minister of the United Kingdom, but he is also Prime Minister of the Empire. That is the position we have got into."

Approaching the King.

In answer to an interjection by Mr. McCallum, Mr. Massey said that the Prime Minister of New Zealand could not approach the King with any recommendation. His Majesty would receive any such communication very courteously, no doubt, but would, if he had anything to say, communicate it to the Prime Minister of Great Britain as *de facto* Prime Minister of the Empire. "I believe," said Mr. Massey, "that amendments may be necessary, and interpretations may be placed on record by which the new arrangement will work out satisfactorily."

Dominion Ambassadors.

It had been suggested that each Dominion might appoint an Ambassador to a foreign country. It could not do anything of the sort: that was the prerogative of the King.

Mr. D. G. Sullivan (Labour, *Avon*): "What happened in regard to Canada?"

The Prime Minister replied that Canada did not appoint an Ambassador to the United States. Canada might have a representative at the British Embassy in the United States, though he did not think one had been appointed yet. He would probably be more like a Trade Representative than anything else. And so it was with treaties; no Dominion could make a treaty with a foreign Power, unless it were a commercial treaty.

Question of Dominions' loyalty.

After dealing with Germany's War debt and the financial position as between the Allied Nations, in the course of which he said he had often wondered why some serious attempt had not been made, possibly it had been made, to induce America to take over the debt owing by France and Italy to Britain in lieu of the debt which Britain owed to America, Mr. Massey said he would like to quote part of an Address presented to the King prior to the end of the Conference. There were actually some doubts, he said, as to the loyalty of the Dominions to the Empire, and to its Sovereign.

An Hon. Member: "Where? At the Conference?"

The Prime Minister: "Not at the Conference; that is quite another story."

Conspiracy against the Empire.

Those doubts, continued Mr. Massey, were raised, and very often expressed, in the Press. When he was in London it was stated openly over and over again (he had seen it in print) that one morning paper was receiving Russian gold in order to support the propaganda of the Bolsheviks. He believed that there was a world-wide conspiracy in existence to break up the British Empire; and it was their duty to put down disloyalty wherever they found it. After quoting at length from the Address to the King, Mr. Massey said: "There is a complete answer to any suggestion that any one of the nations of the Empire, through its representative, will contemplate in any way whatever anything in the shape of disloyalty."

Mr. McCallum: "Or severing the silken thread."

The Prime Minister: "Exactly; or severing the silken thread. . . ."

The Disarmament Conference.

Speaking of the Disarmament Conference, Mr. Massey said he wished it well, but he knew of some of the difficulties, and he could not help thinking that it had not been managed well up to that date. Had it been so, they should have had that preliminary consultation, about which the members of the Imperial Conference were unanimous, not to arrive at any definite decision—that would have been left to the great Conference itself—but in order to have been able to put the position from the point of view of the people of Australia and New Zealand. In years to come the Pacific might be the storm-centre of the world, and it was quite possible that there were no countries so interested in the Conference as those to which they belonged.

An Hon. Member : " Or so little able to resist."

The Prime Minister : " Well, there are some things that are better not discussed in public. I am not going to be one to strike anything in the nature of a discordant note."

Dealing with the question of the reduction that had taken place in the *personnel* of the British Navy and in naval shipbuilding, whilst America and Japan continued, Mr. Massey said that if that building went on, instead of the British Navy being supreme, Britain would have been the third naval Power in the world. He wished Members to think of the position if they allowed any Power in the world to be strong enough in time of war to cut the communications between the different parts of the Empire. It could not exist except by sea-power.

Mr. G. Witty (Liberal, ***Riccarton*****)** : " The other two would not combine, though—America and Japan."

The Prime Minister : " I think not, but it is not well to take risks. I do not say that they would, I express no opinion ; but I do say that the risk was too great to take."

An Empire Navy.

Continuing Mr. Massey said he wanted peace, but as a citizen of one of those countries in the South Pacific, " I could not approve," he declared, " of the state of affairs that was going on at the time we met in London. Of course I was only one, but in the end we were all of one opinion. We decided to back up what had been suggested in the House of Commons—that four battleships of the modern type should be laid down . . . there was no difference of opinion in the Conference with regard to the necessity for maintaining the supremacy of the British Navy."

Mr. A. S. Malcolm (Reform, ***Clutha*****)** : " In what way did the Conference back up the House of Commons ? "

The Prime Minister: "By a resolution; and on the understanding that the ships should be Empire ships." Continuing, Mr. Massey said that Mr. Lloyd George told them that the United Kingdom could not go on bearing the cost of the Navy as she had done prior to the War, and that she must have help from the overseas Dominions; "and," said Mr. Massey, "we agreed."

Mr. Malcolm: "They agreed to accept their share of the liability?"

The Prime Minister: "Yes, the shares will be agreed to at the next Conference. . . ." In each case, he said, the question would be submitted to the Parliaments of the Dominions concerned. The rights of the overseas Dominions had been safeguarded.

The suggestion had been made at the Conference that the cost of the ships should be made a first charge on the German Reparations Fund. He did not say that was agreed to; but he thought it ought to be borne in mind, and especially by them.

After quoting the Resolution of the Conference relating to co-operation in regard to naval defence, Mr. Massey said that he thought that the increase in the size of warships had done away with the local navy idea. Canada and Australia would soon have to consider whether they would continue to maintain a local navy or join in the keeping up of a navy for the whole Empire. Of course that would not prevent Australia or New Zealand from keeping a few light cruisers on their coasts for protection of their commerce.

China.

One of the most difficult and most serious questions the coming Conference would have to decide was in regard to China. He doubted whether any satisfactory arrangement could be made; but something would have to be done. He was not sure that justice had been done to China in past years and it should be their duty and the duty of America, and of Japan for that matter, to see that every justice was done to China, for at present she was in a very bad position.

Cost of League of Nations.

Very brief reference, said Mr. Massey, had been made at the Conference to the League of Nations; but it was felt that the League of Nations was yet on its trial, and that it should be given time to prove whether it could be useful, or until some better arrangement could take its place.

Mr. T. M. Wilford (Leader of the Opposition): "Could there be an alliance between nations already in the League?"

The Prime Minister: "That is rather a difficult question to answer, but I do not know why there should not. . . . I ask the hon. gentleman to take up the Treaty of Peace and see there the names of nations in the League. I ask him how many of them he would trust in case of trouble. . . ." Continuing, he said reference had been made to the cost of administration of the League. The amount that they had been expected to pay would have been an impossible sum for the Dominion. He would suggest to Parliament that they should not go on paying any unreasonable sum. The amount that they might be called upon to pay after that would be very much smaller than was intended at first. He had been told that the amount paid to some of those associated with the League was very large. If it continued, it would smash the League. He did not want to make trouble and was willing to advise Parliament to go on for another year when perhaps they should be able to get some different recommendation from the British Government.

The New Hebrides.

After referring to the apportionment of Reparation payments amongst the various units of the British Empire, Mr. Massey dealt with the position of the New Hebrides. The Condominium was utterly unsatisfactory. The French Government were opposed to parting with any of those islands.

Australia the senior partner in Pacific.

Mr. G. Witty: "Could not an exchange be made?"

The Prime Minister: "That has been tried. Australia comes first; she is the senior partner in the South Pacific. Australia is given control of the New Hebrides and it is for Australia to speak first. . . . I am bound to say," continued Mr. Massey, "that Mr. Hughes and myself worked together very well on the whole. Wherever the interests of Australia and New Zealand were concerned we were found working in sympathy."

Foreign Office Despatches.

It was intended to provide copies of Foreign Office despatches to every Prime Minister of the Empire, Mr. Massey said; and he thought it would mean that a responsible man would have to be appointed whose duty it would be to look after them. The Prime Minister would be expected to express an opinion on important matters dealt with and would thus become acquainted with everything going on at the heart of the Empire.

Imperial Preference.

New Zealand had gone a long way in the direction of Imperial Preference, but they would have to do a great deal more. If he could do anything to bring free trade between the different countries of the Empire a little nearer he would be only too happy to do it. If Parliament would assist him he was willing to go further than they had ever gone in providing Preference for their fellow-citizens in any part of the world.

Mr. A. Harris (Reform, *Waitemata*)**:** " Britain must reciprocate."

The Prime Minister : " Britain does not charge a farthing duty on anything we send to it. . . ."

The Minister of External Affairs (Hon. E. P. Lee) : " The hon. Member means the Empire."

The Prime Minister : " That is another story, and I quite agree."

Mr. Harris : " We impose an extra duty against foreign nations, which Britain does not."

The Prime Minister replied that anything that Britain had done did not affect New Zealand, as their (New Zealand's) products were mostly food products, which the population of Great Britain would not tax.

Mr. Massey concluded his speech at 9.30 p.m., having spoken for two hours.

On October 18th.

The Prime Minister, having brought down the Report of the Proceedings of the Conference of Prime Ministers, and having moved that the same be laid upon the table, and be printed, stated in reply to Mr. T. K. Sidey (Liberal, *Dunedin South*) that he was prepared to agree to extend the time for speeches to one hour. " I want this matter discussed very fully," he said, "and I do not want to limit speeches at all."

Mr. Wilford : " It is not a question of Party."

Features of the Conference.

Mr. Wilford then addressed the House. He said it was refreshing to find a subject upon which he hoped all Parties could agree and one that could be looked at from different angles free from Party. That should be the case on Empire matters. It was impossible for anyone then to foretell the actual advantages to be reaped from the Conference, " but," he said, " the most noteworthy feature of the Imperial Conference, and one which seems to me to be pregnant with possibilities, is that the Imperial Conference made possible the Disarmament Conference." When they came to consider the vastness of the proposal, and that the Conference was not so much for the purpose of reducing armament as for producing a policy of disarmament, they must feel that the Imperial Conference had at least warranted its existence.

The next point he would make was that its deliberations had resulted in absolute unanimity that the Anglo-Japanese relations must be brought into consonance with the League of Nations. It meant that the military clause must be eliminated from the Anglo-Japanese Alliance.

The next point upon which he wished to congratulate the Imperial Conference was that it created an atmosphere favourable towards the settlement of the Irish question; and enabled all the statesmen of the Dominion to arrive at a full comprehension of the principle underlying the British and foreign policy, and the effect which the application of such a principle produced upon the international situation.

The question was whether or not an annual meeting was sufficient to enable them to keep in touch with the foreign policy of the Empire, or whether the time would not arrive when some representative of New Zealand should be regularly stationed in Great Britain merely for the purpose of being able to be in touch personally with those who controlled foreign policy.

Anglo-Japanese Treaty.

He would shortly review what their position was under the Anglo-Japanese Treaty, and then deal with how Japan and Great Britain looked at the Alliance, and how America, China, and the various Dominions had looked at the Treaty. Australia, through Mr. Hughes, agreed to the renewal "in some modified form." The interests of Australia and Canada were not quite identical with those of Africa and Canada.

In Article 2 of the Anglo-Japanese Treaty of 1911 they undertook, by their signature, that if Japan was involved in war in defence of "territorial rights" or "special interests," Great Britain must come to the assistance of its ally.

The Prime Minister: "There is a qualifying clause."

Mr. Wilford: "I know there is a qualifying clause, and I want to refer to it, because it does not answer the point. . . ."

Mr. Wilford then proceeded to say that Clause 4 (the qualifying clause) guaranteed neutrality if there were a war between the United States and Japan, provided the United States entered into a treaty of general arbitration; but in 1912 that question was turned down by Congress, and thereupon Clause 4 had no application in protecting Great Britain from fulfilling its obligations under the Treaty; so that if Japan to-morrow had an unprovoked attack on the part of any Power, in defence of its territorial rights or special interests, they (the British Empire) would have to do whatever was asked of them. They knew the maintenance of the Treaty was the fundamental basis of Japan's foreign policy.

Attitude of China.

How did China look upon that Alliance? If the representatives of Great Britain did not consider the possibility of China linking with America and Japan they would be very unwise indeed. America had laid itself out to obtain the confidence of China. Again, Japan had so increased her powers in China that American prestige had become reduced, and that was one of the things that was hitting the Americans hard. If the Disarmament Conference brought about an alliance between Japan, China, America and Great Britain, the peace of the world was assured.

Contribution to the Navy.

The Prime Minister had said that New Zealand's contribution to the Imperial Navy should be a first charge on their claims under the Reparations. He (Mr. Wilford) would suggest that they should give something solid, that they should give the British Government back the *Chatham*, and let them have as their contribution to the Navy the cash it cost to run the *Chatham* as an earnest of what they must pay. He had always been against the local-navy idea. "If Japan fought us," said Mr. Wilford, "and I do not think that possible, she would have America on her flank; and if America fought us she would have Japan on her flank; and both would have Great Britain."

League of Nations.

Continuing, Mr. Wilford said he was a believer in the League of Nations, for it spelt arbitration as against war..

Reparation Moneys.

Finally, Mr. Wilford said he hoped the Reparation moneys would be paid, but he had his doubts. He would ask the Government not to depend upon them; and to shape their course financially without regard to them at all; and if it turned out that the money did actually come in the end, well, let them look on it as "something from home."

"The Veil of Secrecy."

Mr. H. Holland (Labour, *Buller*) said the one thing noticeable in the discussion was that the House practically knew nothing about what had taken place at the Conference; and he could not find that they had been told anything except that they were practically pledged to a share in financing the Imperial Fleet. The Prime Minister's statement left them almost completely in the dark. If there was one thing more than another it was the veil of secrecy which seemed to have been drawn over all the proceedings of the Imperial Conference.

Anglo-Japanese Alliance.

As late as 30th June, Mr. Lloyd George had been questioned and had refused to give an assurance that the House of Commons would have an opportunity of discussing the renewal of the Anglo-Japanese Alliance. On the 1st July the cables again told them :—

> The Conference is now in the midst of the Japanese problems, which are shrouded with as much secrecy as the foreign debate.

Not only were the proceedings conducted with the utmost secrecy, but when great public meetings were being held to protest against a renewal of the Treaty, no news of those meetings was allowed to filter through to that Dominion. It was not until the Lord Chancellor had suddenly reversed the decision of the Crown Law Officers, and announced that the Note of July, 1920, sent to the League of Nations by both parties to the Alliance did not constitute a denunciation, that the Imperial Conference itself realised the true position. The Prime Ministers of the Dominions seemed to have discussed the Alliance without being aware of what the position was, " and," said Mr. Holland, " they seem, so far as we have been permitted to read of what took place, to have reached at one stage the verge of a deadlock, and were reported to have solemnly discussed a proposal to extend the Treaty for three months to enable the Australian, New Zealand and Canadian Premiers to return home and consult with their colleagues and, if necessary, obtain a referendum vote from their own people upholding or rejecting the proposal which was to be settled by the Imperial Conference."

The Prime M.nister : " Who said that ? "

Mr. Holland : " I say that is what we gathered from such of the reports as were permitted to filter through."

The Prime Minister : " Absolute nonsense."

Mr. Holland replied that what was clear that day was that if either the Prime Minister of the Dominion, or of Australia, or Canada, were to submit the question of the renewal of the present Anglo-Japanese Alliance to the people it would be defeated by an overwhelming majority. Continuing, Mr. Holland said the great Labour Conferences of Australia and the political Labour Conference had both unanimously resolved against the renewal. It was because it was a War Treaty that the working-people generally were opposed to it.

Japan's Policy of Militant Capitalism.

Mr. Holland, after dealing at length with the economic and historic foundations of the present Alliance between Great Britain and Japan, said that the hon. Member for Hutt was not quite correct in saying that there was no general arbitration treaty of peace between America and England. The American Senate had refused to ratify a treaty in 1912, but a general Peace Treaty of Arbitration had been ratified between America and England in 1914. England had notified Japan that she regarded that document as an arbitration treaty under the terms of the Anglo-Japanese Treaty; still, the arrangement did not provide for any final settlement of a dispute which might arise between England and America. It provided for an arbitration tribunal to be set up which should investigate any dispute, and report to the countries concerned; but, when it had reported, the countries were to be free to do what they liked. What was clear was that the Japanese policy was a widening and aggressive policy of militant capitalism. Japan controlled not only the iron and coal of China, but she controlled most of the railway system of Northern China, and was operating it with the aid of British capital. During the War Japan, with the aid of Britain, had forced China to grant her a ninety-nine years' lease in connection with the South Manchurian Railway. American capitalists saw a mighty yellow capitalist civilisation growing up in the East to challenge the operations of Western capitalism.

Continuing, Mr. Holland said he wished to draw the attention of the House to the position with regard to Shantung. While Britain had stood pledged to maintain the integrity and independence of the Chinese Empire, her diplomats had secretly pledged her to the dismemberment of it, to handing over thirty-eight millions of people to be dominated by a foreign Power. That fact constituted a solid reason why all the proceedings of the Imperial Conference should be in the open and in full view of the public. Mr. Hughes, speaking in the Australian House of Representatives on 7th April last—after having backed and filled considerably on the question—said Mr. Holland, had told the House he was in favour of a renewal of the Anglo-Japanese Alliance; but he had also made it clear that Japan would not honour any agreement that she might make with the British Empire unless their navy was sufficiently strong to compel her. That was an extraordinary statement to come from a man in a public position claiming to speak for a whole continent, and to be in favour of making an alliance with a certain other nation, while declaring that such treaty, if made, would not be worth the paper it was written on unless they (Great Britain) had a navy sufficiently strong to compel observance of that treaty.

It was quite clear that America was Japan's potential enemy that day, and anyone knowing the history of the Anglo-Japanese Alliance and the terms of the Anglo-American Peace Treaty would know that it was quite possible for England to be drawn into a war against America on the side of Japan, and if that happened it would bring disaster to the whole human race. But supposing that such a thing could not happen, it could still happen that England could be involved in a war to uphold Japan's right to keep her grip on the people of Eastern Siberia, into a war against France, against China, against Soviet Russia. Obviously the correct attitude for the Conference to have taken up would have been to notify Japan that since both contracting parties recognised that the Treaty was a violation of the League of Nations, and therefore *ultra vires*, Britain could no longer be a party to that international illegality.

Mr. Malcolm said they had for the first time in the history of that Parliament the opportunity to discuss the doings at the Imperial Conference. His fear was that that great Empire of theirs was not at present based on sure foundations. The amity between the Mother-country and the Dominions was so wonderful that it clouded their minds to the real danger of allowing the position to go on just as it was. It must be a question of real partnership, not of any make-believe, if the family was to be kept together. Britain was not going to force any form of Imperial Government upon them, not even going to suggest it. He was confident that if the Dominions did ask that they might be admitted to a full responsibility and a full share of the government of the Empire, they would not be denied it.

Canada's "Ambassador" to the U.S.A.

During the Prime Minister's speech a Member had asked a question as to Canada's probable appointment of an Ambassador to the United States; and the Prime Minister had stated that that Ambassador would be subordinated to the British Ambassador.

The Prime Minister: "He would not be an Ambassador at all."

Mr. Malcolm: "Well, now, that is not borne out by what I have read. The Canadian Prime Minister is not of that opinion."

The Prime Minister: "I do not know anything about that."

Mr. Malcolm, continuing, said the late Prime Minister of Canada (Sir Robert Borden) asserted and insisted that the Canadian Ambassador appointed by the Canadian people, with the approval of the King, not of the British Prime

Minister, would not be subordinate to the British Ambassador, but would be responsible wholly to the Canadian Parliament.

The Prime Minister: "You miss the point. The King can only give consent to anything of the sort, and the Ambassador's Ministers know it would not be constitutional to do it."

The King and the Dominions: "Empire's Prime Minister."

Mr. Malcolm, in answer to the Prime Minister's interjection, said that brought him to the second point, as to the difference of opinion between the Prime Ministers on the constitutional question. Their Prime Minister said, and he (Mr. Malcolm) agreed with his sentiment, that New Zealand had no power to approach the King directly, but they had in the Canadian Parliament an assertion by Sir Robert Borden, in regard to access to the King: "The King, in each Dominion, acts only upon the advice of his Ministers for that Dominion."

The Prime Minister: "I do not think that is quite correct."

Mr. Malcolm: ". . . I say that a situation in which the constitutional position is so badly understood and in which there are such emphatic differences is a situation that is bound sooner or later to cause endless trouble. Some day that difference would become material. . . ."

The Prime Minister: "Do you not see that the Prime Minister of Canada goes to the Governor-General, the representative of the King?"

Mr. Malcolm: "It does not matter how he goes to the King. The question is that as Prime Minister he has access to the King, not through the British Government. . . . The debate in the Canadian Parliament shows that they recognise that they are going very much further than that: they insist that the King is King of Canada as well as King of Great Britain, and that they have a right to approach him as King of Canada, in the same way as Mr. Lloyd George has the right to approach the King as King of Great Britain; and General Smuts is of the same opinion, because in 1919 he said:—

As a result of the Conference in Paris, the Dominions in future would, in regard to foreign affairs, deal through their own representatives."

Going to War.

Continuing, Mr. Malcolm said that since his return the Prime Minister had been replying to the doubts urged by some, whether all the Dominions would be compelled to join in any war made by Great Britain; and in answer to that the right hon. gentleman had said that when the King was at war all his subjects were at war. That did not seem to advance them very much further, because the question at once was : On whose advice does the King go to war ? Of course the Prime Minister later on had said "He goes to war on the advice at present of Mr. Lloyd George, the Prime Minister of Great Britain." But the question was one of fact also : were all the subjects of the King at war when the King was at war ? It had not been always the case. The Georges were Kings of Great Britain and Kings of Hanover.

The Prime Minister : " It is the same King."

Mr. Malcolm : " The King is the King of Great Britain . . . and of the Dominions ; and in recent years it has been urged that the Dominions are independent nations."

The Prime Minister : " Not now. I do not think I would follow that up."

Mr. Malcolm said that in so far as that was concerned he would take the Prime Minister's advice. Continuing, he said he thought there was a danger of over-stressing the King's position. There might come to the Throne a man of strong will, strong character, and immense ability. Such a man might easily have, as King George III. had, Ministers of inability—weak men. When the King found that the Dominions had been inviting him to take a more pronounced part in the affairs of the Empire than he had hitherto been allowed to take, was there not a danger, happily not now but in the future, of that King asserting himself in a way that would be to the injury of the Empire as a whole ?

The Prime Minister : " I explained the other night that that is not possible."

Mr. Malcolm, continuing, said that he entirely agreed with their Prime Minister when he said that Mr. Lloyd George was at present Prime Minister of the British Empire, but with limitations.

The Prime Minister : " In effect."

Mr. Malcolm : " Quite right ; in effect. . . ." But, he said, it was not satisfactory to them to leave the guidance of affairs, well satisfied though they might be with their treatment, entirely to the Prime Minister of Great Britain. Even at present he had not the power that any Governor of the British Empire should have : he had the power to decree, but not to enforce.

The Prime Minister : " Nobody ever claimed that he had."

Mr. Malcolm : " Yet the Prime Minister declared that Mr. Lloyd George was the Prime Minister of the Empire."

The Prime Minister : " In effect."

Mr. Malcolm : " As far as enforcement is concerned, not even in effect, as I shall proceed to show. He can decree, but he cannot enforce. He can declare war for the Empire."

The Prime Minister: "Who can?"

Mr. Malcolm: "The Prime Minister and the Cabinet."

The Prime Minister: "After consultation, and on recommendation to the King."

Mr. Malcolm: "Of course, but it goes through the Prime Minister of the United Kingdom. . . ."

Proceeding, Mr. Malcolm said that the Prime Minister of Great Britain could make war for the Empire, but he could not wage it for the Empire. The Cabinet of Great Britain did make war for them—for the Empire—in 1914. Every part of the Empire was committed to war. But neither Canada, nor New Zealand, nor South Africa could be committed by the British Cabinet to send a single man to the war, or to undertake a shilling's worth of expense. In that way the Government lacked force, lacked strength. There was no individual or body in the Empire which could with authority make a call on the Forces of the whole Empire.

Naval Defence: "sponging" on Great Britain.

Then the Prime Minister told them in regard to naval defence that the Conference decided to back up the proposal of the House of Commons that the building of warships should be commenced. He (Mr. Malcolm) had asked for details—in particular whether the Conference had decided to accept the liability. Mr. Massey had said "Yes," but had later qualified the affirmation by saying that the Dominions would have to be consulted through their Parliaments. But here was the difficulty, that in every Dominion—with one exception, New Zealand—every Parliament urged upon the Prime Ministers that they must not commit their Dominions to anything at the Conference.

The Prime Minister: "Not by resolution; individual Members here and there."

Mr. Malcolm: "And the Prime Ministers accepted that position, and they did so in set terms. They gave positive assurances that the Dominions would not be committed. . . ." And here, Mr. Malcolm said, he would like to ask the Prime Minister a direct question: "Does he wish the Dominions to continue sponging on Great Britain in respect to naval defence?"

The Prime Minister: "I think that is not a proper way of putting it. It is perfectly clear that New Zealand will pay its share. There is no 'sponging' about it."

Imperial Taxation.

Mr. Malcolm said they had not contributed as they ought to have done. But if they had no wish to sponge further on the Mother-country, where came in the objection to taxation under an Imperial Parliament? Surely if they were willing to pay at all it would be better to pay with representative men sitting as their representatives in an Imperial Parliament, after a face-to-face discussion with representatives from other parts of the Empire, than in a round-about way after intricate negotiations here, there and everywhere.

The question of finance—the supposed objection of the Dominions to submit to taxation by a Federal Parliament, which he hoped he had shown was a mere bogey, because in any event that Dominion was willing to pay, brought up the question of the Executive.

The Prime Minister had come back recognising it was simply impossible for the Imperial Conference to sit at regular and frequent intervals. He was confident that their people would not tolerate that much longer. How could a body that met every two or four years call itself an Executive? All the same, until they got a better system and Constitution, by all means carry on the Conference: he would rather see an annual conference than the present biennial or triennial Conference.

Usurpation of power at Conferences.

After stating that no New-Zealander need be afraid that the Imperial Parliament would ever threaten their autonomy, Mr. Malcolm said that, without their knowing it almost, and, he believed without the Prime Ministers meaning it, a certain usurpation of power had grown up in connection with the Conferences. It was being cloaked under the King, largely. Without any constitutional standing at all, the Prime Ministers of the Dominions, acting upon the invitation of the Prime Minister of Great Britain, had met in London without authority from their Parliaments. They had gone Home and had acquired certain powers which, he believed, amounted to usurpation. They should be just as careful that they did not surrender their rights and privileges to their Prime Ministers as they had been that they did not surrender them to any King. Invitations to those Conferences should be addressed by the King, acting on the advice of the British Prime Minister, to the Parliaments of the Empire, and the Parliaments should appoint representatives, clothed with authority by resolution, to go to such Conferences. That procedure, at any rate, would protect them from the danger of usurpation.

Mr. Hughes on constitutional relations.

After the last Conference, Mr. Hughes, Prime Minister of Australia, had been reported to have said something to the effect: "Thank Heaven, they had prevented a Conference in regard to constitutional relations being summoned." Had they not a right to be indignant over such language as that, affecting the very existence of the Empire? That the Empire should, without its Parliaments being consulted, be prevented from attempting to frame a Constitution that might save it! Had they no right to be consulted? At those Conferences, as far as he could recognise, continued Mr. Malcolm, one of the difficulties was that nothing could be done unless there was unanimity. They could never govern an Empire, or anything else, on unanimity. If one single Dominion stood out, that apparently meant that the proposition under consideration must be abandoned.

The Prime Minister: "No."

Mr. Malcolm said he had seen in the reports where certain resolutions had been withdrawn owing to the fact that unanimity could not be obtained.

The Prime Minister: "Not at the recent Conferences."

Mr. Malcolm, continuing, said that if they had an Imperial Federation, the first Cabinet would consist of the Empire Prime Ministers. Then they would be in a position really to rule. They would not go Home as guests, to be advised on foreign affairs as a favour. Owing to the fashion of laying emphasis on autonomy, it might be more difficult to secure Imperial Federation that day than it was, say, twenty years ago, but it could still be done, and he hoped it would be; and he hoped the country and Parliament, and more particularly their Prime Minister, would lend themselves to securing for the Empire such a Constitution as would enable it to stand against the storms that were sure to beat against it.

A Liberal view.

Mr. H. Atmore (Liberal, *Nelson*) said he did not think Mr. Malcolm was representing the opinion of the majority of the people of New Zealand when he pleaded for a formal Constitution of the British Empire. If formalism had sway it would be an expression of the voice of the majority, and the minority would be always big enough to cause trouble and disaster. It was because there was no formal bond, no compulsion in any part, because they might leave it to-morrow if they so chose, because they were absolutely free to work out their own destiny, that they were securely united.

He agreed with Mr. Malcolm that in the past they had sponged on the British nation. Not so many years since they had been paying 1s. 10d. per head for the upkeep of the Navy that made them safe there, whilst in Great Britain the expenditure was £1 per head.

When they criticised the policy of Japan, as the Member for Buller had done, and denounced the Japanese Treaty, it was time to put in a word for the Japanese, who had proved themselves not disloyal to the white race. So long as they retained the right to say who should come within their gates it did not matter what alliances they concluded, so long as they retained their self-respect as a nation, and so long as the objective was to prevent war.

Speaking on the subject of immigration, and of those who took the narrow view that they must keep New Zealand against all comers, Mr. Atmore said the burden of the War on Britain was much greater relatively than in the Dominion, and how could they turn their backs upon a country whence their mothers and fathers came by saying they could not absorb them? Their population was only 1,200,000, and why should any man feel that an incomer might take his job when New Zealand could, with ease and with increased wealth and comfort to all, carry a population of ten million, perhaps twenty million. For their defence they had been long enough a burden on the people of Britain. "Let us tell them frankly and openly," said Mr. Atmore, "that we will not 'sponge' on them any longer, and that we are eager and anxious to carry our share of Empire burdens. . . . We must stand by the British Navy and pay our proportionate share, because it is to all intents and purposes a partnership Navy."

So far as anything Imperialistic was concerned, Mr. Atmore said, he was quite satisfied that there had never been a more Imperialistic House, or a House that was more imbued with desires to live up to the best traditions of the Empire, than the present Parliament of New Zealand.

Partners of equal status.

The Minister of Education (Hon. C. J. Parr) said he disagreed with the Member for Clutha (Mr. Malcolm) when he said the Prime Minister went as a guest to the Conference. The Prime Minister went as a partner to a partnership board meeting; a board meeting summoned, if they would, by the senior partner, to a meeting of the other partners equal in status and authority with the senior partner. The Prime Minister went as a matter of right, and not as a guest. For the first time in the history of the Empire it had been recognised by that Conference that the Dominions should have an effective say in all matters of foreign policy, in all matters which touched the Empire, and that the Dominions had a right, which would never be alienated, to say whether there should be peace or war. And it had been done in that marvellously easy and informal manner which was characteristic of the evolution and growth of the Empire. No written contract was necessary to establish those rights; they had grown, they had come to them without asking, created by the free will of the Home country. He would emphasise it that the events of the last few years had proved incontestably that a written Constitution was unnecessary for the proper government and evolution of the Empire.

Imperial Federation: Future Conferences.

He entirely disagreed with the hon. Member for Clutha, notwithstanding his extremely interesting speech, that it was necessary for the preservation of the Empire that they should have an Imperial Federation and an Imperial Parliament. Lord Milner, in 1916, in giving an address to forty Dominion Parliamentarians, had spoken about a written Constitution and the necessity for an Imperial Parliament. But after he had listened to the views of Delegates from South Africa, Canada, Australia and New Zealand, Lord Milner had modified his opinions and had admitted that the practical difficulties made the proposition one quite out of the question for the time being. To-day he (Mr. Parr) ventured the opinion that it was completely out of the realm of practical politics. He did not think they sufficiently appreciated the opinion of other parts of the Empire. New Zealand was peculiarly loyal, peculiarly Imperialistic. Those feelings were not so strong with other parts of the Empire. South Africa and Canada did not want a written Constitution, nor an Imperial Parliament; they were content with things as they were, and he thought it was well to leave well alone. He could see no evidence at Home of any great desire for an Imperial Parliament; and he very much doubted whether there was any opinion in New Zealand tending in that direction.

Mr. Malcolm: "Then you do not know. I addressed public meetings right throughout New Zealand that declared in favour of it."

Mr. Parr replied that he thought that if the practical difficulties to the proposal had been put before those same meetings, the proposal would have got a very short shrift. The hon. gentleman had overlooked in the idea the difficulty of the Crown Dominions. What was he going to do with India? India would not, he was sure, submit for a moment to be relegated to the position of a Crown Colony if every other part of the Empire had representation in an Imperial Parliament. Hon. gentlemen, the Member for Clutha particularly, were not satisfied with the present machinery of Imperial counsel and Imperial action. He thought they ought to be satisfied. The Conferences did the work, and they did it without creating vexatious bonds between the integral parts of the Empire. It was not easy to attend them every year. Perhaps biennial conferences would be sufficient. To that Conference the Prime Minister would always go. " I do not care," said Mr. Parr, " what the conditions in this country may be, at these Conferences the leading man in the Cabinet should speak. He would make the exception that should it become necessary that those Conferences should become an annual matter, and if the Prime Minister should be unable to go on every occasion, and if the Conference should not involve matters of serious moment, some other Minister might well go. If, however, the business were of most serious consequence to the country, the Prime Minister must always be the Delegate.

Labour view.

Mr. E. J. Howard (Labour, *Christchurch, South*) said that what they wanted to get at was a clear understanding of where they were in regard to the Empire. The Prime Minister had said there was no written Constitution for the Empire, nor did he think there was any necessity for one. It seemed to him (Mr. Howard) that they had arrived at a stage in the history of their Empire when they said: " Put nothing in writing, let no one know what we are aiming at, where we are going, or what end we have in view." It was quite questionable, if they took up any section of the Empire as voiced by its representative men, that they should find that they themselves were in agreement. In spite of the fact that the Prime Minister said that the Conference was unanimous, he doubted it. They probably were unanimous on certain things. They knew they were told about things that did not matter very much, but not about the most important things ; and whether the Conference was unanimous on those they were not told. The sum and substance of the report they had had from the Prime Minister was : " I have been Home ; we have come to an agreement, but I cannot tell you what it is. I have agreed not to put it on paper. Everything is all right. Now, boys, you can talk about it, but do not take too long."

Dominion devolution.

The Hon. J. A. Hanan (Liberal, *Invercargill*) said the conditions arising out of the War had made it imperative for nearly all the Parliaments of the world to take a wider view of their duties and responsibilities, and to possess a deeper knowledge of the problems involved in the work of national reconstruction and the big questions arising out of international relationships. They should have an enlarged form of local government, and he believed the time was not far distant when the country would insist on decentralisation to some extent. Public opinion was growing in Australia in the direction of decentralising certain powers exercised by the

State Parliaments, and he believed that enlarged Councils with greater powers of local government were bound to be adopted in Australia and in New Zealand.

He would like to have had some information from the Prime Minister as to whether anything had been done at the Conference relative to such subjects as copyright, patent rights, trade-marks, nationalisation and weights and measures. They should be independently dealt with by a body of special experts.

Referring to New Zealand's share in foreign affairs, Mr. Hanan remarked that it was said they should have an equal voice in determining the foreign policy of Great Britain. They would not get that voice and no one could reasonably expect it. There were certain powers or responsibilities that the Imperial Government would not share with them, although it might make a pretence of doing so.

Consulting Dominions before War.

Mr. A. Harris said that some hon. Members were of opinion that before Britain declared war the Dominions would have a right to be consulted. He did not think there was any desire on the part of the people of New Zealand to be consulted. As far as he viewed the position, if Britain decided to go to war, she would do so without consulting them, and in that sense he drew a distinction between partnership and actual membership of the British Empire family.

The Prime Minister: "In the event of war being declared, each Dominion will be consulted through its Prime Minister."

Mr. Harris: "Possibly, but purely as a matter of courtesy. It would make no difference if they refused to agree. . . ."

The Prime Minister: "It would then be for the Prime Minister at the other end to make up his mind as to the proper course, and recommend that course to His Majesty."

Mr. Harris, speaking of New Zealand's contribution to the British Navy, said he believed that if the Government consulted Parliament it would declare in favour of New Zealand taking an equal share of the burden of naval defence, and say, "If they are prepared to spend £2 per head we are prepared to spend at least the same amount."

Defence of Mr. Hughes.

Mr. D. Jones (**Reform**, *Kaiapoi*) said the hon. Member for Buller had said in his speech: "Mr. Hughes (Prime Minister of Australia) said that Japan would not carry out her Treaty unless we had a navy sufficiently strong to compel her to carry it out." He (Mr. Jones) had the report of Mr. Hughes's speech in his possession and he had never made any such statement as the hon. Member had attributed to him, nor any approach to it.

Mr. Holland said the words he had used were his interpretation of Mr. Hughes's statement.

The hon. Member for Clutha had taken strong exception to Mr. Hughes coming back (from the Conference) and boasting that they had practically killed the idea of creating a Constitution, but Mr. Hughes, before he went to the Conference, had spoken exceedingly strongly against Imperial federation.

Mr. Jones concluded by saying that what they wanted in connection with the Imperial Conference was a general understanding upon the main lines of foreign policy and their position as far as defence was concerned; but any hard-and-fast Constitution under which resolutions might be carried there, committing the country without Parliament having a final say, he should be bitterly opposed to. The chief source of satisfaction to him in connection with the Conference was the great success it had achieved in coming to a general understanding without committing them to any cast-iron system that might have the effect of destroying the Empire in the future.

The Prime Minister, in his reply, said in regard to the statement of Mr. Malcolm that the present occasion was the first time that the House had had an opportunity of discussing the reports of the Imperial Conference, that it was not the first occasion by any means, and that there had been quite a lengthy discussion on the report in regard to the Conference of 1917, and that Mr. Malcolm had then spoken.

Sharing maintenance of Imperial Navy.

With regard to the criticism of the Leader of the Opposition of H.M.S. *Chatham* which he had designated as an expensive toy, the principal duty of the *Chatham* was to police the islands of the Pacific, and especially the islands in which New Zealand was interested. Not long ago there was very serious trouble at Fiji, and the European inhabitants were in serious danger. When they appealed to the New Zealand Government to assist them, all they could do was to send down the little *Tutanekai* with fifty men of the Permanent Force and one machine-gun. It was a different thing now. On their way back from the Conference one of the first things they saw at Fiji was the *Chatham* flying the White Ensign, and he was very glad to see it. It was a far better arrangement for the country, and for the Empire, though in a very small way, to have that ship in those waters, and to have their young men given the opportunity for sea training that many of them desired. He was glad to hear the expressions from all round the House with regard to paying their share of maintenance of the Imperial Navy.

Open diplomacy impossible.

The hon. Member for Buller, said Mr. Massey, had complained that more publicity was not given to the work of the Imperial Conference. He (Mr. Massey) agreed with the opinion that open diplomacy was absolutely impossible—it could not be done.

Dominion "Ambassadors."

Talking of Ambassadors, Mr. Massey said, let them suppose that four or five of these Ambassadors from countries of the Empire met in some foreign capital city and each one held opposing views——

An Hon. Member: "It would mean chaos."

The Prime Minister: "It might be worse than chaos."

Mr. Wilford: "Every country ought to have an adviser in England."

The Prime Minister: "I agree with the hon. Member; but the Ambassador, as suggested, is impossible."

"Imperial Parliament" impossible.

The old question of an Imperial Parliament had been mentioned by the Member for Clutha. He (Mr. Massey) now believed it was absolutely impossible: that was to say, it was not impossible to bring it into operation—he did not say that for one moment—but he believed the effect would be far worse than most people could possibly imagine. Just think of a Parliament sitting in the United Kingdom and attempting to tax New Zealand—and they were probably not the least loyal of the citizens of the Empire! Neither the people of New Zealand nor of any other Dominion would be satisfied with being taxed by a Parliament sitting outside their own countries. He could not see any improvement in the way that had been suggested of a Parliament responsible to the whole Empire.

Mr. Malcolm: "You would know where the sovereignty resided."

The Prime Minister: "We know that now."

Mr. Malcolm: "Can you tell us where it is?"

The Prime Minister: "If you put the question in an intelligible way I will answer it."

Mr. Malcolm: "Where does the sovereignty of the Empire reside?"

The Prime Minister: "The sovereignty of the Empire is as the heart of the Empire; but the sovereignty of each country of the Empire is in that particular country."

Mr. Malcolm: "Then it is distributed?"

The Prime Minister: "To a certain extent. It cannot be otherwise; but the hon. gentleman cannot suggest that it does not work out well."

League of Nations and Dominion representation.

Continuing, Mr. Massey said the hon. Member (Mr. Malcolm) had referred to Mr. Hughes and his attitude regarding the suggested Conference to consider constitutional changes. He (Mr. Massey) thought the right thing had been done, and he had supported Mr. Hughes. They had made very important changes during the last Conference, and it was well that time should be given for those changes to consolidate. After their experience with the Peace Conference, the League of Nations, and other matters dealt with, he had come to the conclusion that a Conference that dealt with Constitutional matters might be dangerous, and required very careful watching. There was no danger on the last occasion, but he happened to know that matters did not quite turn out under the Peace Conference as many of them had expected. For instance, there was that proposal in the Covenant of the League of Nations by which separate representation was to be given to each Dominion. Most people were inclined to think it was a very good thing; he was very doubtful about it. What was the position, supposing that of four Dominion representatives on the Assembly or League, two were found voting one way and two the other, on the same question? That was possible. What then was the good of special representation? He was strongly of opinion that when they next got together they would have to make some amendments in that particular respect. People who ought to have known better said that, practically, the Dominions had become independent, and that each could do exactly as it liked. They could do nothing of the sort.

Mr. Holland: "General Smuts said that."

The Prime Minister: "I do not care who said it. . . . We should be particularly careful with respect to these loose statements; they do no good, and very often do a great deal of harm."

Monarchy the keystone of Empire.

Continuing, Mr. Massey said he did not agree with the Member for Clutha that the present structure of the Empire was too heavy for the foundation. He believed the Monarchy was the keystone of the Empire, and that as a result of the Imperial Conference the Monarchy had been strengthened rather than weakened, because it was based on enthusiastic loyalty on the one side, and on much sacrifice on the other.

Migration within the Empire.

The question of migration of the different peoples of the Empire, said Mr. Massey, had been discussed very exhaustively at the Imperial Conference. He hoped the existing law would stand, because it asserted the right of the different peoples of the Empire to select their fellow-citizens. In view of the position that there were too many people in the United Kingdom it was only right that they should do all they could to induce their fellow-citizens to live within the Empire—that when they migrated they should keep under the Union Jack. There were people who said that they should not permit immigrants from the United Kingdom when there was depression, and when employment was not plentiful. He did not agree with that—always on the understanding that they got the right class of settler. Every good settler who came there helped them to bear the burden of taxation; he became a producer or a consumer, in many cases both.

Anglo-Japanese Treaty.

In regard to the Anglo-Japanese Alliance, Mr. Massey quoted from the 1911 Treaty, and said that, so far as his interpretation went, Japan was not compelled to support them in the recent War, for the reason that Eastern Asia and India was not affected. He believed that Japan could have stood out had she felt inclined; but she did not, and it was all the more creditable to the Government of that country.

The Round Table and the Samoan Mandate.

There was a question concerning Constitutional matters, said Mr. Massey, which had arisen through an article that had appeared in *The Round Table* for September last, and which was entirely misleading. It referred to Samoa, and stated:—

> "New Zealand received her Mandate direct from the League of Nations, in a letter sent from Geneva on the 11th February last to her Prime Minister, and the correspondence thereon is not being conducted through Downing Street. The course in which Sir James Allen detected danger to the Empire was apparently accepted by New Zealand as soon as his back was turned, and neither Minister nor private Member has had a word to say about it."

He was going to quote from an official document to show that no other course could have been followed:—

> "It was the duty of the League of Nations to prepare the Mandate, and it was the duty of New Zealand to receive the Mandate, because New Zealand had His Majesty's permission and direction to accept and to act under the Mandate. . . ."*

* The remainder of the extract quoted above refers to the terms of the Order in Council issued in London under the Imperial Foreign Jurisdiction Act (*vide* Vol. I., No. 2, of the JOURNAL, p. 365), and to the Treaties of Peace Act passed by the New Zealand Parliament (*vide* Vol. I., No. 1, of the JOURNAL, p. 167).

After quoting a further extract, Mr. Massey said the whole thing (the Mandate) came down to New Zealand from the British Government through the proper channel—that was, through His Majesty—and they had accepted the Mandate instead of sending it back. In the first place, the New Zealand Government had insisted, of course, that the authority to govern the islands should come to them from the British Government; but by the arrangements that were made at the time of the Peace Conference, the League of Nations had been given certain power and authority so far as the conditions were concerned, and it was those conditions they were then dealing with.

Finally, Mr. Massey quoted from a speech of Mr. Lloyd George made at the opening of the Peace Conference, when the British Prime Minister had referred to the Empire outside Great Britain having raised more than two million soldiers, and had said " without these two million men . . . Prussianism would probably have triumphed in the West and the East before American troops arrived on the stage."

The motion was then agreed to.

EMPIRE DEFENCE.

(Question as to General Policy.)

In the House of Representatives on 26th October, 1921,

Mr. George Mitchell (Independent, *Wellington, South*) asked the Prime Minister for a statement as to what had been arrived at by the Imperial Conference in reference to the general policy of Empire Defence; what was to be the policy and the amount of their (New Zealand's) contribution to naval defence; what was the basis of the general policy of military defence agreed to; and whether their land defence was to be in keeping with the general Imperial policy? If so, when was it proposed to put such policy in operation in the Dominion?

The Prime Minister (the Right Hon. W. F. Massey) replied that the question of military defence had not been considered at the Conference. He had, he said, already dealt fairly fully with the Conference's deliberations on naval defence. The Conference had expressed the opinion that each country of the Empire should contribute. The next Conference would probably express an opinion as to what should be New Zealand's proportion of the cost, but it would be for the Parliament of New Zealand to agree.

Mr. Mitchell: " But the basis of the contributions has not been settled yet? "

The Prime Minister said it had not, and that it was a matter not as easy to settle as might appear at first sight. One might think that it could be fixed on a population basis; but there were some Dominions which considered that they were not nearly so vitally interested in naval defence as others were, and, therefore, should not be asked to contribute so much. He only mentioned that point, he said, as one of the difficulties to be overcome in fixing the amount each country would be expected to contribute.

Mr. Mitchell: "Then is our military defence to go on as at present?"

The Prime Minister replied that the question of military defence was left with each country, to act according to its own judgment.

WASHINGTON CONFERENCE.

(Representation of the Dominion; status of Delegate.)

In the House of Representatives, on 11th October, 1921,

Selection of Delegate.

The Prime Minister (the Right Hon. W. F. Massey) said he desired to make a statement about the very important Disarmament Conference to be held at Washington, and as to the necessity of New Zealand being represented there. It was quite out of the question for him or Sir Francis Bell (the Attorney-General) to go, and the Cabinet had come to the conclusion that it was not desirable to send a member of the Government. They had selected Sir John Salmond, one of the foremost authorities in the Empire on constitutional law, to go and he had accepted.

Mr. G. Witty (Liberal, ***Riccarton*****)**: "Surely it would be better for a Minister to represent the country?"

The Prime Minister replied that they had entered upon a very important Session, and that Ministers' hands were full.

Mr. D. G. Sullivan (Labour, ***Avon*****)**: "The appointment is no compliment to Parliament."

Mr. W. A. Veitch (Independent Labour, ***Wanganui*****)**: "He is not a representative at all."

The Hon. J. A. Hanan (Liberal, ***Invercargill*****)** asked whether it would not have been better to have submitted a motion to Parliament, as was done in the Federal Parliament (of Australia)?

The Prime Minister replied that he felt there would be little difference of opinion in the House, because he was confident a huge majority would vote for sending Sir John Salmond on account of his special qualifications.

No power to commit the country.

Mr. H. Holland (Labour, ***Buller*****)**: "Will he have power to make commitments on behalf of New Zealand ?"

The Prime Minister: "No more than any member of the Ministry who went. Even the Prime Minister would not commit the country on any point of importance. He will be able to tell the members of the Conference, especially the members of the British Delegation, the position in which we are to-day from the defence point of view, and the particular ideas of the people of this country."

Status of Dominion Delegate.

Mr. T. M. Wilford (Leader of the Opposition) asked the Prime Minister whether it was not a fact that the British Empire representatives would really be those who would be consulted and dealt with by the representatives of the other great Powers at the Conference, and that any representative from New Zealand would really be there in a kind of consulting capacity to advise the British representatives on matters particularly appertaining to that country ? Was it not also a fact that the Conference was one hoping to evolve a policy of Disarmament, and in no way a Conference of Disarmament ?

The Prime Minister replied that the newspapers had called it a Disarmament Conference, and whether it would lead to that or not no man could say. So far as the other point was concerned—that of the representatives of the Dominions being consulted through the delegation—that was what really took place at such important gatherings, what took place at the Peace Conference. The British Delegation used to meet them, and everyone present from the Dominions, or from Britain, or India had the opportunity of expressing an opinion. Had the Prime Ministers been able to go there (Washington) they would have had the opportunity of sitting in the Conference proper; but he doubted if anything else would be done on the present occasion than had always happened.

TREATIES OF PEACE EXTENSION ACT.

(Chinese Labour in Samoa, etc.)

The Bill for the above Act originated in the Legislative Council, having been introduced by the Attorney-General, and passed through all stages in that Chamber on 26th October, and in the House of Representatives on the following day.

The object of the amending Act is to keep the principal Act (the Treaties of Peace Act, 1919) in force indefinitely, except that portion relating to Western Samoa, which is repealed in view of the legislation introduced in regard to Samoa and to come into force on 1st April, 1922.*

During the passage of the Bill in the Lower House there was a lengthy debate on the question of indentured labour in Samoa, and an amendment moved by Mr. H. Holland (Labour, *Buller*) that "no order in Council shall be made under the principal Act authorising further importations of indentured Chinese labourers into Samoa," was defeated.

The Act consists of only two sections, the main provisions being:—

2. (1) The principal Act shall remain in force until it is specifically repealed:

Provided that no Order-in-Council with respect to the Government of Samoa shall be made under the principal Act on or after the 1st day of April, 1922, and no such Order-in-Council made before the said date shall remain in force thereafter, save pursuant to the provisions of any Act that may be hereafter passed relative to the Government of Western Samoa.

(2) Sections five and six of the principal Act, and the Treaties of Peace Amendment Act, 1920, are hereby repealed.

IN LEGISLATIVE COUNCIL.

The Attorney-General (Hon. Sir Francis Bell), in moving the Second Reading on 26th October, explained that they were proposing that the Treaties of Peace Act, 1919, which would expire on 29th October, 1921, should remain in force until specifically repealed, because it authorised the Government to give effect to the Treaty of Versailles, and steps were still being taken under that Treaty. It was proposed to repeal Section 5 which related to Western Samoa.

DEBATE IN HOUSE OF REPRESENTATIVES.

On the 27th October, 1921,

The indentured labour question.

The Minister of External Affairs (Hon. E. P. Lee), in moving the Second Reading of the Bill, said that it kept aliv

* *Vide* p. 196.

the Treaties of Peace Act, except as to Samoa, and allowed of the Samoa part being continued until the 1st April, 1922. The reason for fixing that date was because the Samoa Bill, just passed, did not come into force until 1st April next, and so it was necessary to extend the existing Constitutional Order under which Samoa was then governed until the Samoa Bill became operative. He moved the Second Reading of the Bill.

Mr. H. Holland (Labour, *Buller***)**: "Mr. Speaker, there is one thing wrong with this Bill, and that is that it makes no provision whatever for ending the system of indentured Chinese labour in Samoa. I suppose one of the main reasons for continuing the legislation is the need for maintaining the legality of the system of indentured labour which is now in existence in Samoa."

The Minister of External Affairs: "It is not the main cause at all."

Mr. Holland proceeded to say that if they were to knock out Chinese indentured labour the desire to hold Samoa would vanish very largely in the minds of some people. The system was no credit to New Zealand, or to the British Empire. It was an opportune time to take the matter into consideration once more and to say whether the stain of that slavery was to remain upon the Administration of New Zealand.*

Mr. Holland also spoke at length on the question of the relations between the Chinese labourers and Samoan women.

Mr. H. Atmore (Liberal, *Nelson***)** said he did not believe there was a Member in the House who was in favour of indentured labour as a settled condition, but if it was a case of saving the Samoans from extinction—because if their cocoa-nut plantations were annihilated by the rhinoceros beetle then one could not doubt that the Samoans were doomed—one must vote for it as a temporary expedient.

The Prime Minister (the Right Hon. W. F. Massey) said there was not an argument used that night, not a statement made, that they had not had in previous years, and especially last Session. Continuing, he said: "I told the House last year that as soon as it was possible to do away with Chinese labour in Samoa, Chinese labour would be done away with. I do not admit the 'slavery' argument at all; there is no slavery about it. The Chinese leave their country as free men. When they arrive in Samoa they are asked to sign a document engaging to work there for three years."

---

* *Vide* Mr. Holland's speech on this subject during the discussion in the House on 28th—31st July, 1920, in regard to the visit of the New Zealand Parliamentary Party to Samoa, summarised in the JOURNAL, Vol. I., No. 4, pp. 720—728.

An Hon. Member: "Supposing they will not sign that document?"

The Prime Minister: "Then they can return to China. . ."

The Minister of External Affairs having replied, the Bill was read a second time.

Mr. Holland's amendment referred to above, having been taken in Committee and defeated, by 38 votes against 17, the Liberal, and all the Labour, Members voting for the amendment, the Bill was read a third time.

SAMOA BILL.

(Provision for future Government; Franchise; Native Petition, etc.)

A comprehensive measure, making permanent provision for the government of Western Samoa, in lieu of the existing government by Order in Council, was presented to the House by the Minister of External Affairs on 23rd September, 1921, and was debated on 11th October, when the Bill passed its Second Reading. It passed the Third Reading on 26th October.

On 12th October, some amendments were made in Committee, the most important being that in respect of Clause 300, prohibiting marriages between Samoans and Chinamen, this clause being struck out on the motion of the Minister in charge of the Bill.

The Bill was read a first and second time in the Legislative Council on 27th October without debate.

The Preamble to the Bill, after reciting the authorities under which temporary provision had been made for the Government of Samoa, proceeds :—

"And whereas it is expedient that permanent provision should now be made for the peace, order, and good government of the aforesaid Territory."

Commencement of Act.

Clause 1 provides that the Act shall come into force on 1st April, 1922.

Part I. (Clauses 4 to 45) deals with the following matters :—

Executive Government of Samoa.

The Executive Government is declared to be vested in the King as if the territory were part of His Majesty's Dominions. (Clause 4.)

The Administrator.

There is to be an Administrator, appointed by the Governor-General, who shall be stationed at Apia, and be under the Minister of External Affairs. (Clause 5.)

The Chief Judge of the High Court is to be *ex-officio* Deputy-Administrator. (Clause 6.)

Samoan Public Service.

Officers of the Public Service are to be appointed by, and hold office during the pleasure of, the Minister of External Affairs, but this authority may be delegated to the Administrator. (Clauses 9 and 10.)

Salaries and allowances are to be paid out of the Samoan Treasury. (Clause 13.)

Officers of the New Zealand Public Service may be appointed to the Samoan Public Service, and various provisions are made as to adjustment of status, etc., in such cases, including a provision that in compiling length of service for superannuation purposes every year served by a New Zealand Public Servant in Samoa shall be computed as one year and a half. (Clauses 14 to 25.)

Treasury.

Provision is made for the establishment of a Samoan Treasury. (Clauses 27 to 33.)

Public Health.

A Department of Public Health is to be set up under a Chief Medical Officer, and the Administrator is to establish and maintain "such hospitals and other institutions as he may deem necessary for the public health." (Clauses 34 to 38.)

Prisons and Police.

Prisons are to be established and police to be appointed. (Clauses 39 to 42.)

Education.

The Administrator is given power to establish public schools "for the education of the Samoan or other inhabitants thereof." (Clause 43.)

Good Government, Restrictions on Imports, etc.

The Governor-General (of New Zealand) may, by Order in Council, make regulations for the peace, order, and good government of Samoa, and may by regulation impose conditions, restrictions and prohibitions upon the export or import of goods from or into Samoa. (Clause 45.)

Part II. of the Bill (Clauses 46 to 62) deals with the Legislative Government of Samoa.

Ordinances.

The Administrator, acting with the advice and consent of the Legislative Council of Western Samoa, may, subject as stated, make laws (to be known as Ordinances) for the peace, order, and good government of the Territory. (Clause 46.)

A Legislative Council.

There is to be a Legislative Council, consisting of :—

(A) Official members (not less than four) of the Samoan Public Service, to be appointed by the Governor-General ;

(B) Unofficial members (not more in number than the official members) also appointed by the Governor-General;

and a Member of the Legislative Council must be either a natural-born British subject, or a Samoan, born in Samoa. (Clauses 47 and 48.)

Governor-General's Veto.

The Governor-General has a veto to be exercised within one year after the assent of the Administrator has been given to an ordinance. (Clause 57.)

Limited Scope of Ordinances.

The scope of Ordinances is strictly limited, and it is provided that it shall not be lawful or competent by any Ordinance: (A) to affect the prerogative of the Crown or the title of His Majesty to any land; (B) to impose Customs or export duties; (C) to establish any body corporate; (D) to establish any form of local government possessed of rating, taxing, or legislative authority; (E) to establish any paper currency; (F) to provide as the penalty for any offence imprisonment for more than one year or a fine of more than £100. (Clause 61.)

Limitation of Powers of Legislative Council.

The Legislative Council or Executive Government may not: (A) maintain any naval or military base or any fortifications in Samoa; (B) provide for the military training or service (except police) of Samoan inhabitants other than Europeans; (C) borrow money except from the New Zealand Treasury.

High Court of Samoa.

Part III. deals with the establishment of a Court of record to be called the High Court of Western Samoa. (Clauses 63 to 79.)

Jurisdiction of New Zealand Supreme Court.

Part IV. extends the jurisdiction of the Supreme Court and provides the machinery whereby the High Court may state cases for the New Zealand Supreme Court. Provision is also made for appeals from the High Court to the Supreme Court. (Clauses 80 to 99.)

Criminal Code.

The Criminal Code and Criminal Procedure of Samoa and Law of Evidence are set forth in Parts V. and VI. (Clauses 100 to 263.)

Criminal Jurisdiction of High Court.

All offences may be tried by the High Court, except where otherwise provided by Ordinance or Regulation. (Clause 213.)

Felonies and Misdemeanours.

The usual distinction between felonies and misdemeanours is not to apply. (Clause 214.)

Assessors (in Lieu of Jury).

The High Court sits with or without assessors (Clause 220); assessors must sit when the trial is for an offence (and the plea is "not guilty") punishable by death or imprisonment for more than five years (Clause 221); for offences punishable only by fine, assessors are not to sit (Clause 222); in other trials the Court has a discretion as to assessors (Clause 223); there are to be four assessors in all cases, and assessors "shall be such fit and proper persons (whether men or women) as the Court thinks fit to appoint, and the consent of the assessor shall not in any case be requisite for his appointment"; and assessors must be gazetted as qualified before they can act (Clause 224); an assessor upon being appointed is compellable to attend and act as such (Clause 225); on a trial with assessors if the Court is against a conviction, or if less than three of the assessors concur in conviction, the accused is to be acquitted (Clause 231); the concurrence of assessors is not necessary to the sentence, nor in any act of the Court except conviction. (Clauses 232, 233.)

Crown Suits.

Part VIII. of the Bill deals with Crown Suits.

Land.

By Part IX. of the Bill, all land is classified as: (A) Crown land; (B) European land; and (C) Native land. (Clause 268.)

Native land is to be vested in the Crown, as trustees for the beneficial owners, subject to the Native title, "and under the customs and usages of the Samoan race." (Clause 278.)

There are restrictions on the alienation of native land; and a contract for the sale of crops, timber, minerals, etc., from land comes under the restriction. (Clause 280.)

Marriage and Divorce.

These subjects are dealt with in Parts IX. and X. There was a prohibition of marriages between Chinese and Samoans in the Bill (Clause 300) but *vide* amendment below.

Intoxicating Liquor.

Part XIII. of the Bill (Clauses 336 to 341) prohibits the manufacture, importation, or sale of intoxicating liquor, and makes it an offence to give liquor to a Samoan except with medical approval (Clauses 336 to 339); but the Administrator may import intoxicating liquor for medicinal, sacramental or industrial purposes. (Clauses 340, 341.)

Laws of Samoa. (General Provisions.)

Part XV. makes general provision in regard to the law of the country. (Clauses 349 to 372.)

The Common Law.

The Law of England as in the year 1840 (being the year in which the Colony of New Zealand was established) is to be in force in Samoa (Clause 349); the statute law of New Zealand (except where specially provided) is not to be in force in Samoa (Clause 351); the Statute of Frauds is not to apply (Clause 352); the English Common Law Rule disqualifying aliens from holding land is not to apply (Clause 353); copyright law and patent law is to be that in force in New Zealand. (Clauses 357, 358.)

No Distress for Rent.

There is to be no distress for rent. (Clause 362.)

Calendar of Samoa.

The Calendar in Samoa is to be one day behind that of New Zealand. (Clause 363.)

Banking.

Banking may not be carried except under Order in Council; and bank notes may not be issued. (Clause 364.)

Currency.

Currency, coinage and legal tender is to be the same as that of New Zealand; the Minister of External Affairs may issue Samoan Treasury Notes of not more than £5 and not less than five shillings. (Clause 365.)

Contracts by Samoans.

The Courts of Samoa are given a discretionary power in regard to enforcing the contracts of Samoans. (Clause 367.)

Powers of Sale.

No security given by a Samoan over property is to be enforceable, whether by power of sale or otherwise, without the leave of the High Court. (Clause 368.)

Succession to Property.

Succession to the property of a deceased Samoan is to be in accordance with Samoan custom. (Clause 369.)

Property of German Government.

His Majesty the King is declared to be the successor in title to all property and rights whatsoever of the Government of Germany in respect of Western Samoa. (Clause 376.)

Amendments.

Samoan-Chinese Marriages.

Clause 300, prohibiting marriages between Samoans and Chinese, was struck out.

Other amendments were made in Committee mainly in the direction of modifications of fines and punishments for criminal offences.

DEBATE IN HOUSE OF REPRESENTATIVES.

On 11th October, 1921,

The Minister of External Affairs (Hon. E. P. Lee), in moving the Second Reading, dealt exhaustively with the provisions of the Bill. He said they (the Government) were endeavouring, as far as possible, to maintain the Public Service of Samoa from that of the Dominion, which was bound to result in a highly essential continuity between New Zealand and Samoa in administration.

The franchise difficulty.

It might be contended that there was not a representative Government. The question which would arise would be: Was the franchise to be British? He did not think the House would consider it expedient in the meantime that the Legislative Council should be elective. In Article 22 of the Peace Treaty it was recognised that those people would be best governed by the laws of the mandatory country.

Mr. H. Holland (Labour, ***Buller*****)**: "What became of the Treaty of Berlin—the 1899 Treaty?"

The Minister of External Affairs: "I should say that it has been scattered to the four winds of heaven. It has served its purpose and has died a natural death. . . ."

Trial by assessors.

Upon the Minister mentioning Part V. of the Bill, dealing with Criminal offences,—

Mr. T. M. Wilford (Leader of the Opposition): "Trial by jury?"

The Minister of External Affairs: "No; trial by Judge, with Assessors. . . ."

The Minister proceeded to explain that trial by jury in Samoa would be very different from New Zealand, the conditions being so entirely novel. In answer to further questions, the Minister said that the Court—with assessors—would have the power of life and death and that an assessor must attend the Court whether he desired to or not, in the same way as a juror.

Mr. Wilford: "Then the Judge selects the jury."

The Minister of External Affairs: "The Judge selects the assessors. I use the words of the Bill."

Mr. Wilford: "Is there any right of challenge?"

The Minister of External Affairs: "No."

Mr. G. Witty (Liberal, ***Riccarton*****)**: "That is a biased jury."

Trusteeship of Native land.

The Minister of External Affairs, dealing with the classification of Samoan land, explained that the land held by German nationals and German companies, under the Peace Treaty and under New Zealand legislation, became Crown Land of New Zealand. They had been valued, and New Zealand would account for their value through the clearing-houses. The amount which New Zealand would have to pay for those estates was taken as part of their Reparations from Germany; but the companies and individuals who had held them received the value of the lands from the German Government. They were worth about £1,000,000. In order to make it clear to the Samoans that they (New Zealand) did not own the native land they had put in the words that they held it "as the trustee of the beneficial owners thereof, and shall be held by the Crown subject to the Native title."

Prohibition in Samoa and Cook Islands.

Proceeding, the Minister said that Part XIII., dealing with the subject of intoxicating liquor, was no alteration of the existing state of affairs, and he had the authority of his colleague, Dr. Pomare (member of the Executive Council representing the Native Race) to say that he proposed to introduce the same system into the Cook Islands.* Speaking a little later in regard to the same subject, Mr. Lee said that the Chief Medical Officer had stated, in regard to a deputation which had asked that a modified system of liquor supply be sanctioned (to white residents and half-castes), that, speaking as a medical man and not as a private citizen, liquor was not required in the country for anyone, and that the people, notwithstanding the circumstances mentioned by them, were better without it.

Minister's visit to Samoa.

Mr. Lee said that he had been to Samoa, and hearing that some members of the community were not satisfied with everything that was going on, he had publicly announced that he would be prepared to meet any member of the community or any deputation and hear what they had to say in regard to the administration. Those residents would not come forward but took the course of sending a general letter just on the eve of his departure. To say: " We recognise the futility of bringing forward our ideas as to the proper management of Samoa " was not a proper way to have grievances remedied, if any existed.

Natives' Petition the King.

There had been a meeting of some of the chiefs—the Faipules—and a Native Petition had been presented to him for transmission to the King. When the proper time came he should be able to show that the Petition did not reflect the general feeling of the Natives.†

---

* The Cook Islands Amendment Bill, introduced into the House of Representatives by the Hon. Dr. Pomare and read a first time on 12th October, contains a clause to the effect stated by the Minister of External Affairs, and the Bill, together with any debate upon it, will be summarised in the next issue of the JOURNAL.

† The general effect of the Petition, the clauses of which were read to the House by the Minister of External Affairs, was one of complaint that the Government of Samoa was not in accordance with the Treaty made by Great Britain, the United States and Germany, called the Berlin Treaty, of 14th June, 1889; that the Samoans were not being consulted in matters of government as formerly, under the German protection and the New Zealand military occupation; that it was not right to enforce the New Zealand Constitution Order of 1920 upon them without their signed approval, as had been done in the case of the Berlin Treaty; that the Samoans did not wish to be heavily indebted to New Zealand as a result of high salaries paid to white officials, etc.; and that things done by some of the white Government officials signified that

This, said the Minister, the Samoans had been led to bring forward. They had been pushed on to take that action by the white residents. The Petition had been forwarded to the Governor-General for transmission to His Majesty. When the Petition was presented,* the High Chief Malietoa had addressed the Faipules advising them not to present it, and explained to them that they were making a mistake in presenting it at all.

Why not an Elective Legislative Council?

Mr. T. K. Sidey (**Liberal**, *Dunedin, South*) said that he failed to see anything in the Mandate which was inconsistent with granting the Samoans some elective power in the constitution of the Legislative Council.

Mr. H. Holland said the Samoans had a very genuine grievance in the manner in which the Treaty of Berlin had been torn up without any reference whatever to the Samoan people.

Indentured Labour.

The New Zealand Government did not want the Chinaman in Samoa as a free man, but only as a slave. It would not have him as a free settler, and it would be a wrong policy to have him there in large numbers as a free settler; but their Government was prepared to have him there bound hand and foot, practically a slave.

Mr. G. Witty said that whilst it had been their duty to take possession of the islands during the War, he really thought it was a pity they remained in possession of them. If he had his way there would not be a Chinaman going into the islands. He would sooner see them revert to the State they were before the Germans took possession than see a mixed race of Chinese and islanders in the Pacific. The Chinese could not marry the Samoan women, but they could co-habit with them. They could leave their progeny behind as a liability to the country, and return to China.

New Zealand had no respect for the Samoans; the prayer of the Petition being: "We humbly pray, also, that Your Majesty King George V. may have pleasure in appointing only a Governor to represent Your Majesty in Samoa. We and our children who have been educated are quite sufficient to perform the various duties of our Administration. In addition, there are a great number of British subjects who have been amongst us for a great many years, and are thoroughly acquainted with our customs, and can therefore make laws for the administration of these small islands which are under the care of Your Majesty and your Empire."

* The Minister is apparently speaking of the presentation made to him by the natives.

The Minister of External Affairs, in his reply, pointed out in regard to the Treaty of Berlin, that the report of the Imperial Treaties Committee stated :—

"That multilateral treaties where all the parties are belligerents (*i.e.*, the Samoan Convention of 1899) should be regarded as terminated by the War and as requiring revival by the Treaty of Peace if they are to remain in force after the conclusion of peace."

The Bill was read a second time.

COMMERCIAL RECIPROCITY WITH AUSTRALIA.

In the House of Representatives, on 13th October, 1921,

Dr. H. T. J. Thacker (**Liberal**, *Christchurch, East*) asked the Minister of Customs : "Whether in our tariff-revision he intends to fully consider reciprocal commercial arrangements with Australia to encourage closer trade relationship ?" There was a note to the question : "In the future, Australia's strength will be our strength. We produce much that she wants, and she produces many things we want."

The Minister of Customs (Hon. W. Downie Stewart) replied that the operation of the Australian tariff as applied to exports from New Zealand had been fully considered in framing the new tariff and the Bill to accompany the tariff. The Prime Minister of Australia had made it clear that he was not prepared to begin any direct negotiations for reciprocity until after the new Australian tariff had become law. It was hoped, Mr. Downie Stewart said, that schedules governing a selected list of items would then be agreed to and prepared during the coming Recess for submission to Parliament.

LICENSING LAW.

(Government intentions if "no-license" not carried; question of a new licensing policy.)

In the House of Representatives on 6th October, 1921,

Mr. R. McCallum (Liberal, *Wairau*) said the Prime Minister had promised that he would inquire into the licensing business at Home, and he now wished to ask what was in his (the Prime Minister's) mind in connection with the suggested amendments of their licensing laws, should "no-license" not be carried at the poll to be taken next year; and would he give some particulars of the knowledge gained by him during his recent visit to London ? He would like the Prime Minister to note that what was aimed at in the question was (1) an improvement of the conditions of the trade for the convenience of the public, and (2) consideration of the whole question from a revenue-producing point of view.

The Prime Minister (the Right Hon. W. F. Massey) said that what was asked was a pretty big order. It would mean disclosing the new policy of the Government on licensing matters. He did not say there was a new policy; but if there was one it would mean disclosing the whole of it. He admitted that last year, when a small Licensing Bill was before the House, he had promised to set up a Committee in the present Session and give him (Mr. McCallum) and his friends an opportunity of appearing before it and making suggestions generally, and the promise would be kept.

With regard to the financial side of the question, it was a matter for serious consideration, and he took it the Committee would have an opportunity of dealing even with that point. Some of the other points, however, were more urgent than the financial point. He would not attempt to predict what might happen at the forthcoming poll, but if "no-license" was not carried it would be the duty of the Government to make a number of important amendments in the Licensing Act of the country.

STATE CONTROL OF LICENSES BILL.

In the House of Representatives on the 21st October, **Mr. R. McCallum (Liberal,** *Wairau*) introduced the above Bill, the object of which is expressed to be to amend the Licensing Act, 1908, by providing for State Control of the Liquor Traffic, ending Monopoly, and providing Security of Tenure, or Compensation to every Licensee who conducts his business creditably.

The Bill was read a first time.

The following are the main provisions:—

Ministry of Licenses.

A "Ministry of Licenses" for the administration of the licensing laws is to be set up, and the Minister is given a power of veto over Licensing Committees, and his consent (and the approval of the appropriate Licensing Committee) is required before dealings affecting licensed premises are entered into. (Clauses 6 to 12.)

Licensing Fees.

The existing annual license fees are abolished and fees are to be calculated on a specified percentage of the amount of liquor purchased by publicans, etc., and on the amount sold by brewers and wholesale licensees. (Clauses 13 and 14.)

Compensation.

Licensees are to be entitled to compensation if "no-license" is carried, and fifty per cent. of all license fees from hotel keepers and accommodation-house keepers is to be set aside as a fund out of which compensation is to be paid for lost licenses. (Clauses 15 and 16.)

Trafficking in Licenses, "Tied Houses," etc.

Trafficking in licenses is prohibited; no person is to have any interest in more licensed premises than one; tied houses are to be prohibited; the owner of licensed premises is to conduct them, except under special circumstances; and no license is to be transferred until it has been held at least three years. (Clauses 18 to 22.)

General Provisions.

Employees in licensed premises are to be under the control of the Minister, and Licensees may form guilds for the improvement of the trade; provision is made in regard to the analysis of liquor, the strength at which liquor is to be sold, hours of sale, etc. (Clauses 23 to 28.)

National Poll to be abolished.

The final clause of the Bill (Clause 29) provides that the national poll on prohibition shall only be taken at every second general election (commencing in 1922), but that local option polls shall be taken as formerly.

TARIFF BILL.

(Government Policy; Revenue.)

Questions having been asked in the House of Representatives as to when the Tariff Bill would come down, and as to whether the tariff would be a revenue tariff or a protective tariff,

On 25th October, 1921,

The Prime Minister (the Right Hon. W. F. Massey), in reply to a question by Mr. E. Newman (Reform, *Manawatu*), said he could not give the House any indication with regard to the details of the tariff until he was in a position to lay his proposals on the table and bring them into operation. If the hon. gentleman wanted to know the policy of the Government he (Mr. Massey) was out for revenue.

BANKING AMENDMENT BILL.

(Fixed banking hours; Bank of New Zealand and Commonwealth Bank of Australia compared.)

The above Bill was introduced in the House of Representatives by the Acting Minister of Finance, and a short debate took place on the Second Reading, when comparison was made between the Bank of New Zealand and the Commonwealth Bank of Australia. The Bill was read a third time in the House on 12th October, and passed its First and Second Readings in the Legislative Council without debate on 18th October.

The object of the Bill is to enable banking hours in the Dominion to be fixed by Order-in-Council.

Clause 2 (1) of the Bill provides that the hours during which banks carrying on business in New Zealand may be fixed by Order-in-Council, notwithstanding anything to the contrary in the charter of any bank.

Clause 2 (2) provides that an Order-in-Council may relate generally to all banks, or specifically to one or more banks, "or to any branch or branches of any such bank, and may fix different hours for different branches."

Clause 2 (3) provides that the hours fixed shall be not less than two hours on one day each week and not less than five hours on other days, except bank holidays.

DEBATE IN HOUSE OF REPRESENTATIVES.

Bill asked for by Bank Officers' Guild.

On 7th October, 1921,

The Acting Minister of Finance (Hon. W. Downie Stewart), in moving the Second Reading, said the banks and their officers were desirous of having power to vary the hours of opening and closing the banks either throughout the Dominion or in special localities according to local circumstances. The Bill was asked for, the Minister said, by the Bank Officers' Guild, and, he understood, concurred in by the banks. The banks apprehended that owing to long custom in the opening and closing of certain hours, it might be held that they were bound by those hours. They therefore asked that a Bill might be put through enabling the banks to open and close at earlier or later hours, according to local circumstances by arrangement between the bank officers and the banks themselves. It was another case of legislation by Order-in-Council Mr. Downie Stewart admitted, but, he said, it was Order-in-Council for the convenience of the banks and at their request.

Mr. T. K. Sidey (**Liberal**, *Dunedin, South*) said there was not much to object to, because the total number of hours that banks were now open was not interfered with.

Commonwealth Bank of Australia.

Continuing, Mr. Sidey said the Bill raised the whole subject of banking. He did not want to start a long debate, but he had had a talk with those in control of the Commonwealth Bank in Australia, and they considered there were two main purposes the (Commonwealth) Bank might be made to serve. One was in the nature of a reserve for the assistance of other banks, and the other was as a regulator of the rates of interest, because there was a restriction upon the rate of interest the Commonwealth Bank could charge by way of overdraft.

A Reserve Bank.

It was suggested, said Mr. Sidey, that the Bank of New Zealand might be made to serve a similar purpose in the Dominion.

The Prime Minister (the Right Hon. W. F. Massey): " We do not need reserve banks in this country. . . ."

Mr. Sidey, proceeding, remarked that how the Prime Minister could say, in the face of recent experience, that there could be no necessity for a reserve bank—an institution on which the other banks might lean in times of stress—in that country he had a difficulty in understanding. Speaking of the Bank of New Zealand, he said there were no restrictions upon it as to the rates of interest it might charge, and it worked in conjunction with the other institutions. The Commonwealth Bank was largely run as an ordinary business concern on banking lines, but it was not a member of the Banking Association.

The Acting Minister of Finance in his reply said that in comparing the relative positions of the Commonwealth Bank and the Bank of New Zealand it had to be remembered that the Government of New Zealand were in the position of controlling the Bank of New Zealand, and the Dominion derived over half a million a year taxation from the Bank, apart from dividends. The Commonwealth Bank paid not a single penny taxation to the Commonwealth Government; and the profits of the Bank so far had not been made available for ordinary revenue.

Whatever might be the merit of a State Bank, their position, so far as the Bank of New Zealand was concerned, was particularly favourable. They were drawing a growing revenue, and were not put to the expense of buying out the shareholders, as would be the case if the country acquired the Bank.

The Bill was then read a second time.

BANK OF NEW ZEALAND.

(Question of State Bank.)

Mr. J. Craigie (Independent Liberal, *Timaru*) said that the Prime Minister had made a promise that he would that Session set up a Select Committee to inquire into the Bank of

New Zealand with a view to (1) reviewing the partnership between the State and the Bank; (2) ascertaining whether the State should take over the Bank; and (3) inquiring whether New Zealand should have a State Bank.

Would the Prime Minister consider the advisability of setting up that Committee, if not that year, in the recess, and if not then, at the beginning of the Session of 1922? There was, said Mr. Craigie, a good deal of talk in the country about a State Bank.

The Prime Minister (the Right Hon. W. F. Massey) replied that the hon. Member had forgotten that last Session the House had considered a Banking Bill* which had been referred to the Public Accounts Committee, of which he (Mr. Craigie) was a member, and of which that Committee had approved, he thought, unanimously. He (Mr. Massey) mentioned that just to show that the relations of the Bank of New Zealand to the Government and the people had been considered by that Committee and Parliament on that occasion, and the present position of the Government's interest in the Bank was that the Dominion owned one-third of the Bank of New Zealand, and stood in a very good position in regard to it, with little cost to the country. The Public Accounts Committee would be set up in a day or two, when important financial proposals would be submitted; and he would take the hon. Member's proposal into consideration. The more publicity obtained in regard to those matters the better it would be for the whole of the people, some of whom talked about a State Bank as though it were going to be the salvation of the country. He ventured to say that they received from that institution (the Bank of New Zealand) by way of taxation and dividends certainly not less than £500,000, which was exceedingly useful to the country at that time.

MAINTENANCE ORDERS (FACILITIES FOR ENFORCEMENT) BILL.†

(Applying Imperial Act to New Zealand.)

The above Bill, introduced into the House of Representatives by the Minister of Justice (Hon. E. P. Lee) and promoted for the purpose of complying with the conditions prescribed by Section 12 of the Maintenance Orders (Facilities for Enforcement) Act, 1920 (Imperial), makes provision for the confirmation

* For reference to Bank of New Zealand Act, *vide* JOURNAL, Vol. II., No. 2, p. 435.

† *Vide* also under "Queensland," p. 147, and note to Introduction, p. viii.

and enforcement in New Zealand of provisional orders for maintenance made in the United Kingdom or elsewhere in His Majesty's Dominions.

The Bill differs materially from the Imperial Act, however, inasmuch as it makes no conditions as to reciprocity with regard to its application.

The Bill was debated in the House on 7th October when it passed its Second Reading. It was subsequently referred to the Statutes Revision Committee when an amendment was introduced in the direction of making provision for the appointment of officers to take proceedings on behalf of persons entitled under maintenance orders for the recovery of moneys payable under such orders.

The following are the main provisions of the Bill :—

Clause 3 provides for the enforcement in New Zealand of any maintenance order made out of New Zealand, on the filing of a certified copy of such order. The clause is an adaptation of Section 1 of the abovementioned Imperial Act.

Clause 4 provides for the making in New Zealand of provisional maintenance orders against persons resident in the United Kingdom or some other part of His Majesty's Dominions. Such provisional orders are dependent for their operation on their confirmation by a competent Court in the place where the defendant is. The clause follows Section 3 of the Imperial Act, except that the powers conferred by Section 73 of the Destitute Persons Act, 1910 (New Zealand), are expressly saved. This is necessary for the purpose of enabling beneficiaries under maintenance orders against absentees to have recourse against property in New Zealand.

Clause 5 is adapted from the corresponding provisions of Section 4 of the Imperial Act, and provides for the confirmation in New Zealand of provisional maintenance orders made elsewhere within the Empire. Before the confirmation of any such provisional order the defendant is given an opportunity of appearing and of raising any defence that he would have been entitled to raise if he had been represented at the original hearing.

Clauses 6 and 7 relate to matters of evidence, and are in conformity with corresponding provisions in the Imperial Act.

Clause 8 enables the Governor-General to make regulations for facilitating communications between Courts and generally for the purpose of giving effect to the Act. In the Imperial Act a similar authority is conferred on the Secretary of State.

Clause 9 is declaratory of the extent of the operation of Section 4[illegible] of the principal Act, as to charging orders on property in satisfaction of maintenance orders.

Amendment (by Statutes Revision Committee).

Clause 10 provides for the appointment of officers to take proceedings for the recovery of moneys payable under maintenance orders, and also makes provision for the manner in which moneys so recovered are to be disposed of.

SOUTH AFRICA.

The following summaries consist of matter held over from previous issues and are in continuation of the summaries dealing with proceedings of the First Session of the Fourth Parliament of the Union of South Africa which opened on 11*th March*, 1921, *and closed on* 4*th July*, 1921. *Summaries of discussions in the earlier part of the Session will be found in Vol. II., Nos.* 2, 3 *and* 4, *of the* JOURNAL.

UNION OFFICES IN LONDON.

(High Commissioner's functions and allowances; Trade Relations with United Kingdom and Foreign Countries; Immigration, etc.)

In the Senate, and in the House of Assembly on the Estimates, the matter of the Union Offices in London and the position and functions of the High Commissioner were discussed and references were made generally to the trade of South Africa both within the Empire and externally, and to such matters as immigration, etc.

IN THE SENATE.

On 14th May,

Senator the Hon. C. G. Marais asked the Prime Minister the reason for granting to the High Commissioner in London an allowance of £1,000 over and above his salary of £3,000 per annum; and how long this allowance would be granted?

The Prime Minister (Lieut.-General the Right Hon. J. C. Smuts) said the Union's representative in London had various large demands made upon him, in his official capacity, by way of entertaining, subscriptions, etc. The allowance, which does not cover all the various expenses, was granted as a contribution towards meeting these demands. The amount was voted annually by Parliament and was provided for in Section 3 (1) of the High Commissioners' Act, 1911 (Act No. 3 of 1911).

On 15th June,

Senator the Hon. F. W. Reitz asked the Acting Prime Minister whether his attention had been drawn to what had appeared in the newspapers or elsewhere concerning the expression of views of the High Commissioner in London with reference to the political position in the Union; whether such views were in accordance with the duties which that official had to perform; and, if not, whether the Government would warn him to confine himself in future to the duties for which he had been appointed.

The Acting Prime Minister (the Right Hon. F. S. Malan) said he did not think any objection could be taken to a reasonable interpretation of his remarks. The High Commissioner was not a member of the Public Service, and the Government did not think that occasion had arisen to make any special representations to him.

DEBATE IN HOUSE OF ASSEMBLY.

Motion to reduce expenditure.

On 30th May, in Committee of Supply on the Estimates, on Vote 10, High Commissioner in London, £73,729,

General the Hon. J. B. M. Hertzog (Leader of the Nationalist Party) moved to reduce the Vote by £50,000. The expenditure in connection with the office of the High Commissioner had, he said, gone up year after year in an alarming manner. Morley's Hotel had been acquired at a cost of £145,000, but, although that money had been expended, the Union had not become the owner of the Hotel, but had only purchased the leasehold for nine years. A further point was that the railway were making preparations for a similar establishment to the High Commissioner's. He contended that the present system was the very worst the Union could have; it was laid down when the Union was under Colonial status and did not enjoy the status which had rightly been laid down by the Prime Minister. In those days the Union of South Africa could do nothing without the British Government.

Representatives on the Continent and in United States.

He held that South Africa should have her representatives on the Continent of Europe as well as in America. It was totally wrong that all affairs regarding South Africa should first go through London. The office of the High Commissioner should be split up, and part should go to the European Continent and part to America. At the same time, he agreed as to the necessity of there being an official of high standing in England. He also argued that Parliament should have greater say about what was done by the High Commissioner, and complained that not a single report had been laid on the Table regarding his work.

On the Chairman ruling that General Hertzog must move reduction on individual items,

General Hertzog moved the deletion of the whole Vote.

Receipts.

The Minister of Finance (Hon. H. Burton) said, in regard to Morley's Hotel, they had fought this thing out on a previous occasion.* Mr. Burton went on to say that although the Vote was for £73,000, the Department got receipts to the extent of £50,000, which were by way of payment by the Railway Department to the Treasury for business which the High Commissioner's office did.

South Africa behind other Dominions.

Even now, Mr. Burton continued, South Africa was a long way behind other Dominions in regard to advancing its interests by way of representation in London. He did not think for a moment that the Government would object to providing for trade representation in other parts of the world when the need justified it. As regards the United States, the Government had business agents in New York with whom they were in constant communication. The reason of their not having Commissioners in other parts of the world was simply that more than 80 per cent. of South Africa's business was done with the United Kingdom, and if they were going to start Trade Commissioners in other countries they were going to land themselves in infinitely higher costs than by having their business centred in London.

"The Business Centre of the World."

He was convinced that they were wise for the present in keeping their Commissioners in London; it was not merely the business centre of England, but of the world. From every country on earth the threads of business went towards London, and even if that were not the Union of South Africa, the business of the country would still have to be done with London if the Government wished to do it in the best way.

Complaint had been made that Union tenders for railway material were also centred in London. That was inevitable. The idea, he supposed, was that British manufacturers had an undue advantage, but this was not the case. Where there was an open tender for the world it went to the world, and in proof of that he would remind the House that the Government had recently entered into large contracts with Canada and the United States, while before the war a good many of their orders were placed in Berlin.

In reply to a question Mr. Burton said the reason why the tenders could not be offered in South Africa was that South Africa was not a business centre, and he felt that until that country had advanced very much further in the direction

* *Vide* JOURNAL, Vol. II., No. 2, pp. 452–3.

of direct contact they must go to the very best place for doing their business. He could assure General Hertzog that there was no idea whatever of not developing trade relations with other countries.

General Hertzog contended that the soundest principle was to make one's purchases on the spot and not merely in London. The Minister's explanation, however, had removed most of his objections, although he still held that there was over-concentration in London.

Progress was reported and leave obtained to sit again.

Advice and warning to Immigrants.

On the resumption of the debate, on 1st June,

Brig.-General the Hon. J. J. Byron (South African Party, *Border, Cape*), referring to the advertisements concerning South Africa which he had seen in papers coming from such distant places as Egypt, India and Mesopotamia, and which contained statements that could not possibly be realised, said that those who were anxious to come to that country were people not only with capital, but of character, and they were the ones who should be encouraged to come. Therefore every effort should be made to attract them and to see that they did not come under false pretences, and to this end the High Commissioner and his offices should be used to a larger extent than at present to give people advice and warning.

"Imperial Air" in London.

Mr. C. W. Malan (Nationalist, *Humansdorp, Cape*) controverted Mr. Burton's statement that nearly all South Africa's business was done in London. Even if his contentions were correct, there was no reason why they should not develop their trade relations in other parts of the world. There was something behind the Minister's attitude and preference for London, and he would refer the House to the happenings at the Imperial Conference. It was the Imperial air which Mr. Burton had breathed in London which had been responsible for the present attitude of the Government. It was the resolution in regard to inter-Imperial trade which had caused it to act as it had done. Mr. Malan declared that they were retrenching officials in South Africa but promoting Imperial schemes. He moved to reduce the item "Trades Commissioner" by £1.

"Morley's Hotel."

Mr. T. Boydell (Leader of the Labour Party) disagreed entirely with the attitude taken up by the Nationalists in regard to Morley's Hotel. If South Africa were to be what these honourable Members wanted it to be—a nation among the other nations of the world—then it was only right and proper that they should have headquarters in London, the business centre of the world, worthy of that country. He hoped, however, that Morley's Hotel would not be used as a sort of unemployment bureau.

Mr. P. van Niekerk (**Nationalist,** *Waterberg, Trans.*) said the High Commissioner in London was interfering too much in political affairs and not following the precedent set by Mr. Schreiner.

A Minister of Foreign Affairs.

Dr. D. F. Malan (**Nationalist,** *Calvinia, Cape*) said the time had arrived when, in South Africa, they should have a Minister of Foreign Affairs under which the work of the High Commissioner in London should then fall. The Mandate over South-West Africa could also fall under that, just the same as their relations with the League of Nations, etc. Trade Commissioners should and could be appointed in other parts, their offices to fall under the Department of Foreign Affairs.

Trade Commissioners in Foreign Countries.

Arguing in favour of appointing Trade Commissioners in Europe and elsewhere, Dr. Malan said that even if a Trade Commissioner meant an expenditure of £3,000 the country would benefit largely from such expenditure. Resolutions had been passed at the Imperial Conference in favour of trade expansion within the Empire. The object was to exclude foreign countries as much as possible, and to foster the inter-Colonial trade, which to his mind would act to the detriment of South Africa. He protested also against the action of the High Commissioner, who had contravened the Immigration Act, and sent large numbers of unemployed to South Africa. He moved to reduce the salary of the High Commissioner by £1,000.

Other Nationalist Objections.

Mr. F. W. Beyers (**Nationalist,** *Edenburg, O.F.S.*) wanted to know whether the accounts of the High Commissioner were ever audited. How many of his staff of 166 were Afrikanders, English, and Dutch Afrikanders ? Further, what were the qualifications of the new High Commissioner ?

Minister of Finance replies to criticisms.

The Minister of Finance said honourable Members opposite seemed to have formed themselves into a voluntary association for the discovery of mares' nests. In reply to Mr. Beyers' question as to the audit of the High Commissioner's Office, he would find in the Auditor-General's report a full account of this. With respect to immigration, Mr. Boydell, not at all from the point of view of the Nationalists, had mentioned a case which had come to his notice of some men who had come to that country. Apparently now the Nationalists objected to any white man coming out to that country. This matter, however, did not belong to the High Commissioner's Vote at all. If there was anything in it, it should be raised on the Vote of the Minister of the Interior. All his (Mr. Burton's) information at the moment was that the Government had nothing whatever to do with it. The money was provided by the Prince of Wales's Fund.

Trade with United Kingdom.

After referring to another point, and to the approval which Mr. Canham, the Trades Commissioner, had won for the work he had been doing, Mr. Burton alluded to the objections that had been taken to figures quoted by him in regard to the amount of business which they did with the United Kingdom instead of with the rest of the world. He spoke broadly at the time, and said he thought the trade with the United Kingdom was about 80 per cent. of their whole trade. However, he had had figures taken out for 1920, and he found that in that year South Africa's trade with the United Kingdom in regard to imports was 54 per cent., and with the British Empire 66 per cent., while in regard to exports it was 80 per cent.—76 per cent. with the United Kingdom alone and 80 per cent. with the Empire as a whole.

Trade with other countries.

What was the position in regard to other countries? They would find that in the matter of imports, out of £92,000,000 in 1920 something like over £60,000,000 was done with Great Britain and the British Empire. Of that amount Holland did trade with South Africa in the way of imports to the extent of £760,000, whereas other foreign countries did £29,000,000, so that Holland so far had done less trade with South Africa than some of the other countries outside the Empire. And yet it was extremely likely that Holland would be the first country with which they should develop trade relations. The Government had organised an exhibition of South African products in Holland—they had not selected New York or France—and if they read an account of the way in which it was conducted they would find it very different from that given by Members on the Nationalist benches. Moreover, they would find that great praise had been accorded to Mr. Canham for his work in this connection.

Advertising South Africa.

Referring to the overseas advertising scheme, Mr. Burton said personally he was not fond of this sort of thing, but it was a modern method and they were drawn into it. Before it was entered upon there was the greatest criticism of the Government for being so slow in the matter. The Dominions Royal Commission had said they were struck by the apparent indifference in bringing the products of South Africa before other countries, and that in this respect the Union compared unfavourably with the other Dominions. The Government was alive to the necessity for warning those who contemplated coming out to South Africa, as was also the new High Commissioner, who would see that proper steps were taken in the direction indicated.

Supplies ordered by High Commissioner.

Mr. Burton dealt with other questions and criticisms that had been raised, and concluded by giving some figures as to the amount of supplies ordered by the Administration in 1920. Through the High Commissioner's Office in London £4,000,000 were purchased, while in South Africa there were purchased over £5,000,000 worth. £1,500,000 was spent on South African products, and that figure continued to progressively increase, so that he did not think anyone need fear that the Administration could not be relied upon to support South African enterprise and products in every possible way.

Labour approval of Trades Commissioner.

Mr. Boydell emphasised the fact that Labour Members were not against either the High Commissioner or the Trades Commissioner, and quite recognised that the latter had done well for South Africa.

After further discussion,

The Minister of Finance moved that the question be put, and this was agreed to by 55 votes to 24. Three amendments moved by Nationalist Members to reduce the salary of the High Commissioner by various amounts were defeated, and progress was reported.

EMPIRE NEWS SERVICE.

(Subscription to Reuter's Agency, etc.)

On 30th May in Committee of Supply on the Estimates, on Vote 9, Miscellaneous Services, £144,221.

Subscription to Reuter's.

General the Hon. J. B. M. Hertzog (Leader of the Nationalist Party) moved the deletion of the £1,200 subscription to Reuter's. The amount had been originally £300, and even at that time Members objected, but the reason of the increase was now known: it was due to the fact that news had to be supplied to South Africa from England and elsewhere which the authorities wished to get rid of.

The Minister of Finance (Hon. H. Burton): "We are going to stop that."

General Hertzog: "Well, I think the whole Vote should go." Continuing, he made allegations as to the partiality and unreliability of the agency.

Subsidy for circulation of Empire news.

Dr. D. F. Malan (Nationalist, *Calvinia, Cape*) protested against the vote being put upon the Estimates without proper information being put before the House. He quoted from a reply given to a question in the House of Commons to show that the Union Government paid two-thirds and the English Government one-third of the cost of official information supplied to South Africa; he also quoted from the Minutes of the Imperial Conference to show that the increased subsidy to Reuter's was in connection with a scheme to circulate news of Imperial affairs through British channels. The object was to do this in such a manner as "to achieve and forward the unity of the Empire," in the words of Lord Beaverbrook. The £1,200 to Reuter's was merely the result of one of the resolutions of the Imperial Conference. He protested against the circulation of news so as to promote the Imperial sentiment.

Omissions, partiality of news, etc.

Mr. C. W. Malan (Nationalist, *Humansdorp, Cape*) complained of the delay in publishing the failure of the negotiations regarding the sale of South African wool in February. It was strange that an agency like Reuter's should not have had information of news that was published broadcast in the English Press. It seemed reasonable to assume that the news was received, and that the Government had censured and postponed publication till after the elections. He also declared that during the Elections Reuter's had been extremely partial in its reports, and moved the deletion of £4,000 for "Contingencies," demanding that more information be given.

Mr. T. Boydell (Leader of the Labour Party) asked whether it was the whole of the item for Reuter's Agency, or only £700 of it, as mentioned in the footnote.

The Minister of Finance: "£700."

Labour criticism.

Mr. Boydell said it seemed to many Members that Reuter's Agency was developing into a South African Party Agency. He did not object to that so much, but the taxpayers should not be asked to contribute towards the cost of it. It was significant that during the last Election Reuter's Agency supplied columns of the speeches of General Smuts, but only a few inches of the utterances of the Labour Leader, Colonel Creswell. He also referred to the biased nature of the news transmitted from England.

When they came to the speeches given in that House they found that the representatives of Reuter took it that it was their duty to report only the South African Party's side of the question in the main. When there were racial quarrels between the two sides, Reuter's reported the other side as well. That was good "copy." When it came to what was said about the economic point of view, then they thought the public should know what was being said from the Labour benches.

All the Labour Party asked was that they should have a square deal. They said that Reuter's concern should be to give the public a true reflex of what took place and what was said in that House without regard to Party. He was opposed to one single penny of taxpayers' money going to subsidise this agency, and Members of those benches would give the amendment their hearty support.

Agency defended.

The Minister of Finance said that the Imperial Conference held in 1918 did pass a resolution, but the special contribution of £700 was made for the first time in 1920, and had nothing to do with the Conference. The hon. Member for Humansdorp said they had done away with it because they had come back to breathe the pure air of South Africa. The Government had not run away from the matter. The amount was being taken off because of a suggestion from the other side. In reply to a question about Canada, Mr. Burton said Canada was not in it at all. The people in it were the Imperial Government, £700; the Union Government, £700; and the East and West African Protectorates, £700. Canada refused to come in. The Vote was made with a view of getting fuller accounts of the world's news than they got before. As to the £500, he thought they should let it remain. It was a very old Vote, and should be maintained because it enabled the Government to have at hand special and expert means of advertising the needs of the country. It also enabled statements like those in connection with the reduction of the price of sugar and the advances on wool to be telegraphed at once to all parts of the country. The Agency was extremely useful to the Government in the manner he had indicated.

Press Gallery reports.

Mr. A. G. Barlow (**Labour**, *Bloemfontein North, O.F.S.*) speaking as a former member of the Press Gallery, said Members should not forget that probably their speeches did not appeal to the " gentlemen up above " as much as to the gentlemen who were making them. He certainly thought, however, that Mr. Boydell, as the Leader of the Labour Party, had not been fairly treated by Reuter's Agency in South Africa. He did not think they had much to complain about so far as Parliamentary reports, prepared by the Press Gallery, were concerned. The Minister of Finance advanced one of the weakest arguments possible when he said they should pay £500 to a news agency because that agency was used by the Government to disseminate Government knowledge. What news agency was there in the world which would not pay them £500 a year to get that knowledge ?

Further criticism by General Hertzog.

General Hertzog argued that the Government was not in the least concerned with what was in the interest of South Africa in regard to this £700 subsidy, and without blushing the Minister of Finance had admitted that it was on the suggestion from Overseas that this sum was to be dropped. He wondered how many other Votes there were waiting for instructions from Oversea.

The Acting Prime Minister (the Right Hon. F. S. Malan) said the £700 had been paid simply in order that good, reliable news might be secured from Europe for circulation in South Africa and in other parts. Similarly reliable news was arranged for from South Africa, for which the Imperial Government paid £700. The Imperial Government now said: " Well, we shall stop paying that £700," and the Union Government agreed to stop paying as well, but if Members desired they could continue paying £700—or even £1,400.

General Hertzog said it was again the old imitation of everything the Imperial Government did, and the interests of South Africa were never considered.

Mr. M. Alexander (**Constitutional Democrat**, *Cape Town, Castle*) also opposed the Vote, because he considered it undignified for the Government to subsidise this partnership between itself and a private news agency. He had nothing to say against those who managed the affairs of the Agency in South Africa. He knew them personally, and believed they conducted their task as honourably as any hon. Member in that House.

General Hertzog's amendment to delete the item, £1,200 subscription to Reuter's Press Agency, was defeated by 59 votes to 41.

NATIVE AFFAIRS.

(Unsettlement of Natives by agitators; Sessional Committee on Native Affairs; Poll Tax; Payment of Native Teachers; Native Policy of the Government, etc.)

During the Session several Debates took place in the Senate and House of Assembly relating to various aspects of Native Affairs. The main discussions are summarised below.

DEBATE IN THE SENATE.

Irresponsible agitators.

On 20th May, in the Senate,

Senator the Hon. G. G. Munnik moved that, in view of the unsettled state of native affairs caused by irresponsible agitators, and the consequent disarrangement of the farm labour system which was so acute as to occasion loss and hindrance to farmers in carrying out their avocations, the Government be requested to take the matter into immediate consideration.

Whatever he might say must not be construed as being directed against natives in general. There were many educated and highly civilised natives whom he respected, but his remarks were directed towards pointing out the danger of the huge bulk of raw natives being influenced by irresponsible agitators. As an example he quoted the "Israelite" movement, which had set the law at defiance, and also a gathering at Pietersburg some few months ago, which was attended by many chiefs, even from so far as Barotseland. This meeting was held without the natives getting any permission from the local magistrates.

They were at present sitting on a smouldering volcano, and the Government should see to it that no meeting was held unless a magistrate was present. His desire was not to infringe any of the rights of the natives, but purely in the interests of the raw natives to protect them from their evil counsellors. He read letters from farmers to the effect that owing to the political unrest among the natives it was almost impossible for them to get labourers.

"Israelite" trouble.

After a short discussion,

The Prime Minister and Minister of Native Affairs (Lieut.-Gen. the Right Hon. J. C. Smuts) dealt with the position so far as the "Israelite" trouble was concerned. The Government, he said, had tried to avoid trouble, and had instructed the Native Affairs Commission to proceed to the spot and investigate matters. He mentioned reasons for some delay in the matter, but added that even since the Government had begun to deal with it the natives had adopted a reasonable attitude, and he did not fear that the whole thing could be adjusted without resort to force, which he thought a bad remedy in such cases. As things were at present the Government had at their disposal sufficient power to deal with any dangerous developments.

The position both in regard to the "Israelites" and the Pietersburg meeting had been much exaggerated. His experience was that the natives were prepared to respect the law, and he hoped the motion would be withdrawn.

The motion was withdrawn.

Sessional Committee on Native Affairs.

On 23rd May, **Senator the Hon. Dr. Roberts** moved:

That a Sessional Committee on Native Affairs be appointed, the Committee to have power to hear evidence and call for papers, and to have power to confer with the corresponding Committee of the House of Assembly.

The Prime Minister and Minister of Native Affairs said that he had no objection to the motion; in fact, he welcomed it. In that House there were Senators who specially represented native interests, and he thought that every means possible which could enable them to gain further information should be afforded them.

The motion was agreed to.

DEBATE IN HOUSE OF ASSEMBLY.

Native Poll Tax.

On 27th May, in Committee of Supply, when Vote 8, Provincial Administrations, £4,643,291, was discussed,

Mr. L. Blackwell (South African Party, *Bezuidenhout, Trans.*) drew attention to the new taxation proposals in the Transvaal Province, which included the levying of a poll tax on every adult male, and the raising of the native poll tax from £2 to £2 10s. per head. The latter was expected to produce £100,000. He thought that of all forms of taxation ever devised the poll tax was the most crude, unjustifiable and unfair. They had a white population living in great luxury and comfort alongside a great mass of people in the Transvaal who were in poor circumstances, and to say that both white and black should pay the poll tax of £2 10s. reached the limit of taxing genius. It meant to a native in the Transvaal a month's salary.

Grant for Education.

Proceeding, Mr. Blackwell said that the natives paid over £400,000 a year in poll tax in the Transvaal already. The Transvaal Provincial Council spent £3,000,000 a year in education, and of that sum every penny except a few thousands was spent on white education. It was proposed to take from the native half a million a year by means of a poll tax, and they only gave him £5,000 or £10,000 a year on education.

Question of exemption.

There was a much more serious aspect of this affair, he added. What was going to happen if the tax could not be paid? An authority had told him that under the new Transvaal Provincial Ordinance, if a man could not pay he could get an exemption from the magistrate if he were a white man, but every black man must pay or go to gaol. In the course of further remarks Mr. Blackwell said the Transvaal teachers were paid at a higher rate than any others in the civilised world. It was quite right to pay these salaries if one could afford them, but when they had to impose additional taxation to do so they should carefully scrutinise this expenditure.

The Right Hon. J. X. Merriman (South African Party, *Stellenbosch, Cape*) thought Mr. Blackwell had done a public duty in calling attention to this gross taxation of natives. When a burden of this kind was put upon them, not for their own benefit, but for the benefit of another class of the population, he considered it was time that Members of the House, who represented these natives and who were supposed to be their guardians, raised their voice against it.

Working-classes in the Transvaal.

Mr. H. W. Sampson (Labour, *Jeppes, Trans.*) said the Transvaal Provincial Council had been constantly hampered by Parliament and this poll tax was an outcome of it. He proceeded to give instances of interference, and went on to say that he also was going to appeal to the Minister to veto the tax on behalf of the working-classes of the Transvaal, upon which it would fall very heavily. Personally, he was of the opinion that those who had imposed the tax had done so to bring the Union Government into disrepute—an act of revenge for its interference.

Inadequate payment of Native Teachers.

Mr. J. S. Marwick (South African Party, *Illovo, Natal Province*) supported the suggestion that the Minister should veto the Native Poll Tax, and said there was no doubt that the Act of Union laid it down most clearly that the control of native affairs should rest entirely with the Union Government. In the Transvaal the natives contributed in revenue 23s., compared with 22s. in Natal, 16s. in the Orange Free State, and only 8s. in the Cape. A similar comparison of native affairs existed in connection with provincial revenue, with the exception that Natal was slightly higher than the Transvaal. The native tax was a very burdensome one, and the natives had made representations for reductions.

Mr. J. Christie (**Labour,** *Langlaagte, Trans.*) considered that the House ought to interfere and stop the poll tax coming into force in the Transvaal. The temper of the people on the Reef was very bitter against such an imposition. Referring to education, Mr. Christie said the teachers were underpaid, and there were not sufficient schools to meet demands. There were between 7,000 and 8,000 children unable to go to school because there was no accommodation for them.

Mr. W. H. Stuart (**South African Party,** *Tembuland, Cape*) said that during the last few years the white teachers had received an increase of salary, but it was only last year that the coloured teachers received an increase. This was by virtue of a promise that had been given to the effect that the native teachers were to receive their long-awaited income. The position was such that it would pay the native teachers to throw up their jobs and become ordinary policemen.

An Amendment.

Mr. R. B. Waterston (**Labour,** *Brakpan, Trans.*) denied that the school teachers in the Transvaal were well paid, and pointed out that Mr. Blackwell had not quoted Australia, Canada, or any of the other Dominions. He would be sorry for the teachers of other countries if they were paid less than those in the Transvaal, and if the natives were taxed in order to pay the teachers, it was in no way the fault of the latter. Subsequently Mr. Waterston moved the reduction of the salaries of each of the four Provincial Administrations by £1,000.

Teachers' salaries "A disgrace to the country."

The Minister of Finance (**Hon. H. Burton**) confessed to the deepest sympathy with what had been said about the salaries of the native teachers. For a long time he had been seriously perturbed about their position because he had no doubt in his own mind that the wages they drew for work which they did comparatively quite as well as European teachers was a scandal to the Union. The maximum salary paid for certificated native teachers was £112 10s. per annum, while the minimum was £42 10s. or £3 10s. per month. For uncertificated teachers it was £1 10s. per month—a wage which was less than domestic servants got. They had a duty to perform to these people which they should regard as an obligation, and which they, as the European race in that country, should feel proud to fulfil honestly. The Government found it difficult to deal with the matter at all, because it was one which was under the control of the Provincial Council, according to the Constitution.

Question of altering the Constitution.

A Member having suggested that the Constitution should be altered, Mr. Burton said there might be a good deal to be said for that, but he could not discuss it then. Such an alteration would be a very important one, and would have to be carefully considered in the House. He had been in communication with the Administrator in the Cape for some time past, and as he was still busy with the matter, he would ask the House to leave it there. Mr. Burton gave his assurance that he would spare no trouble to see if there was any method by which the continuance of this disgrace to the country could be avoided.

Government veto not feasible.

In regard to the Poll Tax, he said he could not dictate to the Transvaal. It might be entirely lacking in equity, but they had to ask themselves whether that was a measure of such a nature that the Government should veto it. Broadly speaking, this Ordinance was within the Council's rights, and the Government had nothing to say about it, but it was impossible not to see that in the clauses of the Ordinance there were provisions which appeared to conflict with the laws passed in the House of Assembly.

Discrimination between Natives and Europeans.

There were attempts, undoubtedly, at discriminating between the native and the European. Referring, for instance, to Mr. Blackwell's contention that if a native could not pay he went to gaol, Mr. Burton said that seemed to be correct. A special process was provided by which the native was brought before the Magistrate on a criminal charge, whereas under another clause a white man went through a civil process. It looked like discrimination. The law adviser had come to the conclusion that the discrimination was not so great as would appear at first sight, because provision was made in another Act exempting indigent natives, and they could plead protection under that Ordinance as well.

Protection of Courts of Law.

It would appear that a native who was old, indigent, or ill, was not liable to pay the tax. He might be indigent without being old or ill: he might be lazy. If so, he would not get off; but a lazy indigent white man would get off. The Minister of Finance went on to say, however, that if a native was made to pay when he should not be made to pay, he had the law behind him and would be protected by the Courts. He thought it would be a mistaken policy if the Union Government interfered with that Ordinance. The Transvaal Provincial Council and the Transvaal people must find their own way out of the trouble. The native mind might be disturbed and so the Government would see that the natives were not inequitably taxed.

Authority with Provincial Council or Parliament?

In the course of further discussion

The Minister of the Interior (Hon. Patrick Duncan) said, personally, he would like to see the Provincial Council deprived of all powers of taxation of natives and the Union Parliament ought to be the sole authority.

Amendment.

Mr. A. G. Barlow (Labour, *Bloemfontein North, O.F.S.*) moved an amendment to reduce the salary of the Administrator of the Transvaal by £500 as a protest against the introduction of legislation into the Council discriminating between whites and blacks.

Progress was reported and leave obtained to resume.

On 30th May, on the discussion being resumed,

Mr. Waterston's amendment was withdrawn in view of that proposed by Mr. Barlow, which was defeated by 85 votes to 10. An amendment by General C. Muller to reduce the salary of the Administrator of the Cape by £750 was negatived.

The vote, as printed, was agreed to.

Native Policy.

During June lengthy debates took place in Committee of Supply on Vote No. 24, Native Affairs, £432,884, when the position of the Government on some aspects of native policy was outlined by the Acting Prime Minister.

DEBATE IN HOUSE OF ASSEMBLY.

On 24th June,

General the Hon. J. B. M. Hertzog (Leader of the Nationalist Party) said that among the native population a consciousness ıad arisen as to a necessity for expression in their national ife. To that the white population should not shut its eyes. The question which concerned the native was what the future vould bring. The speaker pointed to the legislation of 1913 ınd the subsequent steps of 1917. All that had been done n those days had been to lay down certain principles regarding ixed property. But that had not been enough to satisfy either the native or the white man. They had, in fact, only ırrived at the threshold of the segregation policy. There were wo alternatives: social equality and mixing up, or the opposite to that.

European and Native.

South Africa, General Hertzog continued, was developing fast, and he asked that the Government should say definitely whether between the territories to be set apart for natives ınd whites there was to be free industrial competition or ıot. Then there were other questions affecting the native franchise. There was no doubt that the European did not ılways act with that calm justice and fairness towards the ıative that he should, but the European was so often affected by nervousness as to what the native would do in future in South Africa.

In regard to the franchise, General Hertzog asked the House to assume the possibility of the native sending a majority of his representatives to Parliament. Could they imagine what would be the result of such a condition? It would be just to neither the native nor to the white man to extend the franchise to the native. He pointed to the development and civilisation which had taken place of recent years. To-day they counted some hundreds of educated, professional men among them, and these men wanted their influence to be felt just as the educated men among the Europeans did. But in spite of their education these men, because of their colour, were regarded as a sort of pariah.

Three questions.

General Hertzog asked the Acting Minister to say whether the Government aimed at free social intermingling or segregation; whether in industrial and professional respects the native and European territories would be open for inter-competition of whites and natives; and whether the Government intended in the European territory to give the franchise to the native living there and in the native territory to the European living there.

Mr. W. H. Stuart (South African Party, ***Tembuland, Cape*****)** said the policy of the Government had been that native policy should, and must, to a certain extent, as long as the safeguards in the Act of Union existed, vary in the different provinces of the Union. The suggestion that the South Africa Act should be altered by eliminating the native vote in the Cape was infinitely more calculated to disturb native opinion of every class throughout the whole of South Africa than a dozen Bulhoek affairs. General Hertzog had put his finger on the real danger point of contact between black and white in South Africa. The real fear of the white man was that they might not maintain the standard of their civilisation, and set an example which would keep them a white race ahead and always a true example to the subordinate races.

A great forward movement.

Mr. W. S. Webber (South African Party, *Troyeville, Trans.*) said the Government had enunciated a policy on the native question and it was laid down in the Act passed last year. He thought a great movement forward was made by that Act, and that it would lead very largely to a proper solution of the problem if it was carried out in the spirit in which it was introduced into the House. He went on to instance two pressing matters not yet dealt with: the life of the natives in industrial centres and the awful confusion in the Pass Laws.

Western civilisation and primitive races.

The Rev. J. Mullineux (Labour, *Roodepoort, Trans.*) urged the wisdom which lay in keeping the matter outside Parliamentary politics. There appeared still to be a very crude and ill-balanced opinion abroad in the country as to this vast problem. They must remember that they were the guardians of a race of people comparatively in their infancy, and it seemed essential that they should learn to act quickly, firmly and with absolute justice. It took a long time, he continued, to develop and reveal the true life and characteristics of a race.

In this particular connection there was the complication of the entry into the problem of our Western ideas of civilisation: they had introduced these ideas into the development of a primitive people, and this had arrested and turned the natural development of the race in an entirely different direction. There was the question of industrialism, which had had a serious effect upon the natives, and of social life; while religion, good or otherwise, had had an enormous effect in unsettling the native people. In fact, all these things had thrown them into a state of chronic perplexity.

More personal contact needed.

The natives had lost confidence in the Government, and in his (the speaker's) opinion the reason was that the white people were so entirely taken up with their own problems that they had withdrawn themselves to a large extent from the exercise of all the influence which personality brought to bear on the native people. They should be more closely in touch with them than by means of departments, and that was why their (the members') ancestors were able to settle native problems better than they did.

Training in handicrafts and agriculture.

It was not book learning, Mr. Mullineux went on to say, that the natives wanted, and the Government would do far better to encourage them in learning handicraft and matters connected with the land. It was along these lines, perhaps, that they would find a solution of the problem. If the present policy of drift was continued, however, the evil forces would grow, and the natives might put their sinister intentions under the cloak of religion.

Segregation impracticable.

The Acting Prime Minister (the Right Hon. F. S. Malan), referring to the wide range which the debate had taken, to the criticisms of the Government on their action in regard to the " Israelite " trouble and the Native Affairs Commission, said that to have total segregation of the whites from the natives would not under existing circumstances lead them any further. Did they think that it would satisfy the spirit which was awakening among the natives if the Government told the educated native that he must live and practice in the native territory among the raw natives? He contended that the Native Affairs Commission should be given time in which to deal with the questions entrusted to it. As to industrial separation, if the white man was prepared and able to do all the work without the natives, it would be possibly good for natives as well as for whites; but they had not yet arrived at that stage.

Progress was reported.

Further discussion took place on 27th June, and the Vote, as printed, was agreed to.

CHILDREN'S PROTECTION ACT AMENDMENT ACT.

The Bill for this Act was introduced by the Minister of Education (Hon. Patrick Duncan) and passed through all stages during the Session. The Act amends in certain respects the Children's Protection Act, 1913,* with regard to the care,

* The Children's Protection Act, 1913, provided for the better protection of children, the consolidation and amendment of the law relating thereto, and the amendment of the law relating to industrial schools and other similar institutions.

training and maintenance of destitute children, committal to auxiliary homes, etc.

Medical Inspection.

The Act requires the deletion of the word "education" wherever it appears in Section 16 of the Act of 1913,* and provides that any medical officer or practitioner directed to examine the person or clothing of any child may demand admittance to a house or premises where he has reason to believe such a child to be, during the day or at any reasonable hour of the night. Any person refusing him admittance or otherwise obstructing him shall be guilty of an offence.

Lying-in-homes and Advertisements for adoption.

The Act also amends the former Act† so as to secure that a "lying-in-home" shall include any maternity home, premises or portion of premises kept for the purpose of accommodating women during their confinement for any remuneration, whether by way of rent or fees for attendance or otherwise, and makes it unlawful for newspapers in the Union to insert, without the written permission of the magistrate of the district, advertisements from persons desiring an infant to be adopted, or from persons willing to take charge of an infant.

"Disciplinary Powers" for Heads of Industrial Schools.

An amendment of that section in the Act‡ giving the Governor-General power to establish industrial schools for destitute children, under a house-father or mother, gives the title of principal and the disciplinary powers of a parent to the head of a Government industrial school.

Care and training of destitute children.

New provisions are made in addition to those contained in Section 34 of the principal Act for the care of a neglected or destitute child in a Government industrial school or by a relative or other fit person, and his apprenticeship to a useful calling until he reaches the age of eighteen, etc.; it being possible for the orders of judges or magistrates' courts relating to him to be varied by said courts, subject to supervision by (on the application of) persons or societies working for the welfare of children.

Destitution defined.

A new sub-section states that a "destitute" child is one "without sufficient means of existence" or whose parent or other person legally responsible for his support is in indigent circumstances and unable to maintain him or is dead or unknown, and who, through lack of training or control, is liable to fall into crime and become a charge upon the State. (*Sect.* 8, III.)

Instalments of maintenance.

The Act gives added powers to the court in regard to ordering a parent, step-parent or guardian of a child to pay for his maintenance by weekly or monthly instalments and in regard to ordering part of any income payable to such guardian or parent to be attached and paid to the person named by the court; or, in the event of regulations regarding payments not being complied with, exercising such powers

---

* Section 16 of Act of 1913 refers to the "local education authority" directing the inspection of children.

† Section 27, Act of 1913. ‡ Section 33, Act of 1913.

as to the disposal of the child as may be exercised by a judge or magistrates' court under Section 34 of the principal Act as amended and referred to above. (See under "Care and training of destitute children.")

Supplementary provision.

When the mother, step-mother or grandmother of any child regarding whom an order is made is a widow, or her husband through ill-health or other cause beyond his control cannot support the child properly, the court, after inquiry, shall report the facts to the Minister of Education; and it shall be lawful for the latter, in accordance with any regulations made by the Governor-General and subject to such conditions as may be imposed by the Minister, to pay to such mother, etc., out of moneys voted by Parliament, what he deems necessary to supplement the provision made by the mother, etc., for the care and maintenance of the child.

Transference of children.

The Minister may also order a child in a Government industrial school or under the care of a relative, etc., to be transferred to another school, etc.; or one over the age of 12, who exercises an evil influence over others, to be transferred to a juvenile reformatory after the Minister has consulted with the Minister of Justice, or to be apprenticed to some useful calling or occupation until he is 18.

Selling or giving tobacco, cigarettes, etc., to a child.

The prohibition in Section 45 of the Act of 1913 against selling tobacco, cigars, cigarettes or cigarette papers to a child except as therein provided, is extended to lending, giving, supplying, delivering or offering to sell, lend, give, etc., to a child.

Judging the age of a child.

Section 52 of the principal Act (which provided that no child under the age of 12 should take part in entertainments in any circus, theatre, etc., unless authorised by the magistrate by licence issued under certain conditions) is amended by the substitution of the word "fourteen" in lieu of the word "twelve." (*Sect.* 15.)

Another section (58) of the principal Act is amended by the addition of a sub-section providing that in any proceedings under this Act, or any amendment for the purpose of determining any question concerning the care, maintenance, etc., of a person who is apparently a child, it shall be the duty of the court, if the age of such person cannot be ascertained, and is a material fact, to judge his age by his appearance, etc., and no error so made in good faith shall vitiate any part of the proceedings. The said person shall be deemed to have attained on 1st January preceding the date of the finding of the court the age so claimed.

Provision is also made for temporary leave of absence from an industrial school or institution.

DEBATE IN HOUSE OF ASSEMBLY.

On 20th April,

The Minister of Education (Hon. Patrick Duncan), in moving the Second Reading of the Bill, dealt especially with

Clause 6, referring to auxiliary homes to which children over the age of 15 could be sent, and remain under supervision while going out to work like other girls and boys—an important item in what was known as the "after-care" of children who had been brought up in a State industrial home. Clause 9 provided for what was popularly known as "Mother's pensions" which, however, was rather a misleading phrase. No State institution, however well managed, could possibly give to a child that treatment which he would receive in his own home; and if the only objection was that that home was destitute it seemed, in accordance with every one's experience, that the best thing to do was to leave the child in his home under proper supervision. Money spent on work of this kind to give these children a chance of becoming good citizens was money well spent.

General the Hon. J. M. B. Hertzog (Leader of the Nationalist Party) said that it appeared to him that there had lately been an unduly great tendency to interfere with the rights of the parents and to take away the child from its natural guardians. A State institution must be a very good one to have an atmosphere which was not worse than the atmosphere of the home. He urged the Minister to do his utmost to see that children were not too easily removed from the control of the parents.

The Rev. J. Mullineux (Labour, *Roodepoort, Trans.*), referring to some objections, said that so far as he had read through the Bill and made comparisons with the original Act, he found that in practically every case the changes were those which had been found absolutely necessary in practice. He thought there was no interference in the Bill with the home life of the people, and he hoped that the grants would be as liberal as possible in order that children in the homes might be properly clothed, housed and educated, and made into decent citizens of the State.

The Second Reading was agreed to.

IN THE SENATE.

In the course of the discussions in Committee on 17th June, on Clause 3, a question having been raised in regard to the interpretation of "lying-in-homes,"

The Minister of Education (Hon. Patrick Duncan) said the clause stated there must be remuneration. It sought to prevent girls and women going to a certain place to be confined, and the child being secretly removed, so that neither the mother nor others knew, nor cared, what happened to it. He proposed that the wording should be "premises which are kept for the purpose of accommodating women or girls during their confinement."

The amendment was agreed to.

CRIMINAL PROCEDURE AND EVIDENCE ACT AMENDMENT BILL.

(Abolition of Trial by Jury.)

This is a Bill to amend the Criminal Procedure and Evidence Act, 1917, in order to abolish trial by jury in criminal cases, and to make other provision in lieu thereof, and was summarised in Vol. II., No. 2, p. 451, of the JOURNAL. It was introduced on 15th March by Mr. E. Nathan (South African Party).

DEBATE IN HOUSE OF ASSEMBLY.

In the House of Assembly on 31st March,

Mr. E. Nathan (South African Party, *Von Brandis, Trans.*), in moving the Second Reading, said he thought the miscarriages of justice which had occurred were sufficient justification for the introduction of this measure. He had written much on the subject and invited criticisms pro and con from all parts, and so far the criticisms had been few and far between. He claimed that the scheme provided under the Bill would be more expeditious and economical than the existing jury system. The innocent had nothing to fear from what he proposed. He was going to give them a judge.

Qualifications of Jurors.

In regard to the qualifications of jurors, had there been an educational test one might have said there was not so much against the present system. They drew their jurors from the Parliamentary voters, and practically every man who became naturalised had the qualification and was entitled to be placed on the jury list. They had men on juries from all parts of the world, some from countries where certain crimes were not regarded with the same gravity as they were there.

The ordinary man, Mr. Nathan continued, was unfit to weigh evidence or grasp figures; he became weary in long trials ; he objected in many cases to the death sentence, and was more frequently swayed by counsel than a judge was likely to be. He was also apt to be influenced and prejudiced by reading the reports published in the newspapers, of evidence given in preparatory examinations. He proceeded to show that several inroads had already been made upon the jury system in the Union, and went on to quote a number of cases dating back to 1879 which, he claimed, constituted strong arguments against the jury system which had been reduced to a farce and had brought the Courts into ridicule.

The Minister of Justice (Senator the Hon. N. J. de Wet) said that although, speaking personally, he sympathised with many of Mr. Nathan's arguments, he was surprised at his onslaught on the jury system. It was one of the English institutions taken over by that country, and he thought it was one of which Englishmen would be proud. Trial by jury had existed in South Africa for a long time and, with all its defects, he did not think human ingenuity had yet found a satisfactory substitute for it. He attached great weight to the experience of their judges, and had taken the liberty of asking them to express their opinion ; of the 23, not counting the judges of the Court of Appeal, 18 gave their opinions, 14 being decidedly against the abolition, while four were in favour of it. The Minister read extracts from the statement made by one of the judges, and said that he would like to associate himself with that opinion.

Improvements in the Criminal Procedure Act.

They had, he said, tried to make some improvements in the Criminal Procedure Act. They had given an accused person the right to be tried without a jury ; they had also a provision by which the Attorney-General had the right in certain cases to ask for a special court of three judges. The former had been taken advantage of in a good many cases, the latter very sparingly. He thought the suggestion made by a judge that cases under the Insolvency Law and other cases involving figures and book-keeping should be taken from a jury and put before a judge or assessors was worthy of attention. The one great point in favour of the jury system was that it made the community share in the administration of justice, and made them feel that they were part and parcel of the machinery. On the whole, he did not think the time was ripe for taking the very important step contemplated by this Bill.

Trial by one's peers.

Mr. W. H. Stuart (South African Party, ***Tembuland, Cape*****)** pointed out that the system of trial by jury, essentially one which had grown up with the civilisation of Great Britain, had been based upon trial by one's peers, one's equals, and as long as that condition was carefully cherished there could be, normally speaking, no great objection to it. The difference in South Africa was that trial by one's peers very rarely occurred.

In cases where both complainant and accused were white, when the trial took place before a European jury he believed that, subject to a certain consideration due to the conditions in South Africa, they had the elements of a fair trial. Where the parties concerned in the dispute which had led to a criminal action were both natives or coloured, he honestly believed that European juries did their best to, and reasonably did, give a square deal to the accused. The third case, however, was the one where either a white man stood in the dock and the complainant was a coloured person, or where a coloured person stood in the dock and the complainant was a white person. So under those circumstances it required the cream of the white race to adjudicate upon a matter like that if they were going to have the adjudication by the white race.

Mixed Trials, Justice to Natives and Coloured people, etc.

That country, Mr. Stuart continued, was one in which a jury other than a European jury was not practical politics. The choice was between a jury, which gave them the average man, and a judge, who was a picked man in the full sense of the word. Where they had a mixed trial he submitted that they should have a judge and assessors, and have that system only. The ordinary man did not know that every accused person had a right to claim that. Then there was the other side of the shield. They wanted to keep the administration of justice pure and unspotted. Under existing conditions, with a million and a quarter European people governing six million coloured people and natives, the fundamental essential was that any feeling of injustice should be taken away from the subject races, and they should realise that white justice was impartial. In conclusion, whatever might be the case for the jury system in England or America, it failed in that country when it was put to the acid test as between men of different status and race.

The present system defended.

Mr. M. Alexander (Con. Dem., *Cape Town, Castle*) said that the conclusion he had come to from his experience of over 20 years was quite contrary to that which they had heard from the hon. member for Tembuland. Indeed, he would despair of the future of the country if it were true that any one of coloured blood could not get justice there. Mr. Stuart had indicated that it was the colour question that rendered it necessary to do away with the jury system, but were there not judges who made mistakes in regard to matters of law and were not the Appeal Courts kept busy in this very direction? It was hardly fair to say that the question of race always entered into the matter.

Mr. Alexander went on to say, in regard to the statement that the people did not know the law, that it was for the friends of the natives to let them know what the law was, and to inform them that if they wished to be tried without a jury they could do so. He submitted that this was better than doing away with the jury system altogether, which would be to take a backward step. If the people had a share in the administration of justice they had more respect for justice, and it resulted in the promotion of law and order. He moved, as an amendment, "that the Bill be read a second time this day six months."

Mr. D. M. Brown (South African Party, *Three Rivers, Cape*) suggested that an improvement might be made if preliminary examinations of a certain nature should be held in private, and that the accused should know what evidence was going to be brought against them.

Mr. R. W. Close (South African Party, *Rondebosch, Cape*) said that Mr. Nathan had overlooked the great amount of good work which had been done by juries, and the isolated cases quoted did not make out a case for the removal of the system.

If this had been a Bill, he went on to say, for the abolition of trial by jury in civil cases, he would have voted for it with both hands. There was a marked distinction between jury trials in criminal cases and jury trials in civil cases. They had civil juries in the Cape and, he believed, also in Natal. In a very large number of cases a civil jury was sought for one particular purpose only, and that was to pile up the damages, as far as possible, against the Government or against the Corporation.

Other Members having spoken, the amendment that the Bill be read a second time six months hence was carried without a division.

NEWFOUNDLAND.

The second Session of the twenty-fourth Parliament commenced on 30th March, 1921 (vide JOURNAL, *Vol. II., No. 3, p. 695). Parliament was adjourned on 12th August until 12th December, on which date, after the transaction of the necessary business, it was prorogued.*

PRIME MINISTER'S STATEMENT.

(Fisheries; Unemployment; Financial position; Lumber operations, etc.)

On 12th December, 1921, the Prime Minister made the following general statement in the House of Assembly :—

Fisheries.

The Prime Minister (Hon. Sir Richard Squires) said that when the House was in Session in July and August last the decision taken by his hon. friends opposite was that trade conditions were such as to make it quite probable that the merchants would not be financially able to purchase the season's catch of codfish, and even if they were able to make the purchase they might find great difficulty in making satisfactory arrangements for its export and sale. He had informed the House that if a situation arose which made it necessary for the staple industry of the country to be handled by the Government, the Government's programme, before being put into execution, would be submitted to the Legislature. He came to the conclusion that adjournment until this day would be the most expeditious way of handling the situation.

He felt that it was a great satisfaction to every Member of the Chamber that trade conditions had so materially improved and that the pessimistic views which had been expressed by many had been shown by subsequent events to be without foundation. It was expected by all that the price of fish this autumn could not approach War prices. The catch had been an average one; the fish had been rapidly absorbed by the merchants, both of St. John's and the outports, and speedily shipped to the foreign markets. He was reliably informed that there was less fish in the hands of the fishermen unsold at that date than there had been at that period of any year for the last ten or fifteen years at least. This situation having worked out in the ordinary commercial channels without the necessity for legislative interference was a matter for great congratulation and consequently there was no business to submit to the House on this adjournment.

Unemployment relief: construction of roads.

In August the Legislature adopted a programme of special relief work in connection with the construction of roads, both in St. John's and outside the city, and special roadwork to relieve the unemployment situation as it existed in the municipality of St. John's. The value received in work had not been commensurate with the money expended. He had been told that the value secured by the municipal council in connection with unemployment works, and also by the Government, did not represent more than 30 cents in work value given for every dollar expended. In other words, if this work had been put out to contract and the contractor had been at liberty to select his own men, and naturally only such number of men as could be profitably employed, as much work could have been done for one-third of the amount that was actually expended. From the standpoint of giving employment to the needy it was a satisfactory method of relief, but from the standpoint of getting for the amount expended good value it was eminently unsatisfactory. This did not mean that the men employed had deliberately aimed at getting something for nothing, but it was the natural result of the relief work under conditions as they found them in Newfoundland particularly, when the number of men who were employed for relief purposes was far in excess of the number of men who could be satisfactorily handled at any one time on the undertaking.

Financial position.

When in May last he took the responsibility of presenting the Budget to the House (*vide* JOURNAL, Vol. II., No. 3, p. 700) he estimated that they would start the new fiscal year on 1st July, 1921, with a credit reserve of $73,000 on surplus account. The Auditor General had sent him a memorandum saying that in his opinion the credit balance would be in the neighbourhood of $167,000, or $94,000 more than he estimated.

Dealing with customs revenue, the Prime Minister said that 43·18 per cent. was the average percentage of revenue collected during the first five months of one year. The customs revenue actually received from 1st July, 1921, to 30th November, 1921, worked out at 44 per cent. of the total revenue estimated by him to be received for the current fiscal year. Thus it was clear that the Customs returns, including Sales

Tax, was fully up to, if not a little beyond, the expectations of his Budget speech.

It was a matter of great congratulation to feel that the financial position of Newfoundland generally had improved so greatly during the past year. They all knew the feeling which was current in December and January last in the matter of the flotation of the loan which was then needed for railway and other purposes. As a matter of fact, he was expressly accused of having taken advantage of the brokers when he had succeeded in making a sale of six million dollars of bonds at such satisfactory figures. That loan, being 6½ per cent. issue, netted the colony in St. John's about $99.8 per 100. The improvements during recent months had been such that these same bonds were now quoted at $106.38.

Unemployment: lumber operations.

The major problem which was receiving the continuous attention of the Government during recess was the question of unemployment. While it was true that Newfoundland had not suffered from unemployment and labour disorganisation to anything like the extent of other countries which participated in the world-War, yet they found themselves face to face with a situation of considerable magnitude. With the exception of the winter fishery on the south coast and the spring seal fishery on the north-east coast, the avenues of employment were indeed limited. Lumber mills throughout the country, both large and small, found themselves with large stocks of lumber on hand, for which no sale could be secured, even at a price much below the cost of production. Under these circumstances a strenuous effort was made to provide employment for many thousands of men. The only avenue of employment available was the lumber woods. The Prime Minister then described negotiations between the Government and private companies for the cutting of pulpwood. Referring to the programme of relief work decided upon, he said that an arrangement had been made whereby the Anglo-Newfoundland Development Co. cut ten thousand cords of wood on their own limits in addition to the quantity of wood which they were cutting in the ordinary course of business, and also that a considerable quantity of wood should be cut at suitable points along the rail line in accordance with specifications furnished by the Company, the Company agreeing to purchase from the Government the wood cut, both on their own limits and along the rail line. This was a business proposition in connection with which it was scarcely possible for there to be any material loss to the Government. A proposition was worked out between the Horwood Lumber Co. and the Department of

Agriculture and Mines under which the Company were undertaking entirely on their own account lumber operations in the neighbourhood of Gander Bay, the entire capital for the operations being found by the Company, about half of it being advanced to them by their own bankers on Government guarantee. The product of these operations was to be lumber, which it was agreed should not be sold in the local market in competition with the products of other mills, but be sold in the United States. This was a purely business proposition in which there could be no Government loss. Special arrangements had had to be made in connection with the southern section of the country, under which a considerable quantity of pit props was being cut in that section and arrangements made for their sale in England. In this way employment had been secured for a very large number of men at an absolute minimum risk of loss to the Government.

Pulpwood market.

In addition to that, private contractors had been arranging to cut pulpwood in various sections of the island where pulpwood could be readily secured. The price of the wood per cord, when accepted by the Government's scalers and properly piled in suitable approved locations, would be $5 per cord. On this venture there was likely to be some loss. The labour situation in Canada had developed to such an acute extent that thousands of men had to undertake pulpwood operations for the winter merely for their keep and without receiving any wages whatever. Under these circumstances the price of pulpwood in the Dominion of Canada would be very much reduced. If in Canada during the coming winter there were huge quantities of pulpwood so cut, that pulpwood in addition to the surplus already in Canada would have the effect of depreciating the market price with the result that it might not be possible for the Government to come out of the venture satisfactorily on the $5 basis. The accounts of the individual men who worked for the contractors were not guaranteed by the Government, as the contractors handled it in exactly the same way as if they were undertaking the venture in the ordinary course of business. Under these circumstances, the unfortunate conditions which attached to public operations, such as the roadwork of the Government and municipal work during the past summer, were entirely done away with. It was relief work in the sense that the Government had undertaken the responsibility of purchasing the wood and otherwise it was solely a business proposal.

VACHER & SONS, LTD., Westminster House, London, S.W.1.—94570.

JOURNAL OF THE PARLIAMENTS OF THE EMPIRE

Vol. III.—No. 2. April, 1922.

Issued under the Authority of the
EMPIRE PARLIAMENTARY ASSOCIATION
(United Kingdom Branch),
WESTMINSTER HALL, HOUSES OF PARLIAMENT,
LONDON, S.W.1.

Price to Non-Members 10*s. Net.*

CONTENTS.

CANADA.

AUSTRALIA.

Commonwealth Parliament.

State Parliaments.

New South Wales.

Queensland.

Western Australia.

NEW ZEALAND.

CONTENTS.

SOUTH AFRICA.

NEWFOUNDLAND.

INTRODUCTION.

The present number of the JOURNAL is noteworthy for the subjects of International importance concerning which pronouncements or discussions have taken place in the different Parliaments of the Empire. Naturally, the greatest number of subjects of this character have been discussed in the Parliament of the United Kingdom. Besides the important debate on the Genoa Conference (in the course of which it has been thought well to give the text of the principal resolution adopted at Cannes) the views of the Leaders of Parties upon Anglo-French relations, the Washington Conference and other important matters received prominence in the course of the debate on the Address. The problem of the Near East in relation to the prolonged conflict between Greece and Turkey was considered in the House of Lords, and members of the Empire Parliamentary Association in the various Parliaments who are specially interested in the League of Nations will note the proposals put forward in this connection. That the position of Egypt is a matter of common concern to the nations of the British Commonwealth was clearly brought out in the House of Commons debate of 14th March.

The relationship of the Dominions to the big questions of Foreign Policy, and their status in facing the world problems of to-day, have been touched upon in more than one Parliament. In the New Zealand Parliament, for example, the matter of the Anglo-French Pact was raised, when a clear pronouncement upon the necessity of the British Empire speaking with one voice in Foreign Policy was made by the Prime Minister. In the debate on the Address in the Canadian Parliament, the status of the Dominions, particularly in relation to the Washington Conference, was commented upon, and Mr. Meighen's position at the Empire Conference explained; while the Resolution of the Australian Commonwealth Senate on the subject of the Washington Conference showed how keenly alive were the statesmen of the Southern Seas to the great issues involved. Further, the discussion in the Commonwealth Senate on the Mandated Territories in the Pacific is of importance as showing the attitude towards the United States. The Conferences at Washington and Genoa are both referred to in the Governor-General's Speech at the opening of the Union Parliament of South Africa. German Reparations have been the subject of questions in the Canadian and New Zealand Parliaments.

As regards the more intimate matter of the relationship of the nations within the British Commonwealth, a good deal that is of material interest appears in the present number. The declaration of the Secretary of State for the Colonies in the course of the debate on the Irish Free State (Agreement) Act as to the constitutional status of the Dominions and the right of secession from the Empire, is of interest to all Dominions, and particularly perhaps to South Africa, where the matter was debated at length some time ago in connection with a statement of Mr. Bonar Law on the subject.* The attitude of the present Canadian Ministry to the subject of the equality of status of the nations within the Empire was defined by the Prime Minister of the Dominion in discussing the recent Conference of Prime Ministers; and more than one question in the New Zealand House should be considered in this connection.

Apart from the more strictly constitutional aspects, matters of special interest to the Dominions have received a good measure of attention in the United Kingdom Parliament, such, for example, as Empire Settlement, Nationality Laws, Canadian Cattle Embargo, Australian Zinc Concentrates, etc. References to the first-named subject do not, unfortunately, include the discussion on the Second Reading of the Empire Settlement Bill, as no debates have been dealt with which occurred after the adjournment for the Easter recess.† A summary of the Bill introduced by the Government is, however, given in the present issue, together with a statement by Mr. Amery on the numbers and destinations of British families who have been assisted to migrate. The debate on Unrest in India should also be of interest to the Dominions and likewise the discussion on the despatch of the Government of India which recommended a revision of the Treaty of Sèvres and involved the question of Cabinet responsibility and the resignation of the Secretary of State for India.

In addition to subjects to which reference has already been made, other matters of importance to the whole Empire have been considered in all the Parliaments, such as the Irish question in the United Kingdom and Australian Commonwealth Parliaments; National Defence by sea, land and air, in the Parliaments of the United Kingdom, Canada (where a department of National Defence is to be established), the Australian Commonwealth and South Africa; Imperial Communications (Airships and Wireless) in the Australian Commonwealth; the Strike on the Rand, involving prolonged discussion and an Indemnity Bill in the South African Parliament; Industrial

---

* For references *vide* p. 282.

† A summary of the important speech of Mr. Amery in moving the Second Reading of the Bill, and of the discussion which followed, will appear in the next number of the JOURNAL.

Arbitration, in the Parliaments of New Zealand, the Australian Commonwealth and New South Wales; Immigration Policy and Asiatic Immigration in Canada and New Zealand; Proportional Representation in the Parliaments of Canada and New South Wales*; the appointment of a Trade Commissioner in Europe and the question of abolishing appeals to the Privy Council in the Parliament of South Africa.

Matters of more local concern, but still of considerable general interest to the Parliaments of the sister nations, relate to cash grants to returned soldiers in Canada (where the motion in Parliament was treated as one of want of confidence in the Government); Payment of Members, in the Australian Commonwealth; Finance and economy in the United Kingdom, Australian Commonwealth, New Zealand, South African and Newfoundland Parliaments; Tariffs (including Imperial Preference, etc.) in the New Zealand Parliament; the Unemployment Problem, Disabilities of Agriculture, and the Safeguarding of Industries in the United Kingdom.

THE EDITOR.

EMPIRE PARLIAMENTARY ASSOCIATION
(*United Kingdom Branch*),
WESTMINSTER HALL,
HOUSES OF PARLIAMENT,
LONDON, S.W.1.

29*th April*, 1922.

---

* Discussions in the Parliaments of New Zealand and South Africa on this subject are being held over to the next issue through lack of space.

UNITED KINGDOM.

The Fifth Session of the present Parliament was opened by the King in person with full State ceremonial on 7th February, 1922. The summary of the proceedings in both Houses which follows relates to business done up till 7th April.

THE ADDRESS—GENERAL DISCUSSION.

(International Affairs; Anglo-French Pact; Washington Conference; Unemployment; etc.)

The debate on the Address in reply to His Majesty's Gracious Speech from the Throne was commenced in the House of Commons on 7th February, 1922, and came to an end on 14th February. The Address was moved by Captain D. H. Hacking (Coalition Unionist, *Chorley*), and seconded by Captain Ernest Evans (Coalition Liberal, *Cardiganshire*). Their speeches were followed by a general debate.

DEBATE IN HOUSE OF COMMONS.

The Right Hon. J. R. Clynes (Chairman of the Parliamentary Labour Party) referred to the Washington Conference. It had kept rather too closely, he said, to the arithmetic of war instruments, though it was a great advantage to have reached an understanding and agreement upon the definite limitation of naval armaments. The Conference had not dealt with land forces in the general sense of the term, but had discussed questions from the standpoint of reducing the barbarism of war and coming to an understanding as to what war weapons should and should not be used. His view was that war could not be humanised.

He hoped, therefore, that the Washington Conference was neither mid-way, nor at the end, but was only the beginning of conferences leading to definite arrangements founded on the disarmament of the world for the purposes of war. It was their duty to anticipate the differences which would arise by providing the machinery necessary to settle pacifically the quarrels of the nations on the same principles on which for long they had settled quarrels between man and man. "I am entirely without hope," said the right hon. gentleman, "of ever maintaining the peace of the world by any system . . . of merely measuring instruments for war, merely determining what degree or state of preparation for war this, that, or the other nation may hold or hope to hold."

Anglo-French Pact; Unemployment; Lords Reform.

Speaking of the Supreme Council, the right hon. gentleman remarked that it had been supreme largely in the making of failures. The agreement in reference to both France and Belgium did not, and could not, in the judgment of the Labour Party, guarantee French safety for the future, or the peace of the world in the generation to come. Continued quarrelling in any part of the world meant a continuance of their own international difficulties. It brought this country nearer and nearer to a state bordering almost on industrial ruin.

The Labour Party were convinced that French security and prosperity could be found more certainly by gaining the good opinion of the world—by gaining through a world-wide League of Nations or association of peoples a strength and a guarantee against further aggression that could not be provided in the same degree by any arrangement between France and one or two other countries. History had taught that grouping between small rings of nations tended only to a recurrence of war and to counter-grouping. "You can have no guarantee against such wars," Mr. Clynes proceeded, "until you make your organisation world-wide, based not upon present fears or suspicions, but upon a new policy which can look to the future and secure mankind regardless of nationality or location, wherever it might be."

In the course of a reference to unemployment and wage reductions, Mr. Clynes said no action had been taken by the Government to arrest the descent in the level of wages. No word of sympathy had he heard from any Minister for the troubled state of the wage-earner, who, because of the pressure of unemployment, had been compelled to yield in some cases to the most monstrous reduction in wages.

With regard to what was called the Reform of the House of Lords, he asked what was the degree of veto which that House was to enjoy. Were the proposals to strengthen and remodel the House of Lords, to increase its powers in relation to the decisions of the House of Commons, in anticipation of the Labour legislation that would be submitted to the Commons by a Labour Government?

Ireland; Anglo-French Pact; Economy.

As to Ireland, if the Government required assistance to get a clear settlement the Prime Minister might depend upon carrying with him the fullest good-will of Labour, which had a real desire to be as serviceable as it possibly could be.

The Right Hon. Sir Donald Maclean (Chairman of the Independent Liberal Party in Parliament) associated himself with the congratulations on the success of the Washington Conference, and said he hoped the United States would be brought into closer relations with Europe. Nothing could be more disastrous for the general peace of the world than that the United States should maintain the attitude that she could discharge no really useful work by entering into arrangements with the Old World. As to a pact or definite alliance with France, he believed that the feeling of this country was swinging very decisively away from entangling alliances which must lead them into wars that might otherwise be avoided.

On the subject of economy in public expenditure, the right hon. gentleman pointed out that from 1st April, 1919, down to April of this year, the country would have raised £5,627,000,000. Thus more than half the total cost of the War had been spent during those three years. That was the primary cause of the extra and the worst part of unemployment. If those hundreds of millions which had been thrown away had been left in the pockets of the community to be devoted to useful business there would have been hundreds of thousands fewer unemployed walking the streets to-day.

Remarking that they ought to restore trade, Sir Donald expressed regret that one of the most serious omissions from the King's Speech was any indication respecting repeal of the Safeguarding of Industries Act. The President of the Manchester Chamber of Commerce had said that the Act was the worst thing any Government had done for trade. He would scrap the whole Act and burn it beyond hope of resurrection.

Premier's speech; arithmetic of peace.

The Prime Minister (the Right Hon. D. Lloyd George), answering some of the observations of Mr. Clynes, said that the extremists who pledged him to House of Lords reform, included Mr. Asquith, the Marquess of Crewe, and Viscount Grey. As to Washington, the Conference was one of the greatest achievements for peace that had ever been registered in the history of the world. The arithmetic of peace meant reducing the dynamics of war, and that was done at Washington. They had the Hague Conference and great resolutions were passed, but they were never reduced to arithmetic.

"When the War came, when the great quarrel came, those resolutions were swept away like cobwebs, and they did not retard by a single hour or a single second the march of armies, or the steaming of men-of-war. . . . It is only when you come to reduce these propositions to arithmetic that you begin to do the business of peace." Instead of assenting to vague resolutions, which would have ended in nothing, Mr. Balfour* had reduced them to practical

* Now Sir Arthur Balfour, K.G.

proposals which would have the effect of saving millions on the estimates. It was said that the Supreme Council had been a failure, but it disarmed Germany, stopped conscription in Germany, and had arranged that a considerable sum should be paid as reparation to France which was not paid before. No single conference could achieve the whole end. Conferences could only carry things forward step by step, but their great achievement was preventing conflict from developing into war.

Great Britain and France.

"Our policy in reference to France," said the Premier, "is one of friendship and one of co-operation in the interests of peace. Friendship does not mean subordination. It does not mean subservience. Friendship is incompatible with that. Friendship means candour; but it also means co-operation for common ends. Our purposes are alike. Our methods may not always agree; and that is where discussion comes in. I have never known an occasion where we have had a frank discussion where we have not achieved the ends of our methods and work.

"Both my right hon. friends have challenged the guarantee we propose to give to France. They are mistaken from their own point of view. I should be surprised if even Germany regarded that pact with anything but a friendly eye. Why? You have to give to France the feeling that she is not isolated and that she is not left alone. . . . One of the real dangers in Europe, not in five, ten, or twenty years, but, maybe, the next generation—as we know from the results of 1870 when the present generation has to pay the penalty in compound interest—is that the young people may be brought up with thoughts of vengeance, of recovering old possessions, old prestige, old ascendancy, of punishing old defeats and generally ministering to the national pride. That is one of the great dangers to France and Europe in the future. And when you are making peace you must not think only of the moment, but of years to come.

"You must make Germany feel that is a policy which will not pay; that a war of revenge is a war that will bring in not merely France but other lands as well. By that means you will discourage that sentiment at the very outset and you will convince every German that it is a policy which is fatal to his own country.

The advanced Rhine policy; Unemployment.

"This undertaking was given by us in the course of negotiations at Versailles in order to counter what is known as the advanced Rhine policy—a policy which proposed that there shall be something in the nature of annexation of territory on the left bank of the Rhine in order to establish the frontier of France. This was given as a guarantee in order to avert what we regarded as a permanent disaster to the whole of Europe. I myself and President Wilson gave the guarantee, and, upon it, that policy was abandoned. I think the consideration having been paid by France, we are in honour bound."

Turning to the question of unemployment, the Premier said they were spending at the present moment at the rate of over £100,000,000 a year in provision for the unemployed. With reference to a readjustment of international War debts, that did not depend on Great Britain alone. "We have been quite willing," the Premier observed, "to enter into a discussion of that problem, so long as all the creditor nations, as well as the debtor nations, came in; but for us to forego payments when there are heavy claims against this country would not be fair. . . . When all the nations of the world that have claims or debts come together to consider all these War debts, then I do not think that Great Britain . . . . will lag behind any other country in either generosity to others, or in justice."

Speaking of Egypt, the right hon. gentleman said they were willing to meet all the legitimate national aspirations of the Egyptian people. They were prepared to abandon the Protectorate, but it must be on clear fundamental conditions.

Understanding with France; policy regarding Austria

Major-General the Right Hon. J. E. B. Seely (Coalition Liberal, *Ilkeston*) remarked that a possible disagreement with France might have most disastrous results. He pleaded for an understanding with France and pointed out that it would have been impossible to get French assent to many of the provisions of the Treaty of Versailles—namely, that part of the Treaty which included the League of Nations—had it not been for the understanding that if the House of Commons would agree Great Britain would try to prevent France from ever again being subjected to an outrage like that of 1914. The argument was advanced that France ought to be satisfied with the Articles of the League of Nations which applied to these cases, but it was a reasonable proposition that until Germany, and possibly Russia, became a member of the League, France, who ran the greatest risk, was entitled to double insurance.

The Right Hon. Lord Robert Cecil (Independent Conservative, *Hitchin*) asked the Prime Minister to state what was the policy of the Government with regard to Austria.

The Prime Minister said there was a danger of a great collapse in Austria. The British Government had been considering with their Allies what could be done in order to support the position there until, at any rate, the American Senate had removed the difficulties in the way of an advance upon the national security. There was still £2,000,000, or over, unexpended out of the £10,000,000 voted by that House for the purposes of Central Europe. It was proposed to advance that sum to Austria upon, he believed, quite good security for the purpose of enabling her to get through the present crisis. He believed France was also making an advance.

International relations.

Lord Robert Cecil remarked that the line of progress and of advance in international affairs must be in the direction of substituting international co-operation for force. The League of Nations was merely the natural development of Anglo-Saxon policy and was seeking to do that which statesmen had tried to do in the past. They must have co-operation as far as they could between the British Empire and France in order to make European life work smoothly. There was not, therefore, the slightest doubt as to the desirability of preserving the closest possible understanding between England and France; yet he was entirely out of sympathy with the proposal for an Anglo-French-Belgian pact. The position of England and France must never be allowed to degenerate into that of seeking to dominate Europe.

The right course was to bring Germany into the orbit of the Western Powers at the earliest possible moment. That was the line which the League of Nations wished to see followed, and it was the only line of safety in the present condition of affairs. As to Reparations, there was the strongest possible ground for saying to the French, "We are perfectly prepared to submit the question of how much Germany can pay to a tribunal appointed by the League of Nations, or, in some other way, to a really impartial tribunal charged to deal with what, indeed, is the chief financial necessity of the moment, namely, the definite settlement of these reparation arrangements." With the support of the French they could make the League a great instrument of peace.

Danger of sectional Treaties; League of Nations.

The Right Hon. G. N. Barnes (Labour, *Glasgow, Gorbals***)** observed that the results of the Washington Conference had revived the hopes of real peace and world re-settlement. Sectional treaties must be dangerous, because they must lead to sectional treaties in other places, and the danger of setting up two rival forces in the world was again produced. For that reason he was against anything in the nature of a pact on the part of Great Britain guaranteeing France immunity from oppression on the part of Germany.

The Leader of the House (the Right Hon. Austen Chamberlain) said they could not pretend to feel at once for Germany as they might have felt if peace had been maintained. But they recognised that the world needed to return from war conditions to peace conditions and the Government were steadily pursuing that object in their policy, achieving it very gradually and only step by step, but leaving on their part nothing undone in spirit or in act that would contribute to that great end. He wished Lord Robert Cecil would get out of his mind the delusion—for it was a delusion—that there was anything among members of the Government but a profound desire to see the League of Nations succeed, to strengthen it, and to develop it. The noble Lord should not suppose that the Government were not ready and, indeed, anxious to make use of the League whenever it could help to solve any of their difficult problems.

Two sittings were devoted to the general debate on the Address, and four to the discussion of specific amendments dealing with a variety of questions.

DEBATE IN HOUSE OF LORDS.

In the House of Lords the debate on the Address was commenced on 7th February and concluded on the following day. The Address was moved by the Earl of Pembroke and Montgomery, and seconded by Lord Clwyd.

The Marquess of Crewe, referring to Washington, said no one could pretend that international disarmament had reached even a hopeful stage unless some form of agreement was arrived at on the Continent of Europe, including Great Britain, for the reduction of land forces. Regarding Reform of the House of Lords, the noble Marquess said it would be worse than useless to attempt to set up a Second Chamber as a solid bulwark against attacks which might be made upon property, whether in land, in money, or in anything else, by some party in the future. If the institution of property was to be safeguarded from the attacks of those who held wild views on the subject, it could only be by convincing the majority of the people that those wild views were wrong. They would never do it by setting up a privileged body of persons, whether they called that body the House of Lords or anything else, with the idea that they could arrest the onrush of the flood by a breakwater of that sort.

Pact with France.

The Secretary of State for Foreign Affairs (the Marquess Curzon of Kedleston), after discussing results achieved at

Washington, turned to the contemplated agreement between Great Britain, France, and Belgium. Comradeship in war and common interests in peace had convinced every thoughtful man in both countries that the fortunes of France and Great Britain were inextricably interwoven, and that differences of bygone history, or mentality, or political outlook ought never to sever them one from the other. That was a basic principle, as he saw it, not only of the continuance of the Entente, but of European welfare and of the peace of the world.

After the conclusion of the Armistice both Houses of Parliament gave their consent to a Bill which embodied the Treaty of guarantee that it was proposed to give by the Government of this country in conjunction with that of America against unprovoked German aggression upon the Eastern frontier of France. Circumstances in the political life of America rendered the fulfilment of that undertaking impossible, but ever since then Great Britain had remained under a certain unfulfilled moral obligation to France. Had such a form of guarantee existed in 1914, and still more had it been known to the Germans, it might have exercised a very appreciable effect upon the situation. Accordingly His Majesty's Government were prepared to repeat to France the engagement to which that House assented in 1919, both as a proof of their friendship and as an addition to her security.

Peace with Turkey.

Lord Islington considered that in an increasing degree their difficulties throughout the whole of their Eastern possessions, and especially in India, were due to the deplorable failure to make peace with Turkey. The result of the neglect to settle with Turkey was that the whole Moslem community throughout the East were disturbed, and were becoming increasingly alienated from Great Britain—a country with whom formerly they were on the best of terms. India was in a very grave condition. This was due in the main to Moslem unrest, precipitated and accentuated by the failure to make peace with Turkey.

Viscount Haldane moved an amendment relating to the reduction of public expenditure and after this had been negatived without a division,

The Marquess of Londonderry proposed an amendment expressing regret that no assurance had been given by the Government that the integrity of the area of the Government of Northern Ireland would be maintained whatever was the final establishment of the Free State. On a division this was negatived by 46 votes against 39.

The motion for the Address was afterwards agreed to.

INTERNATIONAL CONFERENCE AT GENOA.

(Vote of Confidence; Premier's Statement; European Reconstruction; Reparations; Recognition of Russia.)

A full debate on the Genoa Conference took place in the House of Commons on 3rd April, four days before the departure for Italy of the British delegates. The debate was founded on a resolution moved by the Prime Minister which was treated as a vote of confidence in the Government. The motion was in these terms:—

"That this House approves the Resolutions passed by the Supreme Council at Cannes as the basis of the Genoa Conference, and will support His Majesty's Government in endeavouring to give effect to them."

In connection with the debate the Government caused to be issued as a White Paper the text of the Resolutions adopted at Cannes. The principal Resolution was as follows:—

The Allied Powers in conference are unanimously of opinion that an Economic and Financial Conference should be summoned in February or early March, to which all the Powers of Europe, including Germany, Russia, Austria, Hungary and Bulgaria should be invited to send representatives. They regard such a Conference as an urgent and essential step towards the economic reconstruction of Central and Eastern Europe, and they are strongly of opinion that the Prime Ministers of every nation should, if possible, attend it in person in order that action may be taken as promptly as possible upon its recommendations.

The Allied Powers consider that the resumption of international trade throughout Europe and the development of the resources of all countries are necessary to increase the volume of productive employment and to relieve the widespread suffering of the European peoples. A united effort by the stronger Powers is necessary to remedy the paralysis of the European system. This effort must include the removal of all obstacles in the way of trade, the provision of substantial credits for the weaker countries and the co-operation of all nations in the restoration of normal prosperity.

Essential Conditions for Trade Revival.

The Allied Powers consider that the fundamental conditions upon which alone this effort can be made with hope of success may be broadly stated as follows:—

1. Nations can claim no right to dictate to each other regarding the principles on which they are to regulate their system of ownership, internal economy and government. It is for every nation to choose for itself the system which it prefers in this respect.

2. Before, however, foreign capital can be made available to assist a country, foreign investors must be assured that their property and their rights will be respected and the fruits of their enterprise secured to them.

3. The sense of security cannot be re-established unless the Governments of countries desiring foreign credit freely undertake—

(A) That they will recognise all public debts and obligations which have been or may be undertaken or guaranteed by the State, by municipalities, or by other public bodies, as well as the obligation to restore or compensate all foreign interests for loss or damage caused to them when property has been confiscated or withheld.

(B) That they will establish a legal and juridical system which sanctions and enforces commercial and other contracts with impartiality.

4. An adequate means of exchange must be available, and, generally, there must be financial and currency conditions which offer sufficient security for trade.

5. All nations should undertake to refrain from propaganda subversive of order and the established political system in other countries than their own.

6. All countries should join in an undertaking to refrain from aggression against their neighbours.

If in order to secure the conditions necessary for the development of trade in Russia the Russian Government demands official recognition, the Allied Powers will be prepared to accord such recognition only if the Russian Government accepts the foregoing stipulations.

Purposes of the Conference.

Attention was called by the Prime Minister during the debate to the Press notice issued officially by the Supreme Council at Cannes regarding the purposes of the Conference. Following are some extracts from the document:—

The first condition which is of prime importance in the reconstruction of Europe is to establish the relations of all the countries on the basis of a stable and enduring peace.

The Conference will also discuss the financial conditions which impede revival and the financial measures which might assist it; in particular the financial situation in the several countries in relation to the task of reconstruction; the rapid variation in the amount and purchasing power of the national currencies; the violent fluctuations in the relative value of the currencies of different countries as reflected in the exchanges, and the bearing upon these problems of the position and status of central banks and banks of issue. The Conference will examine the conditions under which public or private credit can best be made available for the work of reconstruction.

The obstacles to revival, however, are economic as well as financial. The Conference will therefore consider how the existing impediments to the free interchange of the products of different countries can be removed, in particular by the abolition, as rapidly and completely as possible, of such new impediments as have resulted from post-War conditions.

The improvement and development of the transport system will engage special attention; and among other questions which might be usefully examined are the security afforded by the laws and by the legal systems and commercial documents in the different countries; the provision of expert and technical assistance by countries specially qualified to give it; the position of consular officers; the protection of copyrights; and the regulations governing the admission of foreigners for the purpose of carrying on business.

DEBATE IN HOUSE OF COMMONS.

The Prime Minister (the Right Hon. D. Lloyd George) said the Conference had been called to consider the problem of the reconstruction of economic Europe, devastated and broken into fragments by the War. International trade had been disorganised through and through. The recognised medium of commerce—exchange based upon currency—had become almost worthless and unworkable; vast areas, upon which Europe had hitherto depended for a large proportion of its food supplies and its raw material, were completely destroyed for all purposes of commerce; nations, instead of co-operating to restore, were broken up by suspicions and creating difficulties and new artificial restrictions; great armies were ready to march, and nations already overburdened with taxation were having to bear the additional taxation which the maintenance of those huge armaments to avoid suspected dangers rendered necessary. The Genoa Conference had been summoned to examine the best method of restoring order out of that welter and recovering prosperity out of that desolation.

Continuing, the Premier denied that in the Boulogne conversations with M. Poincaré new limitations were imposed on the scope of the discussions at Genoa. The limitations were all summarised in the phrase, " Without injury to existing Treaties." He did not believe that such a body as was summoned to meet at Genoa could properly consider the revision of existing Treaties—even assuming that it was desirable. As regarded the re-arrangement of the boundaries of Europe, would they wish to restore Alsace-Lorraine to Germany, to tear up Poland again, to take away the independence of Czecho-Slovakia and Jugo-Slavia? It was no use criticising the Treaty of Versailles or the Treaty of St. Germain because they re-adjusted the boundaries of Europe unless they were prepared to say it was an unjust distribution of Europe. At the same time, those changes added one of the most serious complications to the economic situation of Europe.

Reparations.

" I come," said the Premier, " to another limitation which has been urged with greater force than the one about boundaries. That is the question of reparations. The trouble in Europe has been attributed largely to the reparations exacted by the Treaties of 1919. May I just say that those Treaties did not create the reparations. The trouble is due to the fact not that you are exacting reparations, but that there is something to repair.

"If you alter the Treaty of Versailles you do not wipe out reparations. You simply transfer the burden of them from Germany to France, and to this country, as well as to Belgium, but, in the main, to France. You would transfer the burden from the 60,000,000 of people responsible for the devastation to the 40,000,000 who were the victims of the devastation. So it is no use criticising reparations and saying that this gigantic debt of reparations is what is responsible for the economic disorganisation of Europe. The point is—is the damage there? Has it to be made up? Who is to pay it? If Germany does not pay, France and England and Belgium must pay.

"I admit that there is a difference, and a very considerable difference, between the payment of external debt and the payment of internal obligations; and there are two considerations, undoubtedly, which ought to be borne in mind when you come to deal with the problem of reparations. The first is, that if we insist now upon payments beyond the power of a war-exhausted country it would precipitate a crisis which would be by no means confined to Germany. The second consideration is that Germany's ultimate capacity to pay must not be judged by her capacity at this moment when, in common with the rest of Europe, she is struggling to recover from the exhaustion of war.

French rights.

"Those are two considerations which must be taken into account whenever you judge the problem of reparations, but neither of those questions can properly be dealt with at Genoa. They ought to be judged by the machinery of the Treaty, which is very elastic."

France, he continued, could not possibly forego the right that she had won at so much cost to have an adjudication in accordance with the Treaty, and he did not believe that it would be fair to ask her to forego it. She certainly could not be expected to submit to the judgment of a Conference, not merely of Germany, Austria, Hungary and Russia, but also of neutrals, some of whom during the War did not indicate that they had very much sympathy with her. At any rate, it would be unfair to ask France to submit to their judgment upon something that so vitally affected her existence as her Treaty rights in respect to reparations.

One of the first and most essential problems to be dealt with at Genoa, the right hon. gentleman proceeded to say, was to restore the machinery of international trade. They were often asked, " If you lost your trade in Europe, could you not make it up by trading with the Dominions, with the Colonies, and with other parts of the world ? " The world was one trade unit. Their customers depended on their sales in European countries to pay for goods Great Britain sold them. The purchases of India in this country had gone down very considerably, and the main reason was that India had always paid them for the goods they sold her by the proceeds of her sales to other European countries.

The exchanges; shattered machinery.

" Therefore," said the Premier, " the trade of Europe is of the greatest importance to us, not merely directly, but indirectly; and unless you restore the trade of Europe as a whole, our purchasers will not be in a position to pay for the commodities which they get from us. What applies to India applies to Australia, to the Argentine, and to other parts of the world." Not merely was Europe impoverished, the right hon. gentleman observed, but the machinery of exchange had also been shattered. Currency had gone adrift, and one of the first things to be attended to at Genoa was the question of restoring the exchanges.

Before trade could be fully restored they must be able to establish everywhere the convertibility of currency into gold or its equivalent. That might and would involve a devaluation of currency; but the world could not afford to wait until currency was restored to par. What mattered was to establish the rate at a figure which could be maintained and which would therefore continue a reliable basis for international commerce. In order to achieve that, one of the first considerations was to induce the nations to balance their budgets. Until they did so new issues of currency would debase the currency and the exchange would become wilder and wilder. That was a matter where pressure could be exercised at a great international conference of the leading Ministers of the various nations.

Russia.

Above all, it was essential there should be a real peace between the nations. The trader, the financier, and the merchant were unnerved by the present condition of things—gathering armies on the frontiers, "Red" armies and "White" armies, and armies of many other colours. Perhaps, the most controversial part of the issue which would come before the Genoa Conference was the question of peace in Russia and peace with Russia. The doctrine, the demeanour, and the actions of the Bolsheviks had excited wrath and just anger and made it exceedingly difficult to exercise judgment when they came to deal with the problems of relations with that country.

Pitt was confronted with exactly the same problem over a hundred years ago with regard to France. A revolution, provoked by intolerable wrong and leading to the wildest excesses, created bitter and fierce resentment in England. Pitt had to consider whether it was possible to make peace with men who had been responsible for such things. It was realised by Mr. Pitt that unless peace were made with the French revolutionaries there would be no peace for many a long devastating year, and there was not for eighteen years after that period.

Hon. Members: " We are at peace."

The Prime Minister: " We are not at peace. I am not sure that present conditions are very much better than war, except for the actual fact that war is no longer in progress. But we have the effects of war in many ways, and one is the closing down of Russia. I do not believe you are going to restore trade, business, and employment until you appease the whole of Europe. Until you establish peace over the whole of Europe there will be a standing element of disturbance and trade will not go on. The nerves of commerce will be shaken while there are constant rumours of great armies being built up, of hordes of savage revolutionaries to be let loose upon Europe to reduce the countries of Europe to the same condition of desolation . . . in which Russia is."

Conditions of peace.

Continuing, the Premier said that once the trader was admitted into Russia they would get to know the facts. If trade were introduced it would be to the interests of Russia to retain it and Russia would not do that while these rumours were afloat. The effect of those great revolutionary armies was to provide an excuse, if not a real justification, for huge armies in other countries.

France refused to discuss the question of land armaments in the Washington Conference, and everyone agreed that with that enormous "Red" army in Russia as a menace, no country in Europe could reduce its land army. Europe needed what Russia could supply. The greatest undeveloped country in the world, Russia had labour, but would not get capital without security, confidence, and peace, internal as well as external. Another point was that Germany could not pay the full reparations demand until Russia was restored.

The conditions of peace laid down at Cannes meant in substance that Russia must recognise all the conditions imposed and accepted by civilised communities as the test of fitness for entering into the comity of nations. A country that repudiated her obligations because she changed her Government was a country they could not deal with—certainly not in these days when governments changed so often.

Will Russia accept?

"Where the property of our nationals has been confiscated," the Premier said, "it must, if not destroyed, be restored, and I am told there is a good deal of it still there. . . . Impartial tribunals must be established, with free access to them by the nationals of all countries, and those tribunals must not be the creatures of the Executive.

"There must be a complete cessation of attacks upon the institutions of other countries. . . . The Pact which is embodied in the League of Nations will have to be extended in principle to Russia, so that Russia should undertake not to attack her neighbours, and her neighbours, on the other hand, must undertake a corresponding obligation not to attack her frontiers. The only difference would be this—and I think it is important that I should say so—that I do not think we could undertake the responsibility as a country which we have incurred under Article X. of the League of Nations to defend any frontiers which are attacked in that quarter of the globe.

"Is Russia prepared to accept these conditions? There are indications of a complete change of attitude. The famine has been a great eye-opener to Russia as to her dependability upon her neighbours and as to the futility of the scheme of things which the Soviet Government has propounded as a method of solving the problems of life. The new Decrees recognise private property, set up courts, and acknowledge responsibilities; and I would call the attention of the House to the very remarkable speech in which this new policy was propounded. It was propounded on 1st November, 1921, in a speech by Lenin. It was an admission of the complete failure of the Communist system, and in that respect it is a singularly courageous speech. He admits they have been wrong; he admits they have been beaten. He points out that the result of Communism has been completely to destroy the very proletariat upon whom they were depending.

"With the disappearance of capitalists, the disappearance of workmen. That is the new doctrine which M. Lenin puts before the world. It is a very remarkable admission to make. It is worth anyone's while to read this very remarkable condemnation and exposure of the doctrines of Karl Marx by its greatest exponent—the only man who has ever tried honestly to put these doctrines into operation."

Recognition of Russia; a period of probation.

If such a peace as he had indicated could be achieved it would have to be submitted to the House of Commons for approval and ratification. What recognition of Russia would that involve? After approval, the stages of recognition would be those which ensued after most of the Peace Treaties. "It would involve access by other countries and their nationals to the courts of Russia; it would involve access by Russia and her nationals to our courts. Without this fully legal status, business would be quite impossible. It would involve the establishment of the usual agencies by which the trader in foreign lands is protected.

"A feeling has been very generally expressed that before full and ceremonial diplomatic representation is accorded, a probationary period should be interposed. Some diplomatic representation on both sides is essential, otherwise business cannot be effectively transacted or business men protected. It is, however, felt that the character and extent of the diplomatic representation accorded depends not merely on the conditions Russia is prepared to accept, but upon the actual proof which she gives of her *bonâ fides*. Let me say quite frankly that the way in which some of the more important clauses of the Trade Agreement have been violated has not been encouraging. . . . Until the House of Commons ratifies there can be no change in the representation or in the extent of the diplomatic recognition of Russia.

"If the agreement is ratified, then the course pursued could be that pursued in the case of Germany after the Treaty of Peace. . . . Russia would be represented here by a *Chargé d'affaires*, and we should be represented in Russia by a corresponding official, until such time as we felt that it was desirable to establish full ceremonial diplomatic relations. . . . That would present a period of probation which it would be wise to establish . . . in order to receive the necessary guarantees—not merely on paper but in practice—that the Russian Government intend not only themselves to honour the obligations of the Treaty, but that they have established sufficient control over the extremists and powerful organisations in their midst which are now engaged in challenging the new policy of the Soviet Government."

The alternative.

The alternative, the Premier said, was that they should do nothing until one day it was reported that the Soviet Government had disappeared and a Government of a totally different character had been set up. Was anybody there prepared to stake his political reputation that 1922 would see the last of the Soviet Government, or that 1923 would?

Did his hon. friends imagine that the workmen of this country were prepared to wait, with the present unemployment, while half Europe was practically closed down, if there was a real prospect of making peace? He was convinced they were not.

They were doing their best to work in partnership with France and they had, so far, done their best to keep step with France. In approaching Russia they had taken into account all reasonable prejudices against those people who had outraged every sentiment that was dear to the vast majority of the people of this country. "We propound these measures," the Premier added, "in all consciousness, feeling that the people of England demand them, Europe needs them, the world is crying out for them."

Labour's amendment.

The Right Hon. J. R. Clynes (Chairman of the Parliamentary Labour Party) moved the following amendment:—

"That, whilst approving of an international economic and financial conference, this House regrets that the scope of discussion at Genoa has been so circumscribed that the Conference must fall short of a settlement of the political and economic evils which afflict Europe, and is of opinion that His Majesty's Government, which has clearly not the confidence of the country and which is responsible for the policy the unfortunate effects of which are to be considered at Genoa, is not competent to represent this country."

The right hon. gentleman said he agreed with the conclusion of the Prime Minister that in economic affairs, in general industrial and even fiscal interests, the world was a unit, and the countries which formed it could not detach themselves from what was the common interest without either suffering singly or sharing in the common loss that was certain to follow. Yet it had been the policy of the Government, ever since the end of the War, to erect economic barriers, and to do little to produce any condition of industrial co-operation among the nations that were created as a result of the War itself. Unless the Genoa Conference revised and dealt with many outstanding features of the Peace Treaty, it would fail in its purpose as completely as so many other conferences had failed.

Was it not clear that the motion had been put upon the Order Paper less because of the work to be done at Genoa than because of the Party and personal divisions which had aroused in the country the strong resentment shown in recent by-elections? The spirit of genuine international conference was inconsistent with all they had heard recently about the proposed French Pact, with the operation of allied power through the Supreme Council, and with the treatment by the Government of the League of Nations. Until they reconciled those lines of policy the Prime Minister could not expect, on such a high occasion as that, to get a real and unanimous body of support from the House of Commons. Labour stood for the principle of conferences of that kind, but not for conferences hingeing upon a succession of Party manœuvres. The Genoa Conference was being held three years too late and was surrounded by harmful entanglements and commitments due to other phases of their foreign policy.

Treaty revision.

At the bottom of all the difficulties was the Treaty of Versailles, and until the outstanding features of the Treaty, more particularly in reference to reparations, were substantially revised, no one could expect to put Europe economically upon its feet again. If the Conference was not to deal with reparations, with existing Treaties, or with land armaments, how could the Prime Minister expect any substantial improvement to come from it? They could have no fair peace without a Treaty revision and no economic revival or trade restoration until they had a peace grounded in equity and until peace of mind was established among the populations of the various European countries.

Reparations were in a large degree being paid for now, not by Germany, but by the British working-classes. As to Russia, the Prime Minister proposed a most half-hearted and wholly ineffective way of dealing with the problem. " We are not to shake hands with Russia," remarked Mr. Clynes. " We will go only the length of shaking three fingers with her." Their policy towards Russia must be completely changed even if British Ministers had to go back on their furious condemnation of the present Russian rulers. If they did that they could go forward with a new method which would bring Russia into the company of European nations. After stating that the amendment was moved as an act of opposition to the Government's resolution, Mr. Clynes said the Premier's speech clearly revealed that he had ceased to be a Prime Minister in fact and had become a mere Party prisoner.

Colonel J. Gretton (Unionist, ***Burton-on-Trent*****)** held that the key to a safe, sound, and stable foreign policy was that they should have a firm working agreement with France. It was a delusion to represent to the people of this country that they could obtain any employment for years to come by means of a trade agreement with Russia.

Importance of Reparations issue.

The Right Hon. Sir Donald Maclean (Chairman of the Independent Liberal Party in Parliament) said that, reparations having been ruled out, they were really moving along a plane of minor details compared with what the issue would have been if reparations had been under discussion. The very foundation of the peace of Europe depended on the settlement of the question of reparations, of securing the liquidation of Inter-Allied debts and the separate debts of the Central Empires. Eighteen months ago they sent their experts to Brussels and they were much better qualified to deal with those limited financial details than the plenipotentiaries who were going to Genoa.

The outline of the Conference was a summary of the past failures of the Government. After three years what were they going to try to do? They were trying to restore the economic life of Europe, to re-establish confidence between the nations, to establish the relations between all the countries on the basis of an enduring peace, and they were trying to find out how the existing impediments to the free exchange of the products of the different countries were to be removed. Meantime the Government had passed the Safeguarding of Industries Act and they kept on developing control until the last possible moment, when they were driven from their position by the protests of the country. Then the Prime Minister came down to the House, and, with remarkable assurance, asked them to start off with him all over again—after three years. The country wanted to get back to straight politics, and because the resolution moved by the Prime Minister was only another chapter in the degradation of politics he would vote for the amendment.

Difficult and trying auspices.

The Right Hon. A. Bonar Law (**Coalition Unionist,** *Glasgow, Central*) remarked that anyone who said the Prime Minister was going to Genoa for the sake of political capital was a very foolish person. Whatever else might come out of the Conference it was certain that no political capital could be made in time for any election, no matter how it was put forward. The Conference was undertaken under the most difficult and trying auspices. America was out, and, from the point of view of any attempt to set the exchanges right that was a terrible handicap.

It was perfectly true that, in attempting to restore the economic life of Germany, any scheme which did not take into account reparations was terribly handicapped. Reparation had to be made and the sole question was to what extent could Germany make it without shattering the whole foundation of her trade. There was another handicap. He understood that armaments were not to be considered. That added enormously to the difficulty of making the Conference a success, even from the economic point of view. The essence of an improvement was the balancing of the Budget. There was yet another handicap. Russia was the storehouse of the raw material of the world, but did anyone imagine that by any possible concatenation of circumstances Russia could have her trade renewed for years ?

He had been afraid that in some way or other recognition might be given to the Soviet Government when, in his judgment, it ought not to be given, and also that a quixotic scheme, in the state of their own finance, of lending money to other countries might be a danger. His fears on these points had been removed by a definite assurance given by the Government that the House would be consulted first. Anyone would be foolish in the extreme who belittled the possibilities of a revival in Europe or who, because they could not get everything at the Conference, was not willing to try to get something.

Versailles Treaty condemned.

The Right Hon. Lord Robert Cecil (Independent Conservative, ***Hitchin*****)** said the American and British Governments could have imposed any settlement they liked upon Europe. At Versailles they were responsible, perhaps chiefly responsible, for the miserable, fantastic terms set out. Instead of standing before the world as the great pacificators of the world, they might look back to that Treaty as the worst international document that ever disgraced the diplomatic history of the world.

The Leader of the House (the Right Hon. Austen Chamberlain) remarked that he took the middle view. He neither expected anything from the Conference, nor did he think it a useless proposal to make. " We are not going to create a new world if it succeeds. The utmost desire of those of us who care most about it is that it will have opportunities for usefulness, and that it may enable the world to take one more step forward." Would anyone, not a madman, who desired the readjustment of the Treaty of Versailles, or a modification of the reparation agreement, choose a Conference like that at Genoa in order to open that question ? If they had proposed to put that upon the agenda there would have been no Conference.

As to Russia, there could be no substantial trade with that country until confidence in Russia was restored among the trading community. If Genoa could get from Russia acceptance of the fundamental conditions of civilised government and comity of nations—then indeed the world would have made a step forward.

On a division the amendment of the Labour Party was negatived by 379 votes against 84. The Government's motion was then carried by 372 votes against 94.

NEAR EAST CONFERENCE.

(Foreign Secretary's Statement; Treaty of Sèvres; League of Nations.)

Following the conference of Allied Foreign Ministers in Paris to discuss the Near Eastern problem the Secretary for Foreign Affairs made, on 30th March, a full statement in the House of Lords.

DEBATE IN HOUSE OF LORDS.

The Secretary of State for Foreign Affairs (the Marquess Curzon of Kedleston) said it had long been felt that a peaceful settlement of the prolonged conflict in Asia Minor between the Greeks and the Turks was necessary. For a long while he had held the conviction that only by the closest unity between the Great Allied Powers themselves could that solution be attained. Commenting on the Memorandum drawn up in Paris, the noble Marquess said that the invitation telegraphed both to Greece and to Turkey to agree to an armistice was accompanied by an intimation that the armistice would be followed by steps for the evacuation of Asia Minor by the Greeks. "We felt it only right," Lord Curzon observed, "that, as that was the policy upon which we were united, the Turks should at least have an assurance in advance that this was in contemplation."

Whether it was right or wrong to have invited the Greeks in the first instance to Smyrna in 1919, the Allied Foreign Ministers believed there to be a general recognition at the present moment, even in Greece, that that occupation could no longer be maintained. Conditions had been drawn up by the military authorities under which, supposing the armistice were accepted, the evacuation of Anatolia by Greece would take place. They provided for the progressive retirement of the Greek forces in Asia Minor, under the supervision of Allied officers, from a succession of zones. While this was going on, steps had to be taken to set up again a Turkish civil administration in the successive zones as they were left free. Further, they had to secure the avoidance not only of direct contact, but—what might be much more serious—of collision between the two belligerent armies. Lastly, they had to arrange for the embarkation of the Greek forces from ports either on the Marmora or on the Mediterranean.

It was also obviously desirable to provide for the maintenance of order and security in the regions evacuated, and to prevent any sudden exodus or flight of the populations in that area.

Difficult and prolonged operation.

The task of closely supervising those arrangements would be undertaken by a mixed Commission of Allied Generals and Admirals at Constantinople. It was obvious that the operation would be a difficult and prolonged one. The evacuation process, under most favourable conditions, would occupy about four and a half months. Should the operation be successfully accomplished, the Turkish sovereignty in Asia would exist unimpaired from the Mediterranean on the South to the Straits and the Black Sea in the North, and from the borders of Transcaucasia, Persia and Mesopotamia on the East to the shores of the Ægean.

Assuming the recovery by the Turks of the large areas he had geographically described, the serious question arose of what steps were to be taken for the protection of the minorities left in the regions concerned. They had equally to safeguard the interests of minorities left under Turkish rule in Asia and of Moslem minorities left under Greek rule in Europe. What they wanted to do was to formulate a new code of international observance to be drawn up, in the first place, by an Inter-Allied Conference for future observance by the parties concerned.

League of Nations to supervise.

"Our next step," the noble Marquess proceeded, "was to contemplate placing the execution of this new code of international law under the general and effective supervision of the League of Nations . . . in some respects the only instrument for carrying out the kind of policy to which I am now referring."

They proposed at Paris to invite the League of Nations after consultation with Greece and Turkey—always assuming that after peace had been ratified Turkey would herself be admitted to the League—to appoint Special Commissioners for the supervision of those minority clauses in Europe and in Asia. It would be proposed to the League that they should appoint Commissioners to pay periodical visits to the areas concerned and that their reports should be laid annually before the Assembly of the League. In that way they would hope to give to the protection of minorities in the future an international sanction, and if Turkey herself was represented upon the League she would be able to see so far as she was concerned, while the rest of the Powers would exercise a similar responsibility on their own account, that the conditions were scrupulously observed.

The Straits.

After a detailed reference to the position of the Armenian and Greek minorities in Asia Minor, the noble Marquess passed to the question of the Straits.

There was, he observed, common accord that Turkey could not, in any re-arrangement, be left in command of both shores of the Dardanelles. While the Turks were left at Chanak, on the Asiatic side of the mouth of the Straits, the de-militarised zone which it was proposed to draw in the interior would be thrown back to the boundaries of the Sanjak, a distance of sixty miles or more, so that in that area no Turkish government would be able at any time to prepare positions which might enable them to command, or even menace, the entrance to the Straits. That de-militarised zone would be visited and inspected from time to time by Allied officers.

It was proposed that the European shores of the Straits should be constituted a zone of Allied military occupation as far as Rodosto on the Marmora. In the opinion of the military authorities that would constitute a sufficient guarantee for the safety of the Straits in future against any recurrence of the experience of 1914. As regarded the navigation of the Straits, the control of the traffic, the organisation of harbour works, and other services, the International Straits Commission, as it was proposed under the Treaty of Sèvres, would remain. It was proposed that the chairmanship of that body should be placed in the hands of a representative of the Turkish Government.

Constantinople and Thrace.

It was long ago decided that Constantinople should be given back after the War to the Turks, both as the seat of the Caliphate and the natural and historic capital of the Turkish Empire. The Powers at no time had the desire—for both military and political reasons—to remain in prolonged, still less in perpetual, occupation of that city. A year ago, in London, they offered as part of their terms to evacuate Constantinople when the Treaty of Peace had been ratified. That promise would be fulfilled at as early a date as was practicable after the ratification of the new peace, which they now had in view. The Sultan, who would remain in Constantinople, would be allowed to maintain a force, limited in numbers but sufficient for the purpose, in the city of his Government.

By the decision of the Powers at Paris the Greeks had been placed in occupation of Eastern Thrace, and it was felt that it would not only be unjust but impracticable to call upon them to evacuate not merely Anatolia, but the whole of

Eastern Thrace as well. At the same time there was great force in the contention that, if Constantinople were restored to Turkey, it should, as the seat of the future capital of the Turkish dominions, be free from the military menace or the disagreeable situation of a neighbour close at hand with whom the Turks had recently been at war. He had suggested that this frontier should be thrown back to a distance of about 80 miles from Constantinople to a line popularly known as the Midia-Rodosto line.

The new frontier line.

The problem was referred to the military authorities at Paris. They unanimously recommended a line drawn from the neighbourhood of a place called Ganos on the Marmora to the Bulgarian frontier in the north on the western side of the mountain Massif of Istranja. That was a line of definite geographical and strategical value. With the exception of a small band around Adrianople in which the Greeks would be allowed to maintain certain forces as a guard against the Bulgarian frontier, the whole of the two areas of Eastern Thrace—Turkish and Greece—would be de-militarised, so that neither part could constitute a military danger to the other.

As to the future of the armed forces of Turkey, they started by recognising the principle that they could not admit that Turkey should be permitted to recruit her forces by conscription in the future. At the same time, recognising the difficulty that might be found in constituting straight away a volunteer army in Turkey, they said they would be prepared to consider with the Turkish Government in an amicable spirit a determination of the period within which the voluntary system of recruiting must be established in that country. The armed forces of Turkey would consist partly of *gendarmerie* and partly of certain special elements for the protection of the frontiers and otherwise. The *gendarmerie* would number 45,000, and the special elements 40,000.

Finance.

The financial proposals were in the direction of giving Turkey very considerable control of her finances subject to the recognition by her of her pre-War debts and the payment of charges and indemnities arising directly out of the War. It was proposed to set up in Constantinople within three months of the coming into force of the Treaty of Peace, a Commission composed of the representatives of Great Britain, France, Italy, Japan, and Turkey, to prepare, with the assistance of technical experts representing the other Capitulary Powers, proposals for the revision of the Capitulary *régime* in fiscal matters.

These proposals provided for fiscal equality between foreign and Turkish subjects while safeguarding the former against excessive taxation and abuses in collection, and for any necessary modifications of the Customs taxes with the consent of the Powers concerned. As regarded the Capitulations in judicial matters, they repeated their offer to set up a similar Commission to prepare a scheme of judicial reform to replace the Capitulary system which would continue provisionally pending the introduction of the proposed scheme. That Commission would be at liberty to recommend either a mixed or a unified judicial system.

" We all desire peace," the noble Marquess added, " but a peace which is just to all parties, and which will prevent a renewal of a struggle which is disastrous to both sides."

League of Nations intervention.

The Marquess of Salisbury hoped that the intervention of the League of Nations might be effective in protecting the Armenians and in providing for their future. He thought, however, it would probably be of great assistance to the League if they could know what force they had to rely upon in the event of their making a proposal which the Turks would not accept.

The Archbishop of Canterbury agreed with Lord Salisbury that they were anxious to know by what practical means the League were to give effect to any endeavour they made. It was hardly unfair to say that inadequate help given to a community settled like the Armenians in Erivan and Cilicia had the reverse of a good effect, because it served as an irritant to the Turk.

The Secretary of State for Foreign Affairs remarked that the absence of armed forces did not prevent the League of Nations from having handed over to them the decision of the exceedingly vexed and difficult question of Cilicia, on which the Powers were unable with their armed forces to come to an agreement. It was not the case that because the League of Nations had no armed forces that even their physical influence was small. The influence of the League was, of course, in the first place moral, but the support of the public opinion of the world was in the nature of a physical sanction, very often more effective than that of arms itself.

The plans devised at Paris were not merely to be notified to the League of Nations, but were to be embodied in the conditions the Allied Powers were sending to the Greeks and the Turks. He urged public opinion to concentrate on giving every possible support and authority to the League of Nations in accepting the invitation the Allied Powers were about to address to them.

EGYPT: POLICY OF THE GOVERNMENT.

(Termination of Protectorate; An Independent Sovereign State; The Sudan.)

In the House of Commons on 28th February, the Prime Minister made an important declaration of policy in regard to Egypt. The statement was made in reply to a question by the Right Hon. Sir Donald Maclean (Chairman of the Independent Liberal Party in Parliament).

The Prime Minister (the Right Hon. D. Lloyd George) said that a White Paper was being issued showing what had passed since the declaration of policy made by His Majesty's Government in December after the failure of Adly Pasha's mission to London. It also contained the declaration of policy upon which His Majesty's Government, in pursuance of the principles laid down in December, now proposed to proceed.

"We have long recognised, and said," the Premier continued, "that the Protectorate was no longer a satisfactory form of relationship between the British Empire and Egypt, but we have also said that, owing to the peculiar geographical position of Egypt, the Protectorate cannot be terminated unless British Imperial interests are fully safeguarded. This Adly Pasha and his colleagues were the first to admit, but the difficulty of reconciling these interests with Egyptian aspirations proved insuperable during the negotiations last summer. At the present moment there is no Egyptian Government which could go so far as to commit their country to a treaty relationship with Great Britain of a nature to afford us adequate safeguards in these matters, and His Majesty's Government have, therefore, determined to proceed by a unilateral declaration.

"In this course they enjoy the whole-hearted support of Lord Allenby, and of the British officials of all ranks in the service of the Egyptian Government, and they are confident that their action will be equally endorsed by Parliament and by public opinion in this country.

Points in the declaration.

"There are three points in the declaration:—

"*First*, the Protectorate is terminated and Egypt is free to work out such national institutions as may best be suited to the aspirations of her people.

"*Second*, martial law will be abolished as soon as an Act of Indemnity has been passed. On this a word of explanation is necessary. Martial law has not been used in the main, as some people suppose, to enforce British policy upon Egypt. It has been, on the contrary, the main instrument of government in the hands of Egyptian Ministers for certain important measures arising out of war conditions—such, for instance, as the regulation of house rents and the levying of certain taxes. An Act of Indemnity is, therefore, necessary before any Egyptian Government can dispense with martial law. It is for the Egyptian Government to pass the necessary legislation, but we undertake to impose no obstacles, provided the final Clause of the Declaration is duly observed.

"*Third*, this final clause defines the special relation between His Majesty's Government and Egypt. It declares that the following four matters are absolutely reserved to the discretion of His Majesty's Government:—

"(A) The security of the communications of the British Empire in Egypt.

"(B) The defence of Egypt against all foreign aggression or interference, direct or indirect.

"(C) The protection of foreign interests in Egypt and the protection of minorities.

"(D) The Sudan.

Foreign Powers not concerned.

"We are prepared to make agreements with the Egyptian Government upon these matters in a spirit of mutual accommodation, whenever a favourable opportunity arises for the conclusion of such agreements, but until such agreements, satisfactory both to ourselves and to the Egyptian Government, are concluded, the *status quo* will remain intact.

"I must make another point clear. We regard the special relations between ourselves and Egypt defined in this clause as a matter concerning only ourselves and the Government of Egypt. Foreign Powers are not concerned, and we propose to state this unmistakably when the termination of the Protectorate is notified to them.

"The welfare and integrity of Egypt are necessary to the peace and safety of the British Empire, which will, therefore, always maintain as an essential British interest the special relations between itself and Egypt long recognised by other Governments. The definition of these special relations is an essential part of the declaration recognising Egypt as an independent sovereign State. His Majesty's Government have laid them down as matters in which the rights and interests of the British Empire are vitally involved, and they cannot permit them to be questioned by any other Power. In pursuance of this principle, they would regard as an unfriendly act any attempt at interference in the affairs of Egypt by another Power, and they would consider any aggression against the territory of Egypt as an act to be repelled by all the means at their command.

Independent nation.

"On the other hand, we of course accept the protection of foreign interests and minorities in Egypt as a responsibility inseparable from the special position which we claim in the country.

"These responsibilities have not infrequently been brought home to His Majesty's Government in the course of the last few years, when the passions of the masses in Egypt have been inflamed against all foreigners, and all foreigners alike have suffered. It is to be hoped that, with the recognition of their status as an independent nation, the Egyptians will themselves realise how imperative it is to keep political passions within their proper bounds, and the efforts of any Egyptian Government in this direction will always enjoy the sympathy and support of His Majesty's Government.

The Sudan: status.

"I now come to the Sudan, which is very important to the British Empire. The Sudan calls for more than a passing word. The combined efforts of Great Britain and Egypt were needed to rescue that vast country from the devastation and ruin into which the Mahdist movement had plunged it. Since the reconquest, more than 20 years ago, Great Britain and Egypt have alike contributed men and money towards the restoration of peace and prosperity to what should one day prove a country as fertile and populous as it is now barren and empty.

"His Majesty's Government will never allow the progress which has already been made, and the greater promise of future years, to be jeopardised.

"Service in the Sudan is unpopular with Egyptians, and one of the main reasons why conscription is disliked is due to the fact that it entails such service. On the other hand, Egyptian officials are not welcomed by the Sudanese, in whose minds the memories of Egyptian misgovernment 50 years ago still rankle.

"Nor can His Majesty's Government agree to any change in the status of that country which would in the slightest degree diminish the security for the many millions of British capital which are already invested in its development—to the great advantage of the Sudan.

"Egypt, on the other hand, has undeniable right to the most ample guarantees that the development of the Sudan shall never threaten or interfere with her existing water supply, or with that which she may require in order to bring her own territory under full cultivation. Such guarantees His Majesty's Government will be ready to afford, and there is no reason why they should in any way hamper or retard the progress of the Sudan.

Imperial security; Dominion Governments notified.

"The declaration conforms closely to the policy laid down by agreement at the Imperial Conference, and fully covers all matters there defined as essential to Imperial security. It has been notified to the Dominion Governments, who take a very keen interest in the matter, in a telegram published in the White Paper.

"His Majesty's Government have complete confidence in Lord Allenby. As the correspondence in the White Paper shows, the points on which he was invited home for consultation related to the Imperial and international effect of his proposals, on which His Majesty's Government had to be completely satisfied. As already explained, it was essential that the method of procedure to be adopted should thoroughly safeguard the special relations between His Majesty's Government and Egypt recognised by other Powers and essential to Imperial security.

"Lord Allenby fully concurred in our proposals for this end, and has returned to Egypt in complete agreement with the course of action now recommended to Parliament.

"His character, his achievements, and his handling of a very difficult situation during the past three years in Egypt have given him an exceptional position with the Egyptian people, and His Majesty's Government have complete confidence that the interests of the British Empire and the cause of a good understanding between ourselves and the Egyptian people are equally secure in his hands."

DEBATE IN HOUSE OF COMMONS.

A debate on the Government's policy in Egypt took place in the House of Commons on 14th March. It arose on the Report stage of a vote on account of £148,300,000 for Civil Services and Revenue Departments.

Captain Wedgwood Benn (Independent Liberal, *Leith*) moved to reduce the amount of the Vote by £100. He said that if the Government kept faith in the terms of their own declaration with the people of Egypt they could solve the problem in that country.

General Sir Charles Townshend (**Independent**, *Shropshire, The Wrekin*) contended that the Government were correct in not scuttling out of Egypt in a hurry. So long as there was not peace in the Near East there was the greatest danger in moving out of Egypt. He did not see how they were ever to give up holding the zone of the Suez Canal and also a landing base at Alexandria. He had always said that Australia was as much interested as they were themselves in keeping up and paying for that line of communication.

Earl Winterton* (**Coalition Unionist**, *Horsham and Worthing*) believed that it was possible to arrive at a common policy, and thought that the last set of proposals gave hope of such an achievement.

Lieut.-Col. the Hon. Aubrey Herbert (**Coalition Unionist**, *Yeovil*) hoped that the moment circumstances permitted Zaghloul Pasha would be released. In the past, when they had a different Government in England, Zaghloul was highly spoken of. What they really wanted in Egypt was goodwill and a settlement.

Zaghloul's bad record.

The Leader of the House (**the Right Hon. Austen Chamberlain**) said that Zaghloul's record was a bad one. He continuously exercised intimidation over individuals and the means of the expression of public opinion in Egypt. A sigh of relief went up from all responsible quarters in Egypt when Lord Allenby ordered his deportation. He would not be brought back so long as he was any danger to the peace or good order of Egypt, or to the effective protection of essential British interests in that country.

The right hon. gentleman went on to show that the Government had pursued a policy for the concluding of a Treaty between Egypt and this country which would lay the basis for the abolition of the Protectorate and for the independence of the Egyptians in their own land, and at the same time would give Great Britain the guarantees that were essential for discharging their obligations to Europe, for the protection of British interests in Egypt, and for the security of the vital communications of the Empire. But no Egyptian Government —and for that he thought Zaghloul's agitation was largely responsible—dared make a Treaty giving them the essential securities. Accordingly, when the negotiations with Adly had broken down he went back and received Lord Allenby's proposal that they should give up the idea of a Treaty, and should proceed by way of a unilateral declaration—a policy they had ultimately adopted.

* Now Under-Secretary of State for India in succession to the Earl of Lytton.

Egypt would not be in a position to enjoy an independent existence to-day if it were not that Great Britain had rescued her from disaster and protected her from all other interference. Unless Great Britain preserved that measure of protection Egypt would not long enjoy the independence which they were prepared to give.

An Empire concern.

"It is," said Mr. Chamberlain, "only the guarantee we give by these reservations for the safety and security of the foreign communities in Egypt, and our express determination to allow no interference by any other country except our own, which protects Egypt to-day and will protect her to-morrow from intervention by some other country. It is not only British interests in Egypt, it is not only the foreign communities—all of whom, and especially the British, Zaghloul declared his desire to expel—it is not merely that. This question is of vital concern to our Pacific Dominions. Communication through the Suez Canal, communication through Egypt, is a *sine quâ non* having regard to the way in which communications have developed the cohesion and strength of the British Empire.

"This is one of the subjects which, when the Dominion Ministers were last over here, they discussed with His Majesty's Ministers at home in the Imperial Conference as being a matter of common concern to the Empire, and in order that we might be fully possessed of their views as to the necessity for maintaining their security in this respect, and that we might give them the assurances which were vital to their own safety and their own prosperity."

The Hon. W. Ormsby-Gore (Coalition Unionist, ***Stafford*****)** remarked that if they withdrew their troops and established complete Home Rule in Egypt, inevitably neither the French nor the Italian Governments would tolerate it for long.

Mr. J. E. Mills (Labour, ***Dartford*****)** observed that whatever bitterness of opinion there was in Egypt was due to the fact that when Lord Milner and his colleagues went out to that country their terms of reference were to inquire what could be done under the Protectorate. The Egyptian people looked upon the Protectorate as merely a transient scheme, and thought after the end of the War the claims of Egypt, based upon the consecutive declarations of statesmen ever since 1882, would be recognised.

On a division the amendment to reduce the amount was negatived by 202 votes against 70, and the Report of the Vote on Account was agreed to.

LEAGUE OF NATIONS EXPENDITURE.

Replying in the House of Commons on 22nd February to a question by Sir C. Kinloch-Cooke (Coalition Unionist, *Devonport*),

The Lord President of the Council (the Right Hon. A. J. Balfour) said : " Under the scheme of allocation of expenditure adopted by the Second Assembly last autumn, which is not yet in force, the share of Great Britain will represent approximately 9·55 per cent. of the total expenditure of the League of Nations. The Commission of Control was set up by virtue of a Resolution of the Second Assembly in order to scrutinise the provisional estimates of the League's expenditure during the next ensuing financial year, and to report thereon to the Council. The Assembly considered it desirable that members of the League other than those represented on the Council should be represented on this Commission.

" It is misleading to suggest that the Commission of Control is responsible for the finances of the League. Its functions are to facilitate the tasks of the Council and the Assembly in exercising control over the League's activities. The section of the Report of the Committee on National Expenditure relating to the League of Nations is still under consideration."

FAMINE IN RUSSIA.

(Government Decision : No Grant from Public Funds.)

Questions were addressed to the Government in the House of Commons on 9th March asking what decision had been reached regarding the grant of financial assistance for the relief of the famine districts in Russia.

The Leader of the House (the Right Hon. Austen Chamberlain) said : " We have given serious and renewed consideration to this question, but in view of the large sums which this House has already voted for the relief of Europe, of the very heavy burdens resting upon our own people and the great distress and suffering existing among them, we are unable to propose a grant from public funds, but every effort will be made to add to the supply of medical stores already placed at the disposal of the Red Cross Society. The resources in the possession of the Government are being reviewed for this purpose."

The Right Hon. G. N. Barnes (Labour, ***Glasgow, Gorbals*****)** : " Is the right hon. gentleman aware that the American Government have given 12,000,000 dollars and are at present voting about 7,000,000 dollars, I think, to women and children in Russia as against our £700,000 or less, and also is he aware that there are 5,000,000 poods of seed short for this spring sowing, and if the seed is not forthcoming the Russian people will be faced with a catastrophe next year even worse than this ? "

The Leader of the House : " I am aware that the American Government have devoted a large sum, even larger than my right hon. friend has mentioned, to the purpose of famine relief. I believe the horror of the situation in Russia can hardly be exaggerated, but we must have regard to what we have already done, to the burdens we have put upon our own people, to the possibility and even probability that we shall shortly be asked by the League of Nations to vote a further sum to combat the spread of typhus out of Russia into Europe which menaces all the western nations, and I cannot altogether overlook that the Russian Government have resources of their own which are being applied to matters much less urgent and vital than the relief of famine among their own citizens."

Nation's honour.

The Right Hon. Sir Donald Maclean (Chairman of the Independent Liberal Party in Parliament) : " Is the right hon. gentleman aware that so competent an authority as Sir Benjamin Robertson, who has just returned from this very area, is of opinion that, even on material grounds, as an investment for this country, it would be a wise thing for us to advance a sum of between £400,000 and £5,000,000 ? "

The Leader of the House : " The sums I have been asked to advance vary between £400,000 and three or four millions."

Colonel J. C. Wedgwood (Labour, ***Newcastle-under-Lyme*****)** : " Is the right hon. gentleman aware that he is not only the trustee for this nation's finances but also for its honour in this matter ? "

The Leader of the House : " This nation has never been backward in coming to the relief of distress in other countries. That has been done almost universally through the means of subscriptions given by the charitable in this country, generally on an appeal from the Lord Mayor. I know of no demand that there should be a Vote from public funds in the whole of the last century comparable to that which is asked to-day, under circumstances where the distress of our own people and the burden of our responsibility is incomparably greater than at any other period."

The Right Hon. Lord Robert Cecil (Independent Conservative, ***Hitchin*****)** : " Can the right hon. gentleman say whether there has ever been any instance of distress comparable with this that now exists in Russia, and whether it is not the opinion of Indian experts that in India we do not know what famine means compared to what it is in Russia; and is he aware that the opposition to our advancing money comes solely from the richer classes?"

The Leader of the House: "I am certainly not aware that the opposition to spending our resources at this time, when there is so much distress, and more distress than we can meet, among our own people, comes solely from the well-to-do. I am sorry that my noble friend has made a suggestion of that kind. As regards the state of affairs, I do not think that it can be exaggerated. I believe that the utter disorganisation of the transport and of the ordinary means of commerce and trade in Russia has immensely aggravated, and does immensely aggravate, the situation, and takes it out of the category of anything we have had to deal with, even in the worst times, in India; but I think there have been calamities in the world's history on as large a scale where it has not been thought right, or even proposed, that we should vote public money for that purpose."

IRISH FREE STATE (AGREEMENT) ACT.

(Dominion Status; Right of Secession; Attitude of Dominions; Governor-General.)

The Royal Assent was given on 31st March to the Irish Free State (Agreement) Act, which gives the force of law to the Articles of Agreement for a Treaty between Great Britain and Ireland signed in London by the representatives of the two countries on 6th December, 1921. The full text of the Articles of Agreement was published in the last number of the JOURNAL (*vide* Vol. III., No. 1, p. 7).

The operative clause of the Act provides for the making of Orders in Council transferring to the Provisional Government, established for the administration of Southern Ireland until the constitution of a Parliament and Government of the Irish Free State, the powers and machinery requisite for the discharge of its duties.

It is provided that not later than four months after the passing of the Act the Parliament of Southern Ireland* shall be dissolved, and an election be held for the constituencies which would have been entitled to elect Members to that Parliament. The members so elected will constitute the House of the Parliament to which the Provisional Government will be responsible. That Parliament will, as respects matters within the jurisdiction of the Provisional Government, have power to make laws in like manner as the Parliament of the Irish Free State when constituted.

From the date of the passing of the Act no writ is to be issued for the election of a member to serve in Commons House of Parliament for a constituency in Ireland other than a constituency in Northern Ireland.

* The Parliament elected under the Government of Ireland Act, 1920.

DEBATE IN HOUSE OF COMMONS.

The Bill was debated in the House of Commons on Second Reading on 16th and 17th February.

The Secretary of State for the Colonies (the Right Hon. Winston Churchill), remarking upon the urgency of the Bill, asked, with reference to the Provisional Government, whether it was not fatal to peace, social order and good government to have power wielded by men who had no legal authority. A Provisional Government unsanctified by law, yet recognised by His Majesty's Ministers, was an anomaly unprecendented in the history of the British Empire. Contempt of law was one of the great evils manifesting themselves in many parts of the world at the present time, and it was disastrous to the Imperial Parliament to connive at or countenance such a situation in Ireland for one day longer than was absolutely necessary. Moreover, what chance did such a situation give to the Irish Executive who had assumed the very great burden and responsibility of directing Irish affairs ?

The Bill would enable an election to be held in Ireland at an early date, and thus provide for a national decision upon the Treaty by the Irish people. The view of the Irish signatories of the Treaty was that the Irish Republic was set up by the Irish people at the elections which took place during the Conference, and that this Republic could only be converted into an Irish Free State by the decision of the Irish people. That was not the view of the British Government. They had not recognised the Irish Republic and never would do. Was it not a desirable thing that upon the authority of the Irish people recorded at an election the Republican idea should be definitely, finally and completely put aside ?

Need of early Election in Ireland.

Amongst other objects of the election the right hon. gentleman mentioned the necessity of securing a sensible Parliament in Ireland and ensuring that Ministers in that country were supported by a national mandate. Irish Ministers must know where they stood with the Irish nation. He would be asked, " Supposing Mr. de Valera and his friends win this election in Ireland, what is to happen then ? "

" It is perfectly clear," said the Colonial Secretary, " that the repudiation by Ireland of the Treaty would free all parties from their engagement, and that the position of Great Britain—standing on the Treaty, ready to carry out the Treaty, if others could be found, on behalf of the Irish nation, to do their part—would be one of great moral as well as of undoubted material strength. The position of Southern Ireland, on the other hand, would be one of the greatest weakness and division—absolutely isolated from the sympathy of the world, bitterly divided in herself. The position of Northern Ireland would be quite unaffected." Mr Churchill proceeded to say that he did not think it was prudent or necessary at that stage to assume for a moment such a result. There were those who thought that the present Irish Government might be overturned by a *coup d'état* and that a "Red" Soviet Republic might be set up.

The British Government did not think that was at all likely. If it were it was quite clear that a Soviet Republic in Ireland would ruin the Irish cause for 100 years, but would not in any respect impair the foundations of the British Empire or the security of Ulster. No people in the world were really less likely to turn Bolshevik than the Irish. Their strong sense of personal possession, their respect for the position of women, their love of country and their religious convictions constituted them in a peculiar sense the most sure and unyielding opponents of the withering and levelling doctrines of Russia. But the Irish Ministry ought not to be left in a position in which even the most necessary measures which they took for their own defence or for the enforcement of authority, or even for the maintenance of law and the suppression of brigandage or mutiny, were devoid of formal sanction.

Ought Great Britain to regret?

Surveying the whole position since the Imperial Parliament met in the winter and approved the Treaty, he asked ought they to regret what they then did. He thought they were better off in every respect in that Irish matter than they were six months ago. The tables were turned. Ireland, not Britain, was on her trial before the nations of the world. The position of Ulster was one of great and unshakeable strength—not only material but moral strength. The position of the Imperial Government had also become greatly improved. But the position of Southern Ireland was one of great difficulty and danger. When the men who put their hands to the document in Downing Street last December went back to Ireland, they were practically put on their trial for having betrayed the Irish Republic. As long as they stood by the Treaty and the Imperial Government had confidence in them, those men deserved their help and deserved to be given the means of making good.

The situation on the frontier of Northern Ireland had, he thought, been a little improved by the agreement of both Irish Governments to the establishment of a Border Commission to make sure no hostile attack on a large scale was being organised on the one side or the other. The position in Belfast was terrible. He trusted that in the near future, whatever might have occurred since their last meeting, there would be some form of parley between the heads of the two Governments.* It was most desirable from every point of view to arrive at some method of calming the terrible vendettas and the counter-vendettas which were rife in the streets and alleys of Belfast. Turning to the question of the Boundary Commission, the right hon. gentleman said they had no power, except by tearing up the Treaty, to alter what was prescribed in Article XII.† When the time came that Article would have to be interpreted in the manner prescribed in the Treaty.

After reminding the House that all the trouble was with respect to the boundaries of Fermanagh and Tyrone, the Colonial Secretary went on to argue that it would be much better to take up this difficult question after the Irish elections had been held rather than before. Ulster must have British comfort and protection. Ireland must have her Treaty, her election, and her constitution. There would be other and better opportunities of dealing with the difficult boundary question. The British Government strongly deprecated any attempt to reach a final conclusion upon that subject now.

Ulster's amendment.

Captain C. Craig (Leader of the Ulster Unionist Members) moved the following amendment :—

In view of the fact that the Agreement provides for setting up a Boundary Commission to determine the boundaries between Northern Ireland and the Irish Free State, and that such provision is a direct abrogation of the rights of Ulster as secured by the Government of Ireland Act, 1920, and a breach of the pledges given by the Prime Minister, this House declines to proceed with the Second Reading of this Bill until the Government has given an assurance that the provision in question will be eliminated from the Agreement or that any decision of the Boundary Commission shall only take effect after the approval of the Parliament of Northern Ireland has been given.

---

* An All-Ireland conference took place at the Colonial Office in London on 29th and 30th March, resulting in an agreement between the heads of the two Irish Governments for the preservation of peace.

† Article XII. provides that if Ulster elects to remain outside the Free State a Commission consisting of three persons, one to be appointed by the Government of the Irish Free State, one to be appointed by the Government of Northern Ireland, and one who shall be Chairman, to be appointed by the British Government, shall determine in accordance with the wishes of the inhabitants, so far as may be compatible with economic and geographic conditions, the boundaries between Northern Ireland and the rest of Ireland.

The hon. and gallant Member said the people of Ulster thought the Act of 1920, under which the six counties were selected by the Imperial Government as the area over which the Northern Parliament should have jurisdiction, was the last word. Nobody would ever have suggested that the direction in which they could possibly look for trouble was the boundaries. He contended that the Government negotiators with Sinn Fein had no moral right to include Article XII. in the Treaty. So far as it related to Ulster, the Act of 1920 was just as much a Treaty and had more binding force than any Treaty. The Government had no right to touch the territory of a third party without their being represented in the Conference.

" I say quite plainly," the hon. Member observed, " that if the Boundary Commission were to sit, and if it were to make anything more than the very minutest change in our boundary, the inevitable result would be bloodshed and chaos of the worst description."

Lieut.-Colonel the Hon. W. Guinness (Coalition Unionist, *Bury St. Edmund's*) said he had always been very doubtful whether there was any solution between the Union and separation, but the organised Parties of British politics took the opposite view. Administration of the machinery of the Union in alternating moods of concession and repression had steadily encouraged the extremists. There had been sixteen years of that terrible policy, and it was time to test, by experiment, whether Ireland could attain peaceful self-government within the Empire in some other way. He was convinced that to turn back at this time would be a great disaster.

Attitude of the " Die-hards."

Captain C. T. Foxcroft (Coalition Unionist, *Bath*) said that six months ago the " Die-hards "* and the Government held the opinion that no permanent peace was possible in Ireland unless, first, the law-breaker was punished. Apparently it was now the belief of the majority of the House that it was perfectly possible to obtain a permanent peace in Ireland by elevating the law-breaker into a maker of laws. When they were asked to confirm the Treaty they were told they would have something like peace all over Ireland in a very short time. Instead, they found anarchy in the South and invasion in the North. The only hope was that Mr. Collins and his friends would prove that they had both the will and the power to do two things—to defend all peace-loving inhabitants in Ireland and to maintain the British connection.

* The name popularly applied to the group of Unionist Members who opposed the Treaty with Ireland.

The Attorney-General (the Right Hon. Sir Gordon Hewart)* said that the question of interpretation to be put upon Article XII. was one which the Boundary Commission must decide for themselves. It was no part of the duty of the Law Officers of the Crown to interpret the Articles.

Attacks on Catholics.

Mr. J. Devlin (Nationalist, ***Belfast, Falls*****)** said it was the duty of all patriotic citizens to accept the Treaty and help those who were engaged in carrying it into legislative effect. Referring to the condition of affairs in Belfast, he remarked that for the last twelve months life in that city had been practically impossible for a Catholic. A series of attacks had been made upon the Catholics unparalleled in the story of barbarity in any country of the world. He asked, what did the Northern Government propose to do to end that reign of terror, that saturnalia of destruction and assassination?

Lieut.-Colonel H. Page Croft (Unionist, ***Bournemouth*****)**: "Restore the Union."

Mr. Devlin: "It is the Union that has been responsible for dividing Protestants and Catholics." He challenged hon. Members to say that religious persecution was carried on in Southern Ireland. To pursue Catholics because of their faith was a scandal and a crime. Let them try, as the foundation of a better condition of things in Ulster, to extirpate that horror of religious bigotry.

The Right Hon. J. H. Thomas (Labour, ***Derby*****)** remarked that he was in touch with the working-classes as much as any other Member, and he could say that if there was one thing of which the British people were sick it was the Irish problem. The Labour Party on this occasion would support the Government. They were not prepared to make political capital out of the unfortunate state of affairs in Ireland, and they believed that the Government did right in making the Treaty.

Not a Party triumph.

The Leader of the House (the Right Hon. Austen Chamberlain) declared that the Bill was not the triumph of any Party. It was not the solution which any Party in that House sought or desired. The Unionist policy died, not because it was inherently wrong, but because, if it was to be successful, it needed continuity, patience, perseverance, and their people would not pursue it connectedly through the changes of Party warfare. A new solution had to be sought.

---

*Now Lord Chief Justice of England, his successor in the office of Attorney-General being the Right Hon. Sir Ernest Pollock, lately Solicitor-General.

"We have found it," said Mr. Chamberlain, "in the development of the self-governing Dominions of the Empire, creating a new situation, a position of defined powers and responsibilities, clearly within the Empire, clearly subject to the authority of the Crown, and yet giving immense, almost absolute, liberty within the domestic affairs of each of the countries concerned. We have offered that position to Ireland. We place upon it only these limitations, that Ireland shall remain within this Empire and accept citizenship, that she shall acknowledge allegiance to the King and that she should give us those securities which are vital to our national existence and to the maintenance of the communications of the Empire."

As to the boundaries question, he still hoped that in the time which must elapse before the boundary could be drawn it might be possible for North and South to agree.

On a division the amendment was negatived by 302 votes against 60, and the Bill was read a second time.

Bill in Committee: status of the Agreement.

On 2nd March the House went into Committee on the Bill. This stage of the measure was continued on 3rd March and completed on 6th March.

Colonel J. Gretton (Unionist, *Burton*) moved to omit the words " for a Treaty " [" Articles of Agreement for a Treaty "]. He said that under the Constitution a Treaty could only be made between high contracting Powers and independent States. It was not possible constitutionally for Ministers of the Crown or the Crown itself to make a Treaty with subjects of the Crown. If Ministers maintained that the word " Treaty " was properly inserted they admitted that the State which they were setting up in Ireland was a Sovereign Independent State competent to make treaties and that at the time the agreement was come to the Irish representatives had established independence.

The Secretary of State for the Colonies said the expression " the Treaty " had become the foundation of the position of the political Party in Ireland which was seeking to establish the Irish Free State. The use of the word had a great sentimental advantage and would aid the parties to arrive at a satisfactory result. For a long time after the Boer War there was a difference in official circles as to how the agreement concluded at Vereeniging should be styled. The pedants wished to describe that pact as the "Terms of Surrender," whereas those working for the reconciliation of South Africa always referred to it as the Treaty of Vereeniging. It was on the basis of the Treaty of Vereeniging that General Smuts and General Botha came to their aid and maintained the

popularly known as Dominion Home Rule. The constitutional status to be granted to Ireland was one of absolute equality with Australia, South Africa, or Canada. On 30th March, 1920, the late Leader of the House* made a declaration on behalf of the Government that any nation being given Dominion Home Rule without reservation was entitled to shape its own destinies and to declare itself an independent republic.† When that status had been conferred upon her, Ireland would, under the Treaty, be entitled to declare herself independent and set up an independent republic at the heart of the Empire.

The Secretary of State for the Colonies said the Government rested themselves on Articles I. and II. of the Agreement, which accorded to Ireland

"the same constitutional status in the community of Nations, known as the British Empire as the Dominion of Canada, the Commonwealth of Australia, the Dominion of New Zealand, and the Union of South Africa."

He did not think they would be well advised to try to define that status more precisely than was done in the Articles. The Imperial Conference which met last year gave the most careful consideration to the whole question of the constitutional relations of the different parts of the British Empire and decided that it was a subject which was much better left alone.

Attitude of Dominions.

"We have never admitted and the Great Dominions of the Crown have never claimed the right to secede," said Mr. Churchill. "If the question were raised, I have no doubt it would be pressed in one direction or the other to a conclusion. . . . I do not accept the particular statement which has been referred to as governing the constitutional practice of the British Empire, and I am confident that it would not be so accepted in the Great Dominions.

"But, obviously, is not the question, as far as the Dominions are concerned, much better left to the easy forward movement of unity and comradeship, to good sense, to the avoidance of situations which over and over again have thrown other nations and other powerful organisations into disorder, but which with British common sense, with give and take, making allowances here and not pushing things to a logical conclusion there, have enabled us, year after year, generation after generation, to gather together and keep together and carry forward the great structure and fabric of our Imperial inheritance? Obviously these matters will have

* The Right Hon. A. Bonar Law.
† *Vide* JOURNAL, Vol. I., No. 2, p. 252.

to be interpreted in relation to the particular set of circumstances which prevail at the time, in relation to the resources and position of this country at the time, in relation to the intentions of its people and its Government at the time, in relation to the degree of opinion expressed on the one side or the other in any of the Dominions concerned, and it is impossible, it would be futile and it would be mischievous, to attempt to lay down beforehand a general rule.

" By good and wise administration, by patient contribution by every Party in the State and by each of the succession of Governments which may occupy the place of power, it should be possible to bring the British Empire steadily forward through the next generation in the same manner as it has been brought forward through the extraordinary difficulties of the last generation.

No independent Irish Republic.

" I deprecate very much indeed endeavouring exactly to define these matters, and I hope—and this is an effort which we shall certainly make—it will not be a consequence of the Irish Free State Agreement that an attempt will be made to give us an exact definition of the Imperial relationships between the great Dominions and this country. I should greatly deprecate it, and as far as the Government have any control over events we shall endeavour to direct discussion into other and different channels. We do not wish the august relations of the British Empire to be defined by any narrow and hard-fought-out conditions of the Irish settlement.

" As to the question of the Irish settlement—we are not going to have an independent Republic in Ireland. I have said so again and again. And as far as we are concerned, we should never agree to it in any circumstances whatever. What tactics we should employ, what weapons we should use, what machinery we should bring to bear—moral, political, military, economic—whatever it might be that we should do, whatever it was that we thought the best and most convenient, that we should undoubtedly bring to bear on any attempt to set up an independent foreign Republic in Ireland. There is absolutely no question of accommodation on that subject—none whatever.

" The battle has been joined in Ireland on that issue. There is no weakening on that issue by the men with whom we have signed the Treaty. Only this day they have declared in explicit terms, again renewing their declaration to stand by the Treaty, the whole Treaty, and nothing but the Treaty, that they will put this issue to the Irish people with the constitution so that the Irish people shall choose freely between a Republic and a Free State."

"Dominions cannot separate themselves."

The Right Hon. Sir Henry Craik (Unionist, *Scottish Universities*) said it was well known that although the constitutional point was quite clear that the great Dominions could not separate, yet undoubtedly Great Britain would not allow them to remain against their will. But was the case the same with Ireland? Were they prepared to say that the dangers of the separation of Ireland were not greater than those of Canada and that they could allow the same independence of State to Ireland as they did to Canada?

Mr. Ronald McNeill (Unionist, *Canterbury*) remarked that it was one of the most glorious facts of their Empire that all the Great Dominions of the Crown overseas were characterised by intense loyalty to the Crown and Empire. But they were now going to create a new Dominion which even Mr. Churchill, in his wildest flight of optimistic imagination, could not say was characterised by intense loyalty either to the Crown or the Empire. Two days after the Treaty was signed Mr. Michael Collins declared that the dissatisfaction of Ireland with any sort of control by or even connection with Great Britain was likely to be very much worse than in the Dominions. The hon. Member added that in his opinion there was practically an independent Republic functioning in Ireland now and he had not the smallest doubt that before many years—it might be months—had passed it would be definitely accepted that an independent Republic would be recognised by the British Government.

On a division, the amendment was negatived by 241 votes against 57.

An amendment was moved by

The Right Hon. Lord Hugh Cecil (Unionist, *Oxford University*) declaring that the British Government and Parliament, in approving Article **XII.**, did not intend to agree to the transfer of the main area of any of the six counties of Northern Ireland to the territory of the Irish Free State, but only to such minor adjustments (if any) in the boundary, either in the one direction or the other, as might without economic injury either to Northern Ireland or the Irish Free State satisfy the desires of bodies of persons of homogeneous opinions in respect to their territorial situation.

After lengthy discussion, the amendment was negatived by 199 votes against 63.

Governor-General: Canadian precedent.

Mr. T. Moles (Coalition Unionist, *Belfast, Ormeau*) moved an amendment to the effect that, if Ulster elected to remain outside the Irish Free State, the representative of the Crown in Ireland should exercise no jurisdiction or authority in or relating to Northern Ireland. He said that the Governor-General would really be the nominee of the Southern Parliament and they would take good care to select somebody who was known to be in sympathy with their views. For precisely the same reason, they would choose a nominee hostile to the Northern Parliament, to whom His Majesty's Government owed just as much duty as they did to the Southern Parliament. The Viceroy for the Northern Parliament would be the same person, but the nature of his duty and relationship to that Parliament would be so dissimilar from that he would hold to the Southern Parliament as to constitute a real anomaly.

The Secretary of State for the Colonies said that if Ulster contracted out of the area of the Free State, as she would have a statutory right to do, and unless there was an agreement, the Imperial Government would regard the wishes of Ulster in this respect as decisive. If she did not wish the Viceroy or Governor-General selected by the Free State to discharge his functions over Northern Ireland, some other arrangement would be made.

" The Treaty prescribes that a general adherence to the Canadian precedents shall be followed in these constitutional matters," Mr. Churchill added, " and, of course, in the appointment of a Governor-General for Canada, great pains are taken by those who have that responsibility to discharge to make an appointment in accordance with the legitimate wishes and feelings of that great Dominion. The Dominions do not seek to choose or to decide, but it would be extremely bad Imperial diplomacy and Imperial administration to make appointments which one had not ascertained beforehand to be in accordance with the feelings and interests of the Dominions. These are not matters capable of being reduced to a rigid statutory structure. They are matters relating to smooth, convenient, administrative processes, and similar methods will be followed in dealing with the Irish Free State if, and when, it is fully constituted."

Position of Northern Ireland.

Major the Right Hon. H. O'Neill (Coalition Unionist, *Antrim, Mid.*) remarked that there had been many rumours in Ireland and elsewhere as to whom the Government would appoint as the first Governor-General of the Free State. Lord Shaughnessy's name had been mentioned. " I do not say," the hon. Member observed, " that he or any other prominent Canadian or Australian, or New Zealander might not be quite suitable as Governor-General for the Irish Free State and acceptable to the people of the Irish Free State, but the person who is acceptable to them would not necessarily be acceptable to Northern Ireland, and I venture to think, if any such startling departure from precedent were made, and if some Governor-General who was not accustomed to the constitutional machinery of this centre of the Empire were appointed, it would create an absolutely intolerable position for Northern Ireland."

Following further discussion the amendment was, by leave, withdrawn.

The Bill was discussed on Report on 8th March and the Third Reading stage followed. Mr. Ronald McNeill moved the rejection of the Bill, but his amendment was negatived by 295 votes against 52, and the measure was then read a third time.

DEBATE IN HOUSE OF LORDS.

The Bill came on for Second Reading in the House of Lords on 15th March.

The Chancellor of the Duchy of Lancaster (Viscount Peel*) observed that in the unlikely supposition of Ireland repudiating her bargain she could hardly expect to receive any sympathy from the Great Dominions. She would have proclaimed to the world generally that her desire was not for complete self-government, but for definite separation from the British Empire. She would have given out to all Irishmen in all the Dominions that they were themselves aliens within the Empire.

Lord Sumner held it to be entirely wrong that the proceedings under the Bill were to be conducted by Orders in Council. "You have done enough," he said, "to unloose the bonds of the British Empire by the way you have paltered with the Oath of Allegiance, the terms of the Treaty and the position of Ireland; and you will make a further wide breach in our constitutional practice, take a further step to enthrone the Executive on the shoulders of the Legislature and deprive it of its just rights of control over the Executive, unless you insist that Parliament shall see these Orders in Council and approve them before they become law."

Rights of minorities.

The Marquess of Lansdowne said that one of the blots on the Bill was a signal neglect of any attempt to protect the rights of minorities. It had never been the custom of this

* Shortly before Easter Viscount Peel was appointed Secretary of State for India in succession to the Rt. Hon. E. S. Montagu (resigned), his place as Chancellor of the Duchy of Lancaster being taken by Sir William Sutherland, K.C.B., M.P.

country to hold to the doctrine that minorities must suffer. He was not at all sure that the Sinn Fein leaders themselves, in principle, were not quite prepared to agree to the policy of safeguarding minorities.

Viscount Haldane remarked that there was only one way to protect minorities—that was to encourage the people with whom they were dealing to live together as a whole and to look to the majority for the fair treatment of the minority. They did not venture to protect minorities when they were setting up the Constitution of South Africa and experience had shown they had no necessity to do so. It was said that the Constitution was to be shaped by the Irish themselves. When had they given a Constitution to a new Dominion without leaving it to that Dominion practically to settle what the Constitution was to be ?

The debate was resumed on 16th March, when

Lord Carson said he had frequently been told that he spoke too bitterly upon this surrender in Ireland. He never spoke so bitterly as he felt.

The mischief done.

He was not going to argue before their Lordships that they ought to throw out the Bill. The mischief had been done, hideously done, and done in the worst way. He knew there had been high sounding phrases. " Never," said the Colonial Secretary, " will we consent to the establishment of a Republic in the South and West or any part of Ireland." Proclaim a Republic ! Why, there was a Republic there ! " Do tell the people openly, honestly, and above board," Lord Carson proceeded, " that in creating a Free State, as you are pleased to call it, you did it with the knowledge that these men were going to create a Republic, and that Englishmen must be prepared to look forward to a Republic being constituted within twenty miles of their shores." The Irish Government, which was carrying on affairs in Ireland, had every one of them taken the oath to the Irish Republic.

As to Northern Ireland, they could not set up a Government as they had done in Ulster and then say, " We will take no account of the views that you have." If they attempted that throughout the Empire, the Empire would not last a year. Then why did they do it in relation to Ulster ?

The Marquess of Londonderry remarked that if the British Government launched that experiment with the suggestion that it abdicated its authority in regard to Ireland the experiment was doomed to failure. If, on the other hand, the Irish people knew the concessions they would receive and the limit of the British Government's patience there was a chance of the experiment achieving some slender success.

The Lord Chancellor (Viscount Birkenhead) thought the apprehension which had been expressed during the debate that the use of the term "Treaty" would involve them in friction with, or justify the interference of, the League of Nations need not be seriously entertained. The Constitution to be drafted in Ireland must be within the terms of the Treaty, and, if it was not, complaint could be made in the House. He disputed the statement of Lord Carson that they had a Republic in Ireland now.

No Republic.

"We have not a Republic now in the South of Ireland," the Lord Chancellor continued. "We are not, in my judgment and expectation, going in any event to have a Republic in the South of Ireland, because in my view no Government in this country, not a Labour Government, not even one so guilty as this, could ever propose or will ever propose, having regard to the problems of maritime security and to the peculiar situation of Ulster, to assent to this demand. I rule it out with finality for ever, so far as one can attempt to speak with finality in such a matter." The Imperial Government's advisers in Ireland were confident that when the election took place in that country those who were in favour of the Treaty would be returned to power by a majority which would make them masters of the destinies of Ireland for a very considerable period.

The Bill was read a second time without a division and was further discussed during subsequent stages of its passage through the House, ending with the Third Reading on 27th March. An amendment was inserted in the Upper House to provide that the month which is to be allowed to Ulster to exercise her option with respect to contracting out of the Irish Free State should not run from the date of passing of this Bill, but from the passing of the later Bill, confirming the Constitution of the Free State. This amendment was agreed to by the House of Commons and incorporated in the Bill.

EMPIRE SETTLEMENT.*

Replying in the House of Commons on 22nd February to a question by Mr. Grattan Doyle (Coalition Unionist, *Newcastle, N.*),

The Financial Secretary to the Admiralty (Mr. L. S. Amery†) said: "The numbers and destinations of British families

* *Vide* also p. 329.

† Mr. L. S. Amery is Chairman of the Overseas Settlement Committee.

assisted to migrate during the six months ended 31st January last under the ex-service free passage scheme are as follows :—

"Canada, 679.

"Australia, 4,056.

"New Zealand, 960.

"South Africa and Rhodesia, 428.

"Other parts of the Empire, 225.

"These figures do not include families which have been assisted by Dominion Governments. I am not aware what numbers have received such assistance.

"Only a very small proportion of those who proceed overseas have either the experience or the capital necessary to enable them to obtain grants of land immediately on arrival overseas. A certain number have been settled on the land in Canada under the Canadian Soldiers' Settlement Scheme, but selections under this scheme, though at one time made in this country by a special commission of the Canadian Government, have for some time past only been made in Canada, and no exact figures either as to numbers or acreage are available.

"Similarly in the case of the other Dominions referred to, while a few have proceeded direct to holdings already arranged for them, others of whom no exact records are available have been able to establish themselves on the land subsequently to their arrival."

NATIONALITY LAW.

(Dominions and Amendment of the 1914 Act.)

In the House of Commons on 13th February, Mr. Gershom Stewart (Coalition Unionist, *Wirrall*) asked for information as to the present position of the descendants of British parents born in Japan, and whether the Dominions had agreed to their being accorded the status of British citizens.

The Under-Secretary of State for Foreign Affairs (Mr. Cecil Harmsworth): "The descendants of British parents who were themselves born in Japan are of British nationality, with the exception that such persons as were born after the entry into operation of the British Nationality and Status of Aliens Act on 1st January, 1915, to parents themselves born after 17th July, 1899, the date on which His Majesty's Government renounced their extra-territorial jurisdiction in Japan, would at present have no nationality.

"The Governments of Australia and of the Union of South Africa have already agreed to the amendment of the British Nationality and Status of Aliens Act, 1914,* discussed at the

* *Vide* JOURNAL, Vol. II., No. 2, p. 368.

Prime Ministers' Conference last summer, and it is hoped that the agreement of the remaining Dominions will be forthcoming shortly."

Replying to a question on the same subject in the House of Commons on 16th February,

The Leader of the House (the Right Hon. Austen Chamberlain) said that every effort was being made to obtain the concurrence of all the self-governing Dominions, so that the Bill might be ready for the first suitable opportunity for introduction. It was not proper to hurry the Dominions unduly; they must be allowed to answer in their own time. It was desirable that there should be uniformity in the matter within the Empire.

IMPERIAL ECONOMIC CONFERENCE.

(Resolution of the Canadian Chamber of Commerce in London.)

In the House of Commons on 23rd February the question of an Imperial Economic Conference was raised.

Mr. Percy Hurd (Coalition Unionist, *Frome*) asked the Prime Minister whether his attention had been called to a resolution unanimously adopted by the Executive Council of the Canadian Chamber of Commerce in London, urging that, in view of the far-reaching scheme of economic co-operation unanimously agreed upon at the Imperial Conferences of 1917 and 1918, an Imperial Economic Conference should be summoned at an early date, in which the appropriate British and Overseas Ministers would take part, in order to work out this agreement in further detail and take means to execute it for the complementary development of the resources of the two countries and of the whole Empire on lines of mutual helpfulness; and whether His Majesty's Government would take steps to summon such a conference?

The Prime Minister (the Right Hon. D. Lloyd George): "I have seen the resolution referred to, but unless there is a general desire on the part of the Overseas Governments to hold a conference on the lines suggested, I do not think that there would be any advantage in His Majesty's Government taking action at the present time. So far as I am aware, there is no indication of any such desire."

Mr. Hurd: "Would it not be possible to sound the Dominion Government to see whether there is a desire for such a conference being held?"

The Prime Minister: "I will consider that."

CANADIAN CATTLE EMBARGO.*

(Cabinet Decision; Question to be Debated; Free Vote of the House.)

In the House of Commons on 9th February, **Captain the Hon. E. A. Fitzroy (Coalition Unionist,** *Daventry*) asked whether the Government had considered the Report of the Royal Commission on the embargo on Canadian cattle, and whether they proposed to make any alteration in the Diseases of Animals Act, 1894?

The Minister of Agriculture (the Right Hon. Sir A. Griffith-Boscawen) replied: "The Government have carefully considered the Report of the Royal Commission, but in view of the almost unanimous opinion of agriculturists of all classes in England and Wales that the removal of the embargo would seriously injure the industry, and of the fact that the Commission themselves report that it would have little effect on the price of meat, they do not propose to introduce legislation for the purpose of removing it."

Mr. A. MacCallum Scott (Coalition Liberal, *Glasgow, Bridgeton*): "Is it feared that Canadian cattle would be infected if brought over here?"

The Minister of Agriculture: "No; that has nothing to do with it."

Mr. J. Leng Sturrock (Coalition Liberal, *Montrose Burghs*): "Has the right hon. gentleman given consideration to the opinion of agriculturists in Scotland on this matter, and not merely the opinion of agriculturists in England and Wales?"

The Minister of Agriculture: "Yes, we have given consideration to opinion in Scotland, and there is very great diversity of opinion on this matter among agriculturists in Scotland."

Major Mackenzie Wood (Independent Liberal, *Aberdeen, Central*): "Why were the Royal Commission appointed if it was not intended to abide by their decision? Is it a fact that the Government gave a pledge to the Canadian Government that after the War this embargo would be removed?"

Position of Canadian Government.

The Minister of Agriculture: "No Government is pledged to carry out all or any of the recommendations of a Royal Commission, which are the individual opinions of the Commissioners; and in this case even if we had accepted their conclusions they themselves say that they fully recognise that the opinion of Parliament may be a reason for some delay in taking action.

"Apart from that I believe that in this matter certain pledges were given in 1917 at the Imperial Conference when

* *Vide* also pp. 327 and 344.

this question, and a great many others, were under discussion, but, as I understand, the position which the Canadian Government most properly have always taken is that they do not wish to interfere in our home politics or home affairs, and that if we were convinced that the removing of the embargo was detrimental to our interests they would not press for it."

Replying on 13th March to a question by Mr. Sturrock, who asked whether he would cause the Report of the Commission to be reconsidered by the Cabinet, since the embargo prevented employment in shipping, landing, feeding and tending these cattle,

The Minister of Agriculture said : " The answer is in the negative. Any increase in employment in the direction suggested as a result of removing the embargo would be at the expense of employment in other parts of this country, and such action would not contribute to the solution of the unemployment problem, but rather the reverse."

Mr. Sturrock inquired whether, before the Cabinet resolved to take no action on the Report, the views of the Canadian Government on the embargo were invited and considered.

The Minister of Agriculture : " In considering the Report of the Commission, His Majesty's Government were fully cognisant of the views of the Canadian Government."

Day for discussion and a Free Vote.

Replying in the House of Commons on 3rd April, to Captain W. T. Shaw (Coalition Unionist, *Forfar*),

The Leader of the House (the Right Hon. Austen Chamberlain) said he would try to arrange an opportunity soon after the Easter Recess for a discussion on the Canadian cattle embargo question.

Captain Shaw : " Will the decision be left to the free vote of the House ? "

The Leader of the House : " If a motion be put down we will leave it to the free vote of the House, and not put on the Government Whips."

ZINC CONCENTRATES.

(Government's Contract with the Zinc Producers' Proprietary Association, Australia.)

In Committee of Supply of the House of Commons on 21st February the question of contracts entered into between His Majesty's Government and the Australian Zinc Producers' Proprietary Association, Limited, was discussed on a supplementary estimate for £601,200 for the Committee of Privy Council for Trade and Subordinate Departments.

DEBATE IN HOUSE OF COMMONS.

The Parliamentary Secretary to the Board of Trade (Sir W. Mitchell-Thomson) said the amount in question was the estimated balance of the expenditure over revenue in respect of these contracts. The Association, which comprised practically all the producing companies of this class of mining product in Australia, was founded at the instance of, and in consequence of, negotiations with the Australian Federal Government. The British pre-War consumption of spelter was 200,000 tons a year, and of that quantity 55,000 tons were produced in this country.

The balance of 145,000 tons came almost entirely from Germany and Belgium, and a substantial part of the Belgian production was under the control of German financial interests. Those German interests derived the ore from which they smelted the spelter from Australia by virtue of a series of long-term contracts under which they had acquired practically the whole of the Australian output. The total of the world's production and consumption of spelter in 1913 was 977,000 tons. The hon. Member read a summary of the essential facts of the contracts from the second interim Report of the Geddes Committee :—

"An agreement was concluded in 1917 as regards concentrates and spelter with the Zinc Producers' Proprietary Association, Limited, Australia. This agreement operates until the 30th June, 1930, and is divided into three periods as under :—

1. From the 1st January, 1918, to the 30th June, 1921.
2. From the 1st July, 1921, to the 30th June, 1925.
3. From the 1st July, 1925, to the 30th June, 1930.

The annual quantity of concentrates the Government may be required to take is fixed by the agreement at 250,000 tons per annum in the first period, and 300,000 tons per annum for the second and third periods. The prices are fixed for the first two periods, and a formula laid down for regulating prices in the third period. There is also an agreement giving the Zinc Producers' Association the right to 'put' 45,000 tons of spelter annually with the Government at ruling market price."

Government's losses.

The stock position at the moment was as follows : Concentrates and slimes in hand, 786,092 tons ; spelter, 2,286 tons. That was not a satisfactory stock to hold with the world's markets in their present position. The present level of world prices was below the prices at which the stock stood in the Government books. Roughly speaking, the losses on concentrates up to the present date had been £500,000 and on spelter £2,200. The Geddes Report said :—

"The extent of the loss cannot at present be estimated, but it is almost certain to run into several millions."

That might or might not turn out to be the case. He thought the Report painted the prospect in a little darker colours than it deserved. The production of spelter last year was 600,000 tons, and if they set those figures against the annual pre-War requirements of 977,000 tons it would be seen that there was a certain hole to be filled up. That was why he thought there was a prospect of an appreciation in price. Proceeding to discuss the effect of the contracts on the general position of the zinc industry in this country, the hon. Member said the real trouble was that the home industry could not afford to produce ore at the present level of world prices. The Government were asked whether they would not buy British ore at the Australian price and add the cost of freightage from Australia. They had to decline that suggestion because it was economically unsound and would not have been effective.

German clutches on Australian industry.

He did not think it was altogether reasonable to say that a drop in consumption such as had taken place could have been fairly anticipated by those responsible for the contracts, whether in 1916 or 1917. It should be remembered that the Australian people had realised with disgust and dismay that their little industry had fallen into the clutches of German capitalists. Having cut away from that strangle-hold, the Australian Parliament asked this country to assist them in the way they had tried to do. Was that a request that could lightly be refused by men who a few days before had put their hands to the Economic Resolutions at Paris? The contracts were a legacy to the present Administration, and they could only promise that they would do all they could to produce the best results for the British Exchequer.

Sir W. Pearce (Coalition Liberal, ***Limehouse*****)** hoped that whatever trouble the Government might be in now they would not attempt to bring the raw materials from Australia for treatment in this country. The best chance of an economic solution was to do the work in Australia and produce the zinc on the spot.

Mr. H. B. Betterton (Coalition Unionist, ***Rushcliffe*****)** thought that the Parliamentary Secretary had not given a quite adequate idea of the immense liabilities in which this country was involved. Having regard to all the circumstances, he had not the slightest hesitation in describing the contracts as both reckless and improvident. The total production in Australia last year was about 166,000 tons, but next year, in all human probability, it would be at least 300,000 tons, which this country was under contract to take. It was very likely, therefore, that next year they would have to meet an estimate double the amount of the present one. He failed to see why it was necessary to embark on contracts to run for no less than ten years after the termination of the War, as it was certain, having regard to the limited smelting capacity of this country, that an immense stock of concentrates would be thrown on their hands.

A bad bargain.

Mr. J. Wignall (Labour, *Forest of Dean*) moved to reduce the Vote by £100, and remarked that the Government had made a mightily bad bargain. Was it not a fact that the German contract price for zinc concentrates was 40s. per ton, pre-War, plus cost of transport ? Was it not a fact that the contract which the Government entered into was to accept the production of the Australian mines up to 250,000 tons per annum, the first 100,000 tons at £4 10s. per ton f.o.b. plus transport, and the second 150,000 tons at £4 per ton f.o.b. plus transport, with the option to take any excess at £4 per ton plus cost of transport ? His greatest irritation was at the fact that the bad bargain of the Government had displaced all the workers in the British lead and zinc mines.

Major-General Sir Cecil Lowther (Coalition Unionist, *Penrith and Cockermouth*) remarked that the only equitable course seemed to be to include the home mines in the provisions of the Australian contract. They would be told that it was subsidising an industry. Already they were subsidising an industry, not in this country, but in one of the Dominions.

Captain W. E. Elliott (Coalition Unionist, *Lanark*) said the Government should recognise that patriotism, like charity, began at home, and that the miners in Great Britain did as much for the Empire in the days of its trouble as did those in Australia. Mr. Hughes made his fame as a great man by speaking up for Australians. Let their own Prime Minister realise that his brother Welshman did not make his name by speaking up for British or Welsh miners. When the Cabinet had got the two millions of people back into employment then it could set about helping the Australian miner to get employment.

Policy of the Government.

The President of the Board of Trade (the Right Hon. Stanley Baldwin) observed that at the time the contracts were made there was no doubt the strongest arguments could be used for them. No one in the House of Commons was more strongly against Government trading than he was, but until the contract was cancelled, and so long as he was at the Board of Trade, he had to do the best he could for the taxpayer. If all selling prices, and the markets in which the sales were made, were disclosed it would be impossible for the Government to sell on any reasonable terms. It did not make his task easier to go to the Australians and say: "The whole House of Commons has risen up and said that this is the rottenest contract that ever was made. What will you take to let me out of it?"

"As a matter of fact," the right hon. gentleman proceeded, "this contract at the moment is a bad one, as everybody has said. But I do not think anyone can forecast what the result of the full term working contract would be if the contract is not cancelled in the interval. When spelter rises to a certain point, and not too great a point above where we now are, we shall cease to lose money, and if spelter rises substantially, the contract would show a profit. It was estimated by good judges not so very long ago that with normal trade, with normal ups and downs, the contract in the latter part of its existence ought to show nearly as much profit as it probably will make loss in its earlier years. It entirely depends on the world market for spelter. But, nevertheless, my own view is that, whatever the prospect of the world market may be, the right thing is for the Government to get out of this contract as and when opportunity arises, and that is my policy."

The right hon. gentleman explained that the Government had not subscribed £500,000, or any sum at all, to put up a smelting plant in Australia. As regards the mines in Great Britain, the zinc ores mined in this country would cost considerably more than it cost to bring the concentrates to this country. The only way in which the Government could help the zinc ore miners was not by buying material for the British smelters, or buying their products, but by directly subsidising them. He did not believe the House of Commons would sanction any further subsidies and he was sure the country would not.

On a division the amendment to reduce the Vote was negatived by 167 votes against 79.

Suggested appeal to Australian Government.

On the report of the Resolution relating to the Supplementary Estimate, which came before the House on 22nd February,

Lieut.-Commander the Hon. J. M. Kenworthy (Independent Liberal, *Hull, Central*) moved to reduce the amount of the Vote by £1,000. He did not suggest, he said, that they should break any contract with the Australian Government or with the zinc producers. But since the contract was entered into for purely patriotic reasons, could not the President of the Board of Trade appeal to Mr. Hughes on the same ground to come to some decent arrangement to assist the British taxpayer? If not, they would pay, but they would know what value to attach to protestations of super-patriotism in the future.

They were quite entitled to remind the Australian Government of the spirit in which the contract was entered into and to ask for some relief.

Colonel Penry Williams (**Liberal**, *Middlesbrough, E.*) considered the proper method of dealing with the matter was to approach the Australian Government to see whether some arrangement could not be made by which the contract could be cancelled on payment of reasonable and fair compensation. If that could be done the British Government had far better get out of the contract.

The President of the Board of Trade said that with regard to the transport of the concentrates from Australia the British Government had no great commitments of which he was aware to prevent them taking advantage of the best freights that might obtain at any given time. No one was entitled to say that if it was impossible to cancel this contract it would turn out a dead loss during every year of its course.

On a division the Resolution was carried by 147 votes against 73.

SITUATION IN INDIA.

(Mr. Montagu's Administration; Causes of Unrest; British Policy.)

On the closing day of the debate on the Address in the House of Commons—14th February—a discussion took place on the situation in India. It was raised on the following amendment:—

> And desire to express our view that the present position of unrest and lawlessness leading to constant breaches of the peace in India is the direct result of the administration of the Secretary of State during the last three years, and trust that Your Gracious Majesty's Government will take immediate steps to restore law and order, and to establish the security of life and property in that country.

DEBATE IN HOUSE OF COMMONS.

Sir W. Joynson-Hicks (**Coalition Unionist,** *Twickenham*) said he did not disguise from himself that the amendment was in effect a vote of censure upon the Secretary of State for his actions during the last two years. It was largely the gravamen of his case against Mr. Montagu that he had used his position to govern India in accordance with Liberal and Home Rule ideas. That was not a fair position for a Minister in a Coalition Government to take up. It was the view of a number of Conservatives that in a country like India it was far more important to give good government, though it be autocratic, than to give free government.

His charge against the Secretary of State was that since the reforms were introduced* he had consistently, by his conduct, encouraged the extreme party in India, and had failed to authorise or request the Government of India to take the steps which they might, could, and should have done to maintain law and order. Only the previous week Lord Curzon had said in the House of Lords that the situation was anxious and menacing. "The time has arrived," the noble Lord added, "when respect for the law must be enforced in India." Under the recent Reform Act, as all through the history of India, the responsibility for the Government of India rested with the Secretary of State. He did not deny that Mr. Montagu was the most popular man with the extremists. If Ghandi was a friend of his, he was a friend of Ghandi, and the extremists from one end of India to the other would desire him to remain at the head of the supine policy which had led India to the position it was in that day.

Mr. Rupert Gwynne (Unionist, *Eastbourne*), in seconding the amendment, said that during the last three years there had been in India more bloodshed, more disturbance, and more destruction of property than in the preceding sixty years. Not only the Army, but every service in India had been disheartened and disgusted by the treatment they had received from the Secretary of State.

Statement by Mr. Montagu ; growth of race consciousness.

The Secretary of State for India (the Right Hon. E. S. Montagu) said that no sooner did he become convinced that Mr. Ghandi was dangerous to the Indian Empire than he explained that any friendship which existed must cease. He frankly and freely admitted that India to-day was causing the gravest anxiety, but there were some causes of the present condition of India which could not be affected by whoever happened to be the Secretary of State. There had been a steady growth in India of race consciousness, which received the greatest stimulus from the atmosphere in which the War was waged, from the speeches made about the after-War settlement, and also from the spirit in which India's contributions to the War were accepted.

"I think that race consciousness has been the cause of considerable unrest," said Mr. Montagu, "but I do not think it is something which this House ought to lament. It will, if carefully used, add to the strength and vigour of

* *Vide* Government of India Act, 1920.

he Indian peoples, and if it is used by India for co-operation n the preservation of the Indian Empire, I believe any present lifficulty arising from it will disappear." Proceeding, he bbserved that the next great cause of trouble, for which his presence as Secretary of State could not be held responsible, was the economic situation of the world. Taxation and economic conditions had something to do with the matter. The only cure was in the development of the industrial and agricultural resources of India in order that the people might become richer. That was the work to which Lord Chelmsford and his Government desired to direct their attention.

Treaty of Sèvres; Bolshevik propaganda; etc.

Whether they agreed with the Muhammadans in India or not, the most dispassionate observer, must bear testimony to the fact that Great Britain's rupture with Turkey, the Treaty of Sèvres, and the continued hostility between Greece and Turkey, were profoundly affecting the peace of India. "I have never claimed, and I cannot claim now," said Mr. Montagu, "that the Indians should dictate to us the peace with Turkey. What I do ask the House is to remember that it was largely by the efforts of Indian troops that Turkey was conquered, and that they are entitled to every consideration in the ultimate peace. Nothing could give a greater immediate contribution to peace in India than complete agreement between the Allies which would lead to peace and good relations between Greece and Turkey."

Another cause of the present situation, the right hon. gentleman went on to say, was the unrest occasioned by the general disturbance of the world. Ever since the Russian Government fell into the hands of those who were the exponents of the ruin-producing doctrines of Bolshevism, India had been the object of their propaganda. India was not a fertile soil for Bolshevik doctrines, but it had contributed something to the unrest. Mr. Montagu also mentioned among causes of unrest, discontent in relation to industrial labour, agrarian troubles, and the acute feeling of Indians regarding the difficult problems of their position in the Crown Colonies.

Policy in India.

Turning to the allegation that he was responsible for the fact that the Government of India had not been sufficiently vigorous in dealing with disorder, Mr. Montagu said the way he had discharged his responsibility was to go to the people, as he thought all his predecessors had gone, and tell them that it was impossible to keep law and order in India from London. The next thing was to satisfy oneself, as Secretary of State, that the governments in India recognised their prime and essential responsibility for the maintenance of order.

"No step you can take," the right hon. gentleman observed, "can prevent all disorder, for we have to consider the vast size of India. But the fact is that under the conditions I have described—and there may be others—the governments in India are dealing with these things in the way that seems best to them, and I have every reason to believe that His Majesty's Government repose the utmost confidence in them. I have every reason to believe that they are worthy of that confidence, and that through them we shall win through in India to happier times."

British policy was the maintenance of the integrity of the Empire, coupled with the grant of opportunity of development to full self-government within that Empire. His Majesty's Government announced that policy in 1917 and it was ultimately endorsed by Parliament by the passage of the Government of India Act. He did not think there would ever be any question of going back on that policy; but Parliament would not be justified at the present time in thinking of extending the scope of that policy. Upon Indians themselves depended the view which Parliament would take of future steps. To win their way to self-government under the supreme and continuing authority of the King-Emperor, Indians must show, not merely individually but collectively, a readiness for all that was involved in self-government. At the present moment the absolutely essential condition of any further progress was the successful working of the first instalment that Parliament had given.

Trouble can be settled.

General Sir Charles Townshend (Independent, *Shropshire, The Wrekin*) remarked that India, no doubt, was in a very grave condition, but it could be settled at once very easily. If only the British Government would issue a *communiqué* to India saying that they must stand by the Government of India in maintaining law and order the trouble would disappear at once. If they simply showed firmness, agitators like Ghandi and others would disappear at once. When they governed in the East they must send firm men there.

Sir J. D. Rees (Coalition Unionist, *Nottingham, E.*) said that if the Secretary of State attempted to interfere in the actual restoration of law and order in India he would be unfit for his place. If the present state of India was in any way the result of the individual action of Mr. Montagu, how was it that a similar state of affairs existed in Egypt? The Muhammadans in Egypt were in a state of ferment, almost of rebellion, against Great Britain. Was that due to the

Secretary of State for India ? The causes of the present trouble in India, over and above the world spirit which was the aftermath of the War, were the treatment of the Turkish question and, he would say, the tenure question.

Concern, but not alarm.

The Prime Minister (the Right Hon. D. Lloyd George) observed that there was much in the state of India that justified grave concern, but he deprecated alarm. " There is certainly no cause for panic, and the situation is well within the compass of our strength without adding to our burdens." The disturbance and unrest in India did not begin three years ago. He had been a member of Governments since 1906, and he remembered when Lord Morley, as Secretary of State for India, had constantly to bring to the attention of the Cabinet the serious unrest in India. It was, therefore, idle to attribute it to something which occurred when Mr. Montagu assumed the reins of office.

" The strength of the British rule in India comes," said the Premier, " not because we have given way to one faith, because it was menacing, at the expense of another, but because we have quite fearlessly held the balance even between Muhammadan and Hindu and every other religion, and the principle we have applied in India we must apply in the settlement of the Turkish Treaty. We must be fearlessly just to both religions and both races ; otherwise, in the end no good will be done but much harm will be done. We shall sow the seed of future trouble in order to purchase a temporary solution of our difficulties." India, the Premier continued, had never been a democratic country, and it had yet to be seen whether democratic institutions suited the Indian mind. If the experiment in India was to be a success it must be a gradual one, as it had been in the West.

" We must take care," said the Premier, " not to weaken authority when strengthening liberty. . . . You cannot allow in India a challenge to authority which would not be allowed in this country nor in any civilised country in the world. India owes much to the substitution of law for lawless force. Anyone who reads its history knows that, and it is no kindness to the people of India to permit a subversion of Government authority. . . . Under no circumstances or conditions do we propose to withdraw from or impair the full sovereignty of the King-Emperor in India. In terms no agitator in India puts forward that demand."

The only unity created in India, added the Premier, had been by British rule.

On a division the amendment was negatived by 248 votes against 64.

INDIA AND TREATY OF SÈVRES.

(Manifesto by Government of India; Resignation of Secretary of State; Joint Cabinet Action.)

There was published in the newspapers on 9th March a communication* from the Government of India recommending a revision of the Treaty of Sèvres and the settlement of the Turkish question on certain lines. This telegram formed the subject of questions in the House of Commons on the same date, when

The Leader of the House (the Right Hon. Austen Chamberlain) said: "I understand that this telegram was published by the Government of India, with the sanction of the Secretary of State.† No other Minister was consulted.

"I desire expressly to abstain from any comment upon the subject matter of the telegram, though the terms exceed those demanded even by the warmest friends of the Turks themselves. This, however, is matter for discussion at the Conference, into which it would be highly inexpedient for me now to enter. But the publication of such a pronouncement of policy, without consultation with the Cabinet, and without their assent, raises a different question all the more important because the Conference was just about to meet at Paris, when, as it seemed, there was a fair prospect that in concert with our Allies, we should be able to lay the basis for peace between Turks and Greeks.

Collective responsibility of the Cabinet.

"His Majesty's Government are unable to reconcile the publication of the telegram of the Government of India on the sole responsibility of the Secretary of State with the collective

* The text of the despatch was as follows: "On the eve of the Græco-Turkish Conference we feel it our duty again to lay before His Majesty's Government the intensity of feeling in India regarding the necessity for a revision of the Sèvres Treaty.

"The Government of India are fully alive to the complexity of the problem, but India's services in the War, in which Indian Moslem soldiers so largely participated, and the support which the Indian Moslem cause is receiving throughout India, entitle her to claim the utmost fulfilment of her just and equitable aspirations.

"The Government of India particularly urge, subject to the safeguarding of the neutrality of the Straits and of the security of the non-Moslem populations, the following three points, namely, the evacuation of Constantinople; the suzerainty of the Sultan over the Holy places; and the restoration of Ottoman Thrace, including Adrianople and Smyrna.

"The fulfilment of these three points is of the greatest importance to India."

† The Right Hon. E. S. Montagu.

responsibility of the Cabinet, or with the duty which all the Governments of the Empire owe to each other in matters of Imperial concern. Such independent declarations destroy the unity of policy which it is vital to preserve in foreign affairs, and gravely imperil the success of the impending negotiations.

"The Secretary of State has tendered his resignation to the Prime Minister, and His Majesty has been pleased to approve its acceptance.

"When the Foreign Secretary proceeds to Paris to discuss the Eastern settlement with the Foreign Ministers of France and Italy, it will be his object to arrive at a solution that will be equitable to all parties. Due weight will be given by him to the opinions of the Indian Muhammadans, as expressed by the Government of India. But he cannot hold himself bound to accept any solution that may be put forward by that Government irrespective of its relation to the problem as a whole. The responsibility for the revision of the Treaty of Sèvres and the conclusion of peace in the East rests with the Allied Powers in combination.

IN HOUSE OF LORDS.

In the House of Lords on 14th March, the Secretary of State for Foreign Affairs made a statement dealing with certain references to himself in a speech delivered by Mr. Montagu to his constituents at Cambridge on 11th March.

The Secretary of State for Foreign Affairs (the Marquess Curzon of Kedleston) said that in common with his colleagues he received on 4th March from the Cabinet Office a copy of a telegram from the Government of India in which they sought permission to publish their manifesto about the terms of peace with Turkey. A Cabinet Council was held on 6th March. Before the proceedings began he mentioned the Viceroy's telegram to Mr. Chamberlain and expressed the view that when the permission of the Cabinet for publication was sought it must unhesitatingly be refused. A little later, in the course of a private conversation of a few seconds only with Mr. Montagu, he (the Foreign Secretary) said, "Of course, you will not authorise publication without reference to the Cabinet." To this Mr. Montagu replied, "I have already done so—on Saturday last."

"I was so dumbfounded," the noble Marquess observed, "at the avowal of the Secretary of State that he had already given his sanction—as has since transpired before the telegram from the Government of India could ever have been seen by any of his colleagues—that I closed the conversation and returned to my seat. Had Mr. Montagu given me the slightest hint that there was still time to cancel or to postpone the order which he had sent to India by telegram two days before, or had I regarded such suspension as possible, I should at once have brought the matter before the Cabinet. But I assumed that publication had already, under Mr. Montagu's authority, taken place in India, and the more so as the Government of India had pressed for immediate sanction to publish. I presumed, therefore, . . . that it was too late for me to intervene. Furthermore, the responsibility for the step was not mine. It was for the Secretary of State for India to explain and justify his own action that he had already taken to the Cabinet."

Letter to Mr. Montagu.

The Foreign Secretary read to the House a letter he addressed to Mr. Montagu under date 6th March. In this letter he stated that had he, when Viceroy, ventured to make a public pronouncement in India about the foreign policy of the Government in Europe he would certainly have been recalled. As it was, he was once rebuked for making a casual reference in a speech. If the Government of India, because it ruled over a large body of Moslems, was entitled to express and publish its views about what the British Government did in Smyrna or Thrace, why not in Egypt, the Sudan, Palestine, Arabia and the Malay Peninsula, or any other part of the Moslem world ? Was Indian opinion always to be a final court of Moslem appeal ?

The Marquess of Crewe believed it was the universal opinion that in having sanctioned the publication of that telegram, or manifesto, of the Government of India, expressing views they were known to hold, but were not entitled to give formally to the world, Mr. Montagu committed a breach of the ordinary proprieties of Cabinet Government, for which he could recall no precedent.

DEBATE IN HOUSE OF COMMONS.

In the House of Commons, on 15th March, there was a discussion on the subject, and a statement by the late Secretary of State.

The Right Hon. E. S. Montagu (Coalition Liberal, *Cambridgeshire*), after describing the steps he took on receipt of the telegram from the Government of India to acquaint his Cabinet colleagues with its contents, remarked that between Saturday and Thursday the only action taken was the private letter written to him by Lord Curzon. He had never been given an opportunity, by those who believed so convincedly in the doctrine of joint Cabinet action, of confronting his colleagues or arguing his case to his colleagues. " I have said, and I say it again," Mr. Montagu continued, " that in my view, rightly or wrongly, the publication of this telegram was not a matter that I need bring before the Cabinet."

What the House must remember, the right hon. gentleman went on to say, was that for the purpose of this matter India could not be correctly described as a subordinate branch of His Majesty's Government. India was a State member of the League of Nations. The Treaty of Sèvres was signed on behalf of India independently, as well as on behalf of Great Britain and the Dominions. It was the greatest folly to suggest that a great Dependency, Dominion, or whatever they liked to call it, which had been given Dominion status for that purpose, a party to the original Treaty, should not be allowed to express its views as to modification. If it was allowed to express its views, what was the use of hushing them up ?

India and Turkey.

It was not true to say that the Government of India were dictating to the people or to the Government of Great Britain, or that they sought to determine the terms of the Peace Treaty. What they did seek to do was to have their views given the fullest weight or authority, and taken into the fullest consideration. They would be the first to recognise that their views would have to be harmonised with other and wider views.

" All I have to say," remarked Mr. Montagu, " is that India is entitled to a predominant share in the peace with Turkey, because there is no other country whose well-being is so intimately affected by that peace. There is no country which played so great a part in defeating Turkey as India did. I do not believe it will hamper the British Government ; I believe it will help it. . . . If the Government could have found it possible to publish my telegram in answer they would have seen that I myself recognised that it was impossible for the Allies to fulfil all the terms." Mr. Montagu added that his resignation at that moment did not mean a rejection of the right of consideration of the terms put forward on behalf of the Moslems of India.

The Leader of the House stated that the policy of the Cabinet was unaffected by his right hon. friend's resignation.

The Right Hon. H. H. Asquith (Leader of the Independent Liberal Party) said that this was not an isolated case, but was one of a series of instances of continuous Cabinet disorganisation.

The subject afterwards dropped.

BRITISH EAST AFRICA.

(Kenya Colony: Rights of Indians; British Immigration.)

The question of the status of Indians in Kenya was raised in the House of Commons on 14th February.

Colonel J. C. Wedgwood (Labour, *Newcastle-under-Lyme*) asked the Secretary of State for the Colonies whether he would communicate to the House the arrangements recently come to, or attempted, regarding the Indian question in Kenya, and why the Resolution of Equal Rights made by the Premiers' Conference had not been acted upon in East Africa.

The Secretary of State for the Colonies (the Right Hon. Winston Churchill): "The negotiations conducted locally by the Governor of Kenya have unfortunately failed to reveal any common ground for settlement between the European and Indian communities. I do not think that it would conduce to a settlement if I were to make any detailed announcement at this stage. I have not consulted with the European or the Indian delegation, but the former asked for an interview with me, which I have given, and if the delegation representing the Kenya Indians also desire an interview I shall be happy to meet their wishes.

"The application of the Resolution of the Imperial Conference to any part of the Empire must depend on the local circumstances, and the hon. and gallant Member will be aware that the first part of the Resolution, dealing with the control of immigration, presents, in the case of Kenya, as much difficulty as the second part that deals with the rights of citizenship of Indians already lawfully domiciled in the territory."

Answering a supplementary question, the right hon. gentleman said he did not think there was any serious difficulty in bringing the policy which the needs of Kenya required within the ambit of the very general Resolution passed by the Imperial Conference, to which he was a party.

British immigration.

On 7th March, **Colonel Wedgwood** asked the Secretary of State for the Colonies whether there were any and, if so, what restrictions on the immigration of British working men into Kenya Crown Colony or into the Tanganyika mandated territory.

The Secretary of State for the Colonies: "Any restrictions which exist in the territories mentioned are of general application. In Kenya, if an immigrant is without visible means of support or likely to become a pauper or a public charge, he is a 'prohibited immigrant' and his entry is forbidden. If an immigrant appears to come within this description he may be required to deposit a sum of Fl.375, which is returned to him if within six months he can show that he is not a 'prohibited immigrant.' Immigrants may also be refused entry on the ground of insanity, dangerous disease, criminal or moral obliquity, and the like. The regulations in Tanganyika territory are very similar, except that no sum is specified as a deposit, and all Europeans are required at present to obtain a permit of entry from the Secretary to the Administration."

Colonel Wedgwood: "Is it not a fact that this penalty on British working men entering into Kenya Colony is peculiar to that particular Crown Colony?"

Exceptional conditions.

The Secretary of State for the Colonies: "I really do not think that any of the categories which I have read out are to be taken as describing the British working man, and I am surprised that my hon. and gallant friend should have drawn such an inference. It seems to be a very offensive inference, and it is one with which I should certainly not associate myself. The conditions of Kenya Colony are very exceptional and peculiar, and nothing could be worse than to have a large number of completely destitute persons wandering about that country and, no doubt, coming into collision with the local natives."

Colonel Wedgwood: "Does not the right hon. gentleman know that British immigrants are allowed in Kenya Colony provided that they can put down this sum of money, that that is peculiar to Kenya Colony, and that it is imposed there in order to give an excuse for keeping Indians out of that country?"

The Secretary of State for the Colonies: "I do not think that that is the reason at all, but it is obvious that Kenya Colony, in which nine-tenths of the population are natives, requires to be treated in a special way. We do not want to have incursions of white immigrants who cannot maintain themselves, or of Indians in a similar condition, who will undoubtedly be thrown on the top of the natives of the Colony."

Colonel Wedgwood: "By what right do you say that poor Englishmen shall not go to that Colony, but that rich men may?"

The Secretary of State for the Colonies: "That sounds a very fine sentiment, but all the great Dominions require certain assurances that persons immigrating into their domain will be able to get settled down and earn a livelihood, and not simply become a charge."

NATIONAL EXPENDITURE.

(The Geddes Report; Savings in Public Expenditure; International Peace; etc.)

On 13th February the House of Commons debated an amendment to the Address dealing with the question of taxation. A few days previously the first and second interim Reports of the Committee on National Expenditure, presided over by Sir Eric Geddes, had been presented to Parliament. The committee consisted, in addition to the chairman, of Lord Inchcape, Lord Faringdon, Sir Joseph Maclay and Sir Guy Granet. It was charged with the duty of advising the Chancellor of the Exchequer as to the best method of reducing National Expenditure, and subsequent to the debate on the above-mentioned date a final Report was presented.

The total savings recommended in the three Reports amounted to £86,844,175. These proposals fell short by some £13,000,000 of the total reductions of £100,000,000. which the Government asked the Committee to suggest in addition to expenditure "cuts" of £75,000,000 already carried out by the Departments. Sir Eric Geddes and his colleagues expressed confidence that the full sum could be obtained by further economies :—

(1) In naval expenditure (a) as a result of the Washington Conference, and (b) under the heading of oil stocks and oil storage; and

(2) In military expenditure upon a review of the military garrisons abroad.

List of Proposed Reductions.

Appended is a summary of the full reductions in the estimates proposed by the Committee :—

FIRST REPORT—	
Navy	£21,000,000
Army	20,000,000
Air Force	5,500,000
Education	18,000,000
Health	2,500,000
War Pensions	3,300,000
	£70,300,000
Adjustment on First Report	£1,171,875
SECOND REPORT—	
Trade Group	£538,000
Export Credit	500,000
Agricultural Group	855,000
Police and Prisons	1,595,000
General (24 votes)	102,000
	£3,590,000

THIRD REPORT—

Colonial Group	£2,285,500
Legal Group	94,500
Revenue Departments	2,509,200
Houses of Parliament and certain Civil Departments	935,000
Works and Public Buildings Group.. ..	895,800
Art and Science Group	42,900
Foreign Office, etc.	304,300
Stationery Office and Registrar-General ..	584,300
Miscellaneous Group	1,130,800
	£8,782,300
Further Review of Estimates for War Pensions	3,000,000
Grand total	£86,844,175

DEBATE IN HOUSE OF COMMONS.

The amendment to the Address was in the following terms:—

But humbly regret that the extravagance of Your Majesty's Ministers has imposed upon the country a crushing burden of taxation, and that they have been unable to make a definite promise that taxation will be reduced so as to stimulate trade and decrease unemployment.

The Right Hon. H. H. Asquith (Leader of the Independent Liberal Party), in moving the amendment, remarked that he was far from saying the Geddes Committee had not done very useful work. But its appointment amounted to a delegation to an outside and irresponsible authority of the functions which ought to be discharged by the Treasury, subject always to the ultimate control of the House of Commons. The economies recommended in respect of National Defence, which included the Army, the Navy, and the Air Force, amounted to £46,500,000. The pre-War expenditure for defence purposes, the Committee said, was £80,000,000, but the estimates for 1922-23, with which the Committee were dealing, were £170,000,000. It was pointed out by the Committee that the personnel of the Army was increased by 29,000, as compared with what it was in the year before the War.

Taking a large view of European and international policy, what had the War brought them, Mr. Asquith asked, if they could not assume as one of its permanent results that Europe, and indeed the world at large, would no longer be divided into an array of rival armed camps. With the development of the League of Nations peace between the nations must be, and ought to be, regarded as the normal condition of affairs. He found therefore no justification whatever for a scale of personnel and of expenditure on the Army which in the fourth year after the Armistice exceeded that which was put forward in the year before the War.

Expenditure on Education.

With regard to education, the Committee proposed a total reduction of expenditure amounting to £18,000,000. He did not deny that their expenditure on education was colossal, as it amounted last year to £104,000,000 for England and Scotland together. But it was all-important to economise at the right point and not at the wrong point. The economy of £1,750,000 which the Committee proposed should be effected by raising the age at which children were to go to school to six years would be very dearly purchased. What was worse, it was proposed to raise the number of children per teacher from 32 to 50. That was one of the most uneconomical proposals ever made. Anything in the nature of ill-judged parsimony at any stage of education—elementary, secondary, technical, or university—at the point they had now reached in the evolution of the world was not economy, but a waste of the resources of the nation.

The Chancellor of the Exchequer (the Right Hon. Sir Robert Horne) said the most important factor in public expenditure to-day was the country's obligations in respect of War debt. The amount they had to pay in interest and minimum sinking fund charges and for War pensions reached the formidable total of £500,000,000. That represented nearly one-half of the whole expenditure of the year and so was responsible for nearly one-half of their taxation. It was a portion of public expenditure which the Government could do little or nothing to lighten. When they compared the expenditure of Great Britain with that of other countries they did not find any evidence of extravagance.

Treasury and expert advice.

With regard to the Geddes Committee, he asked, following Mr. Asquith's criticism, when was the precedent first created that the Treasury could no longer summon to their aid expert advice upon matters on which they required it. He was certain that nobody but an outside Committee could have achieved the results which that body had accomplished. To anyone who knew the present financial position of the country it was obvious that large reductions must be made in the services either on the lines of the Committee's recommendations or on some other principle. Grave questions of policy were involved in the recommendations and all of them could not be accepted in their entirety.

It was a mistake to suppose that the size of the British Army had ever been based upon that of armies in other parts of Europe. It had always been based upon the necessities of the British Empire. If they looked at the Empire to-day they would find that, so far from their necessities being less than they were before the War, they were greater than ever they were. "What we have to keep in mind," the Chancellor of the Exchequer remarked, "is that the world at large is in a more unrestful condition to-day than it was then, and that we have difficulties in many parts of the world which make it at least necessary that we should see that the security of our Empire is preserved."

Rationing the Departments.

Mr. J. A. R. Marriott (Coalition Unionist, *Oxford*) said the only possible way to effect a real reduction in expenditure was to define the maximum figure they could afford to spend and definitely ration each Department. That principle was put by the Geddes Committee in the forefront of their report. They said:—

> In our opinion the time has come when the Government must say to these Departments how much money they can have, and look to them to frame their proposals accordingly.

The Right Hon. J. R. Clynes (Chairman of the Parliamentary Labour Party) doubted whether when a Labour Government came into power it would go so far as to govern not on the basis of experience, but on the basis of experiment, which was what the present Government had done in relation to the Geddes Report. Extravagance had been followed by frantic efforts at retrenchment. It was the view of the Labour Party that large sums ought to have been saved which had been spent on totally unnecessary purposes—on armaments and costly forms of government.

The Right Hon. Sir Donald Maclean (Chairman of the Independent Liberal Party in Parliament) declared that the extravagance of the Government had a predominant share in the crushing burden of taxation under which the country was suffering. In the three years to be completed on 1st April, 1922, the Army would have spent £860,000,000, the Navy £384,000,000, and the Civil Service £1,871,000,000. The Army, the Navy, the Air Force and the Civil Service had in these three years spent no less a sum than £3,216,000,000.

The Leader of the House (the Right Hon. Austen Chamberlain) said he had been asked whether the Government approved the action of the Admiralty in publishing a Memorandum regarding that portion of the Geddes Report which dealt with

Admiralty estimates. The Memorandum was issued in pursuance of a general decision of the Government that certain Departmental memoranda or Ministerial statements would be necessary for the full information of the House. The views expressed in the Admiralty Memorandum were not to be taken as the considered decision of the Government upon the whole question.

On a division the amendment was negatived by 241 votes against 92.

Government and economy.

The sitting of the House of Commons on 1st March was set apart by the Government for a debate on the Recommendations contained in the Reports of the Geddes Committee. Speaking on a formal motion for the adjournment of the House,

The Chancellor of the Exchequer made a broad survey of the proposals of the Committee. He said that he asked the Committee to suggest reductions in public expenditure to the amount of £100,000,000, but the statement that this was a confession that waste to that extent was going on in the Government services was a complete travesty of the facts. There was the most acute trade depression that had ever been known in this country, and they were confronted with a falling revenue. In those circumstances many things which in normal times they would regard as necessary objects of expenditure they might not now be able to afford, and the prime object of the inquiry was to discover those services in which, with the least detriment to the efficiency of the country, they could economise.

The Committee recommended a reduction in Votes of £86,000,000 exclusive of what might occur as the result of the conversations at Washington. Deducting the amount of savings which were unspecified by the Committee a total of £71,000,000 was left and the Government accepted in all reductions amounting to £64,000,000. That included £10,000,000 attributable to possible savings as the result of the Washington Conference and £1,000,000 possible savings on the supply of oil. The Government meant to go on with the investigation and see that every possible method was adopted by which Departments could effect further savings in their services. The Departments themselves had practised severe economies and as the whole result he thought the estimates for 1922-23 would be £181,000,000 less than in the year ending 31st March, 1922.

The debate was continued until the end of the sitting, when the motion lapsed.

NAVY ESTIMATES.

(Results of Washington Conference; Reductions of Expenditure; One-Power Standard.)

Navy estimates for the year 1922-23 presented in March showed a further reduction in the amount to be voted. Following are the totals as compared with the estimates for the year ended 31st March, 1922 :—

	Gross.	Net.
1921-22	£91,554,869	£82,479,000*
1922-23	£68,950,000†	£64,883,700
Reduction ..	£22,604,869	£17,595,300

Numbers of officers, seamen, boys and Royal Marines 118,500
Numbers of coastguards and marine police.. 2,900

The numbers of officers, seamen, boys and Royal Marines to be voted is the maximum on 1st April, 1922. They will be reduced to about 98,500—that is, by 20,000—as rapidly as practicable.

First Lord's memorandum.

In a memorandum relating to the estimates the First Lord of the Admiralty (Lord Lee of Fareham) observed :—

As stated last year, estimates can only be based upon policy, and the naval policy of the Government, as approved by Parliament and implemented at Washington, is to maintain a "one-Power standard" —*i.e.*, that our Navy should not be inferior in strength to that of any other Power. The duty of the Admiralty is to carry out that policy with the strictest regard to economy, giving the utmost weight to the changed and improved international conditions which have resulted from the Washington Conference. Indeed, the Admiralty have gone further in accepting drastic economies, and consequent risks, which could only be justified on the assumption that the British Fleet will not be engaged in any great war for many years to come. On purely naval grounds such an assumption could not be justified, but both the financial and the international situation call for an exceptional response, and this the Admiralty have made, although they realise that, in this matter, a very grave responsibility is imposed upon them.

A summary of the economies which are being effected, or will be carried out in the year 1922-23, is given in the memorandum :—

(A) The scrapping of twelve capital ships, in addition to the eight recently sold for breaking up, and the maintenance of only fifteen in full commission (as compared with thirty-eight in March, 1914).

* (The 1921-22 figures exclude the Supplementary Estimate due to calling out the Royal Fleet Reserve for service in the national emergency which arose in the early months of 1921-22.)

† Approximate.

(B) The further reduction of the destroyer flotillas of the Atlantic Fleet.

(C) The abolition of twenty-seven submarines and the reduction of the number in full commission.

(D) The abolition of two of the Home Commands (Coast of Scotland and Western Approaches).

(E) The reduction of the personnel of the Fleet, during 1922-23, by over 20,000 officers and men.

(F) The discharge of over 10,000 men from the Royal Dockyards, and a drastic reduction of civil staffs at the Admiralty and other establishments.

(G) The rigorous pruning of all other Services and Votes.

The cost of the Admiralty Office is given as £365,000 less.

New construction; effect of Washington.

Discussing the influence of the Washington Conference on the provision for new construction, Lord Lee remarks:—

As already announced, the building of the four battle cruisers, which had been sanctioned and commenced last year, has now been abandoned, and no provision is made in these estimates for any new programme beyond the laying down, early in 1923, of the two smaller battleships which are specified in the Naval Treaty concluded at Washington. Under the terms of that Treaty no further capital ships can be laid down by the British Empire before the expiration of ten years from 12th November, 1921. The other restrictions on the building, size, and armament of new vessels of war are fully set forth in the Treaty, and will obviate the great increases in expenditure with which all the great naval Powers would, otherwise, have been faced in the near future—not only for shipbuilding but for the development of docks, harbours, etc., to accommodate the rapidly growing size of individual ships.

In view of the fact that the two new capital ships will not be commenced until early in 1923 it is estimated that only £300,000 will be spent upon them during the financial year beginning 1st April, 1922. This compares with £10,557,800 which would have been the cost of proceeding with the four battle cruisers now abandoned. The sum to be devoted to the armaments of these two ships will be £421,500, as compared with £1,295,000, which would have been spent upon the four battle cruisers. After referring to the scrapping of twenty capital ships, including the Commonwealth battle cruiser *Australia*, in accordance with the agreement reached at Washington, the memorandum states that the battleship *Collingwood*, which the Admiralty retained the right to use for non-combatant purposes, will also be disposed of. On the conclusion of the Prince of Wales's tour the battle cruiser *Renown*, built during the War, will be placed in reserve.

Position in European waters.

When the various measures of economy have been carried out the position in European waters will be as follows:—

The main Atlantic Fleet will then consist of one fleet flagship, two divisions of battleships, each composed of four ships, and two battle cruisers. Any reduction in these numbers would be incompatible with the maintenance of the tactical efficiency of the Fleet. The Mediterranean fully-commissioned Fleet consists of only four battleships, every unit of which is continually employed. Apart from the question of tactical efficiency, the Admiralty are satisfied that the number of capital ships to be retained in commission is the minimum necessary for the training of personnel, both officers and men.

The number of light cruisers attached to the Atlantic Fleet is based primarily on tactical requirements, which in their turn are based upon war experience. But these cruisers are also in constant demand for showing the flag, and for political cruises in the Baltic and Northern and Western European waters and Atlantic Islands, and are frequently detached from the Fleet for long periods. For this reason, and owing to the incidence of refits, it has often happened during the last two years that out of the First and Second Light Cruiser Squadrons not more than three or four vessels have been present with the Fleet when it is carrying out important exercises.

One of the destroyer flotillas belonging to the Atlantic Fleet was, for financial reasons, reduced to two-fifths complement last year In view of the urgent need for economy, another flotilla will now be similarly reduced. The total number of destroyers in full complement with the Atlantic Fleet is thus brought down to forty—the smallest number which can provide for the vital part played by destroyers in all modern Fleet exercises and for the training of officers and men. Twenty-three destroyers of the local defence flotillas, now on a reduced complement, will also be reduced to reserve.

Foreign squadrons.

Reference is made in the memorandum to light cruisers on service in foreign waters where no capital ships are now serving. Lord Lee says :—

The light cruiser strength of the African Squadron will be reduced to two ships by keeping the *Birmingham* in reserve at home. In considering the number of light cruisers retained in commission it has been necessary to bear in mind that the light cruisers abroad are required to carry out a great variety of duties in peace. Apart from the general stimulus which their presence gives to British prestige and British trade in foreign countries, their services are frequently requisitioned for the direct protection of British interests or maintenance of order. Moreover, from the naval point of view, these squadrons are placed well for taking up their war stations, and afford invaluable opportunities to officers and men of becoming acquainted with waters which, at some future date, might be the principal theatre of naval operations.

The King has decided that in future only one yacht, the *Victoria and Albert*, shall be retained, His Majesty dispensing with the *Alexandra*. The Admiralty yacht, *Enchantress*, as well as the special service vessels, *Surprise* and *Alacrity*, hitherto retained for the use of the Admirals commanding in the Mediterranean and China seas, are also to be abolished.

In announcing the Admiralty's decision to reduce the size of crews of certain ships, it is stated that " in order to diminish the numbers absorbed in crossing reliefs, the

Admiralty have decided to abolish the system of two-year commissions for ships abroad and to keep ships two and a half years on their stations (the time away from the home port not to exceed three years)." As a result of this policy, a sum of £4,781,500 will be saved on the pay of the Fleet, victualling and clothing, the medical services, and civilians employed on Fleet services. Under pressure of economy, the Government have decided not to make marriage allowances to officers in the Navy, as is done in the case of officers of the other fighting services.

By excusing Royal Fleet Reservists from drill in the year 1922-23 a saving of £80,000 will be effected, and the discharge of over 10,000 men from the Royal Dockyards will result in an economy of £3,849,800.

DEBATE IN HOUSE OF COMMONS.

In the House of Commons on 16th March the motion to go into Committee of Supply on the Navy estimates was the occasion of a debate.

The Financial and Parliamentary Secretary to the Admiralty (**Mr. L. S. Amery**) said the policy of this country ever since the War had been one of drastic reduction in naval armaments. They had relegated to scrap, or otherwise disposed of, nearly two and a half million tons of warships. Referring to Washington, the Parliamentary Secretary said the result of the Conference was that without any dereliction from the one-Power standard—the recognised minimum of security necessary for their existence as a free Power—they had been able to make far-reaching reductions in their naval organisation. The economies thus won for the long-suffering taxpayers of this country were only a part of the economies gained, in like proportion, by the other naval Powers concerned.

"The total sum liberated," Mr. Amery remarked, "may be reckoned, over the next ten years, in hundreds of millions, and represents a powerful contribution to the economic recovery of a war-spent world. There are other gains, less directly susceptible of measurement, but even more worth their endeavours, that our representatives have brought home from Washington—the removal of suspicion, the growth of sympathy and mutual understanding among nations, and, not least, the increasing proof of the capacity of the British Empire, under its new organisation, to unite in, and give effect to, a single Imperial policy." Proceeding, the hon. and gallant Member discussed at some length the recommendations of the Geddes Committee with respect to naval economies. The reduction on the effective Votes, which was a test of the Admiralty's effort at economy, was £20,791,000. They had reached the limit. Things had been scraped to the bone.

Duty to the Empire.

"Only the effects of a further fall in prices, or the possibility of other navies following up Washington by some yet more advanced policy in the reduction of armaments," the hon. Member added, "would make possible additional economies in subsequent years. We cannot go further unless, indeed, we abandon the one-Power standard altogether, and drop to the rank of the second or third naval Power—and if we drop once we shall do so for all time. We have no right to do that. We owe the maintenance of that standard to our fellow-subjects in the Empire, with whom we formally, by resolution of the Empire Conference, agreed only last summer that the standard of equality with any other Power was our minimum.

"We have collaborated again with them at Washington in these last few months in reaffirming that standard and definitely fixing it in actual terms of ships and tonnage in the Naval Treaty. We owe it in trust to future generations of our people here and across the seas. All else in politics may change; one principle stands firm and beyond question. We live and move and have our being as a nation and as an Empire by our power to keep open and free the highways of the sea. That power we can never surrender even to the best friend or the closest ally. We have agreed at Washington to accept terms of equality in naval power with the one nation with which, above all, we wish to live on terms of friendship. We regard that equality as one not of competition, but of co-operation in maintaining the peace of the world.

"But even for the purposes of that co-operation we, with our traditions and responsibilities for the peace of the world, cannot afford to be less than even."

The Right Hon. G. Lambert (Liberal, *Devon, South Molton*) pointed out that they were spending £14,000,000 a year more on the Navy than when the German fleet was in being and was a threatening menace to the security of this country. Had it not been for the Washington Conference the estimates would have been something like £32,000,000 more.

Naval Air Services.

Rear-Admiral Sir R. Hall (Coalition Unionist, *Liverpool, West Derby*) moved as an amendment to the motion:—

"That in the opinion of this House, the Naval Air Services should be put under the control of the Board of Admiralty for the full development of the efficiency of these services, for their better co-operation with the Navy, and for the most economical administration and expenditure."

He said that there was at sea no place for a separate Air Service. All arms in battle required to belong to one Service, to subscribe to a common doctrine, and to be trained in accordance with that doctrine.

Commander Viscount Curzon (**Coalition Unionist,** *Battersea, S.*), in seconding the amendment, submitted that the employment of aircraft at sea nowadays was of vital moment to the Navy.

The Leader of the House (**the Right Hon. Austen Chamberlain**) announced that the Government. considered it would be a retrograde step at the present time to abolish the Air Ministry and to re-absorb the Air Service into the Admiralty and the War Office. The conclusions which had been come to were as follows :—

(1) That the Air Force must be autonomous in matters of administration and education.

(2) That in the case of defence against air raids the Army and Navy must play a secondary *rôle.*

(3) That in the case of military operations by land or naval operations by sea, the Air Force must be in strict subordination to the general or admiral in supreme command.

(4) That in other cases, such as the protection of commerce and attacks on enemy harbours and inland towns, the relations between the Air Force and the other Services shall be regarded rather as a matter of co-operation than of the strict subordination which is necessary when aeroplanes are acting merely as auxiliaries to other arms.

Naval and Air co-operation.

The Government had decided to appoint a Committee, which would consist either of the Standing Committee or the Sub-Committee of the Committee of Imperial Defence, to examine carefully into the system of naval and air co-operation.

Lieut.-Colonel F. B. Mildmay (**Coalition Unionist,** *Totnes*) : "Does that apply to the Army also ? "

The Leader of the House said the case of the Army had been covered by an inquiry already held. The decision of the Government to establish a separate Air Ministry was based on war experience. What was now required in order to ensure success was close and intimate co-operation between the three Services.

The amendment was withdrawn and the motion to go into Committee on the estimates was agreed to. In Committee the Vote for officers and men, and a Vote on account for £12,000,000, were agreed to.

ARMY ESTIMATES.

The Army estimates for 1922-23 were issued on 13th March. The totals compared with the financial year just ended were:—

1922-23	£62,300,000
1921-22	93,714,000
Reduction	£31,414,000

The estimate regarding establishment shows the following totals:—

	All Ranks.
1922-23	152,836
1921-22	201,127
Reduction	48,291

Adding Colonial and native Indian troops and various additional numbers, the totals are:—

	All Ranks.
1922-23	215,000
1921-22	341,000
Reduction	126,000

The sum of £4,930,000 included in the gross total of Army Estimates in respect of the garrisons of Iraq and Palestine is balanced by a repayment from the Colonial Office (Middle East Department) and does not enter into the net total.

Owing to pressure on space, debates in the House of Commons on the Army Estimates, including a statement by the Secretary of State for War (the Right Hon. Sir Laming Worthington-Evans) have been held over until the next issue of the JOURNAL.

AIR ESTIMATES.

(Reduction of Strength; Air Force in the East; Imperial Communications.)

The net total of the Air estimates for 1922-23 is £9,935,500 for normal services and £959,500 for War liabilities, making £10,895,000 in all, a reduction on the total for the previous year of £6,400,000. In a memorandum by the Secretary of State for Air it was stated that:—

> The active strength of the Air Force will be reduced by the equivalent of two Squadrons. The Geddes Committee contemplated that (failing some equal or greater reduction in the Navy or Army) a reduction of 8½ Squadrons could be made. The Government have not felt able to accept this recommendation, but they have fallen in with the views of the Committee to the extent of directing that, over and above the actual reduction of two Squadrons, the equivalent of three more Squadrons should be withdrawn from Navy and Army co-operation and allocated primarily to Home Defence. These Squadrons will still be available for co-operation work on special occasions when required. They will also be used for training purposes, thus enabling economies to be made in the training establishments.

DEBATE IN HOUSE OF COMMONS.

A debate on the estimates took place in the House of Commons on 21st March on the motion to go into Committee of Supply.

The Secretary of State for Air (Captain the Right Hon. F. E. Guest) claimed that Air Force action was less temporary than Army action. Under certain conditions, such as the patrolling and policing of semi-civilised portions of the Empire, the Air Force was not only quicker in its action, but in its cost it was far less and in its power to take life it was more humane. Moreover, the effects were certainly not less lasting than those obtained by military expeditions.

Military action on the Indian frontier had never achieved finality and there was evidence that in the new dependencies in the Middle East it did not bring about final settlement. " I do not suggest," said Captain Guest, " that we have yet proved that the results of air action are more lasting than the results of army action, but, if properly carried out, they are certainly no less so, and, in addition, where suitable opportunity is afforded for air force action, the evidence would seem to indicate that air action is as effective." In Iraq it was now a question as to whether the effect of Air Force control was not at least as valuable and permanent as that obtained by military expeditions. There had been a number of opportunities in Iraq of proving the value of the Air Force as a means of policing large unsettled areas.

" In this connection operations in the districts of Sularmaniyah and Halabja provide a striking example of the effectiveness of the Air Force in suppressing disorder," remarked the right hon. gentleman. " In May of 1919 a *coup d'état* was attempted by Sheik Mahmud. It took an expedition of two brigades to suppress that outbreak, and it took them two and a half months to do it. An almost exactly similar outbreak occurred in January this year, less than three years after the first. This second outbreak was dealt with by the Air Force and was suppressed in a week by eight aeroplanes.

"The marshy lands lying between the two rivers, the Tigris and the Euphrates, the mountains, which in many places are devoid of roads, could only be dealt with by a military force after long and costly preparation. These areas can be, and are being, daily patrolled by the Air Force and its success in the suppression of incidents where necessary has been frequent and effective."

Airships: decision of the Dominions.*

"The House will remember," said Captain Guest, "that in July last, at the Imperial Conference, the future possibilities of utilising the air fleet for Imperial communications were closely considered. At that time an order to dispose of the airships had been recommended by my predecessor, and I was in process of following that policy, but the order was withheld until the Dominion Premiers had had an opportunity of consulting their Parliaments in order to see what contributions could be obtained from them, and which, added to one by ourselves, would have been sufficient to set on foot an Imperial Air Service.

"Since then replies in the negative have been received from New Zealand, South Africa and India. From Australia a more hopeful message came, but even if that individual contribution had materialised, the inability of the other Dominions to contribute has made the scheme impracticable. Neither has any proposal, during this period of many months, emanated from private individuals which did not involve heavy subsidies in one form or another, and in consequence could not be entertained by the Government. We have therefore reluctantly commenced negotiations for handing over the entire outfit to the Disposals Board.

"This postponement has extended over a period of nearly twelve months, and I think it is at any rate sufficient proof of the reluctance with which we have had to abandon a service which is not only attractive in itself, but with which so many expectations have been connected."

Civil aviation.

With regard to civil aviation, he looked upon the cross-Channel services in some degree as the practising and initial stage in the future development of schemes of Imperial communication.

"In the flying sense, we have almost continuous territory from Europe to Australia, with great distances unbridgeable

* *Vide* p. 361.

except by air—for example, Cairo to Bagdad, or Basra to Karachi. These 2,000 miles have been flown in 18 hours. What we are doing now is that we are making this the practising field for future and further development of the experience we have obtained in regard to these links in our Imperial chain. It is, therefore, the definite policy of the Air Ministry steadily to develop this and further links in the Imperial chain, and as soon as the separate stages of the various routes are safely opened, to hand them over to civil aviation to be progressively developed along commercial lines."

Lieut.-Col. the Hon. W. Guinness (Coalition Unionist, *Bury St. Edmund's*) moved an amendment expressing the opinion that to enable the best use to be made of the Air Service all defence forces should be represented on and their activities co-ordinated by the Committee of Imperial Defence, which should meet regularly and frequently; and that a Minister who is not departmentally responsible for any of the fighting Services should be appointed as permanent Vice-Chairman of the Committee, to take the chair in the absence of the Prime Minister.

The Secretary of State for the Colonies (the Right Hon. Winston Churchill) said that no solution of a harmonious or symmetrical character would be achieved in the co-ordination of the Services except through the agency of a Ministry of Defence, but it was not possible to create such a body at present, nor would it be possible for a considerable time. In the interim the only steps which were open to them were to create machinery for pooling the administrative functions of the three arms, and to create a common staff-brain from whose exertions in the future the responsible advice given to the Cabinet of the day in regard to matters of defence must and could only effectively originate.

The amendment was withdrawn and the motion was then agreed to. In Committee, Votes for men (31,176 of all ranks) and for pay (£3,781,000) were passed.

UNEMPLOYMENT PROBLEM.

(Labour views; International Trade; Government Measures.)

The first amendment to the Address—one put forward by the Labour Party on the subject of unemployment—was debated in the House of Commons on 9th February. The unemployment question was fully discussed in Parliament on various occasions last year, and in previous numbers of the JOURNAL summaries have appeared of the views expressed in different quarters of the House as to the best method of meeting the evil. In the last number of the JOURNAL considerable space was devoted to a description of the special legislation passed in the autumn of 1921 to deal with the situation.

DEBATE IN HOUSE OF COMMONS.

The amendment of the Labour Party now submitted to the House was in these terms :—

> But regret that, in view of the disaster to British trade and of the large number of persons unemployed, there is no indication that the Government are prepared to recognise and deal effectively with the causes of unemployment, or to provide the opportunity for useful productive work for the people of this country ; and further, in view of the exhaustion of national funds provided for the assistance of local authorities and the approaching cessation of unemployment insurance benefit, regret that there is no indication of any intention on the part of the Government to grant substantial financial aid to local authorities who cannot be expected to bear a national burden.

Mr. A. Hayday (Labour, *Nottingham, W.*), in moving the amendment, said the Labour Party believed in working for the State as a whole and not for that section which had vested interests in it. They believed in defending and sustaining the weak in the industrial world. Other hon. Members would send them to blazes and damnation.

The Minister of Labour (the Right Hon. T. J. Macnamara) said that af the end of January there were 1,904,300 persons wholly unemployed and 280,000 on short time. The War had left the whole mechanism of international trade in ruins, and heavy taxation, the direct heritage of the War, added another to the many factors which hampered recovery. The result was that the gravity and duration of the depression were unparalleled in their modern history. The Government had worked double tides at the problem—the gravest of the welter of problems thrown up by the great War. Mr. J. H. Thomas, speaking in the House on 20th October, 1921, said that if the Labour Party, or any other section of the House, were sitting on the Government Benches, they could not get up and say that, with the world position as it was, there was one short simple remedy for the problem.

Sir Frederick Young (Coalition Unionist, *Swindon*): "It is a question which a Queensland Labour Government have answered."

World-wide industrial depression.

The Minister of Labour proceeded to draw attention to the world-wide incidence of the existing industrial depression and passed on to speak of the measures undertaken in Great

Britain to grapple with the situation. Both the Government and the municipal authorities, notwithstanding the grave financial embarrassments with which they were confronted, had made provision for the unemployed on a scale out of all relationship to anything attempted in the past. From the autumn of 1920 to the present time round about £40,000,000 had been voted to provide useful and productive work for men who otherwise would have been unemployed. The only way to find work for the mass of people unemployed in this country was to get the mills, the workshops and the factories going again.

State insurance.

From November, 1920, to November, 1921, the Government were able to dispense £50,000,000 of benefit under the Unemployment Insurance Act. From November, 1921, to round about Easter (1922)—a period of six months—they would dispense another £25,000,000. He reminded those who rather loosely used the word " dole " in connection with those payments that roughly four-fifths of the money came from the employers and the workpeople. Under the Unemployed Workers' Dependants Act* of last November, they were now adding to the unemployed man's 15s. benefit 5s. a week on behalf of his wife or housekeeper, and 1s. a week each on behalf of his little children. Under that provision grants were now being made weekly in respect of 600,000 adult dependants and about 1,000,000 children.

The Right Hon. J. R. Clynes (Chairman of the Parliamentary Labour Party) said they were bidden by the Government to turn their eyes to Genoa and look for improvement in the industrial situation as the outcome of the great economic conference which was to assemble there. The first Party to call for a great economic conference which would undertake the task of financial and economic reconstruction of a ruined Europe was the Labour Party. This, therefore, was an instance of the Government undertaking at last to try to do the right thing when they could no longer continue to do the wrong thing.

Mockeries of conferences; Trade with Russia.

The Government had kept on the mockeries of conferences and partial consultations under the Supreme Council. Having finally seen that that sort of partial meeting of representatives of portions of Europe was powerless to effect any economic or financial reconstruction, they now went to the length of inviting the representatives of Soviet Russia and of Germany.

---

* *Vide* Journal, Vol. III., No. 1, p. 58.

Indeed, they were sending invitations to all those representatives for whom years ago Labour claimed the right of admission to discussions on questions of European reconstruction. They were told that all those who had previously been excluded must be brought together to try to make work that which never would work unless enormously modified—the Treaty of Versailles.

Economic prosperity was impossible until a real peace was established. Real peace depended upon Russia and Germany being brought into that Conference, and linked in their interests with other European countries and with America. Labour wanted a speedy economic recovery more than they wanted a Party victory. They wanted trade revival more than they wanted a General Election. Labour believed that opportunities had been neglected of restoring trading relations with Russia. They were mindful of the financial difficulties, but the problems should not be outside the possibility of successful treatment by Ministers who claimed a monopoly of fitness to rule the State.

Reparations.

Sir Godfrey Collins (Independent Liberal, *Greenock*) contended that reparations, as they knew them, were causing unemployment in this country. The Government of the day were passing tariff measures like Bismarck did in 1878. He hoped that experience would show the necessity of altering the present policy.

The Prime Minister (the Right Hon. D. Lloyd George) said that members of the Opposition had no right to go about the country saying that unemployment difficulties were attributable entirely to German reparations unless they were prepared also to say, " If we are returned, we will cancel all these claims." Had the Independent Liberals committed themselves to the policy of reducing the reparations ? Were they to say to France, " Your richest provinces have been devastated, enormous burdens have been cast upon France causing a huge deficit annually in her Budget ; but you must not ask Germany, who was guilty of the devastation, to pay one penny ? " Why ? Because it was the cause of unemployment. Was that the policy of the Opposition ?

There was no basis for the suggestion of Sir Godfrey Collins. He talked about Germany cutting out British goods in the neutral markets of the world. But at Cannes Dr. Rathenau gave them figures showing that the export trade of Germany was just 25 per cent. what it was before the War. Unemployment was attributable to causes deeper and more far-reaching. They were the impoverishment of Britain's customers throughout the world. China, India, and every part of the world were impoverished. There was a general expectation that prices would come down and a good many orders were being held back purely for that reason.

On a division the amendment was negatived by 270 votes against 78.

DISABILITIES OF AGRICULTURE.

(Burden of Rates; Canadian Cattle Embargo; Conciliation Committees.)

An amendment to the Address relating to agriculture was moved in the House of Commons on 10th February. It was in these terms :—

But regret that in the Gracious Speech from the Throne no reference is made to the urgent necessity for relieving agriculture from some of the disabilities which press unfairly on the industry and which, combined with the depression from which it is suffering, threaten to reduce the food supply of the country and to create further unemployment.

DEBATE IN HOUSE OF COMMONS.

Mr. Murrough Wilson (Coalition Unionist, ***Richmond*****)** moved the amendment.

Mr. M. G. Townley (Coalition Unionist, ***Bedford, Mid.*****)** seconded and said that the repeal last year of the guaranteed prices for home-grown wheat was a staggering blow to agriculture. He complained of the heavy burden of the rates, which, he said, at 12s. in the £ equalled approximately 4s. 6d. a quarter on wheat. With reference to the programme of the Labour Party, he asked how were they going to make land pay better than it did now by handing over the ownership to the State instead of keeping it in private hands. If they nationalised land they would find the State a much harder landlord than the landlords they had now.

Mr. W. S. Royce (Labour, ***Holland with Boston*****)** declared that at a time when agriculture was suffering severely it was called upon to pay railway rates on the highest Wär scales. All the things that the farmer wanted as well as all the things that he sold were subject to those oppressive charges. It was one of the greatest bugbears with which agriculture had to deal. With reference to Empire settlement, the Labour Party would not send a number of young men across the seas to the great detriment of this country. They could probably find them something to do in growing food a little nearer home.

Canadian cattle embargo.*

Captain W. T. Shaw (Coalition Unionist, *Forfar*) referred to the embargo on Canadian cattle. Ever since it was imposed in 1893 people in his part of Scotland had never ceased to advocate its removal. It was generally admitted that it was put on in conditions which did not exist now. It was said that disease came from Canada. Now it was admitted on all hands, among others by Sir Daniel Hall at the Royal Commission, that Canadian herds were freer from disease than any other herds in the world. It appeared to him as if the Government never intended to accept the Report of the recent Royal Commission unless the findings were in favour of maintaining the embargo. They must have a large and early supply of store cattle if they were to keep the land in full cultivation.

The Minister of Agriculture (the Right Hon. Sir A. Griffith-Boscawen) observed that the sudden slump in agriculture was not due to any action on the part of the Government. As to the repeal of the Corn Production Acts,† did anybody contemplate that this country would have to pay a subsidy under those Acts amounting to a great many millions a year in respect of wheat and oats? What the Government expected would amount only to a small annual insurance actually turned out to be a large sum of money. They had got rid of the subsidies and he was certain the soundest plan they could adopt was to interfere with industry as little as possible.

Conciliation Committees.

With regard to the wages of agricultural labourers, it was better that the labourer should be receiving a lower wage than that there should be wholesale unemployment on the farms. The Conciliation Committees which had been set up were a new idea in agriculture and on the whole they had done their work extraordinarily well. The Labour Party had a policy for exterminating landlords. The abolition of landlordism might be a very nice catchword, and a fine cry with which to go to the country, but if they attempted to do it in the case of agricultural land they would take away from agriculture the best friend it had.

As to the rates, in his opinion land always had to bear a greater burden than it ought to do. It was, however, a matter which could only be dealt with broadly when the whole question of rating was taken into consideration.

Regarding the Canadian cattle embargo, he was bound to say that of all the extraordinary remedies for agricultural depression to suggest that the Government should remove

---

* *Vide* also pp. 291 and 344.

† *Vide* JOURNAL, Vol. II., No. 4, p. 772.

that embargo was the most extraordinary. It was laid down specifically in the Report that if the embargo were removed it would be very difficult for the crofters and smallholders in Scotland to carry on their business. What was true of them was equally true of the thousands of farmers and smallholders in England and Wales.

After further debate the amendment was, by leave, withdrawn.

SAFEGUARDING OF INDUSTRIES ACT.

(Leave to bring in a Repealing Bill Refused.)

In the House of Commons on 14th February an attempt was made to introduce under "the ten minutes' rule" a Bill to repeal the Safeguarding of Industries Act, 1921.

DEBATE IN HOUSE OF COMMONS.

Captain Wedgwood Benn (Independent Liberal, ***Leith*****),** in moving for leave to bring in the Bill, remarked that, so far as evidence was available, it was safe to say that the Safeguarding of Industries Act had done little good and much harm. There was no evidence to show that it had resulted in the building up of a chemical trade for War purposes, and even the traders who had sought the shelter of Orders under the Act had found in many cases that the Act was a boomerang.

They were informed, for example, that in the course of the last few months the British gas-mantle market had been flooded with cheap German mantles as a direct result of a threat to impose an Order on mantles. British traders, therefore, stood to gain very little by it. The harm that had been done was manifested in many directions. From the consumers' point of view the Act was bad because it had raised prices, and it also did harm in connection with their foreign policy. It was inconsistent with the Government's well-known endeavours to make Germany pay, because it was intended to stop the flow of reparation goods. It introduced an element of irritation into their relations with the French, whereas a good and honest understanding with France was vital at the present moment.

Impeded reconstruction work.

He contended that the Act impeded the work of European reconstruction. When they met at Brussels the experts said it was necessary that there should be a free interchange of goods. There was to be a meeting at Genoa for the purpose of promoting trade and a repeal of this Act would be at least an earnest of the sincerity of the Government in the matter.

Sir Richard Cooper (Unionist, ***Walsall*****)**, in opposing the motion, said that, at any rate in its principal parts, the Act merely carried out a purely Liberal Free Trade conviction. Captain Benn had made a reference to the unemployment created owing to the importation of a number of gas mantles. What better evidence could be required to show the effectiveness of the Act? It was evidence the foreign manufacturer realised immediately that he was not in future going freely to import his articles and, while he could do it, he took the advantage of sending the maximum that was possible. Whether the Act was good or bad in its operation, at least it must keep production in this country and provide employment.

On a division the motion for leave to bring in a repealing Bill was negatived by 170 votes against 92.

EMPIRE SETTLEMENT BILL.*

A Bill to make better provision for furthering British settlement in His Majesty's Oversea Dominions was presented to the House of Commons on 7th April, by Mr. L. S. Amery (Financial Secretary to the Admiralty and Chairman of the Overseas Settlement Committee).

The Bill provides for the co-operation by the Secretary of State for the Colonies with any Dominion Government, or with approved private organisations in the United Kingdom or the Dominions, in carrying out agreed schemes to assist suitable persons in the United Kingdom to settle in the Dominions.

An agreed scheme may be either :—

(A) A development or a land settlement scheme ; or

(B) A scheme for facilitating settlement by assistance with passages, initial allowances, special training, etc.

The Secretary of State shall not :—

(A) Agree to any scheme without the consent of the Treasury ;

(B) Contribute in any case more than half the expenses of the scheme ;

(C) Be liable to make contributions under the scheme beyond a period of fifteen years after the passing of the Act.

The aggregate amount expended by the Secretary of State under any scheme shall not exceed £1,500,000 in the financial year current at the date of the passing of the Act, or £3,000,000 in any subsequent financial year.

---

* *Vide* also p. 288.

CANADA.

Following the General Election in December, 1921, *the First Session of the Fourteenth Parliament of Canada commenced on 8th March,* 1922.

THE ADDRESS—GENERAL DISCUSSION.

(Governor-General's Speech; Tariff; Reciprocity; Dominion Status; Representation at Washington Conference; Railways; Immigration; Proportional Representation; Ambassador at Washington; Cattle Embargo; etc.)

The Session was formally opened on 9th March, 1922, when the Governor-General, Lord Byng of Vimy, delivered in the Senate a speech to both Houses.

Industrial conditions; Unemployment relief.

Reference was made in the speech to the fact that the Dominion had not escaped the world-wide economic disturbance and industrial depression, but had suffered less from it than other countries. Keen observers of the business barometer felt that the worst was about over and that at an early date they might look for a substantial revival of activity. Whilst of the opinion that unemployment relief was fundamentally a municipal and provincial responsibility, the Government had felt that as conditions had arisen in a measure out of the late War they would be justified in continuing for the period of the winter months the expedient of supplementing by grants from the Federal Treasury the relief contributions of Provinces and Municipalities for the purpose of alleviating actual distress.

Agricultural prices: Government action.

The decline of prices in farm products in 1921, as compared with the prices of previous years, had seriously affected agriculture in many parts of the Dominion. The ill-effects of that inevitable deflation had been emphasised by restricted markets and the absence of any corresponding reduction in the cost of production. The Government had lost no time in seeking to gain more favourable conditions of sale and marketing for the products of the farm. Communications had been opened with the authorities of other countries looking to an extension of trade and a widening of Canadian markets, and conferences had been arranged between the railway authorities with respect to the reduction of rates upon basic commodities.

Customs Tariff; Railways; Immigration.

The speech announced that Parliament would be invited to consider the expediency of making some changes in the Customs Tariff. A reference to the national railways, "now extending through every province of the Dominion," followed. It was intended at an early date to co-ordinate the Government-owned systems in the manner best calculated to increase efficiency and to effect economies in administration, maintenance and operation.

The stream of immigration to the Dominion was much interrupted and restricted during the War. Now that the blessing of peace was with them a renewal of efforts to bring in new settlers must be made. The Government were fully alive to the importance of the question and would use every reasonable endeavour to attract to their country people of the most desirable class, with particular regard to settlement on their undeveloped lands.

Department of Defence; Washington Conference; etc.

Work in connection with the re-establishment, medical treatment and vocational training of former members of the Canadian Forces was being sympathetically and energetically prosecuted. With the object of promoting economy and increasing efficiency, a Bill would be submitted to Parliament providing for a Department of Defence, in which the various branches of the defence forces of Canada would be co-ordinated under one Ministerial head. The speech went on to refer to the Washington Conference, from which, it was remarked, Treaties of far-reaching consequence had resulted. It was the opinion of the Government that approval of Parliament ought to precede their ratification on behalf of Canada. The Treaties, with appropriate explanations, would accordingly be placed before them during the Session. Mention followed of the invitation to the Government to participate in the Genoa Conference and of the appointment of delegates for the purpose.

An invitation had been extended to the Government of Canada by the Government of the United States to take part in a Postal Conference at which all phases of mail communication from one country to the other might be fully discussed. Reciprocating the spirit that had prompted the invitation, the Canadian Government would in due course appoint representatives to meet the representatives of the United States for the purpose mentioned.

DEBATE IN HOUSE OF COMMONS.

On 13th March the debate on the Address in reply to the Governor-General's speech was commenced in the House of Commons.

Mr. E. J. McMurray (Liberal, *Winnipeg, North*), in moving the Address, said that the reference to the Washington Conference in the Governor-General's speech was a matter of satisfaction. He was particularly struck with the intimation that the Treaties there arranged were to be submitted to the consideration of that House. " It is," he remarked, " a vindication of the assertion that has been made by Mr. Lloyd George, by Gen. Smuts, and by Mr. Hughes, that we are a nation in every sense of the term." Turning to domestic problems, the hon. Member observed that their State-owned railroad system, one of the largest in the world, was being operated at an annual deficit of many millions. Not for a year or two, but for a reasonable length of time, having regard to prevailing conditions, to the vastness of the project and to the failure of private ownership, State ownership should be given a reasonable opportunity to demonstrate its capacity to deal with that tremendous problem.

Closely connected with the problems of the national indebtedness and the national railroads was the question of conditions pertaining to agriculture. Agriculture was the basic industry of Canada, and since the War prices had fallen or become unstabilised, though the costs of operation continued high. A high tariff wall had been raised against them in the United States, in the form of the Fordney Bill, and the crops of the West last year suffered from heavy rains. Agriculture in Canada to-day, therefore, was becoming an unprofitable occupation.

Men and capital wanted.

Canada lacked two things. They were short in man power and short in capital. " We must bring immigrants to Canada to fill the vacant spaces of the West and help to develop the country's great resources," said the hon. Member. " The call is for men, men, and yet more men. We must attract capital to Canada ; we must provide conditions under which capital will come to this country and be safe in its investment here."

M. Paul Mercier (Liberal, *Westmount, St. Henri*), in seconding the Address, declared that agriculture was one of the factors that would assure the prosperity of Canada. With reference to immigration, he urged that the Government must take care to prevent the inundation of Canada by foreigners not used to their customs and traditions.

The Right Hon. Arthur Meighen (Leader of the Opposition), after welcoming new Members to the House, including the first lady Member, referred to the paragraph in the Governor-General's speech relating to the commercial and industrial condition of Canada. It was, he said, a matter for congratulation that their population had increased, according to the recent census, from less than 7,250,000 to well over 8,750,000. That increase had been achieved against the handicap of the War, and had been accompanied by an expansion of their trade unprecedented in their history.

He did not refer to the inflated figures that obtained during the War, but to the 1921 figures obtained during, perhaps, the very depths of the post-War deflation. Comparing those figures with the figures for the ten years preceding 1911, their exports had multiplied almost three times over in that decade, as opposed to the increase of less than twice in the fifteen years that went before. Therefore, there was a very considerable basis of fact for the assertion in the Governor-General's speech that the Dominion found itself to-day in the best position of any country in the world.

Customs Tariff.

Turning to the paragraph in the Speech dealing with the Customs Tariff, the right hon. gentleman asked what were the changes in the tariff which the Government proposed to ask the House to consider. It was assumed by Mr. McMurray that what was meant was a revision of the tariff downwards, but Parliament was not advised what would be the character or nature of the subjects dealt with. Speaking at Calgary on 11th October, 1920, the Prime Minister made this statement :—

> "We feel that there is no necessity for a tariff commission or any other like expedients to point the way to what is obviously demanded in the interests of consumers and producers as respects the necessities of life and the instruments of production ; but that a downward revision of the tariff, and, in some instances, its complete elimination should be immediately effected."

Further on the Prime Minister stated that there must be put on the free list, and at once, all farm implements and machinery, as well as other articles. Let hon. Members wait and see how far that was accomplished this Session. In his own mind he had not very much doubt what would be the measure and character of "some changes" in the Customs Tariff referred to in the Speech.

The Railways.

With respect to the railways the most evasive and nebulous terms were used. It was not said that there was to be unification of the roads owned by the Government ;

it was not said that there was to be amalgamation; it was not said all were to be brought together as one system, as was the intention of the last Parliament. It was said there was going to be "co-ordination"—a word chosen because of its elasticity. He hoped it meant there would be actual unification in order that the advantages and economies incident to unity would be provided.

The late Government proceeded on the principle of unification. All that was left to be done was to bring in the Grand Trunk. Let that step be taken. He saw in the ranks of the Government itself, however, the bitterest foes of a continuance of national ownership and control. There were hon. gentlemen elected to support the Government who had declared not only that the acquirement of the railroads never should have taken place, but now that they were acquired the proper policy was to get rid of them at the earliest possible date. He and his friends believed those roads could be made a success under fair trial. But he had distrust of the conduct of those roads when influential men in charge of the country's affairs were the sworn enemies of the very principle entrusted to their care. He predicted that whilst the promised inquiry was taking place the Dominions would be flooded with an anti-Government operation propaganda designed to turn the minds of the people in disgust from the public ownership of railways.

Wider markets; policy of reciprocity.

With reference to the question of wider markets for Canadian products, he asked what advances had been made by the Government in that direction. They saw in the Press that the Minister of Finance made another trip to Washington in the supposed belief that he would achieve some practical result in that respect. They were also told that efforts had been made to establish reciprocal relations with Australia. Apparently the Government had in mind the making of one reciprocity pact with the United States of America and of another with Australia. So far as the United States was concerned he said the desire was only apparent, because he believed on the part of the preponderating element of the Government the only purpose was a mere gesture.

"I do not believe," Mr. Meighen observed, "advantage can be gained for any country, only a fraction the size of its neighbour, the competitor of that neighbour in every field of its enterprise, by tying itself to a trade treaty with that neighbour. . . . Reciprocity with Australia is something which should be obtained if we are able to obtain it for Canada. Reciprocity with the West Indies, who produce goods that we do not produce in surplus, who consume what we produce in surplus, is desirable. . . . The late Government did everything in its power to achieve reciprocity with Australia, and before retirement from office I was instrumental by interviews with the Prime Minister of Australia in securing his influence to have inserted in the legislation of that Dominion power to its Government to negotiate reciprocity treaties with the other Dominions of the Empire.

" The legislation of the Dominion of Australia came into effect, I think, only in the fall . . . of 1921. Consequently the Government of that Dominion was not able to take action upon it during the life of the late Government. I earnestly hope this Government will press for fair terms of reciprocity with that Dominion . . . and will meet with success. But in regard to the United States of America, reciprocity with that country of the nature of that which they achieved, and which the people of this country rejected in 1911, could, I think, lead to no good object for this Dominion. It could, I think, only succeed in tying our hands fiscally, in subordinating us more and more as years go on to the commercial domination of the Republic."

The Prime Minister (Hon. W. L. Mackenzie King) said that to-day they had a Parliament that was representative of the people and a Government that in the truest sense was responsible to Parliament, as well as to the people. He thought, therefore, Mr. Meighen might cease to be alarmed as to how the affairs of Canada would be carried on during the next few years under those new auspices.

Washington Conference; Canadian representation; Dominion Status.

He had been asked by Mr. Meighen when did the late Government not submit its Treaties to Parliament. The Treaties in question happened to be the recent Treaties arising out of the Conference at Washington. He ventured to assert that if it had been left to Mr. Meighen to settle the question as to how those Treaties were to be finally signed in all probability their Dominion would have had no representative at the Conference at all. In a statement made shortly after Mr. Meighen returned from the Conference of Premiers the Prime Minister of Great Britain said :—

" As regards the Dominions and India, it was arranged at the recent Imperial Conference that His Majesty's Government should represent the whole Empire at Washington."

That was the position in which the treaty matter was left at the Imperial Conference attended by his right hon. friend.

Mr. Meighen: "Are you reading the whole statement? I cannot think that the statement was made in that naked form. If so, I would dispute it."

The Prime Minister said on the 18th October his right hon. friend handed out the following statement to the Press of Ottawa:—

> "As the result of recent telegraphic communications between the Prime Minister of Canada and the Prime Minister of the United Kingdom, it has been arranged that a representative of Canada should be appointed as a member of the delegation which will represent the British Empire at the Conference on the Limitation of Armaments and on Pacific and Far Eastern Questions. . . . The Canadian Government have accordingly appointed Right Hon. Sir Robert Borden, G.C.M.G., as the representative of Canada for this purpose."

It was between the time Mr. Meighen was at the Prime Ministers' Conference and the date of his issuing the above that the Prime Minister of England made the statement referred to.

Mr. Meighen: "I wish to state again, that the hon. gentleman has failed to quote such language from any statement of mine, and I was no party to such an arrangement."

The Prime Minister: "Let me then say what will be familiar to many hon. Members of this House, that after the Imperial Conference the Prime Minister of South Africa, the Right Hon. J. C. Smuts, having read the statement I have just quoted from the Prime Minister of Great Britain . . . made the declaration that so far as South Africa was concerned she did not propose to return to the colonial status, but was going to maintain the status which she had won at the Peace Conference at Paris at the conclusion of the Great War, and that South Africa would not be represented by a Delegation to be named by the British Government, to take its instructions from the British Government, but that she would be represented by one of her own Delegates acting under instructions from the Government of South Africa, representing South Africa as one of the countries belonging to the British Empire, or not be represented at all.

"If Canada was fortunate enough to be represented at the Conference at Washington by her own representative we have to thank the Prime Minister of South Africa and not the late Prime Minister of our own country for the fact that we had that representation."

Mr. Meighen's repudiation.

Mr. Meighen: "I stated I was no party to any arrangement at the Imperial Conference that Canada should be represented merely by a Delegation appointed by the British Government, taking its directions from the British Government, nor was such an arrangement arrived at while I was a member of the Conference. Our negotiations took place in this regard by correspondence, and from the first I insisted that we should name our Delegate and that that Delegate should take his instructions from us."

The Prime Minister: "I have no desire in any way to contradict my right hon. friend, but I must confess that when the Prime Minister of England makes a statement which he gives to the entire world, which was accepted in South Africa, and which was accepted in Australia as being a correct statement, I find it somewhat difficult not to accept that statement as correct."

Mr. Meighen said he would remind the hon. gentleman that he was not there to the end of the Conference.

The Prime Minister, continuing, said that the pledge made in respect to changes in the Customs Tariff would be carried out during the course of the present Session. As to the railways, the position they were in to-day was due in large part to excessive construction during a period when construction should have been discontinued altogether. It was due, further, to the fact that the Government which succeeded the Government of Sir Wilfrid Laurier, instead of seeking to carry out in a sympathetic way the large vision which prompted the construction of the Grand Trunk Pacific, did all in its power to make that road a failure.

Government's intentions as to railways.

"So far as this Administration is concerned," said the Premier, "I will not for a moment accept any of the insinuations or suspicions of my right hon. friend in regard to its intentions in administering the national railroads.

"We intend to give Government ownership of the national system . . . the fairest trial under auspices the most favourable it is possible for a Government to secure. We go into it with all sincerity and in the hope that we may make it a success. I will say with perfect candour that there are hon. gentlemen . . . who doubt very much whether public ownership can be made the success which private ownership might. But there are others who believe that it can be made a success, and so far as it is possible for this Government to demonstrate what can be done under Government ownership, it is our intention to see that it is done."

Speaking, in conclusion, of the new Administration, the Premier observed that he was quite sincere when he said during the course of the Election campaign that he thought coalitions were a mistake.. What the country needed most, and he believed British Parliamentary practice had gone far to prove it, was an Administration sufficiently of one mind and sufficiently strong to be able to adopt policies of great national importance and carry them through in a way that would make for good government in the country.

It would be the aim of the present Administration to see that every shade of Liberal and Progressive thought was duly considered in the shaping of the policies of the Government.

Attitude of National Progressives.

The Hon. T. A. Crerar (Leader of the National Progressive Party) remarked that they would wait with interest to see what benefits the change of Government would bring to Canada. The Progressives were in that House as an independent Party, standing for the principles in which they believed and prepared to further those principles by every honest and legitimate means within their power.

"The attitude of the Progressive Party is easily and simply stated," the hon. Member said. "We are here not to oppose for the sake of opposing. We are here prepared to give the Government every assistance in carrying on the government of this country when it gives the country the policies we believe it should have. But we are equally prepared to oppose the Government and to criticise it when we think the Government is doing wrong or not adopting the policies that we think this country should have. . . . My own hope . . . is that the policy pursued by the Government in respect of the great vital questions before the country . . . will be such as to command our support."

Turning to the subjects mentioned in the Governor-General's Speech, Mr. Crerar said there was no doubt that the condition of agriculture throughout Canada to-day was very serious. The real prosperity of the Dominion rested upon agriculture, and a great majority of the farmers of Western Canada conducted their business last year at a loss. He believed that was true also of other portions of the Dominion. What was the result? Their factories were closed, there was unemployment in their cities, and there was lack of business for their railways.

Adequate markets.

It was unquestionably true that adequate markets were a part of the problem. He was not sure that the visit of the Minister of Finance to Washington recently was well timed, but he commended the purpose of his hon. friend in desiring to promote better trade relations with the United States in respect to markets for Canada's agricultural products.

He did not agree with the argument of Mr. Meighen that reciprocity would be of no value to the Canadian farmer. The year before last they exported, if his memory served him aright, 350,000 head of live stock over one year old to the United States. When their American friends passed their Fordney Emergency Tariff that market was shut off. The result was that the farmers of Canada did not have that market for their live stock and the value of that live stock in the markets of the Dominion went down steadily. Reference had been made to the need of improved market facilities. One of the great difficulties in Canada to-day, and one of the causes of the high cost of living, was the expensive system of distribution, not only of farm products, but of the supplies that consumers required.

With respect to the marketing of wheat there was a widespread feeling in Western Canada, shared not only by producers, but by many business men as well, that the Canada Wheat Board should be re-established in a temporary way. He noted a statement by the Prime Minister that the whole question of marketing wheat was to be referred to the Standing Committee on Agriculture, and he suggested this should be done as quickly as possible.

Production costs; excessive freight rates.

The suggestion that production costs should come down was, he sincerely hoped, a forerunner of the wiping out of the duty on agricultural implements. There were those who had said that if the United States raised a tariff against Canada's wheat and live stock, they should raise their tariff against them by way of retaliation. But the sensible thing to do was to endeavour to meet that condition by reducing the cost of the things the farmer needed to carry on his operations. Without question one of the things that were throttling business and industry was the excessive freight rates that the country was labouring under.

He hoped the paragraph in the Speech concerning the Customs Tariff forecasted a revision of duties downwards. "I am convinced," said the hon. Member, "that the principle of Protection is not suited as a fiscal policy for this country. . . . I recognise that it is and will be necessary for a considerable time to raise revenue by Customs duties; but a tariff based upon the principle of revenue is an altogether different thing from a tariff based upon the principle of Protection." As to the railways, if public ownership was to be given a full and fair trial, the roads comprising the Government system must be placed absolutely under one central management. The cardinal defect of the system was that the country was overbuilt with railways. Public ownership was not the deliberate choice of the people, but was forced upon them because of the collapse of private ownership and operation.

Immigration: Canada's needs.

Proceeding to deal with immigration, Mr. Crerar said the last census figures were disappointing. The population at present was 8,774,000. In 1911 it was 7,206,000. They had taken into Canada through the gates of immigration during the last decade 1,812,000. They also had a natural increase in excess of births over deaths during the same period of 1,140,000. On a fair basis, if they had held their people in Canada, they would have to-day a population of at least 10,000,000. What was the use of their spending millions a year in promoting immigration to Canada when they were losing the people almost as fast as they could bring them to their doors? They had sufficient people in their towns and cities. What Canada needed was not artisans or workmen, but a sturdy rural population.

Ambassador at Washington; Representative at Genoa.

Following a reference to the Washington Conference, the hon. Member suggested that the Government might very well carry out the understanding reached a few years ago with the British Government by appointing a Canadian Ambassador to Washington. He was sure that if they had a representative at Washington who could represent the Canadian view great good would come to the Dominion. With reference to Genoa, he expressed regret that the Government had appointed Sir Charles Gordon as one of the Commissioners. Sir Charles was well known as a high protectionist, and he felt that whatever influence he would have in that Conference would be exercised along the line of maintaining artificial barriers between nations.

Redistribution: Proportional Representation.

The hon. Member urged that a measure of redistribution should be passed during the Session. Speaking of proportional representation, he said, "The last Election disclosed, more clearly, I think, than anything else could have done, the need for this reform in our electoral machinery. . . . What do we find as a result of the last Election? We find the Party to my right without any representation from six provinces in this Dominion, and yet the Election figures show that there were a great many people—all misguided, I think—who supported the candidates of the Leader of the Opposition. These people should have some means of expressing their will in this House. The same is true in respect to the Progressives, and in respect to the Party supporting the Government. The Government would not have a great deal of difficulty in counting their supporters from the Prairie Provinces in this House, and yet the support the Government did receive in the Prairie Provinces does not adequately reflect the vote the

Government policies received in those provinces. I am quite aware that had the last Election been conducted on the system of proportional representation, there probably would not be as many Progressive supporters in this House as there are to-day. But I am not so much concerned about that as I am with this fact, that this House should be as nearly as possible a correct and exact expression of the will and wishes of the people of Canada.

"There is another argument in favour of proportional representation. My hon. friend the Prime Minister pointed out yesterday that a good many of the supporters who sit behind my hon. friend the Leader of the Opposition were elected by minority votes. I think that if my hon. friend the Prime Minister examines the Election figures he will find that quite a considerable number of those who sit on his own side of the House were elected in the same way. I am putting this forward simply as an illustration of the need for this reform, and I trust that the Government will see its way clear to give favourable consideration to enacting a measure of proportional representation. Such a measure should apply in my judgment to the large cities of Canada, all those cities that elect two or more Members."

Continuing, Mr. Crerar said he would also like to see the principle of the transferable vote applied to single-Member constituencies. With these reforms they would get as exact a reflection of the will of the people in that Parliament as it was possible to secure.

Public ownership of public utilities.

Mr. W. F. Maclean (Liberal-Conservative, *York, S. Riding*), referring to the railway question, declared himself an absolute believer in public ownership of public utilities. The greatest electrical development in the world to-day was owned by the people of Ontario in the Chippewa hydro-electrical development in connection with the Niagara River. The fundamental problem in the regeneration of Canada after the Great War was the improvement of their transportation. There was a way to do it now that they owned five of the railways, steamships, telegraphs, and express services. But they must canvass for business the same as did the privately-owned railways, and that was what the Canadian Pacific Railway feared would happen.

Mr. R. Forke (National Progressive, *Brandon*) said that if they doubled their immigration they would help to solve their railway and taxation difficulties. But they wanted the right kind of people, and not immigrants from the manufacturing towns of Great Britain. If they got artisans from the banks of the Clyde or factory workers from the towns, when they came to Canada they would inevitably drift to the cities.

Mr. J. S. Woodsworth (**Labour,** *Winnipeg, Centre*) said the Labour group was small and inexperienced, but it represented a section of the community of no small importance. He thought it was admitted by the Minister of Labour that they had something like 200,000 people unemployed in Canada. Probably that meant that 1,000,000 people were either directly unemployed or under-employed. It should be recognised that, under the present system of large-scale industry, unemployment was involuntary. Under those conditions the State was under obligation to provide work, and until suitable work was provided there ought to be adequate maintenance. They were behind any of the European countries in that they had not so far been able to make provision for unemployment insurance.

Transportation problem.

Mr. T. L. Church (**Liberal-Conservative,** *Toronto, North*), speaking on the transportation problem, quoted a statement from the Drayton-Acworth report that Canada had as much railway mileage as Germany with a population of 67,000,000, as France with a population of 46,000,000, and as the United Kingdom with a population of 47,000,000. Canada with a population of 7,500,000, he said, had 40,000 miles of single track, with useless duplication and waste; three transcontinental railways running across the Dominion where one with a double track would have done for many years with lateral branch lines built off the main line.

The Minister of Justice (**Hon. Sir Lomer Gouin**) remarked that circumstances had changed in Canada since the dissolution of the last Parliament. The feeling of security amongst the people which was already so noticeable and their confidence in a general revival of business were due to a large extent to the confidence the nation reposed in the new Government. Mr. Meighen had stated that his Government was defeated by the big interests of Montreal, but the power which defeated the late Administration was the will of the Canadian people.

British Columbia: influence of Japanese.

Mr. J. A. MacKelvie (**Liberal-Conservative,** *Yale*) referred to the immigration problem in British Columbia where, he said, one out of every ten or twelve adult males was an Oriental. The schools were crowded with Oriental children and even if the bars were put up so rigidly that not a single one of the Japanese race could enter Canada for the next decade their natural increase would be such as to give them more by far in that province than they could ever begin to absorb profitably. He hoped they would receive assistance in guarding their Western portals against any further influx of a class of people who could not be considered anything but detrimental and dangerous to their national life.

Mr. A. W. Neill (National Progressive, *Comox-Alberni*) observed that the Asiatics in British Columbia had a throttle-hold upon the fishing industry. They were encroaching on the lumber industry and large sections of the country devoted to fruit and market garden produce were entirely in their grip. The situation was becoming so tense that something would have to be done or there would be a development that would astonish the people in the East. He urged the Government to keep away from the idea of allowing settlers from different countries to establish a colony by themselves in Canada.

The Hon. Sir Henry L. Drayton (Liberal-Conservative, *York, W. Riding*) said that every charter which was responsible for the over-building of railway lines in Canada, where that over-building to-day was burdensome upon the public, was authorised by the Liberal Government. When the Laurier Administration embarked upon the construction of the Grand Trunk Pacific they embarked upon a project which committed Canada to three trans-continental lines.

Settlers wanted.

The Hon. H. H. Stevens (Liberal-Conservative, *Vancouver, Centre*) remarked that Canada wanted settlers, but they must be settlers who would contribute something to the up-building of the national life of Canada and not create within their bounds a little Russia, a little Poland, or a Galicia or some other distinctive nationality. They did not want Canada to be made a mere stepping-stone for immigration to the United States, nor did they desire large numbers of immigrants from industrial centres of Europe. The class of settler they wanted was the uncontrolled individual who would stay on the land.

Mr. W. G. Raymond (Liberal, *Brantford*), alluding to the tariff question, said the Liberal Party believed in the middle course of a revenue tariff. Free trade was not in the field of practical politics. They must face the question of raising the revenues of the country and that was not possible to-day by means of free trade, whatever might be done in the future.

The Hon. R. J. Manion (Liberal-Conservative, *Fort William and Rainy River*) said that after all the abuse heaped upon the late Government during the elections he did not know of one change of policy made by the present Government. He agreed with Mr. Crerar that the type of immigrant they wanted was the one that would settle on the land, but he did not agree with him when he attributed the fact that during the last ten years there had been such an exodus from Canada to the United States to the protective policy which prevailed in the Dominion. Sir Clifford Sifton, an authority on the question, had said that the cause of the exodus was an inevitable drift to the south of that class of immigrant who could not " make good " in Canada and who sought a sunnier clime and a warmer sky, and of old people who could not stand the rigors of a Canadian winter.

There was another reason besides climate to explain why the United States had been built up so much more rapidly than Canada. A great many people went to the United States because they felt they were going to a Republican country which believed that all men were born free and equal. As a matter of fact the democracy in Canada was at least as high, if not higher, than the democracy in the United States, but the people in Europe did not know that.

Mr. O. Turgeon (Liberal, *Gloucester*) contended that the railways must be administered in a manner acceptable to the masses of the people. They could not continue to repeat the deficits of seventy millions or a hundred millions of dollars which had occurred during the last two or three years. It was only by the best possible method of operation that they could wipe out those deficits which threatened to ruin the people of Canada. If under Government ownership the railways proved a success and contributed to the prosperity of the country they could remain permanently the property of the Canadian people.

Cattle embargo.*

Mr. J. L. Brown (National Progressive, *Lisgar*) urged the necessity for the removal of the British embargo upon Canadian cattle. It was now recognised that there was no disease in Canada and the embargo was continued purely for the purpose of giving protection to British interests. Unfortunately there seemed to have grown up in Great Britain an impression that the official attitude of the Canadian Government towards the question was one of indifference. He was prepared to recognise that in any event this was a matter to be dealt with by the Imperial authorities. He was prepared to recognise also that they who had imposed protective tariffs against British goods were not in a very strong position to protest against Britain imposing protection. But it would be very unfortunate if they in Canada should in any measure countenance the impression that they were indifferent in the matter. Great uncertainty existed as to where the market for their live stock was going to be. They were not sure of the American market and they were not sure of the British market.

On 28th March, when the debate had occupied nine sittings of the House, the motion for an Address was agreed to.

---

* *Vide* also pp. 291 and 327.

CONFERENCE OF PRIME MINISTERS OF THE EMPIRE.

(Report of Proceedings; Status of the Dominion.)

On the motion for the adjournment of the House of Commons on 8th March,

The Right Hon. Arthur Meighen (Leader of the Opposition) said he thought the House would expect him to make to them at as early a date as possible a report of the part taken by himself and his colleagues as representing Canada at the recent Conference in Great Britain. He had been favoured with a complete report of the Conference proceedings, but it came to him marked " Secret " and of course it was in some degree necessarily of that character.

For the purpose of making the representation he would like to do it was essential that he should review his own position and to make that understandable the position taken by at least some of the other representatives on various matters of great consequence. He would not feel free to do that unless he had definite word as to what use he might make of the report that was to hand. He therefore asked the Prime Minister to communicate with the Prime Minister of Great Britain and secure as far as possible liberty for him (Mr. Meighen) to quote from the report of the Conference and secure as well a statement of such limitations and reservations, as the British Premier felt in the general interest should be imposed.

The Prime Minister (Hon. W. L. Mackenzie King) replied that he would be very pleased indeed to give consideration to the matter.

On 9th March the subject was again referred to in the House of Commons.

The Prime Minister laid on the Table of the House a copy of the proceedings of the Conference and intimated that on the arrival of a further supply of copies from England each Member would be furnished with a copy. The Leader of the Opposition had asked him to find out what part, if any, of the secret proceedings he would be at liberty to disclose. " A good deal has been said by my right hon. friend," the Prime Minister remarked, " in regard to the equality of status of the different countries comprising the British Empire. I would say that I see no necessity for our asking Great Britain what we may do in reference to any conference of Prime Ministers.

Basis of equality.

"As I look at the proceedings I find that representatives of Australia, New Zealand, South Africa, and India were present, and I should think there would be quite as much reason for communicating with Australia and South Africa as with Great Britain in regard to what part of the proceedings should be made public in this Parliament."

There was equal reason also, the Premier continued, to ask the Government of Canada what their view was as to the proceedings and what action should be taken with respect to regarding any part of them as private. This was a public document and the Leader of the Opposition or any other hon. Member was at liberty to quote any part of it. In regard to any proceedings that were secret, he had no doubt that his right hon. friend was a party to any arrangement as to the secrecy of the proceedings, and he must use his own judgment as to what he would disclose or withhold in regard to that part of the Conference.

Mr. Meighen: "It is true that all parties to the Conference had equal status, but my hon. friend must remember that the Conference was called by the British Government and that the Secretariat has issued the report thereon. It is, therefore, the right of the British Government to say to what extent the part taken by those representatives must be regarded as secret. I have asked my hon. friend to find that out; if he declines, he takes the responsibility."

The Prime Minister: "I wish to make my position perfectly clear. I simply take the ground that the Conference of Prime Ministers was a conference of the representatives of different countries, all of which were met on a basis of equality. For that reason I do not propose to return to the colonial status so far as this country is concerned by asking permission to quote from the report."

WASHINGTON CONFERENCE.

(Limitation of Armaments; Report on Conference.)

In the House of Commons on 9th March, the Prime Minister (Hon. W. L. Mackenzie King) laid on the Table copies of the Treaty concluded at the Conference on the Limitation of Armaments held at Washington and signed on behalf of Canada. He announced that a report on the Conference would be prepared by the Right Hon. Sir Robert Borden (who was Canada's representative at the Conference) and presented to Parliament in due course.

GERMAN REPARATIONS.

(Amount received by Canada.)

In reply to a question in the House of Commons on 27th March by Mr. Michaud (Liberal, *Restigouche and Madawaska*) as to the amount paid by Germany to the Allies up to the end of 1921 and the proportion of the sum paid to Canada,

The Secretary of State (Hon. A. B. Copp) said that Germany had paid to the Allies to 30th November, 1921, 6,424,000 gold marks ($1,528,912,000 par of exchange) in cash and by transfer of property; of this sum Great Britain had received 470,000,000 gold marks ($111,860,000 par of exchange) out of which £29,500,000 was paid over on account of the British claim for cost of Occupation up to 1st May, 1921.

The Canadian Government had received from the British Government $6,314,500 on account of the Canadian cost of the Army of Occupation. No further payment than this had been received.

NATIONAL DEFENCE BILL.

(Department of National Defence.)

On 24th March, in the House of Commons, the Minister of Militia and Defence (Hon. George P. Graham) introduced a National Defence Bill, which was passed by the House on 7th April.

The measure provides for the establishment of a Department of National Defence presided over by a Minister of the Crown. The Minister of National Defence will be charged with all matters relating to defence, including the Militia, the Military, Naval and Air Services of Canada.

A Deputy-Minister of National Defence is to be appointed by the Governor in Council, who may also, on the recommendation of the Minister of National Defence, appoint an officer to exercise the powers of the Deputy-Minister under the Naval Service Act, and another officer, known as Comptroller, to have charge of all financial matters pertaining to the Department.

Provision is made in the Bill for the necessary transfer to the Department of powers conferred by the Naval Service Act, the Militia Act, the Militia Pension Act, the Royal Military College Act, the Air Board Act, and other statutes.

The Bill further enacts that there shall be a Defence Council consisting of the Minister, the Deputy-Minister, the officer appointed to exercise the powers of the Deputy-Minister under the Naval Service Act, and four additional members appointed by the Governor in Council.

The Council is to advise the Minister on all matters of defence.

MILITARY SERVICE ACT REPEAL BILL.

This Bill was introduced in the House of Commons by Mr. James S. Woodsworth (Labour, *Winnipeg, Centre*) on 28th March and read a first time.

The object of the Bill is to repeal the Military Service Act, 1917, which established compulsory military service in the Dominion.

The Bill consists of a single clause providing that the " Act respecting Military Service " of 1917 (Chap. 19) is repealed.

IMMIGRATION ACT AMENDMENT BILL.

(Trial by Jury; etc.)

On 24th March, Mr. J. S. Woodsworth (Labour, *Winnipeg, Centre*) obtained the leave of the House of Commons to introduce a Bill to amend the Immigration Act. He said that in 1919 certain amendments were made to that Act which had the effect of depriving those who were not born in Canada of the right to trial by jury and made them subject to deportation without trial. The purpose of the Bill was to repeal those sections of the Act so that every man in the Dominion, whether a Canadian by birth or one who had lived in Canada, would be assured of the right of trial by jury.

CANADA'S SONS INCORPORATION BILL.

(Help for Canadian-born Men; British Connection; etc.)

A Bill to incorporate "Canada's Sons" was introduced by Mr. G. N. Gordon (Liberal, *Peterborough, W. Riding*) in the House of Commons on 21st March and read a first time.

The measure provides for the incorporation of a society under the name of " Canada's Sons," with the following objects :—

(A) To bring together all Canadian men, born in Canada, and their male descendants, for mutual benefit and support, and for the maintenance of the British connection.

(B) The development and maintenance throughout Canada of a thoroughly Canadian spirit.

(C) To assist in the general advancement of good government throughout Canada.

(D) The assisting of the Government and other authorities in the settling of immigrants according to the occupation for which they may be most fitted.

(E) The encouragement of the cultivation of the land, the development of natural resources, and the establishment of Canadian industries.

(F) The protection of forests, mines and resources, the teaching of immigrants in the art of clearing land, the prevention of forest fires, and other avoidable losses.

(G) The encouragement and helping of Canadian-born men to establish themselves in Canada and the stemming of the tide of emigration to other countries.

The society is to be governed and its affairs managed by a federal council.

ELECTION OF SPEAKER.

(British Practice Commended.)

The election of the Hon. Rodolphe Lemieux to the office of Speaker of the House of Commons took place on 8th March.

The Prime Minister (Hon. W. L. Mackenzie King) observed that the most venerable of the duties of the Speaker was that of being the channel of communication between the Commons and the Crown. " The relations between the Crown and the people were never happier than they are to-day," he continued, " whether this be said of His Majesty the King and British citizens throughout the globe, or of His Majesty's representative in Canada and the representatives of the Canadian people here assembled."

It had been more or less a tradition in that House that in successive Parliaments the Speakers should be chosen alternately from representatives of English and French origin. In the last Parliament the Speaker was of English descent. It was fitting therefore that on the present occasion they should select as Speaker one whose ancestry linked him with the great race who were the pioneers of early discovery and settlement in what was now their Canadian Dominion. Their practice had differed in an essential particular from that followed in the British House of Commons, where the Speaker, once elected, was honoured by being re-elected to the Chair at the beginning of every new Parliament so long as he remained a Member of the House of Commons. He thought they would do well to consider the obvious merit of the British practice.

After paying a warm tribute to the distinguished services Mr. Lemieux had rendered to his country, the Premier concluded by moving that he should take the Chair as Speaker.

Government and choice of Speaker.

The Right Hon. Arthur Meighen (Leader of the Opposition) endorsed the remarks of the Premier concerning the qualifications of Mr. Lemieux for the office. He went on to point out that in the British Parliament it was left to private Members to move and second the selection of a Speaker. In the Dominion Parliament they had not in that special regard followed the British practice. No one would deny that a Member acceptable to the Administration should be selected, but he denied the right of the Administration—the right of the

Prime Minister—to announce to that House and to the country in advance whom they should select as Speaker. It was the Prime Minister's function to choose his Ministers; it was not his function to choose or announce a Speaker.

The Hon. T. A. Crerar (Leader of the National Progressive Party) agreed entirely with the observation that the British practice, whereby the Speakership of the House of Commons did not change with the election of a new Parliament, might well be introduced into their assembly.

The Clerk of the House declared the motion carried *nemine contradicente*. Thereafter, Mr. Lemieux was conducted to the Speaker's Chair by the Prime Minister and the Hon. W. S. Fielding (Liberal, *Shelburne and Queen's*).

The Speaker thanked the House in a brief speech for the high honour they had unanimously conferred upon him. It would be his endeavour, above all, to maintain that freedom of speech and that dignity and decorum in debate which had come down to them through precedent and precedent from the Mother of Parliaments—the British House of Commons.

On 9th March the Speaker and Members of the House of Commons proceeded to the Senate Chamber. The Speaker made the usual formal claim for the privileges of the Commons which were confirmed to them by the Governor-General.

SUPPLY: AN INTERIM VOTE

On 27th March the House of Commons went into Committee of Supply, when

The Minister of Finance (Hon. W. S. Fielding) moved that a sum not exceeding $76,499,371 being one-fourth of the amount of the main Estimates for the year, should be voted on account.

The Right Hon. Arthur Meighen (Leader of the Opposition) said the Government had sought to convey the impression that the axe had been unmercifully wielded and that as a consequence of their economy the people were going to save all sorts of money in taxation. The fact of the matter was that, notwithstanding that all War services were necessarily contracting, they were asked to vote main Estimates amounting, he did not doubt, to $50,000,000 more than the whole expenditure of last year. Comparing the main Estimates with those for last year there was a difference of $113,000,000. Of that reduction $81,000,000 was made up of advances necessarily made last year on account of the Canadian national railway betterments, because the Government had just taken over one great system and had to vote $89,000,000 to put it in shape. Those advances were not needed this year, because the railways had been put into the condition which was necessary in order that the people might get from the system the service to which they were entitled.

Reductions in the Votes for the Soldier Settlement Board, Soldiers' Civil Re-establishment, and the Housing Appropriation, none of them a matter of economy, accounted with the Railways for $111,660,000 of the $113,626,000 reduction. The shipbuilding programme brought down in 1919, and never added to since, was completed within a few dollars. The ships were built and the money did not need to be spent over again. That accounted for $10,000,000 odd. Therefore, aside from those items, to which the word " economy " had no application whatever, the Government was $8,000,000 over the Estimates of last year, and was approximating $50,000,000 over the expenditure of last year all told.

The Minister of Finance said the Government had made no boast of economy and Mr. Meighen was alarmed that the people might on their own account see that there was economy.

After other speeches it was agreed that the resolution should stand over for further consideration.

CASH GRANTS TO RETURNED SOLDIERS.

(Resolution proposed amounting to " Want of Confidence.")

On 28th March, in the House of Commons, on the motion that the Speaker leave the Chair for the House to resolve itself into Committee of Supply,

Mr. James Arthurs (Liberal-Conservative, *Parry Sound*) moved a resolution in amendment to Supply, which dealt with the Liberal policy relating to cash grants to returned soldiers, and was treated as a motion of want of confidence in the Government. The division therefore involved the first test of strength in the new Parliament.

The amendment moved by Mr. Arthurs set out the resolution of the Liberal Party Convention of August, 1919, declaring that the system of cash grants to soldiers and their dependants was the most effective means of civil re-establishment (such grants to be in addition to present gratuity and to any pension for disability resulting from service) and proceeded to point out that the pledge embodied in the resolution was declared to be the policy of the Liberal Party and used widely in the late Election.

The amendment then affirmed that the Liberal Party having been returned to power, the refusal by the Government to fulfil such pledge constituted a repudiation of a solemn obligation and a disregard of political honour.

This was seconded by the Hon. H. H. Stevens (Liberal-Conservative, *Vancouver, Centre*), and after discussion* was rejected on a division by 126 votes to 42, the National Progressive Party voting with the Government.

* It is hoped to find room for some account of this Debate in the next number of the JOURNAL.

COLD STORAGE WAREHOUSE ACT (AMENDMENT) BILL.

(Protection of Public Health.)

A Bill to amend the Cold Storage Warehouse Act was introduced in the Senate on 17th March by Senator the Hon. G. H. Bradbury and was read a first time.

The Bill forbids the placing in cold storage of any article of food which is tainted or otherwise unfit for human consumption.

Articles of food are not to be returned to cold storage, after being taken out, except under conditions specified by regulation.

The maximum period of storage is specified in the Bill, though it may be extended if there is no risk of the food becoming unfit for human consumption. The prescribed periods are :—

Bacon (cured)	Not longer than 12	months.
Beef (fresh)	,, ,, ,, 8	,,
,, (salted or cured)	,, ,, ,, 12	,,
Butter	,, ,, ,, 11	,,
Eggs (April and May)	,, ,, ,, 2	,,
,, (other months)	,, ,, ,, 8	,,
Fish (not for export)	,, ,, ,, 3	,,
,, (frozen, for export only) ..	,, ,, ,, 9	,,
Hams (cured or smoked)	,, ,, ,, 12	,,
Lamb	,, ,, ,, 9	,,
Pork (fresh)	,, ,, ,, 6	,,
Veal	,, ,, ,, 4	,,
Mutton	,, ,, ,, 9	,,
Poultry (Oct., Nov., and Dec.) ..	,, ,, ,, 3	,,
,, (Feb., Mar., and April) ..	,, ,, ,, 9	,,

IN THE SENATE.

On 17th March,

Senator the Hon. G. H. Bradbury, in introducing the Bill, said that its purpose was to deal with two important matters that were within the jurisdiction of the Dominion Parliament, namely—health, and trade and commerce.

The Bill was intended, in the first place, to protect the lives and health of the public by preventing cold-storage warehouses from holding foodstuffs until they became unfit for human consumption; and secondly, to prevent the waste of foodstuffs. He pointed out that tons of precious food were destroyed annually by cold-storage warehouses, either because it had been held too long or because of faulty storage.

The third purpose of the Bill was to restore trade to its proper channels in order to bring producer and consumer more closely together.

AUSTRALIA.

Commonwealth Parliament.

The following Summary is in continuation of the proceedings of the First Session of the Eighth Parliament, which commenced on 26*th February,* 1920, *and concluded on* 10*th December,* 1921. *It has been announced that the Second Session will commence on* 17*th May,* 1922.

WASHINGTON CONFERENCE.

(Senate Resolution: Commonwealth Representation.)

On 3rd November, 1921, in the Senate,

Senator T. J. K. Bakhap (*Tas.*) submitted a motion in the Senate in appreciation of the action of the United States of America in convening the Conference to discuss the question of International Disarmament and matters pertaining to the Pacific Ocean, and as to the attitude of the Australian Senate in the matter.* The motion, which was resolved in the affirmative on 23rd November, reads as follows:—

> That the Senate of the Parliament of the Commonwealth of Australia notes with warm appreciation the action of the Government of the United States of America in convening a Conference to discuss the question of International Disarmament and the problems affecting nations with territories which bound or are included in the waters of the Pacific Ocean, and expresses the most fraternal feelings towards the President, Congress and the people of the United States, and full friendship for all nations which are to be represented at the Conference.
>
> That, while observing that representation at the Conference as a deliberate entity has not been accorded to the Australian Commonwealth, the Senate declares its keen and full consciousness of the fact that the interest of Australia in the questions to be discussed at the Conference, particularly those affecting lands south of the Equator, is not inferior in degree and importance to that of any nation which will be represented by a special delegation.
>
> That the Senate will carefully consider the results of the deliberations of the Conference, and, if it deems any action indicated by the participants at the Conference as conducive to the attainment of the great objectives of world peace and more friendly international intercourse, will accord its full support.

MANDATED TERRITORIES IN PACIFIC.†

(Question of control by United States.)

On 23rd November,

Senator P. J. Lynch submitted a motion in the Senate

* *Vide* also the JOURNAL, Vol. III., No. 1, p. 104.

† For debate as to the acceptance of the Mandate, *vide* summary on Commonwealth New Guinea Act, JOURNAL, Vol. II., No. 1, p. 113.

to the effect that the United States of America should be invited to take over the Mandate of the Pacific Islands from Australia. The motion, which was subsequently withdrawn by leave, read as follows:—

> That, in view of the great area comprised in the Commonwealth and its Dependencies, and the need for constant, undivided and economical attention to its administrative needs, the Senate is of opinion—
>
> That further responsibility for the mandated control of those peoples in the Pacific constitutes an undue strain on our limited resources in properly ministering to communities so far afield.
>
> That, in view of the expressed desire of the United States to act as a Mandatory Power in respect to certain of the Pacific Islands and its special fitness for that office, the Government of that country might be invited to accept responsibility for the whole or part of the Territories now under Commonwealth guardianship.
>
> That the Government be asked to concur in this opinion, and, if concurring, to request Senator Pearce at Washington to give effect to its decision.

DEBATE IN THE SENATE.

Senator Lynch (*W.A.*) in submitting the above motion, said that Australia was of such immense area and required such close attention, in a legislative sense, in order to insure the greatest prosperity for its citizens, that they could not then afford to widen their administrative activities to such an extent as the care of the Mandated Territories would involve. The reason he had not mentioned the Mother Country in the motion was because he felt confident that the question of whether Great Britain rather than the Commonwealth could take charge of those Territories must have been threshed out at the Peace Conference at Versailles. The Mother Country being already overloaded with responsibilities in every part of the globe could not, in the nature of things, accept any further burdens. Australia had a big enough contract in hand in husbanding its own resources and concentrating its attention on that island continent of 3,000,000 square miles without embarking on a scheme of such dimensions as the control of the Mandated Territories. When they realised that they had added to their responsibilities an area equalling one-sixth the territory of the Commonwealth, some idea of the magnitude of the task before them would be gained.

As to the suitability of the United States for the responsibility of the Pacific Islands, all he could say was that it was a white democracy like their own, governed by a Constitution almost identical with theirs, because theirs was modelled on the same lines, and lastly, the people of the United States were largely from British stock. In the main the Republic was distinctly Anglo-Celtic in origin. So was Australia. If they wanted a powerful, friendly neighbour how could they better the position ? If they could get the United States to assume control, it would be a step in the direction of giving Australia a great and friendly neighbour, as well as assuring prosperity and progress to the Territory.

The Minister for Repatriation (Senator the Hon. E. D. Millen), in reply, said he felt it necessary to point out that there were to his mind very fatal objections to the course proposed. First of all, it was a complete reversal of the attitude taken up by that Chamber on three distinct occasions. He ventured to say also that if the motion were carried it would come somewhat as a shock to the people of Australia. When they found themselves participants in the recently concluded Great War, the one idea that he thought was in the minds of most people, so far as these islands were concerned, was that they should seek to obtain them, not as additions to their already broad area, but as additional measures of security. Particularly was the possession of them desired as a means of securing what they knew was their national policy. Australia, surely, had been under no illusion as to what the acceptance of the responsibility would mean. She must have known that she could not take these islands without considerable thought and trouble and possibly great expense ; but as against that she had seen very clearly that they were essential to her safety. He would remind the Chamber that part of his mission to the League of Nations Assembly at Geneva* had been to try to obtain possession of the Mandate for these islands.

Senator Lynch had suggested that America should take over the islands. Honolulu had been taken over by America. Looking into the facts of Honolulu to-day, he (Senator Millen) was not able to discover much assurance there regarding their national policy. As against a total of 186,000 Asiatics in Honolulu, there was a total population of Americans, British, Germans and Russians of only 25,000. The population had increased by 37,908, or 24 per cent., since 1900. He ventured to say that did not offer a very reassuring picture to the people of Australia. America had put forward, not through an irresponsible journal, or out of the mouth of an individual statesman, but in a formal manner, the demand that all Mandated Territories should be open to any member of the

* *Vide* JOURNAL, Vol. II., No. 3, p. 621.

League of Nations. She had made that demand with regard to Mesopotamia in the first instance; but she did not limit it to Mesopotamia. She had put it forward as a principle to apply to all Mandates. She still stood to that principle, and it seemed to him that she was likely to continue to do so. It meant that if she took over those islands and maintained the policy of the "open door" they should have reproduced the position in Honolulu. Some mighty change would have to come over the people of Australia before they would willingly agree to a proposition of that kind. America had not only not asked for a Mandate; she had flatly refused one. Even if America were willing to accept a Mandate, it was not a matter for traffic between Australia, America and any other country as to what became of these islands. They were surrendered to the Allied and Associated Powers, and from them, through the Council of the League of Nations, Australia received a Mandate. If they contemplated surrendering these islands, they could only surrender the Mandate to those from whom it was received. If the Mandate went back to the League, the League would look for some other Mandatory Power. He wanted to remind the Chamber that Germany was still a claimant for the Mandate for these islands. She had addressed a memorial to the League claiming that these Mandates ought not to be issued until she became a member of the League, so that she might be an applicant for them. When the League, at Geneva, declined to assent or wait, Germany wrote saying that in no sense did she surrender her claim, and that in due time—her own good time—she would renew the application. Since then the feeling against Germany had not intensified. If Australia surrendered these islands, and said that it would no longer accept responsibility for them, it must surrender them to the League. If Germany's claim was then again pressed forward, there would be a strong danger that Germany would be given the Mandate. The Mandate might possibly be given to the adjoining Mandatory Power, namely, Japan. Japan held adjacent islands a few miles away, and it was quite conceivable that she might be a claimant for the Mandate, or some other country that did not understand or appreciate their "White Australia" policy. Apart from the impracticable nature of the second paragraph of Senator Lynch's motion, the proposal would constitute such a vital danger and be so inimical to the interests of the Commonwealth, that he (Senator Millen) trusted that the Senate would find no difficulty in rejecting the motion.

Senator Lynch thereupon asked leave and withdrew the motion.

SETTLEMENT OF IRISH QUESTION.

(Senate Resolution.)

On 8th December,

Senator P. J. Lynch (*W.A.*) moved a Resolution in the Senate in approval of the settlement of the Irish question. The Resolution, which was carried, read as follows :—

That the Senate desires to convey to the British Prime Minister (Mr. Lloyd George) its fervent feeling of gratitude and appreciation for his crowning act of statesmanship in reconciling the interests of the Irish people with those of the other communities within the Empire, and thus bringing to an end a long and bitter estrangement.

That the Senate further desires to have conveyed to the leaders of the Convention, through Mr. Lloyd George, its warm greetings on the accomplishment of such a happy understanding, and sincerely trusts that the harmony and goodwill that have always prevailed amongst the sons of England, Ireland, Scotland and Wales in the flourishing Commonwealths overseas will be fully manifested under the new order of things in their ancient homes for the enduring peace and prosperity of the people of the Motherland of these Commonwealths.

IMPERIAL COMMUNICATIONS.

(Wireless Agreement: Direct Communication with Great Britain.)

On 7th December, in the House of Representatives, the Prime Minister moved that the Agreement proposed to be made between the Commonwealth and the Amalgamated Wireless (Australasia) Limited be approved and executed. The main proposals in the draft Agreement, as laid upon the table in the House, were as follow :—

The Company shall increase its capital to £1,000,000,* divided into 1,000,000 shares of £1 each, and shall allot 500,001 shares to the Commonwealth, which shall at all times hold a majority in number and value of the shares. Three-sevenths of the total number of the Directors of the Company shall be nominated by the Commonwealth, such Directors to hold office subject to the pleasure of the Commonwealth.

The Company shall forthwith proceed with the development of wireless services for communication within the Commonwealth and its territories, and for communication with the countries overseas, and in particular will undertake the following programme :—

(A) To construct, maintain and operate in Australia the necessary stations and equipment for a direct commercial Wireless Service between Australia and the United Kingdom ; to arrange for the operation of suitable corresponding stations in the United

---

*In reply to a question, Mr. Hughes said he believed the present subscribed capital of the Company was £200,000.

Kingdom; to provide the main trunk stations in Australia and the United Kingdom; and to arrange that the rates to be charged for messages between Australia and the United Kingdom shall not exceed the following:—Full-rate messages, 2s. per word: Deferred messages, 1s. per word: Week-end messages, 6d. per word (minimum, 10s. per message): Government messages, 1s. per word: Press messages, 5d. per word: and Deferred Press messages, 3d. per word.

(B) To provide and operate feeder stations for wireless connection between the high-power stations and the capital cities of all the States, and equip feeder stations to provide communication with merchant ships around the Australian coast.

(C) To arrange for the erection and operation of a station in Canada capable of commercial communication with Australia and so equipped as to distribute traffic throughout North America.

The Company shall not take any action relating to or affecting the policy of the Commonwealth in Naval, Military or External affairs; or to any proposed sale of the Company's business; or to any change in the status or constitution of the Company without the consent of the Commonwealth. In time of public danger the Company if required shall hand over to the Commonwealth the control of its stations, apparatus and services, etc.

The Company shall not become a party to any commercial trust or combine, and shall always remain an independent British business. It shall also give preference to goods manufactured in the Commonwealth when purchasing plant and supplies.

The Commonwealth shall grant to the Company, free of charge, all permits and licences necessary for the realisation of these objects and for the full development of the industry, and so long as the Agreement is in force will not impose any restrictions on the Company calculated to obstruct its business.

DEBATE IN HOUSE OF REPRESENTATIVES.

The Prime Minister (the Right Hon. W. M. Hughes) said it would be recalled that there were two schemes before the Imperial Conference, one the Norman system of relays, and the other the scheme before them, which was a system of direct communication between Australia and Britain and every part of the civilised world. The Norman system provided for stations at Oxford, Cairo, Poona, Singapore, Hong Kong and Australia, and to cover South Africa from Nairobi and Wyndhoek. The estimated cost of the Norman scheme was £1,243,000; Australia's share of the initial cost, £185,000; the annual charge for Australia, £60,000; the estimated revenue, £40,000; and the annual loss, £20,000. The objections to this scheme, other than financial, were fairly obvious. They would get direct communication with Hong Kong only under special atmospheric conditions. The messages were sent in relays and necessarily the outlying stations, of which Australia was the most remote, would be delayed by any congestion at intermediate stations. They wished to advertise Australia in the East and America, and, above all, to have direct communication with Great Britain. The Norman scheme would not enable them to communicate direct with Canada, South Africa or England. The Commonwealth was losing nearly £60,000 per annum on its present system of wireless. Under the Norman scheme it was proposed to add £20,000 to that, making a net loss of £80,000 per annum. It had been alleged by the Norman Committee that because the relays extended only over 2,000 miles, that scheme could be relied on; but there was proof positive that it was possible to send messages from England, America or France direct to Australia. The Norman scheme would be controlled wholly by the Governments of Great Britain and the various Dominions, and it would be run by the Postal Department. Those hon. Members who had expressed grave doubts as to the wisdom of governmental enterprise might now be able to couch a lance in favour of it but on this occasion he was to be counted on the other side. If they wanted an efficient system of wireless they must look for it in quarters where they should have at their disposal men with scientific training and business capacity, and where they had control of those patents and apparati without which it was impossible to be successful.

Dealing with the proposed Agreement in detail, Mr. Hughes said that the shareholders of the Amalgamated Wireless Company were mainly Australians, and the Company was operating at a profit. It had the Australian rights of all Marconi patents. The Commonwealth would take £500,001 worth of the shares, and would have a proportionate amount of control. In order to control a specialised business of this character they must have trained men. That being so, a majority of the Directors were to be nominated by shareholders other than the Commonwealth Government.

He also wished to refer to a third offer—that by the Radio Communication Company, Limited, which offered to form a company with a capital of £700,000 to erect, equip and operate a high-power station capable of direct communication with Great Britain. He would point out, however, that the Company was not able to guarantee to Australia a high-power station in Great Britain. For all practical purposes, therefore, that proposal must be ignored.

At the Imperial Conference, Mr. Lloyd George had agreed that Australia should have the right to choose either of the two first indicated schemes. There was no doubt but that either of them would be given the support of the British Government. Australia, because of its remoteness, needed advertising, and above all they should have some sure and effective medium, which no one could touch or break, of contact with the Mother Country.

Mr. Matthew Charlton (Leader of the Opposition) said he agreed with the Prime Minister with regard to discarding the Norman scheme, which was not satisfactory and could not be compared with the scheme recommended by the Prime Minister. An argument for the adoption of the proposal of the Government was the fact that the Company with which they wished to make the agreement was an Australian company. As the Commonwealth would provide more capital than the Company, it should have a controlling interest in the concern. Only three-sevenths of the directorate was to be nominated by and to represent the Commonwealth, and holders of shares allotted to the Commonwealth would not be entitled to vote in respect of the election or removal of directors. Were they justified in giving control of the concern to the existing Company? The Prime Minister had alluded lightly to the proposal of the Radio Communication Company. Under that proposition the Commonwealth would not be called upon to provide more than £350,000, so that if the offer should prove satisfactory it would lead to a saving of £150,000 to the Commonwealth. They could not turn down such a proposition without giving it consideration. They were not justified in agreeing to commit the Commonwealth to an expenditure of £500,000 in connection with any offer under any agreement which on the face of it was far from satisfactory. He moved that the whole question of wireless be referred to a Committee of the House for investigation and report.

Dr. Earle Page (Leader of the Country Party) said that a proposition that would really have more support from him was one that would not bring the Government into the business at all, but would permit all wireless communication, under proper guarantees and safeguards, to be in the hands of private enterprise. Wireless development was controlled, to a large extent, by patent rights, and he thought that they were wise in getting in touch with a Company that was in a position to acquire and use these rights in the freest possible way. The Norman proposal was not worth considering alongside that of the Amalgamated Wireless (Australasia), Limited, which was one that deserved favourable consideration. The question was whether there should be an arrangement by which the Commonwealth became a partner, or whether the Company should be permitted to undertake the work itself. Australia was remote from other parts of the world, and it was essential that they should take action before all the big wave lengths were commandeered by other countries. He would be sorry to be the cause of any long delay but, in his opinion, the matter required more consideration.

Agreement referred to Committee.

The motion was subsequently amended to provide for the execution of the Agreement subject to investigation and approval, with such alterations as they deemed necessary, of a Committee consisting of six Members of the House and three Members of the Senate.

(*Cable advice received on 28th March stated that the Committee had unanimously approved of the Agreement with minor amendments, details of which are not yet to hand.*)

EMPIRE AIRSHIP SERVICE.

(Co-operation between Great Britain and Dominions.)

On 8th December, in the House of Representatives, the Prime Minister submitted a motion, which was carried, urging the extension of the period for consideration of proposals which arose out of a decision of the last Imperial Conference for co-operation between Great Britain and the Dominions in a scheme for the establishment of an experimental Airship Service.

IN THE HOUSE OF REPRESENTATIVES.

The Prime Minister (the Right Hon. W. M. Hughes), in moving the following Resolution,

> "That this House, recognising the vital importance to the British Empire of Aerial Communication, views with concern the prospect of abandonment of proposals for the establishment of an Imperial Airship Service, and expresses the earnest hope that the period during which the airships and other existing material will be available will be extended, in order that the Parliament may have an opportunity of discussing the proposal for co-operating with Great Britain and the Dominions in a scheme for the establishment of an experimental two-years' service,"

said that on his return from England after the last Imperial Conference he had pointed out that the British Government had a fleet of airships which it was willing to place at the disposal of the Dominions if they would agree to co-operate in a scheme for the maintenance of aerial communication between the various parts of the Empire. A Committee of the Imperial Conference, joined with experts—airship and aeroplane,—had made a careful investigation of the matter, and had submitted a report which covered a period of two years of experimental operations, which could be conducted, speaking from memory, for £1,200,000, of which Australia's share would be about £200,000. A decision in regard to the Imperial Government's offer was urgent, because, unless the offer was accepted the airships that were available for the experiment would be scrapped after 31st December. These vessels cost to produce £40,000,000. That, of course, was not the value of the airships themselves, but covered the whole organisation, for which there were only these airships to be seen. Workshops, hangars, the provision of spares, and the making of arrangements of all sorts, had involved the British Government in the expenditure of that colossal sum of money. This was the only fleet of airships in the world. There were no means of speedier communication with Europe than through the air. They might increase the rate of progress over the sea, but the increase would be slow, and, at most, the journey was not likely to be cut down by more than four or five days. As a matter of fact, it took as long to travel to England now as it did thirty years ago. Realising that time did not permit the discussion of the proposal that the circumstances warranted, he asked the House to agree to the above motion. The carrying of the motion would enable him to ask the British Government to extend the period during which these airships would be available.

Mr. Matthew Charlton (Leader of the Opposition) said it was a subject which should be debated by Parliament, and he was pleased that the Prime Minister had recognised that the circumstances were not opportune for the discussion. He did not think that anyone could take exception to the motion. It did not bind them to anything. It left the subject open to discussion, and to that he had no objection. Aerial navigation was a big project.

IN THE SENATE.

On the 10th December, a Resolution in the same terms as that introduced in the House of Representatives was passed by the Senate.

AIR SERVICES.

On 2nd December, discussing a proposed Vote of £100,000 for Air Services,

Mr. Matthew Charlton (Leader of the Opposition) said that he did not know why the Committee should be asked to vote this large sum, in addition to the £300,000 they had already voted on the Works estimates. It would be noted that the proposed vote for Civil Aviation was £28,794, and for Military Aviation £71,406. He had no objection to civil aerial services, but he took strong exception to the establishment of a new branch of the defence system.

He realised, however, that it was not much use asking for a reduction of the Vote, unless the Government were prepared to make it. He made this protest because he did not wish to be held in any way responsible when this branch of the Service grew large in the future. He ventured to say that within two or three years' time the amount involved would be £1,000,000.

The Assistant Minister for Defence (Hon. Sir Granville Ryrie) said that he hoped that the Committee would not make any reduction in the Air Forces Vote, which was comparatively small. The estimate for this year was £100,000, whereas for 1920-21 it was £305,000.

Mr. Charlton: " Of which only £62,000 was spent."

The Assistant Minister for Defence: " At all events, it must have been contemplated that there would be a large expenditure on the Air Force in connection with civil aviation." The Government and, he believed, every Member, were favourably disposed towards spending a considerable amount in the encouragement of civil aviation. The Government had authorised an Aerial Mail service from Geraldton to Derby, in Western Australia, a distance of some 800 odd miles, at a cost of £25,000 a year, by way of subsidy. Tenders had also been accepted for aerial mail services between Brisbane and Sydney, and Sydney and Adelaide, while tenders had been called for another service from Charleville to Cloncurry.

The proposed Vote was agreed to.

DEFENCE ESTIMATES.

The following is in conclusion of the summary commenced in the last number of the Journal (*vide* Vol. III., No. 1, page 127). The necessary Parliamentary Reports which are now available show that the Defence estimates have been reduced by £500,000 as promised by the Government. The reductions are :—Military Works, £250,000 ; Naval Works, £80,000 ; Air Works, £100,000 ; and Defence Department, £70,000. This leaves the several Votes as follow :—Military Works, £884,251 ; Naval Works, £419,000 ; Air Works, £300,000 ; Defence Department, £1,623,000 ; Navy Department, £2,340,438 ; and Air Services, £100,000.

DEBATE IN HOUSE OF REPRESENTATIVES.

Compulsory Military Training.

Mr. Matthew Charlton (Leader of the Opposition) on 1st December, during the discussion in Committee of the proposed Vote of £434,302 for universal military training, which was ultimately reduced by £70,000, moved that the whole Vote be left out. Last year, he said, £191,950 had been spent upon universal military training.* This year more than double that sum was sought to be devoted to the same purpose. There might be some Members who were not prepared to authorise the complete cessation of military training. But, in view of the speeches which had been delivered that day in advocacy of the practice of economy in every direction, they should move—in the event of his amendment being unsuccessful—that the amount proposed to be spent upon universal military training be reduced to the equivalent of the sum expended last year. He had directed his efforts in the direction of the inauguration of universal military training; but, in the light of the lessons learned during the War, he was convinced that the time had arrived when all the money proposed to be spent upon teaching the arts of warfare should be saved. The War had very quickly shown that those Australians who had enlisted without previous training could rapidly be turned into as good and efficient soldiers as those who had received training. Methods of warfare to-day were constantly changing. No one had anticipated, in 1914, that the War would have been conducted as it was. Such of their men who had received previous training had to be taught afresh, on the other side of the world, before going to the Front. Australians were very apt, and only a brief period was required to bring their Forces up to a state of modern efficiency.

The Assistant Minister for Defence (Hon. Sir Granville Ryrie): "They were always mixed with trained men, which made all the difference."

Mr. Charlton: "From all I have learned such is not the case."

Hon. J. M. Fowler (Nationalist, *Perth, W.A.*): "Responsible officers have declared that they preferred to handle untrained men."

Mr. G. J. Bell (Nationalist, *Darwin, Tas.*): "Nothing that was taught in Australia had to be unlearned abroad."

Mr. Charlton: "I have not said anything contrary to that view." Apart from that aspect of the question, were they justified in increasing expenditure on defence at the present juncture? The hon. Member for Balaclava (the Right Hon. W. A. Watt), and the Leader of the Country Party (Dr. Earle Page), and other hon. Members, had argued that the Defence expenditure should be curtailed. In face of that, were they going to jump from £191,950 to £434,302 of expenditure upon this particular service? If they had

---

* An outline of the Australian system of Compulsory Military Training will be found in the JOURNAL, Vol. II., No. 1, p. 131.

been able to carry on for the last few years with a much less expenditure than that proposed, there was no excuse for not cutting down the Vote. He did not desire to leave his views in any doubt. He was against expenditure on Defence, and the time had arrived when they could at least cut it down. If the attempts that were being made to bring about a better understanding between the Nations of the world did not happily succeed, and if the country found itself embroiled in war, he felt certain that the Australian people would give a good account of themselves in defending those shores, irrespective of whether they had any compulsory military training or not. If they were to continue piling up additional expenditure in that direction there would be no hope for that country financing necessary works in the near future.

Dr. Earle Page (Leader of the Country Party) said that although he was in favour of universal military training, he thought very strong arguments could be advanced in support of commencing the training of their young men at an older age. If the training were begun at eighteen, instead of fourteen years of age, an expenditure of nearly £126,000, which was set down in the estimates for the provision of Senior Cadet uniforms, could be saved. Without putting many people out of work, and without seriously interfering with the defence of the country, a saving could be made almost approximate to the amount previously suggested.

Mr. Charlton's amendment was negatived by 39 votes to 14. An amendment proposed by the Government for the reduction of the Vote by £70,000 was carried.

FUNDING ARRANGEMENTS ACT.

(War Indebtedness.)

This Act, which was assented to 15th December, approves the Agreement made between the Government of the United Kingdom and that of the Commonwealth of Australia in relation to the repayment of the War Indebtedness of the Commonwealth, viz., £92,480,157 (*vide* JOURNAL, Vol. III., No. 1, p. 138).

AUSTRALIAN SOLDIERS' REPATRIATION ACT.

(War Pensions Extension.)

This Act was assented to 17th December. It amends Section 23 of the principal Act so as to provide for the payment of pensions in the case of death or incapacity arising from latent diseases or constitutional defects which were not manifest before the soldiers were sent abroad, subject to the men having served in camp in Australia for at least six months or embarked for active service with the Forces overseas. Pensions were formerly confined to cases in which it was clearly established that the injuries had arisen as a direct result of the War.

The actual provision is as follows :—

Notwithstanding that the origin of the cause of the death or incapacity of a member of the Forces, who, after enlistment with those Forces, served in camp in Australia for at least six months or embarked for active service with those Forces overseas, existed prior to his enlistment, where, in the opinion of a Board—

(A) the conditions of his War service contributed to any material degree to the death or incapacity of the member ; and

(B) neither the death or incapacity, nor the origin of the cause of the death or incapacity, was due to the default or wilful act of the member, the Commonwealth shall, subject to this Act, be liable to pay to the member or his dependants, or both, as the case may be, pensions in accordance with this Act :

provided that no pension shall be payable under this sub-section except in pursuance of a claim made within six months after the commencement of this sub-section.

PARLIAMENTARY ALLOWANCES.

(Proposed Reduction in Payment of Members.)

On 9th December, in the House of Representatives, Dr. Earle Page submitted the following motion :—

That this House is of the opinion that

(1) the Ministers of State Act, 1917, and the Parliamentary Allowances Act, 1920, should be amended so as to reduce the salary of each Minister of State and the allowance of each Senator and Member of the House of Representatives by the sum of £200 ; and

(2) the Government be instructed to forthwith bring in Bills to give effect to this resolution.

DEBATE IN HOUSE OF REPRESENTATIVES.

Dr. Earle Page (Leader of the Country Party) in submitting the above, said his proposal should form part of a general scheme of economy. He did not move the motion because he thought the allowance to Members of that Parliament was excessive, but because of the slump in the national income and the altered position of the country's affairs since the allowance was increased. It was incumbent on Members to take the lead in a movement for national economy. He had supported the measure which increased the allowance to Members, and because he did not withdraw from the opinions he then expressed, he quoted from the official report of his speech in favour of the increase. He disagreed with the contention that Parliament had no right to fix allowances of Members.

Continuing, Dr. Earle Page said that under present conditions, with the prices of primary products falling rapidly, it was the duty and privilege of Members to give the public a lead in economy by reducing their salaries. He hoped the House would agree to his motion and give a lead to the whole continent.

Mr. Matthew Charlton (Leader of the Opposition) said he was glad that Dr. Earle Page did not question the right of Parliament to fix the remuneration of Members. Persons outside, who had represented their action in increasing the allowance last year to be on a par with the conduct of a burglar, lost sight of the fact that the Constitution empowered Parliament to deal with remuneration.

"Are we," Mr. Charlton asked, "as representatives of the people, worth a salary of £1,000 per annum? . . . Whenever that question has been put to me, I have answered it in the affirmative. When I have been asked whether I am getting a fair remuneration for my services to the country, I have always replied 'No.' . . . Are men not deserving of an adequate salary who hold high and responsible positions . . . who are, in effect, the directors of the affairs of the Commonwealth, and have been chosen by the electors themselves?"

Continuing, Mr. Charlton asked what was the idea that permeated the criticism? It was that they received a net income of £1,000 per annum. They received nothing like that. Deduct the expense of maintaining two homes, the cost of fighting elections, the loss of six weeks' pay at election time and contributions to charities, and more than half the salary was gone. The increase of salaries by £400 per annum distributed over Australia's population of 5,000,000 cost the people less than 2d. per head per annum.

The Hon. W. G. Higgs (Nationalist, *Capricornia, Q.*) said they were told they did not consult the electors before increasing Members' salaries. But they did not consult electors when they fixed the salaries of Justices of the High Court at £3,500 a year. He submitted a statement to the House showing the area of each electoral division and the distance from Melbourne of the chief polling place.

Continuing, Mr. Higgs said: "Members of Parliament make the Commonwealth Laws. Commonwealth Judges Administer them. Members of Parliament who make the laws get £1,000 a year and no allowance for hotel expenses when travelling.

"The Judges who administer the laws receive the following :

Chief Justice	..	£3,500	And up to £4 4s. a day hotel expenses for himself and Associate, and railway, coach and steamer fares when away from home. . . . . . .
Other Judges	..	£3,000	

. . . Members of Parliament fixed the salaries and appointed the Judges for life. Members of Parliament have to go up for election every two or three years and have no fixity of tenure. We could have fixed our salaries at the same amount as that paid the Judges . . . but we did not do so, believing £1,000 was a just and liberal allowance."

In conclusion, Mr. Higgs urged that the sum now being paid to Members should be retained.

The Prime Minister (the Right Hon. W. M. Hughes) expressed his regret at being unable to support the motion, and he said without hesitation that the salaries paid to Members of the Commonwealth Government were inadequate. "Unless we are prepared," said the Prime Minister, "to deliberately shut the door of this Legislature against ability, and to uphold the view that only those who cannot find scope for their talents outside may enter here . . . we should at least adhere to the present payment of Members. . . . Here is a country, the home of a democratic community, of a people who make the laws under which they live, and by which they are conditioned. If, for the future, those laws are to be made by low-priced labour . . . we shall be damning Democracy as effectively as by way of the sword and revolution."

Mr. J. M. Gabb (Labour, *Angas, S.A.*) moved an amendment that the figures "200" be left out and "400" inserted in lieu thereof, explaining that if this was agreed to, the allowance paid to Members would be brought back to £600 per annum.

This was seconded by **Mr. G. A. Maxwell (Nationalist,** *Fawkner, Vic.*), and on a division Mr. Gabb's amendment was lost by 44 votes to 18.

Dr. Earle Page's motion was then put, and on a division was rejected by 40 votes to 21.

PATENTS (AMENDMENT) ACT.

This Act was assented to 15th December. Its principal object is to bring the Australian law into line with English law so far as regards the duration of the original term of a Patent and the extension thereof.

The main provisions of the Act are as follow :—

Original Term of Patent.

The original term of a Patent is extended from fourteen to sixteen years. This applies to any patent the original term of which has not expired, subject to the condition that any existing licence which has been granted for the former term of the patent shall be treated as having been granted for the extended term if the licensee so desires.

Where any party to a contract with the patentee or any other person entered into before 19th November, 1917, is subjected to loss or liability by reason of the extension of the term, the Court is empowered to determine in what manner and by which parties such loss or liability shall be borne.

Extension of Term of Patent.

The period of the extension of Patents is reduced from " seven or, in exceptional cases, fourteen years " to " five years, or, in exceptional cases, ten years."

Effect of War.

Where, by reason of hostilities, the patentee as such has suffered loss or damage (including loss of opportunity in dealing in or developing his invention owing to his having been engaged in work of national importance connected with such hostilities) application for the extension of the term of a Patent may be made by originating summons instead of by petition, and the Court, in considering its decision, may have regard solely to the loss or damage so suffered by the patentee. This does not apply if the patentee is an enemy subject or is a company, the business of which is managed or controlled by enemy subjects or carried on wholly or mainly for the benefit or on behalf of such subjects, notwithstanding that the company is registered within His Majesty's Dominions.

The Court, in its discretion, either before or after the expiration of the term of a Patent, may extend the period in which proceedings may be taken for the extension of the term of the Patent, whether such proceedings are by petition or by originating summons.

Other Provisions.

The protection of the rights of priority of a patentee under international arrangements is extended from the patentee to his legal representative or assignee. The Act is extended to New Guinea. The Patents, Trade Marks and Designs Regulations, 1920 (Statutory Rules, 1920, No 61), which related to the revival of patents, etc., which lapsed during the War are validated.

COMMONWEALTH CONCILIATION AND ARBITRATION (AMENDMENT) ACT.

This Act was assented to on 16th December. Its object is to amend the principal Act by extending the scope of the selection of persons for appointment as Deputy President of the Arbitration Court. The only persons previously eligible for appointment were Justices of the High Court and Judges of the Supreme Court of a State.

This Act by amending the Principal Act (Commonwealth Conciliation and Arbitration Act, 1904-20) makes the following also eligible for appointment as Deputy President of the Arbitration Court, viz., barristers and solicitors of the High Court or of a Supreme Court of a State of not less than five years' standing. It will thus be possible to appoint a larger number of Deputy Presidents than formerly, and so provide means of relieving congestion of business, each Deputy President having power to exercise the jurisdiction of the Court.

Another amendment is the provision under which a fixed period may be inserted in the instrument of appointment of a Deputy President. If no term is expressed the appointment holds during good behaviour for the unexpired period of the term for which the President, holding office at the time of the appointment of the Deputy, was appointed, etc.

Provision is also made so that any agreement under the Act will bind the successor, or any assignee or transmittee of the business of a party bound by the agreement, including any corporation which has acquired or taken over the business of such party.

State Parliaments.

New South Wales.*

INDUSTRIAL ARBITRATION (AMENDMENT) BILL.

(Fixing a Basic Wage; etc.)

A Bill for an Act to fix the basic wages for adult male and adult female employees at the rate of £4 5s. and £2 3s. per week, respectively, with proportionate daily and hourly rates, was introduced in the Legislative Assembly on 6th December. When the Session closed on 28th December, 1921, the Bill had not proceeded beyond the First Reading stage.

The main provisions of the Bill are as follow :—

Basic Wages Declared.

The basic wage to be paid to adult male employees shall be £4 5s. per week, 14s. 2d. per day, or 1s. 9¼d. per hour; and to adult female employees, £2 3s. per week, 7s. 2d. per day, or 10¾d. per hour.

Application to Awards.

Unless hereinafter provided no industrial agreement or award shall be made fixing wages for adult male or adult female employees at less than the declared basic rates, which are deemed to be the living wages payable to adult male and adult female employees respectively. Any agreement, whether verbal or in writing, which provides for the payment of wages lower than the basic wages shall be illegal and void.

Deductions for Board and Lodging.

Employees in receipt of board and lodging or other privilege or payment in kind shall not be bound by the basic wage provisions unless and until the Arbitration Court has assessed the amount to be deducted

---

* A General Election for the Legislative Assembly took place on 25th March, 1922, and resulted in the return to power of a Nationalist-Progressive Coalition, with Sir George Fuller as Premier. The constitution of the new Cabinet will be given in the next issue of the JOURNAL.

in lieu of any such concession, such assessment when made to be taken in part payment of the said basic wage.

Exemptions.

Permits may be granted to aged, slow or infirm employees to work for less than the basic wage.

Power to Enforce Basic Wage.

Employees entitled to the basic wages may enforce payment thereof as if such basic wages had been fixed by an award made under the Industrial Arbitration Act of 1912.

Overtime Rates for Casual Workers.

Employees whose hours of labour are not regulated by any award or agreement, and who are engaged as weekly or daily employees, shall be paid overtime rates at the rate of time and a half for all time worked in excess of 44 hours per week or eight hours per day in the case of industries the ordinary working hours of which have been fixed by proclamation at 44 hours per week, and in respect of all other industries or occupations, 48 hours per week or 8¾ hours per day.

*Abolition of the Board of Trade.**

Such sections of the Industrial Arbitration (Amendment) Acts of 1918, 1919 and 1920 as relate to the constitution, powers and functions of the New South Wales Board of Trade are repealed, the Board being thereby abolished.

PARLIAMENTARY ELECTIONS (CASUAL VACANCIES) AMENDMENT ACT.

(Proportional Representation; Preferential Voting.)

This Act was assented to on 19th November, and amends the Parliamentary Elections (Casual Vacancies) Act, 1920, which provided that where a vacancy occurred in the Legislative Assembly, such vacancy should be filled by the election of the unsuccessful candidate who represented the same Party interest as the late Member at the last General Election for the constituency for which the vacancy had occurred, and who, upon the count of the primary preference votes, was highest on the list of unsuccessful candidates representing such Party interest.

The Amendment Act provides that where there is no unsuccessful candidate representing the same Party interest who can fill the vacancy

* The Board of Trade, which was constituted under the Industrial Arbitration (Amendment Act) Act, 1918, was vested with power, *inter alia*, to declare after public inquiry as to the increase or decrease in the average cost of living, what shall be the living wages to be paid to adult male and adult female employees in the State, it being provided that no industrial agreement or award should be made for wages lower than the living wages thereby declared. In October, 1920, the Board declared the living wage for adult male employees to be £4 5s. per week, and for adult female employees to be £2 3s. per week, which declarations were gazetted accordingly. In October, 1921, the Board declared the living wages for adult male employees at £4 2s. per week, but the finding was not accepted by the Government and gazettal was withheld.

as above prescribed, the recognised Leader of the Party concerned shall nominate a person whose name is enrolled on an electoral roll, and who shall be entitled to be elected in place of the late Member.

Queensland.

CONSTITUTION ACT AMENDMENT ACT.

The Constitution Act Amendment Bill (a summary of which appeared in the JOURNAL, Vol. III., No. 1, p. 142, *et seq.*) provided for the abolition of the Legislative Council, and, having been passed by both Houses, was reserved by the Governor for the King's Assent.

On the 11th March, 1922, the Premier (Hon. E. G. Theodore) announced that the Royal Assent had been given to the Bill.

WORKERS' COMPENSATION ACT AMENDMENT ACT.

This Act was assented to 14th November, 1921. It amends the principal Act by extending the application of compensation to further classes of workers, by increasing the amount of weekly compensation, and by making Workers' Compensation Insurance a State monopoly.

The main provisions of the Act are as follow:—

State Monopoly.

All sections in the principal Act relating to insurance companies are repealed, and Workers' Compensation Insurance becomes a State monopoly. The new provision in the Act is that policies of accident insurance shall be issued only by the Insurance Commissioner and by no other person, company, firm, or association. Every such policy is issued on behalf of and guaranteed by the Queensland Government. Insurance is obligatory, and the penalty applicable to employers in the case of failure to insure their workers is a fine not exceeding £100, and after conviction further penalties not exceeding £20 for every week default is continued. Moreover, in the case of the payment of compensation by the Insurance Commissioner in respect of an uninsured worker the amount of such compensation is recoverable from the employer.

Extension to other Classes and Diseases.

Farmers, prospectors, and any other classes of persons, whether employees or not, may now voluntarily take advantage of this insurance. The term worker is extended to include those receiving up to £10 per week (instead of £400 per annum as formerly); salesmen, canvassers, collectors or persons in receipt of commission; share farmers, and wages men employed thereby.

The industrial diseases provisions of the principal Act are extended so as to provide for compensation in the case of persons employed at or in connection with a hospital or ambulance brigade if incapacitated by such diseases as Asiatic cholera, bubonic plague, diphtheria, measles, mumps, scarlet fever, small pox, tetanus, typhoid or other zymotic diseases. Workers in the baking and milling industries will receive compensation for millers' phthisis.

Compensation.

The minimum weekly compensation to an injured worker, who is the sole or main support of a wife, husband, parent, brother or sister, is fixed at £2. A further provision is made for an allowance of 5s. per week to children of such worker who are dependent upon him, the maximum for all children being 30s. per week. The maximum weekly compensation is therefore increased from £2 to £3 10s. The gross total compensation remains unaltered, viz., £750.

Miners' Phthisis.

Compensation to the worker, or in case of death, to his dependants, in respect of miners' phthisis or suchlike diseases, is extended to workers, whether engaged in mining and suchlike operations prior to 1st January, 1916 (as provided in the principal Act), or subsequently to that date, provided such worker has resided continuously in Queensland during the five years immediately preceding the date of death or incapacity, and was employed in Queensland in such employment for not less than 300 days; or resident in Queensland for five years out of the seven years immediately preceding the date of death or incapacity, and so employed in Queensland for 500 days. The maximum compensation is 25s. per week, or £200 in all.

BANANA INDUSTRY PRESERVATION ACT.

("White Australia" Policy.)

This Act was assented to 4th October, 1921. Its object, which is closely connected with the "White Australia" policy, is to preserve the industry of the cultivation of bananas in Queensland for white Australian citizens as against other races.

The Act provides that no person who has not passed the dictation test shall engage in or carry on the industry or be employed in connection therewith. The "dictation test" consists of not less than fifty words in such language as the Secretary for Agriculture may direct. Regulations which have since been framed exempt from the operation of the Act all persons who, at its commencement, were engaged in or carrying on the industry, and who, before 31st January, 1922, or later approved date, make application of exemption. Other grounds of exemption are also prescribed.

Western Australia.

RECIPROCAL ENFORCEMENT OF MAINTENANCE ORDERS ACT.

This Act was assented to on 21st December. Its object is to facilitate the reciprocal enforcement in Western Australia of Maintenance Orders made in other parts of His Majesty's Dominions and Protectorates. It includes orders of affiliation.*

RECIPROCAL ENFORCEMENT OF JUDGMENTS ACT.

An Act to facilitate the Reciprocal Enforcement in Western Australia of Judgments and Awards obtained in other parts of His Majesty's Dominions and Protectorates, and *vice versa*, was assented to 29th November, 1921.

The provisions of the Act are almost identical with Part Two of the Administration of Justice Act, passed by the Imperial Parliament in 1920, and are reciprocal therewith.

The main provisions are as follow :—

Judgments obtained outside State.

A judgment obtained in a superior Court in any part of His Majesty's Dominions outside the Commonwealth, to which this Act extends, may, on application of the judgment creditor, be registered in the Supreme Court, provided the court decides that the judgment should be enforced in the State, and that application is made within twelve months of the date of the judgment or such longer period as may be allowed by the court. No judgment shall be ordered to be registered if the original court acted without jurisdiction ; if the judgment debtor being ordinarily resident outside the jurisdiction of the original court did not submit to its jurisdiction, or being subject to its jurisdiction was not served with the process of the original court ; if the judgment debtor satisfies the Supreme Court that he intends to appeal against the judgment ; or if the judgment was in respect of a cause of action which for reasons of public policy or similar reason could not have been entertained by the Supreme Court. Where a judgment has been registered it shall be of the same force and effect as if it had been originally obtained in the Supreme Court.

"Judgment" means any judgment or order given or made by a court in any civil proceedings, whether before or after the passing of this Act, whereby any sum of money is made payable and includes an award in proceedings on an arbitration if the award has, in pursuance of the law in force in the place where it was made, become enforceable in the same manner as a judgment given by a court in that place.

Extent of the Act.

The Act extends to the United Kingdom and to such part of His Majesty's Dominions outside the Commonwealth and the United Kingdom where reciprocal provisions have been or are about to be made for the enforcement of judgments obtained in the Supreme Court of the State.

* This Act is reciprocal to that passed by the British Parliament in 1920. The Act passed by Queensland will be found summarised in the last issue of the JOURNAL, Vol. III., No. 1, p. 147. South Australia and Tasmania have also enacted similar legislation.

NEW ZEALAND.

The following summary is in continuation of the Third Session of the Twentieth Parliament, which commenced on 22nd September, 1921 :—

ANGLO-FRENCH PACT.

(Voice of Dominions in Foreign Affairs; Empire Speaking with "One Voice"; British Cabinet as Executive of Empire.)

On 16th January, 1922,

Mr. A. S. Malcolm (Reform, *Clutha*) referred to cabled messages to newspapers with regard to the proposed pact between France and Britain, and the reputed arrangement to allow the Dominions to contract themselves out of any such pact. " In view," said Mr. Malcolm, " of the fact that Britain and the Dominions are a solid Empire, one and indivisible, and considering the danger that is involved in practically inviting any one part of the Empire to refrain from falling in with the rest, and considering the fact that until the Empire has a Parliament representative of the whole Empire and consequently an Executive representing the whole Empire, would it not be well that we should recognise the British Cabinet for the time being as the Executive of the Empire, and recognise that in foreign affairs it can rule for us, seeing that the British Government does so carefully consult the Dominion Government in every possible way? Therefore, I would ask the Prime Minister, at any rate, to say that New Zealand expresses itself as not being desirous to have provision made for its contracting out, but as being willing to allow the British Government to carry out foreign affairs of the whole Empire."

The Prime Minister (the Right Hon. W. F. Massey): " I am sorry the honourable Member did not give notice of this question, because it is worthy of a little more attention than it is possible for me to give on the spur of the moment."

Mr. T. M. Wilford (Leader of the Opposition): "And of careful consideration before you reply."

The Prime Minister: " I do not know that it needs particularly careful consideration. As far as I am concerned, my mind is pretty well made up. I am very strongly opposed to anything in the way of divided counsels in the affairs of the Empire, especially in the cases of conferences such as that now sitting at Washington, or even in connection with the League of Nations. I have always thought from the very beginning that this was one of the dangers we had to confront. I feel that it is very important that the Empire should speak with one voice, and with no uncertain sound, and that there should be no possibility of one Dominion of the Empire voting or speaking one way, and another, or perhaps the British Government, in an opposite direction. I dare say that I shall hear something about this matter in a day or two, and if I get the opportunity, or if I have to make an opportunity, I shall let the Prime Minister of Great Britain know exactly how I feel as representing New Zealand, if he does not know it already, on a question such as this.

On 24th January, the question was again raised when

Mr. H. E. Holland (Labour, *Buller*) referred to a cabled statement to the effect that Britain would be unable to conclude the Pact with France without reference to the Dominions. Mr. Holland asked if the Prime Minister had received any request with respect to the Pact, and if so, what attitude he was taking up; and, further, would the hon. gentleman place the particulars of the new arrangement, when received, before the House for ratification before agreeing on behalf of New Zealand?

The Prime Minister replied that he did not think it was intended that representatives of the Dominions should sign anything in the way of a treaty with respect to the new arrangement that was apparently intended to be made. Members would recollect that when the Peace Conference sat the Prime Minister of New Zealand signed the draft treaty; and he had not the slightest doubt that if it had been gone on with New Zealand would have stood by what had been done. He did not think there had been any change in the sentiment of the people of New Zealand since that time. The Peace Treaty really became null and void, because it was not ratified by the American Legislature. He did not know quite what the position was at the moment in respect to the Pact; in saying this it was only fair to admit that he had received communications on the subject from Mr. Lloyd George. As a matter of fact, communications passed every week between the Prime Minister of Britain and the Prime Ministers of the different Dominions. He did not quite know yet what shape the Pact was going to take, and consequently, was not able to make any definite statement to Parliament; but as soon as anything transpired which he could give to Parliament without being a breach of confidence he would be glad to give it. He had noticed a statement a few days previously in a cablegram to the effect that the Dominions might or might not sign, just as they felt inclined. That sounded very well at first; but it was a very dangerous procedure.

An Hon. Member: "It is loose."

The Prime Minister said it was not only loose, but dangerous. He was very strongly of opinion that when the opportunity offered, which might not be for another year or two, perhaps not until the meeting of the next Imperial Conference—and he did not know when that would be—something should be done to prevent these suggestions of divided counsels among the different countries of the Empire. If the Empire was to stand, the different countries within its boundaries must stand together; and he hoped that the policy of the future would be a policy of unity.

IMPERIAL CONFERENCES.

(Continuity of Representation.)

On 7th December, 1921, in the House of Representatives,

Mr. A. S. Malcolm (Reform, *Clutha*) asked the Prime Minister whether, as continuity of representation at Imperial Conferences was much to be desired, and as the present system of having only one representative from New Zealand meant that in the event of the retirement of the Prime Minister, New Zealand at the following Conference would be represented by one strange to the procedure and previous discussions, as well as to other members of the Conference, he would suggest to the Home Government such representation in the future as would tend to secure continuity?

The Prime Minister (the Right Hon. W. F. Massey) replied: "This matter has not been lost sight of, but the Prime Minister has at present no intention of retiring."

GERMAN REPARATIONS.

(Share of the Dominion.)

On 10th February, 1922,

Mr. W. H. Field (Reform, *Otaki*) having asked the Prime Minister whether the Dominion was likely to receive any portion of the German reparation money at an early date; and whether any proposal that the Dominion be asked to accept a reduced amount would be submitted to Parliament before being agreed to,

The Prime Minister (the Right Hon. W. F. Massey) said he did not think any money would be coming to New Zealand during the present year, for the simple reason that France and Belgium had priority. After that year, he believed, a share would be coming to New Zealand. As to accepting a reduced offer, if the Germans offered £13,000,000 cash down he would certainly recommend Parliament to accept it. Mr. Massey added that he had a pretty strong opinion that the payments would not last for many years. By that he meant, he said, that the peoples to whom the payments were to be made would be willing either to stop the payments or take a great deal less than had been arranged in the first instance.

LEAGUE OF NATIONS.

(Contribution to Expenses.)

On 26th January, in the House of Representatives,

Mr. C. N. Mackenzie (Reform, *Auckland, East*) asked the Prime Minister if New Zealand was still paying £25,000 annually to the League of Nations; and, if that was so, in view of the fact that the League was largely fading from the field of international politics, and that its place was being taken by much more practical Conferences and Pacts, as those at Washington, Genoa and Cannes, and in view of the financial situation, whether he would consider reducing the sum to, say, £2,000 annually.

The Prime Minister (the Right Hon. W. F. Massey) replied that the total payments amounted to £10,209. He did not think he could quite agree with the opinion expressed by the honourable Member, because he was anxious in every way to promote peace as far as it was possible to do so; but he was watching very carefully what was going on, and if he thought it necessary next Session, or any Session after that, to make a recommendation to the House, he would have no hesitation in doing so.

SAMOA ACT.

(Marriages between Samoans and Chinese; Native Petition to the King.)

The Bill for the above Act, a summary of which appeared in Vol. III., No. 1, of the JOURNAL, p. 196, passed its Third Reading in the Legislative Council on 25th November, 1921. That Chamber reinstated in the Bill Clause 300, which prohibited marriages between Samoans and Chinese, and which had been struck out in the House of Representatives. The Legislative Council made other slight amendments in the Bill which were agreed to by the House of Representatives, and the Act received the Governor-General's Assent on 7th December, 1921.

Native Petition to the King.

On 9th November, 1921,

The Prime Minister (the Right Hon. W. F. Massey) announced in the House of Representatives that the King in his reply to the Native petition (summarised in Vol. III., No. 1, of the JOURNAL, p. 202) assured the Samoans that he had great love for them and desired earnestly that they might live in peace and happiness under his protection: that it should be explained to them that Germany having renounced, under the Treaty of Versailles, all her rights and title over her overseas possessions, the Government of New Zealand had, under the Mandate from the League of Nations, full power of administration and legislation over Samoa; that neither His Majesty's Government nor the New Zealand Government had any power to alter that Mandate, and that it was therefore His Majesty's wish that the Samoans should in every way co-operate with and assist the Administration.

ASIATIC IMMIGRATION.

(Success of Method of Regulation.)

On 10th February, 1922, in the House of Representatives,

The Minister of Internal Affairs (the Hon. W. Downie Stewart) in reply to a question by Mr. G. Mitchell (Independent, *Wellington, South*) as to the number of Asiatics coming into New Zealand, said that the return laid on the table showed that the working of the Immigration Restriction Act, 1920, was very successful. His own opinion was that that Act would be copied all over the British Empire, because it was the most ingenious method of regulating immigration yet devised.* Speaking of Hindus, Mr. Downie Stewart said that the regulations were being enforced without causing more inconvenience to India than could possibly be avoided, and the statistics showed that the position was under control.

IMMIGRATION.

(Government Policy.)

The Government policy in regard to immigration was the subject of several questions in the House of Representatives during the Session, and a discussion took place on 27th January in Committee of Supply on the vote of £225,000 for

* The Act referred to substitutes for the education test previously in force, a method whereby an intending foreign immigrant is required to obtain a permit, by previous application from his country of residence, before he may enter New Zealand (*vide* JOURNAL, Vol. I., No. 4, p. 729).

the Department of Immigration. The Minister stated that only one system of immigration was then in vogue, namely, of persons nominated by relatives and friends in New Zealand, who guaranteed to provide such persons with homes and employment.

DEBATE IN HOUSE OF REPRESENTATIVES.

On 30th September, 1921,

The Minister of Immigration (Hon. W. Nosworthy) having moved that the Annual Report of the Immigration Department lie on the table,

Labour Criticism.

Mr. J. McCombs (Labour, *Lyttelton*) asked the Minister to inform them as to what the policy of the Government then was in connection with encouraging immigrants, in view of the fact that New Zealand had not employment to offer them, and that if they were guaranteed employment before they left Great Britain it only meant that a place was to be given them which would otherwise be filled by persons already in the Dominion.

The motion was agreed to, and the report laid on the table, but no statement of policy was made.

On 26th October,

Mr. R. A. Wright (Reform, *Wellington, Suburbs*) having asked whether the Minister would take steps to discourage further immigration until the demand for labour increased,

The Minister of Immigration replied: "Immigrants coming to New Zealand at present belong to three classes: (1) persons nominated by their friends in New Zealand, and who guarantee to provide them with homes and employment; (2) ex-Service men and their families, whose passages are paid by the Imperial Government; (3) domestic servants.* There are thousands of people in Britain who are applying for facilities to come to this country. Among them a considerable proportion possessed of capital."

In Committee of Supply.

On 27th January, 1922,

Mr. P. Fraser (Labour, *Wellington, Central*), in opposing the Vote: "Department of Immigration, £225,000," said the economic condition of the country and the state of the labour market were such that there should be a vast reduction in the Vote. The glowing account in the annual report (of the Immigration Department) to the effect that a large number

* But *vide* the Minister's statement in Committee of Supply, p. 382.

of people had been brought out to the Dominion without in any way affecting the life of the Dominion workers was, he said, absolutely fallacious. He had been informed by the Engineers' Union that there were numbers of its members who had recently come out to that country who were out of work. Under the Government's policy the workers of the Dominion whose wages were being reduced would have to pay to bring workers out to compete with themselves for their jobs.

Mr. G. Mitchell (Independent, *Wellington, South*) said every one knew they had not enough people in New Zealand; but at present, owing to economic conditions, there were a lot of people out of work. He wanted more people brought into New Zealand, but wished to see a clear line of policy laid down so that those immigrants would help to create wealth by land-settlement, secondary industries and mining.

Mr. G. R. Sykes (Reform, *Masterton*) said his experience was that the man who nominated his relatives as immigrants, and paid the passage-money and guaranteed employment, often found on their arrival that he himself was out of work. He urged the Government to apprise people intending to come to the Dominion of the condition of affairs then existing—the serious lack of housing accommodation and the unemployment throughout the country.

Mr. P. Fraser moved the reduction of the Vote by £100, as indicating disapproval of the Government's policy of immigration.

Helping hand to "Old Country."

Mr. H. Atmore (Liberal, *Nelson*) hoped the House would vote solidly against the amendment. It was not only the conditions in the Dominion, but those prevailing in the Old Country, that must be considered. There could be nothing much more disgraceful than to say that because they were better off they would not extend a helping hand to the Old Country, where there were nearly two millions out of work. Considering the stress of circumstances all over the world, New Zealand offered better opportunities than existed in the Old Country; and he was satisfied that if the Government formulated an immigration policy the people of the Dominion would see it through. Even from a selfish, parochial view such a policy would be beneficial to the Dominion. He could not, he said, too strongly deprecate the extreme Party's selfishness.

The Minister of Immigration, in his reply, gave statistics as to immigration, saying that the country was still wanting 23,997 people to make up for the leeway caused by the War.

He assured the House that not one person was coming to the Dominion who had not accommodation and employment to come to. Many of them were doing well and assisting in the development of the country. There was only one system of immigration now in vogue—the nominated. Those on the books would be brought out as opportunity offered, and by the time that had been done he thought that country would be a more desirable place for immigrants.

Mr. Fraser's amendment was negatived by 37 votes against 8, and the Vote of £225,000 agreed to.

COOK ISLANDS AMENDMENT ACT.

(European Representation on Island Councils; Prohibition; Abduction; Child Adoption by Natives; Divorce; Banking; Anti-Profiteering; etc.)

The above Act amends the Cook Islands Act, 1915, its main purpose being to provide for European representation on Island Councils, entailing an alteration in the conditions of annexation of the Islands, to which the natives had agreed on condition that the laws prohibiting the sale to them or consumption by them of intoxicating liquor should be applied similarly to the European population. The Act, therefore, provides for absolute Prohibition.

Other clauses relate to the abduction of girls, adoption of children by natives, divorce, and banking. The Bill passed its Second Reading in the House of Representatives without division on 2nd November, 1921, and was read a third time on 8th November. It went through all stages in the Legislative Council on 23rd November.

Clause 3 provides for the election of one or more European members of an Island Council as representatives of the European population.

Clause 4 renders any one liable to two years' imprisonment who, without the consent of the father, etc., abducts an unmarried girl under 18; and provides that it shall be no defence that the girl was taken with her own consent, or that the offender believed her to be of or over 18 years of age.

Clauses 8 *and* 9 modify certain provisions of the principal Act with respect to the adoption of children by natives.

Clause 10 extends the jurisdiction of the High Court of the Cook Islands in divorce matters.

Clause 12 amends Section 602 of the principal Act (as to sale of liquor), bringing absolute Prohibition into force in the Cook Islands.

Clause 13 makes unlawful the carrying on of the business of banking, except under Order in Council.

Clause 15 makes provision for the sale of island products by the Resident Commissioner on behalf of planters.

DEBATE IN HOUSE OF REPRESENTATIVES.

On 3rd November,

The Minister in Charge of Cook Islands (Dr. the Hon. M. Pomare) said that the Bill had been before the Native

Affairs Committee and had been referred to the Cook Islands, where it had been approved by the local Native Council.

Speaking with reference to Clause 3, dealing with European representation on the Island Councils, Dr. Pomare said that when the Islands were annexed the natives had made a condition that if annexation took place their then form of government by Council should prevail, and, as no European had been elected on the Council it meant that the natives had to alter their condition of annexation. As the Europeans contended that there should not be taxation without representation, the matter was looked into, and the natives had come forward with this proposition :—

> We agree to one white member elected, but he must be a full-blooded white man—he must not be a half-caste Maori; and the European community alone must elect him—one member only; and he shall sit to represent the whites only; he shall not have any *mana* (power, or say, or jurisdiction) over our Maori affairs. As the Europeans want to be level with us, they must therefore be level with us in regard to the law as we are—that is, in law with regard to liquor and immorality. Absolutely no liquor to be sold to them, and they must be fined for drinking liquor or for being drunk, and be fined for immoral living.

That, said the Minister, was the condition on which the natives had given up the right to exclude Europeans from the Native Council, and from that time to the present, nearly two years, he had not had a single objection from the Europeans as to the proposition; on the other hand, he had had approval from the representatives of the natives.

Speaking of Clause 10, Dr. Pomare said the clause made it possible for a native woman who had married a European to sue for a divorce in her own country. Under the Act of 1915 the woman would have had to go to the expense of going to New Zealand and suing in the Supreme Court there.

Absolute Prohibition as in Samoa.

The Minister said that Clause 12 was really the complement of Clauses 3 and 4, because it was one of the conditions under which the natives agreed to the representation of Europeans on their Council—namely, that they should do away with liquor. It meant absolute Prohibition in those Islands, the same as in Samoa.*

American system of selling Island products.

By Clause 14 they were bringing the anti-profiteering sections of the Board of Trade Act (N.Z.) into operation in the Cook Islands. The last Clause (15) provided for the making of agreements between the Resident Commissioner

---

* *Vide* JOURNAL, Vol. III., No. 1, p. 196, *et seq.*

and any planter to sell, on behalf of such planter, copra and other products of the island, on the lines of the American system in Eastern Samoa.

Mr. H. E. Holland (Labour, *Buller*): "Does the last clause apply to the white planter, too?"

The Minister in Charge of Cook Islands: "Yes. I have struck out the word 'Native' in the clause. I move the Second Reading of the Bill."

Question of Administration under Home Government.

Mr. T. M. Wilford (Leader of the Opposition) said that he believed that before many years were passed they would have a big question opened as to whether it would not be better to have direct representatives from Home introduced into the islands. He believed that men skilled and trained in foreign affairs were necessary in those island groups as administrators.

Labour approves submission of Bill to Natives.

Mr. E. J. Howard (Labour, *Christchurch, South*) congratulated the Minister on some of the amendments which would be introduced into the government of the Cook Islands by the passage of the Bill, notably that regarding representation of the white people on the Island Councils. He would like to congratulate the Minister also upon one other point—and he thought it was the main point about the Bill—that the Bill had been sent to the natives, approved by them, and then brought back to that House.

The Bill was then read a second time.

THE BUDGET.

On 3rd November, 1921, the House of Representatives went into Committee of Supply, and the Prime Minister submitted his Financial Statement and his Budget proposals for the current financial year.

The statement disclosed the following position:—

For the Financial Year, 1920-21.

Revenue	£34,260,962
Expenditure	28,128,730
Surplus for Year	£6,132,232
Add Accumulated Surplus at end of Financial Year, 1919-20	£17,538,977
Total Accumulated Surplus	£23,671,209

Estimates for Financial Year, 1921-22.

Estimated Revenue	£28,000,000
Estimated Expenditure	29,266,367
Excess of Expenditure over Revenue.. ..	£1,266,367

Financial Statement by Prime Minister.

On 3rd November,

The Prime Minister (the Right Hon. W. F. Massey) explained that to the estimated revenue of £28,000,000 had to be added the actual cash balance of £4,920,294 carried forward at the beginning of the year—leaving an estimated cash surplus of £3,653,927, which was reducible by the amount which might be appropriated on the Supplementary Estimates. By the aid of the past year's surplus sufficient cash had been in the hands of the Treasury to meet ordinary charges; and although for the current year the chances at that time of fully meeting expenditure out of the year's revenue appeared uncertain, still he was sanguine enough to believe that at the 31st March (1922) they should be able to show a balance of cash in hand, as stated above. Items of special interest in the Budget were:—

Customs Revision.

A departmental Commission had been employed revising the Customs Tariff, and resolutions affecting the tariff would be submitted that evening.

Readjustment of Taxation and Retrenchment.

Legislation would be laid before Parliament with the object of giving effect to the intentions of the Government in the way of economy and retrenchment, which would provide for a readjustment of the revenue so that taxation might press more equally upon the different sections of the community, and so that relief might be given where most urgently required. Customs duties were being increased on certain articles, mostly luxuries. This was not being done for protective purposes, but to assist the revenue.

Public Health: Child Welfare.

An important step had been taken in the creation of the Division of Child Welfare, having mainly for its object the dissemination of information regarding the health of the community, by means of suitable propaganda, lectures and demonstrations.

Censorship of Cinematograph Films.

Films to the number of 3,146 had been examined. Thirty-eight had been rejected, and excisions made in 240. "A" certificates, *i.e.*, recommending the picture as more suitable for adults than for children—had been issued in 105 cases.

Prisons Department (Wages to Prisoners).

After referring to the various prison industries which were being carried on, Mr. Massey said that the increased earning power of the Department had enabled it to meet the additional expenditure caused by the new system of payment of wages to prisoners, which had been of great assistance to those deprived of their bread-winners.

Interest on Post Office Savings Bank Deposits.

Interest was now being paid on deposits up to £5,000. Prior to the 1st January, 1921, interest had not been paid on an account exceeding £1,000.

Automatic Telephone Exchanges.

An automatic telephone exchange, having a capacity of 2,000 lines, had been opened at Hamilton. Five other similar installations were proceeding, and new central automatic exchanges were being considered for Wellington and Dunedin.

State Forest Service.

The preliminary organisation of the State Forest Service had been undertaken.

New Zealand Royal Naval Reserve.

The House would be asked to pass an amending Bill to the Naval Defence Act, 1913, to admit of the formation of this very necessary arm of a Naval Division.

Defence Department.

The New Zealand Military Forces had been reorganised during the past year, unfortunately entailing the abolition or amalgamation of a number of the old regiments and units of the Territorial Force; but this had been found necessary to facilitate economy in administration.

Rebate on Land Tax.

With the object of assisting and encouraging the prompt payment of land tax, a Bill had already been laid before the House providing for a rebate of ten per cent. in the event of the tax being paid within 21 days of due date.

Reference was also made to the subjects of Unemployment, Housing, Coal Control, Immigration, Economies in the Public Service, and other matters.

In conclusion, the Prime Minister said that as a result of the War there had been a greatly increased expenditure in the Dominion. Along with increased expenditure there had been a very serious drop in the prices of their staple products, particularly wool, which had fallen to a lower price than had been reached for twenty years. A change for the better had, however, taken place and the feeling was growing that the Dominion was over the worst of its troubles, and that the prosperity which they had enjoyed for so many years would, by the exercise of economy and industry on the part of their people, soon return to those Islands.

Customs Tariff.

On the same date the resolutions were agreed to abolishing the existing Customs Tariff, and substituting a new tariff, including excise duties on beer and tobacco.

The debate on the Financial Statement, which was very lengthy (more than forty Members addressing the House), began on 9th and concluded on the 18th November.

DEBATE IN HOUSE OF REPRESENTATIVES.

On 9th November, 1921, the Prime Minister having moved (as Minister of Finance) that the House go into Committee of Supply,

Mr. T. M. Wilford (Leader of the Opposition) said he would, at the end of his speech, move an amendment that:—

In the opinion of this House the absence of any policy in the Financial Statement, together with the lack of appreciation of the industrial necessities of the Dominion displayed by the tariff proposals, proclaim the Government to be without any adequate realisation or conception of the needs of the present day.

It was impossible, said Mr. Wilford, to ascertain from the Budget what the policy of the Government was. The Budget gave no statement of the intentions of the Government, but merely admitted that it expected the revenue to reach £28,000,000, and the expenditure to reach £29,266,367. That was to say that the country was told by the Treasurer that it expected a deficit at the end of the financial year of £1,266,367, and to that had to be added the sums that the House would require to put on the Supplementary Estimates.

The Prime Minister: "That is not so, and you ought to know it."

Mr. Wilford: "That is so. . . . It is here in the Budget."

Continuing, he said that the only way in which New Zealand could increase its capital was by keeping expenditure below revenue, and unless its expenditure was below its revenue it could not be suggested that the financial proposals of the Government were sound. After criticising various items of the Budget, Mr. Wilford referred to the unemployment difficulty, which he said was glossed over with a wave of the hand, but the truth was that there were a great many people out of work.

In reference to the tariff alterations, he suggested a permanent Tariff Commission, acting on a defined principle, with power to adjust tariff rates. The principles should be determined by Parliament, and the application of the principle should be a matter of adjustment by specialists.

Mr. Wilford then moved the amendment standing in his name.

The Minister of Education (Hon. C. J. Parr) said the Leader of the Opposition had made as his principal charge the absence of any policy in the Budget. There was scarcely a page, said Mr. Parr, which did not contain reference, clear and direct, to policy matters.

Want of Confidence.

On 10th November, the debate was begun on Mr. Wilford's "Want of Confidence" motion.

Effect of Prime Minister's absence at Imperial Conference.

Mr. T. K. Sidey (Liberal, *Dunedin, South*) said that if every time they had an Imperial Conference the business of the country was going to be disorganised as it had been that year, the Prime Minister would strike a big blow at the popularity of the Imperial Conference. That was not all. The tariff should have been brought down more than a year earlier than it had been; and the position had been further aggravated by the postponement of the Session three months beyond the ordinary time. The Government, by their failure to deal promptly and adequately with the tariff, had aggravated unemployment conditions in the country.

Labour view of retrenchment policy.

Mr. H. E. Holland (Labour, *Buller*) said that while the Government was telling them that its taxation policy was in the direction of making the burden fall on the shoulders of those best able to bear it, Members of the House were faced with proposals for dismissals, reductions and retrenchments in the Public Service. He (Mr. Holland) did not agree that there was any such necessity. If there were to be reductions, they should start at the top, not at the bottom. Before they called upon the wage workers in the Public Service to suffer retrenchment, the first salary that should be attacked was that of the Governor-General. He was quite sure that his (the Governor-General's) own good sense would lead him to voluntarily agree to any reduction. The same principle should apply to the salaries of the Judges, although on the Civil List. He would personally fight against any attack on the wages of the men down below while those above remained untouched. The position the Labour Party was going to take up was that there would be no reduction in the case of the man getting under £500 a year.

While the Government came to them with their cry of retrenchment and their demand for economy, what were they doing in the matter of expenditure on militarism? In 1914 they spent £512,328; the present Estimates provided for an expenditure of £851,940. The German militarists were crushed, but German militarism had made its home not only in New Zealand, but in America, England and Japan.

Mr. Holland concluded by criticising the Government tariff proposals, which, he said, like the general policy of the Government, could not be defended.

Banking legislation criticised.

Mr. C. E. Statham (Independent, *Dunedin, Central*) criticised the statement in the Budget under the heading of Banking, to the effect that the legislation passed in 1920* had resulted in increased revenue to the Crown, and contended that instead of the State giving its prestige to the Bank of New Zealand to enable it to make enormous profits for private shareholders, which it did, it would have been better that the Bank should have been taken over by the State.

Criticising the Budget figures, Mr. Statham said that by applying the cash balance of £4,920,294 at the end of last March, the Prime Minister was going to have a cash surplus of £3,653,927. That meant that the year's operations were going to result in a deficit.

Concerning the Customs Tariff, they had the definite statement in the Budget that it was not being introduced for the protection of industries, but to assist the revenue. In that pronouncement they had the definite policy of the Government. If the Prime Minister was going to raise all that money—£29,000,000 odd—it might be assumed that he was not going to make any savings in his estimated expenditure for the year.

They (the Government) told them that they could save £4,000,000 on their administration, and the Prime Minister had told them last year that the present Minister of Labour, during the first week he was in office, had saved his whole year's salary in certain economies he had effected. Surely, in face of all those statements, there was something radically wrong with the administration of their Departments when such things could happen.

There was no real constructive policy in the Budget, and nothing of any practical value in the way of social and industrial reform.

On 15th November, the House divided, and the amendment was defeated by 37 votes against 21, the Liberal and Labour Members voting together against the Government.

On 18th November,

The Prime Minister, in reply, said he was going to predict that there would be a surplus at the end of the financial year even without including the surplus of last year. He was bound to admit that the financial position of the railways was not satisfactory, but what had happened in that country was as nothing compared with what had occurred in other countries.

Customs.

Replying to Mr. Wilford's suggestion that a Commission should be appointed to deal with Customs,† Mr. Massey said

---

* *Vide* JOURNAL, Vol. II., No. 2, p. 435. † *Vide* p. 387.

that the Parliament of the country either controlled taxation or it did not; and he would do his level best to keep the taxation, and the revenue, and everything connected with the finances of the country under the control of Parliament.

Bank of New Zealand.

In reference to the remarks of the Member for Dunedin, Central, in regard to the Bank of New Zealand,* Mr. Massey said they got from the Bank of New Zealand last year: Dividends, £112,500; income-tax, £306,000; land-tax, £17,000; notes in circulation, £153,148; total, £588,648. The amount paid in income-tax by the Bank was equal to about 14s. 8d. in the pound on the profits of the Bank. It would be one of the biggest mistakes they could make if they ruined the Bank of New Zealand for the sake of enabling anyone to establish a State Bank.

Causes of financial depression.

Continuing, the Prime Minister said they had heard a great deal about the increase of taxation and the hardships of many people throughout New Zealand, but they had not heard very much about the causes of those things. The War had cost New Zealand £80,000,000, and Pensions another £20,000,000 when capitalised. They had to find 1 per cent. sinking fund on the £80,000,000, and interest as well; there were other factors—they had to find increased salaries and bonuses for the whole Public Service on account of the increased cost of living. That was not all. In that country where they owned their own railways, and where they had a great Public Works Department, all of which were using materials which had to be imported from the other side of the world, the cost had gone up enormously.

He had known that depression was coming. He did not think he had expected it to be so bad. But it was there with them, and there was only one thing for them to do, and that was to reduce expenditure and increase their income. Mr. Massey then detailed various savings and economies which had been effected or agreed to, totalling £3,250,000. They could, retrench to the extent of another £2,000,000 besides what he had mentioned, and they could not stop there.

Retrenchment.

He was going to ask Parliament to agree to probably a 10 per cent. reduction on all salaries down to, perhaps, £300 a year, commencing at the top with the highest salaries, with the salaries of Ministers and his own salary, and going right down through the different Departments, and also dealing with

* *Vide* p. 389.

the salaries of Members of the House. The Govenor-General had asked that £500 be taken off his salary, although they had made a contract with His Excellency and he (Mr. Massey) knew that the Govenor-General was spending more than he received by way of salary.

The motion to go into Committee of Supply was then agreed to.

TARIFF.

(Preference within the Empire; Tariff Board; etc.)

A new tariff came into operation in New Zealand by resolutions passed in the House of Representatives on 3rd November, 1921.* Certain amending resolutions were, however, passed on 23rd and on 29th November, and the Tariff is now incorporated in the schedule to the Customs Amendment Act, 1921. A summary of the principal provisions of this Act and of the debate thereon, appears on pp. 395–401. As in the case of the Australian tariff,† three rates of tariff are provided, viz., British Preferential, Intermediate, and General. In the debate the Minister of Customs stated that whereas under the old Tariff, British Preference had been given upon about 100 items, this number had been extended to 300 items under the new tariff. On 23rd November, some aspects of the tariff were discussed in the House of Representatives—in particular, relations between the Dominion and Australia in regard to Customs duties.

DEBATE IN HOUSE OF REPRESENTATIVES.

On 23rd November,

On the question that the House go into Committee of Ways and Means,

Position with Australia.

The Prime Minister (the Right Hon. W. F. Massey), speaking as Minister of Finance, said that a good deal of objection had been taken to the position which Australia was placed in regarding the resolutions which had been agreed to. That point had been reconsidered. Australia had been on the preferential tariff, and was now intended to be placed

* A concise statement setting forth the history of tariff development in New Zealand is contained in the New Zealand Official Year Book for 1919, pp. 427-434.

† *Vide* JOURNAL, Vol. II., No. 4, p. 879.

upon the general tariff. Mr. Massey said he was sorry to do that; but he thought the right thing was being done, because Australia did not show a great deal of consideration to New Zealand in their latest tariff. "We have got to be in a position," said Mr. Massey, "to negotiate with Australia." Continuing, he said he noticed that the Federal Minister of Customs, Mr. Massy Greene, had said to Members of the Federal Parliament a few days ago that he was quite prepared and hoped to make satisfactory arrangements with New Zealand as to Customs duties. "I hope that will be done," said Mr. Massey.

Upon an hon. Member interjecting that Mr. Massy Greene had pointed out that they (in Australia) were badly treated compared with South Africa, the Prime Minister said New Zealand had to admit it. He thought a mistake had been made in connection with the South African Treaty. They had to go back on that to a certain extent; but the Treaty had first to be denounced in the ordinary way before other arrangements could be made.

Canada on preferential tariff.

Asked whether he was putting Canada on the general tariff, as well as Australia, Mr. Massey said: "No, Canada is on the preferential tariff. Canada gives us preference. And I hope that before very long, when we open up these negotiations to which I have referred, we shall be able to place Australia on the preferential tariff as well as those of our own people in other parts of the British Empire."

With regard to the Tariff Board suggested by Mr. Wilford, the Prime Minister said though the arrangement was evidently working in Australia, he was not sure that it would be suitable to conditions and circumstances in New Zealand.

Sir J. P. Luke (Reform, ***Wellington, North*****)** said that the remarks of the Prime Minister with regard to Australia were almost satisfactory. Had the tariff conditions between Australia and New Zealand according to the schedule first brought down been adhered to, Australia would very soon have become the workshop for New Zealand, and those activities necessary to the proper development of the industries of the country would have passed to another country. He agreed with the Leader of the Opposition that there should be a permanent Tariff Commission or Board, and said he thought it was an absolutely sound proposal, and of great advantage, to the Dominion.

Enemy countries.

Speaking in reference to imports from enemy countries, Sir J. P. Luke said there should be a sur-tax. The Prime Minister, he said, had told them that Germany was purchasing their wool. Nevertheless it behoved them to see that manufactures of Germany did not come in without additional duty, because unless they were careful the markets of the country would be flooded with cheap German productions.

Partially-manufactured goods from America.

Further, preference should not be given to America unless there was 50 per cent. of British manufacture in the article concerned. There were many articles shipped from America in a partial state of manufacture, and they came into the country as British goods.

Mr. T. K. Sidey (Liberal, *Dunedin, South*) said they had had a very different story that night from the Prime Minister as compared with that he had given them a few nights ago when he brought down his tariff proposals. A greater back-down in regard to some of them could not have been imagined. He (Mr. Sidey) thought he could take credit for being one of the first to urge the Government to place the Australians on the general tariff, and he was pleased they had at last yielded on that very important point. Otherwise Australia would have become the workshop of New Zealand. He had been amazed, in the face of the unemployment, that the Government should have brought down a tariff which was calculated in many industries to throw numbers out of employment.

Labour criticism.

Mr. H. E. Holland (Labour, *Buller*), in indicating the attitude of the Labour Party towards the tariff, said they should foster and develop industries that New Zealand was specially adapted for, and provide that those things that could not be economically produced there should be brought from abroad on a system of free exchange. Theoretically, he said, all Socialists were free-traders, but they recognised that certain industries had been developed in New Zealand, and now stood where they could only live with assistance. "We do not desire to destroy those industries," said Mr. Holland, "but we do say that when the point is reached where an industry can only live by the aid of an abnormal duty the time has arrived when the State should take that industry over and conduct it in the interests of the people." So far as the tariff was concerned, he continued, the Labour Party were prepared to move in every case for the free admission of articles which were necessaries, and which could not be produced in New Zealand; they would fight to the last ditch to take the duty off tea, which was a specific tax, not an *ad valorem* tax, and therefore a tax on the poorer section of the community.

Mr. Holland also attacked the tax on sugar, tobacco, cotton, kerosene and other articles, and said there was a long list of items, goods that were not produced inside New Zealand and that were to be taxed, and through their taxation the cost of living was to be increased while wages were to be forced down.

Tariff Board proposal criticised.

The Hon. J. A. Hanan (Liberal, *Invercargill*) said he favoured in theory the establishment of a Tariff Board; but knowing something as he did, he said, about Boards and Commissions, not only there but in Australia, and how their proposals were ignored by the Government receiving the reports, he could not agree to the setting up of a tribunal and the creating of a new Department with an army of clerks and an extension of officialism and cost of government. He would venture to say that no Minister would give effect to the recommendations of the Tariff Board unless they suited his Government. He believed in a tariff to protect and encourage industries, to secure command of their own markets, particularly in such commodities for which they had the raw materials to be worked up, and which could be successfully established.

England and German goods.

Mr. C. E. Statham (Independent, *Dunedin, Central*), in referring to the statement of the Member for Wellington, North (Sir J. P. Luke) to the effect that there should be a sur-tax on German goods, said that when they heard people talking on one hand of exacting a big indemnity from Germany, and then saying they would never trade with her again, he did not know how it would be done.

Continuing, he said he was glad to think the Government, after all those years, had come to his way of thinking about the taxation of luxuries. But the way they were doing it now meant putting a very big tax on working people; and, giving as an instance the increased tax on tobacco, Mr. Statham said the working men were entitled to share in luxuries.

Minister's reply.

The Minister of Customs (Hon. W. Downie Stewart), replying to the criticisms of the tariff, said that Mr. Holland had been extraordinarily disingenuous in his attack and had tried to lead the House to believe that the Government were imposing duties on a number of specified items, which he (Mr. Holland) believed were penalising the wage-earners of the Dominion, but had refrained from stating that in respect of those items there was no duty at all so far as Great Britain or reciprocating Dominions were concerned. The whole object of the preferential taxation was to assist British industry, and British workmen, and British capital. Under the old tariff there were only about 100 items upon which British Preference was given, but under the present tariff they had managed to extend the number to more than 300.

In reply to Mr. Sidey, who had referred to the sudden change of front on the part of the Government on the treatment of Australia, the Minister said the facts were simple. He restated them and said that if the effect of putting Australia on the general tariff would be to expedite the desire for reciprocity, that would attain the object they had in view.

The motion having been agreed to, the House resolved itself into Committee of Ways and Means and the further resolutions* mentioned above were considered and agreed to.

CUSTOMS AMENDMENT ACT.

(British Preferential Tariff; Provision for Tariff Agreements, etc.; Anti-dumping; Duties against Countries with depreciated Currencies; Imports from Foreign Countries; Commercial Treaty with South Africa.)

The above Act, which came into force on the 22nd December, 1921, is based mainly on the recommendations of a Tariff Commission set up by the Government, and contains provisions dealing with the economic problems with which the Dominion is faced. The Governor-General is given wide powers in regard to the administration of the Act, to be exercised by Order in Council. Owing to opposition as to the extent of these powers, the clause of the Bill as originally brought down was amended, and the Act provides that all Orders in Council are to be subject to review by Parliament. The new tariff is set forth in a schedule to the Act.

The Bill was debated at length in the House of Representatives on the Second Reading on 29th November and subsequent sittings.

The main provisions of the Act are as follows :—

DEFINITIONS.

The meaning of "British Preferential Tariff," of "Intermediate Tariff" and of "General" is set forth in Section 2.

---

* The following is the text of the tariff resolution affecting Australia :—

"Resolved that there shall be levied, collected, and paid on all goods imported into New Zealand on and after the 1st day of December, 1921, and being the produce or manufacture of or imported from the Commonwealth of Australia, the duties mentioned in column No. 3 of the First Schedule to the resolutions of the 3rd day of November, 1921 (as the same may be amended from time to time), as if the Commonwealth of Australia were not part of the British dominions within the meaning of the said resolutions."

POWERS OF GOVERNOR-GENERAL.

After providing for the abolition of existing Customs duties (Section 3), and for the application of the British Preferential Tariff to the "British Dominions" (which term includes British Protectorates and "Mandated" Territories) and for the application of the General Tariff to other countries (Section 4); the Act proceeds to vest in the Governor-General (*inter alia*) the following powers, viz., by Order in Council, (A) to apply the Intermediate Tariff to any country, whether part of the British Dominions or not, in lieu of the British Preferential or Intermediate Tariff, as the case may be; (B) to apply the General Tariff to any part of the British Dominions (other than the United Kingdom); (C) to impose reciprocal duties with any other country; and (D) to modify the standard tariffs, subject to certain limitations. Duties, called "suspended duties," are only to be levied pursuant to an Order in Council. (*Sections* 5 *to* 9.)

Section 10 provides:—

"10. (1) The powers conferred on the Governor-General in Council by Sections 5 to 9 hereof shall be exercisable for the purpose of giving effect to any agreement or arrangement entered into by or on behalf of the Government of New Zealand with the Government of any other country (whether a part of the British Dominions or not) for the purpose of promoting trade between those countries; or in case of the adoption by any country of a tariff which imposes excessive rates of duty on any goods being the produce or manufacture of new Zealand; or in any case where the Governor-General is of opinion that the exercise of those powers or of any such powers is necessary or advisable in protection or furtherance of the public interest.

"(2) No such agreement or arrangement as is referred to in the last preceding sub-section shall have any effect unless and until it is ratified by Parliament."

THE ANTI-DUMPING CLAUSE.

Section 11 makes comprehensive provision for the imposition of a special Customs duty (referred to as a Dumping duty) for the protection of local industries.

ALTERING TARIFF TO PROTECT LOCAL INDUSTRIES.

Section 12 empowers the Governor-General, if satisfied: (A) that a Customs duty, or exemption from duty operates injuriously, unfairly, or in an anomalous manner in respect to public interest or to industry, trade, etc.; or (B) that trade concessions (by way of freights, special bounty, etc.) are being allowed on goods imported into New Zealand; or (C) that duties payable in any country on the importation of goods from New Zealand are excessive, to suspend by Order in Council the existing tariff in whole or in part, and in lieu thereof to impose on any goods such duties, or create such exemptions from duty, as appear to him just.

COUNTRIES WITH DEPRECIATED CURRENCY.

Section 13 provides for the imposition of a special duty on goods imported from countries having a depreciated currency. Certain goods (*e.g.*, raw materials of any industry carried on in New Zealand) may be exempted from special duty. The Section proceeds to define what constitutes a country with a depreciated currency, and makes special provision for the case of a country not having a mintage rate of exchange.*

GOODS FROM FOREIGN COUNTRIES.

Section 14 makes provision for the imposition of special duty on the importation of goods from foreign countries, not exceeding twenty-five per cent. *ad valorem.*

PRIMAGE DUTY; COUNTRY OF ORIGIN.

Provision is made for the imposition, subject to certain exceptions, of a primage duty of one per cent. on all imports, whether liable to Customs duties or not. (*Section* 15.)

Full provision is made in regard to evidence of the country of origin of goods imported into New Zealand. (*Sections* 16 *to* 18.)

TREATY WITH SOUTH AFRICA.

Nothing in the Act is to conflict with the Customs duties and exemptions under the New Zealand and South African Customs Duties Reciprocity Act, 1906, provided that no higher duties are to be enforced against South Africa than the British Preferential rate now brought into force; and provided further that, on the termination of the Treaty, the British Preferential Tariff shall, unless and until altered in accordance with the present Act, apply in lieu of the duties provided for by the Treaty. (*Section* 21.)

COOK ISLANDS.

The Governor-General is empowered by Order in Council to bring the Act into force in the Cook Islands. (*Section* 22.)

ORDERS IN COUNCIL.

It is provided that all Orders in Council under the Act are to be laid before Parliament within 14 days after being gazetted; and if Parliament is not then in Session, within 14 days after the commencement of the next Session; and any such Order may then be revoked or varied, and provision is made for the refund of duty in cases where an Order is varied or revoked by Parliament. (*Section* 31.)

DEBATE IN HOUSE OF REPRESENTATIVES.

On 29th November,

The Prime Minister (the Right Hon. W. F. Massey), in moving the Second Reading of the Bill, said very important alterations were being made, and suggested that the tariff should be revised at periods of not more than five years. He said they had not had a proper revision since 1907.

They had been able, to a great extent, to avoid increases on necessaries of life. They had kept as closely as possible to luxuries, on which there had been important increases in taxation. What was being done was to a great extent on account of the fall in revenue. They had done something in the way of giving additional protection to promising industries.

* The clause as originally drawn gave the Minister power to give exemptions from payment of special duty under this section. This power was objected to by the Leader of the Opposition and the clause was amended by the Government and the power vested in the Governor-General by Order in Council.

It had become necessary to spread the burden of taxation. It was impossible to go on expecting landowners, farmers and others on the one hand, and payers of income tax on the other, to contribute the amount they had been doing during the War.

Imperial Preference.

One of the most important features, said Mr. Massey, was the additional preference given to British countries. Personally, he was a strong believer in Imperial Preference, and he believed the people of New Zealand from one end to the other were of the same way of thinking. He added that what they were doing was not quite equal to what Canada had done. The principle of Preference had been agreed to by what was called the Imperial Parliament. Though they (in New Zealand) had received no benefit from that protection, it was their duty to help the other countries.

Anti-Dumping; Depreciated currencies.

The provisions against Dumping were as drastic as it was possible to place upon the Statute-book, but in his opinion they were not too drastic. Speaking of the provisions in regard to countries having a depreciated currency, the Prime Minister said he thought when Members looked into the proposals contained in the Bill they would see that there was very little chance of anything going wrong regarding the depreciated currency in other countries affecting the industries of New Zealand.

Reciprocity with South Africa and Australia.

Speaking of the existing Commercial Treaty with South Africa, which had come into operation the year after the end of the South African War, Mr. Massey said that since then the position had completely changed, and he knew that their neighbours in Australia were very sore because South Africa was placed in a better position, as far as the New Zealand market was concerned, than Australia.

Question of reciprocity with Australia.*

But, continued Mr. Massey, the present position gave them an opportunity of negotiating with Australia some reciprocal trade agreement. "I hope," said he, "that these two countries of the British Empire will not continue to wage commercial warfare. I hope we shall be able to make a satisfactory arrangement which will be suitable to both of us, so that the industries in one country will not be used to injure the industries in the other."

* *Vide* p. 391 and JOURNAL, Vol. III., No. 2, p. 204, for previous reference to this subject; also Australian reference, JOURNAL, Vol. II., No. 4, p. 879.

Encouraging industries.

Continuing, the Prime Minister said that in New Zealand there were plenty of opportunities for increasing their industries; and he thought that what was being done would give very great encouragement to their struggling industries. "It has always been very unsatisfactory to me," he said, "to see so much of our raw material going out of this country to the other side of the world to be made up, and then coming back to this country in the shape of manufactured goods."

Report of Tariff Commission.

After remarking that he considered the Report of the Tariff Commission the best report on tariff proposals that he had ever seen, Mr. Massey referred at length to it and quoted (*inter alia*) the principles laid down by the Commission regarding the protection of New Zealand industries.*

Mr. Massey then moved the Second Reading of the Bill.

Mr. T. M. Wilford (Leader of the Opposition) emphasised what he had proposed earlier in the Session, namely, that they should set up through the Bill a Tariff Board, when, he said, there would be no real necessity for a new Tariff Bill

---

* The following is the quotation referred to:—

"We would lay down the following principles regarding the protection of industries in New Zealand:—

"(A) Any protection given should be well devised, and not more than sufficient for the welfare of the industries concerned.

"(B) In addition to ordinary protection under the tariff, effective provision should be made against dumping. Anti-Dumping duties on the lines of the Canadian policy appear to be satisfactory, and are recommended by the Commission.

"(C) The profits of those engaged in protected industries should be subject to periodical investigation by an authority such as the Department of Industries and Commerce.

"(D) Encouragement through protection should be directed mainly to those industries which obtain their raw material wholly or principally in New Zealand.

"(E) Special steps should be taken by the Government to promote scientific research and development in protected industries, and to provide for adequate education of mechanics, engineers and skilled workmen.

"(F) Arrangements should be made for giving due notice of several years of the removal of protection to industries; and as far as possible the protection given to industries—apart from anti-dumping provisions—should be regarded as a temporary measure covering a period long enough to ensure the due development of the industries concerned.

"We believe that all these principles can be followed by the New Zealand Government with the official organisations at present at its command—the Customs Department, the Department of Industries and Commerce, the Education Department, the Labour Department, and the Dominion Laboratory."

every five years. He referred to an Order in Council which had been gazetted in regard to the computation of Customs Duties on imports from countries having an appreciated rate of exchange, saying that the Prime Minister had never mentioned this, and that the methods of dealing with appreciated or depreciated currency in the importation of goods should have been incorporated in the Bill itself. He proposed to move for a reduction on the duty on tea. He had intimated that he intended to test the feeling of the House with respect to the duty on kerosene, but the Cabinet had since decided to take off the duty on kerosene.

American motor-cars.

In regard to duties on motor-cars, it was just as well that they should give what preference they could to British motor-cars. The Americans practically had the run of the country at that time ; it was impossible to get the British manufacturer to make a car that was suitable for the country roads of a place like New Zealand.

Mr. H. E. Holland (Labour, *Buller*) said he was glad the Liberal Party was willing to join in getting the tea-tax taken off. If duties were to be imposed for the purpose of helping certain industries on which they depended, they ought not to leave the lower-paid workers to pay for the increase, and that was what a number of those increases amounted to.

Labour and British Preference.

Referring to Clause 4 of the Bill, Mr. Holland said that the matter of British Preference was made subordinate to the coldest materialism of the profit-making interests of certain industries in New Zealand. Continuing, he said that while the Government told them they were going to make their policy one of British Preference, at the same time they were taking power by Order in Council to apply to goods from any part of the British Empire the same duty as they would apply to Japan, America, or even Germany, if her depreciated currency should become stabilised. The whole of the Bill gave the Government a power which it ought not to possess in the matter of making Orders in Council ; the Governor-General might, by Order in Council, modify the British preferential tariff, the intermediate tariff, and the general tariff. Of course there was the qualification that the modification should not have the effect of imposing a higher duty than was set forth in the general tariff. The whole idea of so concentrating the power in the Cabinet ought to be repulsive to every Member of the House.

In the matter of Dumping, the power was left entirely with the Minister to determine the amount of duty. Why should not the duties be determined by that House ?

The Minister of Customs (Hon. W. Downie Stewart) said in his reply that the Order in Council, referred to by the Leader of the Opposition, dealing with the question of the currency, was passed for the purpose of dealing with the position that had arisen in American trade, whereby the Preference given to Britain by the previous tariff was being largely negatived by the appreciation of the American currency.

The Member for Buller had taken strong exception to the powers conferred on the Minister to modify the tariff. He (Mr. Downie Stewart) recognised that they were far-reaching, but more and more it was being found necessary to confer those powers on a Minister, or on the Government or some authority in order to make the tariff flexible and workable, and adjust it to the rapidly changing conditions of modern industry. They could not have it both ways. If they were not willing to trust the Executive with the administration of a flexible law, then they must submit to many grave difficulties.

The Bill was then read a second time.

On 8th December, the Bill having been dealt with in Committee through several sittings, the debate on the Third Reading was taken; the Bill was then read a third time.

The Journal.

On 8th December, during the debate on the Third Reading of the Bill,

Mr. T. K. Sidey (Liberal, *Dunedin, South*), in supporting the proposal for a Tariff Board, said that if members had taken the trouble to read the JOURNAL OF THE PARLIAMENTS OF THE EMPIRE, which had come to them the other day, they would see that South Africa had been going in the same direction and had decided to appoint a Tariff Board.

IN THE LEGISLATIVE COUNCIL.

On 9th December, the Bill was read a first time in the Legislative Council, and passed the Second and Third Readings on 13th December.

INDUSTRIAL CONCILIATION AND ARBITRATION AMENDMENT ACT.

(Arbitration Court and resignation of Labour Representative; Specialised Assessors to assist Judge; Attitude of Government and Labour.)

The Labour representative on the Arbitration Court having resigned on the 1st September, 1921, and having intimated that he was able to attend sittings of the Court but would not do so,* the Court could not function for the reason that the only provision in the principal Act dealing with the point referred to the inability of a member to attend. The Bill was therefore introduced by the Government for the purpose of enabling the Arbitration Court to function at all times. During the debate on the committal stage of the Bill, questions were raised as to the success or otherwise of the Arbitration Act in New Zealand. The Act became law on 4th November, 1921.

Provision is made in the Act for the appointment of "acting nominated" members to represent industrial unions of employers or of workers on the Arbitration Court in case of vacancies, or in the event of the nominated members not being present at the sitting of the Court; further, the Act provides for the appointment of "temporary nominated" members where there is a vacancy or failure to act on the part either of a nominated member or an acting nominated member.—*Sections 2 and 3.*

DEBATE IN HOUSE OF REPRESENTATIVES.

On 26th October,

The Minister of Labour (Hon. G. J. Anderson), having detailed the circumstances which had led to the work of the Arbitration Court being held up, said that no one individual should have the power to do so, and that the Bill was intended to remedy defects in the Act and enable the Arbitration Court to function. Continuing, he said he was sorry to see that the organ of Labour in New Zealand appeared to think that the Arbitration Court was not necessary. If the workers did not want the Court, why did they not come out in the open and say so straight-forwardly and definitely, instead of trying to "monkey" with the question as had been done during the last few weeks?

Mr. T. M. Wilford (Leader of the Opposition) began by saying he was a thorough believer in the principle of arbitration. As their Arbitration Court was then constituted they had, he said, a Judge and two Assessors. A permanent appointment (an assessor) was made on behalf of the employers, who was supposed to be *au fait* with every class of dispute—and every form of adventure in the industrial world, and no man was born who could possibly understand the technical details of the various trades disputes. As with the employers' representative so with the employees' representative. He personally favoured doing away with any

---

* Mr. McCullough, the Labour representative, was re-elected by an overwhelming majority and was re-appointed, but notified the Judge that he was unable to attend the Court, and wrote a letter to the Registrar of the Court, said the Minister, which clearly showed that he was able to attend the Court, but had no intention of doing so.

permanent appointment on the Arbitration Court except the appointment of the Judge; and, instead of one Judge, he would have two Judges, or even three, to keep up with the continual applications made to the Court for awards. The Arbitration Court had outlived its usefulness as at present constituted; and to attempt to tinker with the Court as was being done in that Bill was going to be not even a palliative, but merely a makeshift. He would ask the Minister to take the Bill back and consider the question of appointing only Judges, and to allow the appointment of Assessors in the industries in which the dispute arose, at the time the dispute arose, and for that dispute only.

Labour views on Arbitration, etc.

Mr. H. E. Holland (Labour, *Buller*) said he thought the Bill might be described as an effort to patch up the patchwork of a previous day. It would still only mean an extra patch on a garment that was already tattered and torn. The trouble that day was that in their society as constituted there were interests that conflicted, and which no arbitration could reconcile. It was apparent to every one that the arbitration system as they then knew it was losing ground; that the workers of that country had practically no confidence in the Arbitration Court; and, said Mr. Holland in conclusion, the Government had not hesitated on occasions to break the Arbitration Court law in the interests of the employing classes, which the Government represented.

Mr. D. G. Sullivan (Labour, *Avon*) said he was inclined to attach deeper significance to the attitude of the Minister and his provocative statements than the Member for Buller had done. When he took in conjunction with that the statements made by the Member for Gisborne (Mr. W. D. Lysnar, Reform) of a similar character, together with the resolutions carried by farmers' unions throughout the country desiring that the Government should introduce legislation to put an end to the preference (to unionists) clause; and also the statements made by the farmers' deputation to the Prime Minister urging interference with the minimum wage, he wanted to put the question to the Minister as to whether he was not, and the Government was not, trying to find an excuse for putting an end to the Arbitration Act. He did not believe there was the slightest intention on the part of the Labour movement of the country, in the incidents that had happened recently, to interfere with or kill the Arbitration Act.

The Minister of Labour in his reply said that the Government as long as he was Minister of Labour, would never dream of abolishing the Act, because he believed is was a safeguard both for the employer and the employee. He believed it stabilised wages—that one employer could not undersell another by cutting wages, as was common before the Act came into operation.

The Bill was then dealt with in Committee, when some amendments were made, after which the Bill was reported.

IN THE LEGISLATIVE COUNCIL.

On 1st November slight technical amendments were made in the Legislative Council, and the Bill was then read a third time.

INDUSTRIAL CONCILIATION AND ARBITRATION AMENDMENT ACT (No. 2).

(Cost of Living; Status of Judge; Voting-power of Unions; Amending of Awards; Status of Railway Servants; Application of Act to Local Authorities, etc.)

The above measure amends the law of the Dominion relating to industrial conciliation and arbitration. The principal provision is that whereby the Arbitration Court may by general order, having regard to any increase or decrease in the cost of living, and having regard to "a fair standard of living," amend awards or industrial agreements in so far as they determine "rates of remuneration to workers."

The Bill was opposed in the House of Representatives by the Labour Members and passed its Third Reading on 7th February, 1922. It passed through all stages in the Legislative Council, after debate, on 9th February.

The main provisions of the Bill, and the amendments made during its passage, are given below.

STATUS OF JUDGE.

The provision in the principal Act, whereby the Judge of the Arbitration Court may be appointed a temporary Judge of the Supreme Court, is repealed. (*Clause* 2.)

ELECTION OF "NOMINATED MEMBERS" OF COURT.

Section 66 of the principal Act dealing with the voting-power of unions in regard to the election of representatives on the Arbitration Court is amended so that "in no case shall a union have more than five votes." (*Clause* 3.)

CURRENCY OF AWARDS.

Section 90 (1) (d) of the principal Act is amended, so that the currency of an award shall run, not, as previously, from the date of the award, but from "the date on which the award is expressed to come into force, or if the award fixes different dates on which different provisions shall come into force, then from the earlier or earliest of such dates."

(*Clause* 4.)

AMENDING AWARDS BY CONSENT.

The special powers conferred by the Court in regard to awards are added to by the provision that "the Court may, if it is satisfied that all the parties to an award are desirous that the award should be reviewed by the Court, amend the provisions of that award for such purpose and in such manner as the Court thinks fit." (*Clause* 5.)

AMALGAMATED SOCIETY OF RAILWAY SERVANTS.

Section 121 (n) of the principal Act, which provides that for the purposes of the appointment of members of the Court the Amalgamated Society of Railway Servants shall be deemed to be an industrial union of workers, is negatived. (*Clause* 6.)

Amendment.

The above clause was struck out in Committee, and a new clause inserted, extending the provisions of the principal Act to the "Engine Drivers', Firemen and Cleaners' Association."

APPLICATION OF ACT TO LOCAL AUTHORITIES.

Section 131 of the principal Act, whereby the Act is declared not to apply to Crown or Government Departments, is amended so as to exempt also from its operation "any local authority or public body." (*Clause* 7.)

Amendment.

The above clause was struck out by the Labour Bills Committee and an amending clause inserted, to the effect that the provisions of any award or industrial agreement should not apply to or affect local authorities or public bodies in respect of relief works carried out by them.

QUALIFICATION OF ASSESSORS.

It was proposed that every person recommended as an assessor under the Act must be "actually and *bona fide* engaged or employed, either as an employer or as a worker in the industrial district, and in the industry or in any one of the industries in respect of which the dispute has arisen." (*Clause* 8.)

This clause was struck out of the Bill.

VACANCIES IN MEMBERSHIP OF COURT.

Provision is made in respect of casual vacancies occurring in the office of a nominated member of the Court. (*Clause* 9.)

AMENDMENT OF AWARDS AND COST OF LIVING.

It was proposed (*inter alia*) that every provision contained in any award or industrial agreement whereby increases in the rates of remuneration of any workers were granted in accordance with any increase in the cost of living, affecting such workers, should cease to operate on 30th April, 1922, etc., etc. (*Clause* 10.)

Amendment.

The above clause, a very comprehensive one, was struck out by the Labour Bills Committee, and a new clause (10A) substituted, the main operative portion (which is contained in sub-clauses 1 to 6) as reported from that Committee being :—

> 10A. (1) At any time and from time to time while this section remains in force the Court of Arbitration shall have power, subject to the conditions hereinafter expressed, to amend in such manner as it thinks fit, the provisions of awards or industrial agreements

under the principal Act, in so far as such provisions determine the rates of remuneration of any workers.

(2) In exercising the powers conferred upon it by this section the Court shall have regard to any increase or decrease in the cost of living since the half-year ended on the thirtieth day of September nineteen hundred and twenty, and to the economic and financial conditions affecting trade and industry in New Zealand, and all other relevant considerations, and may, by general order, make such increase or reduction in the rates of remuneration payable under the provisions of any award or industrial agreement as it thinks just and equitable having regard to a fair standard of living.

(3) Such general order shall be filed in the office of the Clerk of Awards in every industrial district, and shall be deemed to have been incorporated in every award and industrial agreement in force in such industrial district as from the date of the order, or as from such later date as may be specified in the order in that behalf, and shall have affect according to its tenor :

> Provided that no such general order shall be expressed to come into operation before the first day of May, nineteen hundred and twenty-two.

(4) The Court may, by the same or a subsequent order, of its own motion, or on the application of any party to an award or industrial agreement, make such provision as it considers just and equitable for any class or section of workers if it is satisfied that by reason of the special provisions of any awards or industrial agreements affecting such workers, or of economic conditions affecting any trade or industry, or any other relevant considerations, such class or section of workers should be excluded from the operation of any such general order :

> Provided that the Court shall not reduce the rate of remuneration of any such workers to a lower wage than will, in the opinion of the Court, enable such workers to maintain a fair standard of living.

(5) No application under the last preceding sub-section shall be made by any industrial union or industrial association unless and until a proposal to make such application has been approved by the members of the union or of each of the unions comprised in the association, as the case may be, in the same manner as if the application were an application to which section one hundred and seven of the principal Act applies.

(6) Every application under sub-section four of this section shall state the special grounds on which the application is based, and shall be filed with the Clerk of Awards in each of the industrial districts to which the award or industrial agreement relates.

OFFENCES.

Clause 11, dealing with attempts to dissuade two or more workers from accepting work, etc., under the conditions of an award, and with attempts to dissuade employers from employing two or more workers under the conditions of an award, was struck out of the Bill.

On 4th February,

Sir J. P. Luke (Reform, *Wellington, North*) having **moved** that the report of the Labour Committee be laid on the **Table,**

Mr. E. J. Howard (Labour, *Christchurch, South*) said that if they took the original amending Bill, as introduced, they would find some of the most pernicious clauses ever brought down in the history of that legislation. It had been suggested that all local bodies should be exempt from the operations of the Bill, although local bodies had, for the twelve or fourteen years for which the Act had been in operation, always forced their workers under the Act. The Labour Members of the Committee had got evidence from local bodies to the effect that they desired to remain under the Act, and the result had been that the clause was thrown out. Some exceedingly bad clauses had been left in the Bill, one of these being that which wiped out the Amalgamated Society of Railway Servants. It had been argued on the Committee that the railway servants had never used the Court for the settlement of industrial disputes, which was quite true. He regarded that as a tribute to that organisation—that they had been able to settle around the table any disputes between themselves and their employers, and that they had never yet had to go to the Court for a final settlement. He (Mr. Howard) wanted to bring this point before the employers: where an agreement had been entered into by negotiations around the table, whether before the Conciliation Commissioner or without one, the agreement had been always honoured by the working class, even if afterwards they had discovered the agreement had not been to their advantage. But he must admit, he said, that the same thing could not be said with regard to the sentences meted out by the Court of Arbitration When the men had been unable to agree and had found themselves subjected to an unjust sentence by the Court they had not felt themselves so bound.

Proceeding, Mr. Howard said the House was being asked to wipe out all the conciliation machinery from the Act. They (the Labour Members) were going to use every permissible method to retain on the Statute-book the conciliation machinery which the workers had enjoyed for so many years.

The Committee had struck out Clause 11, which was a bad clause, because it made it an offence punishable with a heavy fine, for two men to suggest that the conditions under which they were working were unfair. He congratulated the Minister and the Committee upon having that clause struck out. It would have made a criminal of every worker in the near future.

Speaking of Clause 10,* which was introduced, he understood, at the instigation of the Judge of the Arbitration Court,

---

* Clause 10 of the Bill became Section 9 of the Act as passed.

Mr. Howard said there was some one wishing to issue an order: "You shall have this standard of living." But those who spoke in that way did not give to the working class the same standard of living that they asked for themselves. They were asked to wipe out—or to suspend for eighteen months—the operations of the Act. It was also asked that there should be put into the hands of the Judge of the Court the power to make decrees and pronouncements on the standard of living and the conditions under which the workers should live. He suggested that the present legislation was quite sufficient to give the Court power to review and amend the awards in the same manner as was the case when wages were being raised.

Mr. D. G. Sullivan (Labour, *Avon*), speaking with regard to Clause 3 of the Bill, which limited the voting power of the unions in the matter of electing the workers' representative on the Arbitration Court, said the clause had not been demanded by anyone. As brought down in the first instance the clause had read "but in no case shall a union have more than three votes." The Minister had slightly amended it by substituting "five" for "three," so that as it now stood a union with two hundred and fifty members had exactly the same voting strength as a union with five or ten times that number. Why this interference with what was really an internal affair of the unions? What was at the back of it, in view of the fact that it had never been asked for by anybody? The only conclusion was that the Government wished to put a premium on small unions and to impose penalties on large ones. Probably, Mr. Sullivan continued, it would be correct to say that the Government was aiming at reducing the power of what was known as the Alliance of Labour. The Government had got it into its head that the purpose of the Alliance of Labour was to put an end to the Arbitration Act. The officers of that organisation had stated in evidence before the Labour Bills Committee in the most explicit terms that they did not stand for the abolition of the Arbitration Act. Under the legislation now proposed the anomalous position would be created that a group of small unions in a single industry not federated or amalgamated would have immensely greater power, so far as the election of a representative on the Arbitration Court was concerned, than they would have if they chose to amalgamate. He did not believe that the workers and employers would use the Conciliation Councils if the Bill were passed into law. They would be in no mood to discuss wages and conditions, and certainly employers would not be very ready to make concessions to the employees. Instead of trying to use conciliation, the Government, in conformity with its general attitude towards labour, preferred to rely upon the "big stick," and to use force.

Mr. M. J. Savage (Labour, *Auckland, West*) opposed the Bill, and moved that the report be referred back to the Committee.

Sir J. P. Luke said that he regretted that the altered conditions necessitated a review of the cost of labour in the Dominion. They had had in the debate statements that if the report was adopted the principle of arbitration would be wiped out altogether; but, he said, he could not see that, because the Bill conferred greater, more humane powers of conciliation upon the Court. Hitherto the Arbitration Court when dealing with matters before it, had to consider the well-being of the particular industry concerned. The Bill was not confined to the well-being of any special industry. The new principle in the Bill was that no award or agreement would be considered except in the light of the increase of the cost of living, and that was a safeguard. They had been told that neither the employees nor the employers had asked for the Bill; but if certain matters were not satisfactory the conditions had to be considered, and then it was right for the Government to anticipate public opinion. The voting power in the Bill, said Sir J. P. Luke, had been considerably improved. The opponents of the Bill wanted the big unions to override all the other unions. It had been stated that the Government favoured small unions. Was that any crime? The small unions had a perfect right to voting power, and up to the present their votes had been of no use to them, as they had been swamped by the larger organisation. The Leader of the Labour Party had predicted an industrial upheaval as a result of the Bill. He did not believe there would be anything of the sort. The feeling of the country was in the direction of the elimination of those defects which had brought about industrial upheavals in the past. It had been stated that the Bill if carried would bring them back to the conditions that existed in 1914. Upon an hon. Member interjecting "Below that," Sir J. P. Luke said he would rather go out of Parliament than be a party to anything that would bring conditions below the 1914 standard; his aim, he said, was to maintain a higher standard than pre-War rates.

The motion that the report and evidence lie on the Table was carried by 41 votes against 21.

The Minister of Labour (Hon. G. J. Anderson) in moving the committal of the Bill, said it stood for the protection not only of the worker, but of the honest employer. There had been no departure from any of the vital principles of conciliation and arbitration, or from the legislation which had been on the Statute-book since 1918. One or two clauses had been criticised, and he had struck out certain clauses which he had recognised might not be equitable. The principal condemnation of the Bill was coming from the Alliance of Labour and the real position was that it was not the Government but the Alliance of Labour that wanted to wreck the Court.

The Minister then dealt at length with the reason for the legislation having been brought forward. Coming to the provisions of the Bill, he referred to Clause 2, providing that the Judge of the Arbitration Court cannot act on the Supreme Court, saying that the provision was made so that the Judge should give the whole of his time to the work of the Arbitration Court. In regard to Clause 3, he maintained that the principle underlying the voting for the Labour representative on the Court should not be one unionist one vote, but one union one vote. They had compromised and had given a larger union more consideration than a small one. At present, he said, the large unions could by reason of their voting power, dominate the election of the nominated member.

Clause 5 allowed an award to be altered if both parties so wished, "as the Court thinks fit"; that expression had been inserted because it might not be a wise thing to alter an award, even if both parties agreed to it.

The Railway Servants.

The main bone of contention so far as the clauses that had not been struck out were concerned, the Minister said, had been in regard to Clause 6, dealing with the Amalgamated Society of Railway Servants; but he had the highest authority in the labour world for saying that the majority of the unions considered it absolutely unfair that the Society should have a vote for the election of a workers' representative on the Court, seeing that the union never used the Court, and that they would never have the necessity, as far as he (the Minister) could see, of using it.

Clause 8 of the original Bill (in regard to casual vacancies in the Membership of the Court) had been struck out. It had been very severely criticised, and he admitted there was a great deal in the objection of those gentlemen who gave evidence before the Committee.

The Minister then entered upon a detailed and technical explanation of Clause 10 and of the new clause (10A) substituted for it.

Mr. E. J. Howard said that Clause 10 was brought in to put into the hands of the Judge of the Arbitration Court power to cut down wages without any worker having the right to be heard.

Mr. H. E. Holland (Labour, *Buller*) said that the clause (Clause 10), which bestowed upon the Courts power to step in and interfere with awards that had already been made, on the plea that the time had arrived for the wholesale reduction of wages, could only result in bringing about the gravest dissatisfaction in the ranks of the people.

On 7th February,

The debate on the Third Reading was taken, and the motion carried by 38 votes against 9, the House adjourning at 25 minutes past 5 o'clock a.m. on 8th February.

DEBATE IN LEGISLATIVE COUNCIL.

On 9th February,

The Attorney-General (**Hon. Sir Francis Bell**), in moving the committal of the Bill, explained the various clauses. Clause 6, he said, was one to which exception might be taken, but he trusted not in the Council. Hon. gentlemen were aware that the principal Act provided that it should not apply to employees of the Crown, but there was a special provision in regard to the Amalgamated Society of Railway Servants, and some time ago the then Minister of Railways had promised, if Parliament agreed, the same privileges to the Engine-drivers', Firemen and Cleaners' Association. One of two alternatives had, therefore, to be adopted—either to deprive the Amalgamated Society of Railway Servants of the privilege it already had under the Act, or to grant the Engine-drivers', Firemen and Cleaners' Association similar rights. The latter alternative had been adopted.

Speaking of Clause 9,* Sir Francis Bell said that a few words should make its object and effect clear. The Court, he said, had power to deal with awards under the War legislation, but that power was coming to an end. The awards also were coming to an end. Without some provision such as was contained in the clause the Court could be held up for an indefinite period, dealing with union after union and trade after trade, in separate localities, and determining a single question relevant to all unions and all awards, in the earlier cases coming before it, and not only delaying the effect of its determination of that general question, but creating seething discontent by reason of the difference between cases which had been dealt with and cases of continuing awards remaining to be heard. That was the reason for the clause, and the obviating of that result was the effect of the clause. The detail of it had been before a Committee of the Council. There was a provision in sub-clause (4) of the clause that the Court should not reduce the rate of remuneration of any worker to a lower wage than would, in the opinion of the Court, enable such worker to maintain a fair

* Referred to in the summary of the Bill given above, p. 405, as Clause 10A.

standard of living. Subject to that, the clause enabled the Court to do justice to the employers on the one hand and the workers on the other hand.

Legislation "at point of the bayonet."

Hon. W. Earnshaw (*Wellington*) said the Government had entirely failed to consider the people whom the Bill directly affected, and had thrust it through Parliament at the point of the bayonet, with what one might term a conspiracy of silence on the one side and legislation by exhaustion on the other—legislation which affected the daily life of every worker in that country. Clause 9,* said Mr. Earnshaw, was very difficult reading to him. It might be clear enough to those with legally-trained minds, but it appeared to him to contain many pitfalls, and to give more power than was on the surface apparent.

"Disastrous consequences" to country.

Clause 9 determined, in the first place, he said, that a Court of two or one should fix a fair standard of living. He was saying "two or one," because it was obvious that in a Court of three, where there was one representing Labour and another representing Capitalism in its varied forms and, the Judge presiding, the "man in the street" would never be convinced that the representative of Capitalism was favourable to a high standard of existence. Therefore they were asking the Judge—and, he said, he believed the Judge would be the determining factor—to settle an almost impossible problem. If the standard had to be fixed, he (Mr. Earnshaw) thought it ought to have been done by some tribunal entirely away from the Judge of the Court altogether. He concluded by saying that if his sixty years' practical workshop experience was of any value, he was of opinion that the measure was creating disastrous consequences in the country.

Alliance of Labour attacked.

Hon. J. Barr (*Christchurch*) disputed what had been stated by previous speakers, namely, that there had been a deal of outside criticism of the measure before them; saying that he had followed the Bill very closely from the first moment of its appearance, and, taking into consideration that they were dealing with 406 unions, and that 99 per cent. of the criticism had come from one organisation, representative of only a small number of those unions—the Alliance of Labour—he was entitled to say that they had had no adverse criticism from the large bulk of the unions. He wanted, he said, to go

---

* Referred to as Clause 10A in the summary of the Bill above, p. 405.

further, and to say that with the exception of the representative of the Seamen's Union, those who had given evidence on the Bill had admitted the need for what was contained in Clause 10, now Clause 9.

His experience of trade unions was that if they were utterly opposed to a provision they would have no amendments, and would take such vigorous steps as would prevent it going through. But in every instance, with the exception he had mentioned, emphasis was laid on this fact—that what was desired in connection with that clause was that before a general order was made by the Court an opportunity should be given to the Unions to be heard.

"One Big Union."

Coming to Clause 3, about which, Mr. Barr said, there was a difference of opinion outside among two sections of the trade unions, there had been for a number of years, as they all knew, the extreme Socialist section that had captured many of the offices in trade unions, and that had as one of its objects the ultimate creation of the one big union. They now had it in the Alliance of Labour. The thing to be aimed at was the one big union, not to be used beneficially for the trade unionist as a trade unionist, but for political action so that the political machine would be more easily captured.

Possibility of Labour Government.

Speaking in reference to opposition to the Bill, not because the clauses were not beneficial, but because it was not considered a right thing to allow any other than a Labour Government to bring in any amendment of the Arbitration Act, Mr. Barr said if they had to wait for that day the Act would never be amended, unless a more reasonable and more loyal body of men came forward as the representatives of Labour. "If that were done," said he, "I do believe we should see a Labour Government in this country."

Status of Railway servants.

In regard to the clause dealing with privileges to Railway servants under the Act, Mr. Barr said he joined with Mr. McIntyre in his disagreement with Clause 6 as it appeared in the Bill. Why, he asked, should the Railway servants or any organisation be under the Act with special legislation ? They had too much special legislation for Railway servants and for Civil servants. If they were going to take advantage of the Acts that ordinary unions worked under they ought to toe the line and have no privileges that ordinary unions did not have.

In conclusion, Mr. Barr said that the trade unions realised that in order to get continuity of employment there must be a reduction in wages in the same way as wages had been increased—that was, relative to the cost of living, and he did not believe that the opposition to the Bill had been justified.

The Attorney-General, in his reply, said that Mr. Barr had put the case in such plain and intelligible language that he thought the case he had made was unanswerable. He joined issue on behalf of the Government with the statements made by Mr. McGregor and Mr. Gow in their speeches to the effect that the Arbitration Court had nothing to do with what was a fair standard of living. Every one knew, he said, that the workers' wage fixed by the Arbitration Court had been fixed on what the Court had considered to be a fair standard of comfort for the workers. It had been omitted from the legislation of the past; he welcomed its admission to the legislation of the present; and that was the attitude of the present Government.

The Bill was reported and the Third Reading taken and carried on the same day.

ARBITRATION ACT.

(Question of Abolishing Preference to Unionists.)

On 13th October, 1921,

Mr. J. R. Hamilton (Reform, *Awarua*) asked the Prime Minister whether he would give Members an opportunity to place on the Statute-book legislation abolishing the Arbitration Act and preference to unionists, thereby giving the free man freedom to work, and also give him protection while willing to work?

The Prime Minister (the Right Hon. W. F. Massey) replied that it was hoped to introduce a compilation and a number of amendments of the Industrial Conciliation and Arbitration Act shortly, when the question raised could be discussed.

Later, on 30th November, the question was again raised, when, in answer to a question by Mr. J. A. Young (Reform, *Waikato*),

The Minister of Labour (Hon. G. J. Anderson) said that the question of whether the present system of "voluntary-compulsory" preference to unionists should remain was under consideration, and had been under consideration, he supposed, by every Government. He was advised, he said, that in law there was no such thing as statutory preference, as it was left to the Court to say whether the preference should be given or not. It was in the working out that it became compulsory, because a non-unionist found it very difficult to continue working among unionists. There was one thing clear, he continued—that if it was found impossible to fill any particular manufactory with unionists, the employer had a right to put on non-unionists. But the question whether the Court's discretion should be abrogated was under consideration, because the present position was peculiar in the history of the country. It was necessary that employment should be provided, and that all enterprises should be carried on; and if there was a hold-up those who were willing to work should be given every opportunity of doing so.

EDUCATION AMENDMENT ACT.

(Teachers' Oath of Allegiance.)

The above Act, which came into operation on 13th January, 1922, *inter alia*, requires school teachers to take the oath of allegiance to H.M. The King.

It is provided that—

> 11. (1) On and after the first day of April, nineteen hundred and twenty-two, no person shall be employed or shall continue to be employed in, or shall act as a teacher in, any public school, secondary school, technical school, endowed school, native school, or in any private school, unless, in the case of a British subject, he has since the passing of this Act made and subscribed the oath of allegiance, and, in any other case, he has since the passing of this Act made and subscribed in the prescribed form an oath that he will not directly or indirectly, use words, or be concerned in any act, which would be disloyal to His Majesty, if such words were spoken or written, or such act was committed, by a subject of His Majesty.*

MEAT-EXPORT CONTROL ACT.

(N.Z. Meat Producers' Board; London Agency; Control of Export and Shipping; Levy on Meat Exported; Government Guarantee.)

Adverse conditions in the marketing of New Zealand exported meat having affected the economic welfare of the Dominion, conferences were held between Government representatives and various persons interested; and, as a result,

* In the course of the debate on the Second Reading of the Bill, the Minister of Education (the Hon. C. J. Parr) quoted the case of a teacher who had been proved in the Police Court to be a propagandist of communist and revolutionary opinions, and who, he said, had been discharged from her position. He added that, at that time, inquiry was being held into two complaints with regard to other teachers.

the Prime Minister introduced in the House of Representatives on 2nd February a measure whereby it is proposed to set up a Board of Control, "with power to act as the agent of the producers in respect of the preparation, storage, and shipment of meat, and in respect of the disposal of such meat beyond New Zealand."

The Bill was read a first time on the date above mentioned and a second time on the 9th February. Having passed other stages, it received the Governor-General's assent.

The following is a summary of the main provisions of the Bill as amended in Committee after the Second Reading :—

Constitution of Board.

A New Zealand Meat Producers' Board is to be established, to consist of (A) two Government representatives ; (B) five elected representatives of the producers ; and (C) a member representing stock and station agents. The Government members are to hold office during the pleasure of the Governor-General, and the period for which the other members are to hold office, and the method of their re-appointment and of the election of new members, the filling of casual vacancies, etc., is set forth. (*Clause* 2.)

London Agency.

A London Agency is to be set up by the Board, and is to include one Government nominee. The duty of the London Agency is to keep the Board advised as to prices of meat, and as to other matters relative to the disposal of New Zealand meat in England and elsewhere, and generally to act as the Agent of the Board under its directions. (*Clause* 8.)

Export of Meat.

The export of meat from New Zealand may be prohibited, save in accordance with conditions determined by the Board. (*Clause* 9.) Further, the Board is empowered to determine from time to time the extent to which it is necessary the Board should exercise control over the export of meat, and may assume control of any such meat accordingly. Such control may be either absolute or limited. All meat of which the Board has assumed absolute control is to be graded, shipped and sold by the Board or under its direction. Where the Board has assumed limited control, the extent of its control is to be defined by notice, given in conformity with the Act, or by agreement with the owners of the meat or other authorised persons. Existing contracts, or contracts made before such notice as aforesaid for the purchase and sale of meat, are protected so far as such contracts relate to meat to be exported up to 31st October, 1922. (*Clause* 10.)

Board is Empowered to Determine Shipping Contracts.

The Board may also control (subject to a saving in regard to existing contracts) contracts for the carriage of meat by sea. (*Clause* 12.)

Levy on Meat.

Provision is made for a levy, to be prescribed by Order in Council, on meat to be exported, and for the manner in which moneys, arising from such levy, are to be disposed of. (*Clause* 13.)

Other Powers.

The Board is to have full authority to make arrangements and give directions for the following matters :—

(A) For the grading, handling, pooling and storage of meat in New Zealand prior to shipment.

(B) For the shipment of such meat on such terms and in such quantities as it thinks fit.

(C) For the sale and disposal of meat on such terms as it thinks advisable.

(D) For the insurance against loss if any such meat either in New Zealand or in transit from New Zealand, and until disposed of.

(E) Generally for all such matters as are necessary for the due discharge of its functions in handling, distributing and disposing of New Zealand meat.

The Board is also empowered to give security for advances made to the Board, or to the owners of any meat, at the request of the Board. (*Clause* 14.)

Disposal of Proceeds of Sales.

The manner in which moneys received by the Board as proceeds of sales or otherwise is prescribed by *Clause* 15.

Government Guarantee.

It is provided that the Minister of Finance may guarantee advances made to the Board or made to the owners, etc., at its request. (*Clause* 17.)

DEBATE IN HOUSE OF REPRESENTATIVES.

On 2nd February, 1922, the Bill having been received by message from the Governor-General,

The Prime Minister (the Right Hon. W. F. Massey) shortly outlined its provisions, stating that it was proposed to set up the New Zealand Meat Producers' Board. In answer to Mr. H. E. Holland, Leader of the Labour Party, who asked : " Will there be representation of the employees ? " Mr. Massey said there would not. The business of the Board would be to look after the interests of the producers both in New Zealand and in the United Kingdom—as far as possible to keep down the cost of production at that end (New Zealand) and to look after freights, insurance and other matters. The London Agency was to advise the Board (in New Zealand) with regard to the supply of meat. It was not intended at any time to take any improper advantage of the power that might exist of withholding supplies of meat to increase the price, but to ensure that a regular and sufficient supply of meat would be forthcoming from that end (New Zealand) to the other. Mr. Massey quoted Clause 10, which he said gave very important powers to the Board; but whether, he said, it would be necessary to exercise those powers, remained to be seen. The Board might assume absolute control (over the export of meat from New Zealand) if it found that course necessary, or it might only assume partial control. It was not intended to interfere more than could be avoided with people engaged in the meat trade, but if there was any movement on the part of any section antagonistic to the interests of the producers it would be for the Board to take action under Clause 10. It was intended to give the Board control of freights.

After explaining other provisions of the Bill, Mr. Massey concluded by saying that the freezing companies, the stock and station salesmen and the exporters were all interested; and that he believed nearly all those people, instead of being antagonistic to the Bill, would be supporters of it. If they all pulled together with the producers it would be found to be for their own good and for the good of the whole country.

The Bill was then read a first time.

On 8th February,

The Prime Minister, in moving the Second Reading, said that the cables had advised people at Home of what was on foot, and the British Empire Producers' Association, which, he said, took an intense interest in what was called "Empire Preference," had cabled its hearty approval. Mr. Massey also referred to telegrams supporting the proposals received from Manchester, Hull, Bristol and Liverpool.

"I believe," said Mr. Massey, "that the time is coming when the producers in the United Kingdom itself will join with the producers in the overseas Dominions to bring about preference. What form that preference will take I am not able to say at the moment; it may be by way of Customs Duties, or it may be by way of giving the products of the Dominions a preference as regards transport or sea carriage."

A preference of ½d. per pound or even ¼d. would make, he continued, an immense difference to producers in countries like theirs. Nor did he believe for a moment that it would make any material difference as far as prices to consumers in Great Britain were concerned.

Subsidiary pools.

It was not proposed that there should be one huge pool taking in all the meat produced in New Zealand, but each freezing works would be a subsidiary pool on its own account. As far as that season was concerned, it was not intended to interfere with the exporters in connection with contracts already made.

Freezing companies' petition.

In referring to a statement in a petition intended to be presented to the House from the owners of freezing works to the effect that one of the inevitable results of the Bill if passed would be that freezing companies and meat exporters with a distributing business in Great Britain would be unable to rely upon supplies purchased being available for their trade at any particular time, "as the proposed Board may at any time prevent shipment from New Zealand," Mr. Massey said that was nonsense, and that part of the business of the Board would be to regulate shipments so that anything in the way of a glut should be avoided, and to see that the market was supplied with just that quantity of meat and no more than it required; and when the pool came into operation, he believed it would supply the meat to the London market particularly, and also to some of the other centres from which telegrams had reached them, in a manner that would be more satisfactory than it had been up to that time.

Shipping question.

In referring to the expense of shipping, he hoped it would be quite easy for the organisation to so regulate things that a ship loading meat would be able to pick up her cargo at not more than three ports, and so avoid the waste and loss incidental to going round the coast and picking up supplies at a large number of places in order to complete her cargo.

Opposition of Chambers of Commerce.

Continuing, the Prime Minister said he was sorry to notice that almost the whole of the Chambers of Commerce were up in arms against the pool. He expected that they would have understood that anything benefiting the producer in that country must benefit the people in the cities.

Proposed Australian meat pool.

The pool was not a new thing. There was then a cheese pool in Queensland; they had a wheat pool in Australia, in full operation, and he had received information that day that Australia was following the example of New Zealand, and setting up a meat pool. He hoped the Australian people would go ahead with theirs, and if both were successful, then the two organisations might come together and become a very important and powerful combination of great benefit to both countries.

In conclusion, Mr. Massey said the Government were "out in the open," and they wanted to tell the public exactly what they were doing, and get their criticism, whether they approved of the proposals or not.

Government's distributing ability questioned.

Mr. T. M. Wilford (Leader of the Opposition) assured the Prime Minister that while they on his side of the House were going to be critical, they were helpers of the farmer in marketing his produce. Proceeding, he said they were told that there were markets in Manchester, Liverpool and Bristol for their meat; if there were those markets, why were those big companies in England missing them? Would the Minister tell them that they had provided for the distribution of the meat abroad, or that it could be arranged? He hoped the Minister would let them know whether anything in the past had prevented its fair distribution. Did it mean that the financial trusts so controlled the means of distribution that it was impossible for outsiders to get into Manchester, Liverpool and Bristol without the consent of the trust? The Government ought to be able to tell the producers how they were going to get rid of the goods at the other end. The Prime Minister had stated that night that the Government was not taking any risk. That was a bold statement to make, and he (Mr. Wilford) was afraid it was not backed up by any proof. Concluding, he said that he wished any scheme well that would help the producers, but he feared the big combines and powers at the other end. If they adopted the best methods of grading and distribution, then the scheme might succeed.

Labour criticism: "a private profiteering department."

Mr. H. E. Holland (Labour, *Buller*) said that when the Prime Minister had spoken first on the question they had all understood that the proposed pool was to be a matter of the State marketing of the meat of New Zealand, and consequently he (Mr. Holland) had declared that they on the Labour benches would be in favour of the State marketing of meat. He had also intimated that they would look for representation of the working-men on whatever Board was set up. The present proposal amounted to a private profiteering department of industry having the whole of the credit of the State placed behind it, but the State was not to have control. They were now asked to hold up the price of meat, to use all the machinery of the State to safeguard the interest of the meat-owner, and while they were doing that they were to pull down wages in New Zealand. There must be guarantees, continued Mr. Holland, that if the system operated the prices should not go up to the consuming public in New Zealand. The Labour Party suggested that when distribution was being effected in the Old Country it should be effected either through their own shops or through the British co-operative societies.

Mr. R. McCallum (Liberal, *Wairau*) submitted that the Bill was a transgression against all economic principles. Could anybody say it was not an attempt to increase the price of meat to the consumer in Great Britain ? And if it was, then surely it would directly affect the retail price in New Zealand. The Prime Minister had already said that the talk on the Bill had had the effect of increasing the price of their meat products. They knew that the meat from the Argentine and Patagonia shared the increase, and they had nothing to do with Patagonia or the Argentine. How could anything they did in New Zealand affect the price of meat from Patagonia or the Argentine ? If the Minister of Agriculture had concluded that their action in the matter of a meat pool affected the prices of those countries, he (Mr. McCallum) should be sorry for him.

Ministerial reply.

The Minister of Agriculture (**Hon. W. Nosworthy**), in his reply, stated that early in that year firms in that country had been contemplating a reduction in the price to be given for lamb, and the freezing companies had been actually contemplating an increase in their rates (for freezing). But when they (the firms in question) found that there was likely to be a pool in operation, backed by the Government, they had realised that they must let up, and let up not only there, but in Australia and in England. The action of the Government had resulted in an improvement in the position of the producers to the extent of between £2,000,000 and £3,000,000. If they had not made that move the best meat in the country would have passed into the hands of the buyers at low prices, and the buyers would have marketed it at higher figures, putting the money into their pockets.

The Bill was read a second time.

BANKING AMENDMENT ACT.

(Banking Hours.)

The Bill for the above Act (a summary of which appeared in Vol. III., No. 1, of the JOURNAL, at pp. 206-207), after having passed its Third Reading in the House of Representatives, and its Second Reading (*pro forma*) in the Legislative Council, was greatly altered in Committee by the last-named Chamber, and the whole of Clause 2 of the original Bill was struck out and new clauses substituted.

The Act, which became law on 22nd December, 1921, provides that all banks shall be open for business from 10 a.m. till 3 p.m. on every week-day except Saturday. The banking hours fixed for Saturdays are from 10 a.m. till noon ; but the Saturday hours may be varied with the consent of the Minister of Finance provided that any such variation must apply to all banks, and they must in such event remain open for not less than two consecutive hours.

SOUTH AFRICA.

The Second Session of the Fourth Parliament of the Union of South Africa commenced on 17th February, 1922.

GOVERNOR-GENERAL'S SPEECH.

(Land defences; Conferences at Washington and Genoa; Rhodesia; Strike on Rand; Legislative measures; etc.)

The Speech of the Governor-General, His Royal Highness Prince Arthur of Connaught, dealt with the following matters.

Imperial Conference: Land defences of Union.

In July last a Conference between the Imperial Government and the Governments of the Dominions and India sat in London and was attended, on behalf of South Africa, by the Prime Minister and the Ministers of Agriculture and Defence. Advantage was taken of the presence of these Ministers to conclude an agreement with His Majesty's Government, by which the Union Government had assumed full responsibility for land defences and the Military Command of the Imperial Government had been entirely withdrawn. All lands and buildings occupied by the Imperial War Department had also been transferred on the most generous terms to the Union Government.

Anglo-Japanese Treaty; Washington Conference.

The most important subjects discussed at the Conference were the Anglo-Japanese Treaty and the interests of the Empire and of other Powers in the Far East. The result brought into harmony the views of the Imperial Government and the various Dominions, and at the subsequent Conference at Washington agreements were reached which had removed, he trusted for ever, possible causes of misunderstanding which might have become a menace to the peace of the world. The agreement as to the limitation of armaments was a most notable step towards ensuring the peaceful settlement of international differences.

Irish Free State.

The establishment of the Irish Free State as a sister Dominion in the British Commonwealth of Nations was welcomed, and the hope expressed that it would prove a new source of strength to the Empire and enable the people of Ireland to work together in unity for its progress and happiness.

International Court of Justice; Genoa Conference.

The Speech also referred to the establishment by the League of Nations of an International Court of Justice, and to the proposed Genoa Conference for discussing the many economic problems pressing on Europe as the result of the War, at which the Union had been invited to be represented. The interests of South Africa were closely bound up with a right solution of these most difficult problems, and the invitation had been accepted.

Rhodesia; Mozambique; etc.

The relations of the Union with Rhodesia in connection with the attainment of self-government by that territory would be discussed at a Conference between representatives of the Rhodesian people and the Government. The agreement entered into in 1909 between the Government of the Transvaal and the Portuguese Province of Mozambique would also be discussed at a Conference to which the High Commissioner of the Province had been invited.

Trade depression; transport; etc.

The acute depression in trade and industry referred to at the opening of the last Session continued. The diamond-mining industry had almost entirely ceased; the export of South African coal had been seriously restricted by outside competition; the continual fall in the price of gold threatened with extinction a number of mines which for years past had afforded employment to thousands of European and native workers; the markets for agricultural produce had been uncertain and the prices in many cases unremunerative. The conditions had had an adverse effect on the public revenues. Measures of economy had been put in force in the Public and Railway services, and the serious problems arising from unemployment, etc., continued to receive the earnest consideration of the Government.

Legislative measures.

Among the legislative measures to be laid before Parliament were Bills dealing with the financial relations between the Union and the Provinces; the improvement in certain respects of the conditions of natives residing in urban areas; co-operation between producers and consumers; the regulation of apprenticeship to certain trades and occupations; the provision of accurate standards of weights and measures, etc.

Strike on the Rand.

Referring to the serious effect of the stoppage of mining work throughout the Transvaal, the Governor-General said he intended, on the advice of his Ministers, to appoint a

Board to deal with the issues raised by the strike, and to consider what changes were necessary so as to enable the gold-mining industry to carry on its business on a sound economic basis and afford, under proper conditions, employment to as large a proportion as possible of the community at present dependent upon it.

STRIKE ON THE RAND.

(Statement by Prime Minister; Nationalist and Labour Parties' proposals; Origins of the Strike; Colour bar and *Status quo* Agreement; Martial Law; Revolutionary movement; League of Nations; etc.)

On 17th February, the day of the Opening of Parliament, the strike issue on the Rand was raised before the House adjourned by Mr. T. Boydell (Leader of the Labour Party).

DEBATE IN HOUSE OF ASSEMBLY.

The Prime Minister (Lieut.-General the Right Hon. J. C. Smuts) stated that, up to the present, although the Government had been conferring with representatives of the two parties to the dispute, together and separately, no agreement had been arrived at. He had promised the workers that the Government would appoint an impartial Board to go into the whole matter and report to Parliament, and that Parliament should then arrange the final terms of settlement. Both the Chamber of Mines and the Federation of Trades had failed to assist the Government or suggest members for such a Board, and under these circumstances the Government had not yet taken action. The issues were so complicated and far-reaching that Parliament could not decide until there had been obtained reliable and impartial evidence, and it would not act until after proper inquiry. As this would take time, he had advised the parties to return to work.

The workers, he went on to say, had behaved well, even in spite of provocation. He thought they had shown that they were entitled to the good treatment of the House, and he was sure they would get it. But while they were waiting for a settlement the sands were running out. The sooner work was resumed the better for the country and for the men.

The motion for adjournment was agreed to and the House rose.

Nationalist Leader's motion.

On 21st February,

General the Hon. J. B. M. Hertzog (Leader of the Nationalist Party) moved a Resolution urging that—

While it was desirable that the strike should be terminated as soon as possible, and that as far as possible the causes giving rise thereto should be removed in a manner which should assure also for the future the good understanding between employee and employer, it was not in the interest of the country that any change should be brought about in any law, or established custom or agreement, whereby the sphere of employment at present secured to the European labourers in the mines should be curtailed in favour of native labour; and that if necessary the Government should be instructed immediately to take legislative action in order to prevent this.

It was desirable further that the miners on strike should resume work and that the mine-owners should immediately reinstate them; also that a Select Committee be appointed to report upon the composition of a body entrusted with the decision upon, and the solution of the existing disputes between mine-owners and their employees, and upon the desirability of establishing a permanent body empowered to decide industrial disputes.

The last part of the Resolution set out the conditions under which, should the mine-owners and labourers have notified their readiness for a resumption of work, the Select Committee would report the terms upon which this resumption should be assumed to have taken place, provided, however, that such terms and conditions be only provisional, that the body to be appointed (referred to above) should be entrusted with the revision and fixing of the terms provisionally recommended by the Select Committee, and that any modification in these terms and conditions should be retrospective as from the day upon which work had been resumed, unless otherwise determined by the said body.

An impartial tribunal.

General Hertzog said he wished Parliament now to show that it was that great and important body which could cope with a situation such as had arisen. He was in no way concerned with any of the parties to the present dispute. What his motion aimed at was that both disputant parties should have their case heard before an impartial court or tribunal. If a Commission or Board was appointed by Parliament there should be no fear that the body would be anything but absolutely impartial.

Colour bar.

In order to give absolute confidence in the Board to be appointed, he had in the first part of his motion dealt with the colour bar question, which was an issue of policy—an issue which should be decided by Parliament. The policy laid down in the motion had on more than one occasion been approved by the Minister of Mines and by Parliament; it had been approved by Government and Parliament in their resolutions regarding industrial segregation, and that was what he had intended to convey when he stated some time ago that on the colour bar issue 90 per cent. of South Africa stood behind the miners.

Terms for resuming work.

Dealing with another paragraph of his motion, General Hertzog emphasised that the House was not competent to express an opinion on the question of wages and labour conditions. He also moved, however, that the strike should immediately terminate.

The Prime Minister: " On what terms ? "

General Hertzog replied that if the Chamber of Mines and the workers complied with that request they would know what the position was to be. He proposed giving the Select Committee the power to lay down provisional terms on which work was to be resumed. The Board to be appointed would lay down the final terms.

Mr. W. S. Webber (South African Party, *Troyeville, Trans.*): "How about the mines which will close meanwhile ? "

General Hertzog: " That is really a point we cannot go into at this stage." The Select Committee, he continued, might be expected to act as a common-sense body of men, and would not give work where work could not be carried on. He was proposing, in his motion, something which neither the mines nor the miners would dare reject, and if they did, legislation would have to be passed to cope with that eventuality, and provide for the working of the mines.

He went on to say that until the Board had made its final report the provisional terms to be fixed by the Select Committee would be enforced.

" This is not the place," he declared, " to take sides with either of the disputing parties. I do not desire to make recriminations on either side. But it is the duty of Parliament to take steps such as I propose, and if the motion is agreed to there will be an end to the strike within two days."

Mr. C. W. Malan (Nationalist, *Humansdorp, Cape*) seconded the motion.

Labour amendment.

Mr. T. Boydell (Leader of the Labour Party) moved an amendment

urging the withdrawal of the ultimatum of the Chamber of Mines and other employers of labour ; that the subject matter of the *status quo* agreement be referred to a Select Committee ; that an Arbitration Board be established, to be presided over by a Judge of the Supreme Court ; and that provision should be made for the resumption of work by all the strikers on conditions which prevailed at the time of the strike pending recommendations of the Arbitration Board.

He agreed with the Prime Minister that the strike was not only disastrous, but would have far-reaching effects on the social and economic life of the country. But the Labour Party strongly disagreed with the Prime Minister when he suggested that the men now on strike should practically crawl back to work on any terms which the Chamber of Mines liked to offer. It would not be the strikers who would be beaten in this fight; South Africa would be defeated if the men went back on terms of abject surrender.

Effect of "Commando System."

He was glad to hear the Prime Minister commend the men upon the way they had conducted themselves. Taking the position as a whole, with the exception of isolated outbreaks, the men, in spite of provocation, had conducted themselves very commendably during the whole of the dispute. This was due, in a great measure, to the establishment of what was now known as the "Commando System." Although this was new in industrial warfare, it was going to have a far-reaching effect in other countries. It was responsible for the promotion of the spirit of solidity and discipline, and would further promote a spirit of responsibility as far as was possible.

Police authority exceeded; complaints of Police action.

Continuing, Mr. Boydell said the Government seemed to have come out openly on the side of the Chamber of Mines. As the result of information which he had received, he stated that the police were exceeding their authority, and doing their utmost to drive the people back to work against their will. If the Prime Minister wanted to maintain order he should send a telegram to put a stop to such things. What they wanted was not police provocation but an armistice.

His (Mr. Boydell's) amendment was an honest attempt to try and set up a bridge to bring about the settlement of the dispute. He held that if the industry were treated as a whole all the men who could not go back to the low grade mines could be absorbed in the higher grade and richer mines. If it was not possible to absorb all the men on strike, those left out should be provided with maintenance until such time as employment could be found for them. The interim report of the Unemployment Commission showed that thousands of men could be absorbed in the higher grade mines.

The *status quo*.

Then there was the *status quo*. They wanted to see established a civilised basis, and they did not want to see industries built up on cheap black labour to the detriment of a white population. If the wages were standardised on a civilised basis he would not mind if the *status quo* and the colour bar were abolished to-morrow, for he had worked alongside coloured men, and they had hundreds of coloured men in his own Union. That question should be dealt with by a Select Committee of the House, and ultimately by Parliament.

Civilised conditions of labour.

After criticising the figures put forward by the Chamber of Mines in regard to the low-grade mines, Mr. Boydell said if the low-grade mines could not stand civilised conditions of livelihood for the employees South Africa could not afford to have these mines. He quoted what Mr. Justice Higgins in Australia had said on the subject, to the effect that the Court could not endanger industrial peace to keep unpayable mines going.

An Hon. Member: "What has become of the mining industry in Australia?"

Mr. H. W. Sampson (**Labour**, *Jeppes, Trans.*) replied that there was more white labour there.

Prime Minister criticised.

Mr. Boydell went on to criticise the methods of the Government and of General Smuts, contrasting the attitude of the latter to-day with that he had adopted as Colonial Secretary of the Transvaal, when he had "put up a very fine fight on behalf of the people of South Africa against the same interests they were up against at present."

Mr. J. Stewart (**Labour**, *East London, Cape*) seconded the amendment.

Causes of dispute.

The Prime Minister said that General Hertzog in proposing his motion did not explain its terms and the circumstances which surrounded the case. Neither did he speak of the facts of the strike, the region of the strike and the responsibilities of the parties and people concerned. There were four different sets of people involved in the dispute, viz., the engineering workshops on the Witwatersrand, the Victoria Falls Power workers, the workers on the coal mines in the Transvaal, and the workers on the Witwatersrand. Attempts had been made from time to time to widen the area of the dispute and, if possible, to create a general strike in South Africa; but the atmosphere had never been a good one for the propagation of that object. His conviction was that the workers of South Africa as a whole were dead against this strike.

The Victoria Falls Power Station workers occupied a key

position in the north; the gold mines worked by the power supplied by this Station. A number of other industries were worked on the Witwatersrand and in Johannesburg with the power supplied by it. These workers had struck for higher wages. Last year they met to fix a higher basic rate of pay, and the answer of the Directorate was that it was impossible to even discuss that question. To-day was not the time to discuss higher pay. On the contrary, they had to consider the question of lower pay.

Colliers and reduction of pay; other workers.

The colliers in the Transvaal struck because they declined to submit to a reduction of pay from 30s. to 25s. a day. There was no question of the white position. Reductions, the Prime Minister continued, were taking place all over South Africa. The Government had to make their Civil Servants accept reductions by tens of thousands, and they had surrendered millions of pounds in doing so. No one liked to take lower pay, but the Civil Servants were convinced of the necessity of the Government's action and submitted to it.

Not only the railway workers and the Civil Servants, but the gold miners of the Witwatersrand had submitted to a reduction. The only community who would not accept any reduction were the coal miners of the Transvaal. They were a fine body of men, a good body of men, but they had made a ghastly mistake. Members must recognise facts if they were to do their duty. The great coal fight in England lasted three months, and ended in disaster for the men. Before the strike they got 20s. a day, and now they were getting 8s. or 9s.

Mr. W. B. Madeley (Labour, *Benoni, Natal*): "Do you approve?"

The Prime Minister said it was not for him to approve of the economic factors which the Government and the world to-day had to submit to.

Result of the strike.

The result of the local strike was that their market was placed in jeopardy, they were placed out of the world's competition, they lost huge contracts in India, and the coal-owners went to the Government and asked for assistance. The Manager of Railways had also helped them, as far as possible, by lowering the coal rates, but in the end he asked them if they were not able, by reducing prices or financial arrangements, to compete with other markets. They had said it was impossible, because they had to pay miners 30s. a day. The coal-owners proposed a reduction of 5s. a day, which still left 25s.

The men went on strike. He (the Prime Minister) warned them, and they accused him of being partial. But whatever charges were levelled against him he was prepared to do his duty. Now the men were not on strike but were unemployed. The coal industry had gone. They could not sell a third of the coal they did before. It was no good taking the men back.

Gold miners' grievance.

The gold miners went on strike because the Chamber of Mines had given notice of certain changes which were to come into operation on 8th January, but they were extended to 9th February. They had a clear month in which to conduct any negotiations with the Chamber of Mines, which, in giving them the notice, told them that it was without prejudice to the Association. No strike was necessary at all. During the month Parliament, which was due to meet on 20th January, would have sat till 9th February. That was 20 days. He appealed to them, and a meeting of the Federation was called. He did his best to convince them that a strike would be a fearful thing for the country, and would in no way improve their position. He went further and said if they rushed into this strike a month before it was necessary they would find the attitude of the Government would be one of impartiality, but they would preserve law and order and allow the disputants to fight it out. The strike occurred, and an appeal was made to the Government to take action.

The gold miners went further and ordered the withdrawal of all men from essential services, a terrible thing to do. When the coal miners in England endeavoured to do that there was such an outburst of public opinion that the men were allowed to go back and keep the mines going. There was no such consideration in South Africa. There were thousands of workers in the mines who looked upon that industry not as their main interest in life, but as their enemy, and it seemed to him as if they were bent on destroying the industry that gave them their livelihood.

Government's efforts to save mines.

The Government, "in the interests of the Chamber of Mines," he supposed, issued an appeal to the officers of the mines to keep them going, and promised them all the necessary protection, with the result that if it was possible to resume mining operations again in a large number of mines, it was entirely due to the precautions of the Government.

Decay of gold industry.

"It is said," General Smuts proceeded, "that the strike happened for a great principle, in order to preserve the white position—the colour bar—the *status quo.* I think it is necessary for us calmly and impartially to review the facts.

. . . The position of the gold industry in the Transvaal is like that of all other gold industries in the world; they have been declining industries. Where is the gold industry of the U.S.A. and of Australia to-day ? " For some time past the Transvaal gold industry had been on the down-grade, and it was clear that unless special steps were taken the process of decay might be so rapid as to be a very great and severe shock to the whole of South Africa.

" Our whole policy for years now," the Prime Minister declared, " has been directed to lengthening the life of the mines and keeping them going in one way or another. Before the War a mine had a fair chance, and to-day, though the bulk of our ore is low grade, the mining engineers tell us that if we could come back to pre-War conditions, costs and efficiency, the vast bulk of the Rand could be worked practically for generations, and the mines would continue to be one of the most important groups of industry in South Africa."

Low-Grade Mines Commission.

The position changed very much in the War, and when it became clear to those who understood it that unless drastic steps were taken half, at least, of the mining industry on the Rand was in danger of collapse, the Low-Grade Mines Commission was appointed—a most competent and disinterested body.

Continuing to review the position, the Prime Minister referred to the unexpected rise in the price of gold after the War, when it reached 130s. an ounce, and to the subsequent fall until to-day it was about 95s. an ounce, and once more the great danger which was pointed out by the Low-Grade Mines Commission had come to the fore. They were bound to take a very serious view of the situation. The Witwatersrand not only supported the largest industrial population and industry of South Africa, but it was the market of all their producers. Farmers and producers looked to the Rand as their main market, and if half of the Witwatersrand were to decay, and the mines were to stop, the result would be a terrific and cataclysmic blow to the whole of the rest of South Africa.

Native labour.

Last year he had called a conference to deal with some of the aspects of the Low-Grade Mines Report, and to make better use of the native labour on the mines. That was secured without much trouble. The Chamber of Mines said it was impossible to make the best use of the native labour underground until there was a complete reorganisation there, and it put forward these further claims: firstly, that there should be a new scale of prices for underground contract work; secondly, that there should be a rearrangement to meet the working conditions; and thirdly, an abrogation and a termination of the *status quo* agreement.

This last agreement had been confused even that day in the House with what was called the colour bar, and he wanted to make it perfectly clear what the *status quo* agreement was on the one hand and the colour bar on the other.

Colour bar and *status quo* agreement.

The colour bar was a legal statutory bar or line which was drawn in the mining regulations of the Transvaal. It was an old practice there, and on Union was embodied in the State Regulations, that certain work could only be done by whites—by skilled white labour. It was only in the two interior Provinces that this existed—in the other Provinces there was no such protection of white labour. Seven thousand miners were entrenched under this in the Transvaal.

They had heard the colour bar discussed in the House for years, and he did not think anybody had—he certainly never had—heard of the *status quo* agreement being discussed. There was no proposal to touch the colour bar at all. There was a very great difference of opinion on this differential treatment, and there had been discussions in the House on the matter. The Government made it perfectly clear when these negotiations started between the Federation of Trades and the Chamber of Mines last year that the colour bar was not to be touched. He had said so plainly, and it had been the bed-rock of the whole situation.

In the *status quo* agreement a different proposition was made. In 1918 this arrangement was made on the mines:—On some mines certain work was to be done by the natives, and on other mines the same work was to be done by whites, and the dispute between the Chamber of Mines and the Miners' Union was whether that was a native's or white man's work.

To settle this a little document was drawn up in which it was laid down that employment should continue as it was then; for example, where natives were doing drill sharpening they should continue to do so in future, and where in another mine whites were doing the same work, they should also continue doing so.

White workers under colour bar and *status quo*.

Members would see that there was nothing about this agreement which entrenched the white position at all. For the sake of peace this *modus vivendi* was continued. On the Crown Mine, one of the biggest in the Transvaal, drill sharpening was done by blacks, and there was no doubt that the natives looked upon this *status quo* as their charter.

There was nothing sacrosanct or nothing needing special regulations on this agreement.

The Low-Grade Mining Commission reported two years ago that 4,000 whites were working under this *status quo* agreement, whereas 70,000 whites were working in the mines under the colour bar—the 4,000 men being additional to that. What the Chamber of Mines proposed at various conferences with the men was that in order to reduce costs of the low-grade mines it wanted to get rid of about 2,000 of these 4,000 workers under the *status quo* agreement. If that agreement went, many white men would still be necessary on the mines. The whole fight so far as the agreement was concerned had been whether the mines should have the right to retrench the maximum number of 2,000 white men on these mines, and that the retrenchment should be spread over a certain period.

Government's difficulty.

General Smuts went on to say that the demand under the *status quo* was not accepted by the workers, and they went on strike. The Government had to choose between two evils. Unless drastic economies took place in the lower-grade mines, half of the Witwatersrand mines were in danger, and the closing of these would mean the retrenchment of not 2,000, but from 4,000 to 6,000 white men. The Government had not been advised by the Chamber of Mines, but by a thoroughly able and impartial body. With all the responsibility that he possessed he reasserted that what had happened was not a defence of the whites' position at all.

A White South Africa.

There was nothing more fatal to the white position in South Africa than a false idea of a standard the Government could not maintain. He hoped they all supported the idea of a "white South Africa" and a white civilisation for that sub-continent. But if they attempted to establish that on a false economic basis by endeavouring to bolster it up on a false economic standard the effort was bound to end in a ghastly failure. The miners at Witbank had refused 25s. a day, and he would like to know where in the whole of South Africa did a farmer make 25s. a day ?

Government and the strike; defence of Police.

Referring to the efforts the Government had made to prevent the strike, General Smuts said : "I defy any man to go through the happenings of the last few months and point out to me what could have been done to prevent the strike that the Government did not do." He felt that they had been patient in the face of very great provocation.

It was their duty to take all necessary action in order to uphold the law and protect the peaceful pursuits in this country.

In regard to the police, he knew the bulk of the workers themselves appreciated the action of the Government. A hooligan element existed in every large centre of population, and the workers knew how their whole case was spoilt by these ruffians. He deprecated most strongly the references made in the House to the attitude of the police, who had done their best to be helpful, and he did not think the gibes which had come from some Members should be taken seriously.

Hostile political activity.

The Government had been seriously hampered in its work by political Parties. He was not referring particularly to the Labour Party, whose leaders on the whole avoided the dispute. He was sorry, however, that the temptation proved too much for a number of members of the Nationalist Party. Some of the leaders of that Party had adopted a line which had done a grave and serious disservice to the country.

He did not mind at all being called a paid agent of the Chamber of Mines ; he was entirely beyond that. But when the workers on the Witwatersrand were told from day to day by the Nationalist organs that the Government consisted of scoundrels, when the private characters of members of the Government, and especially the Prime Minister, were blackened to the utmost, it became impossible for the workers to have any respect for the Government. The result had been that it was almost impossible for the Government to effect anything, even when they made attempts, to extricate the workers from their impossible position.

Futility of General Hertzog's motion.

Coming to the motion, which he described as futile and impossible, the Prime Minister said General Hertzog perhaps thought that no change should take place in the colour bar or in the *status quo* agreement, and if necessary Parliament ought to legislate in order to entrench that position. In regard to the former, they had statutory regulations and no legislation was necessary. As to the latter, he was sure very few Members would like to make that the law of the land.

Constitution of a Select Committee.

The hon. Member had proposed the appointment of a Select Committee which should report upon the functions of the body which would settle that matter. He could only see one way in which Parliamentary effect could be given to that Select Committee, which was that it would report to that

House and recommend that such and such persons ought to be appointed a court or tribunal, and that they would have such and such functions to settle the strike. That report neither the workers nor the Chamber of Mines might take exception to.

They were asked to create a statutory dictatorial body and to give it compulsory powers of arbitration to settle the strike. That was the system in Australia and New Zealand. There they had compulsory arbitration, and a Court which administered it. They would have to pass a law. That Court which they would create would give their decision as the law of the land. If he knew one thing about the people of that country they would never submit to any such law.

Compulsory Arbitration in Australia and New Zealand.

The only countries in the world where there was compulsory arbitration were Australia and New Zealand, and there it was a ghastly failure. Accounts continued to be published which showed that it was one of the features which was dragging the whole of the industrial position of those countries down. A decision of the Court, affecting 20,000 or 30,000 workers, was ignored. There was no country where strikes were more rife than in Australia.

Government policy defended.

He put it to the House that the only way to deal with that strike was the way in which the Government had dealt with it so far, the only way it could have been dealt with. He had advised the workers to go back to their work. If they did the Government proposed to appoint an impartial tribunal, which would investigate all issues raised by both sides. That body would try to work out from their study of the case the permanent lines of a solution, and their report would be made to Parliament and dealt with during the Session.

Parliament the final authority.

If large industries, said General Smuts in conclusion, were to be bound in that country it would have to be done by Parliament and not by any dictatorial body constituted for the purpose. They wanted an impartial body of capable men who would come before Parliament and make recommendations about racial questions, financial matters and the economical working of the mines. Any other scheme the Government would never agree to. Any other scheme would be illegal. On those grounds only their policy was right. His side of the House would vote against the motion and the amendment.

The debate was adjourned.

The debate was continued on 22nd, 23rd, 24th, 27th February.

On 22nd February,

Mr. W. B. Madeley, who charged the Prime Minister with "having allied himself with the Chamber of Mines, or rather the executive body of the international financiers who pose as the Chamber of Mines, in their determined effort to depreciate the whole of the South African community," urged that the men had not struck for money, but had fought for a principle that many times before had been fought for in other parts of the world and South Africa—the principle of collective bargaining.

Wage reductions in England.

The Chamber of Mines, he further declared, wanted to reduce wages because wages had come down in England where they had said they must reduce because there had been a reduction in America. If there was a reduction in South Africa the English mine-owners would advocate lower wages still. The eight shillings that men got in England was an average wage.

Arbitration in Australia.

The Right Hon. J. X. Merriman (South African Party, *Stellenbosch, Cape*) referred to arbitration in Australia, where as long as the men got all they wanted it was quite a good thing, and they forced on their employers. But if arbitration was in favour of the employers the men simply refused to carry it out.

Black labour in the mines.

All Johannesburg, he went on, and a great part of that country were living on the labours of the black workers in the mines. A large number of white men had left the mines; there was no employment for the blacks who had also left. Members opposite were doing their best to ruin South Africa. Once they got the natives imitating them they would have the country landed in bloodshed and disaster. The salvation of the mines was getting rid of the uneconomic system of labour which prevailed. They had the finest asset, he supposed, of any country in the world in their native population, which was industrious, and, if treated properly and with justice, worked well; and yet those were the men whom they were treading down, and they thought they were creating a "white South Africa" by putting incompetent fellows to watch these native people work.

Mr. M. Alexander (Constitutional Democrat *Cape Town—Castle, Cape*) said Mr. Boydell had said that he had worked alongside coloured men, who got the same wages as he did, but he knew that in the Transvaal the white worker refused to do this, however civilised the coloured man might be. To lay down the principle that because a man was coloured he would never be able to do skilled work was interfering with the laws of nature. Coloured men could do skilled work, but in the Transvaal no matter how skilled or civilised he would have no claim to rise in the social scale. Any settlement of the strike which did not go into the question of the colour bar could not possibly be a lasting settlement.

Position of mines.

On 23rd February,

Mr. Harry Graumann (South African Party, *Commissioner Street, Trans.*) said he could show that the E.R.P.M. had only made a profit of £559 during December, and yet during the same month it had spent £151,000 among the people, which was equal to about £2,000,000 a year. That went to show the benefit to the counrty of the low-grade mines.

Sir Abe Bailey (South African Party, *Krugersdorp, Trans.*) said Mr. Waterson and Mr. Madeley had done nothing but speak against the Chamber of Mines and the capitalists. If the movers of the motion and the amendment had approached the Prime Minister and tried to arrive at a solution they would have accomplished much more good. They were a peculiar combination of long-windedness and short-sightedness, and they wanted to make political capital out of the question. The workers and the Chamber of Mines would have come to an agreement but for intervention by the politicians.

The men and concessions.

On 24th February,

Mr. H. W. Sampson said that the Prime Minister, who was a fighting man, instead of referring the settlement to the proper courts provided for the purpose, had said : " Put them inside a ring, and we will fight it out." He had forgotten to tell the House that from the beginning of the present dispute, before any strike had taken place, the men had agreed to put these questions to arbitration, and were bound to abide by the result. He had also forgotten to tell them in what manner the ultimatum had been given to the men, and also that in the previous year the men agreed to a big cut in wages after a long conference.

The Prime Minister said that he had spoken about that reduction.

Mr. Sampson went on to say that the concessions that had been made from time to time had been made by the men with a view to preserving industrial peace, and not by the Chamber of Mines.

The low-grade mines had nothing to do with the present strike, which was a phase in the industrial development of South Africa.

Mining in England.

In England mining was divided into occupations which were defined, and there was a scale of wages irrespective of colour. A native would get the same wages as a white man, but he would have to do the same work. In industry there was always a tendency for the employer or the management to cast eyes on the top of the list and reduce occupations by definitions to the lowest limits, and pass that work on to the semi-skilled worker. The struggle in industries had been on these lines of demarcation. The Whitley Report was an attempt to stop petty struggles inside workshops, and recommended the "shop-steward" system, which Members had been condemning. He had never understood the system to be such that a shop-steward could order a man not to do any particular work.

Increase of unskilled labour.

Continuing, Mr. Sampson showed what causes had operated—the introduction of machinery, Chinese labour, the War, native labour, etc.—to give to unskilled the place of skilled labour. Then the *status quo* agreement was introduced; it was a clumsy arrangement, but it had gone through the War, and the men were justified in trying to preserve it. By the employment of more efficient whites in the mines, proper supervision, healthy surroundings, and more attention to the technique of mining, a better condition of things would be brought about. What, he asked, was of more consequence to South Africa—the wages the white man spent, or the few pence which dribbled through to the native? No native had been hurt in this fight; nobody had attempted to interfere with him. He had only been exploited, and had been used to the detriment of the white people in that country.

The Minister of Mines (the Right Hon. F. S. Malan) spoke of the impossibility of making the men realise that there were mines which, on account of high working costs, did not pay, and stated that since 1915 up to November, 1921, no fewer than 17 mines had closed. Of these, some might re-open when working costs came down, involving 2,300 Europeans and 22,000 natives. Other mines were exhausted. There was still a premium on gold, but if that disappeared, on the present working costs, half the existing mines would become unpayable.

The Minister added that there was no doubt that the Nationalist Party was making political capital out of the whole matter. The Labour Party was now very strong on compulsory arbitration, but not on the *status quo*, and General Hertzog also desired certain matters kept out. But the fact of the matter was that the two Parties were not prepared to agree to the proposal of voluntary arbitration. Now it was argued that the Chamber should be compelled to take the men back on pre-strike terms, but what if it were proved that the mines could not be made to pay on those terms? If, as Mr. Roos had said, in that case the State would have to work the mines, it amounted to nothing more than confiscation or nationalisation. How would Nationalist Members like to have that principle extended to their farms?

Colour bar to remain.

Referring to the colour bar he pointed out that in 1921 he had, after discussions and conferences, definitely stated that the Government could not contemplate the alteration of the colour bar regulation. The *status quo*, however, was different. Since 1899 the ratio of whites to natives had always been in the neighbourhood of 8 to 9 to 1, and even the *status quo* had not made any difference. It was degrading to the white man to be artificially protected against the native or coloured man, and figures showed that there was no necessity. The reason why numbers were in danger to-day was that many were not efficient miners.

Amendment.

On 27th February,

Major E. Hunt (South African Party, *Turffontein, Trans.*) moved as an amendment that it was in the best interests of the country and the men that the latter should return to work on the best terms obtainable pending an inquiry by an impartial Board.

Mr. Tielman Roos (Nationalist, *Lichtenburg, Trans.*) said he thought the mines had been the graves of a large portion of the cream of South African manhood. It was necessary for the men to work in these mines because the Government had done nothing for years to open up fresh avenues of employment. Employing classes were conducting a general offensive against the workers all over the country in a most oppressive manner.

Turning to nationalisation he asked why, if it were a right thing to nationalise power, was it a Bolshevik policy to nationalise coal mines? The Prime Minister had talked a good deal about making the world safe for democracy: it was only safe for democracy to starve.

Working for a Republic.

Referring to a resolution which had been presented to him, Mr. Roos said, " Our policy with regard to a Republic remains exactly the same as it was, and when the time arrives and is ripe, we will try to bring it about by constitutional means . . . we will have nothing to do with shooting, and we will never consent to matters of this kind being dealt with by other than constitutional means."

After an all-night sitting, which ended at 9.40 a.m. after 17 hours of debate, a division was taken to delete certain words to allow of the incorporation of the amendments. A decision to retain the words, which meant that the amendments would drop, was agreed to by 70 votes to 54.

Mr. Boydell's amendment was negatived by 70 votes to 54, the majority being the same; Major Hunt's amendment was agreed to by 69 votes to 53.

Treatment of Natives: Military measures.

On 9th March,

The Right Hon. J. X. Merriman (South African Party, *Stellenbosch, Cape*) moved the adjournment of the House:—

on a matter of urgent public importance, *i.e.*, the recent development on the Witwatersrand leading to the loss of life amongst natives and Indians.

The motion was allowed in view of the seriousness of the situation.

Mr. W. H. Stuart (South African Party, *Tembuland, Cape*) said that during these difficult times the natives on the Rand had maintained, for all practical purposes, a complete silence, although some 40,000 of them had, owing to a dispute to which they were not parties, been thrown out of their billets. When their brothers broke the law at Bulhoek they were punished. What the natives wanted to see was that when other people broke the law even-handed justice was meted out to them.

Mr. T. Boydell said the new phase of the position included attempts to try and put down the disturbance by means of aeroplanes and other weapons. It would be almost impossible for military forces to use aeroplanes without doing damage to innocent Europeans and natives. He appealed to the Prime Minister to stop the policy of trying to settle the dispute by the military machine.

The Prime Minister compared the conduct of the white men with that of the blacks in native areas, and said " We whites are on our trial, and I hope that from this House will go the impression all over South Africa that on all the benches here and on all sides of the House we deplore, and deplore bitterly, what has happened on the Witwatersrand, and not only do we deplore it—we denounce it." In reply to a question he added " I do not draw any distinction between the black man who is killed and the white man who is killed. We deplore and denounce all these outbreaks." The ordinary elements on the Rand were in abeyance, and their place had been taken by criminal and lawless elements of the population. These were organised. That was a novel and dangerous feature of the situation. The Government had given instructions of the strongest and most peremptory kind to deal with the situation. If the commandos continued in their lawless careers the responsibility would rest upon themselves.

Martial Law declared.

On 10th March, in reply to a request for a statement made by Mr. Boydell,

The Prime Minister said the Government had been reluctantly compelled to advise the Governor-General to declare martial law on the Witwatersrand and adjoining districts. The position had become graver. That morning the commandos attacked, fighting started and was still going on. Under these circumstances it was impossible for the Government to wait any longer. The country must be prepared for considerable trouble and for bloodshed on a scale which they had not anticipated before.

Conduct of natives; progress of fighting.

The natives were in a state of turmoil; and the friends of those natives who had been murdered in large numbers had appealed to him for protection. It had been stated that some provocation had come from the natives and that they had been armed. Neither of these statements was correct. There had been not the least provocation from the natives. In one or two cases they had been attacked and had defended themselves, but only after they had suffered heavy casualties. The conduct of the natives had been exemplary. It was difficult for them to draw a distinction between the Government and the strikers. To them they were all white people. They had been assaulted and thought that every white man was against them and that they must protect themselves. The Government had an added inducement to proceed forcibly and to say these people were no longer to be subject to assaults.

The fighting which started that morning, the Prime Minister added, was not going in favour of the Government. The commandos were well armed. What the end would be they all knew. He asked the House, which was representative of South Africa, to use all its influence to minimise the bloodshed, which had now become inevitable, and assist the Government by word and deed in order that the trouble might be got over as speedily as possible.

Labour support.

Mr. T. Boydell, in submitting a motion for the adjournment of the House, said they were all fired by a desire to do what they could to assist the Government to bring about peace and law and order at the earliest possible date. He asked the Prime Minister to take that as an offer from the Members on those benches. They would do all they could, and if the Prime Minister would get the Chamber of Mines in a frame of mind to meet the men, they would get the men to meet the Chamber.

The motion was not allowed and the matter dropped.

On 13th March the Second Reading of the Appropriation (Part) Bill was moved by the Minister of Finance (Hon. F. Burton) and the position on the Rand further discussed.

On 17th March, in the course of the debate on the Second Reading of the Appropriation (Part) Bill, further references were made to the strike on the Rand.

"Liberty" under commandos; revolution intended.

Mr. H. S. McAlister (South African Party, *Germiston, Trans.*) said that to say the commandos had been the guardians of the liberty of the people, and were purely peaceful organisations, was trifling with the intelligence of the House and the country. He had had four weeks of the commandos, and the tyranny of martial law was glorious freedom compared with their "liberty, equality and fraternity." No liberty had existed, unless it was the liberty of the leader of the commando and his followers. He believed the Government would realise that it was only because it had failed to prevent these commandos forming, drilling and becoming efficient that it was largely responsible for the loss of life which had taken place.

Surely no reasonable citizen of common sense could believe for one moment those who said there was no intention of a revolution.

Martial Law.

Dr. T. C. Visser (Nationalist, *Vrededorp, Trans.*) said it seemed to him that the Government with their military forces had rounded up and captured nearly every man in Vrededorp, whether they were suspected or not. If the Government could prove there had been a plot to reduce the country to the same state as Russia, he, personally, would say it was their duty to put it down. His side of the House favoured doing things by constitutional means. He did not believe there had been any plot. It was scandalous* that

* At the instance of the Speaker, Dr. Visser substituted the word "undesirable."

the Prime Minister should be making certain representations on the Rand.

On 20th March the Prime Minister made his first appearance in the House of Assembly after the Rand strike, and made a statement as to the position.

The Prime Minister said he did not think the gravity of the situation, as it was when he arrived at Johannesburg, shortly after his last statement, had been sufficiently appreciated. Practically the whole of the Witwatersrand was in possession of revolutionaries with the exception of Boksburg, and a small portion in the centre of Johannesburg.

The Minister of Defence had acted with great expedition as the outbreak took place. He had mobilised the surrounding districts and commandeered the burghers, and the organisation and response were magnificent.

Revolutionary movement; mine workers; Council of Action; etc.

After giving details of the fighting and restoration of order in Johannesburg, the Prime Minister said the country had escaped a tremendous danger. The strike had been submerged in a revolution, and this was recognised by the Mine Workers' Union when they came together and passed a resolution calling off the strike, so far as they were concerned, in the following terms:—

> That this meeting of executive members of the South African Mine Workers' Union wish entirely to dissociate ourselves and the organisations we represent from the revolutionary movement set up without our knowledge or sanction under cover of the real strike issue. We repudiate and condemn such unwarranted action, and dissociate ourselves entirely from those who are responsible.

Continuing, the Prime Minister said it had been clear for some time that the Mine Workers' Union, and the Executive of the Federation of Trades—the augmented Executive—were not entirely free agents, but that there was an influence dominating and in a certain sense controlling them. As soon as the Trade Unions noticed that they were not free agents and that physical force was in the background, they should have taken this step of dissociating themselves from it. A clear opinion should have been given all over South Africa, and much of the trouble and misunderstanding would have been cleared away at once.

The Government had been blamed for not arresting the people who dominated the Council of Action, as they were called, but there was a stage in the business when most of these men were in gaol. They were let go by the magistrates of Johannesburg on the flimsiest possible bail.

It was clear from statements made from time to time by some of their leaders that what they were really out for was revolution of the French Republic type. An attempt was made to establish a Soviet Government. It might be said that these people were mad, but they had a measure of success.

Support for law and order; conduct of natives.

When the appeal was made by the Government for the assistance of the country every part responded. Burghers were commandeered: there was no question about their duty or their politics. It was not a question of the Government, but of public stable authority.

"I am certain," said the Prime Minister, "that all over the world it will be realised that in South Africa, whatever may be its politics or its divisions, there is a vast body of quiet, solid, public opinion which will support law and order."

Continuing, the Prime Minister warmly praised the police. They were a young force, they had not time to build up any *esprit de corps*, and they were full of people who were not in political agreement with the Government. If people read the names of police killed and wounded, they would see that they were men who bore Dutch names.

He wished also to associate with this word of thanks the other forces which came forward, the citizens of Johannesburg and on the Witwatersrand. The burghers came up in their thousands with a rapidity which was an astonishment to him. Many of them had been killed; half of their casualties belonged to the police force, the other half to the other forces,

Continuing, General Smuts said the Government had decided that all who were wounded and the families of all those who fell should be treated on the most generous basis—either on the compensation provided by the Police Laws, or, if it was more favourable, the treatment meted out to their soldiers in the last war.

"Very deep gratitude," said the Prime Minister, "is due to the natives of this country for not getting stampeded. The fear when I left this House on Friday afternoon—the fear that obsessed me above all things—was that owing to the wanton provocation of the revolutionaries there might be a wild outbreak among the natives. They kept their heads, and were the most solid and stable element on the Witwatersrand. The white people of this country are in duty bound to recognise the attitude and law-abiding conduct of the natives in this great crisis."

Martial law: trial of criminals; impartial Board.

Conditions, said the Prime Minister, were gradually becoming normal, and martial law should not be maintained longer than was necessary. It had to be kept in force until an Act of Indemnity had been passed. The Government hoped almost immediately to introduce the Act, and he hoped it would be convenient to get it through the House as soon as possible.

In regard to the very large number of persons who had been concerned with the revolution, and who had committed crimes (General Smuts enumerated a few, such as outrage and murder, blowing up railways, sniping, etc.), the situation could be cleared up rapidly under martial law, and for that there was a good deal to be said. But, on the whole, the Government had thought that would not be the proper course to take. Martial law was disliked, and in the end it left behind it effects just as serious and reprehensible as the revolution itself. The Government had, therefore, thought it best not to try these people under martial law.

Another course open to them was to do what was done after the rebellion, and constitute a special tribunal. In order to follow that procedure they would have to pass an Act through Parliament. In the nature of things they might find it difficult to get legislation of that kind through that House, and it would be months and months before it would be possible to commence the trial of the guilty. The Government thought the feeling would be so great that it would not be in the interests either of justice or the country itself that they should have this delay, and they had therefore decided that the trial of these people should take place according to the ordinary law of the land.

"Let me say a word," the Prime Minister continued, "in regard to a matter which has been referred to in this House before, and that is, the appointment of a Commission, an Industrial Commission, to inquire into the matters in dispute." The House would remember that on previous occasions it was the remedy which the Government proposed as a permanent solution to the industrial issues raised in the strike. They were far-reaching and important, they required very careful inquiry, and the Government at a previous stage put that solution before the House which passed a resolution in favour of an impartial Board to inquire into these issues.

The Government adhered to that policy, and proposed, now that the strike and revolution were over, to appoint the ablest and most impartial Board they could command in that country to go into the issues and guide the House in future in laying down lines of legislation that might secure industrial peace. They were now considering the question of its *personnel*. At one stage they had thought it advisable to have nominees in addition to independent members to be nominated by the Government, both of the Industrial Federation and the

Chamber of Mines. They had, however, abandoned that idea. The Government felt that the body they appointed should be such as to be impartial, able, and in a position to do justice to both sides.

In conclusion the Prime Minister said he would make one appeal. They had been busy in that House for a month, and during most of that time had been discussing the upheaval on the Rand. It was over now; the men had declared the strike off and were going back to work. He submitted that Members would best consult the dignity of the House, and be discharging the best service to South Africa if they turned their attention to the very important task which lay before them. They had a very heavy legislative programme which had to be passed. Not only the finances of the country had to be put right, but they had to pass a number of industrial laws necessary to give work to thousands of unemployed as a result of the upheaval. The eyes of the whole country were upon that Parliament and the problems which were before them.

General Hertzog asked the Prime Minister whether he would be prepared to support the appointment of a Select Committee to conduct an inquiry into what had taken place on the Rand and the events immediately preceding the outbreak.

League of Nations: Commission of Inquiry.

Mr. T. Boydell said the eyes not only of South Africa, but of the whole world were on that country and what had taken place along the Reef. They were all too much mixed up with all the happenings that they thought the Commission to be appointed should be one outside the scope of South Africa, and be appointed by somebody in whom the Prime Minister had great confidence. It would be only right and proper if the Prime Minister would agree to make representations to the League of Nations—to the industrial section that was appointed under the League. If the Prime Minister were to ask the League of Nations to appoint its highest tribunal, they could eventually know exactly the whole of the causes that led up to the trouble.

The Prime Minister said he had a high opinion of the League of Nations, but he had a high opinion of their Government. It would not be necessary to go to the League of Nations and ask for a tribunal to do something that would be outside its functions. He thought they could appoint in that country a body that ought to carry the necessary weight of public opinion and of that House.

In regard to General Hertzog's suggestion, he thought it would be a most inconvenient course to appoint a Select

Committee. Every possible witness would have to be brought from up-country at great expense, and his own opinion was that all these cases would be dealt with in the Law Courts. If simultaneously a Select Committee or Parliamentary Commission were also probing these affairs, it would possibly lead to a serious prejudice of the Courts of Justice. If, as a result of what took place in the Law Courts, it became necessary to appoint a Committee or Commission, he would not say nay, but at the present stage it would be premature.

The House then proceeded with the Orders of the Day.

INDEMNITY AND TRIAL OF OFFENDERS (DISTURBANCES) BILL.

(Strike on the Rand.)

On 24th March, in the House of Assembly,

The Prime Minister (Lieut.-General the Right Hon. J. C. Smuts) asked for leave to introduce a Bill

To provide for the withdrawal of martial law in certain districts of the Transvaal; to indemnify the Government, its officers and other persons in respect of acts in relation to measures taken for the prevention and suppression of disorder in those districts, the maintenance of good order and public safety, and the administration of martial law; and, further, to enable special criminal courts constituted under the existing law to try certain classes of offences committed during the disturbances.

General the Right Hon. J. B. M. Hertzog (Leader of the Nationalist Party) in opposing the motion, said the unfeeling and unsympathetic attitude of the Prime Minister meant that people who had lost relatives would have to be satisfied with evidence which might be produced in the course of the trials. He agreed that the Bill would have to go through the House; in cases where men were called upon to maintain law and order there was always the possibility of their exceeding their powers, accidentally or through ignorance, and indemnity was required for such purpose. At the same time, it was essential that they should see to it that anyone who maliciously exceeded his powers should be rigorously dealt with, and should not benefit from the indemnity. The Prime Minister had told the House that he was not aware of any irregularities under martial law, nor did he (General Hertzog) know of any, but in order to secure that information an inquiry was essential. In refusing an inquiry the Prime Minister was making himself guilty of complicity in the acts complained of.

General Hertzog concluded by moving for

the appointment of a Parliamentary Commission to inquire without delay into and report upon the recent occurrences on the Rand which led to martial law, the extent of the disturbances, and the excesses committed on either side, the number and nature of casualties, arrests, etc.

Mr. J. P. Mostert (**Nationalist,** *Namaqualand, Cape*) seconded.

Judicial Commission.

Mr. T. Boydell (**Leader of the Labour Party**) said that while he agreed with almost everything General Hertzog had said, he thought a Commission appointed by Parliament or consisting of Parliamentarians would be a great mistake. They did not want members of Parties who would be likely to be accused of Party bias. The highest, most weighty and independent tribunal should be set up to go into the whole of the recent happenings, and if they could not get it, they (the Labour Members) said that a Judicial Commission, consisting of three Judges of the Supreme Court, should be set up. They ought to have the inquiry before the Government got indemnity for all those happenings.

The Prime Minister: "How long do you want martial law?"

Mr. T. Boydell: "We agree that martial law should be withdrawn as quickly as possible. But martial law can exist on paper without a single regulation being given practical effect to."

There was no Parliament in the world, he continued—not even in Mexico—where they were so familiar with Indemnity Bills. It was a standing reflection on the public life of South Africa that they always had to use force instead of reason. In addition to a Parliamentary Commission he would like to see a Judicial Commission so that every opportunity might be given to elicit the whole truth.

The Prime Minister made an appeal for true patriotism and impartiality in dealing with the matter. The first point was that it had been necessary to proclaim martial law, and what the Government had been blamed for was that it had waited too long.

The second point was that they could not remain under martial law, and it having been declared, and acts having taken place under it, the next step was to withdraw it. General Hertzog had admitted that such a Bill as was now being introduced was necessary, so that the real matter which he (General Smuts) had introduced was not contentious at all. If General Hertzog's amendment was passed, the Indemnity Act dropped, and remained so until the Session was finished, and he (the Prime Minister) in his plain ordinary duty would not be in a position to withdraw martial law after that.

As to the Commission of Inquiry, in itself, he had no objection; he had an open mind on the question of a Commission ultimately inquiring into certain aspects of the recent affair in the Witwatersrand. The character of the Commission was a matter of difficulty. If it was appointed now, it would have to proceed with its work immediately, and under the amendment it would have to deal with the very questions which they wanted to delegate to the Law Courts. Did General Hertzog contemplate that the two bodies, a Parliamentary Committee and the Courts of the land, could sit simultaneously to discuss the same facts ? He could not conceive anything more absurd or contrary to justice. Referring to the number of arrests and casualties, General Smuts said long before a Parliamentary Commission was in a position to report its findings, the Government would be able to give the House and the country generally all information possible. If it was possible to make out a good case for the appointment of a Commission afterwards, the Government would be quite prepared to do so.

The debate was adjourned.

On 27th March, the motion that the " question be now put " was carried by 57 votes to 45.* The Prime Minister's motion for leave to introduce the Bill was agreed to by 59 votes to 45. General Hertzog's amendment dropped.

The First Reading was agreed to by 60 votes to 45.

Commission of Inquiry to be appointed.

On 1st April,

The Prime Minister, having referred to certain cases of shooting which had been brought to his notice, and to the opinions formerly expressed by him on the subject of a Commission of Inquiry, said certain charges had been made in that House, and charges would continue to be made, and he was afraid the refusal of an inquiry might cause a wrong construction to the effect that the Government had something to hide when things had taken place under martial law, or otherwise which would not bear the light of day. The Government had come to the conclusion that there was nothing on which the fullest light should not be turned, and under these circumstances they had decided to appoint immediately a Commission of Inquiry. It would not be a Parliamentary Commission. The object of the Government was to try and get an impartial Commission to make an impartial investigation. They would make the Judge of the Supreme Court the President; in regard to the rest of the *personnel* they would see that the Commission was so constituted that it would carry weight.

Mr. T. Boydell, asked whether the Prime Minister would suspend any indemnification which he proposed to take until the facts had come to light and the Commission had reported,

* The Nationalist and Labour Parties voted in the minority.

and whether the men who had been committed for sentence would be allowed to give any evidence which they had before the Commission.

The Prime Minister said the Indemnity Bill must in its provisions be of a reasonable character, and Members would see when they came to the provisions that they safeguarded individuals and indemnified them only in respect of what they had done in good faith. Wherever they had transgressed a rule of good faith and done anything opposed to that, they were not protected. In view of that the hon. Member would see that it was not possible for the Government to either suspend the Bill or suspend the indemnity until the Commission had completed its inquiries.

The Second Reading of the Indemnity Bill was then moved, the Prime Minister reviewing the principal incidents of the Rand disturbance.

The debate was adjourned.

On 5th April,

General Hertzog moved,

that the order for the Second Reading be discharged and the subject matter be referred to a Select Committee, to be instructed to inquire into certain telegrams alleged to have passed between the Chamber of Mines and its representative in Cape Town regarding the Chamber's agreement with his (General Hertzog's) motion on 21st February.

The debate was adjourned.

It is reported in a Press cable that the Second Reading of the Indemnity Bill was agreed to on 22nd April after prolonged discussion, and that the Third Reading was carried on 29th April by 57 votes to 44, but the reports of the debates have not yet reached England.

TRADE COMMISSIONER IN EUROPE.

Replying to a question on 23rd February regarding the appointment of Mr. K. Spilhaus as Trade Commissioner for the Continent of Europe,

The Prime Minister (Lieut.-General the Right Hon. J. C. Smuts) said: "Mr. Spilhaus will not represent any South African merchants in England. He has been appointed Commissioner for Commerce on the Continent of Europe where his duties will be to extend the Union's trade relations generally, and any South African merchant may avail himself of Mr. Spilhaus's assistance towards this end."

DEBATE IN HOUSE OF ASSEMBLY.

On 3rd March in the House of Assembly, in Committee on the Additional Estimates, on the High Commissioner's Vote,*

* *Vide* JOURNAL, Vol. III., No. 1, pp. 211—217.

subsistence and transport, £1,000, the appointment of Mr. K. Spilhaus as Trade Commissioner for Europe was debated.

Mr. M. Alexander (Constitutional Democrat, *Cape Town, Castle*) said meetings had been held in Cape Town in regard to that appointment; and from the outset he condemned any racial reference in regard to it. He objected to it purely and solely on its merits. Why was it necessary to make such an appointment at all? If it was to encourage trade with Europe everybody knew what the position was. Was it seriously intended by the Government that Mr. Spilhaus was going to do what the wisest brains of the world had failed to do?

The appointment, he continued, was not going to bring an ounce of additional trade to the country. He would like to know why they did not wait until Parliament met before making an appointment of that kind. At one time they were told that this ambassador of trade was going to be in Europe, and at another time that he was going to support the High Commissioner. The most serious accusation against the Government was that the contract with the Trade Commissioner had not been made public. They did not know how long it was for, or how much he was going to get. After putting various questions Mr. Alexander moved a reduction of the Vote to £500.

The Minister of Finance (Hon. H. Burton) said the real root of the objection to Mr. Spilhaus's appointment was that he was of German birth. Personally, and he spoke for his colleagues and himself, they deeply regretted that objection. He could understand it though he deplored it. The War was over and peace had come, and they must act as though they were still at peace. The sole question had been "Is this the gentleman best fitted for the post that we wish to establish?"

Need of new markets; terms of appointment.

Central Europe had been one of South Africa's best markets, and it was a good thing from the point of view of South Africa that they should endeavour to broaden out their markets for the sake of their agricultural produce, not only in the United Kingdom, but on the Continent. Mr. Spilhaus's operations would not be confined to Germany, but he would operate in Holland, Belgium and France. Prices of agricultural produce were very low, and agriculturists could not sell, and the Government had thought it worth while to attempt to get somebody who would be in touch with Germany and the Continent. The appointment had been made for three years, and if the endeavour of the Government was not justified, they would know how to act. Mr.

Spilhaus had not been a candidate for that office, and he had offered great objection. He had started a very good business of his own in Cape Town and it did not pay him to give it up and go on the Continent.

Functions and pay of Trade Commissioner.

His record was known to them in the town, Mr. Burton continued, as a sound good business man of outstanding ability. He would be a subordinate to the High Commissioner and form part of the High Commissioner's office; but the arrangement made with Mr. Spilhaus was that he acted on the Continent with a free hand and kept in touch with Sir Edgar Walton. On important questions and when emergencies arose, he would be free to act for himself. They were giving him as free a hand as necessary.

Mr. T. Boydell (Leader of the Labour Party): "What is his salary?"

The Minister of Finance: "£2,000 a year."

Mr. Boydell: "And expenses?"

The Minister of Finance: "The expenses of his office. We don't know what they will be."

Sir Abe Bailey (South African Party, *Krugersdorp, Trans.*) said there were men in South Africa equally suitable and qualified for the position. He would say frankly that whether Mr. Spilhaus was a German did influence him. He did not think the choice of a representative of South Africa in Germany or any other country should come, as it were, from the concentration camp. The Minister's reply did not take into account sentiment.

Mr. W. Macintosh (South African Party, *Port Elizabeth—South-West, Cape*) urged the same objection. There were a large number of Germans by birth who during the War had served South Africa. Had Mr. Spilhaus done so?

Mr. R. W. Close (South African Party, *Rondebosch, Cape*) said he believed the Government had acted in this matter with a full regard to the best interests of the country, but he believed also they had acted without the least knowledge of the real strength of the sentiment of a large number of people who had suffered very heavily.

Prime Minister's explanation.

The Prime Minister deprecated Mr. Close's statement, but added that the exhibition of sentiment had been far beyond anything which had recently happened in South Africa, and it certainly came as a complete surprise to them. He personally had no racial feeling in him, but he could understand the sentiments of other people. They were, of course, not far from very great events, and could not forget how people had suffered.

They had been deeply distressed, and although there might have been an apparent disregard of public opinion, it had not been, as a member had said, cynical. It was due to Mr. Spilhaus to say that when this feeling was at its highest and the whole Peninsula and some other parts of the country seemed to be in a wild uproar over the appointment, Mr. Spilhaus offered to resign. He (the Prime Minister) said no. They stood firm because they knew they were right. They had never been more convinced of the rightness of their action in any matter than they had been in regard to this.

The matter caused the Government anxious consideration for months. Members knew that pressure had been brought to bear upon them, not by persons, but by the necessities of the case, to make provision for markets and outlets in Europe. They had sent deputations and officials and done everything they could to get that country out of the morass in which it was.

German market; reasons for selection.

Their principal market in the past was Germany. Most of their wool, and a very large portion of their maize and wattle. bark, etc., went there. A very large portion of their export trade had been done, directly or indirectly, with Germany, and they had made most determined efforts in the last few years to re-establish those markets. They had not been successful, and it appeared to them necessary, finally, to appoint a representative who could do more than any casual expedition or mission to open these markets.

Prima facie, it seemed to him that the appointment of a German by itself might be a good thing. In regard to the post itself, he did not think honestly there could be any real argument about it. They ought to have made the appointment earlier.

Proceeding, the Prime Minister explained how the selection was made after consulting a number of gentlemen in South Africa who could speak about the trade in that country; and, he added, Mr. Spilhaus's name was suggested by people who were entirely loyal and British. The Minister of Railways,* a loyal Britisher, when the list of names was submitted to him, had not the least doubt that Mr. Spilhaus was the best man.

Mr. Spilhaus had written to the Press and denied the charges levelled against him. It was true he had been interned, but only for four days, a mere formality; then he was released and kept under observation, as many others were, and there was not in all that time the least thing that could be said against him. The matter was finished now, General

* The Hon. J. W. Jagger.

Smuts went on, and could not be recalled. He urged that they should give Mr. Spilhaus a chance, and if he were successful it would redound to the interest of South Africa.

Nationalist approval.

Mr. Tielman Roos (Nationalist, *Lichtenburg, Trans.*) said in this case they were entirely in sympathy with the Prime Minister. To push their trade interests in Germany and to be free from the London Office and the High Commissioner was a good thing, and he thought that 100 per cent. of the farmers of the country were very well satisfied. Those who said that the appointment was not necessary should also object to the High Commissioner's office in London. Public opinion in South Africa was not against Mr. Spilhaus's appointment, it was either indifferent, or, with the exception of a few places, it favoured the appointment.

Mr. P. le Roux van Niekerk (Nationalist, *Waterberg, Trans.*) expressed gratitude that the Government had at last agreed to the appointment of a Trade Commissioner for the European Continent, which had been advocated for so many years.

General E. A. Conroy (Nationalist, *Hoopstad, O.F.S.*) said it was clear that the objections raised by some Members were based on the fear that goods would be imported from Germany in competition with goods from England.

After further debate the amendment was negatived and the Vote agreed to.

Duties and relation to High Commissioner.

On 8th March,

The Prime Minister in reply to Mr. J. Henderson (South African Party, *Durban—Berea, Natal*), said Mr. Karl Spilhaus's appointment as Commissioner for Commerce in Europe was for three years; his total salary and remuneration was £2,000 per annum, plus travelling expenses; his office establishment had not yet been determined; his headquarters would be Rotterdam; his specific duties were the extension of the Union's trade relations with Europe; and he would be independent of the High Commissioner in respect of his work on the Continent.

APPEALS TO THE PRIVY COUNCIL.

(Suggested Abolition Rejected.)

IN THE SENATE.

On 24th March,

Senator the Hon. F. W. Reitz moved:—

(A) That it is desirable to delete all the words after the words "King-in-Council" in line 3 of Section 106 of the South Africa Act, 1909, so that in future there shall be no appeal from any judgment given by the Appellate Court of the Union; and (B) that the Government be requested to take the necessary steps to bring about the propcsed amendment.

He maintained that the Judges of their courts were better acquainted with the Roman-Dutch law than oversea Judges, however eminent and learned, could be, and in a better position to adjudicate on questions arising from the special conditions in South Africa. Originally it was not contemplated that any appeal should lie to the Privy Council, but a supplementary clause had been inserted afterwards under which such appeals could be allowed if the Privy Council saw fit to hear them. The Judges of the Appellate Court had to be asked to stultify their own decisions by having to grant leave of appeal to the Privy Council. This was all contrary to the spirit of the South Africa Act, which contemplated a complete South African system of the judiciary.

Senator Reitz further wanted to know when the Privy Council had given a pronouncement as to what machinery existed there (in South Africa) to enforce that decision. On many occasions the Privy Council had rightly refused to hear appeals from the Courts of the Union on the ground that they were matters which their own Judges were properly competent to deal with. Therefore, why continue to retain a clause which was to all intents and purposes a dead letter? In Canada, in spite of the fact that their laws were based on the English common law, the appeal to the Privy Council had been abolished.

The Minister of the Interior (Hon. Patrick Duncan) said on behalf of the Government he could not accept the motion. No one could appeal to the Privy Council without the consent of the Appellate Court. But the supplementary clause was inserted to give a subject a right to appeal in special circumstances. The Privy Council had to determine whether a *prima facie* case had been made out or not. The Privy Council had on many occasions rightly refused to interfere with the judgment of their Appellate Courts, believing that the latter were more competent to deal with domestic matters than they. But occasion might arise when grave constitutional matters would require determination, and the appeal to the Privy Council would be in a more secure position to interpret the points involved.

He further pointed out that although the Roman-Dutch law was the basis of their system of jurisprudence, there was super-imposed on it an enormous mass of statute law, especially relating to matters of daily concern, such as shipping, commerce, insurance, etc., which were really based on the English law. Appeals to the Privy Council were not very numerous, and he believed that their Judges, who sometimes differed from one another, were only too glad to have the assistance of the greatest legal minds of the Empire when important issues were involved.

The motion was rejected on a division by 17 votes to 12.

RHODESIA AND THE UNION.

On 3rd April, in the House of Assembly, in reply to a question by Mr. Boydell (Leader of the Labour Party),

The Prime Minister (Lieut.-General the Right Hon. J. C. Smuts) said the Union Government had not invited a deputation from the Rhodesian Legislature with a view to discussing possible terms of entry by Rhodesia into the Union, but the Secretary of State for the Colonies, in a dispatch forwarding the draft Constitution under Responsible Government for Rhodesia, intimated that he wanted the option put to the people of Rhodesia, by way of referendum, whether they would accept Responsible Government in the terms of the draft Constitution or would rather be incorporated in the Union. If they decided on Union, then the terms and conditions would have to be arranged under the South Africa Act. The Secretary of State wanted a conference between the Union Government and the Rhodesian Delegation by which these terms and conditions might be discussed; the Union Government was approached by the Imperial Government to meet the Delegation which had now arrived and the discussion was proceeding.

The terms or conditions of Rhodesia's entry into the Union had not been drawn up and would not be drawn up until after the conference was completed and there had been a full discussion.

The Prime Minister added that Parliament must be consulted and the proper time for that would be when the addresses were before the House for consideration and ratification, to be passed on to the King. It was premature to discuss the matter in the House at that juncture.

In reply to a further question by General the Hon. J. B. M. Hertzog (Leader of the Nationalist Party) on the same date, as to whether it was the intention of the Government to consult the country as to the proposed terms of Rhodesia's entry into the Union,

The Prime Minister said that the Government proposed to follow the course laid down in the Act of Union, viz., that before Rhodesia was incorporated that House and the other place should send an address to the King. If consulting the country meant that there should be a general election or referendum, it was not the intention of the Government to follow that course. The conference was not for the purpose of concluding an agreement with the people of Rhodesia; it was simply an attempt to find out the terms which, in a unilateral Act, the Government of the Union was prepared to give Rhodesia.

FINANCES OF THE UNION.

(Fall in Revenue; Subscription to League of Nations; Gold and Diamond Mines; Strike and increased Police Vote; etc.)

DEBATE IN HOUSE OF ASSEMBLY.

On 20th February, in the House of Assembly, in moving that the House go into Committee on the Estimates of Additional Expenditure to be defrayed from Revenue and Loan Funds during the year ending 31st March, 1922,

Fall in Revenue.

The Minister of Finance (Hon. H. Burton) said the revenue for the year, particularly the Customs revenue, had fallen very far short of expectations, and the estimates of the principal revenue officers at the close of last year (allowing for additional expenditure which had necessarily been incurred) involved a deficit of one and a quarter millions. The strike on the Witwatersrand and the coal mines had had a particularly detrimental effect on revenue; and Customs and Excise receipts, especially in respect of liquor, had fallen off very heavily.

Decrease in Estimates.

The restriction of the purchasing power evidenced in financial matters was making the question of taxes a very difficult matter for the Government. There had been a decrease in the Estimates of £942,000. Of this, Customs duty accounted for £1,071,000; Excise duty, £439,000, Postal revenue, £375,000; and Diamond-mining revenue was down by £259,000. Export duty on diamonds, £15,000. There had also been a decrease under the heads of Sale of Crown lands, Forest revenue, £28,000; and Departmental receipts, £50,000. These and other falls were due to the depression which had prevailed, and were accentuated by recent industrial troubles.

Income Tax and Excess Profits.

On the other hand, income tax was half a million more than the original Estimates, and excess profits duty another half million. The Estimates were framed on the assumption that settlement of the dispute on the Rand would not be delayed. If a settlement was not achieved in the very near future, the loss of revenue would be substantially bigger.

Gold premium higher.

The position had been saved from being worse by the fact that the gold premium maintained during 1921 was of a considerably higher figure than was originally estimated. There was a net additional expenditure amounting to over £600,000. The accumulated deficit on the Estimate was £1,900,000 for the current year, a deficit amounting to nearly £2,000,000 sterling.

Living beyond means.

Those figures, Mr. Burton said, showed the need for rigid economy in the Government's management of its business. There was no road except the old, safe and sound one of cutting down expenditure. The country was living beyond its means in regard to Government expenditure, public institutions, and even from the point of view of private individuals. It was not the time to embark upon a policy of large additional taxation. The other practical alternative was a reduction on present expenditure. It was only fair to say that their administrative expenditure had been substantially reduced; the work done by the Public Service Commission in this respect would commend that body to the confidence of the country.

Expenses of the Strike.

It was too early to ascertain the expenditure to which the Government was going to be put in connection with the strike. The Police Vote was unchanged. It might be that later they would require additional funds on this Vote,* but in the absence of information that amount would have to be treated as unauthorised expenditure and submitted later on for approval.

Public Debt; Pensions; Telegraphs and Telephones.

The Public Debt was £105,000 up, the amount required being approximately £11,800,000. It was difficult to estimate accurately what was going to be the amount of interest on loan account. Pensions had increased by £275,000, £125,000 of which represented pensions in respect of South African wars. The remainder of the excess—£150,000—was mainly accounted for by additional benefits granted by the Act of 1920.

---

* *Vide* p. 462.

The total number of pensions in respect of these wars was 4,626, and the amount paid for them per annum £211,762. In the Great War they had 11,030 cases of Europeans and 675 of coloured units, involving an expenditure of £722,000 and £198,000 respectively. During the War, 602 cases previously paid by the Ministry of Pensions in London had been included in the South African list for the first time.

The Telegraphs and Telephones Vote was increased by £135,000 ; £33,000, in respect of the Post Office, was required for gratuities to 150 officials who had been retrenched.

Unemployment grants and allowances.

Coming to unemployment, 6,000 men were being assisted, of which number only 700 were coloured persons and natives. The Vote had been used to subsidise works under the control of the Railway Administration, Provincial Administrations, Provincial Councils, Irrigation and Forestry Departments. Some £450,000 was being allocated amongst these various bodies. The amounts granted as loans to the Administrations would be reserved from them. Grants from inland Administrations, like irrigation and forestry, were really additional to the funds provided yearly, so that the Government was spending a much larger sum than £450,000 for the relief of unemployment. Generally speaking, the rate of pay was 7s. 6d. a day for married men, and 4s. 6d. a day for single men, but the question—a very serious one—was whether it would not be more reasonable to house and ration these unfortunate people and make them a monthly payment.

Reductions; League of Nations; Defence.

There had been a decrease, the Minister went on, of nearly £34,000 in their subscription to the League of Nations owing to a re-allocation of expenses to be borne by members of the League ; originally they had to pay as 25 units, and now they were paying under a class which paid 15.

There was also a reduction in expenditure on the Defence Department mainly on training and equipping units of the Active Citizen Force.

Gold and diamond mines.

Referring to the gold and diamond industries, on which to an enormous extent the trade and revenue of the country was dependent, Mr. Burton said that when he made the last Budget speech*, the premium on gold was about 20s. an ounce, and on that basis 13 of the 39 mines showed a loss, and only 14 could show a profit. To-day, the premium was

---

* *Vide* Journal, Vol. II., No. 4, p. 921.

approximately 10s. an ounce. The revenue from the diamond mines, which in 1920 was £2,600,000, was estimated at £750,000 for the present year, and he was afraid they would not get a penny more than £450,000, for which more than half was in respect of profits made for past years.

Last year the revenue from the gold mining industry was £2,250,000 for the Union Government, but the Transvaal Province also took £300,000. For the current year the sum would be £2,400,000, and the Transvaal Province would receive upwards of £200,000. The increase was due to the increased rate on the companies, which had been raised from 1s. to 1s. 6d. in the £, in addition to the amount from taxes on dividends, which were going into the pockets of people paying super-tax.

Effects of Strike.

The strike would seriously affect next year; right throughout the country this stoppage was affecting every branch of industry; unfortunately, too, the market was bad for their agricultural produce. At such a time, the gold-mining industry was becoming even a more important element to the Revenue than formerly. In 1920 its value was about 45 millions, including premium, and in 1921, 43 millions, so that in the latter year it represented 66 per cent. of the value of the exports of South Africa.

The debate was adjourned.

Railway Revenue.

On 20th February,

The Minister of Railways and Harbours (the Hon. J. W. Jagger) said that at the end of the last financial year, 31st March, 1921, there was an accumulated deficit of £2,586,000. The loss on working for the current year had been considerably over £693,000, and the actual loss at 31st December, 1921, was £1,106,000; January, February and March of the present year showed a further loss of £150,000, so that the total loss on the working would be £1,250,000. It was difficult to say what the actual loss would be during the present three months. There was the strike. He believed that had this not occurred they would have been paying their way to the end of the year.

The loss was due, in the first place, to a falling off in estimated railway revenue. They had had a big falling off in goods. In the first nine months of the year they carried less imported goods from the coast to the interior by 70,000 tons. There was a big drop in coal revenue—something like £663,000 in the nine months. No doubt too big an estimate had been made. Their loss would have been heavier if they had not made very considerable savings in working expenses. They would spend, he expected, £25,285,000, making a saving of £953,000. As regards running expenses, they were justified in cutting down the train mileage. They also had had considerably to reduce the staff.

The general manager and his staff had spared no pains to get the country's railways on a sound, financial basis, and the Government much appreciated the way in which the staff generally had received the various reductions in their salaries.

Pending further discussion in Committee, Mr. Jagger said of the additional Estimates there was £263,000 extra expenditure from Revenue Fund and £510,000 from Loan Fund.

The motion was agreed to.

On 2nd March, on the resumption of the debate,

Mr. C. G. Fichardt (Nationalist, *Ladybrand, O.F.S.*) asked what use it was discussing the Estimates in the House; and also if they had tried to run the business of the country on business lines? During the twelve years he had been in Parliament he had only known one Vote that had been removed, and that was when it concerned his own constituency. They wanted to get on a more reasonable financial basis. He would like to see an Estimates Committee formed which would go through the Estimates before they were brought into the House.

Morley's Hotel.

He went on to criticise the expenditure on the upkeep of Morley's Hotel in London, and the cost of expensive Commissions, and asked what the result of the last loan on the London market had been, and whether there was any truth in a statement in a trade paper that the proceeds of the loan were to be spent in England? He also wanted to know why there had been an increase in pensions when the cost of living allowances had been taken away?

Subsistence and transport allowances for the High Commissioner's Office in London had gone up too. Was there any adequate financial control over that Office? Too much was also being spent on Government telegrams. The cost of the High Commissioner's Office would soon be greater than that of the whole of the O.F.S. before the Boer War.

Mr. Fichardt also criticised the Post Office and agricultural Votes, and, referring to the gold and diamond industries, said he would like to know what the Government intended to do to enable other industries to take their place.

Mr. W. Macintosh (South African Party, *Port Elizabeth—South-West, Cape*) entirely disagreed with the suggestion that the Estimates should be sent to a Committee. Such a course would relieve Ministers of all responsibility for the finances of the country. He also criticised the wastefulness of the Government, including the appointment of a Trade Commissioner in Europe. Referring to the sale of wools and mohair, Mr. Macintosh was glad to have something nice to say: Government assistance had proved of great value to farmers, the price had risen steadily and now there was a good demand.

The Minister of Finance in reply said he would have to ask for an item to be added when they went into Committee, namely, £40,000 for the police, entirely due to the strike.

Reductions compared.

Having answered some of the criticism of Members, he said comparison had been made between what the Union Government had done and what had been done in England. Continuing, Mr. Burton said: "The Union Government has done, in the way of deflation and reduction of expenditure, far more in proportion than the British Government has done. In one year we reduced our expenditure by £2,000,000."

Mr. Fichardt: "We did not get the advantage of deflation in the currency."

The Minister of Finance: "Oh, yes—very largely." Concluding, he gave the assurance that the Government would do everything they possibly could to effect economies.

The motion was agreed to.

On 6th March,

The Minister of Finance moved for leave to introduce a Bill to supply a sum of £14,000,000 on account of the services for the year ending 31st March, 1923.

In reply to some criticism, he said they had had so much experience in the past of Part Appropriation Bills, leading to endless debates, that they had decided to save Parliament's time, and ask for four months' supply to carry them over to the end of July. With regard to the Estimates, it would be understood how difficult it was for the Government, under the present conditions, to frame them, and he was afraid they would have to wait beyond the end of the present month.

Leave was granted, and the First Reading agreed to.

On 20th March,

The Right Hon. J. X. Merriman (South African Party, *Stellenbosch, Cape*) said they were asked to vote £14,000,000—only a third of the year's Supply. They had not yet got their Estimates and had no idea what their revenue was expected to be. They knew there was a big deficiency for last year. He thought the House should have more information on these points, and he therefore moved to report progress and ask leave to sit again.

The amendment was negatived.

Mr. C. T. M. Willcocks (Nationalist, *Winburg, O.F.S.*) moved a reduction of £5,000,000 from the amount asked for on revenue account, and £1,600,000 from the loan account, by way of protest against the Government asking for a partial appropriation equal to half of the total annual expenditure.

Both portions of the amendment were negatived, and the Bill set down for Third Reading. This was agreed to on 22nd March, and the Bill was transmitted to the Senate for its concurrence.

WOMAN'S ENFRANCHISEMENT BILL.

This Bill, to enable women to be registered as voters for the election of Members of the House of Assembly and of all Provincial Councils, was introduced by Mr. R. Feetham (South African Party, *Parktown, Trans.*) and debated in the House of Assembly during the last Session.* It was reintroduced on 7th March, 1922, and rejected on the Second Reading on 23rd March, by 55 votes to 51.

NEWFOUNDLAND.

The Third Session of the Twenty-fourth Parliament opened on 14th March, 1922.

GOVERNOR'S SPEECH.

Naval Expenditure; League of Nations; Exchange.

The Governor said that the decisions of the Disarmament Conference at Washington if carried into effect would ease the burden of Naval expenditure, though they could not but feel genuine regret at the dismantling of H.M.S. *Briton* in the Port of St. John's.

The work of the League of Nations, in bringing nations closer together, should greatly assist in creating harmony and good will.

The general improvement in exchange was an important feature in world-trade and should have an encouraging influence on the marketing of the staple product of Newfoundland.

Unemployment.

Continuing, His Excellency said that their experience of the question of unemployment, which had engaged the close attention of his Ministers, had been similar to that of other

*A summary of the Bill was given in the JOURNAL, Vol. II., No. 4, pp. 943-4. It is hoped to give a summary of the Debate in the next issue of the JOURNAL.

lands, though perhaps not to so great a degree. At the close of the last Session, negotiations were being conducted regarding special works to meet unemployment, and discussion of the matter at that moment might have prejudiced the situation. The present position of the matter would now be laid before the Legislature.

War Memorial School.

Referring to the proposed Normal School for Teachers for which an appropriation had been made by Parliament, the Government proposed to proceed as soon as possible with the erection of this School which, while serving its practical purpose, would also stand as a memorial of the service and sacrifice of the brave men from the Colony who gave their lives in the Great War.

Revenue and Expenditure; Loan; Forthcoming Bills.

With regard to the Statement of Expenditure and Revenue for the last fiscal year His Excellency stated that the expenditure was within the amount estimated. The Revenue slightly exceeded the estimate, and it was possible in closing the account to leave a balance to the credit of the Surplus Trust Account larger than the amount set forth in the Budget Speech of last year.* For the purpose of financing certain public operations, including particularly marine works, road construction and railway improvements, etc., it would be necessary for a loan to be procured.

Bills relating to this Loan, to the complete revision of the War Pensions Act, 1919, and probably to the Telegraph and Cable services would be submitted to the Legislature for consideration during the Session.

Operation of Railway.

The contract between the Government and the Reid Newfoundland Company for the operation of the railway had been receiving the close consideration of Ministers. For some time negotiations had been in progress with the object of establishing a definite and permanent basis for the operation of the Railway. Negotiations were still proceeding, but before the end of the Session it was hoped to submit satisfactory proposals.

The Debate on the Address in the House of Representatives took place on 20th, 21st, 22nd and 23rd March. On the last-named date a vote was taken on an amendment moved by the Opposition and was defeated on a strict Party vote by 17 votes to 8.†

---

* *Vide* JOURNAL, Vol. II., No. 3, p. 699.

† It is intended to give a summary of this debate when the necessary Parliamentary debates reach England.

VACHER & SONS, LTD., Westminster House, London, S.W.1.—37182.

JOURNAL OF THE PARLIAMENTS OF THE EMPIRE

Vol. III.—No. 3. July, 1922.

Issued under the Authority of the
EMPIRE PARLIAMENTARY ASSOCIATION
(United Kingdom Branch),
WESTMINSTER HALL, HOUSES OF PARLIAMENT,
LONDON, S.W.1.

Price to Non-Members 10*s. Net.*

CONTENTS.

CANADA.

AUSTRALIA.

Commonwealth Parliament.

CONTENTS.

State Parliaments.

New South Wales.

Tasmania.

NEW ZEALAND.

SOUTH AFRICA.

NEWFOUNDLAND.

INTRODUCTION.

In the present issue of the JOURNAL it is possible again to call attention to the considerable number of matters of international and inter-Imperial importance discussed in the different Parliaments of the Empire.

Dealing firstly with subjects affecting the relations of the British Empire with foreign countries, the discussions in the United Kingdom Parliament upon the Genoa Conference; the Treaty of Versailles, particularly in regard to German reparations; the League of Nations and the Palestine Mandate are of interest to all the Parliaments of the British Commonwealth. Similarly, the discussions in the Canadian Parliament on the Genoa Conference; the League of Nations, involving important references to the representation of the Dominions at the Washington Conference and the constitutional position of the Dominions as sister nations; the Limitation of Armaments; Oriental Immigration; International Labour; the ownership of Wrangel Island, etc., will be read with interest by those members of Parliament who are closely concerned with the attitude of the Empire as a whole towards the international situation.

The approval by the Canadian Parliament of the Washington Conference Treaties and of the Treaties of Peace with Hungary and Turkey, and by the Australian Parliament of the Treaty of Peace with Hungary serve to remind the world once more that, so far as the British Empire is concerned, the issues of peace and war now rest with the elected representatives of the people in each of the free Parliaments of the Commonwealth.

Subjects of first-rate practical importance to the nations within the Empire relate in the United Kingdom Parliament to Empire Settlement, where the speech of Mr. L. S. Amery and the debate in the House of Commons on the Second Reading are summarised, together with the debate in the House of Lords, where several ex-Governors-General took part; to the Imperial Conference and the Cabinet Secretariat, both of constitutional significance; to Imperial cable communications; to naval discipline as applied to the personnel of the British Navy serving on Dominion ships; to the Canadian cattle embargo; to the Safeguarding of Industries and Imperial Preference; and to the conferment of Honours upon residents in the Dominions.

In Canada, the animated discussion on naval policy illustrates the differences between the present and late Governments regarding the part which Canada should play in the naval defence of the Empire. The establishment of a Department of Defence, the discussions on British Tariff Preference, reciprocity with Australia and the cattle embargo question are all of importance from the standpoint of the general interests of the Empire. In the Australian Commonwealth the matter of preference with New Zealand is considered, while the subjects of Imperial Communications and Income Tax Assessment, involving the elimination of double Income Tax, claim attention.

In the New Zealand and South African Parliaments several matters affecting the other nations of the Empire have been discussed, including migration and settlement, Proportional Representation,* and so far as the Union Parliament is concerned, the question of the incorporation of Southern Rhodesia.

In the realm of more domestic affairs, finance has formed the subject of detailed discussion in the Parliaments of the United Kingdom, Canada, South Africa, and Newfoundland, though it has been found necessary to hold over the Canadian Budget discussion to the next issue of the JOURNAL. Labour representatives in all the Parliaments will be interested in the United Kingdom discussions on the Trade Union Act Amendment Bill and the Labour Party's proposals for the prevention of Unemployment. Other subjects of domestic, though general, interest relate to the proposal to limit the length of speeches in South Africa, Parliamentary allowances in New South Wales, and amendments relating to divorce in New Zealand and South Africa.

THE EDITOR.

EMPIRE PARLIAMENTARY ASSOCIATION
(*United Kingdom Branch*),
WESTMINSTER HALL,
HOUSES OF PARLIAMENT,
LONDON, S.W.1.

29th July, 1922.

---

* Owing to pressure upon space it has been decided to hold over to the next issue the discussion on this subject which took place in the Canadian Parliament.

UNITED KINGDOM.

In the last number of the JOURNAL *the proceedings of the Fifth Session of the Third Parliament (which commenced on 7th February,* 1922) *were dealt with up till 7th April,* 1922. *The summary which follows relates to business transacted between that date and* 1*st July.*

GENOA CONFERENCE.

(Statement by Premier; Restoration of Europe; Russian problem; Conference at The Hague.)

On 25th May a statement by the Prime Minister on the results attained at the International Conference at Genoa was made in the House of Commons, and was followed by a debate. The occasion was a Vote of £154,679 for the Foreign Office.

DEBATE IN HOUSE OF COMMONS.

The Prime Minister (the Right Hon. D. Lloyd George) said that there assembled at Genoa probably the largest gathering of nations that had ever met in the history of the world. He felt that if a Conference of that kind had assembled in 1914 the world would have been spared a very tragic experience. The main purpose of the Conference was:—

Restoration of financial and trading relations, and improvement of diplomatic relations.

Removal of disputes which were endangering the peace of nations.

The attainment of normal conditions in Europe was impeded by numerous obstacles, and the removal of those obstacles constituted the aim of the Genoa Conference. They were (1) Currency difficulties and the instability of exchanges; (2) Customs and trading restrictions; (3) Transport difficulties; (4) The absence of a sense of security against war. Four Commissions were set up for the purpose of reporting upon four different branches of the various problems on which the Conference was engaged.

International trade.

The Financial Commission not only defined the conditions under which the currency and exchange problems of Europe could be solved, but it also arranged for the initiation of reforms at a meeting of central banks. The object of the currency code was to anchor paper currencies again, directly or indirectly, to gold and secure for the nation a credit policy in order to prevent fluctuations.

The primary recommendation with regard to exchanges

was that the artificial control of exchange operations should be removed in order that nothing should stand in the way of the recovery of exchanges as currencies recovered and as the exports which supported them improved. Trade was checked by the absence of credit and an invaluable body had been organised in the shape of an international corporation. Restrictions, impediments, unfair conditions in the way of trade were to be found everywhere. It was one of the unfortunate results of the War that it should have ended in an abnormal development of a narrow, selfish and blind nationalism. He was very hopeful that the reports of the various Commissions would have the effect of producing a great improvement in some of those conditions.

Although peace had been established in Europe it was quite clear that to a certain extent the war atmosphere remained—an atmosphere of international suspicion and pending conflict.

Russian problem.

The problem which occupied most attention and excited most controversy was that of Russia. Without the assistance of the other nations it was hopeless to expect Russia, whatever her Government, to extricate herself from the pit of squalid misery. No one at Genoa suggested using force, and as regarded the alternative of leaving Russia to her fate until she wore a more acceptable demeanour, the Conference cast a flash of light on its sinister possibilities. He referred to the Russo-German Agreement.

Pariahs were more gregarious than paragons. Those on whom discredit fell wanted society and friendship. This agreement might ripen into a fierce friendship. "Germany is disarmed, and if necessary you could disarm her still more," the Premier continued. "I will not say you could take every gun away—you find that difficulty in Ireland—but you could take most. You could render her perfectly impotent; but there is one thing you cannot do, and that is prevent the re-arming of Russia if the nations are driven to despair. Germany cannot re-equip Russia economically. She has not the capital. It needs the West. That is not the case with armaments, where you have every natural resource in one country and every technical skill in the other.

"It is necessary that we should look at all the possibilities of the situation, and I hope the warning I have given to-day may not be quoted a few years hence."

Unanimity of Empire Delegation.

The British Empire Delegation met together to consult upon the whole of the facts. They included the representatives of Canada, Australia, Africa, New Zealand, and India.

"There was not a step of any kind taken," said the Premier, "without previous consultation, and the action we took had their unanimous support and was arrived at after the guidance which they gave us. They came to the same conclusion as we did, that, whatever we thought about the Soviet Government . . . some arrangement with Russia was necessary in order to save the misery in Russia itself, necessary in order to enable Russia to make her contribution to the needs of the world, necessary to enable Russia to help in the swelling of that volume of trade upon which so many millions of people depend for their daily bread, necessary in order to give a sense of stability, necessary above all to avert those evils which lurk in the future if nothing is done in order to unravel this tangle of misunderstanding.

"For that reason the British Empire Delegation, all of us, gave the whole of our strength and our minds, day after day, to fight the battle of the peace of the world."

Attitude of Soviet Leaders.

Describing the position taken up by the Leaders of Soviet Russia, the Premier remarked that they said the revolution was a break with the methods and the obligations of the past, but they realised that Russia could not be restored economically without the help of "the capitalistic system" with which they were at war. Although they did not abandon any of their principles, they realised that they could not get the assistance required unless they made terms with the capitalists, and they were prepared to acknowledge debts for money advanced to Russia before the revolution, but until Russia was restored economically they could pay nothing. Therefore they said: "The obligations which we enter into will depend upon the assistance you give us." There was a basis for a business discussion.

The first challenge of principle came in regard to the claim for £5,000,000,000 sterling put forward by the Soviet Government for compensation for ruin wrought in the civil war. They said that the damage was done by Denikin, Koltchak and Wrangel's intervention. The Allies had to tell them that they could not, under any circumstances, acknowledge that claim. Historically it was an unsound proposition, because in revolutions assistance had been given in the past by other countries to one or other of the parties. The Allies said they could not accept any liability, but, in view of the serious economic condition of Russia, they were willing to write down the claims for money advanced by Governments during the War. But they could not accept any claim to be put against the money advanced by any individuals to Russia.

A letter was received from the Russian Delegation which was not wholly satisfactory, but the Powers came to the conclusion that it was good enough to enable them to go on with the discussions.

The Hague discussions.

With respect to debts no insuperable question of principle divided the parties, but when they came to property the division was a more serious one. The position of the European Powers was clearly stated in the Cannes resolutions,* which stated that although a country had a right to do what it chose with the property inside its own jurisdiction, still, if it was seeking credits from the rest of the world, it must either restore the property of foreign interests or give compensation. The Russian Delegation stated that a vast majority of the properties could be restored, and with regard to the rest, they were prepared to discuss the giving of concessions.

Where there had been amalgamations by the State of concerns like the Douetz coal mines, they were prepared to give compensation in the form of shares in the larger combines to the owners of any particular mines, and with regard to the small minority, which he was sure would be left, they were prepared to give bonds. The property owners would consider these matters with the full knowledge that they were dealing with concerns which might not for a great many years to come pay 20s. in the £. These were things to be discussed at The Hague. There would also be the question of what credits would be available. Russia needed money for railways, ports, machinery, agricultural implements, re-equipment of factories and mines, and clothing the people.

He was hopeful that when those questions were considered, in conjunction with the other propositions, at The Hague, something might be achieved.

Truce of peace.

The Premier referred to the strength of the "Red" Army and the danger of conflicts in Europe. "The first thing we had to do if we were to continue the Genoa examination," he said, "was to ensure that the peace of Europe should be maintained during that period. That is why we have the truce of peace, which embodied a solemn declaration on the part of 34 nations that they would be guilty of no act of aggression against their neighbours during the period of these examinations, nor would they be guilty of any act of aggression against the institutions of each other during that period. . . . When The Hague Conference have examined the propositions which are submitted to them—if they make recommendations and the Governments take them up and consider whether

* *Vide* Journal, Vol. III., No. 2, p. 249.

they will adopt them, and if they are favourable and acceptable, then I hope there will be a peace which will be permanent.

"If Genoa were to fail the condition of Europe would indeed be tragic. The channels of international trade would become hopelessly clogged by restrictions and difficulties, artificial and otherwise. Commerce would stagnate into poisonous national swamps of insolvency. There would be quarrels, suspicions and feuds between nations, ending in great conflicts. But if Genoa succeeds even partially, great things will be accomplished for the peace of Europe. We have already captured positions from which further advances may be made. We have established a truce of peace between nations which had armies massing against each other and advancing towards each other.

"If we can go further and make an arrangement by the goodwill and co-operation of these great nations of Europe, the psychological effect on trade will be immediate and incalculable."

Mr. Asquith's criticisms.

The Right Hon. H. H. Asquith (Leader of the Independent Liberal Party) spoke of the results of the Conference as depressingly and even distressingly meagre. Had they advanced one single step, as the result of the Conference, towards a re-opening of economic relations between Russia and the rest of Europe? All had been relegated to The Hague Conference.

"The Hague Conference," the right hon. gentleman observed, "will really start with a *tabula nova*, or, I would say, with a clean slate, upon which nothing is written, and with the memory—the rather discouraging memory—behind it that these great people representing thirty-four Powers spent five weeks in Genoa, and when the Conference rose it was in exactly the same position as when it began." What was the positive achievement which the Conference was entitled to claim? It was the pact between the thirty-four Powers to refrain from flying at one another's throats for a period which was limited by four months from the expiration of the Conference at The Hague.

Who were the parties to the pact? Germany was not one. As regarded the others, with a perfectly negligible exception (leaving Russia out of account) they were all bound by the Covenant of the League of Nations to a much more solemn and enduring pledge to abstain from aggression on one another, or, indeed, carrying any dispute to the arbitrament of war.

Baltic States, Poland, and Russia.

What about Russia? The Premier had not referred to the fact that on the 30th March, the eve of the Genoa

Conference, a meeting was held at Riga at which an agreement was come to between Esthonia and Latvia (the Baltic States), Poland, and Russia, setting forth that it was indispensable to establish along the frontiers a zone to which only a minimum of armed forces would be admitted. It was a complete agreement between those countries to abstain from aggression one against the other. How could it be seriously contended that at that time there was any menace on the Russian frontier?

What was the real reason for the relative failure of the Genoa Conference to take even a substantial step towards the solution of the great problems that were under discussion? The abstention of America was a very serious matter. The half-hearted participation of France, whose Prime Minister was not present at Genoa, was another serious matter. " But what was far more serious and what I will venture with the utmost assurance to predict will wreck all future proceedings of this kind," said Mr. Asquith, " was that it was precluded in advance from dealing with the real problem of the European economic situation. What is the good of passing resolutions . . . in regard to stabilising exchanges and so forth until you have dealt with the fundamental problem of regulating the reparations? That lies at the root of the whole European situation.

" What is the use of the establishment of better economic relations with Russia—which, after all, from our point of view and from the European point of view, is not by any means the most important factor—so long as you ignore and postpone the one thing on which the real re-establishment of credit, free intercourse and interchange, and the ultimate economic restoration of Europe depend, namely, settling reparations, letting everybody know once and for all how the matter stands, and providing, as I think we ought to provide, in a large and generous spirit for a substantial remission of any claims we ourselves may have made? "

Labour criticism.

The Right Hon. J. R. Clynes (Chairman of the Parliamentary Labour Party) said that the method of conference for the settlement of international differences was an old Labour method. His Party's criticism of it in this instance had been that it could not succeed until the programme was ample enough to deal with the big outstanding questions of substance and not limited to matters of secondary importance. Only the persistence of the Prime Minister saved the Genoa Conference in the first week, but even the Prime Minister could not keep alive the spirit of real confidence, which in that week had been killed.

" I do not blame France for her attitude," Mr. Clynes observed. " We are largely to blame for it. We granted to

France all the apparent, if illusory, gains and benefits of the Treaty of Versailles, and, naturally, the French Government and the French Prime Minister now turn round and say, ' All that we ask for is embodied in that Treaty.' The question for us is: Have we reached a stage where boldly we must say that we have guaranteed more than we can deliver; that we have built up hopes and expectations in France which cannot be realised ? "

The Labour view was that these conferences must be held because the Treaties and the so-called settlements embodied numerous crimes and blunders in international relationships. These would be rectified by the use of straightforwardness in diplomacy and openness in discussion, and in wisdom and action which for long they had advised their statesmen to follow.

Militarism or disarmament.

" We have a choice of two paths in the government of Europe in the future," Mr. Clynes remarked. "One is the path of government in the spirit of militarism; the other is the path of government which will tend to disarmament and to that real state of peace for which millions fought throughout the years of the Great War. . . . If we do not live on a footing of friendship with both Germany and Russia those two countries, with their immense populations, will give Europe in due course far more trouble than Europe will find it easy to deal with."

He thought the better policy would be to put no limit of any kind to their recognition of the Russian Government. That Government, like all others, would in due course find its level. They had secured from Genoa something like a pledge of non-aggression for at least a period of eight months, and they had certainly a little closer relations with their good ally Italy. He hoped the Prime Minister would not cease to do his best to arrange terms with Russia. "Russia has no need," said Mr. Clynes, "of this country, or of the other countries of the world, but we are in need of the great opportunities offered by Russian trade. Germany is not blind to these great trade opportunities, and the business men in this House are doing damage to their own trade interests, as I think, because of their stupid political attitude towards Russia."

Political results; Entente with France.

Mr. Rupert Gwynne (Conservative, *Eastbourne*), in moving to reduce the amount of the Vote by **£1,000,** observed that the Conference could not be said to have achieved any economic results. In spite of the warning of the United States of America, the Prime Minister allowed it to degenerate into a political conference, which had resulted only in benefiting the two countries which detested the victory of the Allies in the War, namely, Germany and Bolshevik Russia. He very much feared that when the time came the results of The Hague would not be much better than those of Genoa.

The Right Hon. Lord Robert Cecil (Conservative, *Hitchin*) remarked that all the questions would have had much more chance of being really usefully solved if the United States had taken part in the Conference. He was afraid that Great Britain's relations with France were not so good as they were before Genoa. Any breach of their *entente* with France would be a real disaster to Europe. He did not mean they should always conform in policy to French policy. If French policy was leading towards war that would be too great a price to pay even to avoid a shaking of the *entente;* but they should not underrate the grave disadvantage of so serious a disagreement that the French Government would be unwilling to co-operate with this country in a hearty way in European problems.

The Prime Minister said he was earnestly desirous that France and Great Britain should work together, but they must work together for peace in Europe.

League of Nations.

The Right Hon. G. N. Barnes (Labour, *Glasgow, Gorbals*) believed that if it had been possible to have had a conference of the League of Nations it would have been a rather better method than the methods adopted at Genoa. But the main object of the Conference was to get Russia back into the comity of nations, and Russia had repeatedly declared that she would have nothing to do with the League of Nations. Therefore if the Conference had been convened by the League of Nations they would have had no Russians there at all.

The Secretary of State for War (the Right Hon. Sir L. Worthington-Evans) said the Russian Delegation were definitely told that the British Government would not give them a Government loan or a Government credit. They were told there would be trade credits available for them as soon as they reassured people that when they sold goods to Russia they would be paid for them, and when they lent money they would be repaid. He believed that the holding of the Conference had shown that they were wrong who supposed that the victors in the Great War thought only of themselves and of imposing their will on the rest of Europe. While they had not forgotten the comradeship of the War, they had shown themselves ready to co-operate with all nations in lifting Europe out of the misery into which the War had plunged her.

On a division the amendment was negatived by 235 votes against 26, and progress was reported.

DEBATE IN HOUSE OF LORDS.

On 27th June a debate on the Genoa Conference took place in the House of Lords.

The Earl of Midleton, in moving that certain correspondence with reference to the Conference should be laid before the House, said the new diplomacy, about which so much was heard, was supposed to bring principals together, to make a short cut to decision, and to abjure subtleties. It was claimed that it gave greater information to nations as to what was being done on their behalf. He was not sure that the experience of Genoa had been very favourable in that respect. Having stated that the only important representative of the Foreign Office who was at Genoa, so far as he knew, was the legal adviser, the noble Earl remarked that in the course of the last few years the tendency had been more and more to allow the Secretary of State for Foreign Affairs and the Foreign Office to degenerate, in the eyes of foreign Ministers, into a sort of dull background to the picture in which the Prime Minister and his Secretariat were the only prominent figures. The aim of the motion was, first, to obtain a better knowledge of what occurred at Genoa, and what led to the failure there —failure in the sense that it caused considerable divergence between Great Britain and France; failure in the sense that to a certain extent it divided or began the division of Europe into two camps; failure also in the fact that other nations seemed to have been somewhat shy of further conference. In the second place, they had a right to make a stand for knowledge to be given to Parliament of foreign affairs, a right which had been almost entirely rejected in the course of the last few years. Thirdly, the Secretary of State for Foreign Affairs should have returned to him the transaction of all routine business and of important affairs which might have lapsed from his hands, and those of the Department to which he belonged.

The Marquis of Crewe could not help thinking that His Majesty's Government were mistaken in thinking that entirely new principles of international consolidation had become desirable in the sense in which nobody would have believed them to be desirable twenty or thirty years ago. The only real hope of an entirely novel system of consolidation and co-operation between the Great Powers, and also the small Powers, both of Europe and of the rest of the world, must, after all, lie in the League of Nations. Some of them felt that the recent dealings of the Government with foreign affairs, and, in particular, with the Conference at Genoa, were harmful to the idea of the League of Nations.

Anglo-French Pact.

The Earl of Derby remarked that the new form of diplomacy differed from the old form in that instead of written despatches there were personal discussions. The fact of there being personal discussions rendered it all the more necessary that information should be given to the country, and given quickly, because as a general rule no two people agreed as to what took place at these oral discussions. In the case of the so-called Pact or Alliance between Great Britain and France, the withholding of information had undoubtedly led to a misunderstanding between the people of the two countries.

The man in the street in England would say that the Pact was offered to France and refused by France. The man in the street in France would say, " The Pact was offered as a condition of our going to Genoa. We went to Genoa, we delivered the goods, and you have not delivered them in return." He believed both those replies to be absolutely inaccurate, but they were opinions which were gaining strength simply because people could not get information as to what was the reality of the position. He asked for an answer to the following questions :—

(1) When the Prime Minister offered the Pact to M. Briand at Cannes, did he do so in writing ? Was it accompanied, either in writing or verbally, by any condition, such as that the French should send delegates to Genoa ?

(2) Was the offer of the Pact renewed to M. Poincaré ? Did he, in response, send any despatch making conditions or suggestions ? If he did, what were those conditions, what were those suggestions ?

(3) If M. Poincaré did send a despatch, what was the reply of the British Government, and when was it sent ?

Cannes conversations.

The Lord President of the Council (the Earl of Balfour) said the Prime Minister and M. Briand discussed the subject of the Pact at Cannes. The Pact outlined by the Prime Minister was a mere repetition of the original abortive Treaty in which America was to take a part. It came to this, that the British Empire would guarantee France against aggression and invasion by Germany and would confirm the London Reparation Agreement. In addition to that (not as touching the substance of the Pact, but as touching the time at which it would be useful to discuss it and, if necessary, to carry it out) the Prime Minister and M. Briand were agreed that there were three or four questions, outstanding questions, between the two countries which it would be desirable to settle. The substance of what he had explained to the House was subsequently communicated in writing to M. Briand.

What happened when M. Briand left office and was succeeded by M. Poincaré ? The latter desired, he believed, to take up the negotiations exactly where they had been left. He also agreed with his predecessor, M. Briand, and with the British Government, that the Pact should only follow a general liquidation of outstanding questions. " Broadly speaking," said Lord Balfour, " that is where the matter rests now. These subjects of discussion between the two Governments are still subjects of discussion, and until they have reached, or have nearly reached, a complete settlement it will surely not be worth while to enter into further and minute details upon this most important and interesting subject."

Turning to the Motion of Lord Midleton, Lord Balfour observed that he did not believe any Conference had ever taken place with regard to which completer information had been given. To say that the Foreign Office was not represented at Genoa was wholly inaccurate. Neither the Secretary of State, nor the Under-Secretary, could go, but there were other very able officials who went, whose services were in constant request, whose information was entirely at the disposal of the British Delegation, and whose information was largely drawn upon.

The old and the new diplomacy.

The Earl of Balfour went on to say that if the difference between the old diplomacy and the new was the question of record all the advantage was with the new. Every conversation was recorded, and it would be possible at any future time to find out what was said at Conferences on every occasion by every man of importance. " Let me say," remarked Lord Balfour, " that these confidential records were communicated, as of course, day by day, to the Prime Ministers in the great self-governing Dominions, and I have myself seen a letter from South Africa explaining how grateful the South African Government was for being kept *au fait* with all that was done, day by day, in the Genoa Conference."

He saw a great deal of the British Secretariat, both at Paris and at Washington. He was able to say that it was trustworthy and was trusted ; that it was almost as useful to those with whom they were negotiating as to themselves. He was sure that the attacks made upon the Secretariat were attacks made in pure ignorance. There was no set of public servants from whom the public got more value for its money.

Reconstruction of Europe.

Viscount Grey of Fallodon observed that years had passed since the Armistice and they were really making no progress towards the reconstruction of Europe. He could not think that any substantial progress had been made at Genoa, and, if not, it was a very serious matter. All the Governments agreed that the recovery of Europe was a most important and urgent problem, but they did not seem to have settled down to any clear perspective of the methods by which that progress could be brought about.

"The first thing which seems to me essential to the reconstruction of Europe," Viscount Grey said, "is the co-operation of the Government and the resources of the United States. I ventured to say, when the project of the Genoa Conference was first launched, that it seemed to me a pity that the League of Nations was put aside, because I thought that everything practicable could be better done through the League of Nations than through the Conference. . . . It must be a prime condition of getting the co-operation of the United States that France and ourselves are in cordial co-operation. As long as we differ the United States will not look at European questions."

He believed that so long as the question of German reparation remained unsettled it would be a menace to peace, as well as a bar to financial and economic progress. He felt that Great Britain was drifting and Europe was drifting, in the most perilous way. If the Government had stuck to the League of Nations policy, and if the League had been encouraged instead of leaving everything to the Supreme Council, or inventing Genoa Conferences and so forth, they would be better off than they were now.

After further debate the Motion for papers was, by leave, withdrawn.

TREATY OF VERSAILLES.

(German reparation; Great Britain and France; Premier's statement.)

On 31st May, on the Motion for the adjournment of the House of Commons for the Whitsuntide Recess, a brief discussion took place on international questions.

The Right Hon. J. R. Clynes (Chairman of the Parliamentary Labour Party), referring to the subject of German reparation, said the people of this country were the genuine friends of France. The working-classes were not either last or least in their admiration for the French character and their desire for the maintenance of French friendship. But friendship with France need not rest upon pacts or treaties. Unhappily, there had been differences of opinion on questions of after-war policy and it would be unwise any longer to conceal or underrate the difficulties. All that France desired, he understood, was the execution of the Peace Treaty. It was clear that the Treaty terms had failed, and also the other measures to reduce Germany to a state of military impotence.

His conviction was that safety for France could be found only in the practice of what was provided for in the Covenant of the League of Nations. They could not succeed in crushing Germany economically and dismembering her as a family and at the same time make her pay according to the terms laid down. The Government were largely to blame for the differences with France, for France was misled by the persistent pronouncements and extraordinary electoral declarations in this country in 1918. "We have created in France," said Mr. Clynes, "expectations which now have produced for us difficulties in policy which we must try to remove. In other words, we must go far to unsay much of what we said in 1918."

He asked whether in the opinion of the Government it was not better that they should get reparation from Germany by agreement or arbitration than by the application of force or threats of force.

Armies of Occupation.

Lt.-Comdr. the Hon. J. Kenworthy (**Independent Liberal,** *Hull, Central*) observed that it was no good bringing Russia into the world's market again if Germany was going to fall, weighted down by a reparation demand which her people could not meet. All their endeavours should be used to get the Armies of Occupation withdrawn from German territory. They had not been a really efficient means of coercing Germany and their cost had swallowed up more than all the payments received from Germany.

The Prime Minister (the Right Hon. D. Lloyd George) said that the critical aspect which the case of reparation presented some weeks ago had for the moment passed away. Mr. Clynes attributed a great part of the present difficulty to certain declarations made by the Government in 1918, but he (the Premier) made it clear in the only speech he delivered on the subject that Germany, although morally responsible for paying the whole cost of the War, and of the damage inflicted by her in the course of the War, could only be expected to pay according to her capacity.

It was assumed that the Treaty of Versailles imposed upon Germany burdens which she could not bear—that all that was provided for was that the Reparation Commission should ascertain the total amount of the damage inflicted by Germany, and send in the bill, and if Germany did not pay the Allies were to march to Frankfort, Berlin, or anywhere else and extort it. That was not the Treaty. The Reparation Commission was to act judicially—first of all to ascertain the damage inflicted by Germany within the categories set out in the Treaty, and afterwards to decide, not for twenty or thirty years, but from time to time, what was Germany's capacity to pay at any given moment.

United States and Treaty; British position.

One fact which had upset the balance of the Reparation Commissioners—and it was a fact which had upset the balance of the League of Nations—was the absence of America. There was no doubt that the absence of America from the machinery of the Treaty of Versailles had disturbed its equipoise and made the machine less effective.

"For the moment," the Premier observed, "all I will say about it is that there is no cause of disagreement between France and ourselves. The matter has been submitted to the consideration of the Reparation Commission, and all the reports I have are very hopeful that an arrangement will be arrived at which will be acceptable, not merely to the creditor, but to the debtor countries as well." As to War debts, Great Britain was perfectly prepared to enter into any international discussion for the obliteration of the whole of them, provided she received a benefit which was not unequal to that she was prepared to confer.

"Our interest goes beyond that of a mere creditor," the Premier said. "We have an interest as a great international trader. We realise that it is an advantage to us to forgive the very great amount of money due to us, providing there is a clean slate; but we cannot possibly contemplate entering into a transaction by which we should forgive all the debts due to us, while we are liable for every penny which is owing by us. We want fair play and justice, and I am very surprised to find that in all the proposals which have been made up to the present that aspect of the matter has not been stated."

Policy of moderation and restraint.

He was glad the German Government had made a real effort to meet the requirements of the Reparation Commission. If there were a Government in Germany that came in to resist the Treaty, to refuse to carry out its provisions, France would not be left alone to execute those provisions. Great Britain and France would act together.

"We have stood," said Mr. Lloyd George, "for a policy of moderation and of restraint. We have stood for the policy of considering the difficulties of Germany, and in doing so we have rendered ourselves liable to a good deal of misrepresentation between France and ourselves. Nevertheless, we are pursuing the old traditional policy of this country, of moderation. It was the policy we pursued after Waterloo towards France when we were being urged by Prussia and the other victorious armies to trample upon France.

"In spite of misrepresentation we shall stand still for the policy of moderation, but we shall also stand for the policy of fulfilment. We stand for the fulfilment of the Treaty of Versailles, with the reasonable interpretation which we put upon it, and which I think is incorporated in the very essence of the Treaty itself."

Economic position.

The Right Hon. Lord Robert Cecil (Conservative, ***Hitchin*****)** said they would never get a solution of the economic position until they settled the reparation question. He was sorry to hear the Prime Minister put aside all suggestions that they should remit their War debts.

The Prime Minister: "I hope the whole question of War debts will be considered, and considered very carefully. The only point is that it was unfair to ask that we should remit all debts due to us when we are liable for debts for a very considerable amount of money."

Lord R. Cecil said the Government should make up their minds definitely what their policy in the matter of reparation was and say candidly to the French: "We have arrived at the conclusion that we did try to get too much out of Germany, and that we shall not succeed in obtaining a settlement of the economic position of the world if we insist on that. Let us agree to a more moderate policy, not because Germany is entitled to mercy or pity, but because it is essential that these economic difficulties should be ended."

The subject then dropped.

LEAGUE OF NATIONS.

(Financial contributions of Great Britain and the Dominions; Admission of Germany.)

On 10th April questions relating to contributions towards the expenditure of the League of Nations were asked in the House of Commons.

Maj. the Hon. C. Lowther (Independent, ***Cumberland, N.*****)** inquired why the United Kingdom's share of expenditure for the expenses of the League was to be increased from 4·84 per cent. to 9·55 per cent.?

The President of the Board of Education (the Right Hon. H. A. L. Fisher): "The increased contribution which this country is to make towards the expenses of the League of Nations results from the adoption by the Second Assembly of a revised basis for the allocation of the League's expenses, but the new scale will not become operative until the necessary amendment to Article VI. of the Covenant has been ratified by at least 26 members of the League, including the members of the Council, and it is to be reconsidered by the Assembly of 1923."

Maj. Lowther: "Does that mean that other nations may put up the percentage of our contribution just as they will to any figure without our having the opportunity of voting against it ?"

The President of the Board of Education: "No, that is not a fact."

Sir J. D. Rees* (**Coalition Unionist**, *Nottingham, E.*): "Is not the increase in the British contribution due really to the fact that other nations do not pay their subscriptions ?"

The President of the Board of Education: "No, it is due to the fact that the original arrangement was found to be very anomalous. It had, for instance, the anomaly of requiring contributions from Australia, Canada and South Africa on the same basis as the contributions required from Great Britain and the other great Powers, and it was consequently violently objected to by our own Dominions, and it was very largely owing to their pressure that the new basis was adopted."

Admission of Germany.

On 26th June, in the House of Commons,

The Right Hon. Lord Robert Cecil (**Conservative**, *Hitchin*) asked the Prime Minister whether he could make any statement as to the attitude of the Government towards the admission of Germany to the League of Nations.

The Prime Minister (**the Right Hon. D. Lloyd George**): "This is not a question which concerns Great Britain alone, and it primarily concerns Germany herself; but, as far as His Majesty's Government are concerned, we would support a proposal to admit Germany into the League of Nations."

PALESTINE MANDATE.

(The Zionist Home; Fears of Arab population; Government's pledges.)

On 21st June a debate took place in the House of Lords on the Palestine Mandate. It arose on the following Motion:—

"That the Mandate for Palestine in its present form is inacceptable to this House, because it directly violates the pledges made by His Majesty's Government to the people of Palestine in the Declaration of October, 1915, and again in the Declaration of November, 1918, and is, as at present framed, opposed to the sentiments and wishes of the great

* Sir J. D. Rees was killed in a railway accident during the Session.

majority of the people of Palestine; that, therefore, its acceptance by the Council of the League of Nations should be postponed until such modifications have therein been effected as will comply with pledges given by His Majesty's Government."

DEBATE IN HOUSE OF LORDS.

Lord Islington, in moving the Motion, said it raised issues concerning certain important Articles which dealt with the Zionist Home. The policy embodied in the Mandate, and the administrative methods adopted in pursuance of that policy, had created public concern and apprehension. If his Motion were agreed to it would necessitate a modification of the Preamble of the Mandate and of Articles 4, 6 and 11.

Article 4 dealt with the Palestine Zionist Executive which had been set up. In the Mandate it was called the Jewish Agency, which was a consultative and advisory body to the Administration in Palestine, purely of a Zionist character. Article 6 dealt with the powers and facilities that were to be given to Jewish immigration into Palestine, especially in connection with the advice of the Agency. The second paragraph of Article 11 dealt with the controlling influence that the Jewish Agency was to have in regard to the construction and operation of the general commercial and industrial services and utilities that were to be developed in the country. The establishment of a Zionist Home under the Palestine Mandate, as implied by those Articles, was directly inconsistent with the undertakings in Article 22 of the Covenant of the League of Nations.

The moment it was decided to introduce into the Palestine Mandate the principle of the Zionist Home the whole of the great ideal of leading the people on in their own way and by their own means to a system of self-government in their own country was at once and for ever abandoned.

Zionist political predominance.

"The Zionist Home must and does mean," Lord Islington said, "the predominance of political power on the part of the Jewish community in a country where the population is preponderatingly non-Jewish. And that is what the Palestine Mandate, if it is ratified at Geneva, sets forth permanently to establish. If ratified, it imposes on this country the responsibility of trusteeship for a Zionist political predominance where 90 per cent. of the population are non-Zionist and non-Jewish."

He disclaimed any hostility to the Jewish race. In fact, many orthodox Jews all over the world viewed with the deepest apprehension, not to say dislike, the principle of a Zionist Home in Palestine. It seemed to him that the

Palestine Mandate as it stood was a real distortion of the mandatory system, where a small portion of the population was to be given preferential treatment and where British authority was to enforce that system. One was driven to believe in the truth of the allegation made by many impartial witnesses who had recently visited the country that the Zionist Commission, or as it was now called the Zionist Palestine Executive, had gone a long way towards usurping the position of Government in Palestine.

A modification of this policy would be no injustice to the Jews in Palestine, because they had never asked for it, while the continuance of it would be a growing injustice to the Arab community, who would bitterly resent it.

Breach of faith.

Coming to the allegation that Zionism was a breach of faith, Lord Islington contended that the Proclamations of 1915* by Sir Henry MacMahon, High Commissioner of Egypt, and of 1918* by Lord Allenby, constituted a definite undertaking to the Arab community by Great Britain, whilst Zionism, as embodied in the Balfour Declaration, as implied in the Palestine Mandate, and as given effect in the administrative system now prevailing, could not constitute other than a direct repudiation of those solemn and authoritative undertakings.

"The people of Palestine ask, and I think most reasonably," Lord Islington observed, "for a national form of Government representative of the people in their own country. They will welcome every kind of British assistance to enable them to make effective that form of Government, and under such a Constitution both the Jewish community and the Arab community can live in perfect harmony." The Zionist scheme, Lord Islington added, really ran counter to the whole human psychology of the age, while it was not the proper function of His Majesty's Government to spend the money of the British taxpayer for purposes of that kind.

---

* Extracts from the two Proclamations are as follows :—

Sir Henry MacMahon : "Great Britain is prepared to recognise and support the independence of the Arabs within the territories included in the limits and boundaries proposed by the Sherif."

Lord Allenby : "The object of war in the East on the part of Great Britain was the complete and final liberation of all peoples formerly oppressed by the Turks and the establishment of national Governments and administrations in those countries deriving authority from the initiative and free will of those peoples themselves : . . . Great Britain agrees to encourage and assist the formation of native Governments and their recognition when formed."

The Lord President of the Council (the Earl of Balfour) said the mandatory system always contemplated the Mandate for Palestine on the general lines of the Declaration of November, 1917.* It was not sprung upon the League of Nations, and, before the League of Nations came into existence, it was not sprung upon the Powers that met together in Paris to deal with the peace negotiations. It was accepted in America, it was accepted in this country, it was published all over the world; and, if ever there was a Declaration which had behind it a general consensus of opinion, he believed it was the Declaration of November, 1917.

"The League of Nations," Lord Balfour continued, "has asked His Majesty's Government to continue to carry out the policy of the Mandates. As your Lordships are aware, the Mandates are not yet part, so to speak, of the law of nations. The fact that we have not yet concluded, most unhappily as I think, peace in Eastern Europe and in Western Asia has prevented these Mandates passing through all the stages which will ultimately be required of them, but we are carrying out the policy of the Mandates.

"Only recently, I believe, the whole question came up before the Senate of the United States. They had before them, if I am rightly informed, witnesses competent to give evidence upon every aspect of the case, and they came to the unanimous conclusion that the policy of a Jewish Home was a policy for the benefit of the world, and they certainly, by the very terms of the resolution at which they arrived, were not oblivious of the interests of the native Arab population."

When Lord Islington tried to maintain the paradox that the Powers who adopted the mandatory system were violating all their principles when they established the policy of a Jewish Home in Palestine, he was asking them to accept a proposition which, as men of common sense, they should certainly repudiate.

Political interests of Arab population.

He could not imagine any political interests exercised under greater safeguards than the political interests of the Arab population of Palestine. Every act of the Government would be jealously watched. The Zionist organisation had no attribution of political powers. If it used political powers it was an act of usurpation. Whatever else might happen in Palestine he was confident that under British Government

* The Declaration of 1917 included the following passage :—

"His Majesty's Government will use their best endeavours to facilitate the achievement of a National Home for the Jewish people."

no form of tyranny, racial or religious, would ever be permitted. The whole policy of immigration was subject to the most careful study, and, so far as his information went, no single immigrant had been a charge upon any public fund since he entered the boundaries controlled by the British Administration.

As soon as the Mandate question was finally settled and existing legal difficulties had been got over the Jewish communities throughout the world, he believed, would come forward and help freely in the development of a Jewish Home. As regarded the Rutenberg scheme* not only was there nothing in the nature of undue favouritism, but if that scheme could be carried into effect it would give economic advantages to Palestine which could be obtained in no other manner. Of all the charges made against this country the charge that they had been unjust to the Arab race seemed to him the strangest. He was prepared to maintain that the policy of His Majesty's Government and of the Allied and Associated Powers in Palestine was and would be most helpful to the Arab population. He saw no reason why those who lived, according to Lord Islington, in amity under Turkish rule should insist on quarrelling under British rule.

The ideal he desired to see accomplished was that of giving to the Jewish race an opportunity of developing in peace and quietness under British rule those great gifts which hitherto they had been compelled from the very nature of the case only to bring to fruition in countries which knew not their language and belonged not to their race.

"Zionism will fail."

Lord Sydenham confessed that he disliked and distrusted the mandatory system. Zionism would fail, but the harm done by dumping down an alien population upon an Arab country might never be remedied. The Mandate, as it stood, would undoubtedly in time transfer the control of the Holy Land to New York, Berlin, London, Frankfort, and other places.

Lord Lamington said that if they tried to establish the Zionist settlement in Palestine they were bound to have trouble. If they would only allow time for suspicion to be somewhat allayed he believed it would be perfectly possible to reconcile the Moslems with the Jews.

On a division the Motion of Lord Islington was carried by 60 votes against 29.

---

* A concession (which was referred to by Lord Islington in his speech) has been granted to Mr. Rutenberg with respect to water and electric power works in Palestine.

BRITISH NATIONALITY AND STATUS OF ALIENS BILL.

On 20th June the Home Secretary introduced in the House of Commons the British Nationality and Status of Aliens Bill. The object of the measure is to provide for the continuance, under certain conditions, of the British nationality of successive generations of British descent born abroad. Under the existing law British nationality by descent ends after the first generation (or in the case of persons born before 1915 the second generation) born abroad.

The Bill provides for amendment of the British Nationality and Status of Aliens Act, 1914, in respect of the definition of a natural-born British subject.

It proposes that every child born abroad of a British father shall be a British subject if two main conditions, calculated to show continued connection and sympathy with the British Empire, are fulfilled, viz. :—

(*a*) The birth of the child is at the time registered at a British consulate, and

(*b*) The child, on obtaining majority, asserts his British nationality by a declaration duly registered.

EMPIRE SETTLEMENT ACT.

(Co-operation with the Dominions; A permanent scheme; Assisted migration and land-settlement.)

The Royal Assent was given on 31st May to the Empire Settlement Act.

The Act provides for co-operation by the Secretary of State for the Colonies with any Dominion Government, or with approved private organisations in the United Kingdom or the Dominions, in carrying out agreed schemes to assist suitable persons in the United Kingdom to settle in the Dominions. A summary of the text of the Bill, which was passed practically without amendment, was given in the last number of the Journal. (*Vide* Vol. III., No. 2, p. 329.)

DEBATE IN HOUSE OF COMMONS.

On 26th April the Second Reading debate on the Bill took place in the House of Commons.

The Parliamentary Secretary to the Admiralty (Mr. L. S. Amery), reviewing the successive steps which had led to the introduction of the measure, said the need for a more direct interest on the part of the British Government in the movement of its citizens overseas was strongly urged both by the Dominions Royal Commission appointed as the outcome of the Imperial Conference of 1911, and by the Committee under Lord Tennyson's chairmanship, which in 1917 investigated the problem from the point of view of the interests of ex-Service men. In compliance with their recommendations the present Lord Long, then Secretary of State for the Colonies, set up shortly after the Armistice the Government Emigration Committee, a designation subsequently changed to the Oversea Settlement Committee. Of that Committee he (Mr. Amery) had acted as chairman almost since its inception.

The first duty, and up to the present the main administrative task, of the Committee was to deal with the ex-Service men. They felt that these men had fought for the Empire and ought not to be denied access to any good opportunity which the Empire had to offer. The Committee accordingly persuaded the Cabinet to include among the facilities given to ex-Service men—and to ex-Service women as well—a free passage for themselves and their families. This offer was subject to conditions important from the point of view of both the ex-Service men and the Dominions to which they went. One was that they should have assured employment in prospect. Another was that from the point of view of the Oversea Governments themselves they should be in every respect—both personally and in regard to the local economic situation—desirable immigrants.

Small percentage of failures.

"We have, in fact," said Mr. Amery, "entrusted the whole responsibility of selection in this respect to the representatives of the oversea Governments, and no voucher for a free passage has been issued except upon the express recommendation of these representatives. As several of the Governments have, in view of their own industrial difficulties, practically confined their endorsement to men willing to go upon the land, or to women prepared to enter domestic service, the numbers who might have availed themselves of this scheme have been very much limited. Those who have actually been passed have been less than one-third of the applications, while the numbers of those applying have, of course, been kept down by a knowledge of the conditions laid down.

"Even so, the numbers who have actually gone are not inconsiderable. The total, up to the time when the applications still pending have been dealt with—the scheme itself was closed at the end of last year—will amount to about 50,000 ex-Service men, making, with their families, a total of 100,000 persons. Thanks to the precautions taken, only a very small percentage of these actually have failed, while quite a considerable number are well on their way to substantial prosperity. We have encouraged all those who received free passages to write to us, and, while we have received some letters of complaint and disappointment, we have received a very large number expressing in the most enthusiastic language the gratitude of the writers for the chance in life we have given them."

Money well spent.

Proceeding, Mr. Amery remarked that the free passages were open to all who served, without question of their private means, but the Committee estimated that fully 80 per cent., if not 90 per cent., of those who went were unemployed, or would have come on the unemployment funds. By the time the ex-Service scheme was wound up these free passages would have cost something like £2,700,000. The same people would have cost the community in various forms of relief up to the end of the year about £3,000,000.

The real difference between these figures lay in the fact that in the one case they would have been here, still unemployed, increasingly less employable, a permanent drain on the country and a weakness to the nation. As it was, they were to-day productive workers, many of them on the way to becoming their own masters, supplying this country with goods that it needed, buying this country's goods and keeping its trade under laws which gave these goods a preference over the goods of foreign countries. The scheme had been, he believed, money well spent from the point of view of the British Government, even though it had paid the whole cost of the passages itself. That was a natural arrangement while the resources of the Dominions were completely taken up with the problems of the repatriation and re-settlement of their own soldiers.

Permanent scheme; Dominion co-operation.

But that obviously could only be a temporary arrangement. Any permanent scheme for Empire migration and settlement must clearly be based on the full co-operation of the Dominions concerned, whose need for population to develop their resources, sustain their defence, and build up their standard of progress was at least as great as this country's need for the transfer of surplus population. That was the view of the Dominions as well, and in February of last year a special Conference* took place at which the whole problem was fully discussed.

The subsequent Conference of Prime Ministers, after full investigation, formally by resolution approved the proposals of the special Conference, the Dominions undertaking to co-operate effectively with the United Kingdom in developing schemes based on those proposals, though South Africa made

* The proceedings of the Conference are summarised in Appendix 5 to the Blue-book on the subsequent Conference of Prime Ministers (Cmd. 1474).

it clear that the limited field for white labour in the Union would preclude co-operation on the lines contemplated by the other Dominions. The resolution went on to express the hope

That the Government of the United Kingdom will at the earliest possible moment secure the necessary powers to enable it to carry out its part in any scheme of co-operation which may be agreed upon, preferably in the form of an Act which will make it clear that the policy of co-operation now adopted is intended to be permanent.

The schemes naturally fell into two main categories: schemes of assisted migration and schemes of land settlement and development.

Lack of co-ordination.

The former category represented the natural extension to general migration of the existing ex-Service scheme, with certain modifications due to the altered conditions and the experience gained under that scheme. The Government were now of opinion that not more than one-third of the passage money—at any rate in the case of adults—should actually be given as a free grant, though another one-third, or in special cases even two-thirds, would be advanced as a loan. Again, experience had led them to assign very special importance to juvenile migration, to the migration of women, to hostels for the women and arrangements for reception generally, and to the preliminary testing and training, both here and overseas, of those who intended to go on the land.

Having reminded the House of the valuable experiment carried out before the War by Viscount Elveden at his training farm at Woking, Mr. Amery said that a valuable complement to such farms in this country would be training farms or base camps on the other side to which newcomers would go straight without the risk of being intercepted and diverted to urban pursuits in the great cities while waiting, and where they could learn something of local methods and conditions before being placed out among local farmers. Even with every training facility—and in this respect they were still a long way from an adequate co-ordination throughout the Empire—it was doubtful whether with an adult population of which over 90 per cent. was industrial they would ever get enough men to meet the needs of the Dominions for workers to open up their land.

Juvenile and women migrants.

" But we have here," said Mr. Amery, " a vast juvenile population not yet definitely settled down to industrialism. To rescue these from overcrowded professions and industries, and from even more soul-killing blind-alley occupations, is one of the most hopeful tasks to which we can put our hand.

" A wonderful and still insufficiently appreciated work has been done in this respect by the child migration and settlement work of Dr. Barnardo's Homes and other similar institutions, and I am glad to think that, largely at the instigation of our Committee, Dr. Barnardo's Homes have now begun to extend their sphere of activities to Australia as well as to Canada. A similar and no less hopeful experiment is now being initiated by the South Australian Government, which is proposing to invite out some 6,000 boys between 15 and 18, and start them in life under selected farmers, with special arrangements for looking after their welfare and prospects.

"Another and even more important aspect of this problem is that of the migration of women. There is to-day a surplus in this country of 1,700,000 women. In the Dominions there is a small deficit of women, measured simply by the standard of arithmetical equality of sexes. But measured by the standard of the social need for the services of women in household work there is a far greater deficit, and one that in every direction is having a most prejudicial effect upon the social life of the Dominions. Here, too, much can be done by training, both here and overseas, to enable those without any experience to enter successfully upon domestic work overseas."

Settlement on the land.

" Our experience, and that of all the Dominions, as voiced at the special Conference, convinced us," Mr. Amery continued, " that the capacity of the Dominions to absorb additional industrial and urban population, and, in fact, to deal with any immigration on a really large scale, is strictly conditioned by the opening up of their agricultural resources. The direct settlement of men on the land as primary producers must be the foundation of any broad policy of economic regeneration in the Empire. Consequently, we attach even greater importance to the second category of schemes—those that deal with land settlement and development.

" These will naturally be of very varying kinds, according to the very various conditions which they may have to meet, but, broadly speaking, they will fall either into individual settlement schemes under which men without sufficient capital will receive advances to enable them to set up as farmers overseas, always, as I hope, after the necessary preliminary period for gaining local farming experience, or else development schemes for opening up large new areas to cultivation by the clearing of forests, building roads and railways, and works of irrigation.

" Schemes of this latter type are in many respects the most hopeful from the point of view of dealing with large numbers of men without capital and without experience. They afford abundant local opportunity for wage-earning while the men are being acclimatised to local conditions, and for facilitating settlement in groups and communities. A last, but not least, important consideration is that they ought to be relatively cheap."

Administration.

For the carrying out of the various schemes it was proposed to rely, Mr. Amery explained, upon existing Government and private organisations. It was not intended to set up any elaborate new administrative machinery either in this country or overseas. The actual administration was far better left to the oversea Governments, all of which had existing machinery which could be adapted or expanded to meet new developments, or else to private organisations, whether of a business or philanthropic character. Mr. Amery spoke of the valuable work done in this connection by the Salvation Army, the Church Army, and the Y.M.C.A. By making provision for 15 years ahead, he remarked, the Bill provided that element of permanence and continuity in general policy upon which the Dominions insisted so strongly at the recent Conference.

Finance of the Bill.

" It is not proposed," Mr. Amery observed, " to spend in the present year more than £1,500,000, and in view of the full investigation and discussion which will be required into every scheme that is put before us, I doubt if we shall be in a position to spend even the whole of that sum in the present year. The normal expenditure is fixed at £3,000,000. Of this total I estimate that about £1,000,000 will be required for schemes within the category of assisted migration. The basis of contribution for schemes in this category will normally be half and half, so that the total amount available both from the Dominions and the United Kingdom for this purpose will be about £2,000,000 a year.

" I reckon that the average cost per adult of passages is about £26, though I hope that figure will gradually come down. While the whole of this will not necessarily have to be furnished in every case there will, on the other hand, be many instances where we shall have to spend money on initial training and advances of landing money, and so on. I reckon that a figure somewhere between £25 and £30 will probably represent fairly the average cost per head of a migrant. On that basis £2,000,000 would make possible an annual assisted migration of something between 60,000 and 80,000 persons a year to begin with, and a considerably larger figure eventually if the repayment of advances is added to the fund for fresh assistance.

"The remaining £2,000,000 of United Kingdom money would be available for assistance to land settlement and development schemes.

British contribution.

"Any estimate of the numbers which should be settled under these schemes depends on the particular kind of scheme adopted. It was agreed at the special Conference that the British contribution to schemes of individual settlement should not exceed an advance of £300 a settler, roughly speaking, about one-third of the minimum total amount required. On that basis it would be possible to settle about 3,000 heads of families as farmers for a low expenditure of £1,000,000. On the other hand, block settlement schemes may yield larger results for a smaller immediate contribution.

"We are, for instance, considering at this moment a scheme, already agreed upon between the Australian Commonwealth and the Government of Western Australia, under which the latter undertakes to settle 75,000 persons for an expenditure of £6,000,000, provided that the Commonwealth and the United Kingdom each contribute a sum equivalent to one-third of the interest for five years on the successive instalments raised. This would cost us altogether, over a period of seven or eight years, £600,000, in other words, 10 per cent. of the total expenditure, or only about £8 per settler. These figures are, of course, not strictly comparable.

"In the one case we are dealing with individual owners of farms and with money advanced, which would be recoverable. In the other case we are dealing with the total population, which would be settled in consequence of a scheme of development, and with an outright contribution. Still they suggest that where favourable local conditions exist these larger development schemes may offer the most substantial immediate result for a relatively small contribution."

Co-operation with the Dominions.

The amount provided would enable the problem to be taken in hand seriously, but he believed that before very long they would regard it as quite inadequate for so great and so remunerative a task. "There is, I think, in all the Dominions," said Mr. Amery, "a very keen sense of the need of additional human, as well as material, capital in order to develop their resources and strengthen their national life. Where there is local or sectional opposition to immigration, it is based upon the fear of an influx of unemployed industrial workers into urban centres where there is often serious temporary unemployment. There is nowhere any opposition to the policy of land settlement and development, which is the main object of this Bill and which can only increase employment.

"If the Dominion Governments have not already moved more actively in this matter it has been owing to the very heavy burdens which the War has left upon them and which have been increased by the task of their own soldier settlement schemes—a task which has, however, in many ways prepared the ground for new settlement schemes. The prospect of some measure of co-operation by the United Kingdom means, I believe, that every Dominion will have an opportunity of tiding over the gap between the immediate cost of such schemes and their certain ultimate benefits. . . . Apart from the general pledge of effective co-operation contained in the Conference resolution, several Oversea Dominion Governments are only waiting for the passage of this Bill to enter into definite negotiations."

What Oversea Governments will do.

The Prime Minister of Australia had declared himself prepared in principle to consider schemes involving—of course over a considerable number of years—an expenditure of £50,000,000, subject to securing satisfactory arrangements with the State Governments who owned the land and would actually administer any schemes. The Western Australian scheme to which he had referred, if they could see their way to join in it under the provisions of that Bill, would be only an instalment of a far-reaching policy of Australian development. The Commonwealth was equally ready to join at once in a scheme for assisted passages to any extent that Australia's requirements for population might demand.

Mr. Massey, the Prime Minister of New Zealand, expressed at the time of the Conference his own readiness and that of his Dominion to co-operate both in schemes of settlement and migration on a scale proportioned to the limited area of his Dominion. The case of South Africa was exceptional owing to the fact that there was no opening there for white unskilled or semi-skilled labour. That precluded any idea of large development schemes or of a larger volume of assisted migration.

Colonel J. C. Wedgwood (Labour, *Newcastle-under-Lyme*)**:** "What about Rhodesia ?"

The Parliamentary Secretary to the Admiralty: "Yes, I think a certain amount can be done in Rhodesia for individual land settlement, but, even there, the opening is somewhat limited. The South African legislation, and the Rhodesian legislation too, is very generous in its terms and offers a fruitful though . . . a limited field for co-operation.

Not a panacea for unemployment.

"As regards Canada—perhaps the greatest and certainly the nearest field for settlement—Mr. Meighen was not able at the Conference, in view of the imminence of the General Election, to give any assurance beyond his conviction that Canada would be certain to co-operate effectively in any such policy of Imperial development. The new Canadian Government has, I understand, been giving very serious consideration to the whole subject and will, I have no doubt, take full advantage of the co-operation which we shall be in a position to offer if this Bill passes into law."

Proceeding, Mr. Amery said that for the full success of that policy they would want something more than the co-operation of the Dominion Governments. They would need the whole-hearted co-operation and sympathy of the great public in the Dominions. He was not recommending the policy of Empire settlement as a panacea for the immediate crisis of unemployment with which this country was confronted. " To attempt to solve unemployment here by taking the unemployed, as such, and dumping them down in the Dominions without regard to the conditions there, without regard to their own fitness, would be a policy cruel to the unemployed themselves and in any case impossible because the Dominions would never consent to it. What we are aiming at is only incidentally the relief of the immediate crisis ; our main object is to find a permanent constructive remedy for the enduring problem of the economic situation which the War has left behind it."

The economic task, as he conceived it, was essentially the task of securing a right distribution of their population in the Empire. He commended the Bill as the first step forward on the right road to economic recovery. He would also commend it as a measure of Imperial defence—the most economical, the least provocative, and the surest. He commended it, further, as a measure happily outside their Party controversies and at the same time in the true line of their national tradition and of their historic Imperial policy.

Labour view.

The Right Hon. J. R. Clynes (Chairman of the Parliamentary Labour Party) said all were agreed that it was very desirable to devise some plan for a wiser and fairer distribution of the population within parts of the British Empire. The worst of the population in the old country—the least skilled, the least healthy, the least efficient—were not desired by those who had the general good conditions of other parts of the Empire in their keeping. If they wanted anything, they wanted the best.

Mr. J. A. R. Marriott (Coalition Unionist, *Oxford*) : " Quite right. Why not ? "

Mr. Clynes : " It is right from their point of view. . . . The question is, can we afford to get rid of the best ? Have we got them in such an abundance from the standpoint of our own well-being as to be able to afford any large margin in response to the attractions of this measure ? " While they were all wishful to cultivate greater and improved trade relations with the Dominions, he did not see that they could find any appreciable solution of their state of unemployment unless they competed more effectively with their rivals in the larger markets of Europe.

In other words, to limit themselves to trading relations with their Dominions population would be at the most to try to maintain or expand trade conditions with a population of some 12,000,000 or 15,000,000. It would not do to seek to improve trade with that number and neglect trade with a population approaching 300,000,000.

Use of private organisations.

He had a great deal of sympathy with the main purposes of the measure, but no hon. Member should mislead himself to the extent of thinking that they were solving economic problems, or supplying a real remedy for root troubles, by paying the expenses to the Dominions overseas of certain unemployed or ex-soldiers. How far was it the purpose of the Dominions or of the Home Government to work through private organisations ? In the past there had been a great deal of emigration, in many instances with painful consequences, because people were lured to leave this country by the representations of advertisements and by the promise and prospect of improved conditions when they landed in another country.

Sir C. Kinloch-Cooke (Coalition Unionist, *Devonport*) : " Not by societies."

Mr. Clynes : " By shipping companies and by emigration agents. . . . I hope that it is not intended in any sense to subsidise or support out of taxes private agencies like shipping companies which in the past have had no concern with the future of the emigrant, and whose sole interest has been with the present—with securing for the moment the gain to be derived from payment of the passage money."

Consultation with Labour.

To what extent, if any, had Labour organisations in the Dominions been consulted or considered in connection with the general problem of the distribution of population ? Much of the success of the measure must depend upon securing the goodwill of Labour both in its organised and non-organised aspects, as Labour existed in the Dominions of the Empire. Different parts of the Dominions were at present suffering from the general economic dislocation which existed throughout the world. So far as he knew, their unemployment was centred in the various large towns and cities.

" There is," said Mr. Clynes, " the very natural suspicion on the part of those who are unemployed in the large towns and cities, that to send to the Dominions great drafts of unemployed from this country will only intensify the economic situation, and will make worse the degree of unemployment from which they are now suffering. . . . Therefore I think it is of the highest importance that Labour should be not merely consulted in the Dominions, but should be taken into the confidence of the Dominion Governments, and that the co-operation and goodwill of Labour should be sought in order that as soon as the emigrants arrive in any part of the Dominions they should be properly trained for the general purposes to which they are going to apply themselves."

Government ownership of land.

Whilst very generous terms must be arranged in order to attract people to work and live on the land, those terms should fall short of actually giving away to people of this age a form of property which should be retained by all Governments as the rightful property of the people collectively throughout the centuries. He was certain that opinion was shared by organised Labour in other lands, and he uttered it in order to claim that the view must be considered for what it was worth, and that Labour opinion, particularly in Australia and Canada, must be taken into account by the Governments of the Dominions which were wishful to act with the Government of the home country.

Capt. R. Gee (**Unionist**, *Woolwich, E.*) observed that the decision as to what men and women should be sent out called for careful examination. He suggested that a joint Committee should be set up for the purpose, consisting of business men and women at home, and of the participating Dominions—people thoroughly conversant with the industries in the Dominions and at home. Also, there should be an official of the Home Government and of the Dominion Governments to go into the whole question. Those who had the deciding of the question, however, should be as free as possible from Government control, so that there would be no fear of the scheme being wrecked through interference by successive Governments. By backing the Bill and getting a white population in Australia and in Canada they would be helping to do away with the bogey of the " yellow peril."

Over-population at home.

The Right Hon. Sir Donald Maclean (Chairman of the Independent Liberal Party in Parliament) remarked that it was an integral part of their existence as a world Power that there should be emigration from these shores, particularly to their Dominions. It was obvious that there was over-population in these islands at the moment, and there was an unquestioned case for the Bill.

"We have here," the right hon. gentleman proceeded, "a large or, at any rate, a comprehensive Government scheme. It is essential that there should be Governmental co-operation, linked with efficient voluntary aid, and I am glad to know from the reports which I have read of speeches made by distinguished representatives of the Dominions in this country, particularly those from Australia, that there is not only the intention to co-operate, but that schemes are already in operation or are being formed for efficient co-operation.

"I have been very much impressed by the scheme laid before various Members of this House by the Prime Minister of Western Australia. There is a working model which might be applied to all the Dominions overseas. There is first of all a man who has got his heart in the business in the person of the Prime Minister of that State, and then there is a really efficient machine for bringing the emigrant into touch with the actual position in which he may be expected most beneficially to operate. That is not only done through the official channel, but there is linked up with it an efficient and sympathetic voluntary organisation."

Inadequate expenditure.

Maj.-Gen. Sir Newton Moore (Coalition Unionist, *Islington, N.*) expressed his grave disappointment at the limitation of expenditure this year to something like £1,500,000. That was totally inadequate when it was considered that a small State like Victoria had spent within the last two years something like £2,000,000 in the settlement of 10,000 settlers. During the time he was Agent-General for Western Australia—and by the way, he was representing a Labour Government—he sent out from this country 30,000 to 40,000 emigrants, and he was not aware of half-a-dozen failures.

Practical advantage could be taken of the Bill only by those portions of the Dominions that had some ready-made scheme to deal with the problem at the present time. So far as Labour was concerned, he did not think they need anticipate that there was going to be much objection from Australia. A man who went on the land under the Western Australian scheme, which was practically a land settlement scheme, was not going to do any man out of a job. He was going to make work for others. No country in the world could appeal more to the democrat than Australia, where out of seven Prime Ministers four had been trade union leaders.

Sir C. Kinloch-Cooke stated that the Central Migration Board (of which he had been Chairman for 15 years) had a Settlement Information League. People on this side and on the other side were prepared to act as friends to anyone sent out. That system was now being taken up by the Commonwealth of Australia, and he suggested that it should also be adopted in Canada.

The Under-Secretary of State for the Colonies (Hon. E. Wood) remarked that the reason why the Bill had won a general measure of support was that it had recognised the subject of emigration as an Imperial concern.

The Bill was read a second time without a division, and committed to a Standing Committee. It was read a third time on 22nd May.

DEBATE IN HOUSE OF LORDS.

On 29th May the Bill was debated in the House of Lords on the Order for Second Reading.

Lord Denman said he fully recognised the need for settlers in all the British Dominions overseas, but he thought there was no case so urgent at the present time as that of Australia. Obviously it was desirable that men and women of British birth should emigrate to Canada, but Canada had the advantage of proximity to the United States and comparative proximity to European countries which ensured for her a considerable influx of population from those sources. The great distance which separated Australia from Europe unfortunately prevented her from receiving any considerable number of emigrants from other European countries and she was not so well situated as Canada in that respect. There was also the political aspect to consider. That was not the same for Australia as it was before the War. When the German Fleet was sunk the centre of naval strategy shifted from the North Sea and the Atlantic to the Pacific, and the position of Australia was affected by that change.

"I am a believer in the 'White Australia' policy," said Lord Denman. "I believe it to be right, but it can only be maintained and justified in the eyes of the world if Australia can achieve a great increase in her population and render her now unoccupied territory fertile and productive." He welcomed the appearance of the Bill because he believed it to be a step in the right direction and regarded it as giving a great opportunity to the Australian Commonwealth. Referring to the question of medical examination, Lord Denman said the Commonwealth Government had lately appointed medical referees in this country to whom intending migrants might apply for examination. He understood that other Dominions were following their example. But the migrant had still to pass the medical authorities at the ports of debarkation. He suggested to the Dominion Governments that, unless migrants contracted an illness on the voyage out, the examination by the referee in this country should be regarded by the medical authorities at the ports of debarkation as final.

"Your Lordships are well aware of the power that the Labour Parties possess in the Commonwealth and in the States of Australia," Lord Denman added, "and if you can secure, as I hope you will secure, the co-operation of the Australian Labour Parties for this measure, you will enhance the good work that I hope it is going to achieve."

Position of Canada.

Viscount Long of Wraxall thought it was somewhat erroneous to assume that the difficulties of Canada were not nearly so great as those of any other part of the British Empire because she was able to get a supply of residents which was denied to Colonies and Dominions further afield. No doubt that was an advantage up to a certain point; but from the Empire point of view it was a disadvantage, because there was a constant flow into the fruitful lands of Canada of men who had no sympathy with the British Empire, some of whom were actually opposed to the British Empire, and who, if a moment of difficulty came to the Empire, were not to be found aiding and supporting her as were those of British blood. He looked at this matter far more from the Empire and home point of view than from that of any particular Dominion. If the Empire was to continue to grow in strength, in influence, and in importance, wise methods must be devised by which she could transfer her surplus population from those spots which were already overcrowded to those in which there was, happily, abundant open space.

The Earl of Selborne said that reference had been made to the migration of some of the finest specimens of their congested population to the empty spaces of the Empire. But where was their congested population? It was in the great cities, and so far as he understood the attitude of the Dominion Governments they did not want that kind of population at all. He was told that at the present moment some of those Governments would admit only domestic servants, agricultural labourers, or farmers. "I want to point out," said Lord Selborne, "that the effect of this Bill may be not to migrate from our great cities those whom we should like to see moved but to tempt away from our agricultural population some of our very best agricultural labourers and farmers—in fact, to depopulate still further our rural areas, and still further to diminish our home production."

Public school boys as migrants.

Viscount Novar suggested that most of the information concerning migration could be obtained from the Dominions, especially after the experience they had acquired of settling ex-soldiers on the land. Many of the younger boys leaving public schools in England would probably prefer to go upon the land instead of becoming clerks in the great banks and insurance companies. They would possess a certain amount of capital, and would be in a different position from those who went out from the towns in the old days as emigrants. If those boys were entered in the agricultural colleges in the Dominions and had their training there they would be able to make their way in the Dominions just as well as the boys who were already in those colleges. That was one avenue by which migration from this country could be extended.

The Duke of Devonshire said it was certainly time that steps were taken in the Dominions and the Old Country for dealing in a systematic manner with this big question. He would not like to deprecate the work which could be done by a well-trained and skilful agriculturist in this country, but one of the difficulties he would have to contend with in the Dominions was that there might be a good deal he would have to unlearn before he could adapt himself to the somewhat unusual conditions. The Duke of Devonshire went on to remark that there were many great developments to which they could look forward with confidence in Canada.

Prospects in Canada.

"At the moment," he said, the financial and social conditions are such as to make it undesirable that there should be a large entry of mechanics and artisans, but, in Canada, at no very distant date, there will be a great development of her mineral wealth and of the lumber industry. Great as has been the lumber industry in the past, and still is, Canada will be for many years, as the country gets more and more opened up, a centre from which there will be a still greater flow of finished and unfinished lumber materials.

"There is not the slightest reason why, with a little training and a little practice, a man who may not be qualified for agriculture should not be capable as well as anyone else of doing work in the lumber industry. In the mineral industry, when conditions which are prevalent throughout the world become more stable, there is bound to be a very big development, and I am sure there will be an opening, when that industry is further developed, for other classes of the community besides those connected solely with agriculture."

Medical examination.

The First Commissioner of Works (the Earl of Crawford), replying on the debate, said there was no age limit in the Bill and the words "suitable person" did not preclude a child being sent out. With regard to medical examination, Lord Denman was quite right when he said that in old days it frequently happened that a wretched man with a family was induced by some speculative person to spend his money upon transport overseas and on arrival there found himself rejected. The Oversea Settlement Committee and the Dominions were very conscious of this difficulty, and every effort was being made to prevent any recurrence of the trouble.

The Commonwealth had arranged to appoint medical referees throughout the United Kingdom to give certificates to men before they departed. He assumed that a certificate given by any of those referees appointed by the Commonwealth Government would hold good until the end of the journey, unless, of course, some infectious disease developed in the meantime. The Commonwealth Government alone was appointing 15,000 of those medical referees, and he hoped that the system would be extended.

The Earl of Selborne: "Do I gather that the Dominion of Canada has taken this step?"

The First Commissioner of Works: "I have no record of what the Canadian Government has done, but obviously it is good sense." Reference had been made, Lord Crawford proceeded, to migration from Australia. It must be a very small percentage and if the subject were investigated it would probably be found that people coming back from Australia were people who ought never to have gone there. There would always be unsuitable migrants, and the whole scheme underlying the Bill would tend to reduce undesirable migration to the smallest possible compass. If agricultural labourers and young farmers migrated from rural England to other portions of the Empire the Bill would at least ensure that they would be given a fair chance and would be watched over by the paternal interest of the Overseas Governments.

The Bill was read a second time without a division, and was subsequently passed through its remaining stages.

IMPERIAL CONFERENCES, 1917 AND 1918.

(Publication of Report of Proceedings.)

On 14th June, in the House of Commons,

Mr. Percy Hurd (Coalition Unionist, *Frome*) asked the Prime Minister whether a full report of the proceedings of the Imperial Conferences of 1917 and 1918 could now be published.

The Leader of the House (the Right Hon. Austen Chamberlain), who replied, said: "Extracts from minutes of proceedings and papers laid before the Imperial War Conferences of 1917 and 1918 were published as Parliamentary Papers in May, 1917, and October, 1918. As at present advised, I do not think that the time has yet come for considering the question of publishing full reports, which would, in any event, necessitate detailed examination of the proceedings by His Majesty's Government and reference to all the Dominion Governments represented at the Conferences. The decision to publish, if taken at all, could be properly taken only by the Imperial Conference as a whole."

Mr. Hurd: "Will the right hon. gentleman say whether the decisions of these two Conferences do not now form the basis of policy, not only in this country, but in many of the Dominions, and how can public opinion be properly informed unless the public get something more than the bald publication which has already been made?"

Secrecy must be observed.

The Leader of the House: "These Conferences were in the nature of Cabinet Councils, and for their full usefulness the secrecy usually attaching to the proceedings of Ministers in Council must be observed. I do not think that the time has come when these proceedings should be published in full, if, indeed, as I say, that time should ever come, until the historian deals with that period."

Mr. Hurd: "Have not the Blue Books published in reference to earlier Conferences been the means of giving information to the public as to matters on which policy is now based?"

The Leader of the House: "In the years between the earlier Imperial Conferences and the later meetings, such as those of 1917 and 1918, immense strides forward have been made, and the matters taken into consideration at the later Conferences were in many cases of a much more confidential character, but even as regards the earlier Conferences I think that particular discussions were not published."

Mr. G. A. Spencer (Labour, *Broxtowe*): "Does not the right hon. gentleman think that it would be better for the world at large if there were less secrecy among Ministers in all countries?"

The Leader of the House: "No. I think that the complaint made yesterday was that the Cabinet Secretariat prepared for publication matters which ought to be kept confidential. Without accepting that charge, I think that the proceedings of councils of Ministers, whether in this country alone, or in other parts of the Empire, should be in private."

CABINET SECRETARIAT.

(A constitutional development ; Power of the Prime Minister; Question of secrecy.)

On 13th June in the House of Commons opportunity was taken on a Vote for the Cabinet Offices to discuss in Committee of Supply the question of the Cabinet Secretariat.

DEBATE IN HOUSE OF COMMONS.

The Right Hon. Sir Donald Maclean (**Chairman of the Independent Liberal Party in Parliament**), in moving a reduction in the Vote, said the mere newness of the Cabinet Secretariat was no ground of objection to it, because, if their Constitution was to go on developing as it had done in the past, there must from time to time be changes consistent with and not too far in advance of the needs of the time. The secret of the effectiveness of the British Constitution was its almost complete fusion of the executive and legislative functions, distinguishing it very definitely from the Presidential system, at any rate as that system obtained in America.

It was therefore of vital importance, if they were to preserve intact the distinction between their Cabinet system and the Presidential system, that the House of Commons should lose none of its control over the executive Departments of the State. The power of the Prime Minister was rapidly and, as he thought, not wisely being increased. He wished to know what was the need for the Cabinet Secretariat.

The Leader of the House (**the Right Hon. Austen Chamberlain**) characterised as unbusinesslike the old system under which no agenda was prepared of the business to be laid before Ministers and no record was taken of anything that passed in Cabinet, or of any decision taken by the Cabinet, except such as might be embodied in the letter written by the Prime Minister to His Majesty. He failed to see how the Cabinet Secretariat would remove the Departments, or Ministers, or the Government as a whole from Parliamentary control.

Prime Minister's position.

How on earth could the control of the House of Commons over public affairs be affected adversely by the fact that a record was kept of Cabinet proceedings and that Cabinet decisions were recorded instead of being left to the individual memory of the Ministers ? The position of the Prime Minister had always had special weight in Cabinet deliberations, but his influence and authority depended upon the man himself. Did anybody think that Mr. Lloyd George was more all-powerful in the Cabinet to-day than were Mr. Gladstone, Lord Beaconsfield, or Mr. Asquith ?

The Cabinet Secretariat had no executive function, no administrative function, displaced no other Department, and did the work of no other Department. Its duty was to bring the business of the Cabinet before the Cabinet in proper form, to take such notes of discussions in Cabinet, or Cabinet Committees, as the Cabinet might require, to record the decisions of the Cabinet, and to see that those decisions were communicated to the Departments which had to execute them. When he was Chancellor of the Exchequer he secured that there should always be one official of the Treasury attached to the Secretariat whose business it would be to see that financial questions were not brought before the Cabinet or a Cabinet Committee until the Treasury had an opportunity of considering them.

League of Nations; Dominion preference.

Similarly, the whole of the League of Nations' work was under the charge of an official seconded from the Foreign Office to the Cabinet Secretariat for that particular purpose. The question had been asked, "Why did you put the League of Nations' work under the Secretariat at all ?" In the first place, the League of Nations intimately concerned the Dominions, and the Dominions preferred to correspond with the Cabinet Office. Moreover, the League of Nations was not merely a Foreign Office concern. An immense part—even the larger part—was concerned directly and immediately with other Departments than the Foreign Office. They settled, therefore, that the Cabinet Secretariat was the best Department for the League to correspond with. The same staff which served the Cabinet Secretariat served the Committee of Imperial Defence.

The Right Hon. H. H. Asquith (Leader of the Independent Liberal Party) recalled the practice pursued by Mr. Gladstone (inherited by him from Lord Palmerston and Sir Robert Peel), and adopted by Lord Salisbury and Sir Henry Campbell-Bannerman. All the heads of the great Departments of State, once or twice a week, met the Cabinet in Council to contribute their share of information and advice. So, after discussion, decisions were come to. Secrecy was so well maintained, in theory at any rate, and he thought in fact also, that he believed in practice no one ever opened the door of the Chamber except a Cabinet Minister. No note was kept of the proceedings by anybody except the Prime Minister. He did not believe he had ever known a single instance in which there was any serious subsequent difference of opinion as to what had taken place at the Cabinet.

"I am perfectly certain, if I may venture to say so—for I have not had experience of the new system—that Gladstone and Lord Beaconsfield would have shuddered in their graves at the thought of an outsider being present and taking notes of what was going on. They would have considered it a breach of the fundamental laws of the Constitution."

Labour's approval.

The Right Hon. W. Adamson (Labour, *Fife, W.*) said that a system that provided for no agenda, no record of business done, and no co-ordination was, in the opinion of the Labour Party, not in keeping with the spirit of the times. Trusting to the memory of the individual Minister was a most unbusinesslike proceeding, and the change was a step in the right direction. The keeping of a correct record of the proceedings of the Cabinet would in no sense lessen the individual responsibility of various Ministers.

The Prime Minister (the Right Hon. D. Lloyd George) had no hesitation in saying that whenever there was a change of Government the next Administration would be glad to utilise the services of the Cabinet Secretariat and would continue them more or less in their present form. Not only so, but if they were to do otherwise they would soon find that they had committed a fatal error and would be glad to revert to the present practice. He was perfectly certain that if Cabinet decisions had ever been revealed they had not been revealed by any member of the Secretariat.

Foreign policy: Genoa Conference.

The machinery of the Cabinet Secretariat was the machinery of the Committee of Imperial Defence. If they could trust the Secretariat with matters which involved peace and war between great nations, he thought they could trust them with regard to the questions that came up for discussion inside the Cabinet. There was never a more futile suggestion than that the Secretariat was a machine to enable the Prime Minister of the day to get control over foreign policy. If the Prime Minister wanted to control foreign policy that was not the way to do it. At the Genoa Conference the experts who dealt with the questions were not experts of the Cabinet Secretariat, but of the Departments themselves.

The Secretariat had nothing whatever to do with policy. They dealt with records. They transmitted copies of documents. They summoned the meetings of the experts. They summoned the meetings of the British Empire Delegation when it was desired to have a Conference with all the

Representatives of the Dominions and of India. There seemed to be a fear that they would interfere with the Foreign Office, the Treasury, the Board of Trade, and the War Office. They were doing none of those things. They were quite loyally and fairly discharging their tasks within the limitations laid down. The Cabinet Secretariat was purely a recording machine, and a machine which was an improvement upon the past.

On a division the motion to reduce the Vote was negatived by 205 votes against 111.

IMPERIAL COMMUNICATIONS.

(Cable Rates; Imperial Wireless Chain.)

On 4th April, in the House of Commons.

Mr. Percy Hurd (Coalition Unionist, *Frome*) asked whether the Postmaster-General would take steps to encourage the use of the Imperial cable by granting lower rates for Press and general messages despatched during the slack hours of the day, and so lessen the peak load of the cables.

The Postmaster-General (the Right Hon. F. G. Kellaway): " Specially low rates are already given on the 'Imperial' cable service for non-urgent traffic, which can be held over until the slack hours of the day. The 'Imperial' is the only cable route on which the following reduced rate services are provided: A deferred Press service to Canada at 2½d. a word, and to Australia and New Zealand at 4½d.; a deferred service for general traffic to Canada at 4½d. a word, which is 1½d. less than the rate by other cable routes; a week-end service to Australia and New Zealand at quarter rates. A large amount of traffic is sent by these cheap rate services. It is held over whenever necessary in favour of full-rate traffic, which latter is given a rapid service, even at the busiest hours of the day."

Position of Canada.

Mr. Hurd: " Is it not a fact that no lower rates whatever are given to one Dominion to which the matter is of the greatest importance, namely, Canada, and that the same rate is given by the 'Imperial' cable as by the other cables?"

The Postmaster-General: " I have answered the question which my hon. friend put to me, as to the granting of special rates for a special class of service, and I have shown that these special rates are in fact granted and used."

Mr. Hurd: " Was not His Majesty's Government a party to a unanimous resolution at the Imperial Conference calling for far lower rates than these which the right hon. gentleman now announces?"

The Postmaster-General: "There are demands from all quarters for far lower rates, but I have to have regard to the solvency of the service."

Imperial Wireless Chain.

On 26th April,

Mr. Hurd asked the Postmaster-General whether any, and, if so, what, replies had been received from the Governments of the Dominions and India respecting their attitude towards the Imperial Wireless Chain; and whether any of them, and, if so, which, had entered upon wireless projects of their own, independently of the Post Office scheme.

The Postmaster-General: "The only Dominion which has entered upon any wireless project of its own is Australia, whose representative at the Imperial meetings of last year reserved to the Commonwealth Government full freedom of action to decide in what manner it would co-operate in the Imperial wireless scheme. Precise information as to the project of that Government is not yet to hand, but when it is received its bearing on the remainder of the scheme will be carefully considered.

"The Indian Government have stated that they will have difficulty in finding funds to erect a high-power station of their own, and the position thus created will also be examined. Communications are proceeding with the Union Government, and the Canadian Government are sending two representatives to this country to discuss the matter."

Mr. Hurd: "Is it the position that no Dominion has, up to the present time, taken any part whatever in this Empire wireless scheme?"

The Postmaster-General: "I think that is a very exaggerated way of stating the facts, which I have set out accurately in my answer."

DEBATE IN HOUSE OF COMMONS.

On 4th May, in introducing the Post Office Vote in the House of Commons,

The Postmaster-General made a statement in the course of which he dealt with the carriage of mails by air. The progress made not only in this country, but in most other countries, had not realised anything like the sanguine expectations some of them held a few years ago, but he thought last year had shown greater progress than any other period since man conquered the art of flight. The most successful of all the air mail services with which this country was associated was that from Cairo to Bagdad. A letter sent from London to Bagdad in the ordinary way took from 28 to 30 days. Sent by air service it took only twelve days.

"I visualise the time," said Mr. Kellaway, "when throughout the Empire we shall be able to provide air services which will make just as great a saving in time as that which the Air Ministry has succeeded in making between Cairo and Bagdad. No man can put any limitation to the possibilities of this service, and the fact that accidents have happened, that the percentage of reliability has not, so far, been very great, is no proof that the Air Ministry and those companies which have with great audacity invested their capital in these services will not succeed in doing for the whole of the Empire what the Air Ministry has succeeded in doing between Cairo and Bagdad.

"A Civil Aviation Advisory Board has been formed by the Air Ministry, with a representative of the Post Office upon it, and this is its first business :

'To consider the cost and the practicability of setting up an Imperial Air Mail Service.'

They are first directing their attention to the Cairo-Bagdad and the Bagdad-Bombay sections of a possible future Imperial air route to India and to Australia."

Lower cable rates.

Mr. Hurd urged in relation to Imperial communications the necessity for cheapening and increasing the facilities. He was glad the Postmaster-General had brought the Empire and the United States within the ambit of the new 1½d. letter rate. It was a step towards the restoration of Imperial penny postage. They might, he hoped, look forward in the near future to a lessening of the cost of cable communications overseas. They possessed at the moment an Imperial cable—one of the remnants that came to them as a result of the War. Why could not they reduce the rates on that? It affected Canada, Australia, South Africa, and New Zealand.

The Assistant Postmaster-General (the Right Hon. H. Pike Pease) said the Imperial cable was, he thought, the only cable which had restored the 4½d. rate to Canada at the present time.

Mr. Hurd pointed out that there was the same deferred rate on the Imperial cable as on the ordinary commercial cables. He would like to see the Post Office aim at a penny cable rate to Canada and a corresponding rate to other parts of the Empire.

Wireless chain.

The record of the Post Office in connection with the Imperial wireless chain had been a miserable one—vacillation, indecision, and ineffectual isolation. He did not know whether the Post Office intended to go on with an Empire wireless scheme that had next to nothing of Empire in it, or at all events left out of account the main Dominions of which the Empire was composed. His own impression was that the scheme had gone too far towards desuetude, decay, and dissolution to be restored. The idea of the creation of the chain by State enterprise had broken down and it should be left to private enterprise.

The Assistant Postmaster-General said that, as regards the wireless chain, they had no definite answer from South Africa. They had only just received a reply from India, and consultations were going to take place shortly with the representatives of Canada.

Mr. Hurd: "Does that not prove the futility of the Post Office methods after ten years?"

The Assistant Postmaster-General said they had to take into account what had happened in those ten years. "With regard to the Imperial cable service, which runs from Penzance to Halifax (Nova Scotia) *via* the Azores, it was formerly," said Mr. Pease, "a German cable running from Emden to New York *via* the Azores. It is worked by the Post Office at the Central Telegraph Office, London, and by the Pacific Cable Board at Halifax, the expenses of the Halifax station being borne by the Post Office. The rate is 4½d. to Canada, the week-end service at quarter rates to Australasia, and the deferred Press rates 2½d. and 4½d. to Canada and Australasia respectively. That, in spite of the depression in trade, the load over the cable remains satisfactory is rather surprising. The cable since its purchase has been leased to one of the Atlantic companies, but is now to be taken over and worked by the Post Office."

Mr. Hurd: "Can the right hon. gentleman give us cheaper rates at certain hours to lessen the load?"

The Assistant Postmaster-General said the suggestion was a good one, and he would be very glad if it could be carried out.

The Vote for the Post Office was agreed to.

IMPERIAL PREFERENCE.

(The West Indies.)

On 23rd May, in the House of Commons,

Mr. Percy Hurd (Coalition Unionist, *Frome*) asked the Secretary of State for the Colonies whether he was aware that the Government of Jamaica had published in the West Indian and Canadian Press for general information his despatch of 9th March on the proposal to continue for 10 years the preference on goods at present entitled to preferential rates on importation into Great Britain ; and whether the despatch would be laid before this Parliament forthwith, together with any replies that might have been received from Colonial Governors.

The Secretary of State for the Colonies (the Right Hon. Winston Churchill): "The answer to the first part of the question is in the affirmative. The despatch in question was sent to the Colonial Governments with a view to publication, and it will be laid before the House as early as possible. A notification has been received from the Governments of Jamaica and Barbadoes that publication has taken place; but no other replies have yet been received."

Lt.-Comdr. the Hon. J. Kenworthy (Independent Liberal, *Hull, C.*): "Is it proposed to consult the House of Commons before committing future Governments—a change is expected—to a fiscal policy for ten years ?"

The Secretary of State for the Colonies: "I certainly hold that the Government has not gone beyond what is usual in matters of this kind. It is desirable that the Colonies should have some assurance of a continuance of conditions."

CANADIAN CATTLE EMBARGO.

(Free Vote in House of Commons; Motion for Removal carried.)

On 24th July,* in the House of Commons, a debate took place on the following motion by Captain W. T. Shaw (Coalition Unionist, *Forfar*):—

> "That this House is of opinion that the time has arrived when the embargo on the importation of Canadian cattle should be removed."

This was carried on a free vote of the House by 247 votes against 171. A summary of the debate will be published in the next number of the JOURNAL.

No communication with Canadian Premier.

On 22nd June in the House of Commons,

Sir Harry Brittain (Coalition Unionist, *Acton*) asked the Prime Minister whether he had had any communication with the Prime Minister of the Dominion of Canada with reference to the lifting of the embargo against Canadian cattle.

The Prime Minister (the Right Hon. D. Lloyd George): "The answer is in the negative."

* This being shortly before going to press, it was impossible to deal with the debate in the present issue, which covers only the proceedings up till 1st July.

Sir Harry Brittain: "Is it not possible to find out officially from Canada whether this promise is regarded as a pledge?"

The Prime Minister: "Undoubtedly the late Prime Minister made that clear at the meeting of the Imperial Conference."

Mr. Ronald McNeill (Conservative, *Canterbury*): "Has the right hon. gentleman explained to the Canadian Government that this embargo rests upon a Statute, and that it can only be removed by Parliament?"

The Prime Minister: "It is not necessary to state that, because they are well acquainted with the fact. It is a matter of very great importance to Canada."

Price of beef.

On 23rd May, in the House of Commons,

Capt. the Hon. E. A. Fitzroy (Coalition Unionist, *Daventry*) asked the Minister of Agriculture whether, in view of the statements frequently made that the admission of Canadian store cattle would cheapen the price of meat, he could give any figures to show to what extent, if any, the price of beef depended on the price of store cattle; and whether there was any appreciable increase in the price of beef in the years following the first imposition of the embargo in 1892.

The Minister of Agriculture (the Right Hon. Sir Arthur Boscawen): "There is no evidence to show that the price of store cattle determines the price of home-killed beef, which is mainly governed by the price of imported beef, just as the price of wheat and certain other agricultural products is mainly governed by the price of the imported article. Last year, for example, store cattle were expensive in the spring months, but the price of fat cattle and meat fell in the autumn. With regard to the latter part of the question, Canadian store cattle were, as stated in the question, first excluded from this country in 1892. Official statistics of meat prices were not collected at that period, but records published in trade papers indicate that the average prices of beef at the London Central Market during the five years after this were about a halfpenny per pound less than in the five years before."

Mr. W. S. Royce (Labour, *Holland-with-Boston*): "Does the right hon. gentleman suggest that, because store cattle are dear now, we shall have cheaper meat in the autumn?"

The Minister of Agriculture: "No, Sir; what I suggested was that the price of store cattle has nothing whatever to do with the price of beef."

Protection of cattle in transit.

On 10th May, in the House of Commons,

Sir Robert Newman (Coalition Unionist, *Exeter*) asked the Minister of Agriculture whether his attention had been called to the sufferings which cattle underwent in their transit from Canada and other countries for slaughter at British ports; whether, in view of these cruelties, he would direct his inspectors to investigate and report upon the present condition of the traffic; and, in the event of these reports confirming the allegations of cruelty, would he take measures, in co-operation with the Canadian Government and Governments of other countries concerned, to end these cruelties.

The Minister of Agriculture: " Every possible precaution is taken to safeguard cattle sent across the Atlantic to this country. Provisions are contained in the Foreign Animals Order of 1910 issued by the Ministry for the protection of animals on the voyage, and I understand that the vessels also have to pass Regulations laid down by the Governments of the exporting countries. Reports are made by the Ministry's inspectors as to the conditions of the animals on arrival in this country. There is no evidence of cruelty, but from the nature of the case a certain amount of suffering is unavoidable when prolonged heavy weather is experienced. The number of casualties since the resumption of the traffic early last year has been small, but there was one serious case in September last, when 57 cattle out of 285 on board were lost in the North Atlantic in a very heavy and prolonged gale."

Mr. J. Leng Sturrock (Coalition Liberal, *Montrose Burghs***)**: " Is my right hon. friend aware that, before the Canadian cattle embargo was imposed, shiploads of cattle used to be put ashore in Scotland without any evidence whatever of their having suffered any hardship; and is he further aware that in several cases not only did the number of cattle which left Montreal arrive at a port of destination in Scotland, but even more appeared on the voyage? "

The Speaker (the Right Hon. J. H. Whitley): " The hon. Member is giving information."

DOMINIONS AND HONOURS.

(Sir Joseph Robinson's peerage; Government's pledge for the future.)

On 22nd June, in the House of Lords, the following questions were addressed to the Government:—

(1) Whether the grounds on which Sir Joseph Benjamin Robinson of Wynberg was recommended to His Majesty for the grant of a Peerage were National and Imperial services in connection with his chairmanship of the Robinson South African Banking Company, Limited;

(2) Whether that company was liquidated in 1905; and, if so,

(3) What were the services rendered to the Nation and the Empire by that company and by Sir Joseph Robinson up to or since that date?

DEBATE IN HOUSE OF LORDS.

Lord Harris, in putting these questions, recalled that in October, 1917, the House adopted certain resolutions on the subject of recommendations for honours, and they were accepted by the Government. The first resolution provided that a definite description should be given of the ground on which the honour was granted, and in *The London Gazette* under the heading " Peerages " he found the following :—

Sir Joseph Robinson, Chairman of the Robinson South African Banking Corporation, National and Imperial services.

The Robinson South African Banking Corporation was liquidated in 1905, but he submitted that laymen, reading the *Gazette*, could come to no other conclusion than that the fact of Sir Joseph Robinson being chairman of the Corporation had to do with his recommendation for a Peerage. It seemed to him inevitable that the Prime Minister had not been correctly advised and that, of course, the incorrect advice had been passed on to the Sovereign.

Grant of baronetcy.

There was this additional perplexity. In 1908 Mr. Robinson—as he then was—was made a baronet. That was three years after the liquidation of the Bank, and one would come to the conclusion that whatever services Mr. Robinson had rendered as chairman had been recognised by the grant of a baronetcy. But evidently they were not sufficiently so, or Sir Joseph Robinson—as he became in 1908—had rendered national service to the Nation and the Empire between that date and the present time. He thought he could honestly say that no one who knew Sir Joseph Robinson either in the Cape or in this country knew what those services were.

" During last year, and perhaps preceding last year," Lord Harris said, " Sir Joseph Robinson was concerned in certain cases in the Courts in South Africa. The allegation I believe is contained in the judgment of the High Court. In 1906 Robinson was the chairman of the Randfontein Estates Company, in which capacity he dictated and controlled the policy and operations of the undertaking. There were other directors, but these—and these words are in the judgment—' were completely under his thumb.'

" In the year mentioned it became Robinson's duty to acquire for the company the freehold of certain mining properties. His method of performing this duty was to purchase the freehold for himself, and then to re-sell it to the company at an enormously higher price. He concealed from the shareholders the fact that he had made this illicit profit by means of a certain company promotion which the Court described as a ' device to camouflage the transaction.'

Chief Justice quoted.

"In 1915 S. B. Joel purchased from Robinson all the latter's interests in the Randfontein Estates and thereafter discovered what had transpired in 1906. Thereupon the Randfontein Estates sued Robinson. Under judgment by the Appellate Division of the Supreme Court of South Africa, Robinson has been condemned to pay a sum, including costs, of over £500,000. In giving judgment the Chief Justice declared that—and here I quote the words of the Chief Justice —'It is wholly inconsistent with the obligation of good faith.' I would emphasise to your Lordships the words 'not consistent with the obligation of good faith.' Surely, if that means anything, it means faithless. The Chief Justice's words are:—

'It is wholly inconsistent with the obligation of good faith that the defendant should have made for himself these profits by the method which the evidence discloses.'

"The method is the one I have already read to your Lordships—'A device to camouflage the transaction.' These are facts, and surely these facts were not before the Prime Minister when he recommended Sir Joseph Robinson for distinction at His Majesty's hands. Surely the Prime Minister must have been misled, and consequently His Majesty misled.

"I think I had better state here that in consequence of that judgment Robinson has been described in the public Press in this country as a fraudulent trustee. I should have thought that anyone would prefer to clear his name of such an imputation before taking those steps which are necessary to obtain introduction to your Lordships' House. Robinson petitioned the Judicial Committee of the Privy Council for leave to appeal. His petition was considered in November, 1921, and was dismissed. The Judicial Committee found that Robinson had failed to show any *prima facie* reason why the judgment of the South African Courts should be upset. Therefore, the judgment of the Chief Justice of the Union, which I have read to your Lordships, stands."

In conclusion Lord Harris submitted that the House and the public were entitled to a correct description of the grounds upon which a Peerage was granted.

The South African point of view.

Earl Buxton said it could not be disputed that the matter was one primarily and mainly affecting the Union of South Africa. Sir Joseph Robinson was born there; he lived practically the whole of his life there; all his interests, financial and otherwise, were wrapped up in South Africa; and therefore the matter was one which seriously affected South Africa itself. The question was, "What had been the services which justified the grant of a Peerage to Sir Joseph Robinson?" It might be true that thirty or forty years ago he was a prominent person in South Africa—what was called a pioneer, a magnate. His main activities were in gold and diamonds. That was a long time ago, and as far as those services were concerned he was rewarded by his baronetcy in 1908.

"What has he done since? I have for the last eight years," said Lord Buxton, "had first-hand knowledge of what has been going on in South Africa, and I am in a position to express an opinion with regard to the activities of Sir Joseph Robinson. When I saw this grant, this appointment, in the Press I confess I was astonished. I searched my memory in vain to find any legitimate reason why this Peerage had been conferred. The War, after all, was a touchstone of public and Imperial services. . . . But since 1914, when I went out to South Africa, I have never heard Sir Joseph Robinson's name connected with any public service, either himself or in co-operation with others, and as far as I know—and I am in a position to know—he showed no marked liberality to the various War Funds which were inaugurated for the assistance of the dependents of soldiers and sailors. . . . I will undertake to say that no one of any repute in South Africa recommended that this Peerage should be granted. I will undertake to say that no single person in the Union, white or black, considered that either by his services or by his record he deserved this honour."

There remained, said Lord Buxton, the home services of Sir Joseph Robinson. They had not come to his notice, but he thought, considering his connection with South Africa, he would have heard something about them if they had been of any great character. "Let us hope they were rendered," he remarked, "and that Sir Joseph Robinson is one of those who do good by stealth and blush to find it fame." He thought the House was entitled to a categorical answer as to the actual grounds on which this honour was conferred.

Grave issues raised.

"I take a very serious objection," Lord Buxton proceeded, "to the method under which this Peerage has been conferred. It touches not only the prestige of the House of Lords . . . and the honour of those who conferred the grant, but it raises, in my opinion, very grave issues between the Dominion and the Home Governments. . . . It has, of late years at all events, been fully recognised that when it comes to a question of honours for a citizen of a Dominion they should, in the first place, be recommended by the Prime

Minister of that Dominion to the Prime Minister or other Ministers here for their consideration.

"The Prime Minister and other Ministers here are not, of course, bound to accept the suggestion of the Prime Minister of the Dominion. On the other hand, no citizen of a Dominion who has performed the services for which he is to be rewarded in the Dominion ever, nowadays, appears in the Honours List except at the initial suggestion of the Prime Minister of that Dominion. Indeed, I would go further and say that it was my experience, at least in South Africa, that if the Home Government here desired to recommend a particular person for public services rendered, over here or otherwise, but not in the Dominion itself, they in the first place consulted confidentially the Prime Minister of the Dominion to know if he had any objection to that proposal. That would appear to be only common courtesy and ordinary expediency in the relations between the Dominion and the Home Governments."

What was the case here? The Prime Minister of the Union, said Lord Buxton, denied that he had in any way been consulted, directly or indirectly, in regard to this Peerage. "I can only congratulate Sir Joseph on that fact," Lord Buxton continued, "because my own impression is that if there had been any consultation with South Africa he would not have got his Peerage."

Slight to the Dominion.

"I venture to say that both the reasons given and the method adopted are a slight to the Dominion in question, and a flouting of public opinion in that Dominion, very harmful to the trustful and cordial relations which we desire to exist between the Prime Minister of the Dominion and the Prime Minister, whoever he may be, representing the British Government over here, and deplorable also from the point of view of depreciating the Dominion honours, which we all desire to keep on a very high level indeed." Lord Buxton added that so far in the history of the Union one Peerage and one alone had been given to a South African—Sir Henry de Villiers. When Sir Henry was created a Peer he was quite sure there was no one of any race, or colour, or politics, but felt that he deserved the honour, and that it was a compliment to South Africa. The second Peer was Sir Joseph Robinson.

The First Commissioner of Works (the Earl of Crawford) said he was reluctant to discuss the constitutional issue involved with a Dominion, and the problem of how far a Dominion Minister would be entitled in effect to veto the recommendations made to the Crown by Ministers here, without having had an opportunity of examining with care the statement made by Lord Buxton. He was afraid that if the notices in the *Gazette* gave the impression that Sir Joseph Robinson was recommended to the King in consequence of being chairman of the Robinson South African Banking Company, the description was clearly misleading. In fact, the Bank was liquidated in 1905 owing to the serious hindrance of trade and the depression consequent upon the Boer War. The Bank returned to the shareholders the full amount of their capital in cash. With reference to the judgment in the High Court of South Africa, he (Lord Crawford) did not know if there were qualifications or reservations in the judgment, still less could he tell their Lordships if it was claimed that a different complexion could be put upon the quotation given.

Services in South Africa.

Sir Joseph Robinson had spent the whole of his life in South Africa, and had devoted his energies to developing that part of the Empire. Lord Buxton indicated that he rendered no services of value to the State.

Earl Buxton: " I did not say in the old days. Thirty or forty years ago I think he may have, but he was rewarded for that."

The First Commissioner of Works: "He certainly rendered valuable services to the Government both during and after the war in South Africa."

The Earl of Selborne: " Which war ? "

The Earl of Crawford: " The South African war. I believe that at the request of the home Government he approached President Kruger, and did his best to bring about an understanding, and his influence has persistently been directed towards the removal of racial prejudice and bitterness. He has occupied a public position in South Africa. He was a member of the Cape Assembly when the Cape was a Crown Colony, and was later elected one of the representatives for Kimberley in the South African Parliament. South African statesmen, whatever Lord Buxton indicates, have expressed their appreciation of the services which he has rendered to that country."

The Earl of Selborne was sure Lord Buxton did not say that the Dominion Prime Minister ought to have a veto over the grant of an honour by His Majesty here on the recommendation of the Imperial Prime Minister. What he did say was that the Prime Minister in England ought never to make a recommendation with respect to a British subject domiciled in the Dominions, without first consulting the Dominion Prime Minister. That was a wholly different proposition.

A public scandal.

During the debates he (Lord Selborne) initiated several

years ago he showed their Lordships how very grave a scandal there was in connection with a certain class of honour and since then the evil had become much greater. It amounted now to nothing less than a public scandal of the first magnitude.

"Hitherto," Lord Selborne continued, "there has been no personal corruption in connection with these honours—when money has been taken it has been taken for the benefit of a political Party, be it Conservative, or Liberal, or Coalition—but I do not believe that these immense sums can continue to pass in complete secrecy, with no publicity, no responsibility, and personal corruption not ensue. I think there is a real danger, not of the corruption of Ministers, but of corruption on the part of those who, unknown and in the dark, do this dirty work for the Ministry, and I think it is altogether unconstitutional. I put this question for consideration. Is it really consistent with our Constitution that there should be great sums of money at the disposal of any Ministry, without any control from Parliament ?"

With reference to Sir Joseph Robinson, there had been put into Lord Crawford's hand such a record of services as those who were really responsible for what had taken place could trump up for the occasion.

Lord Selborne's experiences.

"Lord Buxton has told your Lordships his experiences. I will tell you mine," Lord Selborne continued. "I was responsible for South Africa for five years. I never in my mind, in my humble efforts to serve the Empire, was ever conscious that the influence of Sir Joseph Robinson was on my side. I go further, and I say that when I went to South Africa he was known everywhere as a pro-Boer. When I went to South Africa, three years after the war, so far as my information went, his sympathies had never been with this country.

"But there are two other noble Lords in this House who can speak—Lord Milner and Lord Gladstone. Between us we cover more than twenty years of South African history. Why do not the Government produce a testimonial from Lord Milner, or one from Lord Gladstone ? Is public opinion going to be satisfied with this *dossier* from an unknown source, when four High Commissioners and Governors-General in succession, and the Prime Minister of the Union of South Africa, are quite unable to state the national and Imperial services for which this honour has been granted ?"

The Prime Minister here had taken his recommendations from somebody he trusted—he (Lord Selborne) thought a little too carelessly. And that person was so cynical that he had taken no trouble to dress up the gazetted reasons with any approach to accuracy or plausibility.

The debate was adjourned, and was resumed on 29th June when :—

The Lord Chancellor (Viscount Birkenhead) said it was, of course, the fact that the numbers of the House of Lords had increased very greatly in the last hundred years, and more particularly in the last twenty years. At a not very remote period the number of Peers in the House was 126 ; to-day it was more than 700. It was, however, important to consider the immense increase in the population of the country taken as a whole in the period which was under review. As regarded the creations in the last few years, they had taken place in an age in which an opportunity had fallen to a larger number of people to render distinguished services to the State than in almost any equal period of time in English history.

Dominion assent ; Government's determination.

Coming to the case of Sir Joseph Robinson, the Lord Chancellor said that undoubtedly there was a grave omission —and one he hoped not to be repeated—in the circumstances under which that recommendation was made to the Crown.

"The Secretary of State for the Colonies," the noble and learned Lord proceeded, "was not consulted upon this in order to make himself, as constitutionally he ought to make himself, the mouthpiece of the self-governing Dominions, so as to acquaint the Prime Minister with the opinions and desires of the Dominion and generally to advise him in relation to the matter. . . . It is realised, and most plainly admitted and stated, that no citizen of this Empire ordinarily resident in and primarily belonging to one of the great self-governing Dominions ought ever to have an honour in this country except with the assent and approval of the Government of the self-governing Dominion of which he is a member. That determination your Lordships may consider as announced officially by me, and is laid down as a canon which will undoubtedly guide and determine action in the future. If it had been exercised on the present occasion it might have avoided a great deal of embarrassing discussion."

Continuing, the Lord Chancellor said that Sir Joseph Robinson at the present moment was a very old man. He believed he was in his eighty-third year. No one had ever said that he was not an extraordinarily zealous and able pioneer in the development of the diamond and gold industries which had coincided with the prosperity and growth of South Africa. Sir Henry Campbell-Bannerman was advised by General Botha to confer a baronetcy upon Sir Joseph Robinson. General Botha at least knew South Africa, and it was to be presumed that, knowing South Africa, and having become, as he had, a loyal subject of the Empire, he also knew Sir Joseph Robinson.

The grant of a baronetcy: meritorious pioneer life.

When Lord Buxton hinted that in the whole course of Sir Joseph Robinson's career he never did anything either for blacks or whites in South Africa he (the Lord Chancellor) must be allowed to say it was a most amazing thing that in those circumstances General Botha, as Prime Minister, should have recommended to Sir Henry Campbell-Bannerman that Mr. Joseph Robinson, as he then was, should be created a Baronet.

Earl Buxton: "I did not speak of the period up to 1908. My point was that, whatever his services might have been in the past and up to 1908, I questioned the additional services which, after 1908, he had given to South Africa, or elsewhere, which rendered him entitled to a Peerage."

The Lord Chancellor did not think Lord Buxton drew any clear distinction at all, or that he ever made reference to the fifty years of meritorious pioneer life in the development of South Africa. In the year 1907 Sir Henry Campbell-Bannerman did not grant that recognition, but in 1908 the recommendation, as he was informed, was more insistently repeated by General Botha that a baronetcy should be given to Sir Joseph Robinson. He could not believe for a moment that Lord Buxton would be regarded as being entitled, in respect of that period of fifty years, of which everything was known by those who gave the advice, to disclaim any such knowledge, or say that this man had done nothing.

Difficult and laborious as the task would have been, he would have thought it necessary, but for a circumstance to which he was about to call attention, most carefully to study the whole tangled story of the litigation about which the words quoted by Lord Harris were used in the judgment, in order to see whether there was either qualification or explanation which it was possible for him to lay before their Lordships.

The honour declined: Sir Joseph Robinson's letter.

It was not necessary for this reason—that Sir Joseph Robinson had written to the Prime Minister the following letter dated 23rd June, 1922:—

"MY DEAR PRIME MINISTER,—I have read with surprise the discussion which took place yesterday in the House of Lords upon the proposed offer of a Peerage to myself. I have not, as you know, in any way sought the suggested honour.

"It is now some sixty years since I commenced as a pioneer the task of building up the industries of South Africa. I am now an old man to whom honours and dignities are no longer matters of much concern.

"I should be sorry if any honour conferred upon me were the occasion for such ill-feeling as was manifested in the House of Lords yesterday, and while deeply appreciating the honour which has been suggested, I would wish if I may without discourtesy to yourself and without impropriety, to beg His Most Gracious Majesty's permission to decline the proposal."

The Prime Minister had made suitable communication in conformity with the proposal contained in Sir Joseph Robinson's letter. After explaining that a day was to be given in the House of Commons for discussion of the whole question of the submission of names for honours, the Lord Chancellor added that he was able to reinforce and confirm the statement of Sir Joseph Robinson that he did not in any way seek that this honour should be conferred upon him.

A proper and dignified letter.

The Marquis of Lansdowne said that Sir Joseph Robinson's letter struck him, as he thought it must have struck all those who heard it read, as a very proper and dignified letter. To that extent, certainly, he thought it must have raised Sir Joseph Robinson in the estimation of the House. Sir Joseph Robinson, by his own action, had extricated His Majesty's Government from a position which most of their Lordships would, he thought, agree with him in thinking was absolutely untenable. He urged that there should be a distinct and quite categorical pledge on the part of the Government that these most unfortunate mistakes should not be allowed to occur again.

The Marquis of Salisbury intimated that he would on a later date call attention to the whole system of recommendations for honours and make a definite motion for definite action.

Viscount Long of Wraxall mentioned that shortly after he went to the Colonial Office a case occurred in which an honour was conferred upon a gentleman who belonged to one of the Dominions. "I had not been consulted," said Lord Long, "and therefore I had not been able to consult the Prime Minister of that Dominion. I protested at once and pointed out that in these days, when the Dominions are rightly entitled to be described as nations, it is absurd, and indeed impossible, to deny them the right, which each ought to enjoy through its Ministers and its Governor-General, of being able to make their own recommendations for honours. But, apart from that, if the rule then laid down is not accepted with the utmost strictness and severity, it is obvious that you will have difficulties arising in your Dominions which will become extremely grave."

After further debate the subject dropped.

IRISH FREE STATE.

(Draft Constitution; Colonial Secretary and restoration of order.)

On the eve of a debate on Ireland in the House of Commons on 26th June, the Government issued as a White Paper the draft Constitution of the Irish Free State which had been agreed upon as the result of prolonged discussions in London between representatives of the British and Southern Irish Governments. Following are a few of the main points of the Constitution:—

The Irish Free State (Saorstat Eireann) is a co-equal member of the Community of Nations forming the British Commonwealth of Nations.

The National language is the Irish language, but the English language shall be equally recognised as an official language.

The liberty of the person is inviolable and no person shall be deprived of his liberty except in accordance with law.

The dwelling of each citizen is inviolable and shall not be forcibly entered except in accordance with law.

Freedom of conscience and the free profession and practice of religion are inviolable rights of every citizen.

All citizens of the Irish Free State have the right to free elementary education.

The rights of the State in and to national resources, the use of which is of national importance, shall not be alienated.

LEGISLATIVE PROVISIONS.

A Legislature is to be created to be known as the Parliament of the Irish Free State (Oireachtas) consisting of the King and two Houses: the Chamber of Deputies (Dail Eireann) and the Senate (Seanad Eireann).

All citizens of the Irish Free State, without distinction of sex, who have reached the age of 21 years and comply with the provisions of the prevailing electoral laws, will have the right to vote for members of the Chamber of Deputies.

In the case of the Senate the electoral age is thirty years.

Every Member of Parliament will be required before taking his seat to take the following oath:—

> I do solemnly swear true faith and allegiance to the Constitution of the Irish Free State as by law established, and that I will be faithful to H.M. King George V., His heirs and successors by law in virtue of the common citizenship of Ireland with Great Britain and her adherence to and membership of the group of nations forming the British Commonwealth of Nations.

CHAMBER OF DEPUTIES AND SENATE.

The total number of members of the Chamber of Deputies is not to be fixed at less than one member for each 30,000 of the population or at more than one for each 20,000. Members are to be elected upon principles of Proportional Representation.

At a General Election for the Chamber the polls are to be held on the same day throughout the country. That day is to be not later than thirty days after the date of the dissolution and is to be proclaimed a public holiday.

The Senate is to be composed of citizens who have done honour to the Nation by reason of useful public service or who, because of special qualifications or attainments, represent important aspects of the Nation's life.

Every University in the Irish Free State will be entitled to elect two representatives to the Senate. The number of Senators exclusive of the University members is to be fifty-six.

To be eligible for membership of the Senate a citizen must be a person eligible to become a member of the Chamber and must have reached the age of thirty-five years. The term of office of a member of the Senate is to be twelve years.

THE EXECUTIVE.

The Executive Authority of the Irish Free State is declared to be vested in the King. It is to be exercisable, in accordance with the law, practice, and constitutional usage governing the exercise of the executive authority in the case of the Dominion of Canada, by the Representative of the Crown.

The Executive Council (Aireacht) will be responsible to the Chamber and will consist of not more than twelve Ministers (Airi) appointed by the Representative of the Crown. Of these four will be members of the Chamber and a number not exceeding eight will be chosen from all citizens eligible for election to the Chamber, but will not be members of Parliament during their term of office.

Ministers who are not members of the Chamber will, by virtue of their office, possess all the rights and privileges of a member of the Chamber, except the right to vote. They may be required by the Chamber to attend and answer questions.

The Representative of the Crown, styled the Governor-General of the Irish Free State, will be appointed in like manner as the Governor-General of Canada. The salary is to be of the like amount as that now payable to the Governor-General of the Commonwealth of Australia and will be charged on the public funds of the Irish Free State.

DEBATE IN HOUSE OF COMMONS.

On 26th June the debate in the House of Commons took place on the Vote for the Irish Office.

The Secretary of State for the Colonies (the Right Hon. Winston Churchill), in a lengthy review of the situation, stated that everything had been done by Mr. de Valera and his friends to weaken and discredit the Provisional Government, to create disorder throughout the country, and to embroil Southern Ireland with Ulster. For that purpose the mutinous or irregular portion of the so-called Irish Republican Army was always available. Around and behind them gathered those predatory and criminal elements which existed in every society and claimed to lead in times of revolution. The Ulster Government saw themselves confronted with the existence of an active conspiracy in their midst, a conspiracy of which the object was to make their task of maintaining a separate Government impossible, while from over the border serious raids occurred with the threat that raids would be continued.

His Majesty's Government had supplied the Government of Northern Ireland with upwards of 50,000 stands of arms and all the equipment necessary for a defence force organised upon that scale. There would be no excuse in Ulster, now that the Northern Government had been strengthened and was effectually supported, for acts of lawless reprisal against the Catholic population in their midst.

The border—shield of British troops.

The situation on the frontier of Ulster was much easier. The operations undertaken in Pettigo and Belleek* by His Majesty's Forces under the direction of the Government had the effect of clearing the border. A triple agreement had now been reached between the British Government, the Provisional Government, and the Government of Northern Ireland, by which a neutral zone some four or five miles wide was to be established in the Pettigo and Belleek district. Within that zone no person was to be accredited by any Government with the right to bear arms, an unarmed police of a local character was to be established for local purposes, and the maintenance of order throughout the district was to be exclusively confided to Imperial troops.

The Imperial troops would be stationed as a shield between the two hostile and mutually explosive forces of the Irish Republican Army and the Ulster Special Police. Any person in the district found using arms would have no recognition or protection from any Government and would be liable to be shot by the troops on the mere fact being established. If that experiment should succeed it was proposed to extend it along the border, sector by sector, making in each case a local agreement, until at the end a complete shield of British troops and an adequate central zone would have been established between the hostile forces of Orange and Green. If the experiment failed then it would be necessary for the Imperial Forces to draw a military line between Northern and Southern Ireland.

The greedy and criminal design of breaking down the Northern Government, either by disorder from within or by incursion from without, had to die in the hearts of those who nourished it, whatever might be the cost to individuals or to Governments. The Sinn Fein Party had to realise, once and for all, that they would never win Ulster except by her own free will and that the more they kicked against the pricks the worse it would be for them.

---

* Pettigo and Belleek are situated on the western border of Ulster.

Provisional Government warned.

After a reference to the murder in London of Field-Marshal Sir Henry Wilson—a shocking and abominable crime—Mr. Churchill proceeded to speak of the recent elections to the Provisional Parliament in Ireland. If he were to attempt to interpret the will of the Irish nation as expressed unmistakably at the elections he would sum it up as follows: "You have given us our freedom; we wish to give you our friendship. You will help us towards a united Ireland; we will help you towards a United Empire." That indicated the road along which they were marching and were going to march.

But, in the interests of peace, firmness was needed as much as patience. The Constitution satisfactorily conformed to the Treaty. It had now to be passed through the new Irish Parliament. "There is no room," said Mr. Churchill, "for the slightest diminution of the Imperial and Constitutional safeguards and stipulations which it contains. That is not all. Mere paper affirmations, however important, unaccompanied by any effective effort to bring them into action, will not be sufficient. Mere denunciations of murder, however heartfelt, unaccompanied by the apprehension of a single murderer, cannot be accepted. The keeping in being within the Irish Free State by an elaborate process of duality, merging upon duplicity, of the whole apparatus of a Republican Government will not be in accordance either with the will of the Irish people, with the stipulations of the Treaty, or with the maintenance of good relations between the two countries.

"His Majesty's Government do not feel that, after this election has clearly shown what are the wishes of the Irish people, we can continue to tolerate many gross lapses from the spirit of the Treaty, and improprieties and irregularities in its execution, with which we have put up, and in which we have acquiesced, during the last six months."

A stricter reckoning.

The Provisional Government was now armed with the declared will of the Irish electorate. It was supported by an effective Parliamentary majority. It was its duty to give effect to the Treaty in the letter and in the spirit without delay. A much stricter reckoning must rule henceforward. The ambiguous position of the so-called Irish Republican Army, intermingled as it was with the Free State troops, was an affront to the Treaty. The presence in Dublin, in violent occupation of the Four Courts, of a band of men styling themselves the Headquarters of the Republican Executive was a gross breach and defiance of the Treaty.

"From this nest of anarchy and treason, not only to the British Crown, but to the Irish people, murderous outrages are stimulated and encouraged, not only in the 26 Counties, not only in the territory of the Northern Government, but even, it seems most probable, here across the Channel in Great Britain. From this centre, at any rate, an organisation is kept in being which has branches in Ulster, in Scotland, and in England, with the declared purpose of wrecking the Treaty by the vilest processes of which human degradation can conceive. The time has come when it is not unfair, not premature, and not impatient for us to make to this strengthened Irish Government and new Irish Parliament a request, in express terms, that this sort of thing must come to an end.*

"If either from weakness, from want of courage, or for some other even less creditable reasons, it is not brought to an end and a very speedy end, then it is my duty to say, on behalf of His Majesty's Government, that we shall regard the Treaty as having been formally violated, that we shall take no steps to carry out or to legalise its further stages, and that we shall resume full liberty of action in any direction that may seem proper and to any extent that may be necessary to safeguard the interests and the rights that are entrusted to our care."

"You must govern."

The Right Hon. Sir F. Banbury (Conservative, *City of London*) moved to reduce the amount of the Vote by £2,000.

The Right Hon. A. Bonar Law (Coalition Unionist, *Glasgow, Central*) said it was represented in Ireland that England was so sick of the matter that she would not in any circumstances interfere with a Republic. If that was the attitude and state of mind of Irish people it might have some effect if now the Imperial Government said: "We and the English nation long for peace, but if there is to be peace, you must govern." Much time could not elapse before those grave matters were brought to the test. He believed the Imperial Government meant to see them through, but if they did not he would be against them, and he hoped the House of Commons would be against them also.

The Prime Minister (the Right Hon. D. Lloyd George) said that for the first time in the history of Great Britain's treatment of Ireland, if the Treaty was broken by Ireland, the civilised world would say that England was blameless. He was not

* A day or two after the statement in the House of Commons the Irish Provisional Government took military action against the irregulars occupying the Four Courts and other "strongholds" in Dublin. The Free State Forces, equipped by the Imperial Government with all necessary materials, also began a vigorous campaign against the insurgents in many areas of the 26 Counties. These operations have been attended with success.

willing to accept the theory that the Treaty was a failure, but he must say frankly that he was disappointed with the way in which the Provisional Government had gripped the problem. The Irish Parliament was about to meet. What they did now, or failed to do, was the real test of whether they were fit to govern. By that test—a test which the Irish people themselves had made possible, having put them in a position to demonstrate it—the Treaty must stand or fall.

On a division the amendment to reduce the Vote was negatived by 342 votes against 75. Thereafter, the Vote was agreed to.

NAVAL DISCIPLINE BILL.

(Personnel of Royal Navy serving under Dominions.)

On 25th May, in the House of Lords, the First Lord of the Admiralty moved the Second Reading of the Naval Discipline Bill. It was explained in the course of the debate that there are really only two matters of importance dealt with in the Bill:—

(1) The discipline of the Royal Navy *personnel* when serving in Dominion naval ships or establishments.

(2) An increase in the compulsory deduction from the pay of ratings for the maintenance of wife, or children, or illegitimate children.

DEBATE IN HOUSE OF LORDS.

The First Lord of the Admiralty (Lord Lee of Fareham), referring to the Clause relating to the status of *personnel* of the Royal Navy serving under a Dominion, said that under the existing law they were not liable to the Naval Discipline Act of the particular Dominion which they were serving—that was to say, to the law of the Dominion in which they were serving. This had been represented to the Admiralty frequently, particularly by the Canadian authorities, and it was thought desirable that both officers and men—who, after all, volunteered for these services, and had the position explained to them quite clearly before they so volunteered—should come under the provisions of the Naval Discipline Acts of the different Dominions in which they were serving.

Viscount Haldane said the Clause dealing with this matter provided that the officers and seamen in ships of self-governed Dominions were to be under the laws of the particular Dominion " provided such ship is not at the time placed at the disposal of the Admiralty." The point was as to the choice of those words. " One sees the good sense of it," said Lord Haldane, "and I think it is probably what the Dominions would agree to and wish to observe when those ships are the King's ships under the Dominion Minister and Dominion laws. 'Placed at the disposal of the Admiralty' is, perhaps, not enough to take them out of that category. If the Dominion Governments have assented to these words, or raised no objection to them, then it is right enough.

Trenching upon Dominion powers.

"It is certainly legislation under the powers of the Imperial Parliament, but coming in and trenching upon Dominion powers. It may well be that has been found the most convenient way of doing it, and that the Dominions have raised no objection. If so, it is all right. Otherwise, it is using the powers of the Imperial Parliament to trench upon a matter which might come under the Dominion."

The First Lord of the Admiralty: "In reply to the noble and learned Viscount, I can only say that this provision has been drawn up in close conversation with the Dominions. It applies, after all, only to Royal Naval ratings, and if the ship in which they serve is no longer for the time being under the control of the Dominion concerned but under the Admiralty, it is surplus."

Viscount Haldane: "The difficulty is the words 'placed at the disposal.' You may put a ship at the disposal of the Admiralty quite well, and yet it might still remain a Canadian ship."

The First Lord of the Admiralty: "Quite."

Viscount Haldane: "If the noble Lord says that the words have been discussed with the Dominions I should take it that they have said, as they did in reference to the Copyright Act, 'We welcome Imperial legislation as putting everything on a sensible footing.'"

The Second Reading was agreed to and the Bill was subsequently passed through its other stages in the Upper House. On 16th June the Bill was read a second time in the House of Commons after a brief debate and was referred to a Standing Committee for consideration.

BOARD OF TRADE VOTE.

(Shipping discrimination; United front with Dominions; Safeguarding of Industries; New Zealand proposals.)

On 11th May the House of Commons went into Committee of Supply and discussed the Vote for the Board of Trade.

DEBATE IN HOUSE OF COMMONS.

The President of the Board of Trade (the Right Hon. Stanley Baldwin), dealing with the trade position at home, said that though they might not be through the worst of the adverse conditions, they would, with perseverance and with courage, emerge once more into better times. So far as the Dominions, the United States, South America, Holland, Scandinavia and Spain were concerned, there was nothing in the condition of any of those countries which should prevent them again being large buyers in the world's market. One curious result of the War had been an increase in the spirit of nationalism throughout the world and the desire on the part of countries to be self-contained industrially. There had been an increase in tariffs in many parts of the world—a tendency visible alike in the newly-formed countries and in the old countries. Such increases must be felt in a country like Great Britain which, more than any other country, was dependent on the export of its manufactured goods.

"I have had many complaints from traders," Mr. Baldwin said, "particularly in regard to France, Italy and Spain. Our traders are also viewing with considerable apprehension the movement that is at present to be observed in the United States of America for a still further increase of the tariff, which, so far as manufactured goods go, is almost prohibitive at the present day. Lancashire has been viewing with alarm the increase in the duties in India. Those duties were raised from 7½ per cent. to 11 per cent., and subsequently to 15 per cent., and the duties on luxuries were raised to 20 per cent. and subsequently to 30 per cent. It is quite true that a fiscal Commission, set up in India last autumn, is studying this whole question, and I only hope that the result of its labours may bring some comfort to our manufacturers in this country.

Counsel with the Dominions.

"I would only add on this subject that, so far, we should hold our own in the Dominions, because, even in instances where increases have been effected in the tariff, we have been treated with considerable generosity in the matter of preference.

"One other aspect of this same question also causes me anxiety, and that is the attempted discrimination which is now being made in certain maritime countries against our shipping. Our shipping is the vital link in the whole system of our Commonwealth of nations. Anything that imperils it imperils not only this country, but every one of our Dominions, and I hope that the Mother Country and the Dominions will take earnest counsel together on this matter before it is too late, so that we may show, in this respect at least, a united front against any attempt that may be made to discriminate against us to damage the position of our shipping."

Referring to the breakdown of the exchanges, the right hon. gentleman said that if, owing to any unforeseen catastrophe, what was called the restoration of Europe should be delayed it would make the road to prosperity longer and steeper. He believed that this country could face such a condition of things better than any other country, and that in time they would have to do what they had done before—make up for what they had lost by getting something fresh. They would have to get that by an intensified development of their own Empire and by pushing with renewed vigour into the great markets of the East and the markets of South America.

Safeguarding of Industries Act.

Captain Wedgwood Benn (**Independent Liberal**, *Leith*), in moving a reduction of the Vote, criticised the Safeguarding of Industries Act, and declared that trade was hampered by the delay which it caused. The Act encouraged foreign manufacturers at the expense of home manufacturers.

Mr. W. Graham (**Labour**, *Edinburgh, C.*) said it was perfectly plain that while they must strive to drive some new bargains, or make some new arrangements within the Empire, they must also try to get the best arrangements possible with the United States. The hon. Member proceeded to refer to proposals in New Zealand*: (1) To take certain steps in regard to articles offered for sale in New Zealand below the domestic price of those articles in the country of origin; (2) To take similar steps in regard to articles offered for sale in New Zealand below their cost of production in the country of origin; (3) To penalise articles coming into New Zealand which were manufactured in New Zealand, but which went to that country with the advantage of some grant or other, some rebate, bounty, or concession from another part of the world.

Did any hon. Member suggest it was going to be an easy matter for New Zealand, or any other country, to determine accurately what was the cost of production? It was, however, more important to consider how New Zealand or any other country could come to any conclusion regarding the influences upon the other countries of the rebate, or concession, or bounty. Whatever they might do to improve the efficiency of industry in Great Britain would be negatived in practice by devices rapidly growing up after the War, when not the maximum of restriction, but the maximum of freedom was required.

The amendment to reduce the Vote was negatived by 177 votes against 67 and progress was reported.

---

* *Vide* JOURNAL, Vol. III., No. 2, p. 395.

SAFEGUARDING OF INDUSTRIES ACT.

(Working and Administration.)

On 12th April, during a debate on the motion for the adjournment of the House of Commons for the Easter Recess, the subjects discussed included the working and administration of the Safeguarding of Industries Act.

DEBATE IN HOUSE OF COMMONS.

The Right Hon. H. H. Asquith (Leader of the Independent Liberal Party) remarked that the Act, which had been in operation for six months, was stamped from the beginning with the marks of congenital infirmity. No measure so recently carried by such large majorities in Parliament had ever been so forlorn of friends. It was equally scouted by Free Traders, by Protectionists, and by the business community at large. Under Part I., which dealt with what were supposed to be key industries, the Board of Trade had issued a schedule. It enumerated some 6,000 commodities, of which no less than 2,000, or thereabouts, belonged to various processes and products in the chemical trade. He was told that the department had unearthed quite a considerable number of strange products which had for years languished in subterranean obscurity.

Some of them—indeed, he believed, a considerable number—were not being, and never had been, produced in this country. Yet they were to be clothed for the first time with the character of key industries. He was not surprised to hear that there were already 400 or 500 appeals to the referees under the Act against various items in the list. Of these he thought not more than 10 or 11 had been heard and decided. He need not point out what a tremendous obstacle that was to the free course of business in the trades which were, or might be, affected by the application of the list. It was, perhaps, more interesting as showing the practical impossibility of administering legislation of that kind. With reference to Part II. of the Act he was informed that three cases of complaint by people who alleged that their goods had been improperly interfered with by competition of the character of dumping had been dismissed by the Committees with the assent of the Board of Trade.

Serious hardship.

Four reports of Committees had been sent in, but no decision on any of them had yet been given by the Board of Trade. There was consequently great uncertainty in the trades concerned, which was a serious hardship to producers, distributors, and the public.

The President of the Board of Trade (the Right Hon. Stanley Baldwin) said that under Part I. he hoped to see substantial progress made in a number of very valuable industries—so substantial that, by the time the Act lapsed, those industries might be able to face any competition that they might at that time have to meet. When the Act first began to have effect the country was entering upon a period of profound depression of trade and, having regard to all the circumstances, he did not think they had cause to be dissatisfied with the progress made.

"The reports reaching me from the fine chemical industries," Mr. Baldwin observed, "are of a distinctly cheering nature. I hear of firms of chemical manufacturers who, when the Act first became effective, were discharging men and working short time, and the same firms now are fully employed and working full time. I hear of progress made in scientific work, in which a beginning has been made in . . . the creation in this country of a body of skilled investigators and skilled workers in these trades—a new department of work in which we have hitherto been inferior to Germany." The right hon. gentleman went on to say that the manufacture of the latch needle and of optical and scientific instruments was progressing, and one firm had a scheme for the production on a large scale of microscopes.

Little dissatisfaction: few appeals.

Scientific glassware was also being made on a larger scale in this country and the quality of the various articles was improving. The progress generally was such and the goodwill in those industries was such that he felt his most sanguine hopes in regard to them would be justified by the time the Act came to an end. He thought it a remarkable thing that in producing such a complicated schedule there should have been so little dissatisfaction with it and so few appeals. There had been, so far, seven cases brought before the Referee. Of these three were decided in favour of the Board of Trade, three against, and one had not yet been decided. In regard to complaints made as to the exclusion of articles, there were three complaints and in each case the Referee held that they were properly excluded, thus justifying the original action of the Board of Trade. As to Part II. of the Act there had been three cases referred to Committees which had been reported upon unfavourably, and four others in which the decision had not yet been given.

Mr. J. D. Kiley (Independent Liberal, *Whitechapel*) denied that those who objected to the Act were opposed to the development of British trade. The important fact that the greater part of the commodities affected by the Act were the raw materials necessary for the development of British industries was completely overlooked. One result of the Act was that a considerable part of the fine chemicals trade was being diverted abroad. London traders had opened branch establishments in Hamburg and elsewhere.

After further debate the House passed to the discussion of other subjects.

Anti-Dumping Orders.

On 19th June, in the House of Commons, replying to questions by the Right Hon. H. H. Asquith and others,

The Leader of the House (the Right Hon. Austen Chamberlain) announced that an Order under Part II. of the Act in respect of certain classes of goods, as to which Committees had reported that the conditions laid down in the Act were fulfilled, would be placed before the House.

The Order in question was laid on the Table a day or two later. It made provision for the imposition under the anti-dumping provisions of the Act of a 33⅓ per cent. *ad valorem* duty on imports of goods of the following classes or descriptions :—

(1) *Fabric Gloves*, that is to say, gloves made of woven or knitted material, which are cut out and sewn up, termed in the trade fabric gloves, and including Lisle, Suède finish, Duplex, Silk and all other gloves made from Cotton or Silk Fabric.

(2) *Glove Fabric*, in the piece or cut out for sewing.

(3) *Domestic Glassware*, not mounted with silver or other metal, that is to say, Carafes, Celery Jars, Cream and Milk Jugs, Custard Glasses, Decanters and like containers, Desert and other plates, Finger Cups or Bowls, Flower Vases and Glasses, coloured or decorated in colour, Goblets, Ice Glasses, Ice Plates, Jelly Glasses, Liqueur Glasses, Salad, fruit, cucumber and like Bowls and Dishes, Sugar Basins, Tankards, Tazzas and Comports, Trays, Tumblers, Water Jugs, Pitchers and Basins, Wine Glasses.

(4) *Illuminating Glassware*, for use with artificial light, not including Electric Incandescent Lamp Bulbs, Miners' Lamp Glasses, or Oil Lamp Chimneys.

(5) *Domestic Hollow-Ware*, decorated or not : (1) Aluminium ; (2) of Steel or Wrought Iron, Enamelled.

Note.—(*a*) Paragraphs 3 and 4 of Schedule do not include any article of Glassware (whether Domestic or Illuminating) which is only pressed, or any article composed of fused silica, vitreosil, or similar material.

(*b*) Paragraph 3 of Schedule does not include any particular goods falling within the description of Domestic Glassware as defined in the said paragraph in respect of which the importer proves to the satisfaction of the Commissioners of Customs and Excise that the goods in question are in fact to be used for the purpose of mounting with silver or other metal.

THE BUDGET.

(Reductions in Tea Duty and Income Tax; Decrease in Postal Rates; Trade prospects; Suspension of Sinking Fund.)

On 1st May the House of Commons went into Committee of Ways and Means and the Chancellor of the Exchequer made his Budget statement. The position at the close of the financial year ended 31st March, 1922, and the estimate of the position at the end of March, 1923, were as follows:—

PAST FINANCIAL YEAR, 1921—22.	
Revenue	£1,124,880,000
Expenditure	1,079,187,000
Surplus for debt reduction ..	£45,693,000
NEW FINANCIAL YEAR, 1922—23.	
Revenue	£910,775,000
Expenditure	910,069,000
Estimated Surplus	£706,000

At 31st March, 1922, the amounts owing to Great Britain by Dominions and Allies were:—

WAR LOANS.	£	£
Dominions—		
Australia..	91,453,000	
New Zealand	29,623,000	
Canada	13,810,000	
South Africa	12,286,000	
Other Dominions and Colonies ..	3,260,000	
		150,432,000
Allies—		
Russia	655,000,000	
France	584,000,000	
Italy	503,000,000	
Serb-Croat-Slovene Kingdom	25,000,000	
Portugal, Roumania, Greece and other Allies	67,000,000	
		1,834,000,000
RELIEF AND RECONSTRUCTION LOANS.		
Austria	12,100,000	
Poland	3,900,000	
Roumania	2,200,000	
Serb-Croat-Slovene Kingdom ..	2,000,000	
Other States	1,000,000	
		21,200,000
Belgian Reconstruction Loan ..		9,000,000
OTHER LOANS.		
Armenia	829,000	
Czecho-Slovakia	2,000,000	
		2,829,000
	Total ..	£2,017,461,000

Taxation changes.

Announcements were made in respect of taxation changes as follows :—

CUSTOMS AND EXCISE.

	Existing Duties.		Proposed Duties.	
	Full Rate.	Preferential Rate.	Full Rate.	Preferential Rate.
	£ s. d.	£ s. d.	£ s. d.	£ s. d.
Customs :—				
Tea .. .. .. the lb.	0 1 0	Five-sixths of Full Rate	0 0 8	Five-sixths of Full Rate
Cocoa .. .. .. the cwt.	2 2 0		1 8 0	
Husks and Shells .. the cwt.	0 6 0		0 4 0	
Butter .. .. .. the lb.	0 0 4½		0 0 3	
Coffee :				
Not kiln-dried, roasted or ground .. .. the cwt.	2 2 0		1 8 0	
Kiln-dried, roasted or ground .. .. the lb.	0 0 6		0 0 4	
Coffee and Chicory :				
Roasted and ground mixed .. .. the lb.	0 0 6		0 0 4	
Chicory :				
Raw or kiln-dried .. the cwt.	1 19 8		1 6 6	
Roasted or ground, .. the lb.	0 0 6		0 0 4	
Excise :—				
Chicory :				
Raw or kiln-dried .. the cwt.	Five-sixths of 1 18 6		1 1 1	
Coffee or Chicory substitutes or any mixture of such substitutes with Coffee or Chicory .. .. the ¼ lb.	0 0 1½		0 0 1	
Sugar : varying .. the cwt. (According to polarisation.)	Five-sixths of 11s. 2d. to £1 3s. 4d.		Excise duty repealed.	
Molasses : varying .. the cwt.	Five-sixths of 4s. 9½d. to 13s. 6d.			

INLAND REVENUE.

I. *Income Tax : Rate.*—It is proposed to reduce the standard rate of Income Tax from 6s. to 5s. in the £.

II. *Basis of the Income Tax Charge under Schedule B. in respect of the occupation of land.*—Persons occupying lands for the purposes of husbandry only, or mainly for those purposes, are assessed to Income Tax under Schedule B. in respect of the profits of their occupation upon the statutory basis of twice the annual value of the lands occupied. It is proposed to reduce this statutory measure of the profits from twice the annual value of the lands to the single annual value of the lands.

Persons occupying lands for purposes other than the purposes of husbandry are normally assessed to Income Tax under Schedule B. in respect of their occupation upon the basis of the single annual value of the lands. It is proposed to reduce the basis of assessment in these cases to one-third of the annual value of the lands.

III. *Interest received without deduction of Income Tax, and other income assessable under Case III. of Schedule D.*—The principal class of income falling within Case III. of Schedule D. is the interest on a number of Government War Securities and on Treasury Bills, but interest on bank deposits, profits from discounts and some minor items are also included.

The statutory basis of assessment under Case III. of Schedule D. is the amount of the income arising within the year preceding the year of Income Tax assessment. The Courts have, however, recently held in the case of the *National Provident Institution* v. *Brown* and other cases [1921, 2 A.C. 222] that no assessment to Income Tax in respect of income falling within Case III. of Schedule D. can be made for the year of assessment following the year in which the ownership of the source of income ceased, and, inasmuch as no charge of tax can be made for the year of assessment in which the ownership of the source of income commences (the statutory basis of assessment being the amount of the income of the preceding year) a considerable and unjustifiable loss of Revenue would follow from the legal position as it now stands.

To correct this anomaly it is proposed that income falling within Case III. of Schedule D. shall be made assessable for the first year of receipt, on the basis of the amount of the income for that year.

IV. *Employments and Pensions.*—Tax in respect of public offices or employments of profit, and of certain pensions, etc., is assessed under Schedule E. on the basis of the income of the year of assessment; the assessments upon weekly wage-earners though made quarterly are also, in effect, on the same basis; all other employees are assessable under Schedule D. on the average of the preceding three years.

It is proposed to transfer to Schedule E. all employments and pensions which are not already within the scope of that Schedule, and to have one common basis of assessment for all employees, viz., the amount of the emoluments of the year of assessment.

V. *Legal avoidance* (A) *of Income Tax and Super-tax by means of Trusts and Covenants, and* (B) *of Super-tax in connection with the holding of shares in certain Companies of a private character.*—Devices are being adopted under the above heads by an increasing number of taxpayers in order legally to avoid to a greater or less extent the liability to taxation which it has been the intention of Parliament to impose upon them. Legislation is proposed with a view to counteracting this growing loss of Revenue.

Excess Profits Duty.

It is proposed to include in the Finance Bill a provision to give effect to the scheme announced by the Chancellor of the Exchequer in December of last year, under which payment of Excess Profits Duty might, in suitable cases, be spread over a period of five years from the 1st of January, 1922; and as from that date to charge interest at the net rate of 5 per cent. per annum, without allowance for Income Tax, upon all Excess Profits Duty due for payment.

It is also proposed to amend the law as respects the right of recovery of duty in certain cases where a change of ownership of a private trade or business has occurred through gift or bequest.

REDUCTION IN POSTAL RATES.

—	Present Rates.		Proposed Rates.	
Inland Letters ..	Not exceeding 3 oz.	2*d.*	Not exceeding 1 oz.	1½*d.*
			Do. 3 oz.	2*d.*
	For every additional oz.	½*d.*	For every additional oz.	½*d.*
Letters to the British Possessions generally, the United States of America and British Postal Agencies in Morocco.	Not exceeding 1 oz.	2*d.*	Not exceeding 1 oz.	1½*d.*
	For every additional oz.	1½*d.*	For every additional oz.	1½*d.*
Inland Postcards ..	1½*d.*		1*d.*	
Inland Printed Papers*	Not exceeding 2 oz.	1*d.*	Not exceeding 1 oz.	½*d.*
			Do. 2 oz.	1*d.*
	For every additional 2 oz. up to 2 lb.	½*d.*	For every additional 2 oz. up to 2 lb.	½*d.*

In addition, there will be certain reductions in Telephone charges.

DEBATE IN HOUSE OF COMMONS.

The Chancellor of the Exchequer (the Right Hon. Sir Robert Horne), in presenting his financial proposals, spoke of the past year as one of unexampled difficulty for industry and commerce. But they had finished the depressing year, 1921—22, with less misfortune than he had anticipated, and certainly with less disaster than members of the Opposition had predicted. The dead-weight National Debt of the country on 31st March, 1922, was, as near as he could estimate it, £7,654,500,000.

"Apart from a few small market debts in the United States," the Chancellor of the Exchequer said, "our external obligations consist only of our debts to the United States Government and the Canadian Government and to certain Allies who owe us much more than we owe them." At an exchange of 4 Dollars 40 cents to the £, the sterling equivalent of their total debt to the United States was, he stated, about £946,820,000. When the exchange was restored to par the sterling equivalent would be £856,030,000. Dealing with expenditure in the current year, the right hon. gentleman explained that the estimate of £546,631,000 for Supply Services was £242,500,000 below final estimates for expenditure last year. He was confident the Government would succeed in making very appreciable reductions in expenditure in the present year and still more in the year following.

* The reduction in the rate for printed papers will be accompanied by some limitation of the hours of posting at the reduced rate, in accordance with the recommendation of the Committee on National Expenditure.

Speaking of trade prospects, the Chancellor of the Exchequer remarked that unemployment was widespread. It was breaking the hearts and embittering the lives of hundreds of thousands of their workmen. The professional and middle classes were enduring privation to-day such as they never before had to face.

Unparalleled depression.

The unparalleled depression which beset the country throughout the whole of last year was still with them. Happily there were hopeful signs of a revival which with a little encouragement might develop into solid progress.

" The burdens of taxation which have been borne by the British people both during and since the War in a degree that has excited the admiration of the whole world, are now," the right hon. gentleman remarked, " felt to be so oppressive as to check enterprise and deepen despondency. Is it essential that we should maintain this taxation ? Is it not possible by slackening it to give some much needed stimulus to trade, thereby lessening our expenditure and next year at least, if not this, gain some revenue as the result of the augmented profits of revived industry ? The policy of the redemption of debt we have pursued with vigour and success. We have provided £322,000,000 in cash for redemption of Debt during the last two years. I have no doubt we were right in doing so. I have no doubt we benefited by it. It enhanced our credit, and it put back into the hands of industry considerable sums which were unprofitable in the hands of the State.

" Equally, I have no doubt as to the course which we ought to pursue at the present conjuncture in our affairs. We are saddled in the present year with a new burden in the shape of the interest that we have to pay on our debt to the United States of America. That we shall meet without question. It is possible by making too great exactions on the taxpayer to defeat the very object at which you aim, no matter how praiseworthy it is.

Sinking Fund to be suspended.

" I am of opinion that we ought not to ask the taxpayer in this year to redeem Debt. I do not mean to say that he is not to find the revenue to meet the expenditure. That must be. All I say is that after the superhuman efforts of the last few years and in the very exceptional circumstances of the times, we shall offend against no sound canon of finance if we content ourselves in this year with raising the revenue which is necessary to meet our expenditure. What does that involve ? "

Sir W. Joynson-Hicks (Conservative, *Twickenham*): " It involves a fall in the rate of exchange."

The Chancellor of the Exchequer: "I do not think that for a moment. It involves in the first place the suspension of the Sinking Fund, and in the second place that we should, to meet our obligations towards the holders of securities, re-borrow the money necessary for that purpose. I think the Committee understand clearly that that re-borrowing is for the purpose of paying special forms of Debt, and does not in any way result in adding to the general burden of Debt. At the end of the year our Debt will not be decreased, but it will not be any greater."

He claimed for the Budget the merit that in a very trying, anxious, and critical time for the commerce and industry of the country it provided within the limits of legitimate and prudent finance as much relief from the burden of taxation as was possible.

After debates on the Budget Resolutions in Committee and on Report extending over several sittings the Finance Bill, embodying the Budget proposals, was introduced.

Finance Bill; Labour and a capital levy.

On 29th May, in the House of Commons, the Finance Bill was debated on the order for Second Reading.

Colonel J. C. Wedgwood (Labour, *Newcastle-under-Lyme*) moved its rejection on the ground that in the proposed remission of taxation vested interests had been thought of first and the common people second. Further, there was no proper case for any reduction in taxation at all. There should have been a reduction in expenditure and that should have translated itself into a reduction of Debt. Labour suggested that taxation should be so altered as to fall upon vested interests and monopolies, that they should not pass it on to the consumer, and that a definite effort should be made to pay off the capital indebtedness of the country by a general levy upon capital. A capital levy was a reconstruction of the finances of the country wiping out the National Debt.

The Right Hon. H. H. Asquith (Leader of the Independent Liberal Party) doubted whether the forecasts in the Budget, both of revenue and of expenditure, were likely to be realised.

The Chancellor of the Exchequer said, with regard to a capital levy, that nobody could explain to him how it was going to produce any money. Immediately they began to impose such a levy, capital would be so depreciated that, instead of getting something by the levy, they would really decrease the wealth of the country as well as the confidence on which all wealth depended. The capital the Chancellor of the Exchequer sought to reach would always disappear as he attempted to snatch it.

On a division the amendment to reject the Bill was negatived by 163 votes against 21, and the Second Reading was agreed to. The Bill was subsequently discussed at great length in Committee and on Report.

PREVENTION OF UNEMPLOYMENT BILL.

(Labour Party's proposals; Work or maintenance; Measure rejected.)

On 12th May, a Labour Party Bill "to make provision for the prevention of unemployment and to provide for the proper treatment of unemployed persons" was debated in the House of Commons on the order for Second Reading.

The Bill proposed to transfer to the Minister of Labour all powers and duties relating to or connected with the prevention of destitution among, or the relief of the able-bodied poor, including workmen in distress from unemployment and vagrancy.

It laid down that in order, as far as practicable, to maintain at an approximately constant level the national aggregate demand for labour, both by private employers and by public Departments, and thereby prevent irregularity of employment, the Minister of Labour (acting in consultation with Departments ordering works or services) should advise the Treasury how works and services could best be organised and apportioned among the different seasons of each year and spread over different years.

The Minister was also to take steps for the preparation and submission of schemes to enable a national aggregate demand to be maintained for labour of all kinds at an approximately uniform level.

Casual labour.

Power was proposed to be given to the Minister to declare employment in any trade or occupation, either generally or in particular districts, to be casual labour of an undesirable character, and in such case to make it obligatory upon employers who wished to engage any person for a period of not less than one month to enter into engagements with workmen through or with the approval of an Employment Exchange.

The Minister was to establish and maintain such institutions, including receiving houses for temporary accommodation and day and residential colonies, as he deemed fit. Admission to or attendance at any such institution was to be voluntary. The Minister was to be empowered, if he thought fit, to grant financial assistance to a person admitted to an institution and to his wife or other person in charge of his children.

The duty was placed upon borough, urban district, and county councils of establishing an unemployment committee. The committee was to inquire from month to month what was the total number of persons out of employment within its area, and what circumstances were adversely affecting the volume and nature of employment.

Work or maintenance.

The employment committee was to decide how all the work done by the council which involved the employment of manual or clerical labour at wages could best be organised and apportioned among different seasons of the year, and spread over different years, in such a way as without inconvenience to the public service to maintain as nearly as possible at a constant uniform level the aggregate volume of employment of all kinds, both public and private, within its area.

When any unemployed person had applied to any Employment Exchange for employment, and no work had been found for him, and he had not meanwhile been admitted to any institution, the council was required through its employment committee :—

(A) To provide such person with suitable employment under the Act ; or

(B) Within three days to make such provisions as would ensure that the applicant and those legally dependent upon him should not be without such maintenance as the medical officer of health of the council might certify to be necessary to maintain him and his dependents in a state of physical efficiency.

The duty of the council either to provide employment or to secure the provision of maintenance for every person was not to extend to any person who :—

(A) Had refused employment offered under conditions which were not lower as regards wages or hours of labour than those commonly obtaining for such employment within its area ;

(B) Had been offered and had refused reasonable employment in connection with the execution of work provided under the Act ;

(C) Had been offered and had refused without reasonable cause maintenance under training provided in accordance with the Act.

DEBATE IN HOUSE OF COMMONS.

Mr. T. Griffiths (**Labour**, *Pontypool*), in moving the Second Reading of the Bill, said that directly or indirectly it would affect every home and industry in the land. Unemployment was a phenomenon which lay outside the control of the individual worker and, indeed, outside the power of control of the individual employer.

The Labour Party were concerned with the imperative need for a national policy aiming at the prevention of unemployment, so far as possible, and the minimising of its evil effects where it could not be prevented. As a Party they regarded it as one of the fundamental duties of the State to use every possible means to avert the sufferings and miseries which accompanied recurrent periods of unemployment, and the tremendous national waste which the enforced idleness of large masses of willing workers inevitably caused. By national and local action on the lines laid down in the Bill the Labour Party believed that fluctuations in the volume of employment between good and bad years could be largely diminished. If, in spite of all the efforts of the Government and local authorities, unemployment remained, it was the duty of the community to make adequate provision for the maintenance of those who were denied employment.

Precise figures had not been included in the Bill, but the Labour Party insisted on two principles :—

(1) The amount received by unemployed workers should vary according to the number of a person's dependents.

(2) The total figure should be such as to enable the worker to maintain himself and his dependents in efficiency.

Mr. J. Wignall (Labour, *Forest of Dean*), in seconding the Motion, said that a nation's wealth built up on a nation's poverty was a nation's disgrace, and would ultimately result in a nation's disaster.

The Right Hon. Sir F. Banbury (Conservative, *City of London*) moved the rejection of the Bill which he said was more likely to create unemployment than employment.

No permanent solution.

The Right Hon. G. H. Roberts (Labour, *Norwich*) observed that no such thing was known to humanity as an absolute and permanent solution of the unemployed problem. It was impossible so to order a complex state of society as to secure that none should ever be out of work. The primary fact had to be recognised that Great Britain depended largely on foreign trade and the Government could not possibly regulate the conditions in the various countries with which they dealt. His own constituents were largely concerned in the manufacture of boots and shoes. Some of the Dominions were among their best customers—South Africa included.

Recently South Africa had embarked on an intensive campaign with a view to making herself a self-contained Dominion. She had put up barriers against the products of his constituency in order that she might build up an efficient boot and shoe industry of her own. Take the cotton industry. There was a large market in India, but the Indians had now set out on a policy of developing their own textile industry, and in order to assist that project had put up a barrier against Lancashire goods. They would be compelled to rely less and less in the future upon the possibilities of foreign countries, because what had happened in South Africa and India would be repeated elsewhere.

Trade revival needed.

The Minister of Labour (the Right Hon. T. J. Macnamara) said he was convinced that the Labour Party's proposals, and the principles underlying them, would leave the last state of the country worse than the first. If the Bill was designed, as no doubt it was, in the interests of the working classes, then they might well ask to be saved from their friends. What was wanted was a trade revival and a better opportunity for employment under normal conditions. They would not get that by adding to the burdens already pressing heavily on industry.

"We must," the right hon. gentleman said, "peg away at our trade facilities scheme, and our export credits scheme, and meantime we must put in hand such relief work with the cordial and patriotic assistance which we have from the municipalities as is possible and ease the hardships of those for whom relief work cannot be found or is unsuitable by unemployment benefit upon the three-fold principle of contributions from the employer, the employed person, and the State." The maintenance proposals in the Bill were administratively impracticable, and would lead to all sorts of controversy. The Government's efforts might not be the last word in the treatment of this grave and distressing problem, but nobody should suppose that the Bill provided a better way. The right hon. gentleman outlined the financial provision made by the Government and the municipalities to meet the situation.

	£
Relief work	40,000,000
Export credits scheme	12,000,000
Guarantee of loans scheme	16,750,000
Unemployment benefit (since September, 1920)	80,000,000
Relief of distress by guardians	50,000,000

Advocates of State Socialism might sniff at all that, but it represented a common effort that he looked back upon with gratitude and thankfulness.

Right to work.

The Right Hon. J. R. Clynes (Chairman of the Parliamentary Labour Party) said the Labour Party had long claimed the worker's right to work. A Government with any sense would not only recognise that right, but would make every man live up to it—would insist upon his working and not merely asserting a theoretical right. If a workman could not find employment in the ordinary market, try how he would, employers of labour had so far fallen short of their function that the State and the municipal bodies had a right to step in and repair the shortage. It would pay the State to do that, for there was nothing in any country more wasteful than enforced idleness.

"We cannot stand where we are, or where we were, on this problem," Mr. Clynes said. "It is, I know, quite a new and almost revolutionary thing to many hon. gentlemen in this House to have these proposals put forward as items of State responsibility. It is an easy matter for anyone to riddle this or any other Bill on an occasion of this kind. In a problem so big as this, none can claim perfection in offering a solution. But those who are exposed to the most severe censure in such a debate as this are those who propose nothing. Those who cannot go beyond letting things alone, and paying large sums to other people for doing nothing, have the last and the least right to criticise those who make any definite proposals."

On a division the amendment to reject the Bill was carried by 172 votes against 82.

TRADE UNION ACT (1913) AMENDMENT BILL.

(Levy for political purposes; Contributions of Trade Union members.)

On 19th May in the House of Commons a Second Reading was given to the Trade Union Act (1913) Amendment Bill. The measure—an unofficial one—has since been under consideration by a Standing Committee, and throughout this stage was strongly opposed by the Labour Party. It now awaits the Report Stage in the House.

Under the Bill it is proposed so to amend the principal Act as to empower a trade union to raise and apply moneys for political objects in accordance only with conditions prescribed in the measure.

If the furtherance of political objects has been approved as an object of the union by a resolution passed by a majority of the members voting on a ballot, it will be competent for any member to give notice to officials of the union that he is willing to contribute to a political fund.

Any member giving such notice will be liable to contribute to the political fund of the union until the end of the year in which the notice is given.

A member may, for a period of one year only in each case, renew his liability to contribute by giving on or before 31st December in each year notice of renewal for the ensuing year.

The political fund is to be kept separate and distinguished from all other funds or money of the union. The political fund account shall be subject to annual audit and to inspection by members.

DEBATE IN HOUSE OF COMMONS.

Lt.-Col. E. C. Meysey-Thompson (Coalition Unionist, *Handsworth*), in moving the Second Reading, said the Bill was not in any sense an attack upon trade unions and did not attempt to prevent political action.

Under the Bill trade unions could take any political

action they desired on condition that the members expressed the wish that their funds should be used for that purpose. A very large number of members of trade unions had complained to him that it was impossible for them to know how much of the levy went to political purposes and how much was used for the ordinary purposes of the trade unions. The levy should be paid into a separate fund, the accounts of which could be presented to the Registrar for his examination and approval. Members of trade unions claimed very strongly that they should have freedom to give or withhold their consent to the spending of their funds for political purposes.

Mr. G. Balfour (Coalition Unionist, *Hampstead*), in seconding the Motion, claimed that the title of the measure should be " A Bill for the Emancipation of Trade Unions." They did not want trade unionists to be tricked into supporting by their money a political fund for purposes to which they might object. They should not, as under the Trade Union Act of 1913, say that every member of a trade union must contribute to the political fund. The honest and fair course was to say that every man who wished to contribute should express that wish. The Act of 1913 established political Prussianism. It was a crushing blow at individuality and progress.

Labour's hostility.

The Right Hon. J. R. Clynes (Chairman of the Parliamentary Labour Party) moved the rejection of the Bill. Its effect, he said, would be seriously to undermine the political purposes and public work of trade unions. Trade union history was a long record of effort to overcome such forms of resistance as were offered in this measure. If workmen in any organised capacity were to take part in the political and public life of a country they must do it through their trade unions. The law now provided that any contribution resulting from a ballot must be placed in a separate political fund and be used only for the purpose for which it was subscribed.

" It is not fair," said Mr. Clynes, " to compel bodies of workmen to go through the process of arranging a ballot for a definite purpose and then completely to frustrate that ballot by saying that even then any contribution must depend upon the initiative and the voluntary offering of the individual workman. . . . I put it to the House that personal liberty, which is the plea of those who support this Bill, is fully ensured as the law now is, and that any workman who feels deeply upon politics, who in his conscience cannot conform to a ballot vote by his mates, has ample personal freedom and is able to avoid any payment if he will only go to the trouble to announce his unwillingness to pay to his own particular organisation."

Victimisation threats.

Sir George Younger (**Coalition Unionist,** *Ayr Burghs*) said that in many cases the unions had not carried out the law, and men who had contracted out of the payment of a political contribution had been subjected to threats of victimisation. The Bill only meant this change—the man in future was asked to contract in and not to contract out. The Act of 1913 had entirely failed to protect a man against breaches of the Act itself except by having recourse to the law, and unless he had a great organisation of some kind behind him he could not proceed to law.

The Right Hon. J. H. Thomas (**Labour,** *Derby*) said the Act of 1913 provided that every member of a trade union should be entitled to claim exemption from subscribing. If any interference took place a member had the right to go to the Registrar—a public official—who could take action against the union without the intervention of the member himself. The Labour Party were as anxious as anybody to rectify the few abuses that occurred, but the House should not, in order to rectify those abuses, ruin the constitutional trade union and Labour movement.

On a division the amendment for the rejection of the Bill was negatived by 161 votes against 82. The Second Reading was then agreed to.

LAW OF PROPERTY ACT.

On 29th June the Royal Assent was given to the Law of Property Act. The measure was first introduced by the Lord Chancellor (Viscount Birkenhead) in the second Session of the present Parliament and some of its main provisions were summarised in the JOURNAL, Vol. I., p. 305. Although the measure was passed by the Upper House in 1921, time could not be found to deal with it in the House of Commons, and it was necessary to re-introduce it in the present Session. The general principle of the Act, as explained in the summary already published in the JOURNAL, is to assimilate the law of real and personal estate, which involves the repeal of the Statute of Uses.

DEBATE IN HOUSE OF COMMONS.

On 16th June, in the House of Commons, during a brief debate on the occasion of the Third Reading of the Bill,

The Solicitor-General (**Sir Leslie Scott**) said that immediate results must not be expected from the Bill. It was not to come into force until 1st January, 1925, in order to give time for consolidating measures and the preparation of textbooks. At the end of some ten years he believed they would be filled with wonder at the waste of time and energy that had taken place in this country for so many generations in the administration of that branch of the law. It was a tribute to the capacity of their race that it should have worked a system of patchwork incongruities in that way when dealing in such detail with underlying principles. He hoped that as the result of this reform the transfer of land would become both cheaper and easier.

The Right Hon. Sir Donald Maclean (Chairman of the Independent Liberal Party in Parliament) paid a tribute to the work of the Lord Chancellor in connection with the Bill. It was quite true that two or three at least of Lord Birkenhead's predecessors, notably Lord Haldane, had taken a great interest in and done a large amount of work in connection with that scheme. But he was certain that had it not been for the persistence, industry, and ability which the Lord Chancellor had applied to the measure, a really great reform in their system of land tenure would have still remained long overdue. It was because the undoubted tendency of the measure must be to make the user of land much more a part of the social business and a commercial unit in its widest sense that the Bill was so heartily welcomed by all Parties in the House.

Mr. Dennis Herbert (Coalition Unionist, ***Watford*****)** said the Bill was described by the Lord Chancellor in the memorandum as "not revolutionary, but evolutionary." That was true; but it did not alter the fact that the changes were enormous.

The Bill was afterwards read a third time without a division.

CANADA.

The following summary deals with the continuation of the proceedings of the First Session of the Fourteenth Parliament, which commenced on 8th March, 1922, and was prorogued on 27th June.

Owing to the considerable number of subjects discussed, it has been found necessary to hold over some of the material to the next issue of the JOURNAL.

General Election and New Government (*Note*).

In the list of Cabinet Ministers who had been sworn into office as the result of the General Election, which was published in the JOURNAL, Vol. III., No. 1, at p. 70, it is regretted that the names of two Ministers were accidentally omitted. The following names, therefore, should be added to the list already given, viz.:—

Minister of Soldiers' Civil Re-establishment and Health	Hon. Henri S. Béland, M.P.
Secretary of State	Hon. A. B. Copp, M.P.

GENOA CONFERENCE.

(Canada's Representatives; Trade with Russia; Expenses of Delegates; Instructions.)

Questions relating to the Genoa Conference were dealt with on several occasions during the Session.

DEBATE IN HOUSE OF COMMONS.

Canada's Representatives.

On 31st March in Committee of Supply,

The Hon. John A. Stewart (Liberal-Conservative, *Lanark, Ont.*) asked if it was the intention of the Department of Labour to be represented at the Genoa Conference by a Labour Representative of the Dominion.

The Minister of Labour (Hon. James Murdock) replied that if his hon. friend was referring to the Conference in April they would be represented by Colonel Carnegie. He thought the Conference his hon. friend referred to was at Rome, not Genoa. The governing body of the International Labour Office would meet at Rome in April. They (the Labour Department) had had no invitation to be represented at the Genoa Conference.

Mr. Stewart said that the Conference was for the consideration of economic and financial questions which were vital to the interests of Canada—questions in which Labour as well as Capital had a very deep interest. He would like to ask if in the consideration of these matters the interests of Labour would be well taken care of by Sir Charles Gordon.

The Prime Minister (Hon. W. L. Mackenzie King) stated that an invitation was extended to the Government of Canada to be represented at the Genoa Conference. The Government had named Sir Charles Gordon and Professor Montpetit. Professor Montpetit was Professor of Economics in the University of Montreal and was well versed in Labour and other problems. He was sure that in the hands of these two gentlemen the interests of Labour, so far as they were matters of special concern, would be represented at the Conference.

Information brought down.

On 10th April on the Orders of the Day,

The Hon. T. A. Crerar (Leader of the National Progressive Party) asked the Prime Minister if he would bring down for the information of the House the Memorandum presented by Mr. Lloyd George to the Cannes Conference which laid the foundation for the Conference that was being held in Genoa; and also if he would bring down a copy of the Resolutions passed at the Cannes Conference. He thought they were entitled to this information since Canada was being represented at the Genoa Conference.

In accordance with Mr. Crerar's request a copy of the Memorandum on Anglo-French relations and the draft of the proposed Treaty with France presented by the Prime Minister of the United Kingdom to M. Briand at the meeting of the Supreme Council at Cannes, January, 1922, and a copy of the Resolutions adopted by the Supreme Council at Cannes, January, 1922, as the basis of the Genoa Conference, were brought down by the Prime Minister on 11th April and were incorporated in the Hansard of that date.

Trade with Russia.

On 5th May on the Orders of the Day,

Mr. Crerar said that he had noticed in a newspaper, in a report of the proceedings of the Genoa Conference, a statement that the Canadian Government, through its representative, had subscribed **£1,000,000** to the consortium that was being established to deal with the re-establishment of business in Russia.

The Prime Minister replied that the report was not an accurate statement. He understood that there was being sent from Genoa to the Government for consideration the proposal to which his hon. friend referred, but no decision would be reached by the Government until it had had an opportunity of examining it and ascertaining what it involved.

Expenses of Delegates; Instructions.

On 11th May in Committee of Supply on the following item:—

Expenses of the Canadian Delegates to the Economic and Financial Conference at Genoa, $25,000.

Mr. Crerar asked the Prime Minister the circumstances under which the Canadian Government was asked to participate in the Genoa Conference. Did they receive an invitation direct from Italy as he understood the other countries that were sending Delegates to the Conference did ?

The Prime Minister replied that an invitation direct from the Italian Government to the Government of Canada asking them to send Delegates was received.

In reply to a further question by Mr. Crerar as to the nature of the instructions given to the Delegates the Prime Minister stated that generally they were asked to participate in the Conference, and to keep the Government informed as to any matters which it was thought advisable to bring to the Government's attention. The Delegates were instructed to observe those matters pertaining more essentially to the European countries, but to pay particular attention to those matters relating to the Dominion and not to take final action with respect to the signing of any treaties or agreements without fully informing the Government of the nature of the proposed treaties before final action was determined upon.

Mr. Crerar: " And receiving the Government's approval."

The Prime Minister: " Yes, and also to see that all agreements or treaties that were signed were made subject to the approval of Parliament."

Mr. S. W. Jacobs (Liberal, *George Etienne Cartier, Que.*): " I see by the Press that the Conference has determined the question of the Mandate of Great Britain over Palestine. Can the Prime Minister tell us if any instructions have been given our Delegates with regard to their action in the matter ? "

The Prime Minister: " No, they have an absolutely free hand in regard to Palestine."

The item was agreed to.

WASHINGTON CONFERENCE TREATIES.

(Parliamentary approval of Treaties: Limitation of Armaments, etc.)

On 7th April, in the House of Commons,

The Prime Minister (Hon. W. L. Mackenzie King) moved, seconded by the Minister of Finance (Hon. W. S. Fielding) that a resolution to the following effect should be taken into consideration at the next sitting of the House :—

Resolved, That it is expedient that Parliament do approve of the following Treaties, of which copies have been laid before Parliament :—

The Treaty between the United States of America, the British Empire, France, Italy, and Japan, for the limitation of naval armament, which was signed at Washington on 6th February, 1922 ;

The Treaty between the above Powers to protect neutrals and non-combatants at sea in time of war and to prevent the use in war of noxious gases and chemicals, signed at Washington on 6th February, 1922 ;

The Treaty between the United States of America, Belgium, the British Empire, China, France, Italy, Japan, the Netherlands and Portugal, to stabilise conditions in the Far East, signed at Washington on 6th February, 1922 ;

The Treaty between the above Powers relating to the Chinese customs tariff signed at Washington on 6th February, 1922 ;

The Treaty between the United States of America, the British Empire, France and Japan for the preservation of the general peace and the maintenance of their rights in relation to their insular possessions and insular dominions in the region of the Pacific Ocean (and the accompanying Declaration), and the Agreement between the same Powers supplementary thereto, which Treaty and Agreement were signed at Washington on 13th December, 1921, and 6th February, 1922, respectively ; and that this House do approve the same.

On 19th June the Prime Minister moved that the House should go into Committee to consider the above resolution.

DEBATE IN HOUSE OF COMMONS.

The Prime Minister (the Right Hon. W. L. Mackenzie King*) said that by this resolution the House was asked to express its approval of Treaties signed at the Conference on the Limitation of Armaments at Washington. As respected Canadian representation, the procedure followed in relation to other Dominions and Great Britain was similar in the final arrangements to that followed at the Peace Conference at Paris. It was appropriate that there should be an expression from the Canadian Parliament of appreciation of the great service rendered Canada in common with the other countries of the world by the President of the United States in calling the Conference and by the United States Government in co-operating through the Conference with the several Powers in the hearty manner it did, which co-operation helped so effectively to bring the proceedings to a successful issue. He should also like to say a word of appreciation of the services rendered their country and the other countries associated at the Conference by Sir Robert Borden, the Canadian Delegate. The document which Sir Robert had presented, embodying

* In the King's Birthday Honours, published on 3rd June, 1922, Mr. Mackenzie King was made a Privy Councillor of the United Kingdom.

the proceedings of the Conference, would remain one of historic interest.

The Treaties had already been signed by the Canadian Delegate; but they would not be ratified by His Majesty on behalf of Canada until after both Houses of Parliament had approved them. There were five Treaties, two of which were of special interest to Canada: the Treaty on the Limitation of Armaments and the Quadruple Pacific Treaty, which related to matters pertaining to the insular possessions of countries whose territories bordered upon the Pacific.

Treaty for limitation of naval armaments.

The parties to the Treaty were the five great Naval Powers: the United States, the British Empire, France, Italy and Japan. Its chief effect had to do with capital ships, which were for aggressive purposes the main naval weapon. In respect of capital ships an agreed ratio of naval strength was established. As between the United States, the British Empire and Japan, the ratio was 5 : 5 : 3. The ration assigned to both France and Italy was 1·75. The eventual figures in actual capital ship tonnage were to be as follows:—

	Tons.
United States	525,000
British Empire	525,000
Japan	315,000
France	175,000
Italy	175,000

To achieve this result there was also involved in respect of capital ships the renunciation of present building programmes, the scrapping of many existing ships and the declaration of a naval construction holiday of nearly ten years.

In respect of aircraft-carriers also, a limitation upon total tonnage was self-imposed on the five Powers corresponding to the ratio of strength already stated. So far as other auxiliary craft were concerned, the proposal to establish a limitation upon numbers and total tonnage in the same ratio failed to command unanimous agreement; and hence the Powers remained free to build war vessels of these types. Individual cruisers, however, were to be limited in size to 10,000 tons.

With the exception of the two capital ships that might be laid down immediately, the British Empire, or any part of it, could not lay down new capital ship construction until 1931. The Treaty had no effect upon the question of Imperial co-operation. A matter of direct interest to Canada was Article XIX. of the Treaty, which preserved the *status quo* in respect of naval bases and fortifications of certain Pacific islands. The islands adjacent to Canada, however, such as Vancouver Island, were not included in the restriction.

The Treaty was to remain in force until 31st December, 1936, and thereafter unless one of the Powers had denounced it.

It would probably be necessary at a later date to introduce legislation to render effective certain of the provisions laid down for preventing evasions of the intent of the Treaty. This had reference to Articles XV. and XVI., which related to the construction of war vessels for non-contracting Powers within jurisdiction of the contracting Powers. It was understood that the British Government would shortly introduce legislation giving the Admiralty control over the construction and delivery of war vessels in private shipyards. The matter was under the consideration of the Government and a Bill would probably be presented at the next Session after an opportunity had been had to examine British legislation in relation to the existing powers of the Government.

Treaties relating to neutrals and non-combatants at sea and use of noxious gasses, etc.

A proposal made by the British Empire Delegation to the effect that, by international agreement, the submarine should be abolished outright was not accepted by the Conference. Similarly it was impossible to secure unanimous agreement among the five naval Powers upon any proposal to limit either the size of individual submarines or numbers and total tonnage of submarine fleets. In view, however, of the improper uses to which this weapon was put in the War, the Conference took action regarding the laws of war governing the operation of submarines. The purpose of the Treaty was, firstly, to declare briefly the existing international law concerning the protection of neutrals and non-combatants at sea in time of war, and to secure thereto the formal adhesion of all civilised Powers, that there might be a clear public understanding throughout the world of the standards of conduct by which the public opinion of the world would pass judgment upon future belligerents. In declaring the existing rules for seizure or attack of merchant vessels, it was implicitly laid down that submarines were not in any circumstances exempt from the universal laws stated. In order to provide a sanction for these rules it was proposed to introduce a new feature into international law. The five Powers agreed that any person in the service of any Power who should violate any of the existing rules, whether or not under orders of a governmental superior, should be liable, as an act of piracy, to trial and punishment by the civil or military authorities of any Power within whose jurisdiction he might be found. It would probably become necessary to introduce legislation giving power to Courts to enforce this provision.

Recognising the practical impossibility of using submarines as commerce destroyers without violating the rules of international law, the Treaty proposed to prohibit such use altogether. Steps were being taken to secure the adhesion to the Treaty of all the other Powers, so that this prohibition might be universally adopted.

The signatory Powers assented to the prohibition of the use of poisonous gases and other analogous liquids, agreed to be bound thereby as between themselves, and invited all civilised nations to adhere thereto, that prohibition should be universally accepted as a part of the law of nations.

Quadruple Pacific Treaty.

This was the Treaty between the United States, the British Empire, France and Japan for the preservation of general peace and the maintenance of their rights in relation to their insular possessions in the region of the Pacific Ocean. Each Power agreed to respect the rights of the others in relation to these possessions. If there should develop between any of the parties a controversy arising from a Pacific question and involving these rights, which was not settled by diplomacy and seemed likely to affect their existing harmonious accord, there should be a joint conference of all the parties. If the rights were threatened by the aggressive action of any other power, not a party to the Treaty, the parties agreed to consult together fully in order to reach an understanding. Upon the ratification of the Treaty the Anglo-Japanese Alliance came to an end.

The Supplementary Declaration provided that the Treaty should apply to the mandated islands in the Pacific. It also provided that the controversies were not to be taken to embrace questions which, under international law, lay exclusively within the domestic jurisdiction of the respective Powers, *i.e.*, questions such as those relating to immigration and tariff matters. The Treaty did not constitute what was known as an alliance. It imposed no military obligations. The effect was to employ the conference method of diplomacy as a means of settling international disputes.

Far Eastern Treaty.

The parties to each of the two Treaties relating directly to China were the whole nine Powers represented in the Conference under the Treaty signed on 6th February to stabilise conditions in the Far East, to safeguard the rights and interests of China and to promote intercourse between China and the other Powers upon the basis of equality of opportunity. It was also agreed that whenever a situation arose involving, in the opinion of any one of the Powers, the application of the Treaty, there should be full and frank communication between the Powers concerned. Steps were to be taken to secure the adhesion to the Treaty of all the other Powers that had Treaty relations with China.

Chinese Customs Tariff Treaty.

The main purpose of this Treaty was to provide for an immediate revision of the Chinese Customs Tariff in order to bring the rate of duty up to an effective five per cent. It further provided for the creation of a special Conference which was to meet in China in the near future with the object of settling conditions upon which China might be enabled to increase the rate of her customs duties above five per cent. in order to secure adequate revenues.

"Certainly the highest interest of all," concluded the Prime Minister, " demanded the allaying of the sinister discord that has been threatening this area of the world. Such an appeasement seems now fairly promised as the result of the agreement reached, while the perpetuation of the conference method, so successful in this instance, affords the basis of a stable policy to preserve the future peace. It remains for a vigilant and informed public opinion to give reality to the promise. It is a great privilege to have the opportunity of moving a resolution which I am sure will meet with the unanimous support of all Parties and of all groups in this House."

The Right Hon. Arthur Meighen (Leader of the Opposition) said that he fully approved the Prime Minister's Motion for the approval of the Treaties, to all of which the British Empire was a party, to all of which Canada, due to her place in the British Empire and as between the Empire and the world, was a party as well. The treaty-making power was inherent in government and might become effective even without confirmation by Parliament; but though such was the case the practice had always been, virtually without exception in the case of any Treaty of consequence so far as Canada was concerned, and increasingly so as far as Britain was concerned, to bring such Treaties to Parliament for approval. Complaint had been made even in this Session as to the expense incurred by Canada in summoning a special Session in 1919 to confirm the most consequential Treaties resulting from the War. He could not see how the complaint could be made save on the part of those who did not regard the ratification by Canada of a Treaty made in the name of the Empire as a fundamental importance. With the development of their constitutional powers as a portion of the Empire it became of great consequence that Canada's adhesion should be obtained. The adhesion of Great Britain alone, without her Dominions, would have been relatively ineffective.

"The courage of the United States," continued Mr. Meighen, "was equalled, if not excelled, by that of the Government of Great Britain in immediately acquiescing in the suggestions of the United States, and in subsequently advancing proposals that in the direction pointed by the United States Government went further than the United States itself. We are proud as citizens of the British Empire, as a component part of the Empire, that the palm of credit for seeking to go further along the path of Disarmament, much further along the path than any other nation present, was taken by the British Empire. Indeed, had the proposals of Britain's representatives been accepted, much more would have been achieved than has been achieved, and the weight of responsibility for defence resting upon the Empire now would have been much lighter than it is." That they should have taken the lead in that regard, and that Canada's representative in particular should have taken so prominent a part in that noble work was a matter for congratulation to every Canadian.

Referring to the naval Disarmament Treaty, Mr. Meighen said he did not think that any hon. Member would complain of the provisions in so far as it laid out a measure of defence naval forces which the British Empire might sustain.

He joined with the Prime Minister wholeheartedly in regret that a proposal advanced by Great Britain for the complete elimination of the submarine was not accepted by the other Powers. While other nations were building and preparing to use, if war should come, this detestable weapon, Britain would undoubtedly find herself bound to do the same.

One might think at first sight that they were not particularly interested in the stabilisation of Far Eastern conditions; but the area of peril in one part of the universe, though at the very Antipodes to themselves, might threaten their peace as acutely as though it were at the borders of Canada. At the Conference last summer it was felt that the settlement of Far Eastern questions was not only vital to the success of the general Disarmament Conference, but it was the almost unanimous opinion that the settlement of Far Eastern questions was a necessary preliminary to any possible success in the Disarmament question itself.

Mr. Lucien Cannon (**Liberal,** *Dorchester, Que.*) asked whether it was possible to settle any Eastern questions without a proper Chinese Government being fully represented.

Mr. Meighen replied that it was possible to help settle them. Were it not for the inchoate state of China, many questions that were to-day a source of anxiety would never have been allowed to arise at all.

Referring to the Chinese Customs Tariff Treaty, Mr. Meighen said that they who were trying to build up some Chinese trade were interested in that matter, and a considerable part was played by Canada's representatives in arriving at a solution of this vexed question.

" I whole-heartedly support the Motion," concluded Mr. Meighen, " and commend these Treaties to the House, and I commend also to the House approbation on the part of all hon. Members and of the people of Canada of the Conference itself, concurrence in the results achieved and in the part Canada has taken in it; loyalty to the results achieved, loyalty to the provisions of the Treaties, and a determination that Canada shall take her part not only in bringing about this agreement for the betterment of world affairs, but in living up to all the responsibility that that agreement involves."

The Hon. T. A. Crerar (Leader of the National Progressive Party) thought that this Conference marked a great step forward in the settlement of international disputes, and the result achieved at Washington had fully justified expectations. Was it too much to hope that, with the development of this method of settling international disputes, the time would come when common agreement could be reached amongst the great nations of the world to rid themselves of the burden of maintaining armaments, excepting what might be necessary for police purposes internationally? The Conference, while it was called outside of the League of Nations, emphasised in a very direct way the great value that attached to the central idea associated with the League, the idea of settlement of international disputes by friendly means. He hoped to live to see the day when international disputes would be settled in the International Court of Justice, recently set up.

The Treaty having to do with the stabilising of conditions in the Far East was also one that had a very direct interest to Canada. Canada had taken her place slowly, but in a way that no one could deny, in international affairs. The same ocean that washed the coasts of China and Japan washed the western coast of Canada. The present rapid means of transit brought these countries closely together, and they were interested, therefore, in anything that would stabilise conditions in the Far East.

The last Treaty mentioned seemed to have a significance, for Canada at any rate, greater than that attaching to any of the others, because Canada was a Pacific Power. The Treaty had another particular significance to Canada—that when it was ratified the agreement between Great Britain and Japan of 1911 should cease to be further operative. The fact that Great Britain had this Treaty with Japan was, he thought, an irritating factor in the minds of many of their neighbours to the south; in that way the Anglo-Japanese Treaty had a direct bearing on Canada; because there was nothing of greater consequence to Canada than the maintenance of the most friendly relations between themselves and the United States.

The Minister of Marine and Fisheries (Hon. Ernest Lapointe) said he was glad that, although the Dominions had not been invited in the first instance, Britain had seen that they should be represented at that Conference.

Heretofore, Treaties entered into between nations had been for the purpose of forming alliances, either offensive or defensive, or both. This Treaty had for its object the preservation of peace. There was no legal or moral obligation on the part of any of the signatories to take part in a war. When the Treaty of Versailles was discussed in Parliament, he, with others, took a strong stand against Article X. He seconded a Motion to the effect that they should not be bound to any military action except after the previous consent of the Canadian Parliament had been obtained. He hoped that whoever represented Canada at the next meeting of the Assembly of the League of Nations would see that the Motion presented last year was proceeded with and that Article X. was eliminated from the Covenant.

One of the great merits of this Four-Power Treaty was that it made possible the termination of the Anglo-Japanese Alliance, which was a menace to Canada. He hoped that world conditions would so adjust themselves as to permit of the reduction of land armaments as well. Nations had been precipitated in devastating conflicts on account of having made military preparations. He was pleased that in Canada public opinion asserted itself in no uncertain tone against heavy armaments.

The Prime Minister's Motion was subsequently agreed to.

DEBATE IN SENATE.

On 27th June, in moving the resolution,

The Leader of the Senate and Minister without Portfolio (Senator the Hon. Raoul Dandurand) said that if it was a good principle for the five Powers that signed this Treaty in trying to establish peace on the Pacific on a permanent basis, it seemed that it was a principle that could as well be applied to all the Allies—and if it were extended to all the Allies, it would truly be a League of Nations.

Senator the Right Hon. Sir George Foster (*Ont.*) said that the one great thing that had happened through the Washington Conference was that the United States of America had removed a very great obstacle from one of the cardinal aims of the League of Nations, namely, the diminution of armaments. Take naval armaments. That was the difficulty that had faced the League in all its Council meetings and in the two Assemblies which had already taken place. How was it possible to carry out Disarmament under the existing circumstances, when the United States had proclaimed a naval scheme which would make her fleet the most powerful in the wide world ?

The sympathy and confidence that was shown at Washington by the other great nations of the world with regard to the future of China, and the respect which was shown to the national development of Japan, would have a steadying and stimulating effect.

Senator the Hon. W. Roche (*N.S.*) said that he wished he were as optimistic as his right hon. friend that the negotiations at Washington would result in such widespread harmony and brotherly love as he desired. There was not so much security for peace when the most formidable engines for war had not been eliminated and when, under the allowance for tonnage, Great Britain and the United States could each build twenty-one of the most powerful modern ironclads. M. Briand went from the Conference at Washington and on his return journey to Paris was supported in the attitude he had taken regarding the maintenance of the French army at its full strength and the retention of the full strength of submarines. Although they most ardently desired that peace might come, he was afraid the old arbitrament of war would be resorted to.

Senator Dandurand's resolution was agreed to.

HUNGARY AND TURKEY TREATIES OF PEACE ACT.

This Act, for carrying into effect the Treaties of Peace between His Majesty and Hungary and Turkey, was assented to on 27th June.

The Act provides that, whereas on 4th June, 1920, a Treaty of Peace (including a protocol and declaration annexed thereto) between the Allied and Associated Powers and Hungary was signed on behalf of His Majesty acting for Canada by the plenipotentiary therein named; and whereas at Sèvres on 10th August, 1920, a Treaty of Peace between the Allied and Associated Powers and Turkey was signed on behalf of His Majesty acting for Canada by the plenipotentiary therein named, and it is expedient that the Governor in Council should have power to do all such things as may be proper and expedient for giving effect to the said Treaties: Therefore His Majesty, by and with the advice of the Senate and House of Commons of Canada, enacts as follows: (1) The Governor in Council may make such appointments, establish such offices, make such Orders in Council and do such things as appear to him to be necessary for carrying out the said Treaties, and for giving effect to any of the provisions of the said Treaties; (2) Any Order in Council made under this Act may provide for the imposition by summary process or otherwise of penalties in respect of breaches of the provisions thereof, and shall be laid before Parliament as soon as may be after it is made, and shall have effect as if enacted in this Act, but may be varied or revoked by a subsequent Order in Council; (3) Any expense incurred shall be defrayed out of monies provided by Parliament.

DEBATE IN HOUSE OF COMMONS.

On 24th June,

The Prime Minister (the Right Hon. W. L. Mackenzie King), on introducing the Bill, explained that it was simply to provide machinery to enable the Government to deal with former enemy property and debts in Turkey and Hungary in a manner similar to that which was already provided for dealing with former enemy property and debts in Germany, Austria and Bulgaria. The House would remember that Treaties between the Allied and Associated Powers and the latter countries were ratified by His Majesty, and that subsequently legislation was adopted to enable the Government to give effect to certain provisions of those Treaties. A similar enactment was not passed with respect to the Treaties with Hungary and Turkey, for the reason that they were not ratified at the same time as the others. The Treaty with Hungary had been ratified by His Majesty, but not the Treaty with Turkey, although it had been signed.

The Hon. T. A. Crerar (Leader of the National Progressive Party): "Are we likely to get anything out of Turkey?"

The Prime Minister: "That the House may see the significance of the legislation asked for I might mention that one concern in Canada has a claim against these countries amounting to $600,000. I am informed that steps cannot be taken to deal with that claim until machinery is provided which will give the Governor in Council power to act under authority conferred by statute."

DEBATE IN SENATE.

On 27th June,

Senator the Hon. N. A. Belcourt (*Ont.*), on the Second Reading of the Bill said in reference to the Treaty with Turkey, that it was an extraordinary thing that they should pass an Act to provide means for carrying out a Treaty which they had not ratified.

The Leader of the Senate and Minister without Portfolio (Senator the Hon. Raoul Dandurand): "We are now ratifying it."

Senator Belcourt: "This is for carrying it into effect, and assumes that we have ratified it."

Senator the Right Hon. Sir George Foster (*Ont.*): "These Treaties have been passed and have been signed by us, but as I understand, Turkey has not agreed to sign the Treaty in question?"

Senator Belcourt: "Parliament should not ratify a Treaty that one of the parties has not signed."

Senator the Hon. Sir James Lougheed (Leader of the Opposition): "Should not the exercise of these powers be made subject to the ratification of the Treaty and should not the Bill so provide? It seems to me rather a peculiar step to take—to make provision for appointments establishing offices, passing Orders in Council, and doing all other things necessary to the carrying out of the Treaty, if it is not an effective instrument. . . . My recollection is that in the case of former Treaties growing out of the Treaty of Peace, the Government of Canada signed them and we afterwards ratified them. That is to say, effect was given to them and we approved by statute of what was done. It seems to me that that would be the better course to pursue in this case."

Senator Sir George Foster: "Both of these Treaties have really been signed by us and by Great Britain. I imagine the difficulty arises in this respect: The Treaty was with the Turkish Government, but there is an *imperium in imperio* in Turkey and ratification has not been made because of the Kemelites."

LEAGUE OF NATIONS.

(Scope of the League; Work of the Commissions; Armaments; Labour aspect; Canada's participation; Representation at Washington Conference; Constitutional aspect; British Empire Delegation; Amendment to Covenant.)

On 26th April, 1922, Senator Sir George Foster called attention in the Senate to the aims and work of the League of Nations, and inquired whether the Government would furnish various reports of its proceedings for the information of members.

DEBATE IN THE SENATE.

Scope of the League.

Senator the Right Hon. Sir George Foster (*Ont.*) stated that fifty-one of the nations of the world were gathered intact on the basis of the Covenant of the League of Nations, which comprised 75 per cent. of the total population of the world.

There were nine sections in the Covenant devoted to what was the primary object of the League—the prevention of war—by the diminution of armaments, by arbitration, by reference to councils and assemblies, and by a judicial court which had been established. That was the kernel of the whole pact. They had sections dealing with the registration of treaties and with the re-arrangement of treaties which were contrary to the spirit of the League of Nations. They had sections which had to do with mandatories. They had sections with regard to the humanitarian and philanthropic agencies and activities of the League. The Covenant was an amendable document. There was no coercion, no attempt to interfere with national prerogatives or functions. All depended upon the consent of the members of the League.

The League of Nations had nothing to do with the formation of the terms or conditions of peace ; that was a work which was carried on by the Great Powers, and to which work the Conference in Paris had devoted itself. It was the supposition that the League should come into operation after peace had been made. The first organ of activity of the League was the Council. The Council had been functioning up to the present with eight members, made up of one for each of the four great Powers, less the United States, and four selected by the Assembly who represented China in Asia, Brazil in South America, and Spain and Belgium in Europe. The Council might be called upon in any emergency. Before any primary matter could be disposed of by a decision it was necessary that the Council should be unanimous with reference to that decision. That rule had had the test in both the Council and the Assembly, and in no single instance had that condition of unanimity been a bar to the examination and the conclusions arrived at by either the one or the other.

The next great branch of activity of the League was the Assembly which met yearly and was representative of all the nations which were members of the League. Each nation-member had three representatives but only one vote. When he said that that assembly of men from all nations of the world met and organised themselves, chose their president, their rules of procedure, organised six great committees with 42 members upon each, each nation being represented on the grand committees, he gave them a key to the problem. The operation of the Council and of the Assembly had gone on in the best of harmony, and with the best attendant results.

Work of the Commissions.

The Transit and Communications Commission was one of the first projects formed. By constant pressure they were carrying on the work ; "and," declared Sir George Foster, "although there are still troubles in Europe, the amount of amelioration which has been brought within the last year and a half by virtue of such action is very refreshing, and very great in its ultimate results." Austria was close to bankruptcy. The Economic and Financial Commission took it in hand, applied with modification the principles adopted at the Brussels Conference, and saved Austria from immediate bankruptcy and chaos. The effort of the Commission was to get every country to which Austria owed debts to postpone those debts for a period of twenty-five years. At the present Session of Congress a resolution was passed by the Senate and the House of Representatives making the postponement in the case of the United States; and now, all postponements having been made, and Austria having agreed to the conditions upon which the credits should be used, under the supervision of the League of Nations, the financial and economic reconstruction of Austria was well within view.

Saar Basin and Danzig.

Turning to the Saar Basin, which for fifteen years was to go on under the management of the League, Sir George Foster said that on the Administrative Commission of five Canada had a representative in Mr. Waugh, whose work in that administration had been as practical and efficient as that of any other member of the Commission. That Commission had the right to levy taxes, to constitute courts; but it governed according to the German laws, modified if they could or ought to be modified by consultation with the people of the district assembled in a representative capacity. The administration of Danzig was put under the League of Nations, and Danzig was now a great, free, self-governing city with a corridor attached to it.

Aaland Islands.

After dealing with the settlement effected by the League in Upper Silesia, Sir George dealt with the Convention regarding the Aaland Islands. Finland kept her right to the territory, but gave guarantees as to how she should act with reference to the islanders themselves. If anyone violated the pact the League of Nations was to say what should be done to bring the violator to justice. One term of the agreement was that no armaments of war of any kind should be established, made or imported into, or in any way had, in the islands.

Armaments.

"The doing away of armaments," declared Sir George, "down to the minimum of national security—that is all that is contemplated—is the chief duty of the League of Nations, and the League of Nations has not forgotten or been unmindful of that duty. But take into account the circumstances. There was a Russia on one side that boasted of an army of 1,500,000 'Reds' and 200,000 *gendarmerie* in addition. There was the United States which was not a member of the League. Could they ask Japan and Great Britain to dismantle their fleets, and so come within a recognition of the demands of the Covenant of the League of Nations to diminish armaments, when they did not know what the United States were going to do, and when the programme of the United States was for the building of a fleet which would have made it the most powerful in the world? If the United States could have sat with the other 51 Powers of the world, then the question of armaments could have been taken up and settled in Geneva. Nine-tenths of the people of the United States, to every heart-beat, are one with the aspirations and ideals of the League for the destruction of war methods and for the substitution of peace methods; and the Conference called by President Harding, and the stand taken on naval armaments, have cleared one difficulty out of the way of the Armament Commission of the League of Nations, and has made their future work much more easy than it has been in the past or would have been had this not taken place." The legislatures of the world were not in a position to be asked for vast sums of money for equipment of navies and armies. A pressure, economical and material in every nation of the world, was now being exerted, and would hereafter be more and more exerted on that line. Then there was the economic blockade. Any nation that violated the pact could be sent into Coventry. "We are a part of the League of Nations," declared Sir George. "We signed the Treaty, we helped to organise the League; we have been represented in its every meeting; it is part of ourselves. Shall we neglect a child of our own?" What he wanted to ask the Government was to take into account the necessity for organising a small staff in connection with External Affairs to whom and through whom these communications (reports of the League, etc.) should come from the League, and which should serve as a liaison between Canada and the League.

Senator the Hon. G. Lynch-Staunton (*Ont.*): "Is there anything in the constitution of the League of Nations which prevents any member from honourably resigning, thus leaving him free to declare war on the others?"

Senator Sir George Foster: "There is nothing to prevent any member of the League of Nations from severing his connection with the League."

Labour aspect.

On 27th April,

Senator the Hon. Gideon Robertson (*Ont.*) said that the first International Labour Conference was held in Washington in November, 1919, and was attended by representatives of governments, of employers and of labour from thirty-eight countries of the world. The various subjects under consideration were referred to different committees. On some questions, it was obvious, uniformity was not possible. For example, on the question of hours of labour it was obvious that some of the countries represented at that Conference could not adopt a universal eight-hour law. The International Labour Conference was wise enough to realise that a revolutionary action of that sort could not be taken at once; but steps were taken in the proper direction, and the three countries principally concerned—Japan, China and India—all made promises of improvement. As time went by the condition of employment and of life among workmen throughout the different countries of the world, parties to the League, would become more and more standardised; so that the disputes that arose because of the competition of cheap labour in one country as against the labour in their North American Continent, for example, would gradually fade away and the possibilities of international disputes arising out of these industrial questions would disappear.

At the Washington Conference there was a persistent attempt on the part of at least two countries to arrange internationally for the control and direction of immigration in the various countries of the world. Hon. gentlemen could readily appreciate how Canada would view a proposition of that sort. A young country that was receiving immigration and had no emigration to other countries to speak of, Canada necessarily took the position that it must retain local autonomy in the matter of its immigration policy.

The Premier of Canada had taken with him probably the most experienced man in the organised Labour world in Canada —Mr. P. M. Draper, Secretary of the Trades Congress—to Versailles, and Mr. Draper and Sir Robert Borden played an important part in the working out of the details and final consummation of Part XIII. (Labour) of the Treaty of Peace. To the Washington Conference in 1919 the Government sent two Government representatives and the full complement of employer and labour delegates. It participated in the conferences at Genoa and at Geneva, and succeeded in obtaining representation for Canada on the governing body of the International Labour Office. The prestige obtained for Canada at the Washington Conference, largely through the splendid work of Mr. Rowell, who was one of the Government's representatives there, had placed Canadian Labour high in the opinion of other countries of the world.

Canada's participation.

On 8th June,

Senator the Hon. L. O. David (*Que.*) said that he felt that Canada's participation in the work of the League might raise very dangerous complications in their relations with England and the United States. He hoped that their representatives in those international conferences would do what was necessary to reconcile their interests with those of England and of all the Dominions. Hon. Members must remember when "Canada First" was the motto of some of their most eminent political men. They should do everything necessary in order that Canada might continue to grow and develop its resources under the protection of the British flag, under the guidance of British institutions, until its destiny required a radical change in its political status.

Senator the Hon. F. L. Béique (*Que.*) rejoiced at seeing the Dominion of Canada become a separate and independent entity to the Covenants. That was a very great step towards the complete autonomy of the great Dominion.

The Leader of the Senate and Minister without Portfolio (Senator the Hon. Raoul Dandurand) said that although it was claimed in some quarters that their status had not been altered, the question which they were discussing seemed to have enlarged the scope of their interests and to have brought them into world politics. The Hon. Mr. Pearce, who represented the Commonwealth of Australia at Washington, in passing through Canada described that new condition of things in the following terms:—

> At Washington His Majesty King George V. was represented by five plenipotentiaries, two for the United Kingdom, one for Canada, one for Australia, and one for India, respectively appointed on the direct advice of the Executive Council of those four autonomous nations—one same and sole King, but four equal Governments. How illogical! But—another miracle!—it worked.

Canadian representation at Washington Conference.

"While the appointment of Sir Robert Borden to Washington," continued Senator Dandurand, "was made by an Order in Council in Ottawa, he represented His Majesty King George. That Order in Council had to bear the signature of His Majesty. How was that signature obtained? It was obtained through the Secretary of State for the Colonies in London. This, to me, implies an outward sign of subordination. We are sister nations; we all proclaim the fact; yet it was through the Secretary of State for the Colonies that the signature of His Majesty the King was sought. Do we Canadians not appear by this form to be still the subjects of the King's subjects? When the Order in Council was sent to His Majesty the King through the Secretary of State for the

Colonies, did it not imply that the Secretary of State for the Colonies could retain that document, or submit it to his own Cabinet for advice? Does it not carry the idea that His Majesty the King may have been moved by the advice of his Imperial Cabinet to put his signature on that Order in Council from Canada? I long for the day when an Order in Council from the Dominion of Canada will reach the King directly through his representative the Governor-General of Canada."

Turning to the League of Nations, Senator Dandurand said that he believed the League, with the United States included, would be a success; without them there might be chaos throughout Europe. He urged the League to hasten the establishment of a publicity bureau which would tell them weekly the real situation in regard to matters which a certain Press was trying to distort. The Germans would, some day, need part of the outside territories which were open to colonisation. He thought the offer might have been made to them that when they had made sufficient reparation their former colonies would be handed back to them.

Constitutional aspect.

Senator Béique: "I understood the hon. gentleman to say that the Order in Council appointing Sir Robert Borden to represent the Canadian Government at Washington was transmitted to His Majesty through the Secretary of State for the Colonies. I doubt that the fact of the services of the Secretary of State for the Colonies being used for that purpose implied that he had a right to over-ride the Order in Council. I should rather think that constitutionally it would not have been permitted—and that he was used merely as a channel for the purpose of reaching His Majesty."

The Leader of the Senate: "I should surmise that in most instances he could comply with the request conveyed to him; yet it must be remembered that he owes allegiance to the Cabinet of which he is a member, and that in certain cases he may deem it proper to exercise his own judgment as to executing a Mandate which comes from the outside Dominions. I said that in reality the Hon. Mr. Pearce was right in declaring that the representatives of the Dominions were appointed by Orders in Council of their respective executives, but that, as to the form, it would still appear that we were dependents and not equals, since we were using the Department of the Secretary of State for the Colonies instead of reaching His Majesty through his representative, the Governor-General."

Senator the Hon. Sir James Lougheed (Leader of the Opposition) pointed out that his hon. friend overlooked one very important fact: the invitation to the Washington Conference was issued by the United States to the Imperial Government, not to Canada, not to the other Dominions overseas. Consequently it became necessary that the representatives of the Dominions should pass through the channels connected with the State invited to attend that Conference. Assuming that they were a sovereign State and had one Sovereign, King George, would his hon. friend suggest how the representatives of the Dominions would attend that Conference when they were not specifically invited as representatives of those particular Dominions ?

British Empire Delegation.

The Leader of the Senate: " The invitation went from the United States to London, and it was there decided that the Empire should be represented by those nominated from London, constituting a British Imperial Delegation. . . . General Smuts cabled to London that he objected to that procedure —that he did not want the power which had been granted to my right hon. friend and his colleagues, of representing the Dominion, to be diminished at Washington. He desired that the Dominions should be represented directly. And, in spite of the fact that Mr. Lloyd George had made the statement that it was a British Delegation, representing the whole Empire, and appointed from London, he gave way and recognised the claim put forward by General Smuts, and Canada was communicated with. His Majesty appointed the Right. Hon. Sir Robert Borden to go to Washington as his representative for Canada."

Senator Sir James Lougheed: " It would have been a most unseemly thing, and discourteous to the United States, if the Imperial Government had said to Washington : You must change your invitation ; instead of inviting the Imperial Government to the Conference, you must issue invitations to the representative of Canada, the representative of Australia, and the representative of South Africa. . . . If this is an Empire, there must be one head to the Empire ; and in our international relations these communications can be only with one Sovereign or with one head of the entire State."

Senator the Hon. N. A. Belcourt (*Ont.*) said that they had no right to expect, and certainly no right to insist at Westminster, that any Canadian should form part of that Delegation. It was merely an act of grace ; it was merely the doing of something which the Imperial Government was not bound to do.

Senator Lynch-Staunton: " Suppose the Earl of Balfour had disagreed with all the other Delegates, would anything different have happened ? "

Senator Belcourt: " Yes, because he had authority to speak for the one paramount authority of the British Empire. He was speaking for the King."

Senator the Hon. G. W. Fowler (*N.B.*) : " So was Borden. He was appointed by the King as well as Balfour."

Senator Belcourt : " Not in that sense at all. Surely we have to distinguish between the right of the Crown as exercised by the Imperial Parliament and the right of the Crown as exercised by any one of the Dominions."

The Leader of the Senate : " They are sister nations."

Senator Belcourt : " Not at all, except to speak in very loose language. . . . I say we have to have the permission of the Parliament of Westminster when we go outside of our constitution. . . . It is all nonsense to talk about our constitutional development in Canada."

Senator the Hon. J. P. B. Casgrain (*Que.*) declared that the Imperial Parliament said to Canada : Give us a name, and we will appoint him as one of our own ; and Sir Robert Borden went there as delegate or a commissioner of His Majesty King George, appointed on the advice of the Imperial Parliament.

The Leader of the Senate : " No, I challenge that statement. It was upon the advice of the Executive Council of the Dominion of Canada at Ottawa."

Senator Sir James Lougheed : " He went as representing both, and had the status of a British representative just the same as Mr. Balfour, or any other, and likewise represented Canada."

Senator Casgrain : " And King George never put his name on that paper except on the advice of the Imperial Government. What could poor King George do ? Is he going to take advice from Ottawa and from London at the same time ? If the advices differ, how is he our King ? There is only one King, and one Empire, and one Flag."

After further discussion, the Leader of the Senate promised to take up with Sir Herbert Ames, the Financial Secretary of the League of Nations, Senator Sir George Foster's suggestion as to the circulation of the monthly publications of the League.

Approval of Amendment to the Covenant.

On 19th June the Prime Minister moved the following resolution in the House of Commons :—

> That it is expedient that Parliament do approve of the Protocols of Amendment, signed on behalf of Canada at Geneva on 20th May, 1922, of which copies have been laid before Parliament, embodying certain proposed amendments to Articles 4, 6, 12, 13, 15 and 26 of the Covenant of the League of Nations, which were adopted by the Second Assembly of the League at Geneva on 3rd, 4th and 5th October, 1921, and that this House do approve of the same.

The Prime Minister (the Right Hon. W. L. Mackenzie King) explained that for the most part the Protocols were either consequential or procedural in their nature and did not in any way vary the spirit of the Covenant. For this reason the Government might very well have approved the several Protocols and authorised their ratification by His Majesty without coming to Parliament for approval before ratification. Inasmuch, however, as Parliament was in Session at the time the Protocols were referred to the Government, they thought it was fitting that Members of the House particularly should have the opportunity of approving of them.

The amendment to Article 4 proposed that the Assembly should fix rules with reference to the selection of the additional four members of the League to be represented on the Council by a two-thirds majority. The original Article 6 provided that the expenses of the League should be borne by the members in accordance with the apportionment of the expenses of the Universal Postal Union. This had worked inequitably and had been especially hard on Canada, since it had obliged her to contribute on an equal basis with Great Britain, France, Italy, etc. The Amendment to this Article proposed a scheme that would materially reduce Canada's contribution.

Under the original Article 12 the members of the League agreed that if there should arise between them a dispute likely to lead to rupture, they would submit the matter, either to arbitration, or to inquiry by the Council, and they agreed in no case to resort to war until three months after the award of the arbitrators or the report of the Council. The amendment proposed to add submission to " judicial settlement " as a further alternative to submission to arbitration or to inquiry by the Council. This was necessary in view of the creation by the first and second Assemblies of the Permanent Court of International Justice. Canada, having ratified the scheme of the Permanent Court, had also ratified this amendment.

The amendment to Article 26, the Prime Minister explained, related to the procedure for enacting amendments to the Covenant. Amendments must be voted by the Assembly on a three-fourth's majority, which majority must include the votes of all the members of the Council represented at the meeting. Before amendments so voted could take effect, they must be ratified by all the members whose representatives composed the Council when the vote was taken and by a majority of those whose representatives formed the Assembly. If sufficient ratifications were not obtained within twenty-two months after the vote, the proposed amendments remained without effect. All members were to be notified of the taking effect of an amendment, and any member who had not at that time ratified the amendment was free to signify his refusal to accept it, but in that case he should cease to be a member of the League.

There were four other Protocols relating to Article 16. It appeared from the Colonial Secretary's despatch of 31st December, 1921, that the Governments of Great Britain and France had agreed not to ratify these proposed amendments before the meeting of the Assembly in 1922. As they were both represented on the Council, their ratifications were absolutely essential to the taking effect of any amendment. Consequently, there would seem to be no point in signing the Protocols relating to Article 16.

In answer to a question by Mr. Meighen (Leader of the Opposition) the Prime Minister explained that when the Covenant was adopted at the Peace Conference of Paris, the Universal Postal Union was the only international organisation affording a precedent for the purpose of the expenses of the Secretariat and, as it would have been impracticable to work out an elaborate new scheme, the scheme of the Postal Union was adopted. For Canada the matter had a direct interest. At both the first and second Assemblies the Canadian representatives joined with other representatives in the endeavour to secure a re-allocation. It was proposed to strike out the last paragraph of Article 6 of the Covenant and to provide instead that the Assembly should be authorised to fix the allocation of the expenses of the League. The second Assembly was unable to agree upon what should be regarded as a final allocation, but it did arrive at a provisional new allocation, to come into force on 1st January, 1922; under this, Canada appeared in the third class. The Canadian representatives at the second Assembly reported to the Government that they were doubtful as to the ultimate fairness of the new allocation so far as Canada was concerned but that it was impossible at the moment to secure anything better and that it would still be possible to make representations in the future.

The Right Hon. Arthur Meighen (Leader of the Opposition) said that the Prime Minister had observed that the ratio between Canada and Australia was as 35 is to 15. He did not know how that ratio could have been arrived at.

The Prime Minister said that he could not give his right hon. friend any information at the moment.

The Prime Minister's resolution was then agreed to.

INTERNATIONAL LABOUR CONFERENCE.

On 10th April, in the House of Commons, in reply to questions asked by Mr. A. B. Neill (National Progressive, *Comox-Alberni, B.C.*),

The Secretary of State (Hon. A. B. Copp) said that the

Dominion Government was represented at the first International Labour Conference held at Washington in October and November, 1919. The Provincial Governments were not represented in the Conference, as the Provinces were not members of the International Labour Organisation. They were, however, represented in the Canadian Delegation to the Conference, since on the invitation of the Dominion Government each Provincial Government named an adviser to the Dominion Government Delegates. A draft convention in regard to the acceptance of an eight-hour working day by the Governments represented at the Conference was passed, Canada participating as a federal state and subject to the limitations as to federal states in these matters set forth in Article 405 of the Treaty of Versailles. The Department of Justice having decided that the subject dealt with fell within Provincial authority, the Dominion Government referred the draft convention to the several Provincial Governments as the authorities competent in the matter. Consideration was being given at the present time to suggestions which had been received from certain of the Provincial Governments for calling a conference for discussion of this matter between the Dominion and the Provinces.

In reply to the question as to whether, pending legislation, the Government would give instructions to have an eight-hour day put into effect on all Government works, the Secretary of State said that the practice with respect to works performed by the Dominion Government required that the working hours should be in conformity with the practice or law of the locality. Since the Provinces were understood to have the representations of the Convention under present consideration, in the opinion of the Government a change of practice at the present time might only serve to create a misconception or to prejudice the position of the Provinces in dealing with this matter.

WRANGEL ISLAND.

(Dominion and the United States.)

On 12th May the House of Commons discussed the following item in Committee of Supply :—

Patrol of the northern waters of Canada, $15,000.

The Minister of Defence (Hon. G. P. Graham) explained that this item was really to publish the reports of the Stefansson expedition.

The Right Hon. Arthur Meighen (Leader of the Opposition) asked what was the policy of the Government towards the northern islands, with particular reference to those covered by the Stefansson expedition, laid claim to on behalf of Canada, and to Wrangel Island.

The Minister of Defence: "It is a delicate matter to state the policy of the Government on that question."

Mr. Meighen: "Has the Government any policy?"

The Minister of Finance (Hon. W. S. Fielding): "What we have we hold."

Mr. Meighen continued that it was well known that there was a dispute as to Wrangel Island. The question of the proper attitude of Canada towards that Island was doubtless before the Government. He was asking if the Government was in a position to say what its views were with relation to the retention of Wrangel Island or the continuance of Canada's claim thereto; and the same words applied to the other islands covered by the expedition.

The Minister of Defence: "The policy of the Government, as I understand it, is as just expressed by the Minister of Finance—what we have we hold."

Mr. Meighen: "Well, have we Wrangel Island?"

The Minister of Defence: "Yes, as I understand it, and we propose to retain it."

Mr. J. T. Shaw (Independent, *Calgary, W., Alta.*) understood that the United States had published a map in which they showed all the lands north of Melville Island as being a country which did not belong to anybody, and which was consequently open for discovery by any nation whose expedition might happen to locate there. It was a matter of the utmost importance that they should not lose sight of the fact that the extreme northern part of the country should be preserved to Canada.

The Hon. Hugh Guthrie (Liberal-Conservative, *Wellington, S. Riding, Ont.*) stated that within the last month the question had been discussed in *The New York Times* and *The Washington Post*, and there was no doubt that certain interested parties in the United States intended to make a claim to Wrangel Island as United States territory by right of prior discovery. He was satisfied that that claim was unfounded. There was no right of prior discovery beyond the right of Canada or Great Britain in that respect. This matter was going to come to the front in the very near future, and he thought it was high time that the Government should take a stand on the matter and make the stand known to the world. It would be a matter for international discussion very soon unless they were going to forgo their claims and let the United States take over the Island. Whether the Island was of very much practical importance he did not know, but parties in the United States seemed to think it was. One paper said that the mineral wealth of Wrangel Island was far greater than that of Alaska.

That might be problematical, but it was the basis of the claim which was made by certain interests in the United States.

The Prime Minister (Hon. W. L. Mackenzie King) said that the Government had had interviews with Mr. Stefansson. He did not know that it was in the public interest to disclose the full nature of those interviews, but at the present time the Canadian flag was flying on Wrangel Island, and there were Canadians on the island, members of a previous expedition of Stefansson's. The Government certainly maintained the position that Wrangel Island was part of the property of Canada.

Mr. Meighen believed that there might be a claim to the island on behalf of Russia, a claim based very largely on the geographical location of the island. The island of Ellesmere on the west coast of Greenland was also one to which the Government should give some attention. An expedition was about to be launched by a Dane with, he thought, the approval of the Danish Government, designed to make some occupational claim in Ellesmere Island, and it was anticipated, probably, to base on that occupational claim certain rights of Denmark in the island. He called that matter to the attention of the Government, so that whatever position Canada was in with respect to Ellesmere Island would be held because, in his judgment, Ellesmere Island was of greater importance than Wrangel Island.

On the 29th May, on the Orders of the Day,

The Hon. R. J. Manion (Liberal-Conservative, *Fort William and Rainy River, Ont.*) pointed out that *The Washington Times* stated that the United States Government had decided that Wrangel Island was properly the property of Russia and that it should be held in trust until conditions in Russia had become settled.

The Prime Minister replied that the matter was now for the first time drawn to the attention of the Government by the remarks of his hon. friend.

DEPARTMENT OF NATIONAL DEFENCE.

(Amalgamation of fighting Services; Mounted Police; Military position; Defence Council; etc.)

On 4th April the House of Commons discussed the resolution moved by the Minister of Militia and Defence for the creation of a Department of National Defence. The Bill embodying the resolution, which was assented to on

27th June, is summarised in the JOURNAL, Vol. III., No. 2, p. 347.

DEBATE IN HOUSE OF COMMONS.

Amalgamation of the fighting Services.

The Minister of Militia, Defence and Naval Affairs (Hon. G. P. Graham) stated that it was the intention of the Government to bring under one ministerial head what might properly be termed the defence forces of Canada. There were four branches—the Militia, the Royal Canadian Mounted Police, the Naval Service and the Air Service. In the departments referred to there was a large number of temporary employees, and the Government hoped that by the amalgamation of the different branches in question the services could be approximately carried on by the permanent staff. There were other directions in which economy could be promoted; for example in the amalgamation of the various executive forces of these different branches—the purchasing departments.

The Hon. Hugh Guthrie (Liberal-Conservative, *Wellington, S. Riding, Ont.*) thought that the resolution forecasted a Bill which, in general, would be to the advantage of Canada. In a scheme advanced by Sir Frederick Borden, and in another scheme suggested to Parliament in a report by Lord French—made, he thought, in the year 1910 or 1911—the suggestion was advanced that all the military and naval forces of Canada should be brought under one department. Neither in Sir Frederick Borden's suggestion nor in Lord French's report was it proposed that the Mounted Police of Canada should be made part of the Department of National Defence. In his report (1920) Sir Arthur Currie recommended that the military force, the naval force and the air force should be brought under one department and also that there should be a committee of national defence in the Government, but he likewise excluded the North-West Mounted Police. He feared from what he had read and heard in the House that a severe assault was to be made upon the militia system of Canada, and he was greatly gratified to find that substantially the Government proposed to maintain in Canada what they had maintained from Confederation down to the present time. The chief benefit derived in the Dominion from the North-West Mounted Police had been in regard to civil work, and if they now turned that purely civil into part of their military establishment or part of their national defence, they would rob that exceptional force of the distinctly civil character which it had enjoyed heretofore, and by reason of which it had been so useful.

Retention of staff officers.

They had to-day in the Militia Department the most highly-trained men and the most thoroughly experienced staff that they had ever had in the history of the Dominion. Three at least of them had been sent at the expense of Canada to the Staff College in Great Britain, and they had taken brilliant courses there. It was of the highest importance that such men should be retained in the Militia of Canada and that their services should not be dispensed with.

Mounted Police.

The Right Hon. Arthur Meighen (Leader of the Opposition) said that the naval service should be joined to the Militia Department was, in his judgment, a matter for the Government itself to determine, and did not lend itself to criticism. But he did object to the Mounted Police being taken out of a civilian department and made part of the military forces, and he saw no reason for the step whatever.

Gen. the Hon. S. C. Mewburn (Liberal-Conservative, *Hamilton, E. Riding, Ont.*) felt convinced that if the Mounted Police could remain, for administrative purposes, under the Prime Minister, it would be much wiser and sounder. Although under the present Militia Act it was within the power of a municipality to call upon the militia to turn out for the preservation of law and order, that was the very last resort that should be adopted in Canada.

The Prime Minister (Hon. W. L. Mackenzie King) said that if they once opened the door to having the Mounted Police called in aid to the civil authorities on any occasion when there might be alarm on account of industrial disputes, they would in a very short time have the Federal Government discharging a function in the matter of keeping law and order which it was never contemplated it should discharge.

The Hon. T. A. Crerar (Leader of the National Progressive Party) said he was in hearty sympathy with the principle that the different defence arms of Canada should be united under one control and direction. He was among those who believed that the administration of civil law and the maintenance of civil order should be kept away as far as possible from that relating to the defence of the country.

Mr. S. Woodsworth (Labour, *Winnipeg C., Man.*) said that, speaking as a representative of Labour, he believed that there was no other organisation that caused so much friction in their communities as the North-West Mounted Police. To a very considerable extent they were reduced to the position of being a secret service department. He contended that the activities of the Mounted Police should be confined to the unorganised territories, and that each Province should be left to administer its own civil affairs.*

After further discussion the resolution was passed, and the Bill embodying it read a first and second time.

On 6th April the Minister of Militia and Defence intimated to the House in Committee on the Bill that he had decided not to press for the inclusion of the Mounted Police in the Department of National Defence.

DEBATE IN THE SENATE.

On 9th May in Committee,

Senator the Hon. W. A. Griesbach (*Alta.*) said the argument which appealed to him in support of the Bill was that the three departments of the Government, having a common object to fulfil, namely, the defence of the country, would function best if they were all brought under the control of one brain. The total of the three Services (Militia, Navy and Air Force) last year was $17,306,158; this year it would be $14,489,800, an economy of $2,816,358. Military efficiency was based on men, money and leadership; and the greatest of these was leadership. But leadership without money was helpless. Their experience in the War had produced men who knew what ought to be done in things military. But these gentlemen had not been heard; and the matter was being disposed of on a basis of political expediency—and that was the basis of these economies.

Canada's military position.

What was the result of the amalgamation so far, and of the situation which had been brought about by the Government? Positions were being done away with or minimised, and the future of a man in the permanent service of Canada was not worth bothering about. One member of the other House had referred to the officers of the Militia as parasites. How long did they think the military spirit of the country was going to stand up against that sort of treatment, and what did they think was going to be the future of voluntary military service in Canada unless the Government was prepared to support that service in the only way that it could—by adequate grants of money?

---

* On 10th April Mr. Woodsworth moved :—

"That, in the opinion of this House, the activities of the Royal Canadian Mounted Police should be confined to Territories not included in any Province of Canada."

The resolution was negatived by 108 to 47 votes.

There were to-day in the world three times as many men under arms as there were in 1913. There were situations in China, in India, in Germany, in Russia, in Ireland, in France, South Africa, and in scores of other countries which aroused the greatest concern. Against such forms of revolutionary activity as oppressed the world to-day there was only one answer, and that was armed force. They had before them in the public Press fairly definite information of a military treaty between Russia and Germany. The very men who opposed preparation to-day were the men who protested to the country that they were quite certain there never would be war with Germany. While the United States was twelve times greater than Canada in population, her military expenditure was thirty-six times greater.

They had heard of the effects in a battle of running out of bombs. Did they know that in Canada to-day they had not a single bomb? There were no mortars in Canada except a few for demonstration purposes. There was not a single tank in Canada. They had not in Canada any preparation for the making of gas, and nothing to utilise gas. They had an insufficiency of rifles. Their position to-day was worse than it was in 1914; and they dared to occupy that position because in the back of their heads they thought that if ever they got into serious trouble they might rely on Great Britain to get them out. The new commitments following the War—new territories which required to be policed and guarded, and Mandates taken over at the request of the League of Nations—made the demands on the British Army three times as great as they were in 1914. To-day the position, as stated in the House of Commons in England, and not controverted, was that one division could be sent to Europe in the event of war, another division might follow in three weeks, and other divisions could not be secured under several months. The time had come when they should be prepared to paddle their own canoe. If they were to be a nation and give themselves the airs of a nation, this sort of thing could not go on. Of the per capita expenditure of all the civilised countries to-day for army, navy and air forces, that of Canada was the lowest.

Senator the Hon. J. G. Turriff (*Man.*) said that he would like anyone to point out a single case wherein preparedness or the spending of money by the hundreds and thousands of millions had kept any nation out of war. He believed that the policy followed by Britain in the past, of conserving her resources, had done more to bring Great Britain and her Allies out ahead in the recent War than had any other policy that could have been adopted.

Defence Council.

On 17th May,

Senator the Hon. Sir James Lougheed (Leader of the Opposition) declared that there was no more necessity for a Defence Council (Section 8) than there was for a fifth wheel to a coach. The Militia Council was brought into existence for the purpose of giving additional remuneration to the officers who constituted it. If this clause were stricken out, the work of national defence would go on just the same.

Senator Griesbach said that their Militia Council was based primarily on the Military Council in England for the government of the Army. There was also a Military Council in India and in each of the other British Dominions, and the reasons why they had a Militia Council were the same reasons as existed in those other countries.

On 18th May,

Senator the Hon. J. A. Calder (*Sask.*) thought that under Section 6 of the Bill the Governor in Council was given powers to do anything he liked in the way of establishing such organisations as might be thought necessary to the efficient working of the Department. If that was so, he was opposed to Section 8 of the Bill.

Senator Griesbach said that they would probably be having another Imperial Conference in a few years, and before that Conference would come questions of military moment; and representatives of other Dominions would be there to speak with the advice of their military councils. If they rejected this Section, they were putting out of legal existence the Military Council which was to advise their Minister; they were putting themselves out of joint with the rest of the Empire; and they were requiring their Minister to go to that Conference with advice which might be expert, but which was unknown to the public and was irresponsible.

After further discussion Section 8 was rejected by 35 to 21 votes, and the Bill was reported with this and other amendments which were concurred in by the House of Commons on 12th June.

NAVAL POLICY.

(Reduction of armaments; Government's proposals; Dependence on British Navy; Prime Ministers' Conference; Submarines; Labour attitude; Canada's obligations; Expenditure in other Dominions; Liberal policy; Attitude of National Progressive Party; etc.)

On 12th May the House of Commons in Committee of Supply discussed the following item :—

Naval Service—to provide for the maintenance of the Royal Canadian Navy—**$1,500,000.***

The Minister of Militia, Defence and Naval Affairs (Hon. G. P. Graham) said that the subject of the Canadian Navy was one which had interested the people of Canada for some years. In 1910 what was called the Naval Service Act was passed under which Canada established for herself a naval service. In 1911 arrangements were made under which the British Admiralty handed over to the Dominion certain services which the Admiralty had previously performed, particularly those relating to the docks at Esquimalt and Halifax. There was great divergence of opinion as to what they should do under the Naval Service Act. Under it the then Government purchased two ships, the *Niobe* and the *Rainbow*, for the purpose of training young men for naval service. When the War broke out, the *Niobe* was refitted and served one year; the *Rainbow* served during the War. They had no ships to take the place of the *Niobe* and *Rainbow* until the British Government after the War presented to Canada three ships: the *Aurora*, the *Patricia* and the *Patriot*, and two submarines. The records of the British House of Commons disclosed that a question was asked in the House as to whether Canada undertook to maintain these ships in commission when they were accepted, and the answer was that there was no agreement except that implied by the acceptance of the ships. He thought they were all agreed that Canada must maintain something of a naval service, and he thought the opinion now generally expressed as to what Canada must do in the matter was primarily to protect her own coasts and harbours and her fisheries.

Reduction of armaments.

"We showed during the War," declared the Minister, "although we had no Navy, that Canada was ready to do her part just as well as any other portion of the Oversea Dominions, or as thoroughly as the Motherland herself, or any of her Allies; so there can be no question of the willingness and anxiety of the Canadian people to do their duty as a young nation in the making. What has been done in the past will

* In reply to a question by Mr. F. Rinfret (Liberal, *St. James, Que.*) on 20th April, the Minister of Militia, Defence and Naval Affairs (Hon. G. P. Graham) stated that the Royal Canadian Navy consisted of the cruiser *Aurora*, the torpedo-boat destroyers *Patriot* and *Patrician*, and the submarines *C.H.*14 and *C.H.*15, constituting the fleet; a submarine depot at Halifax to which the submarines *C.H.*14 and *C.H.*15 were attached; the Royal Naval College of Canada; officers in training in the Imperial Service; the youths' Training Establishment at Halifax; the Naval Executive Staff at headquarters; the Naval Dockyard at Halifax and Esquimalt.

be continued, I believe, in the future. We are in this position in regard to the question of a Navy. Every country in the world to-day is endeavouring to reduce its armament. At the great Conference in Washington recently, where we were represented, the great nations of the world agreed not only to take a holiday in naval construction, but to scrap many of their fighting ships. All over the world to-day people are anxious to reduce, as far as possible within the limits of safety and without any sacrifice of national dignity, the expenditure on fighting machines and fighting material." Mr. Graham proceeded to quote from Sir Robert Borden's report on the Washington Conference to illustrate the proposals as to the number of ships to be retained by the great Powers concerned.

Mr. A. J. Lewis (**National Progressive,** *Swift Current, Sask.*): " The Minister referred to the number of ships permitted to the British Empire. Would that include Canada ? "

The Minister of Naval Affairs: " It would include, I think, all the Oversea Dominions."

Mr. Lewis: " We would benefit, of course, from having these 26 capital ships in the service of the Empire. Is Canada paying towards the upkeep of those ships ? Is it because all nations in the world are moving to reduce their expenditure on armaments, as the Minister has just said, that he is reducing this item to $1,000,000 ? Or did that apply to Canada, which practically to all intents and purposes has no Navy ? "

The Minister of Naval Affairs: " It applies to Canada, being one of the Oversea Dominions." Canada, he pointed out, had no capital ships. She did not contribute to the upkeep of the British Navy. No man in the world would agree more heartily than himself to the proposition that the British Navy was essential to the peace of the world. The British Navy not only saved Canada, but saved their friends on the other side of the line, and it was a question of policy whether there should be a contribution or that each portion of the Empire should do its own part. " Canada at the present time," declared the Minister, " has taken the ground that we as a young country growing up, having our own service,—the British Government having handed over to us the naval service, which we undertook, and the management of our militia,—should proceed along that line. It may be in the years to come that Canada will have to develop, perhaps, a larger naval service than she has, or has had, but one that will maintain the principle of Canada, within the Empire, being a nation that so far as possible looks after her domestic affairs."

Mr. J. T. Shaw (**Independent,** *Calgary, W., Alta.*) asked whether it was possible for Canada to have a capital ship until the expiration of the Washington Agreement, which would occur in 1940 ?

The Minister of Naval Affairs : " I would rather think not."

The Right Hon. Arthur Meighen (Leader of the Opposition) : " Unless it were in reduction of Great Britain's capital ships."

The Minister of Naval Affairs : " I imagine, as part of the British Empire, we could have one transferred."

Mr. Lewis said that morally he thought they were responsible, and, if Members on the both sides of the House claimed that they were a nation, and they on that side were always saying that they were a nation, and that they wanted to stand on their own feet, he thought they ought to help to pay for the protection they received.

Government's proposals.

The Minister of Naval Affairs said that he wanted to submit to the judgment of the Members of the House that in the Dominion of Canada as they were now constituted a better service on their own behalf, and for the Empire at large, would be obtained by using the voluntary effort of their young men than by having a great permanent force. The proposal that he had to lay before the House, and for which Estimates were asked, was that they should discontinue in commission the ships which they now had ; that they should continue the protection and care of the wharves and docks at Halifax and Esquimalt ; that they should provide a reserve force composed of officers and men, officers who are now in the Navy, the number of them altogether would be 233 ; that they should create on the Pacific coast at Esquimalt an establishment with one small ship and two trawlers of 450 tons ; that they should establish there a portion of their naval force for training in the protection of their shores and harbours, mine-sweeping, mine-laying ; that at Halifax in the East they should have the same services. It must be remembered that the second line of defence, the great reserve of the Dominion of Canada, was their merchant marine. This meant that under the estimate in another year some 1,500 men could be trained during the year on land and on sea for two or three weeks. This would have one benefit, that it would not take a single man out of industrial employment in Canada. Newfoundland had a force of this kind, so had South Africa ; and he believed that in preparing the young men in the way he had outlined, forming a volunteer force, they would instil a better spirit into them. Under this scheme, concluded the Minister, they were retaining four officers from the British Admiralty ; the rest, kindly loaned to them, would be returned to the Royal Navy. The others would be young Canadians.

Dependence on British Navy.

Mr. Meighen declared that the Minister's statement touched a subject that was of paramount consequence to their whole country. He was thoroughly in accord with the sentiment he uttered when he commenced his address, and was only sorry that his concrete proposals had not the remotest relationship to that sentiment. In time of quiet and serenity the five trawlers would be all right, and they would be quite safe in training their Navy in their armouries. But in time of emergency, which was really the time one required to prepare against, then it was that defence was rather more desirable than in sunshine and calm. In such a time they were to depend upon the British Navy and the British taxpayer. He wondered if the Minister was armed with any statement from one acquainted with the needs of Empire defence as to the value of the Government's service. It occurred to him that it would be rather serious for Canada if Great Britain herself prepared for her own and their defence in this manner, if she put a few trawlers on the Atlantic to watch the fish, and put a few boys into their armouries as a sort of diversion. "If she took that course," asked Mr. Meighen, "what would become of our defence in the hour of crisis and peril? Where would Britain be? Where would we be? No, she does not take that course; that indulgence is reserved for Canada. I am afraid the Minister's statement will be received with profound disappointment, if not with poignant humiliation, on the part of this country." The statement, he continued, made some comparison with what South Africa had done. He feared his comparison would not hold good very far. South Africa was a very small country in population and a very young country compared with Canada. He also compared them with Newfoundland. He did not doubt the comparison was likely a very good one in the measure of what they were doing. He had no doubt, too, that possibly Trinidad and maybe Bermuda would be appropriate comparison.

Resolution passed at Conference of Prime Ministers, 1921.

"So far as our freedom of action is concerned," said Mr. Meighen, "it stands to-day where it has always stood throughout our history. The position taken by this country last summer was embodied in a resolution agreed to unanimously by all the representatives of the nations of this Empire. It was a resolution which obviously expressed the right course, because the measure of Imperial Defence could not be known until the measure of world armaments would be dealt with by the Disarmament Conference. The Disarmament Conference is over, and now the time for determination of our policy has come. We are free to decide. This is the resolution that was passed :—

> That while recognising the necessity of co-operation among the various portions of the Empire to provide such naval defence as may prove to be essential for security, and while holding that equality with the naval strength of any other Power is the minimum standard for that purpose, this Conference is of the opinion that the method and expense of such co-operation are matters for the final determination of the several Parliaments concerned, and that any recommendation thereon should be deferred until after the coming Conference on Disarmament.

Mr. Shaw said he would like to know if that resolution was to be taken as implying a contribution to the Empire by Canada for naval purposes.

Mr. Meighen : " Not at all ; it is to be taken as implying just what it says."

The Prime Minister (**Hon. W. L. Mackenzie King**) drew attention to the address delivered by Lord Lee, the First Lord of the Admiralty, who was one of the British Delegates to the Washington Conference, before the Colonial Institute in London :—

> Lord Lee pointed out that the Imperial Conference after a full, prolonged and intimate discussion of the naval needs of the Empire, had agreed that the maintenance of an Empire Navy was the common concern of the whole Empire, and that the extent and form whereto the burden should be shared should be left until after the Washington Conference.

" Is my right hon. friend aware," asked the Prime Minister, " of any understanding arrived at at the Conference which he attended with respect to any obligation upon Canada in relation to an Empire Navy ? "

Mr. Meighen said Lord Lee was doubtless interpreting for himself the resolution. There was no agreement or understanding of any kind whatever save that embodied in the resolution.

Mr. E. M. Macdonald (**Liberal**, *Pictou*, *N.S.*) asked if proposals were not made by the British representatives at that time for a contribution from the Dominions ?

Mr. Meighen, in replying, said : " The Conference published its report, and I am bound to abide by it. These are the conclusions reached by it. I cannot go behind those conclusions until it is agreed that publicity can be given. The Government is in a position to obtain consent for such publicity. It has refused to try. . . ."

The Prime Minister : " I ask the right hon. gentleman the question as one of the representatives of Canada at the Imperial Conference. Is he aware, directly or indirectly, of any obligation resting upon the Government of this country as a consequence of the Conference which he attended with respect to naval defence other than what has already been approved of by this Parliament ? "

Mr. Meighen: " I am aware of none, and there is none arising from that Conference other than what appears in this document."

Mr. Macdonald said that Sir Robert Borden in his report had pointed out that the conclusions arrived at at Washington did not apply to the navies of the Oversea Dominions, because those navies were treated as being part of the entire naval defence of the Empire, and he instanced the fact that the cruiser *Australia*, one of the largest vessels of the Australian Navy, which played such a prominent part in the War, was to be scrapped. The report went on to say that the question of co-operation in the maintenance of the naval power which the British Empire as a whole was permitted to maintain stood exactly where it stood before the Conference, for the decision of the Parliaments of the Empire. The point which Mr. Macdonald wanted to make was that, as the time had arrived for a naval holiday by dismantling a good many ships in commission and stopping construction of others already laid down, participation of the Oversea Dominions in any scheme of Imperial Defence was left entirely untouched. It must therefore form the subject for the next Imperial Conference.

Mr. Meighen thought he had as good a right as any Member of the House to express the fullest sympathy with all the purposes of the Disarmament Conference. As to what might be the residuum of necessary defence for the Empire, after all that was done, and as to what might be their share therein, was another question. " I venture to suggest," added Mr. Meighen, " that he would be a remarkable Canadian who would find our share taken care of in an honourable way by the Estimates presented now, and by the proposals of the Minister."

Mr. Macdonald asked why they should not have a naval holiday, the same as every other country.

Mr. Meighen said that the Minister had made no reference whatever to waiting for another Imperial Conference ; he had announced his policy, such as it was.

Torpedo-boat destroyers ; submarines.

On 16th May,

The Minister of Naval Affairs, after proposing that the two torpedo-boat destroyers should be retained for training purposes, said that there were some, if he remembered the reports of the Disarmament Conference aright, who favoured the total abolition of the submarine in future warfare. In putting the submarines out of commission the Canadian Government was following the exact lead of the

British Admiralty, and its policy was in harmony with the official declarations of the British Government's representatives gathered together in conference with the great nations of the world.

Mr. Meighen asked whether, now that France and the other assembled nations at the Washington Conference had declined the British lead of abandoning the submarine, it was a fact that Great Britain had abandoned the submarine.

The Minister of Naval Affairs replied that he would not say that Great Britain had, but that did not affect the argument that the submarine had been declared by Great Britain not to be a success, either in attack or defence, except against merchant vessels.

Naval policy not final.

This proposal was not a finality on naval policy. While all countries of the world were wondering at the present time what policy they would finally adopt for attack and defence, Canada was proceeding along safe, sane, economical lines, and when the time came that a future policy was to be decided upon, they would have a foundation on which could be built a naval policy worthy of Canada, if the Parliament of Canada decided on development.

The Hon. Hugh Guthrie (Liberal-Conservative, *Wellington, S. Riding, Ont.*) said that the five ships (the gift of the Imperial Government) were in commission in the Canadian Naval Service, under their jurisdiction and their control, only forming a modest beginning for the purpose of training their young men, for the purpose of enabling them to do a little, or begin to do a little, of that which he thought they should do in regard to naval operations within the British Empire. They could not make a sailor by giving him two weeks' training a year for three years. It looked to him as if it were going to be a pure waste of money to spend a million and a half a year on a volunteer service such as described by his hon. friend.

Mr. William Duff (Liberal, *Lunenburg, N.S.*) did not hesitate to say that those ships had been absolutely useless for defensive purposes. His argument was that if they could not spend $100,000,000 a year in order to maintain a sufficient Navy on both oceans to be ready for any eventuality, which was absolutely improbable, then it was useless for them to spend $2,500,000 or $1,500,000 for the purpose of pretending that they had a Navy.

Labour attitude.

Mr. James S. Woodsworth (Labour, *Winnipeg, C., Man.*) said that some of them felt very strongly that they must not do anything whatever that would lead them into any sort of Imperialism or draw them into responsibility for doing something over which they had not absolute control. He would urge that they in Canada, very largely separated from other nations and freer in that respect to work out their own affairs than most of the nations, should begin at once to stop naval expenditure and to recognise that it was only by the cultivation of international good fellowship that they would obtain any security from external attack.

Admiralty Memorandum of 1918.

Mr. Meighen, in reviewing Canadian policy in regard to naval defence, stated that in 1918 the subject came before the Imperial Conference. The Admiralty presented a Memorandum setting out the great advantages from a strategical standpoint of a central Navy, and from an economic standpoint. The representatives of the Oversea Dominions, however, felt that there were difficulties in the way of accepting the Admiralty's conclusions, because of strong local feeling then existing, and, as a consequence, there was presented to that Conference, on behalf of the representatives of the Oversea Dominions, by Sir Robert Borden, Prime Minister of Canada, a Memorandum embodying the conclusions of those Ministers. (*Vide* JOURNAL, Vol. I., No. 3, p. 487.) The wise nation, declared Mr. Meighen, sought to the utmost of its powers compatible with its own safety, to reduce its weapons of defence and then to manfully carry the burden so reduced. That was the course which the Empire had pursued and of all the nations of this Empire there was none that had contributed more ardently and more effectively than Canada to help the Empire towards that end.

Canada's naval obligation.

As a consequence of the Disarmament Conference, they knew now the aggregate responsibility for naval defence that rested upon the British Empire. Therefore they were in possession of all the facts to determine what were the duties of the Dominion. While Canada was a growing nation they had made no effort whatever to assist in that form of defence. They had always recognised the obligation. They did not recognise it as a contractual obligation. They recognised it as a moral obligation binding upon them. They had now passed, said Mr. Meighen, every emergency that then threatened them, they were past imminent and great danger, for the time being, but that there was no possibility of any future danger surely those who confessed the truth would not contend. When they saw Britain taking upon herself the obligation she did; the United States, prior to that Conference, entering upon a squarely designed programme to surpass all the nations of the world; and France to-day insisting on an equality with Britain, bringing down a programme of naval construction and maintenance exceeding by $69,000,000 her programme of last year, it began to dawn upon them that they might be a little premature in concluding that the great new social order had arrived, and that the possibility of war had gone by. Feeling that they must commence some training, knowing what the other Dominions of the Empire were doing, knowing what the Mother Country was doing, they accepted from Great Britain a free gift, not of obsolete vessels at all, but of oil-burning vessels of the most modern type. That duty they fulfilled, abiding the day when they would know what the aggregate obligations of the Empire were. Now that time had come, and the Government of the day came to Parliament and said that their full duty under those aggregate obligations was to spend a million and one half dollars, to scrap one ship, to scrap the two submarines. "If," asked Mr. Meighen, "Britain passes below the one-Power standard and other nations in naval matters get ahead of her—these same nations being much stronger than she is in the matter of military organisation —then where has the security of this Empire gone? Consequently, she is determined that that one-Power standard must be maintained, with the acquiescence of every Dominion in this Empire, and to do it she binds her people to an annual taxation approximating $400,000,000."

Expenditure in other Dominions.

New Zealand, he pointed out, had been expending on naval defence $1,088,400 odd for a population of 1,200,000 people. Australia had been spending for purposes of the navy $14,000,000 odd, or at the rate of about $2.80 per capita. The proposals of this Government was to spend in Canada $1,500,000, or at the rate of 17 cents per capita. South Africa did not distribute between her naval defence and her other defences but her expenditure per capita for all defence was $5.55 as against Canada's for all purposes of $1.69, though the Union of South Africa was a far younger nation than they were. He thought the Minister was under pressure from certain sources in the country, under dictation from them, that compelled him to come down and present this miserable policy to the Parliament of Canada. "How can we stay and hold our heads up," asked Mr. Meighen in conclusion, "within the circle of the Empire and refuse to bear anything like a commensurate share of the cost of the Empire's defence as the other Dominions are doing? . . . There are those who say, 'Oh, we are in favour of British connection because of the traditions of Great Britain, because of this and that glory of Great Britain,' but who follow that by the assertion that we cannot pay any money in discharge of the responsibilities that undoubtedly are incident to British connections, responsibilities far less than we would have had to discharge if we stood independent as a nation, far less than the corresponding obligations would be as an independent nation. 'Oh,' they say, 'if we did anything in the way of assisting in national defence, that is Imperialism,' and they turn in holy scorn from the very thought of Imperialism as they describe it; but when they say, 'nevertheless though we do not do anything, we want British connection,' they call that loyalty. That definition of loyalty I do not understand. . . . I do not think there are any anyway who would not acknowledge that their (Great Britain's) responsibility per capita is justly greater than ours, but surely on the other hand no one will urge that 17 cents per capita for the Canadian people is fair assistance on our part, when the burden resting on England is something like $10 a head for the people of that country."

Naval Service Act and Liberal policy.

The Prime Minister, in referring to the Naval Service Act of 1910, said that it had in view four main objectives. The first was the provision for a Department of Naval Service. The second made provision for a Naval Reserve Force. The third made provision for the organising and maintaining of a force to be called the Naval Volunteer Force. The fourth provision was that in times of emergency the naval service and the members of the naval forces might be placed by the Governor in Council at the disposal of the British Admiralty. "That law," declared the Prime Minister, "embodies the Liberal policy as it was stated at that time, and as we are standing for it to-day." Although the Conservative Party came into power in 1911, and had before them the tenders for various ships, they refused to award a single contract. That was how much attention they paid to naval service and how much they believed in the existence of any emergency. The position the Liberal Party maintained consistently from 1910 until the moment of the War was that Canada should construct fleet units on the Atlantic and on the Pacific, and should do so just as speedily as possible; that there was legislation on the Statutes to enable any Government to do what it pleased in the way of constructing capital ships and to use them as they wished. Had this policy been carried out, there would have been a very different story when the War came on as to the part played by Canada's naval service. The Liberal Party had never wavered in that policy; and some day that policy would become the pride of Canada and of the Party that inaugurated it.

Question for future Imperial Conference.

"We take the position," said the Prime Minister, "that was taken by the Minister of Marine at that time, that there are heavy financial commitments of which this country and this Parliament have to take account, that Great Britain has not yet fully decided on her policy, and that an Imperial Conference is to be held at which the question of naval defence will come up for discussion between the Home Government and the Overseas Dominions. Hon. Members opposite have always contended that we should wait until there has been an Imperial Conference before taking any steps that committed this Parliament very far in the matter of naval expenditure. I think they are right in that. I think they are sound in their view that naval policy, so far as this country is concerned, should have, as one factor meriting consideration, the matter of possible co-operation with the other British Dominions and with the United Kingdom in the event of any great and serious danger arising. Possible co-operation, I say, but thus far, in regard to the question of existing naval armaments, there has been no Imperial Conference held since the War."

Speaking of the five ships presented by the British Government, the Prime Minister said that there were more urgent matters; there were demands for their money to-day greater than any that came within the circumference of this particular contribution for naval purposes. Not only was Canada placed under an obligation by the late Government through forcing these expenditures on the country against its will, but they found that the Members of the British House took exception to the gifts being made without the Parliament of Great Britain having been consulted. Was that the way to bring the British Empire closer together? Was that the way to work out an effective naval scheme of co-operation—a surreptitious method which caused the Parliaments of both countries to take exception to a course of action which owed its origin to their not having been consulted in the matter at all?

Interpretation of Resolution of 1921.

The Prime Minister then referred to the Resolution adopted by the Conference of Premiers in 1921 (*vide* p. 583) and said that if it had any meaning other than reference to co-operation as the word was used in the Canadian Naval Service Act, he would not accept the further meaning. If it implied an obligation beyond that which Parliament itself had been ready to assume in the matter of national defence, then he contended it went beyond rights or powers which the Leader of the Government of the day had any right to assume in giving assent to the resolution. The Government of to-day proposed to accept Mr. Meighen's interpretation of his action while at the Conference, and not to recognise any obligation which might directly or indirectly have been made as respected Canada implying military or naval expenditure beyond what had already been agreed to before his right hon. friend attended the Conference.

Mr. Meighen: "As I have stated, the Resolution could not be worded more clearly. It means precisely what it says. It places no obligation upon us at all. It clearly says that what we do, in point of character and in point of amount, is for us to say. Any obligation we are under is bounded only by our sense of duty and right and honour in the Empire.'"

The Prime Minister said in regard to the submarines, that they did not feel justified, in view of the opinion expressed to the world in the British Memorandum, in having as part of their policy the maintenance of submarines.

Canada's obligations.

"In conclusion," said the Prime Minister, "let me say that the Government is quite as sensible as any of its predecessors of the obligation that rests upon this country as a nation and as part of the British Empire. It is fully cognisant of its obligation of service on land and sea, and its obligations, moral and otherwise, in every other respect. But we feel that every obligation can be rightly discharged only in the light of conditions as they exist, and the conditions to-day are entirely different throughout the world, and in our own country in particular, from those that prevailed prior to the War. . . . The German Navy has been completely destroyed. What menace is there at the present time that threatens any part of the British Empire on sea? Does my right hon. friend think that Canada, or Great Britain, or any other part of the British Empire is going to be attacked by the United States, by France, or by Japan? These countries have recently entered into a solemn agreement together with Great Britain for the very purpose of helping to obviate the possibility of war arising between them. . . . I think the Government is justified in taking . . . . very much into account the changed conditions of the world to-day, and, in addition to that, the changed condition of our own Treasury and the way in which these matters are likely to be viewed by the taxpayers of the country. We can build up the British Empire in no better way than by helping to make a united, a contented, and a happy people . . . . If we are ever to have retrenchment in military and naval expenditure this is the one moment in which it is possible to bring about something of that character. The Government regards that as its first duty, its first obligation. It is sensible of all its larger duties and obligations, but it feels that it will best serve the interests of the British Empire as a whole when it helps to enlist, in the matter of defence, whether on land or sea, the sympathies of all our citizens throughout the Dominion, rather than antagonise their just sentiments by experiments of different kinds which will only tend to increase taxation and render no effective service in the long run."

Cost of efficient Navy.

Mr. Meighen said that Mr. Duff argued, and argued rightly, that if they had, in an independent sense, to protect their own shores and to develop in Canada a Navy which in itself was sufficient for their defence, they would need to spend $200,000,000.

Mr. Duff: "$100,000,000."

Mr. Meighen: "Very well. But as part and parcel of the British Empire, as an autonomous nation within it, we occupy a more fortunate position; the real value of the great League of Nations of the British Empire is that by co-operation we can secure that defence at a much lower cost. But we cannot have co-operation unless there is among the various nations of the Empire a sense of the individual duty of each nation and some honest attempt to discharge that duty."

Mr. Duff wanted to know how much the Leader of the Opposition thought the people of Canada should spend in 1922 on naval defence.

Mr. Meighen: "I would certainly maintain the operation of what we have. . . . Last year it cost $2,500,000. . . . I say one manifest thing: Outside of Great Britain, for Great Britain is not the only country in the Empire, we cannot stand squarely in front of our fellow citizens of other Dominions and say that we are bearing our fair share of the burden under the conditions of to-day."

On 22nd May,

Mr. Meighen agreed that they had more debt than they had before the War. But was the British debt per capita not two to three times what theirs was per capita and British natural resources very much less? Australia's debt would run, he thought, about three or four per capita to theirs, and New Zealand the same. But they found all these countries maintaining naval services on a scale far transcending theirs—by hundreds of per cent. Then the question came: Were the Mother Country and Sister Dominions going anywhere at all beyond the margin of safety itself? They were striving to maintain a one-Power standard as the aggregate Naval strength of the British Empire. They (Canada) were in effect saying this: We don't throw down the burden of defence, we just lay it on somebody else; we just expect "Tommy Atkins" and the "Weary Titan" to carry it. We expect our Australian brother and our New Zealand brother to carry it.

New scheme the most acceptable.

The Minister of Naval Affairs said that if the cost were the same under the scheme that had existed and under the one now proposed by the Government, he would suggest to Parliament to accept the new scheme, because he believed it gave a broader opportunity for doing the thing that Canada in years to come would probably have to do, and for launching on a permanent naval policy.

Mr. Meighen declared that the words of the Prime Minister of Great Britain* were as true as human lips ever uttered. His voice in world's Conferences and among the Powers of the world counted for as much as the muscle behind it as represented in the British Navy.

Attitude of National Progressive Party.

Mr. John Evans (National Progressive, *Saskatoon, Sask.*) was of opinion that they did not want to make Canada a military nation, but she had an obligation to fulfil. He believed that they might well cut some millions off other Estimates rather than be too scant on this one.

The Hon. T. A. Crerar (Leader of the National Progressive Party) supported the reduction made by the Minister of Militia. His regret was that the Minister did not stick to the first programme he laid down, because he thought the second programme involved a further expenditure of money which at the present time the country was not in a position to face. He ventured the prediction that the Minister of Finance, if he discharged his duty to Canada, must find additional taxation; there was no way out if Canada was to meet its obligations. In the face of that situation, were his hon. friends on good ground in arguing that they must spend a million Dollars more on the Navy that year? Mr. Duff had made what was, to his mind, the most sensible suggestion that had been heard in this debate, namely, that if they were going into the naval business they should go into it in earnest and quit playing with it. He thought Canada could well take a naval holiday for five years. "We discovered during the late War," declared Mr. Crerar, "that food, for instance, was just as vital a thing in the waging of war as were munitions and ships. And what has Canada done in that respect? It is not a fair comparison to put Canada on even keel with Great Britain in the matter of these expenditures. We have spent hundreds of millions of Dollars in the building of railways and in the opening up of new country; and every time we built a mile of railway, every time we opened up new parts of this country and brought additional areas under cultivation; every time we contributed to the material wealth of this country, we were adding to the strength of the Empire."

After some further discussion, the item was agreed to.

---

* The words referred to were quoted in the course of the Debate as follows: "My word in Conference is as strong and efficacious as is the muscle represented by the British Navy."

MILITIA ESTIMATES.

On 25th April and subsequent dates the House of Commons in Committee of Supply discussed the various items of the Militia Estimates.

DEBATE IN HOUSE OF COMMONS.

The Minister of Militia, Defence and Naval Affairs (Hon. G. P. Graham) said that not a few of the Members of the British House of Commons and some members of the British Cabinet had opposed Canada being allowed to have control of her Militia, because it was feared it would tend to encourage the idea of too great independence and would weaken the tie that bound them to the Motherland. That fear had been dispelled because the principle enunciated by Lord Grey in 1851 had been fully borne out by subsequent history, namely, that the greater the responsibility they placed on what might be called the subordinate body, the stronger became the attachment to the head. The greater freedom they had to manage their own affairs, the stronger did they grow as one of the great self-governing Dominions of the British Empire.

Were they to have a Militia, and was that Militia to be kept at proper strength ? The answer could only be in the affirmative if they were a self-respecting nation. They must have a permanent militia force, as well as a volunteer force, for conditions that might arise within their own borders. At the present time this force was composed of 3,800 officers and men, and was a very small force indeed to cope with emergencies throughout such a vast country. If they were to realise their aspirations they must accept the responsibilities that went with those aspirations and be prepared to carry on their share of defence work as part of the British Empire, and that share, so far as the militia was concerned, was provided for in the estimates he was now presenting. The estimates were being decreased. When the reorganisation was completed the reduction in the permanent force would be in the vicinity of 400 or 500 all told. The volunteer force was exactly the same this year as last, but they had reduced the amount for annual drill by $100,000.

The Hon. Hugh Guthrie (Liberal-Conservative, *Waterloo, S. Riding, Ont.*) did not believe that if they were going to maintain a militia force that was to be of any practical use, the Minister could cut very much below the figure he had submitted to the House. Comparison showed that Canada was a long way below the lowest of any country of the globe in all classes of expenditure on armaments—so far below the lowest that he was almost ashamed to make the comparison.

Mr. William Duff (**Liberal**, *Lunenburg, N.S.*) congratulated the Minister upon reducing the total Estimate from something over $11,954,000 to $10,788,000, but he thought in the present condition of affairs in Canada, in future this expenditure could be greatly reduced. It seemed to him that the estimate for annual drill ($1,400,000) should not be spent this year at least.

Mr. J. S. Woodsworth (**Labour**, *Winnipeg, C., Man.*) said that he should like to challenge the implication that in order that they might become a self-sufficient nation it was necessary for them to maintain a military force. The best way to bring about international disarmament was by national disarmament. They in Canada were in a particularly good position to accomplish this.

The Minister of Militia explained that the vote for annual drill provided for the training of 60 per cent. of the force for nine days instead of sixteen, and the only criticism that he had heard so far was that the reduction had gone too far.

Gen. the Hon. S. C. Mewburn (**Liberal-Conservative**, *Hamilton, E. Riding, Ont.*) stated that the first contingent mobilised at Valcartier was composed, to the extent of over 98 per cent. of officers, non-commissioned officers and men of the active Militia. Now the active Militia were endeavouring to get on their feet once more. The annual allowance for training was the only means by which these units could rehabilitate themselves.

Mr. C. G. Power (**Liberal**, *Quebec, S.*) moved that the item of $1,400,000 for annual drill should be reduced by $1,100,000.

The Minister of Militia stated that he had put the question squarely to his Chief of Staff, General McBrien : " If we cut out our military training for one year what effect would it have ? " He said : " The effect would be disastrous on any attempt to maintain an organisation of voluntary Militia throughout the Dominion of Canada." Did they propose, as a young nation, to shirk the responsibilities of a nation while asking for all the privileges ? They asked for a seat in the Genoa Conference ; they asked for a seat at the Disarmament Conference at Washington ; they asked for a seat at the meeting of the League of Nations ; they asked to be allowed to take part in the formulation of the Versailles Treaty ; and now when the time came that they should maintain their position as a young nation, were they going to shirk, and go back one hundred and fifty years and become Crown Colonists to be looked after by Great Britain and not by themselves ?

On 9th May,

The Minister of Militia proposed a reduction of $400,000 on annual drill and a total reduction on the Estimates of

$700,000. He said that if the reduction on annual drill was made, the artillery could be trained, city corps, and possibly a portion of the country units.

The Minister of Marine and Fisheries (Hon. Ernest Lapointe) consequently moved an amendment to Mr. Power's amendment in accordance with the Minister's proposals.

Gen. Mewburn said that, after the Minister of a Department, who had prepared his Estimates after consultation with his technical officers and had had those Estimates considered by the Privy Council and approved by them, had presented them to the House and moved their adoption, they had witnessed the extraordinary spectacle of the Estimates being attacked by one of the Minister's own supporters, and being supported by the Opposition. He regretted exceedingly that the Minister had taken anything off the item of " training." In Canada they had not got what was known as a " standing Army." The permanent force was organised for instructional purposes for the Militia of Canada. He believed the permanent force could be used to greater advantage, and in certain military districts in Canada a very considerable saving could be made.

Mr. A. E. Ross (Liberal-Conservative, *Kingston, Ont.*) pointed out that Australia was expending both on military and naval training approximately $24,000,000, while Canada, with almost double the population, was expending only $13,490,000. South Africa had her own unique system of defence. She had the first, second and third lines of defence and upon them she was expending $1,500,000.

The Hon. T. A. Crerar (Leader of National Progressive Party) declared that he would have been gratified if the reduction were greater than it was.

Mr. T. L. Church (Liberal-Conservative, *Toronto, N., Ont.*) said that when he read the debate which had taken place in the Australian Parliament, it seemed almost a repetition of what happened in the Canadian House. Mr. Hughes, the Australian Premier, took very strong ground against reduction. He declared that the Government was responsible for the defence of the country and if there was any reduction he declined to be responsible—the Country Party would have to be responsible for it. The Country Party put up a strong fight, but the Prime Minister of Australia stood by his guns, and the Commonwealth Parliament backed the Hughes Government up.

Mr. William Irvine (Labour, *Calgary, E., Alta.*) said that the desire to seek safety in military preparation made no attempt whatever to deal with the causes of war, and they could not expect to have anything else but war if they permitted the causes to run rampant. He was opposed to this estimate. He was in sympathy with the expressed opinion of organised labour, not only in Canada, but in the United Kingdom, when he said that they looked forward to complete disarmament and would take every step possible to achieve that end.

The Right Hon. Arthur Meighen (Leader of the Opposition) declared that a nation, if it was going to be a nation at all, must just the same as an individual be in a position to take care of itself, both internally against disorder and revolutionary insolence, and externally against aggression. While everyone hoped that there would be no more great wars, he did not think the sensible people of the world were of opinion that the British Empire and other nations of like character were going to hasten that time merely by themselves disarming. " It is for those nations," said Mr. Meighen, " that undoubtedly have no militaristic purposes, that undoubtedly are not animated by sentiments of revenge or by ambitions of conquest, to stand together in a world policy, endeavour to bring other nations into line with themselves, and all as one group be in a position to make their policy and their pacific purposes reign. . . . I do not need to name the nations that are of that temperament . . . that undoubtedly are peace-loving people, but I have not the least hesitation in naming two, and I name the United States of America, and the British Empire, inclusive of all her Dominions." Who was there, he continued, who had any feeling for that Empire at all, who would dare to suggest at this hour that Great Britain throw down her arms and place herself in the position when her word in the councils of Europe and in the councils of the world would mean nothing at all. Such being the case, surely it followed that they, as an integral part of the British Empire, must maintain a fair share and proportion of that means of defence which all the Empire must sustain. Let them never forget that if any portion of the Empire of which they were a part was in peril, it could not be long before that peril was equally right there in Canada. Surely the War taught them that the British Empire could be maintained only to the extent it stood united and that they were secure there as a part of that Empire only to the extent that the whole Empire was secure.

In the judgment of the Minister, the Militia Estimates had been pared down to a point as low as was compatible with national safety. They were now asked to take $400,000 off the appropriation for annual drill and to take corresponding amounts off other services deemed essential, not only by the expert advisers of Canada, but by the Minister of Militia, by the Government itself. They were cutting those services down to 66 or 70 per cent. of the figure which they asserted was the point of safety. He stood by the Estimates as they were.

Mr. A. R. McMaster (**Liberal**, *Brome, Que.*) said that if Great Britain and the United States, more especially the former, would abandon militaristic adventures here and there and everywhere all over the world, the amount of force which they would be obliged to maintain would be very much less than it was now. There was one great outstanding feature in the present European situation which bade them hope, and that was that these two great nations which had been ostracised from European society ever since the War now had their representatives at the council table at Genoa, because there could be no real European accommodation and, therefore, no real world accommodation as long as Germany and Russia were kept out of the society of nations. The world situation was better than it had been two years ago, because at that time there was a danger of naval competition between the United States and Great Britain.

But, said the Leader of the Opposition, some other part of the Empire might get into trouble and that might bring trouble home to them. He disagreed most heartily with that interpretation of the responsibilities of Canada. The Leader of the Opposition at the Conference in London apparently committed Canada, to a certain extent at least, to a different attitude, but so far as he did so he departed from the traditional attitude which Sir Wilfrid Laurier led Canada to adopt, namely, that as long as they flew the flag they were liable to attack, but so far as participation in war was concerned, that was a matter for the Canadian people to decide through their elected representatives.

Mr. McMaster, after stating that according to what Mr. Lloyd George said there grew out of the Imperial Conference a solidarity of responsibility which before that time had not been admitted, asked whether there was anything unfair in his deduction that if a part of the Empire got into war, under this joint responsibility the other parts would have to come to their assistance. He thought that was a very unwise and dangerous policy for Canada to follow.

Mr. Meighen: "Does the hon. Member suggest that at previous Conferences, under Liberal Governments, there were no joint councils and discussions on matters of foreign policy of the Empire?"

Mr. McMaster: "I say there was not. I say that Sir Wilfrid Laurier took the position that he would not be informed as to the foreign policy of Great Britain, because if he was given information there might be an implication of honour that having received the information, and not having protested, he would be liable to support the foreign policy which might eventuate from those facts."

After further discussion, Mr. Lapointe's amendment to the amendment was agreed to.

AIR ESTIMATES.

On 12th May the House of Commons in Committee of Supply discussed the Air Estimates, amounting to $1,000,000.

DEBATE IN HOUSE OF COMMONS.

The Minister of Militia, Defence and Naval Affairs (Hon. G. P. Graham) said that civil aviation consisted almost altogether of work done for the other Departments such as fire ranging, work done for other Provinces, and survey work. It was an experiment in collaboration with the Provinces. The Imperial authorities had presented to the Federal Government five million dollars' worth of aviation equipment. This year they had informed the Provinces, as well as the other Departments of the Dominion Government, that, if they wanted work done, they would be glad to undertake it provided they paid the cost of doing it. The Air Force was comparatively small and must, for a few years at least, be in a merely experimental state. Consequently, it, and the Militia Department, were being brought under the Department of National Defence. There had been a considerable difference of opinion, and not without reason, as to whether it was better to keep the Air Force outside the military branch than to bring it into the Department of National Defence. If they had a large organisation and anticipated a great development in the Air Force, it might be as well to leave it by itself, but he took it for granted that they were not in a position to develop any considerable organisation just now in Canada. Furthermore, when civil aviation had reached a certain point in its development, private companies would largely undertake this work. He believed that the Dominion was not prepared to enter upon any large scheme of Government-owned and operated civil aviation services. They hoped this year to carry on all the civil aviation work they did last year.

The Right Hon. Arthur Meighen (Leader of the Opposition) said that the work was almost wholly experimental and undoubtedly could be done better by the Dominion Government in co-operation with the Provinces than it ever could be done by the Provinces themselves, each acting on its own initiative. He had some confidence that very considerable results would be achieved in the matter of forest fire protection ; in regard to survey work in the Interior and other departments, although he was not sure that it had yet reached the point where it may be described as being a success, it had not yet been brought to the point where failure was evident.

Mr. E. J. Garland (**National Progressive**, *Bow River, Alta.*) stated he had had letters from the Boards of Trade protesting against any diminution on the part of the Federal Government of its activities in this matter.

The Hon. Hugh Guthrie (**Liberal-Conservative,** *Wellington, S. Riding, Ont.*) stated that last year the Air Board performed services for the Department of Marine and Fisheries ; coastal patrols to prevent poaching and fishing out of the season ; transportation of spawn ; rapid transportation to inaccessible points in British Columbia. Certain work was performed for the Department of Agriculture : securing vertical and oblique photographs of mosquito-infested areas in proximity to Vancouver ; for the Department of the Interior : oblique photographs of deltas, lakes, etc., for map purposes ; also forest fire protection work, forest reconnaissance and inspection of burnt areas from the air. All that work was charged to the Air Board so that the people knew what the cost was. Now the Minister proposed to charge it to the Department of the Interior and no one would know what the Air Board cost. Last year the Air Board did work for the Department of Customs : patrols to prevent smuggling of drugs from the East into Canada. The Air Service was now a very important item in the Budget of every country ; last year the Vote for this purpose in the United States was $95,000,000 ; in Great Britain the amount spent was tremendous ; Australia and New Zealand had made their first expenditure in air services, and he thought that every civilised nation had done likewise. They should know what the Air Board was costing Canada.

Mr. Guthrie asked whether the Air Board was to be a separate branch of the Defence Department, and if so, who was to be the presiding genius and what assistance would he have ?

The Minister of Militia said that the Air Board would be an integral part of the Department of Defence. All the technical officers and men of the staff would be taken into the new Department of Defence. They would have a Director of Aviation and perhaps one or two assistants. They believed that when they got the Department properly organised they could perform the essential service that they did last year at much less expense. They were cutting out at the present time training at Camp Borden, but hoped that they would have the Instruction School at Camp Borden later on. They were undertaking to carry on the work with a reduction of $625,000.

Mr. Donald Sutherland (**Liberal-Conservative,** *Oxford, S. Riding, Ont.*) said that the Air Service was one that the majority of people were inclined to underestimate, and at the Conference which took place at Washington some time ago between the great Powers one might have observed how readily the Disarmament proposals that were made were being accepted by some of those countries, and, at the same time, the notion came out, and it was undoubtedly the view of many of those countries, that the Air Force was going to be a much more prominent feature of warfare in the future than it had ever been in the past, and that possibly some of those naval armaments would not be so invulnerable as they had been in the past, and might possibly be a handicap. As far as he could understand from the Minister's explanation, the Air Force as a defensive force was practically going to cease to exist; the civil aviation was going to be continued if some arrangement could be made with the Provinces to employ those people who would be under the Department of National Defence purely as a civil Force; and the services of those men who had attained such wonderful experience and training during the War would be dispensed with. It was essential that a number of these highly-trained experts should be retained so that Canada might benefit from the valuable experience which they had gained from the services they rendered to Canada instead of allowing this to become a purely civil force.

The Minister of Militia said that practically all the aviators engaged in forest protection work were members of the Defence Force. This work was for civil purposes, but it gave, if possible, the best training they could get. For instance, flying over the forests photographing the ground beneath was just the work they would be doing on the battlefield.

Mr. L. H. Jelliff (**National Progressive,** *Lethbridge, Alta.*) said they were very insistent in their part of the country on the patrol system being maintained at the fullest possible pitch and even extended.

Mr. Sutherland suggested to the Minister the advisability of letting this Vote stand over until they had some definition of what "national defence" really was. If national defence in the future was to consist of an Air Force for forest ranging and the detection of smugglers, he thought the House should know it. To his mind, national defence had an entirely different meaning from that of civil aviation for the purposes which had been outlined. They were dragging the service into the mire when they utilised it to detect smugglers and forest fires. The prevention of smuggling was essentially a work for the naval service, one for the ships which were to be returned to the Motherland with the compliments of the Government of Canada.

The Minister of Militia said the amount for civil aviation would be approximately $473,000 odd; the balance would be for military training at Camp Borden by their instructors and the replacement of and procuring of material and equipment.

After further discussion, the item was agreed to.

IMMIGRATION OF ORIENTAL ALIENS.

(Reasons for exclusion; Immigration restrictions; Natal Act; Policy of other Dominions; Indian immigration; Head tax; Japanese Trade Treaty; Dominion power of control.)

On 8th May the House of Commons discussed the following resolution:—

> That in the opinion of this House the immigration of Oriental aliens and their rapid multiplication is becoming a serious menace to living conditions, particularly on the Pacific coast, and to the future of the country in general, and the Government should take immediate action to secure the exclusion of future immigration of this type.

DEBATE IN HOUSE OF COMMONS.

Mr. W. G. McQuarrie (Liberal-Conservative, *New Westminster, B.C.*), in moving the resolution, said that it did not include British subjects such as, for instance, East Indians. It was to prevent the increase by direct immigration of an element in their population which was not only undesirable but dangerous to Canadian interests.

Chinese and Japanese immigration.

Discussing the condition of Canadian immigration laws, Mr. McQuarrie, said that in respect to the Chinese they had an open field: there was no treaty or arrangement of any kind between Great Britain and China dealing with the matter. The different Governments which had been in power had only adopted a policy of restriction so far as Chinese immigration was concerned. In 1885 a head tax of $50 was imposed; in 1901 that tax was doubled and in 1904 it was increased to $500. In 1919 an Order in Council was passed which prohibited the entry into Canada at certain ports in British Columbia of skilled and unskilled labour and that Order in Council applied to the Chinese as well as other classes. Notwithstanding, the Chinese still continued to come into the country.

In regard to the Japanese, there was a treaty, known as the Treaty of Commerce and Navigation between the United Kingdom and Japan, signed at London, 3rd April, 1911. That Treaty provided, among other things, that:—

> The subjects of each of the High Contracting Parties shall have full liberty to enter, travel and reside in the territories of the other and, conforming themselves to the laws of the country, shall in all that relates to travel and residence be placed in all respects on the same footing as native subjects. They shall have the right equally with native subjects to carry on their commerce and manufactures and to trade in all kinds of merchandise of lawful commerce either in person, or by agents, singly or in partnership with foreigners and/or native subjects. They shall in all that relates to the pursuit of their industries, callings, professions and educational status be placed in all respects on the same footing as the subjects or citizens of the most favoured nation.

That Treaty was assented to by Canada in 1913, and was to remain in force till 16th July, 1923. It prevented the Legislatures of the various Provinces from enacting what might be termed discriminatory legislation. He submitted that a request should be made to the British Government that notice should be given to Japan to terminate the Treaty in July of next year. That notice could be given by Great Britain on behalf of Canada without reference to other parts of the Empire involved in the Treaty.

Instead of having the $500 head tax, they should have exclusion altogether of Chinese immigration to Canada.

The Japanese were very fond of protesting against discrimination by Canadians against their people. It might be very interesting to look at the situation so far as Canadians in Japan were concerned. Canadians could not, as individuals, hold land in Japan and might not become owners of ships flying the Japanese flag, and might not as individuals engage in mining.

Oriental population in Canada.

They might assume that they had a total of about 57,133 Chinese in Canada at the present time. The Chinese population of Canada had doubled in the last ten years. They had at least 16,311 Japanese in the country. The Japanese birth rate in British Columbia was very alarming. The demand for exclusion was not limited to the Province of British Columbia but was general and Dominion-wide. In California there was a Japanese population of approximately 100,000 and with the alarming birth rate the situation was very serious.

Reasons for exclusion.

Mr. McQuarrie gave the following reasons why Orientals should be excluded from Canada: (1) They could not be assimilated; (2) their peaceful penetration would eventually lead to racial conflict and international unpleasantness; (3) their standards of living were lower than those of Canadians; (4) their people could not compete with the Japanese and Chinese in certain lines; (5) unemployment would be increased; (6) they were responsible to a certain extent for the drug traffic; (7) they could not become good Canadians because of their dual citizenship; and (8) it was desirable that they should have a " white " Canada.

His answer to the question what should be done was threefold: (1) The Japanese Treaty should be abrogated so far as Canada was concerned; (2) the " Gentlemen's Agreement " (Lemieux Agreement entered into between Canada and Japan in 1908 under which Japan voluntarily restricts the movement of Japanese to Canada to a comparatively small number each year), should be cancelled; (3) the immigration Act should be amended so as to provide for exclusion.

Mr. Alfred Stork (Liberal, *Skeena, B.C.*), said this was a question which very vitally affected the Province of British Columbia. He believed that it was good policy to settle this Oriental problem with the Oriental while the white population was still in possession of the Province of British Columbia rather than to defer settlement of the issue until the time when the Oriental himself was in full and complete possession of that great Province. They found themselves to-day confronted with the silent and steady absorption of the Province of British Columbia by Orientals. Experience had shown that the Japanese were the very incarnation of commercial aggressiveness. The Japanese was the human Terido so far as the organisation of human labour was concerned, because he had created an industrial strata into which the white man could not descend. Unless they dealt with this matter, they were parting with the Province of British Columbia just as effectually as if they gave British Columbia away by signing a treaty.

Mr. W. T. Lucas (National Progressive, *Victoria, Alta.*), in seconding the Motion, said that the time was fast approaching when they on the prairies were going to be confronted with the keen competition of the Oriental. They found the Chinese engaged in the drug traffic which was demoralising the standards of their people.

Mr. George Black (Liberal-Conservative, *Yukon*) declared that countless whites, young men and young women, were being mentally and physically ruined by their contact with these Orientals. Canada wanted settlers, but she only wanted settlers who would adopt Canadian and British ideals, people who would become Canadians; but Asiatics were not of those races, with them naturalisation was nothing more or less than a farce.

A national issue.

Mr. L. W. Humphrey (National Progressive, *Kootenay W., B.C.*) said that the movement eastwards of the Orientals of recent years had been brought home to them with such force as to make them realise that it was not a local question, not even a merely provincial matter, but a national issue with which the Federal authorities must deal. After the War they found that Orientals had secured greater control of their natural resources and had improved their position to such an extent that they were better off financially than the average citizen of British Columbia. He believed they could attribute the unemployment situation to a certain extent to the laxity of their laws in connection with the increase in population of Chinese and Japanese.

Immigration restrictions.

Mr. A. W. Neill (National Progressive, *Comox-Alberni, B.C.*) said that in Canada they allowed aliens of brown or yellow race to be naturalised, to their everlasting regret. An Order in Council stated that immigration of labourers of any kind into certain parts of British Columbia was prohibited owing to lack of employment. That applied as well to the British as to the Oriental. The Immigration Department stated :—

> All Japanese entering Canada are subject to all the provisions of the Immigration Act, with the exception of such provisions as would conflict with the Lemieux Agreement.

Therefore, as regarded the 400 people (under the Lemieux Agreement), they could not exclude them while they were at the present moment restricting immigration of British subjects. The principle was this, that they absolutely prohibited British immigration and then they said that they could not prohibit Japanese immigration.

The Hon. H. H. Stevens (Liberal-Conservative, *Vancouver, C., B.C.*) declared that he treated this as a sociological and ethical and essentially an economic problem. Let them visualise what it would mean if there was even a tremor of immigration unrestricted from such a prolific source of supply as the population of 800 millions to a country the total population of which was eight millions.

Slave system and labour.

Wherever the white man was brought into competition with the Asiatic, the standard of living must be reduced or there was no possibility of successful competition. First in regard to the Chinese. They had in Canada a veritable slave system; Chinese syndicates brought into Canada large numbers of natives, paid their $500 head tax, their passage, their expenses. These Chinamen so brought into Canada remained the bondmen of that syndicate until they had paid off not only every dollar of that expense money, but usurious interest as well. In any community of which a large section consisted of Orientals it was noticeable that that community was a mighty poor market for their manufactured goods and for the white man's food. From other sections of the country there were those who suggested the importation of Asiatic labour in the form of indentured or contract labour. There was not a country in the world where indentured labour had been tried where it had not been found that the labour that was not indentured formed a very difficult problem in the country after the indenture had expired. Canada above all others was not a suitable country for indentured labour.

The Natal Act; Other Dominions.

He thought he could show to the Government that the argument against their position, because of Imperial reasons, was not a well-founded one. He held in the first place that it was the inherent right of Canada in common with all other countries to determine the conditions upon which anyone might be admitted within the bounds of the State. The British Columbian Legislature had passed an Act similar to the Natal Act, whereby they imposed the educational test. This Act was disallowed, but the argument was advanced that they must not deal with this question because of Imperial difficulties. The Imperial Government was officially on record twice in urging them to adopt the Natal Act. The Natal Act had been in force in Natal and in the other portions of what was now the Dominion of South Africa, in Australia and in New Zealand. It had been taken advantage of to restrict Oriental immigration. The Japanese Government in 1886, 1895 and 1913 had admitted their right to restrict their immigration if Canada so chose.

Japanese Alliance; British institutions and traditions.

It had been said that owing to the peculiar manner in which the British Empire was closely allied with Japan that nothing could be done by Canada that might in any way disturb the kindly relations between the two. Only a few months ago in Washington this dual responsibility was ended; Great Britain, France, the United States and Japan entered into a treaty that whenever questions arose of a perplexing or threatening nature, a conference would be held and a solution would be found. That pact of Washington removed from Great Britain a very serious anxiety. He took without reservation the position of exclusion. In Australia, New Zealand and South Africa there were large areas that were semi-tropical, in which perhaps there was some excuse for saying that these areas were not a white man's country, but no man on earth could say that Canada was not essentially, climatically and in every other way a white man's country.

"Shall Canada remain 'white,'" asked Mr. Stevens, "or shall Canada become parti-coloured? Shall British institutions, traditions, ethics and social standards prevail, or shall they by blind neglect and purposeless procrastination submit to a peaceful conquest by the forerunners of the hordes of Asia? Shall Canadianism, which we are always proud to picture as the perfection of British democracy, prevail or shall it recede before the races that are incongruous and incompatible with our mode of life? That is the problem before the House."

The Prime Minister (Hon. W. L. Mackenzie King) said that this was a question of great concern to all parts of the British Empire. "From the point of view of the maintenance of our social and industrial standards," declared the Prime Minister, "from the point of view of the desirability of maintaining a homogeneous population, and from the point of view of avoiding social and industrial unrest and the possibility of international strife . . . I believe strongly in the restriction of Oriental immigration and I think it is the duty of the Government to do all in its power to make that restriction as effective as it can be made, maintaining the goodwill, as far as it can be maintained, of all the peoples that go to make up the vast human family."

Indian immigration.

He thought that the mover of the resolution had very wisely made no mention of the immigration from India because there were special reasons which should incline them to take up that problem with the greatest possible care, but in the last analysis they must remember that the arguments which applied in the case of immigration from China and from Japan were applicable also when it came to matters of industrial competition by the population from India, and for that reason he thought that any position they took up on this question with respect to Japan and China should be regarded as being equally applicable to peoples from other parts of the Orient because they would have that question as well again to deal with sooner or later.

Head tax; Chinese students.

The number of Chinese coming into Canada despite the $500 head tax was very considerable. He would favour the elimination of this head tax altogether and the substitution of a method that would be not only less objectionable, but also more effective. In 1908 he had had the honour of representing Canada at an International Conference at Shanghai. Sir Wilfrid Laurier mentioned to him that it was his desire to do away with the head tax and bring about an arrangement with China whereby emigration from that country to Canada thereafter would be restricted by the adoption of a system of passports. He would like to say on behalf of the Government that they had already taken steps to resume negotiations looking to the restriction of Chinese immigration by a system of passports, the numbers of which the Canadian Government would control. He thought they should make an effort to encourage Chinese students to come to their universities. It was wholly to their advantage that Chinese students should come to Canada, that they should know something of Canadian conditions, and after returning to their country help to make Canadian conditions known to China.

Trade Treaty with Japan.

Mention had been made of the existing Trade Treaty with Japan and it had been suggested that the Government should give notice that twelve months hence the Treaty would be abolished. It might be that such was a wise and desirable course, but before it was taken the Government should consider very carefully the advantages which might thereby be lost. In the present Treaty he found the following clause :—

> Nothing in the said Treaty or in this Act shall be deemed to repeal or affect any of the provisions of the Immigration Act.

He submitted that by negotiation with the Japanese Government it would be possible to ascertain whether the Japanese Government had any objection to that clause being construed as applicable to the immigration laws of Canada. As they might be amended at any time, he was inclined to take that view, but if they should not do this, he thought it would be time to consider whether in the national interest that Treaty should be abrogated. A further step that was suggested was that they should abolish what was called the "Gentleman's Agreement" now existing between Japan and Canada. They had to consider to what extent the prevention of further immigration was likely to be effectively brought about by the abolition of an agreement to which at the present time the Japanese Government was a party and which he believed the Japanese Government had adhered to loyally. He did not think, unless they were very sure of their ground, that they would help to solve this question by imputing any wrong motive to the Government of another country, particularly a country which had been their ally for years, and which rendered Canada vast service at a very critical moment in the course of the last few years. He believed this would only be solved by the Governments of the two countries working together with the one motive of bringing about an effective solution.

Policy of the Dominions: "effective restriction" or "exclusion."

The word "exclusion" in regard to these matters of immigration had come to have a meaning that to peoples of the Orient was most offensive. There was not to-day as regarded any part of the British Empire—South Africa, Australia, New Zealand, or any other part—any Exclusion Act so termed, nor did he know of any Exclusion Act on the part of any nation in the world. He might point out that in 1901 when Australia adopted what was termed the "Natal Act" she applied an educational test. In 1905 the Government of Australia agreed to admit by passport into that country tourists, merchants, students and other classes, the Minister of External Affairs of the Commonwealth undertaking to control the number of passports that were being issued. The same thing was true of New Zealand and South Africa. He contended that the House would make a great mistake if it took a course which, after great care and thought, no other part of the Empire had thus far taken. If his hon. friend was prepared to substitute the words "effective restriction" for the word "exclusion" in his resolution, he would on behalf of the Government agree to accept his resolution, but he would feel that the reasons he had mentioned were sufficiently grave as to constitute a justification for the Government not accepting the resolution in the form in which it had been moved.

The Right Hon. Arthur Meighen (Leader of the Opposition) said that the resolution had to do with the relations between the British Empire and the two great nations, China and Japan. There was a special reason as to both of them why they must be careful that the good relations now existing should continue. As to China, because they had been parties at the recent Disarmament Conference to action looking to the rehabilitation of that country and its elevation again to the front rank of nations. As to Japan, because the intimacy between the Empire of which they were a part and the Empire of Japan had been greater than it had been between that Empire and China. Japan had stood square with all the burdens of the Anglo-Japanese Alliance. He had not heard before that there was any cause of complaint over Japan's fidelity to the "Gentleman's Agreement."

Oriental population increasing.

Nevertheless, they knew that, both in the United States and in Canada, the numbers, by reason of the occupation, modes of life and the habits of the people, were alarming in view of the increase. The rate of propagation was such that in their own Province it appeared probable that the years would not be many before the births from those of Japanese origin in British Columbia would equal the births of the whites. The state of alarm existing in the Western States was at as high a peak as that which existed in their own Province. Was there anything else they could do besides deciding upon exclusion of immigrants ? The point then was to inquire what were the perils about going that length. He recalled a resolution which was passed at a Conference which he attended last summer and in which it was distinctly affirmed that full and unrestricted control of immigration rested in the power of each Dominion of the Empire even as against the inhabitants of another Dominion or of India, and he did not think a stronger resolution on that subject could be possible. There was effective exclusion in Australia and effective exclusion in New Zealand.

Dominion power of control.

The Prime Minister asked whether the word " exclusion " might not imply when the cable reached Japan that Parliament had enacted a resolution in favour of the exclusion of Japanese. It was that danger the Government was seeking to avoid.

Mr. Meighen held that they ought to be able to say without conditions that the time had come for effective exclusion of that class of people from their shores as residents in Canada. It was for the peace and concord of both that they should say to them frankly : " You can keep us from your country if you desire ; we must keep your people from becoming residents in our country ; and we will be better friends if we adopt that policy." Suppose they took that stand. It was quite open to the Government to bring about the result in the method adopted by Australia, but that was not effective restriction, that was effective exclusion. Change the resolution to read " effective restriction," and at once there was no authorisation to the Government to change the present law at all.

" Let it be understood," concluded Mr. Meighen, " that so far as I am concerned I favour exclusion. I think we must have it. I do not care how it is brought about, but I do think it has got to be brought about. Restriction will not do. It must be restriction of such an absolute character that it excludes. That is the position I take on this Motion."

An amendment.

The Minister of the Interior (Hon. Charles Stewart) said he was entirely in sympathy with the object of the resolution, but if that object was to be obtained they must be careful about the methods they employed. Would it not be better in the interests of all parties concerned to bring about the object aimed at without arousing the antagonism of the Japanese by the use of a word that without doubt must be offensive? He therefore moved:

That the word "exclusion" in the fifth line of the resolution be struck out and the words "effective restriction" be substituted therefor.

The Hon. T. A. Crerar (Leader of the National Progressive Party) said that he proposed to support Mr. Stewart's amendment. Under that amendment he thought it would be quite possible for the Government by friendly negotiations to secure almost precisely the same position that existed in South Africa, in New Zealand, in Australia.

Mr. J. S. Woodsworth (Labour, *Winnipeg, C., Man.*) declared that for years Labour had been pleading that something should be done to prevent unfair competition. It was as well that they should recognise very clearly that it was the big corporations and financial organisations that had been responsible for the Oriental immigration to Canada. If they were to maintain their trading and financial interests with other parts of the world, he could not see how they could adopt a rigid policy of exclusion. They claimed the right to go in and dominate India, and yet at the very same time refused to let the races of India come into Canada in any number at all. He was not pleading for permission for them to enter Canada, but they must have regard to the larger international issues.

After further discussion Mr. Stewart's amendment was carried by 130 to 36 votes.

IMMIGRATION OF ARTISANS.

On 29th May, in the House of Commons, on the Orders of the Day,

Mr. J. S. Woodsworth (Labour, *Winnipeg, C., Man.*) drew the attention of the Government to a despatch from London in *The Montreal Gazette* headed, "Many British artisans preparing to make their homes in Canada." He asked whether, in view of the fact that they had such a large volume of unemployment in Canada, there was any protection for the artisans in Canada.

The Minister of Labour (Hon. Charles Stewart) replied that it was true that the money qualification of $250 formerly exacted had been removed, but notwithstanding that fact care was being exercised by the officials of the Immigration Department to impress upon intending immigrants to Canada, who were looking for immediate employment, that no work in the artisan classes was available, but that there was abundant room for agricultural labourers, household workers, and others who were able to purchase land or had sufficient means to support themselves in Canada.

COOLIE LABOUR ON BRITISH SHIPS.

On 22nd May, in the House of Commons, on the Orders of the Day,

Mr. J. S. Woodsworth (Labour, *Winnipeg, C., Man.*) said that according to the official journal of the Marine Engineers of Canada, he noticed that British ships manned by coolie crews were engaged in coastwise port traffic on the Atlantic seaboard. In view of the discussion and the resolutions which were passed in the House on the Oriental question (*vide* p. 601), he should like to know if the Government would take steps to protect Canadian seamen against the unfair competition of coolie labour on board British ships engaged in coastwise trade.

The Minister of Marine and Fisheries (Hon. Ernest Lapointe): " The matter has been engaging the attention of the Department of Marine and Fisheries, and steps are being taken to meet the views of my hon. friend."

TRAFFIC IN OPIUM AND NARCOTIC DRUGS.

On 19th May, the Minister of Health made a brief statement to the House in Committee of Supply on the traffic in narcotic drugs.

DEBATE IN HOUSE OF COMMONS.

The Minister of Health (Hon. H. S. Béland) stated that the work in connection with the enforcement of the Opium and Narcotic Drug Act was being followed very closely. Though the quantity of narcotics entering Canada through ordinary permitted channels had immensely decreased during the last three years, he was sorry to convey to the Committee the information that the illicit introduction of opium and its derivatives, such as morphine, heroin and cocaine, had considerably increased. The smuggling in of opium was carried on particularly on the western coast, whilst the illicit introduction of other drugs was carried on especially through eastern ports. The Minister showed in tabular form that there was a total of 835 convictions (634 Chinese) during last year. It was the intention of the Department to follow up as closely as possible and to prosecute illicit dealers in the year just commencing.

Mr. R. A. Hoey (National Progressive, *Springfield, Man.*) : " Have any Japanese been convicted of dealing in narcotics during the past year ? "

The Minister of Health : " There is no record of any Japanese being prosecuted."

The Hon. R. J. Manion (Liberal-Conservative, *Fort William and Rainy River, Ont.*) asked for information on the statement which was often made that the drug habit in Canada was increasing by virtue of the fact that temperance or prohibition measures had been taken in different Provinces.

The Minister of Health said that he did not believe that the liquor habit and the drug habit had very much relation to each other. It was true that in British Columbia the liquor traffic was permitted under certain legislative regulations; and in that Province that the largest number of convictions for the illicit use of drugs had taken place. But the large number of convictions against illicit traders in narcotics in British Columbia would, he thought, naturally result from the geographic situation of that Province. He was unable to give any reasons for the apparent increase.

The Hon. H. H. Stevens (Liberal-Conservative, *Vancouver, C., B.C.*) said that in British Columbia, where they realised, more than any other part of the country, the connection between Canada and the Orient in the supplying of these drugs, they had been asking that those convicted should, wherever possible, be deported. One of the heaviest blows that could be struck at the traffic would be a vigorous campaign of deportation. He thought the chief cause of the spread of the drug habit lay in the profit which was made by unscrupulous traffickers. The main source of supply for opium was the Orient. The derivatives of opium came chiefly from Germany, although to a certain extent from France also—the two major sources of supply. He thought Canada might well initiate steps to prevent the export of drugs generally from these countries to Canada, except under strict regulations. They might very properly make strong representations not only to Germany, but to all the other countries which participated in the international convention to control the export of those drugs as effectively as possible.

The Minister of Health said that it would be possible for the signatories to the convention entered into in 1912, and ratified by Canada in 1919, to enter into negotiations with the view of ascertaining the exact quantity of drugs exported from any country.

JAPANESE COAL.

(Use by Mercantile Marine.)

On 2nd June, in the House of Commons, on the Orders of the Day,

The Prime Minister (Hon. W. L. Mackenzie King) said he wished to correct a false impression that seemed to exist in regard to the use of Japanese coal by the Canadian Government Merchant Marine on the Pacific. The impression seemed to have got abroad that the Government Merchant Marine intended to use Japanese coal, or were bringing Japanese coal to Canada. Some time ago the coal that came from Japan was merely in the nature of ballast. The Merchant Marine was under the Board of Directors of the National Railways. The Government had not to do with the control of its affairs, or the operation of its steamers, but the following statement had been made :—

As far as they can possibly do so the steamers of the Government Merchant Marine will hereafter use only British Columbia coal on the Pacific Ocean.

Mr. W. G. McQuarrie (Liberal-Conservative, *New Westminster, B.C.*) asked if the Prime Minister was aware that the ships of the Government Merchant Marine were purchasing their coal from mines at Cumberland which employed Orientals underground ; and that these mines were the only mines in Canada where Orientals were so employed ; and if the Government would take action to see that this condition was remedied.

The Prime Minister replied that he would take occasion to inquire into what his hon. friend had represented.

CATTLE EMBARGO.

On 20th April the House in Committee of Supply discussed the question of the removal of the Cattle Embargo by the British Government.

DEBATE IN HOUSE OF COMMONS.

The Minister of Agriculture (Hon. W. R. Motherwell) explained that a Delegate was on his way overseas and that he had dictated a letter instructing him to spend two days in London to call upon the new High Commissioner there with respect to the embargo question and through him to seek an interview with the Right Hon. Winston Churchill, because he had a feeling that there were developments in the air with regard to the embargo question.

Value of British market.

Dr. the Hon. S. F. Tolmie* **(Liberal-Conservative,** *Victoria, B.C.*), after discussing the United States as a market for Canadian cattle, said that another market that was offering to them was the British and that it was a more suitable market for the reason that there was less chance of any tinkering with the tariff. At the present time they could dispose of their live animals at Birkenhead and Glasgow on condition that they were slaughtered within ten days of arrival. This was not a very advantageous way to sell their livestock, but the embargo had not yet been removed and they had, therefore, to sell under those conditions. It might be asked why it did not pay them to kill their cattle in Canada and send them over as chilled beef. The answer was simply because they could not face the competition of the Argentine. Why did they want the British embargo against their cattle withdrawn? For the reason that in Canada they did not possess either the facilities or sufficient trained men for the finishing of their cattle so that they could ship them to the British market in a fat or finished condition.

Pleuro-pneumonia; British Minister's promise.

He was very glad to hear from the Minister of Agriculture that he had been impressing on the British Government the desirability of lifting the cattle embargo. "It has been in operation now for about thirty years," stated Dr. Tolmie, "having been first imposed on the assumption that in the shipment of cattle from Canada to Great Britain one animal was found affected with contagious pleuro-pneumonia. That disease had never been known to exist in this country and it did not exist at the time, nor has it ever existed here since." It was now acknowledged that the diagnosis made at that time by the British veterinarians was erroneous. However, the Canadian Government since the embargo was put on had made all possible efforts to have it lifted. These efforts were abated during the War, but were renewed with increased vigour immediately after the Armistice. The withdrawal of the embargo was strongly urged by Sir Robert Borden, who in 1917 was successful in obtaining a promise from the then British Minister of Agriculture to the effect that the embargo would be lifted. A continuous campaign was carried on during 1919, 1920 and 1921 with the British authorities for the purpose of having the embargo removed. In 1921 the British Commission appointed to deal with the matter gave its decision in favour of Canada. In addition to this, a great deal of very valuable work had been accomplished by various associations in Great Britain.

---

* Dr. Tolmie was Minister of Agriculture in the late Government.

The excuse had been made by the British Government that, if they permitted cattle to come in from Canada, that would necessarily mean that all other countries would have the same privilege in regard to their cattle. It was clearly proven before the Commission that Canadian herds were freer from contagious diseases than any other herds in the world. Therefore it would be a very easy matter to pass regulations on a disease-free basis so that, by naming the various diseases, Canadian cattle could easily be permitted to enter Great Britain without allowing cattle from other countries to get into that market.

Arguments in favour of Embargo refuted.

Canadian steers could be shipped to the United States, France, Belgium, Switzerland and Germany, but they were not allowed the same privilege as regarded Great Britain. Why should they not have the same privilege as Ireland? Ireland was clamouring to be given the same Dominion status as Canada, but still she objected to the entrance of Canadian cattle to Great Britain. The argument had been made that there was a possibility of disease coming in from the United States, but, even though they had had three outbreaks of foot-and-mouth disease in the United States, the last in the year 1914, not one single case was permitted to cross the line and gain a foothold in Canada. So that the fact that they had been able successfully to protect their boundary line against disease from the United States for many years past was sufficient guarantee of what they could do in the future. Another point brought up was that once they got access to the British market the United States might ship their cattle to Canada and then across to the British market as Canadian cattle. But it would be quite easy for the Department of Agriculture to brand permanently every animal coming in from the United States and so make it utterly impossible for United States cattle to be shipped across to the British market as theirs. The next argument was that there was a great danger of Canadians glutting the British market and lowering the prices. The Canadian would be the last one to let that happen, because he was under heavy expense in sending his animals over there. They admitted that the Britisher had every right to protect his own market, but, in the first place, they had had a definite promise to the Prime Minister of Canada that the embargo would be lifted; they had had a favourable finding by the Freight Rate Commission appointed by the Government to inquire fully into the whole embargo question, and in the findings of that Commission they not only declared that Canadian cattle were free from disease, but that there was no danger to British herds from contagious disease from Canada. Their cattle were still kept out of Great Britain by the Animal Diseases Act.

He would like to take the opportunity to thank the British Embargo Commission, headed by Lord Finlay, for the courtesy extended to the Canadian representatives, and Sir George Perley, the Canadian High Commissioner, for the many services rendered. Sir Howard d'Egville, Secretary of the Empire Parliamentary Association, was another gentleman who did everything possible to make their trip to England very pleasant and gave them every assistance and all the information they required in presenting their case.

While in England, he was very pleased to note that there was a strong move to increase trade within the Empire and that in 1923 an Exhibition would be held in London at which an opportunity would be given to all the Dominions to exhibit their products and their manufactures, and he sincerely hoped that the Government would take advantage of that opportunity to make a good and strong exhibit of Canadian products.

Injustice to Canada.

The Right Hon. Arthur Meighen (Leader of the Opposition) said that they had a just grievance while the embargo stood on the present basis, and they were justified in proceeding by legitimate means to get it removed. The embargo in its present form was unjust to Canada, not because Canada was discriminated against in any sense; Canada was not discriminated against in the British legislation, it was equally applicable everywhere. But the embargo was imposed at a time when it was advertised that a case of pleuro-pneumonia had been found among the Canadian herds, and the embargo took the form of a protection of British cattle breeders against all diseases, so that from its very origin it implied a reflection on the health of Canadian herds. As long as the embargo rested on that origin, it constituted in itself an injustice to Canada, whether it was applied generally or whether it was not. There was obtained at the Imperial Conference of 1917 the promise of the British Minister of Agriculture that after the War, although the date was not fixed, the Government would remove that embargo. The Royal Commission found that there had been no case for the maintenance of the embargo in so far as disease was concerned. Considering the subject from the standpoint of the protection of the industry in Great Britain, that was to say, from the standpoint of the British cattle-breeder, certain comment was made as well, but even in that respect the verdict, in so far as it was favourable to that protection and against Canada, was about all that they could expect it to be. At the Imperial Conference he took the subject up and then at the Conference of Prime Ministers he rested his case on the promise of the British Government and asked in the name of Canada that that promise should be carried out.

Mr. John Evans (National Progressive, *Saskatoon, Sask.*) urged the Government to leave no stone unturned to secure the removal of the embargo if by increasing the British preference to at least 50 per cent. that object could be attained.

Attitude of Prairie Provinces.

Mr. A. J. Lewis (National Progressive, *Swift Current, Sask.*) drew attention to an article in the Press which represented the Hon. P. C. Larkin, High Commissioner for Canada, as assuring the British Ministers that the Government's failure to redeem its pledge to remove the cattle ban would place a potential weapon of considerable power in the hands of the Annexationists of the Prairie Provinces and other foes in Canada of the Imperial connection. Mr. Lewis said that they were quite prepared to believe that it was in the interest of all Canadians that the embargo should be removed, but they did not believe that the High Commissioner had a right to make a threat to the British Government at the expense of the Prairie Provinces. It was a reflection upon the integrity and loyalty of the Prairie Provinces, and they on that side of the House took great exception to the remarks he had quoted.

On 5th May,

The Prime Minister (Hon. W. L. Mackenzie King) said that he had received a telegram from the High Commissioner of Canada stating that, whatever opinion he held in private, no public statement of the kind imputed to him had been made.

DEBATE IN SENATE.

On 22nd June, in the Senate, on the Orders of the Day,

Senator the Hon. J. J. Donnelly (*Ont.*) drew attention to an article in the Press to the effect that the British Minister of Agriculture had stated in the House of Commons that it was estimated that 200,000 head of cattle would be imported from Canada at once if the present precautions regarding importation of live cattle were abolished. Senator Donnelly said that the report largely exaggerated the number of cattle that would probably be shipped to England at once if the embargo on cattle were removed. His own idea was that it was better for farmers to finish their cattle before shipping them to the old country. But it had been the experience of stockmen that some cattle did not stand the voyage well, and it would be a great advantage to have the privilege of sending those cattle inland and having them fed awhile before they were sent to market. He would suggest to the Leader of the Government that representation be made to the Minister of Agriculture in England to show that there was no ground for the fear expressed that if the embargo were removed the British market would be flooded with Canadian cattle, or that the people of Great Britain would be put to any great expense in providing quarantine. His own opinion was that if the embargo were removed less than 10,000 of the cattle referred to would be immediately sent to England.

BRITISH TARIFF PREFERENCE AND CANADIAN SEAPORTS.

On 5th April, Mr. Logan moved the following resolution in the House of Commons :—

That, in the opinion of this House, the British tariff preference should be confined to goods brought into Canada through Canadian seaports.

DEBATE IN HOUSE OF COMMONS.

Mr. Hance J. Logan (Liberal, *Cumberland, N.S.*) said that the tariff preference granted by Canada on goods of the Mother Country and most of the Dominions was distinctly a family matter. It created a very favourable impression throughout the Empire. He desired to-day that the gates of a foreign country should be closed to that preference, freely given by the daughter to the mother. He submitted that they could not build a nation upon pure materialism. In order to make a great country, they must create a national spirit. They needed, in Canada, more intense Canadianism. He desired to proclaim to the world that Canada was self-reliant and independent of other nations. Surely it was time for them to declare to the people of England, at any rate, that they had ports in Canada, both on the Atlantic and the Pacific, which were open the year around. The policy which he advocated had been proclaimed ever since Confederation, and even before. One of the leading policies of Canada had been that Canadian trade should be carried through Canadian channels. The English free importation would largely come in through the ports of Quebec and Montreal, and importations from different British possessions, particularly New Zealand, to which the British preference applied, would be brought in *viâ* Vancouver and Prince Rupert. The lack of westbound cargo was the weakness of their transportation system with Great Britain. An objection had been raised to this policy that it might be resented by the people of the United States. Even if this policy were an interference with the bonding privilege, they would only be carrying out the historic policy of the United States which, ever since it had become a nation, had put upon its Statute books the very class of legislation for which he was asking to-day. If "Canada for Canadians" was a good policy, then "Canadian ports for Canadian ships" ought to be equally as good a policy.

Mr. John Evans (**National Progressive**, *Saskatoon, Sask.*) said that the Conservative opposition from 1896 onward never had any policy but that of more protection and less British preference. To-day British preference stood in their tariff schedule just a little better than the favoured nation treatment or the intermediate tariff. But, after all, the greatest preference to-day was on goods that they did not get from Great Britain. He thought that the beneficiaries of protection, realising that it was not possible to further whittle down the British preference and still recognising it in the tariff schedule, were taking other means now to rid themselves of British competition. At all tariff inquiries since 1897 the farmers of the whole Dominion, as well as the importers of textiles in the eastern Provinces, commended the British preference and asked for a repeal of the amendment of 1904 which curtailed it. He thought that it would have been more consistent if his hon. friend had advocated that they should compel all goods that came in free to come through Canadian ports,—and this would apply also to goods coming in under the intermediate tariff or the favoured nation provisions. Why single out goods coming in under the British preference? If the hon. Member wanted to keep trade going east and west, it would have been more consistent for him to advocate that their Atlantic ports be thrown open to the free entry of British goods. The resolution was a camouflage to curtail British competition, and he for one was going to oppose it.

The Hon. John B. M. Baxter (**Liberal-Conservative**, *St. John City and Counties of St. John and Albert, N.B.*) said he would like to go one step further and add to the resolution "and only in British or Canadian-owned bottoms." He believed the Government would do well to think of the possibility of utilising their Canadian Government Merchant Marine for the importation of goods, with a special preference because they were Canadian bottoms owned by the Canadian Government.

The Hon. T. A. Crerar (**Leader of the National Progressive Party**) asked why it was that ocean freights from Atlantic ports in the United States to Great Britain were usually more favourable than from Canadian ports. It was due to the fact alone that vessels plying between American ports and European ports could get return cargoes from Europe for American ports when they could not get return cargoes for Canadian ports. At the present time, with British goods coming in through United States ports in bond, they had the element of competition in transportation costs. That element would be completely eliminated were the resolution of his hon. friend carried. As the years went on the interdependence of nations in matters of trade was growing, and there was an increasing realisation of the fact; and to argue that they must be independent of the United States in respect of any matter of that kind was but to make a sort of patriotic appeal that had no basis whatever in real patriotism. If favourable trade arrangements (reciprocity) with the United States were to be secured, they were to be secured not by taking any step that would antagonise a body of opinion in that country that was now favourable to the proposal but by their cultivating that opinion in the hope that eventually a satisfactory arrangement might be brought about. If goods from foreign countries were coming through the United States now, what was the explanation of the fact? The reason was simply because the Canadian people and Canadian firms could secure those goods more cheaply in that way than in any other way. Were they to set up an arbitrary provision of this Parliament that would compel the people of Canada to purchase the things they needed from Great Britain through an arbitrary channel that would increase the cost to the consumers?

Mr. L. H. Martell (Liberal, *Hants, Ont.*) hoped that he should see the day when they would have absolute free trade with the Motherland. If they passed this resolution to force goods getting the British preference to come through Canadian ports, they were in effect supporting what was practically an argument to bolster up that false principle of protection against which he should always raise his voice.

Mr. W. F. Maclean (Liberal-Conservative, *York, S. Riding, Ont.*) held that no great mistake would be made by enacting legislation of this kind which proposed to build up their ports and, through them, their railways, and to do so in the light of the experience of the United States. The most highly organised nation in the world to-day was that republic, and its success was founded on a national policy.

After further discussion the Motion was withdrawn.

RECIPROCITY WITH AUSTRALIA.

On 12th June, on the Orders of the Day.

The Right Hon. Arthur Meighen (Leader of the Opposition) said that in the Budget Speech the Finance Minister referred to negotiations for reciprocity with Australia commenced by the late Government and prosecuted further by the present Government. He mentioned that no progress had been made since the refusal of a certain proposal advanced by Canada. Mr. Meighen said he had read in *The Times* (London) of 2nd June, a Melbourne despatch of 1st June as follows :—

> The Government has submitted to the Government of Canada proposals for Tariff Reciprocity.

The Times added :—

> This is a sequel to the recent arrangements between Australia and New Zealand reported by our correspondent in *The Times* on 8th April.

Mr. Meighen asked the Government if this report was correct, and, if so, were they in a position to state what advance had been made since Australia's proposal was presented ?

The Prime Minister (the Right Hon. W. L. Mackenzie King) : " It is correct that the Australian and Canadian Governments are at the present time in correspondence by cable respecting the reciprocal tariff arrangements between the two countries. I do not think it would be in the public interest to disclose at this particular moment the nature of the proposals."

Mr. Meighen : " May I ask if it is correct that the proposal has been made, as stated, on 1st June, by the Australian Government ? "

The Prime Minister : " As to its being a sequel to the arrangements with New Zealand ? "

Mr. Meighen : "*The Times* says that the Australian Government has forwarded to the Government of Canada proposals for tariff reciprocity. Is that correct ? "

The Prime Minister : " It is the other way round. Our Government made proposals ; those now alluded to are modifications of an original proposal that was not accepted."

Mr. Meighen : " But the present proposals are from Australia ? "

The Prime Minister : " Yes."

CANADIAN LOAN.

On 24th April, in the House of Commons,

The Minister of Finance (Hon. W. S. Fielding) asked to be permitted to announce a very important financial transaction which had just been closed. The Government had sold $100,000,000 of Canadian bonds to Messrs. J. P. Morgan and Company of New York. The bonds would be placed on the market on 25th April at par, bearing interest at 5 per cent., for a thirty-year period, callable after twenty years.

On 25th April the Minister announced that this Loan was a complete success.

CASH GRANTS TO RETURNED SOLDIERS.

("Want of Confidence" resolution.)

On 28th March, Mr. James Arthurs moved a resolution in amendment to Supply dealing with the Liberal policy relating to cash grants to returned soldiers (*vide* JOURNAL, Vol. III., No. 2, p. 351).

DEBATE IN HOUSE OF COMMONS.

Mr. James Arthurs (Liberal-Conservative, *Parry Sound, Ont.*), in moving the resolution, referred to the pledge given at the combined Liberal Party Convention of August, 1919, and declared that this was a solemn promise to the returned soldiers that the Liberal Party, if they got back to power, would grant cash bonuses and that it was used in every constituency where there was a returned soldier. The late Government, and the Party to which he belonged, were opposed to the granting of $2,000, or any similar bonus, indiscriminately to returned soldiers; but their friends opposite, by this plank in their platform, succeeded in getting thousands of votes, evidently under misapprehension, and in spite of the fact that the present Prime Minister knew that his Party would never implement that promise. While the Conservative Party was opposed to any cash grant of that nature, it was not opposed to doing everything possible for the returned soldier. As Canadians they were proud whether they were on one side or the other that Canada had paid the most liberal scale of pensions of any country that was engaged in the War. It was quite true that certain soldier organisations had passed resolutions advising against any request for a cash gratuity of $2,000, it was quite true that they had moderated their demands; but it was foolish to say for one moment that these men were repudiating a cash grant of any kind.

The Prime Minister (Hon. W. L. Mackenzie King) declared that the resolution was not a pledge on the part of the Liberal Party to give cash grants indiscriminately to all returned men. As the Liberal Convention understood it, the resolution was a declaration that in the opinion of the Convention that was the most effective means at that time of dealing with the question of re-establishment. What the Convention believed was that if the Government would adopt a policy with the returned soldiers of giving to them a cash grant of a certain amount and allowing them to re-establish themselves with the aid of that money, that would be the most effective way of bringing about their re-establishment. What might have been the wise course to take at that time when men were returning from overseas and seeking to get back into their regular vocations would not necessarily be the wise course to take some years later, particularly after Parliament had met and after the House of Commons on two occasions had discussed the whole question in Special Committee and had decided upon certain measures of re-establishment, and when the Government were taking action in accordance with views which were unanimously concurred in by Parliament. What he had said to every deputation of returned men whom he had had the privilege of addressing had been this : One of the first steps he would take would be to refer the whole question of the treatment of returned men to a Committee of the House which would be thoroughly representative of all shades of opinion in the country ; that he would ask the Committee to deal with the questions that came before them and that the Government would be guided into action in the light of the report made. That pledge had already been fulfilled ; there was no reason why the Committee should not consider, if it so wished, the question of cash grants.

The Hon. H. H. Stevens (Liberal-Conservative, *Vancouver, C., B.C.*), in seconding the resolution, declared that they were calling upon his hon. friend (Mr. Béland) either to implement that pledge by legislation providing for cash gratuities, or to admit that his statement, and the statement of his Party, were unfair to them, that they misled the soldiers in regard to the course which his hon. friend intended to pursue.

The Right Hon. Arthur Meighen (Leader of the Opposition) asked whether when they were in office they were or were not frank with the returned soldiers. They told them definitely, once they had gone the extent they thought the country could go in the matter of cash gratuities, that they could go no further, and they took the penalty of certain hostility among them because of that candour. In 1920 the Great War Veterans passed a resolution after the Convention of 1919 in which they affirmed themselves definitely in favour of cash grants and pledged themselves to secure such grants if they could. In face of the position taken by the Great War Veterans the Government of the day declined their request and said to them : We believe we have gone as far in the general cash grants as is in the interests of the country and we think that anything further should be in the way of enabling the soldier to help himself through re-training, seeking out various ways in which specially disabled men may be helped in the struggle for life to overcome to some extent the handicaps they labour under as the result of their War services. In 1921 they passed a general resolution with regard to re-establishment, but took no special position one way or another on the matter of cash grants.

The Minister of Finance (Hon. W. S. Fielding) said that the country accepted the judgment of the Committee of the House presided over by Mr. Cronyn as a settlement of the soldier bonus question. Before that Committee the door was opened to consider any matters that might arise in connection with soldiers, but when his right hon. friend (Mr. Meighen) said that was an issue at the last Election and on that issue they came back to power, his hon. friend was entirely mistaken.

The Hon. T. A. Crerar (Leader of the National Progressive Party) held that if he said to the Government: Because you had a resolution approving the principle of a soldiers' bonus at your Convention in 1919 you must disregard all that has taken place since then and implement that resolution—then he was going a little too far. If public opinion throughout Canada had changed upon that question in the last three years since June, 1919, and if other things had intervened, then in his judgment the Prime Minister and his hon. friends opposite were not acting dishonourably in stating that the time had passed for the giving of a bonus to the returned soldiers. They recognised the fact that three years ago a definite policy was followed by the Government of the day, in his judgment a wise policy, for giving assistance to returned soldiers, and already a sum amounting to almost one hundred million dollars had been spent in the soldiers' land-settlement scheme.

The Hon. R. J. Manion (Liberal-Conservative, *Fort William and Rainy River, Ont.*) pointed out that every soldier who served overseas and who returned received from the Government that was in power at that time a cash grant running anywhere, he thought, from $300 to $600, so that they were giving cash grants, and unless that resolution meant a further cash grant it could mean nothing at all. He thought it was a financial impossibility to give $2,000 to each of the returned men. This was a resolution condemning the principle, or rather the lack of principle, of advocating platforms in the country before election and refusing to carry them out after.

After further discussion, the resolution was rejected by 126 to 42 votes.

DAYLIGHT SAVING.

On 19th April, in the House of Commons, Mr. Kay moved the following resolution:—

That, in the opinion of this House it is desirable that legislation be introduced during the present Session to prohibit the adoption of Daylight Saving Time in any part of Canada.

DEBATE IN HOUSE OF COMMONS.

Mr. F. W. Kay (**Liberal**, *Missisquoi, Que.*) said that during the War daylight saving was introduced in Canada as a War-time measure, in order that the people of Canada should be able to devote an extra hour of the evening to cultivating land, especially in the cities, where, by working on garden plots during this extra hour of daylight, people were able to cultivate a good deal of ground in the aggregate, and so help production. At that time Parliament enacted a measure enforcing daylight saving throughout the country, and the people without exception accepted the change of time. Since the War ended, Parliament had not seen fit to re-enact daylight saving legislation, but many of the cities had adopted the change. As a rule the larger cities, through an order of their municipal councils, adopted daylight saving for themselves, but the smaller towns and villages all went by standard time. The result was there was no uniformity in the clock, and this caused a great deal of confusion. He had received many letters from all parts of the country commending him for bringing the Motion forward and expressing the hope that legislation would be introduced during the present Session to prohibit any municipality from advancing its clocks at will. He was told that, in the city and also in the country, daylight saving time was very injurious to the health of children, for the reason that children could not be made to go to bed by daylight saving time. If Parliament had not power to prohibit daylight saving time or to enforce standard time throughout the country, he would strongly recommend that the British North America Act should be amended to give Parliament that power. The farmers of Canada could not successfully carry on their farm work under daylight saving time.

Mr. T. L. Church (**Liberal-Conservative**, *Toronto, N., Ont.*), stated that in Toronto the people voted on the measure, and it carried by a majority of ten to one. They had had petitions from all classes. Daylight saving had its inception in Germany in 1914. At that time Great Britain also adopted it, the House of Commons and the House of Lords unanimously favouring the principle. France, Holland and twelve other European countries followed suit. Great Britain a short time ago passed a measure making for uniformity with France, and other countries. The principle was thoroughly investigated by a committee of both Houses of Parliament in the Mother Country. This committee made a study of the practical working of daylight saving in England, Germany, France, Holland and other countries which had adopted it of necessity, because of considerations of health and economy, and they unreservedly recommended it for Great Britain as well. The difficulty in connection with the practice of daylight saving in Canada was not due to any inherent defect in the system itself, for all the large cities in Canada adopted the principle by large majorities. The principle was investigated by the United States Senate, the Interstate Commerce Commission, the Chamber of Commerce at Washington, and by various Boards of Trade throughout the country. These bodies were all agreed that from the standpoint of health, of economy, in the saving of light and power, and because of the benefit that accrued to the children of the country, to the farmers, and to the business community, daylight saving was not only desirable, but necessary. If the United States had daylight saving, their time should synchronise with Canada's. If they made it nation-wide in Canada, he had no doubt that its benefits would be appreciated. Any defect in its operation was due to the lack of a nation-wide enactment of co-ordination between the various parts of the country and the United States. The Minister of Finance (Hon. W. S. Fielding) had said that it was not the intention of the Government to adopt a measure of national daylight saving, but that where a municipality had adopted daylight saving, the local government offices would conform.

The Right Hon. Arthur Meighen (Leader of the Opposition) said that Parliament had certain rights in relation to the daylight saving question. They could, for example, establish daylight saving within those institutions under the control of Parliament. But to say or suggest that they had any right to pass legislation putting it out of the power of a municipality to adopt daylight saving was to suggest something that did not admit even of argument or serious consideration.

Mr. Thomas Vien (Liberal, *Lotbinière, Que.*) declared that daylight saving was fraught with evils, so far as the rural population at large was concerned. Even in the cities, where daylight saving had been much advocated, it caused a great deal of inconvenience. He knew as a positive fact that their educational institutions objected to daylight saving.

Mr. W. D. Euler (Liberal, *Waterloo, N. Riding, Ont.*) agreed entirely with the Leader of the Opposition that Parliament should not have the right to dictate to the people of any city, large or small, with regard to this matter.

Mr. L. H. Martell (Liberal, *Hants, Ont.*) submitted that it was not in the best interests of Canada to have the towns, or urban centres, adopting daylight saving when it was not carried out in the country districts.

Mr. O. R. Gould (National Progressive, *Assiniboia, Man.*) thought that when hon. Members attempted to compare these conditions in Canada with conditions in France, Great Britain, and the older countries of Europe, the comparison was unfair.

When daylight saving was introduced in the West and forced upon them, they, as agriculturists, met with many difficulties.

Mr. H. A. Stewart (**Liberal-Conservative,** *Leeds, Ont.*) thought that opinion in Canada was against daylight saving, and if the resolution had been confined to that, he was sure there would have been very little opposition to it. But it involved the other feature, of a prohibitory action on the part of Parliament in a field of doubtful jurisdiction.

The Hon. Sir Henry Drayton (**Liberal-Conservative,** *York, W. Riding, Ont.*) said there was one practical way in which the Government could register its views on daylight saving. The city of Ottawa had adopted daylight saving to go into effect on 30th April, and the only practical thing that could be done with the resolution by gentlemen who had taken their stand upon the subject was to say that the ordinary rules should not apply, and the House would pay no attention whatever to the daylight saving regulation passed by the city government.

Mr. William Duff (**Liberal,** *Lunenberg, N.S.*) said that it seemed to be that the House should express the opinion that daylight saving was not in the best interests of the great majority. He moved the following amendment to the resolution :—

In the opinion of this House it is not desirable that daylight saving time should be adopted in any part of Canada.

On 28th April,

The Minister of Finance (**Hon. W. S. Fielding**) informed the House that daylight saving had come into effect in Ottawa. It was understood, he said, that while it was not proposed to make any general law on the subject, the policy of the Government was to adapt itself to the local decision in the matter of daylight saving.

On 1st May, Mr. Kay's Motion was declared lost.

AUSTRALIA.

Commonwealth Parliament.

The Second Session of the Eighth Parliament opened on 28th June, 1922, but no Parliamentary Debates were available up to the time of going to press with the present number of the JOURNAL. *The following subjects were held over from the proceedings of the last Session which terminated on 10th December, 1921.*

TREATY OF PEACE (HUNGARY) ACT.*

This Act, assented to on 15th December, 1921, empowers the Commonwealth Government to do all things that are necessary and expedient for giving effect to the Treaty of Peace with Hungary, signed at Trianon on 4th June, 1920. The Act applies to the Territories under the authority of the Commonwealth, including the territory governed under the Mandate.

IN HOUSE OF REPRESENTATIVES.

On 6th December, 1921,

The Minister for Trade and Customs (Hon. W. Massy Greene),† in moving the Second Reading, said that the Bill followed the lines of the other measures‡ already passed by that Parliament to give effect to the Versailles Treaty. The only country with which Australia was not yet at peace was Turkey. The measure enabled regulations to be made, and such things to be done as appeared to be necessary for carrying out and giving effect to the provisions of the Treaty, and extended the operation of the Treaty to the territories under the control of the Commonwealth. It was purely a formal measure.

IMPERIAL COMMUNICATIONS.

(Wireless Agreement; Direct communication with Great Britain.)

The proposed Agreement between the Commonwealth and the Amalgamated Wireless (Australasia), Limited, sum-

---

* *Vide* Canada, p. 558.

† Now Minister for Defence and the Navy (*vide* note on the reconstitution of the Cabinet, JOURNAL, Vol. III., No. 1, p. 89).

‡ *Vide* JOURNAL, Vol. I., No. 1, p. 131 (Germany); and Vol. II., No. 2, p. 367 (Austria and Bulgaria).

marised in the last number of the JOURNAL (p. 357 *et seq.*), was signed on 28th March after alteration as recommended by the Parliamentary Committee. A new clause was inserted providing that "so long as the Commonwealth or its nominees continue to hold a majority in the number and value of the shares" there shall be seven directors of the company, consisting of three nominated by the Commonwealth, three elected by the other shareholders, and a seventh selected by a majority vote of the other six directors. If the voting be equal, the seventh director shall be selected by arbitration. The only other material alteration as compared with the proposals originally submitted to Parliament, is the provision for the company to take over, within one month after the signing of the agreement, the existing Commonwealth radio stations, excepting those wholly under the control of the Defence Department. As mentioned in the earlier summary the Amalgamated Wireless Company is empowered forthwith to increase the capital of the company to 1,000,000 shares of £1 each, of which the Commonwealth shall be allotted 500,001, and be required to pay 2s. on allotment, and three further calls of 6s. each, not earlier than 1st July, 1922, 1st January, 1923, and 1st July, 1923.

CUSTOMS TARIFF (NEW ZEALAND) PREFERENCE ACT.*

This Act was passed on 8th December, 1921. It provides for the extension of the British preferential rates under the 1921 Tariff to goods of New Zealand produce or manufacture imported from that Dominion into the Commonwealth and as specified by proclamation.

IN THE HOUSE OF REPRESENTATIVES.

The Minister for Trade and Customs (Hon. W. Massy Greene), in Committee of Ways and Means, in submitting the Motion to the above effect, said that owing to the provisions of the Customs Act, they were obliged to submit to the Tariff Board any proposal for reciprocal Tariff relations between the Commonwealth and other parts of the British Dominions. During the last few weeks they had been conducting negotiations by cable with the New Zealand Government in regard to reciprocal Tariff relations, and they had practically come to an agreement on the basis that New Zealand would concede British preferential rates to the Commonwealth. The Commonwealth would get from New Zealand a much greater advantage

* *Vide* also New Zealand and Australia, Vol. 3, No. 2, p. 391 (New Zealand).

than New Zealand would get from Australia. The Commonwealth's trade with New Zealand was about £2,500,000 per annum, and the Dominion's trade with Australia amounted to £7,500,000 per annum. It was eminently desirable that at the first possible opportunity the agreement with New Zealand should be ratified. He was quite satisfied that the arrangement would be entirely advantageous to the Commonwealth, and that they would run no risk, from a Protectionist point of view, by its ratification.

Mr. A. Hay (Country Party, *New England, N.S.W.*)**:** "Will this proposed arrangement be extended to Fiji and other Dependencies ? "

The Minister for Trade and Customs: "The principle certainly will apply to all other parts of the Empire that care to enter into reciprocal arrangements with us."

(*The Bill was passed through all its stages without amendment or debate.*)

INCOME TAX ASSESSMENT ACT, 1921.

(Elimination of double Income Tax; Primary producers.)

The above Act was assented to 17th December, 1921. It amends the Principal Act by the insertion of new Sections providing, in conjunction with the British Finance Act, 1920, for the elimination of double income taxation on the lines recommended by the Sub-Committee of the Royal Commission on Income Tax; the taxation of the income of Primary Producers on the average amount of taxable income over a period of five years; the taxation of non-residents under certain conditions; and the constitution of Boards of Appeal, etc.

Double taxation, rebate.

Any person who has an amount of income liable to taxation under the Commonwealth Act and in the United Kingdom, or in a State of Australia, and who satisfies the Commissioner as to the amount of the income and the amounts of taxes to which the income is so liable, together with the rate or rates of those taxes, shall be entitled to a rebate of tax at a rate which is ascertainable as follows :—

Commonwealth and United Kingdom—if the Commonwealth rate is greater than one-half of the British rate :—

(A) Where the Commonwealth rate is greater than the British rate, the rate of rebate shall be one-half of the British rate ;

(B) Where the Commonwealth rate is not greater than the British rate—rebate of the excess of the Commonwealth rate over one-half of the British rate.

Treble taxation, rebate.

Commonwealth, State and United Kingdom—if the sum of the Commonwealth and State rates is greater than one-half of the British rate, the proportion which the Commonwealth rate bears to the sum of the Commonwealth and State rates shall be ascertained, and the rate of rebate shall be that proportion of the following rates :—

(A) Where the sum of the Commonwealth and State rates is greater than the British rate—one-half of the British rate ;

(B) Where the sum of the Commonwealth and State rates is not greater than the British rate—the excess of the sum of the Commonwealth and State rates over one-half of the British rate.

"Commonwealth rate" means the rate ascertained by dividing the total amount of income tax (before deduction of the rebate) by the amount of the total taxable income in respect of which the tax has been charged for that year ; except that, where the tax is charged on an amount other than the ascertained amount of actual profits, the rate shall be determined by the Commissioner. "State rate" has a corresponding meaning. "British rate" means the appropriate rate of tax in the United Kingdom upon the amount of income.

Primary Producers.

For the purpose of ascertaining the rates applicable to the income of primary producers the amount of so much of the taxable income as is derived from primary production (*i.e.*, the cultivation of land, or the maintenance of animals or poultry, including dairy produce manufactured by the person who produced the principal raw material used in the manufacture of the produce) shall be taken to be, for the year ending 30th June, 1923, the average of the amounts of taxable income derived from primary production during the last two preceding financial years ; 1924—the average of the last three preceding years ; 1925—four years ; and for all subsequent years—the average of the last five preceding years.

Non-residents.

Where a non-resident person carries on business with a resident person, and it appears to the Commissioner that, owing to the close connection between the resident and the non-resident persons, and to the substantial control exercised by the non-resident person over the resident person, the course of business between these persons can be so arranged and is so arranged that the business done by the resident person in pursuance of his connection with the non-resident person produces to the resident person either no taxable income or less than the ordinary taxable income which might be expected to arise from the business, the non-resident person shall be assessable and chargeable to tax in the name of the resident person as if the resident person were an agent of the other. Where the true amount of the taxable income of the non-resident person cannot be readily ascertained, the Commissioner may, if he thinks fit, assess and charge the non-resident person on the turnover of the business done by him through or with the resident person in whose name he is chargeable. Nothing in the above shall render a non-resident person chargeable in the name of a broker or general commission agent or in the name of an agent not being—

(A) an authorised person carrying on the regular agency of the non-resident person ; or

(B) a person chargeable as if he were an agent in pursuance of this section, in respect of profits or gains arising from sales or transactions carried out through such a broker or agent.

Deduction for children, etc.

The deduction from the taxable amount of income in respect of children is raised from £26 to £30. The exemption in the case of unmarried persons without dependants, which was formerly £100 less £1 for every £5 in excess thereof, is amended to £104 less £1 for every £3 in excess of £104.

Other Provisions.

The definition of "absentee" is amended to exempt residents of Papua from taxation of income derived from sources therein, thus leaving the income fully available for taxation by the governing authority of that territory. Members of co-operative societies are exempted from taxation of the rebates allowed them on their purchases from such societies. Section 10 of the Act provides for the constitution of Boards of Appeal, and the powers of such Boards and the Courts on the hearing of appeals.

DEBATE IN HOUSE OF REPRESENTATIVES.

Double and treble Income Tax.

The Prime Minister (the Right Hon. W. M. Hughes), referring to the provisions of the Bill in connection with double and treble taxation, said that the long and short of the arrangement was that where the British tax was greater than the Commonwealth and State rates combined, the taxpayer would pay in the aggregate only the British rate, but where the combined rates exceeded the British rate he would pay only at the combined rates. The higher rate would always be charged, and the lower tax would be wholly rebated. There would be no adjustment between Governments. The Commonwealth would not have to make an adjustment with the States or with the United Kingdom, nor the United Kingdom with the Australian authorities. The whole matter would be arranged by the Taxing Commissioners. The assessment in the case of the United Kingdom would take note of the liability to taxation under the Commonwealth laws, and, in the case of the Commonwealth, of liability to taxation under the British law and the rate of tax would be fixed accordingly. The Bill, of course, provided only for relief to be given by the Federal Department of Taxation. A full adjustment of the matter would not be effected until the State Legislatures also arranged to rebate a portion of their own taxes.

Non-residents.

Clause 9 imposed income tax upon profit derived by ex-Australian principals from the sale of their goods in Australia.

Hon. Members perhaps had had their attention drawn to a practice which was becoming common, and was notorious in the case of one particular company where an Australian branch house was believed to be debited by the foreign house for goods at a price which left little margin for profit on the sale of such goods in Australia. These allegations had been made from time to time in that House. It had been said that one company in particular had resorted to some such method in order to escape the Australian tax. The proposed new Section would give the Commissioner power to assess and charge tax upon what appeared to be the real profits.

Boards of Appeal.

On the recommendation of the Commonwealth Royal Commission on Taxation provision was being made for the appointment of Boards of Appeal, and they would start by the appointment of only one. As many more could be created as circumstances demanded. It was estimated that each Board would cost £10,000 per annum. It might be necessary, ultimately, to have as many as ten Boards. Where questions of law arose, the taxpayer had the option of appealing to the High Court or to the Supreme Court of a State. Where a question of fact was involved, he could appeal to one of the Boards. When it was a question of law and of fact, he could appeal to the Board in regard to the fact and to the Court as to the law. But he had the option of appealing to the High Court or the Supreme Court of a State on questions of law, and he could go to the Court on questions of law and of fact; but he could go to the tribunal only on questions of fact. There was one class of cases which neither the tribunal nor the Court could deal with. He referred to cases of hardship, which were specially provided for, and which would be heard, as then, before a tribunal composed of the Taxing Commissioner, the Secretary to the Treasury, and the Comptroller-General of Customs.

Mr. Matthew Charlton (Leader of the Opposition) remarked that he had always complained of the taxation imposed on single persons. The exemption was far too low, and the proposed amendment made the position worse. A single person might earn from £150 to £200, and all income over £130 would be more heavily taxed than it then was. He had been under the impression that it was proposed to give relief to single persons; but that was not so. Personally, he believed that the exemption should be largely extended; at any rate, in view of the high cost of living they ought to considerably increase it. In his opinion, it would be only a fair thing to make the exemption at least £200. In the case of married men, who had the care and burden of a family, the exemption was £156; but could it be claimed that this was not then far too low a point at which to start taxation? There was an exemption of £26 for each child under sixteen years of age. In New South Wales the exemption was £250, with an allowance of £50 for each child. He suggested an exemption of £300 with an allowance of £60 for each child. The Bill proposed to increase the child allowance to £30. An extra £4 was infinitesimal.

Dr. Earle Page (Leader of the Country Party) said that though the measure did not give the primary producers exactly what they had asked for or desired, it provided a great improvement on the then system of taxation; and one must be thankful for small mercies. He hoped that on some future occasion a full measure of justice would be meted out. He agreed with the Leader of the Opposition that the child allowance was not sufficiently high. He would like to see it raised to approximately the allowance made in the New South Wales Act.

The Minister for Works and Railways (Hon. Littleton E. Groom), in reply to a question during the Committee stage, said that by increasing the child allowance from £26 to £30, as proposed, there would be a loss of revenue amounting to over £30,000 per annum, and if the exemption were increased to £60 the loss of revenue would be between £300,000 and £400,000.

WAR PRECAUTIONS ACT REPEAL (AMENDMENT) ACT.

(Control of foreign corporations; Foreign capital.)

This Act was assented to on 22nd December, 1921. Its object is to amend Section 7 of the Principal Act (*vide* JOURNAL, Vol. II., No. 2, p. 377) by extending to 31st December, 1922, the War Precautions (Companies Firms and Businesses) Regulations so far as they relate to the control of the registration and activities of foreign corporations and trading and financial corporations formed within the Commonwealth; and to repeal Section 19 which required the agents of overseas companies and firms to furnish the Collector of Customs with full particulars as to the amount of capital, balance-sheet, etc., of their principals.

DEBATE IN HOUSE OF REPRESENTATIVES.

On 8th December, 1921,

The Minister for Works and Railways (Hon. Littleton E. Groom), in moving the Second Reading, said that Section 7 of the original Act provided that the War Precautions Regulations controlling the registration and activities of companies and firms operating within the Commonwealth should continue until the end of 1921. The measure extended their operation until 31st December, 1922, but not in their entirety, because it was proposed to limit their application so far as they affected firms, a matter which could easily be dealt with by the various State laws dealing with the registration of firms; and to continue the regulations for the extended period so far as they remain related to foreign corporations and trading or financial corporations formed within the limits of the Commonwealth. During the War, and for some time afterwards, there was a suspension of the registration of foreign corporations desiring to carry on business in Australia, but latterly about thirty had been registered. The Treasurer in his Budget speech had said:—

> *Foreign Capital.*—Under the War Precautions Repeal Act, 1920, it is an offence to register in Australia any company with capital partly or wholly subscribed outside the British Empire, except with the consent of the Treasurer. Since the beginning of the current year (1921), authority has been issued for the registration in the Commonwealth of twenty-seven foreign companies, with a total subscribed capital of approximately £13,500,000 sterling. The bulk of this capital has been found in the United States of America. Seven of the Companies, with a subsidised capital of about £3,500,000 sterling, have been established to carry on industrial and productive operations in the Commonwealth, two to conduct fire and marine insurance business, and eighteen to carry on trading operations.

The Government were dropping altogether the necessity for the registration of firms as distinct from corporations.

Mr. Matthew Charlton (Leader of the Opposition): "You are reverting to the position that existed prior to the War?"

The Minister for Works and Railways: "Yes, we are leaving the registration of firms to be dealt with by State laws. All we propose is to continue the regulations so far as they relate to foreign companies and trading or financial corporations formed within the limits of the Commonwealth."

The Treasury and the Crown Law Department had for some time had under consideration the question of submitting to the Commonwealth Parliament a comprehensive measure dealing with company law under the present constitutional powers. But at that stage it would be impossible to bring such a big Bill before the House. They were now simply asking for an extension of twelve months of the Commonwealth control over these corporations. In the meantime the matter of exercising more complete control over them could be taken into consideration.

Agents of overseas companies.

The other part of the Bill dealt with the repeal of Section 19 of the War Precautions Act, which required the agents in Australia of all overseas companies and firms to furnish particulars regarding the business of their principals to the Collector of Customs in the State in which their chief place of business was situated. These particulars included the name, address, capital and balance-sheet of the company or firm. But under the Companies and Firms Acts of the States all companies and firms carrying on business in Australia in their own names were required to be registered, irrespective of whether their head offices were established in Australia or abroad. The effect of Section 19 had, therefore, been to require companies and firms already registered in Australia to be practically re-registered with the Department of Trade and Customs. This obligation had imposed a great deal of trouble on firms, and strong objection had been taken by British companies, especially by the provision requiring them to furnish particulars as to their financial position to their agents in Australia for submission to the Department of Trade and Customs. Having given consideration to these representations, the Department had found it practically necessary to suspend the provisions of the section, and in the circumstances they had come to the conclusion that it would be better to repeal it.

COMMONWEALTH ELECTORAL (AMENDMENT) ACT.

Provision has been made by certain State Acts whereby a Member of the State Parliament who resigns his seat to contest a Federal seat may, if he is not elected, resume his seat in the State Parliament. The Commonwealth Act under review, which was assented to 15th December, repeals Section 70* of the Principal Act, and inserts the following section in its stead:—

No person who—

(A) is at the date of nomination a Member of the Parliament of a State; or

(B) was at any time within fourteen days prior to the date of nomination a Member of the Parliament of a State; or

(C) has resigned from the Parliament of a State, and has the right, under the law of the State, to be re-elected to the Parliament of the State without the holding of a poll,

shall be capable of being nominated as a Senator, or as a Member of the House of Representatives.

---

* Section 70 as in the Principal Act reads: "No person who is at the date of nomination, or who was at any time within fourteen days prior to the date of nomination, a Member of the Parliament of a State, shall be capable of being nominated as a Senator or as a Member of the House of Representatives."

IN HOUSE OF REPRESENTATIVES.

On 8th December, 1921,

The Minister for Home and Territories (Hon. A. Poynton), in moving the Second Reading, said a Bill was passed by the Tasmanian Parliament in 1907 enabling a Member of the State Legislature to resign his seat and contest a Federal Election. Provision was made that, on a request from the Member so resigning his seat, the issue of a writ to fill the vacancy should be delayed until after the declaration of the poll of the Election he was contesting. It was not provided that if he did not succeed in winning the Federal Election, his seat in the State Legislature should be kept for him, but that defect was remedied in 1917, when the State law was amended. Following on that, every State in the Commonwealth had passed similar legislation. There were, however, two States in which the Bills had been reserved for His Majesty's Assent, presumably on some constitutional ground.

Supposing there was an Election for the Federal Parliament, and there were three candidates, one, the State Member who had resigned his State seat, the retiring Federal Member, and another candidate nominated from outside—assuming, further, that the outsider won—what was then the position? If there then happened to be a vacancy in the State Parliament, the Federal Member was not eligible to contest it because it was given back to the man who had resigned to contest the Federal seat, and did not succeed.

State Parliaments.

The only State Parliament for which Parliamentary Debates of the present Sessions are available is that of New South Wales.

New South Wales.

General Election and New Government (Note).

The General Election for the Legislative Assembly was held on 25th March, 1922. The results showed the state of Parties as follows: Nationalist 41; Labour 36; Progressive 9; Independent 3; and Democrat 1. In the last Parliament the state of Parties was: Labour 45; Nationalist 28; Progressive 15; and Independent 2.

The constitution of the new Government is as follows:—

Premier	Hon. Sir George W. Fuller, K.C.M.G., M.L.A.
Vice-President of the Executive Council	Hon. Sir Joseph H. Carruthers, K.C.M.G., M.L.C.
Secretary for Lands and Minister of Forests.	Hon. W. E. Wearne, M.L.A.

Colonial Secretary and Minister of Public Health.	Hon. C. W. Oakes, M.L.A.
Attorney-General	Hon. T. R. Bavin, M.L.A.
Colonial Treasurer	Hon. A. A. Clement Cocks, M.L.A.
Secretary for Public Works and Minister of Railways and State Industrial Enterprises.	Hon. Sir Thomas Henley, K.B.E., M.L.A.
Minister of Agriculture	Hon. R. T. Ball, M.L.A.
Minister of Public Instruction ..	Hon. A. Bruntnell, M.L.A.
Secretary for Mines and Minister of Local Government.	Hon. J. C. L. Fitzpatrick, M.L.A.
Minister of Justice	Hon. T. J. Ley, M.L.A.
Assistant Minister of Lands and Agriculture.	Captain the Hon. F. A. Chaffey, M.L.A.
Minister of Labour and Industry ..	Hon. E. H. Farrar, M.L.C.

EMPIRE SETTLEMENT.

On 26th April, in the Legislative Council,

The Hon. J. B. Nash, speaking on a motion for adjournment, referred to the publication in the newspapers that morning of a statement* that the New South Wales Government

---

* The Statement referred to was contained in a Minute adopted by the Cabinet on 18th April, and made available for publication in the Press by the Premier (Sir George Fuller). The Minute provides for the opening of negotiations with the Federal Government for the carrying out of proposals :—

1. For the construction of developmental works to open up areas of Crown lands for settlement.
2. For the survey and laying out of such land, as :—
   - (A) Farm areas.
   - (B) Sites for towns, villages and reserves.
   - (C) Training farms where necessary.
3. For the financing of such work under arrangement with the Federal and British Governments, or with the Federal Government.
4. For the discussion of the terms of an agreement to be entered into by the State with the Federal Government, and, if necessary, with the British Government, such agreement to deal with the following matters :—
   - (A) The security for the financing.
   - (B) Provision of work for New South Wales citizens and for immigrants, and in what proportions and under what conditions.
   - (C) Provision for placing Australians and immigrants on the land, and in what proportions and under what conditions.
   - (D) Control of the works to be carried out.
   - (E) Arrangements for financing the proposals.
   - (F) Any other matters that may arise in the course of the discussion.

was going to join with the British and Federal Governments in bringing about a state of things which, if persevered in and brought to fruition, would help to place the young people of Australia in years to come in a position of prosperity which had only been equalled in any other country by the adoption of methods of the same kind. As proof of what he said, he put to them the present position of the United States of America. What had made that country great? What had made that country pre-eminent, and given it a position which made it command the statesmen and leaders of the greatest nations to go to Washington? It had been the movement of the people during the latter half of last century from the United Kingdom and Ireland to the United States. That was why Australia was to be congratulated upon entering upon a process which would raise the British Empire again to its rightful position as leader of the world. It had had to sacrifice that position. If at the commencement of the War they had had 100,000,000 white people under the Union Jack, there would have been no need to ask for the assistance of any one. There would have been no war, because the British people would not have allowed it. But now, because there was a greater aggregation of white people under another flag, they had to take a second place. If the policy set forth that day was to be the policy of the Government, then Australia would reach its destiny in due time, and their children would live in a world in which their nation and their Empire would play second fiddle to no other country.

(On 1st May, the Premier was officially advised by the Prime Minister of the Commonwealth (the Rt. Hon. W. M. Hughes) that the Federal Government was prepared to assist the State with the scheme.)

---

5. That special attention shall be directed to the following localities, viz.:—

(1) The Murray valley lands within the State of New South Wales.

(2) The Crown lands lying between the Great Northern Railway and the North Coast Railway.

(3) The hydro-electric schemes at Burrinjuck and at the Gorge (Clarence River), which will assist settlement and find employment on reproductive works that will develop good lands.

Such other places as may be reported to be suitable for operations under agreement with the Federal Government.

6. That a special investigation be made into the possibilities of the extension of settlement on the Murrumbidgee irrigation area with a view to suitable action to effect such extension, either by State action alone or under agreement with the Federal Government.

PARLIAMENTARY ALLOWANCES AND SALARIES ACT.

On 27th April, 1922, a Bill for an Act to reduce the allowances to Members of the Legislative Assembly and the salaries of Ministers of the Crown, was introduced in the Legislative Assembly. The Bill was passed with amendments by the Legislative Assembly on 3rd May, and by the Legislative Council the same day.

The Bill, as amended, provides for the reduction of the annual allowance to Members of the Legislative Assembly from £875 to £600.

The sum appropriated for the salaries of Ministers of the Crown is reduced from £23,420 to £18,000 per annum, the salaries of the respective Ministers being reduced as follows:—

Premier, from £2,445 to £2,000;
Attorney-General, from £2,095 to £1,600;
Vice-President of Executive Council, from £1,375 to £900;
Nine other Ministers, from £1,945 each to £1,500.

The salary of the President of the Legislative Council is reduced from £1,200 to £925; the Speaker of the Legislative Assembly, from £1,675 to £1,400; the Chairman of Committees, Legislative Council, from £700 to £500; and the Chairman of Committees, Legislative Assembly, from £1,115 to £840.

Provision is also made for the appropriation of a sum of £1,000 for the salary of Solicitor-General, should such an appointment be made. This is a reduction of £945.

DEBATE IN LEGISLATIVE ASSEMBLY.

The Colonial Treasurer (Hon. A. A. C. Cocks), in moving the Second Reading on 27th April, said that in view of the representations that had been made during the debate on the expediency motion that it would be unfair if the Bill were made to have a retrospective effect, the Government had decided that the Bill should become operative on 1st July. While Ministers had agreed to adopt that course in respect to Members' allowances, they had decided that they were in honour bound to the resolution they had passed themselves that the reduction of Ministers' salaries should operate voluntarily as from 25th March. He would point out that the reduction now proposed was in accordance with the statement made by the Premier in his policy speech that the salaries of Members and Ministers should be reduced by £275 per annum. They must bear in mind that the increase which was made (by the previous

Government) in the allowances of Members represented a very much larger percentage than the increase granted to Ministers. The former had been 75 per cent., and the latter 40 per cent.

Capt. the Hon. W. F. Dunn (Deputy Leader of the Opposition) said that if the Ministers were prepared to take £275 off the £375 increase which had been granted to Members, they should deduct the same proportion from the increases which were granted to Ministers. The deduction of £275 from Members' salaries would represent 31 per cent., and a deduction at the same percentage from Ministers' salaries would amount to £600, and Ministers now receiving £1,900 would receive £1,300. He had always been opposed to any reduction of salaries. Members were entitled to a fair remuneration for the responsible work they did. They ought to be prepared to give the whole of their time to the work of Parliament. At the present time Elections were very expensive matters. In his electorate there were 230 polling booths, and some were 150 miles from a railway station. Proportional representation had brought about a great deal of added expense in connection with Elections, and another result of that system had been that they had had two Elections in two years. He had conducted his electioneering on a reasonable scale, but his two Elections had cost him over £900. The Electoral Act forbade candidates from subscribing to local bodies after the writs had been issued. If the Minister would insert a similar clause in this Bill, it would give relief to Members; and such a provision ought to be made operative during the whole life of Parliament. The proposal that the remuneration of Members should cease when Parliament expired by effluxion of time or a dissolution was unfair, because between the dissolution and the General Election Members did perhaps more work than when the House was sitting. Ministers continued to occupy their offices whether the House was dissolved or not, and received their salaries because they did the work of their offices. He believed the intention was to force salaries down so low that no one but a man with a large private income would be able to enter the House. A great many Members, especially on his side of the House, were wholly dependent on their Parliamentary salaries; and no one could say the remuneration was princely when the expense of winning an Election was considered.

Lt.-Col. M. F. Bruxner (Leader of the Progressive Party) said he was quite prepared to accept the reductions provided in the Bill, though as far as he was concerned they could go back to what they had been prior to the increase two years ago. He was quite prepared to admit that under the proportional system there was perhaps reason why the amounts of £500 a year should be increased. There was to-day a bigger field to cover and more responsibility. The Party to which he belonged stood for the proposed reductions, although he thought the Government should have gone further and reduced the number of Ministers.

Consideration in Committee.

When the Bill was considered in Committee, the following amendments were brought forward:—

Mr. W. G. Ashford (Independent, *Wammerawa*) moved that the allowance to Members be further reduced to £500 per annum. This was rejected, and the original clause approved by 64 votes to 12.

On the motion of the Hon. J. T. Lang (Labour, *Parramatta*), the sum of £1,670 provided in the Bill for the salary of the Solicitor-General was reduced to £1,000. An amendment proposed by the Hon. E. A. McTiernan (Labour, *Western Suburbs*) that the provision be wiped out, was rejected.

The sum of £20,120 provided in the Bill for the salaries of Ministers was reduced to £18,000 on the motion of Lt.-Col. Bruxner. An amendment proposed by Mr. McTiernan to reduce the sum to £16,051 was rejected by 44 votes to 34.

The provision in the Bill that the payment of the allowance to Members should cease at the date of the dissolution or expiration of Parliament was deleted on the motion of the Colonial Treasurer. The allowance will, therefore, continue to be paid until the day appointed for the poll for the next General Election.

Tasmania.

General Election (Note).

The General Election for the House of Assembly was held on 10th June, 1922, the results showing the state of Parties as follows : Nationalist 12 ; Labour 12 ; Country Party 5 ; and Independent 1. The strength of Parties in the last Parliament was : Nationalist 16 ; Labour 13 ; and Independent 1.

(*Particulars as to the personnel of the Cabinet are not yet available in London.*)

NEW ZEALAND.

The following Summary is in conclusion of the Third Session of the Twentieth Parliament, which opened on 22*nd September,* 1921, *and closed on* 11*th February,* 1922. *The Fourth Session commenced on* 28*th June, and will be dealt with in the October issue of the* JOURNAL.

DEFENCE ESTIMATES.

(Naval Estimates; New Zealand branch of British Navy; Admiralty Commission; Land and Air Defences.)

DEBATE IN HOUSE OF REPRESENTATIVES.

Naval Estimates.

On 20th January, 1922,

Mr. T. M. Wilford (Leader of the Opposition), on the proposed Vote of £335,782 for Naval Defence coming up for discussion in Committee of Supply, asked the Minister of Defence whether he was prepared to make a statement in regard to the Washington Conference with relation to naval defence, and generally in regard to naval defence, and what officers and staff the Government had dealing with the Naval Adviser's work.

The Minister of Defence (Hon. Sir R. Heaton Rhodes) said in reply that no official communications had so far been received, and, awaiting them, it was not possible to say what the future policy of the Dominion would be.

Mr. G. Witty (Liberal, *Riccarton***)** moved: that the Vote be reduced by £10 as an indication that the *Chatham* was neither wanted nor warranted. The cost of administration did not give the benefit it should to the Dominion—indeed, it was impossible to keep up a Navy that would do any good to the country. Certainly they must have a ship on which to train boys, but the present cost was too great for a country like New Zealand.

The Prime Minister (the Right Hon. W. F. Massey), in reply to Mr. Witty, said that every country in the Empire must contribute to the Navies of the Empire: that had been laid down at the Imperial Conference and agreed to, though the amounts had not been fixed. With regard to the Washington Conference, he believed, he said, the shadow of war had, as a result of that meeting, passed from the Pacific, for many years at all events; but that was no reason why the Empire's Navy should not be maintained. When New Zealand kept a ship like the *Chatham* it was doing its share in the maintenance of the Navy, and doing all that could be asked from it, and it was better than an annual contribution to the Imperial Government for the purposes of the Navy. He believed that the New Zealanders would be a maritime people in the future.

Mr. Witty: " We can never have a Navy of our own."

The Prime Minister replied that he did not suggest that. The whole position had changed in the last year or two, and what New Zealand was doing at present was enough, and quite satisfactory to the people at the other end. New Zealand might be called on to contribute to the cost of new Empire ships, and no doubt she would do her duty in that matter. He believed that war was far from being at an end. They might not have to face it for another twelve years, but when it came they must not be unprepared, as on the last occasion. He spoke, he said, from the Pacific point of view more particularly. If a ship like the *Chatham* had been in New Zealand waters during the War the raider that did all the damage would never have got away, and probably would never have come there. Mr. Massey concluded by saying that he wanted to save money, but was strongly of the opinion that the money the *Chatham* cost was being quite properly expended.

Mr. P. Fraser (Labour, *Wellington, C.*) said that if there was to be a naval defence policy for New Zealand it should be drawn up in connection with the British Navy.

The Minister of Defence, in reference to the remark of Mr. Fraser, said that the Admiralty had approved of New Zealand's present policy and the establishment of the New Zealand branch of the British Navy. A Commission had been sent out to New Zealand to inquire into naval matters, and the Government was acting on the advice of that Commission, with the entire approval of the Admiralty. It was not contended that the *Chatham* was a match for a battleship, and when battleships were expected in those waters other provisions would have to be made.

Mr. Witty's amendment was negatived by 55 votes against 10.

Land defence.

During the course of the debate on the proposed Vote of £367,043 for New Zealand Military Forces and Cadets on the same date,

Dr. H. J. T. Thacker (Liberal, *Christchurch, E.*) said the defence of the country in future would be the arm of aviation.

Mr. H. Holland (Labour, *Buller*) said that the whole of the Military Estimates for the year represented an increase of £305,000. The amount expended last year had been £579,734; but the House was being asked to vote this year £884,740. He moved that the Vote £467,043 be reduced by £200,000—which, added to the Government's decrease of £100,000, was roughly the total increase for the whole military and naval expenditure.

The Minister of Defence replied that the Vote for the previous year had been £600,000, of which £509,000 had been spent. The estimates (for the present year) of £467,000 for Military defence had not satisfied the Cabinet, and it had then placed them before the Public Accounts Committee, which had recommended a reduction of £100,000, making them £367,000 as against the £509,000 spent the previous year.

Mr. Holland's amendment was negatived by 46 votes against 12.

DISCHARGED SOLDIERS SETTLEMENT AMENDMENT ACT.

(Relief of ex-Soldiers; Power to extend principal Act to South African War veterans.)

The fall in prices of the primary products of the Dominion having seriously affected ex-soldiers who had taken up land under the Discharged Soldiers Settlement Act, the above legislation was passed in order to improve the position of the discharged soldier, and at the same time, where money had been advanced by the Government, to give better protection to its security. The Act, which is retrospective in its operation, came into force on the 11th February, 1922.

The principal provisions of the Act are as follows:—

Where the Crown acquires a mortgagor's interest as mortgagee under the Discharged Soldiers Settlement Act, such interest shall not merge in any other interest possessed by the Crown, but shall enure as a separate interest to be disposed of under the Act in such a manner that the Discharged Soldiers Settlement Account shall be recouped to the amount of the advances made. (*Section* 3.)

Freehold land coming into the possession of the Crown as mortgagee may be disposed of either by way of sale or renewable lease by public auction, public tender, or private contract, and for cash or on deferred payments. (*Sections* 4, 5, 9 and 10.)

There are also provisions as to the disposal of leasehold lands coming into the possession of His Majesty under the Act mentioned. (*Sections* 6, 7, 9 and 10.)

In special cases, with the Minister's approval, land acquired by His Majesty as aforesaid may be disposed of to persons who are not discharged soldiers. (*Section* 8.)

Pending permanent disposal, land may be disposed of under temporary licence to any person, whether a discharged soldier or not. (*Section* 13.)

The consent of the Minister is to be obtained to all transfers, conveyances, etc., of lands mortgaged to the Crown under the Discharged Soldiers Settlement Act. (*Section* 14.)

Deferred payment licences-to-purchase can be exchanged for renewable leases (in order to make the ex-soldier's payments lighter). (*Section* 15.)

The Minister may postpone instalments of principal payable under certain mortgages. (*Section* 16.)

The Governor-General may by Proclamation declare that the provisions of the Discharged Soldiers Settlement Act shall apply to domiciled New Zealanders who have served beyond New Zealand in His Majesty's Forces in connection with any other war than the War with Germany. (*Section* 17.)

DEBATE IN HOUSE OF REPRESENTATIVES.

On 30th January, 1922,

The Minister of Lands (Hon. D. H. Guthrie), on the motion for Second Reading, said the Bill was introduced for the purpose of improving the position of discharged soldier settlers who had been seriously affected by the slump in produce-prices. They had to deal with lands under various tenures. Under the Bill, with the object of protecting the country's money, they were making provision for the transfer or other disposal of any lands mortgaged to His Majesty under the Act to be subject to the consent of the Minister. While it had been stated that there would be a very large number of foreclosures throughout New Zealand, they had had only sixty up to that time. As the advances had been made under the Discharged Soldiers Settlement Act, the properties concerned could not under existing law revert to civilians; and as in some cases the original owners would quite willingly take them back provided they had not to pay off the whole of the mortgage, the Department had considered it wise to provide for such a transfer rather than sell the soldier up and probably make a loss on the property.

Under Clause 4, if the former owner of a property was prepared to take it back, the Land Board might deal with him, or with any other civilian who was prepared to take it over.

After explaining various other Clauses of the Bill, the Minister made reference to Clause 17, which, he said, contained proposals for the redemption of a promise made by the Prime Minister, and also by himself, that when times improved and money became easier they would make provisions for the South African veterans.

Mr. Guthrie, in concluding, said the loss in connection with the foreclosures would be but small in comparison with the good done by putting those settlers on the land. He did not think, he said, that any other country in the world, or any Government, had done for its returned soldiers what New

Zealand had done in placing them on the land, and in repatriation work generally.

Mr. T. M. Wilford (Leader of the Opposition) said that was the first public utterance of the Minister of Lands admitting failure of the Government land policy towards the soldiers.

The Minister of Lands: " I do not admit it."

Mr. Wilford, continuing, said that Clause 13 provided that the Government could take the soldiers' land and give it to ordinary soldiers, if only temporarily. They had a Bill of sixteen clauses to enable the Government to make the best of a bad job. He asked the Minister to tell the House and the country how many poor soldiers had had to walk off their sections and give them up. They were doing it still.

Mr. R. W. Smith (Reform, *Waimarino*) said that as a country Member he welcomed the Bill. It was true it had been framed to meet cases where settlers had failed. It was a good measure, because it would help to minimise the loss of those settlers who had found it necessary to give up their holdings. In addition, it would expedite and simplify the re-settlement of the land upon which other settlers had failed. He welcomed particularly the last clause, which gave recognition to the claims of South African veterans, though he would like to see the clause made very much more definite.

The Minister of Lands in his reply said there was no honest " trier " among the returned soldiers who need have anything to fear from the Government. They were not prepared at that moment to write down values or to forgo interest, except in cases where it was absolutely necessary. They must conduct their business on business lines. The whole country had been suffering, but the future prospects were now better.

The Bill was then read a second time, and referred to the Lands Committee.

PROPORTIONAL REPRESENTATION AND EFFECTIVE VOTING BILL (No. 2).*

This was a private Member's Bill, introduced, by leave of the House, by Mr. J. McCombs, on 25th November, 1921, when it was read a first time. No Reform Members took part in the debate.

---

* Earlier in the Session a Proportional Representation Bill was introduced by Mr. W. Veitch (Labour, *Wanganui*), but was thrown out without debate on the motion for its Second Reading. The Bill was similar to that previously introduced by the same Member, and summarised in Vol. I., No. 1 of the JOURNAL, pp. 187-189, but which did not get further than the Second Reading.

On 25th January, 1922,

Mr. J. McCombs (Labour, *Lyttelton*) asked the Prime Minister whether an opportunity would be afforded him before the Session closed to move the Second Reading, saying that the Bill had been approved by a conference of "Proportionalists," which had met at Wellington, and had been drafted on lines recommended by the British Proportional Representation Society.

The Prime Minister (the Right Hon. W. F. Massey) replied that he would consider the request, but could not hold out much hope that it would be granted.

The Second Reading had not been proceeded with when the Session ended.

The object of the Bill is "to consolidate electoral districts and to secure proportional representation and effective voting in the Dominion."

An explanatory memorandum is attached to the Bill which sufficiently sets forth the scope and provisions of the Bill. The memorandum is as follows:—

> In this Bill the quota of votes necessary to ensure the election of a candidate is that known as the Droop quota, first explained by Mr. H. R. Droop in a paper read before the Statistical Society in 1881. Mr. Hare proposed to ascertain the quota by dividing the number of votes cast by the number of members to be elected. Mr. Droop's method is to divide the number of votes cast by one more than the number of members. His was the method adopted in the Legislative Council Act, 1914. It is preferred by the majority of proportionalists, and its chief advantage probably is that it ensures representation for a smaller minority than is possible under the Hare quota. In a three-member constituency, for example, one-fourth of the electors would be assured of representation.
>
> The elector is left free to mark as many preferences as he pleases. Should he mark only one preference his vote cannot be used (that is to say, transferred) in the event of the candidate he prefers being elected without his vote, and it is apprehended that voters will soon realise that their ballots will be more effective by marking more than one candidate. On the other hand it is not consistent with the principles of proportional representation to compel the voter, on pain of invalidating his ballot-paper, to mark every name on the list, and on the whole the vast majority of proportionalists agree that it is preferable to leave the voter free to record as many transfers as he pleases. In Ireland, where this method was adopted in connection with the local elections held in January, 1920, the number of invalid ballot-papers was 1 per cent., but in New South Wales, where proportional representation was applied at the general election last year, the voter was compelled to mark every name on the ballot-paper, with the result that there were 7 per cent. of invalid votes.
>
> The method of transferring surplus votes provided for in the Bill is that adopted in the English Municipal Representation Bill, 1910, and recommended by the English Proportional Representation Society. The method in force in Tasmania eliminates all possibility

of chance results, but it involves delay in counting, and the possibility of a different result being obtained by counting the surplus votes in manner herein provided is so remote that it may be disregarded altogether.

In the matter of vacancies necessitating by-elections—in this Bill called "particular vacancies"—proportionalists have differed among themselves. The Bill proposes that, on a vacancy arising, the ballot-papers used at the previous general election in the same district should be re-examined, and the next candidate who polls the quota declared elected. This plan presupposes that a sufficient number of unsuccessful candidates is available, and such would no doubt usually be the fact. If, however, by reason of an insufficient number of unsuccessful candidates, this method is impracticable, a by-election must be held, and in that event the voters' task of marking the ballot-papers is precisely the same as at a general election, but the quota is ascertained, unless some candidate has secured an absolute majority on the first count, by eliminating the candidate polling the fewest votes and distributing his votes over the continuing candidates.

DEBATE IN HOUSE OF REPRESENTATIVES.

On 25th November, 1921,

Mr. J. McCombs said he believed there was no more pressing reform that could be urged in New Zealand than the restoration to the people of the right of self-government; and there was nothing more calculated to destroy the prestige and authority of Parliament and undermine their whole Constitution than the knowledge on behalf of the electors that Parliament did not represent the people, and the further knowledge that the Government represented a minority and was opposed by a majority of the electors.

The Prime Minister: "That is not so—absolute nonsense."

Mr. McCombs replied that the statement was on the authority of Fischer Williams.* Continuing, Mr. McCombs said the matter had been receiving considerable attention in the Old Country and on the Continent; and proportional representation was being supported by all shades of political opinion.

It was said that proportional representation had been definitely embodied in the Government of Ireland Act; in Canada it was used in the Parliamentary Elections of Winnipeg, and Municipal Elections in other Provinces; in South Africa it was used in the Election of the Senate and the Executive Committee of the Provincial Councils; in the United States it was in force in some of the towns, and the principle had recently been formally approved for Municipal and State elections by the American Municipal League. It was used in Belgium, in some Swiss Cantons, and also for a portion of the Upper House of Denmark.

* Mr. Fischer Williams, K.C., C.B.E., is one of the hon. Treasurers of the Proportional Representation Society of Great Britain.

New South Wales experiment.

The difficulty that had occurred in New South Wales had been made by the enemies of proportional representation; but the House placed it on the Statute-book in spite of the opposition of Mr. Holman, and the Act allowed the Government of the day to make such regulations as to bring proportional representation into disrepute. Mr. Storey,* who had been at first opposed to proportional representation, when in England a little while ago, had spoken on the platform of the Proportional Representation Society, and had said that he had been converted even by the very bad experiment in New South Wales, and that he and his Party stood definitely for proportional representation. The difficulty had been that the regulations required the elector to indicate his preference right up to the thirty-second preference. After mentioning the tremendous strides proportional representation had taken in Europe, and after giving the House some facts as to the progress which, he alleged, it had made in England, Scotland and Ireland, Mr. McCombs said that the proportional representation movement was becoming world-wide, and New Zealand would be found among the most backward nations of the earth, so far as electoral reform was concerned, unless they soon had an amendment in their present unscientific method of electing representatives to Parliament. In concluding his speech, he said he thought the people of that country felt so strongly about it, with their knowledge that the Government in power had a legal but no moral right to govern, that they were going to organise in order to ensure that the condition of affairs then existing would not continue after the next Elections.

Dr. H. T. J. Thacker (Liberal, *Christchurch, E.*) said that by that day's Press they saw that New South Wales had again adopted proportional representation for next Election, with modifications to make. A fact he wished to bring out was that the Reform supporters in the Province of Auckland, the newly formed political Country Party, stated definitely in the first issue of their journal that they wanted a better system of election. It was significant that the Reform Party's dearest friends in the Province that sent most Reform Members to that House, were dissatisfied with the present method of election.

Labour view.

Mr. H. Holland (Labour, *Buller*) said he was inclined to think that proportional representation would drive the more Conservative elements into one camp and the more Radical elements into the other. The Conservative might outnumber the Radical element: he did not think that would be so, but

* Then Premier of New South Wales.

even if he was assured it was, he would still be an advocate of proportional representation. He had never thought it would be worth while the Labour Party occupying the Treasury benches if it had the same minority following that the Government had at present. He wanted to say that the Labour Party would never enter a Coalition Government.

Other Labour Members having spoken, the Bill was read a first time.

DIVORCE AND MATRIMONIAL CAUSES AMENDMENT ACT.

(Modification of law as to "separation by consent" as ground for divorce.)

The Divorce and Matrimonial Causes Amendment Act, 1920, a summary of which appears in the JOURNAL, Vol. II., No. 2, p. 434, contained a provision (Section 4) to the effect that a divorce decree might be made where the parties had been separated for three years under a decree, order, deed, etc., or where the separation had been by mutual consent.*

On 26th October, 1921, Mr. R. A. Wright (Reform, *Wellington Suburbs*) asked whether the Act referred to which enabled a husband or wife to obtain a divorce after three years' separation by mutual consent, was likely to prove a menace to the State and the Minister replied that some communications had been received as to the effect of the Act and, with the hon. gentleman's question, were receiving the consideration of the Government. Several petitions were also presented to the House, asking for the repeal (*inter alia*) of the section in question, and on the 17th January, 1922, a Bill dealing with the subject was introduced in the Legislative Council by the Attorney-General (Hon. Sir Francis Bell).

Certain objections were raised in the House of Representatives to the Bill as passed by the Chamber, and eventually a compromise was made and the Act became law on the 11th February.

The operative clause of the Bill as originally passed by the Legislative Council was as follows :—

2. (1) Section 4 † of the Divorce and Matrimonial Causes

---

* A question as to the possible effect of this section, in regard to a British marriage where either of the parties subsequently became domiciled in New Zealand, was asked in the House of Commons on 20th July, 1921. *Vide* JOURNAL, Vol. II., No. 4, p. 752.

† Section 4 of the Divorce and Matrimonial Causes Act, 1920, is as follows :—

(4) It shall be lawful for the Court in its discretion, on the petition of either of the parties to a decree of judicial separation,

Amendment Act, 1920, is hereby amended by adding thereto the following proviso :—

"Provided that if upon the hearing of a petition under this section the respondent opposes the making of a decree of dissolution and it is proved to the satisfaction of the Court that the separation was due to the wrongful act or conduct of the petitioner the Court shall not make upon such petition a decree of dissolution of the marriage."

(2) Nothing in this section shall be deemed to apply to any decree *nisi* heretofore made by the Court, or to prevent the making absolute of any such decree *nisi*.

Amendment.

It was eventually decided to omit sub-Clause 2 of Clause 2, the same having been struck out in the House of Representatives, and to substitute the following sub-Clauses (2) and (3) :—

(2) Nothing in this section shall be deemed to apply to any decree absolute heretofore made by the Court.

(3) No decree *nisi* heretofore made by the Court under the provisions of the Divorce and Matrimonial Causes Amendment Act, 1920, shall become or be made absolute except on motion or notice. If the respondent opposes the making of the decree absolute, and it is proved to the satisfaction of the Court that the separation was due to the wrongful act or conduct of the petitioner, the Court may, in its discretion, refuse to make the decree absolute.

The Act was accordingly passed in this form.

LEGITIMATION AMENDMENT ACT.

(Enabling legitimation of child born during existence of legal impediment to parents' marriage.)

The general effect of Section 2 of the Legitimation Act, 1908, is to make provision for the legitimation, by subsequent marriage of the parents, of a child born before marriage. But it was provided by Clause 4 (1) that nothing in the Act should have the effect of legitimating a child if at its birth there existed any legal impediment to the marriage of its parents.

The above Amendment Act, which came into force on 6th February, 1922, repeals Clause 4 and provides further that, in the case of a man who has married the mother of a child born before their marriage dying without availing himself of the provisions of the principal Act to secure the legitimation of such child, the mother may secure its legitimation.

---

or to a separation order made by a Stipendiary Magistrate, or by a Resident Magistrate, or to a deed or agreement of separation or separation by mutual consent, when such decree, order, deed or agreement is in full force, or has so continued for not less than three years, to pronounce a decree of dissolution of marriage between the parties, and in making such decree, and in all proceedings incidental thereto, the Court shall have the same powers as it has in making a decree of dissolution in the first instance.

FINANCE ACT, 1921-1922.

(Customs Amendment: Duty on imports from countries having depreciated currencies; Protection extended to industries within British Dominions.)

It having been found in practice that Section 13 of the Customs Amendment Act, 1921 (summarised in the JOURNAL, Vol. III., No. 2, pp. 395-401) dealing with the importation of goods from countries having depreciated currencies, was not sufficiently flexible, an amending section was introduced and incorporated in the Finance Act (No. 3), 1921-22 (Section 18) whereby greater discretion is given to the head of the Department in regard to such imports. The Act came into force on 11th February, 1922.

The amending Section provides that the special duty on goods from countries having depreciated currencies shall be charged only in respect of goods of a kind of which the importation into New Zealand is deemed by the Minister to prejudicially affect an industry established in New Zealand or in some other part of the British Dominions. Any person aggrieved by the admission of such goods upon which the special duty is not imposed may require the Minister to determine the question as to whether their importation does or does not affect an industry. Lists of goods in respect of which the special duty is made payable are to be gazetted from time to time. The Minister is given a wide discretion to exempt goods where it is "difficult, inequitable or impracticable" to carry out the provisions of the Section.

PUBLIC EXPENDITURE ADJUSTMENT ACT.

(Retrenchment in Government Services: Governor-General, Judges and High Commissioner not affected; Cost of living; "Levy on capital.")

The above Act, which came into force on 30th January, 1922, makes provision for extensive retrenchment in the Government and Education Services of the Dominion.

The retrenchment is to be effected by means of three "cuts":—

One as from 1st January, 1922, one not earlier than three months, and the third not earlier than 1st July, 1922.

The Prime Minister estimated there would be a saving of £800,000 by the first, £700,000 by the second, and £600,000 by the third "cut." The Act affects the salaries of Ministers and Members of the General Assembly, but does not apply to those of the Governor-General, the Judges, or the High Commissioner in London.

Two proposals in Committee by Labour Members that the Act should not apply so as to reduce any salary below £250 and £210 respectively, were each defeated by only four votes, the voting in respect of the first proposal being 37 against 33 and in the second 35 against 31, some Government Members voting for each proposal.

DEBATE IN HOUSE OF REPRESENTATIVES.

On 17th January, 1922, on the question that the Bill be referred to Committee of the whole House,

The Prime Minister (the Right Hon. W. F. Massey), on being asked by the Leader of the Opposition (Mr. T. M. Wilford) to explain the measure, reminded Members that, with the object of meeting the cost of living to people in the employ of the Government, increases had been made; sometimes these had been called bonuses, and sometimes increases in salary or wages. The increases had amounted to £4,500,000; they commenced about 1916, and there had been a number of increases right up to the beginning of last year, at which time they amounted to an average of £45 per annum in addition to the salaries or wages which those people had been receiving in 1914. There had been a very sharp rise in the cost of living in the first quarter of last year and a further increase of £50 in addition to the £45 had been granted. The understanding had been that when the cost of living dropped to 52 per cent.—at that time, said Mr. Massey, it was about 62 per cent. or 65 per cent.—there should be a revision, and a reduction made. The cost of living as compared with the commencement of the War had now dropped to about 50 per cent., or nearer 48 per cent.

Mr. H. Holland (Labour, *Buller*): "That is on the food groups only."

Proposed "cuts."

The Prime Minister replied that the original calculation had been made on the food groups. Continuing, he said the Government had already cut down their expenditure, and they had by reasonable methods got increased revenue. He did not know how long it might be necessary to go on cutting down expenditure. Including the first "cut," to be explained presently, the reduction would be over £4,000,000. The present intention of the Government was to leave the £45—the first bonus—intact; they were only touching the increases made since the beginning of 1920. Coming to the £50, he said they proposed to divide it into three "cuts": one then, one not earlier than three months, and one not earlier than three months after that. In reply to a question by Mr. George Mitchell (Independent, *Wellington South*), Mr. Massey said they expected to save £800,000 in the first "cut," £700,000 in the second, and perhaps £600,000 in the third. He believed the effect of the reduction would be to greatly decrease the cost of living in the country.

Workers' wages; Cost of living.

Mr. J. McCombs (Labour, *Lyttelton*) said the workers had not received an increase in wages commensurate with the increase in the cost of living: so it was idle for the Prime Minister to say that he was only going to tackle the bonuses and not the real wages—the purchasing-power of the money received for services rendered—as, with the bonuses, the workers that day were not receiving (equivalent in value to) the money which they had received in 1914. The figures which were being relied on in support of a reduction in the cost of living only covered one-third of the cost of living budget,—groceries, dairy produce, and meat. But there were fuel, rent, light, clothing, and miscellaneous, which ought to be included in any fair computation. Furthermore, if they took the six-monthly moving average, the very latest figures they had available for the food groups gave the cost of living as 60·19 per cent. That was for the six months ended November—the latest six-months average they had. The figure quoted by the Prime Minister, 50 per cent., was the month's figure (for food groups). The British Statistical Office, said Mr. McCombs, had no difficulty whatever in furnishing the "all-groups" figure for every month. What was being proposed was a general raid on workers' wages; because, he said, it had been voiced by Members on the Government benches that the Government would set the example, and the hope had been expressed that local bodies and other employers would follow.

The Hon. J. A. Hanan (**Liberal**, *Invercargill*) said that no man with any regard to the grave financial position of the country but must recognise that the cost of government in the country must be substantially cut down. If there were a searching examination into the Government services there would be disclosed great extravagance and waste. He hoped the Government would make the blow fall as lightly as possible, particularly upon the low-paid Government wage-earners, upon those who had large families whose incomes were under £300 per annum. Substantial reductions should be made in land-defence expenditure.

On 19th January, the debate on the Second Reading was taken, when—

War Expenditure.

The Prime Minister said he was afraid there were many people in the country to whom the Bill was not welcome, but they had got to make the best of a bad position. The extra (annual) expenditure, arising out of the War, amounted to £14,500,000. In 1920-21 the expenditure out of revenue amounted to £28,128,730, and in 1913-14 to £11,837,264—being an increase of £16,291,460. Then the direct (increased) expenditure due to the War deducted from the sum mentioned left a balance of £1,700,000. Mr. Massey then gave particulars of the last-named sum, saying it included a large sum that was not accounted for in the ordinary way, but arose directly or indirectly from the War. They heard, he said, a lot about extravagance, but he wanted hon. Members to look into those figures and see if they could find a single item of extravagance.

After giving details of the expenditure of £4,500,000 due to increased cost of living, Mr. Massey referred to the very large increases in the cost of materials for public works. In regard to the Railways, he said that for some months before Christmas they had been losing at the rate of £4,600 a day, and were now losing over £4,000 a day.

Primary products below cost of production.

In connection with the drop in the primary products of the Dominion, he said that butter, meat and wool were below the cost of production. In regard to the suggestion he had heard in connection with the Bill that they were not taking as high a percentage from the man with the higher salary as from the man with the lower salary, that was correct to a certain extent; but he wanted Members to recollect that the officer with the higher salary received nothing as compensation for the increased cost of living, and, on the other hand, he had to pay income tax. They could not stop until they got another £1,000,000 or £1,500,000 by way of reduction, in addition to the present recommendations. The number of public servants retrenched last year was 2,719, but he (Mr. Massey) knew there were more, because under the head of "Defence" the number given was 496, and officially he knew the real number was 808, including all retrenched, up to a recent date.

In regard to Mr. McCombs's suggestion that other classes should have been taken into account besides the food-group in granting increases, Mr. Massey said that the Statistician's Office had stated that they were based on the increase in the retail prices of foods between July, 1914, and March, 1920, housing, fuel and lighting not being taken into account owing to the fact that in the absence of complete data regarding clothing and miscellaneous items food-prices alone gave at that time a better indication of the increase in the cost of living.

Mr. T. M. Wilford (Leader of the Opposition) said those with him realised that there had to be some reduction in some salaries, but those who could afford to make a contribution to the State's needs should be required to do it. The method of the Government had neither uniformity nor fairness, and the reductions were harsh and unconscionable in some cases. It was not right that the Government should keep to itself the report of the Economy Committee it had appointed and not hand it to Members before that very important Bill was dealt with. The Prime Minister had given the House figures—with which he (Mr. Wilford) found no fault—from the Government Statistician in regard to the cost of living. How could the Government ask that House to accept for their calculation a foundation which omitted the cost of clothing, fuel, light, and rent? His third point was that the parties who were to have reductions in their salaries had a right to be heard.

The Minister of Justice (Hon. E. P. Lee) said that the report referred to by a Member was that of a committee set up to obtain information for the Government in order that it might bring about economies in administration. It was a confidential document belonging to the Government. In regard to reduction of salaries, Mr. Lee said that the objective of the Prime Minister was, in the first instance, to get £800,000; and it was of no use talking about reducing the higher salaries and leaving the lower salaries alone. Continuing, Mr. Lee said that a 10 per cent. reduction on all salaries of from £500 to £600, and a 20 per cent. reduction on those of £600 and over would amount to an annual sum of £113,499. How were they going to get £800,000 on a graduated scale on those salaries? It must come partly out of the lower grades of salary.

Public servants' "stormy resolutions."

Mr. H. Holland said that the public servants that day were faced with the gravest attack ever made on their standard of living, and that through them all the rest of the wage workers of New Zealand were menaced. What impressed him was the number of stormy resolutions carried throughout New Zealand by the public servants. Never in the history of Australasia had there been such a storm of protest against proposed legislation as that sweeping over New Zealand at the present moment. The Labour Party's position was that no reductions were at all necessary; but if the Government insisted that they should be made, the Labour Party would consent to no reductions in salaries under £500.

"Levy on capital."

On the 31st March last, said Mr. Holland, their accumulated surpluses totalled £23,671,901. Last year their revenue had been under-estimated by over £6,500,000, and he had a suspicion that the same thing had happened this year. If it were a *bonâ-fide* surplus, then where did the excuse come in for wanting to reduce the public servants' salaries? There was scarcely an item of the Government's policy that was not in the interests of the wealthier people of the country.

Continuing, Mr. Holland said there were £200,000,000 worth of mortgages registered in the country, and the primary producers and others were paying from £10,000,000 to £15,000,000 in interest to the mortgagees. The day would come when they would have to get rid of the interest problem one way or another, and the way to get rid of it was not by further borrowing, but by a levy on the accumulated wealth. In conclusion, Mr. Holland said that the Labour Party did not agree with the attitude of the Liberal Party in the matter. It was an occasion on which it must be a fight to a finish.

On 26th January, the Bill was discussed at length in Committee, frequent divisions on various clauses and proposed amendments taking place.

Close divisions in Committee.

At the close of the Committee stage,

Mr. T. M. Wilford moved that the Bill be recommitted for the purpose of reconsidering paragraph (b) of Sub-Clause (1) of Clause 6, dealing with the lower-paid members of the Public Service, stating as his ground for doing so that there had been four very important divisions in Committee in regard to it, two of which had only been lost by four votes. The last amendment, he said, proposed to restrict the cuts to those salaries above £210.

Mr. Wilford's amendment was defeated by 38 votes against 26, and the debate on the Third Reading was then taken.

Prime Minister's reply.

The Prime Minister, replying to various criticisms, said that when he heard suggestions made that instead of a policy of retrenchment and economy they should increase the taxation of the people on the land, he would say that they could not tax the producers without causing trouble, and if they taxed the business men it simply came back on the mass of the community. He believed if things went on as they were doing, and they got round the corner at the 31st March, they should have begun to leave the depression behind.

The Third Reading was carried by 40 votes against 19.

ABOLITION OF CAPITAL PUNISHMENT BILL.

A Bill for the abolition of capital punishment was introduced by Mr. J. McCombs but was defeated on its Second Reading.

The Bill consisted of one operative clause, as follows :—

> "2. Notwithstanding anything to the contrary contained in the Crimes Act, 1908, the penalty of death is hereby abolished, and where by that Act the penalty of death is prescribed for any offence the penalty of imprisonment for life shall be substituted therefor."

DEBATE IN HOUSE OF REPRESENTATIVES.

On 2nd November, 1921, on the question that the Bill be read a second time,

Mr. J. McCombs (**Labour,** *Lyttelton*) said that capital punishment had been abolished in Holland, Finland, Italy, Switzerland, Belgium, Portugal and Roumania, and that in every one of those countries murders had decreased, and that where it had been abolished crime had diminished, and so long as they had the death penalty on the Statute Book and put it into operation the State itself was in the position of committing official murders.

Mr. T. M. Wilford (**Leader of the Opposition**) said that he had had the defence of more than twenty men for murder, and if they abolished capital punishment they would increase the number of murders.

The Minister of Justice (**Hon. E. P. Lee**) said he knew that no more special care could possibly be given than was given to murder trials by the Judges, counsel and the juries. Even after a conviction had been recorded, he said, the utmost care and consideration was given by the Executive Council as to whether the prerogative of mercy should be exercised. If the death sentence was repealed it would undoubtedly lead to an increase of murders, and the safety of the people would be in jeopardy.

The Second Reading was defeated by 61 votes against 7.

MENTAL DEFECTIVES AMENDMENT ACT.

(Extension of powers of Public Trustee; Application to United Kingdom and British Possessions.)

The above Act, which amends the Mental Defectives Act, 1911, and (*inter alia*) extends the powers of the Public Trustee in dealing with the estates of Mental Defectives, came into force on 13th January, 1922.

Special provision is made regarding the application of the Act to the United Kingdom and other British Possessions, the latter coinciding with legislation in force in the State of Victoria (Australia). A " British Possession " is defined as meaning " any part of the British Dominions exclusive of the United Kingdom."

The Governor-General, on being satisfied that the laws in force in any British possession (other than New Zealand) are such as to enable powers to be exercised in that possession in cases of lunatic patients residing in New Zealand substantially similar to the powers contained in the next succeeding Section (Section 12) in cases of lunatic patients residing in that possession, may by Proclamation declare that the said section shall, subject to any specified modifications, apply to that possession. (*Section* 11 (1).)

The Governor-General, on being satisfied that adequate provision has been made by the laws of the United Kingdom or of any British possession for the recognition of lunacy orders made by the Supreme Court of New Zealand, may also by Proclamation declare that Section 13 of the Act shall, subject to any specified modifications, apply to the United Kingdom or any such Possession. (*Section* 11 (2).)

The Public Trustee is empowered, on the certificate of the proper officer of any British Possession (other than New Zealand) charged with the care, administration, etc., of the property of lunatic patients therein, to administer the property in New Zealand of a mental patient confined in the other British possession; but this Section only applies as provided in Section 11 (1) above. (*Section* 12.)

A lunacy order made in the United Kingdom or any British Possession may on certain conditions be resealed in New Zealand. This section similarly only applies as provided in Section 11 (2) above. (*Section* 13.)

MORTGAGES AND DEPOSITS EXTENSION ACT.

(Moratorium extended to mortgages and deposits.)

After the Armistice the Government passed the Mortgages Extension Act, 1919 (*vide* JOURNAL, Vol. I., No. 1, pp. 191-92) whereby the Supreme Court was empowered to extend the currency of mortgages up to 31st December, 1921, and it was hoped that the moratorium on mortgages would end with that piece of legislation; but that which had been anticipated did not happen, and the financial stringency increased, and it therefore became necessary to deal with the position which arose by reason of the termination of the Act of 1919 on 31st December, 1921. It also became advisable to place a restriction on the right of depositors to demand repayment of their deposits, and the above amending Act was accordingly passed and became law on 22nd December, 1921.

The Act provides for the further extension of mortgages, without the necessity of any application to the Court, to 31st December, 1924, the rate of interest in respect of all extended mortgages being fixed at six and a half per cent. per annum, unless a higher rate has been agreed upon.

In regard to deposits, those up to £1,000 are extended until 31st December, 1922, and those over £1,000 until the 30th June, 1923, subject to the conditions that interest in either case is to be at six and a half per cent., and that certain instalments on account of principal, varying as the deposit is over or not exceeding £1,000, are to be paid off on dates fixed by the Act. Where the borrower is a building society, or a company whose principal business is the lending of money on mortgage of lands, for fixed terms of years, the interest is to be 5½ per cent. in lieu of 6½ per cent.

INSURANCE COMPANIES' DEPOSITS ACT.

(Companies favoured within British Empire.)

An explanatory memorandum attached to the above Bill as introduced in the House of Representatives sets forth that the present law requiring deposits by insurance companies is unsatisfactory in many respects. Under the Foreign Insurance Companies' Deposits Act, 1908, as amended by the Act of 1910, (*a*) no deposit whatever is required in respect of the business of fire insurance, and practically none in respect of the business of employers' liability insurance; (*b*) the same deposit is required from companies constituted within the British Empire as from companies constituted in foreign countries, and the term "foreign company" is used as descriptive of British companies; (*c*) the business of life insurance, though dealt with separately by the Life Insurance Act, 1908, is again dealt with in the Foreign Insurance Companies' Deposits Act; (*d*) securities may be deposited in lieu of money, and difficulties may arise in the event of the realisation of such securities being required.

The object of the above Act, which came into force on 6th February, 1922, is to consolidate and amend the law of the Dominion in regard to the requirement of deposits from companies carrying on the business of insurance against Fire, Accident, and Employers' Liability.

The Act repeals the Foreign Insurance Companies Act, 1908, and the Amendment of 1910. No deposit is required from companies constituted in New Zealand under the New Zealand laws, but from companies constituted beyond New Zealand substantial deposits are required in respect of (1) fire-insurance business, (2) employers' liability insurance business, and (3) all other classes of insurance other than life insurance and marine insurance. From such companies established within the British Empire less deposits are required than from companies established in foreign countries, for the obvious reason that recovery under a policy is simpler by process within the Empire than by process in foreign countries. Judgment in either case can be obtained by process under the New Zealand law against the local attorney of the company, but enforcement is more difficult.

A further distinction in the amount of deposit required is made between companies already established in New Zealand and companies desiring to enter into such business in New Zealand in future.

All deposits are required to be in cash, and to be invested in the common fund of the Public Trust Office.

The provisions in the repealed Acts relating to life insurance companies are transferred in substance to a separate Bill amending the Life Insurance Act, 1908.

The following deposits are required under the Act:—

DEPOSITS BY BRITISH COMPANIES NOW CARRYING ON INSURANCE BUSINESS IN NEW ZEALAND.

	£
In respect of fire insurance business	15,000
In respect of employers' liability insurance business	15,000
In respect of all other classes of insurance business	5,000

Deposits by Foreign Companies now carrying on Insurance Business in New Zealand.

	£
In respect of all classes of insurance business, and whether one only or more than one class of insurance business is carried on	35,000

British companies hereafter proposing to carry on any class of insurance business will be required to deposit £50,000 and foreign companies £100,000.

LIFE INSURANCE AMENDMENT ACT.

The above Act, which came into force on the 6th February, 1922, provides (*inter alia*) that:—

Consolidating Act.

Every company now carrying on or hereafter commencing to carry on the business of life insurance in New Zealand shall deposit with the Public Trustee money or securities to the amount of £5,000, and a further amount of £5,000 for every £100,000 or part of £100,000 by which the total amount assured by its policies current in its New Zealand business exceeds £100,000 up to a maximum deposit of £50,000.

COMPANIES' TEMPORARY EMPOWERING ACT.

(Empowering Issue of "Deposit Preference Shares"; Income Tax; Application to trustees.)

Certain companies in New Zealand holding moneys on deposit having found difficulties, "by reason of the financial conditions consequent upon the late War and of the depreciation in market selling values of the principal products of the Dominion," in making payments to their depositors, and depositors having been willing in certain cases to acquire preference shares in such companies in exchange for their deposits, the above Act was passed as a temporary measure with the object of enabling companies to do this, and without increasing their liability in respect of income tax.

The operation of the Act, which came into force on the 11th February, 1922, is limited to five years, and Trustees are empowered to accept "deposit preference shares."

The principal provisions of the Act are as follows:—

A company holding deposits is (notwithstanding anything in its memorandum or articles of association) empowered by special resolution within one year after the commencement of the Act to increase its capital by the creation of deposit preference shares. The denomination of the shares and the rate of preferential dividend is to be determined by the special resolution creating them, and they must be issued as fully paid. (*Section* 3.)

A company issuing deposit preference shares is for the period of five years from the commencement of the Act to be entitled to deduct each year from its assessable and taxable income the dividends payable by the company on deposit preference shares, and the liability for income tax is placed upon the holder of the shares. (*Section* 6.)

SOUTH AFRICA.

The following Summary is in continuation of the proceedings of the Second Session of the Fourth Parliament of the Union of South Africa which commenced on 17th February, 1922, and was prorogued on 20th July.

UNION DEFENCE FORCES BILL.

(Registration and exemptions; Training; Air Service; etc.)

The further provision made for the Permanent Defence Force and the assumption by the Union Government of full responsibility for land defences formed the subject of various discussions in the House of Assembly during May and June. As the South African Defence Act Amendment Bill and the Defence Endowment Property and Account Bill had not been received at the time of going to press, the discussions upon these have been held over.

DEBATE IN HOUSE OF ASSEMBLY.

On 4th May,

The Minister of Defence (Col. the Hon. H. Mentz) explained that the Union Defence Forces Bill* had been amended in Select Committee, and the amendments as agreed to were now before the Committee of the House. On the clause relating to the Registration of Citizens,† he himself moved an amendment to substitute " 1920, 1921, 1922, 1923, or 1924 " for " 1919, 1920, or 1921," and to substitute " 1924 " for " 1922." He had met his friends opposite, and proposed to only start to pick up registration from the year 1920.

Exemptions.

General J. C. G. Kemp (Nationalist, *Wolmaransstad, Trans.*) said the Minister of Defence should also exempt recruits for 1922-23, because it was not their fault that they had not been mobilised, and he moved an amendment accordingly.

The Minister of Defence said he would change his amendment so as to exempt the recruits for 1921. Replying to other Members, he said there had been no registration since the War owing to the disturbed state of affairs. The endeavour of the Bill was that those who became 17 in 1921 should register in 1924. They would start training in 1924 the boys

---

* Provisions of the Bill and debate on the Second Reading were given in the JOURNAL, Vol. II., No. 3, pp. 681-8. The Bill lapsed by reason of prorogation last Session, and Clauses 1, 2 and 3 were amended in Select Committee.

† *Vide* JOURNAL, Vol. II., No. 3, p. 682.

who became 17 in 1920. Exemption would be given on educational and other grounds, but if these youths did not make their choice of the unit in which they propose to serve before they became 21, the Department would step in and allocate them.

General Kemp having withdrawn his amendment, and the Minister of Defence's amendments having been agreed to, the clause (5) as amended was agreed to.

Peace training.

On the clause (6) dealing with peace training,*

The Minister of Defence said the Nationalist objections were removed by his proposals. Centralised camps were done away with, and youths could be trained in the camps and units which they chose for themselves. Every possible care had been taken that the camps were not too near to the large towns, but one difficulty was to say what constituted a large town. He thought this matter might safely be left to the military authorities, who would always be willing to listen to representations. Where a cadet made full use of his facilities of training between the ages of 17 and 21, he would put in at the most about 30 days in the training camp. It was only the man who had never undergone any training during those years who would be kept 60 days. The military authorities would not hold camps at a time of year when the youths were needed on the farms.

Mr. P. W. G. Grobler (Nationalist, *Rustenburg, Trans.*) wanted to know why a change in the Act of 1912 was necessary at all. The only warfare they were threatened with was against natives, and for that such a prolonged period of training was unnecessary. On the other hand, if it was sought to bring their cadets up to European standard, the training proposed would not be really adequate.

On 8th May, on the resumption of the debate, Dr. Forsyth (Labour, *Capetown, Gardens*) having raised the question of training on Sundays,

The Minister of Defence gave the assurance unreservedly that there would be no training on Sundays.

Air Service proposals.

On another clause (9), in reply to a request for a statement as to the Government's air-service policy, the Minister said if the country wanted, as he believed it did, an air service, there was no reason why the personnel and material at present in the possession and control of the Department should not be used for that purpose. He would support it, but somebody else would have to foot the bill. If there were any loss, as he

* *Vide* JOURNAL, Vol. II., No. 3, p. 682.

was afraid there was bound to be, judging by the experience of other countries, then Parliament should know that it was voting a special sum of money for an experiment.

The amendments were agreed to, and the Bill set down for Third Reading.

MOZAMBIQUE CONVENTION.

(Notice of renunciation.)

On 6th April, in the House of Assembly, replying to a question by Mr. W. Greenacre (South African Party, *Durban, Point, Natal*),

The Prime Minister (Lieut.-General the Right Hon. J. C. Smuts) said the Government had given notice of its intention to renounce the Mozambique Convention as from 1st April, 1923. Twelve months' notice had to be given of any such intention between the two parties, and the Union Government had given that notice. Some time ago the Administration of Mozambique informed the Union Government that they were dissatisfied with the Convention, which they considered no longer applicable to the circumstances existing between the two countries. They did not renounce the Convention, but informed the Government that they were going to do so; and before actually taking that step they intended to have a Conference between the two countries.

Portuguese Government and Conference.

The Conference was welcomed by the Union Government, and was to have been held in March in Cape Town, and the Portuguese Delegates had been invited; but owing to various causes it was not held, and as the Union Government was just as much dissatisfied with the existing Convention, they came to the conclusion that the proper course, in the interest of the Union, was to take the step themselves and give notice of renunciation, which was done.

The notice had to be given before the end of March in order to become operative from 1st April of 1923. At the same time, they had informed the Portuguese Government that in giving notice they were not proceeding with the idea of abandoning the Conference, but welcomed it, and renewed invitations to the Delegates to visit Cape Town to discuss fully the terms of the new Convention.

The Prime Minister said he had every reason to think that course would be pursued by the Portuguese Government, and that at an early date a Conference would take place.

In the course of subsequent negotiations in Cape Town between the Union Government and representatives of the Portuguese Government no agreement was reached, and it was announced by the Prime Minister on 23rd June that General Freire d'Andrade, the head of the Portuguese Delegation, was returning to Lisbon to lay the position before his Government.

(*The Parliamentary Debates in which this statement is reported did not arrive in time to be adequately dealt with in the present number of the* JOURNAL.)

INDIANS IN THE UNION.

(Census figures; Repatriation.)

On 1st March, in the House of Assembly, in reply to a question by Mr. L. Blackwell (South African Party, *Bezuidenhout, Trans.*) in regard to the figures of the Indian population of the Union as revealed by the recent census,

The Minister of the Interior (Hon. Patrick Duncan) gave the following figures: Cape Province, 4,827 males, 1,650 females; Natal, 78,868 males, 59,889 females; Orange Free State, 58 males, 21 females; Transvaal, 9,316 males, 4,028 females. Totals: 93,069 males; 65,588 females.

On 6th March, in the House of Assembly, when the Additional Estimates of Expenditure from Revenue and Loan Funds were under consideration in Committee, on Vote No. 20, Interior, £31,775,

Mr. T. Boydell (Leader of the Labour Party) asked for information in regard to the sum of £16,000 for the repatriation of Asiatics.*

The Minister of the Interior said that the item appeared on the Estimates because a large number of Indians were going back to India, and many of them were indigent, and it was necessary to render them some assistance. The number of Indians who had gone back under this scheme since July, 1920, was about 4,400. Since the Act was passed in 1914 up to the end of this month some 12,600 had gone, "or will have gone," under that scheme. It was quite possible that a considerably greater number would go back.

The Vote was agreed to.

MIGRATION.

(Conditions of entry into the Union; Restrictions against undesirable aliens; etc.)

On 1st March, in the House of Assembly,

Mr. C. W. Malan (Nationalist, *Humansdorp, Cape*) asked the Prime Minister for information on (1) special benefits

* *Vide* JOURNAL, Vol. II., No. 2, p. 439.

granted to ex-Service men who emigrate to South Africa from the United Kingdom under the Imperial Oversea Settlement Committee Scheme; (2) the obligations undertaken by the South African Government in connection with this scheme; (3) who was the representative appointed by the Government who undertook the responsibility of deciding as to the suitability of each applicant and the assured prospects of employment awaiting him, and what were his emoluments; (4) what steps were taken by the Government to find employment in South Africa for these immigrants; (5) whether special railway facilities were granted to these and other immigrants from the United Kingdom, and the exact nature thereof; and (6) when was the scheme started, and how many immigrants had been admitted to South Africa under it.

The Prime Minister (Lieut.-General the Right Hon. J. C. Smuts) replied: (1) None so far as the Union Government was concerned; (2) None; (3) No one, but the High Commissioner was consulted in each case to see that the persons selected could comply with the Immigration Laws on arrival in the Union; (4) No such immigrants were afforded special facilities to find employment, the persons concerned either having sufficient capital to maintain themselves or come to definite employment; (5) No special railway facilities were granted; and (6) In May, 1919; 2,304 males and 718 females had arrived since that date up to 31st December, 1921.

Immigration Statistics for 1921.

On 14th March, in the House of Assembly, in reply to Major G. B. van Zyl (South African Party, *Cape Town, Harbour*), who asked how many immigrants arrived in South Africa during the year ended February, 1922,

The Minister of the Interior (Hon. Patrick Duncan) said the figures could not be given without a great deal of clerical labour. The following, however, represented the statistics for the calendar year 1921, and the months of January and February, 1922:—

For 1921: British, 16,784; South America, 31; United States, 394; Austria, 7; Belgium, 941; China, 63; Holland, 431; France, 152; Germany, 277; Greece, 74; Italy, 194; Japan, 5; Spain, 10; Portugal, 149; Roumania, 114; Russia, 1,416; Denmark, 38; Switzerland, 120; Turkey, 9; Scandinavia, 171; others, 600.

January and February, 1922: British, 2,099; South America, 25; United States, 25; Austria, 1; Belgium, 118; China, 2; Holland, 29; France, 29; Germany, 36; Greece, 7; Italy, 23; Japan, 1; Portugal, 26; Roumania, 2; Russia, 92; Denmark, 4; Switzerland, 10; Scandinavia, 21; others, 132. The figures in regard to China were those of wives and children of Chinese domiciled in the Union.

British Naturalisation.

In reply to a further question by Major van Zyl, the

Minister gave the number of persons who were naturalised as British subjects during last year as follows:—

Russians, 701; Germans, 402; Italians, 40; Austrians, 34; Danes, 20; French, 5; Turks, 19; Swiss, 17; Greeks, 41; Hollanders, 22; Americans, 10. Total, 1,311.

DEBATE IN THE SENATE.

On 27th March, the subject of alien immigration and the need of greater safeguards against the unrestricted entry of undesirable aliens into the Union was discussed.

Senator the Hon. Sir Jacobus Graaff (*Cape*) asked the Minister of the Interior: In view of the large number of undesirable aliens who are finding their way into the Union, does the Government propose to amend the present immigration law with a view to providing more stringent provisions restricting the immigration of such aliens?

The Minister of the Interior said that the Government had the matter under consideration with a view to providing greater safeguards if at all possible to control undesirable immigration.

Upon the House resolving into Committee on the Appropriation (Part) Bill,

Senator Sir Jacobus Graaff said it was the duty of the Government to take strong action to prevent the immigration of undesirable aliens; he feared that a good many came through non-British ports. South Africa was at present the dumping ground for these people and from recent events they knew what it had cost them.

Senator the Hon. E. R. Grobler (*Nom.*) said it was difficult to decide who were undesirables. He would like to see the Deportation Act more rigidly applied.

The Minister of Posts and Telegraphs (Hon. Sir Thomas Watt) said the law was somewhat elastic. It was an exceedingly difficult thing to keep these people out, because the undesirable was very often a well-educated man, and, therefore, the education test was not perhaps the best way of excluding them.

Imported "political sympathy."

Senator the Hon. C. J. Langenhoven (*Cape*) thought the Immigration Act placed too great powers in the hands of the Government to show favours to any particular class of immigrants. For instance, they had looked with the greatest favour towards a certain class of immigrant who would swamp the existing voters. He referred to the 1820 British Settlers' movement, which had a full measure of Government sympathy. He thought it a dangerous thing for a Government to import political sympathy from outside. The evil might work both ways. To-day the Government might flood the country with English voters, and next a pernicious Nationalist Government might introduce large numbers of Hollanders and Germans to swamp the other side. The arguments which the Minister had produced for continuing the present immigration laws were sufficient reason for their amendment, inasmuch as it gave too arbitrary power to officials.

British Settlers' Association, 1820.

Senator the Hon. Sir Walter Stanford (*Nom.*) said that, as far as he knew, the names mentioned in connection with the recent upheaval on the Rand were those of South Africans. The settlers being brought out there by the 1820 Settlers' Association were carefully selected men who would be a valuable asset to the country. The Association had even received two applications from Hollanders which had been favourably considered. There was at present a stream of immigration flowing to Canada, Australia and other countries. He ridiculed the idea that the introduction of British settlers was intended to dominate the Dutch. The British Settlers' Association had sought no assistance from the Government and worked on their own responsibility.

References desirable.

Senator the Hon. I. W. B. de Villiers (*O.F.S.*) said it was to be suspected that after the War there would be a large influx of people from the more unsettled countries. What America had done was merely to foresee matters and frame laws accordingly. They should act on similar lines.

Senator the Hon. W. Cochrane (*Natal*) maintained that as long as they allowed sedition to be preached at street corners they would have trouble. There was an Act in existence dealing with the suppression of such things, and he asked why it had not been applied.

Senator the Hon. W. K. Tucker (*Trans.*) thought that immigrants should be required to produce references from their country of origin and that they should not be allowed to settle in South Africa until these had been confirmed.

OVERSEAS ADVERTISING.

Replying in the House of Assembly on 2nd May to Mr. C. W. Malan (Nationalist, *Humansdorp, Cape*),

Expenses.

The Minister of Railways and Harbours (Hon. J. W. Jagger) said: "Contributions towards overseas advertising during the period of 34 months ending 28th February, 1922, were made up as follow:—South African Railways and Harbours, £27,434; Union Government, £21,337; public bodies and private individuals, £9,765; Total, £58,536. Overseas advertising is under the jurisdiction of the High Commissioner in London. Mr. Tatlow, who is an officer of the Railways and Harbours Administration, visited Europe in connection with the inauguration of the advertising scheme, but returned to South Africa nearly a year ago. The scheme was financed from the contributions shown above. Immigrants may get advice from the High Commissioner's Office; but giving advice to intending immigrants is not the only function of any section of the High Commissioner's Office. The reasons advanced by the hon. Member for discontinuing the overseas advertising scheme are good reasons for continuing it and encouraging the diversion of capital to the development of industrial and agricultural activities in South Africa as a means of extending the scope for employment."

Objects of the scheme.

The main objects of the scheme were: (1) to disseminate authentic information relating to South African industries, manufactures and farming; (2) to extend the demand and the markets for South African products; (3) to attract capital for mining, industrial and farming activities, and make known to prospective investors the opportunities for industrial development and for increased activity in mining, especially in base minerals and metals; and (4) to attract tourists to the South African route.

RHODESIA AND THE UNION.*

(Negotiations with Chartered Company and Imperial Government; Fiscal Policy.)

On 22nd May, in the House of Assembly, in reply to a question by Mr. T. Boydell (Leader of the Labour Party), regarding statements which were being made in the Legislative Council of Rhodesia,

The Prime Minister (Lt.-Gen. the Rt. Hon. J. C. Smuts) said that when the Rhodesian Delegation were there, the Government had informed them that they would be prepared to offer terms of union as soon as they (the Government) could come to an agreement with the Chartered Company. To offer them before would, of course, be a very great blunder indeed, because it would put the Union in these negotiations regarding expropriation, very much at the mercy of the Chartered Company; the latter would be able to say,

* *Vide* JOURNAL, Vol. III., No. 2, p. 456.

"The Union Government is bound, and we shall raise our terms."

Negotiations with the Chartered Company.

They therefore made it perfectly clear that before they could offer terms to Rhodesia they must first be *ad idem* with the Chartered Company and know exactly on what terms they should expropriate. As soon as the Conference with the Rhodesian Delegation was over they started negotiations with the Chartered Company, and it did not seem impossible that they might come to terms, but the questions were very difficult. They involved practically the whole history of Rhodesia, and the negotiations had been very protracted.

Imperial Government involved.

But that was not the only difficulty. The Imperial Government was also involved. In the Union's efforts to come to a settlement with the Chartered Company they had, at a certain point, required the consent of the British Government, and they wanted the British Government to take part. That had raised a difficulty of considerable dimensions. Under these circumstances it was entirely wrong to accuse the Union Government of delay. They had urged on day and night in connection with these negotiations, because he (the Premier) foresaw quite early that a charge would be made against them that they were holding up the impending change in Rhodesia.

The difficulties would be overcome, too, in regard to the Imperial Government, and the people would find that long before it was possible to hold a referendum in Rhodesia all the obstacles would be cleared away, and the Rhodesian people would know exactly where they stood and be able to give a free and unbiased decision in regard to the future.

Fiscal Policy.

On 26th April, in the House of Assembly, the Minister of Finance moved :—

> That the two Protocols to the Customs Agreement between the Union of South Africa and Northern and Southern Rhodesia, which were laid upon the Table of this House on the 13th March, 1922, be ratified and confirmed.

DEBATE IN HOUSE OF ASSEMBLY.

Duties paid to Northern and Southern Rhodesia.

The Minister of Finance (Hon. H. Burton) said that under the agreement which existed prior to 1915 the Union Government paid to the Administration of Northern and Southern Rhodesia, first of all, the actual duties collected on goods removed into these territories, and, secondly, duties paid on imported material of goods manufactured in the Union, and subsequently removed into Rhodesia. This system was afterwards superseded by an arrangement to pay a lump sum in commutation of the duties, the first arrangement being to pay Northern Rhodesia £5,000 and Southern Rhodesia £58,000.

Since this arrangement was made in 1915, in succeeding years upon consideration of the trade statistics the sum to Northern Rhodesia had been increased from time to time. It rose to £10,000. In 1921 the trade statistics were examined, and it was ascertained that the sum of £10,000 was unfair, and it was agreed it should be £12,500. A protocol giving effect to this arrangement was entered into last year.

As to Southern Rhodesia, the payment was raised in 1918 to £100,000. The provisions of this particular protocol expired in 1920, and it was agreed that the payment of £100,000 should go on, and that, thereafter, the Union might give twelve months' notice to change. At the end of 1920 the position was reviewed, and the Union Government recognised that the amount should be increased to £125,000.

The Administrations of Northern and Southern Rhodesia desired to increase the duty on Union spirits by 2s. 6d. per imperial proof gallon, and had asked the Union Government to allow them to apply in their territory the same tobacco excise as in the Union. They had been able to levy a duty on Union spirits up to 21s. 3d., and on imported spirits up to 30s. The Union duty had been increased since then, and Rhodesia simply asked to be allowed to increase the duty on Union spirits, provided the duty on imported spirits was increased proportionately. In reply to a question as to the period the protocols would cover, Mr. Burton replied "Twelve months."

Influx of Rhodesian cattle.

Mr. N. C. Havenga (Nationalist, *Fauresmith, O.F.S.*) alleged that the Minister of Finance only recently told the House that the Union exported much more to Rhodesia than it imported from that territory, and that the Union would come off worse in a customs war with Rhodesia. The Government should have clinched the opportunity to guard against the influx of Rhodesian cattle to the Johannesburg market to the detriment of farmers in the Union.

Mr. A. S. van Hees (Nationalist, *Christiana, Trans.*) moved as an amendment that the Protocols be referred back to the Government with a view to consulting the Rhodesian Government, and a settlement regarding the import of live stock from Rhodesia.

The Minister of Agriculture (Hon. Sir Thomas Smartt) discussing the meat question and the farmers' position, gave some details in regard to the Co-operative Association, which was formed, not to raise the price to the consumer, but to secure a better price for the producer. Grain-growers in South Africa knew that now there was a drought in Rhodesia, there was a big demand for forage. Large quantities of produce was going forward to Rhodesia, and if they struck a balance it would be in favour of the producer in South Africa by 2 to 1. The idea of preventing goods going backwards and forwards between Rhodesia and the Union was one of the most churlish propositions that could possibly be made.

Free interchange of products.

The Minister of Finance hoped they were not going to accept the amendment of Mr. van Hees, because by so doing they were going to tear up their agreement with Rhodesia. They had an agreement, such as they had had between the Transvaal and Rhodesia for the last twenty years, which provided—he thought wisely—for free interchange of products. They could not alter the Customs agreement until June, 1923, and then six months' notice would have to be given. If ever the country was going to make a mistake in its fiscal policy it would do so if it tore up, or altered, or interfered with the fiscal policy between the Union and Rhodesia. No doubt the farming community were affected for the time being, but if they attempted to deal with what was only a present difficulty, they would immediately raise repercussions in all directions which would leave them very sorry for having attempted it.

Export figures.

In 1921 the Union sent goods worth £2,881,000 to Rhodesia, South African produce and manufactured articles amounting to £1,049,000. Rhodesia sent to the Union £477,000 worth of goods. The position was that the South African manufactured article was beating the foreign one out of the Rhodesian market.

The difficulty in which their cattle breeders were placed was, Mr. Burton believed, only temporary. In 1920, 14,000 cattle, valued at £148,000, had been imported into the Union from Rhodesia, and in 1921 this had decreased to 8,000, valued at £74,000. Evidence seemed to show that the number was being reduced. If they put an import tax on Rhodesian cattle, would not the Rhodesian people come along with reprisals ? There was a more severe drought in Rhodesia now than in the Union, and the Rhodesian people fully expected that they would have to come to the Union for maize. It was a decided advantage to the producers of the whole of South Africa that there should not be reprisals, and that there should be free trade between Rhodesia and the Union.

The amendment was negatived by 67 to 31 votes, the Labour Party supporting the Government, and the resolution, which was agreed to, was forwarded to the Senate for its concurrence.

PROPORTIONAL REPRESENTATION.

On 4th April the question of applying Proportional Representation in connection with Elections to the House of Assembly was debated in that House, on the motion of Mr. D. M. Brown.

DEBATE IN HOUSE OF ASSEMBLY.

Mr. D. M. Brown (South African Party, *Three Rivers, Cape*) moved

That the Government be requested to consider the desirability of appointing a Commission during the ensuing recess to inquire into and report upon the expediency of introducing and applying the principle of proportional representation in connection with the election of Members of the House of Assembly.

Position in O.F.S.

He pointed out that under the present system nearly one-third of the electors of the Orange Free State who were of the opposite political colour to the present Members representing that Province were, with one exception, unrepresented in that House, and Members of the Orange Free State to whom he had spoken on the matter admitted it was wrong. Of course, it was somewhat unfair to single out only that one Province, but if they took the position for the whole of the Union, the Nationalist Party under proportional representation would be in no worse position, as far as the number of its Parliamentary representatives was concerned, than was the case at present.

The men who sat in the National Convention had come to the conclusion that proportional representation was a fair and just system. He asked where would the representation of the Senate have been without it, as a result of which Natal had obtained one Labour Senator. In the Cape the Nationalist minority were represented in the Senate, but would not have had a representative without proportional representation.

The Prime Minister, Mr. Brown went on to say, had stated that they ought to have proportional representation so as to give fair play to the Free State. He (Mr. Brown) did not want fair play for the Free State only, but for the Union. He wanted a minority to be represented in that House. No system yet devised was perfect, but he claimed that proportional representation was more perfect than the present system.

Present Parliament unrepresentative.

Mr. Sampson (Labour, *Jeppes, Trans.*) said he did not see how Parliament could be a representative body unless the system embodied in the motion were followed. He thought the present Parliament a most unrepresentative body.

Mr. L. Blackwell (South African Party, *Bezuidenhout, Trans.*) said that in the North they had had considerable experience of proportional representation, but it had been weighed in the balance and found wanting. There were cases where proportional representation elections were the only fair ones, as in connection with the Senate. But there were other cases in which it fell away. It had been found wanting in Johannesburg. The average back-velder would not be able to grasp the intricacies of it.

The Minister of Posts and Telegraphs (Hon. Sir Thomas Watt) said the matter had been thrashed out at the National Convention, where it was adopted, but was afterwards thrown out, and for good reasons. That showed that it had broken down. Then came the question of larger constituencies, and they had constituencies in the Cape Province almost as large as Natal itself. It followed that it was almost impossible for a candidate to visit all the centres between nomination day and polling day. It would necessitate the prolongation of the election period, and that was undesirable. If they had larger constituencies it would give an old candidate an advantage over a newcomer.

The system had been introduced in the Transvaal, he continued, in the hope that it would be a workable proposition in the various Provinces, but nobody was satisfied. It was an undoubted fact that it was complicated in working out the result of the voting, and even intelligent people were puzzled when they were expected to vote for 15, 20, or 30 candidates at an election.

Mr. J. H. H. de Waal (Nationalist, *Piquetberg, Cape*) pointed out that in the old Cape days the "plumping" system, which was to some extent a kind of proportional representation, had been as great a failure as the experiment in the Transvaal.

Election on population basis.

Mr. A. S. van Hees (Nationalist, *Christiana, Trans.*) anticipated all kinds of trouble in regard to nomination of candidates under the Party system, and feared that in South Africa, with its large constituencies, the proportional system would prove impossible. He moved an amendment to the effect that the election of Members should be on a population basis. His object was that the whole of the population in the country should be counted and divided up into equal numbers, each of which totals would elect a representative.

Mr. J. Christie (Labour, *Langlaagte, Trans.*) said that the whole object of proportional representation was to see that every section was represented. It also did away with the misuse of the direct vote. The position in Johannesburg during the period of proportional representation was quite as good as it was now, and he believed the percentage of voters was higher. He did not think the system had been tried and found wanting, but, on the contrary, regarded it as a success.

Mr. van Hees's amendment was negatived on the voices. Mr. Brown's Motion was negatived by 74 votes to 15.

INDUSTRIAL EXPANSION.*

(Development of South African industries; support for Protection; Government policy outlined—preference for copper, bounty for iron and steel; help for farmers.)

On 2nd May,

Mr. N. G. Mackeurtan (South African Party, *Durban—Umbilo, Natal*), in moving

That this House recognises that the encouragement and development of South African industries are essential to the future prosperity of the country and requests that the Government at the earliest possible date will take further and active steps to that end.

said he had no interest in any industry of any kind in that country and no axe to grind. He wanted to see local industries prosperous and encouraged by definite and direct means.

Problem of unemployment.

They needed these industries in order to solve the problem of unemployment. There were thousands of young men and women coming on, and there were poor whites for whom they had no work. They had a unique opportunity for producing industries. They had been sending their hides and wool out of the country and receiving back the manufactured products. That was not economy. It was the same thing with wattle bark. They had plenty of raw material and an abundant cheap labour supply; they also had the start which the War had given them and a splendid geographical position with unlimited resources.

Government policy.

The expressed policy of the Government, Mr. Mackeurtan continued, was one of protection for local industries. The question was, how would they protect? Some assistance had been given. The Act of Union said that the railways must be

* *Vide* Journal, Vol. II., No. 4, p. 928.

run on business lines with a view to developing South African industries. The Minister's policy of preferential rates had not yet been abolished. That meant that any help in respect of local industries in the way of railway rates for the future was insecure. The policy was a policy of preferential tariff on South African made articles. That meant that there would be no protection in that direction. At present some South African articles did get help in that way, but others did not. The railway rate might be put down to-morrow and raised the day after; therefore, they could not look to the railways to assist South African industries.

Customs tariff; licence system; etc.

Referring to the Customs tariff, Mr. Mackeurtan said it was not a Customs tariff, but a revenue tariff, framed and treated as such. They had quite recently the licence system in regard to boots and shoes, which he was satisfied had been the salvation of the boot trade in that country. Another way in which it was said that local industry was helped was by fixing the exchange on articles from Germany at 400 marks to the £. Lastly, they had the Board of Trade and Industries, which came in last Session. It was a genuine attempt to effect improvement, but had not been a success, one reason for that being that there was no manufacturer represented on it at all.

The manufacturers of South Africa had been for years trying to get adequate protection. The result was that people were not inclined to invest money in their industries. They had natural resources which were untapped. Manufacturers were working with labour that was not fully skilled in many occupations, under climatic and other difficulties, against highly-skilled labour, mass production and no local prejudice, so far as the overseas manufacturers were concerned.

Protection in Australia and Canada.

Dwelling on the value of protection, Mr. Mackeurtan cited the cases of the tobacco, wine and sugar industries, and spoke of the growth of industries in Australia and Canada under the protective system.

A number of suggestions had been made. First, they must abolish the Board of Trade and Industries and supplant it with a whole-time Board of Experts, as they had in Australia, New Zealand and elsewhere. The Tariff Board should have representatives of the various interests involved. They should also consider other means of protection. They did not want protection for every mushroom industry. He wanted the Board he had suggested to be a recommendatory Board, and to act promptly.

Mining and agriculture.

Sir Abe Bailey (South African Party, *Krugersdorp, Trans.*) said he believed in the Government carrying out a protective policy. The two basic industries of the country were mining and agriculture. If by protecting these industries they raised the price of the article they would also raise wages and the spending power of the people. As an instance of a high tariff cheapening the cost, he mentioned the case of chemicals in England. He also showed that the buying power of the £ during the War was lower in South Africa than in Australia or New Zealand, both of which were highly protected countries.

Sir Abe Bailey further said that they produced tin and copper and other things in South Africa and sent abroad for their supplies. In regard to coal, 18 months ago the industry was killed by the action of the railways, and it was hit on the head again through the strike. The railways should assist if they were going to develop industries. All great countries, he continued, had been built up by protection—for instance, Japan, Germany, America, Australia and Canada. Personally, he thought the abolition of preferential rates a good one. Properly speaking, the money should come through the Customs.

On the Rand they had more unemployment than ever before in their history, and it was increasing. The farming industry was depressed, and large numbers of bijwoners were leaving the farms and going to the relief works on the Rand. They wanted to encourage a spirit of private enterprise. The cry should be for a bold and forward policy of development.

Nationalists advocate protection.

General the Hon. J. B. M. Hertzog (Leader of the Nationalist Party) said his Party had always advocated a definite protective policy. Even England had built up its industries on a policy of protection and industrial independence. He condemned the *laissez-faire* policy of the Government, which made the position worse from year to year, and, while fully concurring in the Motion, moved an amendment to the effect that legislation should be introduced during the Session by the Government with a view of making the country more independent industrially.

Mr. J. Stewart (Labour, *East London, Cape*) moved to add to General Hertzog's amendment :—

> Such proposals to make provision for the extension of State and municipal enterprise in the production and distribution of the necessaries of life.

Mr. C. Pearce (Labour, *Liesbeck, Cape*) seconded the amendment.

The debate was adjourned.

On 22nd May, in the course of the Budget debate, the Prime Minister outlined the Government's programme in regard to industrial expansion.

Good prospects for mining industry.

The Prime Minister (Lieut.-General the Right Hon. J. C. Smuts) said the mining industry now had the chance to re-organise itself on a really efficient basis, and he hoped the Commission which was then sitting would contribute materially to that end. The gold mines would enter upon a new era, and prosperity would come not only to those immediately concerned, but to every one else outside. He was hopeful that nobody would be permanently out of employment, and that they would see fresh employment opening out in many other directions.

Coal exports.

Unless they could supply proper outlets for the export of their coal to the Indian Ocean the coal industry would become throttled. Every effort was being made with the Portuguese Delegation now in South Africa* to obtain that outlet, and he hoped that in a few years the coal industry would become one of their greatest industries. The position on the Witwatersrand was painful and lamentable, but at the rate at which native labour was coming back to the Rand the coal industry ought to be working at its full level, and the artisan class absorbed as a whole, next September.

Industrial transformation.

In regard to the industrial position of the Union, the country looked to Parliament and the Government in order to bring about, on sane and wise lines, the transformation awaiting them. He did not believe there were free traders there or that the old issues concerned them. They were all industrialists, and their only problem was how to reasonably bridge the transition from the old South Africa to the new.

The Prime Minister pointed to some of the difficulties they were faced with. In other countries farming and agriculture had been opponents of a policy of protection; if they went to the North of America or to Canada they found that a great battle for free trade was put up by the farming classes. High protection meant high prices, high prices meant high wages, and the circle at once started round again. But there was no reason why they should not steadily and moderately move forward in shaping their industrial position.

Australian tariff; Dumping.

After giving as an instance what had been done in the boot and shoe industry by the permit system instead of by

* *Vide* p. 665.

Customs tariff, import dues and high protection, the Prime Minister said that in Australia, where very high tariffs had been adopted, industries were falling to pieces in large numbers. This showed how careful they had to be in the matter of protection.

One of the gravest dangers to which they were exposed was dumping, due to the cheapness of production in countries with depreciated currency. The Minister of Finance proposed to widen the scope of the dumping clause and give it a form which would provide against the danger mentioned.

Investigation by Board of Trade.

Their Customs tariff, the Prime Minister went on to say, was in a very anomalous condition, and the position required a thorough overhauling; but investigation should be made into a number of questions before they asked Parliament to take action and revise the whole tariff, and the Board of Trade had been instructed to make that investigation. It was a judicial body, not interested in one way or the other, whose opinion could be accepted on the facts. He thought they had made an immense step forward, the magnitude of which was not yet appreciated, in the constitution of the Board. Australia had at last been forced to copy that example and had appointed a Tariff Board, but the chairman of it was the Director of Customs, while in their country (South Africa) they had put at the head of the Board a man of impartial judgment who, under the instructions of the Government, would give his best time and attention to the consideration of the evidence brought before him. The Board would make recommendations to them next year, and the House would be in a position with the full investigations before them to arrive at an impartial judgment.

Preference to South African copper.

There were other ways in which their industrial condition might be, and was being, strengthened. The provision in the tariff that the Tender Board should give a 10 per cent. preference to South African industries in tendering to Government requirements was being broadly carried out. The tenders for electrifying a large portion of the railways, for which a great deal of copper was necessary, were called for in London, however, where there was world competition, and not before the Tender Board in South Africa. The Minister of Railways had, therefore, given instructions in London, in calling for these tenders, that a preference of £5 a ton should be given to South African copper, and they were told that this would materially help some of their copper mines to proceed with, or resume, operations. On the present price this would be something like 9 per cent.

Bounty for iron and steel: Canadian example.

Coming to the iron and steel industry, which was of fundamental importance in their future industrial development, the Prime Minister showed how it was suffering from want of working capital, and said the Government had decided in principle to give a bounty to all iron and steel produced from native South African ores. The enormous iron and steel industry in Canada started with that initial advantage of a bounty, which was given over a period of ten years, and that was how Canada succeeded. That was what they were doing in Australia. In South Africa they were resorting to this endeavour, which had been successful in other countries.

Assistance for farmers.

The farmers, who had passed through a period of the greatest trial and difficulty, suffering especially from two great calamities, unprecedented droughts and the plague of locusts, would also have to be assisted. One method which had been suggested was through the Land Bank; that was under investigation. If the co-operative Bill passed* and farming became a much more organised institution than at present, he hoped it would then be possible for the Land Bank to be more liberal in supporting the farming industry, and that before the end of the Session means could be effected and alterations made which would materially help the farmers.

Meat problem.

The question of meat was one of the gravest problems before them. South Africa was very largely a ranching country, and yet the position was one of total chaos and disorganisation. The great percentage of their meat must be exported, but there was no system whatever in fixing prices. They exported meat which had made their name stink in the markets of Europe; and they had certainly lost the chance of building up the export trade in meat with the Argentine, New Zealand and Australia.

What they wanted was not monopolies but organisation. A hue and cry had been raised about monopolies and a document produced which was laid on the Table,† but they (the Government) had had nothing whatever to do with that document. He asked the members not to look out for corrupt deals between the Government and other interests in the

---

* The Co-operative Societies Bill, to assist Co-operation among the farming population.

† This refers to a document purporting to be a draft agreement between certain companies, with references to the Government, commented upon by Mr. M. Alexander (Constitutional-Democrat, *Capetown, Castle*), who made allegations against the Government, in the course of the debate on the Budget on 19th May.

country, but to let them all put their heads together in order to solve one of the greatest problems before their farming industry.

THE BUDGET.

On 5th May, the Minister of Finance made his Budget statement in the House of Assembly, the position being as follows :—

Expenditure, 1921-22	£30,225,000
Revenue	28,864,000
Deficit	1,361,000
Deduct surplus, 1919-20	460,000
	901,000
Deficit, 1920-21	400,000
Total accumulated deficit	£1,301,000
(To be carried forward.)	
Expenditure, 1922-23	£28,718,000
Strike expenditure	225,000
	28,943,000
Revenue, 1922-23	27,900,000
Excess of Expenditure over Revenue	1,043,000
Less Loan Revenues, Land Sales, Mining Leases ..	640,000
Deficit	403,000
Less Amount from New Taxation, Estate Duties, etc. ..	195,000
Deficit, 1922-23..	£208,000
(To take care of itself.)	

The Minister of Finance (**Hon. H. Burton**) said the estimate of revenue was £29,150,000 ; they had actually received £28,864,000. Customs, estimated to yield £6,315,000, only brought £5,300,000, and Excise, estimated to yield £2,151,000, had been reduced to £1,695,000. There was a reduction of £310,000 on Posts, Telegraphs and Telephones. The yield from diamond export duty, estimated at £300,000, only gave £143,000. Stamp duties yielded only £874,000. In regard to Income Tax, however, the normal and dividend tax, which was estimated to give £4,952,000, had produced £5,584,000 ; the super-tax, estimated at £1,000,000, had produced £1,390,000 ; excess profits duty, estimated at £1,300,000, had yielded £1,814,000 ; interest, estimated at £4,825,000, gave £5,113,000 ; and on the total inland revenue figures there was a net increase of £1,429,000. The final position as to the revenue was substantially better than they expected, and fortunately the gold premium was maintained during the year 1921 at a considerably higher figure than they had anticipated. The large increase in expenditure was due to their increased payments in respect of the public debt.

Other items referred to were as follows :—

Loans Account.—Of the money available for capital expenditure from the loans account, £657,000 had been spent on public works ; on telephones and telegraphs, £500,000 ; land and settlements, £443,000 ; on irrigation, £1,100,000 ; on local works and loans to the Provinces, £1,943,000 ; to the Land Bank an additional £500,000 ; on Forestry, £53,000 ; and Miscellaneous, £263,000.

Public Debt.—The public debt had been increased by £13,169,000, and now stood at £191,770,000.

Importations.—The total value of importations into the Union amounted to £58,201,000, compared with £105,927,000 in 1920. In accounting for this fall in values, falling prices, and the fact that 1920 was a decidedly abnormal year, had to be borne in mind. If the position in regard to trade was compared with 1918 and 1919, it would be seen that it was not so bad. They continued to import less and less of foodstuffs and drink, the total imports of food and drink last year being £3,394,000, as against £13,099,000 in the previous year. The figures for boots and shoes were interesting in view of the embargo on the import of these articles last year. In 1920 boots and shoes to the value of £5,359,000 were imported into the Union ; in 1921 the value was £769,000.

Exports.—Exports had decreased from £83,632,000 in 1920, to £62,381,000, this being due first of all, undoubtedly, to the collapse of the diamond market (which had fallen from £11,597,000 in 1920 to £1,355,000 last year) ; and also to the fall in the price of wool, hides and skins (total export value being £10,700,000 less than in 1920). In spite of the fall in prices, however, the tonnage weight or measurement had risen during this bad year from 2,763,000 to 3,577,000. The exports of food and drink had increased from £3,820,000 in 1920 to £7,218,000 in 1921.

Mining Industry.—The gold production for 1921 was 30,000 ounces less than 1920, but if the gold premium were maintained at about the present figure for the calendar year, and reductions could be made in working costs, it was estimated that the gold mines would contribute in 1922 and 1923 £1,620,000. They were allowing for the stoppage of work for three months, the reduced labour supply, etc.

Diamond Industry.—The diamond mining position was well known, but Mr. Burton thought he was justified in anticipating a revenue in export duty for 1922-3 of £360,000.

Banking.—The Banking position had improved very materially. Deposits were contracting far less rapidly than in 1920. Advances, which represented 88 per cent. of the deposits at the end of 1920, now represented 79 per cent. ; the note circulation had been reduced, and the gold value increased, by over a million. The Reserve Bank had commenced operations, but until it was in a position to issue its own notes it could not function properly and take its place as it should in the commercial world. The Pretoria Mint would be opened during the current financial year, and it was proposed to introduce a distinctive Union silver coinage.

New Estimates : Revenue.—The total revenue for the new year was estimated at £27,900,000. An increase in Customs and Excise had been anticipated, but the receipts from diamonds would probably be some £58,000 less than last year, and the collection on normal income tax less, while the excess profits duty had run dry and only £400,000 was expected as against £1,814,000 last year.

Expenditure.—Against the sum, £27,900,000, for revenue, expenditure had totalled £28,718,800.

These estimates made no special provision in connection with the cost of the strike on the Rand, which would be submitted at a later date in a Supplementary Estimate. For the last year these industrial disturbances had cost £200,000, and in the present year the figure would be much the same. When the present debit amount was added to this extra expenditure the deficit would be brought up to £1,043,000. In these circumstances they would be acting contrary to the country's interests if they did not call upon the revenues of land, sales and mining leases as they did last year. This would be about £640,000 next year, and that left a final deficit of £403,000. That result was certainly very much better than one was led to expect a few months ago. It was satisfactory when they remembered that they arrived at this final stage in spite of the expenditure incurred through the strike which could not reasonably have been calculated upon. But for this they might very well on those figures have been running on an even keel that year.

The estimates on administrative and clerical expenditure, establishments, services, etc., had been reduced very considerably, but they had not been obliged to interfere with the salaries of public servants

Some of the proposals made by the Board of Trade and Industry were going to be incorporated in the Budget, amongst them a measure against the dumping of goods imported from a country whose coinage has depreciated at prices detrimental to South African industries. This principle had been adopted in various ways in Canada, Australia, New Zealand and the United States. Estate Duty anomalies were also to be dealt with. Except in the Transvaal the levies in respect of death duties were almost nominal. In the United Kingdom the death duties, according to their latest information, averaged 11 per cent. of the property. They estimated that the £300,000 which they had got that year would be increased next year by 50 per cent.

DEBATE IN HOUSE OF ASSEMBLY.

Amendment.

On 12th May,

Mr. C. G. Fichardt (Nationalist, *Ladybrand, O.F.S.*) regarded the Budget as " entirely contrary to the facts." After criticising various items of expenditure, he said that the Imperial Forces at Simonstown got a rebate on Customs of £12,850, and he asked why the Union should not obtain the full benefit of that. He ultimately moved an amendment to the effect that in the opinion of the House it was not desirable to proceed with the Estimates without a full explanation as to the financial position of the country and the submission of the Government policy in regard to a programme for the effective development of the natural resources of the country.

In deference to an objection by Mr. Speaker, who said that he could allow a free discussion on the policy of the Government but could not accept the latter portion of the amendment, Mr. Fichardt withdrew that portion.

Mr. C. W. Malan (Nationalist, *Humansdorp, Cape*) seconded the amendment.

The burden of the poor.

Mr. T. Boydell (Leader of the Labour Party) said Mr. Fichardt and his Party had put forward no alternative proposals to those of the Government. He ought to be under a deep debt of gratitude to the Minister of Finance for not taxing the rich man more. The Government had tried to restore financial equilibrium by means of wholesale dismissals throughout the country, and the burden of the poor had been increased, not for the benefit of the State coffers but in order to benefit certain large industries in that country. The average family of the Union, in food, clothing and other requirements, paid something like 24s. or 25s. a month on Customs duty. That was indirect taxation which fell on the great mass of the people.

Taxation of land values.

Referring to revenue, Mr. Boydell said that South Africa got £450,000 from death duties, whereas Australia got £3,700,000 and New Zealand £1,000,000. South Africa should get at least £1,000,000. There was no country in the world where the income tax was so light as in South Africa. He then went on to advocate the adoption of a tax on land values, and claimed that it would benefit the landowner himself, as well as the country. They had 250,000,000 acres of farm lands, of which just over 13,000,000 acres were cultivated, or 4½ per cent. of the whole, as against 40 per cent. in New Zealand, where they had a land tax. He also urged the need of a State Bank, and, dealing with the vote for the League of Nations, said not a thing had been done in that House which would make the League or the Labour Convention under its auspices a success.

Labour amendment.

Mr. Boydell moved as a further amendment to add to the end of the Motion :—

Until a definite assurance is received from the Government that it would this Session introduce legislation providing for (1) the raising of revenue and the opening up of the country ; (2) a steeper grading of the income tax and death duties; (3) a differentiation between earned and unearned incomes for taxation; and (4) more adequate provision for the relief of unemployment by pushing forward relief work and other schemes for the national benefit.

The debate was adjourned.

Markets in Germany.

On resumption of the debate on 15th May,

Mr. W. R. Burch (**South African Party**, *Uitenhage, Cape*) spoke of the serious agricultural position. They had not the markets now that they used to have. When he was in Berlin last year he was particularly struck with the activities of other countries with regard to the German market. The British Government had a staff of fourteen men trying to foster trade between Great Britain and Germany. The Argentine had also a big staff. Personally he welcomed the action of the Union Government in endeavouring to open up a market there. There might have been personal feeling in regard to the appointment made,* but the principle was right, and every step in that way was a step in the right direction.

Educating public opinion.

The Right Hon. J. X. Merriman (**South African Party**, *Stellenbosch, Cape*) spoke of the need for educating public opinion, but asked what chance had they to do that? He thought that was the only Assembly in the world that managed to carry on without a Hansard. Was that because they were ashamed of what they said?

He did not think they would improve that country by introducing bastard industries. A few people in England might make millions out of them, but not the people as a whole. A great deal had been heard about finding occupations for their sons and daughters, but were there no people out of work in Australia and Canada, where high wages were paid? In Canada the average earnings of a man in a factory were £154 a year. That would be called starvation wages in Johannesburg.

The Navy in South Africa.

Mr. W. Macintosh (**South African Party**, *Port Elizabeth, S.W. Cape*) referred to the rebate of Customs to the Navy. That concession was also given to foreign Consuls. They did not allow the Navy to vote or take part in the Government of the country. The men of the Navy were welcome visitors. They were there for their (South Africans') pleasure and profit. and in welcoming them the Government was only doing what was done by every State in the world.

The debate was adjourned.

---

* *Vide* Journal, Vol. III., No. 2, pp. 450-454.

"White South Africa" impossible.

On 18th May,

Sir David Harris (South African Party, *Beaconsfield, Cape*), referring to the "absurd doctrine" of a "White South Africa," said that by substituting in the gold, diamond and coal industries, for a coloured man, whose wage might be put down at 2s. 6d. per day, a white man at 15s. per day, which was not too much, the difference would amount to £44,024,488 per annum. To that must be added the amount of the present wages paid to white men in these industries—£12,225,000. It was utterly impossible for the mining industry to carry on only with white men, and what to-day was a great asset to the country would naturally, if white men only were employed, become a burden on the State.

Contribution to the Navy.

Mr. J. Henderson (South African Party, *Durban—Berea, Natal*) said he could not congratulate the Minister of Finance upon the deletion of the contribution to the Navy, £85,000. It behoved the Government to make up its mind in regard to its policy of naval defence.

The debate was adjourned.

On 22nd May, the Prime Minister, in the course of debate on the Budget, delivered a speech dealing with the development or assistance of industries, which is summarised under "Industrial Expansion" on pp 679–682.

On 24th May the Minister of Finance (Hon. H. Burton) and the Minister of Railways and Harbours (Hon. J. W. Jagger) replied to criticism; and Mr. Boydell's amendment having been negatived by 73 votes to 10, and Mr. Fichardt's negatived without a division (which meant that one proposed by Mr. A. J. P. Fourie, as an amendment to the latter, dropped), the motion of the Minister of Finance was agreed to.

INDEMNITY AND TRIAL OF OFFENDERS ACT.

The Indemnity Bill, which was introduced by the Prime Minister in the House of Assembly on 24th March,* was discussed at great length on the Second and Third Reading, passed through all stages, and has been promulgated, thus putting an end to martial law on the Rand.

The Bill† provided for the withdrawal of martial law in every district which was placed under it by Proclamation; it also provided that no

* *Vide* JOURNAL, Vol. III., No. 2, p. 447.

† The text of the Act as passed by both Houses had not reached this country at the time of going to press so a somewhat fuller summary of the Bill is given than that published in the last number of the JOURNAL.

action or legal proceeding should be brought against the Government or its officers for certain acts "in good faith, advised, commanded, etc.," for the suppression of disorder or the maintenance of public safety on or after 10th March, 1922, and prior to the promulgation of the Act. The sentences pronounced and convictions made under martial law were by the terms of the Bill confirmed and rendered lawful; but if the Attorney-General of the Transvaal decided to indict certain persons upon a charge of murder, or assault with intent to commit murder, etc., the Governor-General might constitute a special Criminal Court to try such offences under Act No. 31 of 1917 (Criminal Procedure and Evidence Act).

DEBATE IN HOUSE OF ASSEMBLY.

On 7th April, in the course of the debate on the Second Reading,

The Minister of Lands (Col. the Hon. Deneys Reitz) said that in every crisis that South Africa had passed through the Nationalists had failed their country time after time. During the War those members had never risen above petty political intrigue; throughout the strike they played the part of wreckers. He further questioned the sincerity of the Nationalist Party's support of the Labour Party on the colour bar. The Nationalist Party was a racial Party; it believed, rightly or wrongly, that it represented a very great race. The Labour Party, on the other hand, did not believe in national boundaries, patriotism, or separate nationalities. In its origin the Nationalist Party was a conservative land-owning Party. The Labour Party was a land-taxing Party. The former objected to the South African Party joining the Unionists because the latter represented, broadly speaking, the English-speaking section of the population. When he looked round at the Party to which the Nationalists were allied to-day he did not think a single Member among them had been born in South Africa.

It was unfortunate, Col. Reitz continued, that a large section of the Dutch-speaking element of South Africa—he was speaking of the Nationalists—was so obsessed with the lust for politics that it had become their be all and end all. He was a Dutch-speaking South African, and proud of it; but if the Members opposite did not feel a chill of foreboding as regards the future of a large section of these people, he certainly did. The feeling was being deliberately encouraged that rebellion and revolution were short-cuts to political promotion. He knew it to be a fact that some 90 per cent. of the revolutionaries on the Rand were Dutch-speaking Nationalists, and he believed these men joined the revolution because they thought they were going to be supported from the country. The Nationalist Party had never pulled its weight in South Africa, but had always been a clog on the wheel.

On 11th April,

Mr. H. W. Sampson (Labour, *Jeppes, Trans.*) hoped that the terms of reference to the Judicial Commission would be amended so that the matter of the Press, and its reports of the affair on the Rand and what led up to it, might be inquired into.

In regard to the present "peaceful position" on the Rand, which had been referred to, some 10,000 men were out of work; and he wondered if the Minister of Justice would get the House to believe that when the prisoners were released they were going to make good citizens. Almost before the dead were buried they saw both sides preparing for the next struggle year after year, with intervals; these things would go on, and they were going on a royal road to real revolution. Parliament should pay more attention to these matters and try to remedy the grievances. If the Wages Bill of last year had been passed there would have been no strike on the Rand, because it contained the force necessary to make people abide by agreements.

On 12th April,

Major G. B. van Zyl (South African Party, *Cape Town, Harbour*) alluded to the regrettable way in which Party capital had been made during that debate out of the difficulties in which the country had been plunged, and appealed to General Hertzog, who had a vast influence, to lay aside his personal injury and take up the position which he did in 1914 when, in speaking to a Motion regarding an Indemnity Bill, he said the House neither could nor ought to withhold its protection from the Government. If the latter had been obliged through necessity to exceed the law, then it was their duty to protect it.

The Government, Maj. van Zyl continued, was getting tired of preserving law and order and having no time for developing the interests of the country. He appealed to Members to think more of their country and less of their personal hurts. Once they had been able to boast of the purest Civil Service in the world. They were still proud of their Law Courts, and Parliament was conducted on the most democratic lines. He asked if they were to sacrifice all these by the continuation of petty squabbles which were driving moderate men out of public life.

Brig.-General the Hon. J. J. Byron (South African Party, *Border, Cape*) said Members must realise that they now had a Commission,* and they had to face facts as they were and see, when they knew the causes, what was the best for them to do.

Having quoted from speeches made by Nationalist Leaders in December and January, General Byron remarked that when the strike had developed to the necessary extent, when the native mind was thoroughly upset, and conditions in Johannesburg were reaching " boiling point," a general strike was proclaimed by the heads of the S.A.I.F. They seemed to have been oblivious of the fact that a general strike in any country was a declaration of war by a section of the community against the whole community. The only duty of the Government was to declare martial law. The strike was a consequence of the epidemic of Bolshevism which had afflicted the whole world. The Labour Party was largely responsible for the spread of Communism.

On 18th April,

The Minister of Finance (Hon. H. Burton) stated that the Government did not come there as suppliants, but to claim an indemnity as a right, under circumstances which arose.

Alluding to a reference to the British Government and industrial strikes, Mr. Burton pointed out that the British Government had intervened, as they had intervened. What, he asked, was the result in England ?

An hon. Member : " No bloodshed."

The Minister of Finance : " No, because the English people are not given to that sort of thing. But have they escaped disastrous economic difficulties in England ? Have the extremists in England not succeeded in ousting the moderate men among their ranks ? We know that the British Labour Leaders did their duty, and that the acknowledged Leaders there warned their men that they were on the path to ruin. The advice was not taken, and we know the results.

" What is the wage position in England to-day compared with South Africa ? Your worker in South Africa is infinitely better off. Has Mr. Lloyd George been out to destroy organised Labour ? The truth is that he did not destroy it any more than we did here. They are in the process of destroying themselves by their policy."

The Minister added that they could not dodge the law of supply and demand. The root cause was the failure of Labour

---

* The Prime Minister stated on 11th April that a Judicial Commission would be appointed to investigate the causes and aims of the revolutionary movement, irregularities or excesses in connection with it and their suppression, the behaviour of the natives, etc. It would consist of Sir Thomas Graham, Judge-President of the Eastern Districts, and Sir John Lange as members.

to appreciate the fact that wages must fall with falling commodity prices. It was a phase of the world-wide necessity of getting back to normal.

On 21st April,

The Minister of the Interior (Hon. Patrick Duncan) made a statement in regard to the Government's proposals for compensation for personal injury or damage to property during the disturbances. A committee would be appointed to receive and investigate statements of such injury or damage.

On 23rd April,

The Prime Minister (Lieut.-General the Right Hon. J. C. Smuts) after referring to the two Commissions which the Government had appointed, said the danger he saw to-day was that the employers refused to take any account of organised Labour. The Government must see that Labour did not tyrannise and dominate everything, and it was for the Commission to find a way.

Continuing, General Smuts said that the workers had nothing to be grateful for to the political Leaders of the Labour Party, in whom the workers would even more lose their confidence. The Nationalists were now co-operating with the Labour Party and with the International Socialists. He would attack Nationalist and Labour Parties to the best of his ability.

After a division on an amendment proposed by **Mr. T. Boydell** (Leader of the Labour Party) to alter the wording of the Motion for the Second Reading, which was defeated by a majority of eighteen (65 votes to 47), the House further divided on the question " that the Bill be now read a Second Time," the result being the same. The Bill was set down for Committee Stage.

Certain amendments were agreed to in Committee, and on 28th April the Bill was again discussed at length on the Third Reading, which was carried by 57 votes to 44.

PROCEDURE IN HOUSE OF ASSEMBLY.

(New rules adopted for limitation of speeches and debates.)

On 26th April in the House of Assembly the first report of the Select Committee on Standing Rules and Orders was considered. The recommendations aim at shortening the time given to debates and speeches so as to permit of more business being transacted.

DEBATE IN HOUSE OF ASSEMBLY.

The Prime Minister (Lieut.-Gen. the Right Hon. J. C. Smuts) in moving the adoption of the report, said that unless Parliament were to sit practically for the whole year, the House must face a reform in its procedure such as would make that body a more efficient and more rapidly working instrument than it had been hitherto. He did not wish to belittle for a moment the importance of the events which the House had been discussing during the last two months, but with the single exception of the Financial Relations Bill they had been discussing nothing but the state of affairs in Johannesburg through the strike and the disturbances. Finally, they had had the Indemnity Bill, and he might say that on the Second Reading 82 Members spoke for 74 hours and 28 spoke for more than one hour each. He was very much afraid that if the present state of affairs continued Parliament would fall into great discredit. All over the world Parliamentary institutions were now on their trial.

Budget debate proposals.

Describing the Committee's recommendations, the Prime Minister said it was proposed that the House should revert to the old rule (altered in 1919) and have one general Budget debate, embracing both the general financial situation and the railway finances. It was also proposed that the rule that a Member should not speak for more than forty minutes be abolished. In addition to the time taken up by the Government in introducing the debate, five full days would be allowed for discussion and the reply of the Government. Under these circumstances about 38 hours would be given to the whole debate.

Speeches in Committee of Supply; General business

As regards discussion in Committee of Supply, a new Standing Order provided that, with one exception, there should be no general debate, and while in Committee no Member should speak for more than ten minutes at a time, though no limit was laid down as to the number of times he might speak. The exception would be when the question of a Minister's salary had been raised in reference either to the general policy of the Government or that of the Minister's Department. In that case, provided that not more than two Members spoke for forty minutes, that would be allowed. The Minister in reply would not be limited as regards time. Members might speak fifteen minutes at a time in Committee of Ways and Means but then only twice. On each question put from the Chair a Member might speak twice for fifteen minutes.

Coming to general business, Bills, Motions, etc., when Mr. Speaker was in the Chair, Members would be limited by a forty-minute rule, and when the House was in Committee by a ten-minute rule. The only exception was when Ministers had to introduce matters or other Members introduced a Motion, when they were not limited as above stated. A debate should not continue when there had been a Ministerial reply.

System in British House of Commons.

Referring to the practice adopted in other Legislative Chambers, the Prime Minister drew attention to the system of Closure by compartments adopted by the House of Commons in Great Britain. This, he said, was a drastic system. He thought it would be a salutary rule to resort more frequently to the Closure in that House. In the British House of Commons work was got through more rapidly than with them, and the debates were much shorter; on that account they were not less efficient or less able. No Member would dare to speak over an hour there.

Having alluded to what took place in Canada and New Zealand, General Smuts said the amendments were reasonable and ought to meet the approval of the House.

Nationalist Amendment.

Dr. D. F. Malan (**Nationalist**, *Calvinia, Cape*) welcomed the proposal for reverting to a single Budget debate, but was opposed to all the other proposals, and moved as an amendment the deletion of the whole report except the first sub-section (which lays down that there should be a full debate on the Motion for the House to go into Committee of Supply on the Estimates of Expenditure for the consolidated Revenue of Railway and Harbour Funds). If the restrictions were adopted there would be a number of matters to which the House would be unable to do justice—for instance, the "higher status" of the Union, the effect of which was that the latter shared with the rest of the Empire responsibility for every conference on foreign affairs from "Greenland to Erebus and from San Francisco to Timbuctoo." He feared that the limitation of speeches in Committee would not make for brevity, because a Member who might ordinarily have finished his speech in eleven minutes but was stopped after ten minutes would avail himself of the opportunity to make another speech of ten minutes later on. Dr. Malan quoted figures to show that the present Parliament had not been so uneconomical of its time, and pointed out that during the War the House had never given that consideration to money matters which it would otherwise have done. There were also fourteen more Members than in previous years. He suggested as an alternative to the proposals that there should be more frequent recourse to the old system of consultation between the Whips of the various Parties.

Labour views.

Mr. T. Boydell (Leader of the Labour Party) said he did not think the Parliament of any country which had gone through such an upheaval as theirs would have discussed and handled the situation in less time than the House had devoted to it. He was not surprised at the Prime Minister. "I think," Mr. Boydell declared, " he would prefer to have no Parliament at all. I think Parliament is to him a sort of national excrescence or constitutional encumbrance." These proposals were drastic and revolutionary, and he claimed that reasonable facilities should be given for debate. If necessary, the House should sit right through the year, and if Cape Town were too distant for most of the Members, let the House sit in a more central place. He maintained that they had not got in that Parliament one quarter of the disorder which was found in other Parliaments of the Empire. His Party were in favour of combining the two Budget debates, but they would oppose the other proposals.

The debate was adjourned.

On resumption on 1st May,

Mr. W. Macintosh (South African Party, *Port Elizabeth, S.W. Cape*), who said the Select Committee deserved the thanks of the House for having grappled with the matter in the way it had, said the aim was twofold : one was to limit time, and the other to make the Budget debate a real finance debate. At present it was a debate on the general affairs of the country.

An hon. Member : " That is the only chance we have."

An annual general debate.

Mr. Macintosh said he thought they should transfer the debate to some other item, which could be automatically arranged every year for a general debate on the affairs of the country. He further said he would like to see an opportunity afforded of having a debate on the Speech from the Throne. That might be limited to the first week of the Session. Everyone could speak, and it would not delay Parliament.

"Party Government" at fault.

Mr. C. G. Fichardt (Nationalist, *Ladybrand, O.F.S.*) thought the fault lay in a system of Party Government. No suggestions made on his side of the House were ever accepted. He objected to the rights of Members being whittled down any further, and submitted that 45 hours per year was not too much time to devote to the finances of the country. He suggested that considerable economy in time could be effected if the reading of Ministerial replies to questions could be dispensed with and the replies were simply printed. Again, notices of Motions, reports and papers could be handed in without any formal reading, and the record printed in the Order Paper. He also urged that Bills to be introduced during the Session should be printed and circulated among Members in advance.

Mr. H. Graumann (South African Party, *Commissioner Street, Trans.*) looked upon the new proposals as a Members' protection measure which would save many of them from tedious repetition. He reminded them that in other parts of the world the tendency was to curtail debates.

Amendments.

Mr. J. Stewart (Labour, *East London, Cape*) joined in the protest against the restrictions upon Members' speeches, and moved as an amendment that the period of the Budget debate be restricted to ten days.

Mr. T. G. Strachan (Labour, *Pietermaritzburg, Natal*) seconded the amendment.

Mr. A. J. Werth (Nationalist, *Kroonstad, O.F.S.*) moved a series of amendments, the effect of which was to remove the limitations proposed to apply to the Committee stage of financial Bills and to substitute eight days for five on the Budget debate.

Suggested changes.

Mr. H. S. van Hees (Nationalist, *Christiana, Trans.*) said the system of their Constitution was wrong. To begin with, they had First, Second and Third Readings on which the same things were said over and over again. They should ask themselves whether they should not limit the time devoted to such a procedure and make a radical change in the system of legislation. Ministers or private Members wishing to introduce a Bill should do so in the form of a Motion which could be dealt with in detail and referred to the Senate, and ultimately brought before the House in the form of a report. He thought there should be no limitation whatever to the discussion of financial details, and was of opinion that if a Bill had been thrown out in one Session it should not be allowed to come up again during the same Parliament.

It was decided by 59 votes to 46 that the Select Committee's report be adopted.

Mr. Stewart withdrew his amendment, and Mr. Werth's amendment was negatived by 60 votes to 47.

The report was adopted by 60 votes to 48.

The new Standing Orders were to be put in operation the following day.

WOMEN'S ENFRANCHISEMENT BILL.

On 23rd March, the Women's Enfranchisement Bill, which was introduced by Mr. R. Feetham in the House of Assembly last Session, was debated on the motion for the Second Reading, and rejected.

DEBATE IN HOUSE OF ASSEMBLY.

Mr. R. Feetham (South African Party, *Parktown, Trans.*), in moving the Second Reading, said that the Bill was again introduced in response to the constant and growing demand on the part of the Women's Union and because the reformers and supporters of the Bill believed it to be in the interests of the whole country, and regarded it as a measure that had been too long delayed. He proceeded to deal with the basis of representation, and said the extension of the franchise to women in no way endangered any of the provisions of the South Africa Act. Women's Suffrage had been submitted to the House on many occasions. Bills had been introduced in 1914, 1920 and 1921. The feelings of Members had been very much stirred, but they had never actually reached the point of a decision. He asserted that the demand for women's suffrage was based on justice and public policy, and he asked the House to face the issue fairly and squarely, and give a decision on the merits of the case.

Mr. M. L. Malan (Nationalist, *Heilbron, O.F.S.*) held that not more than 20 per cent. of the female sex in South Africa were in favour of the Bill, and of that 20 per cent. the great majority were in the urban areas, while the overwhelming majority of women in the country districts were opposed to it.

Gen. the Hon. J. B. M. Hertzog (Leader of the Nationalist Party) said he did not think one could say that the existence of the female franchise anywhere had led to greater happiness or better conditions. The fact was that the family bonds had grown looser and looser. Until the native and coloured races had been placed on a proper footing, he added, he would not vote in favour of the extension of the franchise anywhere. That was the attitude of the majority of the people in the rural districts, and, he took it, of everyone on the Nationalist side.

The Minister of Mines (the Right Hon. F. S. Malan) did not agree that the loosening of family bonds had any connection with women's franchise; the reason for that must be looked for elsewhere. He claimed that every time women had been given greater power and responsibility it had proved to be to the benefit of the community.

The question of the native races raised by General Hertzog was emphasised by other Members; and further general objections to the Bill having been stated,

The Prime Minister (Lt.-Gen. the Right Hon. J. C. Smuts) urged that the time to plead for women's franchise had passed. The most progressive countries in the world, where political opinion had gone ahead, had given the vote. The women of South Africa were no less worthy than the women of England, America, or any other country, and there was no reason why they should not have the vote. In regard to the view that it should not be given to them until the native question had been settled, he thought it unfair to couple the two questions. The native question would take years to solve; must the women of South Africa remain in an inferior position till that time? That kind of thing would create all kinds of bitter political propaganda.

A Motion to adjourn the debate, by Mr. H. H. de Waal (Nationalist, *Piquetberg, Cape*) was negatived by 54 votes to 52. The motion for the Second Reading was negatived by 55 votes to 51, the voting not being on Party lines except that the Labour Party voted for the Bill.

DIVORCE BILL.

(Extension of grounds for divorce.)

Upon the order for the Second Reading of this Bill* the question of the extension of the grounds for divorce was discussed in the House of Assembly on 27th April. The measure aroused considerable opposition, and did not pass the Second Reading.

DEBATE IN HOUSE OF ASSEMBLY.

On 27th April,

Mr. A. S. van Hees (Nationalist, *Christiana, Trans.*), who introduced the Bill last year, said he asked for an extension of the grounds for divorce only where one of the parties was a leper, an habitual criminal or a lunatic. In these cases the Courts of Law were on their own responsibility separating the parties, and that being the case, it could not be contended that he sought to make it easier to obtain divorce.

Commdt. B. J. van Heerden (South African Party, *Ventersdorp, Trans.*) argued that these three grounds, urged by Mr. van Hees, were not necessarily permanent, because leprosy and insanity could be cured, and there were good

* For provisions of the Bill, *vide* Journal, Vol. II., No. 2, pp. 450-1.

authorities who held that even hardened criminals could mend their ways. If divorce were given on these grounds, then it would not take long before it would be possible to dissolve marriages on the grounds of blindness and rheumatism, and the solemn pact of marriage would become a farce.

The Minister of the Interior (Hon. Patrick Duncan) said it was a monstrous thing that people could be divorced merely on the grounds of desertion, and not in the case of incurable insanity. He felt very strongly about the sanctity of the marriage tie; but he did not think they should make themselves slaves to words, and he supported the Bill.

Mr. R. W. Close (South African Party, ***Rondebosch, Cape*****)** thought that an officer should be appointed in South Africa analogous to the King's Proctor in England. He held that the exemptions specified in the Bill should not be allowed.

Mr. M. Alexander (Constitutional Democrat, ***Cape Town—Castle, Cape*****)** pointed out that it was the law of South Africa that if a person were imprisoned for life the other spouse could obtain a divorce. He regarded the argument in favour of divorce on the ground of incurable insanity as unanswerable.

Other Members having spoken, an amendment that the Bill be read that day six months, proposed by Mr. J. G. Keyter (Nationalist, *Ficksburg, O.F.S.*), was agreed to by 44 votes to 40.

GIRLS' AND MENTALLY DEFECTIVE WOMEN'S PROTECTION ACT AMENDMENT BILL.

(Sexual offences with girls under 16.)

On 27th March, in the House of Assembly, a Bill was introduced by Mr. R. W. Close to amend Section 2 of the Girls' and Mentally Defective Women's Protection Act, 1916, by the deletion of the first proviso to that section which established certain defences to charges of indecency with girls under 16:—

Section 2 of Act No. 3 of 1916, provided that every male person who has unlawful carnal connection with a girl under sixteen, or solicits or entices a girl under that age to immoral or indecent acts, etc., shall be guilty of an offence, and liable on conviction to imprisonment with or without hard labour for a period not exceeding six years, with or without whipping not exceeding twenty-four lashes, and with or without a fine not exceeding £500 in addition to such imprisonment and lashes.

The first proviso to the above section which the Bill proposes to delete, made it a sufficient defence to a charge under the section if it appeared to the Court that the girl at the time of the offence was a prostitute or that the person charged was under 16.

DEBATE IN HOUSE OF ASSEMBLY.

On 16th March,

Mr. R. W. Close (South African Party, *Rondebosch, Cape*) in moving the Second Reading of the Bill, said the object was to repeal in two very important respects the provisions of Act 3 of 1916, which had to deal with the amendment of the criminal law in respect to the protection of girls under the age of 16. When the Bill came forward in the House it contained a proviso enabling a person charged with a very serious offence created under the law to take two defences. One was that the girl with whom the unlawful act was committed was a prostitute, and the other that the accused person himself was under the age of 16 years.

Mr. Close quoted largely from the laws in other Provinces that were in force before the existing Act was passed, and which did not contain any such provision, and he submitted that it was a sad and horrible state of affairs that they should have such a law on the Statute book. The law was intended to prevent a very definite evil of the day, and it had gone a good way in doing so. But they must remove the blot from it in order to protect the young. He further argued against males between 14 and 16 being entitled to a special protection when found guilty of an offence against a girl under 16, where there was consent.

Mr. W. B. Madeley (Labour, *Benoni, Natal*) would have liked to see the age of consent raised to 18, but he had no desire to jeopardise the passage of the Bill.

Mr. W. Macintosh (South African Party, *Port Elizabeth, S.W., Cape*) said he felt that boys should have a measure of protection in the same way as girls had at the hands of the law.

The Minister of Agriculture (Hon. Sir Thomas Smartt) pointed out that if the parents did their duty, it would not be necessary to go so far as Mr. Close asked them to go, and which was further than he could go. He hoped the House would not endorse the Bill.

Mr. C. G. Fichardt (Nationalist, *Ladybrand, O.F.S.*) said he saw in the proposal the possibility of a boy being led into temptation and then being sent to his doom. There should be protection all round. In the case of men he did not think the death penalty too drastic.

The Second Reading was agreed to by 45 votes to 37, the division being on non-Party lines, though none of the Labour Party voted against the Bill.

NEWFOUNDLAND.

GOVERNOR-GENERAL'S SPEECH.

(Address in Reply.)

On 22nd March, in the House of Assembly, the closing debate on the Address in Reply took place.

Unemployment.

The Attorney-General (Hon. W. R. Warren) said that the Government had come in for the bitterest condemnation for their relief work policy. The Government had been faced with the situation where they had to give out relief, and it was better that the men did something for the money than that they should be pauperised. He admitted that in some cases both road inspectors and the Government were imposed upon and men were working who were not in need of any relief, but where the thing was of such magnitude this was to be expected.

Fisheries.

Dealing with the fishery needs of the South-West coast, the Attorney-General said that what the South-West coast needed was cold storage depots, and it was his intention to bring the matter forward for the serious consideration of the Government in the very near future. In England, where trade conditions were enormously worse than they were in Newfoundland, the Government had stepped in with guarantees of various kinds to encourage projects so that the people might have a means of earning sufficient for their immediate needs. In Canada there were grave problems arising out of unemployment, and even in the United States, with all their boasted wealth, unemployment victims could be counted by the million. In Newfoundland practically everything depended upon the success of the fishery, and when this, their chief industry, went wrong, everything else was bound to go wrong. In his opinion the real trouble was to be traced to the cut-throat methods pursued by the merchants in the disposal of their fish in the foreign markets. Their agents waged a bitter campaign of competition, the only result of which was the cutting of prices. Until there was co-operation of some kind among the fish merchants of the country, they could not hope to derive from this industry the best it had to give.

The Prime Minister (Hon. Sir Richard Squires), after dealing with criticisms on the financial situation, said that the Government had handled the serious question of unemployment in the best and only way calculated to bring about the required results. No one pretended for a moment that full value had been received for the moneys expended on relief works. The only thing that could be done was to devise the best means under the circumstances to relieve the situation that called for immediate attention. What had been done was done to prevent starvation stalking throughout the land. As to the manner in which the relief work had been handled, no more enthusiastic or fair-minded body than the citizens on the Employment Committee could be found to lend their aid to this work. They were free from political considerations and could be relied upon to use their discretion in apportioning the work. He was certain that in the great majority of cases the money expended was earned by men whose families were in want and who had only this means of keeping the wolf from the door.

Railway situation.

Dealing with the railway problem, the Prime Minister said that this Government, like its predecessors, was doing its best to grapple with it. The branch lines were a veritable sinking pot into which the earnings of the whole system were disappearing. Taken as a whole, the railway system could never be expected to pay.

THE BUDGET.

On 5th April, in the absence of the Minister of Finance and Customs owing to illness, the Annual Financial Statement was delivered by the Prime Minister in the House of Assembly.

Revenue and Expenditure.

The Prime Minister (Hon. Sir Richard Squires) said that a year ago in the Budget Speech for the fiscal year 1921-22 (*vide* JOURNAL, Vol. II., No. 3, p. 699) he submitted estimates, both as to revenue and expenditure, which the opponents of his Administration ridiculed as entirely impossible of realisation. It was now, however, a matter of satisfaction to find that the figures then submitted, though at that time they were for the most part estimates, had proved, not only to be fully justified, but quite conservative ; the present financial condition of the Colony was substantially better than that anticipated in his Budget Speech of last year. He had estimated that the revenue for the current fiscal year expiring on 30th June, 1922, would be a total sum of $8,903,803 ; but the revenue which was now practically assured was $499,303 more than that estimated as probable a year ago. The amount of money voted by the Legislature at its last Session under the head of General Estimates was the total of $8,522,569. In the case of current revenue there was, with the Supplementary Supply Bill fully provided for, an estimated surplus of $24,311. He felt that no one could appreciate better than the Leader of the Opposition how difficult it was to reduce expenditure and inaugurate retrenchment in the public services of the Colony. The Government had, however, during the past year bent its energies in this direction with the result that an expenditure of $10,951,488 for the fiscal year 1920-21 had been reduced to an expenditure of $8,879,492 for the current fiscal year. In other words, the public services of the Colony had been maintained with some curtailment, but without curtailment so severe as to affect the business of the Colony, for the sum of $2,071,956 less than the previous year. In this connection it must be remembered that during the current financial year there had been the added expenditure of $422,500 as interest on last year's loan, and approximately $100,000 on account of War Pensions, which were not liabilities on the previous year's accounts. He could assure the House that the concerted efforts of all departmental heads, and the co-operation of the representatives of the various constituencies, both Government and Opposition, would make possible during the coming year a further substantial reduction in the cost of the public service.

Savings deposits.

Dealing with the Savings Deposits in Newfoundland, the Prime Minister pointed out that, while the amount of savings deposits was not by any means an invariable index of prosperity, yet it was very encouraging to note that in spite of the depression through which Nowfoundland had passed during the year 1921, the people found it necessary to lessen their total savings deposits by the sum of $406,979 only.

Income and Business Excess Profits Taxes.

It was interesting to note the effect upon the Income Tax of the discontinuance of the Business Excess Profits Tax. During the years 1917-1920 there was collected under the head of Business Excess Profits Tax a total sum of $3,005,300; during the same period the Income Tax amounted to $300,789. The Assessor of Taxes reported that the estimated collection for the fiscal year 1921-1922, the Business Excess Profits Tax not being in operation, was the sum of $182,050, which was an increase in Income Tax collection above the average for the previous four years of $106,853. The net result of the discontinuance of the Business Excess Profits Tax was an annual reduction of $644,000 in taxation imposed directly on the business community. There were substantial arrears outstanding in connection with the Business Excess Profits Tax. A Bill had already been submitted to the Legislature dealing with this matter, so that there could be no discrimination between those who during the War made large profits and paid their taxation gladly and those others who during the War likewise made large profits but had, up to the present, succeeded in evading payment of the amounts due by them. Resolutions had already been submitted to the House in reference to some necessary changes in Income Tax law. In the matter of the collection of Income Tax the Assessor had been faced with many difficulties and was seeking legislation to make it possible for him to enforce the law more effectively. He had been informed that an agitation was being developed in some quarters against income taxation. In the past, taxation which had devolved upon their business people had been such as they could readily transfer to the consumer by increasing the price of their merchandise. Direct taxation, however, was not so easily transferable. Direct taxation in a community such as this had, however, certain advantageous features in that the person paying the taxation was more likely to take a personal interest in the administration of affairs and the expenditure of public funds and to co-operate with the Government of the day to secure the most efficient administration possible.

Postal Rates.

The Minister of Posts and Telegraphs had called the attention of the Government to the fact that the recognised rate of foreign letter postage throughout the British Empire was 4 cents. This rate had recently been adopted by the Dominion of Canada. He had also pointed out that Newfoundland was unique in that they provided free postage for newspapers. The Minister of Posts and Telegraphs had consequently recommended that their foreign letter rate be raised from 3 cents, as at present, to 4 cents; also, that the postage charge of ½ cent per lb. on newspapers be levied.

Customs Tariff.

The Minister of Finance and Customs had undertaken the chairmanship of a Commission for the revision of the Customs tariff. The Commission, which would consist of a total of nine members, would be a body of citizens prominently identified with the trade of the country and as fully representative of the various business interests as possible. The whole question of tariff revision and adjustment would be submitted to them for consideration and their recommendations would be laid before the Legislature at its next Session. No general tariff reorganisation was contemplated pending the report of the Commission.

"Newfoundland," declared the Prime Minister, "has passed through many periods of depression, some much more severe than that of the past and present year. The Colony has always rapidly recovered from these periods and has risen to a greater height of prosperity and success than existed prior to the depression. I have no reason to believe that the generation of to-day has less buoyancy, less industry, less integrity, and less enterprise than those who have preceded us."

On 10th April,

Government's extravagance.

The Hon. Sir Michael Cashin (Leader of the Opposition) declared that the Budget Speech dealt merely with the state of affairs covered by the ordinary revenue and expenditure accounts, and it carefully and purposely avoided any reference whatever to the tremendous burdens imposed upon the country through the policy of utter extravagance in which the Government had persisted from the day it assumed office, when it doubled the salaries of the heads of departments and increased the burdens of the Colony by millions. Here was a document, miscalled a Budget Speech, which contained no reference to the railroad which was costing the country 2½ million dollars a year; not a reference to the iniquitous distribution of money for so-called relief purposes; not a reference to the loss of $400,000 on supplies to the fisheries; to nearly $200,000 on pit props; to $235,000 on the notorious fish deals; to $35,000 on salt; and would probably mean another $50,000 on the Anderson Housing scheme. Never at any time in the past history of the country had there been anything like such a carnival of corruption. At the very hour that the Premier was making his Budget Speech the newspapers were appearing with full reports of a mass meeting held by the Board of Trade in which resolutions were passed that were in fact a denunciation of the Government's policy and a demand that drastic and sweeping reductions be made in the scale of expenditure in order to render possible a reduction of taxation, without which, the meeting declared, it would be impossible to carry on the general business of the country.

Another evidence that the Government's policy was not beneficial was the fact that so many business concerns had gone to the wall within the past two years. The Government had spent at the rate of over 15 millions a year, and in spite of all that there was destitution all over the country. There were thousands of men being kept alive by the pauper's dole or by the giving out of relief work, either by snow shovelling, pit prop cutting, or some other form of labour, which was only an alternative for feeding them through the Poor Commission. The amount the Government had expended in these two years and a half was as a matter of fact more than the value of the exports of the country for the same period. The exports for this year would bring into the Colony about 16 million dollars in money; the loan would bring in about 6 million dollars more, making 22 million dollars altogether, which might be described as the country's income for the twelve months. Against that the Premier estimated to get 9 million dollars of revenue. This was just 41 per cent. of the income represented by the cash value of the exports and the cash from the loan—out of every 100 dollars earned by their people, 62 dollars went into the Customs House and only 38 were left for their support.

Housing scheme.

After criticising the Government's policy in regard to railways, the sale of pulpwood and fish, and road construction, Sir Michael said with regard to the Government's Housing scheme that all the fifty-nine people who had invested in it would lose every cent of their investment unless the Government came to their relief. The Government under the Act passed two years ago merely guaranteed these people the interest on their money for twenty-five years at 5 per cent.; at the end of the 25 years they would lose their principle entirely unless the Government helped them out. Mr. Anderson and his fellow philanthropists started to build 30 houses. His estimate was that the houses were to cost $1,500 each; when the houses were built it was found that they cost roughly $3,000 each. He thought he was safe in saying that the Colony would lose between $30,000 and $40,000 as the result of the Government giving its endorsement to this crazy scheme.

The loan.

But for the loan of six million dollars obtained at the last Session, the Prime Minister would not have had a revenue within millions of what he received. He would in the same way be able to do the same thing for the coming year with another six million dollars to spend throughout the Colony on railroads, roads, and other works, especially public doles. They would keep on borrowing money at the rate of six million dollars a year indefinitely, and the longer they kept at it the sooner must the crash come and the whole country go down together.

The larger portion of the public revenue was being supplied to-day for no other purpose than to keep alive people who would starve if relief was not given to them. The business community was likewise on its beam ends.

Public Debt.

Sir Michael stated that the Prime Minister had shown the net funded Debt as at 52 million dollars in round figures, but suppressed altogether the fact that they owed the British Government two million dollars loaned to them during the War, which was as much a part of the Colony's Debt as any other of its obligations.

"The outlook for the future of the country," concluded Sir Michael, "its industries and its people, is the gloomiest perhaps of the whole history of Newfoundland since the day it attained responsible government."

On 11th April,

Mr. John R. Bennett (Opposition, ***St. John's, West*****)** declared that the Vote for public charities and able-bodied poor relief was charged up on Loan Account. So was the expenditure on the railroad, so with pit props, so with fishery supplies and other expenditure, when every item of this should have been charged to current account. But to deceive the people into believing that the Government was living within its income these despicable tactics were resorted to. It was preposterous to suggest that the Government was living within its income when not a single public service was in any way curtailed. How came it that the Board of Trade was passing resolutions asking the Government to reduce the tariffs? What had the Prime Minister done in relation to the Board of Trade's request? Nothing was told in the House about complying with the request and reducing taxation. The whole public service was run by the present Government for political purposes. The Education Department was one that could be very well done without. One of the ways to reduce the cost of living of the average citizen was to have the duty taken off sugar. The country was being bled to the tune of half a million dollars per year to pay for the blunder of the Food Control Board of last year. They were closing down their factories and allowing the factories of Canada to operate against them and they were buying Canadian goods.

GOVERNMENT'S RAILWAY POLICY.

On 19th May and subsequent dates the situation with regard to the railway was discussed in the House of Assembly.

The Prime Minister (**Hon. Sir Richard Squires**), in moving the adjournment of the House on 19th May, stated that the Reid Railway Company had informed the Government that they would sell the railway for $2,400,000 and release all their claims, and that, further, they were going out of the transportation business altogether, both on land and sea, and could not now undertake to offer any hope that they would ever again be operating the railway as they had not the money to do it.

On 22nd May,

The Prime Minister said that litigation, arbitration or some settlement was necessary for the purchase of the railway. The Government would have to take over the road, as the Reid Company had retired absolutely from the railway. Financial difficulties prevented them from carrying on further railway operations in Newfoundland. No matter what happened, the Government must take over and operate the railway.

Mr. John R. Bennett (**Opposition,** *St. John's, West*) asked if the Attorney-General had taken steps to obtain any outside legal opinion as to the Colony's position and liabilities. If the Reid's claims should be substantiated the country ought to be independent enough to pay them. He could not see, however, why the country should pay anything for the Reid's assets if they had defaulted.

The Prime Minister said that the Colony had always been financing the Reids. When Mr. Morgan returned he would operate the line temporarily. Later the line would be leased out to some firm of contractors.

The Hon. Sir Michael Cashin (**Leader of the Opposition**) thought it would be best to adjust the present dispute and let the Reids carry on until the end of the fiscal year.

Mr. W. J. Walsh (**Opposition,** *Placentia & St. Mary's*) was convinced that the whole thing was a plot to ruin the country and bring it into confederation.

Sir Michael Cashin read messages from several settlements which stated that if food did not soon arrive the people would starve.

On 15th June,

The Prime Minister informed the House that a provisional agreement for the operation of the railroad during the summer and the early autumn had been entered into between the Government and the Reid Company. The Government assumed operation from 15th June to 15th November of the Reid railway line, steamboats and express business, the actual loss in operation for the period to be borne by the Government.

EDUCATION VOTE.

On 20th April the House of Assembly, in Committee of Supply, discussed the Vote for Education.

The Minister of Education (Hon. Dr. Arthur Barnes) said that he could not recommend to the Government any reduction in this Vote of over $800,000 for various reasons. The teachers' salaries could not be reduced. They were not paid now anything like they should be paid. The carpenters, policemen and even the ordinary sanitary men on the streets were being paid far better than the school teachers. The reduction in the Vote meant the closing of the schools. The education of the youth was the surest way to prevent the spread of Bolshevism. He thought Newfoundland was deplorably behind in education. In 1911 the percentage of illiteracy was seventeen, but he thought it was up to thirty-three or thirty-four per cent. His Department was now engaged in finding out how the retardation of the children compared with certain standards. The country was indifferent on education. It was hard to awaken it. The only Vote he could recommend for deletion was that of the summer school.

Mr. James MacDonnel (Opposition, *St. George*) declared that they should wipe out the Department root and branch. They should do away with inspectors entirely. The thing was only a farce. The schools were never inspected. To remedy the ills Dr. Barnes spoke of they should pass a Bill here and now to enforce compulsory education in Newfoundland. Until they did that they would never get results.

Mr. C. J. Fox (Opposition, *St. John's, East*) said he was disappointed that Dr. Barnes did not see fit to make any reduction in his Department. The Minister talked of Bolshevism and was trying to educate the youth to prevent it. He asked who was responsible for Bolshevism that they had in their midst to-day if it was not the Government? They took office over a happy and prosperous people in 1919 and look at the contrast to-day. The condition of the country was deplorable. Unemployment was rampant. He asked the Government to move the wheels of trade and thereby stamp out the curse of Bolshevism. Take off the Surtax, the Super Tax and the Sales Tax and they would begin to do something. Cut out the waste of the Department of Education which was an ornate department which had not, would not, and could not justify its creation.

The Minister of Education defended the Normal School Vote and the Vote for inspection of schools, and compared the percentage grant for education in Newfoundland with some of the Canadian provinces, to the disadvantage of Newfoundland. The dispensing with his Department would only save the country $9,280. The amount, he thought, was too insignificant to discuss.

UNEMPLOYMENT AND UNREST.

On 11th April, in the House of Assembly,

Mr. N. J. Vinicombe (Opposition, *St. John's, East***)** asked the Prime Minister whether it was the intention of the Government to retain the warship *Cambrian* then in port, and if it was further intended to order another one in the contemplation of any trouble arising?

The Prime Minister (Hon. Sir Richard Squires) replied that the warship was not retained there at the request of the Government, neither did the Government request another warship to come there. He did not contemplate any rioting taking place unless the suggestion of the Board of Trade last week that men should be paid off from relief work caused such rioting.

TARIFF REDUCTIONS.

On 19th May the Prime Minister, having moved the House of Assembly into Committee on Ways and Means, made an announcement in regard to certain reductions in the tariff.

The Prime Minister (Hon. Sir Richard Squires) tabled resolutions with reference to reductions on the Export Tax on fish and the import duties on certain fishing supplies. These reductions comprised:—(A) 10 cents off the 40 cent per quintal export on fish shipped in foreign bottoms; (B) 10 cents off the 20 cent tax on fish shipped in British bottoms; (C) 5 cents off the 15 cent tax on salt bulk fish. The super tax of 25 per cent. and the sales tax of 5 per cent. were removed from kerosene oil, gasolene, long rubber boots and oil clothes. The total reductions amounted to between $250,000 and $300,000. Last year, said the Prime Minister, the Government entered into a fishing supplies policy which should not be repeated this year. The estimated loss last year on this policy was $300,000.

The Hon. Sir Michael Cashin (Leader of the Opposition) said he was glad to see that there were some reductions made in the tariff on fishing supplies. His only regret was that they did not go far enough.

CUSTOMS AMENDMENT BILL.

This Bill, which seeks to amend Chapter 22 of the Consolidated Statutes entitled "of the Customs," provides that:—

Whenever any duty *ad valorem* is imposed on any goods imported into Newfoundland, the value for duty shall be the current domestic value thereof in the principal markets of the country whence and at the time when the same were exported directly to the Colony.

It is further provided that duties shall be payable in all cases on the quantity and value of goods in the warehouse as ascertained on first entry; provided that an allowance not exceeding 2 per cent. per annum, nor exceeding 8 per cent. in the whole, may be made for deficiencies in measurement arising from evaporation or other natural causes, after liquids have been entered for warehouse.

The Bill also provides that any person who smuggles into the Colony any goods subject to duty, or passes or attempts to pass through the Customs House any false invoice, or in any way attempts to defraud the revenue by evading the payment of the duty on any goods, such goods if found may be seized and forfeited; or if not found, but the value thereof has been ascertained, the person so offending shall forfeit the value as ascertained. Further penalties, on summary conviction, including a fine or imprisonment or both, are also imposed.

DANGEROUS DRUGS BILL.

This Bill is to regulate the importation, exportation, manufacture, sale and use of opium and other dangerous drugs.

Raw opium.

The Bill makes it unlawful for any person to import into or export from Newfoundland any raw opium except under licence and into or from approved ports. For export it must be in packages marked to indicate the contents. If the importation of raw opium into a foreign country is prohibited or restricted by the laws of that country, there shall be attached to every licence issued by the Colonial Secretary under this Act authorising its export from the Colony, conditions necessary for preventing or restricting its exportation from the Colony to the country in question. The Governor-in-Council is empowered to make regulations for controlling or restricting the production, possession, sale and distribution of raw opium.

Prepared opium.

The import and export of prepared opium is forbidden. Any person shall be guilty of an offence against this Act who (*a*) manufactures, sells or otherwise deals in prepared opium; (*b*) has in his possession any prepared opium; (*c*) permits his premises to be used for the preparation of opium for smoking or for the sale or smoking of prepared opium; (*d*) is concerned in the management of any premises for such purposes; (*e*) has in his possession any pipes or other utensils for use in connection with the smoking of opium or its preparation for smoking; (*f*) smokes or otherwise uses prepared opium, or frequents any place used for opium smoking.

Other drugs.

The import or export is forbidden, except under licence, of morphine, cocaine, ecgonine, diamorphine (heroin) and their respective salts, medicinal opium, and any preparation or extract containing not less than one-fifth per cent. of morphine or one-tenth per cent. of cocaine, ecgonine or diamorphine. The Governor-in-Council is empowered to make regulations for controlling the manufacture, sale, possession and distribution of these drugs; and to declare that this part of the Act shall apply to any new derivative of these drugs which is likely to be productive, if improperly used, of ill effects substantially of the same character to those produced by morphine or cocaine.

The Bill further provides, *inter alia*, that any constable or other person authorised by the Colonial Secretary shall, for the purposes of the execution of the Act, have the power to enter the premises of any person producing or selling any drugs to which the Act applies and to inspect books and stocks. Any constable may arrest without warrant any person who has committed or is suspected of having committed an offence against the Act, if he believes that person will abscond unless arrested or if his name and address are unknown.

The penalty for the first offence is a fine not exceeding $1,000 or imprisonment with or without hard labour for a term not exceeding six months, or both; and for any subsequent offence a fine not exceeding $2,000 or imprisonment for two years, or both.

LOAN BILL.

This Bill is for the purpose of raising a loan on the credit of the Colony for the general purposes of the Colony.

The Bill empowers the Governor-in-Council to raise upon the credit of the Colony a loan not exceeding the sum of $6,000,000, by the issue and sale of securities dated 1st March, 1922, bearing interest at a rate not exceeding $5\frac{1}{2}$ per cent. per annum, which loan and securities shall be chargeable upon and repayable out of the funds of the Colony on or before 1st July, 1942. The loan is to be applied to one or more of the following purposes:—

(1) Public works throughout the Colony.

(2) The liquidation of the Railway Commission Account and for railroad purposes generally.

(3) The general purposes of the Colony.

It is also provided that any stock issued in accordance with this Act may, with the consent of the holders of the stock, issued under the provisions of the Act 58 Victoria (1895), be made available for the sinking fund connected with that issue.

The obligations represented by securities of the Colony issued in accordance with this Act and all payments in discharge thereof shall be exempt from all present and future taxes imposed by the Legislature, including any Newfoundland income tax, and the payment of the interest and the principal thereof shall be made in time of war as well as of peace.

SEALFISHERY BILL.

This Bill is for the purpose of regulating the Sealfishery during 1922.

It is provided that, subject to the provisions of the Sealfishery Act respecting the hours and days upon which seals may be killed, it shall be lawful to kill seals at any time during the present year after 13th March, while no export duty shall be payable in respect of skins of seals taken during the Sealfishery for the present year.

VACHER & SONS, LTD., Westminster House, London, S.W.1.—99147.

JOURNAL OF THE PARLIAMENTS OF THE EMPIRE

Vol. III.—No. 4. October, 1922.

Issued under the Authority of the
EMPIRE PARLIAMENTARY ASSOCIATION
(United Kingdom Branch),
WESTMINSTER HALL, HOUSES OF PARLIAMENT,
LONDON, S.W.1.

Price to Non-Members 10*s*. *Net*.

CONTENTS.

UNITED KINGDOM.

CANADA.

AUSTRALIA.

Commonwealth Parliament.

CONTENTS.

State Parliaments.

New South Wales.

Queensland.

Western Australia.

Tasmania.

NEW ZEALAND.

SOUTH AFRICA.

NEWFOUNDLAND.

INTRODUCTION.

Though the present issue of the JOURNAL constitutes the fourth and last number of Volume III., it will, probably, be the first number to reach a great many new Members of the Empire Parliamentary Association, who have entered Parliament as a result of General Elections in the United Kingdom, the Australian Commonwealth and New Zealand.

Under these circumstances it is a matter for congratulation that the contents of the present number provide a good example of the wide range of legislative proposals, enactments and discussions which from time to time are concisely summarised in the pages of the JOURNAL from the Bills, Acts and Hansards of the sister nations of the British Commonwealth. Thus, it may serve to illustrate how essential a piece of machinery the JOURNAL has become to those Members of all Parties in all Parliaments who wish to follow, with a minimum of effort, the proceedings and ideas of the leaders of opinion in each Parliament of the Empire. It may, perhaps, be possible, at some future date, to estimate the number of occasions that Bills introduced into one Parliament have been based upon information supplied in the JOURNAL as to the terms of a Bill introduced into another Parliament; in any event there is no room for doubt that the summarised discussions provide the only reliable data which admit of a ready comparison between the views of leaders of Parties on the problems, great and small, which are constantly calling for the joint consideration of all the nations of the British Commonwealth.

Perhaps the discussions of most vital interest to the whole Empire which are summarised in the present issue relate to the approval by the various Parliaments of the Washington Conference Treaties. Apart from the value of a perusal of these discussions from the standpoint of International affairs, the references to the constitutional status of the Dominions in the domain of Foreign Policy by the leaders of different Parties in different Parliaments deserve close attention and careful comparison, with a view to securing the smooth working of the machinery of inter-Empire consultation at all future gatherings of a similar nature. The discussions on this subject in the Parliaments of the United Kingdom, the Australian Commonwealth, New Zealand and South Africa* affect not only matters of common interest to the Empire, but to the League of Nations and the world in general.

* For discussion in the Canadian Parliament on this subject, *vide* JOURNAL, Vol. III., No. 3, p. 549.

Other subjects in the sphere of international relationship have reference in the United Kingdom Parliament to the Near East (a full summary of Mr. Lloyd George's momentous speech being given), The Hague Conference, War Debts and Reparations, the Mandate for Palestine, etc.; in the Australian Commonwealth and New Zealand Parliaments to the League of Nations and to Mandates in New Guinea and Western Samoa; in the South African Parliament to the Mozambique Convention.

Of matters more particularly concerning the nations of the Empire *inter se*, the discussions in Canada, Australia (Commonwealth and State Parliaments), New Zealand and South Africa relating to Migration are of first-rate importance; while the subject of Defence is considered in Australia, New Zealand and South Africa. Of particular interest in the latter connection is the Bill enabling the South African Government to take over from the United Kingdom the responsibility for the land defences of the Union, and the arrangements made in substitution of the contribution to the Navy.

Other questions of general Empire significance relate to India, the Canadian Cattle Embargo, and the West Indies, in the United Kingdom Parliament; to Indian enfranchisement in the Canadian Parliament; to a reciprocal Tariff agreement in the Australian and New Zealand Parliaments; and to Asiatic settlement and the incorporation of Rhodesia in the Union, in the South African Parliament.

Matters of more domestic concern, but which are, nevertheless, of general interest to the various nations of the Commonwealth, have reference to Proportional Representation (in the Parliaments of Canada and New Zealand), Finance (in the Parliaments of Canada and Australia), the abolition of Capital Punishment and the introduction of Voting by Proxy for Members of Parliament (in the Parliament of Queensland), the Constitution of the Senate (in the Parliament of South Africa), Railways and Prohibition (in the Parliament of Newfoundland), and Railways and the establishment of a Wheat Board (in the Parliament of Canada).

THE EDITOR.

EMPIRE PARLIAMENTARY ASSOCIATION
(*United Kingdom Branch*),
WESTMINSTER HALL,
HOUSES OF PARLIAMENT,
LONDON, S.W.1.

30th October, 1922.

UNITED KINGDOM.

In the last number of the Journal *the proceedings of the Session, which began on 7th February, 1922, were summarised up to 1st July. The business transacted between that date and 4th August, when Parliament adjourned, is now dealt with.*

The adjournment motions passed in both Houses at the beginning of August provided for the re-assembling of Parliament on 14th November to continue and complete the work of the Session.

But the resignation of the Government on 19th October was followed in the course of a few days by a Royal Proclamation dissolving Parliament, and the Session was thus automatically brought to an end.

It is announced that the General Election will take place on 15th November, and the new Parliament will meet on 20th November.

Formation of New Government: Mr. Bonar Law's Ministry (Note).

Mr. Lloyd George handed his resignation to the King on the afternoon of 19th October. His Majesty, thereupon, sent for Mr. Bonar Law, and invited him to undertake the formation of an Administration. On 23rd October, Mr. Bonar Law was unanimously elected leader of the Conservative and Unionist Party at a representative meeting in London.

The same evening he was again received in audience by the King, and, having signified his readiness to form a Ministry, kissed hands on his appointment as Prime Minister and First Lord of the Treasury.

On the advice of the new Premier, Parliament was dissolved by Royal Proclamation on 26th October, and a new Parliament was summoned. Down to the time of going to press the following appointments to the principal offices in the new Ministry had been announced:—

Prime Minister and First Lord of the Treasury	The Rt. Hon. A. Bonar Law.
Lord President of the Council and Deputy Leader of the House of Lords	The Marquess of Salisbury.
Lord Chancellor	Viscount Cave.
Chancellor of the Exchequer	The Rt. Hon. Stanley Baldwin.
Secretary of State for Home Affairs ..	The Rt. Hon. W. C. Bridgeman.
Secretary of State for Foreign Affairs and Leader of the House of Lords	The Marquess Curzon of Kedleston.
Secretary of State for the Colonies..	The Duke of Devonshire.
Secretary of State for India	Viscount Peel.
Secretary of State for War	The Earl of Derby.
Secretary of State for Air	The Rt. Hon. Sir Samuel Hoare.
First Lord of the Admiralty	The Rt. Hon. L. C. M. S. Amery.
President of the Board of Trade ..	The Rt. Hon. Sir Philip Lloyd-Greame.

Minister of Health	The Rt. Hon. Sir Arthur Boscawen.
President of the Board of Education	The Rt. Hon. Edward Wood.
Minister of Agriculture and Fisheries	The Rt. Hon. Sir Robert A. Sanders.
Minister of Labour	The Rt. Hon. Sir Montague Barlow.
Minister of Pensions	The Rt. Hon. G. C. Tryon.
First Commissioner of Works ..	The Rt. Hon. Sir John Baird.
Postmaster-General	The Rt. Hon. Neville Chamberlain.
Attorney-General	The Rt. Hon. Douglas M. Hogg, K.C.
Solicitor-General	Mr. T. W. H. Inskip, K.C.
Secretary for Scotland	Viscount Novar.
Lord Advocate	The Hon. William Watson, K.C.

NEAR EAST.

(Greece and Turkey; Premier on British policy; Protection of minorities; Conditions of peace.)

On 4th August, on the motion for the adjournment of the House of Commons for the Recess, a debate took place on the situation in the Near East and included a statement by the Prime Minister with respect to the Government's policy.

DEBATE IN HOUSE OF COMMONS.

Lt.-Comdr. the Hon. J. M. Kenworthy (Independent Liberal, *Hull, Cent.*) reminded the House that in the spring of 1918 the Prime Minister gave a pledge to a meeting of trade union leaders that they were not fighting to deprive Turkey of her capital, or of the rich and ancient lands of Thrace and Anatolia—the homelands of the Turkish race. That message mollified the trade union leaders and was of great value to the Moslem dependencies of Great Britain in India. But Greece was sent to occupy Smyrna and the excesses committed there had roused all Turkey. They brought thousands of men to the banner of Mustapha Kemal, who had become the great national hero of Turkey and was looked upon as the wielder of the sword of the Faithful.

Armenia, he was sorry to say, was being used as an excuse for Greek Imperialism. But all the killings of Turkish peasants in the vilayet of Smyrna by the Greeks, the bombarding of Turkish ports by Greek warships, the blusterings of Constantine at the gates of Constantinople, did not protect the Armenians. The British Government had issued a very stern warning to the Greeks against any such venture as an attempt to occupy Constantinople, but the fact that there should have been such a demand showed the effect of British policy. A much more serious matter was the apparent intention to imitate the example of D'Annunzio and Zilogowski in an attempt to set up an independent Ionian State in Smyrna. He hoped it would be made clear to Athens that any announcement of that sort would bring severe retribution on the Greeks.

He asked the Prime Minister to recognise that the atrocities committed by the Turks were not sufficient to warrant encouragement of a continuance of war in Asia Minor.

League of Nations and a settlement.

Maj. R. Glyn (Coalition Unionist, *Clackmannan*) said it was the business of the Government to try to find some common ground by which peace could be re-established and trade set going. It was a little ingenuous of Members of the House of Commons to throw stones at the British Government, because, so far as he could understand, they had endeavoured over a very long period to bring about peace in Asia Minor.

It might be a defeat for this country, although he rather doubted it, if the Greeks gained a victory. But he was perfectly certain that if the Turks gained the victory it would not be a victory for Christianity. He hoped it might be possible for the League of Nations to take some part in the settlement of that most difficult problem. He would like to see a branch of the League of Nations established at Constantinople with control up to the Maritza, forming a buffer State between Greece and Turkey. If the British wished to have a strong policy, it was high time that this country, which had taken such a prominent part in guiding the nations of the Middle East, should again come to the front and help to establish prosperity among those people.

Brig.-Gen. H. C. Surtees (Coalition Unionist, *Gateshead*) claimed that in the interests of tranquillity and trade an end should be put to the unsatisfactory state of affairs in the Near East.

Government's desire for peace.

The Prime Minister (the Right Hon. D. Lloyd George) said the Government had no other desire than that peace should be established in Asia Minor. There was, however, one important consideration. It was that the peace must be a just and fair peace, and one which was likely to be enduring. Lieut.-Commander Kenworthy seemed to present the case to the House of a friendly Turkey alienated by the policy of His Majesty's Government.

" I know," said the Premier, " it is only a few years ago since this country had such a large influence in Turkey, but the hon. and gallant Member for Hull seems to have forgotten the very recent history of that country. He has forgotten that eight years ago, when we were engaged in a very deadly struggle with the Central Powers of Europe, when the Dardanelles, the Bosphorus, and free access to the Black Sea was very vital to us, this very friendly Power slammed the gates of the Dardanelles in the face of the two countries without whose continuous assistance the Turkish Empire would not have been in existence. We fought one great war to preserve Turkey against her enemies. Before that we had constantly intervened to protect her against those who attacked her, and, as late as 1878, the whole power of this country was mobilised to protect and save Turkey from the consequences of a disastrous defeat inflicted upon her by her old enemy.

"In August, 1914, when we were engaged in a struggle of life and death, when Turkey should have assisted us without hesitation, as a result of a conspiracy which she entered into before the War with our greatest enemy she did us the greatest dis-service any country could have done; and I have no hesitation in saying, from my knowledge of the War, and I am sure that I am confirmed in it by everybody who has ever read the history of the War, that the action taken by Turkey then had the effect of prolonging the War by probably a couple of years."

The Sèvres Treaty.

Continuing, the Premier said the collapse of Russia was almost entirely due to that. It would probably never have happened if the Black Sea had been free. The same applied to Roumania, because, under other circumstances, Great Britain would have poured a sufficient amount of ammunition into those countries. What was the use of talking of the friendliness of Turkey a few years ago?

"There is," the Premier proceeded, "another illusion under which the hon. and gallant Gentleman seems to be labouring, entirely through ignorance of the facts. He is under the impression that the occupation of Smyrna and the proposals of the Sèvres Treaty were entirely the work of Great Britain. He clearly cannot have acquainted himself with the facts. What was done there was due to a Commission appointed by the Great Powers, upon which France, Italy, Japan and ourselves were represented. We were represented by one of our greatest Dominion statesmen, Sir Robert Borden, who, in addition to being a man of very great breadth of mind, was a great jurist. He represented Great Britain with the aid of the officials at the Foreign Office. We never interfered with that Commission. We left it to them to recommend, and they recommended, upon the facts, that Smyrna and the adjoining vilayets ought to be handed over to Greece, because they were predominantly Greek in population, in interest and in industry.

"That was not our decision. France took the same view. America took the same view. The only Power that expressed no opinion was Italy, for very obvious reasons. Italy was claiming Smyrna herself at that time. That was why this part of Asia Minor was assigned to Greece. It is perfectly true, for reasons which are thoroughly well known, that France has changed her mind since, but it was not our action alone. It was action in which the jurists and experts of France agreed with ours to put Smyrna under the control of Greece which led to the occupation."

British policy unchanged.

The only change, the Premier observed, had not been a change of policy on the part of Great Britain. Such change of policy as there had been had been a change entirely on the part of other Powers.

The fall of M. Venizelos and the accession of King Constantine had produced a certain chilliness of opinion in France, and also undoubtedly in this country, towards Greece. It made a very considerable difference to French opinion. He did not believe that there would have been any of this trouble if M. Venizelos had remained at the head of affairs. His influence as one of the greatest democratic statesmen in Europe would have been sufficient to keep French public opinion loyal to its original decision in this respect. But King Constantine had been responsible for certain acts of hostility to the Allies which hurt France very deeply, and he was not at all surprised at the fact that French opinion felt angry with Greece because she elected to stand by her King. If Greece was loyal to her King, that was her business; we must judge the whole question upon its merits. But it did produce a modification of the Treaty of Sèvres.

Efforts to secure agreement.

Two efforts had been made to get the parties to agree. The first was made in London, where very considerable modifications were introduced into the Treaty of Sèvres, and there was good reason to believe that the representative of Angora was, on the whole, in favour of accepting. No doubt, had Angora accepted, Greece also would have accepted the terms then proposed; but the Angora Government repudiated its representative, and the failure to come to terms was entirely the failure of Angora. Then another effort was made in Paris by the Foreign Secretary to secure another modification which would secure peace and tranquillity in the region. It was proposed that there should be a meeting of all the parties somewhere in the East—Turkey and Greece, as well as the Great Powers; but, as a preliminary, it was stipulated that there should be an armistice. That was a most obvious condition to impose. How could the representatives sit in Constantinople or anywhere else to discuss terms of peace when the belligerents were engaged in cutting each other's throats somewhere down in Busra.

An armistice had been the condition of every conference of peace that had ever been held, and without any hesitation the Powers were unanimous in imposing that condition upon the parties. Greece accepted; the Angora Government refused. The Constantinople Government, he believed, were prepared to accept, and it was in Constantinople that the Sultan was. Mustapha Kemal might be a great general and a great patriot, but the head of Islam was in Constantinople. Mustapha Kemal refused, with the result that nothing had been accomplished. He insisted upon preliminary evacuation by the Greek Army. He professed to desire peace, but the Turks were encouraged in their refusal of the one condition which the Powers sought to secure from them. That was not the road to peace.

Atrocities.

The Greek Army said, "We cannot evacuate the position, and leave our people behind, until we know what provisions have been incorporated in the Treaty for the protection of those people." That was not unreasonable. Lieut.-Commander Kenworthy admitted that there had been atrocities committed by the Turks.

"He has dwelt with great indignation," the Premier said, "upon one or two isolated instances of Greek atrocities, but I did not notice the same tone of indignation when he referred to the Turkish atrocities. His anger is reserved for the Greeks. Has he read the official reports? It is perfectly true that in some cases there have been deplorable outrages by Greek soldiers. It is almost inevitable in that part of the world when there is war. It happened in Macedonia, in conflicts between various nationalities there. There have been inquiries instituted by the French, Italian and British Missions. There is no doubt there have been a large number of atrocities and that those on the part of the Turks have been more considerable and more ferocious than those on the part of the Greeks. But all the indignation the hon. and gallant Member had was reserved for the atrocities committed by Greek soldiers.

"I wonder whether the hon. and gallant Member has acquainted himself with the Report of the American Mission with regard to the atrocities at Pontus. There have been individual cases of outrages by the Greeks in the war region, but at Pontus there was not the slightest suggestion there was any rebellion or preparation for rebellion, and, indeed, it would have been an act of supreme folly on the part of the population to have acted in such a manner. Under the conditions that obtained I cannot imagine they would have done so, for whatever the Greeks lack, they do not lack intelligence.

"Extermination."

"What has happened there? Not individual instances, but tens of thousands of men, women and children have been deported, and tens of thousands have died. The reports with regard to the women are perfectly horrible, and all these outrages were committed without any rebellion, and without any provocation. It was pure deliberate extermination. 'Extermination' is not my word. It is the word used by the American Mission.

"It was open to the Greeks to say: 'Before our troops retire from the lines which we have occupied after driving the Turks out with great loss, there are 500,000 men, women and children of our race behind us, and we want some guarantee that the same thing may not happen here as happened at Pontus. Our business is to hold the balance justly and fairly between both parties. It is not a question of Mussulman *versus* Christian. I want to make that perfectly clear. Supposing the Armenians were in control of Asia Minor, and supposing they had been guilty of these atrocities, these wholesale atrocities against Mussulmen, we should have been bound to intervene. We should have been bound to use the whole of our influence as a great Muhammadan Power. Scores of millions of Muhammadans are our fellow-subjects, and we should have been bound to intervene on their behalf. It is a pure question of humanity.

"After all, the responsibility for the defeat of the Turks was our responsibility. They were our troops who overthrew the Turks, and, therefore, the responsibility for the establishment of peace in Turkey must be our responsibility. We cannot abrogate the predominance which has been won by the sacrifice of our own people. We have a right to say we will make no peace which will place hundreds of thousands of poor defenceless people who are looking to us for protection at the mercy of those who have been guilty of the deportations and outrages at Pontus without some guarantee."

Turkish diplomacy.

"These outrages have undoubtedly modified and profoundly modified the position. First there is the fact that the Turks have refused to accept the conditions imposed by all the Powers quite unanimously with regard to an armistice.

"We could not allow the war to go on in that very important quarter. We could not afford to allow the trade of the district to be kept in a condition of disturbance and uncertainty. But the Turks have deliberately insisted on it. In addition to that, they have disturbed the balance of the Paris proposals, after having shown that they cannot be trusted with complete sovereignty and sway in a quarter like the Smyrna vilayet, where there are hundreds of thousands of Christians who would be entirely at their mercy.

"The Turk is an Oriental. He knows many things. He does not always know, perhaps, the value of time, but he always plays for time in diplomacy. He hangs on in the hope that the other party will give way first. It ought to be made quite clear that the terms I have mentioned are not indefinitely open to the Turk, who is saying to himself, 'If I hold out I may have a chance of getting everything I want, and if I do not the worst that can happen to me will be that I shall get the Paris terms offered to me.' That cannot be the case."

A fair and just offer.

"The hon. and gallant Gentleman quoted what I said at the end of 1917 or the beginning of 1918, about a year before the end of the War. That was a definite offer to Turkey to go out of the War, and she did not. The same offer was made, I believe, privately. . . . Turkey went on for a year. She went on until she was completely beaten, and had added scores of millions to our debt and tens of thousands to the casualties. Turkey thinks she is entitled to the same offer a year later, after all that has happened, as that made to her at a time when there was a good deal to be gained by getting her out, and it was worth our while to give her better terms.

"The question whether it was a just offer was tried by a perfectly fair, reputable and honourable Commission which gave a decision and we abided by it.

"I forget who it was that said we were not fair as between the parties. I am not sure that we are. What has happened? Here is a war between Greece and Turkey. We are defending the capital of one of the parties against the other. If we were not there, there is absolutely no doubt that the Greeks would occupy that capital in a very few hours, and that would produce a decision. There is only one way now in which the Greeks can have a decision and that is by marching through almost impenetrable defiles for hundreds of miles into the country. I do not know of any army that would have gone as far as the Greeks have. It was a very daring and a very dangerous military enterprise. They established a military superiority in every pitched battle. They were barred by the conformation of the country and the fact that they had to maintain lines of communication that no other Army in Europe would ever have dreamed of risking.

Greeks not unduly favoured.

"If we were simply holding the ring between them and said: 'There you are, fight it out,' they would have marched to the capital and taken it . . . in a week. Who is preventing that? British troops, French troops, Italian troops, and the British, French and Italian navies. It is quite right that we should do so; but do not let us say that we are unduly favouring the Greeks, that we are giving them some sort of preferential treatment.

"There are even suggestions, not altogether, perhaps, without foundation, that the Kemalist forces are being re-equipped from Europe. The Greeks under other conditions would have been entitled to blockade the coast of Asia Minor. If it had been any other belligerent they would have been entitled to search ships and to prevent arms from going to the Kemalists. They are not allowed to do that. That is what the hon. and gallant Member calls preference for the Greeks. On the contrary, one of the unfairnesses of the situation is that we are driven by the position we occupy there into not giving a fair field and no favour to fight the issue out. We cannot allow that sort of thing to go on indefinitely in the hope which the Kemalists entertain that they will at last exhaust this little country, whose men have been in arms for ten or twelve years in one war or another, and which has not indefinite resources. We only want to see a just peace established. Facts that have occurred during the last few months have made it clear that whatever happens there must be adequate and efficient protection of the minorities in this part of Asia Minor as an essential part of any settlement which Great Britain can accept. By these guarantees I do not mean the word of anger. That was given in Armenia. What has it been worth? It has not saved the life of a single Armenian or Greek. The protection must be an adequate one, which will take form and effect in the very constitution of the government of this particular province.

"The hon. and gallant Gentleman talked about events in the past history of Turkey, when the Greeks were not massacred and the Armenians were not massacred. Yes; that is the change which has come over the policy of Turkey in the last 30 years. There is no doubt at all, in the mind of anyone who has watched what has happened there, that a sentiment has grown up that there is only one way by which Turkey can get rid of her embarrassments with non-Mussulman populations, and that is by deportation or extermination. Abdul Hamid was very largely responsible for that policy.

Turkish history written in blood.

"Millions of Armenians have been exterminated, and the same policy is being applied to the Greeks. What does the Turk say? He says: 'As long as these people are here, Europe will interfere. I shall be receiving diplomatic Notes. I have been threatened constantly. I cannot always control my Pashas and my Beys. Therefore, the best thing is to get rid of them, and to get a homogeneous population.' There is no doubt that that is the policy which is governing and controlling a great many Turkish officials, and it is written in blood in the history of the last thirty years in Turkey. It is now extending to the Greeks.

"It is no use referring to the Turkey of a hundred years ago, or even of fifty years ago—certainly not to the Turkey of 200 or 300 years ago. There has been a complete change in their attitude. I agree that there was a Turkey which was tolerant, which, on the whole, was indulgent in its treatment of people of a different religion and race. There is a new spirit which is inspiring a good many of those who direct the policy of the country, and we must take that into account in every settlement that is made."

It had been pointed out, the Premier added, that Greece was suffering from unfortunate division among her people—the division between the followers of Venizelos and Constantine—which was paralysing her activities. It was remarkable that she had been able to accomplish what she had. He earnestly trusted that, whatever happened, this country would see that the Christian populations of Asia Minor were adequately protected against a repetition of such horrible incidents as had disgraced the annals of that land.

The Right Hon. Sir Donald Maclean (Chairman of the Independent Liberal Party in Parliament) said that he was glad the sitting closed not on the note of mere pounds, shillings, and pence, but on the note of humanity and of their obligations towards the oppressed races of the Near East under the heel of a nation which, after all the lessons which had been read to it during the past few years, had learned little if anything at all.

At the close of the debate the House adjourned for the Recess.

TREATIES OF WASHINGTON ACT.

(Limitation of Navies; Submarine warfare; etc.)

On 20th July, the Royal Assent was given to the Treaties of Washington Act. The measure vests in the Government the legal powers necessary to enable them to carry out the provisions of the two Treaties signed at Washington on 6th February, 1922.

The Act provides that no person shall, without a licence from the Admiralty, within any part of His Majesty's Dominions to which the Act applies, build any vessel of war, or alter, arm or equip any ship, so as to adapt her for use as a vessel of war, or despatch or deliver such a ship. For the purpose of the Act the Admiralty is empowered to give instructions for the inspection of any dockyard or shipyard and for the search of any ship.

The penalty for an offence against these provisions is imprisonment with or without hard labour for a term not exceeding two years, or a fine not exceeding £100, or both imprisonment and fine, while the ship in respect of which the offence has been committed is liable to be forfeited. In the case of a company or corporation every director and manager will be held to be guilty of the offence unless he proves that it took place without his knowledge and consent.

Violation of Rules of War.

Provision is also made in the Act with respect to the violation of rules as to warfare against commerce. It is laid down that any person in the service of any Power who violates any of these rules, whether or not he is under a Governmental superior, shall be deemed to have violated the laws of war, and be liable to trial and punishment as if for an act of piracy. If found within His Majesty's Dominions he may be brought to trial before any civil or military tribunal possessing jurisdiction to deal with acts of piracy.

The Act extends to the whole of His Majesty's Dominions, except India and the self-governing Dominions, that is to say, the Dominion of Canada, the Commonwealth of Australia (including Papua and Norfolk Island), the Dominion of New Zealand, the Union of South Africa, and Newfoundland, and, after the constitution of the Irish Free State, the Irish Free State. Where the Act is applied to parts of the Empire outside the United Kingdom, the Governor of the possession, instead of the Admiralty, is made the authority responsible for its execution.

Size of Ships and Armament.

Appended to the Act are two schedules setting out Articles of the Treaties which the Act enables His Majesty's Government to make effective. Among other matters, the Articles provide that no capital ship exceeding 35,000 tons standard displacement shall be acquired by, or constructed by, for, or within the jurisdiction of, any of the Contracting Powers; that no capital ship of any of the Contracting Powers shall carry a gun with a calibre in excess of 16 inches; and that no aircraft carrier exceeding 27,000 tons standard displacement shall be acquired by any of the Contracting Powers.

It is also provided that no preparations shall be made in merchant ships in time of peace for the installation of warlike armaments for the purpose of converting such ships into vessels of war, other than the necessary stiffening of decks for the mounting of guns not exceeding 6-inch calibre. Each of the Contracting Powers undertakes not to dispose by gift, sale or any mode of transfer of any vessel of war in such a manner that such vessel may become a vessel of war in the navy of any foreign Power.

Neutrals and Non-Combatants.

The second Schedule relates to the Treaty to protect neutrals and non-combatants at sea in time of war, and to prevent use in war of noxious gases and chemicals. It is as follows :—

The Signatory Powers declare that among the rules adopted by civilised nations for the protection of the lives of neutrals and non-combatants at sea in time of war, the following are to be deemed an established part of international law :—

1. A merchant vessel must be ordered to submit to visit and search to determine its character before it can be seized.

A merchant vessel must not be attacked unless it refuse to submit to visit and search after warning, or to proceed as directed after seizure.

A merchant vessel must not be destroyed unless the crew and passengers have been first placed in safety.

2. Belligerent submarines are not under any circumstances exempt from the universal rules above stated ; and if a submarine cannot capture a merchant vessel in conformity with these rules the existing law of nations requires it to desist from attack and from seizure and to permit the merchant vessel to proceed unmolested.

The Signatory Powers, desiring to ensure the enforcement of the humane rules of existing law declared by them with respect to attacks upon and the seizure and destruction of merchant ships, further declare that any person in the service of any Power who shall violate any of those rules, whether or not such person is under orders of a governmental superior, shall be deemed to have violated the laws of war, and shall be liable to trial and punishment as if for an act of piracy and may be brought to trial before the civil or military authorities of any Power within the jurisdiction of which he may be found.

DEBATE IN HOUSE OF COMMONS.

On 7th July, in moving the Second Reading of the Bill in the House of Commons,

The Parliamentary Secretary to the Admiralty (the Right Hon. L. S. Amery) said the Treaties to which the Bill related represented the greatest measure of agreement in their international relations that had been achieved in their time. The credit of that achievement would rest equally with the Governments of the United States and the British Empire. The execution of the agreement was writ large in every line of their Navy estimates. " We have thought it our duty," said Mr. Amery, " to act in that respect as if the Agreement had been ratified by all the contracting Powers, and we have gone ahead with all the necessary measures for the reduction of our Fleet on the assumption that it was our duty to trust those who have framed Agreements with us, and give a fair lead to other nations in this matter."

There were, he proceeded, several respects in which the execution of this Agreement demanded fresh powers to be placed in the hands of the Government as against the private citizen. For example, they had undertaken under the Treaty for the Limitation of Naval Armaments that their total tonnage of capital ships should not exceed a certain amount. They had undertaken that individual capital ships and ships of war should come within certain limitations. In the main those were undertakings which they could fulfil by administrative action, but they had also given certain other undertakings. The Government did not possess power at the present moment to prevent any private citizen or firm building ships of any size or character they might wish to build. Therefore, the first thing which was essential if they were to fulfil their obligations under the Treaties was to give themselves power to prevent ships being built in this country in contravention of the terms of the Treaty.

Submarine warfare.

It was necessary, Mr. Amery said, that the penalties provided for should have a wide range, because contravention of the Bill might vary from a deliberate conspiracy on the part of all the directors and managers of a company to violate the Treaty at one end of the scale, to some small technical violation, to be dealt with by a comparatively small fine, at the other end of the scale. It was made clear that the grant of a licence did not in any sense absolve a shipowner or a ship-contractor from the obligations of the Foreign Enlistment Act, 1870. That was to say, a licence which enabled the building of a ship within the limitations of the Washington Treaty did not form any justification, if war should subsequently break out between two foreign Powers, for the sale of such ship to one of the belligerent Powers.

There was a further Treaty defined in the preamble to the Bill as:—

> A Treaty to protect neutrals and non-combatants at sea in time of war and to prevent use in war of noxious gases and chemicals.

One of the endeavours of the British Delegation at Washington was to get rid of submarine warfare altogether, in view of the manner in which that warfare had been carried on by their enemies in the late War. "That particular proposal," Mr. Amery said, "did not commend itself to France, or, I think, to some of the other Powers at Washington. But the feeling against the manner in which Germany had employed her submarines was so strong, both among the members of the Conference itself and the general public in the United States, that the American Government brought forward the second Treaty. The object of that Treaty was to make it quite clear that submarines must conform absolutely with the ordinary laws of war."

Commerce destruction: Use of noxious gases.

"The House will notice," Mr. Amery remarked, "that there are certain things in that Treaty which the contracting Powers undertake to observe as between themselves and to endeavour to establish as part of the law of nations. One is the complete prohibition of the use of submarines as commerce destroyers and the use of noxious gases and chemicals. There are certain other things, namely, the proper conduct of interference with merchant vessels by any craft, whether submarine or surface craft, which are re-asserted as part of the existing law of nations, and the violation of which it is proposed shall be treated within the jurisdiction of this country and any other country as an act of piracy."

Col. J. C. Wedgwood (Labour, *Newcastle-under-Lyme*)**:** "It does not include the use of noxious gases, but only submarines."

The Parliamentary Secretary to the Admiralty: "No; I thought I had made that clear. The use of submarines against commerce and the use of noxious gases are among the things which we undertake administratively not to do, and which we hope to see established as part of the law of war. But the use of submarines as they were used in the late War without a proper opportunity for women, children, and other passengers to get into safety is laid down as a violation of the existing law of war, and it is that violation . . . which, in future, is to be treated in the law courts of this country and of His Majesty's Dominions as an act of piracy, liable to be punished in the same way as piracy."

Universal approbation.

The Right Hon. H. H. Asquith (Leader of the Independent Liberal Party) said the two Treaties enacted at Washington were instruments that commanded universal approbation. He congratulated Mr. Amery that he had the privilege of being the first of the statesmen of all countries concerned in that Pact to introduce in his own Legislature a measure to give practical effect to the Agreement concluded at Washington. With regard to the term "capital ships," he thought it was wise that this vague phrase, used in a different sense at different times, should receive an authoritative interpretation. The Article which provided that no capital ship should carry a gun with a calibre in excess of 16 inches would put a stop to the reckless and ruinous competition in the ever-increasing size of guns and ammunition.

As to the second of the two Treaties, he had always thought that the action of the German submarines was a distinct and flagrant violation of the established code of international law. "Unless we had been able," Mr. Asquith said, "to obtain, as I thought we should have been able, an agreement for the abolition of submarine warfare altogether, even with the strongest paper safeguards such as we have here it would be difficult to prevent these violations. If submarine warfare is to be allowed at all, everyone will agree that these provisions or Articles to prevent these acts by submarines are not in any circumstances a departure from the universal rules as to piracy, and are necessary to make logically complete the well-established principles of international law."

The right hon. Gentleman added that it was high time similar agreements were come to with regard to disarmament on land. It was the fervent prayer of the whole House and the country that that happy consummation might not be long delayed.

Co-operation with America.

Capt. Walter E. Elliot (Coalition Unionist, *Lanark*) said these international instruments were the first fruits of co-operation between America and themselves, in which the only hope for the peaceable development of the world was to be found.

Col. Wedgwood remarked that everybody in England would believe that the Admiralty would prevent any sort of infraction of the first Treaty, but it was important that everybody outside England should have faith in the inspection and in the carrying out of the Treaty. Was it not possible, therefore, to use the League of Nations to do that work? There they had the only body that would secure in future a general agreement. International inspection and international authorisation was the next stage towards what the Labour Party wanted to see—the abolition of the right to manufacture all instruments of war in private yards.

The Right Hon. G. N. Barnes (Labour, *Glasgow, Gorbals*) welcomed the Bill as a great step forward in the reduction of armaments generally throughout the world. It was said that they had not done what they ought to have done and might have done in regard to land and air armaments. "It was not our fault," Mr. Barnes remarked, "that these things were not discussed. So far as my memory serves me, the Delegates of this country expressed their willingness to discuss the question of limitation of land armaments, and also armaments in the air."

After further debate the Second Reading was agreed to without a division. The further progress of the Measure was uneventful and it became law on the date stated.

THE HAGUE CONFERENCE.

(Question of Russian settlement; Prime Minister and recognition of Soviet Government.)

On 26th July, the House of Commons went into Committee of Supply and discussed the Vote for Diplomatic and Consular Services. The occasion was utilised for a debate on The Hague Conference which had taken place in June for discussion of a settlement with Russia.

DEBATE IN HOUSE OF COMMONS.

The Parliamentary Secretary to the Department of Overseas Trade (Sir P. Lloyd-Greame) said that at Genoa a serious attempt was made for the first time, by frank discussion, to arrive at a Russian settlement. That settlement was impossible at Genoa, partly because of the unwillingness of the Russian representatives to face economic facts and partly through the impossibility of reconciling conflicting political principles. Those who took part in The Hague Conference were entitled to say that it served its purpose, for it marked a further step on the road. The next and final step rested with the Russian Government.

The hon. Gentleman gave a detailed account of the negotiations at The Hague. Though the Conference was unable to recommend any basis of immediate agreement, he said, the final phase offered a real hope of concrete results. The Russian Delegation were definitely prepared to invite their Government to consider a policy which included a formal acknowledgment of Russia's debts and of an obligation to pay compensation where property was nationalised by the Russian Government. That was a great advance by the Russian Delegation upon the position they had previously taken up and showed a real appreciation of the realities of the position. Appreciation was also shown of the fact that credit must rest on confidence, and the obligations which it was suggested the Russian Government might undertake were, according to the suggestion of the Russian Delegation, to be undertaken irrespective of any question of granting credits.

The non-Russian Commission passed a resolution stating that, although it could not find the basis of an agreement within the terms of the declaration of the Russian Delegation, it considered that the line of conduct indicated, if accepted by the Russian Government and loyally carried out, contributed to the re-establishment of the confidence which was necessary for the co-operation of Europe in the reconstruction of Russia.

Question of accommodation.

The Right Hon. J. R. Clynes (Leader of the Parliamentary Labour Party) observed that Russia could not afford to stand by a policy which alienated her from the rest of the world, and Great Britain could not afford to stand by a policy which Russia was determined to resist. Therefore, this was a question of accommodation, and, so far as Russia was concerned, of a complete departure from the methods she had followed.

"Her internal condition," said Mr. Clynes, "no matter what sacrifices for the moment her people may be able to endure, cannot be improved in any large measure unless she does recognise the methods by which the world is governed, unless she comes more nearly to the point of amicable agreement between herself and the Allied countries." To some substantial extent, Mr. Clynes proceeded, Russia had done that. Great Britain's interests lay in arranging substantial credits, if they were to secure Russian recognition of the debts and of the compensation which they claimed should be made to cover property in Russia of which British citizens had been dispossessed.

Lord Eustace Percy (Coalition Unionist, *Hastings*) asked whether Great Britain was going to use the machinery of her representation at Moscow or strengthen the machinery of that representation, so that it would be possible to conduct, in however non-committal a manner—he asked for no official communications—continuous relations and discussions with the Russian Government. That seemed to him to be the most important question at the present time.

Statement by the Premier.

The Prime Minister (the Right Hon. D. Lloyd George) thought The Hague Conference represented a very distinct advance towards a final solution. Whether it would be a final solution or not would depend, not upon the action which was taken by Great Britain or by her Allies and Associates, but upon the action which was taken by the Russian Government. Things would not get better in Russia, and it was no use pretending they would, until Russia fell in with the civilised world. Unless something was done, and done soon, Russia would be reduced to something like primeval conditions, and it was idle to talk about recognition until the country was restored.

Labour asked, "Why do you not give recognition to Russia first, and all the rest will follow? Send an Ambassador to Moscow to be followed by a train of bankers and financiers and manufacturers and traders, and so on." If they sent out the best Ambassador they had he would not be followed by a single banker or trader until the necessary conditions were established. To say otherwise was to mislead the public. Russia should understand the only conditions under which it was possible for the West to come to her aid, and until she comprehended that fact there was no business to be done.

With regard to property, Russia must either put the owners of private property back into their old position under some workable terms, or she must give real compensation in one form or another. "The time for recognition," the Premier said, "is when the Russian Government has not merely given an undertaking and verbal guarantees, but has given some practical example of her intention to carry out such an undertaking. Then that will be the time to accord to Russia full diplomatic recognition. Until then it will be impossible for us to do that."

After further debate, the Vote was agreed to without a division.

WAR DEBTS AND REPARATION.

(Statement by the Chancellor of the Exchequer; Germany and Treaty obligations.)

On 3rd August, a debate took place in the House of Commons, on the Order for the Third Reading of the Consolidated Fund (Appropriation) Bill, on the question of War Debts and Reparation.

DEBATE IN HOUSE OF COMMONS.

The Chancellor of the Exchequer (the Right Hon. Sir Robert Horne) said it had often been erroneously stated that the Treaty of Versailles finally fixed the amount of reparation that had to be paid by Germany. That was an error. No final fixation was made by the Treaty. On the other hand, the Reparation Commission was set up, and its duty was to fix first the total liability of Germany, and thereafter, from time to time, as circumstances changed, the amount which it was then obvious that Germany could pay. In the year 1921, the Reparation Commission fixed as the total liability the amount of 132 milliards of gold marks, which, converted into pounds sterling, represented £6,600,000,000. That sum was exclusive of the cost to be attributed to Armies of Occupation.

The House would want to know what Germany had actually paid since the Armistice. There had been paid in cash to the Reparation Commission £77,000,000 sterling, and locally there had been paid in paper marks to the Armies of Occupation a sum which was the equivalent of £30,000,000 sterling, making in all in cash £107,000,000 sterling. There had been certain further payments in supplies to the Armies the value of which he did not find it possible to compute. To these there had to be added the following items :—

Value of ships, coal, and payments in kind, £160,000,000.

Value of Government properties in ceded territories, for example, in Poland, Dantzig and Czecho-Slovakia, £125,000,000. These properties had all gone to the countries in which they were situated.

The Saar mines, which France obtained, and some minor items, £23,000,000.

In all, the figures he had given represented £415,000,000.

What Great Britain has received.

"Of this sum of £415,000,000 sterling," said the right hon. Gentleman, "Britain has obtained £56,000,000 sterling. Practically the whole of that has been spent on the Armies of Occupation." Continuing, he referred to the arrangement by which individual creditors in Great Britain and France obtained payment through the German Government of debts due to them by individual debtors in Germany. Those sums passed through a clearing-house, both in England and in Germany. The amount which Germany had paid under that system in all was, up to the present, £38,000,000 sterling. Of that sum, Britain had received £22,000,000 sterling; France, £12,000,000; and Belgium, £2,500,000. There was still due to the Allies £35,000,000, of which £12,500,000 was due to Great Britain.

After describing the conditions in Germany as they have developed since the Armistice and the evil results of the policy of inflation, the Chancellor of the Exchequer said Great Britain had for a long time strenuously represented to Germany that until she made a change in her procedure no real progress could be made. There was a very great improvement already as the result of new measures which had been undertaken. During the months from May to December, 1921, tax receipts were sufficient to cover only 63 per cent. of Germany's domestic expenditure. During the six months from January to June, 1922, after some of the reforms suggested had been put into operation, the tax receipts fully covered Germany's domestic expenditure and left a balance over—a small one only—towards the expenses which were required by the Peace Treaty. That change was due to some extent to getting rid of the subsidies and to a more rigid enforcement of the Income Tax.

Ability to pay.

"I dare say the House will appreciate the great difficulty with which the German Finance Minister is confronted in raising the requisite taxation when the medium in which he works varies with such extraordinary rapidity from one day to another," said the right hon. Gentleman. "In the result, I venture the opinion that Germany can pay very considerable sums in the shape of reparation. I have come to that deliberate conclusion after examination of all the circumstances. But I am equally clear that she requires some respite."

Lt.-Comdr. the Hon. J. M. Kenworthy (Independent Liberal, *Hull, Central*) : "Right at last."

The Chancellor of the Exchequer : "I think the action taken last year and at the beginning of the present year shows that we thought it necessary that Germany should have some respite in the present year. Nobody wishes that Germany should be derelict through too strenuous action on the part of the Allies. On the other hand, everybody must wish that Germany shall not escape the results of her own wrong, and I have no doubt at all that in Germany itself there would be a desire to pay that which is reasonable and proper, according to her capacity. That, at least, ought to be exacted from her."

Inter-Allied debts.

Turning to the subject of inter-Allied indebtedness, the Chancellor of the Exchequer, after a reference to the dispatch issued by Lord Balfour to the Allied nations, said he wished to make it clear beyond all possibility of misapprehension that Great Britain realised and recognised to the full her obligations to pay her debt to the United States of America.

"While this is so," he proceeded, "we have never been blind in this country to the colossal burden which is imposed upon the nations of the world at the present time because of the indebtedness of one nation to another, and we hold very strongly the view that no greater impediment exists to-day to the recovery of the world from the disastrous consequences of the War than that burden of debt. The real significance of what I have said is not in any way weakened by the comment that, while we undoubtedly are in a position to pay our creditors, we might not be able to collect our debts from our debtors. The true aspect of the position is that in addition to the £850,000,000 which we borrowed from the United States of America for the benefit of our Allies, £2,000,000,000 of our War debts of £7,700,000,000 sterling represents money not spent by us or on our own behalf, but lent in the course of the War by us to our Allies.

"In any proposal which we might have been inclined to make, we would still for all time be enduring the burden of that large portion of our debt while, at the same time, our agreement or willingness to forgo what Germany owes us by way of reparation would obviously make it much more easy for our Allies to obtain from Germany reasonable payment for that which they have suffered in the course of the War.

Great Britain's sacrifices.

"We hold the view very strongly that to get rid of these indebtednesses as between the nations would be the first thing to bring about a revival in the world, to give a new impetus to the reconstruction of the world, and a new stimulus to enterprise. In my view, history will not put any inglorious estimate, either upon the stupendous sacrifices which Britain made during the War, or on the great concessions which she has been willing to make since the peace, for the purpose of the reconstruction of the world. But we cannot be expected in this matter to stand alone.

"We cannot forget the condition of our own people, the hardships they are suffering at the present time, the distress and the agonies they are enduring, and the great financial burdens which they, nevertheless, have got to bear. As the result, already, of our sacrifices in the War, we have a burden of debt, which is, I think, greater than that of any other nation of the world. . . . While our Debt is £181 per head of the population, that of the French citizen is £162 and of the American citizen, £47. . . . The British nation is taxed at £17 17s. per head as against £9 in France. Similarly, if a comparison is suggested with America, and every allowance is made for State imposts in that country, taxation is twice as heavy here as in the United States.

"I say in those circumstances it is impossible to ask the British taxpayer alone to shoulder the burden of the payment of War debts."

Two things essential.

The Right Hon. H. H. Asquith (Leader of the Independent Liberal Party) said that in his judgment two things were absolutely essential if they were to deal adequately with the situation. They were promptitude and certainty. Not from any tenderness for Germany, but in their own interest, in the interest of their late Allies, and above all in the interest of international trade, the claim to reparation should be definitely ascertained, should be scaled down to what was really fair.

"We should be ready, I think," Mr. Asquith remarked, "to forgo our share, and, in regard to indebtedness, to remit what is due to us." To remit, in his opinion, was not an act of magnanimity. It was an act of good business. He would deprecate any suggestion, direct or indirect, in the United States of America that they were under any obligation, moral or even sentimental, to abate in any way their just and righteous claim. But he would be more than glad to see the question of American indebtedness kept quite apart from the pressing and urgent European situation.

The Right Hon. Lord Robert Cecil (Conservative, *Hitchin*) said he was satisfied that his fellow-countrymen were wise enough to see that the settlement of the European situation was of far greater importance than any question as to what exact amount they were going to claim from the Germans. The margin of economic safety, which to his mind had always been very small, had now become so small that it was very doubtful whether anything they could do would save Germany and Europe at large from the catastrophe that threatened.

Driving Germany too far.

The Prime Minister (the Right Hon. D. Lloyd George) remarked that Mr. Asquith had said with respect to inter-Allied indebtedness that he was in favour of an absolutely clean slate. That was what Lord Balfour proposed in his Note. " It is not a clean slate," the Premier observed, " when you wipe off every debt which is due to us, but engrave more deeply on the slate the debts which are due by us to other people." As regarded reparation, there was the danger, and he did not conceal it, that they might drive Germany into despair. " Whether she throws herself into the hands of reactionaries or of Communists there is very little to choose from our point of view," Mr. Lloyd George proceeded. " There would be no reparation in either case. There would be lots of trouble, but no cash—none." Therefore, from every point of view it would be a mistake to press Germany beyond the limit of endurance and capacity. But he wanted to put the other point of view. It was a mistake, because of these risks and dangers, to run away from a fair and just claim. Germany quite understood that she had to pay.

After further debate the House took up the consideration of another subject.

ALLIES AND GERMANY.

(Progress of disarmament; Reparations; etc.)

On 5th July, in the House of Commons,

Comdr. Carlyon Bellairs (Coalition Unionist, *Maidstone*) asked, in view of the exaggerated ideas as to the armaments now at the disposal of Germany, for the latest figures of the

Commission of Control as to the aeroplanes, guns, machine-guns, and rifles destroyed; and how these compared with the full expectations of the Commission?

The Financial Secretary to the War Office (Lt.-Col. the Hon. G. F. Stanley): "The latest report from the Inter-Allied Military Commission of Control shows that 33,484 guns and barrels of all kinds have been surrendered, and 33,410 have been destroyed up to date. In addition, 6,051 guns under construction were destroyed by the Germans prior to control. The records have been checked by the Commission. 87,377 machine-guns have been surrendered and 87,351 have been destroyed up to date. 4,382,839 rifles and carbines have been surrendered and 4,369,330 have been destroyed up to date.

"The Commission consider that all important stocks or surplus war material in Germany have been surrendered for destruction, and that only a negligible number of guns, machine-guns and rifles may still be hidden by extremist parties. The Inter-Allied Military Commission of Control have accomplished far more than the members of the Commission themselves considered possible at the outset of their work.

"The aeronautical disarmament of Germany was recognised as complete by the Allies on the 5th February last. On that date, 14,731 aeroplanes had been surrendered and 14,260 destroyed. The Aeronautical Commission of Control has since been withdrawn."

Reparation payments.

On 24th July, in the House of Commons,

Sir W. H. Davison (Conservative, ***Kensington, S.*****)** asked what was the total sum (British currency value) which had been paid by Germany to this country since the Treaty of Versailles; and what was the total cost incurred by this country to date in respect of the Army of Occupation on the Rhine?

The Chancellor of the Exchequer (the Right Hon. Sir Robert Horne): "The total amount debited to this country in respect of receipts from Germany available for the cost of occupation from 11th November, 1918, to 30th April, 1922, is 956,662,000 gold marks. This is equivalent to £50,351,000 at the present rate of 19 gold marks to £1 sterling, but owing to the varying rates of exchange at which receipts have been brought to account, and to the fact that certain cessions of property have not been brought into the Exchequer account at all as money payments, it is not possible to give an exact British currency figure. In addition, about 600,000,000 paper marks have been received locally by the Army.

"The total cost of the Army of Occupation during the same period is approximately £54,000,000. The valuation of certain deliveries is, however, still provisional, and the only statement which can safely be made is that the debit in respect of receipts to date is nearly equal to the cost of the Army of Occupation to date."

Sir W. Davison : " In general terms, are we to understand that we have received, on balance, nothing from Germany since the Armistice ? "

The Chancellor of the Exchequer : " The answer is that the Army of Occupation has cost us practically what we have received."

MANDATE FOR PALESTINE.

(Pledges to Jews and Arabs; Development of the country; the Rutenberg concession.)

On 4th July, the question of the Mandate for Palestine was discussed in the House of Commons in the course of the debate on the Vote for the Colonial Office.

DEBATE IN HOUSE OF COMMONS.

Sir W. Joynson-Hicks (Conservative, *Twickenham*) moved to reduce the salary of the Colonial Secretary by £100, and explained that the real object was to secure a debate on the following motion which he had placed on the Order Paper :—

> That, in the opinion of this House, the Mandate for Palestine, the acceptance of which must involve this country in financial and other responsibilities, should be submitted for the approval of Parliament; and further, that the contracts entered into by the High Commissioner for Palestine with Mr. Pinhas Rutenberg should at once be referred to a Select Committee for consideraton and report.

Having urged that the House should be given an opportunity of deciding whether it wanted the Mandate in its present form, or desired amendments to it, the hon. Baronet proceeded to set out the Arab as against the Zionist contention. The real trouble, he said, was the way in which the Zionists had been permitted by the Government, or with the connivance of the Government, practically to control the whole of the Government of Palestine. Sir Herbert Samuel went out to Palestine with the knowledge of all the people in that country that the Zionists claimed him as their representative. It was not sufficient for an English Governor to be above suspicion, as Sir Herbert Samuel was, but it was necessary that the people of the country, 90 per cent. of whom were Arabs, should believe him to be above suspicion.

A Jewish commonwealth.

If they looked at the proposals of the Zionists before the Versailles Conference in 1919 it would be seen that they used the expression that the Jewish national home was to lead up to a Jewish commonwealth in Palestine. The Arabs could hardly be expected to sit still when they knew that this great organisation was trying to organise Palestine as a Jewish commonwealth. If the sane view of Zionism prevailed he did not think there would be any great trouble from the Arab people. If they wanted only the sane view, the agricultural view, the commercial view, there was no need to turn Palestine into a Judaic country.

The draft Mandate itself foreshadowed something in the nature of the Rutenberg scheme. Article XI. said :—

> The Administration may arrange with the Jewish Agency mentioned in Article 4 to construct or operate on fair and equitable terms any public works, services, and utilities and to develop any of the natural resources of the country, in so far as these matters are not undertaken directly by the Administration.

The Government policy was to block all applications for concessions or otherwise except from the Zionists. He asked that a Select Committee should be appointed to consider the Rutenberg contract, because witnesses could be called to show the attempts which had been made, both by Englishmen and Arabs, to promote schemes of development of various kinds, all of which were turned down because the Treaty of Peace had not been concluded. He had had some experience of contracts in the City, but the Rutenberg contract contained the most astonishing concessions he had ever seen or read of. It gave over the development of the whole country to Mr. Rutenberg. He had two years in which to form a company and during that period no other concession in Palestine could be granted.

Feeling of uncertainty.

Lord Eustace Percy (Coalition Unionist, *Hastings*) said he had always had grave misgivings as to certain provisions of the Mandate, but, Great Britain having accepted certain responsibilities, there was nothing for this country to do except to give its whole-hearted support to the British administration in Palestine. The bloodshed, disturbances and vendettas in Palestine flowed from one thing alone—the feeling of uncertainty whether Great Britain might not be forced to refuse the Mandate in a certain degree, or even to give it up altogether.

Sir John Butcher (Conservative, *York*) remarked that one of the complaints was that it was not British administration in Palestine they were advancing, but Zionist administration.

Pledge to Zionists.

The Secretary of State for the Colonies (the Right Hon. Winston Churchill) said two issues were raised :—

(1) Were they to keep their pledge to the Zionists made in 1917 to the effect that His Majesty's Government would use their best efforts to facilitate the achievement of a national home for the Jewish people ?

(2) Were the measures taken by the Colonial Office to fulfil that pledge reasonable and proper measures ?

No doubt individual Members who had always opposed the Zionist policy were perfectly consistent in opposing it now, but the House as a whole had definitely committed itself on more than one occasion to the general proposition that they should use their best endeavours to make good their pledges and facilitate the achievement of a national home for the Jewish people in Palestine.

The fulfilment of the Balfour Declaration was an integral part of the whole mandatory system as inaugurated by agreement between the victorious Powers and by the Treaty of Versailles. When the Zionist policy was announced by Lord Balfour, then Mr. Balfour, almost every public man in Great Britain supported the Declaration. He appealed to the House not to alter its opinion on the general question, but to stand faithfully to the undertakings which had been given in the name of Britain and interpret in an honourable and earnest way the promise that Britain would do her best to fulfil her undertakings to the Zionists.

Development of Palestine.

At the same time the pledge was made to the Zionists, an equally important promise was made to the Arab inhabitants in Palestine that their civil and religious rights would be effectively safeguarded, and that they would not be turned out to make room for newcomers. " If that pledge was to be acted upon," said Mr. Churchill, " it was perfectly clear that the newcomers must bring their own means of livelihood, and that they, by their industry, by their brains and by their money, must create new sources of wealth on which they could live without detriment to or subtraction from the well-being of the Arab population.

" Were we wrong in carrying out the policy of the nation and of Parliament in fixing upon the development of the waterways and the water power of Palestine as the main and principal means by which we could fulfil our undertaking ? I am told the Arabs would have done it themselves. Who is going to believe that ? Left to themselves, the Arabs of Palestine not in a thousand years would have taken effective steps towards the irrigation and electrification of Palestine.

They would have been quite content to dwell—a handful of philosophic people—in the wasted sun-scorched plains, letting the waters of the Jordan continue to flow unbridled and unharnessed into the Dead Sea."

The Rutenberg concession.

The Rutenberg concession, the Colonial Secretary went on to say, followed in every respect the regular lines of Colonial Office procedure. It had been framed in exactly the same manner and spirit as if it related to East Africa, Nigeria, Ceylon, or any other of the Crown Colonies. It had been scrutinised and executed by the Crown Agents. Technical matters were submitted to the examination of consulting engineers.

The concession provided for strict Government control of the prices to be charged to consumers for electricity, and for the severe limitation of profits. After the company had earned 10 per cent., the profits were to be equally divided between them and the Palestinian Government until 15 per cent. had been received. After that the whole profit reverted to the Palestinian Government. After 37 years the Palestinian Government had the full right of repurchase on certain well-established lines, and that right recurred thereafter every 10 years. It had been stated that streams of applications were coming in from Arabs and British. At the time the Rutenberg concession was granted no other application was before them.

Mr. Rutenberg was a man of exceptional ability and personal force. He was a Zionist and his application was supported by the influence of Zionist organisations. He presented letters from Mr. Edmond Rothschild, the founder of the Zionist colonies, who offered to place at his disposal from £100,000 to £200,000 on absolutely non-commercial terms for long periods for the development of these irrigation and electrical schemes. Profit-making in the ordinary sense had played no part at all in the driving force on which they must rely to carry through this irrigation scheme in Palestine.

Vote of confidence.

"I am bound," Mr. Churchill said, "to ask the Committee to take the Vote which is about to be given as a vote of confidence, because we cannot carry out our pledges to the Zionists, with which the House is fully familiar, unless we are permitted to use Jews, and use Jews freely, within what limits are proper, to develop new sources of wealth in Palestine. I am bound also to ask the Committee to attach significance to this vote because of the adverse vote* recorded in the House of Lords a few days ago."

---

* *Vide* JOURNAL, Vol. III., No. 3, p. 480.

The vote in the House of Lords, the Colonial Secretary thought, was a very unfortunate one and it might have a serious result in Palestine. They were doing their best to carry out their pledges both to the Jews and the Arabs. They were doing their best to develop the resources of Palestine in order to recoup the expenditure made in this country. The year before last they were faced with charges amounting to £8,000,000, but Sir Herbert Samuel had promised that next year the amount would not be more than £1,500,000 and the year after that only £1,000,000. Palestine was all the more important to them in view of what was happening, in view of the ever-growing significance to the British Empire of the Suez Canal, and he did not think that £1,000,000 a year, even if further reductions could not be obtained, would be too much for Great Britain to pay for the control and guardianship of that great historic land, and keeping the word she had given before all the nations of the world.

On a division, the motion to reduce the Vote was negatived by 292 votes against 35, and progress was reported.

IMPERIAL CONFERENCE.

(Discussions on Empire policy: question of publicity.)

On 10th July, in the House of Commons,

Mr. Percy Hurd (Coalition Unionist, *Frome*) asked the Prime Minister whether in accordance with the practice followed in the case of earlier conferences, he would cause to be issued, for the information of the public, the statistical and other papers concerning the resources of the Empire which were submitted to the Imperial Conferences of 1917 and 1918 in so far as they were not deemed to be confidential ?

The Prime Minister (the Right Hon. D. Lloyd George): " The statistical information laid before the Conferences of 1917 and 1918 could not properly be separated from, or published apart from, the confidential discussions with which it was connected."

Mr. Hurd: " In all the previous Conferences has there not been detailed publication, subsequent to the Conference, of proceedings which were not confidential ? "

Confidential information.

The Prime Minister: " In the case of some of the Conferences that is so, but the Conferences are assuming quite a different character. Each successive Conference is more in the form of Cabinet discussions on the policy of the Empire. That makes it increasingly difficult to publish part of the discussions without the whole, and to publish the whole would be destructive of the very object we have in view, which is to secure confidential discussion between the Dominions and the Mother Country as to the policy which the Empire is to pursue."

Mr. Hurd : "Is it not almost impossible to get people to take an interest in these things here and overseas if the essential facts are not disclosed ?"

The Prime Minister : "I do not see why essential facts should not be disclosed, but there is a great difference between that and publishing information which has been given in the course of confidential discussion."

Imperial Economic Conference.

Mr. de F. Pennefather (Coalition Unionist, *Kirkdale*) asked if any steps were being taken to appoint a Cabinet Committee to prepare the way for an Imperial Economic Conference ?

The Prime Minister : "The answer is in the negative."

IMPERIAL RESOURCES.

(Question of development; Imperial Conference resolution.)

On 31st July, in the House of Commons,

Viscount Wolmer (Conservative, *Aldershot*) asked the Prime Minister whether it was the intention of the Government to carry out the definite pledge given on behalf of the Cabinet at the Imperial Conference on 26th April, 1917, and embodied in a resolution of the Conference, that the time had arrived when every possible encouragement should be given to the development of Imperial resources, and especially to making the Empire independent of other countries in respect of food supplies, raw materials, and essential industries ?

The Prime Minister (the Right Hon. D. Lloyd George) : "My noble friend has quoted only the first and not the second part of the resolution passed on the 26th April, 1917. The second part deals with two specific matters, though giving effect to the general principles expressed in the first part, namely, the introduction of preference and the encouragement of inter-Imperial migration. His Majesty's Government have already taken steps in both directions.

"I would refer to the terms of Section 8 of the Finance Act, 1919, dealing with Imperial Preference and to the Empire Settlement Act passed during the present Session, as well as to the administrative action taken since the termination of the War to develop migration within the Empire. I would also remind my noble friend that during the last three years numerous Dominion and Colonial Government loans have been raised, of which the proceeds are being devoted in large measures to the development of Imperial resources."

Viscount Wolmer: "Are we to take it that the Government consider Imperial Preference on tea, sugar and wine will make the Empire independent in respect of food supplies, raw material and essential industries; and if not, may we infer the Government are going in for Tariff Reform?"

The Prime Minister: "I think my noble friend has not taken the answer as a whole. If he does that, he will find it is full and complete."

COLONIAL OFFICE VOTE.

(Crown Colony problems; Future of Rhodesia; West Indies and representative government.)

On 4th July, the House of Commons went into Committee of Supply on a Vote for £306,637 in respect of the Colonial Office, a sum of £367,000 having previously been voted on account.

DEBATE IN HOUSE OF COMMONS.

The Under-Secretary of State for the Colonies (Hon. E. Wood), confining his remarks to what he termed "the older Colonial Empire," said there had probably never been any Empire in the world's history so economical in its encroachments upon public cost or public time in proportion to its size. For the Colonies, not less than for themselves, the last twelve months had been coloured by the hard pressure of severe economic stress. In countries that depended almost wholly, if not wholly, upon a simple staple product, when that staple product had fallen into the universal slump the difficulty of balancing Budgets was far more severe than any they had in Great Britain.

That had been the case in almost every Colony in the last twelve months, but notably in Malaya where the conditions of the rubber industry had been responsible for a period of extreme distress and difficulty. A meeting of the Dutch Rubber Growers' Association had decided in favour of the principle of Government restriction of outputs. The subject had also been engaging the attention of a Committee appointed by the Colonial Secretary, which had issued a very instructive and very valuable report, but as all further progress in the matter depended upon contingent co-operation with the Netherlands authorities he was not in a position to say more at that moment.

Capital expenditure.

The West Indies had suffered as a result of the collapse of the sugar industry. All the African Colonies, West and East, in similar conditions, had been compelled to curtail their expenditure, but in all the Colonies it had been possible either to balance the Budget, or to meet such small deficits as remained out of surplus balances accumulated in prosperous years by prudent finance.

He had seen it stated that in the circumstances it would have been wise on the part of the Colonial Secretary to suspend all extraordinary capital expenditure until times were better. He could not take that view. Great as might be the need of prudence, there was a point at which prudence became pusillanimity, and if that policy were urged to the extreme it would be likely to place them in a position where they would be unable to take advantage of trade revival when it came, and thereby recoup themselves for the present difficulty.

He had made a simple arithmetical calculation as to the comparative value of human labour in transport and railway trucks. An ordinary human being, he was advised, could carry on his head 60 lbs. over 10 miles in one day. A railway truck on a railway could carry 30,000 lbs. 100 miles in one day. The moral was that, as they developed railway transport in countries where head transport was all they had, they were making a very practical contribution towards developing the labour supply and rendering it available for further useful purposes.

Railways and harbours.

Therefore, while many works had to be postponed, the Colonial Secretary had thought it right to sanction the commencement of certain additional public works—railways and harbours in Kenya, Nigeria, the Gold Coast, and other places. When completed those works would place these great producing countries in more direct and immediate relationship with the consuming markets on which they depended.

During the past year, several Colonies and Protectorates had obtained in London, through the Crown Agents for the Colonies, loans for various public works up to a total of something like £23,000,000. In addition, the Government of British Guiana had itself raised a loan of £1,000,000, fully subscribed, and those figures showed what confidence, generally speaking, the investor had in the wisdom of colonial administration. With regard to the recovery of the African Colonies, he was advised that they had touched the bottom, and that in some cases there were already signs of improvement. Referring to the criticism that taxation in the African Colonies had been unduly burdensome, Mr. Wood proceeded to speak in particular of the difficult position in Nigeria.

The difficulty was due principally to a philanthropic effort under which they prohibited the importation of spirits into Nigeria, which affected the Nigerian Exchequer to the extent of £900,000. A part of that sum had been made good by increased import duty, as to which, with the present level *ad valorem* of 15 per cent., he could not think there was any solid ground for complaint. With regard to export duties, the Nigerian Government had recently suggested a reduction of from 50 to 75 per cent. on hides and skins, which had been approved by the Colonial Secretary. A special Committee of Inquiry into the West African trade had unanimously advised the abolition of the preferential duty on palm kernels and the Colonial Secretary, acting on the advice of those immediately affected, had decided to abolish the duty forthwith.

Kenya: Rhodesia.

Turning to the problems of Kenya, the hon. Gentleman said there had recently been appointed a strong unofficial Committee with a wide reference that would enable them, he thought, to render material assistance to the Government in the task of retrenching expenditure and endeavouring to lay the burdens of taxation where they would least be felt. As to the franchise question, while it had not yet been possible to find agreement, he thought there was little doubt that, with the full assent of the white community in Kenya, it would not be impossible for the Colonial Secretary to secure such representation for the Indians as would enable them actively and effectively to participate in the public affairs and government of the Colony

The question of the future of Southern Rhodesia was necessarily in suspense pending the intimation by General Smuts of the terms on which incorporation in the Union might be possible. Those terms, in turn, depended upon negotiations between General Smuts and the British South Africa Company. As soon as those terms were available it was proposed to submit the two alternatives of responsible Government or incorporation in the Union to the Rhodesian people to select by way of the Referendum.

Col. J. C. Wedgwood (Labour, *Newcastle-under-Lyme*): "To all the people ? "

The Under-Secretary of State for the Colonies: " To those who enjoy the franchise, black and white. . . . These matters involve very difficult legal questions, and, so far as the Imperial Government are concerned, I have only to add that on various occasions in the past assurances have been given to Parliament that His Majesty's Government would not commit themselves to any payment to the British South Africa Company in respect of the deficits incurred in the administration of Southern Rhodesia without the sanction of Parliament, and the draft Letters Patent are, in fact, drawn up on the basis that the Company are entitled for the reimbursement of their administrative deficits only to the proceeds of the unalienated lands as and when they accrue."

The West Indies: Representative government.

Speaking of his visit to the West Indies,* the hon. Gentleman said it was in the nature of an experiment in Colonial administration. He endeavoured to appraise the force of the movement for representative government as it existed in different islands, and to discuss the conditions under which and the limits within which it was, in his judgment, right at the present day to meet the demand that had been made. "I am quite satisfied," the hon. Gentleman observed, "that while you have, as you have there, the universal foundations of loyalty, confidence in British administration, and goodwill, that is the time to meet the demands to the utmost legitimate extent."

He was extremely pleased that this course of action had been approved by the Colonial Secretary. It was possible that as time went on wisdom might suggest and events might warrant further advances along those lines. That was for the future. "For the present," said Mr. Wood, "and for so long a future as I personally can foresee, I deem it is essential to maintain in some form or other the ultimate control that is exercised on behalf of Parliament by the Secretary of State for the Colonies over these growing and developing communities, and I have made suggestions how that security can be maintained in conformity with constitutional growth and evolution."

He was at present driven to admit that public opinion in these Colonies was far too centrifugal to make West Indian Federation immediately practicable, and he was disposed to think that the grant of representative institutions was likely to be the most effective instrument by way of education towards the broader policy.

* The Under-Secretary of State for the Colonies, accompanied by Hon. W. Ormsby-Gore, M.P., and Mr. R. A. Wiseman, of the Colonial Office, visited the West Indies and British Guiana between December, 1921, and February, 1922. The voyage was undertaken in consequence of representations made to the Colonial Secretary from the House of Commons which expressed the growing demand in several of the West Indian Colonies for the bestowal of a measure of representative government. A lengthy and interesting report by the Under-Secretary was subsequently published as a Command Paper (No. 1679).

Rhodesia and the Union.

Col. Wedgwood considered it undesirable that a Colony like Rhodesia should be forced for financial reasons to go into the Union of South Africa. It would be far better if it became an independent Dominion. The Under-Secretary seemed to suggest that if the question were put to a vote in Rhodesia the blacks would be consulted.

The Under-Secretary of State for the Colonies : " I said the voters would be consulted."

Col. Wedgwood : " Does the hon. Gentleman know there are probably not more than 50 black voters in the whole of Rhodesia ? It is futile to talk about consultation with the blacks when there are 5,000,000 or 6,000,000 of them and only about 50 have votes." The question would be put to the white inhabitants of Rhodesia, the hon. Member said, and he thought it was unfair, even to the white inhabitants. It was certainly undesirable to give over a Colony, where there were so many natives, probably against the wish of those natives. There was probably not a native who would not sooner be under the direct rule of the Colonial Office than under the Union of South Africa.

Why not follow the decisions of Lord Cave's Committee and Lord Buxton's Committee and find out what was owed to the Chartered Company ? Undoubtedly if the question had gone to the Privy Council, the Chartered Company would have discovered that their claim in respect of Northern Rhodesia was far less than that in respect of Southern Rhodesia. It was now proposed to rush Northern Rhodesia as well as Southern Rhodesia into the Union. As regarded Kenya, they had there the acid test of whether the British Empire was worth while. If they were going into that country to set up a colour bar between Indian and European, by that colour bar they would be judged by 315,000,000 Indians.

West Indian federation.

The Hon. W. Ormsby-Gore (Coalition Unionist, *Stafford*) believed that Kenya Colony was economically doomed by its past history, and by the way the development of that Colony was proceeding. What all the Crown Colonies wanted was a reduction of Government expenditure and a reduction of taxation. He took the view very strongly that the right place for Southern Rhodesia was a province in the Union of South Africa. The future of Southern Rhodesia as a self-governing concern was a very gloomy picture, whereas its union with South Africa was very hopeful and likely to make it a most prosperous province.

As regarded West Indian federation, in the Imperial Parliament they had always regretted that the various West Indian

Colonies were so different, and had not shown that homogeneity which alone would enable them to play the part in the councils of the Empire their importance entitled them to. The mere fact that 16 or 17 separate Parliaments existed was naturally a great disadvantage from the point of view of the Imperial Parliament. The various Parliaments should be encouraged to co-operate and work along similar lines. He believed that before long federation would grow in the West Indies. The Under-Secretary for the Colonies had admirably sketched the first act of development in his Report, namely, that some effort should be made to unify the medical service. So long as every Colony was quite separate and had its own little Civil Service, with promotion practically out of the question, they would not get the same administrative advantages as if they pooled the whole of their Services.

The West Indian people felt that Great Britain had not done all it might do to help the British West Indies economically. When travelling back from British Guiana and Trinidad an American on board the ship said to him, " You in England have too many Colonies. You do not take the trouble to use them. Why not hand them over to some one who will develop them ? " They did not want that sort of thing said against them.

Principle of preference.

Mr. Percy Hurd (Coalition Unionist, *Frome*) said it was an enormous advantage that there should have arisen in recent times so close an economic association between Canada and the West Indies. It was based on the principle of preference, and he cordially welcomed the decision to which the Government had come that some attempt should be made to create a greater stability for the principle of preference. It was impossible for anyone going to the West Indies to fail to appreciate how much they realised there the advantages that the preferential system of the United States was bringing to the American Colonies, and it was extraordinarily difficult to avoid feeling the desirability of following that example.

If the British West Indies were to be brought more thoroughly into accord with one another and more intimately into association with this country, it was essential that the cable problem should be resolutely faced. Moreover, the usefulness of wireless in Colonies like the West Indies was incalculable, and he asked the Under-Secretary if he would bear in mind the possibility of bringing the British West Indies within the Empire wireless project. They were face to face with a growing problem in the attempt to establish far greater intimacy between the various parts of their scattered Empire and the wireless chain was one of the best means of getting the personal touch.

They had made a hopeless bungle of the Empire wireless chain, largely because they did not consult those in the various Dominions who knew the problem.

After other speeches the Committee turned to the discussion of the position in Palestine. A summary of that debate will be found at page 736 of the present issue.

CANADIAN CATTLE EMBARGO.

(Free vote of House of Commons; Motion for abolition carried.)

On 24th July, in the House of Commons, a debate took place on the subject of the Canadian Cattle Embargo.* It arose on the following motion :—

That this House is of opinion that the time has arrived when the embargo on the importation of Canadian cattle should be removed.

The Government left the question to the free decision of the House, and in the division at the close of the debate the official Whips did not act as tellers.

DEBATE IN HOUSE OF COMMONS.

Capt. W. T. Shaw (Coalition Unionist, *Forfar***)**, in moving the motion, said that all the great municipalities and corporations in the country had forwarded resolutions asking that the embargo should be removed. These people recognised that it was vital to the interests of the Empire and to the maintenance of the honour of the country that the pledge given to Canada should be honoured. For the thirty years the embargo had been in operation there had been a fight for its removal. It was admitted by all experts that the herds of Canada were to-day, and had been for 30 years probably, the freest from disease and the healthiest in any country in the world. Having heard and weighed all the evidence, the finding of the recent Royal Commission was :—

We are of opinion there is no substantial ground for the apprehension that such admission would introduce disease among the cattle of this country.

As far as Canada was concerned, all the talk about protecting the herds of this country was absolute eyewash. Properly interpreted, it meant protection of certain people's pockets. Even if the embargo were taken off the breeders in this country would have the protection which arose from the cost of transport, amounting to from £10 to £14 per head.

* *Vide* also JOURNAL, Vol. III., No. 3, p. 509.

Question of quarantine.

He thought supporters of the embargo had for some time recognised that they were beaten in this controversy, but they hoped, by insisting on a period of quarantine, to retain the substance while conceding the shadow. They had to admit there was no disease among Canadian cattle, and, when they did that, upon what could they found their demand for quarantine? It was said that the Canadians insisted upon quarantine for cattle coming from this country, but they could not give the Canadians anything like the same bill of health as the Canadians could give them.

Mr. C. Percy (Coalition Unionist, *Tynemouth*), in seconding the motion, said the British breeders could not supply the demand of the British feeders, and the position was getting worse. The stocks in this country were declining in proportion to the population, and, since they had to import, surely it was a matter of common sense that they should import from the safest quarters. He urged the Government to keep carefully before them the Imperial point of view. As the matter now stood, they were allowing importations from Ireland and refusing them from Canada.

Were they going to refuse Canada equal rights and equal privileges with Ireland? Were they going to send their children to Canada and yet refuse to help them by declining to deal with them in the products of their labours? If they alienated Canada's sympathies, it would not be a misfortune for England only—it would be a calamity to the world.

Opposition to removal.

Mr. Ernest Evans (Coalition Liberal, *Cardiganshire*) moved the following amendment to the motion:—

> This House, while taking note of the recommendations of the recent Royal Commission, is of opinion that it would be inadvisable to repeal or to alter the Diseases of Animals Act, 1896, at the present moment for the following reasons: that this legislation has given a measure of security and stability to stock-breeding unknown under the conditions which prevailed before that legislation was passed; that there is severe depression in agriculture which any interference with existing legislation would tend to aggravate; and that the opinion of the Royal Commission is definite that the interests of the consumers are not involved in this question, the effect of the admission or non-admission of Canadian cattle on the price of meat being in their view immaterial.

The hon. Member said the present law dated from 1896 and was the result of 30 years' anxious effort to frame a policy which would give to every stock-breeder in this country that feeling of security which was essential to the successful conduct of the industry. The House ought not to abandon that policy unless very urgent reasons could be shown. It was said that a pledge had been given. If that pledge was given by anybody, it was given by Lord Ernle, and it was given by him speaking on his own responsibility, without previous consultation with the Government. Lord Ernle himself said that the words which he used did not bear the interpretation which it was now sought to put upon them.

"Stud farm of the world."

They had been told that the removal of the embargo would reduce the price of meat, but the Royal Commission said they were quite unable to accept that argument. There could be no doubt that the policy which had been pursued had done infinite good to the interests of agriculture and the interests of the country generally. Before 1890 on many occasions the country was ravaged by disease, causing untold loss to the farmers and imperilling the food supplies of the country. Since then they had been comparatively free from the most serious diseases of cattle plague and pleuro-pneumonia, with the exception of a few occasional outbursts of foot-and-mouth disease. To-day, as a result of that policy, this country produced better stock than any other country in the world and was generally accepted as "the stud farm of the world."

Capt. W. Elliot (Coalition Unionist, *Lanark*), in seconding the amendment, said that in the 20 years before the passing of the Act of 1896 there were 850,000 animals in Great Britain affected with either pleuro-pneumonia or foot-and-mouth disease. In the 20 years subsequent to the passing of that Act there were just over 4,000.

Imperial Conference pledge.

The Right Hon. H. H. Asquith (Leader of the Independent Liberal Party) remarked that this had been a burning, or, at any rate, a smouldering political question almost ever since he had been in political life. The legislation for the prohibition of the admission of foreign cattle was proposed by a Government of which he was a member, not for the protection of the British farmer against foreign competition, but for obtaining the immunity of their herds and flocks against the possible importation of foreign disease. In the years which followed a growing agitation arose for the removal of those restrictions as regarded the Canadian source of supply.

Although for many years he had been firmly convinced that Canadian cattle ought to be and might be freely admitted to this country without any real danger to their own herds and native sources of supply, he had always been ready to concede that there was a very strong case to be made upon the one side as well as upon the other. There were, however, two new factors which ought to be conclusive to the House. The first and more important was what took place at the

Imperial Conference in 1917. He could not conceive how anyone who had read the proceedings of that Conference, and the authorised and official comments subsequently made upon them by no less an authority than the Prime Minister himself, could seriously maintain that they were not bound in honour to one of the greatest of their own Dominions to implement the solemn promise which was then given.

Explicit and direct pledge.

The conference was presided over by the then Colonial Secretary (Mr. Long*), who was accompanied by the then President of the Board of Agriculture (Mr. Prothero†). The latter said :—

" As far as I personally am concerned, and so far as the English Board of Agriculture is concerned, after the War is over . . . we shall, I consider, be wise to remove the embargo. We do not believe that there is now, or has been for a great many years past, the slightest ground to exclude Canadian cattle on the score of disease."

The President of the Board of Agriculture was followed by Mr. Long, who said :—

" As far as I am concerned . . . I can only say I entirely agree with Mr. Prothero's policy. I think the time that has elapsed has shown that Canada has had a complete and clear bill of health during that time, and now the position is that the restriction is to be removed. The Board of Agriculture will take such steps as are necessary for this purpose.

" Mr. Rogers : Do not you think that we should have a resolution ?

" Mr. Long : You do not want a resolution, do you ? Or, if you like, you can simply move that the embargo on Canadian cattle be removed as speedily as possible.

" Mr. Rogers : I beg to move that.

" Mr. Long : Mr. Prothero accepts that, and there is an end of it."

Could they be surprised, asked Mr. Asquith, that every Canadian statesman from Sir Robert Borden onwards took that as an explicit and direct pledge, given with the full authority of the Imperial Government, that the embargo would be removed as speedily as possible ?

Comdr. Carlyon Bellairs (Coalition Unionist, *Maidstone*) : " It did not bind the House of Commons."

The Premier's words.

Mr. Asquith : " You can repudiate it if you like. But consider the effect of a pledge given as far back as 1917 to one of your principal Dominions. Is the House of Commons going to go back on that ? " Proceeding, Mr. Asquith quoted the language of the Prime Minister on 16th March, 1921, when promising the appointment of a Royal Commission :—

" The pledges given to Canada at the Imperial Conference in 1917 were very definite pledges on behalf of the Cabinet. I agree it is a matter for the House of Commons to decide."

---

* Now Viscount Long of Wraxall. † Now Lord Ernle.

The amendment asked the House to repudiate, after five years, pledges which had been understood by Canada, by the whole of the Dominions, and, indeed, by the whole world as definite and binding pledges given on behalf of the Government of the day.

Capt. Stanley Wilson (Coalition Unionist, *Holderness*) said the House ought to have been consulted first.

Mr. Asquith: "Does the hon. Gentleman really say that, when an Imperial Conference is held, no pledge must be given which is not first submitted to the House of Commons?"

Capt. Wilson: "Not of that character."

Mr. Asquith: "Then I should like to know what is the value of an Imperial Conference. If you cannot enter into a friendly, intimate discussion on the basis of equal membership of this great Imperial partnership, if the accredited representatives cannot enter into such a Conference with confidence upon all sides that pledges given by the authoritative representatives of the various Governments concerned have got to be honoured, there is an end of the whole system."

Even apart from the findings of the Royal Commission, Mr. Asquith added, they would be taking a very grave responsibility upon themselves as a House of Commons in going back upon pledges given by the Imperial Government through its accredited agents to one of their great Dominions. He earnestly trusted that the House of Commons would show to their Canadian fellow-countrymen, who had relied upon those pledges, that they were not going to break faith with them; and if any reason of policy were required to enforce that determination it would be found in the findings of the Commission that the carrying out of those obligations would not be in any way injurious to British agriculture or to the British consumer.

Minister of Agriculture.

The Minister of Agriculture (the Right Hon. Sir Arthur Boscawen), speaking not for the Government as a whole, but for his Department, and, as he claimed, for the great bulk of agriculturists, agreed that, so far as Lord Ernle was concerned, there was an absolute pledge to remove the stigma on Canadian cattle. But in the House of Lords during the previous week Lord Ernle denied that he ever gave any pledge to admit Canadian stores. Even if there had been a definite pledge to admit these cattle as stores, such a pledge, given by an individual Minister who was not a member of the Cabinet, and who had not consulted the Cabinet, could not in any way be binding on the House of Commons. Mr. Asquith did not read the passages where Mr. Rogers and Sir Robert Borden, the Canadian representatives, distinctly laid it down that they had no desire to interfere in the domestic agricultural policy of this country.

In view of those facts, he held that the House of Commons was absolutely free to deal with the question from the agricultural standpoint, and no other. There was no real stigma on Canada. How could there be ? The Act of 1896 did not apply only to Canada ; it applied to every country. From no country, for very good reasons, was it permissible to send live cattle as stores—that was, to be distributed throughout Great Britain. What was the good of stamping out disease by slaughtering here if they ran the risk of importing it from outside? They had in this country 200,000 more cattle under one year old this year than they had last year, and they had only to maintain confidence among the producers for them to produce all the stores the country wanted.

Unscientific and retrograde.

It was not only a question of immunity from disease, but a question of the purity of the blood of their flocks and herds. They had been doing a great deal, especially in recent years, to try to grade up and improve the commercial cattle of this country. The fact was that to remove the embargo would be a thoroughly unscientific and retrograde act. If they were going to allow any number of scrag bulls and heifers to come here and breeding took place, then it was good-bye to all they had been trying to do during the last twenty years. Would anyone tell him that the Canadian animals were free from tuberculosis ? They had only to read the reports of the veterinary department of the Canadian Government to know perfectly well that they had tuberculosis.

"They are making the most laudable and successful efforts to stamp it out," the right hon. Gentleman remarked, "but what on earth is the good of the Minister of Health bringing in a Milk Bill, one object of which is to stamp out tuberculosis in cattle in this country, if you are going to allow animals to be brought in which may have tuberculosis ?" He gathered that the people who were so anxious to remove the embargo would not hear of quarantine. "I am willing to say," he proceeded, "that the Canadian animals are to-day exceedingly healthy. They have been so for 30 years, and it reflects the greatest credit on the Canadian veterinary service.

Need for quarantine.

"But Canada has a 3,000-mile land frontier with the United States, and for us to allow animals to come from the American Continent without quarantine is simply to invite a reproduction of what occurred in the latter part of the last century, when cattle diseases of all kinds were constantly being imported into this country. I state freely that Canada has been very free from diseases, but I say also that she has been very fortunate, because she has not had foot-and-mouth and other diseases for over 30 years.

"When you have a 3,000-mile land frontier, it does not say that you are not going to have disease. Scotland until lately had not had foot-and-mouth disease for many years. It came across the English border the other day, and Scotland had it very badly. The United States had foot-and-mouth disease very badly four years ago. It came very near to the Canadian border. How do we know that it will not cross it next time, notwithstanding any precautions which the Canadian Government may take?

"Yet without any kind of restriction, qualification, or regulation our friends here invite us to play ducks and drakes with the splendid cattle industry which we have built up, and to take risks that no nation would ever think of taking."

Experience in the past.

Mr. James Wilson (Labour, ***Dudley*****)** remarked that when they were told that the importation of Canadian cattle would tend to discourage breeding in this country, and consequently to diminish their own home supplies, one would have thought that such a result would have made itself evident during the years when Canadian stores were coming in. The facts were all to the contrary. From 1886 to 1892, when Canadian stores were coming to this country in comparatively large quantities, the herds in the United Kingdom rose from 10,830,000 to 11,475,000. Therefore, concurrently with the importation of Canadian cattle, their own home supplies in the short period of six years increased by no less than 750,000 head.

Captain H. Dixon (Coalition Unionist, ***Belfast*****)** spoke against the removal of the embargo on behalf of the Ulster Government and the farmers of Southern Ireland.

The Secretary of State for the Colonies (the Right Hon. Winston Churchill) observed that every Party in the State was split to its foundations upon that issue except, he believed, the Labour Party. His view was that there was not nearly so much to be got out of the removal of the embargo, either for this country or Canada, as was expected. On the other hand there would be not nearly as much injury to British agriculture, or disturbance of existing conditions, as was apprehended by those whose lives were wrapped up in that industry. He thought it was common ground between both sides that no large importation was to be expected, and it would seem that inferior Canadian scrub cattle would not pay for transportation.

An Imperial question.

Arguments had been used about cruelty to animals on board ships. That must be a matter of strong regulations and there would be no dispute with Canada about it. He agreed that the effect of removing the embargo would be from the point of view of prices beneficial to the general public, but not by any means revolutionary, and not likely seriously to affect the prices which might be realised by the agricultural producer. It was upon the Report of the Royal Commission, and on the scientific merits of the agricultural problem, that those who were in favour of the removal of the embargo necessarily took their stand.

The argument that they were shutting out Canadian cattle because they were afraid those cattle would infect British herds with disease was mere pretence. He was entitled to say to the House, "This is an Imperial question." Canada had never challenged their rights. Canada had never said, "You ought not to put a tariff on the cattle." On the contrary, Sir Robert Borden and Mr. Meighen repeatedly said, "If we put a tariff on your goods, if you like to tax ours that is your business; but what we do object to is your putting a slur and a stigma upon our herds, which injures them not only in your markets but in the markets of every other country in the world." If that slur were not removed, if that stigma were not taken away, then he was bound to tell the House that undoubtedly they would have committed an injustice to Canada which would rankle and offend Canadian sentiment far out of proportion to the actual material injury she would suffer.

Working for unity.

"Canada does not threaten," Mr. Churchill proceeded: "All those who are our friends in Canada, the great mass of vigorous men and women who are working for the well-being of the British Empire, say: 'Whatever you do, we shall continue to work for the unity of the British Empire'; but they also say this: 'There are many new elements in Canada, there are many unassimilated elements in Canada, there are many interests in Canada which undoubtedly would be served by all kinds of tariff and other arrangements with the great Power which lies over the border. Do not place on our shoulders an unnecessarily heavy burden, do not hamper us unnecessarily in the work we have to do to promote the general and permanent unity of the British Empire.'

"I think the House, in view of all that has been said, would make a very grave decision if it decided, by refusing all redress of this undoubted grievance and injustice, to place a stumbling block in the path of weaker brethren in Canada and hamper our strongest friends in working for Imperial consolidation."

On a division the amendment was negatived by 247 votes against 171, and thereafter the resolution was agreed to.

DEBATE IN HOUSE OF LORDS.

The question was also debated at two sittings of the House of Lords and a decision was come to on 26th July.

Viscount Chaplin moved a resolution in these terms :—

That this House declines to remove what is wrongly described as "the embargo," on cattle which come to our shores from Canada or from other countries for the following reasons :—

(1) The term itself is very misleading, and purports to be used because of its injurious effect on the price of meat. On the other hand, to abandon the policy of slaughter at the port would reopen the door at once to the risk of the ravages of pleuro-pneumonia from which we have suffered so severely in the past, and compels us to relinquish a safeguard which has given us absolute security against that pestilential disease for upwards of thirty years.

(2) There is no embargo on the importation of live cattle for slaughter from any country in the world, Canadian or otherwise, and they have been so imported from Canada and other countries in thousands, and can be so imported now, provided they come from countries which are not suffering from any cattle disease.

(3) Pleuro-pneumonia, unlike many other cattle diseases, can only be conveyed by the immediate contact of one animal with another, therefore, so long as the provision for slaughter remains, and contact is impossible, we are safe.

Quarantine precautions.

Viscount Long of Wraxall proposed an amendment as follows :—

That this House accept the conclusions of the Royal Commission that the Dominion of Canada is free from cattle plague, pleuro-pneumonia and foot-and-mouth disease, and is of opinion that steers from the Dominions might be admitted as store cattle to Great Britain, subject to precautions, by means of quarantine, being taken.

It was not, said Lord Long, a question of doing justice to Canada or to any other Dominion. It was a question of doing what was right by themselves. He did all he could when he was at the Colonial Office to secure the adoption of Imperial Preference, and succeeded. "Therefore," Lord Long continued, "it is in conformity with what has been since 1917 the adopted policy of this country and of the whole Empire that I ask your Lordships to affirm, first, in answer to the request, or indeed, as one noble Lord rightly called it, the demand of Canada, that Canada is free from disease;

and, secondly, that being so, the Department of Agriculture here shall be charged with the same power that every other Department of Agriculture has, including that of Canada, and shall admit store cattle from the Dominions in accordance with the Regulations which they will frame and for which they will be responsible."

At the close of the debate the amendment was agreed to, and was passed as a substantive resolution.

SOUTH-WEST AFRICA.

(Military action in the mandated area.)

On 25th July, in the House of Commons,

Col. J. C. Wedgwood (Labour, *Newcastle-under-Lyme*) asked whether the attention of the Secretary of State for the Colonies had been drawn to the proceedings in the mandated area of South-West Africa, which included the bombing of Hottentot villages containing women and children, and of one 'plane dropping from a low altitude no less than 40 bombs and spraying with 2,000 rounds of ammunition a party of 500 Hottentots, involving heavy losses; and whether His Majesty's Government proposed to take any steps to put a stop to these proceedings?

The Secretary of State for the Colonies (the Right Hon. Winston Churchill): "I am aware that the Administration of South-West Africa have found it necessary to take military action against one of the native tribes. As regards the second part of the question, I would remind the hon. and gallant Member that the Mandate for South-West Africa is held by the Government of the Union of South Africa."

Col. Wedgwood: "Will the Government holding the Mandate make a report to the League of Nations on these occurrences in South-West Africa?"

The Secretary of State for the Colonies: "It is, surely, not a matter in which I am concerned. The Government of the Union of South Africa hold the Mandate, and they are responsible to the League of Nations. There is no *locus* either for me or for the hon. and gallant Member to interfere in the matter."

Col. Wedgwood: "Is there no *locus standi* in the matter by reason of the fact that we are members of the League of Nations?"

The Secretary of State for the Colonies: "I hope we shall find something better to do on the League of Nations than to attack our own Dominions."

POOLING OF WHEAT IN THE DOMINIONS.

On 24th July, in the House of Commons,

Mr. Percy Hurd (Coalition Unionist, *Frome*) asked the Minister of Agriculture what information he had in his Department as to the movement now in process of development among the farmers' co-operative societies of Australia, Canada and the United States for the pooling and marketing of wheat for the British market; and whether his attention had been called to the announcement made at a conference of Australian co-operative farmers that eleven Australian co-operative distributing companies made a turnover of £2,000,000 by one year's operations in flour on the London market?

The Minister of Agriculture (the Right Hon. Sir Arthur Boscawen): "I have no information on this subject, apart from statements which have appeared in the Press.

"I understand that in Australia there is a movement for the establishment of a voluntary wheat pool for the marketing of wheat on the lines of the Wheat Board set up by the Commonwealth Government during the War. In Canada, it appears that the Law Officers of the Crown have decided that the re-establishment of the Wheat Board, with compulsory powers, which operated during the War, would be *ultra vires*, but a Bill for the establishment of a Wheat Board without such powers has recently been introduced into Parliament.* I have no information as regards the United States.

"My attention has been drawn to the announcement referred to in the last part of the question."

INDIAN CIVIL SERVICE.

(Premier's statement; Constitutional changes; Empire's responsibilities.)

On 2nd August, in the House of Commons, during the debate on the Second Reading of the Consolidated Fund (Appropriation) Bill, the present position and the prospects of the Indian Civil Service were discussed.

DEBATE IN HOUSE OF COMMONS.

Sir Samuel Hoare (Coalition Unionist, *Chelsea*) said he was certain that one of the most important factors that would contribute to the success of the policy embodied in the Government of India Act was an efficient and contented Indian Civil

* *Vide* under "Canada," p. 822.

Service. At present, however, there was very grave anxiety and discontent in the ranks of the Civil Service. It was a serious fact that at the recent examinations fewer Europeans were presenting themselves, and if good recruits did not continue to come forward in sufficient numbers year after year the Indian Civil Service could not possibly maintain its efficiency.

A general feeling of insecurity was sapping the efficiency of the Service. In spite of repeated assurances a great many members of the Service genuinely believed that their pay was no longer as secure as it was before, that their pensions were not so certain, that it was doubtful, as constitutional developments took place in India, whether the appointments that they now held would continue, and, if they ceased to continue, whether they would obtain just compensation for having their careers brought to an end. Debates and questions in the new Assemblies suggested that a great many Members considered the Civil Service was no longer wanted in India, and that the civilians had better pack up and go home.

He asked for a clear statement that in spirit and in letter the Government would abide by the pledges that the individual Indian civil servant should not suffer from the constitutional changes which had taken place.

Home Rule for India: no "cutting of the painter."

Sir W. Joynson-Hicks (Conservative, *Twickenham*) remarked that a real difficulty was that attacks were being made upon the British Service of all grades and ranks by Indian extremists and, he was sorry to say, by members of the moderate section of Indian opinion as well. Whatever view might be taken as to the development of Home Rule for India, he was sure the British Government did not intend that in any way the painter should be cut between this country and India. If the Indianisation of the Services went on to the extent that many Indian politicians desired, namely, to 100 per cent., the British Government might just as well say they were no longer going to be responsible for India, as they would not have their own British servants in India to help them to maintain that position.

The Prime Minister (the Right Hon. D. Lloyd George) said that no doubt there was a great deal of uneasiness among British civil servants and British officials in India with regard to the future. There was an apprehension that the great constitutional changes which had been introduced in the course of the last few months would affect their position prejudicially and they wanted, possibly they needed, reassurances.

The changes were in the nature of an experiment and they must be treated as an experiment—a great and important experiment, but still an experiment. Difficulties had arisen and weaknesses had been exposed in the working of the new system, but that was inevitable. "On the whole," said the Premier, "I think it may be said, taking into account the fact that the experiment has been in operation only for a year and a half, that there has been a very considerable measure of success in spite of drawbacks which have manifested themselves. India has never been governed on these principles before. The native States are not governed on these principles now, and it remains to be seen whether a system of this kind . . . a system which the West has perfected for its own conditions, is suitable for India."

They must not, the Premier proceeded, have precipitate judgment on these experiments. On the other hand, he hoped that the Indian leaders would not force a precipitate judgment by their action. It was a case in which a great deal of patience was required on both sides.

Britain's responsibility.

It was important to realise that the most serious and testing time had probably not yet been reached. Before the last election, and until recently, there was a very considerable non-co-operative movement. What influence the non-co-operators and men of that kind would exert upon the elections in a year or 18 months' time he could not predict. It would be a cardinal principle with any Government that could command the confidence of this country that Britain would in no circumstances relinquish her responsibility to India.

"It is important that should be known, not so much in this country . . . but in India, where, for many reasons," the Premier observed, "there seems to be doubt disseminated, sometimes fortuitously, sometimes quite unintentionally, sometimes from facts which seem for the moment to justify conclusions of that kind. . . . We stand by our responsibilities; we will take whatever steps are necessary to discharge or to enforce them." There were, he continued, innumerable divisive forces in India, and if Britain withdrew her strong hand nothing would ensue except division, strife, conflict and anarchy. If they were to do so it would be one of the greatest betrayals in the history of any country.

Co-operation of India.

"I am one of those who believe in getting the co-operation of India in the government of the country. I believe it strengthens the Empire. . . . It would be a mistake to make India regard the Empire as something which is outside. . . . Therefore, I approach this question from the point of view of one who believes in getting Indians to assist us in discharging the very great trust and obligations which we have inherited and which I hope we shall transmit to our descendants in generations to come.

"Whatever the success of Indians, whether as Parliamentarians or as administrators, he could see no period when they could dispense with the guidance and the assistance of the 1,200 British civil servants, 700 British police officers, and 600 British medical officers—a total of 2,500 British officials in a population of 315,000,000. These men were placed at India's disposal, and Indians ought to feel a deep sense of gratitude. He hoped when it was thoroughly realised that there was no idea of winding up the British Civil Service in India, that they considered it essential to the very life of the system, and that they would consider everything that affected conditions in the Service, it would be an encouragement for young men once more to turn their attention to that great career.

They had undertaken the responsibility for India. They had undertaken to guide India. They had undertaken to establish and maintain law and good government throughout its vast domains. They had undertaken to defend its frontiers and to protect its peoples against internal and external foes. The British Empire meant, at all costs, to continue to discharge that sacred trust and to fulfil that high destiny.

A new declaration.

Col. J. C. Wedgwood (Labour, *Newcastle-under-Lyme*) described the Premier's speech as a new declaration with regard to India. Their responsibility for India consisted in assisting the formation of democratic self-government in India. He hoped, now that Mr. Montagu was no longer conducting the India Office, they were not going to have a change from a perfectly steadfast, settled policy to a policy of alternate threats and concessions. The only chance was to see that the Prime Minister and the Secretary of State for India* had definitely in view the same goal, namely, Dominion Home Rule, although that would unseat, from their power at any rate, the present Civil Service.

The Right Hon. Sir Donald Maclean (Chairman of the Independent Liberal Party in Parliament) said he did not read the note of threat or the shaking of the fist in what the Prime Minister said. They could not stop the progress of India. It was a world movement to a different, and, he hoped, a better state of things. If they were sympathetic, full of understanding, and judicious in their language, he was certain the day would come, though it might be distant, when India would perform an even better and nobler part in the great circle of

* Viscount Peel.

self-governing Dominions within the Commonwealth which they called the British Empire.

The Under-Secretary of State for India (Earl Winterton) declared that to read into the statement of the Prime Minister a threat to India was really to make a most mischievous accusation. The Premier had appealed for the fullest co-operation between the many diverse races in India and the British race in carrying out the destinies of India. They had given the tools of statesmanship to India and it was now for India to use them.

The House afterwards passed to the consideration of other subjects.

AIR DEFENCE.

(Decision of the Government.)

On 3rd August, in the House of Commons,

Viscount Curzon (Conservative, *Battersea, S.*) asked the Prime Minister whether the Government had yet been able to consider the question of the control and provision for the air arm of the Royal Navy; whether the Government were satisfied that adequate provision was being made to meet the Admiralty requirements for fighting, reconnaissance, and spotting planes; and whether better provision in these respects and actual economies could be made if a reorganisation of the branch of the Royal Air Force operating with the Royal Navy was carried out and the Royal Navy made responsible for and be given control of its air arm.

The Prime Minister (the Right Hon. D. Lloyd George): "The Government, as the result of an inquiry by the Committee of Imperial Defence, have decided to adopt a scheme submitted by the Air Ministry providing a force of 500 machines for home defence at an increased cost of £2,000,000 per annum. £900,000 out of the total of £2,000,000 will be found by economies in the Estimates of the Air Ministry.

"The inquiries of the Cabinet Committee on Economy in the Fighting Services have advanced sufficiently far to enable me to state that the addition to the Air Estimates will not prevent a reduction in the total Estimates of the three fighting services for the year 1923-24. Considerable orders in execution of this programme will be placed with private firms in the current calendar year.

"The foregoing decisions will not prejudice a further expansion of the Royal Air Force if later on this is found necessary to our national security. This question will be considered in the light of the financial situation next year and of the air policy adopted by other Powers. The inquiry into the system of naval and air co-operation, and as to the best method of securing that the Air Force should render to the Navy the aid it may require, has not yet been completed."

Col. J. C. Wedgwood (Labour, *Newcastle-under-Lyme*): "Is the enormous increase in the expenditure on the Air Force due to the enormous development of the Air Service in France?"

The Prime Minister: "Well, we have to take all the circumstances into account."

HOUSE OF LORDS REFORM.

(Government's proposals; Reduction in numbers; An elected element.)

On 11th July there were tabled in the Upper House on behalf of the Government five Resolutions relating to reform of the House of Lords. They were as follows:—

I. That this House shall be composed, in addition to Peers of the Blood Royal, Lords Spiritual and Law Lords, of—

(*a*) Members elected, either directly or indirectly, from the outside;

(*b*) Hereditary Peers elected by their Order;

(*c*) Members nominated by the Crown, the numbers in each case to be determined by Statute.

II. That, with the exception of Peers of the Blood Royal and the Law Lords, every other member of the reconstituted and reduced House of Lords shall hold his seat for a term of years to be fixed by Statute, but shall be eligible for re-election.

III. That the reconstituted House of Lords shall consist approximately of 350 members.

IV. That while the House of Lords shall not amend or reject Money Bills, the decision as to whether a Bill is or is not a Money Bill, or is partly a Money Bill and partly not a Money Bill, shall be referred to a Joint Standing Committee of the two Houses, the decision of which shall be final. That this Joint Standing Committee shall be appointed at the beginning of each new Parliament, and shall be composed of seven members of each House of Parliament, in addition to the Speaker of the House of Commons, who shall be *ex-officio* Chairman of the Committee.

V. That the provisions of the Parliament Act, 1911, by which Bills can be passed into law without the consent of the House of Lords during the course of a single Parliament, shall not apply to any Bill which alters or amends the constitution of the House of Lords as set out in these Resolutions, or which in any way changes the powers of the House of Lords as laid down in the Parliament Act and modified by these Resolutions.

DEBATE IN HOUSE OF LORDS.

On 18th July and on various subsequent occasions the Resolutions were the subject of debate.

The Secretary of State for India (**Viscount Peel**), in moving that the House should go into Committee on the resolutions, said the Government were pledged to bring forward proposals on the subject. He thought it would be agreed that if any Party or Government was capable of dealing with the question it was a Coalition Government. The Labour Party, so far as its views were known, was resolute on the lack of necessity for a Second Chamber at all. Many of the Independent Liberals were indifferent and many of them also would rest in plethoric contentment on the bosom of the Parliament Act. The charge had often been made against the Coalition Government that their besetting sin was a love of compromise, but in a question of that kind, when they wished to carry with them the general assent of Parliament, that besetting sin might become a besetting virtue.

The Resolutions were a general sketch, laying down principles only, which would afterwards have to be filled up. "It is well known," said Lord Peel, "that we have had in the past no written Constitution, but we have latterly attempted to write one. Other States, of course, have established a very solemn and elaborate procedure, which distinguishes the methods applied to constitutional changes and the procedure which is prevalent in the case of ordinary Bills. We, in our usual piecemeal and haphazard manner, have stumbled into a written Constitution, and we have made no such provision for these distinctions. Therefore, to get something of that permanence which one hopes for from a changed Constitution we have to secure, so far as we can, if not a general assent, yet a very large measure of assent.

"Nothing, I think, could have been worse than the atmosphere in which the Parliament Act was passed. It was one of hostility, of storm and even violent Party debate."

Construction of a Second Chamber.

Proceeding, Lord Peel laid down briefly some of the principles which should govern those who were approaching the construction of a Second Chamber.

"First of all," he said, "a Second Chamber should not have equal powers with, or become a rival of, the House of Commons, nor have the power of dismissing Governments or making the Executive equally responsible to both Chambers. Secondly, the Second Chamber should be powerful enough, self-confident and fearless enough, to oppose the House of Commons when it is convinced that the other House does not respect, and turns away from, the settled opinion of the people. It must, again, be composed of persons so weighty and experienced as to command public confidence and to influence public opinion. I may add, perhaps, that in these days it is rather important to have in any House a certain number of people of marked and powerful peculiarities and idiosyncrasies, to engage the attention of cartoonists and the Press, and enlist the popular ear. Perhaps, too, in these days of rapid shift and change some admixture of the youthful element is necessary among the sedater persons of settled reputation and conviction."

With regard to numbers, Lord Peel said that a House composed of over 700 persons was too large for the volume of business to be transacted, always assuming that the House did not deal with taxation or with the voting of Estimates. There were some who argued that if they were making a change they should make a complete change from the hereditary to the elective principle. But he thought the majority of their Lordships and, he believed, of people outside would oppose that complete cut with the past, and the loss of that respect and dignity which came from tradition and from history.

Not a replica of the House of Commons.

Looked at as a whole, the Resolutions constituted a House different from, and not a mere replica of, the existing House of Commons. Further, they retained in considerable measure the old historic links with the past. They strengthened the position of the House by a popular element, and they gave the opportunity to all ranks of His Majesty's subjects to find a place in the Second as well as in the Representative Chamber.

The Earl of Selborne recalled the recommendations of the Bryce Conference with regard to the powers of the Second Chamber. It was agreed by the Conference that a Second Chamber ought not to have equal powers with the House of Commons, nor aim at becoming a rival of that Assembly.

> "The Second Chamber should aim at ascertaining the mind and views of the nation as a whole, and should recognise its full responsibility to the people, not setting itself to oppose the people's will, but only to comprehend and give effect to that will when adequately expressed.
>
> "It should, by the exercise of this authority, and especially by evincing a superiority to factious motives, endeavour to enlighten and influence the people through its debates and be recognised by the people as qualified, when a proper occasion arose, to require the reconsideration of important measures on which their opinion had not been fully ascertained."

If he saw real powers such as Lord Bryce had laid down as essential to the constitutional stability of this country once more granted to the Second Chamber, reluctant as he would be, he would vote for very great and even drastic reforms in the constitution of that House. If they were going to be put off with a sham he would have nothing to do with the wrecking of the ancient constitution of that House.

Lord Lansdowne's criticism.

The Marquess of Lansdowne described the Resolutions as "a very half-baked scheme." He did not think its production had really brought them an inch nearer the solution of the problem. The real blot of the scheme was that it left ordinary legislation exactly where it stood now under the illogical and ill-conceived Parliament Act. The real feeling of the country when that Act was passed in 1911, and probably now, was not that the House of Lords had exceeded its rights, or deprived the country of useful legislation; the real feeling was that in these democratic days people did not like a Second Chamber composed almost entirely of hereditary Peers.

Most of them were quite ready to respect that feeling at the present time and to make suitable changes in the direction of the Resolutions. But if they were going to assume that they were, sooner or later, to have a Second Chamber not based upon pure heredity, but constructed on scientific and democratic lines, what right had they to assume that that Chamber, when the two Houses disagreed, was always in the wrong and was to be automatically overruled by the mere lapse of time? The House of Lords had never desired to destroy legislation; it had desired to prevent legislation being hurriedly forced upon the people.

The Marquess of Crewe said the Parliament Act was passed owing to the difficult circumstances in which the Government of the day found themselves placed in being unable to deal with legislation as they desired, because the House of Lords, as it then was, appeared to make a claim to deal on a large scale with questions of finance—though not in detail—and also claimed to be able, in effect, to force the dissolution of Parliament whenever it chose. How far the Act needed modification depended greatly upon the conclusion as to the composition of that House and the intention there might be of setting up a Second Chamber which was to be something of a rival of the House of Commons.

Power of revision.

Viscount Burnham said the basis of the discussion on the Constitutional Conference,* of which he was a constant member, was that there was to be drastic amendment of the Parliament Act so as to rescue that House from its present impotence. The real test was whether the Resolutions and the scheme they incorporated would make or re-make the House into a real legislative Chamber. What the Conference of Lord Bryce fully ascertained was that, without question, that was the weakest legislative Chamber in the whole of Europe. Everybody admitted that they were coming to government by

* Generally referred to as the Bryce Conference.

groups, and as the government by groups was increased so the power of the Executive was increased. That made it all the more necessary that in respect of legislation there should be some power of revision, giving time to the electorate and the country for second thoughts on reflection.

The Archbishop of Canterbury said it was perfectly reasonable, and, indeed, in fairness, necessary largely to reduce the number of bishops in a House largely diminished as a whole. The condition of things had entirely changed during the course of centuries so far as the proportion, and, possibly, even the work of the Spiritual Lords of Parliament were concerned. He had been asked whether he would not agree that it would be eminently desirable if persons whose qualifications were of what were called the spiritual kind were to sit in that House the practice should be extended beyond members of the Church of England. He was entirely in favour of that view in theory, but it became an extremely difficult matter when they tried to reduce it to practice. If, however, a plan could be produced which would work fairly for practical purposes he would support and welcome it.

Afraid of a Labour Government.

Earl Buxton asked whether it was intended that the new House, which was to be more or less on terms of equality with the House of Commons, and was to be a strong and efficient body, should be a House which, apart from legislative matters, was to meet the precipitate action of the Lower House, or to act as a buffer against progress—if they liked, revolutionary progress ?

He was afraid that one of the main reasons why the Government entered into the question was that they were afraid of a Labour Government coming into office at some time or other. Nowadays the Upper House, however constructed, could be no real bulwark against a Labour, or any other Government controlling and maintaining a majority in the other House. No such Government and no such House of Commons would allow their measures to be perpetually thwarted and delayed by any Upper House.

Lord Islington said that anything in the nature of drastic reform of that House was neither desirable nor, at the present juncture, feasible. But there were certain changes in the constitution of the House and a certain extension of powers which, if adopted, would materially strengthen the efficiency of their whole Parliamentary system. An increase of powers on a really material scale—it would mean the restoration of the legislative veto—would inevitably necessitate the substitution of a complete elective system for that which at present obtained. He believed there was nobody in that

House and very few outside who were at the present time prepared to see that substitution carried out.

Electors should decide.

The Marquess of Salisbury said it was because on occasions, and very often of late, a greater sense of responsibility was felt in the House of Lords than in the Lower House, and because the House of Lords was a truer exponent of public opinion, a more sympathetic and more independent representative of national feeling, that the power to pass Bills over the head of the Upper House was not in the interests of the country and might often be contrary to the wishes of the electors.

It was essential there should be some effective safeguard so that no Bill could be passed over their heads until the electors had been given an opportunity of applying their considered judgment to the proposed change. In the case of a deadlock between the two Houses, he believed that ultimately they would come to the Referendum, but it might be doubted whether that plan could be carried here and now. They should, in his opinion, be cautious how they changed the constitution of that House, and they must maintain in large measure its hereditary character.

The Lord Chancellor (Viscount Birkenhead) remarked that as a member of the Cabinet Committee which examined this question, he came to the conclusion that they could not even conjecture what powers the country would ultimately be prepared to concede to the Second Chamber until they had reached a clear conclusion as to what was to be the character of that Assembly.

Confiscatory legislation.

"While," said the Lord Chancellor, "an unscrupulous Government, returned to office, perhaps, as the result of a blind, momentary and fugitive expression of popular excitement, might, if you have an unreformed Second Chamber, or even such a Second Chamber as this, sweep away everything upon which the security of our government and our polity depend—while this is undoubtedly true, let us recognise this, that though no one proposes that this House shall re-assert its right to reject Money Bills, if we have in this country a Socialist or a Communist Government they do not, believe me, need to travel the long and statutory road in order to effect the destruction of our liberties, and, indeed, to bring down the whole of our civilisation.

"They can do it by printing an unlimited number of Treasury Bills or by passing confiscatory legislation through this House, which would be rightly enough pronounced by any Committee you may set up a Money Bill."

The House would be ill-advised if it did not correct the present right possessed by every hereditary Peer to take part in the legislative functions of that Chamber. He thought that a number of 300 or 350 might well be chosen as a body which numerically would be extremely adaptable to the efficient discharge of Parliamentary business, would exclude those Peers whose qualifications for legislative contribution were least conspicuous, and would at the same time absolve the Second Chamber from the general charge that it was alike unwieldy and absentee. He did not believe that they could ever set up a hybrid assembly, partly hereditary and partly elected, which had the slightest chance of survival. They were threatened, or they were flattered, with the prospect of the advent to power of a Labour Government.

The hereditary principle.

No more formidable objection could be stated to the constitution of any Second Chamber than that a great Party in the State, likely to obtain office in the not very remote future, ceased to find in that Second Chamber as constituted to-day an efficient or even a possible instrument of government. Besides the desirability of maintaining the hereditary principle, there was the absolute necessity of so dealing with that House that it would become a possibly available instrument of government should the Labour Party assume office. When once the people of the country saw in the House of Lords a body not unwieldy in numbers, constituted in its personnel of the wisest and most experienced men in the House, he believed they would find an immense reaction against the restrictive legislation to which all the Peers so much objected.

After a debate extending over four sittings, the motion to go into Committee on the Resolutions was agreed to. Their consideration in Committee was, thereafter, deferred until the Autumn.

BESTOWAL OF HONOURS.

(Royal Commission to advise on procedure.)

In the last number of the JOURNAL (*vide* pp. 511 to 520) a summary was given of a debate in the House of Lords which raised the question of the Dominions and the grant of honours.

On 17th July a debate took place in the House of Commons on the following motion :—

That it is expedient that a Select Committee of seven Members of this House be appointed to join with a Committee of the Lords to consider the present methods of submitting names of persons for honours for the consideration of His Majesty, and to report what changes, if any, are desirable in order to secure that such honours shall only be given as a reward for public service.

On behalf of the Government the Prime Minister (the Right Hon. D. Lloyd George) announced that a Royal Commission would be appointed "to consider and advise on the procedure to be adopted in future to assist the Prime Minister in making recommendations to His Majesty of the names of persons deserving of special honour."

In accordance with the Government's decision a Royal Commission was subsequently appointed and is now sitting.

CRIMINAL LAW AMENDMENT ACT.*

(Indecent Assaults on Young Persons: Age of Consent, etc.)

On 4th August the Royal Assent was given to the Criminal Law Amendment Act, which was introduced by the Government to amend the law with respect to offences against persons under the age of sixteen and to effect other changes in the Statutes.

The Act provides that it shall not be a defence to a charge or indictment for an indecent assault on a child or young person under the age of sixteen to prove that he or she consented to the act of indecency.

Reasonable cause to believe that a girl was of or above the age of sixteen shall not be a defence to a charge under Sections 5 or 6 of the Criminal Law Amendment Act, 1885. The Act, however, contains a proviso that in the case of a man of 23 years of age, or under, the presence of reasonable cause to believe that the girl was over the age of 16 shall be a valid defence on the first occasion on which he is charged with an offence.

A person convicted of an offence under Section 13 of the principal Act (which relates to summary proceedings against brothel keepers, etc.) is rendered liable on summary conviction to a fine not exceeding £100, or to imprisonment, with or without hard labour, for a term not exceeding three months. A second or subsequent conviction is made punishable by a fine, not exceeding £250, or imprisonment for a term of not more than six months.

Section 5 of the Punishment of Incest Act 1908 (which requires that all proceedings under that Act are to be held *in camera*) is repealed.

DEBATE IN HOUSE OF COMMONS.

On 5th July the Bill was debated in the House of Commons on the Order for Second Reading.

The Home Secretary (the Right Hon. Edward Shortt) said the Government had come to the conclusion that the age of consent for indecent assault ought to be made sixteen, which was the same as the age of consent for carnal knowledge.

* *Vide* also JOURNAL, Vol. II., No. 2, p. 292.

The main dispute in connection with the Bill arose over the Clause providing that reasonable cause to believe that the girl in question was over 16 should no longer be a defence. On the one hand, a very large body of people interested in these subjects was very strongly in favour of the provision as it stood. On the other hand, there was a very considerable body of opinion which thought it was an unfair thing to take away that defence. He thought he was correct in saying that the people who opposed taking away that defence were, comparatively speaking, a small minority.

Protection of young men.

There had been much negotiation about the exemption from that provision of young men who might be tempted by girls who were more to blame than they. Those who were very strongly in favour of the clause were willing to consent to some such exemption as this : where the accused person was under a certain age, say, for the sake of argument, 21 or 23, the magistrate before whom the charge was heard might, instead of committing him for trial, treat the case under the Summary Jurisdiction Act and merely bind him over.

That was not satisfactory to many of those who were opposed to the clause and who desired that a young man under the specified age, whether 21, 23, or whatever it might be, should still have the defence open to him, so that it might be said of him that he had not been guilty of a crime at all.

Sir John Butcher (Conservative, *York*) : " Would that be only in the case of a first offence ? "

The Home Secretary : " One of the suggestions was that it should only apply to a case of first offence."

Mr. Howard Gritten (Independent, *The Hartlepools*) : " In the alternative of binding the person over, I take it that the conviction would still be recorded against him for life ? "

The Home Secretary: " It would be under the Probation Act, under which there need be no conviction. The ordinary powers under that Act will be available for the magistrate to exercise in the circumstances."

Rejection moved.

Maj. the Hon. Christopher Lowther (Independent, *Cumberland, N.*) moved the rejection of the Bill. He said there was a country where the law was held in contempt and was daily mocked. That was the United States of America. The reason was that the legislators of that country had paid attention to such agitations as had gone on in respect of this Bill by loud-voiced, unreasoning societies, and had not attended to what should be their proper duty—the consideration of the merits of the case. People in this country were sick to death of "stunt" legislation, of which, perhaps, this was the most unlovely example.

Lt.-Col. J. Moore-Brabazon (Coalition Unionist, *Chatham*) said the Bill was the thin end of the legislative wedge with regard to eugenics in this country. Eugenics was very admirable on paper; in practice it was particularly difficult. Another ground of opposition was that it was legislation against one sex more than another. All education in this country was really a conspiracy to delay the sexual growth of the boy. At the bottom of the Bill was the fundamental assumption that one sex was vicious and the other was entirely pure. If he thought for a moment that the Bill would stop one assault upon one girl he would be in favour of it. But he was convinced what would happen was that they would make criminals of many boys who did not deserve it.

"Reasonable cause to believe."

The Right Hon. Sir Donald Maclean (Chairman of the Independent Liberal Party in Parliament) said the broad general position was settled by the Criminal Law Amendment Act, 1885. They were making progress much too slowly for his taste, but still they were moving on, and they now said that no young person under 16 should be deemed to be able to consent to an act of indecency to him or her. As regarded the proposal to amend the law by taking away the "reasonable cause to believe," organised opinion in favour of the change came most powerfully and substantially from those who had most to do with the administration of the law. As far as his experience—and he had personal knowledge of not fewer than 200 cases of that special kind—there was no serious danger of blackmail.

Maj. Sir G. Hamilton (Coalition Unionist, *Altrincham*) observed that by the Bill they would put temptations to blackmail in the way of a certain class of the most objectionable criminals in the country, namely, the people who encouraged young girls to go about and entice young men into wickedness. Those were the people whom they should get hold of and legislate against. With reference to the abolition of the "reasonable cause to believe," was it right to pass legislation which had the effect of making a young man a criminal without allowing him to show to a jury that, although he committed a moral offence, he had reasonable cause, which he could justify before a judge and jury, to believe that he was not committing a criminal offence?

Mrs. Wintringham (Independent Liberal, *Louth*) thought the Bill, which was based on the principle of the protection of the weak, was a reasonable one. Girls between the ages of 15 and 16 needed protection. At that age they developed a desire for individuality and independence, and it was just at that time the State ought to step in and give them protection.

The amendment was negatived without a division and the Bill was read a second time. It was sent to a Standing Committee for consideration and subsequently passed through its other stages in the House.

DEBATE IN HOUSE OF LORDS.

On 27th July the Bill was debated in the House of Lords on the Order for Second Reading.

The Parliamentary Secretary of the Ministry of Health (the Earl of Onslow) referred to an amendment which had been made in the Lower House providing that "reasonable cause to believe" should be a valid defence in the case of a first offence up to the age of 23. In the first instance the Government favoured the course that a court of summary jurisdiction should be empowered in suitable cases to deal with young offenders under the Probation Act instead of committing sick persons for trial. They accepted the amendment of which he was speaking not as an ideal solution, but as a compromise on a question which gave rise to very strong and divergent opinions.

The Bishop of London, who reminded the House that it was he who originally brought the proposals to amend the law before Parliament, said he had consulted all the various societies which had been behind the Bill and they had agreed to accept the amendment, though they would rather it had not been inserted.

Lord Sempill complained of the inadequacy of the penalties provided in the Bill.

The Bill was read a second time, and, after full consideration at subsequent stages, was duly passed.

Additional Note: Mr. Bonar Law's Cabinet.

At the moment of going to Press with the JOURNAL, it was officially announced that of the Ministers named on pp. 713-714, the following would constitute the Cabinet, viz.: The Prime Minister, the Lord President of the Council, the Chancellor of the Exchequer, the Lord Chancellor, the Secretaries of State for Home Affairs, Foreign Affairs, the Colonies, War, India, the First Lord of the Admiralty, the Secretary for Scotland, the President of the Board of Trade, the Minister of Health, the Minister of Agriculture and Fisheries, the President of the Board of Education and the Minister of Labour.

CANADA.

The following summary deals with matters held over from the two previous issues of the JOURNAL, *including the Budget statement and some further Acts of the First Session of the Fourteenth Parliament (which commenced on 8th March,* 1922, *and was prorogued on 27th June), and is in continuation of the summaries published in Vol. III., Nos.* 2 *and* 3.

THE BUDGET.

(Annual Financial Statement; British Preference; Trade with Germany; Reciprocity with United States; etc.)

On 23rd May, 1922, the Minister of Finance presented the annual financial statement to the House of Commons.

DEBATE IN HOUSE OF COMMONS.

The Minister of Finance (Hon. W. S. Fielding) said that it was well understood by all close students of their public affairs that Canada had built up a very large Public Debt; that the interest alone on that Debt called for an enormous sum of money, greater than the total expenditure of Canada but a few years ago; that they had a large pension list; and that in various ways they had added enormously to their obligations. He must present two thoughts which were of paramount importance. The first was as to the deep and earnest need of economy. The second thought was that, with all the economy that they could practise, there would still be need of severe examination into their taxation system.

Income and Expenditure; Public Debt.

For the year 1920-21 the public accounts showed what was called a surplus of $73,268,391. Yet as a matter of fact during that year there was actually an increase in the Public Debt of $92,000,000, the difference representing the charges to capital and special account and that now ever-growing account, the railway service of the country. The total Revenue from all sources (1921-22) they placed at $381,271,000, against in 1920-21 $434,386,000. There was, therefore, a very large decrease in the revenue of the year. The Expenditure charged to Consolidated Revenue Fund was $348,145,000, a decrease of $12,972,000. For the fiscal year 1922-23, on the basis of their present taxation he would estimate that the Revenue would be $332,629,000. They received last year from income tax and from arrears of Business

Profits tax $101,500,000. They would not feel justified in estimating for the coming year more than $60,000,000 from that source. With a loss of Revenue last year as compared with the previous year of $53,000,000 and with the prospect of a shortage of $40,000,000 in the Income Tax for the current year, the House would see that the situation was a very serious one indeed. The estimates of Expenditure called for a total of $466,983,359. From their present sources of Revenue they could provide for all their ordinary Expenditure and have a modest surplus, but there would still be a large expenditure on Capital Account and for the Railways, and this would have to be provided for by additions to the Public Debt. They must soon begin to consider the question of the reduction of their Public Debt rather than aim to increase it. Great Britain with all her troubles had since the War paid off £50,000,000 of her Public Debt. They had not only made no reduction, but they had to acknowledge a steady increase in the Public Debt every year since the War. They should endeavour to balance their Budget. Even if their estimates of Revenue should be exceeded, they would find themselves short by a considerable sum. If they were to avoid that situation they must accept the responsibility of additional taxation.

As against a little less than $336,000,000 in 1914, their estimated net Debt on 31st March, 1922, was $2,427,296,798.

Loans.

During the year four Canadian Government Loans had been floated. They would probably need for their financial operations some further borrowing at no distant date. He hoped that when the moment arrived the condition of the money market in Canada would be such that they could have a domestic Loan. Last year had not been a good business year. Not many men had money to invest in Government Bonds to-day, and there was no longer the patriotic zeal for the War. Canada was still but a partially developed country; Canada would still have to be a borrowing country for many years. On 31st August, 1919, the British Government owed them the enormous sum of $330,000,000. On 31st March, 1922, subject to some questions of readjustment with regard to exchange, Great Britain owed them $117,859,630. Arrangements had been made by which this account was to be paid off in instalments of $5,000,000 per month.

Trade.

The effects of the depression of the past year were clearly seen in the returns of their Import and Export Trade. As compared with 1921 their imports from the United Kingdom fell from $213,000,000 to $117,000,000, and their imports from the United States from $856,000,000 to $516,000,000. Their exports to the United Kingdom held better, the amount for 1922 being $299,000,000, and for 1921, $312,000,000. Their exports to the United States showed the course of the decline, being $293,000,000 against $542,000,000 in the previous year.

Trade agreements with West Indies and Australia, etc.; Preference.

An agreement was made by the late Government with the British West Indies (*vide* JOURNAL, Vol. II., No. 4, p. 813, and Vol. III., No. 1, p. 76). One of the islands which remained outside for a considerable period was Jamaica, but she had now joined the arrangement.

Soon after the Australian Commonwealth was formed, a new tariff was adopted which was less favourable than that of New South Wales (which previously had received the benefit of the Canadian preference), and from that time forward Australia had not had the benefit of their preference. They proposed to the Australian Government that they should give them the preference which the United Kingdom enjoyed, and they would in return give them the benefit of their preference. That proposal had not been accepted, nor had they received any counter-proposal. Their hope was that they would be able to make a satisfactory arrangement with the Australian Commonwealth.

Not many months ago the House ratified a Treaty that had been made in France. It seemed to have been of a temporary character, contemplating a larger Treaty at a later date. They had recently been asked by the French Consul-General to take up the matter and had intimated their willingness to do so.

Tariff revision; British preference.

The line upon which they intended to deal was expressed in a resolution he had moved in the House a year ago. This resolution declared for tariff reduction—a tariff reduction that would be made with great care, guarding against any interference of a serious character with the business of the country. With the exception of one item, an increase for strictly revenue purposes, any change he should propose to-day was a reduction in the Customs tariff.

They adhered to the British preference in the arrangement they made, and the effect of the change that they made would be to increase, in some respects, that preference.

Trade with United States.

The flood-tide of goodwill in trade matters from their American neighbours came to them in 1910-11, but unhappily the Canadian people did not accept the agreement. Since the Republican Party was restored to power they had introduced the Fordney Emergency Bill which dealt largely with agricultural products. That Bill unquestionably worked great harm to the Dominion of Canada, and especially to their Western Provinces. Now there was another Tariff Bill at Washington which proposed to enlarge on the Fordney Emergency Bill. They had no right to complain of their American friends for doing that; but they could not expect them in Canada to be as willing as they otherwise would be to deal liberally with them. They had intimated to the American Government that they were quite ready to reopen negotiations with every desire to make a friendly arrangement. They proposed to hold their hands and to await the turn of events at Washington. The reductions which they were going to make were almost entirely in the British preference. They were not going, except in a few cases, to reduce duties on American goods, which came to them under the operation of the General Tariff.

Marking and valuation.

The Budget of last year introduced a number of features which did not work out well. One of those provisions was an Amendment to the Customs Tariff providing that all goods that were imported should, where possible, be marked, and penalties were imposed for failure to do this (*vide* JOURNAL, Vol. III., No. 1, p. 76). The Government which passed that regulation evidently had occasion to reconsider their judgment on the matter; at any rate, they were reluctant to enforce it. Their opinion was that, as a general law, this provision should be repealed.

Another provision of that kind was with regard to the valuation of goods. The time-honoured custom in Canada was that the value of goods for Customs purposes was the fair market value in the country of production. A proposal was made last year that the Customs officer must determine the value; that the value for duty must not be less than the cost of production in the country which produced the goods plus a fair profit (*vide* JOURNAL, Vol. III., No. 1, p. 75). They were of opinion that that also was an unnecessary interference with trade, and they proposed to wipe it out.

Another regulation of a somewhat similar character dealt with the question of depreciated currency. The German mark was normally worth nearly 24 cents; it was actually worth to-day one-third of a cent.*

* The Act of last year provided that in no case should depreciation of currency be recognised below 50 per cent. (*vide* JOURNAL, Vol. III., No. 1, p. 75.

"If," said Mr. Fielding, "you want to say that German goods shall be prohibited, say so; . . . but do not humbug the world at large by pretending that we have a duty of 35 per cent. when the real duty is about 1,000 per cent." The late Government had not succeeded in shutting out German goods. What they had succeeded in doing was in shutting out the Canadian merchant from an opportunity of doing direct trade and in obliging him to pay tribute to somebody else.

Another regulation at that time contemplated the establishment of commercial agencies abroad and the requirement that a commercial agent of Canada should have his certificate attached to every invoice of $100 in value (*vide* JOURNAL, Vol. III., No. 1, p. 75). To-day it was a dead issue and they proposed to make it doubly dead by wiping it out.

Tariff reductions.

They were proposing to make a numerous list of reductions. His recollection was that there were forty-nine or fifty items in the tariff that were affected. Explaining various items, the Minister said that they proposed that the druggists of the country should be allowed to obtain alcohol for their own legitimate purposes at the same rate enjoyed by the large manufacturing concerns. The Excise duty on all weights of cigarettes was increased $3 per thousand. It was proposed to increase the rate of the Customs Tariff on imported cigarettes from $4.10 and 25 per cent. to $5.25 and 25 per cent. It was estimated that the increase in both Excise and Customs Tariff would give an additional revenue of over $5,000,000 per annum. It was proposed to re-adjust the duties on cigars. This would have the effect of reducing the duties on the low-priced and increasing it on the higher priced cigars. They proposed to abolish the duty on raw leaf tobacco when the tobacco was taken into a licensed tobacco or cigar factory.

Reductions and the industries.

The Minister proceeded to enumerate various articles for the farming industry in relation to which reductions of 2½ or 5 per cent. were made. There was a corresponding reduction on these articles under the British Preferential Tariff, but practically all were imported under the General Tariff. Tractors for farm purposes valued at $1,400 or less were now free by Order in Council; it was proposed to make those articles free by Act of Parliament. Further lists, furnished by the Minister, of articles for industrial and general public use, showed reductions of 5 or 2½ per cent., 2½ per cent. being the usual rate of reduction under the Preferential Tariff.

New rates of taxation.

It was quite certain, continued the Minister, that if they did not adopt some other method of taxation they would be adding enormously to the Public Debt. So they were proposing some new rates of taxation. (*Vide* Minister's amendments, p. 786.)

Sales Tax.—The sales tax they proposed to increase by 50 per cent.

Excise Taxes.—They proposed that automobiles up to $1,200 should pay an Excise tax of 5 per cent., and those above $1,200 10 per cent. On confectionery they proposed an Excise tax of 5 per cent.; on ale, beer, etc., 15 cents per gallon; on mineral waters and other soft drinks, 10 cents per gallon.

Cheques.—Cheques now paid 2 cents. They maintained that 2 cents up to $50, but they imposed a tax of 2 cents on each additional $50.

Insurance Premiums.—They proposed a small tax of 5 per cent. on certain classes of insurance premiums which were not at present reached.

Telegrams.—Telegrams and cables which were now taxed 1 cent should hereafter pay 5 cents.

Stock.—On transfers of stock which now paid 2 cents per $100 share, they proposed 5 cents.

Beet sugar.—Beet sugar was to be subjected to an Excise duty of 49 cents per 100 pounds.

Banks.—There was at present a nominal tax of 1 per cent. on the circulation of the Banks, but they found that by another Act that tax was exempted because when they came to deal with the income tax they took whatever the Banks had paid as tax on their circulation. They proposed to abolish the exemption and say that the 1 per cent. tax on circulation should be paid.

In conclusion, the Minister declared that he had deemed it proper to present very clearly what he had regarded as the gravity of the financial situation. There was, happily, a brighter side. He had unbounded faith in the resources of their country, and in the intelligence and patriotism of the Canadian people. If one thing more than another was necessary, it was the establishing of better relations between Labour and Capital.

Dumping clause.

On 26th May,

The Hon. Sir Henry Drayton (**Liberal-Conservative,** *York, W. Riding, Ont.*) believed that his hon. friend desired to enforce his dumping provisions in the interests of Canadian labour, but he was afraid he would find that the results of the proposed change would not be what he expected. He had pointed out that it had become a practice to ship through Holland instead of direct from Germany, or through some other country where the currency provision would not apply. That was an evasion of the law, and it could have been provided against; the practice of indirect importation could have been made illegal. That would be the course to follow, if his hon. friend had the idea that they ought to protect their markets and their working men from the effects of German competition. This Budget might well be called a 2½ per cent. British Preference and German Free Trade. His hon. friend pointed out that business was so bad, that out of business he could only get a much reduced revenue. Yet the Budget was full of little nuisances and pin-pricks, all adding to the cost of doing business, all making business a little more difficult. Apart from the absolute necessity of obtaining proper markets for their farm produce, their chief difficulty was the one-sided trade which they had with the United States and which they were determined to make still more one-sided. This Budget had to turn around and help the American out just a little, in cases when they bought from the American, by cutting down the duties that they now charged upon his materials coming into Canada. This Budget seconded the efforts of Mr. Fordney and his associates.

The Minister of Trade and Commerce (**Hon. J. A. Robb**) declared that they offered Great Britain a preference in the hope, they might frankly put it, that Great Britain would offer still greater concessions to the products of Canada. The ex-Minister of Finance (Sir Henry Drayton) apparently forgot that the Government still retained the right to the Marking Act and that they still had the dumping clause. He also forgot that Germany could not sell to Canada unless she was willing to buy from Canada. In 1922 they imported from Germany $2,000,000 worth of goods and sold her $4,500,000 worth. Did his hon. friend wish to stop this export trade with Germany?

Mr. R. S. Woods (**National Progressive**, *Dufferin, Ont.*) said that if nearly 75 per cent. of the general commodities of life which were dutiable and which had added to the Customs revenues of Canada came from the United States, the people who used those commodities were not going to be benefited to such a wonderful extent with the reduction of the Preferential Tariff. A sales tax was an added burden to the consumer. Referring to the dumping clause, he thought it unfair to deprive the masses of an opportunity of purchasing in the open market.

Labour attitude.

On 29th May,

Mr. J. S. Woodsworth (**Labour**, *Winnipeg, C., Man.*) declared that it had happened several times in Canada that when a Liberal Government had succeeded a Conservative administration it was almost inevitably driven to adopt similar fiscal policies. The sales tax was inherently vicious in principle. It was becoming increasingly difficult, especially in the cities, for the ordinary labouring men, who composed a very large proportion of the population, to provide even the barest necessities. There were no real economic changes proposed as far as he could see. It simply meant they were going to continue a principle which had been followed for a good many years, that of financing by fresh borrowings. Unfortunately they were mortgaging their home to no small extent to outsiders. Gradually American capital was gaining control of their great industries. Not all the mortgages were held outside Canada. There had been in the past few years a remarkable shifting of the wealth of the country from a large group to a comparatively small group. They had had the alienation of millions upon millions of acres of land and of the most valuable natural resources of the country. There had been no effort made by the incoming Government to recover from the profiteers that blood money which they laid up during the time of the War. In Great Britain 81 per cent. of the taxes were taken out of property and income, while in Canada, and that only in the last year of the War, 11 per cent. of the taxes came out of property and income. In regard to Canada's huge debts, he could see nothing for it but repudiation or a capital levy.

On 1st June,

Miss Agnes Macphail (National Progressive, *Grey, S.E. Riding, Ont.*) asked whether Protection had been good for the basic industries of Canada? Could the manufacturing industries continue to flourish, if the very roots that nourished them died? They looked with hope to a day when the indirect method of collecting taxation would be abandoned and the direct method adopted.

Mr. T. L. Church (Liberal-Conservative, *Toronto, N., Ont.*) pointed out that not only the various countries in Europe and the United States but Australia, New Zealand, and the countries of South America were all increasing their protective tariffs. Was it to be argued that these countries were all wrong and the Progressives of Canada were all right?

Trade with Germany.

On 2nd June,

The Hon. Edmund Bristol (Liberal-Conservative, *Toronto, C., Ont.*) stated that there was practically nothing that was manufactured in Canada that Germany could not to-day put on the Canadian market under the present tariff and easily undersell its Canadian competitors. The British people had passed what they called the Safeguarding of Industries Act.

If the agricultural implement factories were shut down and could no longer compete with the American agricultural implement factories, the American factories would be able to sell those implements to Canada at such prices as they might demand. Australia had a Labour Party; they wanted Free Trade and they got it, but they had now gone in for high Protection—60 per cent. on agricultural implements.

Mr. Andrew McMaster (Liberal, *Brome, Que.*) declared that any idea that they could put 70,000,000 Germans in a corner of the world and ostracise them completely for ever, or for any considerable term of years, was mere preposterous nonsense, and any attempt to do it would just result in this, that Germany and Russia would be driven into each other's arms. In 1921 Great Britain imported £20,549,999 worth of goods from Germany, and exported to Germany no less than £17,831,000 odd. The total trade of the United States with Germany for the last year was $452,605,175. The amount of goods which came under the Safeguarding of Industries Act was infinitesimal compared with the amount which went free into the Old Land. The interests of the consumer were well guarded under the Act.

National Progressive Criticism.

On 5th June,

The Hon. T. A. Crerar (Leader of the National Progressive Party) believed that their governmental expenditure was altogether too much. A sales tax was unsound for the reason that it did not bear fairly upon those who had to pay it. Taxes of this kind always discouraged trade and industry. In regard to the tax on cheques he thought the burden imposed would be a very heavy one indeed. The time had come when some attempt should be made to co-ordinate the financial policy of Canada. Under the British North America Act the Provinces had all the powers of taxation except that relating to Customs; and the result was that citizens of some Provinces paid three income taxes, one to the Dominion, one to the Province, and one to the Municipality. Perhaps the most important improvement was the wiping out of that antediluvian provision that foreign currencies should be taken at half their pre-War value for the purposes of Customs assessment. He could not agree that they should have no part or parcel with anything German. A group of men from both the United States and Great Britain was conferring with a view to extending credits to Germany so that her manufacturing and purchasing power might be increased, and the whole trade of the world stimulated thereby. This Budget was a Protectionist Budget. Did they find anything of free agricultural implements. One of the amazing things in the situation was the fact that even in the Government itself there were men who professedly held almost diverse views on the question of the Tariff and Protection. He was not at all sure that the Minister was taking the wisest course in making a discrimination against the United States in favour of Great Britain at the present time. He was more convinced than ever that trade with the United States was necessary. He ventured to predict that within a few years the United States would have its face set definitely against the principle of a Protective Tariff. They of the Progressive Party stood unalterably opposed to the principle of Protection in the fiscal policy.

Reciprocity opposed.

On 6th June,

The Right Hon. Arthur Meighen (Leader of the Opposition) said that when the existing system of nations was abolished, and when the control of markets external to their country was under a common control, then there would be some reason in the theory of Free Traders. He did not think it far-sighted policy that the all but universal practice should be for distinct sections of Canada to trade by themselves with those States immediately to the South; such States in turn pressing on their surplus further towards the sea-coast; and those in turn pressing their surplus, so augmented, of the same goods on to the ultimate consumers of Europe and Asia. The right course for Canada was not to enter into any extensive reciprocal arrangement with the United States. He as a Canadian, loving Canada, loving their association in the Empire, would not welcome the treaty in the least even though he believed it was going to be permanent. What was the explanation of the Fordney Tariff? Was it not chiefly the effect of the importations from Canada, the effect there of the large surplus of their agricultural products? If they entered Reciprocity on a big scale, Canada, as years went on, would reach a position of virtual subjection to the legislation of the United States. The Liberals had stated, as related to seventeen named articles and classes of articles: "If we are returned to power, we will make those free." Seven were dutiable at that time and ten free, of these specific articles; and now they were in power, seven of them were free and ten were dutiable. As regarded the promised increase of 50 per cent. in the British Preference, they had taken off 2½ per cent. on certain goods of which they got a portion from Great Britain. The duty on not one article of food was reduced. He believed that the absence of all special restrictions due to the depreciation of German and Austrian exchange was a mistake on the part of the Minister of Finance, which he ought to correct.

Liberal pledges fulfilled.

The Prime Minister (the Right Hon.* W. L. Mackenzie King) said that the Budget proposals showed that the Government had made an effort to relieve the burdens of taxation where they bore upon the great body of the people, and that the Government had recognised the superior obligation of the well-to-do to bear a larger measure of the taxation which was necessary in order to raise the required revenues of the country. It was impossible to attempt to satisfy the different shades of opinion in a country as large as Canada. It was only reasonable to expect that the Government should be guided by caution, taking only those steps which were most in the interests of the country as a whole, and avoiding anything which would tend to have a disturbing influence on the country's affairs during this period of reconstruction. Every proposal that had been made by the Minister of Finance was in the direction of freer trade. The question that was before the people (at the elections) was not a question as between Protection and Free Trade, but of the revision of the Tariff; that the Liberal Party had stood for Tariff revision on the basis of a tariff for revenue. It was further stated that the revision should be downwards, in the interests of producers and consumers, and that in such downward revision they would seek to lower the duties on the instruments of production in the basic industries and on the necessaries of life, with a view to increased production and the lessening of the cost of living to the masses of the people. He contended that in the Budget proposals those pledges had been fulfilled.

Cautious policy advocated.

On 7th June,

The Minister of Marine and Fisheries (Hon. Ernest Lapointe) was of opinion that the question of adopting absolute Free Trade in Canada was rather an academic one; it was a condition which could not be realised in their lifetime—at least as long as the country would need import duties for revenue. On the other hand, to proclaim Protection as a basis of economic policy was an economic heresy. Since the War sixteen countries had increased import tariffs for revenue. Even export taxes had been imposed. It was their duty to act cautiously and not to enter too deeply on the path which other countries felt compelled to recede from temporarily.

Trade relations with Australia.

The Hon. S. F. Tolmie (Liberal-Conservative, *Victoria City, B.C.*) pointed out that it was suggested that they should

* As mentioned in the last number of the JOURNAL, Mr. Mackenzie King's name appeared in the Honours List published on 3rd June, 1922, as a Privy Councillor of the United Kingdom.

have better trade relations with Australia. When this question was being discussed there were some items which should not be lost sight of. Among these he might mention beef, mutton and lamb, which could be produced in Australia and New Zealand at a cost lower than Canada. Their animals were sold for almost a song and they could be dumped into Canada on an enormous scale, thus seriously handicapping the development of their live-stock industry.

Unemployment and German trade.

On 8th June,

The Hon. H. H. Stevens (Liberal-Conservative, *Vancouver, C., B.C.*) said that during the last three years Germany had encouraged the creation of deficits. During last fall Great Britain had unemployment to the extent of 2,000,000 people, the United States 5,000,000, Canada 200,000. Germany had 150,000, which was below normal for Germany. He thought Germany should have an opportunity to sell her goods abroad, but only to do so on a fair basis, and not at the expense of the Allied countries. If they paid any attention to France with $1,860,000,000 to find for reparations, pensions, and to make up her internal deficits, the situation was appalling. He continued : " Be neutral ; do not pay a premium on German goods and thus force France deeper into the mire than she is at the present time." There was owing to them on reparation 4·35 per cent. of the 22 per cent. due to the British Empire, but apparently they had small chance of ever getting it. Australia passed an Act, called the Preservation of Industries Act, under which the value of all goods landed in Australia from Germany was raised to the cost of a similar article made in Australia.

On 12th June,

The Minister of Finance said that there was now coming in Germany an increase in the price of commodities and wages, and there could be no doubt that as the months rolled on that increase would be very pronounced, and they would not hear such glowing accounts of German prosperity. As a nation they had no right to legislate against Germany. They (the Conservative Government) had wasted $1,000,000 of the money of the people of Canada in a special Session of Parliament for the purpose of approving the Treaty of Versailles—about as useful and necessary proceeding as the fifth wheel of a coach. In view of their action at Versailles he did not like to see his hon. friends denouncing Germany. They had made their peace with Germany, and they ought to treat her decently ; and that was all he proposed to do.

Alterations in taxation proposals.

The Minister proceeded to enumerate certain alterations in his original proposals, namely: (1) tax on soft drinks, 5 cents instead of 10 cents per gallon; (2) tax on ale, beer, etc., 12½ instead of 15 cents per gallon; (3) tax on cigarettes $7.50 instead of $9 per thousand; (4) fertilisers and dried beet pulp to be exempted from the sales tax; (5) the maximum tax on cheques to be $2; (6) stock transfers, including bonds, to be 3 instead of 5 cents per share; (7) tax on beet sugar to be 24 instead of 49 cents per 100 lbs.; (8) a tax of 2 cents to be levied on every receipt of $10 or upwards.

In regard to the valuation of the mark, the Minister explained that they proposed to have the value of the article determined by the standard of the English value. Where the articles were not made in England, they took the value in a neighbouring country where the currency had no substantial depreciation.

After further discussion, Mr. Fielding's motion was agreed to on 13th June by 119 to 101 votes.

CUSTOMS ACT AND DEPARTMENT OF CUSTOMS AND EXCISE ACT AMENDMENT.

This Act, which received the Royal Assent on 27th June, 1922, repeals, in accordance with the Budget statement, the sections in the Department of Customs and Excise Amendment Act respecting the certification of invoices for foreign goods entering Canada by consular officers, the valuation for duty of foreign goods, and depreciated currency (*vide* JOURNAL, Vol. III., No. 1, p. 75); and amends the Customs Act by providing that:—

In the case of importations of goods, the manufacture or produce of a foreign country, the currency of which is substantially depreciated, the value for duty shall not be less than the value that would be placed on similar goods manufactured or produced in the United Kingdom and imported from that country. If similar goods are not made or produced in the United Kingdom, the value for duty shall not be less than the value of similar goods made or produced in any European country the currency of which is not substantially depreciated. (*Section* 2.)

If at any time it appears to the satisfaction of the Governor in Council, on a report from the Minister of Customs and Excise, that the natural products of a kind produced in Canada are being imported into Canada, either on sale or consignment, under such conditions as prejudicially or injuriously to affect the interests of Canadian producers, the Governor in Council may authorise the Minister to value such goods for duty, and the value so determined shall be held to be the fair market value thereof. (*Section* 3.)

Whenever the value of a currency has not been proclaimed or there is no fixed standard value, or the value of a currency has become depreciated or appreciated, there shall be attached to the invoice of the goods imported the certificate of some Consul or Canadian Trade Commissioner resident in such country or the certificate of a bank showing the extent of such depreciation or appreciation, or the true value at the time of the exportation of the goods of the currency in which such invoice is made out as compared with the standard dollar of Canada. Provided that the collector of Customs and Excise may compute the value for duty at the rate of exchange certified by the bank through which the same is drawn as current at the time and place when the goods were exported to Canada. (*Section* 4.)

CUSTOMS TARIFF AMENDMENT ACT.

This Act, which received the Royal Assent on 27th June, 1922, amends the Customs Tariff so as to provide for the tariff reductions outlined in the Budget statement. It also repeals the clause enforcing the marking of imported goods contained in the amendment made to the Act in 1921 (*vide* JOURNAL, Vol. III., No. 1, p. 76), and, instead, empowers the Governor-in-Council to order that goods imported into Canada shall be marked to indicate the country of origin, as he deems fit.

INLAND REVENUE AMENDMENT ACT.

This Act, which received the Royal Assent on 27th June, 1922, amends the Inland Revenue Act so as to carry out the Budget proposals in connection with the Excise duties on cigars and cigarettes, the rebate on spirits used by licensed druggists, and Excise duties on sugar made from sugar beets.

SPECIAL WAR REVENUE AMENDMENT ACT.

This Act, which received the Royal Assent on 27th June, carries out the Budget proposals in regard to the imposition or increase of taxes on insurance with unlicensed British or foreign companies or with unlicensed inter-insurance associations; cables and telegrams; cheques; receipts; bills of exchange and promissory notes; bank overdrafts; transfers of stock; money orders; sales (except sales of bread, flour, meats and poultry, dairy products, vegetables, fruits, fish, and other articles of consumption, feed for animals, ores of metals, fuels, British, Canadian and foreign coin, unmanufactured timber, newspapers and magazines, repairs for ships, radium, certain articles to do with returned soldiers and settlers, fertilisers, dried beet pulp, etc.); automobiles; confectionery; also beverages and cigars.

IMMIGRATION.

(Statement by the Minister ; etc.)

On 23rd May, the Minister of the Interior and Mines made a statement to the House in Committee of Supply on the Government's policy in regard to Immigration from Europe.

DEBATE IN HOUSE OF COMMONS.

The Minister of Immigration (Hon. Charles Stewart) said that during the past winter the Committee had had evidence with regard to conditions in Canada in the amounts they were being asked to vote, and would be asked to vote in the future, for unemployment relief, from one end of Canada to the other. Furthermore, in what they fondly called these reconstruction days, they found a great many people apparently dissatisfied with conditions as they found them, a great many who were loath to engage in enterprises that would provide employment, and on the part of Labour they found no desire to accept a reduction in wages and thereby help them to get back to normal times. Then when they looked abroad to the countries from which they hoped to secure immigration, they found that by far the larger proportion of the people who would be willing to immigrate were men desirous of obtaining employment. Probably not for some time to come would they be able to receive all those who would be willing to come to Canada and who would make desirable citizens, and by that he meant those who were mentally and physically fit and were desirous of finding employment in Canada and becoming Canadian citizens.

Class of immigration required.

He thought at the moment it would not be wise to encourage any large numbers of people who had to maintain themselves particularly by manual labour, but he hoped that period would pass very rapidly. With respect to their policy for immigration some criticism had been offered inasmuch as apparently they had been closing the doors to all but the people with means to become agriculturists, agricultural labourers and household workers. But taking into consideration the situation he had outlined, these apparently were the only classes of individuals that they could absorb in Canada at the moment. Let him say in passing that he sympathised very much with his hon. friends in British Columbia in their desire to have a larger percentage of the population in British Columbia of the white race. An allegation that frequently appeared in the Press of Great Britain was that they in Canada were setting up too rigid an inspection of the immigration that would come to them. Clearly there was no use in augmenting the ranks of the unemployed; they were making the endeavour to get every agriculturist from Great Britain that they could induce to come to Canada.

Child immigration.

He wanted to mention one other class of immigration that had been found very desirable in the past, and which he thought that they could very well encourage to the fullest extent—that was the child immigration coming into Canada. He was astounded to hear that last year 1,500 children were brought to Canada, and that there were applications for 15,000 more. The policy of the Government would be to secure a large proportion of the "teen-age" boys and girls who would come to Canada and fill the demand that appeared to be prevalent for these children. Mr. Smart was about to leave for England on this mission. Australia had become a very strong competitor with Canada, and South Africa as well, for the immigration of adults as well as of children. Ever-increasing inducements were being offered for British immigration to these two countries; and in some measure they would have to meet that competition. It was possible, therefore, that he would ask for increased grants for the purpose of encouraging the assistance of the people who were engaged in this class of work in the Old Land. It was the class that appealed to him very much because these children would go to their Canadian homes, grow up in their schools, and become thorough Canadians.

Foreign immigration.

In the countries of Scandinavia and Iceland—indeed, in Holland and Belgium as well—although he was told that a year ago immigration and immigration propaganda was not looked upon with favour, they to-day found that condition changing. He was hopeful that they would get from Iceland this year a fair amount of the Icelandic people who made splendid settlers upon their western lands. They also entertained the same hope with respect to Scandinavia which had also furnished many fine settlers to Western Canada. Whereas a year ago the Dutch Government were unwilling that their people should leave that country and come to Canada, to-day they were assisting them in a very large way in bringing a splendid class of people to Canada, and they were working that field for all it was worth. Referring to the possibility of getting immigration from the United States, the Minister said they were trying to get as many as they could of the

Canadians who left Eastern Canada, particularly Quebec and the Maritime Provinces, who were now settled in the New England States, and were showing a desire to return to Canada, to come back and once more take up farming in the Dominion.

There had been a regulation in force providing that each immigrant must be in possession of at least $250. They had now altered that provision in so far as it affected Oriental immigrants, but they had removed what was claimed to be to a certain extent a disability in another connection. By "visé-ing" of passports by their own agents they hoped that when people sold up their homes on the other side and embarked for Canada there would be the least possible difficulty in their passing the test at the Canadian port of entry.

Mr. Robert Forke (National Progressive, *Brandon, Ont.*) believed that in the United States could be found the very best class of people they were likely to get, because they could adapt themselves readily to their social and political conditions. He thought quite a large percentage of immigration could be got from the British Islands if they went the right way about it. Canada was only seven days from Great Britain, but to go to Australia meant a long sea voyage, and that militated to a large extent against Australia and in favour of Canada.

Miss Agnes Macphail (National Progressive, *Grey, S.E. Riding, Ont.*) thought that immigration to Canada had now reached a point when it was no longer a question of getting people on the land but a question of keeping them there. The difficulty with the Canadian farmers had been that their standard of life had not been high enough. They had been willing to work long hours and to receive from their investment far less return than any other class of people; and if those people who came to Canada were willing to work longer hours and receive less than the existing farmers were, then the conditions of affairs instead of being improved would rapidly be rendered worse.

Mr. J. H. Harris (Liberal-Conservative, *York, E. Riding, Ont.*) said that his experience had been that immigrants from Central European countries drifted very quickly into the large centres, and the result was that they took hold of the rougher class of work in those centres and deprived their English, Irish and Scotch Canadians of the opportunity of doing that work.

The Hon. T. A. Crerar (Leader of the National Progressive Party) cordially supported the Government in the efforts they might make to bring to their shores immigrants of a desirable type who would go on the land and in time be assimilated into the Dominion as good citizens of it. The best immigration agent they could have in Canada was the contented and prosperous settler. It was a fact that in the finest agricultural countries of Ontario there had been an actual and very serious decline in the rural population in the last ten years. To have a permanently successful policy of immigration, one of the vital factors was to reduce their cost of production in agriculture so that they might successfully compete with other countries in the markets of the world. The Slav was one of the most adaptable of their immigrants. He submitted that they could take a considerable number of wisely selected settlers of that type and they would be a useful asset to the Dominion. But when they brought people to Canada, let them do a little bit more for them than they had done in the past in holding out the hand of welcome to them. There was no one who did not see the great possibilities and the enormous potential wealth of Canada, but they must pay more attention to the building up of homes in Canada so that the people would stay, and until they did that it was not much good trying to bring more people there.

Mr. G. G. Coote (National Progressive, *Macleod, Alta.*) said that if immigrants were going to remain with them they must be of the class that had enough money to start in the farming business ; and so far as he knew nearly all the immigrants that came to Western Canada with any money to speak of and made a success of farming were people from the United States.

The Hon. John B. Baxter (Liberal-Conservative, *St. John City and Counties of St. John and Albert, N.B.*) declared that the immigration policy ought to be for the whole of the Dominion, and that Eastern Canada should not be neglected. It was no use asking the East, with its slender population, to assimilate a large population from Central Europe. He would suggest immigrants from France, Great Britain, or the Scandinavian countries. They did not want Germans.

On 16th June,

The Minister of Immigration said that with a view to inducing as great a number of desirable immigrants as possible to come to Canada during the year 1922-23 a special committee composed of Ministers of the Crown had been formed with the object of studying the immigration situation and laying down a policy which would be to the greatest advantage of Canada. They had been making special efforts in the Old Land. They were trying to make the examination a little more rigid both in Great Britain and on the Continent, in order that they might not have to return so many who were unable to pass the test on this side of the water. However, he thought they must insist that the medical inspection should be at the port of disembarkation and by their own medical officers.

They had not so far taken down the barriers against German immigrants. However, he was quite prepared to give consideration to what appeared to be deserving cases.

The Hon. Hugh Guthrie (Liberal-Conservative, *Wellington, S. Riding, Ont.*) stated that a good many people came into Canada ostensibly as farm labourers who were not farm labourers and on reaching Canada they disavowed any intention of ever becoming farmers. If more stringent regulations were adopted, many of those who now came in breach of the regulations might be excluded. In speeches, according to the Press, the Bishop of Birmingham and Sir Rider Haggard suggested that not only Canada but the Dominions in general should be used as countries to send those of the British people who were not physically up to the mark as a method of "reinvigorating" them. He believed it was the duty of the Government at the present time to advise publicly the people of Great Britain as to the Government's attitude on the matter, because men of the prominence of Sir Rider Haggard and the Bishop of Birmingham should be made aware of the fact that the Dominions did not wish people, whether British or otherwise, who were not physically fit to make their way to come to Canada. Mr. Guthrie proceeded to draw the Minister's attention to a method by which Australia was obtaining a very good class of citizen, and which was called the "nomination system." Citizens who had come from the Old Land and who had made good in Australia had the right to nominate to the Department of Immigration of Australia certain friends of theirs whom they could recommend as good citizens to come to Australia.

Mr. A. W. Neill (National Progressive, *Comox-Alberni, B.C.*) asked whether immigrants had to produce a certificate from the Government of the country they came from that they had been engaged in agricultural life?

The Minister of Immigration replied that that was the very reason why they had men at Bucharest and Warsaw at the present time. A considerable number of farmers were coming from Poland, but to say there were large numbers of immigrants coming into their cities was not in accordance with the facts. Speaking on the subject of immigrants (*e.g.*, the Mennonites) settling in colonies the Minister said that these people would have to assume all the obligations of a Canadian citizen, with respect to military service and everything else.

Mr. John Evans (National Progressive, *Saskatoon, Sask.*) declared that at the present time, particularly since the War, they had a class of people in the West who were not content with the Canadian form of government, and there were foreigners there to-day from the south-eastern part of Europe, foreigners, settled in colonies, who were continually advocating Sovietism. These people who would not allow themselves to be assimilated and would not assume the duties and responsibilities of full Canadian citizenship should be debarred from entering the country.

IMMIGRATION ACT AMENDMENT BILL.

(Deportation of undesirable persons; etc.)

A Bill, introduced by Mr. Woodsworth, sought to amend the Immigration Act so as to prevent the deportation by the Department of Immigration of undesirable persons, with special regard to British subjects, without trial in the Canadian courts. On 3rd May the Bill was referred to a Special Committee which recommended, *inter alia*, a general revision of the Immigration Act. This Report was concurred in, and the Bill was not proceeded with.

DEBATE IN HOUSE OF COMMONS.

On 10th April, on the Second Reading,

The Minister of Marine and Fisheries (Hon. Ernest Lapointe) stated that last year he had himself introduced a Bill to amend the legislation which was passed during what was known as the panicky Session of 1919 while the strike in Winnipeg was on. There was no doubt that provisions were enacted at the time which were of a very serious character, especially when British subjects could be deported from Canada without the right to be tried before suffering deportation, which was the right of all British subjects under British law. Two years ago the then Minister of Labour introduced a Bill in the Senate to amend that legislation of 1919 and to enact that a British subject could not be deported summarily in that way without having a trial in due form. That Bill was rejected by the Senate and never reached the House of Commons during that Session. He should not like to oppose the principle of this Bill, because it embodied what he himself proposed last year and what was then accepted by the Government, and passed by the House of Commons, although it was blocked in the Senate again. This Bill, however, contained provisions which he could not accept, although he agreed with that portion of it that embodied the principles of the Bill he introduced last year. He thought it would be wise for the House to refer it to a Special Committee.

On 3rd May, in Committee,

Mr. J. S. Woodsworth (Labour, *Winnipeg, C., Man.*) said that the effect of the existing amendment to the Immigration Act was really to deprive a very large section of their people of the right to trial by jury—a very serious consideration. This Act was designed, primarily, not, as one might imagine from its being an Immigration Act, to keep out undesirable immigrants, but rather to deal with people who were already in Canada. He submitted that, if they were going to deal with undesirable people in Canada, or people who had committed crimes in Canada, in connection with an immigration law, the provision ought not to be brought in. He should like to appeal to his fellow-Canadian-born Britishers, whether French or English, to relieve the British-born of the disabilities under which they were placed in Canada. Dealing with the various Sections of the Bill, Mr. Woodsworth said that the first one had to do with domicile, and this could be understood only as they remembered that the idea was to get rid of certain undesirable classes. The first provision made it impossible for anyone, later classed as an undesirable, to obtain domicile in Canada. These people could come into the country and they might live in Canada for a certain period of time; but if they were declared to be undesirable, it was as if they were not living there; their residence in Canada gave them no claim whatever, no right to trial in the courts of the country. The fact that they had been living in Canada ceased to have any value. His plea was that, before anybody who had been living in Canada for any length of time was declared undesirable his case should be presented to a regular court and decided by that court and not by the Immigration Department.

Sub-Section (iii.) of the Act in part read:—

> When any citizen of Canada who is a British subject by naturalisation, or any British subject not born in Canada having Canadian domicile, shall have resided for one year outside of Canada, he shall be presumed to have lost Canadian domicile.

That was, if a man who had been living in Canada for a considerable number of years should, for instance, return to Great Britain for a year and then come back to Canada, he would cease to have Canadian domicile. Although a British subject he would cease to have any rights before the courts of Canada.

The amendment to the Act added a number of classes to those who had previously been regarded as undesirable. The objectionable feature was contained in these words:—

> Persons . . . (N) who disbelieve in or are opposed to organised government . . . (O) persons who are members of or affiliated with any organisation entertaining or teaching disbelief in or opposition to organised government.

and :

(P) Enemy aliens or persons who have been alien enemies, and who were or may be interned on or after 11th November, 1918, in any part of His Majesty's Dominions or by any of His Majesty's Allies.

He was not there to advocate, in any way whatever, disbelief in organised government, but this question of belief or disbelief in organised government, and the decision whether people did or did not believe in it, should not be left to an Immigration Department. The question should be left to the courts. The paragraph (p) worked a gross injustice to a large number of their fellow-citizens who were technically classed as alien enemies. They found this Section dealing with these people (*e.g.*, former Austrian subjects) who were in the country, many of whom had been living exemplary lives, the very class of people whom perhaps they most needed as immigrants to go on the land.

The whole question as to whether or not a man was undesirable, or whether or not he belonged to organisations that were supposed to teach doctrines not in harmony with the welfare of the country, was left to the Department of Immigration to decide. They would be in keeping with the very best British practice if they condemned men only when they committed some overt act and not for merely thinking this or the other thing. It had been taken for granted in British countries that a man might believe whatever he liked so long as he did not in any way interfere with his fellow-citizens or imperil the country.

In Section 16, Mr. Woodsworth took exception particularly to the following :—

Any person suspected of an offence under this Section may forthwith be arrested and detained without a warrant by any officer for examination and deportation.

He might without trial be deported, though he might happen to be a British subject. Section 17 provided :—

Whenever any person other than a Canadian citizen or a person having Canadian domicile—

had done so and so. That was where it touched the British-born. Most of them had not realised that in order for a Britisher to obtain rights before the courts of Canada, he had to be naturalised. Most of their English immigrants coming to Canada took it for granted that they had certain rights in the country and would receive full protection from the law. They did not consider it necessary to become naturalised, and this clause, therefore, placed them in a far more difficult and helpless position than in the case with persons born in Germany, Austria or Russia. Every man, Canadian-born and non-Canadian-born, if he was doing anything in any sense detrimental to the best interests of the community, should be regularly tried in open court, and, if found guilty, deported—but given a fair trial first.

The Hon. Hugh Guthrie (Liberal-Conservative, *Wellington, S. Riding, Ont.*) said that it was just possible that the present law was in some respects too drastic. It was placed on the Statute Book at a critical time in the history of the country. That critical period had more or less passed away, and it was quite possible that the law should be modified.

The Hon. T. A. Crerar (Leader of the National Progressive Party) declared that the amendments to the Immigration Act, particularly those drastic amendments which were passed in 1919 giving power to the officials of the Department of Immigration to deport people without any fair trial, were not in accord with British practice and should not remain on their Statute Book. The question, however, was a large one. The Bill sought to repeal a good many Sections of the Act, and he thought it could well be referred to a Special Committee for report.

The Prime Minister (Hon. W. L. Mackenzie King) moved, and the motion was agreed to, that the Bill should be referred to a Special Committee.

On 21st June,

Mr. Joseph Archambault (Liberal, *Chambly and Verchères, Que.*), Chairman of the Special Committee, presented the final Report of the Committee to the effect that a general revision of the Immigration Act was desirable, and that pending such revision the Bill should not be proceeded with, and moved concurrence therein.

Mr. Archambault explained that the Committee had come to the conclusion that the whole of the Immigration Act should be revised. First in importance was the Section regarding a Canadian citizen. Section 41 of the Act gave the definition of undesirable citizens who could be deported by an officer of the Immigration Department, which applied to practically every citizen, except any person who was a British subject, either by reason of birth in Canada, or by reason of naturalisation in Canada. That excluded many British subjects. Their suggestion was that this proviso should be replaced by the following:—

Provided that this Section shall not apply to any Canadian citizen.

Sub-Section (2) read:—

Proof that any person belonged to or was within the description of any of the prohibited or undesirable classes within the meaning of this Section at any time since 4th May, 1910, shall, for all the purposes of this Act, be deemed to establish *prima facie* that he still belongs to such prohibited or undesirable class or classes.

The Committee was of opinion that this Section should be abrogated. It was contrary to the British principle of justice which said that a man was not supposed to be guilty until it was proved that he was guilty; and proof *prima facie* that he was guilty seemed to him to be against the principle of British and Canadian justice. Although Section 41 enumerated those persons who "seek to overthrow by force or violence the Government of or constituted law and authority in the United Kingdom of Great Britain and Ireland or of Canada," they found the following words in this Section:—

or is suspected of belonging to any secret society or organisation.

The Committee was of opinion that the mere fact of a person being suspected of belonging to one of these societies or classes was not sufficient to permit the application of this legislation.

Mr. Woodsworth said, with reference to the last recommendation, that it would still leave the amendment untouched. There was a further recommendation that these clauses should not apply to Canadian citizens. They did not apply to-day, and that was the very point of the Bill. It was barely possible that relief might be given to one particular class, the British citizen who had been naturalised in Canada. He moved (seconded by Mr. Irvine) an amendment to the effect that the Report should not be concurred in, but should be sent back to the Committee to amend the Bill by providing that no one should be deported for any political offence committed in Canada without being granted a trial by jury.

The Right Hon. Arthur Meighen (Leader of the Opposition) said that Mr. Woodsworth's amendment instructed the Committee to amend the Report, and to make it read that all guilty of political offences, no matter from what country they had come, should be deportable only after conviction by a jury. Virtually all he (Mr. Woodsworth) had urged in favour of the striking out of the original Immigration Act Amendment of 1919 was an argument in favour of changing the whole basis of the deportation law and placing upon the authorities the burden of conviction as a necessary precedent to the deportation of a man even coming from Poland. Among the undesirable classes was the class known as anarchists, whose professed principles were against government of every kind. They had not, as far as he could remember, ever had a law making it necessary to get a conviction through process of law and the decision of a jury before such a man could be deported if he came from an outside country.

Mr. William Irvine (Labour, *Calgary, E., Alta.*): "Is the hon. Leader of the Opposition correct when he states that this law places the British immigrant and the immigrant from other countries on the same basis? . . . If a man from, say, Russia, who has been naturalised here commits a crime after he receives his citizenship, he cannot be deported, but if a British subject commits such a crime after living in this country as long, say, as the Russian, he can be deported."

Mr. Meighen replied that after the Russian was naturalised he did not come in under the regular law, and a British subject would consequently be in a different position under the amendment. He was not one of those who felt that immigrants to Canada from the Motherland should, under normal conditions, be treated the same way as immigrants from other countries. He thought they must have regard to the unity of the Empire; they must have some regard to citizenship within the Empire in the determination of all their laws. It had relation to immigration, perhaps, more than anything else. But this law was framed because they were then having very considerable difficulty with just that class of immigrants. The Committee recommended that the course pursued but not carried to successful termination because of the negative action of the Senate in 1920 and 1921 be pursued again. He concurred in the Report of the Committee.

Mr. Woodsworth's amendment was negatived, and Mr. Archambault's motion was agreed to, and the Report concurred in.

PROPORTIONAL REPRESENTATION.

On 10th May the House of Commons discussed a resolution moved by Mr. Good to the effect that, the findings of the Special Committee on Proportional Representation being favourable to the adoption of the Alternative Vote method of election and true Proportional Representation and the recent General Election having demonstrated the serious anomalies of the existing electoral system,

in the opinion of this House the Alternative Vote method should be adopted for use in future Elections for this House in all single-Member constituencies where more than two candidates are running for election.

Also that for the purpose of demonstrating the working and effect of the true Proportional Representation System, one or more multi-Member constituencies should be constituted as early as possible in which that system should be applied at the next General Election.

DEBATE IN HOUSE OF COMMONS.

Alternative vote system.

Mr. W. C. Good (National Progressive, *Brant, Ont.*) said that he was not asking the House on the present occasion to give an unqualified endorsation to the principle of Proportional

Representation, or to authorise its application in any definite number of places, or in any particular constituencies in Canada, but to authorise the trying out of Proportional Representation in certain constituencies. It had already been tried with great success in Winnipeg, and Toronto, he thought, was another place where it could be tried to great advantage. Mr. Good then gave lists showing a total of 140 constituencies in which more than two candidates ran and a total of 74 constituencies where the present representatives sat in the House of Commons as minority representatives. In a few instances, he said, Members were elected who received barely one-third of the total vote. In the report of the Committee of the Ontario Legislature there was an unqualified endorsation of the Alternative Vote method where more than two candidates were running and a Bill was, he understood, being introduced into the Ontario Legislature that year to give effect to that recommendation. Under their present system, every voter in a three-, four- or five-cornered contest was placed in a most unfair position, and a grave injustice was done to him. In the Election of 1917 there were three men running in his constituency, and he (Mr. Good) had to consider which one of the two candidates whom he preferred above the third had the better chance of being elected. No voter ought to be compelled, by an electoral system, to consider a matter of that sort which, in the nature of the case, was utterly irrelevant. If they had any regard for the principle of democracy, they must surely go to the extent, at all events, that the representatives of the electorate in the House should be returned by a majority of their constituents. Therefore, with respect to the alternative or transferable vote, quite regardless of any system of Proportional Representation and having reference only to their present system of single-Member constituencies, they ought to provide that, when more than two candidates were running, every elector should have the privilege of recording his second or third choice, as the case might be, so that in the event of his first choice not having any chance of being elected, he should not lose his vote, but should be privileged to record his vote and to have it counted in the final result.

Statistics.

Why should they not stop there and say : That is sufficient ? Because even if they went that far, inevitable inaccuracies would occur under the single-Member constituency system. The Alternative Vote would bring them back again only to that situation which they had before there were more than two Parties, when a representative sat in the House by reason of the fact that he was elected by a majority. In the British

Columbia Provincial Elections of 1912 the Conservative Party polled a vote of about 51,000 and got 31 representatives and also an additional nine by acclamation. The Liberal Party polled about 21,000 votes and they did not secure a single representative. The Socialist and Independent Party, with a total vote of about 12,000, secured two representatives. Take the Canadian Federal Elections of 1908: the Liberal Party secured a vote of 594,000, getting a representative in the House of 135; the Conservatives, with a vote of 552,000, secured a representation of 86, so that the representation of Conservatives at that time was disproportionately decreased. In the Federal Elections of 1911 the Conservative vote was 669,000 and the representation 134; the Liberal vote was 625,000, almost as great, and the representation only 87—a reversal of the situation in 1908. The returns for the General Election in Great Britain of December, 1918, gave the following results:—

Coalition Groups.	*Votes polled.*	*Seats obtained.*	*Seats in proportion to votes.*
Coalition-Liberal ..	1,500,000	103	73
Coalition-Labour ..	48,000	3	3
Coalition-Unionist ..	3,500,000	285	184

The total of the votes polled by the Non-Coalition groups was slightly over 4,000,000 and the representation secured was 81, although they were entitled to 217. In the last Federal Election the representation should be as follows: Liberals, 96 Members; Conservatives, 73; Progressives, 55; Labour, 4; Independents, 7.* The Liberal Party in the House of Commons was disproportionately represented. In Australia a few years ago there were two main Parties in a General Election, the Labour Party and the Anti-Labour Party. If his memory served him right, the Anti-Labour Party secured a disproportionate amount of representation. But the next Election reversed the situation with a vengeance, and the Labour Party was able to snap its fingers at the defeated Anti-Labour Party. It was wrong for them to allow any system to remain in existence which might cause such extraordinary and unfair results.

Proportional Representation abroad.

Turning to the results which followed under Proportional Representation, Mr. Good stated that in the Tasmanian House of Assembly in 1909 Labour was entitled to 11·69 representatives and secured 12; Anti-Labour was entitled to 18·31 and secured 18. In the Belgian Parliament, in the Elections of 1908, the Catholics secured 37 seats and were

* The actual results were: Liberals 117; National Progressives, 65; Conservatives, 51; Labour, 2.

entitled to 36; the Liberals and Socialists secured 43 and were entitled to 44; the Christian Democrats secured 1, the number to which they were entitled. Mr. Good then proceeded to enumerate those countries where some system of alternative voting or Proportional Representation was in force, including New South Wales, Queensland, Victoria, Tasmania, New Zealand (to be used in 1922), South Africa (for the Senate and the Executive Council and the Executive Committee Provincial Councils), India (single transferable vote in several of the Provinces), Switzerland, Belgium, Bulgaria, Denmark, Holland, Sweden, Norway, Germany (since 1918-19), Austria (since 1919), Luxemburg (since 1919), Poland, Czecho-Slovakia, Italy, France (in part), and several Canadian cities.

Speaking of the advantages and disadvantages of Proportional Representation, Mr. Good said that it provided for a reasonable security of tenure of office in the case of outstanding men. The allegation that Proportional Representation encouraged small Government majorities and was therefore not to be desired, could not possibly be sustained. The evidence was wholly to the contrary. He now came to the greatest objection which had been levelled against Proportional Representation, that it encouraged the formation of groups. He wished to submit the considered opinion of a Committee appointed in 1909 or 1910 by the British Parliament in connection with this matter. The Committee stated:—

> "We are inclined to think that the multiplication of small Parties, feared by opponents, and the encouragement of the independent Member, hoped for by advocates, are alike exaggerated in the evidence given before us."

Some people were staggered at the prospect of holding by-Elections in multi-Member constituencies. It would not be necessary to poll the whole constituency. Although it might be a little expensive, it would not in some cases be a bad thing to reconsult the people. Then again the statement had been made that a tremendous amount of labour would be involved under Proportional Representation in canvassing a large constituency. He submitted, however, that the difficulty was imaginary rather than real. The last point he wished to deal with was the charge that Proportional Representation would be difficult, if not impossible, to carry out in large, sparsely-populated areas. In Australia the Senate was elected by Proportional Representation, each State being polled as a single constituency, and they had not any particular difficulty there with the system.

Mr. Andrew McMaster (Liberal, *Brome, Que.*) stated that they (the Committee of the House of Commons, of which he was a member) had come to the conclusion, unanimously, if he did not forget, that they should adopt the Alternative

Vote in connection with single-seated constituencies in which more than two candidates presented themselves for election; they offered no definite statement as to the wisdom or unwisdom of true Proportional Representation. It was Burke who said that the virtue, the spirit and the essence of the House of Commons consisted in its being the express image of the nation, and they wanted to get a House of Commons which would accurately reflect every important strain of public opinion in the country. That was practically what Mr. Asquith also said. The Alternative Vote would help to a certain extent, but Proportional Representation, he believed, would help even further. In order to get the full benefit of the results of Proportional Representation, they should have a constituency electing at least five Members. The work of the voter was simplicity itself. He had only to indicate on his ballot paper by the figures 1, 2, 3, 4 and 5, as the case might be, the order of his preferences among the candidates, and the counting of the votes merely consisted in giving effect to what was really in the voter's mind.

Gladstone was supposed to have suffered an overwhelming defeat when he went before the people with his Home Rule proposals in 1886, but, as a matter of fact, he had a popular majority of over fifty thousand. If that popular majority had been reflected in the representation of the House of Commons of that day, it was quite possible that the last half-century almost of strain and bloodshed in Ireland might have been avoided. He was inclined to believe that in Canada, as in Belgium before they had Proportional Representation, their present system served to accentuate sectional, religious and racial differences. There were Liberals in the West whose voices could not be heard in the House—they were unrepresented. There were Conservatives in Quebec whose voices could not be heard in the House because they were unrepresented.

Incompatible with responsible government.

Mr. L. J. Ladner (Liberal-Conservative, *Vancouver, S., B.C.*) contended that Proportional Representation was not adaptable to the British system of responsible government. As to Proportional Representation in municipal affairs he was thoroughly in support of it; but in the case of the Federal Constitution of Canada it certainly was not sound. The idea of the system was to give representation to groups of people. But when they got into Parliament how were they going to form a Government that would be able to control the majority of the House, and carry out the system of responsible government as it had been developed under the British Constitution primarily since the time of Charles I.?

The Hon. T. A. Crerar (Leader of the National Progressive Party) declared that Proportional Representation sought to advance one step further in carrying out the idea of getting as exact a representation of the people's will in the matter of government as it was possible to do. It had been adopted by Belgium, Holland, Denmark, Sweden and Switzerland in Europe. While these particular countries had had this method in effect for many years, they had less disturbance, and the fullest and freest functioning of democracy as regards the rights of the people in their government. The Overseas Dominions of the British Commonwealth had, in effect and practice, the British form of government, and that principle had been applied in some of those States. It had been applied in municipal elections in Great Britain, and with very great success. The outstanding men in all political Parties in Great Britain had given their adherence to the furtherance of this reform. He found in the Speaker's Conference of 1916 the outstanding men of the British House of Commons, men drawn from all political Parties, and that Conference recommended precisely the reforms which the Member for Brant had submitted to the House.

Government's attitude.

The Prime Minister (Hon. W. L. Mackenzie King) said that he found himself in entire sympathy with the resolution and would like to express himself as supporting it as it stood. If the House approved the resolution the Government would do all in its power to give effect to it as opportunity afforded. Responsible government was based primarily upon a representative parliament, and any measure that would help to make Parliament more truly representative of the public will must necessarily be furthering responsible government rather than in any way limiting it. The Government would be formed in precisely the same way under this system as it was at present—out of a body of representatives of the people who could command the confidence of the House. He confessed that as he studied the question more and more, it was his view that instead of adding to the numbers of groups in the House, the adoption of what was proposed here might tend to limit the groups. It was to ensure representation based upon a majority that the proposals had been made and that this reform was so much needed.

Opposition from Quebec.

The Hon. Charles Marcil (Liberal, *Bonaventure, Que.*) was confident that the French-Canadians of Montreal would be a unit against Proportional Representation. He was afraid that in such a cosmopolitan city as Montreal was getting to be, if they had this system they would see every nationality wanting representation, and they would have racial candidates running, which would not be an improvement on their present system, but rather the reverse. For that reason he was opposed to the principle of Proportional Representation.

On the motion of Mr. Marcil the debate was adjourned.

ENFRANCHISEMENT OF ALIEN WOMEN.

On 29th March, 1922, Mr. Euler moved a resolution in the House of Commons declaring that it was desirable to strike out the Sub-Section of the Dominions Election Act which provided that the allegiance or nationality of a person as it was at birth, should be deemed incapable of change merely by reason of marriage, etc., or otherwise than by personal naturalisation (*vide* below for terms of Sub-Section, and *vide* also JOURNAL, Vol. I., No. 2, p. 337).

DEBATE IN HOUSE OF COMMONS.

Mr. W. D. Euler (Liberal, *Waterloo, N. Riding, Ont.*) moved :—

> That, in the opinion of this House, it is desirable that Sub-Section 2 of Section 29 of the Dominions Election Act be struck from the Act in its entirety.

He said that that clause of the Act disenfranchised many thousand people. The section first recited the general qualifications of a voter. It stated that the franchise rested with British subjects who were so by birth or naturalisation. They must have resided in Canada for at least twelve months, and two months in the constituency in which they were to vote. Then the following clause (Sub-Section 2 of Section 29) appeared :—

> For the purposes of this Act, the allegiance or nationality of a person, as it was at the birth of such person, shall be deemed incapable of being changed, or of having been changed, merely by reason or in consequence of marriage or change of allegiance or naturalisation of any other person, or otherwise than by personal naturalisation of such first-mentioned person. Provided, however, that this sub-section shall not apply to any person born on the Continent of North America, nor to any person who in person applies to and obtains from any judge having jurisdiction in naturalisation proceedings, a certificate under the hand of such judge, and the seal, if any, of his court, to the effect following. . . .

The effect of the certificate was this, that the judge should certify that the person who made application for the certificate had proved to him that he or she was qualified for personal naturalisation. He then granted a voting certificate. The person who made application was already legally naturalised, but in order to obtain the right to vote she must obtain a voting certificate. If a woman of foreign birth married a man who was a British subject, she herself immediately became a British subject. If her husband was also of foreign birth and he became naturalised she at the same time automatically became naturalised. Moreover, the minor children of such a man became naturalised with him. It followed then that foreign-born women married to foreign-born men, who were legally naturalised, were just as truly and legally Canadian citizens as were their foreign-born husbands. If the right to the franchise was based on citizenship, his contention was that the woman who was naturalised legally should have the right to vote just as unrestrictedly as her husband, who also was foreign-born. The Bill, as originally drafted, disfranchised something like 100,000 British subjects, who happened to be born in Germany and Austria-Hungary. The judge could not grant them voting certificates for the simple reason that they were not qualified for naturalisation, the Naturalisation Act at that time absolutely forbidding the naturalisation of persons who originally came from the countries with which they were at war. The then Government brought in an amendment placing these foreign-born women on exactly the same plane as other foreign-born women, making it necessary for them, however, as for others, to obtain this voting certificate before they could vote, although they were naturalised British subjects. He knew in his own riding women who had lived in Canada for fifty years, who were good Canadian citizens, and they resented the necessity of appearing before a judge and showing cause why he should issue to them voting certificates. As a matter of fact they did not go before him, and he was of the opinion that of the women affected by this clause perhaps 75 to 80 per cent. were thus virtually disfranchised. Their Naturalisation Act provided distinctly that the wife of a British subject was herself a British subject ; but this clause in the Election Act stated that the wife of a British subject was not a British subject when it came to voting. These two Laws were absolutely irreconcilable, and the illogical one ought to give way.

The Hon. Hugh Guthrie (Liberal-Conservative, *Wellington, S. Riding, Ont.*) pointed out that the object of this Section of the Statute was to place the male and female voter upon the same plane and to surround each with the same conditions in respect to the franchise. The naturalised male subject was entitled under the Franchise Act to vote, but before being naturalised he had to meet the requirements of their naturalisation law. Under the Naturalisation Act a woman married to a naturalised British subject became by operation of law a British subject, but no examination was required of her. There was a discrimination as between the male and female voter at that time, and the object was to surround the right to use the Canadian franchise with every reasonable precaution. They had done so in regard to men who became naturalised, and they desired to do the same thing in regard to female voters. As another year had now lapsed, there might not be quite as much reason for this restriction as there was two or three years ago. It might be that as time went on there would be less reason for it. But in his judgment the restriction then adopted was a reasonable and proper one, and it met with the approval of the House of Commons at the time.

Miss Agnes Macphail (National Progressive, *Grey, S.E. Riding, Ont.*) thought that what women really wanted to-day was perfect equality with men, and, therefore, if the striking out of Section 29 of the Dominions Election Act in its entirety did not confer upon women entirely equal rights with men, it was not going far enough. It seemed to her that if a woman herself were a naturalised Canadian it would not matter whom she married, or whether she was married at all, because she would still be permanently a naturalised Canadian. She thought women just wanted to be individuals, as men were individuals—no more and no less. And so she would like to see that principle embodied in the law, rather than that a woman should be made a citizen by marriage to a man who was himself a citizen.

The Right Hon. Arthur Meighen (Leader of the Opposition) said that if they passed the motion, brought in a Bill and made it law, there would still be a distinction between the rights to the franchise on the part of British subjects in Canada, and a very great distinction and discrimination. A man coming from another country to that Dominion, in order to secure citizenship by the law of their land, must, for example, now show that he had lived in Canada for five years; he must show certain qualifications of citizenship; he must take a certain oath. There was not equality in the admission to citizenship. Were there equality, there would be no reason in the world for inequality in the admission to suffrage. Their contention was that perhaps the woman came from a country in which the people lived under conditions which would justify the presumption that she would know little of their institutions, of the obligations of their citizenship. Possibly within the first week in which she arrived in Canada, the first day—for there were many such cases—or the first year she married a naturalised subject. That moment she was a Canadian citizen, and she had reached that status without having met any of the tests whatever which Canada had placed around the admittance to that status of naturalisation. There had been inequality in the admission to the status of citizenship all through the history of the Dominion, of the British Empire, and of every other civilised country under the sun. If the mere admission to the status of citizenship in itself gave the right of suffrage, then necessarily there would be inequality. Then necessarily, in the case of women, there would be an absence of those safeguards that had been thought wise in the case of men.

Mr. A. R. McMaster (Liberal, *Brome*, *Que.*) said that in 1919 they had a Naturalisation Law whereby a married woman had a right to be personally naturalised and receive her naturalisation certificate, but that was taken away by the legislation which was passed in the same year. So the only way in which a woman born out of the British Dominions and married in Canada could get naturalisation was through the naturalisation of her husband. Once they allowed marriage to a British subject to open the door to the franchise, that door should be opened to any woman no matter in what part of the world she was born.

Mr. A. W. Neill (National Progressive, *Comox-Alberni*, *B.C.*) charged the late Government with proceeding against the wishes of the people of British Columbia by enfranchising Orientals in the last election. Quite a number of Japanese enlisted from that Province during the War and went overseas with their troops. When they came back they made application to the Legislature of British Columbia for permission to vote. The application of the Asiatics to vote was disallowed and the Act remained as it was before, disqualifying them. When the Dominion Government came to pass this Franchise Act, they were advised that it might be expedient to allow these Japanese to vote ; therefore it was so arranged. He strongly hoped that when the Act was revised—and the Leader of the Government had indicated that there would be revision—this provision and many others of a similar character would be eliminated.

The Prime Minister (Hon. W. L. Mackenzie King) thought that, as to the relation between the franchise and citizenship, they ought to do all they could to see that their citizenship was kept strong and well-selected ; but once a person became a British subject, he thought they should do all in their power to instil in him or her a pride in British citizenship, and the first duty of every citizen was to take an intelligent part in the affairs of government. No one could exercise the full privilege of citizenship if he was deprived of the right to vote under the conditions prescribed in an electoral law. If the House would approve of this motion, the Government would at a later stage bring in an amendment to the

Elections Act with a view to giving effect to the intention of the resolution.

After further discussion, Mr. Euler's motion was agreed to.

INDIAN ACT AMENDMENT.

(Fitness of Indians for enfranchisement; Land for Settlement; etc.)

A Bill to amend the Indian Act was assented to on 27th June, 1922. It deals with the method of instituting inquiries as to the fitness of Indians for enfranchisement and the acquirement of land for Indian settlement.

The Act provides that upon the application of an Indian of any band, or upon the application of a band on a vote of a majority of its male members of the age of twenty-one at a meeting summoned for the purpose, according to the rules of the band and held in the presence of the Superintendent-General or an authorised officer, a Board may be appointed by the Superintendent-General to consist of two officers of the Department of Indian Affairs and a member of the band to inquire into and report on the fitness of any Indian to be enfranchised. In the course of such inquiry it shall be the duty of the Board to take into consideration and report upon the attitude of any such Indian towards his enfranchisement, which attitude shall be a factor in determining the question of fitness. The Report shall contain a description of the land occupied by the Indian, the names, ages and sex of every Indian whose interests it is anticipated will be affected, and such other information as the Superintendent-General may direct such Board to obtain (Sect. 1).

The Act also provides that the Deputy Superintendent-General may acquire for an Indian settler land as well without as within an Indian reserve, and shall have authority to set apart for such settler a portion of the common lands of the band without the consent of the council of the band. In the event of land being so acquired or set apart on an Indian reserve, the Deputy Superintendent-General shall have power to take the said land as security for any advances made to such settler, and the provisions of the Soldier Settlement Act, 1919, shall, as far as applicable, apply to such transaction. It shall, however, be only the individual interest in such lands that is being acquired or given as security, and the interest of the band in such lands shall not be in any way affected by such transactions.

DEBATE IN HOUSE OF COMMONS.

On 15th June, on the First Reading,

The Minister of the Interior (Hon. Charles Stewart) explained that the purpose of the Bill was to repeal Section 7 dealing with the compulsory enfranchisement of Indians, which Section was added to the Act last Session. This feature met with a great deal of opposition from the Indians themselves. It was bitterly resented by the Six Nations Indians, with whom they had some little difficulty during the past month. The amendment simply repealed the section which gave the Deputy Superintendent-General power to enfranchise an Indian with or without his consent, and reverted to the former practice under which an Indian desiring enfranchisement must make personal application.

The second Section was intended to clarify the situation in regard to the ownership of land remaining in the control of the band, particularly land upon which returned Indian soldiers had been re-established. They were making it absolutely clear that the ownership of the land, whether occupied by a soldier-settler or by any other Indian, remained under the control of the band.

On 19th June, in Committee,

The Right Hon. Arthur Meighen (Leader of the Opposition) said that the principle of compulsory enfranchisement was accepted by the last Parliament, the idea being the same as had underlain their whole Indian law and administration, namely, that they should seek to bring the Indian gradually, by slow and sure degrees, out of the state of wardship and into the status of citizenship. And now, if the Minister gave the ground that he was giving under a certain measure of coercion from certain bands of Indians themselves, then they might as well abandon all hope of the day when they would ever have any substantial enfranchisement of the Indians of Canada. The old law provided, after the most careful examination, under all sorts of restrictions and under proper supervision, that the Indians who were felt to be wholly capable of looking after themselves should take their share of the property that belonged to them and administer it themselves.

The Minister of the Interior said they were trying to educate the Indians. It seemed to him that they would make far greater progress with these wards of the Government if they tried to instil in them the real essence of their manhood, allowing them to take upon themselves the responsibility that was theirs, rather than forcing it upon them. Up to date no Indian had been enfranchised who had not expressed the desire for citizenship. The one outstanding difficulty was that the franchise carried with it, in their minds—as it did, in fact—a certain share of the land that constituted the reserve, and in many cases the reserves were accordingly becoming restricted; and unless these men were taught to cultivate their lands in those areas a greater burden would have to be assumed by the people with respect to them.

DEBATE IN THE SENATE.

On 23rd June, on the Second Reading,

Senator the Hon. G. W. Fowler (*Ont.*) declared that the Indian question was becoming very acute. The Indians, particularly those belonging to the Six Nations, claimed to be allies and not subjects, and therefore not subject to the laws of the country. They were at present defying the Government and everybody connected with it. The sooner they were taught that they were subjects of Canada, and that they were Canadian citizens so far as the moderate kind of citizenship they had, without the franchise, was concerned, the better. The Indian Department had not handled these people with sufficient firmness. There was a statute passed for the purpose of enfranchising them. Many Indians desired to take advantage of it, but in the bands the opposition was so strong that an Indian who wanted to be enfranchised could not do so. Any legislation tending towards easing up on those people made them think they were masters of the situation.

Senator the Hon. Sir James Lougheed (Leader of the Opposition) thought that the law of 1920, which they were weakening, was a very salutary Statute. The whole trend of treatment by the Government of the Indians of Canada had been to make the Indian self-sustaining. Because of that fact the policy of the Canadian Government had been far superior to that of the United States. They had always proceeded on the assumption that the Indian could be made a citizen of Canada ; that he could be so educated as to be able to discharge all the responsibilities of citizenship. Thousands of Indians were to-day amongst the citizens of Canada discharging their duties most satisfactorily. Upon every reserve there were always a certain number of dissatisfied spirits who would oppose the Government's policy of placing the Indian upon a self-supporting basis. They wanted to continue in the position of wards of the nation ; they wanted to be supported by the State for all time ; and if they gave recognition to that spirit of dependence on the Government, they would never be able to develop their administration of Indian affairs to that stage at which they would finally solve the Indian problems of Canada by absorbing the Indian population on the basis of citizenship. He therefore regretted that the Government had seen fit to depart from the policy which they had embodied in the Act of 1920.

The Leader of the Senate and Minister without Portfolio (Hon. Raoul Dandurand) thought that Canada had reason to be proud of its treatment of the Indians. There had been very few occasions when they had shown discontent or excitement.

Strange to say, the Indians generally seemed to be opposed to their own enfranchisement. They were slow in claiming Canadian citizenship. They resented any action on the part of the Government to enfranchise them against their will. They had constantly been protesting against any idea of breaking up the bands. They claimed their autonomy. They had claimed that they had obtained from the Imperial authorities assurances which should protect them against the legislation (compulsory enfranchisement) which it was sought to introduce. He was informed that, although this power was given to the Department, not one Indian was enfranchised under the Act. The machinery which the Department of Indian affairs had sought was never put into operation. The principal grievance of the Indians against being forced to take their enfranchisement was that the Superintendent could name any Indian, enfranchise him against his will, have him take his share of the band money and land, and place him in a position in which he might subsequently sell the land to a white man if he so desired, thereby breaking up the reserve.

OPIUM AND NARCOTIC DRUG AMENDMENT ACT.

This Act, which was assented to on 27th July, 1922, amends the Opium and Drug Act so as to strengthen in certain details the law for preventing the drug traffic.

The Bill, as passed by the House of Commons, provides that any person licensed under the Act to deal with any drug who gives or sells any drug to any person other than an authorised physician, veterinary surgeon or dentist, or to a *bonâ fide* druggist, without a written order therefor, and any druggist who gives or sells any drug to any person other than a physician, veterinary surgeon, dentist or druggist, except upon a written order or prescription, or who uses any prescription to sell any drug on more than one occasion, except when the preparation covered by the prescription might lawfully have been sold in the first instance without a written order or prescription, shall be guilty of a criminal offence, and shall be liable upon summary conviction to a fine not exceeding $1,000 and not less than $200, or to imprisonment not exceeding 18 months, or to both fine and imprisonment. The same penalty is incurred by any physician, veterinary surgeon or dentist who prescribes, gives or sells any drug or who signs any prescription for the filling of which any drug is required, except for medicinal purposes. (Sect. 1.)

Whipping.

The Bill also provides that any person importing, being in possession of, manufacturing or distributing any drug shall be liable upon indictment to imprisonment not exceeding seven years, or upon summary conviction to a fine not exceeding $1,000 and not less than $200, and to imprisonment not exceeding eighteen and not less than six months, provided that any person who unlawfully sells, gives away or distributes any

H 2

drug to any minor shall be proceeded against by indictment and not summarily, and shall, at the discretion of the judge, be liable to whipping. Any person who manufactures, imports, exports, sells or distributes any drug and neglects to keep the record required by the regulations, or refuses to produce such record for inspection, is liable to the lesser penalty. (Sect. 2.)

No person shall, without lawful authority, import or have in his possession any opium pipe, lamp or other device designed for the purpose of preparing opium or smoking or inhaling opium. (Sect. 4.)

Appeals.

It is further provided that appeals, under the Criminal Code, shall not apply to any conviction or proceedings in respect of any offence under the Act. (Sect. 5.)

Deportation : (Senate Amendment).

Notwithstanding anything to the contrary in the Immigration Act any alien who, at any time after his entry, is convicted under Section 2 above shall, upon the termination of imprisonment, be kept in custody and deported in accordance with Section 43 of the Immigration Act. (Sect. 6.)

In the Senate an amendment was carried adding to this section the words "unless the Court before whom he was tried shall otherwise order."

DEBATE IN HOUSE OF COMMONS.

On 15th June, in Committee,

The Minister of Health (Hon. Henri S. Béland), on Section 2, said that the fine of $500 had been reduced to $200, not because they wanted to make it easier for licensees or for physicians and dentists to evade the law, but because in the case of physicians and dentists, the associations to which they belonged had certain regulations to which they were subject, and any physician who engaged in the illicit sale of cocaine, morphine or opium was liable to suspension by his association.

Mr. L. J. Ladner (Liberal-Conservative, *Vancouver, S., B.C.*) moved the penalty of whipping to Section 2 as read the first time. He contended that the man who induced a minor to indulge in the drug habit should not be relieved of such a penalty as whipping. He had examples of the most monstrous action on the part of men engaged in this traffic, involving young girls of fifteen and sixteen. The effect of the carrying on of the drug traffic upon the moral qualities of manhood and womanhood was to bring about diseases of the vilest kind and crimes of all sorts. The court records disclosed the interesting fact that in the majority of cases the people engaged in these criminal enterprises were followers of the drug traffic.

The Minister of Health said that by the Bill which was now under consideration they provided more severe penalties than had hitherto been applied in the case of those who carried on illicit trade in narcotics. It was his intention to move that all aliens convicted under the Act should be deported. The Committee would have some idea of the effect of a deportation clause upon the traffic when he said that for the year ended 30th September, 1921, there were in Canada 1,864 convictions, and of that number 1,211 were Chinese. Possibly they should not adopt the provision embodied in the amendment, at least until they had seen, in the course of the next twelve months, what the result would be of the new provisions made for stricter punishment.

Mr. W. G. McQuarrie (**Liberal-Conservative,** *New Westminster, B.C.*) stated that a great many of their Chinese in British Columbia came from Hong Kong and other British Possessions. What would they do in a case of that kind? He was extremely doubtful if they would be able to deport a great number of those persons if convicted.

The Hon. H. H. Stevens (**Liberal-Conservative,** *Vancouver, C., B.C.*) thought that the clause the Minister was adding providing for the deportation of aliens would very materially strengthen the Bill. He would ask him, however, most earnestly to accept the amendment, and add the penalty of flogging in the case of those trafficking in drugs to minors.

Mr. O. R. Gould (**National Progressive,** *Assiniboia, Man.*) thought that they should first exhaust all other means of punishment before resorting to the lash. It seemed to him that they were reverting to the Dark Ages when they asked for punishment of that kind.

The Hon. S. F. Tolmie (**Liberal-Conservative,** *Victoria City, B.C.*) said that these men adopted the most ingenious methods of evading the law and carrying on this traffic. He could not understand any argument which proposed to give any quarter to a trafficker in narcotics, particularly to one who supplied narcotics to a minor.

Mr. McQuarrie declared tha these people would pay a fine without any hesitation; they could afford to do so because there was a very large profit made in this traffic. There were men who would take imprisonment with a smile on their face. But when a man was faced with a sentence that would subject him to whipping he had seen the most hardened criminals cringe, and it was the greatest deterrent that could possibly be placed in the Criminal Code.

The Minister of Health said that the traffic was very large in Montreal. He pointed out that in the United States the laws provided for very severe penalties in fines and imprisonment, and also for the deportation of aliens, but, as far as whipping was concerned, they did not inflict it.

The Solicitor-General (**Hon. D. D. McKenzie**) hoped

that they would be able to carry out criminal laws to the extreme, without using the lash.

Mr. A. W. Neill (**National Progressive,** *Comox-Alberni, B.C.*) said that the situation in British Columbia fully justified the amendment.

Mr. Ladner's amendment was agreed to.

The Minister of Health moved two amendments. The first had reference to the appeal that could be taken under the present law from a judgment of the inferior court to the higher court (*vide supra,* Section 5). He was informed by the Minister of Justice that those Sections referred only to appeals from decisions of lower courts in criminal cases.

The Hon. J. B. M. Baxter (**Liberal-Conservative,** *St. John City & Counties of St. John & Albert, N.B.*) said that he had no sympathy with merely technical appeals; and yet the right to appeal was, he thought, inherent in the administration of justice as they knew it. It had always been the boast of their jurisprudence that the meanest criminal had the right to be heard and the right to the punctual observance of all the forms of law.

The Minister of Health stated that appeal in most cases was taken in order to gain time and find the money wherewith to pay the fine and escape imprisonment. The principle was not a new one, at least so far as the Province of Quebec was concerned, where there was no appeal in the case of conviction for keeping a disorderly house.

Mr. W. F. Carroll (**Liberal,** *Cape Breton, S., & Richmond, N.B.*) said that they had the same thing in liquor legislation; in their Province a man who was convicted of an offence against the Prohibition Act might not take an appeal. It looked as if they were putting the machinery of the law in Canada into the hands of magistrates, who very often misconducted trials.

After further discussion Dr. Béland's amendment was agreed to.

The Minister then moved the insertion of the clause (Section 6) dealing with deportation.

Mr. Baxter was afraid that some of these people might not be aliens, and yet they might be persons who had come into Canada from somewhere else, in fact be what they called Hong Kong British subjects. He would very much like to see the provision wide enough to bundle them out of the country too, and treat them just as aliens. He would be very glad if the Minister would consider extending this provision to make it apply to anyone not a native of Canada.

Dr. Béland's amendment was agreed to, and the Bill was read the third time and passed.

IN THE SENATE.

On 22nd June, 1922, in the course of the consideration of the Bill in Committee in the Senate,

Senator the Hon. W. Proudfoot (*Ont.*) pointed out that in Section 6 (Convicted aliens subject to deportation) a man might be convicted of an offence for which even the Immigration Department would not think it fair to deport him. He thought it would be very much better to leave some discretion to the trial judge. He moved to add at the end of Section 6 the words: "unless the Court before whom he was tried shall otherwise order." After discussion, this amendment was agreed to.

TEMPERANCE ACT AMENDMENT BILL.

(Importation of Intoxicating Liquor.)

This Act, which was assented to on 27th June, 1922, amends the Canada Temperance Act so as to facilitate the prohibition of the export of intoxicating liquors from Provinces; the amendment to Part V. of the Act, mainly in the interests of British Columbia and Quebec, was struck out by a Senate Amendment.

Part IV.: Importation of Intoxicating Liquor from Provinces.

The Bill, as passed by the House of Commons, provides, *inter alia*, that upon the receipt of an Order in Council, passed by the Lieutenant-Governor in Council of any Province in which the importation of intoxicating liquor is prohibited, requesting that the keeping of intoxicating liquor in such Province for export, and its exportation therefrom by persons other than brewers and distillers duly licensed by the Government of Canada, be forbidden, the Governor in Council may, by Order in Council, declare that such prohibition shall come into force in such Province on a day to be named in such Order. Upon such prohibition coming into force: (A) no person other than a brewer or distiller licensed by the Government of Canada shall have in his possession or control intoxicating liquor for sale in or exportation out of such Province, nor shall he export it out of the Province; (B) the carriage or transportation through such Province of intoxicating liquor which may lawfully be exported shall only be by means of a common carrier by water or railway, excepting for delivery direct to and from such common carrier, and during the time any intoxicating liquor is being so transported, no person shall open or break open any package or vessel containing it, or drink or allow any of the liquor to be drunk. Provision is also made for warrants to search any premises, including Government railways, etc., where there is reasonable cause to suspect intoxicating liquor is or has been dealt with contrary to the Provisions of the Act.

Part V.: Importation of Intoxicating Liquors in Certain Cases.

The Act further prohibits the importation of intoxicating liquor into any Province in which the prohibitions of this sub-section are in force. This prohibition, however, does not apply to (A) intoxicating liquor purchased by or consigned to His Majesty or the Executive Government of the Province; or any Governmental Agency which, by the laws of the Province, is vested with the right of selling intoxicating liquors; (B) its carriage into and through a Province by means only of a common carrier by water or railway, if the package containing it is not opened; (C) its importation into a Province by a person carrying on the business of exporting intoxicating liquor from the Province, where the intoxicating liquor is imported solely for the purpose of his export business, and is kept in a liquor warehouse which conforms to the requirements of the law, and when sold is actually exported from the Province. The burden of proving the right to import, etc., intoxicating liquor shall be on the person accused.

DEBATE IN HOUSE OF COMMONS.

On 9th June, in introducing the Bill,

The Solicitor-General (Hon. D. D. McKenzie) explained that in British Columbia they had to some extent control of the sale of intoxicating liquors, and under the proposed legislation any liquors imported into that Province must be imported by the local Government and nobody else, with the possible exception of liquors imported by parties who were licensed to take them in for purposes of export. In Quebec the business was handled by a Commission appointed by the local Government. This would bring the Commission under the law, as well as the Government of British Columbia. There were certain sections of the Doherty Act which the temperance people of New Brunswick, Ontario, and Nova Scotia thought should be made a part of Part IV. of the Canadian Temperance Act, and this the Bill proposed to do.

On 15th June,

The Solicitor-General said that the Act could not come into force in any Province until the local Government of the particular Province in which it was asked for passed an Order in Council bringing it into force. All that Parliament was doing was passing a law and making it optional for any Province to put it in force. Practically nothing had been done in the House in regard to intoxicating liquor for a number of years unless it was approved by the Province. He was satisfied that for the last year and a half no person, either in Nova Scotia, New Brunswick, Ontario, Saskatchewan or Alberta could import any intoxicating liquor legally, nor could they manufacture it legally.

The Minister of Agriculture (Hon. W. R. Motherwell) stated that in 1917 the Province of Saskatchewan passed an Act—and so did the Province of Alberta—attempting to get rid of the export houses and failed, because the Act was declared by the Court *ultra vires*. They wanted to be dry, and they had not been dry largely because of the existence of those export houses. In order to carry out the will of the people, in so far as Provincial law was ineffectual for the purpose, it was proposed to pass this supplementary legislation. British Columbia wanted to handle wet goods and they were facilitating the people there in carrying out their wishes. He suggested that those houses should be given three months to get rid of their liquor.

Mr. A. J. Lewis (**National Progressive**, *Swift Current, Sask.*) was in favour of the Bill being passed without amendment, leaving it to the Provincial authorities who knew the whole situation to grant any extension of time that might be necessary to enable the owners to get rid of this stuff which was destroying the moral fibre of their life.

Mr. John Millar (**National Progressive**, *Qu'Appelle, Sask.*) declared that if hon. Members had an opportunity of becoming acquainted with the methods pursued by these liquor importers they would not spend five minutes sympathising with them. They were not exporting to Europe, but they were supplying bootleggers in the Province and conveying the liquor across the International Boundary line into the United States.

The Hon. Sir Henry Drayton (**Liberal-Conservative**, *York, W. Riding, Ont.*) said that this legislation conformed to the policy of the late Government, which was to give effect to the wishes of the different communities which had adopted laws dealing with this liquor question.

Mr. W. G. Mitchell (**Liberal**, *St. Antoine, Que.*) pointed out that under the old Canada Temperance Act, any Province or County could, by a vote, put that Act into force. Under the old Act, however, importation was allowed into all the Provinces, notwithstanding the fact that the Canada Temperance Act was in force. Subsequently the Doherty Act was passed, which was an endeavour to extend to the Provinces the right to prohibit importation. This legislation was an endeavour to go a step further and to give to the Provinces exactly what they wanted.

After further discussion, the Bill was read a third time and passed.

DEBATE IN THE SENATE.

On 20th June, on the Second Reading,

The Leader of the Senate and Minister without Portfolio (**Hon. Raoul Dandurand**) explained that the second part of the Bill had for its object control by the Provinces which had taken the monopoly of the liquor trade. Liquor could be exported, for instance, from Saskatchewan to British Columbia and Quebec.

Senator the Hon. Sir James Lougheed (**Leader of the Opposition**) said that the Province of British Columbia apparently asked the Government to exercise a most arbitrary power, one that did violence to a reasonable construction of the British North America Act with regard to the exercise of their right respecting trade and commerce, namely, the power of delegating to the Province a right which should be exercised by the Government. Previous to the War, in legislation touching the liquor question, the right of importation was a right exercisable by the Government of Canada alone.

Senator the Hon. G. W. Fowler (*N.B.*) held that the Federal Government could not delegate its powers to the Provinces. This Act was opposed to the interests of temperance. It was proposed in order that those Provinces might have not only the sole right to sell, but also the sole right to adulterate, the sole right to dispose of any sort of stuff they made, so that their profits might be greater.

Senator the Hon. G. Lynch-Staunton (*Ont.*) declared that this legislation had no temperance basis, it had no moral basis at all, but was simply an arbitrary exercise of power to deprive people of their acknowledged right to buy anything they chose.

Senator the Right Hon. Sir George Foster (*Ont.*), after tracing the history of temperance measures, said in respect to the first part of the present Act, that if they had taken the first step of local option in small areas, if they had taken the second step of local option in large areas, and if they had taken the third step and aided these areas by bringing as to importation the force of the Dominion Government to bear in their aid, what reason was there that they should not take the final step, and give them the opportunity of the best chances that they possibly could have for enforcing the law? In that respect (Part IV.) he was in favour of the legislation. The second part of the Act had a very different aspect. They had the Province of Quebec and the Province of British Columbia which had not passed prohibitory laws, and which sought to carry on the liquor business through control, going from control of a more modified form in Quebec to a control which became an absolute Government monopoly in British Columbia. He was afraid they were putting it into the hands of a Government, and consequently a party, to debauch the public conscience, and to make the case that it gave to the taxpayer an excuse for allowing the system to go on from year to year.

Amendments.

In Committee, on 23rd June, at the suggestion of Senator Pardee (*Ont.*), **Senator Dandurand** moved an amendment to the effect that the Order in Council declarating prohibition (Part IV.) should not be made prior to 1st October, 1922. This amendment was agreed to.

On 24th June.

Senator the Hon. G. H. Barnard (*B.C.*) moved that Section 3 (*i.e.*, Part V.) be struck out. The amendment was agreed to by 37 to 31 votes.

On 27th June, a conference was held between representatives of the House of Commons and the Senate to consider the Bill. No agreement was reached, and the Prime Minister (the Right Hon. W. L. Mackenzie King), in order not to lose the benefit of the legislation contained in the amendments to Part IV. by dropping the Bill, moved that the Senate amendments should be agreed to.

CRIMINAL CODE AMENDMENT ACT.

This Act, dealing with sexual offences, etc., was passed by the House of Commons on 14th June, 1922. Three important clauses, similar to Sections 1, 5 and 7 of the Criminal Code Amendment Act of 1921, which were passed by the House of Commons on 26th May, 1921, and subsequently struck out by the Senate, again failed to pass the Senate. (*Vide* JOURNAL, Vol. III., No. 1, p. 86.)

CANADIAN NATIONAL RAILWAYS.

On 11th April the Minister of Railways and Canals presented the Annual Statement to the House of Commons on the operations of the Government railways.

DEBATE IN HOUSE OF COMMONS.

The Minister of Railways and Canals (Hon. W. C. Kennedy) said that, although a year of depression in trade, with decreased tonnage and less travel, and with reduced rates when contrasted with the previous year, the nationally-owned roads were able, largely owing to drastic curtailment of expenditures, to make an improved showing over 1920. The outstanding feature of 1921 operation was the improvement of the position of the Canadian National-Grand Trunk combination. These roads comprised approximately 52 per cent. of the railway mileage of Canada, and in 1920 they did 52·21 per cent. of the railway business of the country as reflected in the gross earnings of the trans-Continental lines.

Canadian National railways.

The National system was said to be the only trans-Continental system in America whose earnings in 1921 from the increased freight and passenger rates established in September, 1920, were not entirely offset by the loss in tonnage and passengers. The year saw a big slump in railway traffic following the decline in trade which set in during the closing months of 1920. There was a decline in the movement of all commodities with the exception of wheat. The greatly improved showing of the Grand Trunk Pacific was attributed to the fact that for a full year it had been operated as an integral part of the Canadian National System, and was one of the results of co-ordinated operation of those lines under one management. The total advances to the Canadian Northern Railway Company and the Grand Trunk Pacific Railway Company to 31st December, 1921, were respectively $251,088,248 and $82,480,303. Wages and fuel still remained the principal charges on railway revenues. At the present time negotiations were under way looking to a modification of some of the working conditions that the railways felt to be difficult of application, resulting in excessive wages in some classes and the placing of expenses on the railways which were claimed to be unduly burdensome. While the trend in prices of materials and supplies was generally downward, the movement was slow, and the prices continued greatly in excess of pre-War figures. No work was done on eastern lines in the construction of new branches during 1921. All such work during the year was confined to Western lines. There was in the West alone construction projected which would entail an expenditure of $25,000,000 to bring to completion. In view of the financial condition of the country and the impending general reorganisation of National Railway management, it was felt to be better to conhne construction and betterments for the present to the minimum and leave to the new Board to advise as to what was essential in the matter of extensions.

Grand Trunk Railway system.

The Minister pointed out that there was a net loss for the year 1921 of $15,672,299 as against a net loss for 1920 of $6,527,243. The decision of the United States Labour Board, known as the 12½ per cent. decrease, produced to 31st December, 1921, on Grand Trunk Canadian lines a saving of $3,035,112.

Estimates.

The amount to be voted on account of the railways for the fiscal year ending 31st March, 1923, as provided for in the Estimates, was $97,220,000 compared with $179,065,760 last Session.

Freight rates.

A number of conferences had been held, but, because of the uncertainty of the entire rate situation, the executive of the various railways felt that it was inadvisable, at this time, to reduce rates on basic commodities. He proposed, at an early date, to ask the House to appoint a special and representative committee to examine into the question of rates.

Reorganisation.

The first step in the reorganisation of the railways would be the establishment of a single representative Board of Directors for the unified control and co-ordinated operation of the Government-owned Lines, now directed and controlled by two separate Boards and two different managements. This Board would be thoroughly representative and would include in its number the most competent railway men. It was intended to turn over to this Board properties in which the public and the Government had invested $1,582,500,000, and this did not take into consideration cash subsidies amounting to $41,000,000, nor land grants. What would be aimed at would be centralisation of general direction and control and decentralisation in matters of local detail.

Hon. J. A. Stewart (**Liberal-Conservative,** *Lanark, Ont.*) said that the policy of the late Government was to try out, perhaps for the first time in the history of railway economics, Government ownership with independent control of management. The policy adopted at that time provided for the complete removal of the management of the national-owned railways from political control. That condition prevailed down to 1919, when the arrangements for taking over the Grand Trunk were completed, and in order to continue the policy that had been adopted in 1917 the Canadian National Railway Act of 1919 was passed. That Act provided for a new Board which would take over the combined systems. There must be a ruthless co-ordination of these systems if they were to see daylight through their railway problem.

The Solicitor-General (**Hon. D. D. McKenzie**) declared that if the road had not been a success during ten years of administration by hon. gentlemen opposite, that was no fault of theirs (the Liberal Government). They had promised to give Government ownership a fair trial, and that they were bound to do. He was not in favour of Government ownership, because he had always believed that they could not get the same results from Government ownership and management that they got under private ownership and enterprise. He condemned the idea of linking up their railways with the railway systems of the United States and with United States ports, as was done by the Leader of the Opposition.

The Right Hon. Arthur Meighen (**Leader of the Opposition**) thought that the statement presented of the operations in 1921 before the change of Government would strengthen the hands of those who had consistently believed that they could, if they followed the right lines such as had been pursued, make these roads a success. In comparison with the record of Government operation in other countries, it established the system of management which the late Government put in as the best yet devised for the operation of Government Lines. Although there was still a very substantial deficit in operation and fixed charges, a deficit of some 56 millions, they could put the result alongside of corresponding results by privately-owned systems in other countries, and they would find that result reflect credit upon operations in Canada, a favourable result as compared with the results in the United States for the same period.

CANADIAN WHEAT BOARD ACT.*

This Act, which was assented to on 27th July, 1922, provides for the appointment of a wheat Board consisting of not more than ten members.

The Chairman of the Board, nominated by the Governor in Council, is the chief executive officer and is assisted by an Assistant Chairman (Sect. 2). The Chairman and Assistant Chairman are paid such salaries as the Governor in Council may direct; the other members receive allowances for days actually engaged, also travelling and living expenses while in the business of the Board, but otherwise no remuneration (Sect. 3). The Board, which is a corporation, may appoint an Executive Committee of not less than three of its members, including the Chairman, and may assign to it any duties competent to the Board (Sects. 4 and 5).

The Board is empowered throughout Canada to receive and take delivery of wheat for marketing; to buy and sell, store, transport and market wheat, and to sell any quantity of wheat it may possess in excess of domestic requirements to purchasers Overseas or in foreign countries (Sect. 6). Sales of wheat to Canadian millers must be on the same basis as to foreign millers, provided such wheat is to be milled in Canada (Sect. 7). The Board may receive advances of money from any Province, or bank, corporation or individual on terms approved by the Governor-General (Sect. 9). The Board shall have capacity to exercise powers in respect to the marketing of wheat conferred upon it by any Province (Sect. 10). The Board may make advances to producers and others delivering wheat according to approved schedules, and may issue to such person certificates of participation in the proceeds (Sect. 11). Deliveries of wheat may be taken through agents, grain companies or organisations at such points in Canada as the Board may direct (Sect. 12), and disbursements for the expenses of the Board are deducted from the proceeds of the season's operations (Sect. 13). The Board may make regulations, including the appointment of representatives in Canada and abroad, for carrying out the objects of the Act, and must use its best endeavours to dispose of its wheat for the best price obtainable (Sects. 14 and 15). The Government of Canada is not responsible for deficits. Should a surplus occur, it is to be divided among the concurring Provinces on a *pro rata* basis (Sect. 16). The Board is empowered to prohibit or impose conditions upon the export of wheat from any Province (Sect. 20).

* *Vide* also p. 758.

AUSTRALIA.

Commonwealth Parliament.

The following is the summary of the proceedings of the Second Session of the Eighth Parliament, which commenced on 28th June, 1922, and closed 14th October, 1922. The proceedings of the concluding stages of the Session will be summarised in the next issue of the JOURNAL.*

GOVERNOR-GENERAL'S SPEECH.

(Address in Reply: Washington Conference: New Guinea Mandate: Migration: German Trade, etc.)

His Excellency the Governor-General (**the Right Hon. Lord Forster**) opened the Second Session of the Eighth Parliament on 28th June, 1922. The following is a summary of His Excellency's Speech.

Washington Conference.

Universal satisfaction was felt at the successful outcome of the Washington Conference, which had been attended by Senator the Right Hon. G. F. Pearce on behalf of the Commonwealth. International agreements had been reached of the greatest importance to the peace of the world, especially to those countries whose shores were washed by the Pacific Ocean. The six Treaties signed at the Conference, and since ratified by the United States of America, namely, the Quadruple Treaty relating to the Pacific, the Supplement to the Quadruple Treaty, the Naval Treaty and the Chinese Customs Treaty, would be submitted for approval. Such legislation as was needed to enable the Commonwealth to carry out its obligations under the Treaties would be introduced.

Navy and Army reductions; etc.

In view of the results attained at the Washington Conference, which, his advisers believed, guaranteed peace in the Pacific for some time to come, it was proposed to reduce the establishment of the Navy and Army, and to postpone the expansion of the Air Force. The reduction in the establishment of the Defence Forces would necessitate the compulsory retirement of a large number of officers and men, and also of the civil staff. A Bill would be introduced to provide compensation for those persons who were compulsorily retired.

* Cable advices state that Parliament will be dissolved on 6th November, and that the General Elections will be held on 16th December.

Migration.

In view of its importance to the Commonwealth, the subject of migration had been receiving the close attention of Ministers. Large schemes were being negotiated with the Government of the United Kingdom and the Governments of several of the States in accordance with the Empire Settlement Act. An agreement making provision for the passages of migrants under the Act had been made between the British and Commonwealth Governments, and, in pursuance of the agreement made for joint co-operation between the Commonwealth and the States, approval had recently been given to measures for the assistance of the immigration of boys, and of British ex-military officers from India.

New Guinea Mandate.

Steps had been taken to provide the necessary machinery for the administration of the Mandated Territory. A number of ordinances had been framed enacting laws for its good government. Provisions had been made for the development of the Territory, and, throughout, the greatest care had been taken to secure the protection of the natives and their interests, and to comply in every respect with the terms of the Mandate.

Unification of railway gauges.

The report made by the Commissioners appointed by the Commonwealth and State Governments on the subject of the unification of the railway gauges presented a definite and practical scheme for the solution of a problem of vital importance. Each day of delay intensified the evils resulting from the breaks of gauge and added to the ultimate cost of the carrying out of a work which must be accomplished. The Government proposed to press on with this question and to take all possible steps so that the scheme outlined by the independent experts might be proceeded with.

Civil aviation.

The Government had taken steps towards linking up the more remote parts of the Commonwealth with the centres of population by subsidising civil aviation companies formed to provide regular and speedy services. Four contracts* had been let for the conveyance of passengers, mails and parcels. The service between Geraldton and Derby had now been in continuous and successful operation for five months. Aeroplanes had been ordered for the other services, and construction works were well advanced in connection with the

---

* (A) Between Geraldton and Derby in West Australia (1,195 miles), subsidy, £25,000 ; (B) Brisbane and Sydney (550 miles), subsidy, £11,500 ; (C) Sydney and Adelaide (760 miles), subsidy, £17,500 ; (D) Charleville and Cloncurry, both in Queensland (575 miles), subsidy, £12,000 ; the period in each case covered by the subsidy being twelve months.

aerodromes on the routes to be traversed. The Government proposed to extend this modern method of communication, being convinced of its inestimable value.

Extension of Federal powers.

The experience of the War, the general expansion of internal trade and commerce, the growth of the population, and the development of the Continent, had emphasised the need for an early amendment of the Constitution to enable Parliament to cope more adequately with the national problems of Australia. A series of measures would be introduced to provide for an extension of Federal powers, having due regard to the proper functions of the States.

Northern Territory.

It was proposed to introduce a Bill to give representation in the Commonwealth Parliament to residents of the Northern Territory. Proposals for the development and settlement of the Territory would also be submitted.

Federal capital.

The works in connection with the construction of Canberra were in progress in accordance with the reports of the Advisory Committee. Further proposals would be submitted to secure the more rapid development and settlement of the Federal Capital and Territory.

Legislation.

Bills would be submitted for (A) placing the Commonwealth Government Line of Steamers under independent and non-political control and management, (B) the re-organisation of the Commonwealth Public Service, (C) a superannuation scheme for the Public Service based on a just contributory system.

Measures would also be introduced relating to Naval and Air Defence, Lands Acquisition, Bankruptcy, Patents, Trade-marks, Service and Execution of Process, Crimes, Declarations, Navigation, Customs, Beer Excise, and Nationality.

DEBATE IN HOUSE OF REPRESENTATIVES.

Trade with Germany.

On 29th June,

Mr. D. S. Jackson (Nationalist, *Bass, Tas.*), in moving the Address-in-Reply, said that German trade was a matter which affected Australia very vitally. The Customs Tariff (Industries Preservation) Act, 1921,* would certainly go a

* For summary of this Act *vide* Vol. II., No. 4, p. 893, and Vol. III., No. 1, p. 138.

long way towards helping the Australian manufacturer to combat German trade, and the Government had stated definitely that if the Australian trader was not already afforded sufficient protection they would certainly see that it was given to him. For the past seven or eight years they had managed to get along with practically no importations from Germany. Their great aim should be to make their great continent as self-contained as possible, but they could not do that unless they helped its industries to grow.

Migration.

On 5th July,

Mr. Matthew Charlton (Leader of the Opposition) said that to his mind there was no justification for the expenditure of large sums of money on the encouragement of immigration until some proper scheme of land settlement had been devised. Australia needed more population ; but the first duty of its legislators was to provide for the employment and settlement of its own people. To-day in the various States there were thousands of persons who for years had been trying in vain to obtain land on which to settle. The duty of the Commonwealth and State Governments was to see that land was made available, first, for the people already in Australia, and, afterwards, for immigrants. If necessary, legislative action should be taken to throw open the large estates which were now not being put to the best use.

Old Age Pensions.

He was surprised that there was no intimation that the Government had determined to liberalise the invalid and old-age pension system. He did not know how the aged and infirm had contrived to carry on during the last six or seven years, in view of the high cost of living. Some years ago invalid and old-age pensions had been increased from 10s. to 15s. per week* ; but nothing had been done to help pensioners since prices first began to rise.

As the result of the alterations to be made in their defence system, largely as an outcome of the Washington Conference, the Government would have at their disposal this year £1,750,000 more than they had during the last financial year. If they cut down the Defence expenditure, as proposed, they would be to that extent better off. That being so, what was there to prevent the invalid and old-age pensions being increased by 5s. a week ? On 1st July there were 105,172 old-age pensioners and 38,941 invalid pensioners. An increase of 5s. per week would involve an additional expenditure of £1,873,476. Such people should at least be given sufficient

---

* *Vide* Vol. I., No. 2, p. 355, and Vol. II., No. 2, p. 383.

to keep the wolf away from the door. He therefore moved that words be added to the proposed Address regretting that no provision had been made to liberalise these pensions.

Migration: reply to criticism.

On 6th July,

The Prime Minister (the Right Hon. W. M. Hughes), in reply to the criticism by the Leader of the Opposition, said that the foundation of the immigration policy of the Commonwealth Government was the resolution agreed to at the Premiers' Conference in 1920, which gave the Commonwealth charge of immigration affairs overseas, and of the transport of immigrants from overseas to Australia, and left to the States the responsibility of dealing with immigrants when they reached their shores and the right to determine the number and class of immigrants to be admitted into each State. If fewer immigrants were arriving than they should like, it was solely the States that were to blame, unless it could be shown that the transport facilities provided by the Commonwealth were insufficient. But that was not alleged.

Immigration as a practical policy must be considered under three or four heads. The Commonwealth was co-operating with the States in every one of these. The lines of its co-operation were very definite, and the co-operation was as complete as the circumstances permitted. The Commonwealth had a very clear and practicable policy, which it had endeavoured, and was still endeavouring, to carry out.

First of all there were concrete schemes, with which he would deal in detail later. Then there was the scheme of nominated immigrants, under which persons now resident in Australia nominated their friends in Britain or elsewhere. These were brought to Australia by assisted passages. This was an excellent form of immigration, if it were on a wide scale, because the immigrants had friends to go to, and these gave them counsel and aid, and set their feet upon the right road. Assisted passages were granted under various minor schemes. For example, the Commonwealth Government were recruiting agricultural trainees, known as "Dreadnought" boys, at the rate of sixty a month, for the State of New South Wales. In connection with the Fairbridge Farm School, in Western Australia, the Commonwealth Government had recently decided to co-operate with the Western Australian Government by providing portion of the maintenance cost of the school.

About 2,000 British officers of the Indian Army would shortly be retired owing to the intended reduction of the Army establishment in India. These officers were young men in the prime of life, and they would each receive as compensation a sum of between £1,000 and £1,500. Victoria had sent a representative to India. New South Wales had definitely offered to set aside 300 irrigated farms for these officers.

These constituted what might be termed subsidiary schemes of their immigration policy. There were the nominated immigrants, who were given assisted passages, and those other schemes, such as Dr. Barnardo Homes boys, the "Dreadnought" boys, and the Fairbridge Farm. Then they had the scheme of the South Australian Government, who were bringing out 6,000 boys, with a view to placing them with farmers and training them for the work of land settlement. In all these schemes the Commonwealth was co-operating with the State Governments.

Now he came to the greater schemes which aimed at developing the great resources of Australia by bringing out large numbers of immigrants from Britain and settling them on Crown lands. With Western Australia a draft agreement had been drawn up. Broadly speaking, the agreement was one for settlement in which the States and the Commonwealth and, since the passage of the Empire Settlement Act, the United Kingdom were to co-operate in bringing people to Australia and settling them on the land. Land settlement was a *sine qua non* of the Commonwealth immigration policy. He was also in negotiation with the Governments of New South Wales and Victoria. The High Commissioner (the Rt. Hon. Sir Joseph Cook) had recently signed an agreement with the British Government relating to providing portion of the passage money for approved immigrants. Under this agreement the British Government bore half the cost. The liability of both parties was limited in the agreement.

The rate at which immigrants were coming in this year showed a great improvement over last year. The total number of assisted immigrants who arrived during 1921 was 14,677; while the number this year, if the present monthly average were maintained, would be 24,652. This, of course, was still very far from satisfactory, but they anticipated that when the Western Australian scheme was in full operation the number would be doubled. And he did not hesitate to say that only in this way could Australia be developed, and they should be able to obtain results from the co-operation of the British Government and State Governments with the Commonwealth, which would, he hoped, mark a turning point in Australia's career, and indicate to the world their settled determination to show themselves worthy of the inheritance of a continent.

The responsibility of dealing with unemployment in the various parts of the Commonwealth belonged to the States, and not to the Commonwealth Government.

Mr. Charlton's proposed amendment was subsequently defeated by 36 votes to 17.

Two other motions of amendment, one against the action of the Government to dispose of the Commonwealth Government Cloth Factory at Geelong; and the other in connection with Clause 12 of the agreement between the Amalgamated Wireless, Limited, and the Commonwealth, having been negatived, the Address-in-Reply was agreed to by the House of Representatives on 20th July. It was passed by the Senate on the same date.

WASHINGTON CONFERENCE TREATIES.

(Parliamentary approval: Enabling Bill; Limitation of armaments; Submarines and poison gas; Naval defence; Empire Relations; League of Nations.)

On 27th July, 1922, Senator Pearce, who represented Australia at the Washington Conference,* moved the approval of the Treaty between the United States of America, the British Empire, France and Japan relating to their insular Possessions and insular Dominions in the Pacific Ocean, signed at Washington on 13th December, 1921, the declaration signed on that date accompanying that Treaty, and the Treaty between those Powers supplementary to that Treaty signed at Washington on 6th February, 1922. (*Vide* p. 836.)

The Prime Minister moved the approval of the Treaties in the House of Representatives on 26th July.

DEBATE IN HOUSE OF REPRESENTATIVES.

On 26th July,

The Prime Minister (the Right Hon. W. M. Hughes) moved the approval of the Treaties. He said that the position of Australia under the Quadruple Treaty was that it had cleared away all those difficulties that made for war in the Pacific; it had, so far as human effort could achieve such things, brought about peace where there had been war, and it had given them for, at any rate, ten years, an assurance of peace. If they required assurance to be doubly sure, if they were not satisfied with that, as, indeed, some of them might not be, then there was only one sure and certain defence for Australia, and that lay in a virile and sufficiently numerous population. Their present safeguard lay wholly where it had always been —in the fact that they were a partner in the British Empire. That was the beginning and end of their safety.

* For debate as to the representation of Australia at the Conference, *vide* JOURNAL, Vol. III., No. 1, p. 104.

Naval Armament Treaty.

Turning to the Naval Armament Treaty, Mr. Hughes said it was one that profoundly affected the destinies of mankind. It was, perhaps, the most hopeful sign that the world had seen that man had learned something from the Great War. Nothing had come from the high-flown and ambitious projects of The Hague Tribunal, or from any project which had preceded it, nor had the League of Nations itself been able to take any definite step towards disarmament. The Treaty marked the definite abandonment by Great Britain of the two-Power standard. It would not be out of place for him to remind Members what that meant, and to pay some tribute to Great Britain for her great sacrifice in the cause of the peace of the world. Their Empire had been built up upon sea-power. Its splendid history rested upon that solid and enduring foundation. Other nations of the world, and particularly the United States of America, were continental nations. Their seaboard might be attacked, but the foundations of their temple could not be undermined by attacks from the sea, whereas to their Empire, scattered as it was over the four quarters of the earth, sea-power was essential to its very existence. This being so, they might well take legitimate pride in the thought that Great Britain, being confronted with this proposal at the Washington Conference, accepted it not only without demur, but had the proud satisfaction that her Delegates zealously strove to widen its scope. It was to the eternal credit of the Representatives of the British Empire that they had sought to apply the principle to submarines. Unhappily, for the welfare of mankind, this had been found to be impossible, owing to the attitude taken up by certain Powers.

The effect of this Treaty was to give an assurance of peace to a world weary and sick of war. It was true that it did not go so far as some of them would like, but it was a step farther than had ever been taken before in the history of mankind. Its application was limited to capital ships—that was to say, battleships of the first and second class. As to all other vessels, light cruisers and the like, the Treaty was silent; but as, in the opinion of those best qualified to judge, naval battles were now, as ever, decided by capital ships, it gave to the world an assurance of peace. It was a Treaty full of hope to the peoples of the world. It fixed the ratio amongst the various naval nations, and put an end to naval rivalry, so far as this could be effected by any human instrument.

Submarines and poison gases.

In what was known as the Submarine and Poison Gases Treaty there were imposed upon submarines prohibitions which revolutionised their concepts of submarine warfare. They remembered the *Lusitania* and those other vessels whose number was legion. They remembered the women and children who had been sent unwarned and unprepared to the bottom of the ocean. The day of such things was gone, so far as this agreement between the great naval nations could banish it, for ever. Submarines were now prevented from attacking a merchant vessel in time of war until there had been an inspection and search to ascertain the character of the vessel, and if it were found, after inspection and search, that the ship came within the rules of warfare which rendered it liable to destruction, it could not be destroyed until all the passengers and crew had been placed in a position of absolute safety. If the Washington Conference had done nothing but this they should hail it with glad satisfaction.

Fortifications and naval bases in Pacific.

The Treaty provided also for the maintenance of the *status quo* of fortifications and naval bases in the Pacific. It put a period to that growing menace where naval bases were gradually being pushed out farther and farther, converging on each other, and upon a point of which Australia was the very apex. These limitations did not apply to the mainland of Japan nor to Australia nor New Zealand. The Treaty left them free to make what preparations they liked in their own defence, but prevented them from pushing, under any pretext at all, into that wide expanse of the Pacific outside the Commonwealth and its unmandated Territories, in which every advance they made was an encroachment upon the rights and liberties of others. What it did to Australia it did to all others. It respected the *status quo* and made provision for its maintenance.

Rules of war.

The Treaty stated clearly the rules of civilised war. It did more than any other instrument which had emanated from the brain and hand of man to prevent war; but if war took place, then the rules under which it should be waged were laid down. How great an advance this was upon the conditions under which war had been waged by the Central Powers would be appreciated on a perusal of the Treaty. It was a veritable milestone in human progress, a beacon light in a dark place, over-illuminating a sky covered with gloomy and menacing clouds. If the Treaty fell somewhat short of those ideals which they all cherished, the fault lay not upon the British Empire nor upon its Representatives.

China.

The Far-Eastern Treaty represented an earnest effort to assist China to recover from her present state of disintegration and weakness. It guaranteed the territorial integrity of China. This was a noble achievement. It was the first outward and visible sign of the power of world-opinion. The Treaty was of vital importance to Australia ; the problems of the Pacific were intimately bound up with China and with the differences between her and Japan. These were now settled. The terms of settlement had not been forced upon either party by the sword, but had been mutually accepted as the outcome of frank and open discussion.

The Customs Tariff Treaty was complementary to the Far-Eastern Treaty. It abolished the internal Tariffs of China, and would give her vastly increased Customs revenue.

Results of Conference.

In conclusion, Mr. Hughes said that the Washington Conference had achieved great things. Its decisions were very material to Australia. They guaranteed peace in the Pacific, as far as any effort of man could guarantee it. They might rely on the moral support of the signatories, but there was no force behind the Treaties, and they were not in the nature of an alliance. They did not guarantee to Australia material support if she were attacked. They insured merely moral support and the public opinion of the contracting countries. So far as material support was concerned, they were as dependent as ever on the Navy of the British Empire. They welcomed the Treaties, and would loyally abide by them. They rejoiced at the success of the Washington Conference. It had borne fruit abundantly and had achieved much more than even its most ardent advocates had believed possible.

The Conference had brought them great material benefits. It had enabled them to achieve immediate and substantial savings. Were it not for the Treaties they would now be contemplating additional naval expenditure. They must hope that all the world would follow the good example set by the Treaties, and that, although the Washington Conference had stopped short, and had not attempted to limit war in the air, or war upon land, it had taken a substantial step forward. They hoped that that example would not be lost upon civilisation, and that they might yet have an opportunity of ratifying Treaties which would be complementary to these, and which would give greater assurance of lasting peace to them and to the whole world.

On 2nd August,

Mr. M. Charlton (Leader of the Opposition) said that the proposals which had emanated from the Washington Conference would, he felt sure, meet with the approval of all Members, because, first of all, they provided for such a limitation of naval armaments as would considerably lessen the load of taxation carried by the Commonwealth, and also by other nations.

Plea for League of Nations.

Many people said that they could not end war, that wars were capitalistic enterprises and so forth, and that the only method of procedure was on the lines of the League of Nations Covenant. The influence of every public man should be directed to galvanising the League of Nations into life. The Prime Minister had told them that the Washington Conference had accomplished more than the League of Nations. But that was not to say that the League of Nations could not accomplish more than the Washington Conference. Unless they used every ounce of influence they had in the direction of disarmament, they could not hope to achieve much ; and even if they could not bring about total disarmament, they might be able greatly to limit the cost of defence. These were the directions in which he thought they ought to move. If the President and the people of the United States of America could see their way to link up with the other powerful nations in the League, some great results might be seen. A union of the four nations: America, Great Britain, Japan and France would not, of itself, prevent future wars; all nations must be linked up. Some good had already been done, and it had relieved them considerably. They could be further relieved if they used all their influence in the direction of making the League of Nations what it ought to be—a real entity.

Naval defence of the Empire.

Dr. Earle Page (Leader of the Country Party) said the motion which placed the Treaties before them for ratification indicated to him the permanency of the change in the internal relations in the British Commonwealth of Nations. That change had come for good or ill, and it seemed to him that it might be for ill. If it were necessary to have ratification of all Treaties in every independent Dominion, they might create a force which might ultimately lead to disruption within the Empire. There were some who thought that the sense of responsibility was merely a new toy ; but they were now making themselves responsible for Treaties, and that of itself showed their willingness to bear their share of the burden of defence ; and that they must cease henceforth to " sponge," as it seemed to him they were now doing to a large degree, on the Mother Country, for the defence of the continent. They must henceforth take their full share in the defence of the Empire. At the Imperial Conference the Prime Minister (Mr. Hughes) had said that he believed that the British Navy was essentially the first line of defence, and that Australia's contribution to that first line of defence must take the form of a Dominion Navy. Last year they had budgeted to spend £2,340,000 on naval defence, whereas Great Britain had budgeted for £82,000,000 in respect of her full share. When he heard others boast about taxation in Australia being less per head than in the Old Country he felt rather ashamed of the fact that while they paid only £13 per head by way of taxation, as against £24 per head in Great Britain, they left the people there to carry a burden something like forty times as great as their own in respect of this matter of naval defence. Their contribution to the naval defence of the Empire should be commensurate with their weight and influence as one of the Dominions of the Empire.

Empire Relations.

If they were to continue to take part in the foreign affairs of the Empire, they needed some machinery very much better than they had to inform themselves of what was actually taking place. The best course to follow, it seemed to him, would be to secure the establishment of a Committee of that Parliament—a Committee of External or Imperial Relations—consisting of all Parties, which would be enabled to keep itself fully informed of what was happening in the Old Country as well as in the other Dominions. It would thus be in a position to make public pronouncements and so keep public opinion in the Commonwealth practically the same as in all the other Dominions. He trusted that the outcome of the debate would be to lift the consideration of their Imperial and external policies above the Party arena. Irrespective of the general political news of the Party in power, there should be an unbroken effort to develop a tradition for Australia respecting Imperial and external relationships. One factor which would assist in bringing this about would be the establishment of a permanent Committee, from both Federal Houses, upon Imperial and external affairs. The best interests of Australia were bound up with the maintenance of the Imperial connection, and in Australia taking her place as an independent unit of the Empire in the affairs of the world. In order to make themselves secure it was essential that their people should be provided with the fullest information.

The Washington Conference had been very valuable from every point of view. In these Treaties there were to be found definite practical results. There had been created some degree, at least, of world-opinion which should go to the making of better international understandings, so that war in future should be much more difficult of precipitation. The Empire was to be congratulated upon the results which had been achieved. Limitation of naval armaments would relieve them of heavy financial burdens, and if the savings in respect of the construction of battleships could be utilised in developmental and productive directions, there would be achieved a vast amount of good. The attitude of Great Britain and the self-governing Dominions at the Washington Conference had been such that it maintained, throughout, the British tradition of magnanimity that was in conformity with their Empire traditions, and the position it had held for the last hundred years as the most advanced leader of thought and freedom in the world.

The Hon. Sir Robert Best (Nationalist, *Kooyong, Vic.*) remarked that they should be very gratified, indeed, with the unanimity, which was hardly characteristic of the House, shown in the adoption of the various resolutions as submitted by the Prime Minister. He ventured to say that few events in history had been more pregnant with possibilities of fruitful achievement than the Washington Conference. As a consequence of the War the Dominions' status had been changed. "The position is," said Sir Robert, "that we are either within or without the Empire." If they were within the Empire it practically meant that, while they had their separate status, which entitled them to consultation as to the foreign policy of the Empire, etc., yet not one of the Dominions could fairly claim any representation outside the Empire. The change lay in giving to the various Dominions the separate right to consultation and to representation as Empire delegates.

League of Nations.

He confessed frankly that he was one who believed most firmly in the League of Nations, and what it was capable of accomplishing. They were sincerely hopeful that the Conference would prove a substantial step towards bringing into the League not only the United States of America, but also those nations with whom they had fought in the recent War—Germany, Russia and Austria.

The motion was agreed to.

Enabling Bill: Dominions and Treaties.

On 17th August, in the House of Representatives,

The Prime Minister (the Right Hon. W. M. Hughes) moved the Second Reading of a Bill to enable effect to be given to two Treaties signed at Washington on behalf of His Majesty and certain other Powers. With the other Treaties, he said, they were not concerned. The obligation in respect to them required no statutory authority. But their obligation in respect to certain provisions in the Treaty for the Limitation of Naval Armaments and in the Treaty to protect neutrals from submarines, and to prevent the use of noxious gases and chemicals in war, needed that authority. The Bill provided that no person shall, without licence from the Minister for Defence, build any vessel of war, or alter, arm or equip any ship so as to adapt her for use as a vessel of war; or allow to be despatched or delivered any such ship. It also provided for the carrying out of Article 3 of the Submarine and Poison Gas Treaty. The penalty for contravention of these provisions of the Bill was £500, or imprisonment for two years, or both, and the ship in respect of which the offence was committed and her equipment were liable to forfeiture.

Mr. F. Brennan (Labour, *Batman, Vic.*) asserted that the Commonwealth was not a party to the Treaties, and was not qualified to become a party to any Treaty. Only sovereign States might make Treaties, and it was not pretended by those overseas, who had been really the parties to these Treaties, that it was for Australia to either give or refuse ratification. It was only the British Parliament, speaking for and on behalf of the Empire, which was qualified to ratify Treaties as between nations. If they were to assert their unalienable loyalty to the Imperial connection, and to the principle of Imperial solidarity, it was idle, on the other hand, to claim for themselves the rights of a sovereign people as between nations. They did not possess, and it was useless for them to assert, any such privilege.

The Bill passed through both Houses without amendment.

DEBATE IN THE SENATE.

On 27th July,

The Minister for Home and Territories (Senator the Right Hon. G. F. Pearce*), in introducing the motion, said that it was an indication of the enhanced status of Australia as one of the nations that made up the British Empire that the Senate, as on a previous occasion when they had dealt with the Versailles Treaty, was called upon to express its views concerning the ratification of these Treaties. It was an indication that the Commonwealth, as a result of the Great War and the part they had played in it, had taken upon itself great responsibilities, and it marked a very important advance in their growth as a nation. It was only the second occasion upon which that Parliament had been asked to ratify such Treaties. On the first occasion they had been asked to ratify a Treaty in which terms had been dictated by the victors to the vanquished. When they remembered all the trouble that

* When appointed to attend the Conference, Senator Pearce was Minister for Defence, but was appointed Minister for Home and Territories on the reconstruction of the Cabinet, which took place in December, 1921.

had ensued, and was still present throughout the world in consequence of the Great War, and which that Treaty so far had failed to eliminate, it was an omen of great promise that they were then asked to ratify Treaties which made the greatest step towards peaceful relation between the nations which had ever been made.

There were many who during the progress of the Great War had honestly believed that it was a war to end war; but there were many who must have looked upon the world with feelings of misgiving when they saw the turmoil and chaos that had since ensued, and must have almost despaired of the future of civilisation and humanity. When they remembered the atmosphere in which the Conference at Washington had assembled, and took their minds back to the feelings and prognostications which had prevailed during 1921, it seemed difficult now to realise that the nations that had emerged from the terrible blood-bath of 1914-1918 were already not only contemplating the possibility of another great war, but were even speculating as to the date upon which an outbreak would occur. Perhaps not so much in the journals or Press of the Commonwealth, but certainly in those of the United States of America and Japan, war was being referred to and fore-told, and those two nations in particular were obsessed with the possibility of war, and were feverishly making preparations for an outbreak.

If they looked up the long roll of International Conferences, with the possible exception of the meetings of the League of Nations, it would be found that this was practically the only occasion in history when nations had met together and each had made a very important sacrifice in the general cause of peace, and for the welfare of humanity.

The Conference had dealt with two separate sets of questions. One of those was the limitation of armaments, and this had been dealt with by a Conference at which five Powers, Great Britain, the United States of America, France, Japan and Italy, were represented. The second set referred to the Pacific and Far Eastern questions, and that Conference consisted of representatives of the five Powers and also of Belgium, China, Holland and Portugal. It was no exaggeration to say that the nations which made up the Conferences were potentially the greatest naval and military Powers of the earth, and that an agreement arrived at by such Powers could practically dictate the conditions under which the world was to continue to carry on its government.

There had been six Treaties drawn up and agreed to; they were:—

(1) A four-Powers Treaty, between Great Britain, Japan, the United States of America and France relating to the Pacific.

(2) A supplementary Treaty to that.

(3) The Naval Treaty, which was a five-Powers Treaty between Great Britain, the United States of America, France, Italy and Japan.

(4) The Treaty relating to the use of submarines and poison gas in war, which was a five-Powers Treaty.

(5) A general Treaty relating to China, which was a nine-Powers Treaty.

(6) A Treaty relating to China's revenue, which was also a nine-Powers Treaty.

Shantung question; Yap.

There were two other Treaties, one of which, at any rate, was of first-class importance. They in Australia could hardly realise how big the Shantung question loomed in the United States of America. It was safe to say that to millions of people in the United States of America "Shantung" and "war" were synonymous terms; and whilst the Washington Conference did not directly deal with Shantung, there was not the slightest doubt that it was the assembling of the Conference and the spirit it evoked that led the Representatives of China to bring forward the question of Shantung, and later stimulated the action of Japan in meeting the Representatives of China. Subsequently, through the good offices of Lord Balfour, on the part of Great Britain, and Mr. Hughes, on the part of the United States, an agreement was arrived at in regard to that province which was satisfactory to all parties.

There was a little island in the Pacific which, he supposed, not one per cent. of their population in Australia had ever heard of. He referred to the island of Yap, which, in itself, constituted a danger point in the relations between the United States of America and Japan, and might, at any time, have been the flash that would have exploded the powder magazine between those two countries.

These two questions arose out of the Conference, and two Treaties had been negotiated and signed by the Representatives of the two countries directly concerned. These Treaties had removed those danger points, and Japan, to her credit be it said, before the Treaty had been ratified either by the United States of America or Japan herself, had already taken the first steps towards evacuation of the territory, and fulfilment of the terms of the Treaty.

In addition to these Treaties there were twelve sets of resolutions dealing with such matters as rules for the conduct of war, and questions affecting China, to which these nations all subscribed, and which constituted obligations of honour entered into between them for their observation. All the resolutions dealt with questions of first importance, and at almost any other period prior to the War would have been the subject of Treaties. He did not hesitate to say that the nations that had subscribed to those resolutions regarded them as morally binding to the same extent as if they were Treaties. He would like to say that in dealing with those Treaties Australia had accepted the responsibilities of a nation. They had hitherto been so obsessed and busy with their own affairs that they had had little time to lift their eyes to the wider horizon of international questions ; but the very fact that that Parliament was now being called upon to ratify those Treaties showed the immensely important part that Australia would play in the future, when she would take a live and active interest in the wider scope of international politics.

Pacific Treaty; Anglo-Japanese Alliance.

In quoting the Pacific Treaty and the supplement thereto, Senator Pearce said that it constituted a declaration of friendship and mutual interest, forbearance and consultation. There was another important aspect of this question that should not be lightly regarded—the fact that the Treaty took the place of the Anglo-Japanese Alliance. Whilst the Treaty did not constitute an alliance—and there was a sense in which the Anglo-Japanese Alliance was an offensive and defensive one—its place had been taken by a declaration of mutual friendship between not only Britain and Japan, but also the United States of America and Japan. He well remembered, when the discussion was taking place in that Parliament on the question of the renewal of the Anglo-Japanese Alliance,* how from all Parties the opinion had been expressed that Britain should seek a friendly understanding with the United States of America. It was, embodied in that Treaty. They had achieved that end without in any way offending Japan. That, he thought, was of great importance to Australia. As a nation, living on the shores of the Pacific, it was of immense value to have a mutual declaration of friendship and protection of the rights of the nations in the Pacific.

Limitation of Naval Armaments.

He had heard some criticisms in regard to the operation of the Naval Treaty. It was said that the nations, in agreeing to it, had made no real sacrifice, and that it did not amount to effectively doing away with the means of making war. It was also stated that the day of the capital ship was past, and that aircraft would be superior. When they remembered that the British Empire for centuries had enjoyed naval supremacy over all other nations, would anybody say that it meant no real sacrifice to Great Britain when she accepted, for the first

* *Vide* summary on " Conference of Prime Ministers of the Empire," JOURNAL, Vol. II., No. 3, p. 609 ; and Vol. II., No. 2, p. 354.

time in her history, naval equality with another nation? Did Great Britain give up nothing when she, the Empire that lived by sea-power, agreed not to construct any capital ships for a period of ten years, and to limit her naval construction in the way set out in the Treaty? Did it involve no real sacrifice to the United States of America? It was interesting to note that in the Act of Congress dated 29th August, 1916, when the United States of America adopted by far the largest naval programme in her history, mention was made of a Conference to consider the question of the limitation of armament and the President was authorised, in a proviso to the Act, to call together representatives of the nations to consider this question. According to the former naval programme the United States, on paper (taking the class of ships into consideration), would have had in 1923-24 the most powerful battle fleet in the world. So much for those who would say that Great Britain and the United States had made no real sacrifices.

In illustration of the saving to the Commonwealth as a result of the Treaty, Senator Pearce remarked that the battle-cruiser *Australia* had cost that country something like £2,000,000 to construct. She was, at the time of her construction, an up-to-date ship, able to take her place in line of battle with battle-cruisers. To construct an equivalent ship to-day which might occupy a corresponding position in the present-day fleets, embodying the experience of the War, would cost not £2,000,000, but from £8,000,000 to £10,000,000.

Submarines and poison gas.

This Treaty had an interesting history. During the discussion of naval armaments, the British Empire Delegation, through Lord Balfour and Lord Lee, proposed the total abolition of the submarine. That did not find a single supporter at the Conference at the time. But, so strong was the appeal on the humanitarian side whilst the Conference was sitting, that a tremendous storm of public opinion was aroused in the United States backing up the British proposal. So strong was the feeling aroused by the rejection of that proposal, and so much alive were the people of America to the outrages committed by German submarines during the War, that, before the Conference had proceeded far after the submission of the British proposal, the American Delegates themselves brought forward proposals which had the effect of rendering them useless as ships of war.

This Treaty also dealt with the use of asphyxiating, poisonous, or other gases, and this was also condemned. He ventured to say that although the British Delegation was not able to secure, directly, the abolition of the submarine, no nation that intended to abide by these rules and laws of war was going to build submarines in the future, because it was obvious that they could be of little or no use unless these laws were violated. It had been put forward by Lord Lee, on the authority of the British Admiralty, that as an offensive weapon used against warships, the experience of the last War had shown that the submarine was practically useless. Its use was principally, and almost wholly, against merchant ships.

Advantages to Australia.

After explaining the Treaties relating to China, Senator Pearce concluded by saying that there was not the slightest doubt that the ratification of the Treaties would enable them to devote their energies to the arts of peace and development to a greater extent than heretofore. Had it not been for these Treaties, one was appalled to contemplate what Australia would have had to take on its shoulders in the way of naval and military defence.

Senator B. Benny (*S. Aust.*) congratulated Senator Pearce on the success of his mission to Washington. Since the Battle of Trafalgar there had been one nation that had exercised the functions of mistress of the seas *de facto*,—that was Great Britain. Yet she had never violated her obligations nor permitted any injustice to be done in the seven seas of the world.

In the time of Monroe, the United States had very few more people than the Commonwealth had to-day, yet that country arrogated to itself the power to control the destinies of the whole of the New World. It had to be acknowledged that the Monroe Doctrine had made for peace more than anything that had been promulgated in recent years and prior to the Washington Conference. He hoped that at the next Assembly of the League of Nations Senator Pearce might be able to put forward some suggestion for the control of the oceans of the world by America and Great Britain conjointly, and he thought it would have a desirable influence on the maintenance of perpetual peace, because the nations which controlled the seas were in a position to influence and control all other nations.

Senator T. J. K. Bakhap (*Tas.*) said he saw nothing in connection with all the series of Treaties that was calculated to have a baleful tendency, except, perhaps, a weak China. There could be no doubt whatever that it was the particular seriousness of the Far-Eastern position that constrained the Government of the United States, as represented by its President, to take the step which had resulted in this memorable, and he hoped happy, understanding.

After one other Senator had addressed the motion, it was resolved in the affirmative.

DEFENCE RETIREMENT ACT.*

(Reductions in Defence Forces through Washington Conference; etc.)

An Act relating to the retirement or discharge of certain persons from the Permanent Services of the Defence Department was assented to on 14th September, 1922.

The main provisions of the Act are as follow :—

Compulsory Retirement.

Any member of the Permanent Naval, Military or Air Forces, or any employee holding a classified office in the Defence Department, may be retired or discharged on or before 30th June, 1923, notwithstanding that the member or employee has not attained the prescribed age for retirement or completed his term of enlistment.

Compensation.

To any such member of the Forces or employee there shall be payable compensation in the proportion of one month's pay for each year of service, provided that the amount payable shall be not less than its equivalent of six months' pay, and shall not exceed the equivalent of twelve months' pay plus pay for the unexpired period of the service of the member or employee.†

Voluntary Retirement.

Any member of the Forces or any classified employee may make application to retire with compensation as hereinbefore prescribed.

Compensation payable under this Act shall not be claimable or recoverable, but shall be deemed to be a free gift by the Commonwealth.

IN THE HOUSE OF REPRESENTATIVES.

On 18th August,

The Minister for Defence (Hon. W. Massy Greene) in moving the Second Reading, said that it was a great pity that long before then the Commonwealth had not made provision, such as had been made by almost every other civilised country, for the granting of retiring allowances to members of the Naval and Military Forces. Members of the Forces, if they had not risen to a certain rank after a certain period of service, automatically passed out of the Service. All that the Commonwealth had done in the past, when certain members of the permanent Defence Forces had reached the retiring age, had

* At the date of the last Hansard to hand the Bill had not proceeded beyond the Committee stage in the House of Representatives.

† On the Second Reading the Minister, explaining this clause, said that whichever sum—one month's pay for each year of service, or twelve months' pay plus pay for unexpired period of service—was the lesser, would be paid.

been to place a sum of money upon the Estimates and ask Parliament to vote it as compensation to the retired officers. The Bill, however, was designed to deal with a very large number of officers and men of the Army, and a smaller number of the Navy, who were being compulsorily retired owing to a reduction in the Defence Forces. The results of the Washington Conference had enabled the Government to bring about that reduction.

In reply to Mr. W. A. Watt (Nationalist, *Balaclava*), who asked what were the calculations as to the cost of the scheme and the number of men involved, the Minister said he thought they should be able to provide for the Army and Navy retirements at a cost of £300,000. In the permanent Forces, 460 men would be affected in addition to 60 or 70 clerical officers, and also some people in the Navy. He was not quite certain of the number involved in the Navy, but it would not be large, because they were reducing in the Navy by reverting men to the Imperial Navy.

THE BUDGET.

(Annual Financial Statement.)

On 17th August, in the House of Representatives, the Commonwealth Treasurer delivered his Budget statement, the position being shown as follows :—

FINANCIAL YEAR, 1921-22.	£
Revenue	64,897,046
Expenditure from Revenue	65,106,949
Deficit after providing £300,000 for compensation to Defence Officers retired	£209,903

FINANCIAL YEAR, 1922-23.	£	£
Surplus brought forward from the previous year ..	6,408,424	
Estimated Revenue on basis of taxation then in operation	62,518,250	
		68,926,674
Estimated Expenditure from Revenue	62,023,693	
Proposed reduction of Taxation, etc.	3,200,000	
		65,223,693
Estimated surplus to be carried forward to the following year		£3,702,981

The Treasurer (Hon. S. M. Bruce), in introducing the Budget, claimed that it was based on the correct principles of finance, as expressed at the Brussels Conference, particularly as to balancing the Budget; a reduction of armaments compatible with national security; a reduction of expenditure, meeting recurrent ordinary expenditure out of revenue; loans for capital purposes to be met only out of the savings of the people; and deflation of currency. He was optimistic as regards future prospects. He emphasised the necessity for stable government and sound finance, thus inducing capital expenditure for the development of Australia's primary and secondary industries. Trade production was then promoted and a reduction of taxation might be hoped for, together with abundant employment. The financial proposals submitted would establish an atmosphere of confidence in Australia's future stability.

Reduction of taxation.

Although the present taxation was not excessive in comparison with that of other countries, the Federal Government proposed, in view of the large surplus, to remit taxation, to stimulate trade and industry, to promote development, to reduce the cost of living, and to attract capital from overseas. £3,200,000 would be remitted by granting relief as follows:—Increase of the general exemption to £200 in the case of all taxpayers, diminishing £1 in every £3 in excess thereof; reduction of existing graduated income-tax rates by 10 per cent.; reduction of companies' rates from 2s. 8d. to 2s. 5d.; removal of the War surcharge of 20 per cent. on Land Tax; removal of the Entertainments Tax where price of admission was under 1s.; reduction of the duty on galvanised iron, iron and steel wire, wire netting and tractors, and provision of a bounty to local manufacturers of such goods. Allowing for the £3,200,000 mentioned, the surplus estimated to be carried forward at the close of this financial year was £3,702,981.

Accumulated surplus, £6,408,000.

The figures for the year 1921-1922 were:—Revenue, £64,897,046; Expenditure from Revenue, £65,106,949; Deficit, £209,903, after providing £300,000 for compensation to Defence Officers retired. Allowing for the surplus of £6,618,327 brought forward from the previous year, the surplus carried forward to 1922-1923 was £6,408,424. This pronounced improvement in the position indicated that the recuperative powers of Australia were greater than had been recognised a year ago. Notwithstanding the unparalleled dislocation resulting from the War and the world-wide trade depression, the results of the past year showed the stability of the national finances.

Expenditure.

The expenditure from War Loan included Soldier Land Settlement, £6,478,003; War Service Homes, £1,247,466. The total expenditure on Soldier Land Settlement to date amounted to £33,153,273. Altogether 27,858 soldiers had been settled on the land. The total expenditure on Soldiers' Homes was £14,864,766. The expenditure from Loan for Works last year amounted to £5,246,503. The total expenditure from revenue and Loan was £77,930,429, which was less than was estimated by £2,967,000. The proposed Loan expenditure for 1922-1923 totalled £17,250,924, including £6,000,000 for Soldier Land Settlement, £4,000,000 for War Service Homes, £2,100,000 for Ship construction, £2,700,000 for Postmaster-General's Department, £309,015 for the new Federal Capital, £517,000 for the River Murray Water Scheme, and £200,000 for Immigration—the last-mentioned in respect of the arrangement between the Governments of the United Kingdom and the Commonwealth for the provision of assisted passages to Australia of intending immigrants.

Loan expenditure and National Debt.

The proposed Loan expenditure, amounting to £17,250,924, though large, was of a reproductive nature, and was justified by the necessity for developing the country. This would increase the National Debt, which during the past year had increased by £14,350,484, to £416,070,509. After allowing for indebtedness raised for the States and other advances repayable in cash and cash balances, the net Debt amounted to £341,120,778. That sum should be further reduced by assets and properties transferred by the States to the Commonwealth, valued at least at £32,490,617. The net Debt of the Commonwealth and the States after deducting the amount included in both Commonwealth and State Debts was £784,166,600, against which tangible Government assets, amounting to probably £450,000,000, might be set. The increase in the Australian gross Debt since pre-War compared favourably with that of other nations, being only 148 per cent. as compared with France 303 per cent., United States 799 per cent., and the United Kingdom 984 per cent.

It was proposed to vest in trustees a permanent sinking fund of half per cent. on all debt, thus providing redemption in fifty years. In this way a fair share of the burden would be borne by present and future generations of taxpayers.

Expenditure from Revenue.

The estimated Expenditure from Revenue for the year 1922-23 is £62,023,693, being a decrease on the previous year of £3,083,256. Included therein was an expenditure for War services which totalled £29,465,411, as against £31,337,164 in the previous year. These War services included interest and sinking fund, £20,582,810; War pensions, £6,750,000; Repatriation of soldiers, £1,771,000.

Pensions, etc.

War pensions showed a decrease of £278,379 compared with the previous year, but the Australian scale was more generous than that of any other country. The total number of pensioners, including dependants, numbered 225,372. The invalid and old age pensions showed an increase of £167,444 to £5,457,500; the cost in 1913-1914 was only £2,593,501, which increase was due chiefly to an increase from 10s. to 15s. per week. Higher pensions had been urged. The Government, while sympathetic, could not face the additional expenditure, but would endeavour to reduce the cost of necessaries of life, thus increasing pension values. For maternity allowances £690,000 were estimated. The Government was satisfied that the maternity allowance had not achieved the great object of preservation of child life, which object the Government considered would best be dealt with in relation to general questions of national health and by co-operating with the States. A subsidy of £150,000 on the export of beef was provided for. £25,000 was being contributed towards Australia's participation in the British Empire Exhibition, as well as £24,000 in respect of a Superannuation Scheme for the Public Service of a contributory character, the principle now being recognised as essential to the efficient conduct of private enterprise was equally applicable to Public Service.

Reduced Defence expenditure.

The estimated expenditure for the Defence Department, both Revenue and Loan, showed a reduction of £1,787,503 as compared with the past year. This reduction would not have been possible but for the Washington Conference.

Comparison with pre-War conditions.

The Treasurer dealt at length with the increase in the Expenditure over that of the years 1913-1914, showing that the increase was due to higher wages, increased costs now ruling, and new Government functions. He hoped that reduction would be brought about by better organisation of the Departments through the appointment of the Public Service Board contemplated by the Bill then before the House.

Government trading.

Mr. Bruce, replying to criticism as to Commonwealth Government trading, stated that where the output of a factory was absorbed by Government Departments it was a legitimate Government function, but that was not the case if custom must be sought outside. Following that principle, the woollen mills were being handed over to private enterprise, while the Commonwealth line of steamers would be placed under independent control, properly capitalised, and competing with other shipping companies. Shipbuilding as a Government enterprise was also to cease.

Revenue, 1922–1923.

The estimated revenue for 1922-1923, on the present basis of taxation, totalled £62,518,250, of which £28,000,000 represented Customs and Excise duties, while the Income Tax was expected to realise £15,250,000. An increase on the Customs and Excise revenue of the past year was anticipated owing to the marked increase in importation. A lessened yield from the wool, dairying and meat industries, owing to decreased profits would cause a reduction in income tax receipts.

Government Note Issue.

The Australian Note Issue was then £6,285,592 less than its highest point, namely, £59,676,401 in October, 1918. This indicated deflation and an approach towards normal condition. The Consolidated Revenue Fund transactions, on the present basis of taxation for 1922-1923, were expected to show a surplus of £494,557, and compared with 1921-1922, receipts showed an increase of £730,900, and expenditure a decrease of £2,080,765.

Loans.

Mr. Bruce referred to the steady fall in interest rates for loans during the last twelve months, to which he attributed the tendency, owing to the world-wide stagnation of trade, for investments to be made in Government securities rather than in commercial undertakings. He stressed it as the policy of the Government that in future loans as far as possible would be raised only in the local market, regard being paid to capital requirements for other local purposes. The Government proposed to confer with the State Governments in regard to putting Commonwealth and State Loans on a uniform footing as to taxation by both Commonwealth and States.

Taxation.

Negotiations were in progress with a view to the amalgamation of the taxation departments, and to the co-ordination of activities of the Commonwealth and the States in regard to public health, electoral rolls, statistics, etc. Taxation laws were to be consolidated, more important points being the assessment of incomes on five years' average, and the fixing live stock values permanently within a minimum and a maximum selected by the taxpayer. It was also intended to provide that bonus shares were not to be regarded as income. As to the taxation of the undistributed profits of companies, it was proposed so to amend the Income Tax Act, first, that where a prescribed percentage of profits was distributed, no further distribution would be required; secondly, that the Commissioner of Taxation would be empowered to determine what proportion of profits should be distributed where he found that an insufficient proportion had been allocated by way of dividend to shareholders; thirdly, that appeals should in all cases be to the Taxation Appeal Board.

Reduction of Parliamentary allowances.

Mr. Bruce announced that, in view of the necessity for reductions both inside and outside the Public Service, to correspond with decrease in the cost of living, the Government believed that obligation rested upon Parliament to set an example, and he accordingly proposed to submit an amendment to the law whereby Members' salaries should be reduced from £1,000 to £800 per annum.*

CUSTOMS TARIFF (NEW ZEALAND PREFERENCE) AGREEMENT.

On 28th July, 1922, the Minister for Trade and Customs laid on the table of the House of Representatives a copy of the agreement between the Commonwealth and the Dominion of New Zealand providing for a Reciprocal Tariff.

The Minister for Trade and Customs (Hon. A. S. Rodgers), in explaining the agreement, said that it would be remembered that this question of reciprocal tariff treatment between the two countries had engaged the attention of both Parliaments as far back as 1906, but the attempt then made to arrive at an agreement proved abortive. Prior to an amendment of the New Zealand Tariff towards the end of last year, the Commonwealth did enjoy British preferential treatment, but following on the determination of the New Zealand Government to encourage the development of secondary industries, a substantial increase in Customs duties was made towards the end of last year. In order that the Commonwealth might be in a position to negotiate with New Zealand in regard to tariff treatment an enabling Bill had been passed through that House;† and had those negotiations been successful, they should automatically have been able to make operative the British preferential tariff for New Zealand goods. The

* Telegrams to the Press indicate that this proposal was rejected in the House of Representatives by 35 votes to 26.

† *Vide* JOURNAL, Vol. III., No. 3, p. 629.

Commonwealth Government had offered the Dominion preference on this scale, and in turn asked for similar treatment, but New Zealand had been unable to accept the offer. They had therefore been faced with the necessity to negotiate item by item up to a certain stage. New Zealand, like the Commonwealth of Australia, was a primary producing country that had recently turned its attention to the development of secondary industries, but the Commonwealth, having been longer in the field of secondary production, had advanced much farther. In view of the fact that the policy of the New Zealand Government was to secure the development of secondary industries in the Dominion, it could not be expected that a one-sided bargain should emerge from the negotiations. The principle of give and take had to be the foundation of any such agreement, which, to be equitable, must be mutually advantageous. Copies of the agreement and Tariff schedule were being placed before the New Zealand Parliament that day.

An agreement was in existence between the New Zealand and South African Governments in respect of certain items, one of which was particularly affected by this reciprocal arrangement. New Zealand had made an arrangement that was very favourable to South Africa, but greatly to the detriment of the wine industry of the Commonwealth, and that arrangement had been to some extent a barrier in their negotiations. However, as evidence of good faith, New Zealand had already given notice to South Africa of the termination of that arrangement as from the 1st August, thus enabling Australia vastly to improve the protection of its wine industry. Previously they had been in a very bad position, but through the concession made by New Zealand that had been rectified.

Everyone knew that the balance of trade between Australia and New Zealand was overwhelmingly in favour of Australia. The latter was an older manufacturing country, it was more populous, and had had a better start than New Zealand.

Mr. Rodgers claimed that, on the whole, the agreement was sound; that it would advance very substantially the commercial and trading interests of the Commonwealth, and give to both its primary and secondary industries the best measure of help that could be obtained.

Imperial Preference.

Mr. Rodgers hoped that preference to products of the British Empire would be the policy that would prevail in the future. During the testing period of the War they had been able rightly to gauge the value of that policy, and he ventured to say that the effort, particularly on the part of the United Kingdom, to resuscitate Europe for the sake of improved trade relationships, could not be as advantageous to the British Empire as would be a policy of peopling the Dominions and building up Empire industries. He knew of no subject of more outstanding interest than that of thus developing the Dominions, for they were the best customers of the Empire and the greatest guarantee of its preservation. Only by adopting a spirit of reasonable compromise between the Dominions was it possible to make reciprocal agreements.

Agreement ratified.

An Act to give effect to the Agreement was assented to on 23rd August, 1922.

NATIONALITY ACT 1920 AMENDMENT BILL.*

This Bill was introduced in the Senate on 27th July, 1922. Its main object is to extend the provisions of the Nationality Act 1920,† to the Territories of Papua and Norfolk Island and to any other Territories under the authority of the Commonwealth to which the Governor-General by proclamation declares them to extend.

IN THE SENATE.

On 28th July,

The Minister for Home and Territories (Senator the Right Hon. G. F. Pearce), in moving the Second Reading, said that the measure was being introduced owing to some slight disability which rested upon persons resident in their Territories in respect to naturalisation. As regarded Papua and Norfolk Island, the Commonwealth had adopted Part II. of the British Nationality and Status of Aliens Act of 1914, and for the purposes of that Act the Commonwealth of Australia was deemed to include the two Territories mentioned, as shown by the second schedule of the Nationality Act 1920. There was already an Ordinance in force in Papua, entitled the Aliens Ordinance 1911, which empowered the Lieutenant-Governor to grant certificates of naturalisation, but naturalisation granted under that was local only. That Ordinance had to be repealed by the Legislative Council of Papua ; but its repeal would not take effect until the provisions of the Bill

* The Bill passed through the Senate without amendment, but at the date of the last Hansard to hand had not proceeded beyond the First Reading Stage in the House of Representatives.

† *Vide* JOURNAL, Vol. II., No. 2, p. 368.

became law. The rights of persons naturalised under that Ordinance would be safeguarded in the present measure.

There was no law in force in Norfolk Island at present under which naturalisation could be granted to an alien. This measure would overcome the difficulty.

Clause 7 contained an amendment to Section 12 of the principal Act, and substituted "Minister" for "Governor-General." The object of this amendment was to obviate the necessity of notices under the Section being issued by the Governor-General in Council, which was an unusual procedure. Another amendment was to remove any inconsistency in the provisions of the Act relating to the revocation of certificates of naturalisation, and to make it clear that the Governor-General might revoke a certificate granted under a State Act or an Ordinance of a Territory.

COMMONWEALTH ELECTORAL (AMENDMENT) ACT.*

A Bill was introduced in the Senate on 26th July, 1922, to amend in many directions the Commonwealth Electoral Act. Most of the amendments aim at remedying defects which experience has shown to exist.

An important new principle is the introduction of the grouping of candidates for the Senate† according to political Party or otherwise, the elector nevertheless retaining the right to vote according to his own selection if he so desires.

Another important amendment is that by which an elector is prevented from enrolling in a division unless he is a *bona fide* resident therein, thus preventing the possibility of itinerant workers concentrating on an electoral division and seriously influencing the result of any election therein.

LANDS ACQUISITION ACT (AMENDMENT) BILL.

This Bill was introduced in the Senate on 26th July, 1922, and its object is to improve the procedure in regard to the

---

* The Bill passed the Senate on 23rd August, but had not proceeded beyond the Second Reading stage in the House of Representatives at the date of the last Hansard to hand.

† The Senate consists of thirty-six members, six from each State. Members are elected for a term of six years, but a certain number retire at the end of every third year. In elections for Senators, each State is counted as a single electorate. The House of Representatives consists of seventy-five members, each State being represented on a population basis. Members are elected for the duration of Parliament, which is limited to three years. For the election of Members to the House of Representatives each State is subdivided into electorates, and since 1919 Elections have been conducted on a preferential voting system.

acquisition of land by the Commonwealth and the payment of compensation in respect thereof, and to remove certain defects from the existing Act.*

IN THE SENATE.

On 27th July, in the Senate,

The Minister for Home and Territories (Senator the Right Hon. G. F. Pearce), in moving the Second Reading, said that the Bill was somewhat of a technical character, because the main legislation stood, and the measure was designed only to remove defects which had been discovered as a result of litigation or administration. The Act had been found to be seriously defective as regards the acquisition and disposal by the Commonwealth of interests in land less than the fee-simple. The High Court had decided that the power to "sell and convey" in Section 8 did not include the power to lease, and that persons under disability could not lease land to the Commonwealth. Doubt had also arisen as regards the power of the Commonwealth to dispose of less than the full estate in any land which it had acquired. Numerous amendments were accordingly proposed with a view to enabling the Commonwealth to acquire and dispose of any interest in land. It was also desired that this full power to acquire lands should be deemed to have been vested in the Commonwealth from the date of the commencement of the original Act, and suitable provision had therefore been made. They frequently had to resume land in some of their large cities, which lands were sometimes the subject of various tenures and leases. Under the present Act they had practically to determine them. That was not desirable. It was sometimes necessary and desirable that a lease should not be disturbed when they did not require to terminate it for the purposes of the Commonwealth. It was sought to make the law more elastic in the directions he had indicated.

At the present time, on the compulsory acquisition of land which was subject to a lease, the lease ceased and the remainder of the term of the lease was converted into a claim for compensation. It was not always desirable from the point of view of the Commonwealth that the lessee should cease occupation. It was therefore proposed that power be given to include in the notification of acquisition a declaration that the lease should continue, subject to conditions stated in the notification, until it expired by effluxion of time, or was otherwise lawfully determined.

---

* At the date of the last Hansard to hand the Bill had not proceeded beyond the Committee stage in the Senate.

Another important part of the Act which required simplification was that relating to the compensation of mortgagees of land compulsorily acquired by the Commonwealth. At the present time the mortgagee might either (A) join with the owner in making a claim; (B) make a separate claim; or (C) waive his right to compensation and rely on his right against the mortgagor under the mortgage. Considerable difficulty had been experienced in determining the compensation payable to the mortgagee and adjusting the respective rights of the mortgagee and mortgagor. It was therefore proposed to give the mortgagor two alternatives, namely, (A) to claim compensation; (B) rely on his rights under the mortgage.

At the present time a notification of the acquisition of land under compulsory process could only be avoided by a resolution of either House of Parliament passed within thirty days after the notification had been laid before it. Further, this provision did not apply to all lands acquired. It was therefore proposed to give power to Parliament so to avoid the notification of acquisition of any lands whatsoever, and, in addition, to give the Governor-General power to revoke any notification, in whole or in part, within six months after the publication of the notification in the *Gazette*.

After referring to less important amendments and others of a minor or drafting character, Senator Pearce said that it would be seen that the Bill was a technical one, the consideration of which could best be taken in Committee.

State Parliaments.

New South Wales.

EMPIRE SETTLEMENT.

On 4th July, 1922, in the Legislative Council, in his speech, delivered at the Opening of Parliament,

His Excellency the Governor (Sir Walter E. Davidson) said, *inter alia:* "My advisers believe that it is an imperative necessity to rapidly and considerably increase our population, not only for the future safety of Australia, but in order to diminish the burdens of government that at present are relatively too high for our small population. Efforts are being made, and with every apparent prospect of success, to enlist the co-operation and financial support of the Federal and Imperial Governments in the carrying out of a well-devised scheme for the development and utilisation of large areas of the Crown Lands, under a system of community settlement, in the benefits of which our own citizens will participate with selected immigrants from the United Kingdom."

DEBATE IN LEGISLATIVE ASSEMBLY.

On 5th July,

Mr. J. Dooley (Leader of the Opposition), speaking on the Address-in-Reply, said it had been stated, and rightly so, that one of the great needs of Australia was population. One of the problems they had to solve was to see by what practicable means they could enable their country to carry its rightful share of the population of the world. America was often pointed out to them as an example, but he hoped they should never populate Australia on the same lines as America had done. In America there were over 100,000,000 of people, but the number of them that belonged to the British race was infinitesimal. A great mistake made by America was in allowing people coming from foreign countries to settle there in their own way, and to continue the same life as they had previously led. He hoped that in Australia, if they were going in for a system of peopling the country, and if they were going to get people from races outside their own, they would endeavour as quickly as possible to bring them up as Australians. He said emphatically that the only way in which they could do that was by doing something fairly drastic. The Government must be game to tackle boldly the question of opening up the lands of Australia by taking the land out of the control of the people who were holding it for speculative purposes, and put it to use.

The Premier (Hon. Sir George Fuller) said that as far as he and the Government were concerned they would take very great care that they did not follow the lead of America in connection with the class of emigration which flowed into the great United States. In many respects the class of emigration which trended towards the United States consisted of the refuse of Europe, but in Australia they wanted, if possible, to get immigrants from their own homeland. They wanted as many of those men who stood side by side with their men in the defence of the Empire's flag as they possibly could. They would use every means to get those men out, and there would be no necessity to train them as Australians. He would like to point out that, although the Government had been in power only a little over two months, immediately on assuming office they had initiated action towards the carrying out of a vigorous policy of land settlement, particularly including the Murrumbidgee irrigation areas. They knew that in the northern portion of the State there was available a large area of the best land in New South Wales.

And in other portions of the State there was splendid country awaiting settlement. They were out to open up these portions of the State in order to give people who wanted to get on the land an opportunity of doing so. They also wanted to give desirable immigrants from the Old Country an opportunity of settling upon their lands.

EVIDENCE (AMENDMENT) ACT.

(Communications during Marriage; Limits of Cross-examination.)

A Bill for an Act to alter the law as to the competency of a husband or wife to give evidence as to communications passing between them during marriage; to impose certain limits on cross-examination; and to prevent the publication of questions prohibited by the judge, was introduced in the Legislative Assembly on 26th July, 1922, and received assent on 16th August.

The main provisions of the Act are as follows:—

Communications during Marriage.

A husband and wife shall be competent but not compellable to disclose communications passing between them during the marriage. Where a husband and wife are both parties to a proceeding under the Matrimonial Causes Act, 1899, each of them shall be competent and compellable to disclose such communications.

Section 11 of the Evidence Act, 1898, is repealed.*

Limits of Cross-examination.

The Court is empowered, at its discretion, to disallow any question put to a witness in cross-examination which is not relevant to the cause or proceeding, except so far as the truth of the matter suggested by the question affects the credit of the witness; to forbid any question or inquiry, unless it relates to the facts in issue, which it regards as indecent or scandalous, although it may have bearing on the questions before the Court; and to forbid any question which appears to be intended to insult or annoy. The publication of any such prohibited question or inquiry, without the express permission of the Court, is disallowed.

The Attorney-General (Hon. T. R. Bavin), in moving the Second Reading, said that the position to-day in New South Wales was, although a husband or wife could be called as a witness in proceedings in which the other partner to the marriage was concerned, they could not give evidence, either in civil or criminal cases, as to communications passing between them during the existence of the marriage state. That had led to serious failures of justice in some cases. It

---

* This section provided that no husband or wife shall be competent to disclose any communication passing between them during the marriage.

had only been possible to carry on so long by the neglect of that law, because under the Women's Property Act provision was made for the possibility of disputes arising between husband and wife, and it was necessary, in order to adjust these disputes, that evidence should be given about communications which had passed between husband and wife. The proposal in the Bill in this regard had been part of the law of England for a very long time, and no difficulty had arisen out of its existence. They went a little further than the law of England in one respect. Under the criminal law of England a wife could not give evidence of communications with her husband in proceedings as a witness for the prosecution except in a certain limited class of offence. But under the Bill a woman would be competent to give evidence—though not a compellable witness—against her husband in any class of proceedings, just as she was then in divorce proceedings.

The second part of the Bill dealt with the right of cross-examination. The position to-day was that when a witness went into the box to testify as to matters that were in issue, the right of cross-examination extended to allowing the representative of the party against whom he was giving evidence to cross-examine him as to the whole of his past life and conduct. The Bill gave the Court a discretion to disallow these questions if it thought that the answers to them did not really bear on the credibility of the witness. At the present time the Court had some discretion, but its extent was somewhat doubtful. They wanted to clear up the matter and make definite what at present was indefinite.

FEMALE EMPLOYEES' WAGES BILL.

(Equal rates of pay; etc.)

On 25th July, in the Legislative Assembly,

Mr. W. R. C. Bagnall (Nationalist, *St. George*) moved that leave be given to bring in a Bill to provide that there shall be no discrimination in the rates of pay of males and females performing work of the same character. He said that he believed that there was a general appreciation of the necessity for doing something to bring about the establishment of the principle of equal pay for women who were employed in occupations in which they did the same class of work as men, but received very much lower rates of pay. In their country a "White Australia" policy was the corner-stone of their nationhood; and one of the reasons why they had adopted that policy was to remove the danger of cheap labour in opposition to their own white workers. He could not understand why it was that they had not very much earlier seriously taken up the question of removing a blot on their national life, whereby they permitted their industrial conditions to be injured and the prospect of the men of their community securing employment lessened because of the fact that by legislation they permitted women to come in and do the same work for lower pay.

He realised that if legislation were brought in to make the conditions of pay equal immediately it would inflict a very serious hardship upon large numbers of their women workers. He had made provision in the Bill that a period of five years should elapse before the equal conditions fully applied, and that annually one-fifth of the difference should be added to their wages until at the end of the fifth year the pay of female employees would be equal to that of male workers. There were some 50,000 women workers in their various industries. More and more the young girls of the community were going into the various avenues of industry, and were shoving the manhood of the country out of many industrial occupations. There was no question that one of the principal reasons for this was that the labour of women was cheaper. It seemed strange that up to that time they had permitted their women-folk to go into their industries and, so to speak, be made the slaves of their economic position. He believed they were called upon to move in the matter, so that that state of affairs should be remedied.

There being no seconder, the motion lapsed.

Queensland.

COTTON GROWING.

(Governor's Speech: Co-operation with United Kingdom.)

On 4th July, in the Legislative Assembly, in his speech, delivered at the Opening of Parliament:—His Excellency the Governor (the Right Hon. Sir Matthew Nathan) referred to cotton growing in the State, and said that of the many crops that could be profitably grown on the large areas to be opened up to agricultural enterprises, one at least was of Empire concern, and its cultivation was worthy of all the encouragement the Imperial Government could give. He referred to cotton, which was admirably adapted to Queensland soil and climatic conditions, and the successful culture of which would not only benefit the British manufacturer, but provide a comfortable livelihood for their own intending settlers and for many thousands of British people, forced by economic circumstances to emigrate, and yet laudably anxious to remain under the British flag. The action of his advisers in undertaking during a three years period ending 30th June next, to pay 5½d. a pound at the railway or on the wharf for all Queensland grown seed cotton of good quality, had stimulated the cultivation of the plant far beyond their expectations. It was estimated that this season four million pounds of seed cotton would be treated at the local ginneries, which was more than four times the quantity available last year. The whole of the cotton would, under an agreement between the Queensland Government and the Australian Cotton Growing Association, be ginned locally; and the bulk of the ginned product would be shipped to England at a minimum price of 1s. 6d. a pound, offered for a limited period by the British Cotton Growers' Association. His advisers were endeavouring to secure the British Government's co-operation in the proposal to guarantee growers a remunerative return for at least an additional five years.

CRIMINAL CODE (AMENDMENT) ACT.

(Abolition of capital punishment.)

An Act to abolish capital punishment, and to amend the Criminal Code accordingly,. was assented to on 31st July, 1922.

DEBATE IN LEGISLATIVE ASSEMBLY.

On 20th July,

The Attorney-General (Hon. John Mullan), in moving the Second Reading, said that the Bill substituted for the death penalty imprisonment for life without mitigation by any Court. The offences then punishable by death were treason, wilful murder, piracy or attempted piracy, accompanied by assault or danger to life. Philanthropists and philosophers in every age had contended that the penalty of death was less efficacious in deterring crime than the continued imprisonment of a culprit. He would submit sufficient argument to justify that contention. Most countries had come to look upon the infliction of the death penalty as a barbarous method of dealing with crime, and as a result when juries were confronted with the alternative of finding a man guilty of an offence for which he might be hanged or of acquitting him, they frequently acquitted him. On the other hand, if they knew that a man could not suffer the death penalty, they would probably find him guilty. During the period between 1850 and 1879 in England, of the men arraigned for capital offences only 33 per cent. were convicted, whereas for non-capital offences 76 per cent. were convicted. In 1910 in America, there were 8,975 murders, and only 104 men were brought to justice, and America stood for capital punishment. The whole history of criminology went to show that harsh punishment did not stamp out crime. Over a century ago there were in England 250 offences punishable with death penalty. The abolition of capital punishment for 246 of these offences, instead of increasing crime, had diminished it. In Italy capital punishment had been abolished entirely since 1889, and for the ten years succeeding the abolition the number of murders showed a decrease of 32 per cent. Saxony abolished capital punishment in 1868. Belgium had not carried out the death penalty since 1868, although the law was still in existence. The Netherlands abolished capital punishment in 1870; Norway in 1876; Roumania in 1864; Portugal in 1867; and Sweden had recently passed a law abolishing capital punishment. In Queensland the death penalty had not been carried out during the last seven years—the seven years that the Labour Party had been in power. In Queensland in 1915 there were 5·1 per cent. serious offences tried in the Superior Courts for every 10,000 of the population; and in 1919 only 3·6 per cent., representing a reduction of 30 per cent.

The Attorney-General referred to the Report presented to the British Parliament in 1868 by the Royal Commission appointed to investigate the question of capital punishment. That Commission, he said, recommended the abolition of capital punishment in a number of cases. The objection which Lord Hobart had then raised to the death penalty, on the ground of its being irrevocable and irreparable, was as sound to-day as ever it had been. If an innocent man was hanged, the act was irrevocable and the loss was irretrievable. But if a man was imprisoned for life, there was always a possibility of liberating him, and to some extent repairing the injury inflicted upon him.

Mr. J. W. Vowles (Leader of the Opposition) said that the object of imposing penalties was to deter a person from doing wrong, and the magnitude of the penalty was mostly in accordance with the nature of the crime. If a man could be convicted on circumstantial evidence of murder that man could be just as easily convicted on circumstantial evidence for petty larceny. The only thing was that, if the death penalty had been put into effect, it was irrevocable and irretrievable. The Attorney-General had not informed the House that there was such a thing as the prerogative of mercy.

In every case where a man was sentenced to death the Governor in Council in Queensland had the last say as to whether the sentence should be carried out or not. Capital punishment was a deterrent. It was a warning that, if people would insist on taking the lives of their fellow-beings, then they had to suffer the penalty of death. The tendency of the Government, ever since they had come into power, had been to make things lighter for the criminal classes. The law said: "If you do kill, you have to suffer the penalty of death, if you do it wilfully." That had been the practice throughout English-speaking countries from time immemorial. He did not know why, in Queensland, they should want to lead in the direction of making the conditions better for murderers and criminals of the worst type.

LEGISLATIVE ASSEMBLY ACT (AMENDMENT) ACT.

(Voting by proxy.)

An Act to make provision for the voting by proxy of Members of the Legislative Assembly, absent through illness, was assented to 21st August, 1922.

The Act provides that if two or more medical practitioners certify that a Member of the Assembly is medically unfit to attend any sittings of the House for a specified period, and if the Member notifies the Speaker of his inability to "secure a pair," and that he desires to vote as a Member at every sitting of the House and of every Committee of the whole House by means of a named proxy, who is also a Member of the House, or in default by another named proxy; and if the Speaker is satisfied that the matters stated in the notification are true, the first or the second proxy may vote for the absent Member during the period specified, and the votes be recorded among the "Ayes" or the "Noes" as the case may be.

The absent Member may by notification to the Speaker substitute as his first and second proxy or either of them, two Members or one Member of the Assembly as the case may be.

Provision is also made for the certificate of ill-health of the absent Member to be renewed from time to time as may be necessary.

DEBATE IN LEGISLATIVE ASSEMBLY.

On 16th August,

The Premier (Hon. E. G. Theodore), in moving that the Bill be introduced, said that hon. Members might claim that it was a novelty; but he would remind them that Members who were away at the present time had their names included in the division list. By the simple process of securing the courtesy of a "pair," their names were recorded on the

Division list; but in the event of a refusal to give a "pair" to a sick Member, his name could not be included in the list. He was sure that neither on logical or any other grounds could there be any serious opposition to the proposal.

Mr. W. J. Vowles (Leader of the Opposition) said that the Bill was an innovation of the very worst form. It was going back to the old practice which was discarded sixty years ago by the House of Lords. The Government were initiating a principle by which they were going to get right away from the intention of the Constitution that Members should be in the House. Was the proposal simply introduced in order to save the situation as far as the Government were concerned ?* He thought that really it was brought in to save the Speaker from an unfortunate position. Public opinion had become so strong upon the question of compelling the Speaker and the Chairman of Committees on every occasion to take up a partisan position and vote on Government measures, that in order to get them out of that position the Premier was introducing legislation unheard of in any other English-speaking community.

Western Australia.

EMPIRE SETTLEMENT.

On 27th July, in the Legislative Council,

His Excellency the Lieutenant-Governor (Sir Robert McMillan), in his speech at the Opening of Parliament, said that his advisers had long felt that not only the material prosperity of Western Australia, but its safety as a white State in the Imperial Commonwealth of Nations depended upon a rapid increase of population and production. The recess had been devoted to the preparation of a comprehensive policy of immigration. Following upon the initiation of that policy the Premier (Sir James Mitchell) had placed certain proposals before the Prime Minister of the Commonwealth (the Rt. Hon. W. M. Hughes). These proposals were accepted by Mr. Hughes and Sir James Mitchell then proceeded to London to seek the co-operation of the Imperial Government. In that mission also he had been entirely successful, and before he had left London a Bill was passed by the Imperial Parliament authorising His Majesty's Government to render assistance in a policy of migration within the

* The state of Parties in the Legislative Assembly is :—Labour, 37; Country Party, 24; and Nationalists, 11.

Empire, and an agreement was completed under which Western Australia would be the first country in the Empire to secure the advantages of that legislation.

The Agreement.

The arrangement contemplated the taking from Great Britain of 75,000 men, women and children in a period of three to five years, the direct aim being an annual total of 25,000 souls. Under the Agreement entered into with the Commonwealth Government the whole cost of propaganda work, examination and passages would be borne by the Commonwealth Government, whilst the State maintained control of the selection of immigrants. The Commonwealth Government further undertook to return to Britain, at its own cost, any immigrants who on or shortly after arrival were found to be mentally or physically unfit.

The Agreement between the Imperial, the Commonwealth and the State Governments provided that in respect of these 75,000 immigrants £6,000,000 should be made available to the State in annual instalments in the proportion of £2,000,000 to each 25,000 immigrants. The interest on that money for the first five years after each moiety was raised would be borne by the Imperial, the Commonwealth and the State Governments in equal parts. The *per capita* payment of 25s. annually by the Commonwealth to the State under the Surplus Revenue Act would be augmented on account of the 25,000 new arrivals by a sum almost sufficient to pay the State's third of the interest Bill. Thus not only would the immigrants be landed in the State free of all cost, but each loan raised under the arrangement would be free of interest charge to the State for a period of five years.

The money so raised would be employed to strengthen the funds of the Agricultural Bank in order that improvements might be put in hand by existing holders to increase the capacity of their farms; to provide for the housing of people in country towns and districts; and to settle 6,000 additional people on the land, and to bring their holdings to a productive stage by clearing, fencing, etc., and providing railways and other facilities to enable them to market their products.

Tasmania.

*New Government (Note).**

Following on the General Election held on 10th June, 1922, a Nationalist Government was formed under Sir Walter Lee. The con-

* *Vide* JOURNAL, Vol. III., No. 3, p. 642.

stitution of the Ministry, which was sworn in on 28th June, was as follows :

Premier, Treasurer, and Minister for Education	Hon. Sir Walter Lee, M.H.A.
Chief Secretary	Hon. R. Eccles Snowden, M.H.A.
Minister of Lands and Soldiers' Settlement	Hon. A. Hean, C.M.G., M.H.A.
Minister of Works, Agriculture and Mines	Hon. J. B. Hayes, C.M.G., M.H.A.
Attorney-General and Minister of Railways..	Hon. W. B. Propsting, C.M.G., M.L.C.
Honorary Ministers	Hon. Tasman Shields, M.L.C. Hon. J. C. Newton, M.H.A.

Resignation of Government.

On 6th August, following a Vote of Censure in the House of Assembly, brought in by the Country Party, the Ministry resigned, and the following day a Coalition (Nationalist and Country Party) Government was formed with the Hon. J. B. Hayes as Premier. The new Ministry is composed as follows :—

Premier, Minister of Works and Agriculture	Hon. J. B. Hayes, C.M.G., M.H.A.
Treasurer and Minister for Education	Hon. Sir Walter Lee, M.H.A.
Chief Secretary and Minister of Railways..	Hon. J. C. McPhee, M.H.A.
Minister of Lands, Soldiers' Settlement and Mines	Hon. E. F. B. Blyth, M.H.A.
Attorney-General	Hon. W. B. Propsting, C.M.G., M.L.C.
Honorary Ministers	Hon. Tasman Shields, M.L.C. Hon. A. Hean, C.M.G., M.H.A.

NEW ZEALAND.

The Fourth (and last) Session of the Twentieth Parliament of New Zealand began on 28th June, 1922, *and concluded on 31st October,* 1922.

GOVERNOR-GENERAL'S SPEECH.

(Address-in-Reply; Genoa and The Hague Conferences; Economy measures; Defence and Foreign Affairs; Proportional Representation; Immigration and Land settlement; Unemployment; Customs reciprocity with Australia; Reciprocal enforcement of judgments within the Empire; Agricultural banks.)

The Speech of the Governor-General, Admiral Viscount Jellicoe, was delivered in the Legislative Council on 28th June, 1922.

Genoa and The Hague Conferences.

In the course of the speech Lord Jellicoe said that important affairs in the Dominion had prevented his Prime Minister from attending the Genoa Conference, and that the Attorney-General (Sir Francis Bell) had been appointed to represent New Zealand but had been able only to attend the later stages, and that in his absence the members of the British Delegation had been asked to act for the Dominion. Sir Francis Bell had, he said, also been appointed to represent New Zealand at the Conference at The Hague.

League of Nations.

Papers would be laid before them relating to the Conference of the League of Nations at Geneva, at which the High Commissioner had represented them, and they would be asked to pass resolutions confirming certain of its decisions.

Land settlement: finance.

In addressing the House of Representatives on financial matters, Lord Jellicoe said much more would have to be done in curtailing public expenditure. The Speech also referred to the signal success of the 5 per cent. five-million Loan recently floated in London at par as being a gratifying indication of the prestige and credit the Dominion enjoyed. It was essential that development should proceed vigorously by making more land available for settlers and by increasing the facilities for internal transport, and the greater part of the Loan would be used for those purposes.

Customs reciprocity with Australia.*

The tentative agreement entered into for a reciprocal tariff arrangement between the Dominion and the Commonwealth of Australia would be submitted to Parliament.

Other legislation foreshadowed.

At the request of the Imperial Government, Lord Jellicoe said, legislation would be introduced making provision for the reciprocal enforcement of judgments obtained in the Superior Courts within the Empire;† also for the establishment of Agricultural, or people's banks, which operated by means of a system of co-operative credit, and which had proved highly successful in several European countries and also in Canada and the United States.

DEBATE IN HOUSE OF REPRESENTATIVES.

The debate on the Address began in the House of Representatives on 4th July, when

Mr. D. Jones (Reform, *Kaiapoi*) moved the Address-in-Reply.

Mr. Jones said they recognised that the problems confronting the Supreme Council in Europe could scarcely be exaggerated, and brought home to them the fact that the problems of peace seemed perhaps even more difficult of solution than those of war. Speaking of the Washington Conference, he remarked that the spirit of sacrifice with which America met the Conference was worthy of all praise. The importance of the Treaty to them (in New Zealand) was that Britain and America had ten units of naval power to six or seven for the rest of the world. So that they had the satisfaction of knowing that the English-speaking people that day controlled the seas; and he believed that was one of the big factors in the future peace of the world. Speaking of the naval subsidy from New Zealand, Mr. Jones said he thought they all recognised it should be substantial, because the sea-way was vital to them. He believed there was a better way than helping simply with cash. After all, he said, what was an amount of £250,000 or £500,000 gift in a Budget of £900,000,000? One important aspect was the fact that in the preference in trade that they gave to Great Britain was a very important concession. Mr. Jones then dealt with the financial position of New Zealand, saying that it was sounder than anyone had expected twelve months ago to have found it.

Speaking of the American market, Mr. Jones said that one of the undertakings given to them by Armour and Co.

* *Vide* p. 897, and also under "Australia," p. 848.

† *Vide* JOURNAL, Vol. III., No. 2, p. 374.

was that they would develop the lamb trade in America; and if the allotments went on board (ship) as provided for, over 80,000 lambs would have been shipped into the American market that year, thus opening up a new market for their lamb. The Board of Control had secured sufficient control over Armour and Co. to grant them a licence with absolute safety to the Dominion.

On the question of the settlement of the returned soldier, he thought no belligerent country had treated its soldiers as well as New Zealand had treated hers. Up to the 20th June, he said, the Department had placed 27,392 men in positions, and at that date there had been only 295 men left on the register as wanting employment. In Canada they had had 82 per cent. of successes with the men they trained in occupations; in New Zealand they had 91 per cent. of successes. In Canada it cost £190 to train each man, in Australia £150, and in New Zealand £55 per man.

Trade representation in United States; Immigration.

Mr. Clutha Mackenzie (Reform, *Auckland, E.*) seconded the Address, and, in referring to general economic conditions, said that they lived in an era of high tariff walls. Australian trade, he said, had been considerably restricted by the high tariff that prevailed between the two countries. America had reinstated high tariffs, and they (in New Zealand) most likely should lose one of the very best customers for their wool. America was, and should be in the future, one of their greatest clients, and they wanted to see to it that they were properly represented there in matters of trade. The other factor affecting their trade was the ordinary agricultural rivalry of other countries. It seemed, he said, hardly likely, for example, that they should be able to resume their old place as sellers of beef in the London market. Their displacement had been largely brought about by the operation of trusts, but principally by their greater distance from London. In time they might have great rivalry from, perhaps, Russia and other butter-producing countries. Excluded from some markets by high protective tariffs and menaced in others by foreign competition, probably by recently hostile countries, he thought they should be justified in calling upon the Imperial Government before very long to institute a higher Imperial preference than existed at that time.

Speaking of immigration, Mr. Mackenzie said they had an immigration policy, but it was not one which would make of New Zealand what they wanted to see it. Land-settlement must be the key to the development of New Zealand. One of the greatest drags upon the development of the country, said Mr. Mackenzie, was the high price of land.

If they were to get young men from the Old Country they must guarantee to them that they would be able to get land at reasonable prices.

Want of confidence motion; Proportional Representation; Immigration.

On 5th July the debate on the Address was resumed, when **Mr. T. M. Wilford (Leader of the Opposition)** moved a want of confidence motion against the Government on the grounds that:—

It had failed (1) to redeem its promise that on the repeal of the Second Ballot another method of election would be substituted; (2) to efficiently administer the finances of the country, thereby imposing upon the people additional burdens, and had failed to curtail or control gross extravagance and wasteful expenditure in the administration of public Departments, and to run such Departments on sound business lines; (3) to lay on the table the Economy Committee Report, upon which was said to be based the supposed Government economies; (4) to prevent aggregation of land, which was a menace to the well-being of the State; and (5) to deal satisfactorily with the problem of unemployment.

Mr. Wilford said he was a convert absolutely to Proportional Representation, with the maintenance of the country quota. In 1910 and in 1911 he had been, he said, an opponent of the scheme. He believed the reason why proportional representation was not the law in every country in the world was that in many countries it had to be wrung from the parties that were in power, for they feared the results of fair representation of the people. There was that day a Party holding office in the country merely representing 206,000 of the electors out of 546,000, whilst 340,000 of the electors' votes were cast against them.

Coming to his next point, Mr. Wilford said, that just on a quarter of a million had been spent on immigration.

The Prime Minister (the Right Hon. W. F. Massey): "Do you object to that?"

Mr. Wilford replied that it was a scandalous waste of money in times like the present and that immigration at such a cost should cease while it affected local labour conditions. Turning to another point, he said they had been refused the report of the Committee in regard to necessary economies that had had to be made in the country. Further, the Prime Minister had worked out a balance at the 31st March, 1922, of surpluses of £7,531,367. He (Mr. Wilford) asked the Prime Minister if he would explain what had become of that £7,531,367?

Dealing with the purchase of land for soldiers' homes, he said the Government were absolutely answerable for the fictitious value of land that day. The cash they had handed over to a few land-holders had produced gross inflation. Had the Government required those holders to accept bonds in payment instead of cash, they would not have had that inflation. Referring to the question of aggregation of land-ownership in the Dominion, Mr. Wilford said it was clear that there were a number of places in New Zealand where this was going on, and that aggregation was a menace to the country, and no attempts were made to stop it. Finally, he spoke of the burden of taxation and the tremendous amount of unemployment, saying that the Government had failed in its duty to provide help for those entitled to ask for it, and who were not going to pray or beseech the Government for that assistance.

Liberals in agreement with Labour.

The Minister of Agriculture (Hon. W. Nosworthy) said the Leader of the Opposition had openly declared himself an advocate of proportional representation, and that he was opposed to the immigration policy of the Government. He (Mr. Nosworthy) would ask what difference there was between the Opposition and the Labour Party in the main planks of their platforms ? It appeared that the main planks of the Labour Party's platform were also planks in the so-called Liberal Party's platform. The Leader of the Opposition was a supporter of a State bank, he believed, and the Leader of the Labour Party was also. So that on three cards the two Leaders were in agreement.

Proportional Representation; etc.

The Prime Minister, in replying to the speech of the Leader of the Opposition, dealt at length with the question of Proportional Representation. He said he had changed his mind so far as proportional representation for the House of Representatives was concerned, and was not ashamed of it. He saw clearly now that would be no good to New Zealand. They had heard a good deal about the country quota. He had no hesitation in saying that they could not work the country quota satisfactorily in connection with proportional representation. They would be going to the country at a General Election in a few months, and how, he asked, would any Member of the House feel about it if, instead of having to contest an election as at present—in a single electorate where most of the people were acquainted with him—he had to contest one in an electorate as large as five of their present electorates ? It would take a man with a very long purse to pay the necessary expenses incurred in the canvassing of his district under a system of Proportional Representation.

They were told that Proportional Representation was

going to do away with minority Government. It would not. At the 1920 election in New South Wales there were 1,154,437 electors on the rolls; of those 648,709 recorded their votes. The others apparently were afraid of Proportional Representation and kept away. The number of votes recorded in support of the Labour Government of that day was 285,752 out of 648,709 votes cast—not half.

The New South Wales Labour Party on 16th June affirmed the desirability of abolishing the Proportional Representation system and reverting to single electorates and to use their best endeavours to bring it about. Even the Labour people were turning it down.

The hon. Gentleman had, he said, talked about the extravagance of the Government, but was not honest enough to admit the additional cost of the Departments from causes arising out of the War.

Immigration: financial position.

Proceeding to the question of immigration, Mr. Massey said: "The British people sixty or eighty years ago gave our forefathers the right to come to this country, and the British people have defended us ever since. . . . What should we be like in our own eyes, in our own estimation, or in the estimation of the nations of the world, if we turned round and said to British people, 'Get out; we do not want you in New Zealand'?" It was certain, said Mr. Massey, that if they could get half a million industrious people into the country within the next few years they would be of great value, "and," he concluded, "we should have the satisfaction of feeling that we had done our duty."

Mr. R. McCallum (Liberal, *Wairau*): "With means."

The Prime Minister: "With means, if possible. But do not forget when you say 'with means': that the best wealth that a British immigrant can bring to this country is health, strength, and industry."

Mr. McCallum: "He wants more than that."

The Prime Minister: "So much the better if he has it; but if he is healthy, strong, and industrious he will make a good citizen for the benefit of the whole community."

In his concluding remarks the Prime Minister said he knew there had been a tremendous amount of capital attempted to be made out of the financial position, and out of the reductions (in expenditure) that had become necessary. They were going to get the finances of the country right, he said, and when they had done that they should be a very long way on the road to prosperity.

Mr. Wilford's want of confidence motion was defeated by 37 votes against 20.

Labour motion of "want of confidence"; Wages and cost of living; International relationship.

On 14th July,

Mr. H. E. Holland (Leader of the Labour Party) moved:—

That the following words be added to the Address-in-Reply: "Whereas the Arbitration Court during the War period did not increase the minimum wage in proportion to the increase in the cost of living: And whereas wages measured in purchasing power have not been restored to the pre-War level, this House recommends that legislation be passed requiring the Arbitration Court to amend existing awards, so that the nominal increase in wages over the 1914 standard shall not be less than the present-day increase in the cost of living. The computation to be made on the principle always accepted by the Court—namely, six-monthly moving averages for 'all groups,' including food, rent, fuel, light, clothing, and miscellaneous: And whereas the Act placed on the statute-book last session requires the Court of Arbitration not to reduce wages below an amount sufficient to maintain a fair standard of living: And whereas it has not yet been determined what amount of wages is necessary 'to maintain a fair standard of living,' this House further recommends that the Government appoint a Basic-wage Commission to take evidence and report on what amount of wages is necessary to maintain a fair standard of living: And whereas the Judge of the Arbitration Court has determined that the average increase in the whole cost of living is to-day 62 per cent. beyond the pre-War level: And whereas the last bonus granted to the public servants was granted on the Statistician's figures for March, 1920, when, according to the Statistician, the average increase for the whole cost of living (all groups) was 63 per cent.: And whereas now, according to the Judge of the Arbitration Court, the cost of living at March, 1920, was 73 per cent., and not 63 per cent., above the pre-War level: And whereas the cost of living went still higher, but has now returned to the level on which the final bonus was granted this House recommends that legislation should be passed this session restoring the bonus to the public servants. This House wishes to draw Your Excellency's attention to the fact that according to a *Gazette* issued on the 25th May, 1922, there was, according to the Secretary to the Treasury and the Acting Accountant to the Treasury, no less than a sum of £7,531,366 in 'Ordinary Revenue Account' on the 31st March, 1922, available for ordinary revenue expenditure purposes, and of this sum there was in actual cash £4,824,951. These figures were certified to by the Controller and Auditor-General, and they show conclusively that, from the point of view of the public finances, there was no excuse whatever for reducing the salaries of the public servants. We further maintain that had the state of the public finances required an increase in revenue the Government was not justified in remitting land and income tax for the year ending the 31st March, 1922, amounting to nearly half a million, while the reductions in the bonuses of the public servants for the same period were £177,000. Furthermore, this House wishes to draw Your Excellency's attention to the grave breach of faith involved in your Government's failure to fulfil its promise to confer full political and civil rights on the public servants of the Dominion. Finally, we would submit that Your Excellency's Government, by reason of its failure to appreciate the importance of international relationships and its inadequate representation at both

Washington and Genoa, and, further, by reason of its class legislation, has forfeited the confidence of this House and the country."

Speaking of the Arbitration Court and the wages reductions, Mr. Holland said he did not think there was a Member on the Government or Opposition benches who would deny that the wages of the worker that day, measured in purchasing-power, were not restored to the pre-War level. They (the Labour Party) were taking up the attitude that the House should give the Arbitration Court a mandate to amend existing awards, to restore wages to the equivalent of the 1914 standard of living. He wished to draw attention to the remissions of taxation which had amounted to well on towards £500,000, and to put them beside the wage-reductions in the Public Service, which had amounted to £177,000. In doing that he wished to point to the position of the railway men, even in contrast with that of the workers outside that service. The workers outside had suffered reductions which they ought never to have been asked to suffer and were altogether out of proportion. Before the reductions in the Public Service the Government had given remissions in taxation to the land- and income-tax payers. The big landowners and the big business houses with city properties had benefited to the extent of hundreds of pounds, while the small men benefited by a few shillings.

Mr. Holland then proceeded to criticise the mortgage system of the country, giving instances of cases which, he said, were mostly those of returned soldiers—men due to be driven off the land because of the burden of the mortgages which they were carrying.

Washington and Genoa Conferences; etc.

Speaking of the Washington Conference, Mr. Holland said the Government had thought so little of it that it had sent a gentleman who had no representative capacity—who held no elective position. To the Conference at Genoa they had sent another gentleman (Sir Francis Bell) who had no representative capacity. He was not an elected representative of the people: he was a nominated Member of the Legislative Council.

In conclusion, Mr. Holland said that the Government had given a very distinct promise that it would introduce legislation for conferring full political rights upon the Public Service. The public servants wanted full political and civil rights, including the right of the Post and Telegraph men to join up with the Alliance of Labour.

The Hon. G. J. Anderson (Minister of Labour), in replying to speeches of Labour Members who had, he said, stated inferentially that the Government had influenced the Arbitration Court to reduce the workers' wages, remarked that after all it came to this : that in times of depression the Arbitration Court and the Government had got to meet the situation and make reductions. The Labour Party, he said, had done their best to kill the Arbitration Court. He (Mr. Anderson) was satisfied that if the Arbitration Court had not been in existence, and if the legislation passed last Session had not been enacted, wages that day would have been considerably lower than they were.

Mr. Holland's motion was negatived by 43 votes against 9.

Labour Party and Liberals.

Mr. Jones, in his reply, said that he thought the contention advanced at first had not been shaken—that the general administration of the Government had advanced the prosperity of the country, and left them, though temporarily with a certain amount of financial stringency, in a very sound position. Continuing, he said they had seen a new movement in the House that night—that was, the movement of the Labour Party towards the Liberal benches.

The Address was agreed to without division on 25th July.

DEBATE IN LEGISLATIVE COUNCIL.

Russia and Germany and the League of Nations.

On 5th July,

Col. the Hon. W. E. Collins (*Wellington*) moved the Address-in-Reply, and in speaking of the Conference at The Hague said he took it that one of the things to be considered would be whether the present form of government in Russia should be recognised by other nations, and whether any great financial assistance would be rendered to the people of Russia ; also, whether, how, and when, she and Germany should be allowed to enter as members of the League of Nations, adding that he did not see how it ever could function properly until Russia and Germany were admitted. After speaking at length on the League of Red Cross Societies, which he described as a much greater factor than they had ever possessed before for the promotion of peace, Colonel Collins said that immediately they were back to normal conditions he hoped the first thing the Government would do would be to put the peace organisation of the New Zealand Military Forces upon the highest possible footing.

Colonel Collins also spoke at length on questions of public health.

Col. the Hon. G. J. Smith (*Christchurch*) in seconding the motion said that in his opinion the Washington Conference had simply achieved a breathing space for the nations of the earth. He considered that the Defence Forces had been cut down to an absolutely dangerous degree. Speaking on the question of the proposed agricultural banks, Col. Smith said that if they had these they must expect to have a demand for industrial banks; and if they had industrial banks, then was the last stage of the farming and trading community not going to be worse than the first? He thought they were indebted to the banks of the Dominion for the way they had stood by not only the farmers but the manufacturing and commercial people during the War.

The Hon. W. Earnshaw (*Wellington*) in speaking of social and industrial matters said there was a great movement, under pressure—it might be among the farmers and the manufacturers of the country—to declare for the abolition of preference to unionists. This frontal attack would be disastrous to the country, which could not afford, he said, to have a labour conflagration at the present time.

Defence expenditure.

The Hon. J. Barr (*Christchurch*) differed from Col. Smith as to the cutting-down of Defence expenditure. He (Mr. Barr) was inclined to think it would have been better to have cleaned out the Defence Department entirely. The great defence of the country would be future legislation that would enable their children to be physically fit, properly trained as to health, physique, morality, and loyalty to that country, which included the Empire to which the country belonged.

Navy and Foreign Affairs; Dominion status; etc.

The Hon. W. H. Triggs (*Christchurch*) said that for the results that had been achieved at the Washington Conference they had every reason to be grateful. They had secured—for a time at any rate—a respite from the heaviest expenditure for naval construction, and they had also secured, he thought, for a time the adjustment of questions that were vitally affecting the peace of the Pacific. No one, he said, could feel more strongly than he did about the need of maintaining the supremacy of the British Navy. He would prefer to see no limitation placed upon the Navy, but that they should extend it to any extent they felt necessary for the effective defence of the Empire. Whatever other nations might do or leave undone their duty was clear—they must stand by the Mother-Country in the matter of naval defence for the prevention of war as loyally as they had done in the prosecution of the late War.

Referring with approval to the attitude taken up by Sir John Salmond, the representative of New Zealand at the Washington Conference, Mr. Triggs said it was quite right that the British Government should keep in constant consultation with the self-governing Dominions in regard to foreign affairs. He could not conceive, he said, that the British Government would ever venture into any war unless it was sure beforehand not only of the approval but also of the support of the self-governing Dominions, and it would be absolutely suicidal for it to do so. And he could not conceive that the British Government would enter into any treaty affecting a self-governing Dominion unless a reservation were made in favour of that Dominion if it objected to being included in the treaty. With that they should be satisfied, and the less talk there was of a sovereign status, and of the Dominions being represented by their own Ambassadors at Foreign Courts, the better. That way danger lay, he thought—serious danger of the disruption of the British Empire. In his concluding remarks, Mr. Triggs said that when they looked at the vast spaces of Canada few of them would doubt that in the course of time the population of that great Dominion would outnumber that of Great Britain, but he could not believe that there would be any transfer of the seat of Government. The veneration and affection of the rest of the Empire for the Mother-Country were too deeply rooted to admit of any such transfer.

Col. Collins in his reply said that he entirely disagreed with the remarks of Mr. Barr with respect to doing away with their Defence Force. In reference to the Washington Conference, he said that the idea of settling matters of importance by round-the-table conferences was the best method of settling disputes. There was another factor which he thought was operating for peace, and that was the great love of the English-speaking people for peace. In regard to land settlement Col. Collins said if they could settle the people in the country on small areas it would be of the greatest benefit to the country financially, and would be the best answer to anything like socialism and communism.

The debate in the Council concluded on 14th July, and the Address agreed to.

WASHINGTON CONFERENCE TREATIES.

(Parliamentary approval; Constitutional position; Procedure at Washington compared with League of Nations; Admiralty and Dominion Naval policy; Annual Empire Conferences; Privy Council as Imperial Council.)

The report of Sir John Salmond, New Zealand's representative at the Washington Conference, was laid on the table by the Prime Minister on 16th August, and a discussion took place in the House of Representatives on 18th August, when Mr. Massey moved for purposes of record the formal assent of New Zealand to the ratification by His Majesty of the Treaties negotiated at Washington, though pointing out that the ratification required was that of His Majesty, and that no action in New Zealand was legally required. In dealing with the report generally, Mr. Massey referred to the procedure adopted at the Washington Conference and drew a distinction between the position of the Dominions there and that which they occupied at an Assembly of the League of Nations, expressing his preference for the procedure at Washington. He also dealt with New Zealand's naval contribution, and outlined the naval policy recommended by the Admiralty.

In regard to Imperial Conferences, Mr. Massey suggested a modification or rearrangement of the present scope of the Privy Council so that it might do the work now done by the Empire Council in London.

DEBATE IN HOUSE OF REPRESENTATIVES.

On 18th August,

The Prime Minister (the Right Hon. W. F. Massey) in moving that the House take into consideration the report of Sir John Salmond, as the representative of the Dominions at the Conference on the limitation of Armaments held at Washington, said the people of the country had good reason to congratulate themselves on the very able and efficient manner the Dominion had been represented. In referring to the statement in the report to the effect that the ratification of the Washington Treaties required by the constitutional law of the British Empire was that of His Majesty, and that no action in New Zealand was legally required, Mr. Massey said that, in view of the direct participation of New Zealand, it might well be thought expedient that the Treaties should be submitted to both Houses of the Legislature in order that resolutions might be passed approving of their ratification by His Majesty; and in order, he said, to prevent any misapprehension, or any dispute in years to come over what that Dominion had done, he should move a little later on:—

> That the House of Representatives of New Zealand in Parliament assembled assents to the ratification by His Majesty of the Washington Treaties as negotiated by the plenipotentiaries at the recent Washington Conference.

Proceeding, Mr. Massey said they had to be thankful that it had been possible to bring about a better understanding than had existed for some years previously between the three great naval Powers of the world—Britain, America, and Japan; and there was no doubt in his mind that the probability of war in the Pacific had been made very much less for quite a long time to come than they had anticipated as likely even a year ago. But there were many things which the Washington Conference did not do: there was, he said, nothing to prevent the naval Powers or any country building as many ships as they felt inclined to build up to 10,000 tons, carrying 8-inch guns: neither had they done away with submarines or airships in any form. He did not say, he continued, that he looked forward to war in the immediate future; but they could not afford to take risks. Speaking of the prohibition whereby Britain, the United States and Japan could not create new fortifications within certain areas in the Pacific, which prohibition, the report of Sir John Salmond stated, extended, in the case of the United States, to the whole of the present or future possessions of that Power in the Pacific Ocean, with the exception of the Hawaiian Islands, Mr. Massey said that he had had the opportunity of visiting the American naval base there, and experts had informed him that it was absolutely impregnable. In the case of the British Empire the prohibition extended to Hong Kong. That was rather an important matter for Britain, but he (Mr. Massey) was not able to enter into reasons for it.

Continuing, he said, the time might come when one of the Powers—Britain, America, Japan, France or Italy—might wish to give notice that it desired to terminate the Treaty. That would probably come in time, although he hoped that it would be a long time; but when the time did arrive the first thing that would happen would be that the representatives of the different Powers would be called together, and an attempt would be made to renew the Treaty in, perhaps, a more satisfactory form. He believed that the time would come when war would be no more. If that ever did come it would be by a combination of the great Powers of the world, who would say to the others who were inclined for war, that they must refer their disputes to a Court of International Justice, such as that which had been set up in connection with the League of Nations.

Dominion constitutional position; New Zealand attitude.

Mr. Massey then quoted from Sir John Salmond's report about the constitutional position, as follows:—

> The procedure of the Washington Conference was in itself a clear indication that the Dominions were there not in their own right as quasi-independent States, but merely as constituent portions of an undivided Empire. When any question came to be voted upon for the purpose of ascertaining whether there existed that unanimous consent which was necessary for a Treaty, the question was put to the British

Delegation as a whole, and was answered "Yes" or "No" by Mr.* Balfour as the head and spokesman of that Delegation and on behalf of the British Empire as a whole. Although in the process of discussion and negotiation the representatives of the Dominions had, and exercised, the same right of audience as any other Delegates, they never voted separately on behalf of their own Dominion on any question. The final decision in every case was that of the British Empire as an indivisible unity.

The position of the Dominions at Washington was essentially different from the position which they occupy as an Assembly of the League of Nations. By the special and peculiar organisation of that body, self-governing Colonies are admitted as members in their own right as if they were independent States. Although by constitutional and international law such Colonies are merely constituent portions of the Empire to which they belong, they are entitled by express agreement to be treated, so far as practicable, as if they were independent. But no such principle was recognised at Washington, or exists except for the special purposes of the League of Nations.

Commenting on this part of the report, Mr. Massey said he was bound to say that he had never liked the arrangement made in connection with the League of Nations. There was one dangerous feature in it. He did not agree with everything that had been said, that in signing the Peace Treaty they had become independent nations. That was absolute nonsense, he added, and the wish of many people who had so expressed themselves was in many cases the father to the thought. The idea at the back of the minds of many people at the time when the arrangement had been made in connection with the representation of the Empire and the Dominions at the Council or Assembly of the League of Nations was that by placing the Dominions in a semi-independent position, and giving each of them a vote, it strengthened the influence of the Empire as a whole. He (Mr. Massey) would call attention to the point that there might be a difference of opinion on the part of the Dominion representatives, and there was nothing to prevent two of such representatives voting one way, and two another way, and he did not need to say that was a weakness, and a weakness which ought to be remedied. In consequence, he was pleased at what had taken place at Washington.

It was not well, he proceeded, to advertise that sort of thing too much, but it was known that certain of the Dominions were very strongly opposed to going to the Washington Conference without special invitations being given in each case. He (Mr. Massey) had had several communications on the subject, but it was not well to make correspondence like that public, though in no sense had confidence been imposed upon him. He would read one short telegram sent by him to the Prime Minister of another Dominion in reply to a communication, wherein a request had been made to him as Prime Minister

* Now Earl Balfour.

of New Zealand to decline to go to Washington, or at all events, to protest emphatically against the fact that no invitations were forthcoming for the individual Dominions of the Empire.

Mr. T. M. Wilford (Leader of the Opposition): "It only takes one guess to tell where that came from."

The Prime Minister, continuing, said his telegram was :—

Replying to your telegram of 19th instant, our representative had sailed before your telegram came to hand, but while the point you raise is important from certain points of view, I consider it to be much more important that the Empire should speak with one voice and with no uncertain sound.

Naval defence: Admiralty advice.

In reference to a statement in Sir John Salmond's report that: "It is the right and duty of every State to make proper provision for its national safety," Mr. Massey said he did not think it was possible for them to forget the lessons of the War. The British Empire stood for peace; but it might be called upon in the future to defend some part of its territory, or some of its people, or some one of its Allies, and it could not defend them unless it was properly prepared. Quoting from a document which, he said, was not confidential, Mr. Massey said the Admiralty had outlined the naval policy by which New Zealand could best assist in Empire naval defence as follows, giving the various points in order of relative importance :—

1. During the period of financial stringency, maintenance by New Zealand of a nucleus of a sea-going squadron which when times are better can be rapidly expanded. Expansion to consist of light cruisers and ocean-going submarines.
2. Provision of oil reserves in New Zealand.
3. Assistance in equipping Empire naval bases by financial contribution or supply of material manufactured in New Zealand.
4. Providing bases, docks, depôts, and reserves of stores and fuel in New Zealand for vessels maintained by New Zealand.
5. Providing for local protection of trade and storage of guns for merchant ships and their escorts, and providing trained personnel for them.
6. Providing mobile defence organisations for ports, including mine-sweeping organisation.

There, said he, they had the opinion of the men in the Empire best qualified to judge what was necessary for the defence of the Empire. He did not suggest that they should attempt anything like what was suggested under the circumstances existing at that time. That was for the future, but it was clearly necessary that a commencement should be made. He had no doubt but that a similar form of communication was passing between the British Government and other parts of the Empire. At the time he had referred to the subject previously, they had all expected there would have been something coming from Germany in Reparations. The outlook now was somewhat gloomy, and he could not predict what might eventuate in the way of Reparations. If they were going to do their duty in the matter of providing their share for naval defence, they had got to find the cash. If, he said, they had succeeded in recovering some millions from Germany, he would have been quite prepared to suggest that it should all have been spent on naval defence. It was clear they could not expect to sponge on the United Kingdom for the defence of their Dominion.

Dominions and Foreign Affairs; Annual Conferences; An Empire Council.

Turning to the question of the status of the Dominions, Mr. Massey said they were acknowledged as partners, and it was admitted that they had a right to a say—not only to a consultation, but a right to a say—in the management of the affairs of the Empire, and especially in its foreign policy. " When I say ' the public affairs of the Empire,' " Mr. Massey said, " I refer, in the first place, to the possibilities in connection with the making of war or of peace, the making of treaties, inter-Empire communication, foreign policy, and anything in which the Empire as a whole is concerned."

Referring to a speech made by Mr. Lloyd George at the winding-up of the last Imperial Conference, Mr. Massey said a great deal had been done in connection with those Conferences, but there was a great deal yet to do. He did not know when it was going to be done, because in every country of the Empire they had their own domestic affairs to attend to, and they must come first; but some definite understanding would have to be arrived at with regard to what he would call, for the time being, a continuity of Conferences. He did not mean that the Conferences should meet every week, every month, or every three months, but he did think that those Empire Councils, or whatever they were to be called, should meet not less than once a year.

Mr. G. W. Forbes (Reform, *Hurunui*): " They could not meet once a year if the Prime Ministers are to be present."

The Prime Minister in reply said that the Prime Minister could not in every instance leave his own country, and that was one of the difficulties; but, he added, they had managed to find an able and efficient representative to look after their interests at Washington. It ought, he said, to be the Prime Minister, because questions were continually cropping up which only he could answer; but he did not think it would always be possible. If they were not going to lose the effect and benefits of what had been done up to that date they would have to arrange for those meetings to take place in London—or wherever the Conference met—not less frequently than once a year. The whole trip could be done in four or five months as far as representatives of Australia and New Zealand were concerned. That would be a great improvement upon what had taken place in the past.

Then there was another difficulty. He thought it would come to a modification of the Privy Council, with the object of forming an Empire Council. One of their difficulties was the continual overlapping of the affairs of the United Kingdom itself in connection with the business of the Conference. Only the setting-up of a separate conference or council could, he thought, avoid that sort of thing. Something could be done by way of rearranging or modifying the Privy Council, so as to do the work that was now done by the Empire Council in London.

League of Nations; Empire and peace.

Speaking of the League of Nations, Mr. Massey said that the danger was that it might lead to a false sense of security on the part of some countries. There was no power behind it—nothing to enforce its decisions. Unless the stronger nations joined it he did not think anything of the sort was possible. He would like to see a combination of nations, led by Britain and America, which would be able to say to all the other nations of the world that they must keep the peace.

In conclusion, Mr. Massey said he believed they (the Empire) had been specially protected by Providence and preserved for some great purpose which had not been revealed up to the present; but he believed that a part of that purpose would be to assist in bringing peace to the whole world.

Mr. T. M. Wilford, in seconding the Prime Minister's motion, said that Members on his side of the House yielded to no Members on the other side when it came to Imperialistic sentiment, or to standing for Empire and constitutional methods, and quoted at length from a speech he had made in the House in 1910, on the Defence Amendment Bill, in which he had referred to the imminence of war with Germany and had pointed out that the flag of the British Navy was their protection and that if the Navy were annihilated their chief defence was gone.

Washington Conference.

Speaking of the Washington Conference, Mr. Wilford said that the perils of Anglo-American conflict had been averted by frank consultation. The British and American Governments had admitted that they had joint responsibilities, and for the first time in the history of Great Britain and America there was a sincere and spontaneous identity of purpose achieved between four great naval Powers.

The Conference had, he continued, banished the fear of naval competition between Great Britain and the United States of America, which must have grown from the Anglo-Japanese Alliance had it continued. They wanted to remember that nothing achieved at the Conference was going to banish for all time the race for armaments, but only to banish for all time, or at least for ten years under the conditions of the pact, the race for building certain armaments. What had appealed to him was the simplicity of the Conference, the absolute absence of pomp or show and the business-like propositions which were placed before the Conference by the Chairman, Mr. Hughes. He (Mr. Wilford) disagreed entirely with the Prime Minister in what he had said about the non-menace of the submarine, and quoted from Sir John Salmond's report to the effect that Great Britain had had to keep aircraft, submarines, destroyers, and various other vessels, to the number of 3,000, to meet the menace of nine or ten submarines. In reference to aircraft Mr. Wilford said that whatever amount they might consider they should subscribe by way of naval contribution towards the Empire's defence, they had to recognise that all the experts laid it down that the future efficiency of those fleets was rendered absolutely uncertain by the menace of aircraft.

Dominion representation: India and Newfoundland.

In regard to the Conference, Mr. Wilford said he was thoroughly satisfied with the status New Zealand had possessed, and that sending a Delegate to be under the British representative was quite sufficient for that Dominion, and that it was quite right that the British Delegation should speak on behalf of the Dominions. But, he said, some curious things had happened at the Conference in regard to representation—contradictory things that could hardly be reconciled; for while one of the Dominions had no representative there at all, and that a self-governing Dominion—Newfoundland—they found India, which was not self-governing, had a representative. There seemed, to be no basis of representation on behalf of the far-flung parts of the Empire, whether they were self-governing or otherwise.

League of Nations; Near East and Foreign Affairs.

Speaking of the League of Nations, Mr. Wilford remarked that it was a tribunal that was handicapped from the fact that it had no policemen—that was, no force to give effect to its decrees. He added that it was a League of Allies instead of a League of all Nations.

Referring to the Near East, Mr. Wilford said the world was menaced that day. The menace of the Treaty of Sèvres and the possibility of the Greeks entering Constantinople was one of the greatest menaces of the world. They should not overlook the fact, he continued, that there were seventy-two million Muhammadans in India, and Muhammadans in various countries of the world, and those people would suffer anything rather than see Constantinople fall to the Greek army. There was still a menace in the possible military development of Germany, who, if she thought of going to war that day, would not have the menace of 1914, of Russia on her flank, but on the contrary would have an armed force from Russia with munitions. In conclusion, Mr. Wilford said: "I believe from my reading that we have to trade with Germany and Russia or fight them."

Mr. H. E. Holland (Leader of the Labour Party) said he regretted, as he supposed every Member of the House regretted, that there were not greater achievements at the Washington Conference in the direction of ending war.

He thought it was a pity that the invitation to the Conference had not gone to all the nations of the earth. They were, he proceeded, in the unfortunate position that night of discussing a motion to approve a Treaty which had already been ratified, and in the approval or rejection of which they had no voice whatever. The Treaty, he said, imposed no limitations, either in numbers or in aggregate tonnage on the cruiser fleet of any of the Powers. That was one of the failures of the Treaty.

On the question of submarines, Mr. Holland said it was both regrettable and disastrous from the viewpoint of humanity that the British Delegation's proposal had not been accepted, and, after referring to the fact that a French official naval journal had published an article in which the sinking of the *Lusitania* was justified, he remarked that if he were asked to say where the real danger of the world's peace lay that day, he would say that France was the greatest menace, largely because of the lack of balance on the part of those at the head of her affairs.

In regard to Allied War-debts to Great Britain, Mr. Holland said that one of the best and most effective moves in the direction of a world peace and the readjustment of world conditions was Britain's recent suggestion for the cancellation of the Allied Debts and her offer to forgo her share of the reparations. That was, he said, one of the most statesmanlike things that had been done by Britain in modern times, and, if adopted, would rapidly pave the way for the peace of the world. After dealing fully with the origin and history of poisonous gases in warfare, saying that the whole world had been filled with horror because of it, and expressing his disappointment that the Conference had not recognised that aerial warfare was going to be far more disastrous than naval warfare, Mr. Holland referred to the Pacific Treaty, which, he said, was in some respects good, but he thought that the absence of Russia, which had supreme interests in the Far East and bordering on the Pacific was a calamity. It was now a different document from what it had been when the Labour Party had raised a determined protest against it. The new Treaty, he said, imposed no obligation of military or naval action in support of any party thereto, and that was a good thing.

When they came to consider wherein the Conference had failed, he thought they should find the proof in Sir John Salmond's own words, when he said that the primary purpose and significance of the work of the Conference was financial. Was it not a pity that the agreements had not been based on an ethical significance? If Sir John Salmond's views were correct, all the Conference would have resulted in doing would be to prepare the way for the next war—to make war cheaper—to make it possible for nations to engage in the destruction of life at the least possible cost.

Passing to what he termed the achievements and failures of the Conference, Mr. Holland said that the achievement of the four-Power pact for ten years, under which there would be peace in the Pacific, for that period, providing no outside Power aggressed, was good; its failure was that it divided up the Pacific into territories mandated—that was, he said, owned—by the "Big Four," to exploit for themselves—for example, Nauru, Samoa, New Guinea, etc.

After mentioning what he considered the achievements in regard to China, Mr. Holland said the failure was that the treaty presumed to dictate to China as to her government and administration. It in no sense secured peace for China, nor did it protect her against aggression, the only things that mattered. Mr. Holland then enumerated what were in his view the achievements in regard to disarmament, saying that the failures were that the Treaty said nothing about the abolition of armaments; the limitation or prohibition of aircraft or submarines; nothing about the use of deadly microbes in war.

In conclusion, he said that the present League of Nations was not really a League of Nations: it was a League of the Allied Powers in the late War. What was wanted was a League of Nations that would include every people under the sun, that would in reality be a league of peoples able to set up an international organisation which would not only proclaim that it existed to encourage all the acts of peace, but which would not hesitate to use all the international force at its command to forbid the occurrence of any war in the future.

Pacific pact; Dominion's external policy.

The Minister of Education (Hon. C. J. Parr) said that the abrogation of the Anglo-Japanese Treaty in favour of the new arrangement for the Pacific had, with regard to New Zealand and Australia, a significance of even greater import than the naval treaty, and was going to be one of the best things that had happened for those countries since they had become British communities. The great factor was that, whilst they had not lost the friendship of Japan, they had by the pact enlisted the future moral support of the United States in any question that concerned Australia and New Zealand in the Pacific. The States would sympathise, he said, with the ambition of Australia and New Zealand to build up in those southern seas a great white civilisation, which was clearly the policy of the future with regard to Australia and New Zealand. They should see in the years to come not six or seven million people in those southern lands, but ten times that number—people, he hoped, of their own race and blood, from the Home-land and possibly from the States. The four-Power pact established at Washington would tend in some way in that direction. It enabled them in that little country to see what their foreign policy should be. Clearly, the first object for New Zealand in its outside relations should be brotherly friendship and amity with their kin in Australia. Secondly, while there was no reason why they should not retain the friendship of Japan and of the East, there was every reason why they should seek a closer unity with their white brethren, largely their kin of North America—Canada and the United States.

Naval contribution and Conference; Pacific fleet.

Speaking of the naval treaty, Mr. Parr said the danger to Great Britain was not invasion, but was the great risk of its food supply being cut off in war by cruisers and submarines. Therefore the position brought them into partnership with the Old Land in regard to naval defence. They required protection for one reason and Great Britain for another. The time was ripe, he proceeded, for the meeting in London of the best expert minds of the Dominion and the Mother-land to take counsel as to what should be the exact nature of their contribution. Continuing, he said it would seem that a fleet stationed in the North Sea was of little use to Australia or New Zealand against any possible aggression in those southern seas. There must be a Pacific fleet, and towards the cost of it Canada, Australia and New Zealand must contribute largely.

Mr. Balfour and the "Spirit of Sacrifice."

Mr. H. Atmore (Liberal, *Nelson***)** said that the leader of the Labour Party had very properly pointed out that the summary given by Sir John Salmond did not show much result in the way of making for peace. It was a damning statement when he (Sir John Salmond) had said that the Conference had no ethical significance. There was, Mr. Atmore said, no ethical significance in the attitude of America, who, ever keen on the dollar, had seen where the capital competition was leading all the nations. The outstanding figure, in his opinion (at the Conference) was not the President of the United States or Mr. Hughes, but Mr. Balfour. It had been his wonderful tact that had smoothed away so many difficulties, and he (Mr. Atmore) was pleased, as a Britisher, to see that the Britisher led the world when they came to the spirit of sacrifice. America could not be named in the same breath when it came to the spirit of sacrifice. Mr. Atmore stated that America's loss in man-power was less than that of Australia and compared America's war expenditure with that of Great Britain.

Naval contribution.

On the question of New Zealand's naval contribution, Mr. Atmore said it was not honest on their part to sit down and talk platitudes about the British Navy and the necessity of keeping it up to a certain standard when with £33 per head of their population in the savings banks as compared with £6 per head in the Old Country, they (in New Zealand) were only paying 6s. per head per annum for the upkeep of the Navy, while the hard-up Britisher with much unemployment was paying £1 16s., and he hoped the Prime Minister would take the necessary steps to remedy that by making some definite proposal for an increased contribution, which he quite believed Parliament would second. They were not entitled to raise a voice on questions of Empire, he continued, until they paid their share.

The Minister of Internal Affairs (Mr. W. Downie Stewart), in speaking of the status of the British Dominions at the Washington Conference, said that the attitude of the American Government in inviting only Great Britain to send what Delegation she liked, indicated clearly that so long as a great democracy like America refused to recognise any independent status for the Dominions it was useless for them under the terms of the League of Nations to assume that they had acquired independence. Mr. Downie Stewart said that the effect of the Washington Conference seemed to him, from the legal point of view, to have clearly established that while the position of the Dominions had been greatly enhanced, and their authority greatly increased by the proceedings following on the War, they had not acquired the status which some writers had claimed for them.

The Prime Minister did not make any speech in reply, and his motion was agreed to.

MANDATED TERRITORY OF WESTERN SAMOA.

(First Report (1920-21); Consent of League of Nations before publication.)

The report on the Mandated Territory of Western Samoa for the period from 1st May, 1920, to the 31st March, 1921, was laid on the table of the House of Representatives on 8th August by the Minister of External Affairs, when Mr. T. M. Wilford raised the question of the necessity of obtaining the consent of the League of Nations before the report could be published.

DEBATE IN HOUSE OF REPRESENTATIVES.

The Minister of External Affairs (Hon. E. P. Lee), in moving that the report chronicling the affairs of the territory up to the 31st March, 1921, lie on the table, mentioned that it was the first report that had been presented to the League of Nations. A further report up to 31st March, 1922, was almost ready. The practice adopted was to send the report to the Council of the League of Nations, and not to publish it until the Government had the authority of the Council to do so. He proposed to ask the Council to consent to the publication of the second report immediately after it had been despatched to the Council. Should there be no objection—and, he said, he did not think there would be—hon. Gentlemen would then be in possession of full information of the affairs of Samoa up to 31st March last.

Mr. T. M. Wilford (Leader of the Opposition), in reference to Mr. Lee's remark about getting the consent of the League of Nations before publishing the report, said, did they understand that their Mandate included the fact that they had to make a secret report to the League of Nations? Were they such reports that they were not to have publicity unless the League of Nations said they might be published. Was New Zealand in the position that, having the Mandate, it should not know what the Government's report was in regard to the care of Samoa unless the League of Nations said "Yes"? He could not believe, he said, that any country had to hold a Mandate under such conditions, and that the report should only be given to the League of Nations, and not to Parliament.

The Minister of External Affairs explained that the Government considered that, under the Mandate, until the report had reached the Council of the League of Nations it should not be published in that country. That course had been followed in regard to the first report. It was now proposed, as he (Mr. Lee) had said, to publish the report—and this applied to the second report then being completed—after it had been despatched and before its receipt by the Council.

Mr. Wilford said that what he was objecting to was the principle that, unless the League of Nations said they could see the Government's report on Samoa, they were not to have it. If it was so, it should be got over by the Minister preparing a report for Parliament, because the country, and the House, had a right to demand that there should be an annual report on Samoa presented to Parliament. Even that would be better than saying that the country was going to be denied the right to discuss the report sent to the League of Nations until it said "Yes." Did that statement bar their discussing Samoa? If so, it was a wrong principle. They were not used to mandates; but it seemed to him, if they made representations to the League of Nations that a copy of the annual report should be laid on the table of the Parliament of the country holding the Mandate, that would be a reasonable and proper course to pursue. It was quite impossible to discuss the matter just then, and he hoped the Minister would not take advantage of the majority he had behind him to bar them during the Session from having a discussion on Samoa, even though they were losing the opportunity on this occasion.

The Minister of External Affairs replied that he would give the House that opportunity, and the motion was then agreed to.

NAVAL DEFENCE AMENDMENT BILL.

(Status of Warrant Officers; Period of enlistment modified; Naval policy discussed.)

The above Bill was introduced into the House of Representatives by the Minister of Defence and contains some technical amendments to the Naval Defence Act, 1913. A debate on Naval Policy took place on the Second Reading in the House on 1st August, 1922.

The Bill (as passed in Committee) provides for amendments of the Principal Act in the direction of:—

(i) Raising the status of Warrant Officers from the class of non-Commissioned Officers and Petty Officers, and placing them under the classification of Officers. (*Clause* 2.)

(ii) Permitting enlistment under the Act, for a period of less than two years, whilst preserving the maximum period of enlistment at 12 years. (*Clause* 3.)

(iii) Permitting enlistment for 12 years of a man more than 18 years of age. (*Clause* 3.)

The remaining clauses of the Bill are merely re-enactment clauses for the purpose of consolidating the provisions of the Principal Act, and for enabling the Governor-General to delegate to the Minister of Defence certain powers under the Act.

DEBATE IN HOUSE OF REPRESENTATIVES.

On 1st August,

The Minister of Defence (Hon. Sir R. Heaton Rhodes), in moving the Second Reading, said that while the Bill dealt only with technical amendments of the law, he was fully aware that it was open to any member to let loose the flood-gates of his eloquence in a general discussion of naval policy.

Mr. T. M. Wilford (Leader of the Opposition): "What is it?"

The Minister of Defence: "This Bill?"

Mr. Wilford: "No; the naval policy."

The Minister of Defence said that he did not himself propose to touch upon policy matters, leaving that, he said, for the Prime Minister when he opened the debate on the Financial Statement. Clause 2, he explained, gave a better status to the warrant officer. Also, he said it might be convenient to appoint an officer for less than two years; certainly in case of a war likely to be of short duration they would not need to enlist a great number of men for two years; they would enlist them for the period of the War. The Bill also allowed for a man being enlisted for a period of 12 years though he might be more than 18 years of age. Stokers and others, he said, were enlisted at upwards of eighteen, and the amendment would enable them to enlist for a term of years similar to other members of the crew—namely, 12 years. Clause 7 enabled the Governor-General to delegate his authority to accept or make transfers from the King's Naval Forces to the New Zealand Naval Forces, or *vice versa.*

Mr. Wilford said that he could quite understand the Minister's anxiety that Members on that side of the House should discuss naval defence, because as the Government policy was to come down a week or two thence it would be a distinct advantage to the Government if some of the Members gave them a policy. It seemed to him that the proper procedure was for the Government to bring down their policy and the Opposition to criticise it: and he proposed to take that course and refrain from discussing what he believed should be the policy consequent on the Washington Conference, until either the Washington Conference report came from Sir John Salmond, or the Government brought down some policy and nailed its colours to the mast. The Bill was nothing more than a method whereby the various sections of various Statutes should be put in one Bill. It was really an index to the Naval Defence Acts of the country, which was quite useful, but beyond that it was of no use whatever.

Mr. H. E. Holland (Leader of the Labour Party) said he thought they should say that a boy of eighteen should not enlist for any period that would carry him over 21 years of age, and after he had attained manhood it should be open to him to make any new arrangement for himself. A boy enlisting at eighteen could not resign, even in time of peace. He was tied up until thirty years of age. A commissioned officer could resign in time of peace. There was where the class distinction was drawn. There was, Mr. Holland said, altogether too much power given to the Government to act by regulation.

Proceeding, Mr. Holland said they had a Navy at that time—a one-ship Navy, the *Chatham*—and how effective that would be in the event of war was not for him to say. Anyhow, while all the world was talking of peace and the reduction of armaments, and the New Zealand Treasurer was pleading that he was short of money, they were going to be asked to commit the country to a further expenditure in connection with a naval scheme that was just a laughing-stock as far as defence was concerned. Expenditure on the naval policy—or, said Mr. Holland, to put it more correctly the lack of a naval policy—outlined in that Bill seemed to him to be absolute waste.

Mr. A. S. Malcolm (Reform, *Clutha*) said he took the opportunity of speaking on naval policy in the hope that something he might say might have influence on the Government. The Empire, he said, was founded on the Navy. It was the Navy that maintained it. In New Zealand they were protected in such an efficient manner that they were apt to forget their dependence on the Navy. And yet when they came to study the question they all agreed that if the protection of the British Navy were withdrawn the whole Empire must fall to pieces. It was with some concern, therefore, that the British people found that at the Washington Conference the British representatives had agreed to forego British supremacy, exercised for so many years. The agreement left Britain and America with a naval supremacy that the rest of the world dared not challenge, and the British people had in that way put a great trust and confidence in the American people. He hoped that confidence and belief would be justified.

New Zealand's Naval contribution.

Coming to the question of New Zealand's share in maintaining the Navy, Mr. Malcolm said that for many years he had felt that New Zealand had not done herself justice, and had not done the right thing by the Empire, in failing to make a proper contribution towards the maintenance of the British Navy. Continuing, Mr. Malcolm said: "New Zealand has fallen short of her responsibilities, and, I think I might say, of her privileges. She has fallen short of her responsibilities in common with other units of the Empire. No one of the other Dominions, with the honourable exception of the Australian Commonwealth, has fully done its duty in this respect. But it is time the whole of the Dominions were awaking to their duties in this case. Unfortunately, these Dominions, blessed as they are with resources of almost illimitable value, with all this handed to us and preserved for us by Britain, have not recognised that Britain is bearing practically the whole burden of defence. We have been content to let her do it; and even to-day, although Britain is staggering under the weight of the loss caused by the War, we are not coming forward as I hoped we would to offer to take our fair share of the burden and responsibility."

Representation of Parties at Imperial Conferences.

Proceeding, Mr. Malcolm said that while he maintained that the Navy must be kept up, he welcomed all other efforts that might be used to keep the peace. He believed, he said, for instance, in the Conferences occasionally held between the Premiers of the different parts of the Empire. These Conferences should be held more frequently, though he objected to the domestic loss that often arose from the absence of the Premiers. His opinion was that whether or not they went for Imperial Federation—which he would look to—the time had most certainly arrived when they should have a special Conference of representatives of all parts of the Empire; and by a Conference he meant a Conference not only of the Prime Ministers but of representatives of all the responsible Parties. For instance, he considered that New Zealand should send to the Conference not only their Prime Minister or somebody nominated by him, but the Leader of the Opposition and the Leader of the Labour Party. Let them work out the constitutional and other difficulties that concerned them, and try to devise some means of coming to a solution that would keep the Empire strong and firm. It was such a Conference that led to the establishment of the Federal Government in Australia. It was such Conferences that had led to the establishment of Federations elsewhere. All Parties throughout the Empire should get some idea of the difficulties that confronted them, and be allowed an opportunity of attempting to solve those difficulties.

Voice in policy: An Imperial Navy.

In regard to policy, his idea was this: while he would like the Dominions to have a say in the general policy of the Empire—a policy that at present was dictated by the British Government, and must be dictated by it so long as it paid practically the whole cost of defence—he also would say that the Dominions should contribute such a proportion to the upkeep of the Imperial Navy as they were entitled to by their populations.

He would devote to the Navy all the money that was at present spent on the military department. He was satisfied that would be sound sense and good finance.

The Hon. J. A. Hanan (Liberal, *Invercargill*) said he would like to know from the Prime Minister, if he told the Imperial Conference that the people of New Zealand were in favour of a local Navy, or that the Dominion favoured an Imperial Navy, which he (Mr. Hanan) believed had the general support of the inhabitants of the Dominion. He submitted with confidence that the local-Navy theory had now been discredited, although, to remind them of the fact that the Government did believe in a local Navy, they had the *Chatham* that day in those waters. If they went to Australia, said Mr. Hanan, he ventured to say that they would find that they (in Australia) had learned a very severe lesson upon the policy of having a local Navy. What had become of their local Navy? What were they doing with their ships? It was a policy of "scrap" that day. The need of the Empire, and of New Zealand in particular, was for a strong Navy, and there was just ground for paying an increased subsidy towards its maintenance.

New Zealand Naval Reserve.

Turning to the provisions of the Bill, Mr. Hanan said they were asked to support a Bill in the direction of creating a Reserve. If that Reserve was to support a local Navy he was against it, and he believed the people of the country were very strongly opposed to the idea.

Mr. C. E. Statham (Independent, *Dunedin C.*) said if they were going to be taxed *per capita* for their share towards the upkeep of the Navy they should have to be granted proper representation, and there would be difficulty in that. That involved another question: Was Great Britain prepared at the present time to allow a Dominion such as theirs to have a definite say in matters of peace and war? His own feeling was, he said, that a contribution to the funds of the Imperial Navy from that Government, with a stipulation, if they could possibly make it, that certain ships should be kept somewhere in the vicinity of New Zealand, would meet the bill as far as they were concerned.

The Minister of Defence replied briefly, saying that the Prime Minister had promised the opportunity of a full discussion when the financial statement was before the House, and he thought they would leave it at that.

The Bill was then read a second time.

IMMIGRATION.

(Government policy; Immigration from Great Britain; Empire Settlement scheme; Annual Report of Immigration Department; Indian settlers.)

The immigration policy of the Government was the subject of questions and discussion in the House on 21st and 27th July, and 1st August, a debate taking place on the last-named date on the Annual Report of the Immigration Department.

DEBATE IN HOUSE OF REPRESENTATIVES.

Immigration from Great Britain.

On 21st July, 1922,

Mr. H. E. Holland (Leader of the Labour Party) said he wished to ask the Prime Minister, without notice, if he had seen the cables with reference to the luncheon tendered to Lord Birkenhead in London wherein it was stated that:—

> Lord Birkenhead congratulated Sir Joseph Cook upon having that day attended the Colonial Office and signed a document under which Britain and the Dominions were committed to the expenditure of £3,000,000 per annum upon emigration, of which Britain had undertaken the responsibility for half.

Mr. Holland wished to ask whether New Zealand was a party to that arrangement, and to what extent, if any, the Dominion was financially involved?

The Prime Minister (the Right Hon. W. F. Massey) replied that he had read the paragraphs referred to, and it seemed to him—he was not quite clear—that they were not strictly in accordance with the understanding arrived at about that time last year. The understanding was just this: Britain was anxious that the people who desired to improve their position by migrating to some other country or countries should go to or remain in countries that were under the British flag, and that every possible inducement should be offered them by the British Government and by the Governments of the different Dominions. There was no definite number fixed upon.

Mr. Holland: "And no definite sum?"

The Prime Minister: "No definite sum."

Speaking from memory, Mr. Massey continued, the proposal was that Great Britain, in addition to what she had been doing at the time, was willing to advance approximately £300 per head for selected emigrants going from the United Kingdom to the Overseas Dominions, the £300 in each case to be under the control of the Dominion Government and to be expended to the best advantage of the immigrants, if possible in settling them upon the land. They had taken the immigrants as they thought New Zealand would be able to absorb them. They were mostly nominated immigrants, and men selected by the Imperial Government from men who had served in the Army during the War. Of course there was the other class, domestic servants, for whom the New Zealand Government paid.

Mr. Holland: "Do you not know anything about the signing of documents?"

The Prime Minister said there were no such things as documents as far as New Zealand was concerned. He knew, he said, that certain Australian States had been very anxious to take advantage of the fact that a number of suitable immigrants were offering from the United Kingdom, and he thought the Australian people were quite right in doing so.

Ministerial statement.

On 27th July,

The Minister of Immigration (Hon. W. Nosworthy) in making a statement in reply to certain remarks made by Mr. A. Spencer, President of the New Zealand Immigration and Land Settlement League, said that the Government had successfully absorbed over 19,500 souls during the last two years and four months. Only a small proportion of that number had remained in the cities: the balance had been absorbed in the country districts. After stating that the Government policy had been to assist in placing returned soldiers on the land, and that for that reason it had not been possible to offer any assistance in placing immigrants as settlers on the land on their arrival in New Zealand, the Minister said that the Government had made special provision whereby skilled labour for the primary industries had been secured for the Dominion, and that in time those same immigrants would become farmers on their own account. It was the intention of the Government to take advantage of the State-aided Empire Settlement Scheme in such a manner as would produce the best results for the benefit of New Zealand. The statement that immigrants were leaving New Zealand in shoals, and in despair, was absolutely incorrect.

Annual Immigration Report.

On 1st August,

The Minister of Immigration, in moving that the Annual Report of the Department of Immigration do lie upon the table, dealt with strictures passed on the Government in regard to heavy expenditure of the Department, quoting figures to prove that the average expenditure on immigration for the past four years had been £41,285 per annum. He added that the number of immigrants who had arrived in the Dominion from 1918-19 to 1922, both years inclusive, totalled 21,829, at a cost of approximately £8 per head.

Mr. T. M. Wilford (Leader of the Opposition) said he hoped the Minister would give an explanation of the public accounts statement which showed that £247,000 had been paid out of loan-moneys in the last twelve-monthly period for immigration. He moved:

> That while approving the necessity for a strong policy of immigration for New Zealand, it is considered at the present time, while unemployment is acute, that the bringing out of immigrants is unwarranted.

He moved that amendment because, while he thought nothing was wanted more than immigration, while they should open their doors to the Mother Country and, if necessary, subsidise the passage money of those who came there, while they wanted to do all they could to carry out the immigration scheme laid down by the British Government in connection with the Dominions, while they should in every shape and form encourage their cousins from across the seas to come there and settle down and form part of what was undoubtedly a very prosperous section of the Empire—he thought the Government should call a halt at that time, with so many unemployed in the country. The relief works being carried out by the Government were in themselves strong evidence that they could not at the present time find work for immigrants, no matter how much they might wish that they should come.

Mr. P. Fraser (Labour, *Wellington, C.*) said he would second the amendment to test the feeling of the House. To express the full opinion of the Labour Party he would have added something about the shortage of housing; but there was a great deal to be said for confining the amendment to the one point of how the immigration policy was likely to affect the existing acute unemployment. No matter how the Minister might try to camouflage the position by the statement that all the immigrants then coming in were found employment, it still remained true that either they remained unemployed or else somebody already in a job was put out of work to make room for them. There would be no dissent from any portion of the House if two things were first attended to—namely, the unemployment evil and housing shortage. If the Cabinet would put before the House and country a scheme whereby they could give an opportunity to the people of New Zealand and from the Old Country to settle on the land and engage in primary production, then any common-sense person would support the Minister.

Mr. W. D. Lysnar (Reform, *Gisborne*) said that behind his own district there were between five and six million acres of virgin country waiting for settlement, and it was some of the finest country in the Dominion. There was plenty of land; what they wanted was labour to develop it.

The Hon. J. A. Hanan (Liberal, *Invercargill*) recognised they were discussing under present conditions a very controversial question, and before long he believed they should have a grave and more difficult proposition to consider, namely, whether that country was willing to open its doors wider to those who came from India. There had been some talk in New Zealand lately regarding that subject and it behoved the people of that country to study the question seriously. He had not the slightest doubt that it would be before the people in different parts of the Empire before many years. He believed they would have no difficulty in making up their minds. In the first place they were opposed to such a policy because they did not favour the standard of living and social conditions being lowered in that country. It was right that their opinions should be made known, and that no erroneous impression should go abroad in regard to the policy that the people of New Zealand believed in with reference to the question. It was urged that they wanted more population; but they should consider what would be the effect on social and industrial conditions of the country if they were to open their doors widely to an influx of population from other countries, even from their Empire.

Turning to the existing financial and industrial situation, Mr. Hanan said it was not for the benefit of immigrants or the country to bring them there unless they could settle them prosperously on the land or find them steady employment in secondary industries. If the Government's policy was being pursued in order to provide very cheap labour, then they were inviting trouble.

Mr. Holland said he thought there was no Member in that House who would not agree that the country could carry ten times its present population, but before it could do that there would have to be a revision of land policy.

They were still in the dark, he said, as to what arrangements had been made in connection with the agreement with the British authorities. On looking up the Australian papers of 6th April he found a report from Melbourne to the effect that Mr. Hughes, the Prime Minister of the Commonwealth, had received a communication from the British Government stating that the British Cabinet had now agreed to co-operate with the Commonwealth in a scheme of migration along the lines of the proposals Mr. Hughes had submitted for their consideration. The report went on to say that the scheme submitted was that the British Government should join with the Federal Government in obtaining loans, and should pay one-half of the interest for a period of, say, five years. While the Imperial Government had not been prepared to accept the suggestion to pay one-half, they were willing to pay one-third of the interest. Mr. Hughes's proposal was for a loan of £50,000,000 to be raised over a term of years—he (Mr. Hughes) had suggested five. The main provisions of the scheme were that many thousands of immigrants were to be settled on Crown lands made available in Western Australia. In the development of these lands the Imperial Government was prepared to co-operate. Under the arrangement, as it then stood, the British Government would pay one-third, the Commonwealth Government one-third, and the State on whose Crown lands the moneys were to be spent would pay the remaining one-third.

Continuing, Mr. Holland said that hon. Members would remember that when the cable message came out first with respect to Sir Joseph Cook having signed the agreement, that cable was followed by another which said that Sir James Allen* had signed a similar agreement. Neither the Members of that House nor the people of the country yet knew in full the details of the contract made between the New Zealand Government and the Government of Great Britain with respect to immigration into New Zealand. He hoped that in replying the Minister would make that clear, so that the mystery which surrounded the matter might disappear.

The Minister of Immigration: "There is no mystery. No agreement has been made yet."

Mr. Holland, after referring to the risk of unemployment that immigrants ran in coming to New Zealand and to the lack of housing, concluded by saying that the Government carried a heavy responsibility with respect to the conditions that had arisen out of its immigration policy, and the sooner that policy was revised the better it would be for New Zealand as a whole.

The Minister of Immigration in his reply gave particulars of the number of immigrants who had come into the country

---

* Col. the Hon. Sir James Allen is the High Commissioner for New Zealand in London.

in the financial year which closed on 31st March. Of a total of 7,005 immigrants, 1,056 were domestic workers, he said, 172 were fiancées (of soldiers), 1,256 were wives coming to join their husbands, and 2,085 were children—making a total of 4,569. That left 2,436 individuals to be accounted for, who would, they were told, flood the labour market. Of those 2,436 persons, 566 went on the land, 179 were miners, and the remaining 1,691, represented practically every skilled trade. It was absurd to suggest that that comparatively small number had assisted in bringing about the existing industrial conditions.

Mr. Wilford's motion was then put, and defeated by 34 votes against 17.

TARIFF AGREEMENT (NEW ZEALAND AND AUSTRALIA) ACT.

By various provisions of the Customs Amendment Act, 1921, powers are conferred on the Governor-General* to alter the Tariff by Order in Council. Pursuant to this authority the General Tariff was, by Order in Council of 22nd December, 1921, applied to goods being the produce or manufacture of the Commonwealth of Australia in lieu of the British Preferential Tariff.

On the 11th April, 1922, a reciprocal Tariff Agreement (as set out in the Appendix to the Act) was arrived at between the two countries. By Section 10 of the Act above referred to it is expressly provided that no such Agreement shall have effect unless and until ratified by Parliament. The object of the Act is to ratify the Agreement accordingly.

The provisions of the Act are practically contained in a single Section (Section 2) whereby the Agreement above referred to is ratified and confirmed, and the alteration of rates and duties is to be effected by means of an Order in Council issued under the authority conferred by the Act of 1921, and operating from a date to be fixed in terms of the agreement.

Section 2 also provides that any subsequent agreement for the modification of the present Agreement may come into force without ratification. Any such modifying agreement can only be made operative by means of an Order in Council under the Amendment Act of 1921, and such Order in Council will still require to be submitted to Parliament as provided in Section 31 of that Act.

The principal provisions of the Tariff Agreement are:—

1. The Schedule of Customs duties between the Commonwealth and the Dominion is to come into force on a date to be proclaimed after the Parliaments of both countries have accepted

---

* *Vide* Journal, Vol. III., No. 2, p. 395.

it, and is to remain in force until six months' notice of its termination shall have been given by either party.

2. There is a reciprocal agreement that neither party shall impose or increase any Customs duty against the other except by mutual agreement without giving six months' notice.

3. The agreement does not affect the right of either party to impose new duties upon any articles for the protection of any new industry in either country; but such new duties are not to exceed those on similar articles imported from the United Kingdom into the Commonwealth or the Dominion as the case may be.

4. Both parties have the right to bring into force suspended or deferred duties, or dumping duties, or special duties to meet abnormal conditions.

5. The agreement is not to affect the right of the Commonwealth to impose primage duties, provided that such duties on imports from New Zealand do not exceed the duties imposed on similar goods from the United Kingdom.

6. All goods enumerated in the Schedule to the Agreement are to be liable to primage duty upon entry into the Dominion, provided it does not exceed the primage duty upon similar goods from the United Kingdom.

7. Imports to the Commonwealth transhipped to the Dominion, which if they had been imported direct from the country of origin to the Dominion would have been entitled to the British Preferential Tariff of the Dominion, are to be entitled to be entered under last-named tariff.

8. The same applies to such goods imported into the Dominion and transhipped to the Commonwealth, that is to say, they would be entitled to be entered under the British Preferential Tariff of the Commonwealth.

9. The provisions of Clauses 7 and 8 became operative on the 1st May, 1922.

10. No special rebate or bounty is to be granted by the Commonwealth or the Dominion in respect of the sugar contained in any goods exported from one country to the other.

DEBATE IN HOUSE OF REPRESENTATIVES.

On 28th July, 1922,

The Bill was introduced by message from the Governor-General, and referred to Committee of Ways and Means.

The Minister of Customs (Hon. W. Downie Stewart) explained the proposals in the Agreement for reciprocity with Australia so that, as he said, Members might know what were the principles which had guided them in arriving at the terms of the Treaty, the concessions they had obtained, and as to how they had succeeded in giving effect to what the House had in view when it put Australia on the foreign tariff.

There had always been, he said, a vital difference between the policy of Australia and that of New Zealand so far as granting British preference was concerned. Australia had never allowed other Dominions preferential rates unless as a matter of negotiation for a separate trade agreement. New Zealand, on the other hand, had always accorded to the other Dominions the same privileges as she granted Britain. Canada was in the habit of granting reciprocity to those Dominions which extended it to her: so also with South Africa. The policy of New Zealand gave rise to the feeling that it was hardly fair that they should continue it if they did not meet with satisfactory reciprocal treatment from the other Dominions. When Australia had been completing her revision of the Tariff last year they could get no definite assurance that more liberal treatment was going to be extended to New Zealand. As a result of representations made from all over New Zealand, and of the opinion of that House, they came to the conclusion that it would be advisable to force the situation somewhat, and they had therefore placed Australia on the foreign tariff while their (the New Zealand) Customs Bill was going through the House.

After detailing the course of the negotiations with the Federal Government, Mr. Downie Stewart said that the main features of the agreement arrived at were that Australia had taken New Zealand off the foreign tariff, which was, he stated, the primary object aimed at, and this had removed a long-standing grievance, and New Zealand was granted admission to Australia on terms better than those granted to any other country, including Great Britain. Australia had also granted them free entry for several important items, and in addition had substantially reduced their rates in cases where New Zealand manufacturers so desired. New Zealand, on its part, had reduced the foreign rate, temporarily imposed, so as to correspond with the Australian reduction, but, in the cases he was about to mention, had not come down to the British rates where New Zealand industry appeared to require more protection. The new duties were to take effect from a date to be agreed upon. After both Parliaments had ratified them a Proclamation would issue, bringing the duties into force, and there was a provision for termination by six months' notice on either side. There was also a clause in the Agreement which saved the right of either country to impose suspended, deferred, or dumping duties to meet abnormal trading conditions, and a clause which enabled either country to impose new duties where a new industry was started, provided the new duty did not exceed the duty imposed on such articles from Great Britain into the Commonwealth or the Dominion, as the case might be.

There were provisions of minor importance, as to primage duty, and so on; but one provision which had been urgently required was that relating to goods such as tea, sago and other items which came from some country entitled to British preference rates, and which were being subjected to foreign duties because they had technically become part of the commerce of Australia or of New Zealand. In the interests of consumers it was imperative that relief should be granted in that direction as quickly as possible and they had brought that into operation on 1st May in both New Zealand and Australia.

After dealing with items as to which special provision had been made in the Agreement, Mr. Downie Stewart said that on the negotiations he thought they had reasonably protected the interest of New Zealand manufacturers. It was extraordinarily difficult to arrange reciprocity, because both countries were developing along the same lines, and particularly difficult from the New Zealand standpoint owing to the fact that the Australians were building up such huge industries that an export trade was necessary, and that New Zealand manufacturers had more apprehension as regarded Australia than any other country in many lines. He hoped the Treaty would commend itself to that House and to the Australian Parliament. The only way to come to a conclusion was to consider the detailed proposals, and on the balance of advantage to say, " Yes " or " No " to the Treaty. It seemed to him that should an attempt be made to vote on the individual items, or to amend the Treaty in any way, the whole matter was at large, and there was no agreement. He had cabled to the Australian Government to know their view, and it was what he had expressed.

The Prime Minister (the Right Hon. W. F. Massey) said there was no question that those two countries must commercially and financially, and in every other respect, stand or fall together. They could not afford to be at war commercially or financially. Both Parliaments must accept the proposals as they were, or reject them.

The Bill was then read a first time.

On 3rd August,

The Minister of Customs moved the Second Reading, saying that if the House could see its way to ratify the proposals *in globo*, it might be possible thereafter to make certain minor amendments.

Mr. T. M. Wilford (Leader of the Opposition) referred to the suggestion he had made to the Government that the proper thing to have done would have been for the Government to have appointed a permanent Tariff Board. That proposal had been turned down, and that day they saw the folly of the rejection when the Minister had admitted that he went forth on his mission (to Australia) without representation from a number of men vitally concerned in the new tariff proposals. After those admissions one could not be surprised, he said, if there might be points in the Tariff Bill which he (the Minister) and his departmental head had overlooked, and which were still of vital importance to a large section of the people of the country. He would ask the Minister whether it was not a fact that in connection with certain articles or products " not otherwise enumerated " the British-preference rate for Australia would be the toll rates in Australia for the introduction of New Zealand goods; and did not the difference in those rates of preference apply against New Zealand and in favour of Australia? Was it not a fact that because Australia had a higher preference rate for Great Britain than New Zealand there was going to be a distinct advantage to Australia in the exchange of imports?

Speaking of woollens and textiles, Mr. Wilford said that the surplus of those products of Australia under the new Tariff would be sent to New Zealand. He wanted to ask the Minister, he said, whether he was satisfied that, under the arrangements made, Australia, on account of its great mass production, could not do them (in New Zealand) serious injury, and quoted a statement of Mr. Jenkin, President of the New Zealand Industrial Corporation, who had said that a fair adjustment would be to adopt the same tariff for Australia as Australia adopted for Great Britain, and that anything less than that would be a disadvantage to New Zealand. Mr. Wilford also discussed the questions of butter, cheese, timber, oats, and other products and manufactures as affected by the tariff.

Mr. T. K. Sidey (Liberal, *Dunedin, S.*) said that they should treat Australia just as she treated them, but that what had been done with regard to a large number of items was that on goods they exported to Australia she charged against them her British Preferential Tariff, while as regarded goods they imported from her, they did not charge the same tariff, but their (the New Zealand) British Preferential Tariff, which was very much less than hers (Australia's). The position was that the Agreement, while it might in one or two directions offer a little advantage to them, taking it as a whole there was no doubt that Australia was going to get by far the better of the deal as far as the manufactures of the country were concerned.

Mr. R. McCallum (Liberal, *Wairau*) said the Minister had failed to show them that the financial advantages (of the agreement) were about the same. The Government came down with its measures, saying " We are going to put this through at lightning speed without investigation and without inquiry." If they had a duty at all, surely it was that they should demand closer investigation, and allow all interests to be heard. Where was the hurry? He moved:

That the Second Reading of the Bill be postponed, in order that a Special Committee be set up for the purpose of taking evidence and submitting a report thereon to the House within ten days from this date.

The Prime Minister said that if the Committee were set up it meant that they should have evidence from every part of New Zealand, and should be there for a month deliberating, while the people on the other side of the Tasman Sea would be trying to pick holes in the Treaty. In that way they might lose it. He considered it, he said, the best Treaty that had ever been placed before the Parliament of New Zealand. Continuing, Mr. Massey said that the Bill, when it passed into law, would have the effect of increasing the trade with Australia, and that it would increase the exports from that country to Australia. He admitted, he said, that in all probability, seeing that Australia had about four times the population of New Zealand, the balance of trade would always be with Australia, but he believed that the Agreement was going to remove the feeling of soreness between the two countries which had existed for some time past.

Mr. H. E. Holland (Leader of the Labour Party) said the Labour Party had had no protest whatever (against the Agreement) from any of the trade unions, which went to show, he said, that there was not any strong objection on their part. The whole of the interests of that country and Australia, he remarked, were, and must be, linked up together, and any reciprocal arrangement between them must in the end make for the benefit of the people of both countries. They (the Labour Party) did not propose to offer any opposition to the passage of the measure.

Mr. McCallum's motion was negatived.

The Minister of Customs, in his reply, said he realised that it was asking a good deal of the House to accept the Treaty *in toto*, but it was difficult to adopt any other course. After traversing the speeches that had been made, he said that he had had representations from a Christchurch firm asking to delay the coming into operation of the Treaty until March next, but it would not be wise. It would be better, he thought, to wait really until the Australian Government had finally dealt with the matter, and then fix a reasonable date.

The Bill was then read a second time, and passed the Third Reading after a short debate on 4th August.

BRITISH EMPIRE EXHIBITION.

(Ministerial statement.)

On 24th August, 1922, in the House of Representatives **The Minister of Industries and Commerce (Hon. E. P. Lee)** made a statement to the effect that the Cabinet had decided that New Zealand would expend £60,000 on the enterprise, spread over three Budgets, to provide for the erection of a New Zealand Pavilion, and for all incidental expenses. The Government, he said, had also intimated that it would participate in the proposed Imperial Sections of the Exhibition, for which no charge would be made. Steps had also been taken by the Government, said the Minister, to organise Committees throughout the Dominion to insure the success of New Zealand's participation in the Exhibition.

INDIA AND THE DOMINIONS.

(Visit of the Right Hon. V. S. Srinivása Sástri to New Zealand.)

Reference was made in the House of Representatives on the 12th July, 1922, to Mr. Sástri's visit to the Dominion, when,

Mr. R. McCallum (Liberal, *Wairau*) asked the Prime Minister if he could see his way to have the very eloquent address delivered on the previous day by their friend from India, the Right Hon. V. S. Sástri, circulated amongst Members, a number of whom could not be present when the speech was delivered; also amongst members of Chambers of Commerce and, indeed, all the thinking people of the Dominion. Mr. Sástri had, he said, certainly done much to link the people of New Zealand with India, and to show that they had very much in common with the people there—that India was an integral portion of the Empire, and that without India the British Empire would not be what it was that day.

The Prime Minister (the Right Hon. W. F. Massey) replied that if it was possible to get a verbatim report of the speech he would be glad to comply with the request of the hon. Member. He added that he had been pleased to see so many Members of Parliament present at the luncheon to Mr. Sástri, showing by their presence that they welcomed the distinguished visitor.

SOUTH AFRICA.

The following Summary is in continuation of the proceedings of the Second Session of the Fourth Parliament of the Union of South Africa which commenced on 17th February, 1922, and was prorogued on 20th July.

WASHINGTON CONFERENCE TREATIES.

(Parliamentary approval; Limitation of armaments; Submarines; International status of Dominions; etc.)

On 18th July a Resolution was agreed to in the House of Assembly in favour of the ratification of the Treaties signed at Washington relating to the Limitation of Armaments, etc.

IN THE HOUSE OF ASSEMBLY.

The Prime Minister (Lt.-Gen. the Right Hon. J. C. Smuts) moved:—

That the following Treaties signed at Washington be ratified and confirmed:—

(A) Quadruple Pacific Treaty and Declaration of 13th December, and Supplementary Treaty, 6th February.

(B) Naval Treaty, 6th February.

(C) Treaty regarding Submarines and Noxious Gases, 6th February.

(D) Two Treaties regarding China, 6th February.

The consideration of this matter, he said, was long overdue. He believed they were one of the last, if not the last State, to ratify the Washington Treaties. The Washington Conference led to the conclusion of five Treaties with the Powers enumerated above, and which were ratified; two of them were of very far-reaching importance; the three others referred to under (C) and (D) were of lesser importance.

Importance of the Conference.

Before dealing with the substance of them the Prime Minister said he wished to say a word about the Conference itself. It was one of the most important held in recent years, and second in importance only to the Peace Conference in Paris in 1919. In some respects the results were more fruitful than those of the Peace Conference. For the British Empire the Washington Conference was very far-reaching and effected a change in the direction of its former policy. For twenty years—from 1902 to 1922—the foreign policy of the British Empire had been based on the Japanese Alliance, and only now at the Washington Conference that was changed, and for the Alliance between the British Empire and Japan something much more far-reaching in relation to the Pacific had been arranged.

With regard to the world situation generally, this Conference saw the first attempt on a really large scale to limit armaments between the Great Powers, and these two matters —the substitution of a Pacific arrangement for the Japanese Alliance on the one hand and the limitation of naval armaments among Great Powers on the other—constituted the basis of the Pacific Treaty under (A) and the Naval Treaty under (B).

After dealing with the Pacific situation and the considerations which led to the drafting of the Quadruple Pacific Treaty, the Prime Minister said that Treaty provided for the Pacific a system very much like that in the League of Nations. If differences arose between those four Powers they should come together and go to conference, thrash out the difficulties and find a solution of their differences. If differences should arise, not between these four Powers, but owing to the attitude of some third Power, these four Powers would consult with each other and try, as far as possible, to secure the best arrangement. That was according to the Quadruple Pacific Treaty which provided for a settlement. The Treaty was to last for ten years and was, in many senses, perhaps, the most important of its kind. As Members would see, it had been arranged before the others. Since that arrangement had been come to, and if trouble in the Pacific arose, the way was open for some settlement.

Limitation of Naval armaments: American proposal.

On the question of the limitation of armaments, America came forward with a very bold suggestion which took the Conference by storm. Instead of bargaining on the "give-and-take" principle, the Government of the U.S.A. announced that they would drop 28 battleships, as large as any that had ever been built or were being built, on which vast millions of money had already been spent. They offered to drop these outright, and their whole programme of naval construction, to dismantle ships which had cost millions each, and in that way give a most conclusive pledge of their good faith. The condition was that England should similarly write off 20 ships. A further condition was that Japan should in proportion make some specific sacrifice.

The effect of this bold declaration by America was such as to transform the whole atmosphere of that Conference. After consultation, it was finally settled that the Navies of the Great Powers should consist of certain types, that certain ships should be retained by them, that others should be destroyed, and that their naval strength should be on a certain ratio.

Land armaments.

An effort was made to extend this limitation of armaments to land warfare, but owing to the position taken up by the French Delegation, mostly by the Prime Minister of France himself, who pointed out the uncertainties and difficulties of the European situation, it was found impossible to come to any agreement as to limitation of land armaments.

Submarines and poison gases.

The British Delegation made a great effort to eliminate the submarine altogether from naval warfare, but that was not achieved. There was great opposition to this complete elimination of the submarine, and in the end a third Treaty was made, which dealt with the use of noxious gases and the submarine in warfare. That Treaty laid down, firstly, that the submarine should no longer in warfare be used as a commercial destroyer, and, secondly, that whatever destruction it might do, it should first secure the safety of the passengers and crew of any ship which it was going to sink. Whether this provision would be of any use it was difficult to say.

Another provision in this Treaty was that no poison gases should be used in future. What the value of that was they did not know at all. He was told that, in spite of this third Treaty, the great Powers were still busily prosecuting their researches in poison gases, and he might point out that poison gas was rendered illegal at The Hague Conference in 1907. He therefore had to put this third Treaty on a very much lower level than the first two.

Serious omissions.

Several questions of first-rate importance were left open besides the question of the submarine. One was that no limitation whatever was put on the construction of war vessels below the battleship type. It was therefore open to any Power to construct what they called "light-cruisers" to any extent. That certainly was a very serious omission from this general provision for the limitation of naval armaments.

Another serious omission, the Prime Minister continued, was that there was no limitation in the construction of aeroplanes, and, as it is generally expected that, if there is to be a great war in the future, it will be a war very much more in the air than either on land or sea, they would realise what a great omission that was. These questions were discussed but it was found impossible to come to any agreement as to limitation. It was the policy of one of the Great Powers on the Continent of Europe to have an enormous air service. "I think," Gen. Smuts said, "the whole flank of the Washington Conference may be turned by this great omission."

Treaties regarding China.

Two Treaties were also made regarding China. One dealt with financial matters and the other with a group of well-known questions such as the integrity of, and the "open door" in, China, etc. He was afraid, however, that like so many other political and international instruments, this was more a matter of pious wishes than of political reality, and the terms of the Treaty were so vague and general and almost abstract that it was very difficult to know what specific meaning to attach to it. The Treaty was supplemented by a number of declarations by the Powers.

South African status; Dominions and Foreign Affairs.

The Conference, continued the Prime Minister, besides being of great importance to the world in respect of the above matters, was of great constitutional importance to South Africa and other Dominions. The U.S.A. in issuing invitations to the Washington Conference addressed an invitation to the British Government in set terms. The British Government thereupon proceeded to appoint its Delegates, and asked Representatives from the Dominions to join them as the Delegates of the British Government to the Conference. At the time he (Gen. Smuts) thought that a long step backward was being taken from the position which they had achieved at the Peace Conference in Paris. This position was that in diplomatic matters, in matters of international relations, the British Government should no longer speak for the Dominions, but that they should speak for themselves, and have their own Delegates with instructions from their own Governments.

It was clear that the procedure which was being adopted in connection with the Washington Conference was a derogation from the status which they claimed had been attained in Paris. He (the Prime Minister) gave public expression to that and addressed his protest to the various parties concerned. The Union of South Africa occupied a very important position, and it was difficult for the British Empire to make any agreement for the limitation of armaments if one of the Dominions were not a party to it. Unless the position was made right, the British Empire would thus have been placed in a grave position at Washington. In the end the attitude taken up by South Africa had to be recognised, and the position was put right.

The British Government and the Dominions which happened to be represented not directly at Washington consulted with the American Government, which agreed that the position should be restored and that the Dominion Representatives should not be the British Representatives or part of the British Delegation, but should be agents and representatives of their own Dominions under the authority of their own Governments, and should sign whatever Treaties were concluded on behalf of their Dominions. It was most important that the Union should take a firm stand at that stage, because, although it was contended—and he thought correctly—that the international status of the Dominion had been settled at Paris, so far as the U.S.A. were concerned they could always say that they had not abided by that arrangement, that they were not parties to the Peace Treaty, and, therefore, they (the U.S.A.) had nothing to do with the recognition given to the Dominions by the other Powers.

At Washington, America was bound, in consequence of the attitude taken up by South Africa, to fall into line and give them the same recognition, so far as she was concerned, as had been given by the other Powers at Paris. In connection with the next Conference at Genoa, the Union received its invitation direct from the Italian Government in Rome, and it became clear that there was no longer any doubt whatever about the international status and standing of the British Dominions. Although he could not say that all difficulty had been removed from their status, yet he did say that in principle the international status of the British Dominions had been fully recognised by all the Great Powers concerned, even by America in full measure now, and they might claim the credit in South Africa that they had, through their action, through their stand on a critical occasion, contributed very solidly to that result.

In conclusion, the Prime Minister referred to the constitutional position with regard to the ratification of Treaties under the British Constitution, and said that the course the Government had pursued and intended to pursue when any Treaty of real importance was concerned, was to submit that Treaty to Parliament for ratification.

Opposition view of Foreign policy; League of Nations; etc.

Dr. D. F. Malan (Nationalist, *Calvinia, Cape*) said he was glad the Prime Minister had thought fit to submit the Treaties to the House for ratification. He denied that Parliament had ever ratified the Treaty of Versailles to any full extent, and thought that in that respect some progress had been made—thanks, perhaps, to the lead given by Canada.

He deplored the absence of suitable opportunity to discuss foreign policy, and hoped that the Prime Minister would still realise the necessity of instituting a Department of Foreign Affairs, which would allow of a discussion of their foreign policy every year in connection with the estimates.

Proceeding, Dr. Malan said he agreed with the aims of the Washington Conference. The Nationalist Party stood for the fullest measure of freedom, not only for South Africa, but for all countries, and therefore for international peace. They were at the core anti-militarists. They only deplored that the Washington Conference had not gone further by deciding to limit land armament.

He condemned the chauvinistic and vindictive attitude displayed by France, and hoped that the League of Nations, after having been ignored by America, would broaden its basis so as to admit Germany and Russia, because it would remain an important body as long as it was under the tutelage of the Supreme Council. He regretted that the results of the Washington Conference bore no signs of any idealism or new spirit. It had been called together solely because another catastrophe was threatening the world and because the Great Powers were on the verge of bankruptcy.

Dominion Status; International position.

The Nationalist Party, Dr. Malan continued, did not want to see the people misled by vague definitions of Dominion Status. He was afraid there was much more uncertainty about their status than the Prime Minister was prepared to admit. He referred to a statement by Mr. Lloyd George immediately after the Imperial Conference last year, to the effect that the Dominions would be represented by the British Delegation, and maintained that it was of the greatest importance that the House should know what the decision of the Conference had been, in regard to their [South African] representation, in order that it might be known what the feelings of British statesmen were towards a higher status for the Dominions, and who the enemies of any advancement of the Dominions in that direction were.

Dr. Malan then referred to the Constitutional Conference which had been advocated by the Prime Minister as an alternative to the procedure suggested by the Nationalists, and which should have followed the Imperial Conference of last year. Now that that Conference was not going to be called, he asked whether the Prime Minister was going to accept the situation, or would he follow the course advocated by the Opposition, and allow the House to state for itself what the status of the Union should be ? He contended that the latter was the only dignified course for the Union to follow.

In order to pacify the Dominions a doctrine was being preached, amongst others, by the Colonial Secretary (Mr.

Churchill), that the Dominions were no longer subject to England, but to the British Empire. As for the Opposition, they accepted the disappearance of the state of subjection to England, but declined to become subject to half a dozen other masters instead. He maintained that their equality with England was a mere domestic understanding, which carried no international weight whatsoever. He held there was no international acknowledgment of the Union in the manner of Liberia or any other small independent State. They could only expect to gain an international status when the Union was allowed to conduct its foreign affairs free and untrammelled by the British connection, and was allowed to attend international meetings independently and not as a member of the British Commonwealth of Nations.

Labour standpoint.

Mr. T. Boydell (Leader of the Labour Party) said the matter was too important to squeeze into a short space of time. Every right-thinking man favoured limitation of armaments. He agreed with the attitude of Gen. Smuts regarding the Conference, but regretted that South Africa had not sent its own representatives the same as the other Dominions. The Conference had missed a great opportunity. He asked what was the use of scrapping 28 battleships if they were going to build thousands of aeroplanes for war purposes? However, he welcomed the innovation as an instalment. He expressed the hope that in future all treaties would be submitted to Parliament. That was the first one they had been asked to ratify, and he welcomed it on that account.

The Prime Minister said that America had nothing to do with the League of Nations, but in the matter of naval disarmament it had led the way. The Union, he added, was not under subjection to Britain; the Dominion status was perfectly clear.

The resolution was agreed to, and on the proposal of the Prime Minister was ordered to be referred to the Senate for concurrence.

MOZAMBIQUE CONVENTION.

(Negotiations with Portuguese Government: issues involved.)

On 23rd June, in the House of Assembly, the Prime Minister made a statement in regard to the temporary suspension of negotiations between the Union and the Portuguese

Government concerning the question of a new Mozambique Convention.*

IN THE HOUSE OF ASSEMBLY.

The Prime Minister (Lt.-Gen. the Right Hon. J. C. Smuts) said the negotiations for a new Mozambique Convention, which had been going on for some time, had not resulted in any agreement being reached between the representatives of the Union and Portuguese Government. General Freire d'Andrade, the head of the Portuguese Delegation, was returning to Lisbon to lay the position before his Government, and there was a possibility that negotiations might again be resumed before the present Convention lapsed on 31st March, 1923. The Government would, in the meantime, consider the policy which they deemed necessary in the interests of the Union in case no new Convention was concluded before that date, and would lay their proposals before Parliament at its next Session.

Important issues involved.

Replying to a request made by Gen. Hertzog for a more detailed statement, the Prime Minister outlined the three large topics with which the Mozambique Convention dealt. The first was the railway agreement, by which traffic between Lourenco Marques and the Transvaal was regulated, and which was concluded before Union between the Transvaal Government and the Mozambique Government. The second was the recruiting of native labour in Mozambique for the gold mines on the Rand; and the third was the equal and unhampered exchange of products between the two countries. The present negotiations had been confined almost entirely to the first of the three subjects, viz., the conclusion of a new railway agreement between Delagoa Bay and the Union.

Transvaal Coal—Delagoa Bay.

Referring to the further great developments which were expected in the future in the coal industry in the Eastern Transvaal, Gen. Smuts said, "Last year we exported *viâ* Delagoa Bay about a million tons of coal, and the colliery owners assure us that they are in a position almost immediately to treble that exportation. But the railway and the port facilities at Delagoa Bay are entirely inadequate to cope with such development. . . . In recent years it has been found that the coal beds in the Eastern Transvaal form among the greatest in the world, and probably one of the greatest assets of this country." The Government and the country had to face the fact that as the gold industry proved more and more a wasting asset, and the country still continued

* *Vide* JOURNAL, Vol. III., No. 3, pp. 665-6.

to some extent dependent on mining, they should develop mining in other directions.

New Board of Control needed.

The existing Board, the Prime Minister explained, established under the present Convention, had proved unable to be a real instrument for developing their transport and traffic. They had claimed that the Board should be re-formed and become an independent Board of both Governments ; that the Governments should appoint members to a real Board of control and management, responsible for its own affairs very much as the Suez Canal Commission was responsible for running the Suez Canal. The Union's interests were vastly predominant in this matter, and they had contended that, in order to make the Board really efficient, the Union Government should nominate the majority of members on it. On neither of these points had they been able to succeed. General d'Andrade was in possession of the Union Government's views and understood now the difficulties and urgency of the whole situation. If his Government was prepared to meet their (the Union's) point of view, it would be possible to come to a conclusion before the 31st March. If this was impossible, it would be necessary for them to regulate their affairs without such a Convention as that which had existed for a long number of years.

Native recruiting.

Mr. C. G. Fichardt (**Nationalist,** *Ladybrand, O.F.S.*) : " Does the native recruiting lapse ? "

The Prime Minister, replying, said that if there was no agreement, then the Government made no further provision for native recruiting. The arrangement under the present Convention would lapse. It would be possible for the mines, if so advised, to make their own arrangements with the Portuguese Government, but that would be entirely outside any legal measure taken by the Government of the Union.

DEFENCE OF THE UNION.

(Defence Department; Air Forces; Naval Defence: Substitution for contribution; etc.)

On 19th June, the House of Assembly in Committee of Supply on the Estimates discussed the Defence Vote: £915,846.

DEBATE IN HOUSE OF ASSEMBLY.

Brig.-Gen. the Hon. J. J. Byron (South African Party, *Border, Cape*) asked, was the Army of South Africa fit or able to fight the battles of the State ? He was sure there was not efficiency in their defence forces, and was doubtful that there was a policy concerning them.

Mr. R. B. Waterston (Labour, *Brakpan, Natal*) asked the Minister of Defence to hold over the Vote in view of the absence of the Nationalists.

The Minister of Defence (Col. the Hon. H. Mentz) regretted he could not do this, as he was not responsible for the absence of the principal Opposition.

Gen. Byron dealt with tactics, administration, etc., and complained of the increase in the number of civilian clerks in the Defence Department, saying that all the money which did not go towards the training of men to defend their country was so much money wasted.

Mr. W. Greenacre (South African Party, *Durban, Point, Natal*) spoke of the excellent work done by the Durban Light Infantry during the recent upheaval.

Gen. Byron said that that military excellence did not arise through accident. It was fortunate that no military leader of eminence had arisen amongst the insurgents, or the result might have been different. He contrasted the policy of the Prime Minister when he had been Minister of Defence with that of the present Minister. In those days they trained a large number of men and had an efficient headquarters staff, men with regimental experience. He considered that economies were now not being effected in the best way.

The Air Force.

The Air Force, Gen. Byron continued, should be treated as another Department, an adjunct if they liked, and they should make it an air force pure and simple, and not check its probable expansion. He could not see any essential difference between an air force as he would like to see it and the railway service, which both functioned in peace in their respective spheres, but were able to be switched off in national emergencies. To have a half-starved air force did not make for efficiency. If the Minister of Defence compared the number of men available with the number of highly-trained, efficient men he would have at his beck and call if it had been an air service, he must admit that there was something in his (General Byron's) contention. In the meantime the Air Service had to be usefully employed, and he hoped it would not be long before they had an aerial mail between Cape Town and the interior, their country being, above all countries in the world, an ideal one for flying.

Coastal defence.

Referring to the problem of coastal defence, Gen. Byron said it was largely in the hands of aerial and submarine craft, and they should rely more on a highly-trained, highly organised air service adapted for war services, just as they could rely on the railway service, in times of emergency.

The Naval contribution.

Mr. M. Bisset (**South African Party**, *S. Peninsula, Cape*) asked the Minister what the Union proposed to do with regard to the naval contribution.

On 20th June, the debate was resumed, and certain criticisms having been brought against the Defence Department,

Lt.-Col. G. M. Claassen (**South African Party**, *Standerton, Trans.*) made an appeal for the maintenance of the salaries of Burgher officers who did useful peace time work and were the first to come to the aid of the country in time of trouble.

The Right Hon. J. X. Merriman (**South African Party**, *Stellenbosch, Cape*) said that this was one of the most important votes that the Committee could have before them. He regretted that there was no Opposition present. What would the country think when it saw all the brave fellows who came to that House as an Opposition slink out when the question of defence was raised ?

Defence of the Cape Peninsula.

He rose particularly to draw attention to two things; one was the defence of the Cape Peninsula. They were in a position of the greatest danger. They held one of the keys of the world in regard to the trade to the East and the Eastern possessions. The Cape had always belonged to the Mistress of the Seas. Now the Union had been left to its own resources. What were they doing to protect the coast ? He was sorry that the Prime Minister was not in the House so that he might have dealt with the question of their contribution to the Navy. He (Mr. Merriman) regretted very much indeed that no notice had been taken of the naval side of the question, which was intimately connected with the defence of the Cape and of South Africa.

"At the present moment," continued Mr. Merriman, "there is nothing to prevent any Navy sailing into Durban Harbour and holding it to ransom—blowing the whole thing to pieces. Here we sit, ignorant, uncaring what happens to a thing like that. It is of the utmost importance. I regret very much indeed the absence of the Opposition, so-called. They are neglecting their duty in a way which I did not believe they would do." Some things, he added, had come out in that debate which seemed to show that all was not yet well with their defences.

Gen. Byron said many things wanted explaining. Last year 423 persons in the Department were retrenched, 137 of whom were temporary civil servants, leaving a net reduction of

286. In the same year, in spite of these drastic reductions, over which many tears were shed, there were 322 appointments, a quarter of whom were women, leaving a net number of appointments of 241 ; so they could see that on the one hand they had 423 retrenchments, and on the other 322 appointments.

More money needed for coastal services.

The Minister of Defence said he had no objection to criticism ; in fact, he very much encouraged it. One thing, however, was certain, and that was that in view of the country having taken over the responsibilities of the coastal services, the House must be prepared to vote the money for them. Next year an extra million might be necessary for these purposes. The defences had to be overhauled, guns to be obtained, salaries to be paid. Notwithstanding what had been said, he maintained that in regard to retrenchment and economising, the Department had been cut down to the bone, and yet he was able to claim that it was as efficient to-day as it ever had been in the course of its existence, irrespective of any period.

Efficiency of the Defence Department.

On one occasion, the Minister of Defence proceeded, the Department had to make provision for 16,000 men at 48 hours' notice, and it made good in this respect. That in itself was a tribute to its efficiency. He admitted that mistakes had been made, but contended that the Department had stood the test during the dreadful years of the War. The country would have to pay for its defences.

Air Service.

In regard to aeroplanes, it had been asked why they did not use them for flying purposes, say, between Cape Town and Johannesburg. That was all very well, but where was the money ? If the House wanted the Air Service, and they of the Defence Department would heartily welcome it, why should it be carried out at the expense of the Defence Department ? He did not see why the latter should be saddled with the expenses of this venture.

Reduction of the Estimates.

They had reduced the Estimates this year, Colonel Mentz went on to say, by over £400,000, because the Minister of Finance had asked that Department, along with others, to cut down. The machinery was still there, and members who were business men would know that it was as expensive to run an establishment with 30 or 40 per cent. of staff as it would be with 100 per cent. With £1,000,000 or so more they could bring the service to full strength.

Naval Defence: substitution for Contribution.

As Members knew, the Vote of £85,000 to the Navy had disappeared. During the Prime Ministers' Conference this question was very closely examined. First of all the question was discussed as to what were called the Cape defences. He served on a Sub-Committee presided over by the First Lord of the Admiralty and the First Sea Lord, with other Dominion representatives. The position of each Dominion in regard to coastal defence was considered, and when they came to South Africa they had to admit that the contribution was an insignificant one. It was then asked what could be done in place of it. The question, went on the Minister of Defence, was divided into two parts. There was, first of all, the question of what was called local coast defence, and what could be done by the Dominions concerned, and then there was the question of Empire Naval Defence. He had to do with the question of Dominion defence. The first question was the matter of supplying oil tanks. When the House came to the loan estimates they would see that provision was made for two oil tanks now, with a capacity of 12,000 tons each. That was the oil storage required for the present. These tanks would be filled with oil in the first instance.

The next question was that of naval defence. Mr. Merriman had referred to a hostile navy coming and blowing these oil tanks to eternity. One of the first things that Earl Beatty, who was present, said that they should deal with was the question of coastal surveys, not only for what they might call the regular ports, but for the whole of the coast line. The Admiralty had under consideration the question of this survey. One of the first things then asked was whether the Union would undertake that. It was agreed to. The Admiralty authorities were to assist the Union to get a survey ship. As Members knew, the *Crozier* had been sent out. It was hoped that an arrangement would be made with the railways and harbours section and the fishery survey so as to combine the three.

The next question was that of mine sweepers. He now came to a more important question, the training of personnel. It was agreed that the Union should increase the naval section to seven, and possibly more companies, and that they should have more Royal Naval Volunteer Reserves. The scheme was to train a number of men for these mine sweepers, and at the same time train further Royal Naval Volunteers for the Reserve, so that in time of war and when they were required they could provide at least seven companies. It was purely now a matter of funds to be provided for that purpose.

These were the main requirements, and he had to admit that it was certainly a necessity that, as far as their local defences were concerned, these things should be done. He could give them an assurance that the Government's undertakings to the Admiralty would be carried out and were being carried out to the fullest extent. The scheme lent itself to expansion as fast as was necessary, and to any extent for which money was provided by Parliament. Step by step they could increase until they had sloops, convoy ships and, ultimately, cruisers, etc., to any extent that the necessities of the country might demand.

Mr. Bisset thought no one need regret the disappearance of the contribution of £85,000 if something adequate were to take its place. The barest beginning had been made now, and without expansion and development at a fairly reasonable rate, it could only be regarded as a very pitiful contribution for South Africa to make to naval defence. He hoped this would be an earnest of better and greater works which would be carried out in the not distant future.

Mr. Greenacre deplored what he considered was the breaking of a link with the British Navy. Nevertheless, he realised that things must change, and that South Africa had received a new status.

The Vote was agreed to.

DEFENCE ENDOWMENT PROPERTY AND ACCOUNT BILL.*

(Transfer from United Kingdom to Union Government of lands, etc. ; Union responsibility for land defence.)

The object of this Bill is to make provision for the transfer from the Government of the United Kingdom to the South African Government of certain lands and buildings necessary for defence purposes as a result of the assumption by the Union Government of the responsibility for the land defences of the Union.

The Bill provides that the Union of South Africa having assumed, as from 1st December, 1921, responsibility for its land defences and for any military measures which it may be necessary to take for its defence and security; and the Government of the United Kingdom having agreed to relinquish in favour of and transfer to the Government of the Union on its assumption of the above responsibilities all the right, etc., to certain lands and buildings situate in the Union, to be used exclusively for the benefit of its defence organisations, establishments, etc., all land

---

* Though the Bill was passed through both Houses before the rising of Parliament, information as to any amendments made had not reached England at the time of going to press with the Journal. The summary, therefore, relates to the Bill as presented.

and buildings hitherto held by His Majesty's War Department shall be deemed to have been transferred to the Government of the Union as from the dates specified in the Schedule, and shall be held by it, subject to the provisions of the Bill, to the conditions, as far as applicable, imposed by the title deeds, etc., and also to any obligations and liabilities incurred by the War Department existing at the date of transfer. All such lands and buildings shall be defence endowment property.

Provision is made (Sect. 2 (1)) for the record of the transfer of the endowment property by the registrar of deeds or the Surveyor-General without charge.

Subject to certain powers of appropriation, reservation, sale, etc., which are specified, the endowment property shall be maintained for the use of the Union Defence Forces, or any portion thereof. Whenever the Minister of Defence certifies that any endowment property is not required for this purpose (Sect. 3 (2)), the Governor-General may, subject to the provisions of the Bill, and notwithstanding anything contained in any law relating to the disposal of Crown land (A) appropriate such property to the use of any department of State (other than the Railways and Harbours Administration), for any public purpose for which it may be required; (B) cause the property to be sold or leased to (i) the Railways and Harbours Administration; (ii) any provincial administration; (iii) any local authority empowered to hold a lease of land, etc.; or (iv) any person or body of persons corporate or unincorporate. The value of property so reserved is to be determined by a method of assessment approved by the Minister of Defence and Treasury, and when property is sold or leased (*vide* (B) above), the purchase price (in case of sale) or, in case of a lease, the rent payable, terms of lease, etc., shall be likewise approved.

A special defence "endowment account" is to be established (Sect. 4 (1)), to which shall be credited the value of any endowment property appropriated, or reserved as above mentioned (Sect. 3 (2A)), the amount of the purchase price of any such property sold under this Bill, interest on mortgage bonds, rents received under a lease, any rentals of buildings, being endowment property, or deductions from the pay of members of the Union Defence Forces in respect of quarters, provided in kind when the pay of such members is at a rate inclusive of lodging; interest on moneys accruing to the account, etc. The moneys shall be applied to permanent defence works and buildings, repairs, structural alterations and renovations of existing buildings, up to an amount not exceeding in the aggregate the amount paid in respect of the above-mentioned rents and deductions; and no moneys shall be withdrawn from the account without an Appropriation Act.

The sum of £150,262 shall be debited to the defence endowment account, the sum agreed by the Union Government to be due to the Government of the United Kingdom in respect of certain particular lands and buildings included in the Schedule, but not to pass to the Union without payment. To discharge the debit of that sum there shall be set off the first credits to a like amount in respect of any appropriation or reservations of endowment property above-mentioned (Sect. 3 (2A)). Interest (at the current rate at which money is borrowed by the Union for public purposes) shall be credited to the account in respect of endowment property appropriated or reserved (under Sect. 3 (2A)) for departments of State, etc.

Certain Admiralty lands which the Lords Commissioners of the Admiralty are willing to transfer to the Union Government shall, upon transfer, be regarded in all respects as endowment property. This does not apply to the so-called "Admiralty Reserve" along the coast-line of Natal, which has never been claimed by the Admiralty, and shall not be treated as endowment property under the Bill.

DEBATE IN HOUSE OF ASSEMBLY.

On 1st June,

The Minister of Defence (Col. the Hon. H. Mentz) in moving the Second Reading of the Defence Endowment Property and Account Bill, called the attention of the House to two White Papers which he laid on the Table a little while ago, one dealing with the taking over of the command in the Cape Peninsula and South Africa, and the other with lands, buildings, etc., taken over by the Union Government from the Imperial Government. He thought Members would agree that the solution of the question of taking over the command that had been arrived at was a satisfactory one.

Looking at the question purely from the material side, the Imperial Government was most generous in its terms to South Africa in connection with the taking over of these assets. Above and beyond that, he had no doubt that they would feel proud of the fact that the supreme command of South Africa was now vested in the manhood of that country. That immediately created a greater responsibility and imposed a great trust in them.

Naval station at Simon's Town.

Ever since Union, South Africa had felt that every possible step should be taken to qualify itself to take the supreme command, because no self-respecting and self-governing Dominion could for all time look to the Imperial Government for its protection. It would have been foolish for them at the very inception of Union to have been too persistent about taking over the command because, so far, more particularly as concerned the Cape Peninsula defences, they had these fortifications manned by heavy guns requiring the most expert knowledge in handling, and a big naval station at Simon's Town, where the dockyard cost over £3,000,000, the Naval Station for the southern section of the Fleet, all of which, in time of war, as in the last War, required the very best protection. The Union Government, therefore, decided to go slowly, but to steadily qualify itself to take over the command, and more particularly in regard to the training of the *personnel* for artillery.

After detailing the further steps which had been taken in regard to the new forts at Lion Battery, etc., the Minister said that although the Cape did not now necessarily play that important part as a world's strategical point, the centre of gravity was an ever-changing one, and one never knew when it might shift from one ocean to another, or from one part of the world to another, so that at all times it would be their duty to keep that station properly protected and take all necessary steps to cope with dangers that might arise.

The Union Government would naturally maintain a much smaller force in the Peninsula than the Imperial Government did. On the Estimates provision was made for about 300, costing something like £75,000, whereas the Imperial Government had at least 2,000 regulars in the Peninsula practically the whole time. But South Africa could not possibly satisfy itself wi h that small number, however highly trained and efficient they might be.

An endowment fund for fortifications.

Colonel Mentz said that under the Bill which the House had passed last month* provision was made for some five regiments, and in addition they would, of course, have the Citizen Forces. The measure before the House was to provide largely for the material side of that scheme. He would ask the House to consider placing the proceeds of such of this property as might not be required for defence purposes into an endowment fund, from which they could draw for the necessary permanent fortifications, fixed establishments, etc.

Negotiations with Imperial Government.

The Minister then proceeded to explain the position in regard to the taking over of lands, buildings, etc., from the Imperial Government, and the complicated negotiations which had been carried on since 1894, when the arrangement known as the Colonial Lands System was made, up to the time when representatives of the Union proceeded to England to place before the Imperial Government what the Union required. He (the Minister) accompanied the Prime Minister, and the Minister of Agriculture, and when he told the House that they had to deal with a matter involving £2,000,000, that had behind it a history of centuries, and that five Imperial departments were concerned in it, they would see that the task was a big one.

He knew that there was some talk about the huge staff taken over to England by the Defence Department, but not only did he require the whole of them, and also the splendid services of Mr. Sloane, but Mr. Burch, the Member for Uitenhage, was also in London and helped them considerably.

A free gift.

They wanted to press their claims not only for what they could show was immediately required for defence purposes, but

* Union Defence Forces Bill, *vide* JOURNAL, Vol. II., No. 3, pp. 681-2, and Vol. III., No. 3, pp. 663-5.

what the country would require probably for the next quarter of a century. Had not the Imperial Government accepted that view, it would not have given them what was practically a free gift, including the cantonments at Potchefstroom, which the Department was particularly anxious to get for a Mental Hospital; he hoped it would be possible to take over that land at a fair valuation, which could be credited to the Endowment Fund.

He hoped Members would not shirk taking the step, *i.e.*, that all the proceeds of such property sold should not go into ordinary Revenue. If the Imperial Government had insisted on the sale, the Union Government would have had to find the money, and the taxpayer would have had to pay it. The Bill would mean that when the Defence Department came to the House and money was voted it would be spending its own money.

Conditions for assistance by Imperial Government.

If they set about placing their defence in order, then would they carry out the trust that had been reposed in them. They were left with an entirely free hand as to how they would apply the proceeds of the assets, with the exception that they gave a guarantee that they would in particular consult with the Imperial authorities as to the defences around Simon's Town, where warships would go. Provision was made that if at any time the Admiralty or the War Office asked the Union to spend a greater amount than the Union Government intended, the Imperial authorities would then be prepared to spend the additional amount.

Colonel Mentz added that he intended to move that the Bill be referred to the Public Accounts Committee. The Defence Department had no idea of using a single penny of the fund until and unless it was voted by Parliament. As to the property itself, Members would see that £150,000 had to be paid, but that was for certain and specific property. For the rest, there had been a free gift in the fullest sense of the word. He thought that House, representing the people of South Africa, was indeed grateful to His Majesty's Government for the way in which they had dealt with their representatives.

Nationalist suspicions.

Gen. J. C. G. Kemp (Nationalist, *Wolmaransstad, Trans.*) was anxious lest promises might have been given to the Imperial Government in the event of future European wars, and he wanted to know why the secret despatches between the Union and Imperial Governments were not laid before the House. With all the reservations of the Imperial Government he doubted whether the transaction was going to prove such a great boon to the Union.

A step towards higher status.

Mr. T. Boydell (Leader of the Labour Party) said he was surprised that Nationalist Members opposed a Bill of this description because, as far as he could see, it was a very big step forward in giving effect to South Africa's policy of the higher status. The remarks he had been listening to seemed like suspicion gone mad. It was so unusual for anybody or any country to get something for nothing nowadays that perhaps that might account for some of the fears entertained. There was no doubt the attitude of the Imperial Government had been an exceedingly generous one, and he was only sorry that it should be generous in defence and military matters and not in others. He detected in the attitude of the Minister of Defence a strong spirit of militarism and wanted to warn the country against that. They talked a lot of peace, but the whole tendency appeared to be in the opposite direction. However, he regarded the measure as a big step forward in giving South Africa control of its own affairs. The less outside interference they had the better it would be for the country.

British Navy an agency for peace.

The Right Hon. J. X. Merriman (South African Party, *Stellenbosch, Cape*) said Mr. Boydell must know that the course the world was making now was not for peace. It was making for war. The British Navy was the greatest agency they ever had in the making of peace, and he regretted that the contribution to it was so small. Where the British warships floated there they had peace. It was the police of the world, and they should rise to their duty and help to maintain it, as they would have to look to it to help them when the time came. He heartily supported the Bill, and added that the House owed a debt of gratitude to the Minister of Defence for the able, self-respecting way in which he had dealt with the matter.

Gen. the Hon. J. B. M. Hertzog (Leader of the Nationalist Party) moved the adjournment of the debate in view of the fact that the White Paper and the Bill had so recently been laid on the Table of the House, but subsequently, on the assurance that the Bill would be thrashed out in Committee, withdrew his motion.

The cost of the gift.

Mr. P. G. W. Grobler (Nationalist, *Rustenburg, Trans.*) wanted to know what the generosity of the Imperial Government was going to cost the Union. The gift of aeroplanes had cost the country £125,000 for transport,—more than the machines were worth. He was afraid that there was some unpleasant obligation attached to the donation, because even Canada had shown itself reluctant to accept donations from the Imperial Government.

The Minister of Defence having replied, the Second Reading was agreed to and the Bill referred to the Public Accounts Committee.

RHODESIA AND THE UNION.

(Terms of incorporation.)

On 17th July, in the course of the debate on the Second Reading of the Appropriation (1922-23) Bill in the House of Assembly, the Prime Minister, replying to Col. Creswell* who asked that the terms regarding the incorporation of Rhodesia in the Union† should be made public, explained the position and stated that a referendum would be taken in Rhodesia before the end of October.‡

DEBATE IN HOUSE OF ASSEMBLY.

Col. F. H. P. Creswell (Leader of the Labour Party) referred to a cable in the Press regarding the question of a provisional agreement between the Chartered Company and the Union Government. This matter of the incorporation of Rhodesia into the Union had been attracting a good deal of attention outside, and he thought it was common cause that they should have it considered on its merits, and entirely apart from any view which the Government of the day might have as to the technical strengthening of their position by introducing what might be a favourable factor for themselves.

The position appeared to be that after the House was prorogued, the terms upon which Rhodesia was to enter the Union would be communicated by the Union Government to the people of Rhodesia who, under the Ordinance, would have an opportunity of expressing their views. Curiously enough, the House would be prorogued without the people of the Union being informed through the House what those terms were. Col. Creswell thought that before they prorogued, the Prime Minister should take Parliament and the country into his confidence as to the actual terms upon which he was proposing to incorporate Rhodesia in the Union.

Party tactics deprecated.

When they came to financial matters with the Chartered Company he confessed to a certain degree of fear. If the

* Col. F. H. P. Creswell, having been returned to Parliament for Stamford Hill, Natal, at the by-election consequent upon the death of Mr. J. G. Hunter, has resumed the Leadership of the Labour Party.

† *Vide* Journal, Vol. III., No. 3, pp. 670-1.

‡ The referendum was held on 27th October, and resulted as follows :—For Responsible Government, 8,774 ; for incorporation in the Union, 5,989 ; majority for Responsible Government, 2,785.

Prime Minister and the Government looked at this matter too much from a Party tactical point of view, they might try to make arrangements with the Chartered Company which would, perhaps, commit the Union to obligations for the purpose of securing to the Union the immense privilege of continuing to be governed by the present Prime Minister and his Cabinet, that the people would not be prepared to pay. His own view was that the ultimate destiny of Rhodesia was to be incorporated in the Union, but whether at the present time it was advisable or whether it was acceptable to the people was quite a different matter.

The Prime Minister (Lt.-Gen. the Right Hon. J. C. Smuts) said he had frequently explained what the position was. One thing Col. Creswell could banish from his mind: no consideration of Party tactics at all would influence the Government one iota in dealing with that matter. He did not believe there was any Party advantage for anybody in the incorporation of Rhodesia in the Union. The matter was much more important than that.

"A business proposition."

The Government, continued the Prime Minister, had dealt with the question so far as the Chartered Company were concerned purely as a business proposition, apart from all politics. The question in dispute was very complicated, and involved not only the Chartered Company, but the Imperial Government; and the result was that there had been prolonged delay, and it had not been possible to arrive at that position at which they could publish their terms.* When they published them to the people of Rhodesia they must know exactly where they stood with the Chartered Company and what the

---

* The principal terms for the entrance of Southern Rhodesia into the Union were published in the Press early in August as follows:—

Southern Rhodesia will be the fifth province of the Union and will be known as Rhodesia. English and Dutch will be the official languages and will enjoy equal rights.

Rhodesia will send ten representatives to the House of Assembly, but provision is made for increasing this number to seventeen as the population of the new province increases. Rhodesia will at first have four elected and one nominated Senators, but provision is made for an ultimate representation in the Senate of eight elected and two nominated members.

The Provincial Council will consist of twenty members and will be similar to the Councils of the other provinces comprised in the Union.

In addition to the usual provincial subsidy Rhodesia is to get a special subsidy of £50,000 a year for ten years as compensation for the abolition of the Rhodes Clause. [This clause guaranteed lower Customs duties on goods of British origin (other than tobacco and intoxicating liquors), than those now existing in the Union.] The Union taxation system will apply, but for a period of three years income-tax exemption as at present granted in Southern Rhodesia will remain in force.

Union must pay. He had hoped to conclude the business before Parliament was prorogued, but he saw no chance of that now.

Referendum in October.

If things worked out correctly, a referendum would have to be taken in Rhodesia before the end of October, and the people of Rhodesia would see the terms before they voted. The Parliament of South Africa would have to finally decide if incorporation would take place except in terms of their Constitution. The final judgment would rest with the people of South Africa. That was laid down in the South Africa Act which they were following.

Not the terms of Parliament.

Mr. T. Boydell (Labour, *Durban, Greyville*) said the terms that would be submitted to Rhodesia would not be the terms of Parliament, not even the terms of the South African Party, but of the Prime Minister and the Cabinet. When Parliament had risen the terms would be submitted and the people in their referendum would be influenced by them. After the referendum the whole thing would be flung on the floor in the House, which would be told that they must be accepted. That was government by dictatorship. The House would not be consulted.

A development grant of not less than £500,000 a year for ten years is to be devoted to capital expenditure on development such as railways, public works, irrigation, land settlements, telegraphs, roads, bridges, and other development purposes. The Rhodesia and Mashonaland railways are to be taken over and also the other railway rights of the Chartered Company. The Union rates and fares will be charged throughout Rhodesia. Special attention will be devoted to the port of Beira as the principal outlet for Rhodesian traffic.

Crown lands will be freed at once of charges in respect of the debt due to the Chartered Company, and a Land Settlement Board consisting of Rhodesians will be appointed, the funds for which will come out of the development grant. The mineral rights of the Chartered Company will be acquired by a mutual agreement with the company at a later date. In the meantime the present royalties will continue to be paid to the Company. The Rhodesian mining law and regulations will continue in force after the incorporation of the province in the Union.

The public service will become part of the Union service. All its existing and accruing rights will be secured, and additional rights and assurances as to the future will also be granted. The same provision applies to the Chartered Police and railway servants.

The existing defence system will continue until there has been time to consider how best to apply the Union system. There will be no restriction on the movement of Europeans as between Rhodesia and the other Provinces of the Union. With regard to the movements of other than Europeans, the existing restrictions in force in the Union will apply.

No recruiting in Rhodesia of labour for other parts of the Union will be allowed. The existing municipalities will get as a free endowment the transfer of land set aside for them as commonages.

MIGRATION AND UNEMPLOYMENT.

(Criticism of Government; Migration and industrial development; Weakness of white population; Need of capital; Right type of settler; etc.)

On 14th June the House of Assembly, in Committee of Supply on the Estimates, discussed the Vote: Prime Minister, £34,429.

DEBATE IN HOUSE OF ASSEMBLY.

Gen. the Hon. J. B. M. Hertzog (Leader of the Nationalist Party) moved a reduction of the Prime Minister's salary by £500 (from £3,500 to £3,000). He attacked the Prime Minister for having "failed to deal with the problem of unemployment," which it was his first duty to tackle. New factors had arisen recently in regard to the problem: the returned soldiers, also railway men who were being retrenched indiscriminately. The Government was mainly responsible for that new class of unemployed, and was merely trifling with the matter.

The Prime Minister had urged that railway development would ease the situation, but was the man who had been retrenched from the Civil Service going to work for 7s. 6d. per day with a pick and shovel on the railways? He feared that even that class of unemployed who were going to be assisted by railway development would derive only a temporary benefit, and when those works were completed they would be unemployed as before.

Migration and industrial policy; Agriculture.

The Government, Gen. Hertzog continued, was aggravating the evil by assisting immigrants to come and help to swell the ranks of the unemployed. Its industrial policy was also calculated to make matters worse. He congratulated the Prime Minister on his decision to assist the iron industry, but added that there were other industries which were as promising which required only a few years of encouragement to be a proved success. He advocated preferential treatment for South Africans on the railways and in other Government departments.

Mr. H. W. Sampson (Labour, *Jeppes, Trans.*), in moving that the Vote be reduced by £1,000, criticised the Government for having adopted a partial attitude in regard to the strike on the Rand and of neglecting to introduce industrial legislation. The strike would never have occurred if they had had the proper machinery for dealing with industrial disputes.

The Government was not doing much to alleviate unemployment. He wanted to know why it had not introduced legislation to deal with miners' phthisis, and referred to the work of the Commission some years ago, which body had now been dissolved without the Bill which it had advocated having been brought forward. They were by no means at the end of their troubles. Their industries would always be held up unless proper machinery were provided in regard to trade unions.

The Right Hon. J. X. Merriman (South African Party, *Stellenbosch, Cape*) pointed out that unemployment had been going on for twenty years. The great industry in South Africa, agriculture, was not worked at. It had been said that the Government had done nothing in the matter. It had, as a matter of fact, done a great deal. It was employing people at double the wages of coloured people to plant trees, etc. A Bill had just been introduced to spend £4,000,000 on the building of new lines of railway. That would find work for white men.

Gen. Hertzog: "And when the railways have been finished?"

Mr. Merriman: "The men will then have learnt the dignity of labour. The men here are good enough if you can only get them to work."

Unemployment; Attracting settlers.

Mr. C. G. Fichardt (Nationalist, *Ladybrand, O.F.S.*) described the steps which had been taken in Germany to deal with unemployment. Under these schemes a private contractor was selected by the Government to carry out the works, instead of the works being executed departmentally. A certain percentage of the men engaged had to be obtained through the Government Bureau. The authorities started with an unemployed problem of 800,000, which, by the end of March last, had been reduced to 20,000.

Mr. C. W. Malan (Nationalist, *Humansdorp, Cape*) contended that the Government had spent £50,000 upon advertising for immigrants from overseas, etc. Mr. Tatlow had not concealed the fact that he had sought to attract settlers, and the High Commissioner in London was doing his best to obtain immigrants.

Voluntary reduction of Ministers' salaries.

Mr. J. G. Keyter (Nationalist, *Ficksburg, O.F.S.*) said the Prime Minister had given a misleading answer to a question at a meeting in the Free State when he asserted that since the War Ministers had voluntarily foregone a part of their salaries. He (Mr. Keyter) denied that there had been any such reduction.

The Prime Minister (Lt.-Gen. the Right Hon. J. C. Smuts) said that unemployment, which had been most discussed that evening, was a matter of considerable gravity to-day, but they could easily over-rate its importance. He was thankful that notwithstanding the very great difficulties through which they had passed—difficulties which in one sense were world-wide and in another sense were peculiar to South Africa—they were coping with unemployment in a way which he thought was not ineffective. He was assured by the Administrator of the Transvaal, where most of the unemployment was, that everything was being done that could be done. At Hartebeestpoort, he was told, men were not coming forward in sufficient numbers to fill all the vacancies which had been created there.

The question of unemployment was being coped with fairly and effectively by way of relief works, and the immediate difficulties of the situation were all that the Government could be responsible for. There were thousands of people in Johannesburg who were unemployed, but who did not want to go to relief works, and he did not blame them. They were waiting for their jobs to be opened again on the mines when the native labour complement was once more restored. Then the skilled men who had been in employment before would be re-employed.

A Labour Member: " Four thousand must be out."

The Prime Minister said he was not speaking of victimisation now, but of employment. He thought there would be sufficient work for every skilled man who was employed before on the Witwatersrand when the native labour was there. " We have no reason to blame ourselves," he added, " for the results of our efforts."

The "poor whites"; Financial difficulties.

Gen. Hertzog, he continued, took unemployment as being co-extensive with " poor whites." He did not agree that the " poor white " was an unemployed person. The vast number of the people whom they called " poor whites " were employed at a very low wage. Gen. Hertzog said that the Government were not taking effective measures to deal with the situation. What must they do ? Gen. Hertzog's answer was that the Government must go in for an industrial policy. He (the Prime Minister) had said so before. When he said it during the last General Election, Gen. Hertzog said that in all industrial countries you have the poor and unemployed. That was perfectly true.

Gen. Smuts admitted that, as a permanent cure for the problem of " poor whites," and to some extent also of unemployment, they must very largely develop South Africa on broader lines than hitherto. They could not restrict the development simply to mining and agricultural employment. He had explained the policy of the Government on this matter within the last four weeks.* But to expect that they could in a fortnight or four weeks turn that country into an industrial country was a very grave mistake.

The difficulty they were faced with was a financial difficulty, which enterprise had to meet. Most industries that had come to him for assistance had not come with a request for protection; they could not obtain the necessary finance either to get started or carry on if they were started. They [in South Africa] had to work, as the rest of the world had to work, through this state of financial stringency. He agreed that relief measures would only tide them over the immediate difficulties, and that for a permanent cure a broader policy was necessary than they had followed so far. He hoped the House would support the Government in working out that policy. They would then broaden the basis of employment in South Africa, and have more opportunities for the skilled training of "poor whites."

Migration; Small white population.

It was said, the Prime Minister continued, that the immigration policy of the Government stood in the way of the industrial employment or employment in the Government service of the sons of South Africa. The immigration policy of the Government was perfectly simple. Except the money they were spending on advertising the country, they were to-day, to his deep regret, doing nothing for immigration. He had this feeling—he might be wrong—that one of the things which told against the white man in South Africa, that kept him down, was just the smallness of their white population. The struggle was not between one white man and another; the real fundamental struggle was between the white man and the black man, who was being gradually trained up and taking the place of the white man at a cheaper wage. The smaller the white population the more dangerous its position would be. In his opinion, whatever increased and strengthened the white population would help to reduce white unemployment, and would really help a white South Africa.

Overseas advertising.†

An hon. Member had said that advertising meant an immigration policy. He wished it did. They had put Mr. Boshoff with the High Commissioner practically to warn people away from South Africa. They found that a situation

---

* *Vide* JOURNAL, Vol. III., No. 3, pp. 679-682.

† *Vide* JOURNAL, Vol. III., No. 3, pp. 669-670.

had grown up which was dangerous for South Africa and to many people who were coming there. People who had ground to sell were advertising South Africa in London and elsewhere, and misrepresenting the facts. Mr. Boshoff was there to warn people that, unless they had capital, South Africa was not the land for them. Mr. Tatlow was advertising the country very effectively and well,* and he and other agencies were bringing into South Africa fair numbers of people—hundreds per annum.

Mr. C. W. Malan: "As settlers?"

The Prime Minister: "Yes, as settlers. Let us be honest and fair to this country. The man who comes to this country with £10,000 or £15,000, you may call him a settler if you will."

The right type of settler.

What was being done, he continued, through the advertising policy of the Government and the Railways and Mr. Boshoff, was to get a type of man there who could settle in South Africa, buy farms, and was not likely to be an incubus on the State. He was sorry it was so little. He would have been glad if it went further, but their means did not allow. The British Government, notwithstanding all their financial difficulties, were prepared to spend millions per annum over a long period of years to assist emigration to other parts of the Empire. Other parts of the Empire were availing themselves of this; unfortunately they (in South Africa) were out of it.

Nationalist Members: "Why?"

The Prime Minister: "Because the people they are sending out are not the class of people that we can absorb here." They were advertising the country in order to attract, he would not say the better type, but the richer type of settler. If the Government was to be blamed, it was blameworthy only in one respect, that they were not doing more to settle white people in that country. He saw nothing but disaster in this policy of trying to build a wall round South Africa: nothing but unemployment, more "poor whites," and the community as a white community sinking deeper and deeper if the policy adumbrated by Members opposite was followed.

"No, let them come," said the Prime Minister. "We have come here; our forefathers came to this country. Let us build up this country on sound lines. I admit, and we all admit, there is no place in this country for the poor immigrant at present. In coming generations the position may be

* *Vide* Journal, Vol. III., No. 3, p. 670.

different. . . . But the man who brings technical skill, the man who brings education, the man who brings capital, I think that everyone of us will stand with open arms to welcome him."

Migration and the coloured man.

On 15th June,

Gen. Hertzog contended that there was no logic in the Prime Minister's statement that immigration would increase avenues of employment in the Union, and asked whether there was any justice in a policy of depriving the coloured man of his means of existence by introducing white men from oversea.

The Prime Minister: "What happens when you start on economic segregation ?"

Gen. Hertzog said the coloured man would then at least have justice. Moreover, the black man was in favour of segregation even to the extent of economic segregation.

Mr. Fichardt criticised the Prime Minister's "callous" declaration the previous night. The Nationalist Party never wanted to give the natives the franchise, they always said the natives had a right to be in the country, and should have an opportunity of living and rising, but now the Prime Minister said, "Let us import as many people as possible from overseas so as to kill out and crush the natives." He had, in the most emphatic manner, announced that they must encourage as much immigration as possible because of the fight between black and white; that they must strengthen the white man so that the black man should go down. That bastard policy was the result of the alliance between the S.A.P. and the Unionists.

Prime Minister supported.

Mr. Merriman said that with regard to immigrants the Prime Minister seemed to him to have said a very sensible thing. He said that the class whom they wanted were people with capital who could support themselves. To bring out English people and put them down in the towns would be a fatal disaster.

In regard to the native population he heard a very eloquent speech with the greatest pleasure from General Hertzog some time ago, in which he went beyond anything he (Mr. Merriman) had heard in regard to what should be done with the coloured people—that they should be put on a level with the white people, so he understood, and that the coloured or native population should be segregated. Now he had changed his policy. He was attacking the Prime Minister because the Member for Ladybrand had an idea that the Prime Minister was anxious to drive the black people out.

It was a poor compliment to his intelligence to think they could do that. They could not do it, and would not be allowed to do it if they wanted. The natives were too useful in that country for anything of the kind. In South Africa they had got the cheapest, the most intelligent and the most docile people in the whole world. They had built their railways, they had dug all their mines, they had been contented and in a way prosperous.

In conclusion Mr. Merriman drew the Prime Minister's attention to a report of a "Workers' Rally on the Rand" which appeared in *The Cape Times*, specially emphasising the statement in the report that a large proportion of those present were aliens. He would like to ask the Prime Minister or the Minister of the Interior who was responsible for importing these aliens into their midst.

Cheap labour; Repatriated Germans.

Mr. R. B. Waterson (Labour, *Brakpan, Trans.*) said that if they had, as Mr. Merriman had stated, the most intelligent, efficient and docile body of workers in the world, he would like to know why it was that the manufacturers of South Africa were continually asking for protection against overseas competition. As a matter of fact, this so-called cheap labour was not cheap, in the long run it was most inefficient, and, if it were "docile," that was its only qualification. The Government had, he admitted, done something in the direction of helping the lot of the worker, but their efforts were on too small a scale to effectively deal with the problem. The Prime Minister had said that the real difficulty was one of finance. Then why didn't the Government do something to get the country out of the grip of the banks?

Mr. A. P. J. Fourie (Nationalist, *Somerset, Cape*), said if the Nationalists had a grievance against the Government it was that it had sent out of the country men who had been an asset to the Union. If ever a blow had been struck at immigration of the right kind it was when the Germans were repatriated. He asked what the Government had done to give effect to the recommendations of the Unemployment Commission and pointed out that one of the findings in the Report was that unemployment was in a large measure due to the lack of education.

Causes of unemployment; Opposition to migration.

Mr. W. J. Snow (Labour, *Salt River, Cape*) said that the Railway Department was employing 12,000 people less than it did. Where had these men gone? The Government ought to deal with the causes rather than the effects of unemployment. It was far better economy to keep men in the service of the Government and go on with development works, than provide relief works for men to go to after they had been driven out of their billets.

Mr. L. Blackwell (South African Party, *Bezuidenhout, Trans.*) suggested from his observation that a great deal of the unemployment in South Africa was due to the policy of limited production—"going slow on the job"—that had been so persistently advocated.

Capt. P. S. Cilliers (South African Party, *Hopetown, Cape*) said the Prime Minister had a simple panacea for the "poor white" problem, namely, industries. The whole basis of industries was poverty. The greater the industrial development of the country the greater poverty. There were in England twelve million people on the verge of starvation.

Mr. C. A. van Niekirk (Nationalist, *Boshdf, O.F.S.*) urged sympathetic consideration of the difficulties of the farmers, and expressed the fear that all immigrants who might be induced to come at the present time would only help to make the economic conditions worse.

Mr. F. J. du Toit (Nationalist, *Victoria, W., Cape*), who advocated emulation of the policy pursued by Mr. Sauer in the old Cape days, viz., that no immigrant should be given a job while there was a son of the soil without one, referred to what Lord Northcliffe and Colonel Amery had said about emigration to the Dominions, and argued that at the bottom it was a scheme intended to serve Imperialistic ends. He could not understand why the Union Government was encouraging immigration at such a time of depression as the present.

1820 Settlers' Movement.

Brig.-Gen. the Hon. J. J. Byron (South African Party, *Border, Cape*) said that for the first time all Parties were agreed that a certain sort of immigration was necessary to South Africa. He referred to the 1820 Settlers' Movement which was introducing settlers of the most desirable kind. A proof of the carefulness with which the Selection Committee in Britain performed its duties was found in the fact that up to the present there had been no failures. Two hundred and fifty settlers had arrived there and were doing well. Many more were on the books, and 400 farmers were ready to prepare them for the conditions of South Africa. The handful of men who had arrived had brought in no less than three-quarters of a million of money to the country, so they would see it was a movement which should be encouraged. Next year he thought they would have 1,000 settlers with not less than £3,000 each, which would mean bringing not less than £3,000,000 into the country, and the following years would see even more arriving.

League of Nations and eight-hour day.

The Prime Minister said Mr. Waterston had asked why the Government were not carrying out the eight-hour day policy of the League of Nations. They were, as far as they were able, carrying out the eight-hour day principle laid down in the Peace Treaty. The Covenant of the League of Nations brought this up as an ideal towards which they should work, and, so far as lay in their power, the Government had acted up to that principle, but it was not possible in every respect to carry it out. They had made a statement to the League as to what they had done, and the League had replied, generally expressing satisfaction at the course adopted.

"Poor whites" and land settlement; Need of capital.

In reply to Members who had asked if the Government were not carrying out the Report of the Unemployment Commission, the Prime Minister said if they had made a study of the Report they would see that the fundamental recommendation of the Commission was a great land settlement scheme. They calculated that there were so many "poor whites," a very large number (150,000), which he considered a gross exaggeration. The recommendation of the Commission was that these "poor whites" should be placed on the land. It cost thousands to settle a man on the land, and if they had to take these people in their tens of thousands and settle them on the land, it would work out to an enormous figure; not the £15,000,000 which the Commission mentioned, but probably more than double that.

South Africa, continued General Smuts, craved for capital in all directions. They wanted it to build railways, for irrigation works and other necessary expansion; and was it possible that while they spent those millions every year on necessary development, they should spend another £20,000,000 or £30,000,000 now in order to try to solve the "poor white" question? Ever since he had been a member of the Government they had been doing nothing but settle "poor whites" on the land, and if the sum of money which had been expended in this connection were added up Members would be appalled at the figure; and yet they had not touched the fringe of the question.

Continuing, the Prime Minister said he had nothing to alter or subtract from what he had said the previous night.* It was the weakness of the white population in a community of millions of black people which constituted their fundamental weakness, and that was the source of the poor white and many other questions. It seemed to him to be absolutely axiomatic in their politics.

---

* *Vide* pp. 928–9.

Advice to settlers; the future.

The scheme of "advertising the good points of this country," the Prime Minister added, in reply to a question, was to attract people to it. "Believe me, if we are patriotic South Africans, if we love this country and want to see the development of the white races of our civilisation in South Africa, we have been discussing since yesterday one of the greatest issues that could be raised in South Africa. . . .

"There are to-day, under the conditions of Europe as they now exist, tens of thousands of people who want to clear out of the old countries. . . . Let us attract these people. They are leaving Europe, they are leaving the old countries, not only the British Islands, but many other parts of the Continent, They are going to Australia and America, and here is a much better country for them to come to. I believe there is no country so good as South Africa to live in."

Gen. Smuts went on to explain what the Government had done when they found that "wild-cat schemes in connection with land purchase were being hawked about in London," and the advice which Mr. Boshoff was giving to people: that they should not buy land in London, but that they should go to South Africa first, and that they should not do that unless they had a sufficient sum of money to start with. If they had less than £2,000 they need not think of going further into the matter.

In conclusion the Prime Minister said there was no reason why they should sit down in pessimism and despair. He was sure that if they went in very largely for that industrial policy which he had preached, if they broadened the basis of their industrial system, they would work through that phase. When they came to deal with the evils which afflicted white South Africa, he thought there was really no dispute between parties. If they faced the position resolutely and made up their minds not to go in for patent remedies or panaceas of doubtful character, but for a sound policy of development along all lines, agricultural, mining and industrial, he was sure that they would see the same success that had been witnessed under similar conditions in the Southern States of America.

In reply to a question by Gen. Hertzog the Prime Minister said he was for State-aided immigration "if circumstances allowed it."

Gen. Hertzog: "In other words, if you have enough money?"

The Prime Minister: "When the 'poor white' question is out of the way."

Gen. Hertzog said he was glad to hear that the statement of the Prime Minister the previous night was not to be interpreted as purporting to favour unlimited State-aided immigration.

The motion to reduce the Prime Minister's salary by £1,000 was then put and negatived without a division, as was the motion to reduce it by £500.

On 20th June, on Vote 20 : Interior, £186,675.

Mr. M. Alexander (**Constitutional Democrat**, *Cape Town, Castle*) moved a reduction of £5 in the Minister's salary, and asked the Minister to make a clear statement as to why the Government was not content to carry out its immigration policy which was indicated in 1913. If immigrants were unsuitable on economic grounds the Minister had adequate powers to restrict them under the Act.

Mr. T. G. Strachan (**Labour**, *Pietermaritzburg, N., Natal*) said he was more concerned how to get rid of certain elements which were in the country. He was very much in favour of the Government's voluntary repatriation scheme "with a dash of compulsion in it."

Naturalisation laws.

Mr. Alexander declared that the administration of the naturalisation laws was now made a matter of money.

The Minister of the Interior (**Hon. Patrick Duncan**): "Nonsense."

Mr. Alexander said that until recently it cost 2s. 6d. to become naturalised, but the Government increased the fee to £11 at one jump. There was a deputation to the Government, and they came down to £5, but he submitted that even £5 was an exorbitant fee.

Mr. W. B. Madeley (**Labour**, *Benoni, Trans.*) said he hoped that the Minister would considerably mitigate the harshness of some of his decisions, and make a full declaration of policy. The discretionary clause in the Immigration Act placed a dangerous political weapon in his hands. Mr. Madeley also criticised the administration of the naturalisation laws.

Policy of restriction.

The Minister of the Interior said that a year ago he was constantly being assailed by Members sitting round Mr. Madeley for not prohibiting immigration into that country when unemployment was rampant. Now he was being attacked because they imposed restrictions solely with the intention of keeping out people who would aggravate the conditions of unemployment. That was the policy which the Government followed of restricting immigration by the application of what was known as Clause 4 (1) (A). He knew that the clause gave the Minister autocratic powers and that there was no appeal, but he had asked the Appeal Board in Cape Town to hear the case of every man restricted under it, and unless the Board agreed that he was unsuitable, the man was allowed to land.

He denied that naturalisation was made dependent on money. It depended on several things—the character of the person who applied, the question of residence and education to some extent. In regard to fees, he really did not think that a man who desired to obtain privileges as a citizen of South Africa could complain that it was too much to ask him to pay £5, and he (Mr. Duncan) could not hold out any hope that the fee would be reduced. He added that he hoped to see an amending Naturalisation Law introduced into the House next year.

Repatriation of Indians.

In regard to the voluntary repatriation of Indians, the Minister said the Government had done their best to make this known and had increased the amounts payable to those who desired to be repatriated, because they realised that there were a number who were anxious to get back to India, and that it was to the advantage of South Africa that they should be helped and encouraged to go back. This had, however, aroused a considerable amount of opposition amongst the Indians themselves, and a great agitation was now being carried on by the Natal Indian Congress, warning people not to accept any offer from the Government to go back to India. Organisation, he continued, was better, and ships were sailing more frequently. The latest figures of Indians who had returned to their country were 4,800 since the scheme of July, 1920, was inaugurated, and 13,000 since 1914.*

Mr. Waterston said the Labour Members protested, not against immigration, but against men being brought to South Africa under contract at lower wages than were being paid in that country.

Mr. Alexander's motion was negatived and the Vote was agreed to.

ASIATICS IN THE UNION.

(Asiatics in Natal; Repatriation or segregation; Citizen rights; British reputation for justice; Attitude of Indian Government; etc.)

On 9th May, in the House of Assembly, the question of the segregation of Asiatics was discussed, when a resolution advocating this policy was moved by Mr. Mackeurtan.

* *Vide* JOURNAL, Vol. III., No. 3, p. 666.

DEBATE IN HOUSE OF ASSEMBLY.

Mr. N. G. Mackeurtan (**South African Party,** *Durban-Umbilo, Natal*), in moving—

That this House requests the Government to consider the advisability of the early introduction of legislation which will provide for the allocation to the Asiatic community of any one or more of the Provinces of the Union, separate and distinct areas, rural and urban, within its Province, where that community may develop in accordance with its needs and standard of civilisation, due regard being had to the interests of the present and future European native population,

referred to the race antagonism that existed, and quoted a statement by Lord Milner in regard to the position. There were two classes of civilisation living side by side, and racial antagonism had been deepened during the last twelve months. The Provincial Council of Natal had passed two Ordinances in an endeavour to deal with the matter, and owing to the unsatisfactory position which had arisen at Stangar, where it was found that the Municipal voters of Asiatic origin outnumbered the Europeans, it was decided to put the Municipal franchise on the same footing as the political. There was also an endeavour on the part of the Provincial Council to deal with the question of Asiatic licences.

Indian house-owners.

The largest number of people, Mr. Mackeurtan continued, who had been called upon to reduce rents in accordance with the Rents Act were Indians, one of whom owned no fewer than 200 houses in the Borough of Durban. That operated in the minds of people and caused antagonism. A more significant feature had occurred when the Town Council of Durban held a land sale in Umbilo, in what had hitherto been a white residential neighbourhood. One or two lots were bought by Europeans. One or two men then went to the front, and it was discovered that the purchasers were Asiatics. The Europeans walked up and stopped the sale.

Mr. T. Boydell (Leader of the Labour Party): "Direct action."

Mr. Mackeurtan: "Yes, direct action, in a good cause." He went on to say that people in Natal were looking for a lead in trying to deal with matters of that kind. Nothing had been done by the Government. The Municipal Council had tried to do something, and so had the Provincial Council; but Parliament had done nothing.

Repatriation or segregation.

Of course, he realised that there was another factor, and that was the position of India. He did not under-estimate its gravity. In this state of affairs, he continued, they had three courses open to them. The first was to endeavour to repatriate the Indians. They might be able to repatriate under compensation those who were not born in South Africa, but it was impossible to repatriate the Indian who was born there. He had become a South African national. Over half the Indians in Natal were South African born. They had 160,000 Indians in Natal to-day as against 138,000 whites. The second alternative was to do nothing.

There seemed to be a middle course. That was segregation. He did not advocate absolute segregation; there was no desire whatever to interfere with liberty of movement and personal freedom. The idea was social and trade segregation. He suggested that the municipalities should be asked whether they were prepared to set aside segregation areas.

Mr. J. S. Marwick (South African Party, *Illovo, Natal*) supported the motion.

An amendment.

Sir Abe Bailey (South African Party, *Krugersdorp, Trans.*) moved as an amendment to add at the end:

> and also (a) materially to increase its efforts to ensure the departure of Asiatics from the Union, and (b) to tighten up the operation of the immigration laws as regards Asiatics, and to resist by all means within its power any attempt to relax their operation in this respect.

Taking the place of white men.

He did not think these Asiatics were desirable and beneficial as residents of South Africa, and they were a source of weakness and danger to the country. Every Indian in South Africa took the place of a white man, took his livelihood away and forced him to leave the country. What was to become of the 43,000 children born last year? What was their future, and what hope was there for them? Were they to be the salaried clerks of Asiatics or the aliens of South Africa? They certainly would not be able to grasp an opportunity, because there would be no opportunity for them if the Indians were allowed to remain. The only thing the people of South Africa would then be able to say to the people from India was: "You are the winners, we are the fools."

Voluntary segregation.

The Commission recommended voluntary segregation. What was voluntary segregation? They also recommended that they should settle from 20 to 30 miles from the coast. The position was that they were taking up the best land in Natal for the development of the sugar industry. A policy of segregation had been laid down by Lord Milner, who also laid down that certain areas should be reserved for white people. " My policy," said Sir Abe Bailey, " is to reserve the whole of South Africa for white people and the natives."

Indians and citizen rights.

Brig.-Gen. the Hon. J. J. Byron (**South African Party**, *Border, Cape*) said that although he supported the motion and the amendment, in his judgment neither of them went far enough. The question was, were they prepared to give full citizen rights to the Indians in their midst who had thrown in their lot with South Africa ? He did not think there was any political Party that would agree to that. He did not think the remedy would be found in segregation. That was only a very small instalment in dealing with a big question, and he thought they must face the matter as an international question greatly affecting them in South Africa, and come to a definite arrangement that the Indians must be repatriated from South Africa *en masse.* They were not satisfied to have them there as equal citizens with themselves. Would it not be a wise thing if they could exchange the 168,000 Indians in South Africa for the 2,000 or 3,000 men of their own race who were now in India, men of very high standing likely to make first-class citizens in South Africa, and not likely to reduce employment but to give employment in South Africa ?

A further amendment.

Mr. C. P. Robinson (**South African Party**, *Durban, C., Natal*) moved as a further amendment to add at the end :—

Provided that there shall be compulsory segregation or repatriation of Asiatics, but that Government shall proceed on the lines laid down in recommendations 2, 3, 4, 5 and 6 of Section 225 of the Report of the Asiatic Inquiry Commission.

Asiatics in Natal.

The seriousness of the menace was so patent that it seemed to him almost unnecessary that it should be argued. He thought, however, that too much stress was usually laid on the question in so far as the Arab trader was concerned. The real trouble came with reference to the balance of these men, the 130,000 Asiatics in Natal who were not traders. There were not more than 10,000 so-called Arab traders. It was from the ranks of Indians born in Natal that the clerks, solicitors, advocates and doctors were growing up.

Segregation an unsatisfactory policy.

Mr. Robinson asked how they were going to ship 160,000 people from their shores, many of whom had been born in the country ; and said the people who spoke about segregation utilised the services of those Indians, but when they entered into commerce, then they talked about segregation. Where people were segregated they were bound to become degenerate.

He had more sympathy with the amendment that wanted to make a clean sheet of them than with the half-hearted policy of segregation. The present was a period of conferences and they must try to get a conference with these people. Some time ago the Government induced a good many to go back to India; but something had happened to stop that. If a serious effort were made by the Government to induce these people to leave or to keep them in certain trading and living districts, they would go a long way towards ameliorating the position and save themselves from the ignominy of attempting an undertaking that would not be successful.

Britain's reputation for justice.

Mr. J. G. Hunter (South African Party, *Stamford Hill, Natal*) said if people agreed not to sell property to Indians they would help materially. He added that the Indians had been brought there and they could not be sent away against their will. They had established themselves and had families, and they should take care that they did nothing unjust. Britain was always justly proud of the fair play and justice and freedom she extended to colonists, and South Africa must see that she did nothing to injure that fair name.

Asiatics and sugar traders.

The Right Hon. J. X. Merriman (South African Party, *Stellenbosch, Cape*) said that many of them had said over and over again that it was not a good thing for the country to have the Indians there, and had urged the people in Natal to send them back again. But the latter said, "No, the Asiatic must stay; we cannot turn out sugar unless we have the Asiatic." Now, having got all they could out of him, they would kick him out. "Perish the Empire, but save Natal," now seemed to be the cry. He would urge Members not to be led away by the wild and whirling words of the Member for Krugersdorp. They had brought those people there and must treat them in a humane and reasonable way. The idea of a small community on a question like this raising issues which might be of the greatest moment struck him as one of the most foolish things in the world.

Bonuses for Indians.

Mr. P. W. le Roux van Niekerk (Nationalist, *Waterberg, Trans.*) thought the matter was capable of settlement without compromising the interests of the Imperial Government or causing any concern outside South Africa. He urged the repatriation of Indians not born in South Africa and suggested that a substantial bonus might be offered to those willing to go. There was a chance to do something to-day whereas in ten years' time the difficulties would become insurmountable.

Indian Government and Asiatic Powers.

The Minister of the Interior (Hon. Patrick Duncan) said they should not think they were dealing only with British India. In South Africa undoubtedly the majority of the Asiatic population came from British India, but they did not all come from there. Members could be quite sure that if any action were taken against the Asiatic population in South Africa which was unjust, they would have to deal not merely with protests from the Government of India, which was one of their fellow Governments inside the Empire, but also with protests from other Asiatic Powers.

The Government of India naturally showed great interest in the welfare of the Indian people in South Africa, and took up what seemed to him a perfectly logical and intelligible point of view. They said, " If you are prepared to give these Indians political rights in South Africa, then we shall wash our hands of them; they can protect themselves like other citizens of the country; but as long as you deny them political rights "—as Mr. Duncan pointed out they did outside the Cape Province—" then we think it our duty, if they have grievances in regard to the manner in which they are treated which they have no means of redressing themselves, to hear their grievances and make representations in regard to what we think right oı just."

Claim to political equality; Problem in Natal and elsewhere.

The question of political equality had been raised. The Indians in South Africa requested to be accorded full political rights. He did not think the European people in South Africa were prepared to accede to that, anyhow for a very long time to come, and the only answer they had to give to that demand was a negative one.

South Africa, the Minister went on to say, had to take up a different stand to other countries. Members were apt to forget that the proportion of population between the Asiatics and the Europeans of Natal was far less serious than it was ten years ago. Then the former outnumbered the latter by about 60 per cent.; now they were about equal. Outside of Natal, the proportion was negligible. It was not true that the system of repatriation had been stopped by the sugar industry. As a matter of fact, it was being pressed more vigorously than ever. The Indians were assisted in the way of free passages and a little money, up to £20. Last year, 3,427 had been repatriated under the voluntary scheme, and this year 719. Immigration was now stopped except in the case of the wives and children of some of the residents. It was not the sugar planters, but the Indian Association, that stopped the repatriation. They had to remember that this was a world-wide problem.

Outside of Natal, Mr. Duncan said in conclusion, the Asiatic problem was not of urgent pressure, and the commission that had inquired into the position of small traders in many towns reported that it was not as grave as had been made out. Had those who suggested segregation gone into that solution ? Suppose they got the land—and that was not easy—would the Asiatics go there ? Compulsory segregation was an illusion. Was it conceivable that they were going to send out men born in the country—whose fathers and grandfathers had been born there ? Where could they send them ? Would India take them ? Two-thirds of the Indians of Natal were born there. He was in favour of encouraging a measure of urban segregation, provided proper arrangements could be made. But complete segregation or compulsory expulsion were out of the question. He did not agree with the idea of setting all moral considerations aside. They wanted a more sympathetic attitude.

Mr. T. G. Strachan (Labour, *Pietermaritzburg, N., Natal*) said he thought the Minister of the Interior had made out a good case for the Government doing nothing at all in tackling a difficult problem. He moved the adjournment of the debate, which was agreed to.

CONSTITUTION OF THE SENATE.

(Select Committee of 1918 ; Representations to Prime Minister ; Speaker's Conference ; Present Constitution ; Demand for reform ; etc.)

On 30th June a discussion took place on the constitution of the Senate and the position of the Government was explained in relation to the suggested reforms.

DEBATE IN THE SENATE.

Senator the Hon. H. G. Stuart (*O.F.S.*) moved :—

That this House, having regard to the fact that a Select Committee of the House was appointed in 1918 to consider and report on the future constitution of the Senate,* and that the said Committee reported in favour of a new constitution for the Senate to take effect at the end of ten years from the commencement of Union, which report, without any opinion being expressed thereon, was by resolution of the House referred to the Government for consideration ; that on various occasions after the year 1918, both within and outside of the House, representations were made to the Right Hon. the Prime Minister by Members of the Senate, asking for the appointment of a Commission or Conference to

* *Vide* JOURNAL, Vol. I., No. 2, pp. 387-8 ; Vol. I., No. 3, pp. 581-590.

draw up in terms of Section 25 of the South Africa Act, 1909, a new constitution for the Senate; and that, finally in 1920, the Government appointed a Conference under presidency of the Speaker to examine and report upon the question of the future constitution of the Senate, and that this Conference did duly sit in October, 1920, and reported in favour of a new constitution for the Senate, expresses regret that the Government has now declared in a reply given by the Hon. the Minister of Justice to a question put by Senator the Hon. F. W. Reitz on the 15th ult., that it is not prepared to carry out the recommendations of the Conference.

He said that Section 25 of the South Africa Act clearly contemplated the possibility of a new constitution of the Senate after the first ten years following Union. When the report of the Select Committee appointed in 1918 was presented several Members did their best to induce the Government to bring about the desired reconstitution. When Gen. Botha (then Premier) returned from Europe he made sympathetic references to this Committee. He (Senator Stuart) was at a complete loss to understand Gen. Smuts's indifference in regard to the constitution of Parliament. His motion was not one of a loss of confidence, but the least they could do in the interests of that House was to express regret at the attitude of the Government.

Senator the Hon. P. Whiteside (*Trans.*), in seconding the resolution, said that in view of the General Election, which had resulted in greater support being given to the Government, they could understand why Gen. Smuts was satisfied with the present constitution of the Senate. He (Senator Whiteside) considered that the Chief Justice should be the King's representative in South Africa, which change, he believed, would prove more economical. He seconded the motion *pro forma*, but he could not support it unless Senator Stuart was prepared to embody in his resolution further suggestions respecting a new constitution which he (Senator Whiteside) wished to incorporate.

Nominated members objected to.

Senator the Hon. I. W. B. de Villiers (*O.F.S.*) considered that the Senate had been transformed into a political institution like the House of Assembly, and contended that there should be no nominated members, but all should be elected. The Nationalist Members did not participate in the Speaker's Conference, and the discussion was confined to the Ministerialists. He moved an amendment to delete all the words after " House " in the second line and substitute words expressing the undesirability of there being nominated members, and regret at the reply given to Senator Reitz by Mr. de Wet on 15th May.

Senator the Hon. G. G. Munnik (*Trans.*) seconded.

No support for the motion.

The Prime Minister (Lt.-Gen. the Right Hon. J. C. Smuts) said the Government were quite satisfied with the trend of the discussion. Senator Stuart, in so far as the Government was concerned, stood entirely alone in his motion. He had found a seconder with very great difficulty who had taken express care to dissociate himself from the motion. The Government felt that the House was with them in repudiating what amounted to a vote of censure.

This question of re-constituting the Senate had been previously before the two Houses of Parliament. All sides of the House would agree with him that the matter should be approached in no frivolous spirit. The question of the Legislature of South Africa and of the Second Chamber was one of the most important matters which the country had to deal with. Ten years ago the National Convention dealt with the question. He had said in the Assembly, and he repeated that there was not a single question dealt with at the Convention which gave them more trouble than the constitution of the Second Chamber. In all countries it was a difficult subject. They wanted a Second Chamber which was different in character from the First Chamber. A solution was reached after more than a month's debate in the Convention. He considered that wisdom grew in a country and views matured from generation to generation.

Present constitution explained.

What was the constitution laid down? continued the Prime Minister. It was said that the Senate should be equally representative of the four Provinces, and eight members should be elected by an indirect method—not by the people directly. Beyond that there should be the principle of eight nominated members—four of whom should be elected by virtue of their special qualifications to deal with native affairs. The South Africa Act then went on to lay down that these nominations and indirect elections should last for a period of ten years, and thereafter Parliament might re-constitute the Senate if it so wished. If Parliament did not take any action then, the National Convention went on to lay down a permanent constitution for the Senate, and that constitution was in operation to-day.

During those ten years several steps had been taken to bring about the necessary reform of the Senate. The House appointed a Select Committee, which made due inquiry, and reported. The Senate was entirely uncommitted to any view, and expressly declined to record any opinion in regard to this matter. It had acquiesced in the constitution as laid down by the National Convention.

Referring to the Speaker's Conference, the Prime Minister pointed out that the first Senate of the country was to expire on 31st October, 1920, and the Conference made its recommendations almost at the end of that period. It was quite impossible after that Report within the very short time still at the disposal of the Government to call a special Session of Parliament to deal with the legal constitution of the Senate. The Senate expired in due course the following year, and the new Senate had to be elected in terms of the new South Africa Act. Early in 1921 a General Election was held, and as soon as it had taken place, and the Assembly had been re-constituted, the provisions of the South Africa Act were carried out and the Senate was re-constituted on its present lines. He had been asked by Senator Reitz whether he disapproved of that body, but how could he, occupying his responsible position, say that he disapproved of the Senate as at present constituted ?

Eight Senators elected for ten years.

The Senate as constituted in 1921 was as good as it was possible to obtain in that country. They had eight Senators who were nominated and who could not be touched. As many amendments as might be wished could be moved from the other side of the House against those Senators—and most of the remarks made about them that afternoon had been ungenerous and unfair—yet those Senators were elected for the next ten years. Senator de Villiers could move his motion with impunity because he sat there secure for the next decade. The Prime Minister quoted Section 25 of the South Africa Act, and said that whatever constitution was laid down, provision would have had to be made for the nominated members. The House might be dissolved by the Government in the same way as the House of Assembly, and when it was dissolved the elected Senators would have to disappear, but not the nominated Senators.

Senator de Villiers: " If we get a majority we will alter that constitution."

The Prime Minister said it would be a serious matter if they did that. Apart from the sporadic movements two years ago, he continued, there had been no movement in the country for the re-constitution of the Second Chamber. When it had been elected in 1921 everybody was satisfied. So far as they could judge from indications of public opinion, they could safely assume that the country was satisfied with the Senate, and there was no reason for making any change. Under present circumstances it would be frivolous of the Parliament of South Africa, without any call being made upon it, to go in for an innovation. The Speaker's Conference recommended that the nominated members should be elected by the public under the scheme of Proportional Representation, each Province acting as one constituency, but he looked upon that as an impossible proposition. The canvassing of the constituencies and the voting by the electorates would be a farce.

Senator Stuart: "What about Ireland ?"

The Prime Minister said that Ireland was not one constituency. Concluding, he claimed that the course followed by the Government had been amply vindicated.

On a division Senator de Villiers' amendment was lost by 20 votes to 12, and the original motion by an overwhelming majority, Senator Stuart, who had moved it, being the only one voting for it.

DOMINIONS AND HONOURS.

(Honours for services to the State; Attitude of other Dominions; Peerages in England; Sir J. B. Robinson and South Africa.)

On 14th July, in the Senate, the subject of titles bestowed on citizens of South Africa from outside the Union was discussed.

DEBATE IN THE SENATE.

Senator the Hon. F. W. Reitz moved :—

That in view of the recent scandals in connection with the granting of titles of honour, this House is of opinion that, in future, the Government should neither recommend, consent to, nor recognise titles of whatever sort bestowed from outside the Union on citizens of this Dominion.

He was not in any way influenced in bringing the motion, he said, by any private antagonisms, but he believed that only those who had done signal service to the country should be rewarded. As a democrat he was opposed to titles, and, indeed, thought that the only aristocracy which should exist should be the aristocracy of labour. Other Dominions, especially Canada, had set their faces against the granting of titles, and he thought they should follow suit. In England, it was said, titles could be bought for a certain sum ; therefore they found brewers amongst others ennobled.

The Minister of Justice (Hon. N. J. de Wet) could not accept the motion. The Government did not recommend honours, but the Prime Minister was consulted. The Minister mentioned a number of persons who had been honoured in this way, and who richly deserved it. He was not going to condemn a man for accepting a title, but he had other opinions as regards hereditary titles.

Senator the Hon. C. J. Langenhoven (*Cape*) cast ridicule on the whole system of titles. He objected to titles being flung about South Africa. Titles in England had depreciated in the same way as the German mark.

Defence of Sir J. B. Robinson.

Senator the Hon. G. G. Munnik said that newspapers on that side and in England had assailed the promotion of Sir J. B. Robinson to the peerage in most contemptible fashion. At least Sir J. B. Robinson was South African born, and who were Lord Selborne, Lord Buxton and Lord Harris to assail this worthy man ? Just because the two former were ex-Governor-Generals, they thought they had a right to assail a very worthy man.

Referring to recent creations, Senator Munnik said that there were Lord Waring, an upholsterer, and Lord Harmsworth, a bookseller ; and Sir J. B. Robinson had gained the regard of his fellow-citizens by opposing the introduction of Chinese labour on the mines, had done great service to the country, and was an Africander. He had been a Member of Parliament, and had, financially and morally, helped the poor of South Africa.

Amendment.

Senator the Hon. H. G. Stuart thought that titles should only be bestowed on those who had rendered eminent service to the State, and moved an amendment that they should not be granted unless recommended by the Prime Minister of the Union.

Senator the Hon. P. Whiteside supported the motion. If honours must be bestowed they should be by merit.

The question was put and declared to be lost on the voices. Senator Reitz having challenged a division, the motion was rejected by 20 votes to 9.

NEWFOUNDLAND.

The following summary is in continuation of the proceedings of the Third Session of the Twenty-fourth Parliament, which opened on 14th March, 1922, and concluded on 21st June, 1922.

RAILWAY AGREEMENT.

On 15th June, 1922, an Agreement was made between the Government of Newfoundland and the Reid Railway Company for the operation of the Company's rail and steamship services. (*Vide* also JOURNAL, Vol. III., No. 3, p. 706.)

The Agreement, after setting forth the previous Agreements between the Government and the Company, lays down that the Government shall provide the funds necessary to meet the regular pay-roll cheques of the Company's employees for the months of May and June, 1922, and, in addition, a sum not to exceed $70,000 to assist the Company to meet present liabilities to parties other than the Bank of Montreal on account of railway, steamship and express business (*Sect.* 1). The Company assigns to the Government by way of security for the sums to be provided under paragraph 1 and also as security for the amount, if any, by which the sums hitherto paid by the Government to the Company under the 1921 Agreement shall be found to exceed the actual loss of operating under that Agreement, all its book debts and accounts receivable on railway, steamship and express services, and those which might become due to the Company between the date of this Agreement and 30th June, 1922, including in each case amounts accruing from the Canadian and Newfoundland Governments in connection with any of the said services (*Sect.* 3). New accounts are to be opened and all amounts earned by the railway, steamships and the express Company from 1st July and 15th November placed to their credit (*Sects.* 4 *and* 5). The Government is to provide all funds necessary to operate the Company from 15th June to 15th November and shall keep in force the fire and marine insurance at present maintained by the Company (*Sect.* 6). It is entitled to receive on demand all sums placed to the credit of the new accounts and all moneys earned during the period of operation contemplated by the Agreement, and shall pay all debts contracted during that period (*Sects.* 9 *and* 10). The services shall be operated under the management of Richard C. Morgan and Robert G. Reid.

DEBATE IN HOUSE OF REPRESENTATIVES.

On 15th June,

The Prime Minister (Hon. Sir Richard Squires) explained that under the Agreement entered into in May, when the Government had guaranteed the pay roll up to $74,500 up to a few days ago, the amount had been practically liquidated and within a few days more the Government expected to be reimbursed for the full amount as only between $5,000 and $6,000 were outstanding. The present position was that the May and June pay roll with certain bills for coal, and amounting to $50,000 represented by income bills payable, inventories and engine parts, was outstanding, and the Government proposed to finance the amount as was done in May, the Government hoping that it would be liquidated by the Reid Company. The situation being covered up to 30th June, the Government assumed operation from 15th June to 15th November of the Reid railway line, steamboats and express business, the actual loss on operation for the period to be borne by the Government.

Mr. Frank Archibald (Independent, *Harbour Grace*) asked what the programme of the Government would be after 15th November.

The Prime Minister replied that this was a five months' armistice.

On 17th June, in Committee of Supply,

The Hon. Sir Michael Cashin (Leader of the Opposition) described the Vote of $250,000 to finance railway operations from 1st July to 15th November as camouflage, as past experience had shown that a much larger sum would be required. There was no mention of the wharfage of steamers at the dock premises in the Agreement.

Mr. M. S. Sullivan (Opposition, *Placentia*) was of opinion that the Government, while putting Mr. Morgan in as General Manager, were yet tying his hands, as he could make no change in the operating policy without the consent of Mr. R. G. Reid, the Vice-President of the Company. He was opposed to the Agreement as it stood, because he believed it to be unworkable. He did not think it was at all necessary to bring down an outside rail-roader to operate the line as there were several quite capable men in the country.

Mr. J. R. Bennett (Opposition, *St. John's, W.*) declared that the present arrangement was most unsatisfactory. What did the Government intend to do after 15th November? In 1920, the losses for the period of this Agreement had been $489,000. Apparently the Government were not going to try and unravel the situation. It gave him great fears for the future.

PROHIBITION.

On 15th June in the House of Representatives, in reply to a question by Mr. W. J. Walsh (Opposition, *Placentia*),

The Prime Minister (Hon. Sir Richard Squires) stated that he did not know of any petition of 20,000 voters asking for an amendment to the Prohibition Law. He did know of two petitions presented last year, one of which asked for Dry Laws and the other Moderation. Both were considered by the House. It was afterwards intimated that no plebiscite was desired. Since then the Bills had not been considered. The Government as a Government had not considered if an amendment to the law was necessary. No amendments had been submitted to the Government during recent months, and the Government as a Government was interested only in the enforcement of the present Act. It was not the intention to introduce any legislation dealing with this matter during the present Session. This was plebiscite legislation, and the spirit or policy must be determined by the people who put the Act into force. His personal opinion was that no radical change from the present law should be effected. The Social Service Congress desired a Board of Control with an official paid a substantial salary, who would look after the enforcement of the Act. At a special meeting of the Congress he had informed the meeting that there was sufficient time for amendments to be considered by the House at the present Session. Should either Committee submit any amendments or regulations they would be laid before the House, and every Member would be free to vote as he pleased on them.

VACHER & SONS, LTD., Westminster House, London, S.W.1.—100196.

Lightning Source UK Ltd.
Milton Keynes UK
UKHW050842241218
334233UK00008BA/737/P